HarperCollins

ATLAS OF THE WORLD

HarperCollins Atlas of the World

Published by HarperCollins in association with
Borders Press, a division of Borders Group, Inc.
100 Phoenix Drive, Ann Arbor, Michigan, 48108.
All rights reserved

Borders Press is a trademark of Borders Properties, Inc.

First published 1996 as Collins Atlas of the World,
reprinted with revisions 1997

Maps © HarperCollins*Publishers*

This edition printed 1998 for Borders Group, Inc.

All rights reserved. No part of this publication may be
reproduced, stored in a retrieval system, or transmitted,
in any form or by any means, electronic, mechanical,
photocopying, recording or otherwise without the prior
written permission of the publisher and copyright owners.

The contents of this edition of the HarperCollins Atlas of
the World are believed correct at the time of printing.
Nevertheless the publisher can accept no responsibility for
errors or omissions, changes in the detail given or for any
expense or loss thereby caused.

Printed in Italy

ISBN 0 00 448922 5

Globe images : data © 1995 The Living Earth, Inc.
Cover photograph: Zefa Pictures

HarperCollins

ATLAS
OF THE WORLD

CONTENTS

THE WORLD

MAPS *6–24*

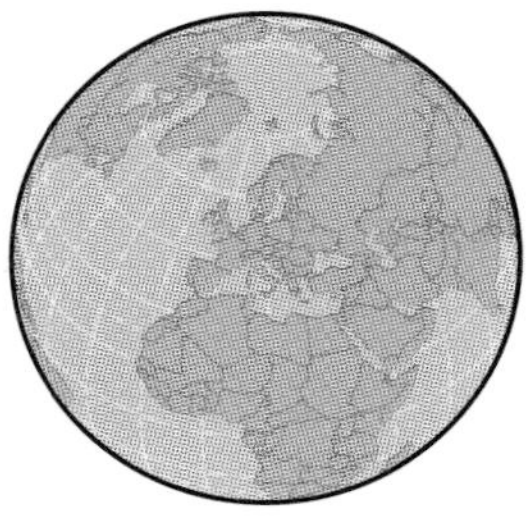

EUROPE

MAPS *2–29*

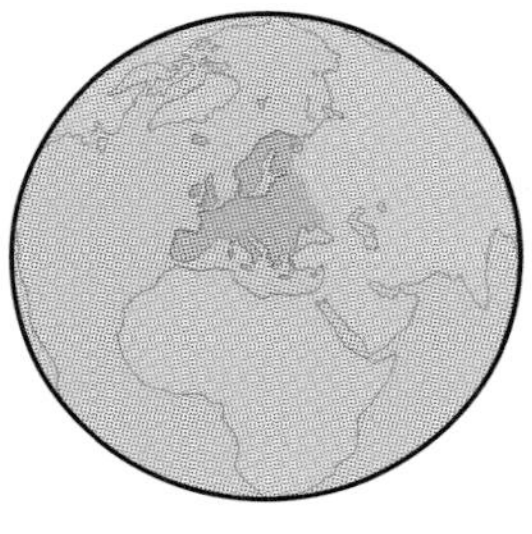

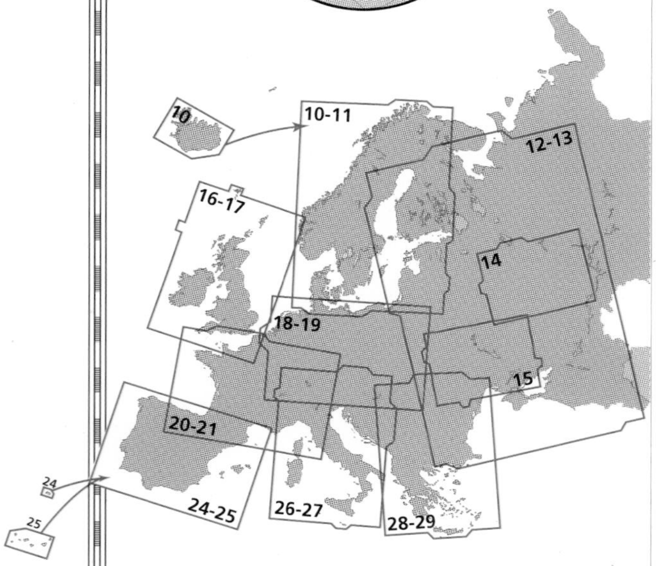

ASIA

MAPS *30–65*

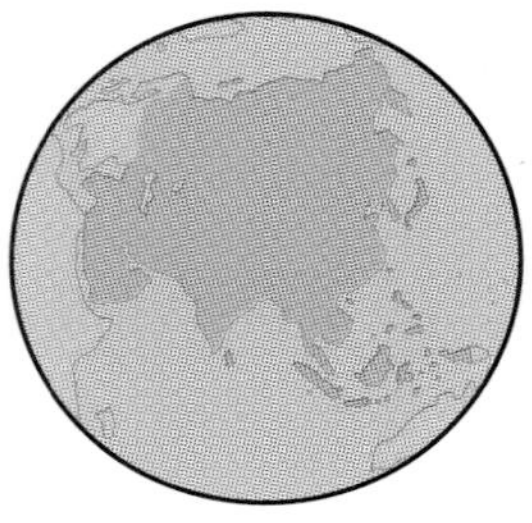

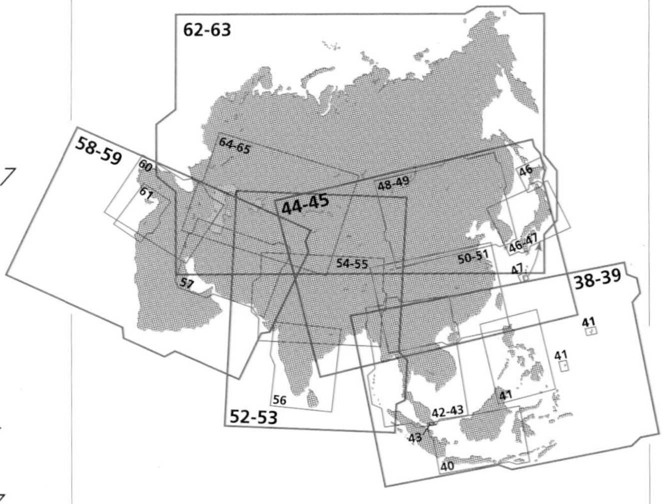

AFRICA

MAPS *66 – 83*

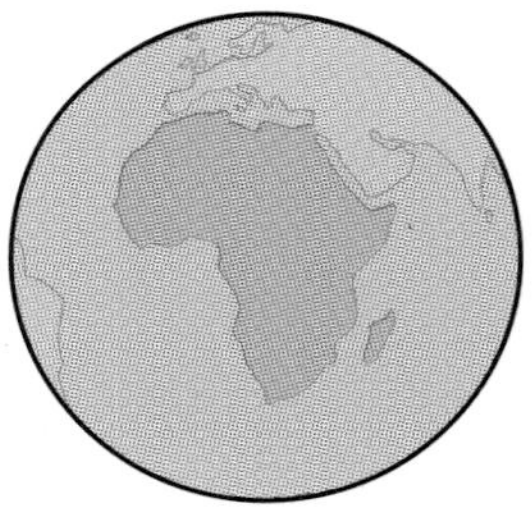

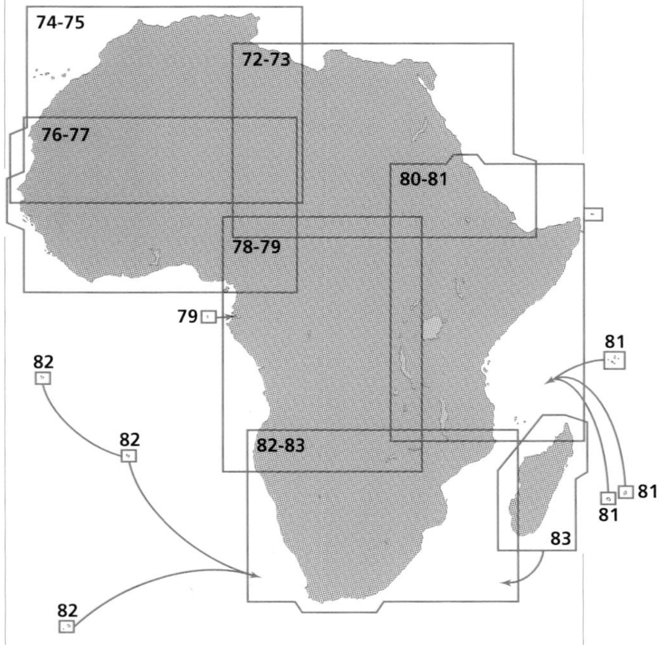

OCEANIA

MAPS *84 –101*

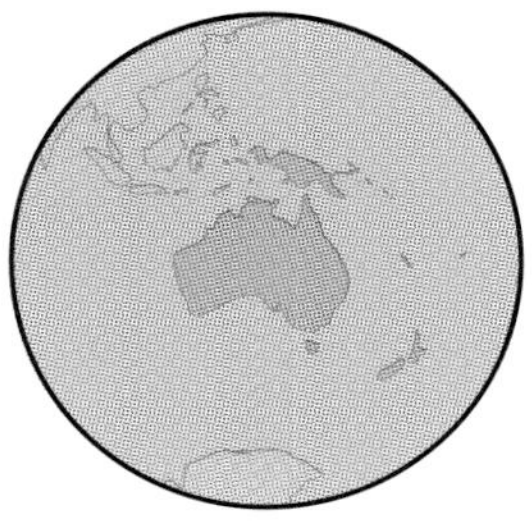

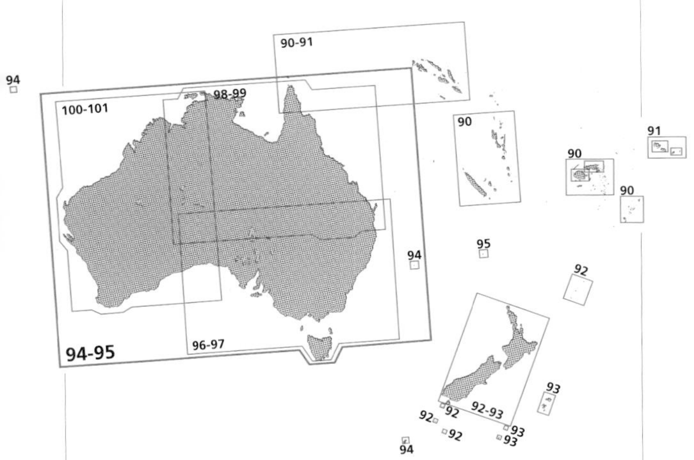

NORTH AMERICA

MAPS *102 –133*

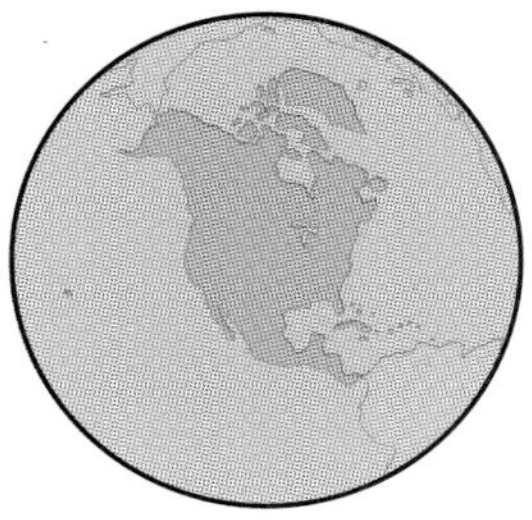

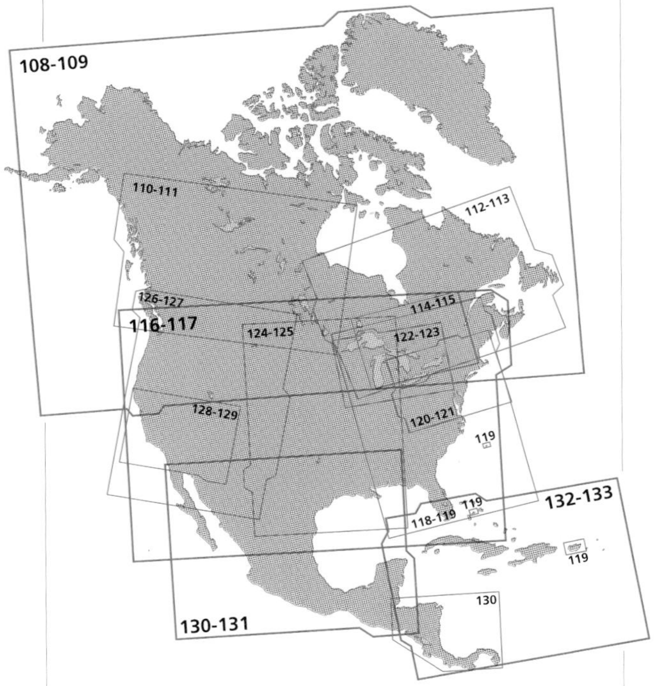

SOUTH AMERICA

MAPS *134 – 147*

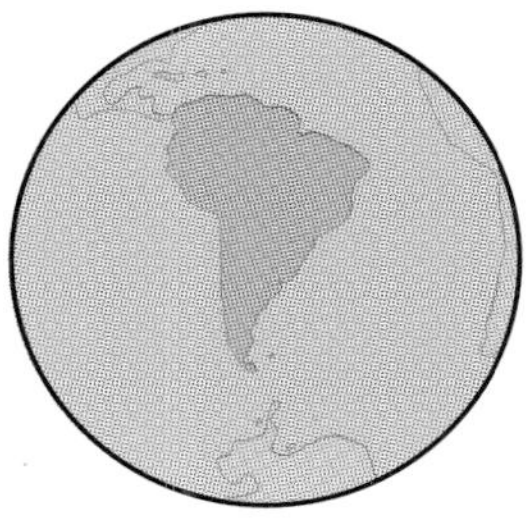

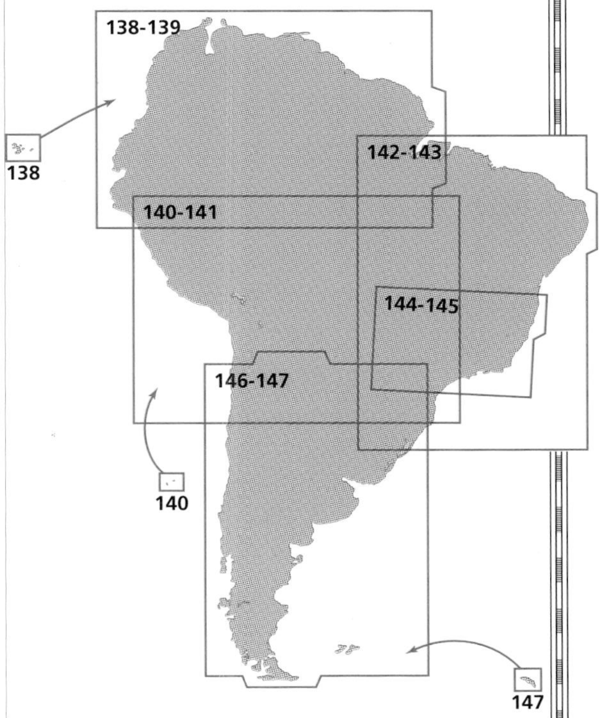

OCEANS & POLAR

MAPS *148 –152*

INDEX

PAGES *153–199*

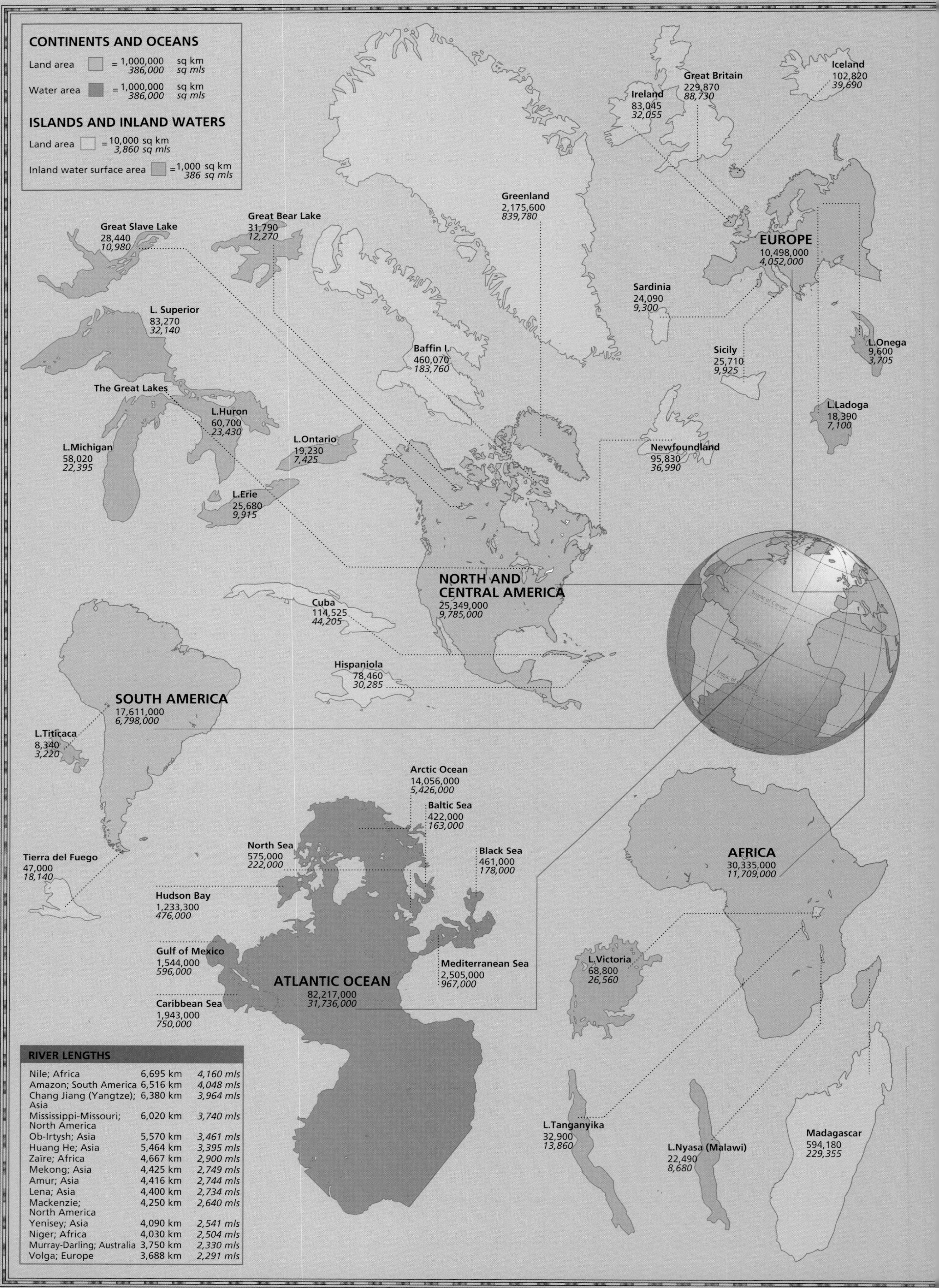
CONTINENTS AND OCEANS
Land area = 1,000,000 sq km 386,000 sq mls
Water area = 1,000,000 sq km 386,000 sq mls
ISLANDS AND INLAND WATERS
Land area = 10,000 sq km 3,860 sq mls
Inland water surface area = 1,000 sq km 386 sq mls
Great Slave Lake 28,440 10,980
Great Bear Lake 31,790 12,270
Greenland 2,175,600 839,780
Ireland 83,045 32,055
Great Britain 229,870 88,730
Iceland 102,820 39,690
EUROPE 10,498,000 4,052,000
Sardinia 24,090 9,300
L. Superior 83,270 32,140
Baffin I. 460,070 183,760
Sicily 25,710 9,925
L.Onega 9,600 3,705
The Great Lakes
L.Huron 60,700 23,430
L.Ladoga 18,390 7,100
L.Michigan 58,020 22,395
L.Ontario 19,230 7,425
Newfoundland 95,830 36,990
L.Erie 25,680 9,915
NORTH AND CENTRAL AMERICA 25,349,000 9,785,000
Cuba 114,525 44,205
Tropic of Cancer
Equator
Tropic of Capricorn
Hispaniola 78,460 30,285
SOUTH AMERICA 17,611,000 6,798,000
L.Titicaca 8,340 3,220
Arctic Ocean 14,056,000 5,426,000
Baltic Sea 422,000 163,000
North Sea 575,000 222,000
Black Sea 461,000 178,000
AFRICA 30,335,000 11,709,000
Tierra del Fuego 47,000 18,140
Hudson Bay 1,233,300 476,000
Gulf of Mexico 1,544,000 596,000
Mediterranean Sea 2,505,000 967,000
L.Victoria 68,800 26,560
ATLANTIC OCEAN 82,217,000 31,736,000
Caribbean Sea 1,943,000 750,000
L.Tanganyika 32,900 13,860
L.Nyasa (Malawi) 22,490 8,680
Madagascar 594,180 229,355

RIVER LENGTHS

Nile; Africa	6,695 km	*4,160 mls*
Amazon; South America	6,516 km	*4,048 mls*
Chang Jiang (Yangtze); Asia	6,380 km	*3,964 mls*
Mississippi-Missouri; North America	6,020 km	*3,740 mls*
Ob-Irtysh; Asia	5,570 km	*3,461 mls*
Huang He; Asia	5,464 km	*3,395 mls*
Zaïre; Africa	4,667 km	*2,900 mls*
Mekong; Asia	4,425 km	*2,749 mls*
Amur; Asia	4,416 km	*2,744 mls*
Lena; Asia	4,400 km	*2,734 mls*
Mackenzie; North America	4,250 km	*2,640 mls*
Yenisey; Asia	4,090 km	*2,541 mls*
Niger; Africa	4,030 km	*2,504 mls*
Murray-Darling; Australia	3,750 km	*2,330 mls*
Volga; Europe	3,688 km	*2,291 mls*

MOUNTAIN HEIGHTS (Selected)

Everest; Nepal/China	8,848 m	*29,028 ft*
K2; Jammu & Kashmir/China	8,611 m	*28,251 ft*
Kanchenjunga; Nepal/India	8,586 m	*28,169 ft*
Dhaulagiri; Nepal	8,167 m	*26,794 ft*
Annapurna; Nepal	8,091 m	*26,545 ft*
Aconcagua; Argentina	6,960 m	*22,834 ft*
Ojos del Salado; Argentina/Chile	6,908 m	*22,664 ft*
Mt McKinley; Alaska, USA	6,194 m	*20,321 ft*
Mt Logan; Canada	6,050 m	*19,849 ft*
Kilimanjaro; Tanzania	5,895 m	*19,340 ft*
Elbrus; Russian Federation	5,642 m	*18,510 ft*
Kirinyaga; Kenya	5,199 m	*17,057 ft*
Puncak Jaya; Indonesia	5,029 m	*16,499 ft*
Vinson Massif; Antarctica	4,897 m	*16,066 ft*
Mt Blanc; France/Italy	4,808 m	*15,774 ft*

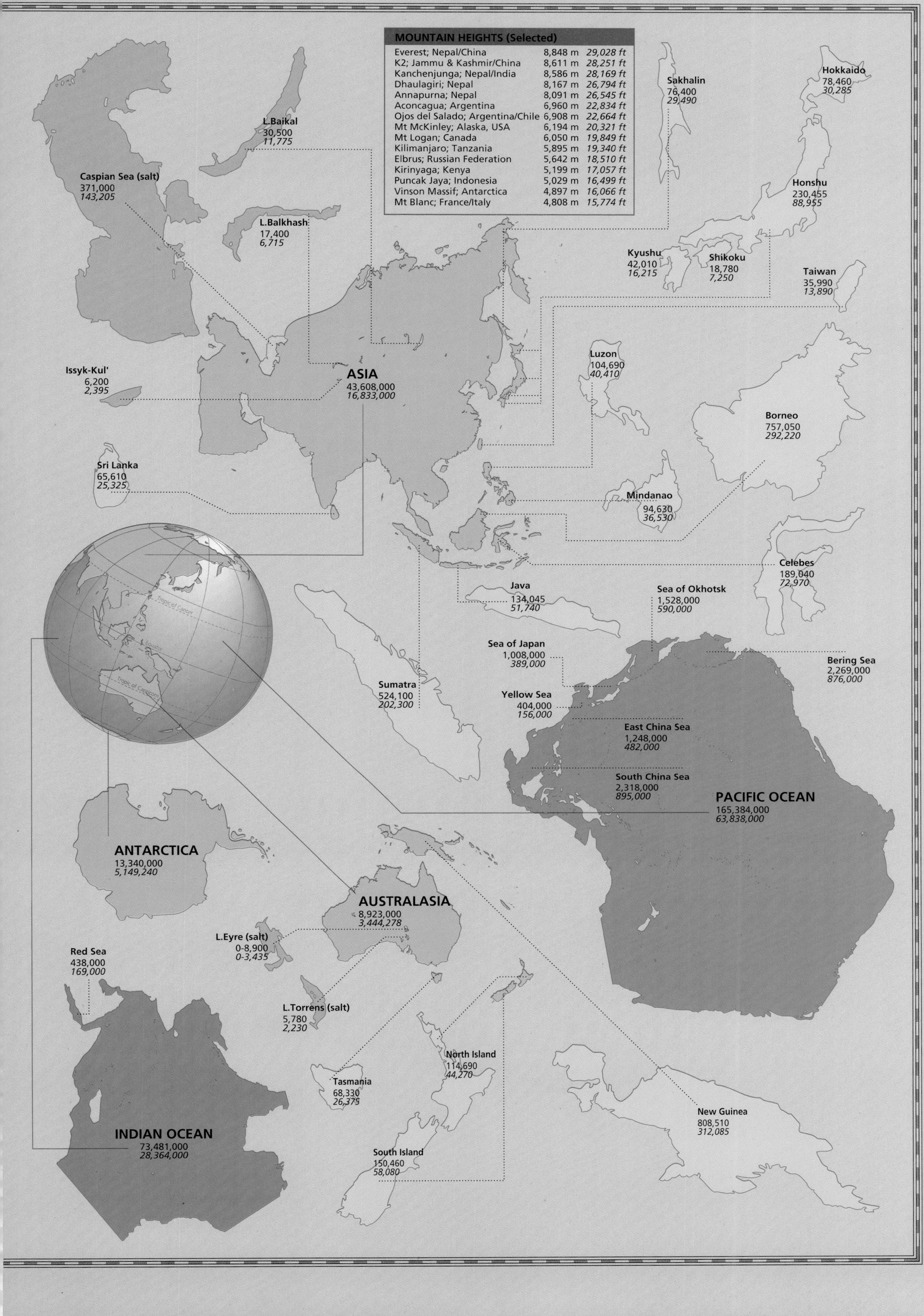

L.Baikal 30,500 11,775
Caspian Sea (salt) 371,000 143,205
L.Balkhash 17,400 6,715
Sakhalin 76,400 29,490
Hokkaido 78,460 30,285
Honshu 230,455 88,955
Kyushu 42,010 16,215
Shikoku 18,780 7,250
Taiwan 35,990 13,890
Luzon 104,690 40,410
Issyk-Kul' 6,200 2,395
ASIA 43,608,000 16,833,000
Borneo 757,050 292,220
Sri Lanka 65,610 25,325
Mindanao 94,630 36,530
Celebes 189,040 72,970
Java 134,045 51,740
Sea of Okhotsk 1,528,000 590,000
Sea of Japan 1,008,000 389,000
Bering Sea 2,269,000 876,000
Sumatra 524,100 202,300
Yellow Sea 404,000 156,000
East China Sea 1,248,000 482,000
South China Sea 2,318,000 895,000
PACIFIC OCEAN 165,384,000 63,838,000
Tropic of Cancer
Equator
Tropic of Capricorn
ANTARCTICA 13,340,000 5,149,240
AUSTRALASIA 8,923,000 3,444,278
L.Eyre (salt) 0-8,900 0-3,435
Red Sea 438,000 169,000
L.Torrens (salt) 5,780 2,230
North Island 114,690 44,270
Tasmania 68,330 26,375
New Guinea 808,510 312,085
INDIAN OCEAN 73,481,000 28,364,000
South Island 150,460 58,080

CLIMATIC REGIONS

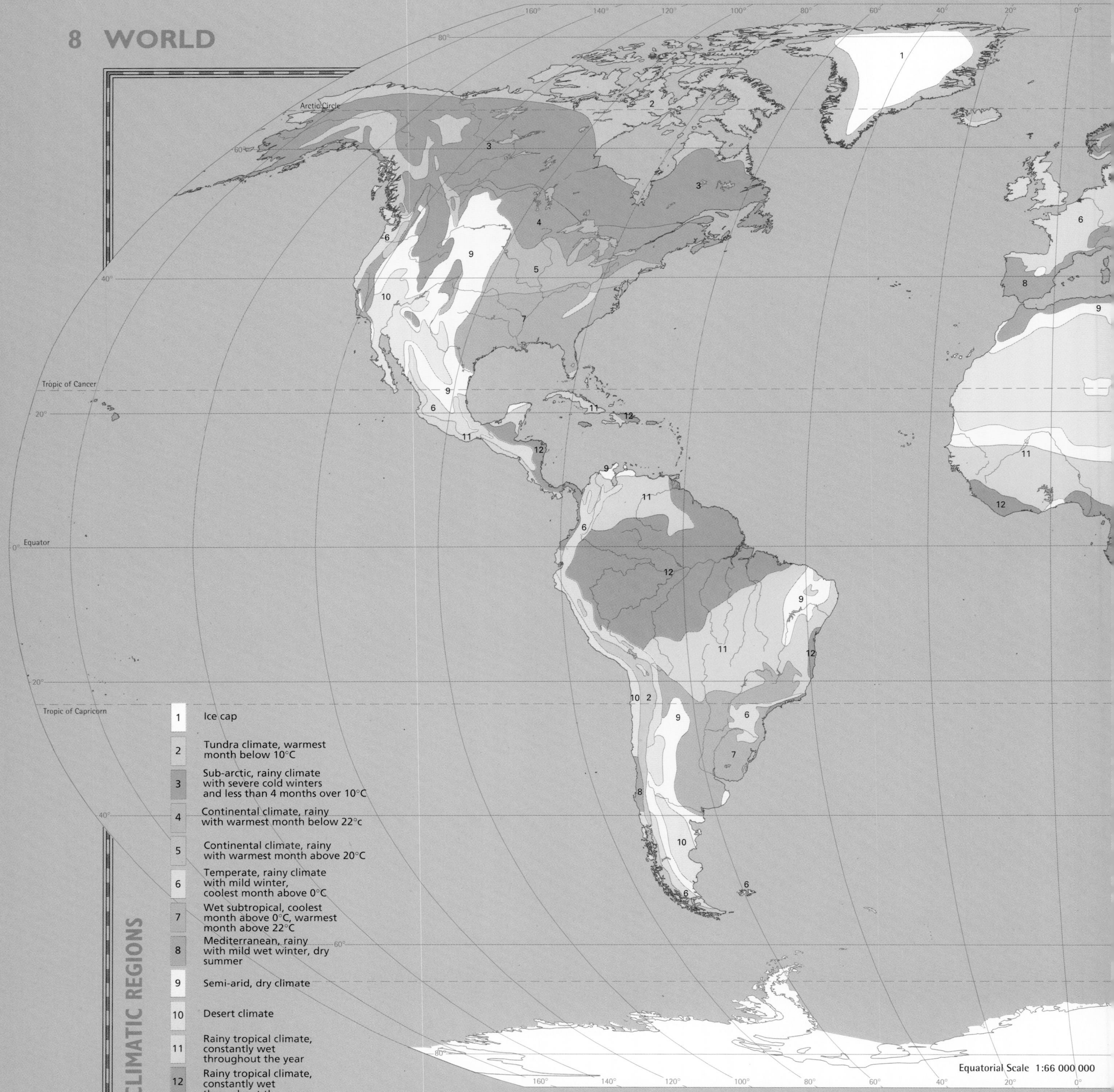
Arctic Circle
Tropic of Cancer
Equator
Tropic of Capricorn
Equatorial Scale 1:66 000 000

1	Ice cap
2	Tundra climate, warmest month below 10°C
3	Sub-arctic, rainy climate with severe cold winters and less than 4 months over 10°C
4	Continental climate, rainy with warmest month below 22°c
5	Continental climate, rainy with warmest month above 20°C
6	Temperate, rainy climate with mild winter, coolest month above 0°C
7	Wet subtropical, coolest month above 0°C, warmest month above 22°C
8	Mediterranean, rainy with mild wet winter, dry summer
9	Semi-arid, dry climate
10	Desert climate
11	Rainy tropical climate, constantly wet throughout the year
12	Rainy tropical climate, constantly wet throughout the year

OCEAN CURRENTS

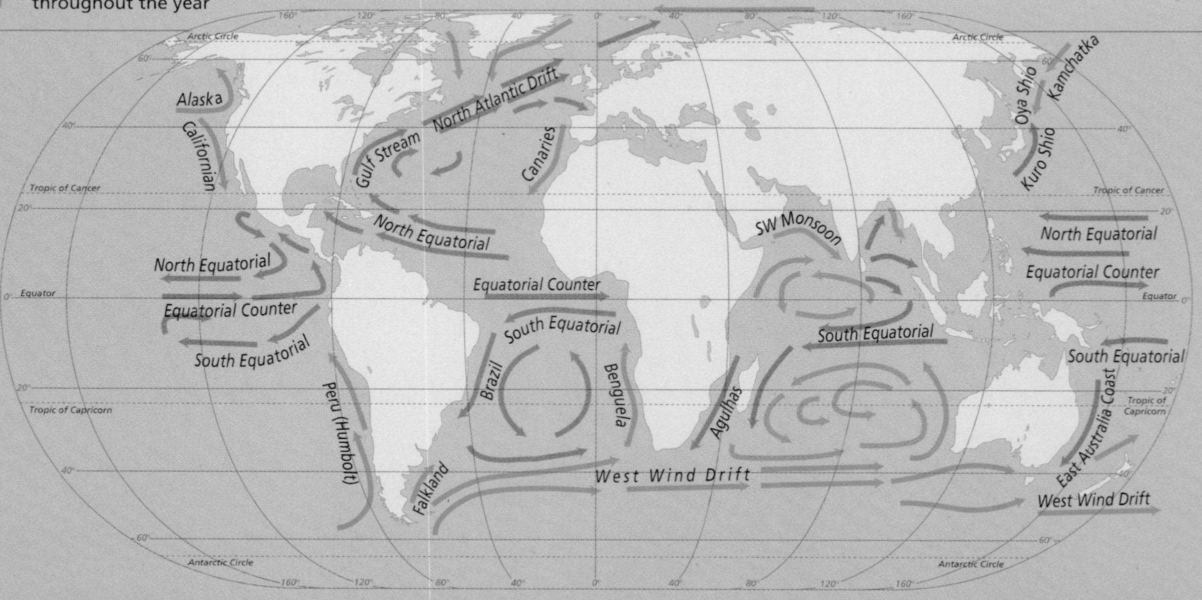
Arctic Circle
Alaska
Californian
Gulf Stream
North Atlantic Drift
Canaries
Oya Shio
Kamchatka
Kuro Shio
Tropic of Cancer
North Equatorial
SW Monsoon
Equatorial Counter
Equator
South Equatorial
Peru (Humbolt)
Brazil
Benguela
Agulhas
East Australia Coast
Tropic of Capricorn
Falkland
West Wind Drift
Antarctic Circle

Ocean Currents

Cold Ocean Currents
Warm Ocean Currents
Seasonal Ocean Currents

Robinson Projection

© HarperCollinsPublishers

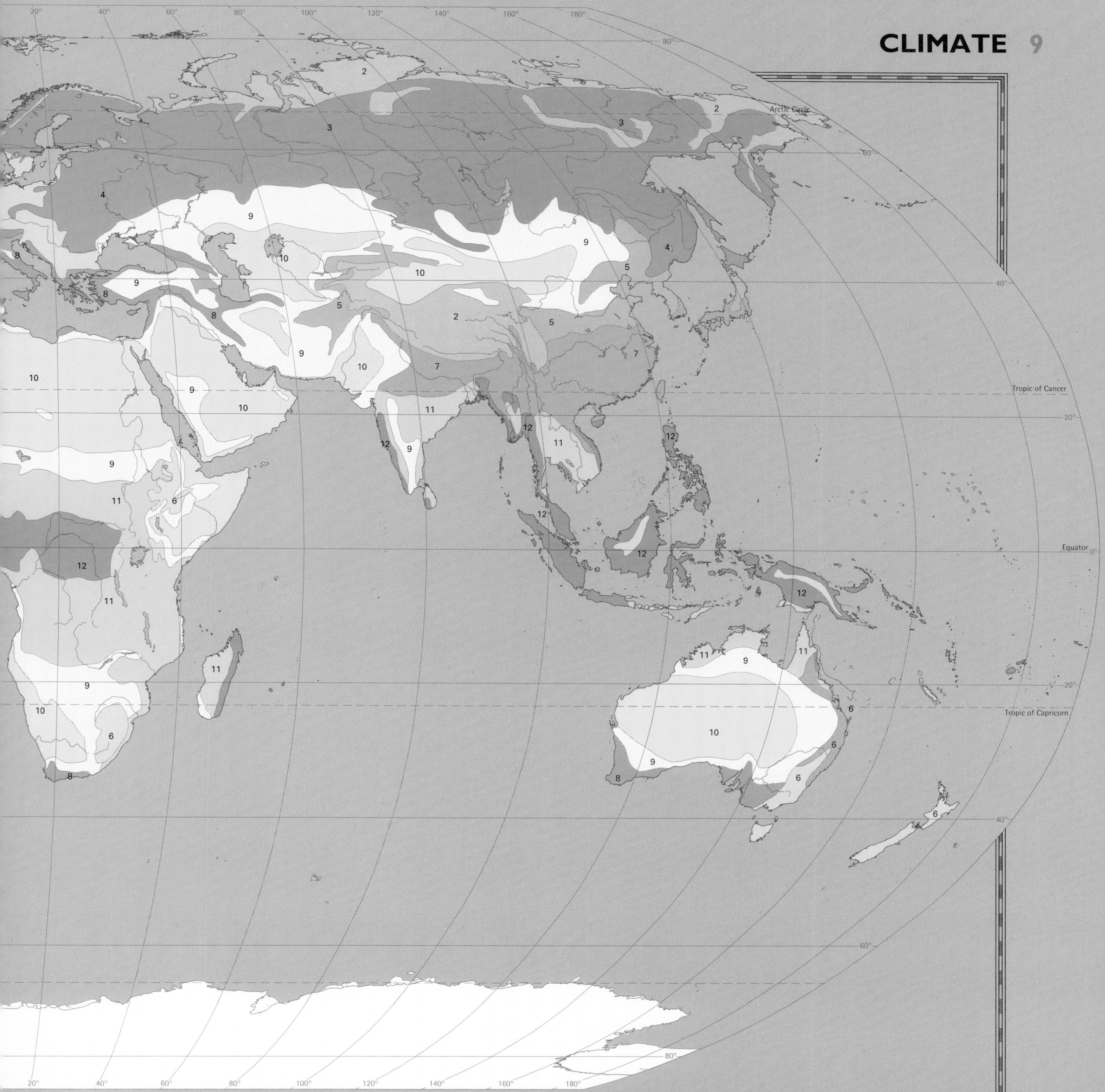
Arctic Circle
Tropic of Cancer
Equator
Tropic of Capricorn
20° 40° 60° 80° 100° 120° 140° 160° 180°

TROPICAL STORMS

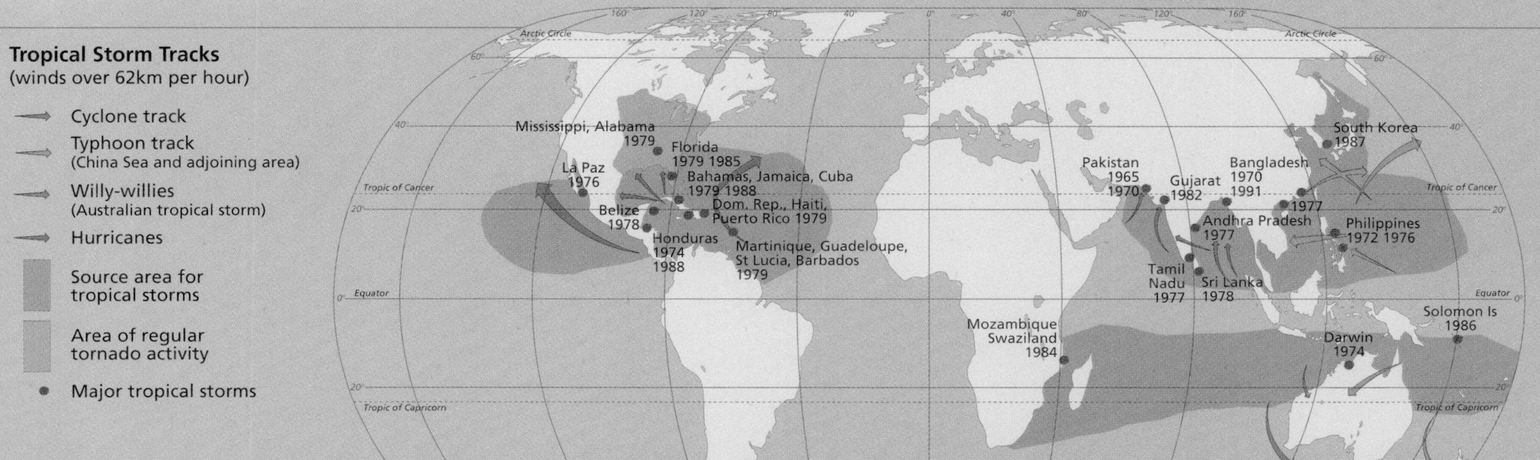
Tropical Storm Tracks
(winds over 62km per hour)
Cyclone track
Typhoon track
(China Sea and adjoining area)
Willy-willies
(Australian tropical storm)
Hurricanes
Source area for tropical storms
Area of regular tornado activity
Major tropical storms
Mississippi, Alabama 1979
Florida 1979 1985
La Paz 1976
Bahamas, Jamaica, Cuba 1979 1988
Dom. Rep., Haiti, Puerto Rico 1979
Belize 1978
Honduras 1974 1988
Martinique, Guadeloupe, St Lucia, Barbados 1979
Pakistan 1965 1970
Gujarat 1982
Bangladesh 1970 1991
South Korea 1987
Andhra Pradesh 1977
Tamil Nadu 1977
Sri Lanka 1978
Philippines 1972 1976
Mozambique Swaziland 1984
Darwin 1974
Solomon Is 1986
Arctic Circle
Tropic of Cancer
Equator
Tropic of Capricorn
Antarctic Circle

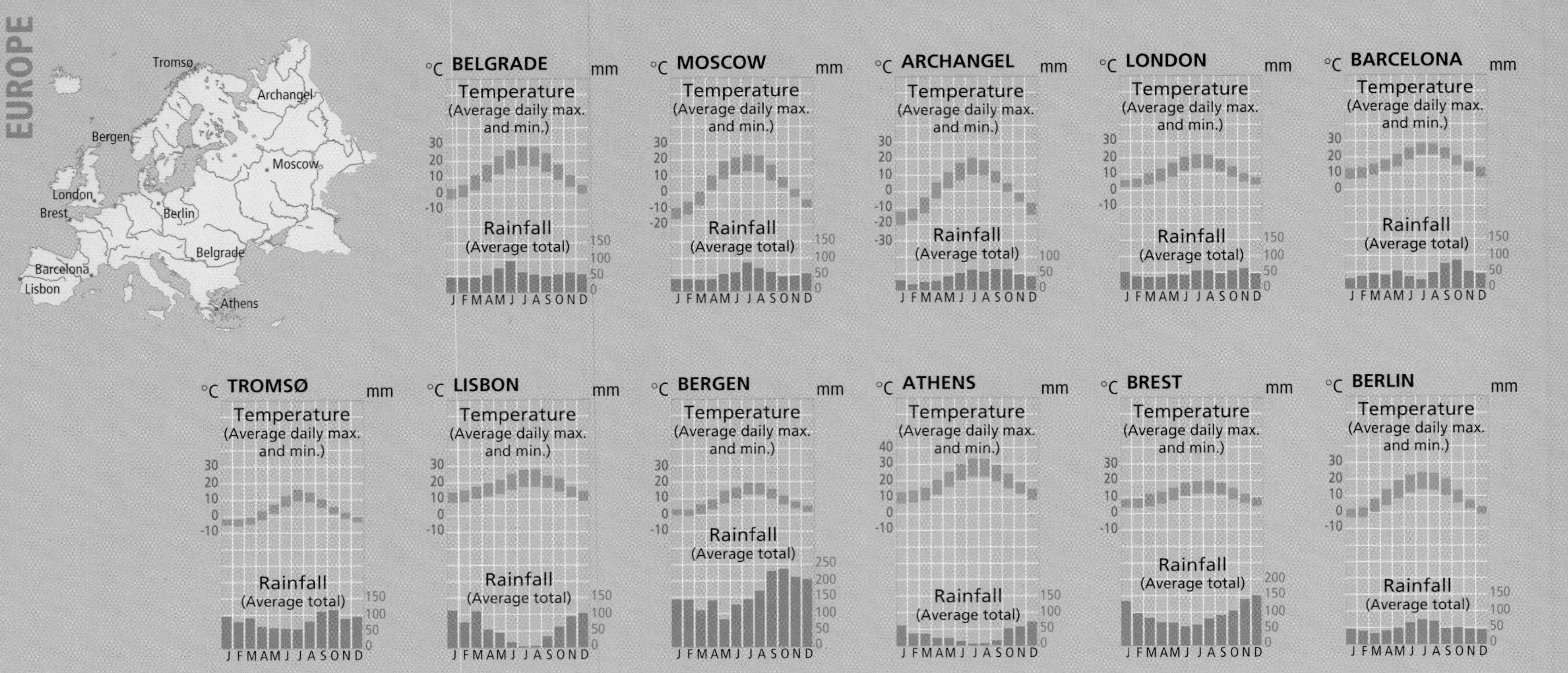
EUROPE
Tromsø
Archangel
Bergen
Moscow
London
Brest
Berlin
Belgrade
Barcelona
Lisbon
Athens
BELGRADE
MOSCOW
ARCHANGEL
LONDON
BARCELONA
TROMSØ
LISBON
BERGEN
ATHENS
BREST
BERLIN
°C
mm
Temperature
(Average daily max. and min.)
Rainfall
(Average total)
J F M A M J J A S O N D

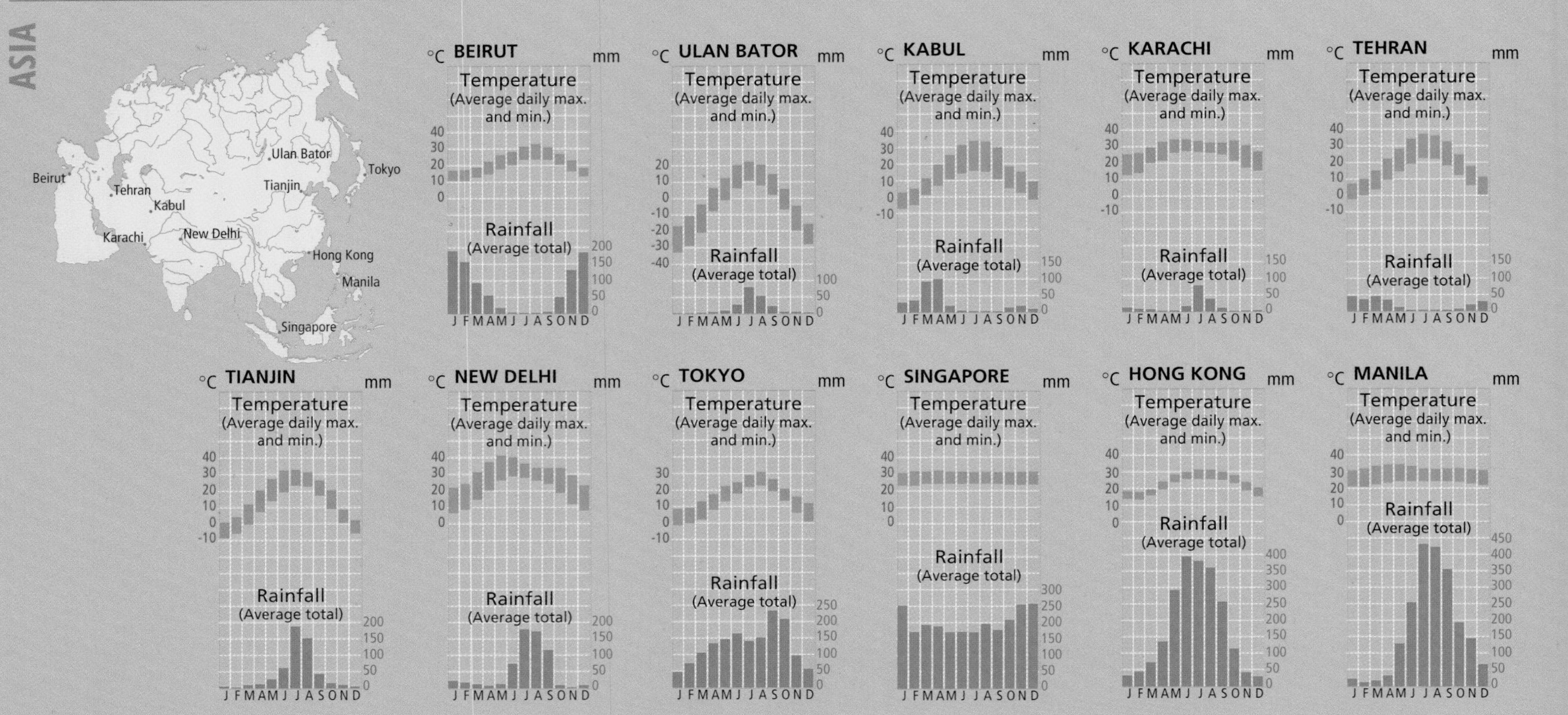
ASIA
Beirut
Tehran
Kabul
Karachi
New Delhi
Ulan Bator
Tianjin
Tokyo
Hong Kong
Manila
Singapore
BEIRUT
ULAN BATOR
KABUL
KARACHI
TEHRAN
TIANJIN
NEW DELHI
TOKYO
SINGAPORE
HONG KONG
MANILA
°C
mm
Temperature
(Average daily max. and min.)
Rainfall
(Average total)
J F M A M J J A S O N D

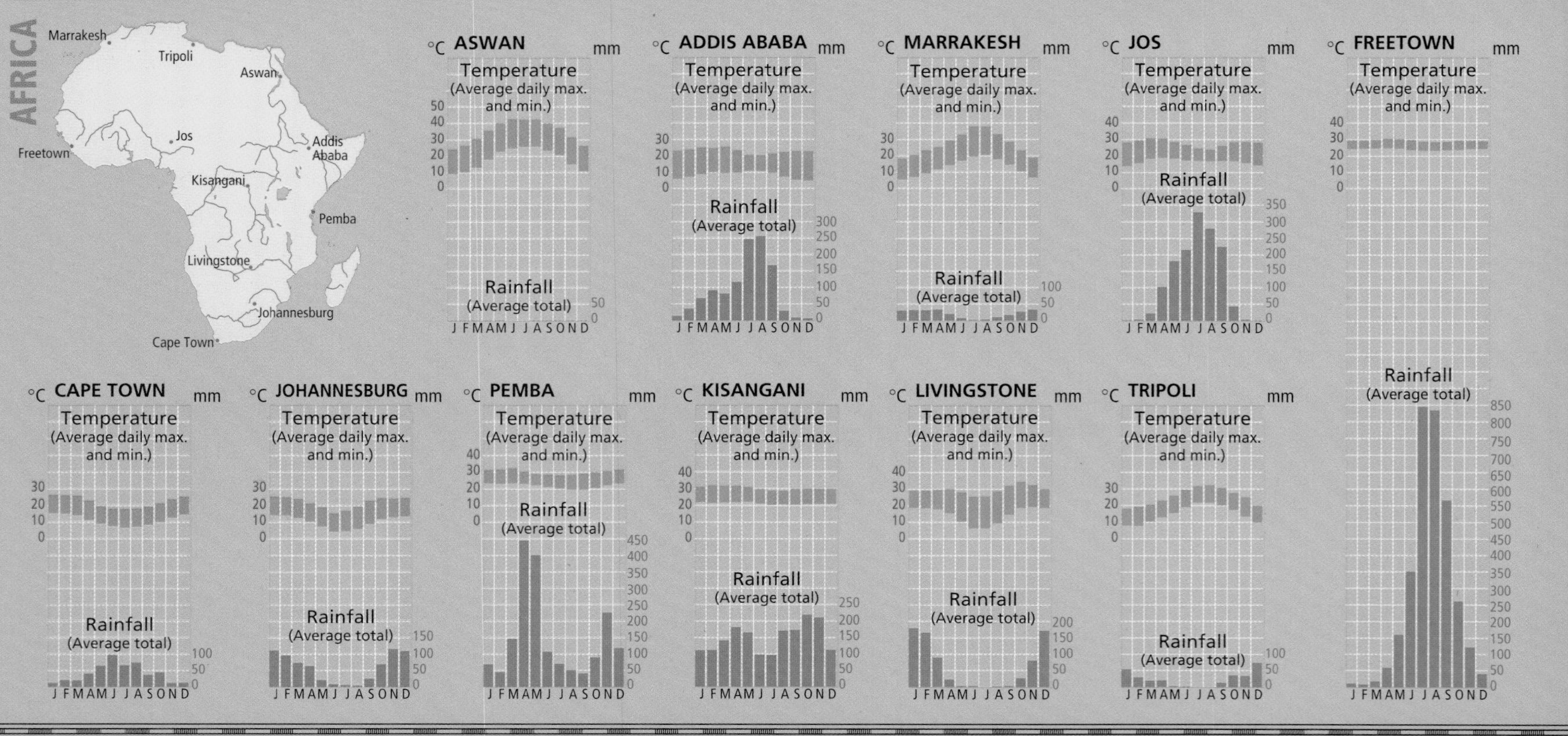
AFRICA
Marrakesh
Tripoli
Aswan
Jos
Freetown
Addis Ababa
Kisangani
Pemba
Livingstone
Johannesburg
Cape Town
ASWAN
ADDIS ABABA
MARRAKESH
JOS
FREETOWN
CAPE TOWN
JOHANNESBURG
PEMBA
KISANGANI
LIVINGSTONE
TRIPOLI
°C
mm
Temperature
(Average daily max. and min.)
Rainfall
(Average total)
J F M A M J J A S O N D

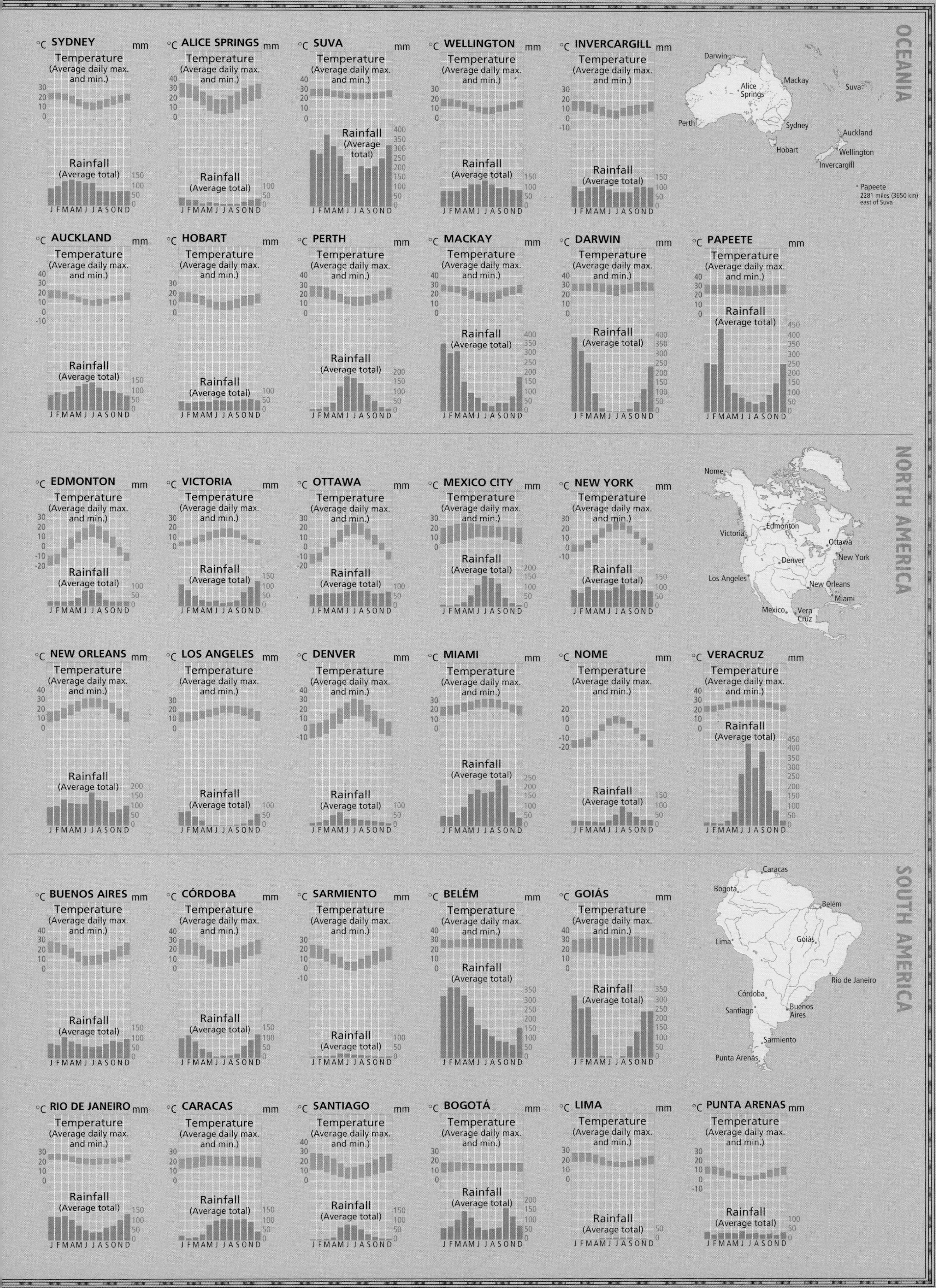

OCEANIA
SYDNEY
ALICE SPRINGS
SUVA
WELLINGTON
INVERCARGILL
AUCKLAND
HOBART
PERTH
MACKAY
DARWIN
PAPEETE
Darwin
Alice Springs
Mackay
Suva
Perth
Sydney
Auckland
Hobart
Wellington
Invercargill
Papeete 2281 miles (3650 km) east of Suva
NORTH AMERICA
EDMONTON
VICTORIA
OTTAWA
MEXICO CITY
NEW YORK
NEW ORLEANS
LOS ANGELES
DENVER
MIAMI
NOME
VERACRUZ
Nome
Victoria
Edmonton
Ottawa
Denver
New York
Los Angeles
New Orleans
Miami
Mexico
Vera Cruz
SOUTH AMERICA
BUENOS AIRES
CÓRDOBA
SARMIENTO
BELÉM
GOIÁS
RIO DE JANEIRO
CARACAS
SANTIAGO
BOGOTÁ
LIMA
PUNTA ARENAS
Caracas
Bogotá
Belém
Lima
Goiás
Rio de Janeiro
Córdoba
Santiago
Buenos Aires
Sarmiento
Punta Arenas
°C
mm
Temperature (Average daily max. and min.)
Rainfall (Average total)
J F M A M J J A S O N D

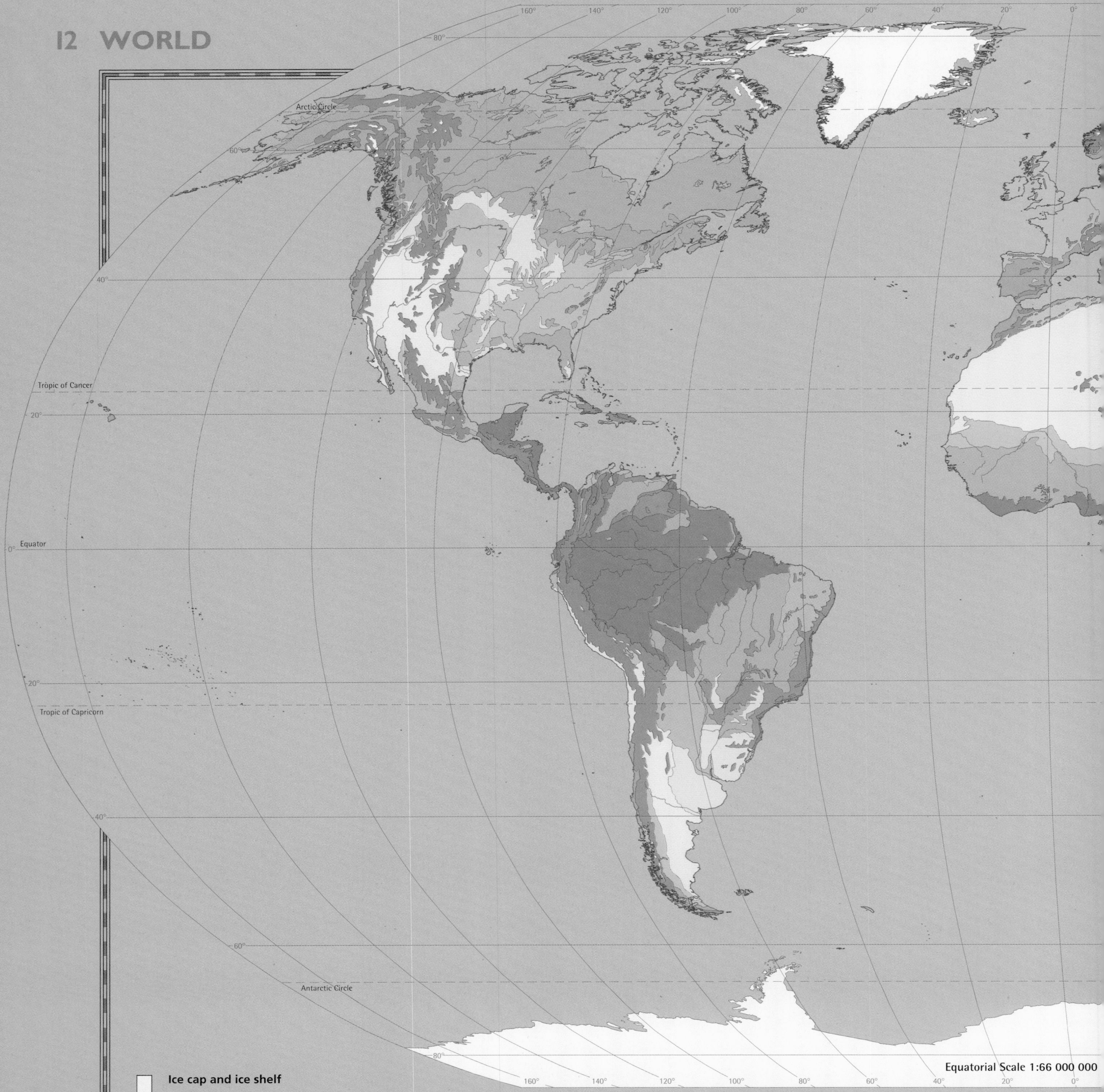

Ice cap and ice shelf

Mountain vegetation
Stunted vegetation growth found on mountains of mid- and high altitudes and at very high altitudes in tropical latitudes. Absence of trees apart from low growing forms of birch and willow. Mosses and lichens are abundant.

Tundra
Region of restricted plant growth confined mostly between latitudes north of 60° N and south of the polar ice cap. Vegetation is characterised by mosses, lichens, rushes, grasses and flowering herbs.

Boreal forest (Taiga)
Continuous zone in northern hemisphere found between latitudes 50° N and 70° N. Characteristic form of vegetation is the coniferous tree with the dominant species being pine, larch, spruce and fir.

Conifer forest
Different formations of coniferous forest to that of the boreal forest, found in western North America, southeastern USA and southern Brazil. Pine, spruce and larch are dominant.

Mixed forest, mid-latitudes
Transition zone in north-central Europe, east-central North America and eastern Asia with a mixture of areas of broadleaf trees and areas of conifer trees in almost equal numbers.

Broadleaf forest
Deciduous forest found mainly in the mid-latitudes of the northern hemisphere. Before 1500 a wide variety of species existed eg. oak, ash, beech, elm, maple, hickory, alder, and birch, but due to exploitation little original forest remains.

Mediterranean scrub
Areas of shrub dominated vegetation located in the Mediterranean basin and similar bio-climatic regions in coastal parts of California, Chile, South Africa and southern Australia. A variety of aromatic herbaceous plants grow beneath low shrub thickets, pines, oaks or gorse.

Prairie
Areas of grassland where long grasses are dominant, found in central North America, the Veld of eastern South Africa and the Pampas of Argentina. Sward grasses and bunch grasses grow up to 1 metre high.

Robinson Projection

© HarperCollinsPublishers

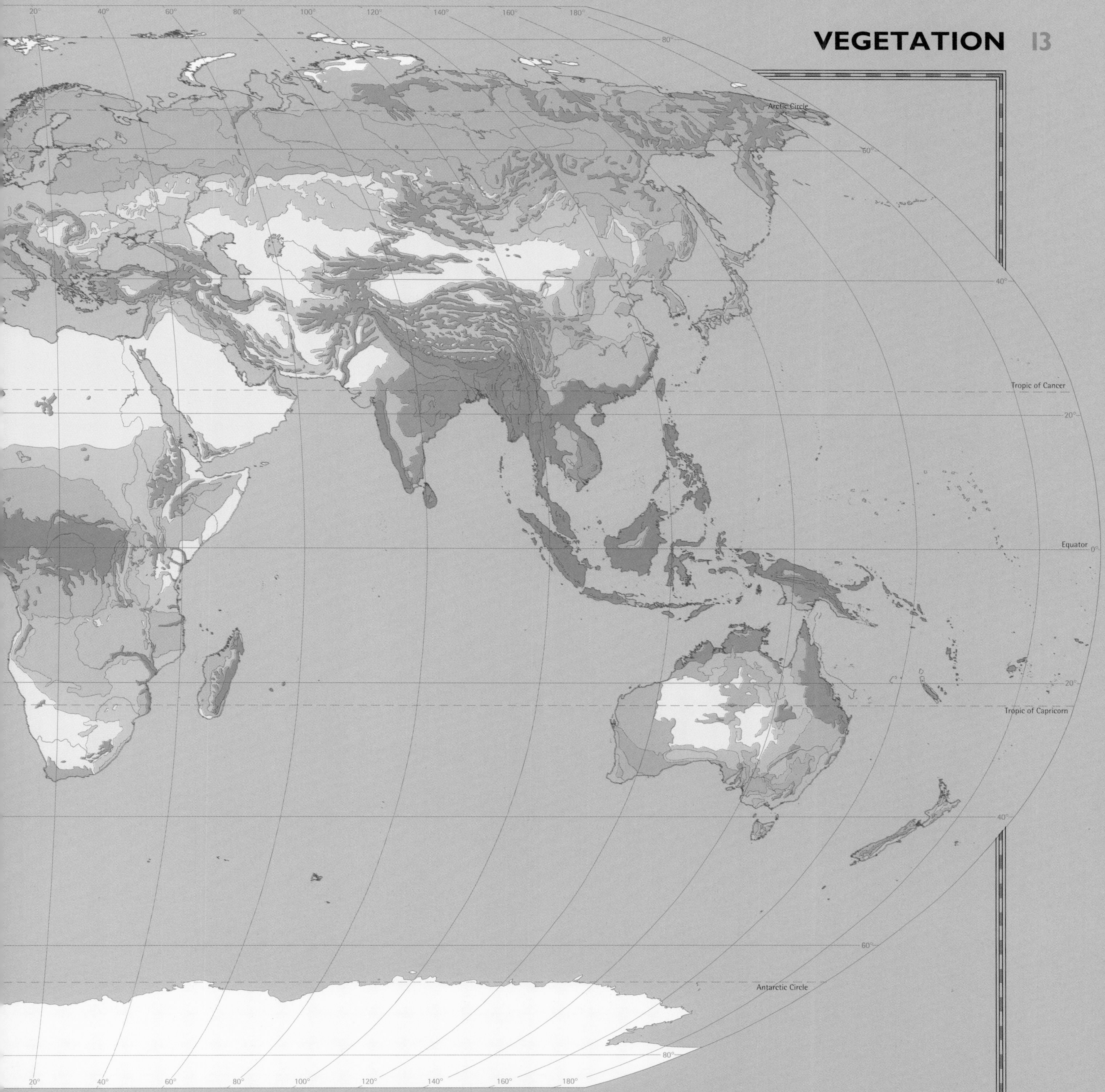
20°
40°
60°
80°
100°
120°
140°
160°
180°
80°
Arctic Circle
60°
40°
Tropic of Cancer
20°
Equator 0°
20°
Tropic of Capricorn
40°
60°
Antarctic Circle
80°

Steppe
Areas of grassland where short grasses are dominant, traditionally the wild grasslands of Euroasia but also found extensively in central North America, central and southern Africa and Australia. Drought resistant grasses grow with colourful flowering herbs.

Savannah
Grassland found in the tropics to the north and south of the tropical rain forests of South America and Africa and around the desert fringes of Australia. Grasses are interspersed with scattered thorn bushes or deciduous trees such as acacia in Africa and eucalypts in Australia.

Tropical rain forest (Selva)
Dense forest located in tropical areas of high rainfall and continuous high temperature, particularly Central America, northern South America, west-central Africa and southeast Asia. Up to three tree layers grow above a variable shrub layer.

Monsoon forest
Deciduous forest mostly occuring in eastern India, parts of Southeast Asia and northern and northeastern Australia, growing in association with the monsoon climate.

Dry tropical forest
Semi-deciduous forest growing in semi-desert areas of South America and the Indian sub-continent where rainfall is usually less than 250mm per annum. Thorny scrub and low to medium sized trees with thick bark and deep roots characterise the vegetation.

Sub-tropical forest
Hardleaf evergreen forests growing between the latitudes of 15° to 40° north and south of the equator in China, Japan, Australia, New Zealand and South Africa.

Dry tropical scrub and thorn forest
Low-growing widely spaced shrubs, bushes and succulents are characteristic of this vegetation growing in extensive areas of Central and South America, Africa, the Indian sub-continent and Australia.

Desert vegetation
Limited vegetation growth in the harsh, dry conditions of desert areas. Xerophytic shrubs, grasses and cacti adapt themselves by relying on the chance occurence of rain, storing water when it is available in short bursts and limiting water loss.

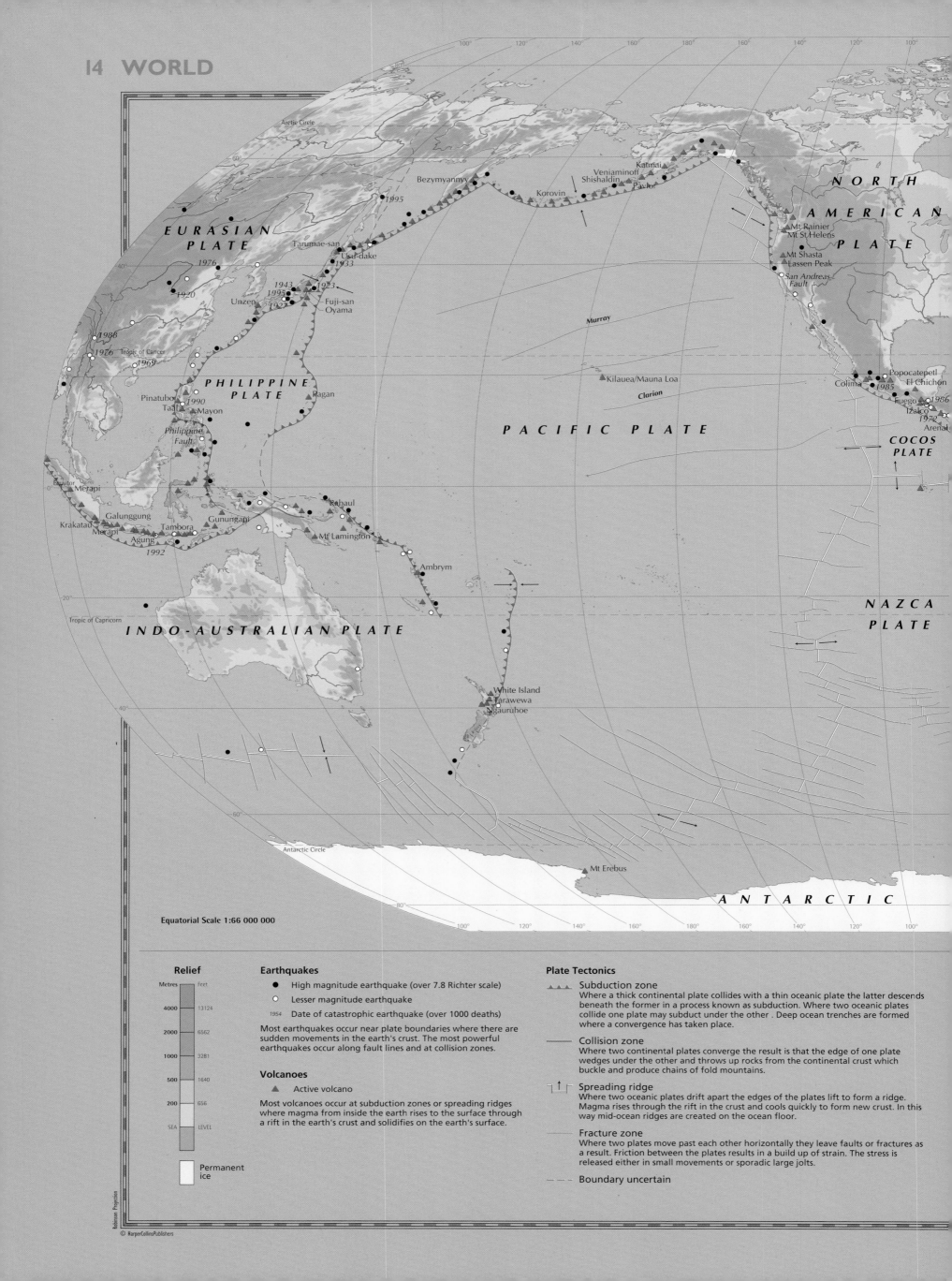

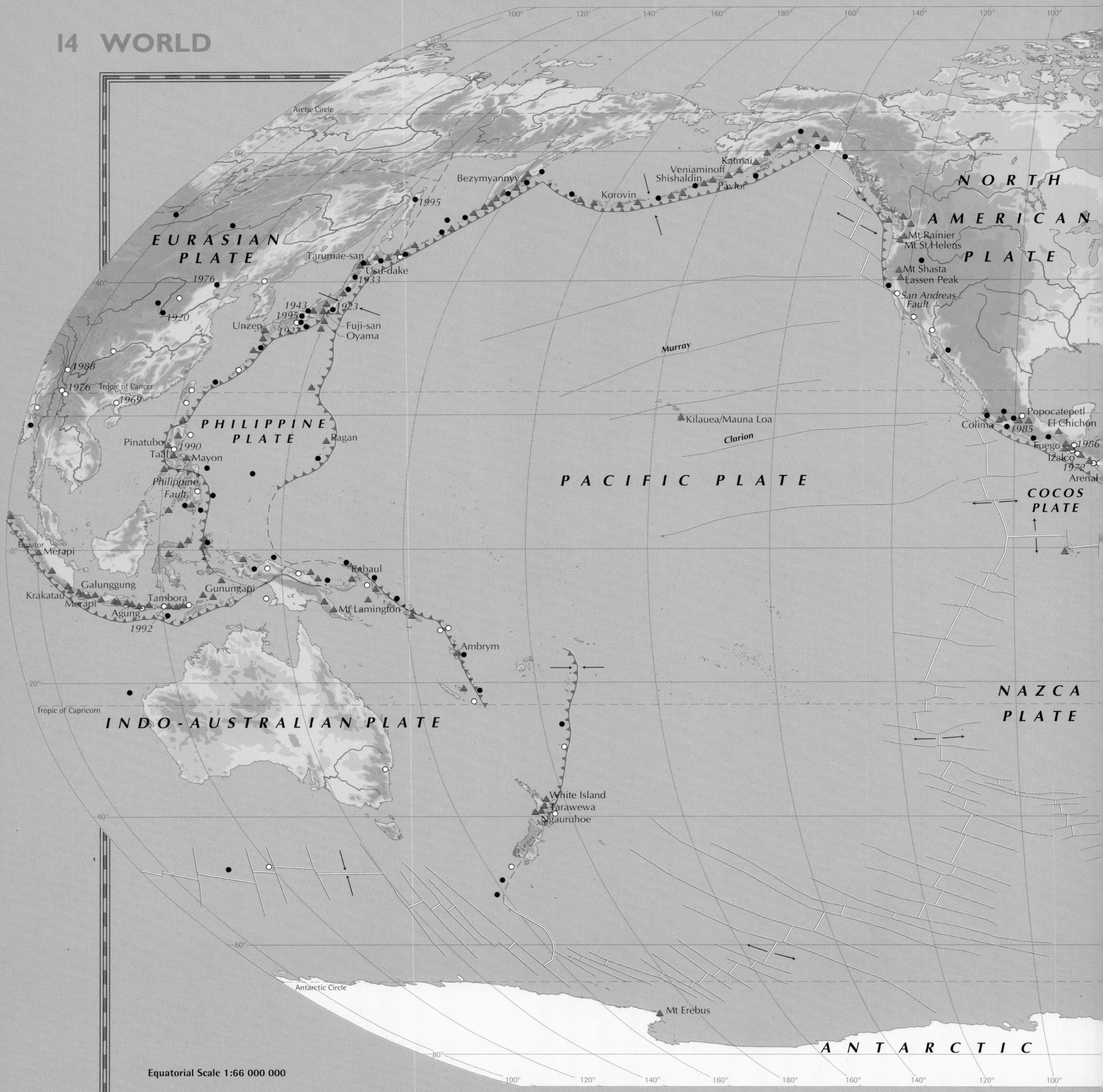
Arctic Circle
Bezymyannyy
Veniaminoff
Katmai
Shishaldin
Pavlof
Korovin
1995
EURASIAN PLATE
NORTH AMERICAN PLATE
Mt Rainier
Mt St Helens
Mt Shasta
Lassen Peak
San Andreas Fault
Tarumae-san
Usu-dake
1933
1976
1920
1943
1995
1923
1927
Unzen
Fuji-san
Oyama
Murray
1988
1976
Tropic of Cancer
1969
PHILIPPINE PLATE
Pinatubo
1990
Taal
Mayon
Pagan
Philippine Fault
Kilauea/Mauna Loa
Clarion
Popocatepetl
Colima
1985
El Chichon
Fuego
1986
Izalco
1972
Arenal
PACIFIC PLATE
COCOS PLATE
Equator
Merapi
Rabaul
Galunggung
Krakatau
Merapi
Gunungapi
Tambora
Agung
1992
Mt Lamington
Ambrym
NAZCA PLATE
Tropic of Capricorn
INDO-AUSTRALIAN PLATE
White Island
Tarawewa
Ngauruhoe
Antarctic Circle
Mt Erebus
ANTARCTIC
100°
120°
140°
160°
180°
160°
140°
120°
100°
80°
60°
40°
20°
0°
-20°
-40°
-60°
-80°

Equatorial Scale 1:66 000 000

Relief

Metres	Feet
4000	13124
2000	6562
1000	3281
500	1640
200	656
SEA	LEVEL

Permanent ice

Earthquakes

- ● High magnitude earthquake (over 7.8 Richter scale)
- ○ Lesser magnitude earthquake
- *1954* Date of catastrophic earthquake (over 1000 deaths)

Most earthquakes occur near plate boundaries where there are sudden movements in the earth's crust. The most powerful earthquakes occur along fault lines and at collision zones.

Volcanoes

- ▲ Active volcano

Most volcanoes occur at subduction zones or spreading ridges where magma from inside the earth rises to the surface through a rift in the earth's crust and solidifies on the earth's surface.

Plate Tectonics

Subduction zone
Where a thick continental plate collides with a thin oceanic plate the latter descends beneath the former in a process known as subduction. Where two oceanic plates collide one plate may subduct under the other . Deep ocean trenches are formed where a convergence has taken place.

Collision zone
Where two continental plates converge the result is that the edge of one plate wedges under the other and throws up rocks from the continental crust which buckle and produce chains of fold mountains.

Spreading ridge
Where two oceanic plates drift apart the edges of the plates lift to form a ridge. Magma rises through the rift in the crust and cools quickly to form new crust. In this way mid-ocean ridges are created on the ocean floor.

Fracture zone
Where two plates move past each other horizontally they leave faults or fractures as a result. Friction between the plates results in a build up of strain. The stress is released either in small movements or sporadic large jolts.

Boundary uncertain

Robinson Projection

© HarperCollinsPublishers

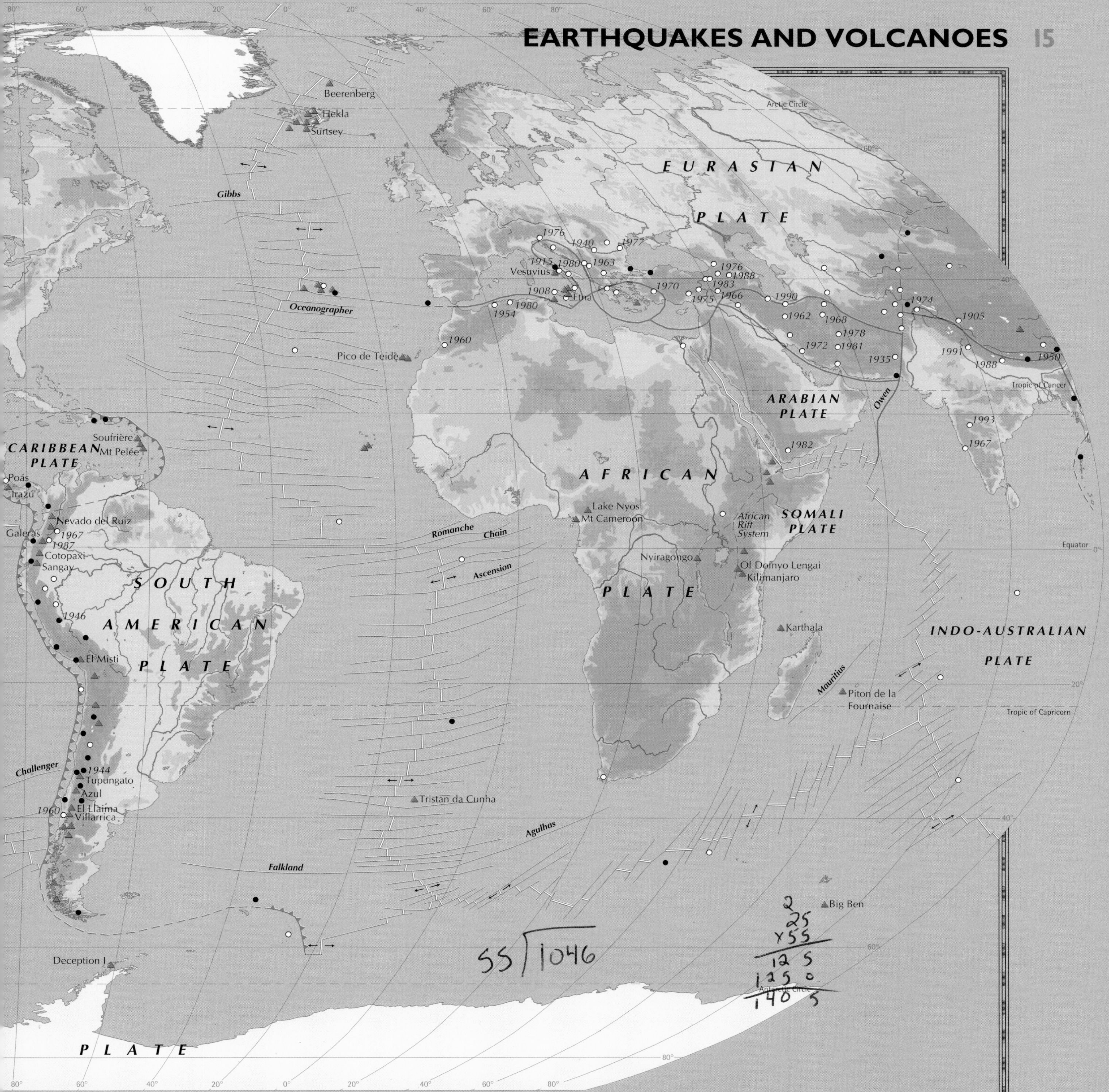
EURASIAN PLATE
ARABIAN PLATE
AFRICAN PLATE
SOMALI PLATE
INDO-AUSTRALIAN PLATE
SOUTH AMERICAN PLATE
CARIBBEAN PLATE
PLATE
Arctic Circle
Tropic of Cancer
Equator
Tropic of Capricorn
Antarctic Circle
Beerenberg
Hekla
Surtsey
Gibbs
Oceanographer
Pico de Teide
Vesuvius
Etna
Soufrière
Mt Pelée
Poás
Irazú
Nevado del Ruiz
Galeras
Cotopaxi
Sangay
El Misti
Tupungato
Azul
El Llaima
Villarrica
Challenger
Romanche
Chain
Ascension
Lake Nyos
Mt Cameroon
African Rift System
Nyiragongo
Ol Doinyo Lengai
Kilimanjaro
Karthala
Mauritius
Piton de la Fournaise
Owen
Tristan da Cunha
Agulhas
Falkland
Big Ben
Deception I
1976
1940
1977
1915
1980
1963
1908
1954
1960
1970
1988
1983
1975
1966
1990
1962
1968
1978
1972
1981
1935
1974
1905
1991
1950
1993
1967
1982
1944
1946
1987
80°
60°
40°
20°
0°

Plate Tectonics

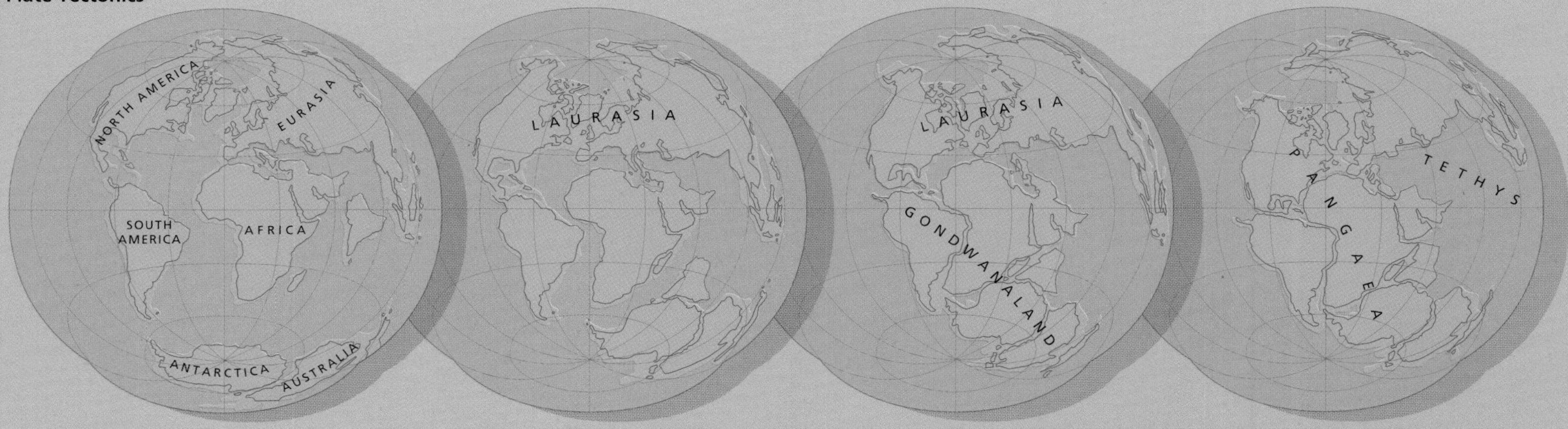
NORTH AMERICA
EURASIA
SOUTH AMERICA
AFRICA
ANTARCTICA
AUSTRALIA
LAURASIA
GONDWANALAND
TETHYS
PANGAEA

50 MILLION YEARS AGO — 100 MILLION YEARS AGO — 150 MILLION YEARS AGO — 200 MILLION YEARS AGO

ENERGY RESOURCES

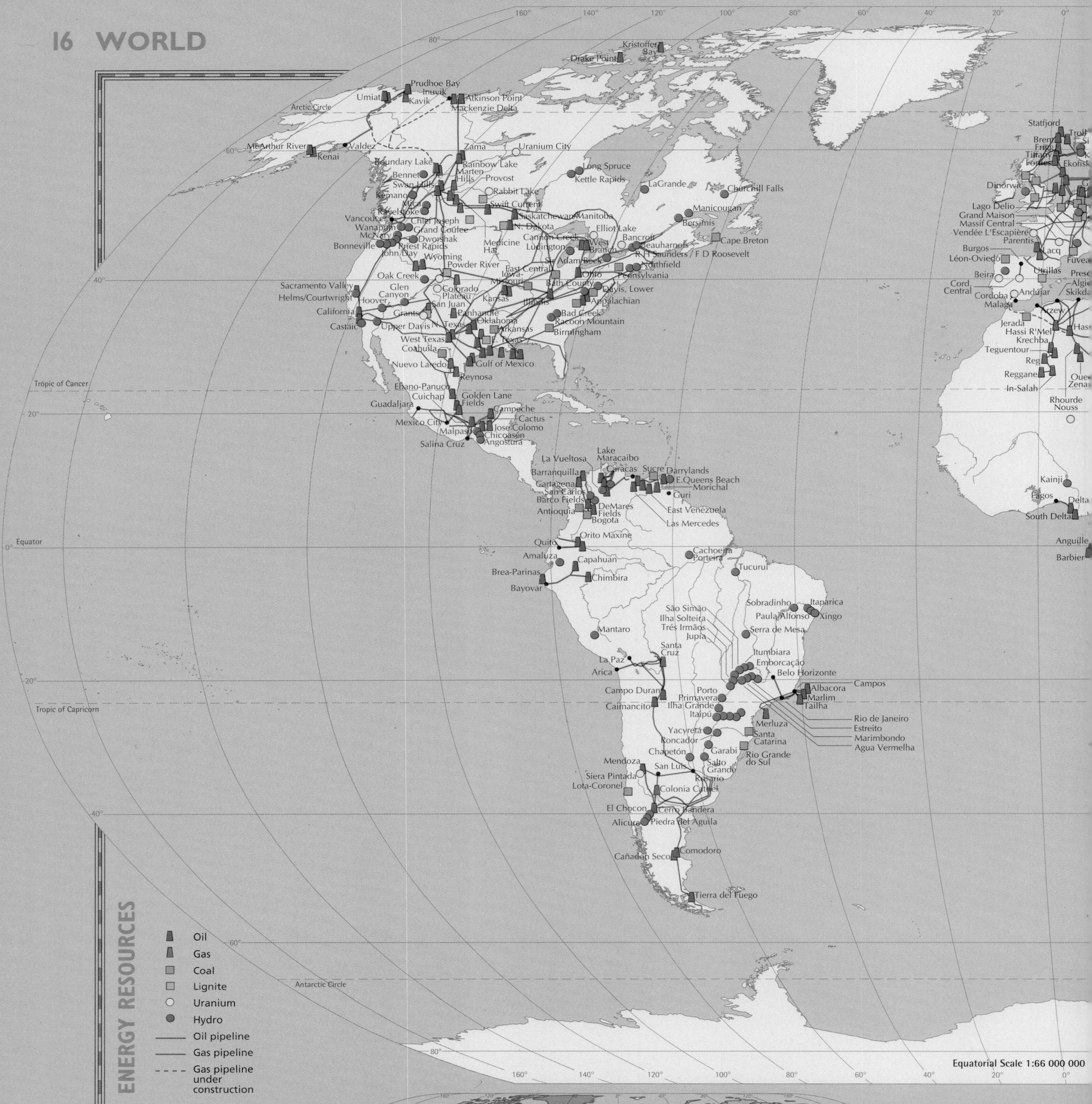

- Oil
- Gas
- Coal
- Lignite
- Uranium
- Hydro
- Oil pipeline
- Gas pipeline
- Gas pipeline under construction

ENERGY PRODUCTION

OIL PRODUCTION 1995

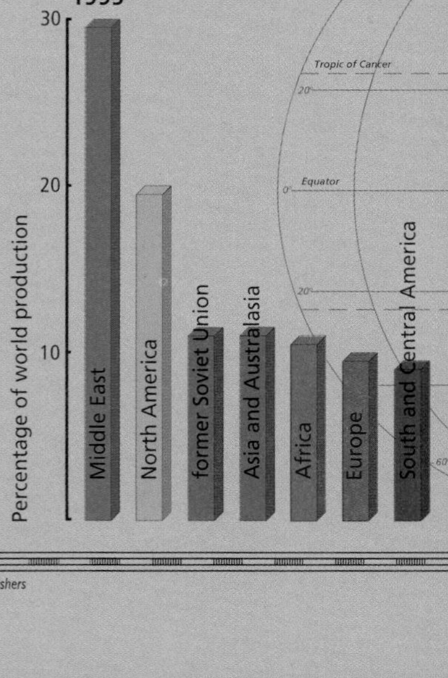

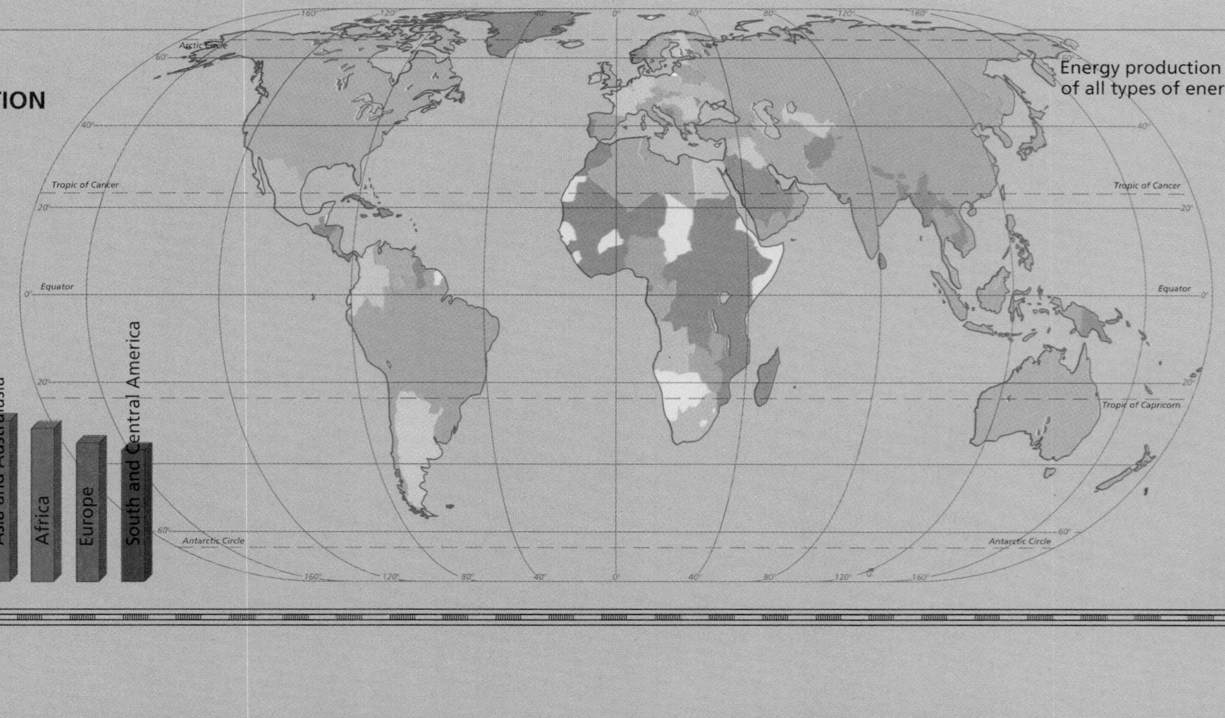

Energy production in kilogram equivalents of all types of energy produced per capita, per year, by country.

kg per capita
- 25000 - 105000
- 2500 - 24999
- 2000 - 2499
- 1454 - 1999
- World average
- 1000 - 1454
- 100 - 999
- 0 - 99
- No data available

Robinson Projection

© HarperCollinsPublishers

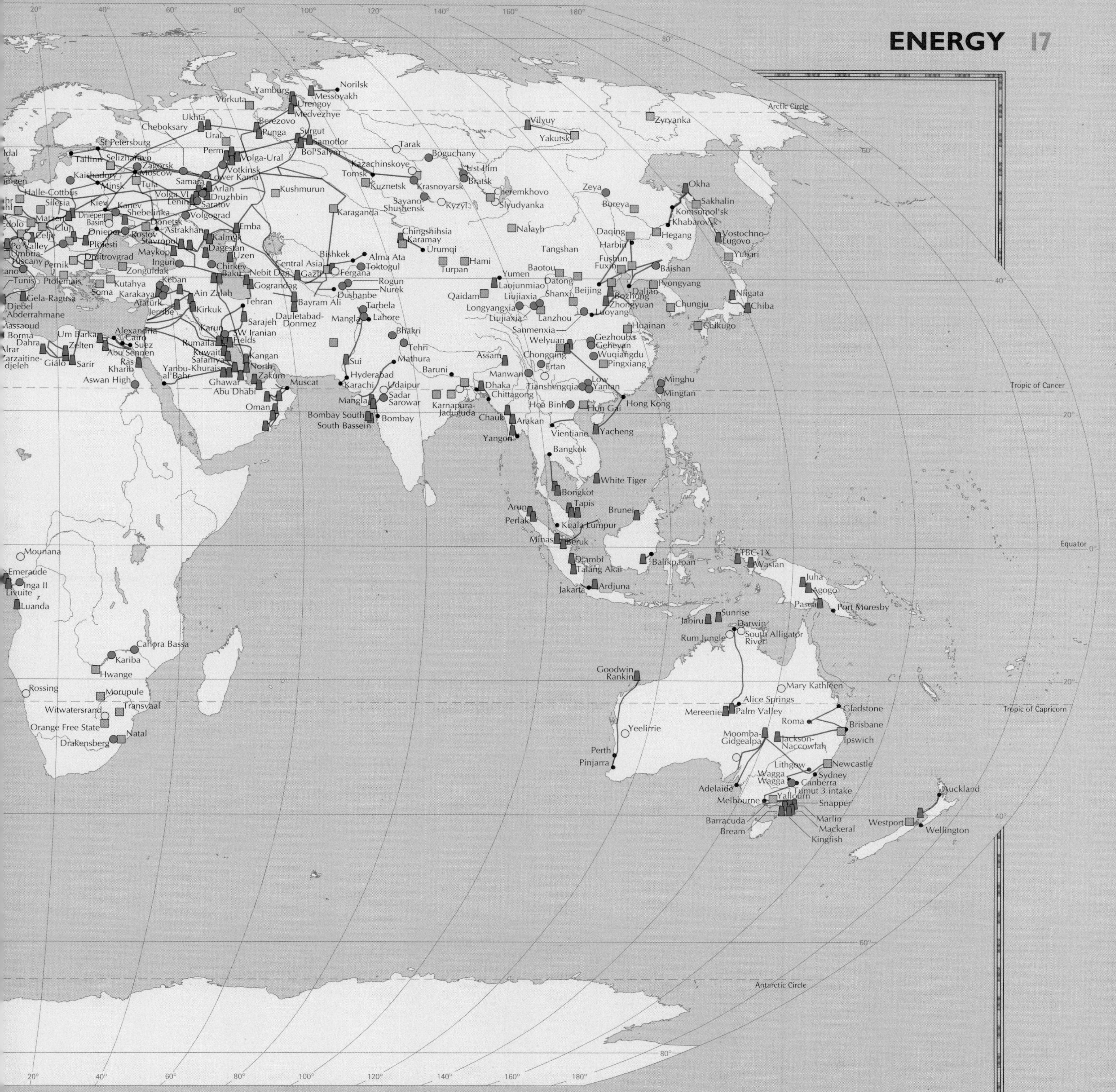

Energy consumption in kilogram equivalents of all types of energy used per capita, per year, by country.

kg per capita

- 25000 - 50000
- 10000 - 24999
- 5000 - 9999
- 1400 - 4999
- World average
- 1000 - 1400
- 500 - 999
- 0 - 499
- No data available

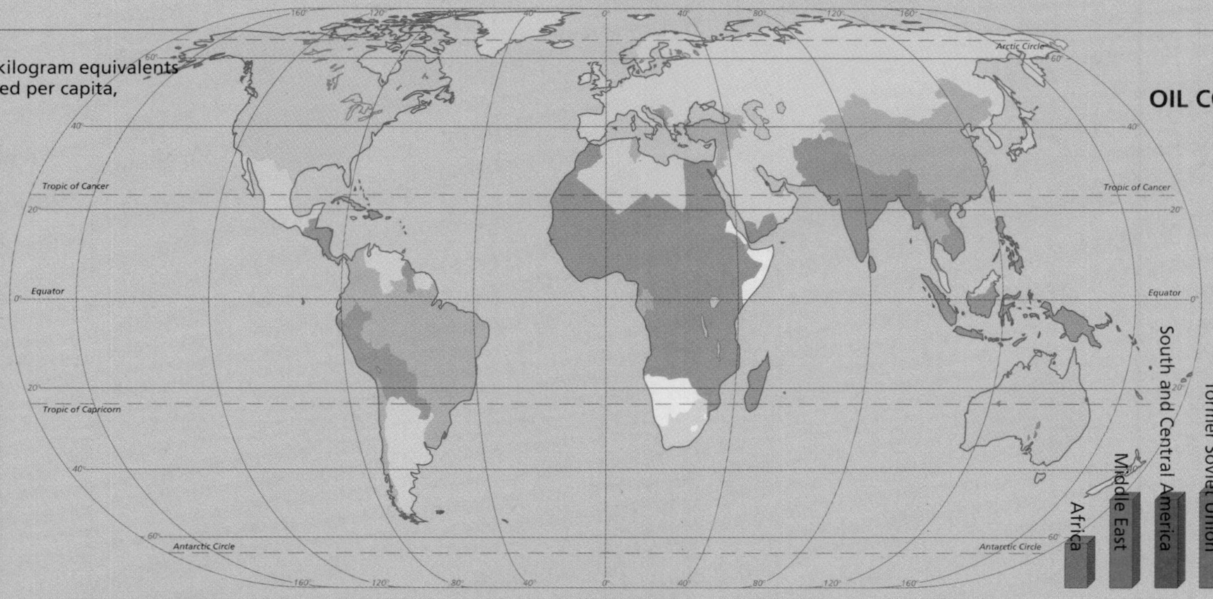

ENERGY CONSUMPTION

OIL CONSUMPTION 1995

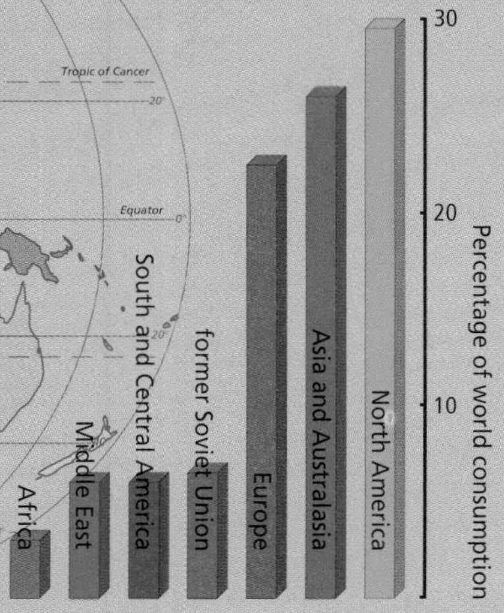

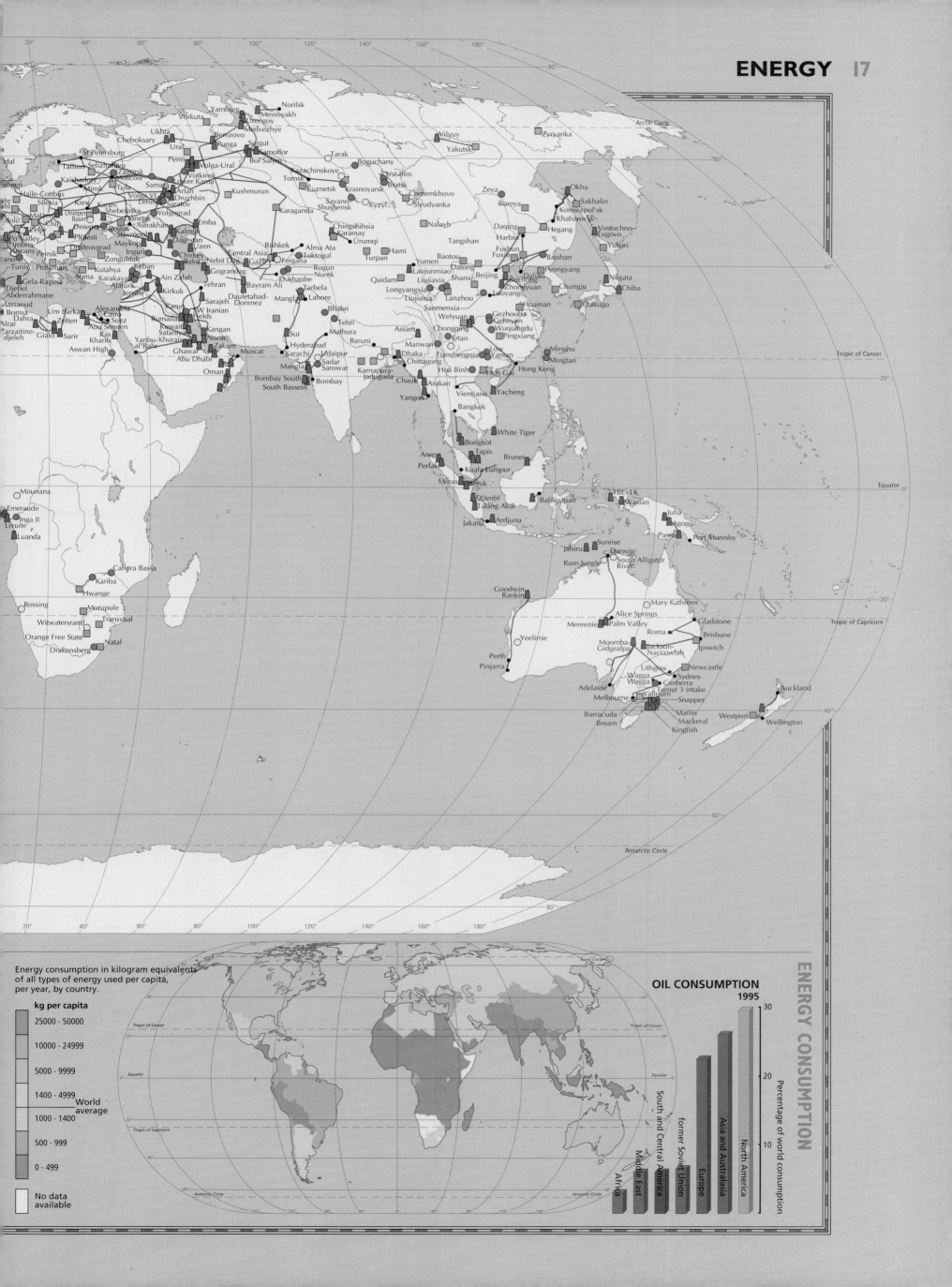

POPULATION DENSITY

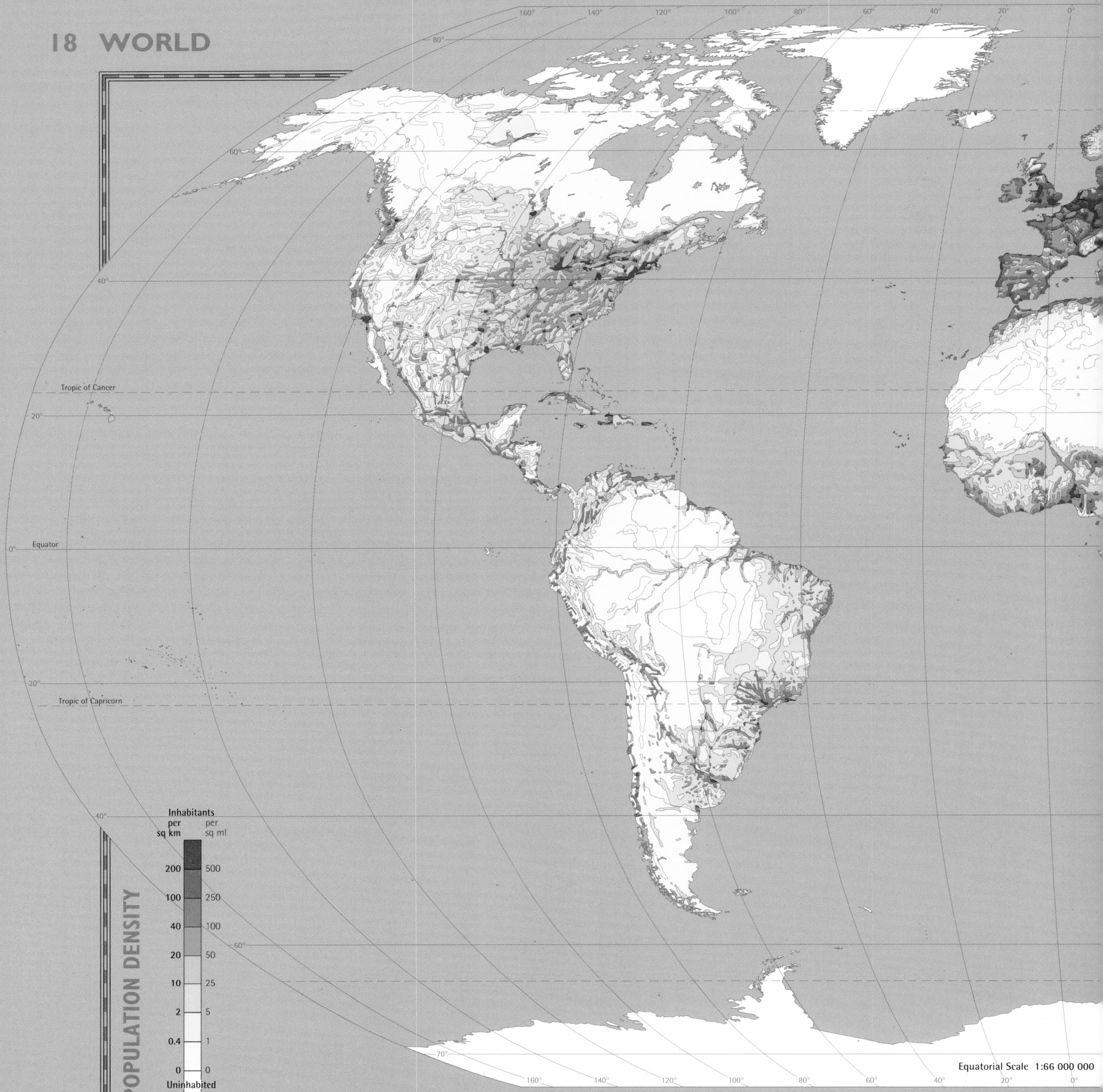

160° 140° 120° 100° 80° 60° 40° 20° 0°
80°
60°
40°
Tropic of Cancer
20°
Equator
0°
20°
Tropic of Capricorn
40°
60°
70°
Inhabitants
per sq km
per sq ml
200 500
100 250
40 100
20 50
10 25
2 5
0.4 1
0 0
Uninhabited
Equatorial Scale 1:66 000 000

POPULATION GROWTH

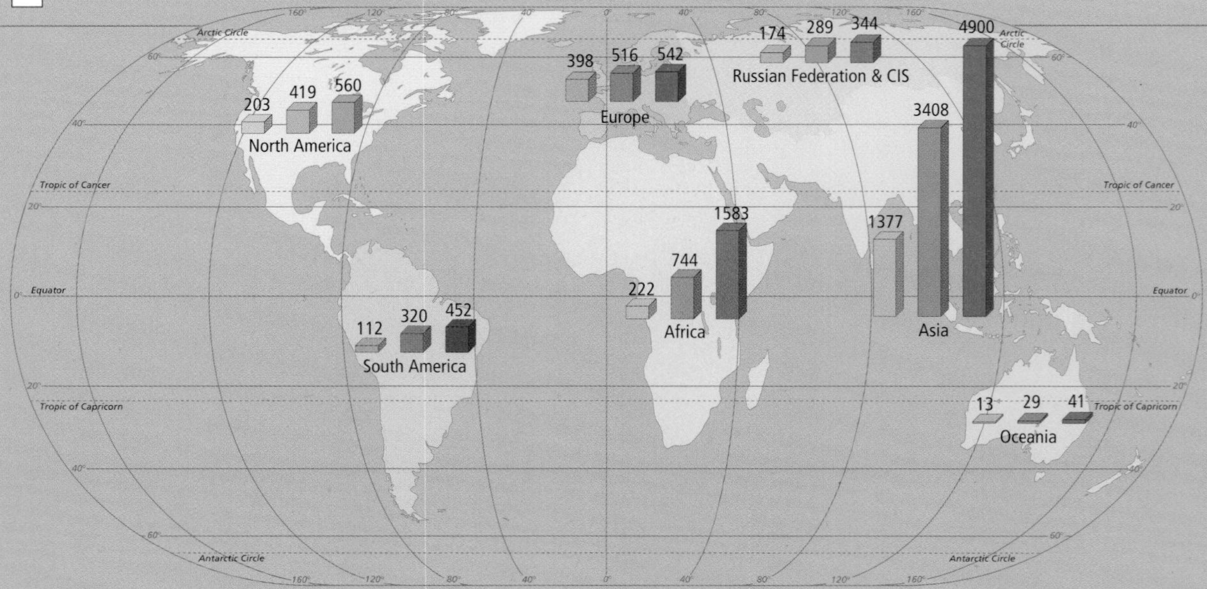

Arctic Circle
Tropic of Cancer
Equator
Tropic of Capricorn
Antarctic Circle
203 419 560
North America
112 320 452
South America
398 516 542
Europe
222 744 1583
Africa
174 289 344
Russian Federation & CIS
1377 3408 4900
Asia
13 29 41
Oceania

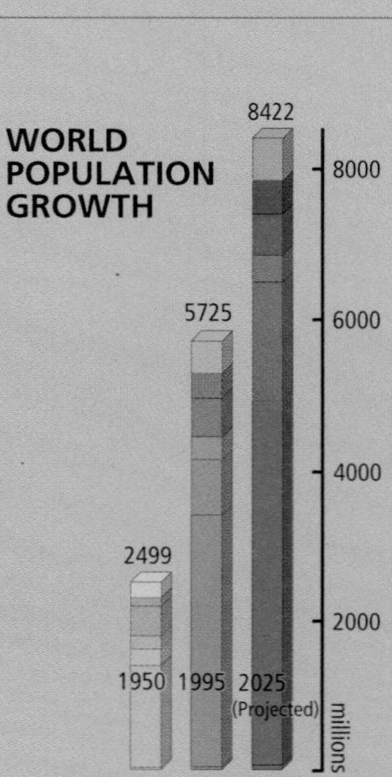

WORLD POPULATION GROWTH
2499
5725
8422
8000
6000
4000
2000
1950 1995 2025 (Projected)
millions

Robinson Projection

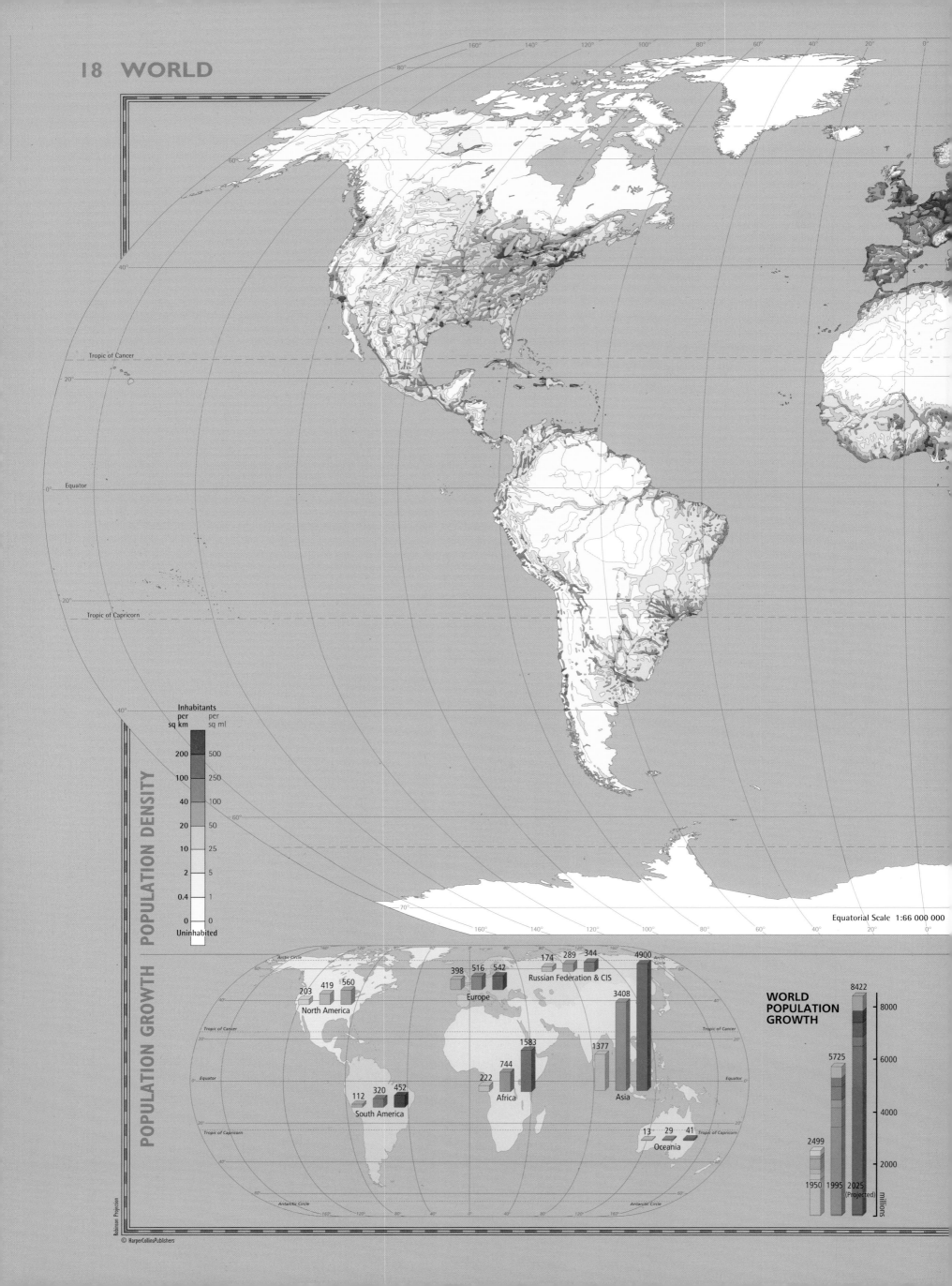

POPULATION CHANGE

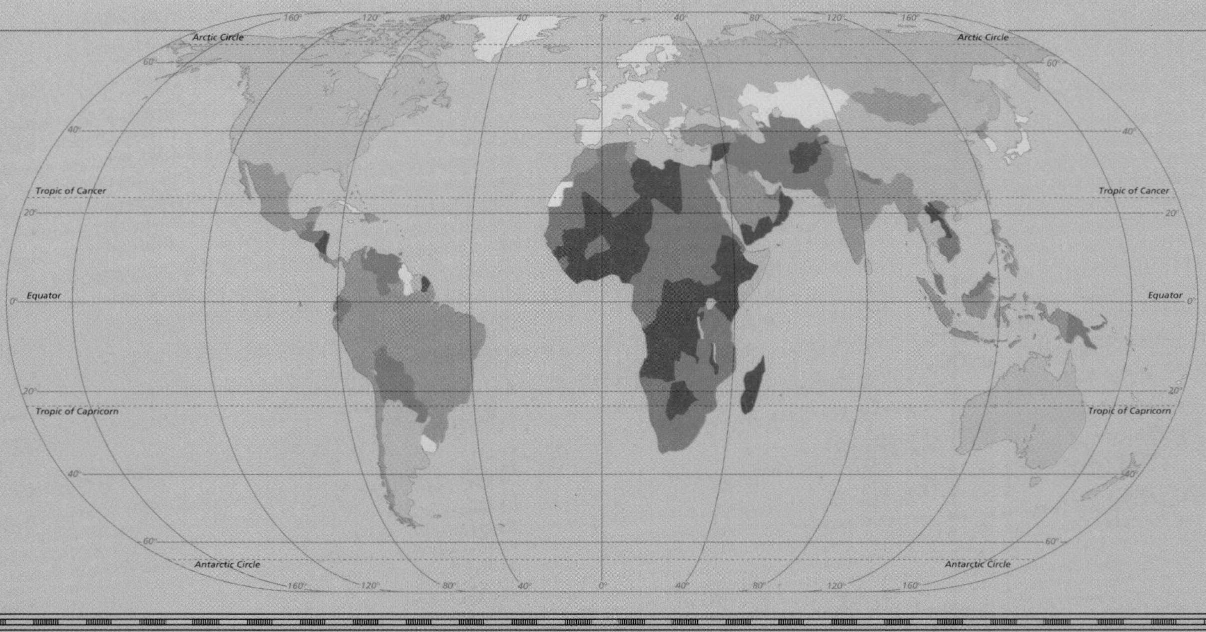

Population change is the average annual percentage increase, or decrease in the population of a country

increase

- 3.0 - 6.0
- 2.2 - 2.9
- 1.5 - 2.1
- 1.0 - 1.4
- 0 - 0.9
- -6.0 - -0.1

decrease

- No data available

GROWTH IN CITY POPULATIONS

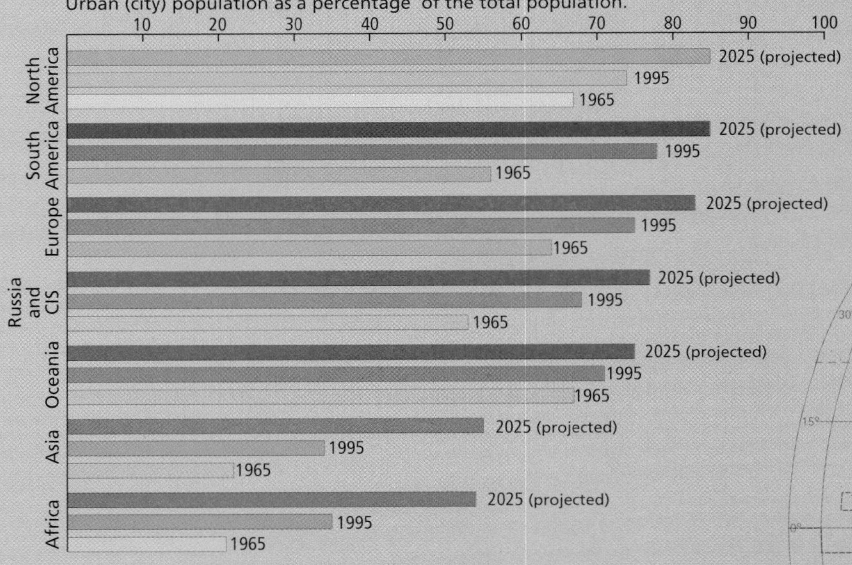

TOTAL CITY DWELLING POPULATION

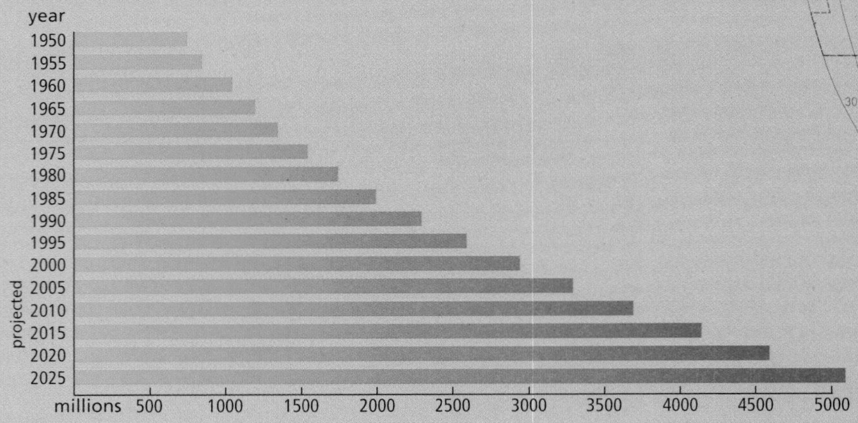

CITY POPULATIONS

The populations given are for metropolitan areas, which may include a number of smaller cities or towns, together forming a mega-city. The total combined population is given either as an estimate or from census returns.

AFGHANISTAN
2,000,000 KABUL

ALGERIA
3,033,000 ALGIERS

ANGOLA
1,717,000 LUANDA

ARGENTINA
12,200,000 BUENOS AIRES
1,179,067 CÓRDOBA
1,078,374 ROSARIO

ARMENIA
1,200,000 YEREVAN

AUSTRALIA
1,065,000 ADELAIDE
1,386,000 BRISBANE
3,178,000 MELBOURNE
1,215,000 PERTH
3,700,000 SYDNEY

AUSTRIA
1,565,800 VIENNA

AZERBAIJAN
1,779,500 BAKU

BANGLADESH
2,040,663 CHITTAGONG
6,105,160 DHAKA

BELARUS
1,633,600 MINSK

BOLIVIA
1,234,000 LA PAZ

BRAZIL
1,334,460 BELEM
3,461,905 BELO HORIZONTE
1,596,274 BRASÍLIA
1,975,624 CURITIBA
2,294,524 FORTALEZA
3,015,960 PÔRTO ALEGRE
2,859,469 RECIFE
9,600,528 RIO DE JANEIRO
2,472,131 SALVADOR
15,199,423 SÃO PAULO

BULGARIA
1,221,000 SOFIA

CANADA
3,127,000 MONTREAL
3,893,000 TORONTO
1,603,000 VANCOUVER

CHILE
4,628,320 SANTIAGO

CHINA
1,370,000 ANSHAN
1,257,000 BAOTOU
10,819,407 BEIJING (PEKING)
2,214,000 CHANGCHUN
1,362,000 CHANGSHA
3,004,000 CHENGDU
3,151,000 CHONGQING
2,543,000 DALIAN
1,420,000 FUSHUN
1,361,000 FUZHOU
3,671,000 GUANGZHOU (CANTON)
1,587,000 GUIYANG
1,412,000 HANGZHOU
2,966,000 HARBIN
1,170,000 HUAINAN
1,327,000 JILIN
2,415,000 JINAN
1,718,000 KUNMING
1,566,000 LANZHOU
1,227,000 LUOYANG
1,415,000 NANCHANG
2,265,000 NANJING
2,040,000 QINGDAO
1,460,000 QIQIHAR
13,341,896 SHANGHAI
4,763,000 SHENYANG
1,352,000 SHIJIAZHUANG
2,199,000 TAIYUAN
1,590,000 TANGSHAN
9,371,000 TIANJIN
3,921,000 WUHAN
2,859,000 XIAN
1,759,000 ZHENGZHOU
2,430,000 ZIBO

COLOMBIA
1,033,951 BARRANQUILLA
5,025,989 BOGOTÁ
1,655,699 CALI
1,594,967 MEDELLÍN

CÔTE D'IVOIRE
2,168,000 ABIDJAN

CROATIA
1,174,512 ZAGREB

CUBA
2,099,000 HAVANA

CZECH REPUBLIC
1,214,174 PRAGUE

DENMARK
1,342,679 COPENHAGEN

DOMINICAN REPUBLIC
2,055,000 SANTO DOMINGO

ECUADOR
1,508,444 GUAYAQUIL
1,100,847 QUITO

EGYPT
3,380,000 ALEXANDRIA
11,642,000 CAIRO
2,096,000 EL GIZA

EL SALVADOR
1,522,126 SAN SALVADOR

ETHIOPIA
1,891,000 ADDIS ABABA

FRANCE
1,230,936 MARSEILLES
9,318,821 PARIS

GEORGIA
1,400,000 TBILISI

GERMANY
3,447,916 BERLIN
2,720,400 ESSEN-DORTMUND
1,669,000 HAMBURG
1,236,500 MUNICH

GREECE
3,097,000 ATHENS

GUATEMALA
1,132,730 GUATEMALA CITY

HAITI
1,402,000 PORT-AU-PRINCE

HONG KONG
5,448,000 HONG KONG

HUNGARY
1,992,343 BUDAPEST

INDIA
3,297,655 AHMADABAD
4,086,548 BANGALORE
12,571,720 BOMBAY
10,916,272 CALCUTTA
8,375,188 DELHI
4,280,261 HYDERABAD
1,514,425 JAIPUR
2,111,284 KANPUR
1,642,134 LUCKNOW
5,361,468 MADRAS
1,661,409 NAGPUR
2,485,014 PUNE

INDONESIA
2,056,915 BANDUNG
9,253,000 JAKARTA
1,730,052 MEDAN
1,249,230 SEMARANG
2,473,272 SURABAYA

IRAN
1,484,000 ISFAHAN
1,882,000 MASHHAD
6,773,000 TEHRAN

IRAQ
4,044,000 BAGHDAD

ISRAEL
1,135,800 TEL AVIV

ITALY
1,358,627 MILAN
1,071,744 NAPLES
2,723,327 ROME
1,002,863 TURIN

JAPAN
1,214,122 FUKUOKA
1,071,898 HIROSHIMA
1,167,604 KAWASAKI
1,015,431 KITAKYUSHU
1,394,964 KYOTO
2,095,393 NAGOYA

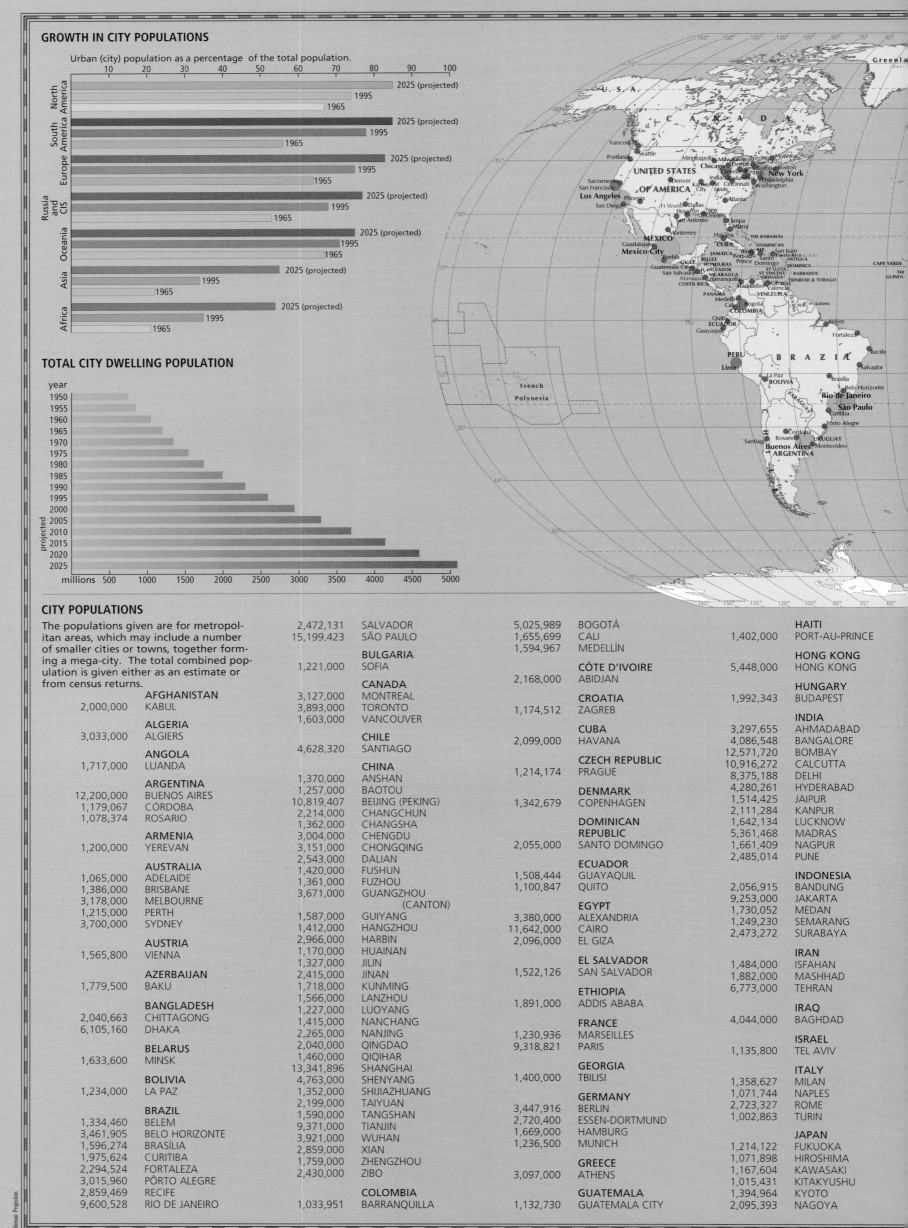

Robinson Projection

over 20 million
10 to 20 million
5 to 10 million
1 to 5 million

Country name abbreviations

AL.	Albania
ARM.	Armenia
AUST.	Austria
AZER.	Azerbaijan
BEL.	Belgium
B.-H.	Bosnia-Herzegovina
BULG.	Bulgaria
B.	Burundi
CR.	Croatia
CZ. R.	Czech Republic
DK	Denmark
EQ. G.	Equatorial Guinea
EST.	Estonia
GEOR.	Georgia
GER.	Germany
GUAT.	Guatemala
HUN.	Hungary
ISR.	Israel
JOR.	Jordan
KYRG.	Kyrgyzstan
LAT.	Latvia
LEB.	Lebanon
LITH.	Lithuania
L.	Luxembourg
M.	Macedonia
MOL.	Moldova
NETH.	Netherlands
NOR.	Norway
PORT.	Portugal
ROM.	Romania
R.	Rwanda
S. T.	São Tome & Principe
SL.	Slovenia
SLA	Slovakia
SUR.	Surinam
SW.	Switzerland
TAJIK.	Tajikistan
TURKMEN.	Turkmenistan
U.A.E.	United Arab Emirates
UZBEK.	Uzbekistan
YU.	Yugoslavia

MILLION CITIES

- 8,520,000 OSAKA-KOBE
- 1,704,135 SAPPORO
- 11,609,735 TOKYO
- 3,250,548 YOKOHAMA

JORDAN
- 1,272,000 AMMAN

KAZAKHSTAN
- 1,151,300 ALMA-ATA

KENYA
- 1,503,000 NAIROBI

KOREA, NORTH
- 2,230,000 PYONGYANG

KOREA, SOUTH
- 1,818,293 INCHON
- 3,797,566 PUSAN
- 10,627,000 SEOUL
- 2,228,834 TAEGU

LEBANON
- 1,500,000 BEIRUT

LIBYA
- 1,500,000 TRIPOLI

MALAYSIA
- 1,711,000 KUALA LUMPUR

MEXICO
- 2,846,720 GUADALAJARA
- 20,200,000 MEXICO CITY
- 2,521,697 MONTERREY
- 1,267,000 PUEBLA DE ZARAGOZA

MOROCCO
- 3,210,000 CASABLANCA
- 1,472,000 RABAT

MOZAMBIQUE
- 1,098,000 MAPUTO

MYANMAR
- 3,295,000 RANGOON

NETHERLANDS
- 1,091,338 AMSTERDAM
- 1,069,356 ROTTERDAM

NICARAGUA
- 1,012,000 MANAGUA

NIGERIA
- 5,689,000 LAGOS

PAKISTAN
- 1,507,000 FAISALABAD
- 7,702,000 KARACHI
- 4,092,000 LAHORE
- 1,099,000 RAWALPINDI

PERU
- 6,483,901 LIMA

PHILIPPINES
- 7,832,000 MANILA - QUEZON CITY

POLAND
- 1,655,700 WARSAW

PORTUGAL
- 1,742,000 LISBON
- 1,314,794 OPORTO

PUERTO RICO
- 1,390,000 SAN JUAN

ROMANIA
- 2,350,984 BUCHAREST

RUSSIAN FEDERATION
- 1,143,000 CHELYABINSK
- 1,104,000 KAZAN
- 8,957,000 MOSCOW
- 1,441,000 NIZHNIY NOVGOROD
- 1,442,000 NOVOSIBIRSK
- 1,269,000 OMSK
- 1,099,000 PERM
- 1,027,000 ROSTOV-ON-DON
- 1,239,000 SAMARA
- 5,004,000 ST PETERSBURG
- 1,097,000 UFA
- 1,006,000 VOLGOGRAD
- 1,371,000 YEKATERINBURG

SAUDI ARABIA
- 1,800,000 JEDDAH
- 1,500,000 RIYADH

SENEGAL
- 1,492,000 DAKAR

SINGAPORE
- 2,874,000 SINGAPORE

SOUTH AFRICA
- 2,350,157 CAPE TOWN
- 1,137,378 DURBAN
- 1,916,063 JOHANNESBURG

SPAIN
- 1,652,542 BARCELONA
- 2,909,792 MADRID

SUDAN
- 1,947,000 KHARTOUM

SWEDEN
- 1,669,840 STOCKHOLM

SYRIA
- 2,769,000 ALEPPO
- 2,913,000 DAMASCUS

TAIWAN
- 1,400,000 KAOHSIUNG
- 2,720,000 TAIPEI

TANZANIA
- 1,657,000 DAR-ES-SALAAM

THAILAND
- 5,876,000 BANGKOK

TUNISIA
- 1,636,000 TUNIS

TURKEY
- 3,022,236 ANKARA
- 6,407,215 ISTANBUL
- 2,665,105 IZMIR

UK
- 2,329,600 BIRMINGHAM
- 1,784,000 LEEDS
- 1,440,900 LIVERPOOL
- 9,227,687 LONDON
- 2,578,900 MANCHESTER

UKRAINE
- 1,187,000 DNEPROPETROVSK
- 1,117,000 DONETSK
- 1,618,000 KHARKOV
- 2,616,000 KIEV
- 1,106,000 ODESSA

URUGUAY
- 1,383,660 MONTEVIDEO

USA
- 3,051,000 ATLANTA
- 2,414,000 BALTIMORE
- 4,497,000 BOSTON
- 1,193,000 BUFFALO
- 7,498,000 CHICAGO
- 1,539,000 CINCINNATI
- 2,213,000 CLEVELAND
- 1,370,000 COLUMBUS
- 4,135,000 DALLAS - FORT WORTH
- 1,668,000 DENVER
- 4,285,000 DETROIT
- 3,437,000 HOUSTON
- 1,406,000 INDIANAPOLIS
- 1,602,000 KANSAS CITY
- 11,420,000 LOS ANGELES
- 3,264,000 MIAMI
- 1,446,000 MILWAUKEE
- 2,583,000 MINNEAPOLIS - ST PAUL
- 1,295,000 NEW ORLEANS
- 16,972,000 NEW YORK
- 4,941,000 PHILADELPHIA
- 2,287,000 PHOENIX
- 2,404,000 PITTSBURG
- 1,570,000 PORTLAND
- 1,073,000 ROCHESTER
- 1,388,000 SACRAMENTO
- 1,348,000 SAN ANTONIO
- 2,549,000 SAN DIEGO
- 5,240,000 SAN FRANCISCO
- 2,078,000 SEATTLE
- 2,507,000 ST LOUIS
- 2,101,000 TAMPA - ST PETERSBURG
- 4,293,000 WASHINGTON D.C.

UZBEKISTAN
- 2,094,000 TASHKENT

VENEZUELA
- 4,092,000 CARACAS
- 1,400,643 MARACAIBO
- 1,274,354 VALENCIA

VIETNAM
- 1,447,523 HAIPHONG
- 1,056,146 HANOI
- 3,924,435 HO CHI MINH

YUGOSLAVIA
- 1,168,454 BELGRADE

ZAIRE (CONGO)
- 3,505,000 KINSHASA

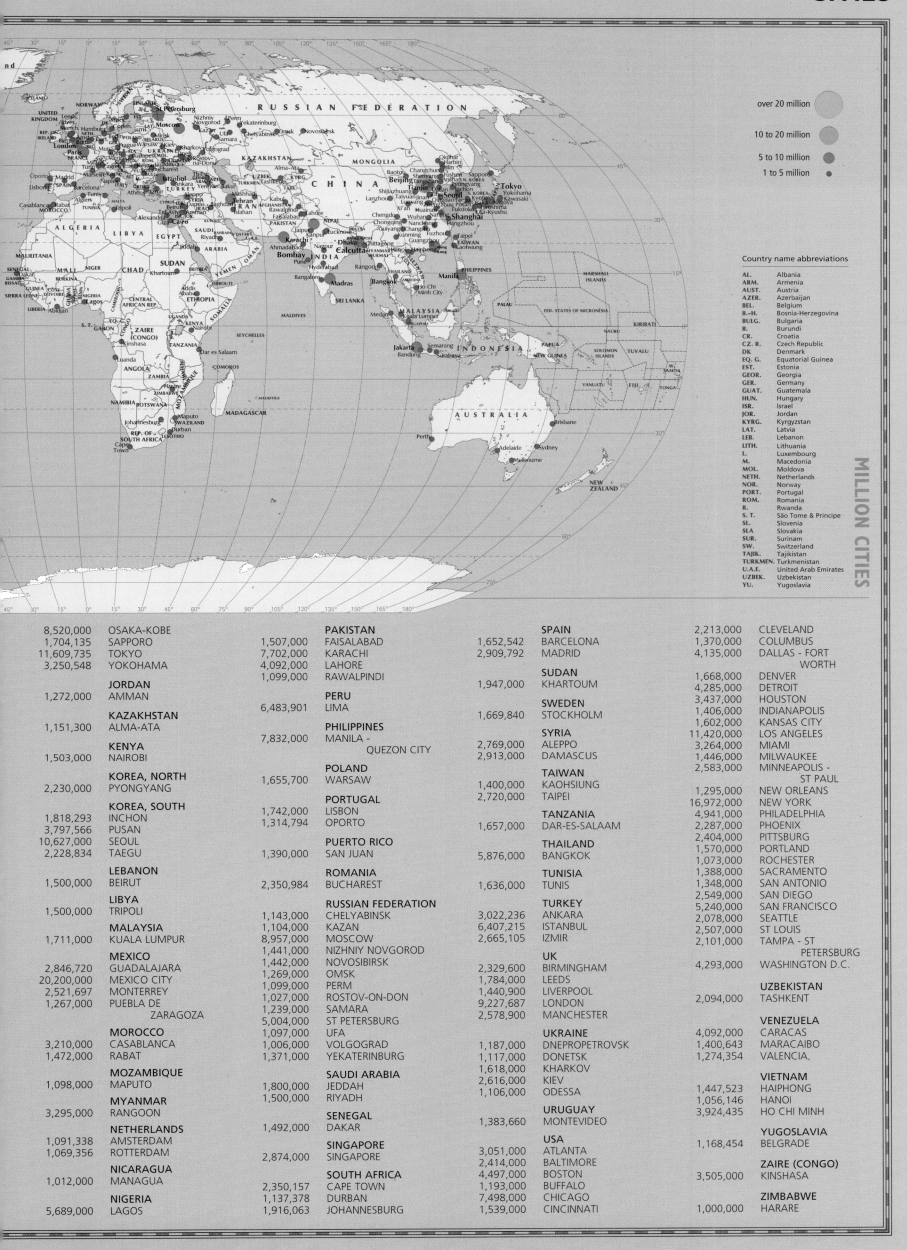

ZIMBABWE
- 1,000,000 HARARE

ARCTIC OCEAN
Greenland (Den.)
Parry Islands
Melville I.
Devon I.
Ellesmere Island
Dundas
Banks I.
Victoria Island
Beaufort Sea
Baffin Bay
Baffin Island
Davis Str.
Scoresbysund
Jan Mayen (Nor.)
Arctic Circle
Denmark Str.
Tasiilaq
Godthåb
ICELAND
Reykjavík
Faeroes (Den.)
NORWAY
Bergen
Barrow
Point Hope
Bering Strait
Nome
Yukon
Fairbanks
U.S.A.
Inuvik
Coppermine
Mackenzie
Great Bear L.
Great Slave L.
Anchorage
Seward
Whitehorse
Juneau
Hay River
Churchill
Hudson Bay
Ivujivik
Frederikshåb
UNITED KINGDOM
North Sea
Glasgow
Edinburgh
DK
Dublin
REP. OF IRELAND
Birm.
NETH.
Amst.
London
BEL.
Brussels
Paris
Aleutian Is
Prince Rupert
CANADA
Edmonton
Fraser
Saskatoon
Regina
Winnipeg
Schefferville
Fort Rupert
Sept-Îles
Goose Bay
Newfoundland
St John's
Vancouver
Victoria
Calgary
Seattle
Portland
Duluth
L. Superior
Quebec
Ottawa
Montreal
Toronto
St John
Halifax
Minneapolis
Lake Michigan
Detroit
Buffalo
Boston
UNITED STATES OF AMERICA
Omaha
Chicago
Pittsb.
New York
Philadelphia
Washington
Indian.
Cincinnati
Salt Lake City
Sacramento
San Francisco
Denver
Kansas City
St Louis
Colorado
Mississippi
Memphis
Norfolk
Oklahoma City
Los Angeles
Phoenix
Atlanta
Birmingham
San Diego
El Paso
Ft Worth
Dallas
Houston
New Orleans
Jacksonville
Grande
San Antonio
Tampa
Miami
Gulf of Mexico
Bermuda (U.K.)
NORTH ATLANTIC OCEAN
Azores (Port.)
Madeira (Port.)
Canary Is (Sp.)
Bay of Biscay
Bordeaux
FRANCE
SW.
Bern
Marseille
Oporto
Bilbao
Madrid
PORT.
SPAIN
Barcelona
Valencia
Lisbon
Tangier
Gibraltar (U.K.)
Algiers
Tunis
TUNISIA
Rabat
Casablanca
MOROCCO
Marrakesh
ALGERIA
Laâyoune
Western Sahara
Tamanrasset
NORTH PACIFIC OCEAN
Guadalupe I. (Mex.)
Torreón
Monterrey
MEXICO
Tampico
Nassau
THE BAHAMAS
Havana
CUBA
Hawaiian Is
U. S. A.
Honolulu
Hawaii
Hilo
Revillagigedo Is. (Mex)
Guadalajara
Mexico City
Veracruz
Puebla
Belmopan
BELIZE
JAMAICA
Kingston
HAITI
DOMINICAN REP.
Santo Domingo
San Juan
Puerto Rico (U.S.A.)
ANTIGUA
Acapulco
GUAT.
Guatemala City
HONDURAS
Tegucigalpa
Caribbean Sea
DOMINICA
ST LUCIA
ST VINCENT
BARBADOS
GRENADA
TRINIDAD & TOBAGO
Port of Spain
EL SALVADOR
NICARAGUA
Managua
Barranquilla
COSTA RICA
San José
PANAMA
Panama City
Caracas
VENEZUELA
Orinoco
Georgetown
GUYANA
Paramaribo
SUR.
Fr. Guiana
Medellín
Bucaramanga
Cali
Bogotá
COLOMBIA
Clipperton I. (Fr.)
MAURITANIA
Nouakchott
CAPE VERDE
SENEGAL
Dakar
THE GAMBIA
GUINEA-BISSAU
Bissau
GUINEA
Conakry
Freetown
SIERRA LEONE
Monrovia
LIBERIA
Bamako
MALI
Mopti
BURKINA
Ouagadougou
CÔTE D'IVOIRE
Yamoussoukro
Abidjan
GHANA
TOGO
BENIN
Accra
Lomé
NIGERIA
Lagos
Abuja
Niamey
NIGER
Gao
Arlit
Equator
Galapagos Is (Ecuador)
Quito
ECUADOR
Guayaquil
Macapá
Belém
Amazon
Manaus
São Luís
Fortaleza
Fernando de Noronha (Braz.)
Libreville
S. T.
Port Gentil
GABON
Marquesas Is (Fr.)
Samoa (U.S.A.)
Tuamotu Islands (Fr.)
Cook Islands (N.Z.)
Society Islands (Fr.)
Tahiti
French Polynesia
Rarotonga
Porto Velho
PERU
BRAZIL
Callao
Lima
Cusco
Recife
São Francisco
Salvador
Arequipa
La Paz
BOLIVIA
Brasília
Iquique
Sucre
Belo Horizonte
St Helena (U.K.)
SOUTH ATLANTIC OCEAN
Martin Vaz Is (Braz.)
Trindade (Braz.)
Rio de Janeiro
São Paulo
Antofagasta
PARAGUAY
Asunción
Curitiba
Pitcairn I. (U.K.)
I. Sala y Gómez (Chile)
Easter I. (Chile)
San Félix (Chile)
Tucumán
Paraná
Coquimbo
Pôrto Alegre
SOUTH PACIFIC OCEAN
Córdoba
Valparaíso
Santiago
Rosario
URUGUAY
Juan Fernandez Is (Chile)
Buenos Aires
Montevideo
ARGENTINA
CHILE
Concepción
Bahía Blanca
Tristan da Cunha (U.K.)
Gough I. (U.K.)
Puerto Montt
Falkland Islands (U.K.)
Stanley
Shag Rocks (U.K.)
South Georgia (U.K.)
Bouvet I. (Nor.)
Punta Arenas
Ushuaia
Cape Horn
Scotia Sea
South Sandwich Is (U.K.)
Drake Passage
South Shetland Is (U.K.)
South Orkney Is (U.K.)
Antarctic Peninsula
Thurston I.
Bellingshausen Sea
Alexander I.
Amundsen Sea
Ellsworth Land
Marie Byrd Land
Weddell Sea
Queen Maud Land
Equatorial Scale 1:66 000 000

Country name abbreviations

AL.	Albania	LITH.	Lithuania
A.	Andorra	L.	Luxembourg
ARM.	Armenia	M.	Macedonia
AUST.	Austria	MOL.	Moldova
AZER.	Azerbaijan	NETH.	Netherlands
BEL.	Belgium	NOR.	Norway
B.-H.	Bosnia-Herzegovina	PORT.	Portugal
BULG.	Bulgaria	ROM.	Romania
B.	Burundi	R. F.	Russian Federation
CR.	Croatia	R.	Rwanda
CZ. R.	Czech Republic	S. T.	São Tome & Principe
DK	Denmark	SL.	Slovenia
EQ. G.	Equatorial Guinea	SLA	Slovakia
EST.	Estonia	SP.	Spain
GEOR.	Georgia	SUR.	Surinam
GER.	Germany	SW.	Switzerland
GUAT.	Guatemala	TAJIK.	Tajikistan
HUN.	Hungary	TURKMEN.	Turkmenistan
ISR.	Israel	U.A.E.	United Arab Emirates
JOR.	Jordan	U. S. A.	United States of America
KYRG.	Kyrgyzstan	UZBEK.	Uzbekistan
LAT.	Latvia	YU.	Yugoslavia
LEB.	Lebanon		

LANGUAGES

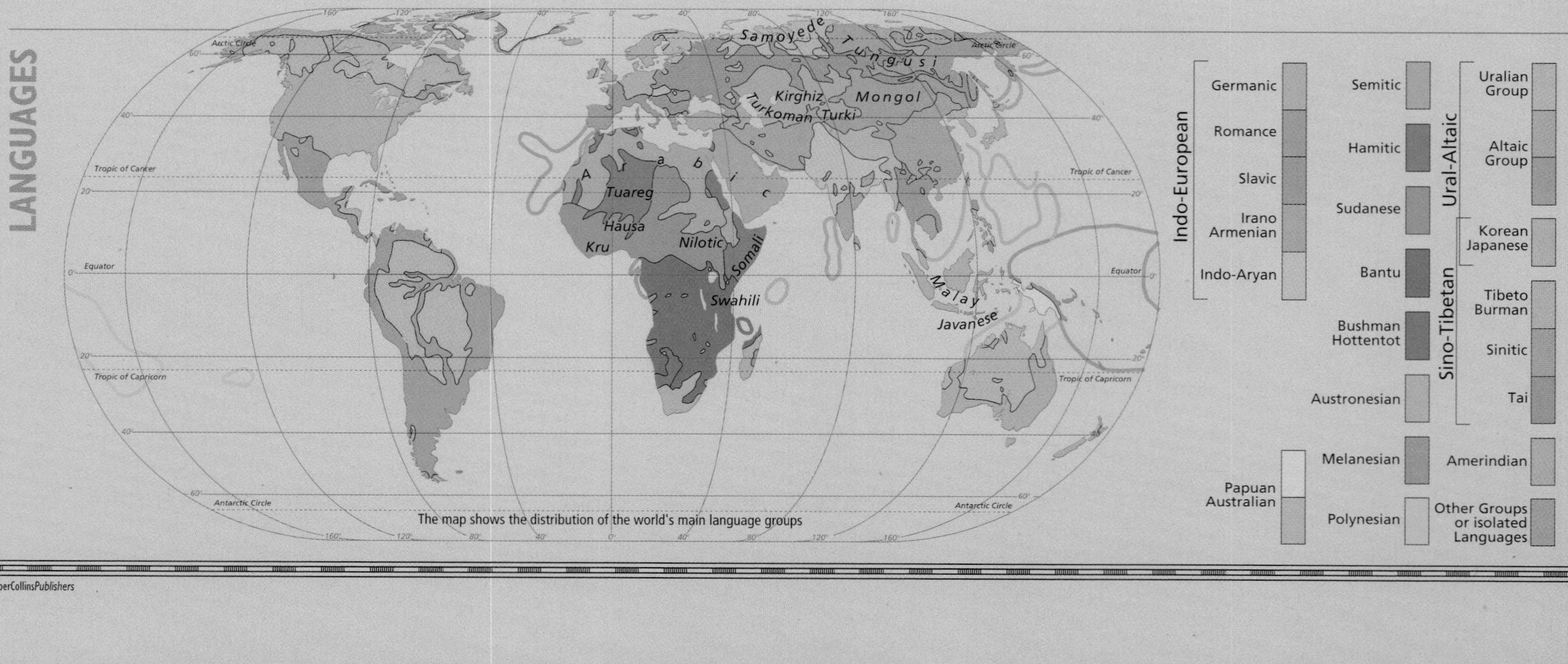

Arctic Circle
Tropic of Cancer
Equator
Tropic of Capricorn
Antarctic Circle
Samoyede
Tungus
Kirghiz
Mongol
Turkoman
Turki
Arabic
Tuareg
Hausa
Kru
Nilotic
Somali
Swahili
Malay
Javanese
Germanic
Romance
Slavic
Irano Armenian
Indo-Aryan
Indo-European
Semitic
Hamitic
Sudanese
Bantu
Bushman Hottentot
Austronesian
Melanesian
Papuan Australian
Polynesian
Uralian Group
Altaic Group
Ural-Altaic
Korean Japanese
Tibeto Burman
Sinitic
Tai
Sino-Tibetan
Amerindian
Other Groups or isolated Languages

The map shows the distribution of the world's main language groups

Robinson Projection

© HarperCollinsPublishers

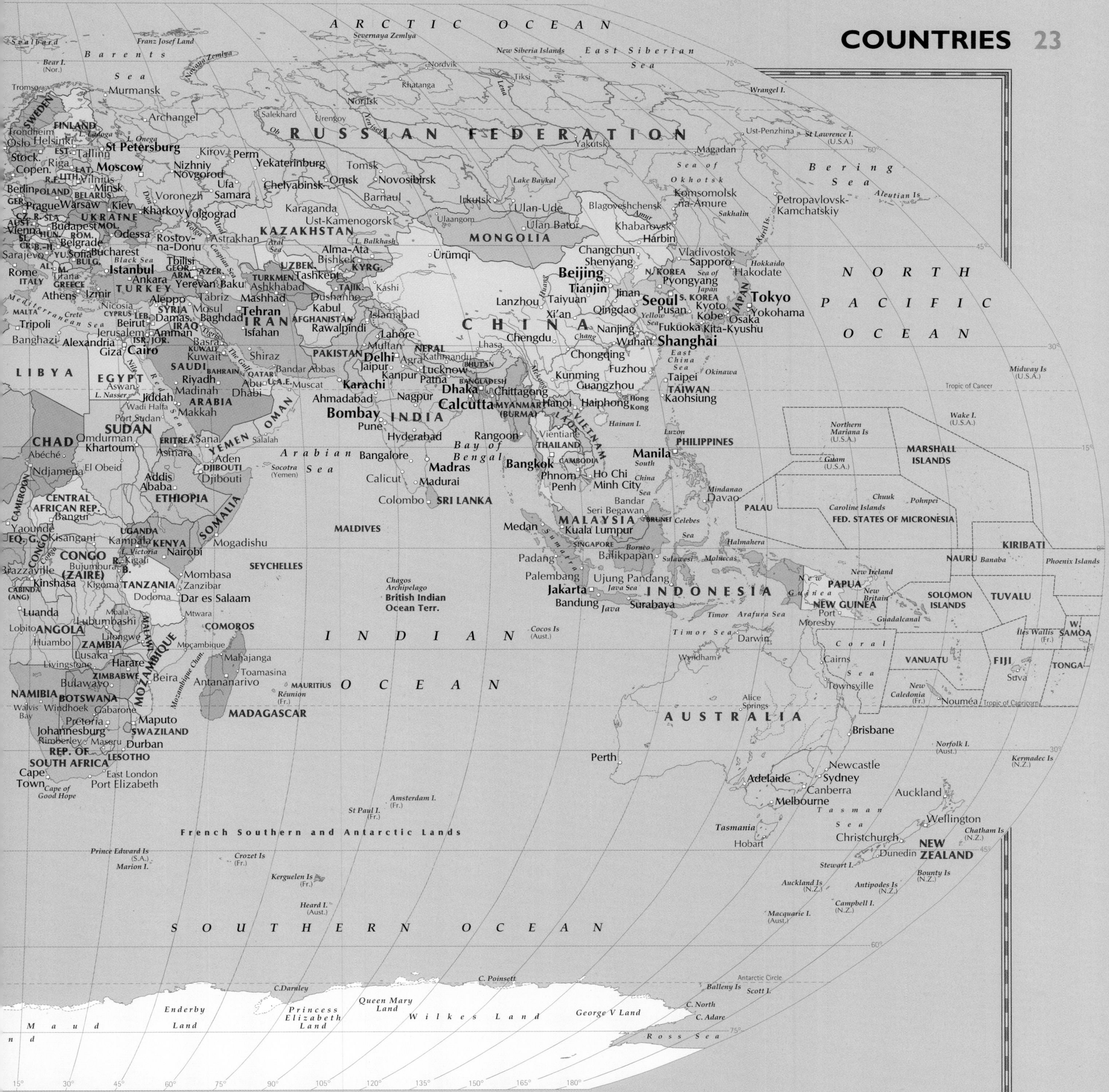
ARCTIC OCEAN
Severnaya Zemlya
Franz Josef Land
Svalbard
Barents Sea
Bear I. (Nor.)
New Siberia Islands
East Siberian Sea
Wrangel I.
Nordvik
Tiksi
Khatanga
Murmansk
Tromsø
Norilsk
Salekhard
Urengoy
Archangel
RUSSIAN FEDERATION
Yakutsk
Ust-Penzhina
St Lawrence I. (U.S.A.)
Magadan
Bering Sea
Sea of Okhotsk
Aleutian Is
Petropavlovsk-Kamchatskiy
Komsomolsk-na-Amure
Sakhalin
Kuril Is.
SWEDEN
FINLAND
Trondheim
L. Ladoga
L. Onega
Oslo
Helsinki
St Petersburg
EST.
Tallinn
Stock.
Riga
LAT.
Copen.
LITH.
Vilnius
Moscow
Kirov
Perm
Nizhniy Novgorod
Yekaterinburg
Tomsk
Berlin
POLAND
BELARUS
Minsk
Ufa
Samara
Chelyabinsk
Omsk
Novosibirsk
Lake Baykal
GER.
Prague
Warsaw
Kiev
Voronezh
Kharkov
Volgograd
Barnaul
Irkutsk
Ulan-Ude
Blagoveshchensk
Khabarovsk
Amur
UKRAINE
Budapest
MOL.
Karaganda
Ust-Kamenogorsk
Ulaangom
Ulan Bator
Vienna
HUN.
ROM.
Odessa
Rostov-na-Donu
KAZAKHSTAN
MONGOLIA
Harbin
Belgrade
Bucharest
Astrakhan
Aral Sea
L. Balkhash
Sarajevo
BULG.
Sofia
Black Sea
Alma-Ata
Bishkek
Ürümqi
Changchun
Vladivostok
Shenyang
Sapporo
Hokkaido
Hakodate
Rome
ITALY
Tirana
GREECE
Istanbul
Tbilisi
GEOR.
ARM.
AZER.
Yerevan
Baku
Caspian Sea
UZBEK.
Tashkent
KYRG.
Beijing
N. KOREA
Pyongyang
Sea of Japan
NORTH PACIFIC OCEAN
Ankara
TURKEY
TURKMEN.
Ashkhabad
TAJIK.
Kashi
Tianjin
Jinan
Seoul
S. KOREA
JAPAN
Tokyo
Yokohama
Athens
Izmir
Aleppo
Tabriz
Mashhad
Dushanbe
Lanzhou
Taiyuan
Qingdao
Pusan
Kyoto
Kobe
Osaka
Mediterranean Sea
MALTA
Crete
Nicosia
CYPRUS
SYRIA
Mosul
Tehran
Kabul
Xi'an
Nanjing
Fukuoka
Kita-Kyushu
Tripoli
LEB.
Beirut
Damas.
Baghdad
IRAN
AFGHANISTAN
Islamabad
CHINA
Yellow Sea
Banghazi
Alexandria
Jerusalem
ISR.
JOR.
Amman
IRAQ
Isfahan
Rawalpindi
Lahore
Chengdu
Wuhan
Shanghai
LIBYA
Giza
Cairo
Basra
KUWAIT
Kuwait
Shiraz
Multan
NEPAL
Lhasa
Kathmandu
BHUTAN
Chongqing
East China Sea
Okinawa
EGYPT
SAUDI ARABIA
BAHRAIN
QATAR
Bandar Abbas
PAKISTAN
Delhi
Jaipur
Agra
Lucknow
Kanpur
Patna
Fuzhou
Taipei
TAIWAN
Aswan
L. Nasser
Riyadh
Madinah
U.A.E.
Abu Dhabi
Muscat
Karachi
BANGLADESH
Dhaka
Chittagong
Kunming
Guangzhou
Hong Kong
Kaohsiung
Tropic of Cancer
Midway Is (U.S.A.)
Wadi Halfa
Jiddah
Makkah
OMAN
Ahmadabad
Nagpur
Calcutta
MYANMAR (BURMA)
Hanoi
Haiphong
Hainan I.
Port Sudan
SUDAN
Red Sea
Bombay
INDIA
Pune
LAOS
Wake I. (U.S.A.)
CHAD
Omdurman
Khartoum
ERITREA
Asmara
YEMEN
Sana
Salalah
Arabian Sea
Hyderabad
Rangoon
Vientiane
THAILAND
VIETNAM
Luzon
PHILIPPINES
Manila
Northern Mariana Is (U.S.A.)
MARSHALL ISLANDS
Abéché
Aden
Socotra (Yemen)
Bangalore
Bay of Bengal
Bangkok
CAMBODIA
South China Sea
Guam (U.S.A.)
Ndjamena
El Obeid
DJIBOUTI
Djibouti
Addis Ababa
Madras
Calicut
Madurai
Phnom Penh
Ho Chi Minh City
Mindanao
Davao
CAMEROON
CENTRAL AFRICAN REP.
Bangui
ETHIOPIA
SOMALIA
Colombo
SRI LANKA
Bandar Seri Begawan
BRUNEI
PALAU
Chuuk
Pohnpei
Caroline Islands
FED. STATES OF MICRONESIA
MALDIVES
Medan
MALAYSIA
Kuala Lumpur
Celebes Sea
Yaounde
EQ. G.
UGANDA
Kampala
KENYA
Mogadishu
SINGAPORE
Borneo
Halmahera
KIRIBATI
CONGO
Kisangani
L. Victoria
Kigali
Nairobi
Sumatra
Padang
Balikpapan
Sulawesi
Moluccas
NAURU
Banaba
Phoenix Islands
Brazzaville
CONGO (ZAIRE)
Bujumbura
Kinshasa
SEYCHELLES
Mombasa
Zanzibar
Palembang
Ujung Pandang
New Ireland
PAPUA NEW GUINEA
New Britain
CABINDA (ANG)
Kigoma
TANZANIA
Dodoma
Dar es Salaam
Chagos Archipelago
British Indian Ocean Terr.
Jakarta
Java Sea
Bandung
Java
Surabaya
INDONESIA
New Guinea
Port Moresby
SOLOMON ISLANDS
TUVALU
Luanda
ANGOLA
Lubumbashi
Mtwara
Guadalcanal
Timor
Arafura Sea
Lobito
Huambo
ZAMBIA
Lilongwe
MALAWI
COMOROS
INDIAN OCEAN
Cocos Is (Aust.)
Timor Sea
Darwin
Coral Sea
Îles Wallis (Fr.)
W. SAMOA
Lusaka
Harare
Moçambique
Mahajanga
Wyndham
Cairns
VANUATU
FIJI
TONGA
Livingstone
ZIMBABWE
Beira
Mozambique Chan.
Toamasina
Suva
Bulawayo
MOZAMBIQUE
Antananarivo
MAURITIUS
Réunion (Fr.)
Townsville
New Caledonia (Fr.)
Nouméa
Tropic of Capricorn
NAMIBIA
BOTSWANA
Walvis Bay
Windhoek
Gaborone
Alice Springs
AUSTRALIA
Pretoria
Maputo
MADAGASCAR
Johannesburg
SWAZILAND
Kimberley
Maseru
Durban
Brisbane
REP. OF SOUTH AFRICA
LESOTHO
Norfolk I. (Aust.)
Perth
Kermadec Is (N.Z.)
Cape Town
East London
Port Elizabeth
Cape of Good Hope
Newcastle
Sydney
Adelaide
Canberra
Auckland
Melbourne
Amsterdam I. (Fr.)
St Paul I. (Fr.)
Tasman Sea
Wellington
Chatham Is (N.Z.)
French Southern and Antarctic Lands
Tasmania
Hobart
Christchurch
Dunedin
NEW ZEALAND
Prince Edward Is (S.A.)
Marion I.
Crozet Is (Fr.)
Stewart I.
Kerguelen Is (Fr.)
Auckland Is (N.Z.)
Antipodes Is (N.Z.)
Bounty Is (N.Z.)
Campbell I. (N.Z.)
Heard I. (Aust.)
Macquarie I. (Aust.)
SOUTHERN OCEAN
Antarctic Circle
C. Poinsett
Balleny Is
Scott I.
C.Darnley
Enderby Land
Princess Elizabeth Land
Queen Mary Land
Wilkes Land
George V Land
C. North
C. Adare
Maud Land
Ross Sea
15°
30°
45°
60°
75°
90°
105°
120°
135°
150°
165°
180°

RELIGIONS

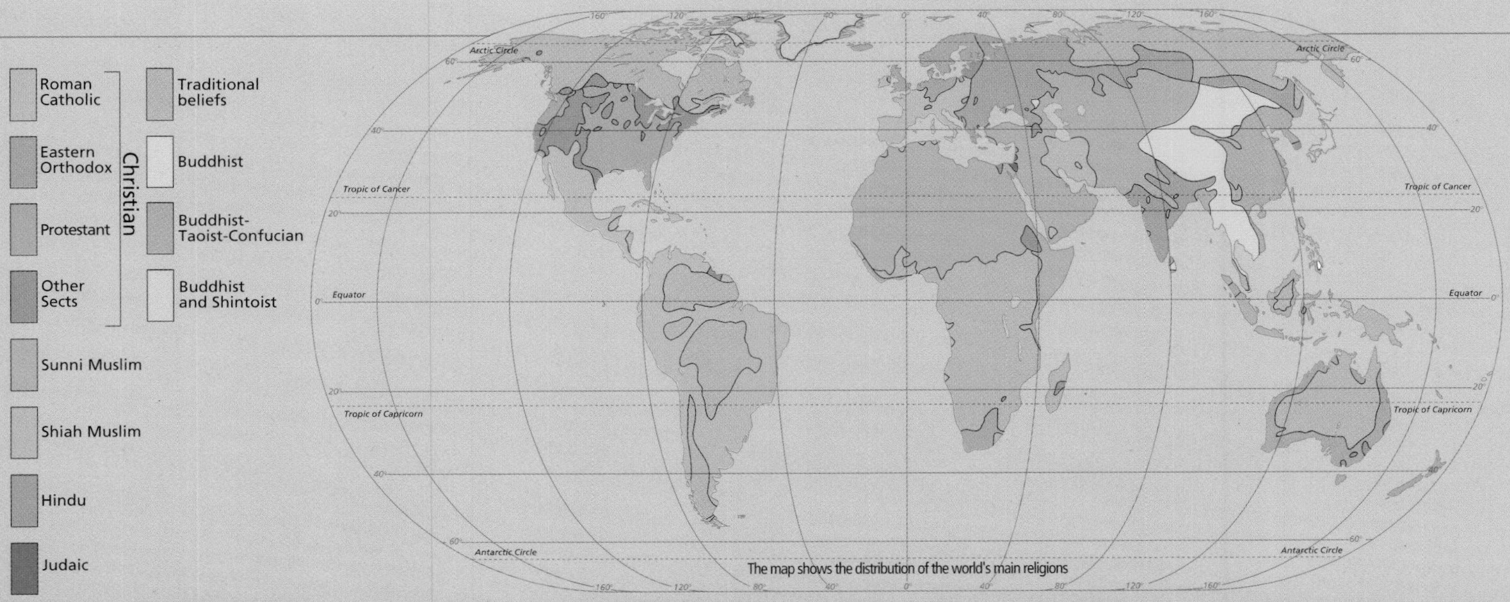
Roman Catholic
Eastern Orthodox
Protestant
Other Sects
Christian
Sunni Muslim
Shiah Muslim
Hindu
Judaic
Traditional beliefs
Buddhist
Buddhist-Taoist-Confucian
Buddhist and Shintoist
Arctic Circle
Tropic of Cancer
Equator
Tropic of Capricorn
Antarctic Circle

The map shows the distribution of the world's main religions

TIME ZONES

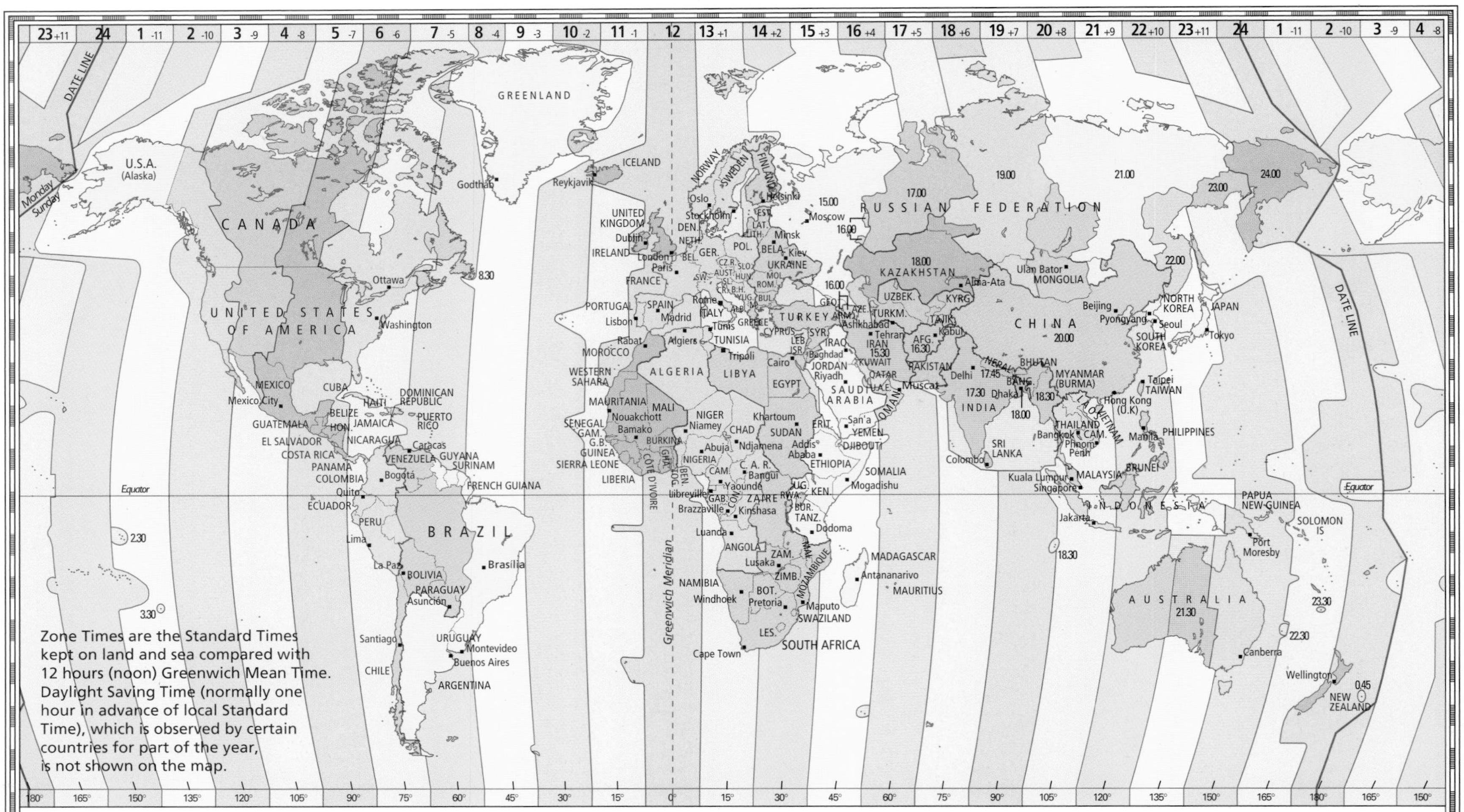

23 +11 | 24 | 1 -11 | 2 -10 | 3 -9 | 4 -8 | 5 -7 | 6 -6 | 7 -5 | 8 -4 | 9 -3 | 10 -2 | 11 -1 | 12 | 13 +1 | 14 +2 | 15 +3 | 16 +4 | 17 +5 | 18 +6 | 19 +7 | 20 +8 | 21 +9 | 22 +10 | 23 +11 | 24 | 1 -11 | 2 -10 | 3 -9 | 4 -8
DATE LINE
GREENLAND
U.S.A. (Alaska)
Monday Sunday
CANADA
UNITED STATES OF AMERICA
Ottawa
Washington
Godthåb
Reykjavík
ICELAND
NORWAY
SWEDEN
FINLAND
Oslo
Stockholm
Helsinki
UNITED KINGDOM
Dublin
IRELAND
London
Paris
FRANCE
PORTUGAL
SPAIN
Lisbon
Madrid
Rome
ITALY
Algiers
Tunis
TUNISIA
Tripoli
Rabat
MOROCCO
WESTERN SAHARA
ALGERIA
LIBYA
EGYPT
Cairo
MAURITANIA
MALI
NIGER
CHAD
SUDAN
Khartoum
ERITREA
YEMEN
DJIBOUTI
ETHIOPIA
SOMALIA
Mogadishu
Nouakchott
Bamako
Niamey
Abuja
NIGERIA
Ndjamena
Addis Ababa
SENEGAL
GUINEA
SIERRA LEONE
LIBERIA
CÔTE D'IVOIRE
C. A. R.
Bangui
Yaoundé
CAM.
Libreville
Brazzaville
Kinshasa
ZAIRE
KEN.
Nairobi
TANZ.
Dodoma
Luanda
ANGOLA
ZAM.
Lusaka
ZIMB.
NAMIBIA
Windhoek
BOT.
Pretoria
Maputo
SWAZILAND
LES.
SOUTH AFRICA
Cape Town
MOZAMBIQUE
MADAGASCAR
Antananarivo
MAURITIUS
Greenwich Meridian
RUSSIAN FEDERATION
Moscow
Minsk
Kiev
UKRAINE
TURKEY
Ankara
SYRIA
IRAQ
IRAN
Tehran
Baghdad
JORDAN
KUWAIT
Riyadh
SAUDI ARABIA
QATAR
OMAN
Muscat
KAZAKHSTAN
Alma-Ata
UZBEK.
TURKM.
KYRG.
TAJIK.
AFG.
Kabul
PAKISTAN
Delhi
INDIA
NEPAL
BHUTAN
Dhaka
Colombo
SRI LANKA
MONGOLIA
Ulan Bator
CHINA
Beijing
NORTH KOREA
Pyongyang
Seoul
SOUTH KOREA
JAPAN
Tokyo
Taipei
TAIWAN
Hong Kong (U.K.)
MYANMAR (BURMA)
THAILAND
Bangkok
CAM.
Phnom Penh
VIETNAM
Manila
PHILIPPINES
Kuala Lumpur
MALAYSIA
Singapore
BRUNEI
INDONESIA
Jakarta
PAPUA NEW GUINEA
Port Moresby
SOLOMON IS.
AUSTRALIA
Canberra
Wellington
NEW ZEALAND
MEXICO
Mexico City
CUBA
HAITI
DOMINICAN REPUBLIC
PUERTO RICO
BELIZE
JAMAICA
GUATEMALA
HON.
EL SALVADOR
NICARAGUA
COSTA RICA
PANAMA
Caracas
VENEZUELA
GUYANA
SURINAM
FRENCH GUIANA
COLOMBIA
Bogotá
Quito
ECUADOR
PERU
Lima
BRAZIL
Brasília
La Paz
BOLIVIA
PARAGUAY
Asunción
Santiago
CHILE
URUGUAY
Montevideo
Buenos Aires
ARGENTINA
Equator
Zone Times are the Standard Times kept on land and sea compared with 12 hours (noon) Greenwich Mean Time. Daylight Saving Time (normally one hour in advance of local Standard Time), which is observed by certain countries for part of the year, is not shown on the map.
180° 165° 150° 135° 120° 105° 90° 75° 60° 45° 30° 15° 0° 15° 30° 45° 60° 75° 90° 105° 120° 135° 150° 165° 180° 165° 150°

ABBREVIATIONS AND GLOSSARY

A. Alp Alpen Alpi *alp*
Alt *upper*
Abbe Abbaye *abbey*
Afr. Africa African
Ag. Agia Agioi Agion Agios *saint*
Aig. Aiguille *peak*
Akr. Ákra Akrotírion Akrotirion *cape, point*
Anch. Anchorage
Appno Appennino *mountains*
Aqued. Aqueduct
Ar. Arroyo *water course*
Arch. Archipel Archipelago Archipiélago *archipelago*
Arr. Arrecife *reef*
Ay. Áyioi Áyion Áyios *saint*

B. Baai Bahía Baía Baie Baja Bay Bucht Bukhta Bukt *bay*
Bad *spa*
Ban *village*
Bayou *inlet*
Bir *well*
Bc Banc *(sand) bank*
Bca Boca *mouth*
Bg Berg *mountain*
Bge Barrage
Bge. Barragem *reservoir*
Bgt Bight Bugt *bay*
Bi Bani Beni *tribe (sons of)*
Bj Burj *hills*
Bk Bank
Bn Basin
Bol. Bol'shoy Bol'shoye Bol'shaya Bol'shiye *big*
Bos. Bosanski *town*
Br. Bredning *bay*
Brüke *bridge*
Burun Burnu *point, cape*
Bt Bukit *bay*
Bü. Büyük *big*

C. Cabo Cap *cape, headland*
Cape
Col *high pass*
Ç. Çay *river*
Cabo Cabeço *summit*
Cach. Cachoeira Cachoeiro *waterfall*
Can. Canal Canale *canal, channel*
Cañon Canyon *canyon*
Cat. Cataract
Catena *mountains*
Cd Ciudad *town city*
Ch. Chaung *stream*
Chott *salt lake, marsh*
Chan. Channel
Che Chaîne *mountain chain*
Cma Cima *summit*
Cno Corno *peak*
Co Cerro *hill, peak*
Cor. Coronel *colonel*
Cord. Cordillera *mountain chain*
Cr. Creek
Cuch. Cuchilla *chain of mountains*
Czo Cozzo *mountain*

D. Da *big, river*
Dag Dagh Dağı *mountain*
Dağları *mountains*
Danau *lake*
Darreh *valley*
Daryācheh *lake*
Diavlos *hill*
-d. -dake *peak*
Dj. Djebel *mountain*
Dr Doctor
Dz. Dzong *castle, fort*

Eil. Eiland *island*
Eilanden *islands*
Emb. Embalse *reservoir*
Equat. Equatorial
Escarp. Escarpment
Est. Estuary
Etg Etang *lake, lagoon*

F. Firth
Fj. Fjell *mountain*
Fjord Fjördur *fjord*
Fk Fork
Fl. Fleuve *river*
Fte Fonte *well*

G. Gebel *mountain*
Göl Gölö Göl *lake*
G. Golfe Golfo Gulf *gulf, bay*
Góra *mountain*
Guba *bay*
Gunung *mountain*
-g. -gawa *river*
Gd Grand *big*
Gde Grande *big*
Geb. Gebergte *mountain range*
Gebirge *mountains*
Gen. General
Gez. Gezira *island*
Ghub. Ghubbat *bay*
Gl. Glacier
Gob. Gobernador *governor*
Grp Group
Gr. Graben *trench, ditch*
Gross Grosse Grande *big*
Gt Great Groot Groote *big*
Gy Góry Gory *mountains*

H. Hawr *lake*
Hill
Hoch *high*
Hora *mountain*
Hory *mountains*
Halv. Halvøy *peninsula*
Harb. Harbour
Hd Head
Hg. Hegység *mountains*
Hgts Heights
Hist. Historic
Ht Haut *high*
Hte Haute *high*

I. Île Ilha Insel Isla Island Isle *island, isle*
Isola Isole *island*
im imeni *in the name of*
In. Inder Indre Inner Inre *inner*
Inlet *inlet*
Inf. Inferior Infrieure *lower*
Is Islas Îles Ilhas Islands Isles *islands, isles*
Isr. Israel
Isth. Isthmus

J. Jabal Jebel *mountain*
Jibāl *mountains*
Jrvi Jaure Jezero Jezioro *lake*
Jökull *glacier*

K. Kaap Kap Kapp *cape*
Kaikyō *strait*
Kato Káto *lower*
Kiang *river or stream*
Ko *island, lake, inlet*
Koh Kūh Kūhha *island*
Kolpos *gulf*
Kopf *hill*
Kuala *estuary*
Kyst *coast*
Kan. Kanal Kanaal *canal*
Kep. Kepulauan *archipelago, islands*
Kg Kampong *village*
Kompong *landing place*
Kong *king*
Kh. Khawr *inlet*
Khirbet *ruins*
Khr Khrebet *mountain range*
Kl. Klein Kleine *small*
Kör. Körfez Körfezi *bay, gulf*
K. Küçük *small*

L. Lac Lago Lake Liman Limni Liqen Loch Lough *lake, loch*
Lam *stream*
Lag. Lagoon Laguna Lagôa *lagoon*
Ldg Landing
Lit. Little

M. Mae *river*
Me *great, chief, mother*
Meer *lake, sea*
Muang *kingdom, province, town*
Muong *town*
Mys *cape*
Maloye *small*
Mf Massif *mountains, upland*
Mgna Montagna *mountain*
Mgne Montagne *mountain*
Mgnes Montagnes *mountains*
Mon. Monasterio Monastery *monastery*
Monument *monument*
Mt Mont Mount *mountain*
Mt. Mountain
Mte Monte *mountain*
Mtes Montes *mountains*
Mti Monti Munţi *mountains*
Mtii Munţii *mountains*
Mtn Mountain
Mth Mouth
Mths Mouths
Mts Monts Mountains

N. Nam *south(ern), river*
Neu Ny *new*
Nevado *peak*
Nudo *mountain*
Noord Nord Nörre Nørre *north*
Nos *spit, point*
Nac. Nacional *national*
Nat. National
Nic. Nicaragua
Nizh. Nizhneye Nizhniy Nizhnyaya *lower*
Nizm. Nizmennost' *lowland*
N.O. Noord Oost Nord Ost *northeast*
Nov. Novyy Novaya Noviye Novoye *new*
Nr Nether
Nva Nueva *new*

O. Oost Ost *east*
Ostrov *island*
Ø Østre *east*
Ob. Ober *upper, higher*
Oc. Ocean
Ode Oude *old*
Ogl. Oglat *well*
Or. Óri Óros Ori *mountains*
Oros *mountain*
Orm. Ormos *bay*
O-va Ostrova *islands*
Ot Olet *mountain*
Öv. Över Övre *upper*
Oz. Ozero *lake*
Ozera *lakes*

P. Pass
Pic Pico Piz *peak, summit*
Pulau *island*
Pou *mountain*
P.P. Pulau-pulau *islands*
Pass. Passage
Peg. Pegunungan *mountain range*
Pen. Peninsula Penisola *peninsula*
Per. Pereval *pass*
Phn. Phnom *hill, mountain*
Pgio Poggio *hill*
Pl. Planina Planinski *mountain(s)*
Pla Playa *beach*
Plat. Plateau
Plosk. Ploskogor'ye *plateau*
Pno Pantano *reservoir, swamp*
Por. Porog *rapids*
P-ov Poluostrov *peninsula*
Pr. Proliv *strait*
Przylądek *cape*
Pres. Presidente *president*
Presq. Presqu'île *peninsula*
Prom. Promontory
Prov. Province Provincial
Psa Presa *dam*
Pso Passo *dam*
Pt Point
Pont *bridge*
Petit *small*
Pta Ponta Punta *cape, point*
Puerta *narrow pass*
Pte Pointe *cape, point*
Ponte Puente *bridge*
Pto Porto Puerto *harbour, port*
Pzo Pizzo *mountain peak, mountain*

Q Qala *castle, fort*

R. Reshteh *mountain range*
Rūd *river*
Ra. Range
Rca Rocca *rock, fortress*
Reg. Region
Rep. Republic
Res. Reserve
Reservoir
Resp. Respublika *republic*
Rf Reef
Rge Ridge
Riba Ribeira *coast, bottom of the river valley*
Rte Route

S. Salar Salina *salt pan*
San São *saint*
See *lake*
Seto *strait, channel*
Sjö *lake*
Sör Süd Sud Syd *south*
sur *on*
Sa Serra Sierra *mountain range*
Sab. Sabkhat *salt flat*
Sc. Scoglio *rock, reef*
Sd Sound Sund *sound*
Seb. Sebjet Sebkhat Sebkra *salt flat*
Serr. Serranía *mountain range*
Sev. Severnaya Severnyy *north(ern)*
Sh. Shā'ib *watercourse*
Shaţţ *river (-mouth)*
Shima *island*
Shankou *pass*
Si Sidi *lord, master*
Sk. Shuiku *reservoir*
Skt Sankt *saint*
Smt Seamount
Snra Senhora *Mrs, lady*
Snro Senhoro *Mr, gentle-man*
Sp. Spain Spanish
Spitze *peak*
Sr Sönder Sønder *southern*
Sr. Sredniy Srednyaya *middle*
St Saint Sint
Staryy *old*
St. Stor Store *big*
Stung *river*
Sta Santa *saint*
Ste Sainte *saint*
Store *big*
Sto Santo *saint*
Str. Strait Stretta *strait*
Sv. Sväty Sveti *holy, saint*

T. Tal *valley*
Tall Tell *hill*
Tepe Tepesi *hill, peak*
Terr. Territory
Tg Tanjung Tanjong *cape, point*
Tk Teluk *bay*
Tmt Tablemount
Tr. Trench Trough
Tre Torre *tower, fortress*
Tte Teniente *lieutenant*

Ug Ujung *point, cape*
Unt. Unter *lower*
Upr Upper

V. Val Valle Valley *valley*
Väster Vest Vester *west(ern)*
Vatn *lake*
Ville *town*
Vorder *near*
Va Vila *small town*
Vol. Volcán Volcan Volcano *volcano*
Vdkhr. Vodokhranilishche *reservoir*
Vdskh. Vodoskhovshche Vodaskhovishcha *reservoir*
Vel. Velikiy Velikaya Velikiye *big*
Verkh. Verkhniy Verkhneye Verkhne *upper*
Verkhnyaya *upper*
Vost. Vostochnyy *eastern*
Vozv. Vozvyshennost' *hills, upland*

W. Wadi *watercourse*
Wald *forest*
Wan *bay*
Water *water*
Wr Wester

-y -yama *mountain*
Yt. Ytre Ytter Ytri *outer*
Yuzh. Yuzhnaya Yuzhno Yuzhnyy *southern*

Zal. Zaliv *bay*
Zap. Zapadnyy Zapadnaya Zapadno Zapadnoye *western*
Zem. Zemlya *land*

© HarperCollinsPublishers

RELIEF

METRES	FEET
6000	19686
5000	16409
4000	13124
3000	9843
2000	6562
1000	3281
500	1640
200	656
SEA	LEVEL
200	656
2000	6562
4000	13124
6000	19686

Contour intervals used in layer colouring in the insets

METRES	FEET
4000	13124
3000	9843
2000	6562
1500	4921
1000	3281
500	1640
200	656
100	328
SEA	LEVEL
100	328
200	656
1000	3281
3000	9843

213 Summit
height in metres

PHYSICAL FEATURES

Freshwater lake

Seasonal freshwater lake

Saltwater lake *or* Lagoon

Seasonal saltwater lake

Dry salt lake *or* Salt pan

Marsh

River

Waterfall

Dam *or* Barrage

Seasonal river or Wadi

Canal

Flood dyke

Reef

Volcano

Lava field

Sandy desert

Rocky desert

Oasis

Escarpment

Mountain pass

Ice cap *or* Glacier

COMMUNICATIONS

Motorway

Motorway tunnel

Motorways are classified separately at scales greater than 1:4 million, at smaller scales motorways are classified with main roads.

Main road

Main road
under construction

Main road tunnel

Other road

Other road
under construction

Other road tunnel

Track

Car ferry

Main railway

Main railway
under construction

Main railway tunnel

Other railway

Other railway
under construction

Other railway tunnel

Train ferry

Main airport

Other airport

BOUNDARIES

Reference maps

International

International
through water

International
disputed

Ceasefire line

main administrative (U.K.)

main administrative (U.K.)
through water

main administrative

main administrative
through water

Continent maps

International

International
disputed

Ceasefire line

main administrative

OTHER FEATURES

National park

Reserve

Ancient wall

Historic *or* Tourist site

SETTLEMENTS

POPULATION	NATIONAL CAPITAL	ADMINISTRATIVE CAPITAL	CITY OR TOWN
Over 5 million	▣ **Beijing**	◉ **Tianjin**	◉ **New York**
1 to 5 million	▣ **Soul**	◉ **Lagos**	◉ **Barranquilla**
500000 to 1 million	▣ **Bangui**	◎ **Douala**	◎ **Memphis**
100000 to 500000	▢ Wellington	○ Mansa	○ Mara
50000 to 100000	▢ Port of Spain	○ Lubango	○ Arecibo
10000 to 50000	▫ Malabo	○ Chinhoyi	○ El Tigre
Less than 10000	▫ Roseau	○ Áti	○ Soledad

Urban area

STYLES OF LETTERING

Country name	**FRANCE**	**BARBADOS**		
Main administrative name	PORTO			
Area name	*ARTOIS*			
Physical feature	**ISLAND**	**LAKE**	**MOUNTAIN**	**RIVER**
	Gran Canaria	*LAKE ERIE*	*SOUTHERN ALPS*	*Zambezi*

Greenland
(Den.)
King Christian X Land
King Christian IX Land
King Frederick VI Coast
Frederikshåb
C. Farewell
Shannon I.
Traill I.
Scoresbysund
Labrador Sea
Greenland Sea
Svalbard
(Nor.)
Spitsbergen
Longyearbyen
Bear I.
(Nor.)
Denmark Strait
Jan Mayen
(Nor.)
ICELAND
Ísafjörður
Húnaflói
Siglufjörður
Keflavík
Reykjavík
Vatnajökull
Höfn
NORWEGIAN SEA
Faeroes
(Den.)
Tórshavn
Shetland
Orkney
Outer Hebrides
Tromsø
Vesterålen
Lofoten
Narvik
Kiruna
Mo i Rana
NORWAY
SWEDEN
Trondheim
Kristiansund
Östersund
Härnösand
Gulf of
Bergen
Voss
Lillehammer
Falun
Uppsala
Stavanger
Drammen
Oslo
Stockholm
Karlstad
Vänern
Vättern
Örebro
Norrköping
Egersund
Kristiansand
Arendal
Larvik
Skagerrak
Skagen
Borås
Jönköping
Göteborg
Gotland
Kattegat
Ålborg
Århus
Kalmar
Öland
DENMARK
Copenhagen
Esbjerg
Helsingborg
Malmö
Odense
Bornholm
Baltic
UNITED KINGDOM
SCOTLAND
Inverness
Aberdeen
Dundee
Edinburgh
Glasgow
Londonderry
N. IRELAND
Belfast
I. of Man
Sligo
REP. OF IRELAND
Tralee
Limerick
Dublin
Cork
Irish Sea
Manchester
Newcastle
York
Leeds
Liverpool
WALES
ENGLAND
Swansea
Cardiff
Birmingham
Norwich
London
Bristol
Plymouth
Southampton
Dover
Isles of Scilly
NORTH SEA
ATLANTIC OCEAN
English Channel
Channel Is
Brest
Cherbourg
Caen
Calais
Lille
Amiens
Rouen
Seine
Reims
Paris
Rennes
Le Mans
St-Nazaire
Angers
Loire
Orléans
Nantes
Tours
FRANCE
La Rochelle
Limoges
Clermont-Ferrand
Bordeaux
Lyon
St-Étienne
Grenoble
Rhône
Toulouse
Nîmes
Montpellier
Marseille
Nice
Toulon
Perpignan
Corsica
Ajaccio
Groningen
NETHERLANDS
Amsterdam
The Hague
Rotterdam
Brussels
BELGIUM
LUXEMBOURG
Luxembourg
Essen
Düsseldorf
Cologne
Bonn
Koblenz
Rhine
Hamburg
Bremen
Hannover
Kiel
Lübeck
Rostock
Elbe
Berlin
GERMANY
Leipzig
Dresden
Frankfurt
Mannheim
Saarbrücken
Nancy
Strasbourg
Nürnberg
Stuttgart
Freiburg
Mulhouse
Dijon
Munich
Zürich
Bern
Lausanne
Geneva
SWITZERLAND
LIECHTENSTEIN
Mt Blanc 4808
Salzburg
Innsbruck
AUSTRIA
Vienna
Bratislava
Danube
Graz
Maribor
Ljubljana
SLOV.
Zagreb
CROATIA
Trieste
Bolzano
Milan
Brescia
Turin
Genoa
La Spezia
Parma
Venice
Bologna
SAN MARINO
MONACO
Pisa
Livorno
Florence
Ancona
Perugia
Civitavecchia
VATICAN CITY
Rome
ITALY
Apennines
Adriatic Sea
Naples
Salerno
Bari
Taranto
Foggia
Sardinia
Cagliari
Cosenza
Reggio di Calabria
Messina
Palermo
Sicily
Mount Etna 3323
Catania
Siracusa
Ionian Sea
MALTA
Valletta
Sicilian Channel
MEDITERRANEAN
Rijeka
Zadar
Split
BOSNIA-HERZ.
Sarajevo
Dubrovnik
Podgorica
Tirana
ALBANIA
Corfu
Gdańsk
Szczecin
Bydgoszcz
Toruń
Poznań
POLAND
Płock
Kalisz
Łódź
Legnica
Wrocław
Prague
CZECH REP.
Katowice
Plzeň
Ostrava
České Budějovice
Brno
SLOVAKIA
Budapest
HUNGARY
Balaton
Kecskemét
Szeged
Bay of Biscay
A Coruña
C. Finisterre
Gijón
Oviedo
Santander
Bilbao
Vigo
Ourense
León
Donostia-San Sebastián
Pyrenees
Pamplona
Burgos
Logroño
Oporto
Braga
Douro
Coimbra
PORTUGAL
Valladolid
Salamanca
Zaragoza
Ebro
ANDORRA
Andorra
Lleida
Barcelona
Tarragona
Lisbon
Setúbal
Tajo
Toledo
Madrid
SPAIN
Castelló de la Plana
Badajoz
Ciudad Real
C. St Vincent
Valencia
Balearic Islands
Menorca
Palma
Mallorca
Ibiza
Huelva
Sevilla
Córdoba
Granada
Alicante
Murcia
Cartagena
Cádiz
Málaga
Algeciras
Almería
Gibraltar (U.K.)
Str. of Gibraltar
Ceuta (Sp.)
Tangier
Tétouan
Melilla (Sp.)
Oran
Algiers
Annaba
Tunis
Rabat
Casablanca
Meknès
Fez
Sidi Bel Abbès
Sétif
Sousse
Marrakesh
MOROCCO
Béchar
ALGERIA
TUNISIA
Gabès
Tripoli
LIBYA
Banghazi
São Jorge
Pico
Terceira
Azores
(Port.)
São Miguel
Santa Maria
Madeira
(Port.)
Funchal
Canary Islands
(Spain)
La Palma
Tenerife
Santa Cruz
Gran Canaria
Las Palmas
Lanzarote
Fuerteventura
Chamberlin Trimetric Projection

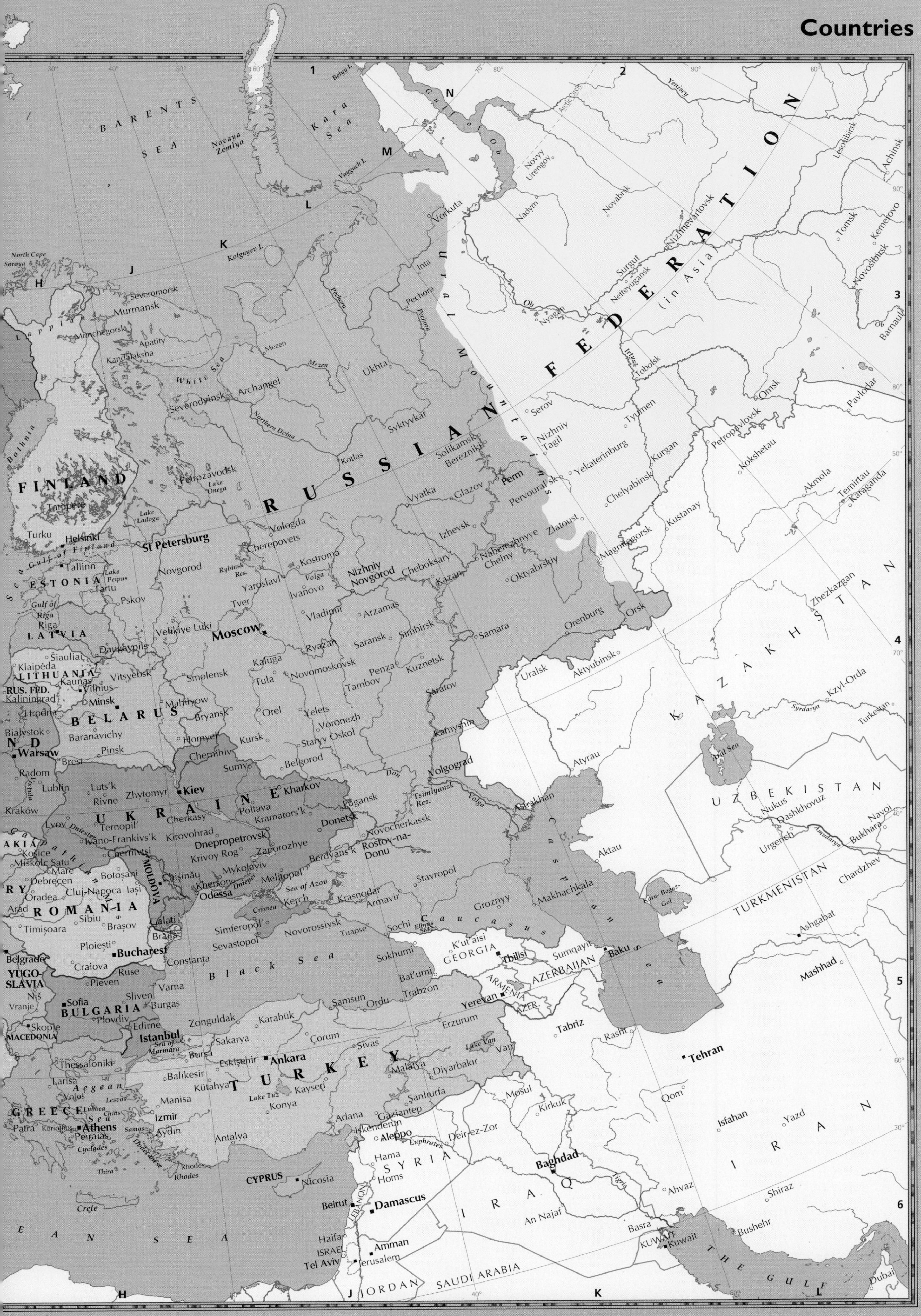
BARENTS SEA
Kara Sea
Novaya Zemlya
Gulf of Ob
Vaygach I.
Belyy I.
Kolguyev I.
North Cape
Sørøya
Lappland
White Sea
Bothnia
FINLAND
Tampere
Turku
Helsinki
Gulf of Finland
Tallinn
ESTONIA
Lake Peipus
Tartu
Gulf of Riga
Riga
LATVIA
Daugavpils
Šiauliai
Klaipėda
LITHUANIA
Kaunas
Vilnius
RUS. FED.
Kaliningrad
Hrodna
Minsk
BELARUS
Białystok
Baranavichy
Pinsk
Brest
Warsaw
Radom
Lublin
Kraków
Vitsyebsk
Mahilyow
Homyel'
UKRAINE
Kiev
Luts'k
Rivne
Zhytomyr
Chernihiv
Sumy
Kharkov
Poltava
Cherkasy
Kramators'k
Donetsk
Luhansk
Kirovohrad
Dnepropetrovsk
Krivoy Rog
Zaporozhye
Mykolayiv
Kherson
Odessa
Melitopol'
Berdyans'k
Crimea
Simferopol'
Sevastopol
Kerch
Sea of Azov
Ternopil'
L'vov
Ivano-Frankivs'k
Chernivtsi
MOLDOVA
Chișinău
Dniester
Dnieper
Košice
Miskolc
Satu Mare
Debrecen
Oradea
Cluj-Napoca
Iași
Botoșani
Arad
ROMANIA
Timișoara
Sibiu
Brașov
Ploiești
Craiova
Bucharest
Galați
Brăila
Constanța
Belgrade
YUGOSLAVIA
Niš
Vranje
Skopje
MACEDONIA
Ruse
Pleven
Sofia
BULGARIA
Plovdiv
Sliven
Varna
Burgas
Edirne
Istanbul
Sea of Marmara
Thessaloniki
Larisa
Volos
Aegean Sea
Lesvos
Chios
Euboea
GREECE
Patra
Korinthos
Peiraias
Athens
Cyclades
Samos
Dodecanese
Rhodes
Thira
Crete
Black Sea
Zonguldak
Karabük
Sakarya
Bursa
Eskişehir
Ankara
Çorum
Samsun
Ordu
Trabzon
Sivas
Erzurum
Balıkesir
Kütahya
TURKEY
Manisa
Izmir
Aydın
Lake Tuz
Konya
Kayseri
Malatya
Diyarbakır
Lake Van
Van
Şanlıurfa
Gaziantep
Adana
Antalya
İskenderun
CYPRUS
Nicosia
Aleppo
Hama
Homs
SYRIA
Euphrates
Deir-ez-Zor
Beirut
LEBANON
Damascus
Haifa
ISRAEL
Tel Aviv
Jerusalem
Amman
JORDAN
SAUDI ARABIA
IRAQ
Mosul
Kirkuk
Baghdad
Tigris
An Najaf
Basra
KUWAIT
Kuwait
THE GULF
Dubai
IRAN
Tabriz
Rasht
Tehran
Qom
Isfahan
Yazd
Ahvaz
Shiraz
Bushehr
Mashhad
GEORGIA
K'ut'aisi
Tbilisi
ARMENIA
Yerevan
AZERBAIJAN
AZER.
Sumqayıt
Baku
Sokhumi
Bat'umi
Sochi
Tuapse
Novorossiysk
Krasnodar
Armavir
Stavropol
Groznyy
Makhachkala
Caucasus
Elbrus 5642
Caspian Sea
Kara-Bogaz-Gol
Aktau
Astrakhan
Atyrau
Volgograd
Volga
Don
Tsimlyansk Res.
Novocherkassk
Rostov-na-Donu
Kamyshin
Saratov
Belgorod
Staryy Oskol
Voronezh
Kursk
Orel
Bryansk
Yelets
Tula
Kaluga
Smolensk
Novomoskovsk
Tambov
Penza
Kuznetsk
Ryazan'
Saransk
Arzamas
Simbirsk
Samara
Moscow
Velikiye Luki
Pskov
Novgorod
St Petersburg
Lake Ladoga
Lake Onega
Petrozavodsk
Rybinsk Res.
Tver'
Yaroslavl'
Ivanovo
Vladimir
Kostroma
Nizhniy Novgorod
Cheboksary
Kazan'
Vologda
Cherepovets
Vyatka
Izhevsk
Glazov
Perm
Pervoural'sk
Naberezhnyye Chelny
Oktyabr'skiy
Orenburg
Orsk
Severomorsk
Murmansk
Monchegorsk
Apatity
Kandalaksha
Severodvinsk
Archangel
Northern Dvina
Mezen
Ukhta
Syktyvkar
Kotlas
Solikamsk
Berezniki
Pechora
Inta
Vorkuta
Ural Mountains
RUSSIAN FEDERATION
RUSSIAN FEDERATION (in Asia)
Arctic Circle
Ob
Yenisey
Novyy Urengoy
Nadym
Noyabrsk
Nizhnevartovsk
Surgut
Nefteyugansk
Nyagan'
Irtysh
Tobol'sk
Serov
Nizhniy Tagil
Yekaterinburg
Tyumen
Kurgan
Chelyabinsk
Zlatoust
Magnitogorsk
Kustanay
Petropavlovsk
Kokshetau
Omsk
Pavlodar
Akmola
Temirtau
Karaganda
Tomsk
Kemerovo
Novosibirsk
Barnaul
Lesosibirsk
Achinsk
KAZAKHSTAN
Uralsk
Aktyubinsk
Zhezkazgan
Kzyl-Orda
Syrdarya
Turkestan
Aral Sea
UZBEKISTAN
Nukus
Dashkhovuz
Urgench
Amudarya
Bukhara
Navoi
TURKMENISTAN
Chardzhev
Ashgabat
MEDITERRANEAN SEA
30°
40°
50°
60°
70°
80°
90°
1
2
3
4
5
6
H
J
K
L
M
N

1:15 500 000

MILES	0	100	200	300	400	500

KM	0	100	200	300	400	500	600	700	800

National Statistics

COUNTRY	AREA sqml	AREA sqkm	POPULATION total	density per sqml	density per sqkm	Form of Government	Capital City	MAIN LANGUAGES	MAIN RELIGIONS	CURRENCY
ALBANIA	11 100	28 748	3 414 000	308	119	republic	Tirana	Albanian (Gheg, Tosk dialects), Greek,	Muslim, Greek Orthodox, Roman Catholic	Lek
ANDORRA	180	465	65 000	362	140	principality	Andorra la Vella	Catalan, Spanish, French	Roman Catholic	French franc, Spanish peseta
AUSTRIA	32 377	83 855	8 031 000	248	96	republic	Vienna	German, Serbo-Croat,	Roman Catholic, Protestant	Schilling
AZORES	868	2 247	237 800	274	106	Portuguese territory	Ponta Delgada	Turkish Portuguese	Roman Catholic, Protestant	Port. escudo
BELARUS	80 155	207 600	10 355 000	129	50	republic	Minsk	Belorussian, Russian, Ukrainian	Belorussian Orthodox, Roman Catholic	Rouble
BELGIUM	11 784	30 520	10 080 000	855	330	monarchy	Brussels	Dutch (Flemish), French, German (all official), Italian	Roman Catholic, Protestant	Franc
BOSNIA-HERZEGOVINA	19 741	51 130	4 459 000	226	87	republic	Sarajevo	Serbo-Croat	Sunni Muslim, Serbian Orthodox, Roman Catholic, Protestant	Dinar
BULGARIA	42 855	110 994	8 443 000	197	76	republic	Sofia	Bulgarian, Turkish, Romany, Macedonian	Bulgarian Orthodox, Sunni Muslim	Lev
CHANNEL ISLANDS	75	195	147 000	1952	754	UK territory	St Helier, St Peter Port	English, French	Protestant, Roman Catholic	Pound
CROATIA	21 829	56 538	4 777 000	219	84	republic	Zagreb	Serbo-Croat	Roman Catholic, Orthodox, Sunni Muslim	Kuna
CZECH REPUBLIC	30 450	78 864	10 336 000	339	131	republic	Prague	Czech, Moravian, Slovak	Roman Catholic, Protestant	Koruna
DENMARK	16 631	43 075	5 205 000	313	121	monarchy	Copenhagen	Danish	Protestant, Roman Catholic	Krone
ESTONIA	17 452	45 200	1 499 000	86	33	republic	Tallinn	Estonian, Russian	Protestant, Russian Orthodox	Kroon
FAROE ISLANDS	540	1 399	47 000	87	34	Danish territory	Tórshavn	Danish, Faeroese	Protestant	Danish krone
FINLAND	130 559	338 145	5 088 000	39	15	republic	Helsinki	Finnish, Swedish	Protestant, Finnish (Greek) Orthodox	Markka
FRANCE	210 026	543 965	57 903 000	276	106	republic	Paris	French, French dialects, Arabic,German (Alsatian), Breton	Roman Catholic, Protestant, Sunni Muslim	Franc
GERMANY	138 174	357 868	81 410 000	589	227	republic	Berlin	German, Turkish	Protestant, Roman Catholic, Sunni Muslim	Mark
GIBRALTAR	3	7	28 000	11157	4308	UK territory	Gibraltar	English, Spanish	Roman Catholic, Protestant, Sunni Muslim	Pound
GREECE	50 949	131 957	10 426 000	205	79	republic	Athens	Greek, Macedonian	Greek Orthodox, Sunni Muslim	Drachma
HUNGARY	35 919	93 030	10 261 000	286	110	republic	Budapest	Hungarian, Romany, German, Slovak	Roman Catholic, Protestant	Forint
ICELAND	39 699	102 820	266 000	7	3	republic	Reykjavik	Icelandic	Protestant, Roman Catholic	Króna
ISLE OF MAN	221	572	73 000	331	128	UK territory	Douglas	English	Protestant, Roman Catholic	Pound
ITALY	116 311	301 245	57 193 000	492	190	republic	Rome	Italian, Italian dialects	Roman Catholic	Lira
LATVIA	24 595	63 700	2 548 000	104	40	republic	Riga	Latvian, Russian	Protestant, Roman Catholic, Russian Orthodox	Lat
LIECHTENSTEIN	62	160	31 000	502	194	monarchy	Vaduz	German	Roman Catholic, Protestant	Swiss franc
LITHUANIA	25 174	65 200	3 721 000	148	57	republic	Vilnius	Lithuanian, Russian, Polish	Roman Catholic, Protestant, Russian Orthodox	Litas
LUXEMBOURG	998	2 586	404 000	405	156	monarchy	Luxembourg	Letzeburgish (Luxembourgian), German, French, Portuguese	Roman Catholic, Protestant	Franc
MACEDONIA, Former Yugoslavian Republic of	9 928	25 713	2 142 000	216	83	republic	Skopje	Macedonian, Albanian, Serbo-Croat, Turkish, Romany	Macedonian Orthodox, Sunni Muslim, Roman Catholic	Denar
MADEIRA	307	794	253 000	825	319	Port territory	Funchal	Portuguese	Roman Catholic, Protestant	Port. escudo
MALTA	122	316	368 000	3016	1165	republic	Valletta	Maltese, English	Roman Catholic	Lira
MOLDOVA	13 012	33 700	4 350 000	334	129	republic	Chişinău	Romanian, Russian, Ukrainian, Gagauz	Moldovan Orthodox, Russian Orthodox	Leu
MONACO	1	2	31 000	41174	15897	monarchy	Monaco	French, Monegasque, Italian	Roman Catholic	French franc
NETHERLANDS	16 033	41 526	15 380 000	959	370	monarchy	Amsterdam	Dutch, Frisian, Turkish, Indonesian languages	Roman Catholic, Protestant, Sunni Muslim	Guilder
NORWAY	125 050	323 878	4 325 000	35	13	monarchy	Oslo	Norwegian	Protestant, Roman Catholic	Krone
POLAND	120 728	312 683	38 544 000	319	123	republic	Warsaw	Polish, German	Roman Catholic, Polish Orthodox	Złoty
PORTUGAL	34 340	88 940	9 902 000	288	111	republic	Lisbon	Portuguese	Roman Catholic, Protestant	Escudo
REPUBLIC OF IRELAND	27 136	70 282	3 571 000	132	51	republic	Dublin	English, Irish	Roman Catholic, Protestant	Punt
ROMANIA	91 699	237 500	22 731 000	248	96	republic	Bucharest	Romanian, Hungarian	Romanian Orthodox, Roman Catholic, Protestant	Leu
RUSSIAN FEDERATION	6 592 849	17 075 400	148 673 000	23	9	republic	Moscow	Russian, Tatar, Ukrainian, many local languages	Russian Orthodox, Sunni, Muslim, other Christian, Jewish	Rouble
RUSSIAN FEDERATION IN EUROPE	1 527 343	3 955 800	106 918 000	70	27					
SAN MARINO	24	61	25 000	1061	410	republic	San Marino	Italian	Roman Catholic	Ital. lira
SLOVAKIA	18 933	49 035	5 347 000	282	109	republic	Bratislava	Slovak, Hungarian, Czech	Roman Catholic, Protestant, Orthodox	Koruna
SLOVENIA	7 819	20 251	1 989 000	254	98	republic	Ljubljana	Slovene, Serbo-Croat	Roman Catholic, Protestant	Tólar
SPAIN	194 897	504 782	39 143 000	201	78	monarchy	Madrid	Spanish, Catalan, Galician, Basque	Roman Catholic	Peseta
SWEDEN	173 732	449 964	8 781 000	51	20	monarchy	Stockholm	Swedish	Protestant, Roman Catholic	Krona
SWITZERLAND	15 943	41 293	6 995 000	439	169	federation	Bern	German, French, Italian, Romansch	Roman Catholic, Protestant	Franc
UNITED KINGDOM	94 241	244 082	58 395 000	620	239	monarchy	London	English, South Indian languages, Chinese, Welsh, Gaelic	Protestant, Roman Catholic, Muslim, Sikh, Hindu, Jewish	Pound
UKRAINE	233 090	603 700	51 910 000	223	86	republic	Kiev	Ukrainian, Russian, regional languages	Ukrainian Orthodox, Roman Catholic	Karbovanets
VATICAN CITY		0.44	1 000	5886	2273	ecclesiastical state		Italian	Roman Catholic	Ital. lira
YUGOSLAVIA	39 449	102 173	10 516 000	267	103	republic	Belgrade	Serbo-Croat, Albanian,	Serbian Orthodox, Montenegrin	Dinar

EUROPEAN FREE TRADE ASSOCIATION (EFTA)

Founded in 1960 by the Stockholm Convention, the original members were Austria, Denmark, Norway, Portugal, Sweden, Switzerland and the United Kingdom. Denmark and the United Kingdom left in 1972 to join the EU, as did Portugal in 1985. The original objectives were to eliminate tariffs and other trade restrictions between members, and to create a free-trade area throughout Western Europe. The formation of the EEA virtually achieves this.

Headquarters : Geneva, Switzerland

EUROPEAN ECONOMIC AREA (EEA)

On 1 January 1994 the EU nations and the EFTA nations (except Liechtenstein, who later joined in April 1995), formed the European Economic Area, the World's largest multi-lateral trading area.

EUROPEAN UNION (EU)

Originally the European Economic Community, founded by the Treaty of Rome in 1957, which was signed by Belgium, France, West Germany, Italy, Luxembourg and the Netherlands. Denmark, the Republic of Ireland and the United Kingdom joined in 1973; Greece joined in 1981 and Spain and Portugal in 1986, the former East Germany became a part of the EU following the reunification of Germany in October 1990. The objectives, under the Treaty of Rome, are to lay the foundations of an ever closer union among the peoples of Europe, and to ensure economic and social progress.

Headquarters : Brussels, Belgium

COMMONWEALTH OF INDEPENDENT STATES (CIS)

Established by the Minsk Agreement signed by Belarus, the Russian Federation and Ukraine on 8 December 1991 following the collapse of the U.S.S.R. The Alma-Ata Declaration was signed on 21 December 1991 by these countries and Armenia, Kazakhstan, Kyrgyzstan, Moldova, Tajikistan, Turkmenistan and Uzbekistan; Azerbaijan also signed the declaration but did not formally join until September 1993; Georgia was admitted in December 1993.

Headquarters : Minsk, Belarus

ORGANIZATION FOR ECONOMIC CO-OPERATION AND DEVELOPMENT (OECD)

Established in 1961 as the successor to the Organization for European Economic Co-operation (OEEC) which was set up in 1948 to administer the Marshall Plan for the post-World War II reconstruction of Europe, the OECD's objective is to promote economic and social welfare throughout the OECD area. It does this by assisting member governments in the formulation and co-ordination to policies to meet this objective; it also aims to stimulate and harmonise members' efforts in favour of developing countries.

Headquarters : Paris, France

© HarperCollinsPublishers

St Petersburg
Moscow
London
Amsterdam
Brussels
Berlin
Paris
Vienna
Madrid
Rome
Athens

KEY TO MAPS

- Built-up areas
- Park or open space
- Open water
- Important building
- Cemetery
- Lake
- River or canal
- Main road
- Road
- Other road
- Railway
- Airport

AMSTERDAM 1:25 000
0 METRES 250
0 YARDS 250
Het IJ
IJhaven
DE RUIJTERKADE
PRINS HENDRIKKADE
Central Station
Anne Frankhuis
Westerkerk
Nieuwe Kerk
Oude Kerk
Museum Amstelkring
CENTRUM
RAADHUISSTRAAT
ROZENGRACHT
Koninklijk Paleis
Nationaal Monument
Waaggebouw
Oosterdok
Ned. Scheepvaartmuseum
Amsterdams Historisch Museum
Allard Pierson Museum
Rembrandthuis
Madame Tussaud
Bijbels Museum
Stadhuis en Muziektheater
Mozes-en Aaronkerk
Hortus Botanicus
Artis
PLANTAGE MIDDENLAAN
AMSTELSTRAAT
VIJZELSTRAAT
UTRECHTSESTRAAT
KERKSTRAAT
MAGERE BRUG
Amstel
WEESPERSTRAAT
SARPHATISTRAAT
MAURITSKADE
OOST
Vondelpark
Rijksmuseum
Van Gogh Museum
Stedelijk Museum
MUSEUMSTRAAT
STADHOUDERSKADE
WETERINGSCHANS
OUD ZUID

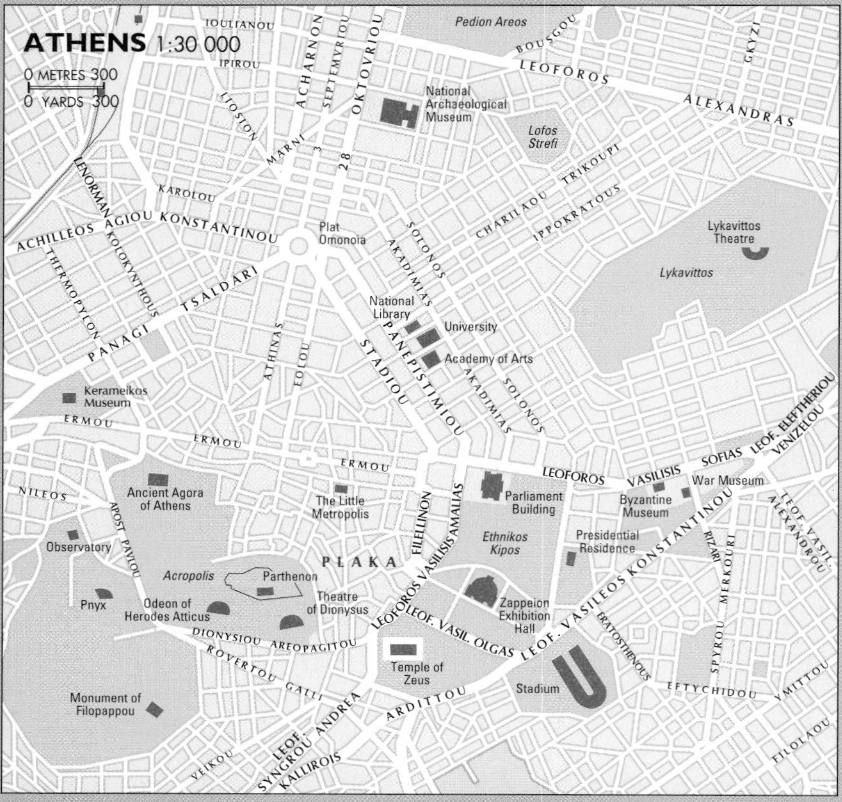
ATHENS 1:30 000
0 METRES 300
0 YARDS 300
Pedion Areos
National Archaeological Museum
Lofos Strefi
LEOFOROS ALEXANDRAS
Plat. Omonoia
Lykavittos Theatre
Lykavittos
National Library
University
Academy of Arts
PANEPISTIMIOU
STADIOU
Kerameikos Museum
ERMOU
Ancient Agora of Athens
The Little Metropolis
Parliament Building
Byzantine Museum
War Museum
Ethnikos Kipos
Presidential Residence
PLAKA
Observatory
Acropolis
Parthenon
Pnyx
Odeon of Herodes Atticus
Theatre of Dionysus
Zappeion Exhibition Hall
Temple of Zeus
Stadium
Monument of Filopappou
LEOF. VASILISSIS SOFIAS
LEOF. VASIL. OLGAS

BERLIN 1:65 000
0 METRES 650
0 YARDS 650
Schiffahrtskanal
MOABIT
CHAUSSEESTRASSE
Museum fur Naturk. und Zoologischer
ALT-MOABIT
INVALIDENSTRASSE
Lehrter Bahnhof
Museumsinsel
Kongresshalle
Reichstag
Staatsbibliothek
Humboldt Universität
Rotes Rathaus
UNTER DEN LINDEN
Staats Oper
Nikolaikirche
Brandenburger Tor
Akademie der Künste
Schloss Bellevue
Siegessäule
STRASSE DES 17 JUNI
TIERGARTEN
Technische Universität
Philharmonie
St Hedwigs Kathedrale
Hochschule f. Musik
Schiller Theater
CHARLOTTENBURG
KANTSTRASSE
Zoologischer Garten
Neue Nationalgalerie
Staatsbibliothek
Aquarium
Europa Center
Landwehrkanal
Anhalter Bahnhof
Berlin Museum
KURFÜRSTENDAMM
Bundeshaus
WILMERSDORF
Amerika Gedenk Bibliothek
KREUZBERG
SCHÖNEBERG
Rathaus Schöneberg
TEMPELHOF
Schöneberg Sporthalle
Zentralflughafen Tempelhof

BRUSSELS 1:30 000
0 METRES 300
0 YARDS 300
Gare du Nord
Ste Maria
BLVD BAUDOUIN
BLVD D'ANVERS
RUE ROYALE
Jardin Botanique
ST JEAN
ST JOSSE
St Jean Baptiste
Ste Catherine
Théâtre de la Monnaie
Cathédrale St Michel
Bourse
CHAUSSÉE DE LOUVAIN
Institute des Arts et Métiers
Palais de la Nation
Théâtre du Parc
Palais des Beaux Arts
Parc de Bruxelles
Palais des Académies
RUE DE LA LOI
Bibliothèque Albert I
Musée d'Art
Palais Royal
Palais d'Egmont
N. D. de la Chapelle
Palais du Midi
Gare du Midi
Gare du Quartier Léopold
Parc Léopold
Musée Wiertz
Palais du Justice
ELSENE
St Boniface
BOULEVARD DE WATERLOO
AVENUE LOUISE

LONDON 1:100 000
0 METRES 1000
0 YARDS 1000
HIGHBURY
HAMPSTEAD
KILBURN
ST. JOHN'S WOOD
London Zoo
Regent's Park
Lord's Cricket Ground
St Pancras Station
Kings Cross Station
Euston Station
SHOREDITCH
Marylebone Station
British Museum Library
Smithfield Market
Liverpool St Sta.
PADDINGTON
Paddington Station
HOLBURN
St. Paul's Cathedral
Fenchurch St Station
NOTTING HILL
BAYSWATER ROAD
Hyde Park
Blackfriars Sta.
Cannon St Sta.
Charing Cross Sta.
The Tower
Kensington Palace
Kensington Gardens
KENSINGTON
Holland Park
Green Park
St. James's Palace
SOUTHWARK
London Bridge Sta.
Albert Hall
Nat. History Mus.
Victoria & Albert Mus.
Buckingham Palace
Westminster Abbey
Houses of Parliament
Waterloo Station
Olympia
CROMWELL ROAD
Victoria Station
Imperial War Museum
BERMONDSEY
LAMBETH
EARLS COURT
Earls Court Exhibition Centre
Tate Gallery
CHELSEA
Chelsea Bridge
The Oval
Burgess Park
Football Stadium
Battersea Park
CAMBERWELL
PECKHAM RD
PARSONS GREEN
Putney Bridge
Thames
Clapham Junction
Clapham Common
BRIXTON
Ruskin Park

© HarperCollinsPublishers

MADRID 1:25 000
0 METRES 250
0 YARDS 250
Parque de la Montaña
Estación del Norte
Palacio del Senado
CUESTA DE SAN VICENTE
GRAN VÍA
Palacio Real
Campo del Moro
Teatro Real
Nuestra Señora de la Almudena
CALLE MAYOR
Plaza Mayor
CALLE DE SEGOVIA
CENTRO
San Isidro
San Francisco el Grande
RONDA DE SEGOVIA
PASEO IMPERIAL
RONDA DE TOLEDO
RONDA DE ATOCHA
Museo Municipal
Palacio de Justicia
Biblioteca Nacional
Museo Arqueológico Nacional
Palacio de Buenavista
Real Academia de Belles Artes
Círculo de Bellas Artes
CALLE DE ALCALÁ
Congresso
Palacio de Comunicaciones
Bolsa
Palacio de Villahermosa
Museo del Prado
Jardín Botánico
Centro de Arte Reina Sofía
Estación Atocha
Puerta de Alcalá
CALLE DE LAS HUERTAS
CALLE DE ATOCHA
PASEO DEL PRADO
PASEO DE RECOLETOS
PASEO DE LA CASTELLANA
CALLE GENOVA

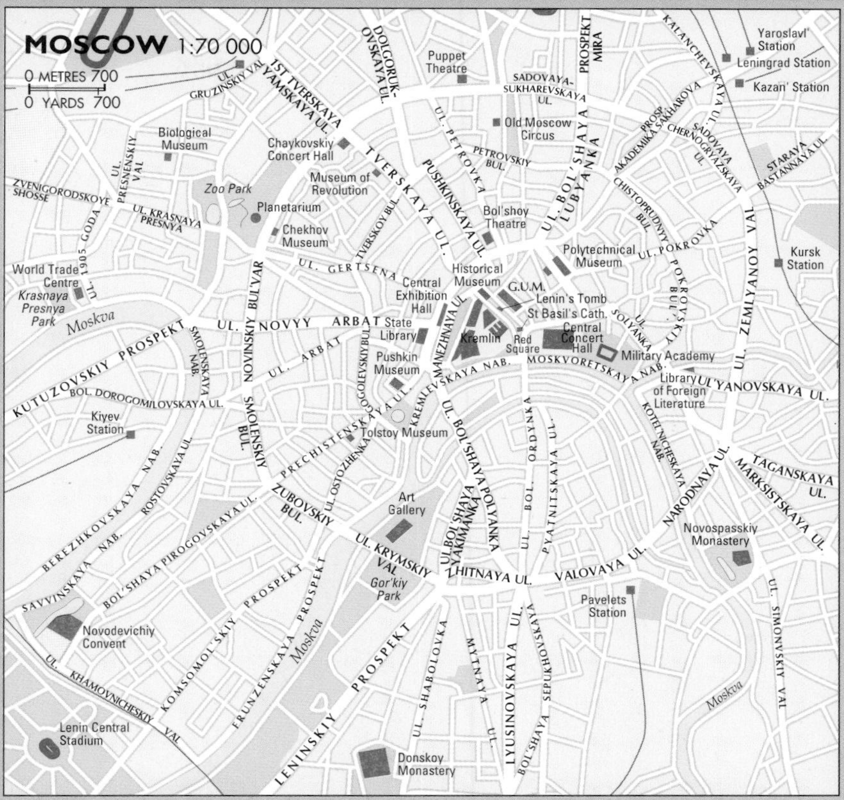
MOSCOW 1:70 000
0 METRES 700
0 YARDS 700
Puppet Theatre
Yaroslavl' Station
Leningrad Station
Kazan' Station
Old Moscow Circus
Biological Museum
Chaykovskiy Concert Hall
Museum of Revolution
Zoo Park
Planetarium
Chekhov Museum
Bol'shoy Theatre
Polytechnical Museum
Kursk Station
World Trade Centre
Krasnaya Presnya Park
Historical Museum
G.U.M.
Lenin's Tomb
St Basil's Cath.
Central Exhibition Hall
State Library
Kremlin
Red Square
Central Concert Hall
Military Academy
Library of Foreign Literature
Pushkin Museum
Kiyev Station
Tolstoy Museum
KUTUZOVSKIY PROSPEKT
UL. NOVYY ARBAT
Art Gallery
Gor'kiy Park
Novospasskiy Monastery
Paveletz Station
Novodevichiy Convent
Lenin Central Stadium
Donskoy Monastery
LENINSKIY PROSPEKT
Moskva

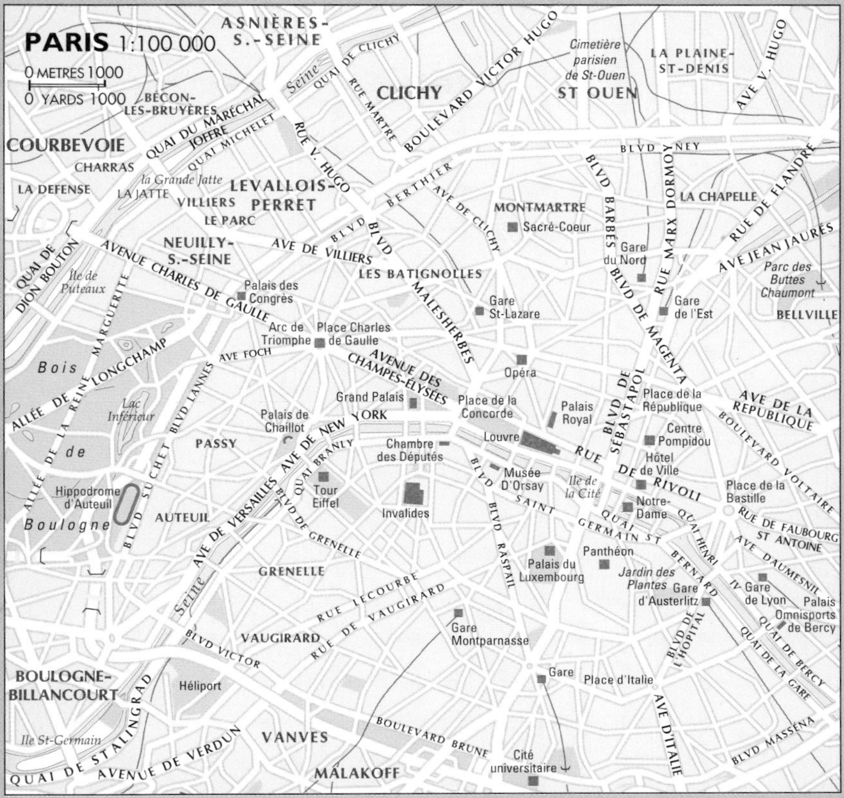
PARIS 1:100 000
0 METRES 1000
0 YARDS 1000
ASNIÈRES-S.-SEINE
CLICHY
LA PLAINE-ST-DENIS
ST OUEN
COURBEVOIE
LA DEFENSE
LEVALLOIS-PERRET
NEUILLY-S.-SEINE
MONTMARTRE
Sacré-Coeur
LA CHAPELLE
Gare du Nord
Gare de l'Est
BELLVILLE
Palais des Congres
Arc de Triomphe
Place Charles de Gaulle
Gare St-Lazare
Opéra
Bois de Boulogne
Grand Palais
Place de la Concorde
Palais Royal
Place de la République
Louvre
Centre Pompidou
Hôtel de Ville
Notre-Dame
Place de la Bastille
Musée d'Orsay
Chambre des Députés
Tour Eiffel
Invalides
PASSY
AUTEUIL
GRENELLE
Panthéon
Palais du Luxembourg
Jardin des Plantes
Gare d'Austerlitz
Gare de Lyon
Palais Omnisports de Bercy
Gare Montparnasse
VAUGIRARD
BOULOGNE-BILLANCOURT
Héliport
Place d'Italie
VANVES
MALAKOFF
Cité universitaire
Ile St-Germain

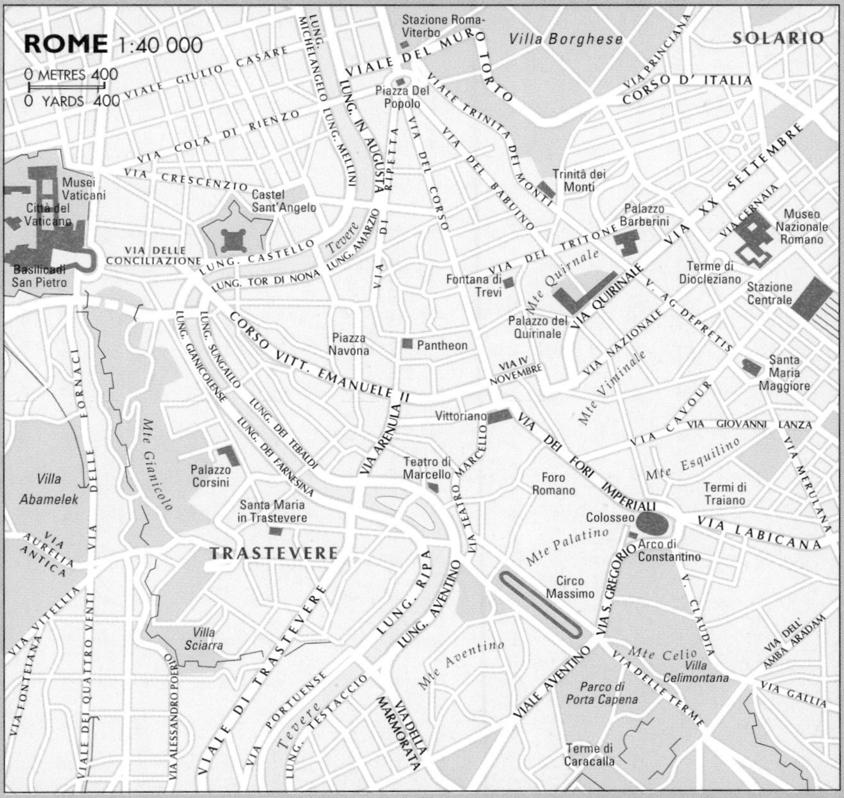
ROME 1:40 000
0 METRES 400
0 YARDS 400
Stazione Roma-Viterbo
Villa Borghese
SOLARIO
CORSO D'ITALIA
Piazza Del Popolo
Musei Vaticani
Città del Vaticano
Basilica di San Pietro
Castel Sant'Angelo
Trinità dei Monti
Palazzo Barberini
Museo Nazionale Romano
Terme di Diocleziano
Stazione Centrale
Fontana di Trevi
Palazzo del Quirinale
Piazza Navona
Pantheon
CORSO VITT. EMANUELE II
Santa Maria Maggiore
Vittoriano
Teatro di Marcello
Foro Romano
Colosseo
Arco di Constantino
Villa Abamelek
Palazzo Corsini
Santa Maria in Trastevere
TRASTEVERE
Circo Massimo
Villa Sciarra
Villa Celimontana
Parco di Porta Capena
Terme di Caracalla
Tevere

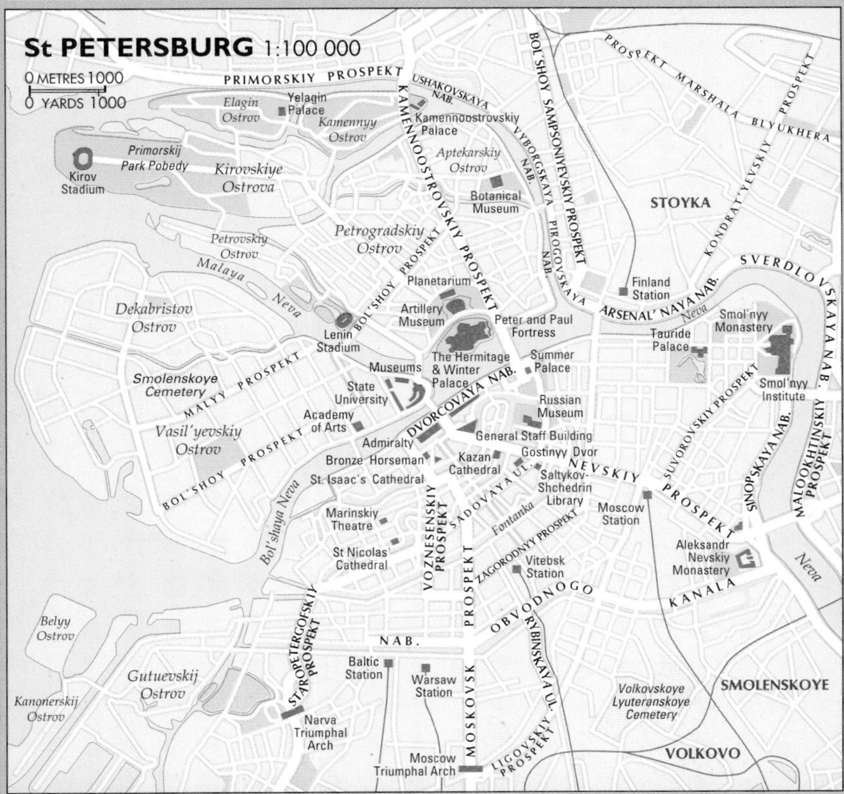
St PETERSBURG 1:100 000
0 METRES 1000
0 YARDS 1000
PRIMORSKIY PROSPEKT
Yelagin Palace
Elagin Ostrov
Kamennyy Ostrov
Kamennoostrovskiy Palace
Primorskij Park Pobedy
Kirov Stadium
Kirovskiye Ostrova
Aptekarskiy Ostrov
Botanical Museum
STOYKA
Petrogradskiy Ostrov
Petrovskiy Ostrov
Finland Station
Dekabristov Ostrov
Planetarium
Artillery Museum
Peter and Paul Fortress
Lenin Stadium
Tauride Palace
Smol'nyy Monastery
Smol'nyy Institute
The Hermitage & Winter Palace
Summer Palace
Smolenskoye Cemetery
State University
Academy of Arts
Russian Museum
Vasil'yevskiy Ostrov
Admiralty
General Staff Building
Gostinyy Dvor
Bronze Horseman
Kazan Cathedral
St. Isaac's Cathedral
Saltykov-Shchedrin Library
NEVSKIY PROSPEKT
Moscow Station
Mariinskiy Theatre
St Nicolas Cathedral
Vitebsk Station
Aleksandr Nevskiy Monastery
Belyy Ostrov
Gutuevskij Ostrov
Kanonerskij Ostrov
Baltic Station
Warsaw Station
Volkovskoye Lyuteranskoye Cemetery
SMOLENSKOYE
Narva Triumphal Arch
Moscow Triumphal Arch
VOLKOVO
Neva

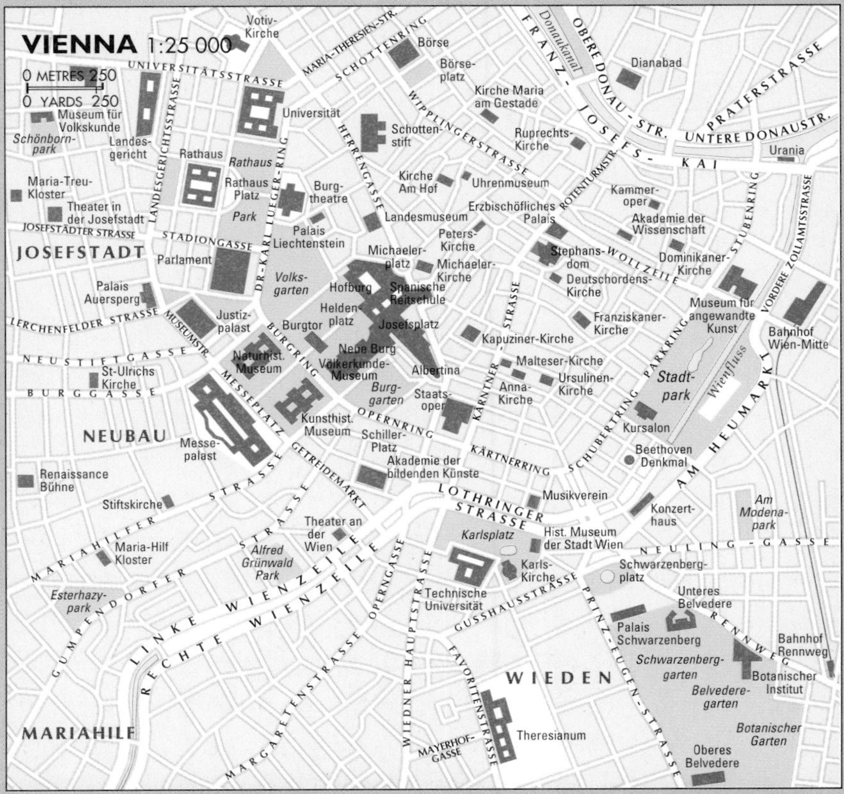
VIENNA 1:25 000
0 METRES 250
0 YARDS 250
Votiv-Kirche
Börse
Dianabad
Museum für Volkskunde
Schönborn-park
Universität
Kirche Maria am Gestade
Ruprechts-Kirche
Urania
Landesgericht
Rathaus
Maria-Treu-Kloster
Theater in der Josefstadt
Burg-theater
Kirche Am Hof
Landesmuseum
Akademie der Wissenschaft
JOSEFSTADT
Parlament
Palais Liechtenstein
Stephans-dom
Dominikaner-Kirche
Palais Auersperg
Volks-garten
Hofburg
Spanische Reitschule
Deutschordens-Kirche
Justiz-palast
Burgtor
Heldenplatz
Josefsplatz
Franziskaner-Kirche
Museum für angewandte Kunst
Bahnhof Wien-Mitte
Naturhist. Museum
Neue Burg
Völkerkunde-Museum
Albertina
Kapuziner-Kirche
Malteser-Kirche
St-Ulrichs Kirche
Ursulinen-Kirche
Anna-Kirche
Stadt-park
NEUBAU
Kunsthist. Museum
Messe-palast
Akademie der bildenden Künste
Kursalon
Beethoven Denkmal
Renaissance Bühne
Stiftskirche
Musikverein
Konzert-haus
Theater an der Wien
Mariа-Hilf Kloster
Karlsplatz
Hist. Museum der Stadt Wien
Karls-Kirche
Schwarzenberg-platz
Unteres Belvedere
Esterhazy-park
Technische Universität
Palais Schwarzenberg
Bahnhof Rennweg
Botanischer Institut
Belvedere-garten
WIEDEN
Theresianum
Botanischer Garten
Oberes Belvedere
MARIAHILF
RINGSTRASSE

© HarperCollinsPublishers

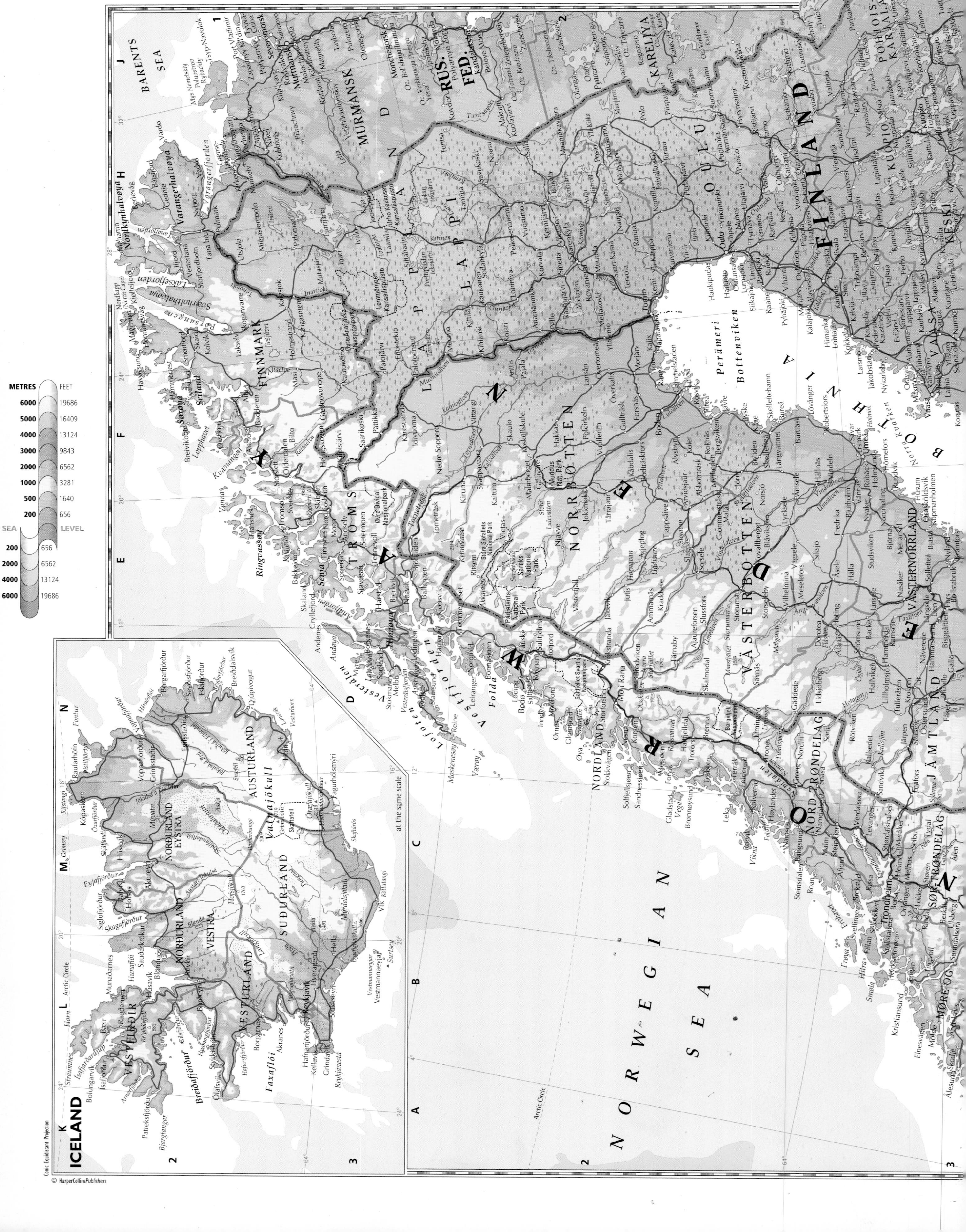
METRES
FEET
6000
19686
5000
16409
4000
13124
3000
9843
2000
6562
1000
3281
500
1640
200
656
SEA
LEVEL
200
656
2000
6562
4000
13124
6000
19686
BARENTS SEA
FINLAND
NORWEGIAN SEA
ICELAND
LAPPI
OULU
FINNMARK
TROMS
NORDLAND
NORRBOTTEN
VÄSTERBOTTEN
VÄSTERNORRLAND
JÄMTLAND
NORD-TRØNDELAG
SØR-TRØNDELAG
MØRE OG
MURMANSK
KARELIYA
RUS. FED.
Gulf of Bothnia
Bottenviken
Perämeri
Lofoten
Vesterålen
VESTFIRÐIR
VESTURLAND
NORÐURLAND VESTRA
NORÐURLAND EYSTRA
AUSTURLAND
SUÐURLAND
Vatnajökull
Reykjavík
Akureyri
Arctic Circle
at the same scale
Conic Equidistant Projection

© HarperCollinsPublishers

SCANDINAVIA and the BALTIC STATES

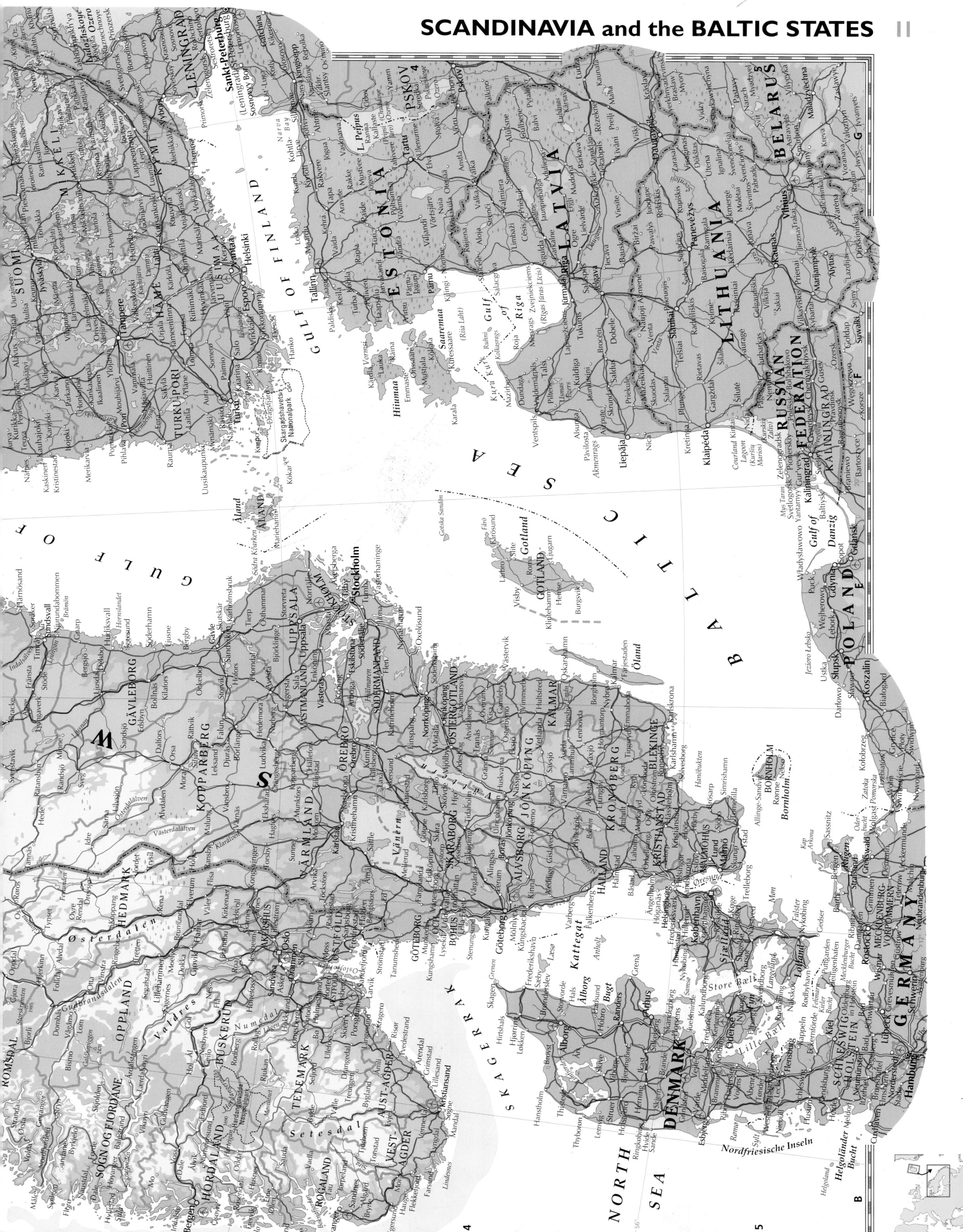

1:4 000 000

0 25 50 75 100 125 150 MILES

0 50 100 150 200 250 KM

RUSSIAN FEDERATION
FINLAND
SWEDEN
ESTONIA
LATVIA
LITHUANIA
BELARUS
RUS. FED.
KARELIYA
ARKHANGEL'SK
VOLOGDA
KOSTROMA
KIROV
NIZHNIY NOVGOROD
LENINGRAD
NOVGOROD
PSKOV
TVER'
SMOLENSK
KALUGA
MOSKVA
YAROSLAVL'
IVANOVO
VLADIMIR
RYAZAN'
TULA
PENZA
MORDOVIYA
CHUVASHIYA
TATARSTAN
MARIY EL
ULYANOVSK
SAMARA
BELOYE MORE (WHITE SEA)
Onezhskaya Guba
Kandalakshskiy Zaliv
Dvinskaya Guba
GULF OF BOTHNIA
GULF OF FINLAND
Gulf of Riga
BALTIC SEA
Ladozhskoye Ozero (Lake Ladoga)
Onezhskoye Ozero (Lake Onega)
Sankt-Peterburg
Moskva
Helsinki
Tallinn
Riga
Vilnius
Minsk
METRES
FEET
6000
5000
4000
3000
2000
1000
500
200
SEA
LEVEL
19686
16409
13124
9843
6562
3281
1640
656
Transverse Mercator Projection

© HarperCollinsPublishers

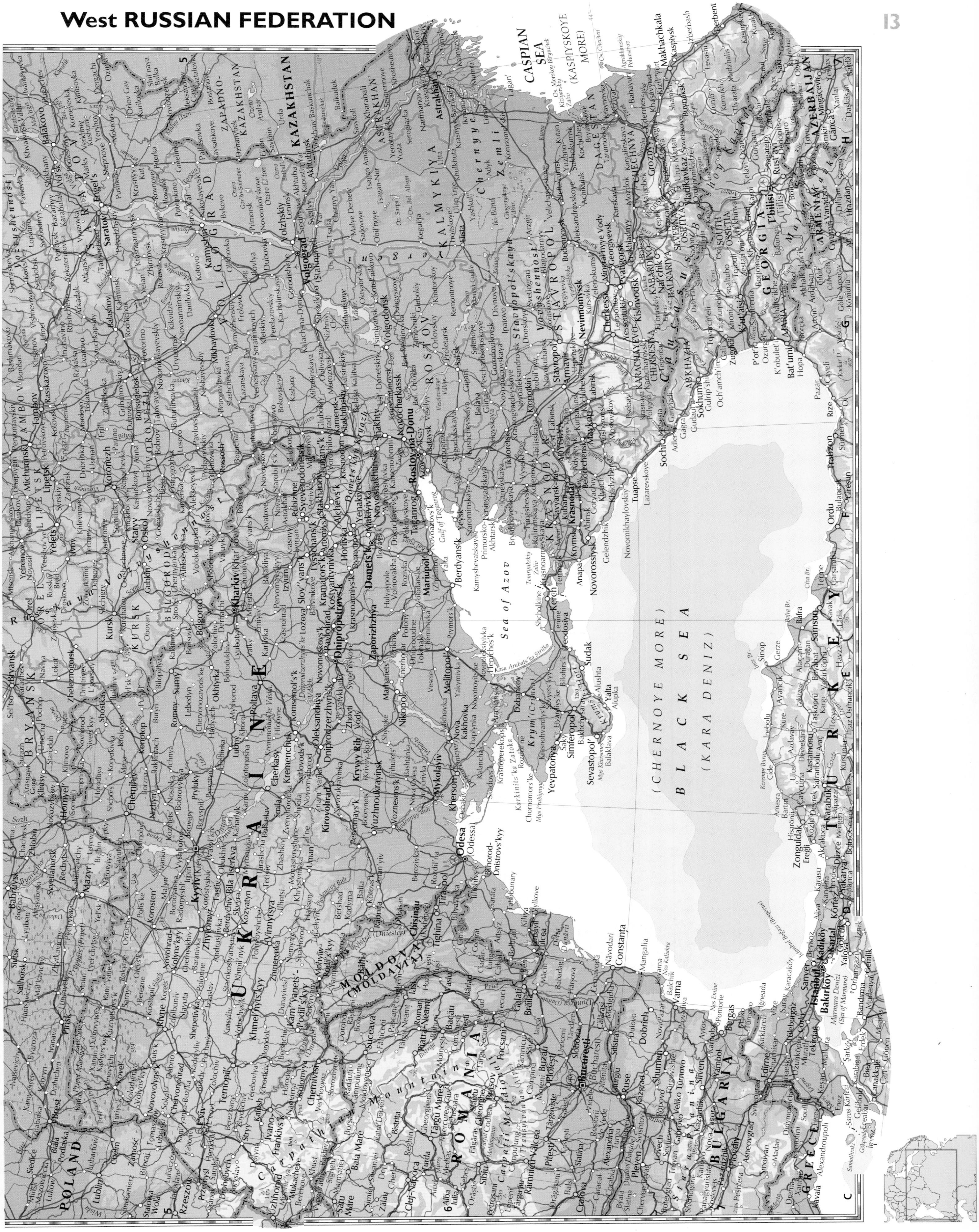

1:6 000 000

0	40	80	120	160	200 MILES

0	40	80	120	160	200	240	280	320 KM

MOSCOW REGION

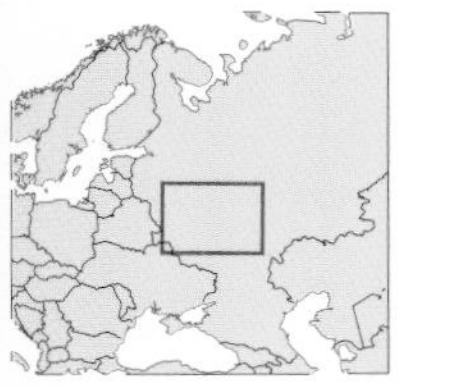

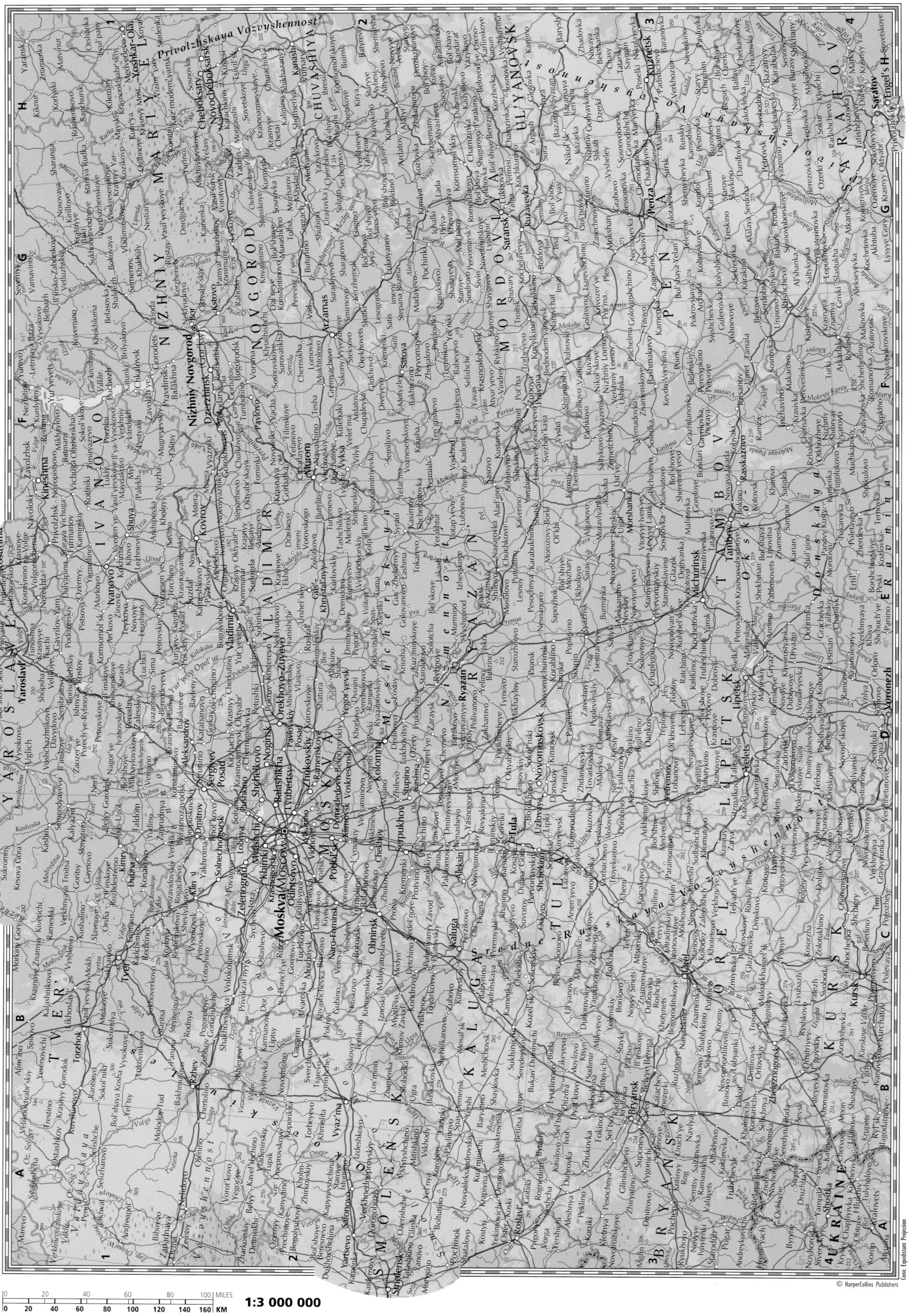

© HarperCollins Publishers

UKRAINE and MOLDOVA

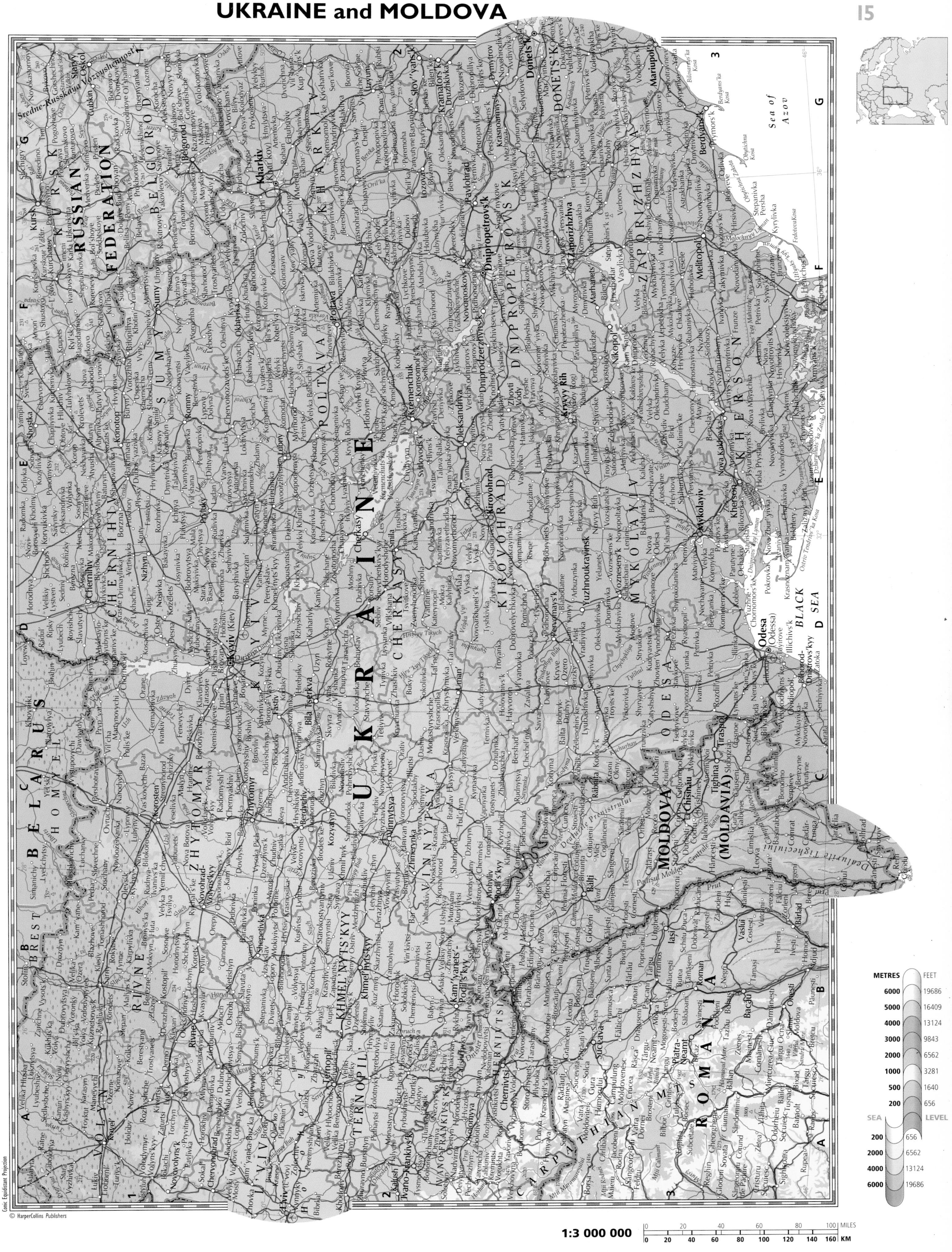
RUSSIAN FEDERATION
BELARUS
UKRAINE
MOLDOVA
(MOLDAVIA)
ROMANIA
Sea of Azov
BLACK SEA
Kharkiv
Kyyiv (Kiev)
Odesa (Odessa)
Chişinău
Dnipropetrovs'k
Donets'k
Zaporizhzhya
Mykolayiv
Kherson
Mariupol'
Poltava
Vinnytsya
Kirovohrad
Cherkasy
Zhytomyr
Chernihiv
Sumy
Rivne
Ternopil'
Chernivtsi
L'viv
METRES
FEET
6000
19686
5000
16409
4000
13124
3000
9843
2000
6562
1000
3281
500
1640
200
656
SEA
LEVEL
1:3 000 000
MILES
KM
Conic Equidistant Projection

© HarperCollins Publishers

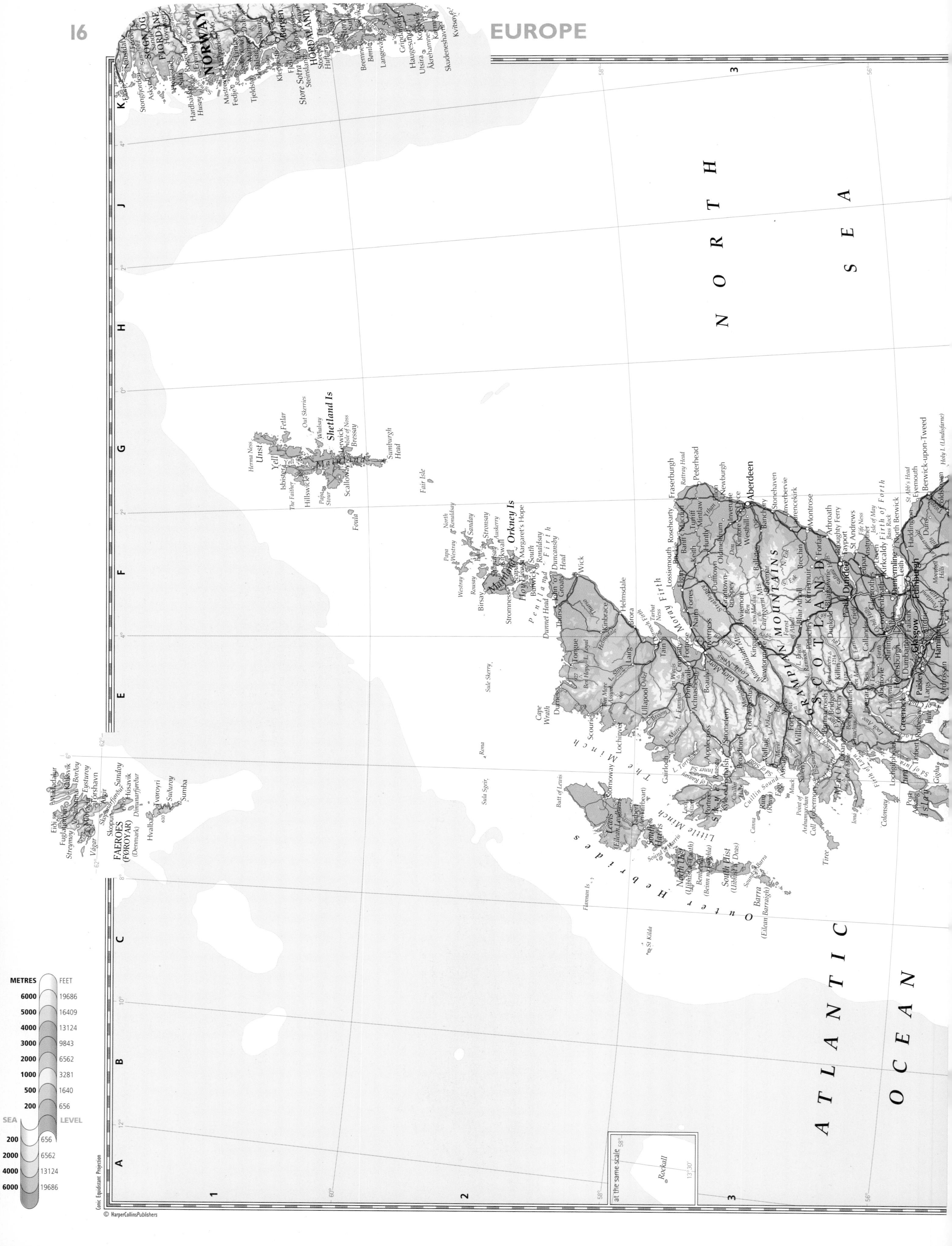
METRES FEET
6000 19686
5000 16409
4000 13124
3000 9843
2000 6562
1000 3281
500 1640
200 656
SEA LEVEL
200 656
2000 6562
4000 13124
6000 19686
Conic Equidistant Projection
NORTH SEA
ATLANTIC OCEAN
NORWAY
Bergen
HORDALAND
SOGN OG FJORDANE
Shetland Is
Mainland
Unst
Yell
Fetlar
Lerwick
Sumburgh Head
Fair Isle
Foula
Orkney Is
Kirkwall
Stromness
Pentland Firth
Dunnet Head
Thurso
Wick
Cape Wrath
Sule Skerry
Rona
FAEROES (FØROYAR) (Denmark)
Tórshavn
Suðuroy
Sandoy
Vágar
Butt of Lewis
Stornoway
Lewis
The Minch
Little Minch
Outer Hebrides
North Uist
South Uist
Barra
Flannan Is
St Kilda
Skye
Tiree
Coll
Colonsay
Islay
SCOTLAND
GRAMPIAN MOUNTAINS
Moray Firth
Inverness
Fraserburgh
Peterhead
Aberdeen
Stonehaven
Montrose
Arbroath
Dundee
Perth
St Andrews
Firth of Forth
Edinburgh
Glasgow
Paisley
Greenock
Stirling
Falkirk
Dunfermline
Kirkcaldy
Oban
Fort William
Ullapool
Lochinver
Berwick-upon-Tweed
Eyemouth
Holy I. (Lindisfarne)
Rockall
at the same scale

© HarperCollinsPublishers

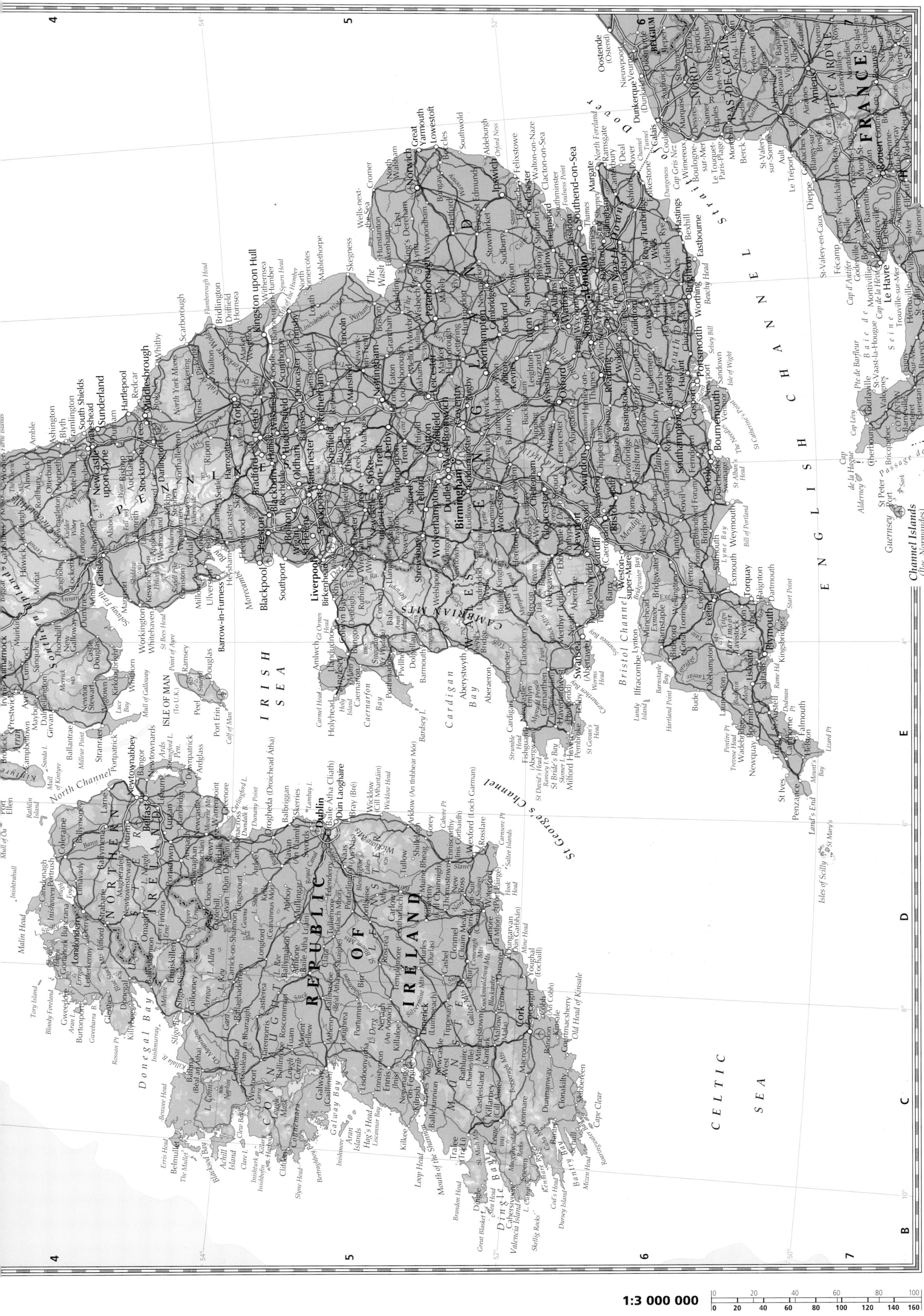

1:3 000 000

0	20	40	60	80	100 MILES			
0	20	40	60	80	100	120	140	160 KM

NETHERLANDS,

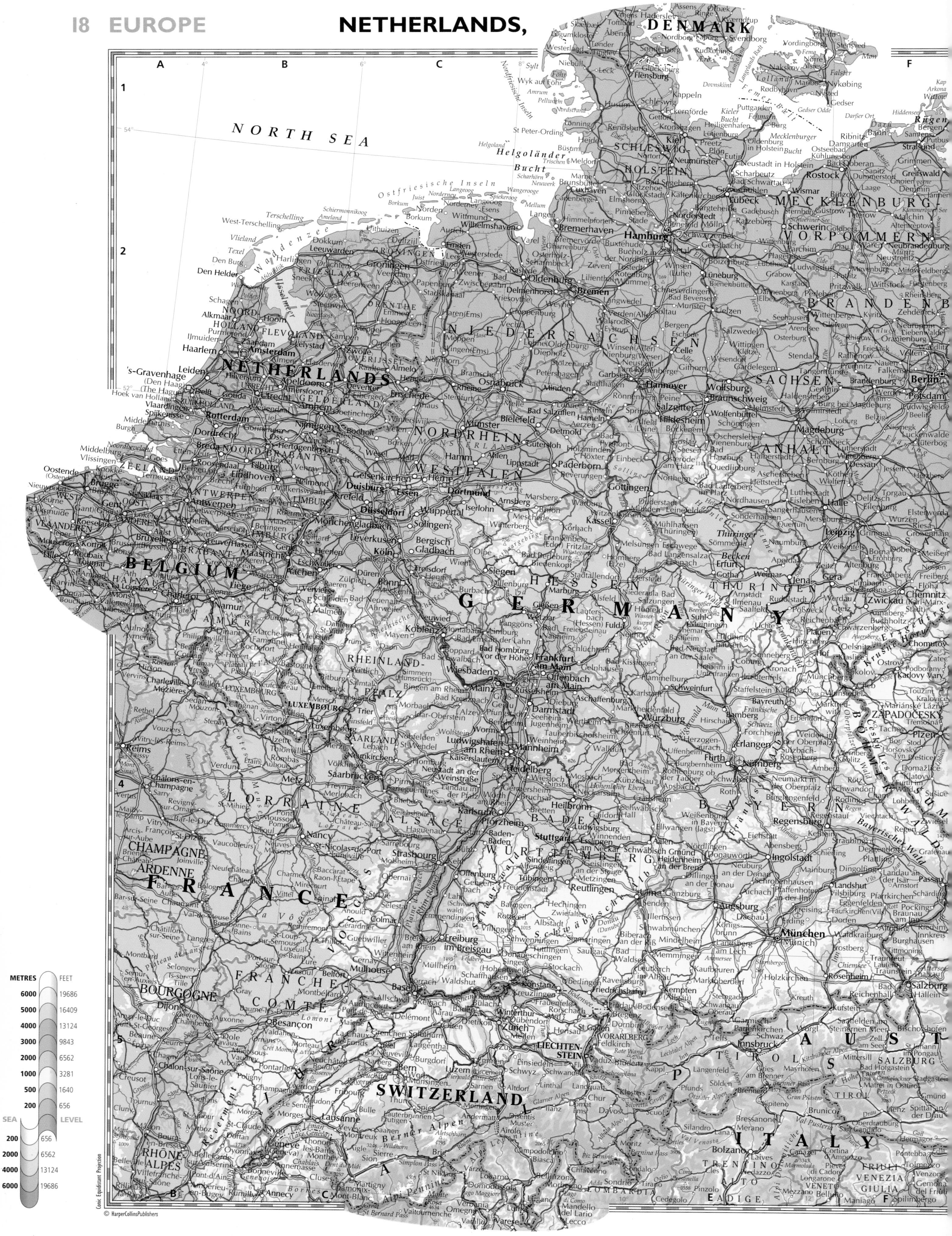

© HarperCollinsPublishers

BALTIC SEA
GULF OF DANZIG
RUS. FEDERATION
LITHUANIA
BELARUS
UKRAINE
ROMANIA
YUGOSLAVIA
CROATIA
SLOVENIA
HUNGARY
SLOVAKIA
CZECH REPUBLIC
POLAND
NIZINA
CARPATHIAN MTS
STEIERMARK
KÄRNTEN
NIEDERÖSTERREICH
BURGENLAND
VÝCHODOČESKÝ
STŘEDOČESKÝ
SEVEROČESKÝ
SEVEROMORAVSKÝ
JIHOMORAVSKÝ
JIHOČESKÝ
Gdańsk
Gdynia
Kaliningrad
Koszalin
Słupsk
Szczecin
Bydgoszcz
Toruń
Olsztyn
Białystok
Warszawa (Warsaw)
Poznań
Łódź
Wrocław
Kraków
Katowice
Częstochowa
Lublin
Radom
Kielce
Rzeszów
Opole
Praha (Prague)
Brno
Ostrava
Olomouc
Bratislava
Košice
Žilina
Wien (Vienna)
Graz
Linz
Budapest
Debrecen
Szeged
Pécs
Győr
Miskolc
Oradea
Arad
Subotica
Maribor
Dresden
Frankfurt (Oder)
Cottbus
Hrodna (Grodno)
Brest
Uzhhorod
1:3 000 000
0 20 40 60 80 100 MILES
0 20 40 60 80 100 120 140 160 KM

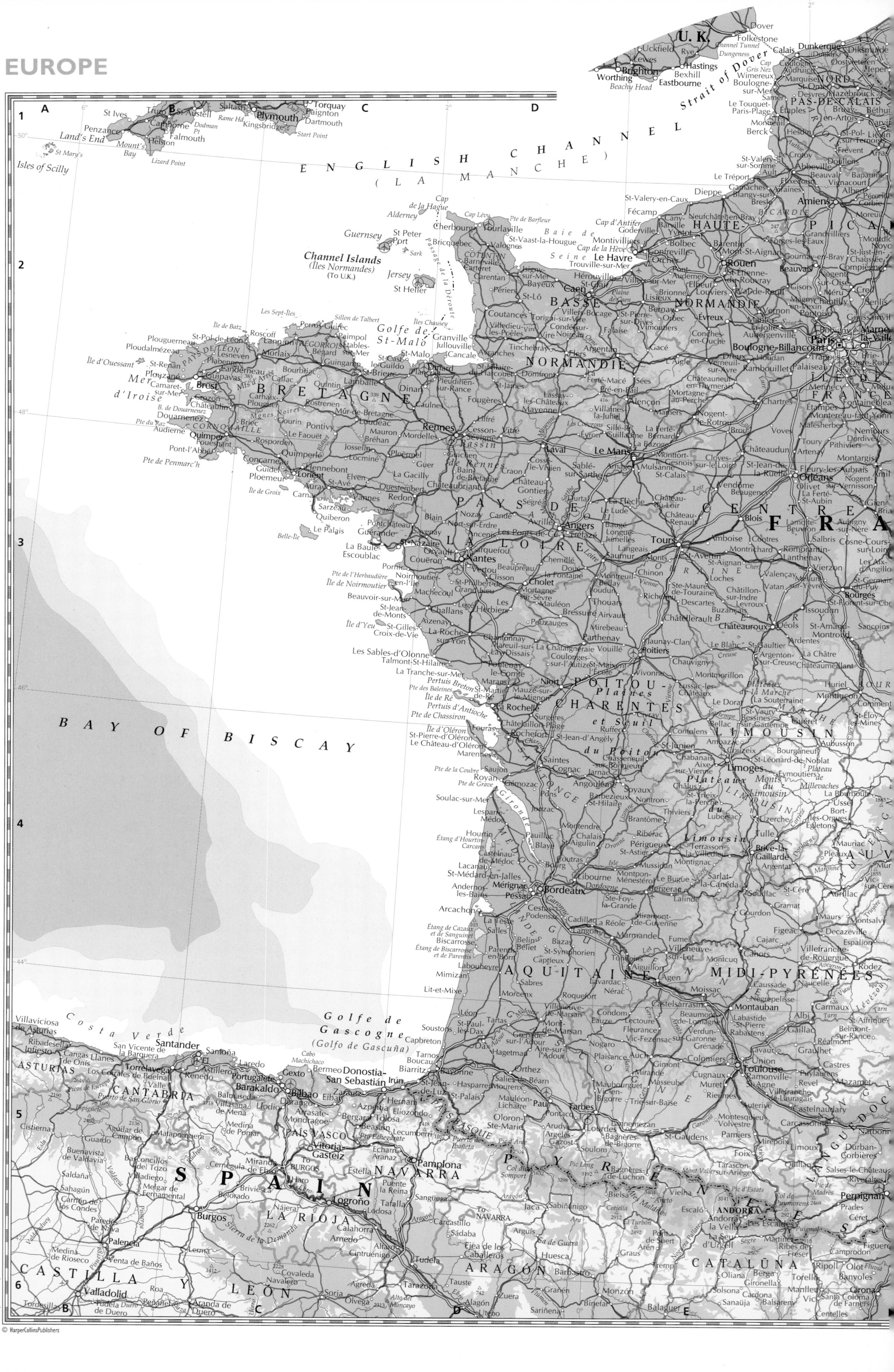
U.K.
Dover
Folkestone
Hastings
Brighton
Worthing
Eastbourne
Calais
Dunkerque
Strait of Dover
ENGLISH CHANNEL
(LA MANCHE)
Plymouth
Torquay
Penzance
Land's End
Falmouth
Isles of Scilly
Channel Islands
(Îles Normandes)
(To U.K.)
Guernsey
Jersey
Alderney
Cherbourg
Le Havre
Rouen
Caen
Amiens
Beauvais
Dieppe
HAUTE-NORMANDIE
BASSE-NORMANDIE
PAS-DE-CALAIS
PICARDIE
Paris
Boulogne-Billancourt
Chartres
Orléans
Tours
Le Mans
Laval
Rennes
Brest
Quimper
Lorient
St-Brieuc
St-Malo
Golfe de St-Malo
BRETAGNE
PAYS DE LA LOIRE
Nantes
St-Nazaire
Angers
Cholet
Poitiers
Niort
La Rochelle
Rochefort
Angoulême
Limoges
LIMOUSIN
POITOU-CHARENTES
CENTRE
FRANCE
Bourges
Châteauroux
Vierzon
Blois
Bordeaux
Mérignac
Pessac
Arcachon
AQUITAINE
MIDI-PYRÉNÉES
Toulouse
Montauban
Agen
Pau
Tarbes
Bayonne
Biarritz
Perpignan
ANDORRA
BAY OF BISCAY
Golfe de Gascogne
(Golfo de Gascuña)
Costa Verde
Santander
Bilbao
Donostia-San Sebastián
Vitoria-Gasteiz
Pamplona
Logroño
Burgos
Valladolid
Palencia
ASTURIAS
CANTABRIA
PAÍS VASCO
NAVARRA
LA RIOJA
ARAGÓN
CATALUÑA
CASTILLA Y LEÓN
SPAIN
PYRENEES
Conic Equidistant Projection
© HarperCollinsPublishers

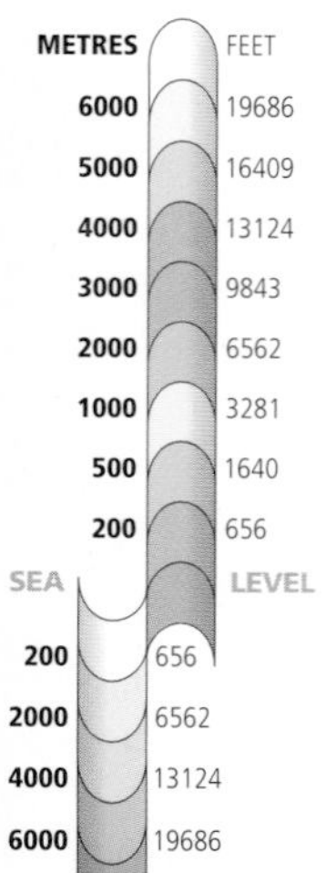
METRES
FEET
6000
19686
5000
16409
4000
13124
3000
9843
2000
6562
1000
3281
500
1640
200
656
SEA
LEVEL
200
656
2000
6562
4000
13124
6000
19686

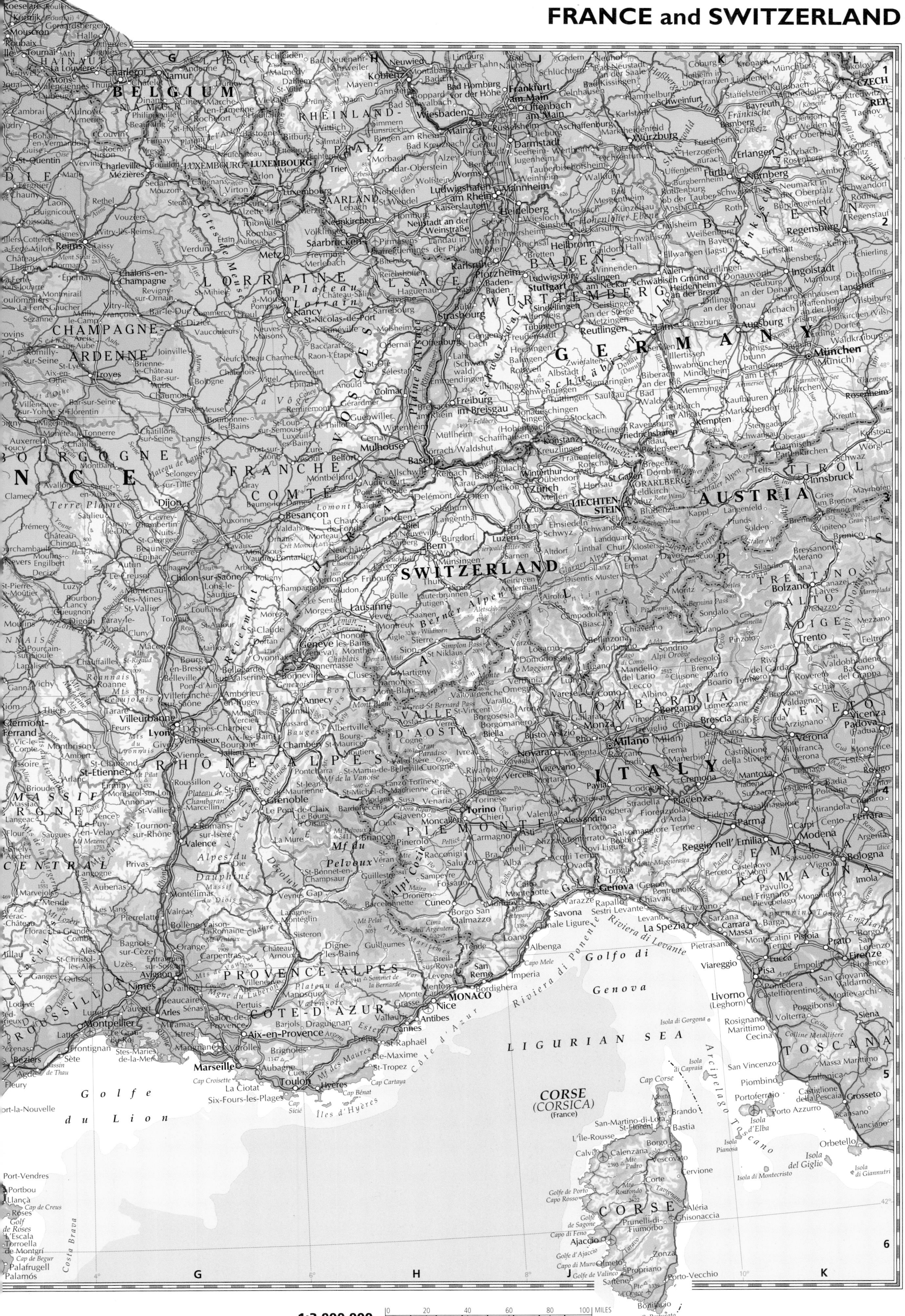
BELGIUM
LUXEMBOURG
RHEINLAND-PFALZ
SAARLAND
LORRAINE
ALSACE
CHAMPAGNE-ARDENNE
BADEN-WÜRTTEMBERG
GERMANY
BAYERN
CZECH REP.
AUSTRIA
TIROL
LIECHTENSTEIN
BOURGOGNE
FRANCHE-COMTÉ
SWITZERLAND
RHÔNE-ALPES
MASSIF CENTRAL
PROVENCE-ALPES-CÔTE-D'AZUR
VALLE D'AOSTA
PIEMONTE
LOMBARDIA
VENETO
TRENTINO ALTO ADIGE
EMILIA ROMAGNA
TOSCANA
ITALY
LIGURIA
MONACO
CORSE (CORSICA) (France)
LIGURIAN SEA
Golfe du Lion
Golfo di Genova
Arcipelago Toscano
Strasbourg
Frankfurt am Main
Stuttgart
München (Munich)
Zürich
Bern
Genève (Geneva)
Lyon
Grenoble
Marseille
Nice
Torino (Turin)
Milano (Milan)
Genova (Genoa)
Innsbruck
Dijon
Besançon
Nancy
Metz
Reims
Avignon
Montpellier
Toulon
Ajaccio
Bastia
Firenze (Florence)
Bologna
Verona
Parma
Livorno (Leghorn)
Pisa
G
H
J
K
L
1
2
3
4
5
6
4°
6°
8°
10°
42°

1:3 000 000

METRES
6000
5000
4000
3000
2000
1000
500
200
SEA
200
2000
4000
6000
FEET
19686
16409
13124
9843
6562
3281
1640
656
LEVEL
656
6562
13124
19686
Lambert Conformal Conic Projection
REPUBLIC OF IRELAND
Cork
Waterford
Wexford
WALES
ENGLAND
Birmingham
Wolverhampton
Derby
Nottingham
Lincoln
Leicester
Norwich
Great Yarmouth
Northampton
Cambridge
Gloucester
Luton
Swansea
Cardiff
Newport
Bristol
London
Southend-on-Sea
Margate
Reading
Southampton
Bournemouth
Brighton
Portsmouth
Exeter
Plymouth
Penzance
English Channel
Channel Islands (Îles Normandes) (To U.K.)
Guernsey
Jersey
Bay of Biscay
Golfe de Gascogne (Golfo de Gascuña)
FRANCE
Paris
Cherbourg
Le Havre
Caen
Rouen
Amiens
Dieppe
Abbeville
Brest
Quimper
Lorient
St-Nazaire
Rennes
Laval
Le Mans
Orléans
Tours
Angers
Nantes
La Roche-sur-Yon
Niort
La Rochelle
Poitiers
Limoges
Bordeaux
Clermont-Ferrand
Lyon
St-Étienne
Grenoble
Dijon
Besançon
Mulhouse
Strasbourg
Metz
Nancy
Reims
Toulouse
Montpellier
Nîmes
Avignon
Marseille
Toulon
Nice
Perpignan
Massif Central
Golfe du Lion
Corse (Corsica) (France)
Ajaccio
Bastia
BELGIUM
Bruxelles (Brussel) (Brussels)
Antwerpen (Antwerp)
Brugge (Bruges)
Lille
Charleroi
LUX.
Luxembourg
NETHERLANDS
Amsterdam
Rotterdam
's-Gravenhage (Den Haag) (The Hague)
Utrecht
Haarlem
Den Helder
Groningen
Arnhem
Breda
Eindhoven
GERMANY
Hamburg
Bremen
Bremerhaven
Hannover
Berlin
Potsdam
Magdeburg
Leipzig
Dresden
Chemnitz
Essen
Düsseldorf
Dortmund
Köln (Cologne)
Bonn
Frankfurt am Main
Mannheim
Heidelberg
Karlsruhe
Stuttgart
Nürnberg
München (Munich)
Augsburg
Freiburg im Breisgau
Regensburg
Saarbrücken
SWITZERLAND
Bern
Basel
Zürich
Genève (Geneva)
Lausanne
Praha (Prague)
CZECH
AUSTRIA
Salzburg
Innsbruck
Klagenfurt
SLOVENIA
Ljubljana
ITALY
Milano (Milan)
Torino (Turin)
Genova (Genoa)
Venezia (Venice)
Verona
Bologna
Firenze (Florence)
Pisa
Livorno
Roma (Rome)
Napoli (Naples)
Trieste
Ancona
Perugia
SAN MARINO
MONACO
Ligurian Sea
Tyrrhenian Sea
Sardegna (Sardinia) (Italy)
Cagliari
Sassari
Sicilia (Sicily)
Palermo
Trapani
Marsala
Agrigento
MALTA
Valletta
SPAIN
Madrid
Barcelona
Valencia
Sevilla (Seville)
Zaragoza
Málaga
Bilbao
Santander
Gijón
Oviedo
A Coruña
Vigo
Valladolid
Salamanca
Burgos
León
Pamplona
Logroño
Toledo
Córdoba (Cordova)
Granada
Almería
Murcia
Cartagena
Alicante
Albacete
Cádiz
Huelva
Badajoz
Mérida
Tarragona
Lleida
Girona
Palma de Mallorca
Menorca
Eivissa (Ibiza)
Islas Baleares (Balearic Islands)
Cordillera Cantábrica (Cantabrian Mountains)
Sierra Morena
Pyrenees
ANDORRA
Gibraltar (U.K.)
Strait of Gibraltar
PORTUGAL
Lisboa (Lisbon)
Porto
Coimbra
Braga
Setúbal
Faro
Lagos
Cabo de São Vicente (Cape St Vincent)
MEDITERRANEAN
MOROCCO
Rabat
Casablanca
Tanger (Tangier)
Tétouan
Fès (Fez)
Meknès
Oujda
Marrakech
Moyen Atlas
HAUT ATLAS (HIGH ATLAS)
Ceuta (Sp.)
Melilla (Sp.)
ALGERIA
Alger (Algiers)
Oran
Constantine
Annaba
Sétif
Blida
Tlemcen
Batna
Biskra
Laghouat
Ghardaïa
Ouargla
Touggourt
El Oued
Béchar
Atlas Saharien
Hauts Plateaux
Grand Erg Occidental
Grand Erg Oriental
Plateau du Tademaït (Tademaït Plateau)
Hammada du Drâa
In Salah
El Goléa
TUNISIA
Tunis
Sfax
Sousse
Kairouan
Gabès
Bizerte
Tarābulus (Tripoli)
TRIPOLITANIA
Al Hamādah al Hamrā'

1:9 000 000

MILES	0	60	120	180	240	300
KM	0	60	120	180	240	300	360	420	480

BAY OF BISCAY
(MAR CANTÁBRICO)
ATLANTIC
OCEAN
GOLFO DE CÁDIZ
Costa Verde
Costa de la Luz
Costa del Sol
PORTUGAL
SPAIN
MOROCCO
GALICIA
ASTURIAS
CANTABRIA
CORDILLERA CANTABRICA
CANTABRIAN MOUNTAINS
CASTILLA Y LEÓN
EXTREMADURA
ANDALUCÍA
SIERRA MORENA
VIANA DO CASTELO
BRAGA
VILA REAL
BRAGANÇA
PORTO
AVEIRO
VISEU
GUARDA
COIMBRA
LEIRIA
CASTELO BRANCO
SANTARÉM
LISBOA
PORTALEGRE
SETÚBAL
ÉVORA
BEJA
FARO
A Coruña
Ferrol
Santiago
Lugo
Ourense
Pontevedra
Vigo
Oviedo
Gijón
Avilés
Santander
León
Burgos
Palencia
Valladolid
Zamora
Salamanca
Segovia
Madrid
Alcalá de Henares
Móstoles
Fuenlabrada
Toledo
Talavera de la Reina
Cáceres
Badajoz
Mérida
Ciudad Real
Puertollano
Córdoba
Jaén
Granada
Sevilla
Huelva
Cádiz
Jerez de la Frontera
Málaga
Marbella
Algeciras
Gibraltar (U.K.)
Ceuta (Spain)
Tanger
Tetouan (Tetuán)
Porto
Coimbra
Lisboa (Lisbon)
Amadora
Setúbal
Évora
Faro
Braga
Strait of Gibraltar
MADEIRA
(Portugal)
Ilha de Porto Santo
Ilha da Madeira
Funchal
Ilhas Desertas
METRES
FEET
6000
19686
5000
16409
4000
13124
3000
9843
2000
6562
1000
3281
500
1640
200
656
SEA
LEVEL
200
656
2000
6562
4000
13124
6000
19686
Conic Equidistant Projection

© HarperCollinsPublishers

1:3 000 000

0 20 40 60 80 100 MILES

0 20 40 60 80 100 120 140 160 KM

SLOVAKIA
HUNGARY
CROATIA
BOSNIA-HERZEGOVINA
YUGOSLAVIA
SLOVENIA
AUSTRIA
CZECH REP.
GERMANY
SWITZERLAND
LIECHTENSTEIN
FRANCE
ITALY
ADRIATIC
LIGURIAN SEA
CORSE (CORSICA) (France)
MONACO
SAN MARINO
Budapest
Wien
Zagreb
Ljubljana
Sarajevo
München
Milano
Venezia (Venice)
Genova
Firenze
Bratislava
METRES
6000
5000
4000
3000
2000
1000
500
200
SEA LEVEL
200
2000
4000
6000
FEET
19686
16409
13124
9843
6562
3281
1640
656
656
6562
13124
19686
Conic Equidistant Projection

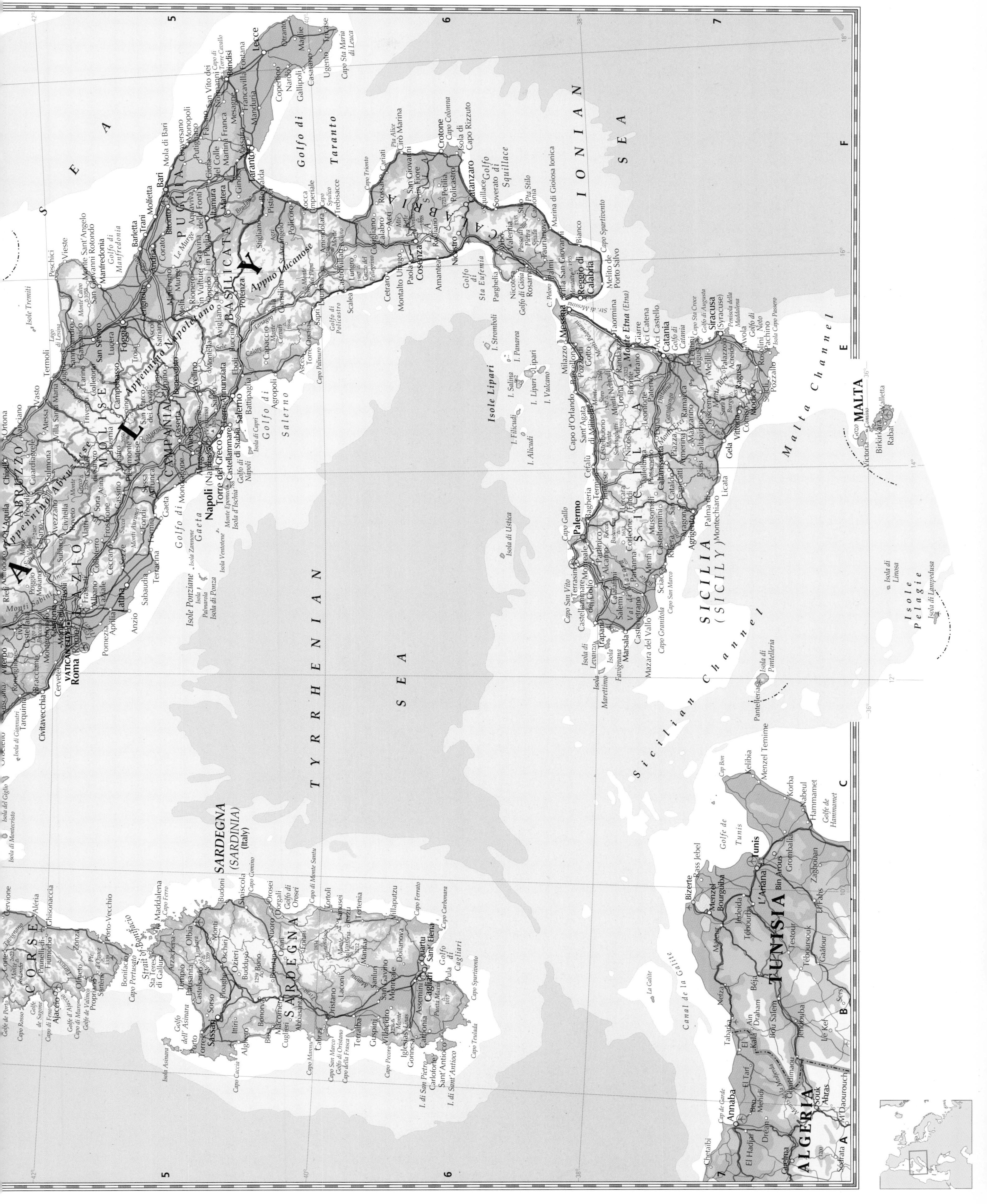

1:3 000 000

0	20	40	60	80	100	MILES			
0	20	40	60	80	100	120	140	160	KM

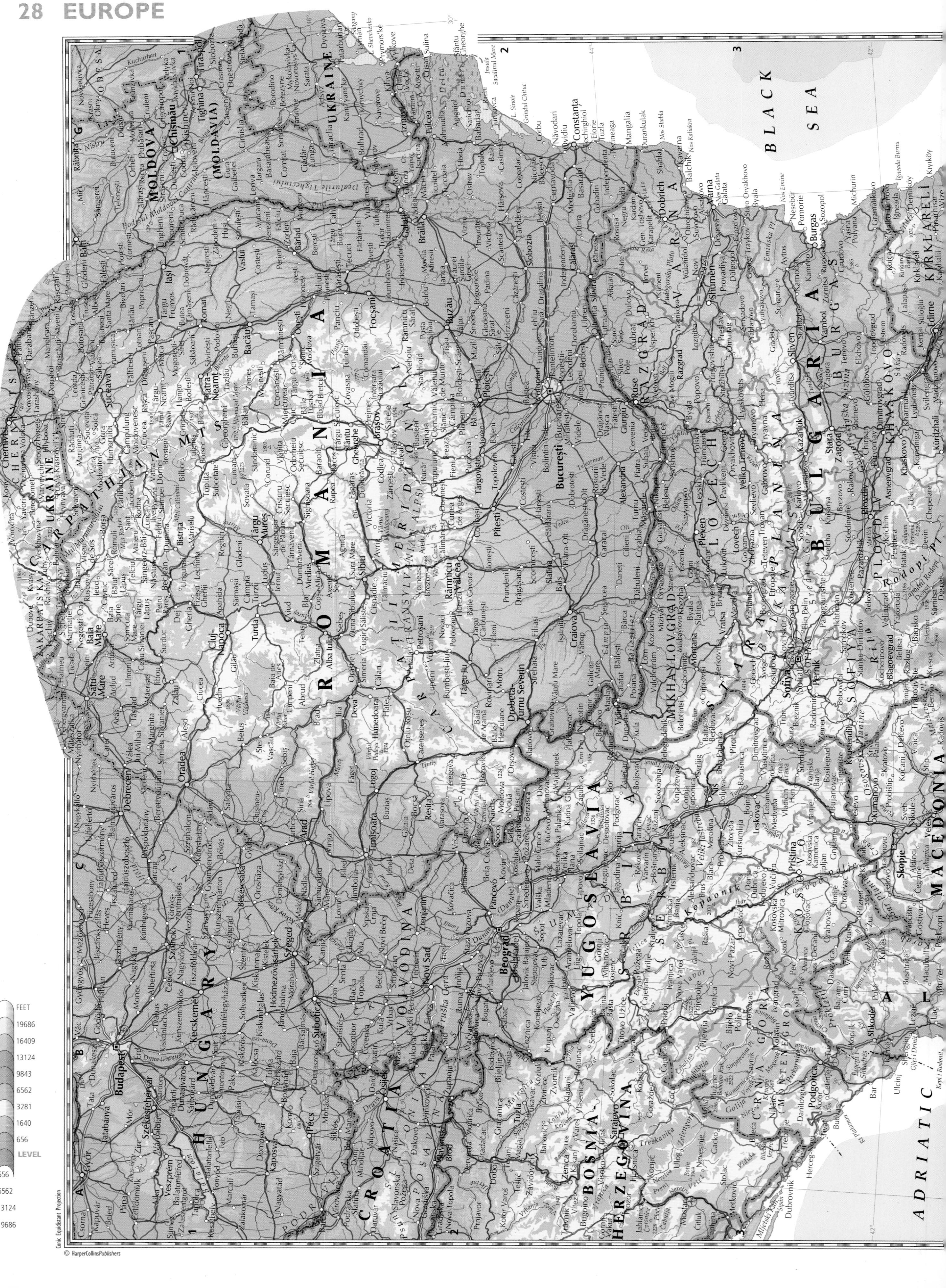
METRES
FEET
6000 19686
5000 16409
4000 13124
3000 9843
2000 6562
1000 3281
500 1640
200 656
SEA LEVEL
200 656
2000 6562
4000 13124
6000 19686
Conic Equidistant Projection
© HarperCollinsPublishers

1:3 000 000

MILES 0 20 40 60 80 100

KM 0 20 40 60 80 100 120 140 160

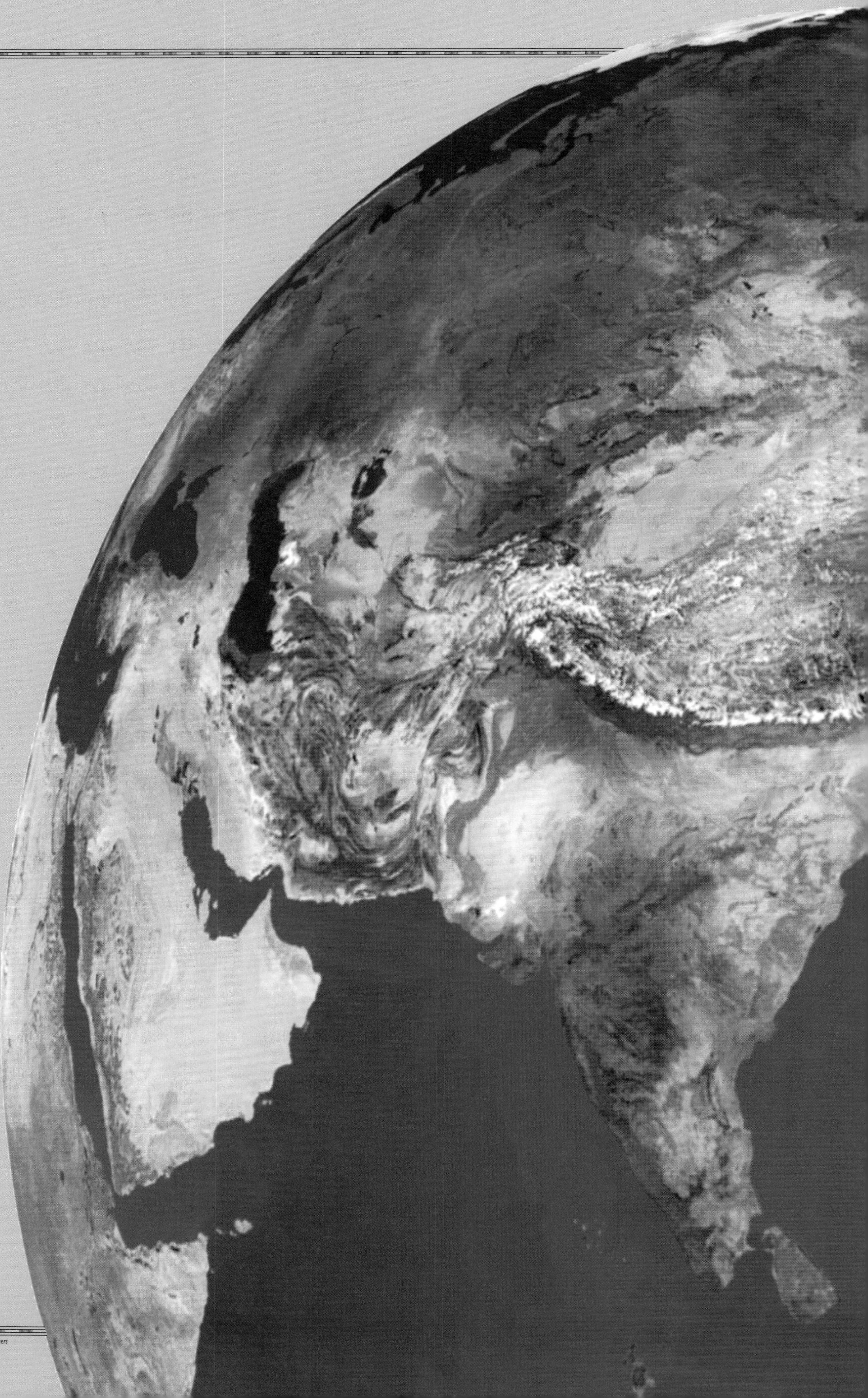

ARCTIC OCEAN
Norwegian Sea
Barents Sea
Kara Sea
North Sea
Bay of Biscay
Baltic Sea
Gulf of Bothnia
White Sea
Pechora Sea
Mediterranean Sea
Black Sea
Caspian Sea
Red Sea
The Gulf
Gulf of Oman
Gulf of Aden
ARABIAN SEA
BAY OF BENGAL
INDIAN OCEAN
Rub' al Khali
North Pole
Komsomolets I.
October Revolution I.
Bolshevik I.
Novaya Zemlya
Svalbard (Nor.)
Spitsbergen
Jan Mayen (Nor.)
Faeroes (Den.)
North Cape
Yamal Pen.
Gydan Pen.
Taymyr Pen.
Ural Mountains
Caucasus
Altai Mts
Tien Shan
Hindu Kush
Karakoram
HIMALAYA
Kunlun Shan
Pik Kommunizma 7495
K2 8611
Mt Everest 8848m (29028ft)
TIBET
SINKIANG
PORTUGAL
SPAIN
FRANCE
UNITED KINGDOM
REP. OF IRELAND
NORWAY
SWEDEN
FINLAND
DENMARK
NETH.
BELG.
LUX.
GERMANY
SWITZ.
AUSTRIA
CZECH REP.
SLOVAKIA
HUNGARY
POLAND
SLOVENIA
CROATIA
BOSNIA HERZ.
YUGO.
ALBANIA
MACE.
BULGARIA
ROMANIA
MOLDOVA
UKRAINE
BELARUS
LITHUANIA
LATVIA
ESTONIA
ITALY
GREECE
RUSSIAN FEDERATION (in Europe)
TURKEY
CYPRUS
GEORGIA
ARMENIA
AZERBAIJAN
SYRIA
LEBANON
ISRAEL
JORDAN
IRAQ
IRAN
KUWAIT
SAUDI ARABIA
BAHRAIN
QATAR
U.A.E.
OMAN
YEMEN
KAZAKHSTAN
TURKMENISTAN
UZBEKISTAN
KYRGYZSTAN
TAJIKISTAN
AFGHANISTAN
PAKISTAN
BALUCHISTAN
INDIA
NEPAL
BHUTAN
BANGLADESH
SRI LANKA
MALDIVES
ALGERIA
TUNISIA
MALTA
LIBYA
EGYPT
SUDAN
ERITREA
DJIBOUTI
ETHIOPIA
SOMALIA
KENYA
TANZANIA
MOZAMBIQUE
COMOROS
SEYCHELLES
Lisbon
Oporto
Sevilla
Madrid
Barcelona
Marseille
Lyon
Paris
London
Birmingham
Liverpool
Dublin
Edinburgh
The Hague
Amsterdam
Brussels
Bonn
Hamburg
Berlin
Copenhagen
Oslo
Stockholm
Helsinki
Tallinn
Riga
Vilnius
Minsk
Warsaw
Prague
Vienna
Bratislava
Budapest
Munich
Bern
Milan
Rome
Naples
Ljubljana
Zagreb
Sarajevo
Belgrade
Skopje
Tirana
Sofia
Bucharest
Chisinau
Kiev
Dnepropetrovsk
Odessa
Kharkov
Donetsk
Rostov-na-Donu
Volgograd
Moscow
St Petersburg
Nizhniy Novgorod
Kazan
Perm
Samara
Saratov
Ufa
Orenburg
Yekaterinburg
Chelyabinsk
Magnitogorsk
Tyumen
Tobolsk
Omsk
Novosibirsk
Barnaul
Tomsk
Krasnoyarsk
Novokuznetsk
Surgut
Salekhard
Norilsk
Murmansk
Archangel
Astrakhan
Guryev
Aktyubinsk
Uralsk
Pavlodar
Semipalatinsk
Ust-Kamenogorsk
Karaganda
Balkhash
Dzhambul
Chimkent
Tashkent
Alma-Ata
Bishkek
Samarkand
Dushanbe
Kokand
Andizhan
Ashkhabad
Krasnovodsk
Baku
Tbilisi
Yerevan
Tabriz
Rasht
Tehran
Mashhad
Hamadan
Qom
Bakhtaran
Isfahan
Ahvaz
Abadan
Shiraz
Yazd
Kerman
Zahedan
Bandar Abbas
Istanbul
Ankara
Izmir
Bursa
Konya
Antalya
Samsun
Sivas
Erzurum
Kayseri
Adana
Malatya
Gaziantep
Aleppo
Homs
Tripoli
Beirut
Damascus
Haifa
Tel Aviv
Jerusalem
Amman
Port Said
Cairo
Alexandria
Mosul
Kirkuk
Baghdad
An Najaf
Basra
Kuwait
Riyadh
Madinah
Jiddah
Makkah
Manama
Doha
Abu Dhabi
Dubai
Muscat
Sana
Aden
Mukalla
Salalah
Masirah
Socotra (Yemen)
Algiers
Tunis
Tripoli
Banghazi
Khartoum
Port Sudan
Asmara
Hodeidah
Taizz
Djibouti
Addis Ababa
Mogadishu
Nairobi
Mombasa
Dar es Salaam
Kabul
Herat
Kandahar
Peshawar
Rawalpindi
Islamabad
Quetta
Lahore
Amritsar
Ludhiana
Multan
Chandigarh
Delhi
New Delhi
Karachi
Hyderabad
Jodhpur
Jaipur
Agra
Gwalior
Kanpur
Lucknow
Kathmandu
Darjeeling
Shillong
Patna
Varanasi
Allahabad
Asansol
Jamshedpur
Calcutta
Dhaka
Chittagong
Ahmadabad
Jabalpur
Indore
Nagpur
Surat
Bombay
Pune
Hyderabad
Cuttack
Vishakhapatnam
Vijayawada
Kurnool
Panaji
Bangalore
Mangalore
Mysore
Madras
Calicut
Madurai
Tiruchchirappalli
Trivandrum
C. Comorin
Jaffna
Trincomalee
Kandy
Colombo
Dondra Head
Bassein
Urumqi
Turpan
Yining
Kashi
Shache
Hotan
Korla
Golmud
Lhasa
Ulaangom
Uliastay
Laccadive Is (India)
Andaman Islands (India)
Nicobar Islands (India)
Amirante Islands
Mahé
Aldabra Is
Gan
Addu Atoll
Salomon Is
British Indian Ocean Terr.
Chagos Archipelago
L. Nasser
L. Turkana
Lake Balkhash
L. Issyk-Kul
Aral Sea
Lake Ladoga
Lake Onega
Kara Bogaz Gol
L. Van
L. Urmia
Bosten Hu
Lop Nur
Nile
White Nile
Blue Nile
Volga
Ural
Ob
Yenisey
Lower Tunguska
Angara
Danube
Rhine
Indus
Ganges
Brahmaputra
Jumna
Godavari
Krishna
Euphrates
Tigris
Syrdarya
Amudarya
Helmand
Chenab
Tarim He
Equator
Two Point Equidistant Projection

NORTH PACIFIC OCEAN
BERING SEA
Sea of Okhotsk
Sea of Japan
East China Sea
South China Sea
Yellow Sea
Philippine Sea
Celebes Sea
Sulu Sea
Banda Sea
Java Sea
Flores Sea
Arafura Sea
Coral Sea
Bismarck Sea
Solomon Sea
Laptev Sea
East Siberian Sea
Chukchi Sea
RUSSIAN FEDERATION
MONGOLIA
CHINA
NORTH KOREA
SOUTH KOREA
JAPAN
TAIWAN
PHILIPPINES
VIETNAM
LAOS
THAILAND
CAMBODIA
MYANMAR (BURMA)
MALAYSIA
BRUNEI
SINGAPORE
INDONESIA
PAPUA NEW GUINEA
AUSTRALIA
PALAU
FED. STATES OF MICRONESIA
Northern Mariana Is (U.S.A.)
Guam (U.S.A.)
Caroline Islands
Kuril Islands
Aleutian Islands
Kamchatka
Sakhalin
Hokkaido
Honshu
Kyushu
Shikoku
Luzon
Mindanao
Borneo
Sumatra
Java
Sulawesi
New Guinea
Beijing
Tokyo
Seoul
Pyongyang
Shanghai
Hong Kong
Taipei
Manila
Hanoi
Ho Chi Minh City
Bangkok
Rangoon
Kuala Lumpur
Jakarta
Ulan Bator
Vladivostok
Tropic of Cancer
Equator
1:30 000 000
0 250 500 750 1000 MILES
0 250 500 750 1000 1250 1500 KM

National Statistics

COUNTRY	AREA		POPULATION			Form of Government	Capital City	MAIN LANGUAGES	MAIN RELIGIONS	CURRENCY
	sq ml	sq km	total	density per sq ml	sq km					
AFGHANISTAN	251 825	652 225	18 879 000	*75*	*29*	republic	Kabul	Dari, Pushtu, Uzbek, Turkmen	Sunni & Shi'a Muslim	Afghani
ARMENIA	11 506	29 800	3 548 000	*308*	*119*	republic	Yerevan	Armenian, Azeri, Russian	Arm. Orthodox, RC, Muslim	Dram
AZERBAIJAN	33 436	86 600	7 472 000	*223*	*86*	republic	Baku	Azeri, Armenian, Russian, Lezgian	Shi'a & Sunni Muslim, Russ. and Arm. Orthodox	Manat
BAHRAIN	267	691	9 568 000	*35863*	*13847*	monarchy	Manama	Arabic, English	Shi'a & Sunni Muslim, Christian	Dinar
BANGLADESH	55 598	143 998	117 787 000	*2119*	*818*	republic	Dhaka	Bengali, Bihari, Hindi, English, local lang.	Muslim, Hindu, Buddhist, Christian	Taka
BHUTAN	18 000	46 620	1 614 000	*90*	*35*	monarchy	Thimphu	Dzongkha, Nepali, Assamese, English	Buddhist, Hindu, Muslim	Ngultrum
BRUNEI	2 226	5 765	280 000	*126*	*49*	monarchy	Bandar Seri Begawan	Malay, English, Chinese	Muslim, Buddhist, Christian	Dollar (ringgit)
CAMBODIA	69 884	181 000	9 568 000	*137*	*53*	monarchy	Phnom Penh	Khmer, Vietnamese	Buddhist, RC, Sunni Muslim	Riel
CHINA	3 691 484	9 560 900	1 208 842 000	*327*	*126*	republic	Beijing	Chinese, regional lang.	Confucian, Taoist, Buddhist, Muslim, RC	Yuan
CYPRUS	3 572	9 251	726 000	*203*	*78*	republic	Nicosia	Greek, Turkish, English	Greek Orthodox, Muslim	Pound
GEORGIA	26 911	69 700	5 450 000	*203*	*78*	republic	Tbilisi	Georgian, Russian, Armenian, Azeri, Ossetian, Abkhaz	Orthodox, Muslim	Lari
Hong Kong	415	1 075	6 061 000	*14603*	*5638*	Special Administrative Region of China		Chinese, English	Buddhist, Taoist, Protestant	Dollar
INDIA	1 269 219	3 287 263	918 570 000	*724*	*279*	republic	New Delhi	Hindi, English, regional lang.	Hindu, Muslim, Sikh, Christian, Buddhist, Jain	Rupee
INDONESIA	741 102	1 919 445	190 676 000	*257*	*99*	republic	Jakarta	Indonesian, local lang.	Muslim, Protestant, RC Hindu, Buddhist	Rupiah
IRAN	636 296	1 648 000	59 778 000	*94*	*36*	republic	Tehran	Farsi, Azeri, Kurdish, regional lang.	Shi'a & Sunni Muslim, Baha'i, Christian, Zoroastrian	Rial
IRAQ	169 235	438 317	19 925 000	*118*	*45*	republic	Baghdad	Arabic, Kurdish, Turkmen	Shi'a & Sunni Muslim, RC	Dinar
ISRAEL	8 019	20 770	5 399 000	*673*	*260*	republic	Jerusalem	Hebrew, Arabic, Yiddish, English	Jewish, Muslim, Christian, Druze	Shekel
JAPAN	145 841	377 727	124 961 000	*857*	*331*	monarchy	Tokyo	Japanese	Shintoist, Buddhist, Christian	Yen
JORDAN	34 443	89 206	5 198 000	*151*	*58*	monarchy	Amman	Arabic	Sunni & Shi'a Muslim, Christian	Dinar
KAZAKHSTAN	1 049 155	2 717 300	17 027 000	*16*	*6*	republic	Alma-Ata	Kazakh, Russian, German, Ukrainian, Uzbek, Tatar	Muslim, Russ. Orthodox, Protestant	Tanga
KUWAIT	6 880	17 818	1 620 000	*235*	*91*	monarchy	Kuwait	Arabic	Sunni & Shi'a Muslim, Christian, Hindu	Dinar
KYRGYZSTAN	76 641	198 500	4 473 000	*58*	*23*	republic	Bishkek	Kirghiz, Russian, Uzbek	Muslim, Russian Orthodox	Som
LAOS	91 429	236 800	4 742 000	*52*	*20*	republic	Vientiane	Lao, local languages	Buddhist, trad. beliefs, RC, Sunni Muslim	Kip
LEBANON	4 036	10 452	2 915 000	*722*	*279*	republic	Beirut	Arabic, French, Armenian	Shi'a & Sunni Muslim, Protestant, RC	Pound
MACAU	7	17	403 000	*61398*	*23706*	Portuguese terr.	Macau	Chinese, Portuguese	Buddhist, RC, Protestant	Pataca
MALAYSIA	128 559	332 965	20 097 000	*156*	*60*	federation	Kuala Lumpur	Malay, English, Chinese, Tamil, local lang.	Muslim, Buddhist, Hindu, Christian, trad. beliefs	Dollar (ringgit)
MALDIVES	115	298	246 000	*2138*	*826*	republic	Male	Divehi (Maldivian)	Sunni Muslim	Rufiyaa
MONGOLIA	604 250	1 565 000	2 363 000	*4*	*2*	republic	Ulan Bator	Khalka (Mongolian), Kazakh, local lang.	Buddhist, Muslim, trad. beliefs	Tugrik
MYANMAR	261 228	676 577	43 922 000	*168*	*65*	republic	Rangoon	Burmese, Shan, Karen, local lang.	Buddhist, Muslim, Protestant, RC	Kyat
NEPAL	56 827	147 181	21 360 000	*376*	*145*	monarchy	Kathmandu	Nepali, Maithili, Bhojpuri, English, local lang.	Hindu, Buddhist, Muslim	Rupee
NORTH KOREA	46 540	120 538	23 483 000	*505*	*195*	republic	Pyongyang	Korean	Trad. beliefs, Chondoist, Buddhist, Confucian, Taoist	Won
OMAN	105 000	271 950	2 096 000	*20*	*8*	monarchy	Muscat	Arabic, Baluchi, Farsi, Swahili, Indian lang.	Muslim,	Rial
PAKISTAN	310 403	803 940	126 467 000	*407*	*157*	republic	Islamabad	Urdu, Punjabi, Sindhi, Pushtu, English	Muslim, Christian, Hindu	Rupee
PALAU	192	497	17 000	*89*	*34*	republic	Koror	Palauan, English	RC, Protestant, trad.beliefs	US dollar
PHILIPPINES	115 831	300 000	68 624 000	*592*	*229*	republic	Manila	English, Filipino, Cebuano, local lang.	RC, Aglipayan, Muslim, Protestant	Peso
QATAR	4 416	11 437	593 000	*134*	*52*	monarchy	Doha	Arabic, Indian lang.	Muslim, Christian, Hindu	Riyal
RUSSIAN FEDERATION	6 592 849	17 075 400	148 673 000	*23*	*9*	republic	Moscow	Russian, Tatar, Ukrainian, local lang.	Russ. Orthodox, Muslim, other Christian, Jewish	Rouble
RUSSIAN FEDERATION (IN ASIA)	5 065 506	13 119 600	41 755 000	*8*	*3*					
SAUDI ARABIA	849 425	2 200 000	17 451 000	*21*	*8*	monarchy	Riyadh	Arabic	Sunni & Shi'a Muslim	Riyal
SINGAPORE	247	639	2 930 000	*11876*	*4585*	republic	Singapore	Chinese, English, Malay, Tamil	Buddhist, Taoist, Muslim, Christian, Hindu	Dollar
SOUTH KOREA	38 330	99 274	44 453 000	*1160*	*448*	republic	Seoul	Korean	Buddhist, Protestant, RC, Confucian, trad. beliefs	Won
SRI LANKA	25 332	65 610	17 865 000	*705*	*272*	republic	Colombo	Sinhalese, Tamil, English	Buddhist, Hindu, Muslim, RC	Rupee
SYRIA	71 498	185 180	13 844 000	*194*	*75*	republic	Damascus	Arabic, Kurdish, Armenian	Muslim, Christian	Pound
TAIWAN	13 969	36 179	21 074 000	*1509*	*582*	republic	Taipei	Chinese, local lang.	Buddhist, Taoist, Confucian, Christian	Dollar
TAJIKISTAN	55 251	143 100	5 933 000	*107*	*41*	republic	Dushanbe	Tajik, Uzbek, Russian	Muslim	Rouble
THAILAND	198 115	513 115	59 396 000	*300*	*116*	monarchy	Bangkok	Thai, Lao, Chinese, Malay, Mon-Khmer lang.	Buddhist, Muslim	Baht
TURKEY	300 948	779 452	60 576 000	*201*	*78*	republic	Ankara	Turkish, Kurdish	Sunni & Shi'a Muslim	Lira
TURKMENISTAN	188 456	488 100	4 010 000	*21*	*8*	republic	Ashkhabad	Turkmen, Russian	Muslim	Manat
UNITED ARAB EMIRATES	30 000	77 700	1 861 000	*62*	*24*	federation	Abu Dhabi	Arabic, English, Hindi, Urdu, Farsi	Sunni & Shi'a Muslim, Christian	Dirham
UZBEKISTAN	172 742	447 400	22 633 000	*131*	*51*	republic	Tashkent	Uzbek, Russian, Tajik, Kazakh	Muslim, Russ.Orthodox	Som
VIETNAM	127 246	329 565	72 510 000	*570*	*220*	republic	Hanoi	Vietnamese, Thai, Khmer, Chinese, local lang.	Buddhist, Taoist, RC, Cao Dai, Hoa Hao	Dong
YEMEN	203 850	527 968	12 672 000	*62*	*24*	republic	Sana	Arabic	Sunni & Shi'a Muslim	Dinar, rial

ASSOCIATION OF SOUTH EAST ASIAN NATIONS (ASEAN)

Established at a meeting in Bangkok in 1967, ASEAN replaced the Association of South East Asia (ASA) which had been established in 1961. The objectives of ASEAN are to promote economic, political and social co-operation. The founder members were Indonesia, Malysia, the Philippines, Singapore and Thailand; Brunei joined in 1984 and Vietnam in 1995. Cambodia, Laos and Myanmar have applied for membership.

Headquarters : Jakarta, Indonesia

BRUNEI	JORDAN	AZERBAIJAN
KUWAIT	BAHRAIN	GEORGIA
QATAR	DJIBOUTI	MOLDOVA
SYRIA	PALESTINE	
LEBANON	ARMENIA	

ASIA PACIFIC ECONOMIC CO-OPERATION FORUM (APEC)

see page 88 for information

COMMONWEALTH OF INDEPENDENT STATES

see page 7 for information

ORGANIZATION OF PETROLEUM EXPORTING COUNTRIES (OPEC)

Established in 1960 at a meeting in Baghdad, to co-ordinate the price and supply policies of oil-producing states, and to provide member countries with economic and technical aid. Member countries are Algeria, Ecuador, Gabon, Indonesia, Iran, Iraq, Kuwait, Libya, Nigeria, Qatar, Saudi Arabia, U.A.E. and Venezuela.

Headquarters : Vienna, Austria

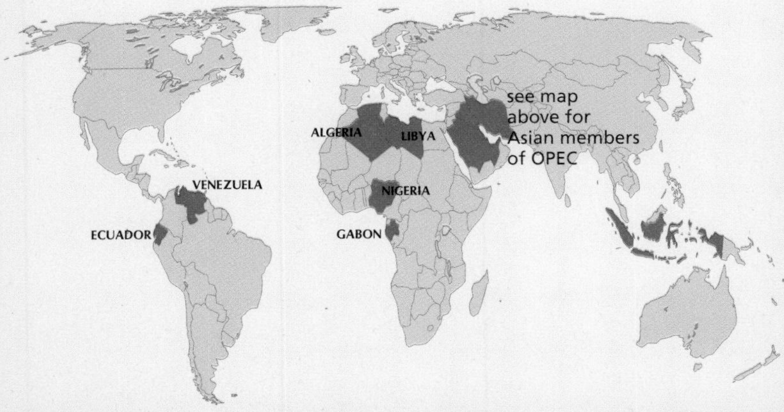

ARAB LEAGUE

The Arab League was founded in 1945 in Cairo, by Egypt, Syria, Iraq, Lebanon, Jordan, Saudi Arabia and Yemen. Egypt's membership was suspended in 1979 because of its peace treaty with Israel; Egypt was re-admitted in 1989.

The membership has now been extended to include Algeria, Bahrain, Djibouti, Kuwait, Libya, Mauritania, Morocco, Oman, Palestine, Qatar, Somalia, Sudan, Tunisia and U.A.E.

Headquarters : Cairo, Egypt

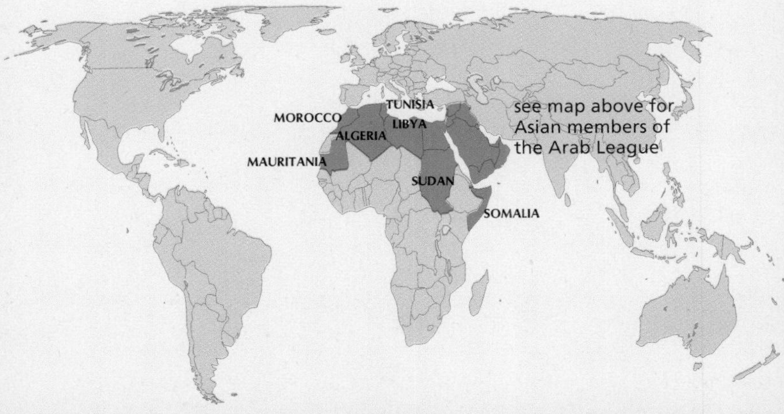

KEY TO MAPS
Built-up areas
Park or open space
Open water
Important building
Cemetery
Lake
River or canal
Main road
Road
Other road
Railway
Airport
Istanbul
Beijing
Seoul
Tokyo
Shanghai
Delhi
Calcutta
Guangzhou
Bombay
Bangkok
Jakarta

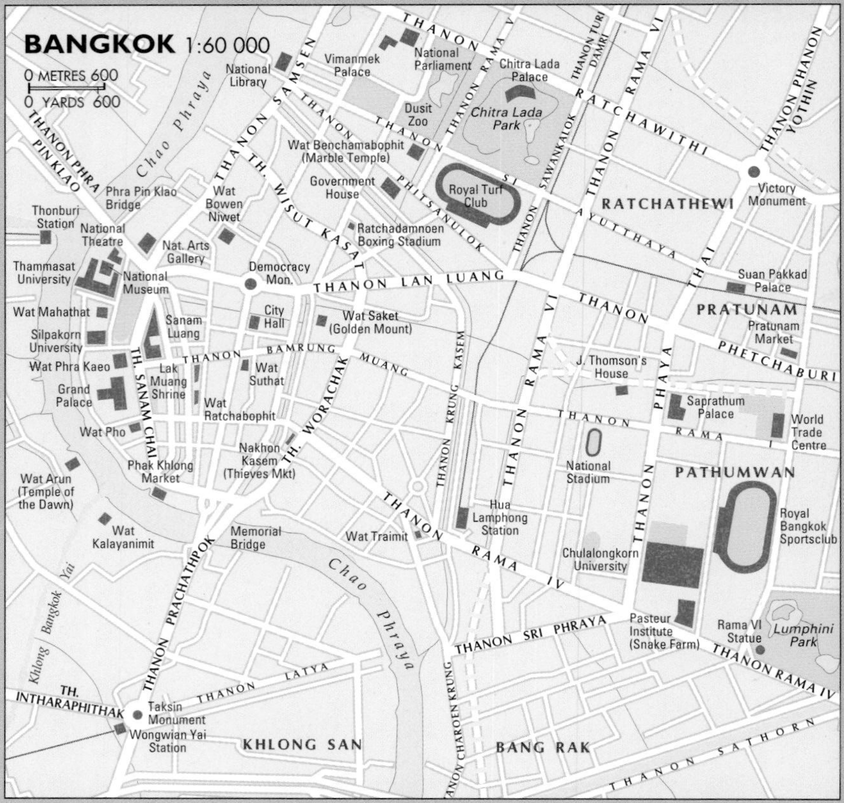
BANGKOK 1:60 000
0 METRES 600
0 YARDS 600
Vimanmek Palace
National Parliament
National Library
Chitra Lada Palace
Chitra Lada Park
Dusit Zoo
Wat Benchamabophit (Marble Temple)
Government House
Royal Turf Club
Victory Monument
RATCHATHEWI
Thonburi Station
National Theatre
Phra Pin Klao Bridge
Wat Bowen Niwet
Ratchadamnoen Boxing Stadium
Thammasat University
National Museum
Nat. Arts Gallery
Democracy Mon.
THANON LAN LUANG
Suan Pakkad Palace
PRATUNAM
Pratunam Market
Wat Mahathat
Sanam Luang
City Hall
Wat Saket (Golden Mount)
Silpakorn University
Wat Phra Kaeo
Grand Palace
Lak Muang Shrine
Wat Suthat
Wat Ratchabophit
J. Thomson's House
Sapratthum Palace
World Trade Centre
Wat Pho
Phak Khlong Market
Nakhon Kasem (Thieves Mkt)
National Stadium
PATHUMWAN
Wat Arun (Temple of the Dawn)
Hua Lamphong Station
Royal Bangkok Sportsclub
Wat Kalayanimit
Memorial Bridge
Wat Traimit
Chulalongkorn University
Chao Phraya
Pasteur Institute (Snake Farm)
Rama VI Statue
Lumphini Park
THANON SRI PHRAYA
THANON RAMA IV
Taksin Monument
Wongwian Yai Station
KHLONG SAN
BANG RAK
THANON SATHORN

BEIJING 1:100 000
0 METRES 1000
0 YARDS 1000
North China Jiaotong University
Xizhimen Station
Beijing Exhibition Centre
Beijing Zoo
XIZHIMENWAI DAJIE
Planetarium
Ditan Park
Temple of the Earth
Beijing Wax Museum
DESHENGMENDONG DAJIE
ANDINGMENDONG DAJIE
Yonghe-Lama Temple
Capital Museum
Bell Tower
Drum Tower
Shisha Lake
DONGSI 10-TIAO
Worker's Stadium
Lu Xun Museum
White Temple
Beihai Lake
White Dagoba Temple
Jingshan Park
National Art Gallery
CHAOYANGMENWAI DAJIE
Yuyuantan Park
FUCHENGMENWAI DAJIE
Zonghai Lake
Palace Museum
Ritan (Temple of the Sun) Park
Cultural Palace of the Nationalities
Military Museum
Nanhai Lake
Gate of Heavenly Peace
FUXING LU
FUXINGMENWAI DAJIE
FUXINGMENNEI DAJIE
XICHANG'AN JIE
JIANGUOMENNEI DAJIE
Great Hall of the People
Tian'anmen Sq.
Chinese Revolution and History Mus.
Ancient Observatory
Monument to the People's Heroes
Chairman Mao Memorial Hall
Beijing Station
XUANWUMENXI DAJIE
QIANMENDONG DAJIE
CHONGWENMEN DONG DAJIE
Tianning Temple
Xibianmen Station
GUANG'ANMENNEI DAJIE
XUANWU
Niujie Mosque
Fayuan Temple
CHONGWEN
Guang'anmen Station
Museum of Natural History
Tiantan Park (Temple of Heaven)
Taoranting Park
Longtan Lakes
Moat
YOU'ANMENDONGBINHE LU
ZUO'ANMENXIBINHE LU

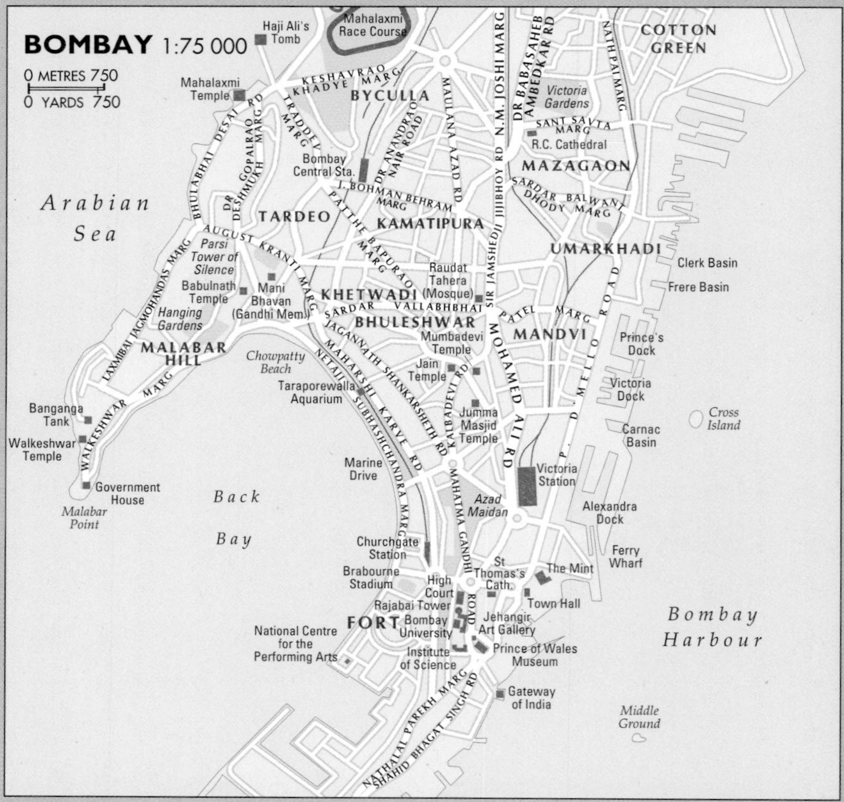
BOMBAY 1:75 000
0 METRES 750
0 YARDS 750
Haji Ali's Tomb
Mahalaxmi Race Course
Mahalaxmi Temple
BYCULLA
COTTON GREEN
Victoria Gardens
R.C. Cathedral
Bombay Central Sta.
MAZAGAON
Arabian Sea
TARDEO
KAMATIPURA
UMARKHADI
Parsi Tower of Silence
Clerk Basin
Frere Basin
Babulnath Temple
Mani Bhavan (Gandhi Mem.)
Raudat Tahera (Mosque)
KHETWADI
BHULESHWAR
MANDVI
Hanging Gardens
MALABAR HILL
Mumbadevi Temple
Prince's Dock
Chowpatty Beach
Jain Temple
Victoria Dock
Taraporewala Aquarium
Jumma Masjid
Cross Island
Banganga Tank
Walkeshwar Temple
Carnac Basin
Marine Drive
Victoria Station
Government House
Back Bay
Azad Maidan
Alexandra Dock
Malabar Point
Churchgate Station
Ferry Wharf
Brabourne Stadium
St Thomas's Cath.
The Mint
High Court
Town Hall
Rajabai Tower
Bombay University
Jehangir Art Gallery
FORT
National Centre for the Performing Arts
Institute of Science
Prince of Wales Museum
Bombay Harbour
Gateway of India
Middle Ground

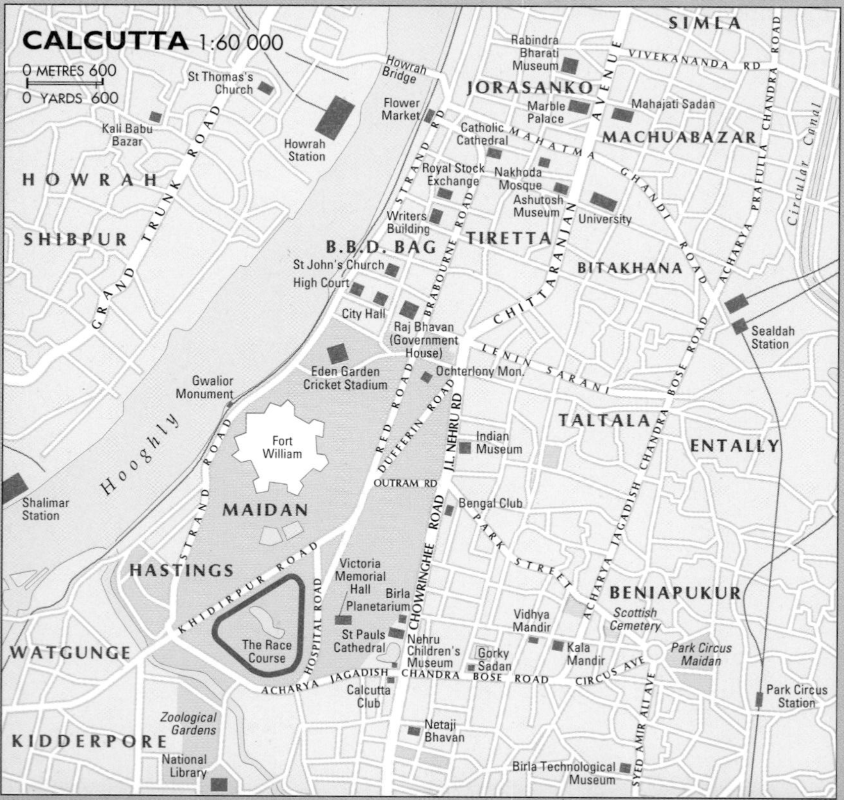
CALCUTTA 1:60 000
0 METRES 600
0 YARDS 600
SIMLA
St Thomas's Church
Howrah Bridge
Rabindra Bharati Museum
JORASANKO
Kali Babu Bazar
Flower Market
Marble Palace
Mahajati Sadan
Howrah Station
Catholic Cathedral
MACHUABAZAR
HOWRAH
Royal Stock Exchange
Nakhoda Mosque
Ashutosh Museum
University
SHIBPUR
Writers Building
B.B.D. BAG
TIRETTA
St John's Church
BITAKHANA
High Court
City Hall
Raj Bhavan (Government House)
Sealdah Station
Eden Garden Cricket Stadium
Ochterlony Mon.
Gwalior Monument
TALTALA
Fort William
Indian Museum
ENTALLY
Hooghly
Shalimar Station
MAIDAN
Bengal Club
HASTINGS
Victoria Memorial Hall
Birla Planetarium
BENIAPUKUR
The Race Course
Scottish Cemetery
WATGUNGE
St Pauls Cathedral
Nehru Children's Museum
Vidhya Mandir
Gorky Sadan
Kala Mandir
Park Circus Maidan
Calcutta Club
Park Circus Station
Zoological Gardens
Netaji Bhavan
KIDDERPORE
National Library
Birla Technological Museum

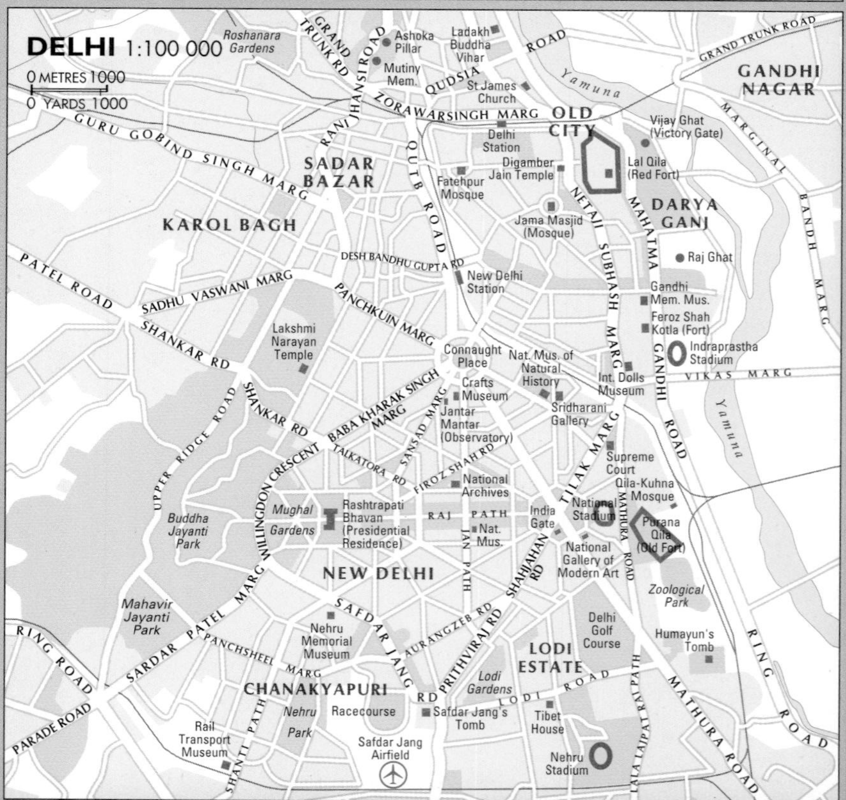
DELHI 1:100 000
0 METRES 1000
0 YARDS 1000
Roshanara Gardens
Ashoka Pillar
Ladakh Buddha Vihar
Mutiny Mem.
St James Church
GANDHI NAGAR
Yamuna
OLD CITY
Delhi Station
Vijay Ghat (Victory Gate)
SADAR BAZAR
Digamber Jain Temple
Lal Qila (Red Fort)
Fatehpur Mosque
KAROL BAGH
Jama Masjid (Mosque)
DARYA GANJ
Raj Ghat
New Delhi Station
Gandhi Mem. Mus.
Feroz Shah Kotla (Fort)
Lakshmi Narayan Temple
Connaught Place
Nat. Mus. of Natural History
Indraprastha Stadium
Crafts Museum
Jantar Mantar (Observatory)
Int. Dolls Museum
Shriharani Gallery
Supreme Court
Qila-Kuhna Mosque
National Archives
Buddha Jayanti Park
Mughal Gardens
Rashtrapati Bhavan (Presidential Residence)
India Gate
National Stadium
Purana Qila (Old Fort)
Nat. Mus.
National Gallery of Modern Art
Zoological Park
NEW DELHI
Mahavir Jayanti Park
Nehru Memorial Museum
Delhi Golf Course
Humayun's Tomb
LODI ESTATE
CHANAKYAPURI
Lodi Gardens
Racecourse
Safdar Jang's Tomb
Nehru Park
Tibet House
Rail Transport Museum
Safdar Jang Airfield
Nehru Stadium
RING ROAD

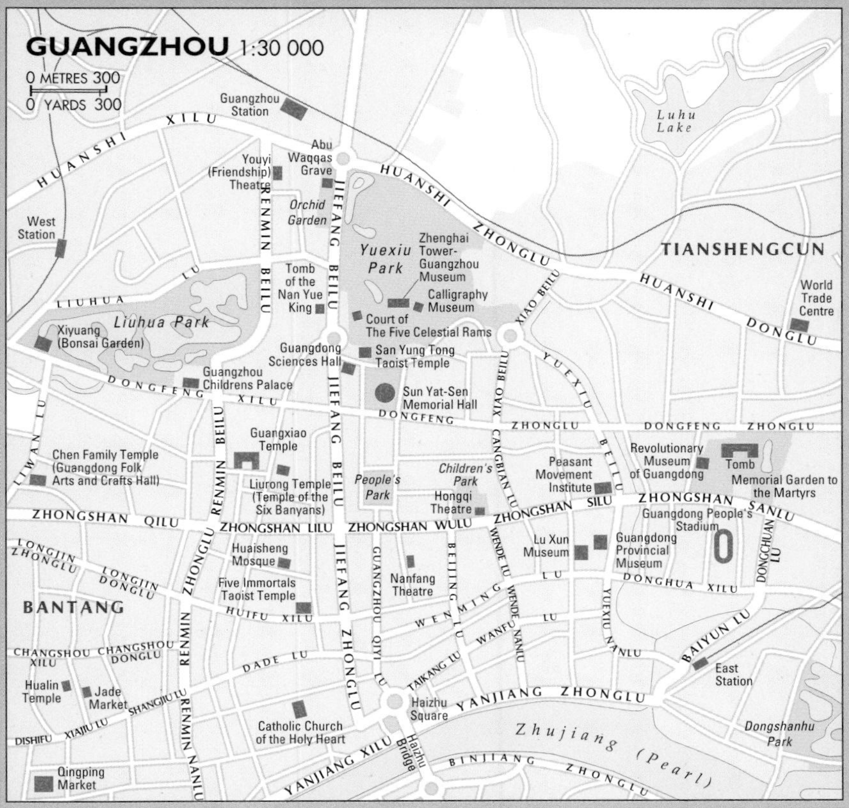
GUANGZHOU 1:30 000
0 METRES 300
0 YARDS 300
Guangzhou Station
Luhu Lake
Abu Waqqas Grave
Youyi (Friendship) Theatre
West Station
Orchid Garden
Yuexiu Park
Zhenghai Tower-Guangzhou Museum
TIANSHENGCUN
Tomb of the Nan Yue King
Calligraphy Museum
Court of The Five Celestial Rams
World Trade Centre
Liuhua Park
Xiyuang (Bonsai Garden)
Guangdong Sciences Hall
San Yung Tong Taoist Temple
Guangzhou Childrens Palace
Sun Yat-Sen Memorial Hall
Chen Family Temple (Guangdong Folk Arts and Crafts Hall)
Guangxiao Temple
Liurong Temple (Temple of the Six Banyans)
People's Park
Children's Park
Hongqi Theatre
Peasant Movement Institute
Revolutionary Museum of Guangdong
Tomb Memorial Garden to the Martyrs
Guangdong People's Stadium
Lu Xun Museum
Guangdong Provincial Museum
Huaisheng Mosque
Nanfang Theatre
Five Immortals Taoist Temple
BANTANG
East Station
Hualin Temple
Jade Market
Haizhu Square
Haizhu Bridge
Catholic Church of the Holy Heart
Zhujiang (Pearl)
Dongshanhu Park
Qingping Market
HUANSHI XILU
HUANSHI ZHONGLU
HUANSHI DONGLU
JIEFANG BEILU
RENMIN BEILU
DONGFENG XILU
DONGFENG ZHONGLU
ZHONGSHAN QILU
ZHONGSHAN LILU
ZHONGSHAN WULU
ZHONGSHAN SILU
ZHONGSHAN SANLU
YANJIANG ZHONGLU
YANJIANG XILU
BAIYUN LU
DADE LU
RENMIN NANLU
JIEFANG ZHONGLU

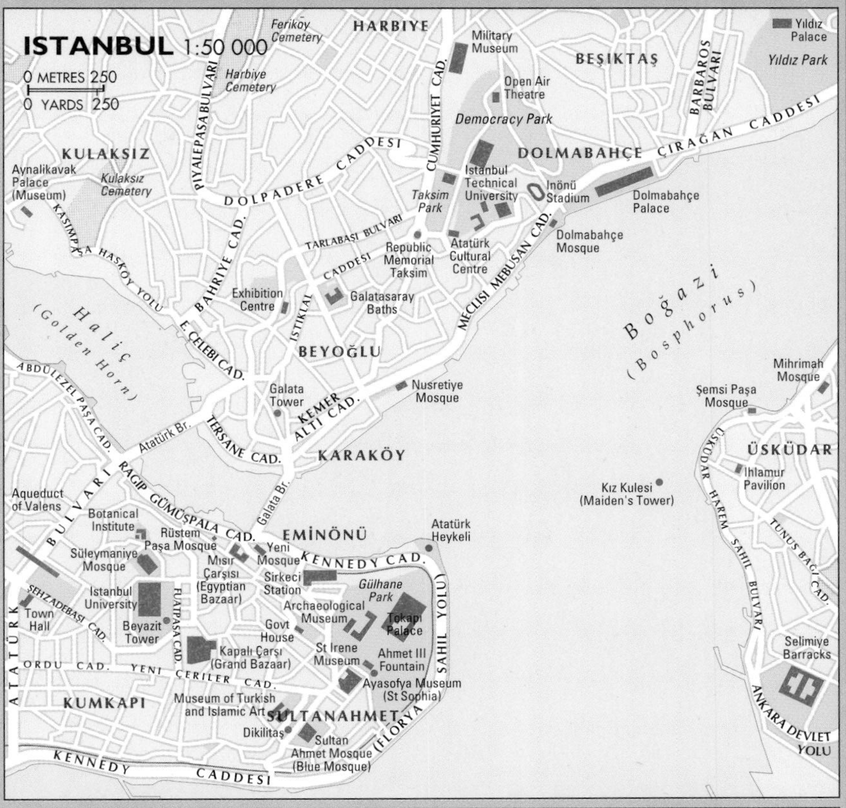
ISTANBUL 1:50 000
0 METRES 250
0 YARDS 250
Feriköy Cemetery
HARBIYE
Military Museum
BEŞIKTAŞ
Yıldız Palace
Yıldız Park
Harbiye Cemetery
Open Air Theatre
Democracy Park
KULAKSIZ
Kulaksız Cemetery
Aynalıkavak Palace (Museum)
DOLMABAHÇE
Istanbul Technical University
İnönü Stadium
Dolmabahçe Palace
Dolmabahçe Mosque
Taksim Park
Republic Memorial Taksim
Cultural Centre
Exhibition Centre
Galatasaray Baths
Haliç (Golden Horn)
BEYOĞLU
Boğazi (Bosphorus)
Galata Tower
Nusretiye Mosque
Mihrimah Mosque
Şemsi Paşa Mosque
ÜSKÜDAR
İhlamur Pavilion
KARAKÖY
Kız Kulesi (Maiden's Tower)
Aqueduct of Valens
Botanical Institute
Atatürk Heykeli
Süleymaniye Mosque
Rüstem Paşa Mosque
EMİNÖNÜ
Mısır Çarşısı (Egyptian Bazaar)
Yeni Mosque
Sirkeci Station
Gülhane Park
Istanbul University
Archaeological Museum
Topkapı Palace
Town Hall
Beyazıt Tower
Kapalı Çarşı (Grand Bazaar)
Govt House
St Irene Museum
Ahmet III Fountain
Ayasofya Museum (St Sophia)
Selimiye Barracks
KUMKAPI
Museum of Turkish and Islamic Art
SULTANAHMET
Dikilitaş
Sultan Ahmet Mosque (Blue Mosque)
KENNEDY CADDESİ
CUMHURİYET CAD.
DOLPADERE CADDESİ
ÇIRAĞAN CADDESİ
BARBAROS BULVARI
ATATÜRK BULVARI
ORDU CAD.
KENNEDY CAD.
ANKARA DEVLET YOLU

JAKARTA 1:45 000
0 METRES 450
0 YARDS 450
TAMAN SARI
Gajah Mada Plaza
Kemayoran Station
Chinese Temple
JALAN K.H. HASYIM ASYHARI
GAMBIR
State Palace
Bina Graha
Istana Merdeka (Presidential Palace)
Catholic Cathedral
Lapangan Banteng
JL. M. MERDEKA UTARA
Istiqlal Mosque
Irian Jaya Liberation Mon.
Baharata Theatre
Senen Station
Medan Merdeka (Merdeka Square)
National Museum
Fountain Park
Monas (National Monument)
Gereja Immanuel Church
Gambir Station
SENEN
JL. M. MERDEKA SELATAN
Arjuna Wijaya
City Hall
Tanah Abang Station
Jakarta Theatre
Textile Museum
Taman Ismail Marzuki Culture Centre
Selamat Datang Statue
MENTENG
Christian Cemetery
Suropati Park
Adam Malik Museum
Kartini Statue
JL. IMAM BONJOL
JL. DIPONEGORO
JL. M.H. THAMRIN
JL. JEND. SUDIRMAN
JALAN KRAMAT RAYA
JL. CIKINI RAYA
JL. S. PRANOTO
JL. K. CARINGIN
JL. TOMANG RAYA
Banjir Kanal

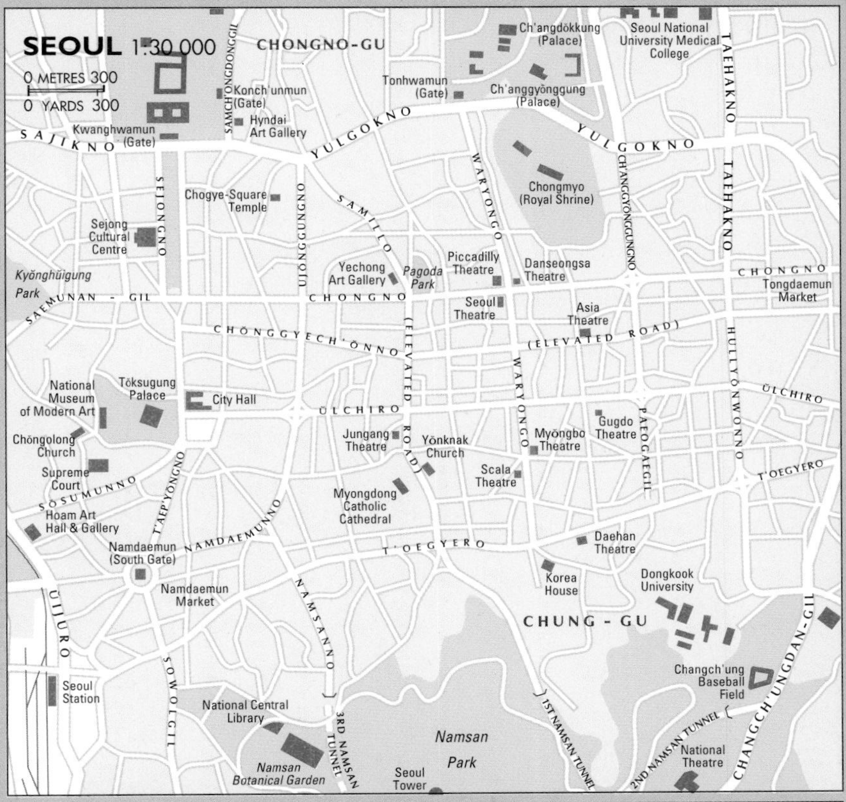
SEOUL 1:30 000
0 METRES 300
0 YARDS 300
CHONGNO-GU
Ch'angdŏkkung (Palace)
Seoul National University Medical College
Konch'unmun (Gate)
Tonhwamun (Gate)
Ch'anggyŏnggung (Palace)
Kwanghwamun (Gate)
Hyndai Art Gallery
SAJIKNO
YULGOKNO
Chogye-Square Temple
Chongmyo (Royal Shrine)
Sejong Cultural Centre
Kyŏnghŭigung Park
Yechong Art Gallery
Pagoda Park
Piccadilly Theatre
Danseongsa Theatre
Tongdaemun Market
Seoul Theatre
Asia Theatre
National Museum of Modern Art
Tŏksugung Palace
City Hall
Chŏngdong Church
Jungang Theatre
Yŏnknak Church
Myŏngbo Theatre
Gugdo Theatre
Supreme Court
Scala Theatre
Hoam Art Hall & Gallery
Myongdong Catholic Cathedral
Namdaemun (South Gate)
Daehan Theatre
Namdaemun Market
Korea House
Dongkook University
CHUNG - GU
Changch'ung Baseball Field
Seoul Station
National Central Library
Namsan Park
National Theatre
Namsan Botanical Garden
Seoul Tower
CHONGNO
ŬLCHIRO
T'OEGYERO

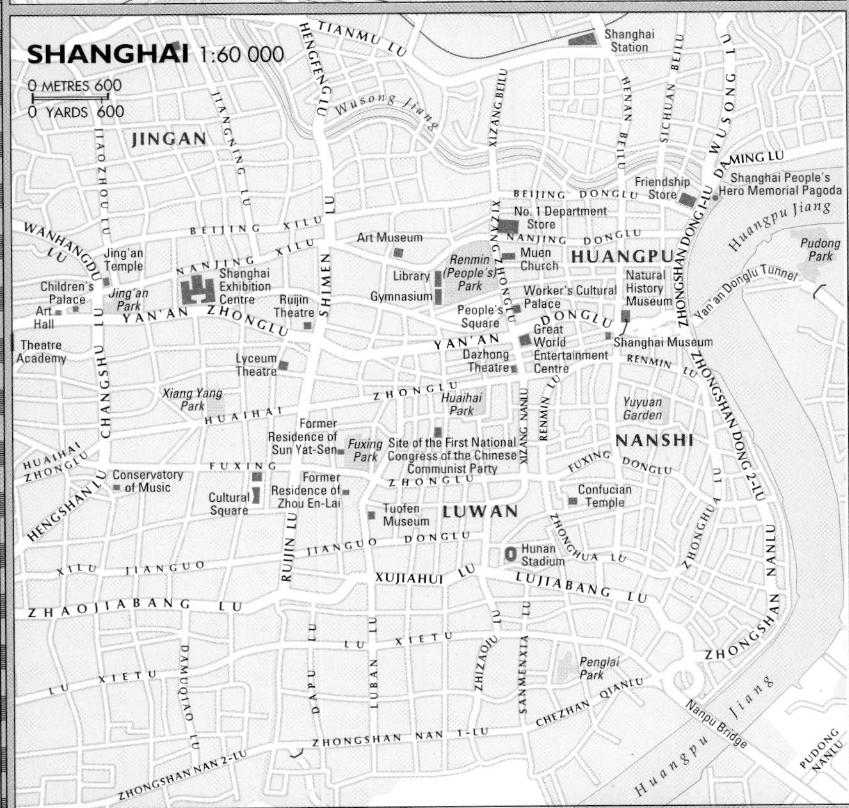
SHANGHAI 1:60 000
0 METRES 600
0 YARDS 600
Shanghai Station
Wusong Jiang
JINGAN
Friendship Store
Shanghai People's Hero Memorial Pagoda
No. 1 Department Store
Huangpu Jiang
Pudong Park
Jing'an Temple
Art Museum
Shanghai Exhibition Centre
Renmin (People's) Park
Muen Church
HUANGPU
Children's Palace
Jing'an Park
Library
Gymnasium
Worker's Cultural Palace
Natural History Museum
Art Hall
Ruijin Theatre
People's Square
Theatre Academy
Great World Entertainment Centre
Shanghai Museum
Lyceum Theatre
Dazhong Theatre
Xiang Yang Park
Huaihai Park
Yuyuan Garden
Former Residence of Sun Yat-Sen
Fuxing Park
Site of the First National Congress of the Chinese Communist Party
NANSHI
Conservatory of Music
Cultural Square
Former Residence of Zhou En-Lai
Confucian Temple
Tuofen Museum
LUWAN
Hunan Stadium
Penglai Park
Nanpu Bridge
Huangpu Jiang
PUDONG NANLU
NANJING XILU
YAN'AN ZHONGLU
HUAIHAI
ZHAOJIABANG LU
ZHONGSHAN NAN 1-LU
ZHONGSHAN NAN 2-LU

TOKYO 1:100 000
0 METRES 1000
0 YARDS 1000
Toshimagaoka Cemetery
Kishibojin Shrine
Kisshoji Temple
Asakusa-Chosokan Gallery
Koishikawa Botanical Centre
Daimyo Clock Museum
National Museum
National Science Museum
Metropolitan Art Gallery
Ueno Zoo
St Mary's Cathedral
BUNKYŌ-KU
Ueno Station
Sensoji Temple
Asakusa Station
Tokyo University
Ueno Royal Museum
TAITŌ-KU
Torigoe-jinja Shrine
SHINJUKU-KU
Science University of Tokyo
Kanda Myojin Shrine
Hōsenji Temple
Transportation Museum
CHUO-KU
Yasukuni-Jinja Shrine
Science and Technology Museum
Shinjuku Station
National Museum of Modern Art
Historical Museum
Japanese Sword Museum
Communications Museum
Suitengu Shrine
Shinjuku Gyoen Garden
Geinin-Kan (State Guesthouse)
National Theatre
New Imperial Palace
Fukagawa Edo Museum
Tokyo Station
Meiji Jingu Shrine
National Noh Theatre
National Stadium
CHIYODA-KU
Tokyo Stock Exchange
Suntory Museum of Art
National Diet Building
Mullion
Fukagawa-Fudoson Temple
Yoyogi Park
Ota Mem Museum of Art
Aoyama Cemetery
Okura Shukokan Museum
Kabukiza Theatre
Riccar Art Museum
Tsukiji-Honbanji Temple
Tokyo University of Mercantile Marine
NHK Broadcasting Museum
Nezu Art Museum
Hamarikyū Garden
Shoto Museum of Art
Tokyo Tower
Zojoji Temple
World Trade Centre
The Furniture Museum
MINATO - KU
Riccar Art Gallery
Tokyo International Trade Centre
Meguro Art Gallery
National Park for Nature Study
Sengakuji Temple
Rainbow Bridge
Daienji Temple
Hatakeyama Collection

© HarperCollinsPublishers

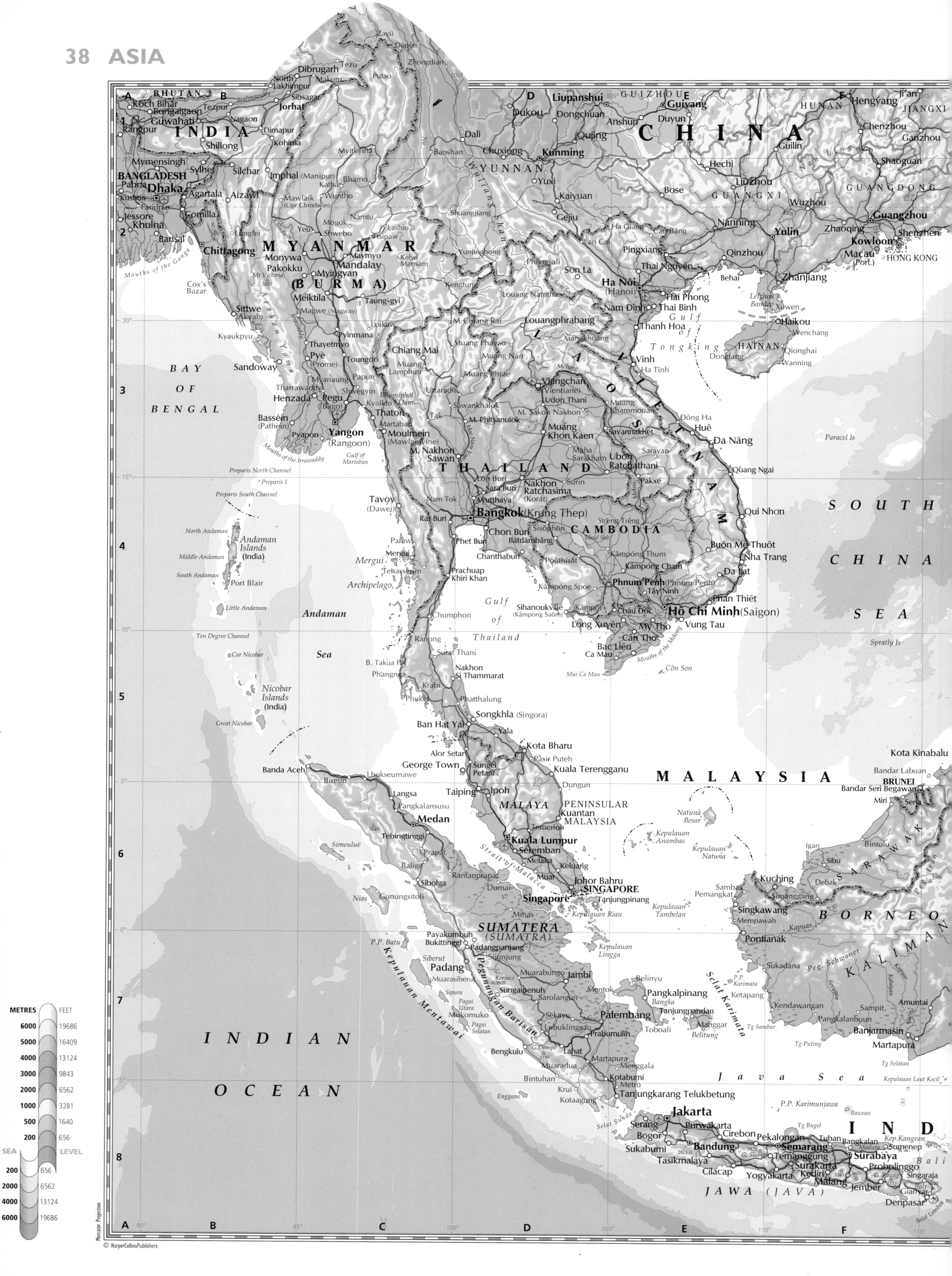
CHINA
INDIA
BANGLADESH
BHUTAN
MYANMAR (BURMA)
THAILAND
LAOS
VIETNAM
CAMBODIA
MALAYSIA
BRUNEI
SINGAPORE
GUIZHOU
HUNAN
JIANGXI
GUANGXI
GUANGDONG
YUNNAN
HAINAN
HONG KONG
BAY OF BENGAL
Andaman Sea
Gulf of Tongking
Gulf of Thailand
SOUTH CHINA SEA
INDIAN OCEAN
Java Sea
Strait of Malacca
Selat Karimata
Selat Sunda
Gulf of Martaban
Mergui Archipelago
Andaman Islands (India)
Nicobar Islands (India)
North Andaman
Middle Andaman
South Andaman
Little Andaman
Car Nicobar
Great Nicobar
Ten Degree Channel
Preparis North Channel
Preparis South Channel
Preparis I.
Paracel Is
Spratly Is
Mouths of the Ganga
Mouths of the Irrawaddy
Mouths of the Mekong
MALAYA
PENINSULAR MALAYSIA
SUMATERA (SUMATRA)
Pegunungan Barisan
Kepulauan Mentawai
BORNEO
KALIMANTAN
SARAWAK
JAWA (JAVA)
Kepulauan Anambas
Kepulauan Natuna
Natuna Besar
Kepulauan Riau
Kepulauan Lingga
Kepulauan Tambelan
Bangka
Belitung
Simeulue
Nias
Siberut
Sipura
Enggano
Kota Kinabalu
Bandar Seri Begawan
Kuching
Pontianak
Banjarmasin
Jakarta
Bandung
Semarang
Surabaya
Yogyakarta
Denpasar
Bali
Palembang
Jambi
Padang
Medan
Banda Aceh
Pangkalpinang
Bengkulu
Tanjungkarang Telukbetung
Kuala Lumpur
Johor Bahru
Singapore
George Town
Ipoh
Kuala Terengganu
Kota Bharu
Kuantan
Malacca
Bangkok (Krung Thep)
Chiang Mai
Nakhon Ratchasima (Korat)
Songkhla (Singora)
Hat Yai
Phuket
Surat Thani
Yangon (Rangoon)
Mandalay
Moulmein (Mawlamyine)
Pegu (Bago)
Bassein (Pathein)
Sittwe (Akyab)
Tavoy (Dawei)
Mergui
Vientiane
Louangphrabang
Savannakhet
Pakxé
Ha Nôi (Hanoi)
Hai Phong
Hô Chi Minh (Saigon)
Đa Năng
Huê
Nha Trang
Đa Lat
Qui Nhon
Vinh
Phnum Penh (Phnom Penh)
Batdâmbâng
Sihanoukville (Kâmpong Saôm)
Kunming
Guiyang
Nanning
Guangzhou
Kowloon
Macau (Port.)
Shenzhen
Zhanjiang
Haikou
Liuzhou
Guilin
Dhaka
Chittagong
Guwahati
Shillong
Imphal (Manipur)
Dibrugarh
Mercator Projection
METRES
FEET
6000 19686
5000 16409
4000 13124
3000 9843
2000 6562
1000 3281
500 1640
200 656
SEA LEVEL
200 656
2000 6562
4000 13124
6000 19686

© HarperCollinsPublishers

PACIFIC OCEAN
PHILIPPINES
TAIWAN (FORMOSA)
JAPAN
PALAU
FEDERATED STATES OF MICRONESIA
Northern Mariana Islands (U.S.A.)
PAPUA NEW GUINEA
IRIAN JAYA
ONESIA
MOLUCCAS
MALUKU
Nanping
FUJIAN
Fuzhou
Yong'an
Putian
Longyan
Quanzhou
Xiamen
Meizhou
Chaozhou
Shantou
T'ai-pei
Hsin-chu
Hua-lien
Chang-hua
T'ai-nan
T'ai-tung
Kao-hsiung
Taiwan Strait
Okinawa
Naha
Nansei-shotō
Sakishima-guntō
Okinawa-guntō
Ogasawara-shotō (Bonin Is) (Japan)
Kazan-rettō (Volcano Is.)
Iō-Jima (Iwo Jima) (Japan)
Tropic of Cancer
Luzon Strait
Batan Islands
Babuyan Islands
Laoag
Aparri
Vigan
Tuguegarao
Ilagan
Bontoc
San Fernando
Dagupan
San Jose
Tarlac
Cabanatuan
LUZON
Polillo Islands
Olongapo
Quezon City
Manila
San Pablo
Daet
Batangas
Lucena
Naga
Catanduanes
Calapan
Mindoro
Legaspi
Sorsogon
Mindoro Strait
Romblon
Masbate
Catarman
Calbayog
Catbalogan
Samar
Calamian Group
Roxas
Visayan Sea
Tacloban
Panay
Iloilo
Bacolod
Ormoc
Cebu
Leyte
Taytay
Cuyo Islands
Negros
Puerto Princesa
Tagbilaran
Surigao
Palawan
Tanjay
Bohol Sea
Butuan
Brooke's Point
Dipolog
Oroquieta
Cagayan de Oro
Sulu Sea
Pagadian
MINDANAO
Cotabato
Davao
Balabac Strait
Zamboanga
Moro Gulf
Mati
Davao Gulf
Basilan
Isabela
Jolo
Sulu Archipelago
General Santos
Sandakan
SABAH
Lahad Datu
Tawitawi
Tawau
Tarakan
Tanjungselor
Tanjungredeb
Celebes Sea
Karakelong
Kepulauan Talaud
Kepulauan Sangir
Manadao
Tondano
Molucca Sea
Morotai
Tobelo
Ternate
Halmahera
Sao-Siu
Minahasa Semenanjung
Tolitoli
Moutong
Gorontalo
Sangkulirang
Sidoan
Teluk Tomini
Kepulauan Togian
Samarinda
Makassar Strait
Donggala
Balikpapan
Palu
Luwuk
Poso
Banggai
Taliabu
Mangole
Kepulauan Banggai
Sula
Obi
Tenteno
Kolonedale
Babana
Sulawesi (Celebes)
Mamuju
Wotu
Malili
Palopo
Makale
Teluk Bone
Kotabaru
Majene
Malamala
Kendari
Parepare
Singkang
Kolaka
Wowoni
Watampone
Muna
Buton
Ujung Pandang
Sinjai
Bulukumba
Baubau
Kepulauan Tukangbesi
Bontosunggu
Benteng
Salayar
Flores Sea
Banda Sea
Buru
Seram Sea
Seram
Namlea
Piru
Wahai
Bula
Ambon (Amboina)
Saparua
Kepulauan Banda
Kepulauan Watubela
Waigeo
Selat Dampir
Sorong
Salawati
Jazirah Doberai
Manokwari
Biak
Numfor
Yapen
Serui
Misoöl
Fakfak
Teluk Berau
Bomberai Peninsula
Fafanlap
Inanwatan
Babo
Cenderawasih
Teluk Cenderawasih
Ransiki
Sarmi
Tg d'Urville
Pegunungan Van Rees
Jayapura
Vanimo
Kaimana
Nabire
Enarotali
Wamena
Pegunungan Maoke
Pk Jaya
Pk Trikora
Pk Mandala
Aitape
Adi
Amamapare
Central Ra.
Kepulauan Kai
Tual
Kai Besar
Kai Kecil
Dobo
Wokam
Kepulauan Aru
Kobroör
Trangan
Tg Deyong
Tg Vals
P. Dolak
Merauke
Morehead
Lake Murray
Tari
Fly
Torres Strait
Arafura Sea
Kepulauan Barat Daya
Damar
Wetar
Kepulauan Tanimbar
Yamdena
Saumlakki
Kepulauan Babar
Kepulauan Leti
Kepulauan Sermata
Timor
Dili
Manatuto
Kupang
Kefamenanu
Sawu (Sawu)
Rote (Roti)
Sawu Sea
Sumba
Waikabubak
Waingapu
Flores
Ende
Maumere
Ruteng
Reo
Larantuka
Kalabahi
Alor
Sumbawa
Sumbawa Besar
Raba
Dompu
Bima
Lombok
Mataram
Kep. Bonerate
Tanahjampea
Ulithi
Fais
Yap
Ngulu
Sorol
Koror
Farallon de Pajaros (Uracas)
Maug Islands
Asuncion
Agrihan
Pagan
Alamagan
Sarigan
Anatahan
Saipan
Tinian
Rota
Guam (U.S.A.)
Agana
Equator
1:12 900 000
MILES 0 100 200 300 400 500
KM 0 100 200 300 400 500 600 700 800

Central INDONESIA

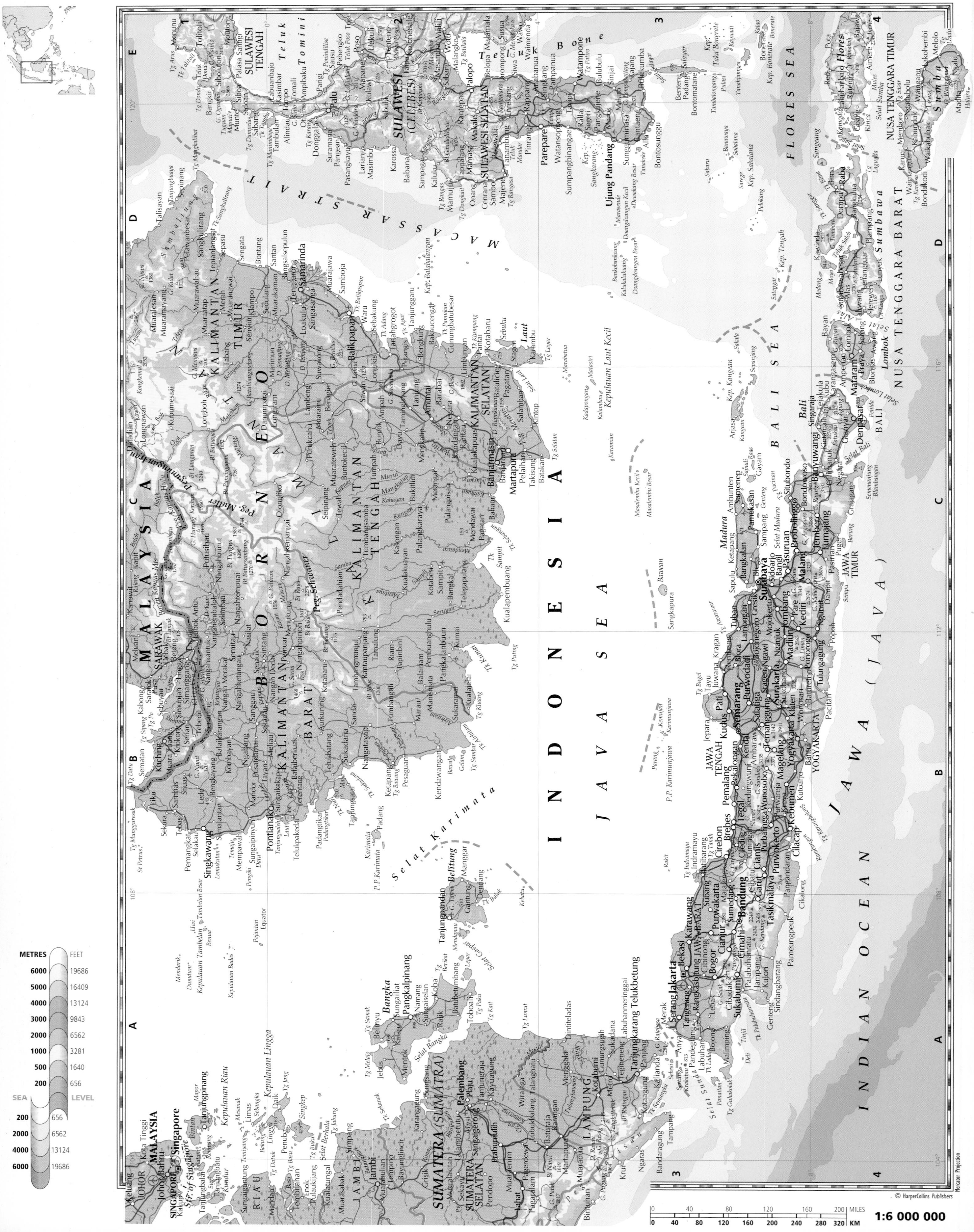

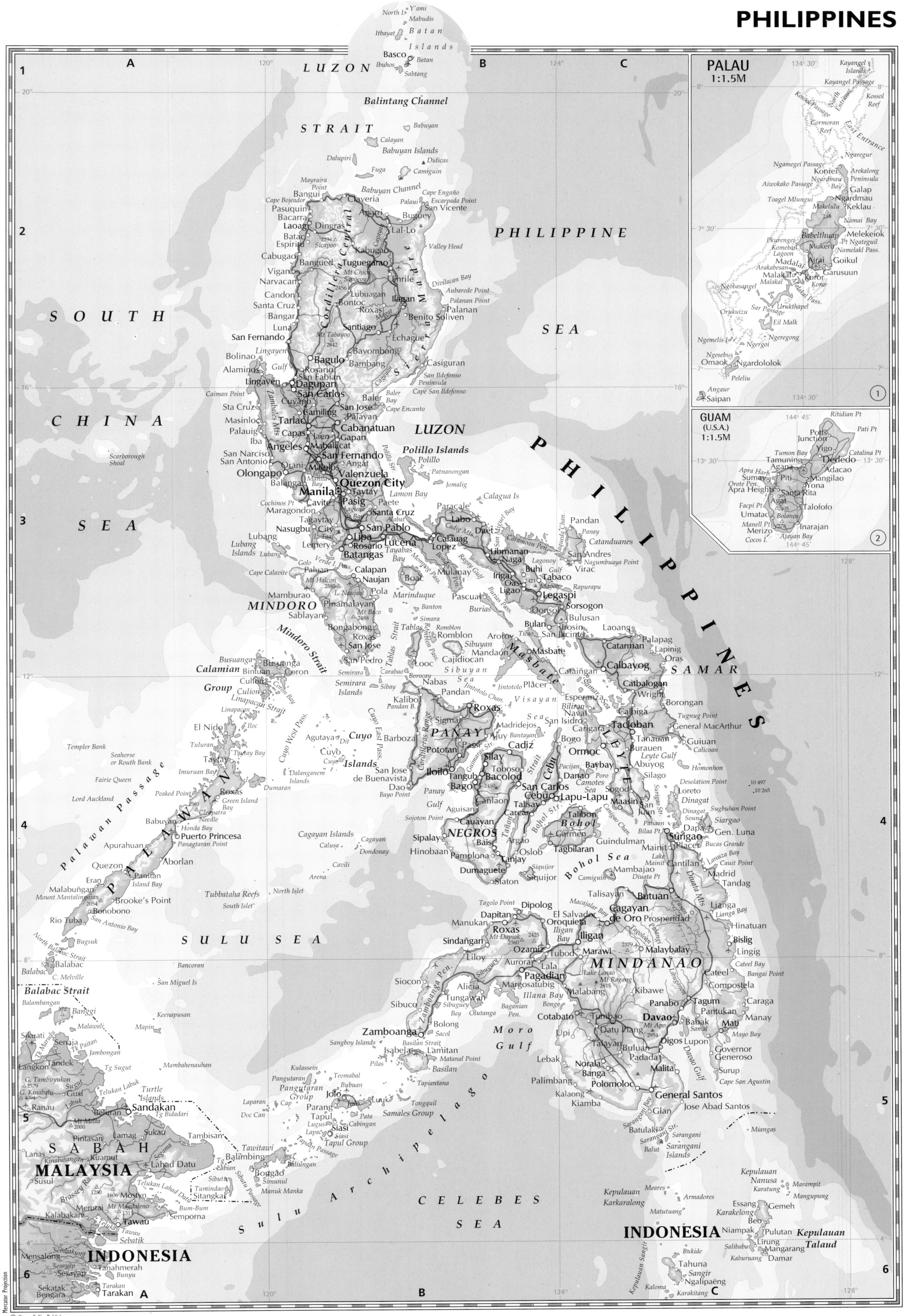
LUZON STRAIT
Batan Islands
Basco
Balintang Channel
Babuyan Islands
Babuyan Channel
PHILIPPINE SEA
SOUTH CHINA SEA
LUZON
Laoag
Vigan
San Fernando
Lingayen Gulf
Dagupan
Baguio
Tuguegarao
Cordillera Central
Sierra Madre
Polillo Islands
Manila
Quezon City
Batangas
Lucena
Naga
Legaspi
MINDORO
Mindoro Strait
Calamian Group
Sibuyan Sea
Masbate
SAMAR
Catbalogan
Tacloban
LEYTE
PANAY
Roxas
Iloilo
Bacolod
NEGROS
Cebu
Bohol
Visayan Sea
Cuyo Islands
Bohol Sea
Surigao
Butuan
Cagayan de Oro
Iligan
MINDANAO
Zamboanga
Davao
General Santos
Moro Gulf
Cotabato
PALAWAN
Puerto Princesa
Palawan Passage
SULU SEA
Tubbataha Reefs
Balabac Strait
Sulu Archipelago
Jolo
CELEBES SEA
SABAH
MALAYSIA
Sandakan
Tawau
INDONESIA
PHILIPPINES
PALAU 1:1.5M
GUAM (U.S.A.) 1:1.5M
Mercator Projection

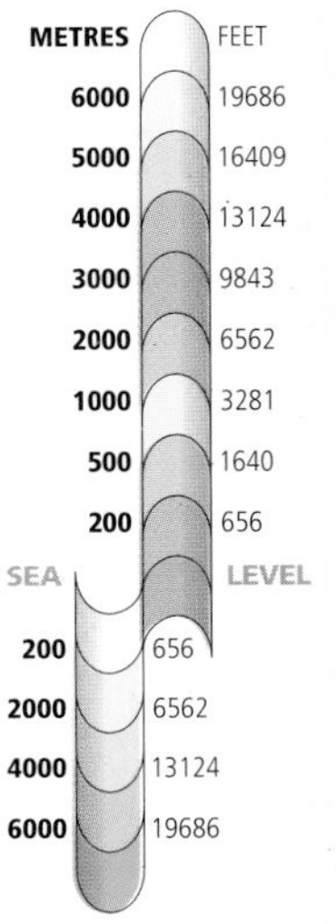
METRES FEET
6000 19686
5000 16409
4000 13124
3000 9843
2000 6562
1000 3281
500 1640
200 656
SEA LEVEL
200 656
2000 6562
4000 13124
6000 19686

1:6 000 000

0 40 80 120 160 200 MILES
0 40 80 120 160 200 240 280 320 KM

© HarperCollinsPublishers

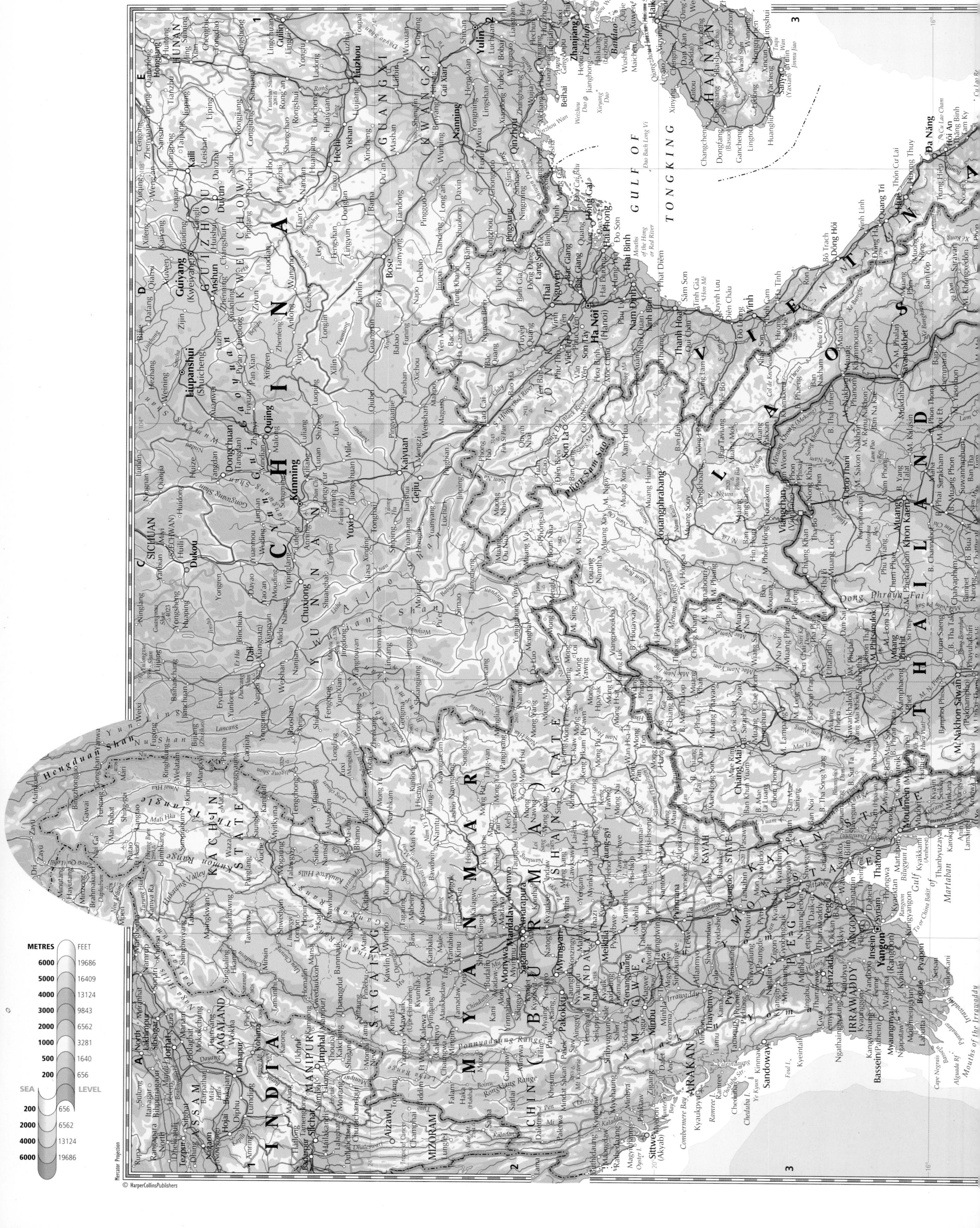
METRES
FEET
6000
19686
5000
16409
4000
13124
3000
9843
2000
6562
1000
3281
500
1640
200
656
SEA
LEVEL
200
656
2000
6562
4000
13124
6000
19686
Mercator Projection
GULF OF TONGKING
HAINAN
CHINA
YUNNAN
GUANGXI
GUIZHOU
SICHUAN
VIETNAM
LAOS
THAILAND
MYANMAR (BURMA)
SHAN STATE
KACHIN STATE
INDIA
ASSAM
NAGALAND
MANIPUR
MIZORAM
Gulf of Martaban
Mouths of the Irrawaddy

© HarperCollinsPublishers

1:6 000 000

MILES	0	40	80	120	160	200
KM	0	40	80	120	160	200	240	280	320

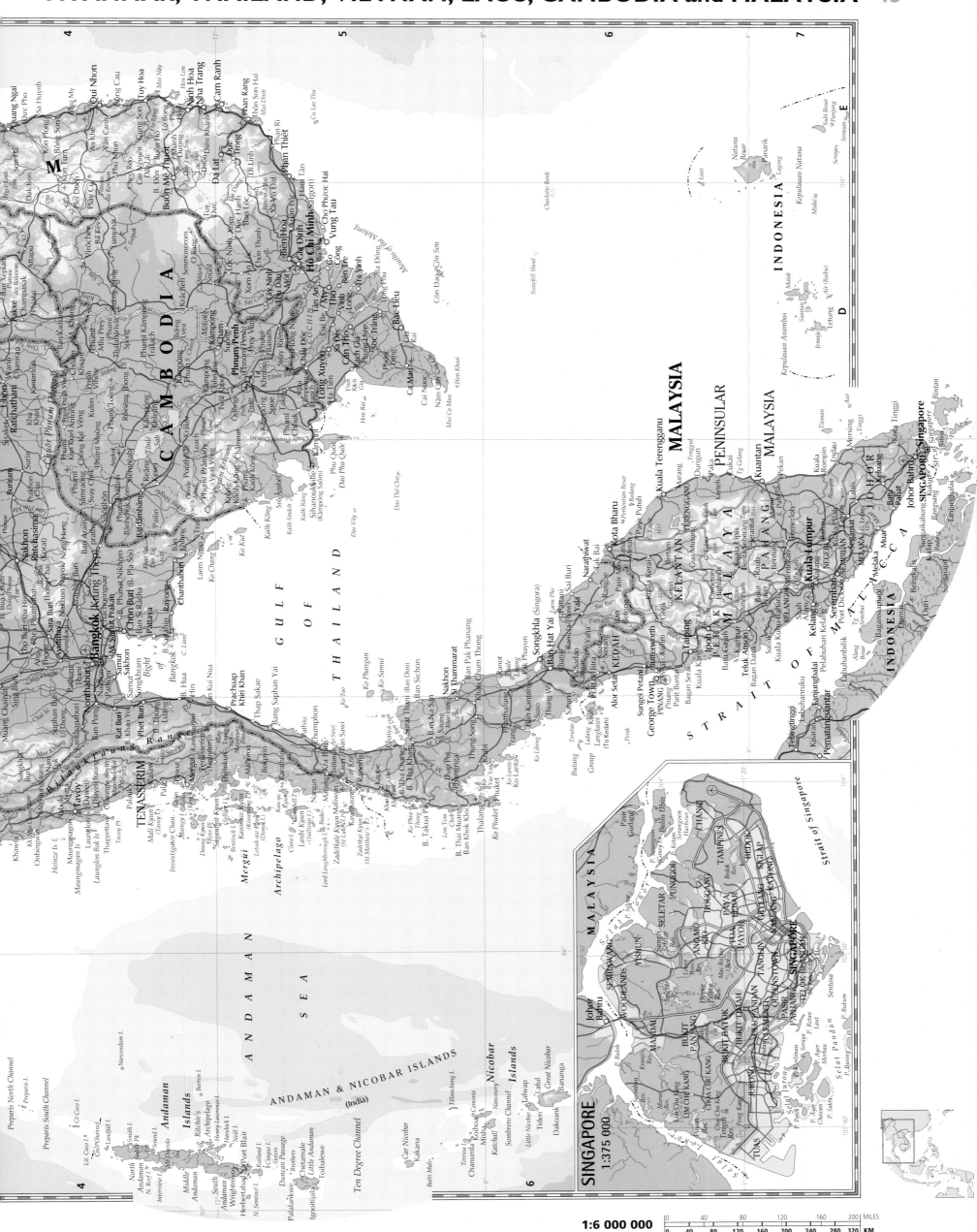

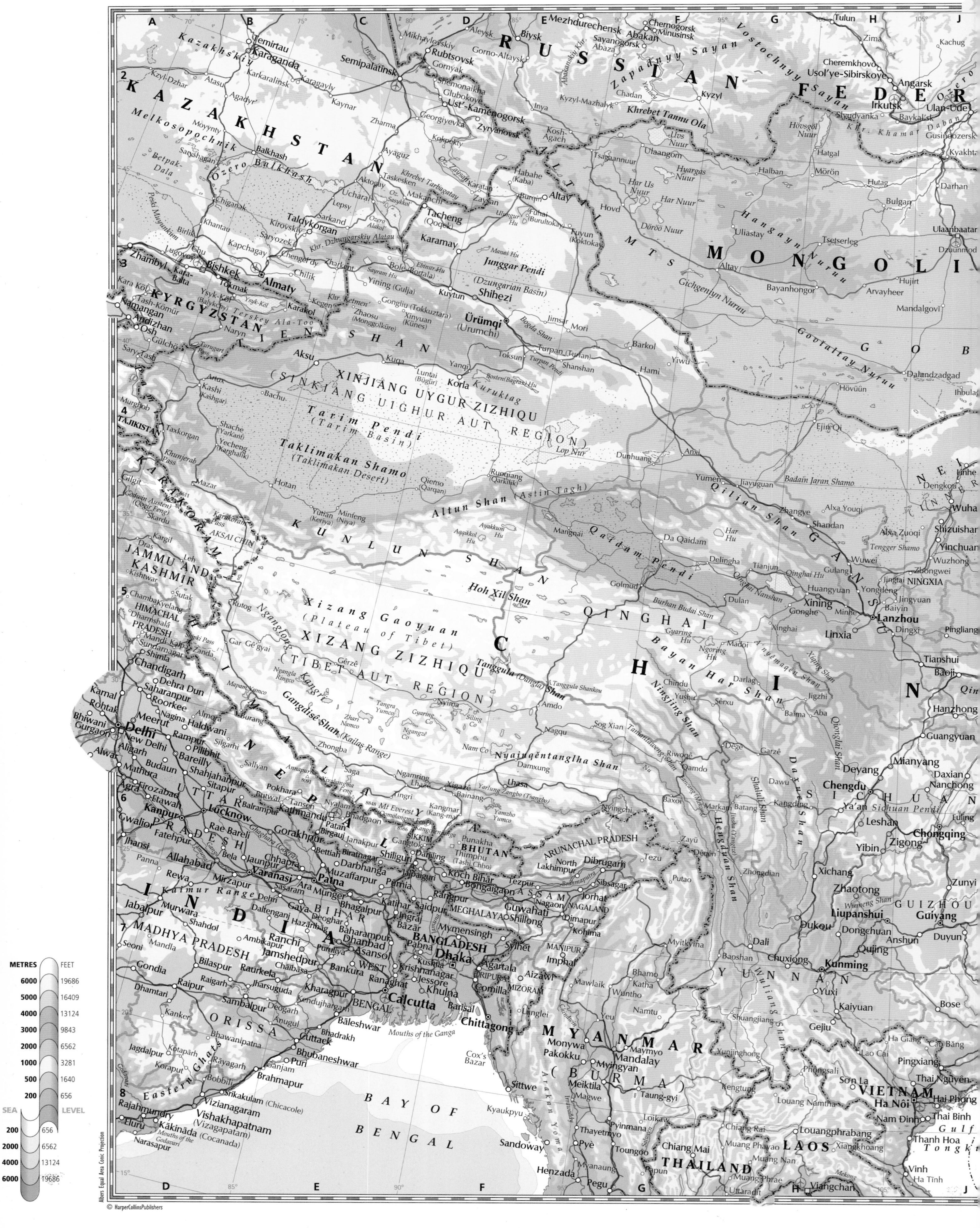
RUSSIAN FEDERATION
KAZAKHSTAN
KYRGYZSTAN
TAJIKISTAN
MONGOLIA
CHINA
XINJIANG UYGUR ZIZHIQU
(SINKIANG UIGHUR AUT. REGION)
XIZANG ZIZHIQU
(TIBET AUT. REGION)
QINGHAI
GANSU
SICHUAN
YUNNAN
GUIZHOU
NINGXIA
JAMMU AND KASHMIR
HIMACHAL PRADESH
UTTAR PRADESH
MADHYA PRADESH
BIHAR
WEST BENGAL
ORISSA
ARUNACHAL PRADESH
ASSAM
MEGHALAYA
NAGALAND
MANIPUR
MIZORAM
TRIPURA
SIKKIM
INDIA
NEPAL
BHUTAN
BANGLADESH
MYANMAR (BURMA)
THAILAND
LAOS
VIETNAM
BAY OF BENGAL
Mouths of the Ganga
TIEN SHAN
KUNLUN SHAN
KARAKORAM
ALTAI MTS
GOBI
Altun Shan (Astin Tagh)
Tarim Pendi (Tarim Basin)
Taklimakan Shamo (Taklimakan Desert)
Junggar Pendi (Dzungarian Basin)
Qaidam Pendi
Xizang Gaoyuan (Plateau of Tibet)
Hoh Xil Shan
Tanggula Shan
Nyainqêntanglha Shan
Gangdisê Shan (Kailas Range)
Bayan Har Shan
Qilian Shan
Hengduan Shan
Eastern Ghats
Kaimur Range
Ozero Balkhash
Lop Nur
Mt Everest (Qomolangma Feng) 8848
Ürümqi (Urumchi)
Almaty
Bishkek
Lanzhou
Xining
Chengdu
Chongqing
Kunming
Lhasa
Kathmandu
Thimphu
Dhaka
Calcutta
Delhi
New Delhi
Lucknow
Kanpur
Patna
Varanasi
Chittagong
Mandalay
Ulaanbaatar
Irkutsk
Hanoi
Semipalatinsk
Karaganda
Kyzyl
Golmud
Hotan
Kashi
Aksu
Korla
Hami
Dali
Guiyang
METRES FEET
6000 19686
5000 16409
4000 13124
3000 9843
2000 6562
1000 3281
500 1640
200 656
SEA LEVEL
200 656
2000 6562
4000 13124
6000 19686
Albers Equal Area Conic Projection

Sea of Japan
Yellow Sea (Huang Hai)
EAST CHINA SEA
SOUTH CHINA SEA
Bo Hai
Korea Bay
Luzon Strait
JAPAN
NORTH KOREA
SOUTH KOREA
TAIWAN (FORMOSA)
PHILIPPINES
MANCHURIA
HEILONGJIANG
JILIN
LIAONING
HEBEI
SHANDONG
SHANXI
HENAN
JIANGSU
ANHUI
HUBEI
HUNAN
JIANGXI
ZHEJIANG
FUJIAN
GUANGDONG
GUANGXI
HAINAN
Beijing (Peking)
Tianjin
Shanghai
Harbin
Shenyang
Dalian
Qingdao
Nanjing
Wuhan
Guangzhou (Canton)
Kowloon
HONG KONG
Macau (Port.)
P'yŏngyang
Sŏul
Pusan
Tōkyō
Ōsaka
Nagoya
Yokohama
Sapporo
Hiroshima
Fukuoka
Vladivostok
Khabarovsk
Yuzhno-Sakhalinsk
T'ai-pei
Kao-hsiung
Hokkaidō
Honshū
Shikoku
Kyūshū
Okinawa
HONG KONG 1 : 600 000

1:12 600 000

0 100 200 300 400 500 MILES

0 100 200 300 400 500 600 700 800 KM

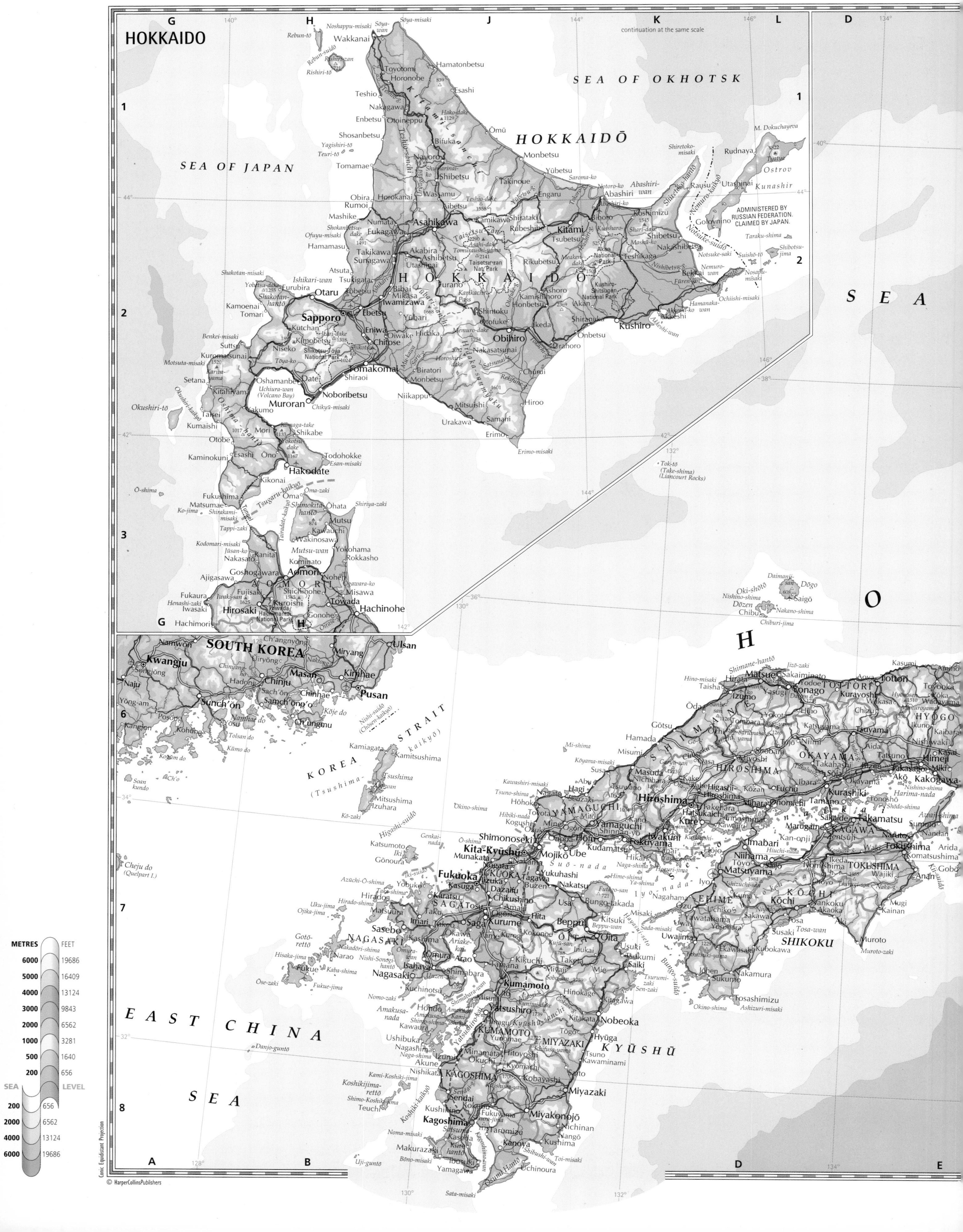
HOKKAIDO
continuation at the same scale
SEA OF OKHOTSK
SEA OF JAPAN
HOKKAIDŌ
ADMINISTERED BY RUSSIAN FEDERATION. CLAIMED BY JAPAN.
Wakkanai
Sapporo
Otaru
Asahikawa
Kitami
Abashiri
Kushiro
Obihiro
Tomakomai
Muroran
Hakodate
Aomori
Hachinohe
Hirosaki
Towada
Mutsu-wan
Tsugaru-kaikyō
Uchiura-wan (Volcano Bay)
Kunashir
Rishiri-tō
Rebun-tō
Okushiri-tō
SOUTH KOREA
Kwangju
Pusan
Ulsan
Masan
Chinju
Cheju do (Quelpart I.)
KOREA STRAIT
Tsushima
EAST CHINA SEA
SEA
O
H
Oki-shotō
Tok-tō (Take-shima) (Liancourt Rocks)
Shimonoseki
Kita-Kyūshū
Fukuoka
Nagasaki
Kumamoto
Kagoshima
Miyazaki
Miyakonojō
Nobeoka
Ōita
Beppu
KYŪSHŪ
SHIKOKU
Matsuyama
Kōchi
Tokushima
Takamatsu
Hiroshima
Okayama
Himeji
Matsue
Tottori
Yamaguchi
Tosa-wan
Bungo-suidō
METRES
FEET
6000
19686
5000
16409
4000
13124
3000
9843
2000
6562
1000
3281
500
1640
200
656
SEA
LEVEL
Conic Equidistant Projection
© HarperCollinsPublishers

1:3 300 000

MILES	0	30	60	90
KM	0	30	60	90	120	150	180

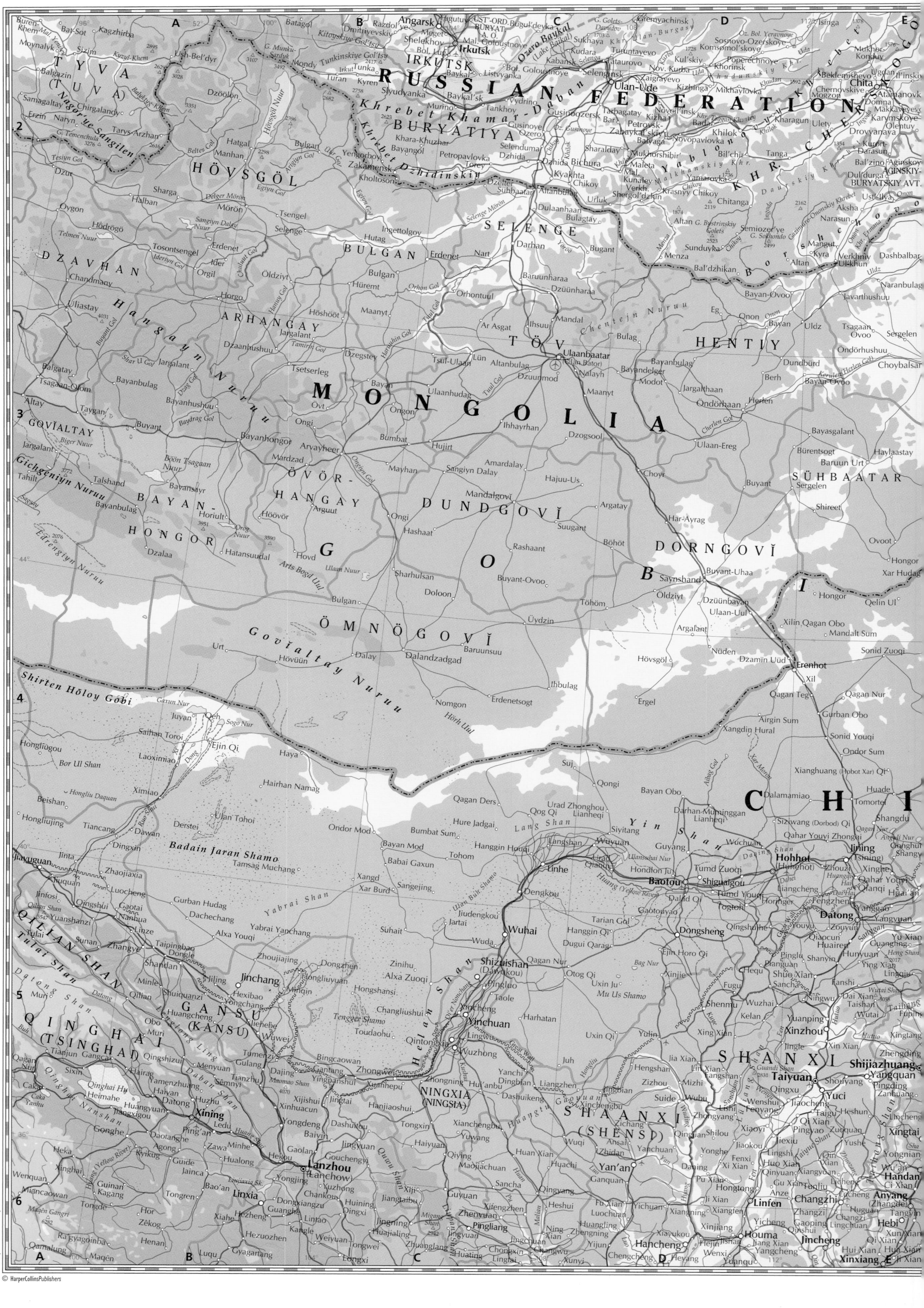

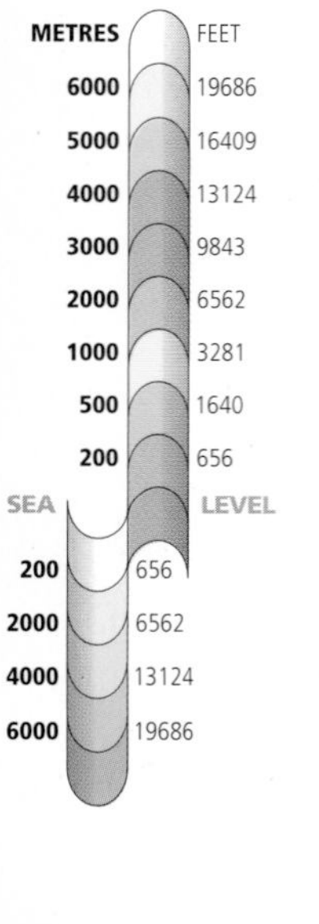

Albers Equal Area Conic Projection

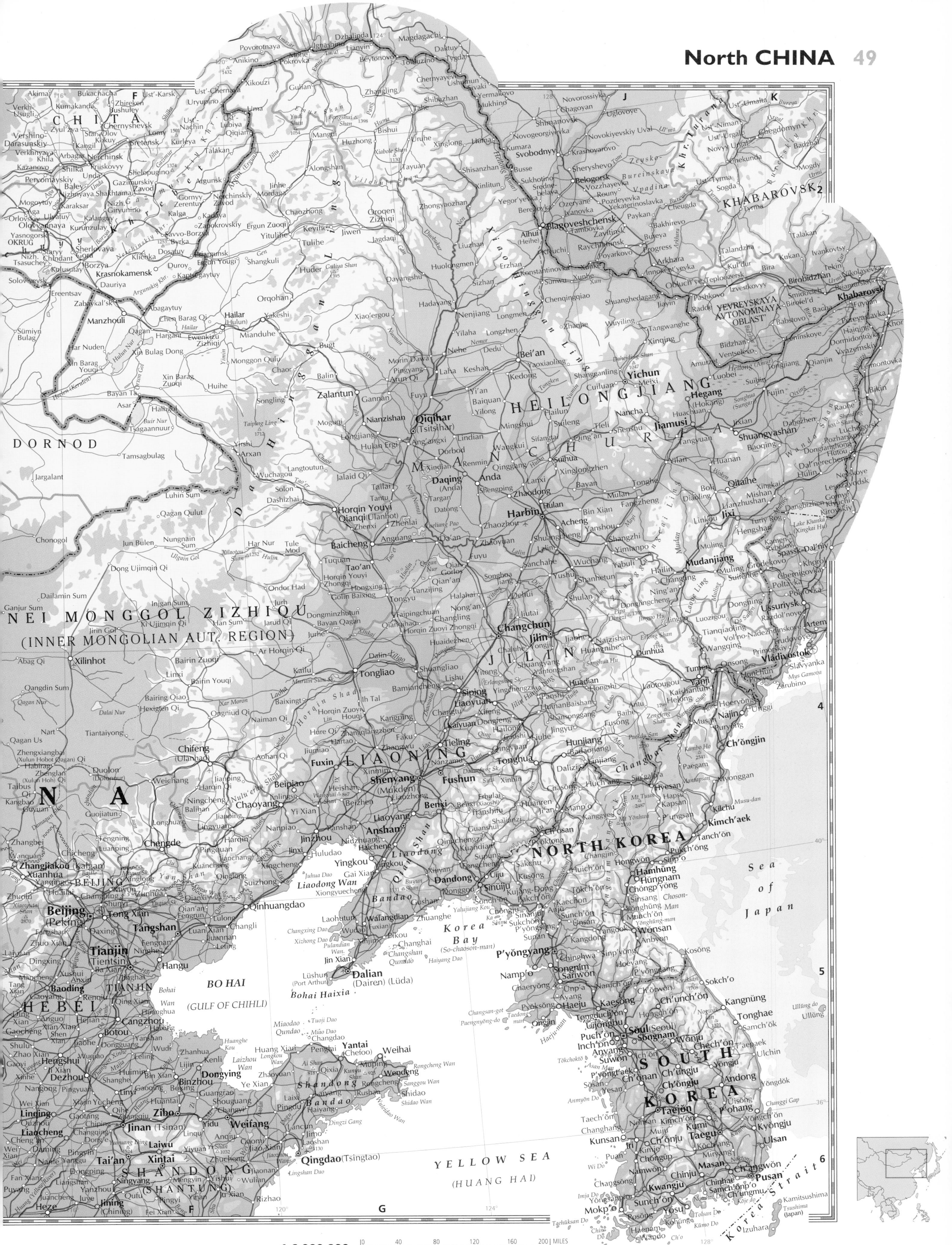

1:6 000 000

0 40 80 120 160 200 MILES

0 40 80 120 160 200 240 280 320 KM

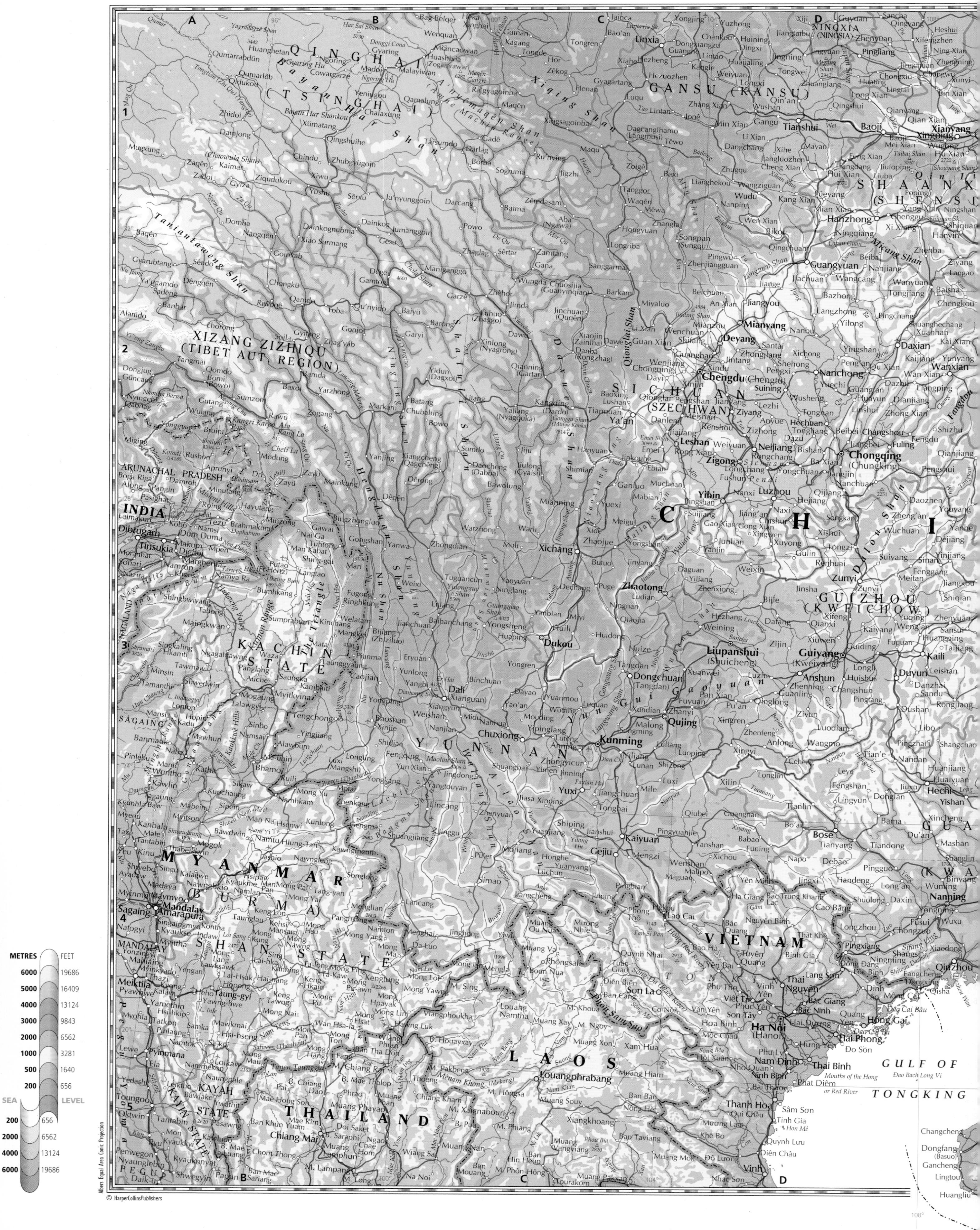
QINGHAI (TSINGHAI)
GANSU (KANSU)
NINGXIA (NINGSIA)
SHAANXI (SHENSI)
SICHUAN (SZECHWAN)
GUIZHOU (KWEICHOW)
YUNNAN
XIZANG ZIZHIQU (TIBET AUT. REGION)
CHINA
INDIA
ARUNACHAL PRADESH
NAGALAND
MYANMAR (BURMA)
KACHIN STATE
SHAN STATE
KAYAH STATE
KAYIN STATE
SAGAING
MANDALAY
PEGU
VIETNAM
LAOS
THAILAND
GULF OF TONGKING
Bayan Har Shan
Xiqing Shan
Hengduan Shan
Daxue Shan
Chengdu
Chongqing (Chungking)
Kunming
Guiyang
Lanzhou
Tianshui
Baoji
Xianyang
Hanzhong
Mianyang
Deyang
Nanchong
Leshan
Zigong
Neijiang
Yibin
Luzhou
Xichang
Dukou
Zhaotong
Liupanshui (Shuicheng)
Anshun
Qujing
Dali
Gejiu
Kaiyuan
Yuxi
Zunyi
Nanning
Hechi
Bose
Qinzhou
Ha Noi (Hanoi)
Hai Phong
Hong Gai
Nam Dinh
Thanh Hoa
Vinh
Lao Cai
Louangphrabang
Chiang Mai
Mandalay
Amarapura
Sagaing
Maymyo
Meiktila
Taung-gyi
Pyinmana
Myitkyina
Dibrugarh
Tinsukia
Yushu
Qamdo
METRES
FEET
6000 19686
5000 16409
4000 13124
3000 9843
2000 6562
1000 3281
500 1640
200 656
SEA LEVEL
200 656
2000 6562
4000 13124
6000 19686
Albers Equal Area Conic Projection

© HarperCollinsPublishers

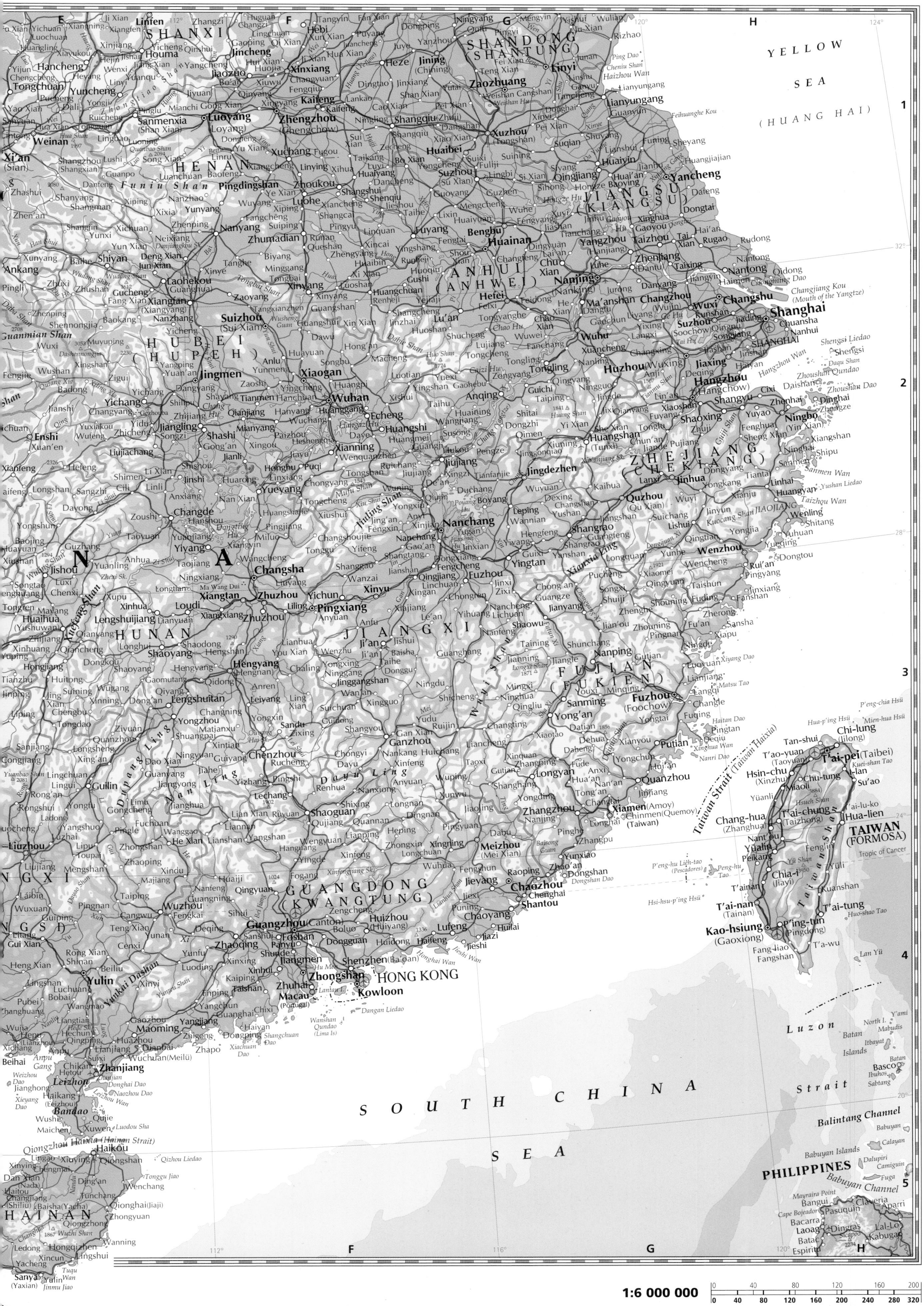
YELLOW SEA (HUANG HAI)
SOUTH CHINA SEA
SHANXI
HENAN
SHANDONG (SHANTUNG)
JIANGSU (KIANGSU)
ANHUI (ANHWEI)
HUBEI (HUPEH)
HUNAN
JIANGXI
ZHEJIANG (CHEKIANG)
FUJIAN (FUKIEN)
GUANGDONG (KWANGTUNG)
HAINAN
TAIWAN (FORMOSA)
PHILIPPINES
Shanghai
Nanjing
Wuhan
Changsha
Nanchang
Fuzhou (Foochow)
Guangzhou (Canton)
HONG KONG
Kowloon
Macau (Portugal)
Xiamen (Amoy)
Hangzhou (Hangchow)
Zhengzhou (Chengchow)
Hefei
T'ai-pei (Taibei)
Kao-hsiung (Gaoxiong)
Haikou
Taiwan Strait (Taiwan Haixia)
Qiongzhou Haixia (Hainan Strait)
Luzon Strait
Balintang Channel
Babuyan Channel
Babuyan Islands
Batan Islands
Tropic of Cancer
Xi'an (Sian)
Luoyang
Kaifeng
Xuzhou
Lianyungang
Yancheng
Wuxi
Suzhou
Ningbo
Wenzhou
Quanzhou
Shantou
Zhanjiang
Guilin
Hengyang
Ganzhou
Jingdezhen
Anqing
Yichang
Xiangfan
Zhuzhou
Xiangtan
Shenzhen
Zhuhai
Zhongshan

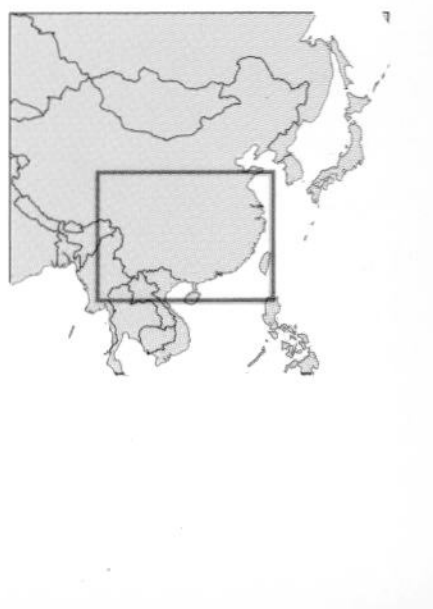

1:6 000 000

0 40 80 120 160 200 MILES

0 40 80 120 160 200 240 280 320 KM

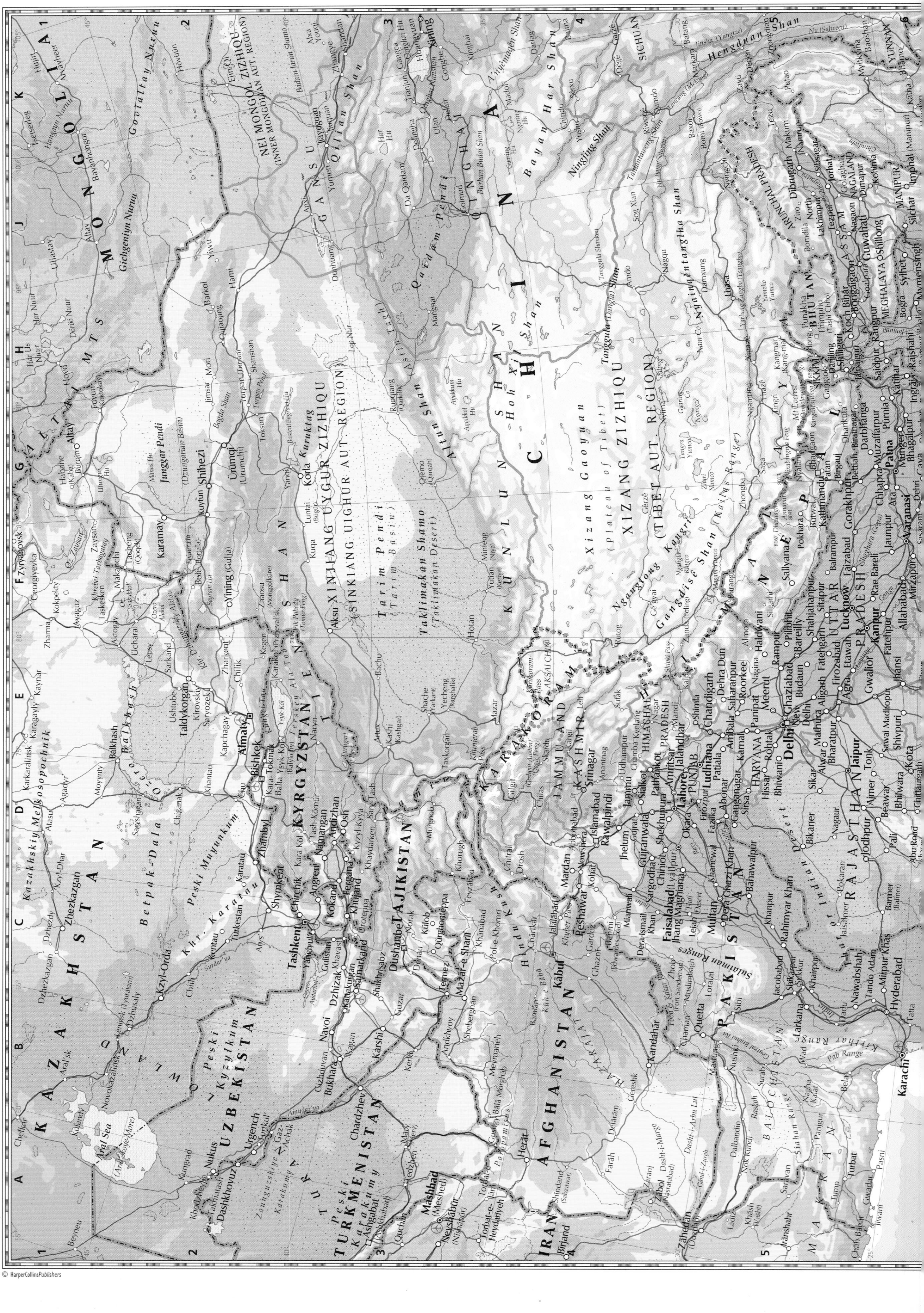

Transverse Mercator Projection

© HarperCollinsPublishers

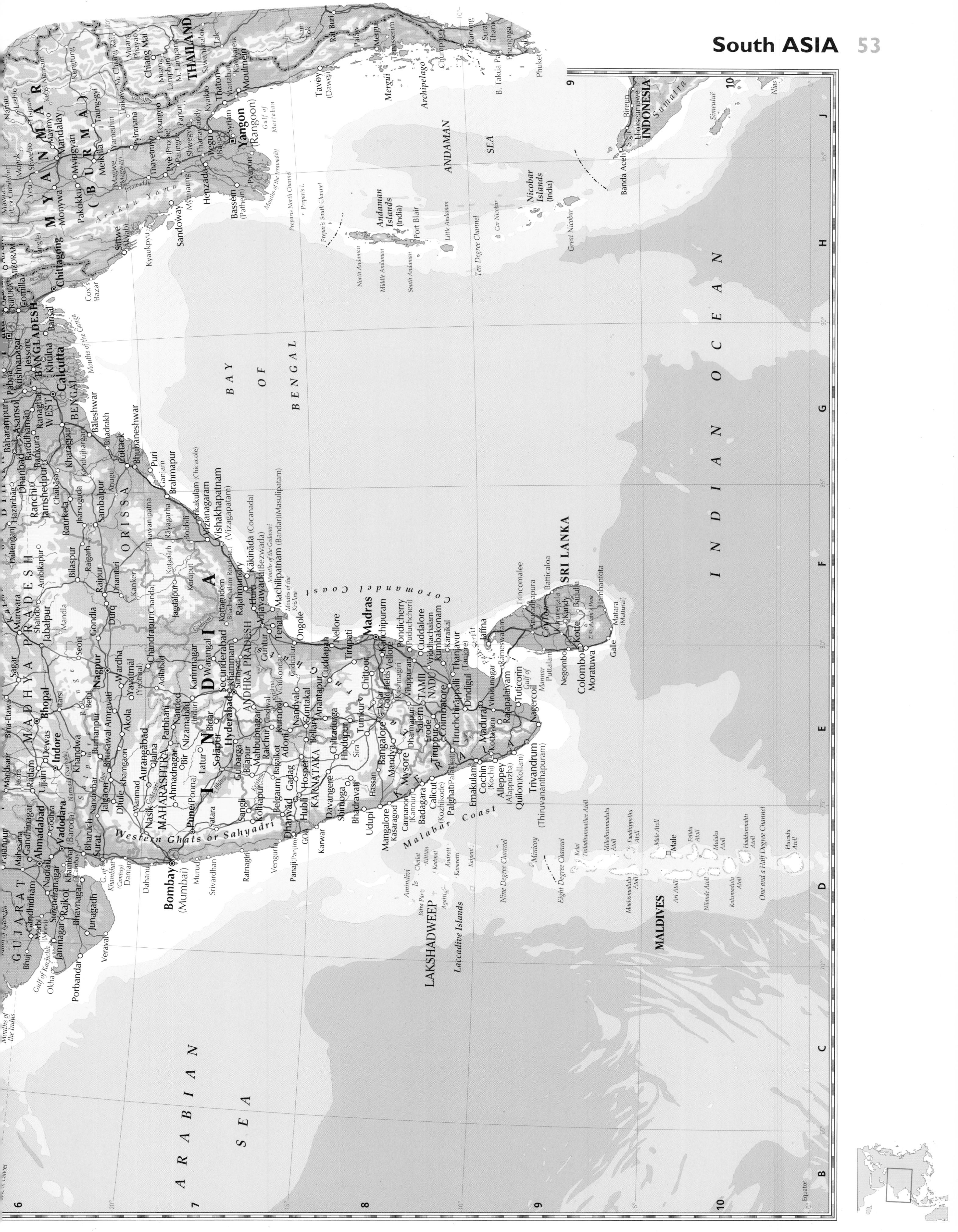
MYANMAR (BURMA)
THAILAND
BANGLADESH
INDIA
SRI LANKA
MALDIVES
INDONESIA
LAKSHADWEEP
Laccadive Islands
Andaman Islands (India)
Nicobar Islands (India)
BAY OF BENGAL
ARABIAN SEA
ANDAMAN SEA
INDIAN OCEAN
Gulf of Martaban
Mergui Archipelago
Coromandel Coast
Malabar Coast
Western Ghats or Sahyadri
Palk Strait
Gulf of Mannar
Ten Degree Channel
Nine Degree Channel
Eight Degree Channel
One and a Half Degree Channel
GUJARAT
MADHYA PRADESH
MAHARASHTRA
ORISSA
ANDHRA PRADESH
KARNATAKA
KERALA
TAMIL NADU
WEST BENGAL
Bombay (Mumbai)
Calcutta
Madras
Hyderabad
Bangalore
Yangon (Rangoon)
Mandalay
Chittagong
Colombo
Kotte
Male
Pune (Poona)
Ahmadabad
Nagpur
Bhopal
Indore
Vishakhapatnam
Vijayawada
Trivandrum (Thiruvananthapuram)
Cochin (Kochi)
Madurai
Coimbatore
Jaffna
Kandy
Trincomalee
Port Blair
Banda Aceh
Sumatra
Equator
Tropic of Cancer

1:12 000 000

MILES	0	80	160	240	320	400
KM	0	80 160	240 320	400 480	560 640	

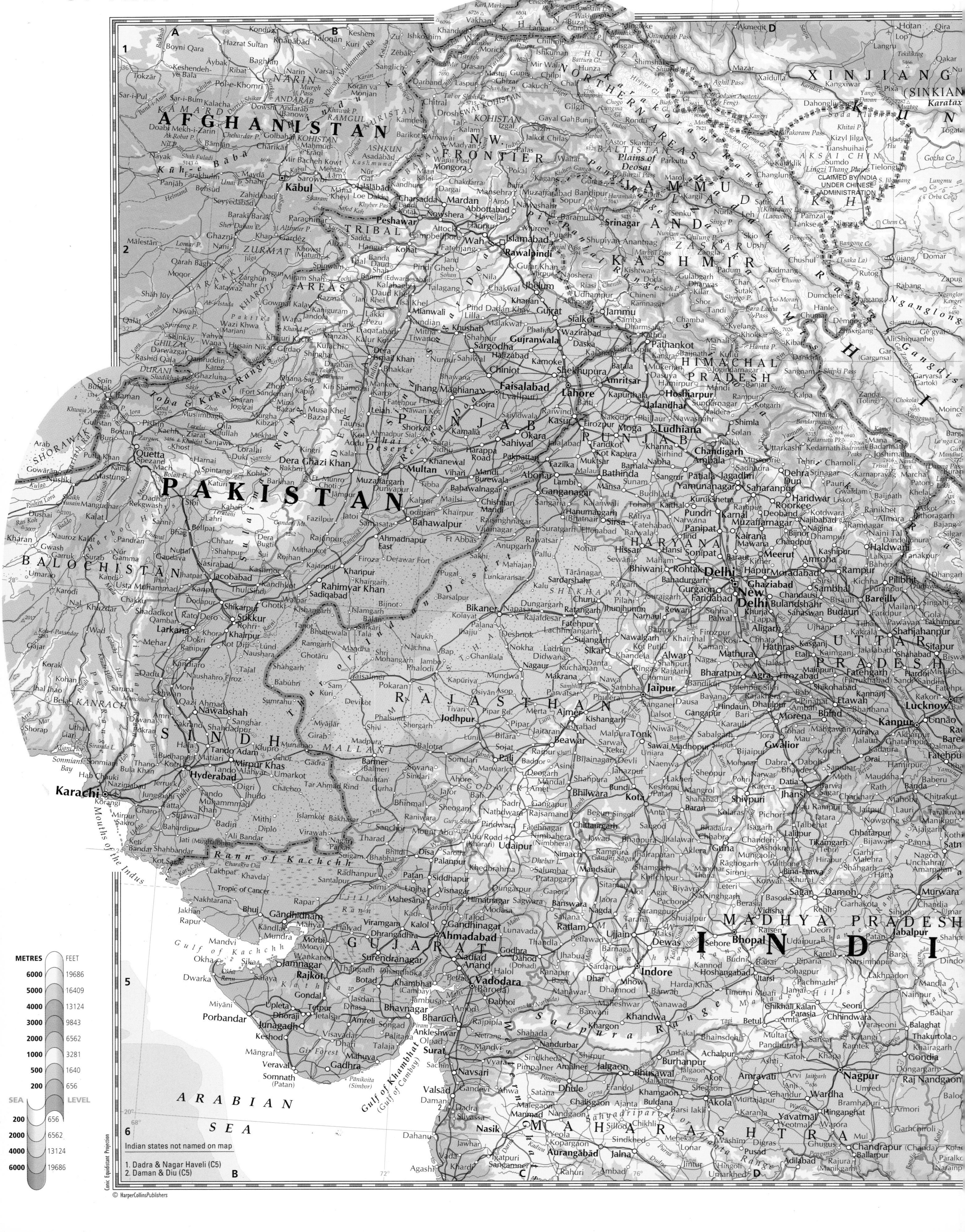
AFGHANISTAN
PAKISTAN
INDIA
XINJIANG
N.W. FRONTIER
TRIBAL AREAS
NORTHERN AREAS
JAMMU AND KASHMIR
PUNJAB
HIMACHAL PRADESH
HARYANA
UTTAR PRADESH
RAJASTHAN
GUJARAT
MADHYA PRADESH
MAHARASHTRA
BALOCHISTAN
SINDH
ARABIAN SEA
Gulf of Kachchh
Gulf of Khambhat (Gulf of Cambay)
Rann of Kachchh
Mouths of the Indus
Thar Desert
Tropic of Cancer
CLAIMED BY INDIA UNDER CHINESE ADMINISTRATION
Kābul
Peshawar
Islamabad
Rawalpindi
Lahore
Faisalabad
Multan
Quetta
Karachi
Hyderabad
Srinagar
Delhi
New Delhi
Jaipur
Jodhpur
Ahmadabad
Vadodara
Surat
Indore
Bhopal
Lucknow
Kanpur
Agra
Nagpur
METRES
FEET
6000 19686
5000 16409
4000 13124
3000 9843
2000 6562
1000 3281
500 1640
200 656
SEA LEVEL
200 656
2000 6562
4000 13124
6000 19686
Indian states not named on map
1. Dadra & Nagar Haveli (C5)
2. Daman & Diu (C5)
Conic Equidistant Projection
© HarperCollinsPublishers

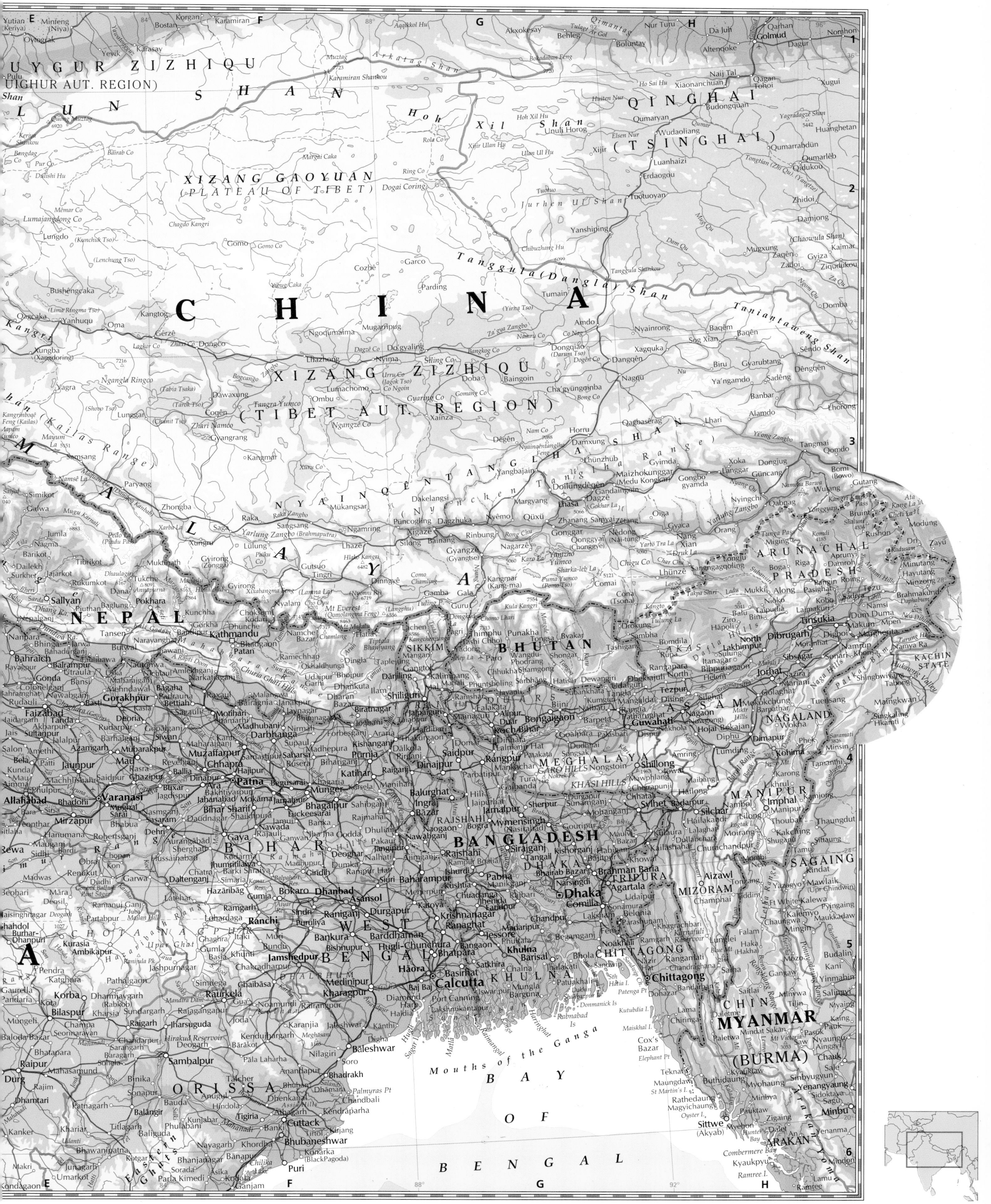

1:6 000 000

0 40 80 120 160 200 MILES

0 40 80 120 160 200 240 280 320 KM

South INDIA and SRI LANKA

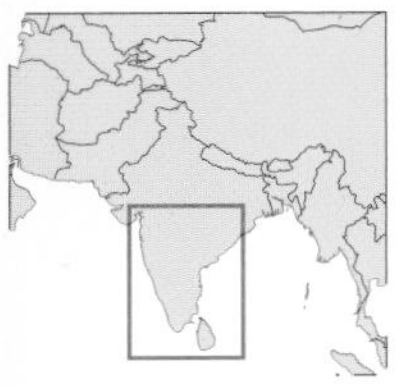

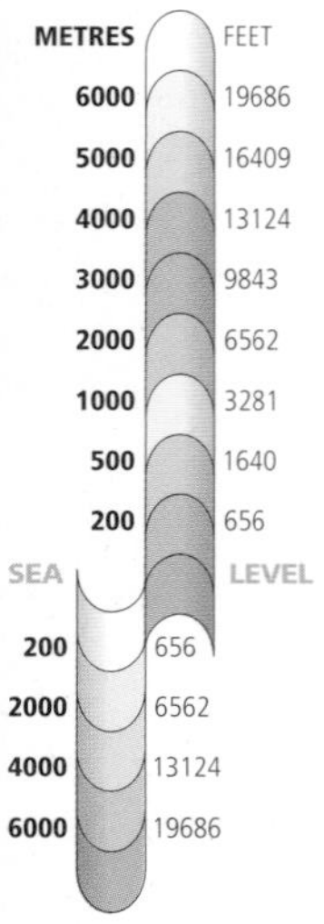

0 40 80 120 160 200 MILES
0 40 80 120 160 200 240 280 320 KM
1:6 000 000

© HarperCollinsPublishers

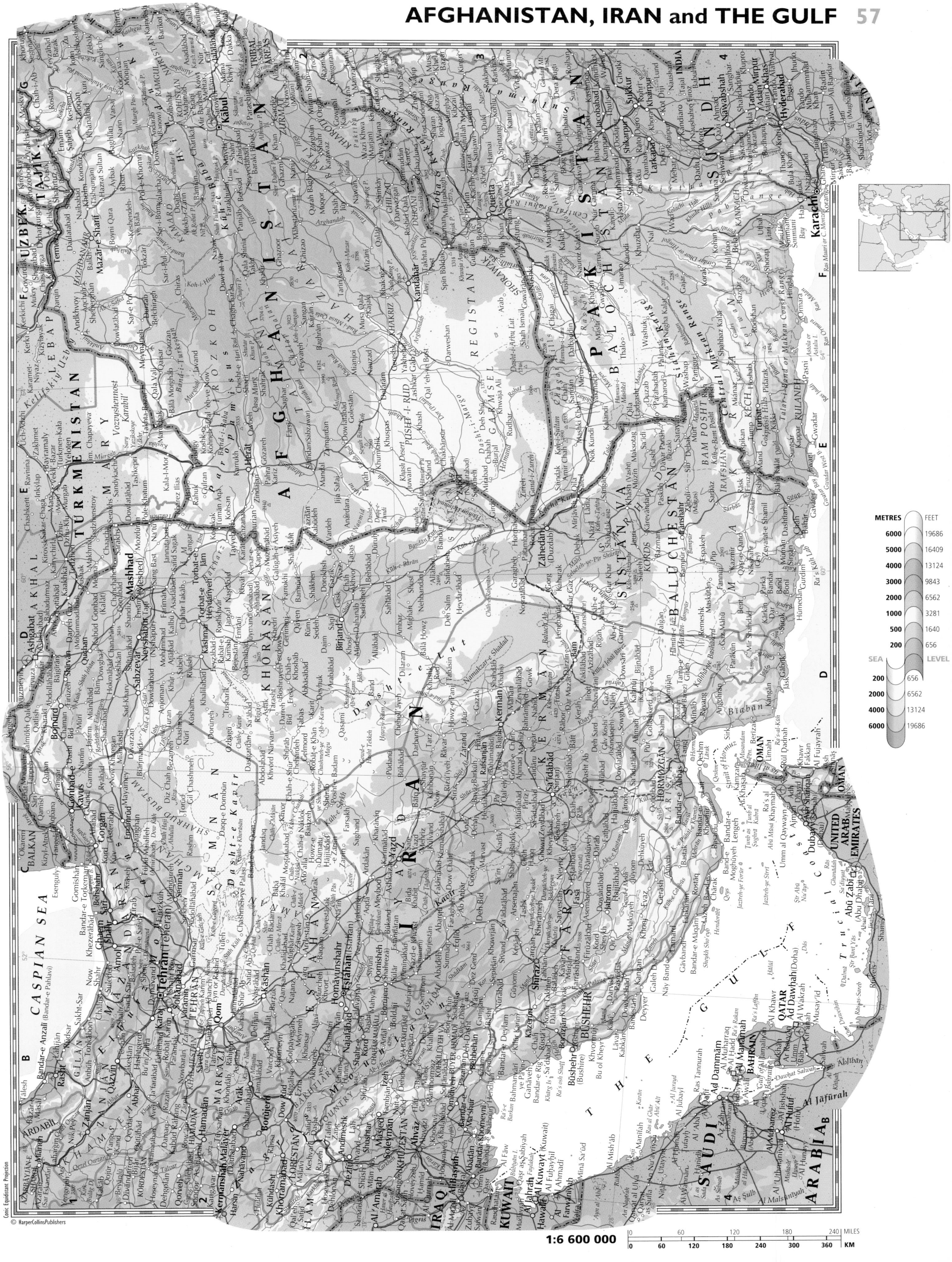
METRES
FEET
6000
19686
5000
16409
4000
13124
3000
9843
2000
6562
1000
3281
500
1640
200
656
SEA
LEVEL
200
656
2000
6562
4000
13124
6000
19686
Conic Equidistant Projection
1:6 600 000
0
60
120
180
240
MILES
0
60
120
180
240
300
360
KM

© HarperCollinsPublishers

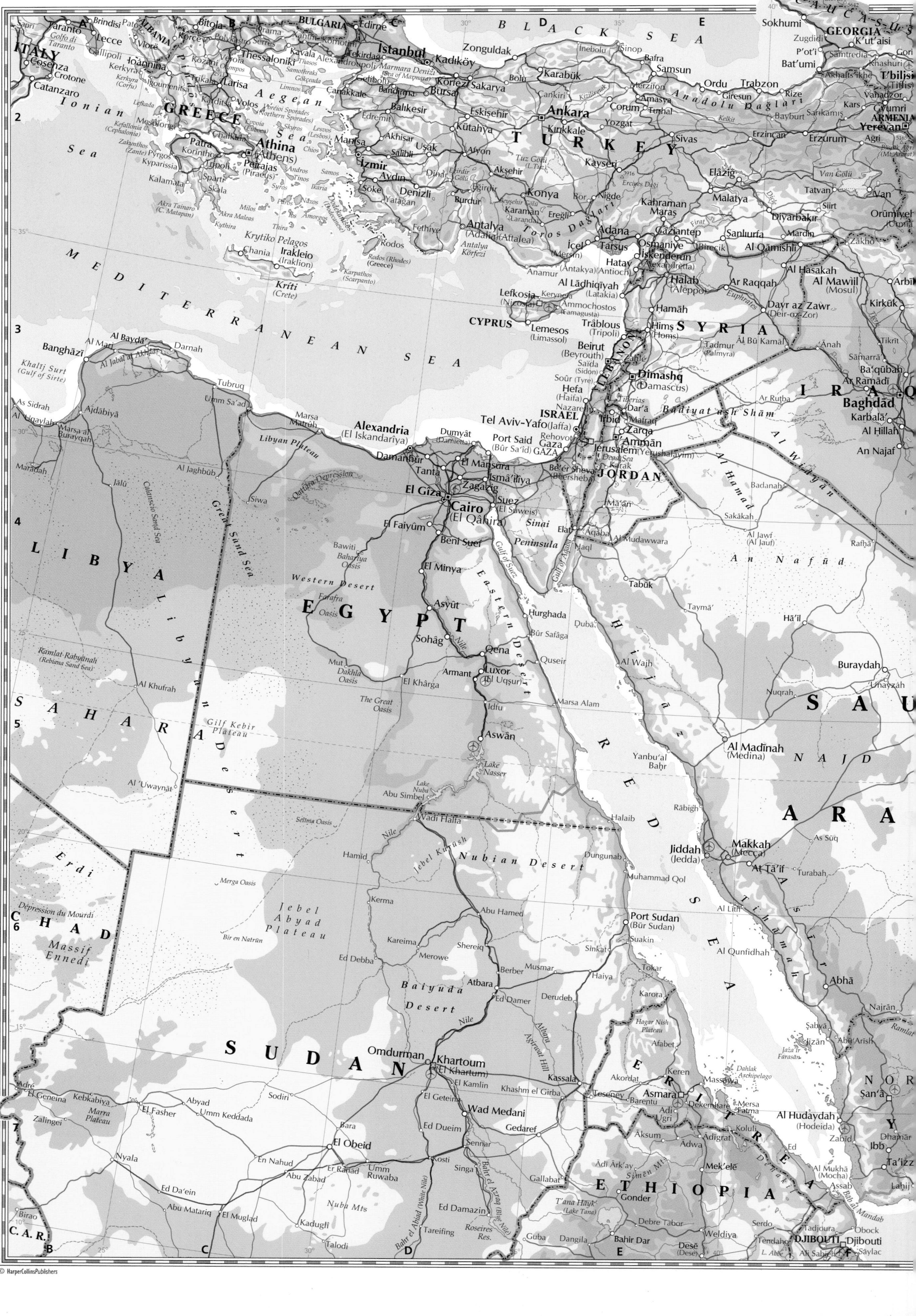

METRES / FEET: 6000 / 19686, 5000 / 16409, 4000 / 13124, 3000 / 9843, 2000 / 6562, 1000 / 3281, 500 / 1640, 200 / 656, SEA LEVEL, 200 / 656, 2000 / 6562, 4000 / 13124, 6000 / 19686

Albers Conic Equal Area Projection

© HarperCollinsPublishers

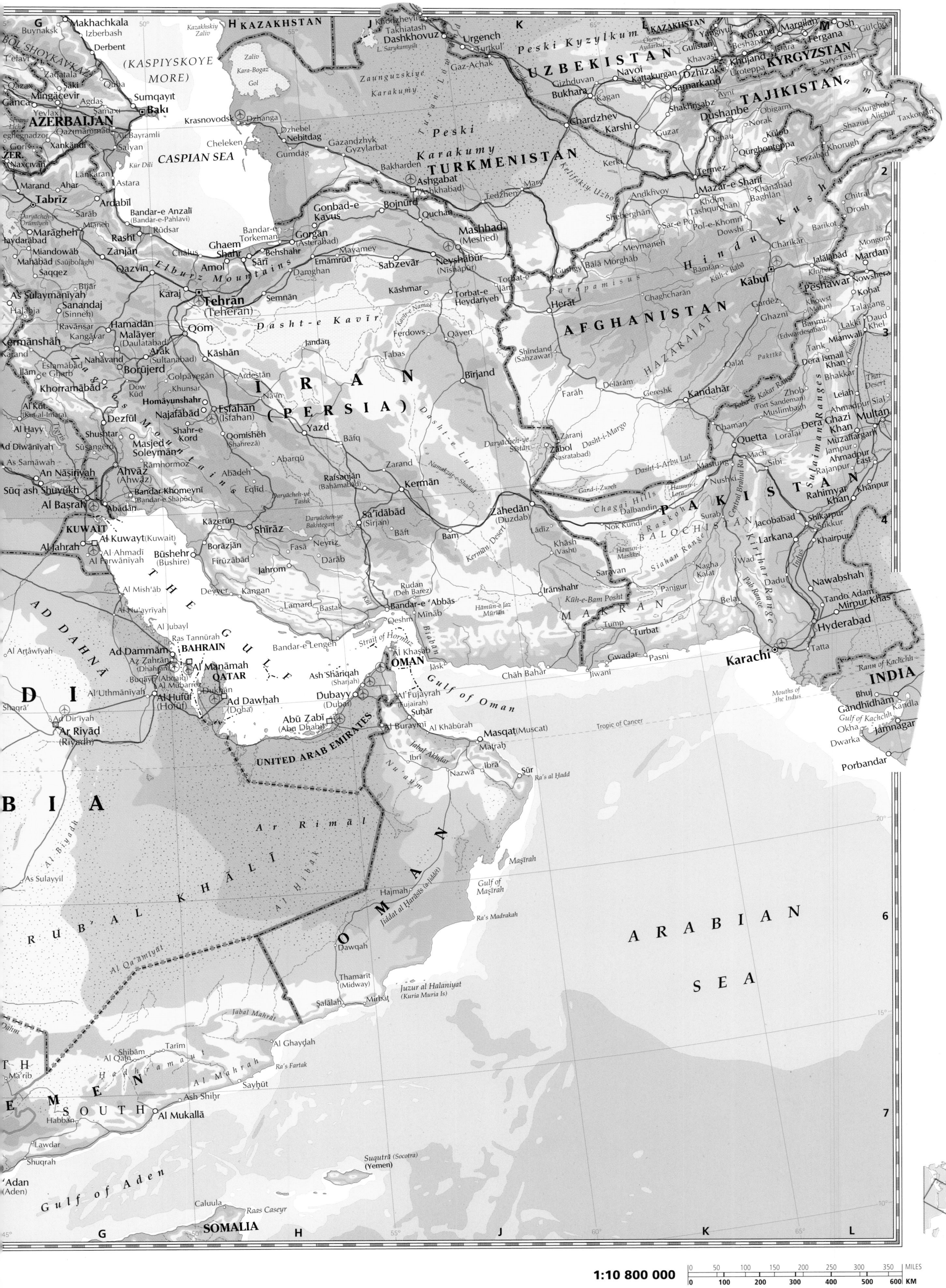

1:10 800 000

0 50 100 150 200 250 300 350 MILES

0 100 200 300 400 500 600 KM

TURKEY, IRAQ, SYRIA, JORDAN and TRANSCAUCASIAN REPUBLICS

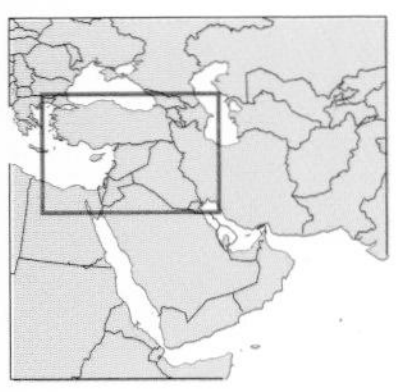

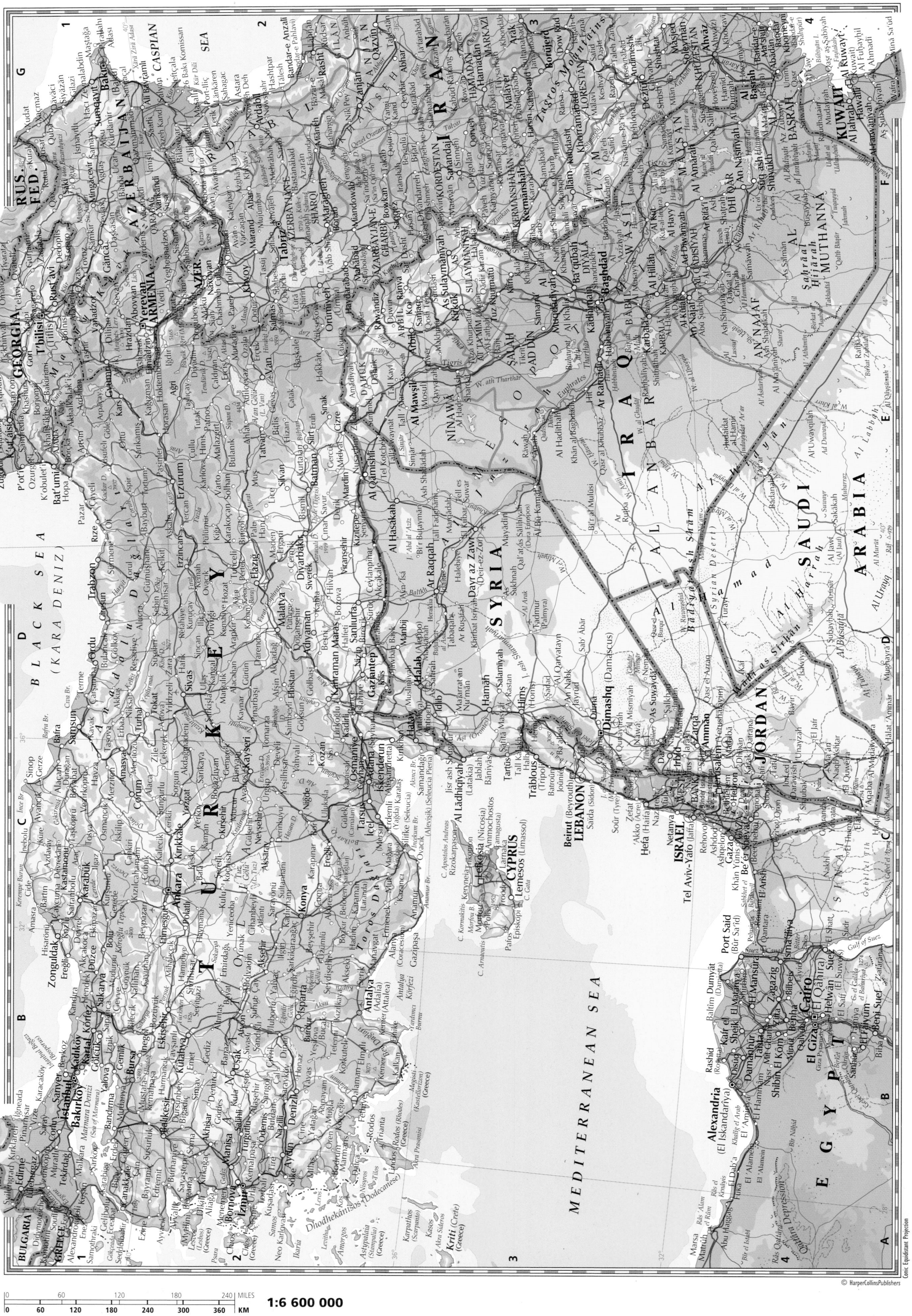
BLACK SEA
(KARA DENIZ)
MEDITERRANEAN SEA
CASPIAN SEA
TURKEY
SYRIA
IRAQ
JORDAN
SAUDI ARABIA
EGYPT
GEORGIA
ARMENIA
AZERBAIJAN
CYPRUS
LEBANON
ISRAEL
KUWAIT
Conic Equidistant Projection
© HarperCollinsPublishers

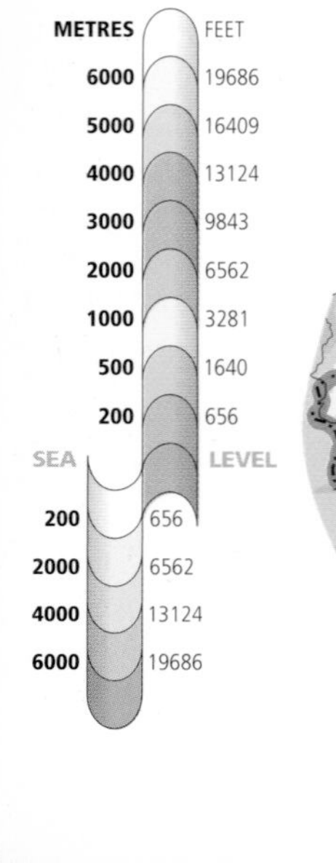
METRES
FEET
6000
19686
5000
16409
4000
13124
3000
9843
2000
6562
1000
3281
500
1640
200
656
SEA
LEVEL
200
656
2000
6562
4000
13124
6000
19686

0 60 120 180 240 MILES
0 60 120 180 240 300 360 KM

1:6 600 000

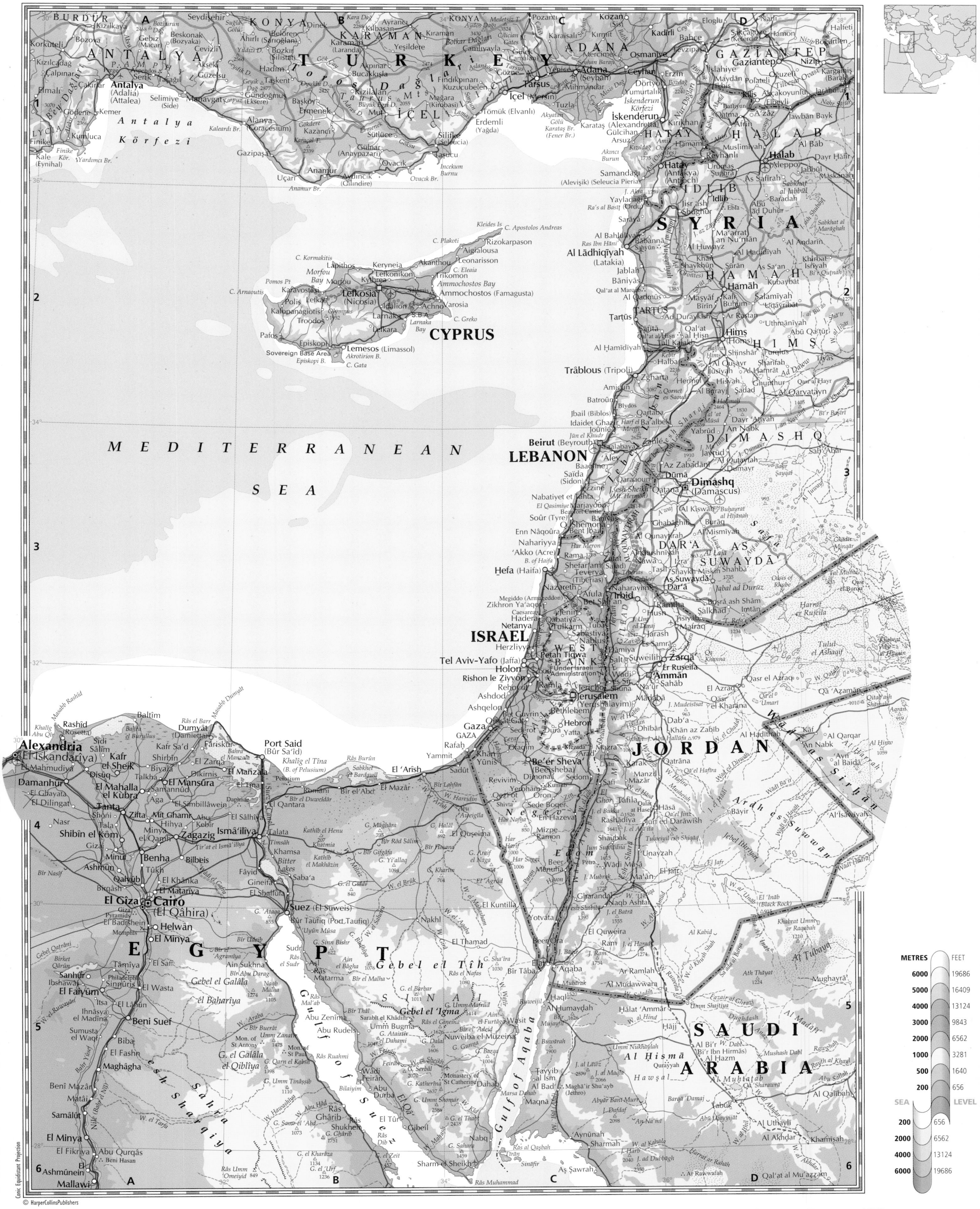

1:3 300 000

MILES 0 30 60 90

KM 0 30 60 90 120 150 180

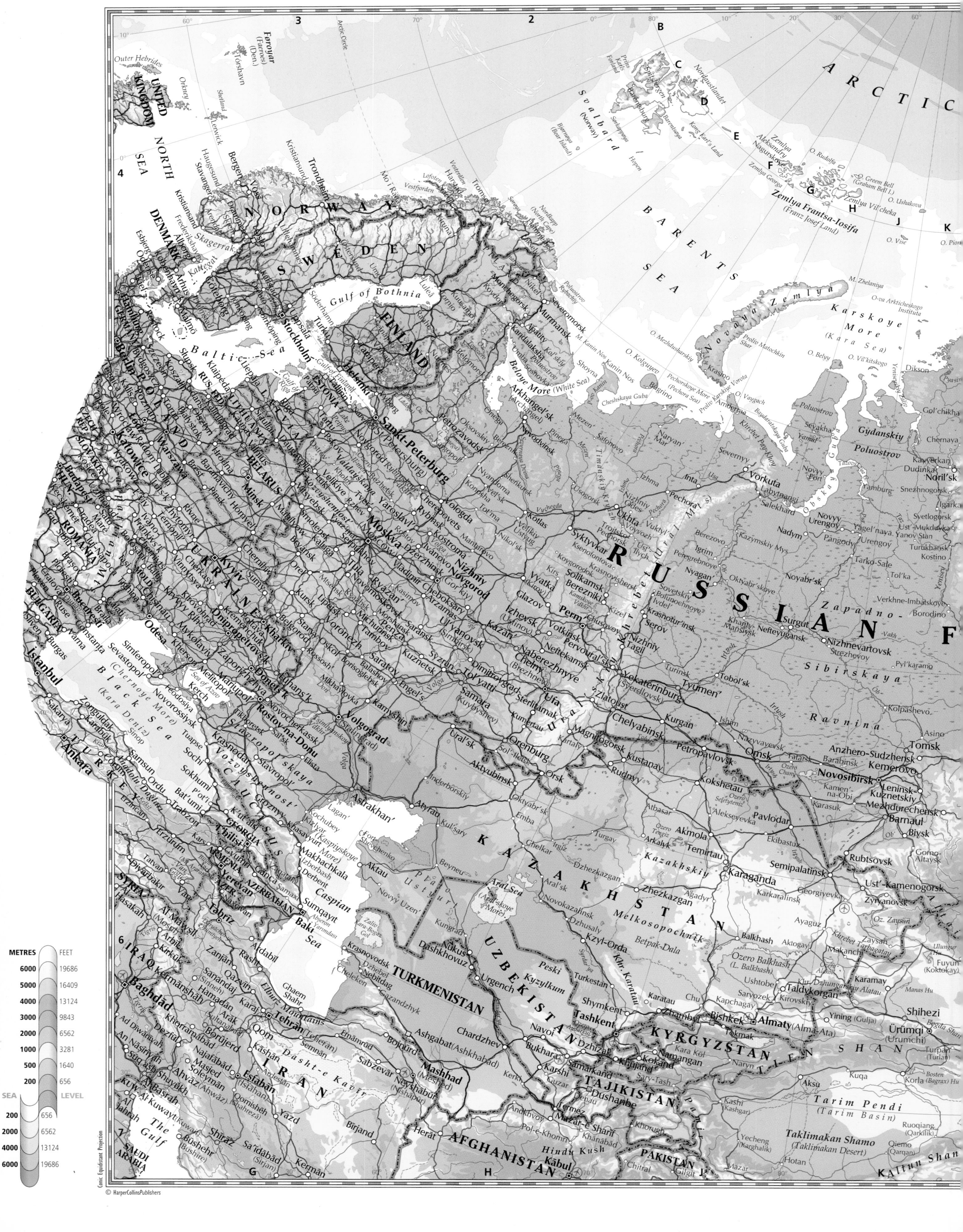

Conic Equidistant Projection

© HarperCollinsPublishers

1:18 000 000

0 120 240 360 480 600 MILES
0 120 240 360 480 600 720 840 960 KM

RUSSIAN FE
KAZA
UZBEKIS
TURKMENISTAN
IRAN
GEORGIA
ARMENIA
AZERBAIJAN
IRAQ
CASPIAN SEA
(KASPIYSKOYE MORE)
Aral Sea
(Aral'skoye More)
Zaliv Kara-Bogaz Gol
ZAPADNO-KAZAKHSTAN
ATYRAU
MANGISTAUZ
AKTYUBINSK
KZYL-ORDA
DASHKHOVUZ
BALKAN
AKHAL
LEBAP
MARY
ORENBURG
BASHKORTOSTAN
TATARSTAN
SAMARA
SARATOV
VOLGOGRAD
ASTRAKHAN'
KALMYKIYA
STAVROPOL
ROSTOV
VORONEZH
TAMBOV
LIPETSK
RYAZAN
PENZA
UL'YANOVSK
MORDOVIYA
CHUVASHIYA
SVERDLOVSK
CHELYABINSK
KUSTAN
DAGESTAN
CHECHNYA
Volgograd (Stalingrad)
Saratov
Samara (Kuybyshev)
Kazan'
Ufa
Orenburg
Chelyabinsk
Yekaterinburg (Sverdlovsk)
Astrakhan'
Atyrau (Gur'yev)
Ural'sk
Aktyubinsk
Aktau (Shevchenko)
Makhachkala
Groznyy
T'bilisi (Tiflis)
Yerevan
Bakı (Baku)
Tabrīz
Tehrān (Teheran)
Ashgabat (Ashkhabad)
Mashhad (Meshed)
Nukus
Urgench
Dashkhovuz
Chardzhev
Bukhara
Krasnovodsk
Kamyshin
Penza
Ul'yanovsk (Simbirsk)
Tol'yatti
Syzran'
Engel's
Balakovo
Magnitogorsk
Orsk
Novotroitsk
Kustanay
Rudnyy
Sterlitamak
Zlatoust
Miass
Qom
Hamadān
Kermānshāh
Qazvīn
Rasht
Ardabīl
Gorgān
Semnān
Elburz Mountains
Dasht-e Kavīr
Karakumy
Ustyurt
Plato Ustyurt
Mangyshlak
Ryn Peski
Prikaspiyskaya Nizmennost'
Obshchiy Syrt
Turgayskaya Stolovaya Strana
Kyzylkum
Vozvyshennost' Karabil'
Khrebet Kopet Dag
Caucasus
Chernyye Zemli
Privolzhskaya Vozvyshennost'
METRES
FEET
6000
19686
5000
16409
4000
13124
3000
9843
2000
6562
1000
3281
500
1640
200
656
SEA
LEVEL
200
656
2000
6562
4000
13124
6000
19686
Conic Equidistant Projection

© HarperCollinsPublishers

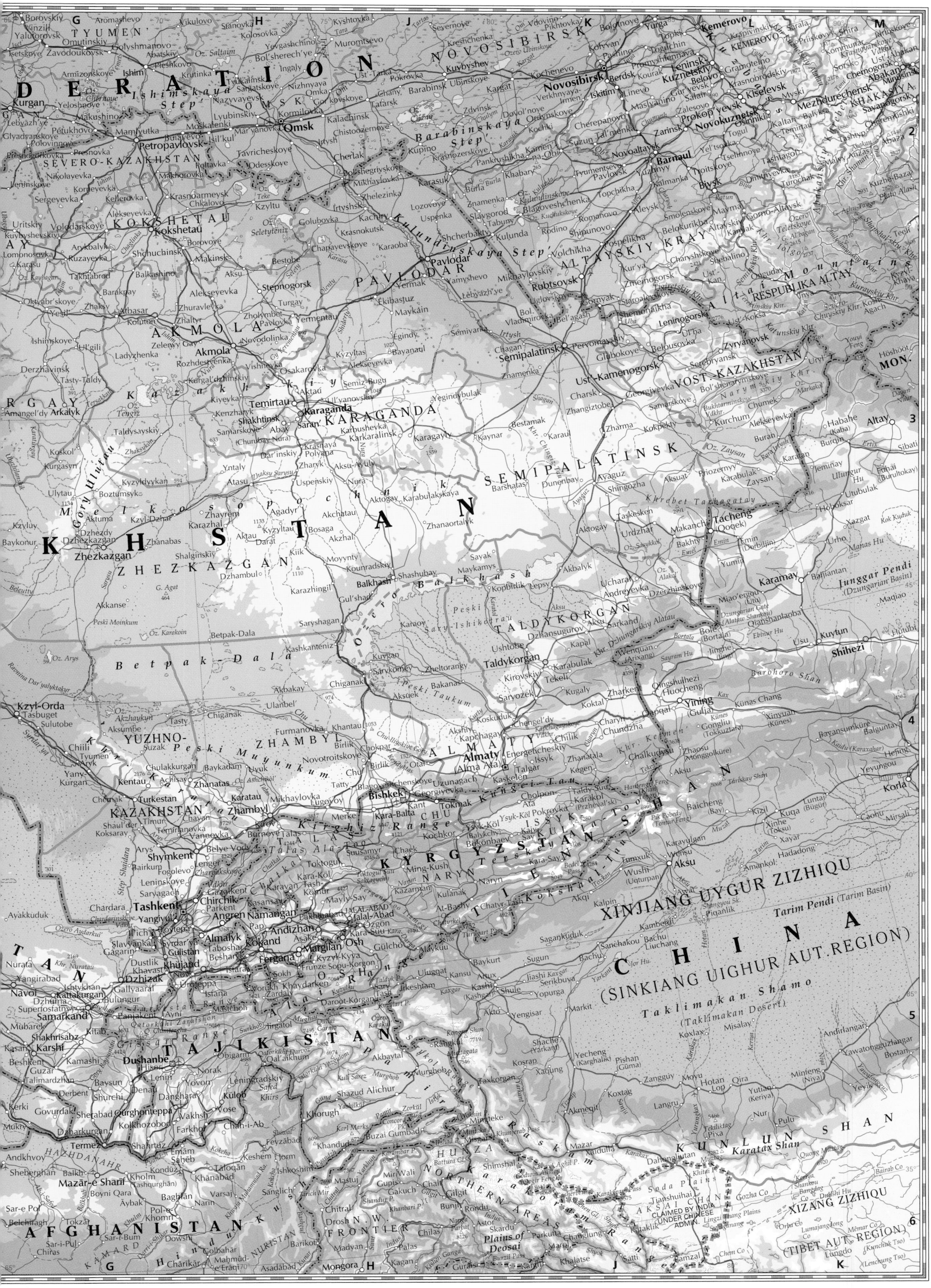

1:7 500 000

0 75 150 225 300 MILES
0 75 150 225 300 375 450 KM

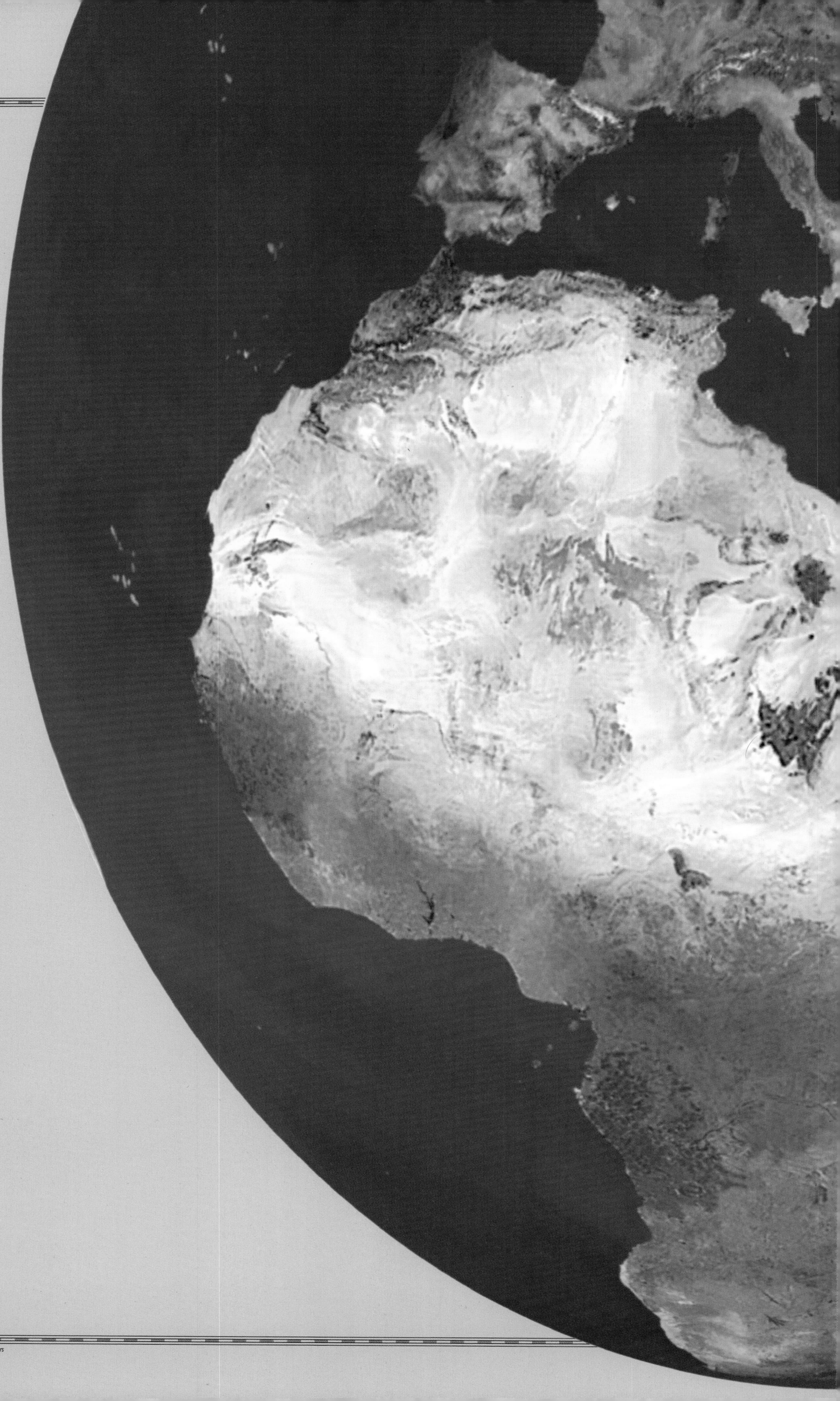

Countries

SPAIN
ITALY
GREECE
TURKEY
SYRIA
LEBANON
ISRAEL
JORDAN
CYPRUS
MALTA
Mediterranean Sea
Tyrrhenian Sea
Ionian Sea
Aegean Sea
Madeira (Port.)
Canary Is (Sp.)
Str. of Gibraltar
Gibraltar (U.K.)
MOROCCO
Atlas Mountains
WESTERN SAHARA
ALGERIA
TUNISIA
LIBYA
EGYPT
Libyan Desert
SAHARA
Hoggar
Tibesti
MAURITANIA
MALI
NIGER
CHAD
SUDAN
ERITREA
SENEGAL
THE GAMBIA
GUINEA-BISSAU
GUINEA
Fouta Djallon
SIERRA LEONE
LIBERIA
CÔTE D'IVOIRE
BURKINA
GHANA
TOGO
BENIN
NIGERIA
CAMEROON
CENTRAL AFRICAN REPUBLIC
EQUAT. GUINEA
SAO TOME & PRINCIPE
GABON
CONGO
CONGO (ZAIRE)
UGANDA
RWANDA
BURUNDI
TANZANIA
ANGOLA
CABINDA (Ang.)
ZAMBIA
MALAWI
MOZAMBIQUE
ZIMBABWE
NAMIBIA
BOTSWANA
SWAZILAND
LESOTHO
REPUBLIC OF SOUTH AFRICA
Namib Desert
Kalahari Desert
Great Karoo
Gulf of Guinea
Bight of Benin
SOUTH ATLANTIC OCEAN
Ascension I. (U.K.)
St Helena (U.K.)
Annobón
Tropic of Cancer
Equator
Tropic of Capricorn
Cape of Good Hope
C. Agulhas
Tangier
Rabat
Casablanca
Fez
Meknès
Marrakesh
Oujda
Algiers
Oran
Tunis
Tripoli
Benghazi
Cairo
Alexandria
Khartoum
Dakar
Bamako
Niamey
Ouagadougou
Abuja
Lagos
Accra
Abidjan
Monrovia
Freetown
Conakry
Bissau
Nouakchott
Ndjamena
Bangui
Yaoundé
Libreville
Kinshasa
Brazzaville
Luanda
Lusaka
Harare
Windhoek
Gaborone
Pretoria
Johannesburg
Cape Town
Durban
Maputo
Nairobi
Kampala
Kigali
Bujumbura
Dodoma
L. Chad
L. Victoria
L. Tanganyika
L. Malawi
Nile
Niger
Congo (Zaïre)
Zambezi
Orange
Limpopo
1:25 000 000
MILES 0 150 300 450 600 750
KM 0 150 300 450 600 750 900 1050 1200
Oblated Stereographic Projection
© HarperCollinsPublishers

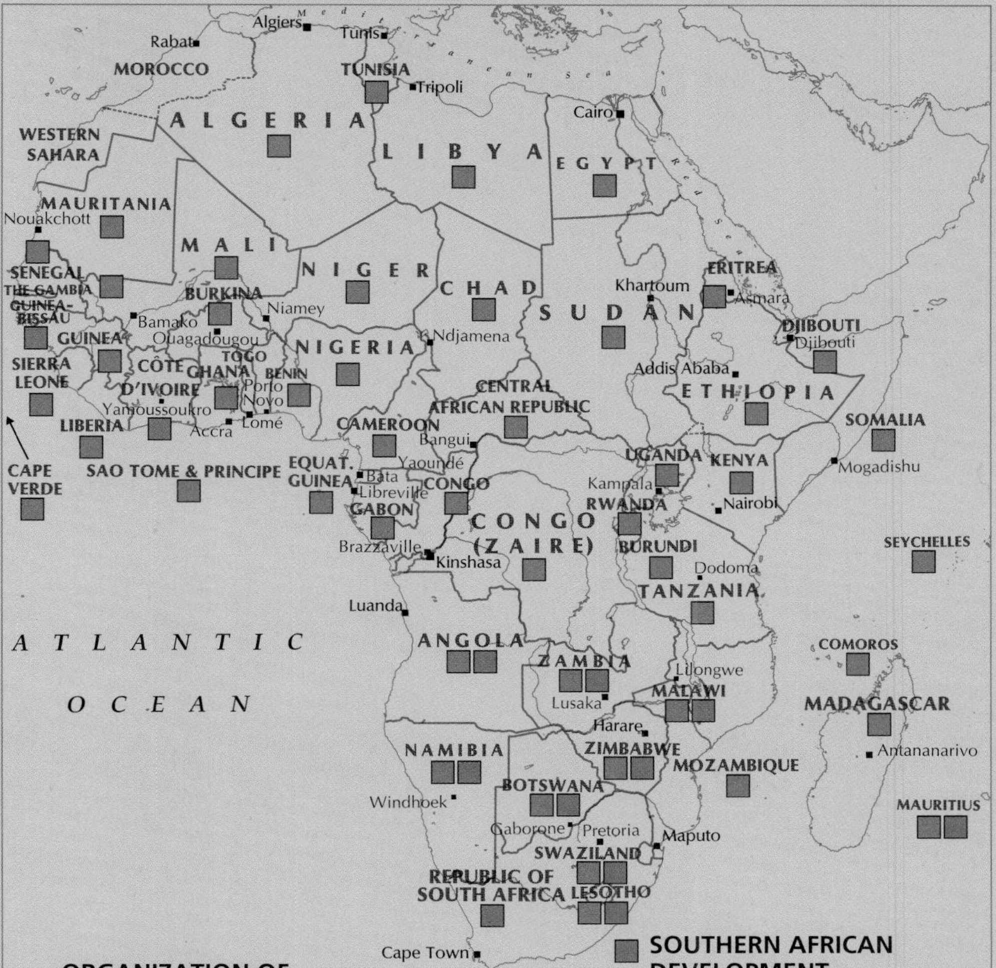

ORGANIZATION OF AFRICAN UNITY (OAU)

The OAU grew out of the Union of Africa states which was founded at a conference in Casablanca in 1961; 19 African states then met in Liberia in 1961 and in Nigeria in 1962, paving the way for the founding of the Organization of African Unity at the Addis Ababa conference in 1963. The objectives of the OAU are to promote African unity and solidarity; the co-ordination of policies on the basis of non-alignment; the defence of the independence and sovereignity of African states; the improvement of living standards, and the eradication of all forms of colonialism. All continental African countries are now members together with Cape Verde, the Comoros, Sao Tome and Principe, and Seychelles. The Sahrawi Arab Democratic Republic (Western Sahara) was admitted in 1982, but blocked by Morocco. Morocco withdrew over the issue of Western Sahara in 1984.

Headquarters : Addis Ababa, Ethiopia

SOUTHERN AFRICAN DEVELOPMENT COMMUNITY (SADC)

Formerly the Southern African Development Co-ordination Conference, formed in response to a conference in Arusha, Tanzania in 1979, called to discuss South Africa's economic dominance of the region. The founder members were Angola, Botswana, Lesotho, Malawi, Mozambique, Swaziland, Tanzania, Zambia and Zimbabwe. Namibia joined in 1990, South Africa in 1994 and Mauritius in 1995. The objectives of SADC are deeper economic co-operation and integration and the promotion of political and social values, human rights and the alleviation of poverty.

Headquarters : Gaborone, Botswana

ORGANIZATION OF PETROLEUM EXPORTING COUNTRIES (OPEC)

see page 35 for information on OPEC

ARAB LEAGUE

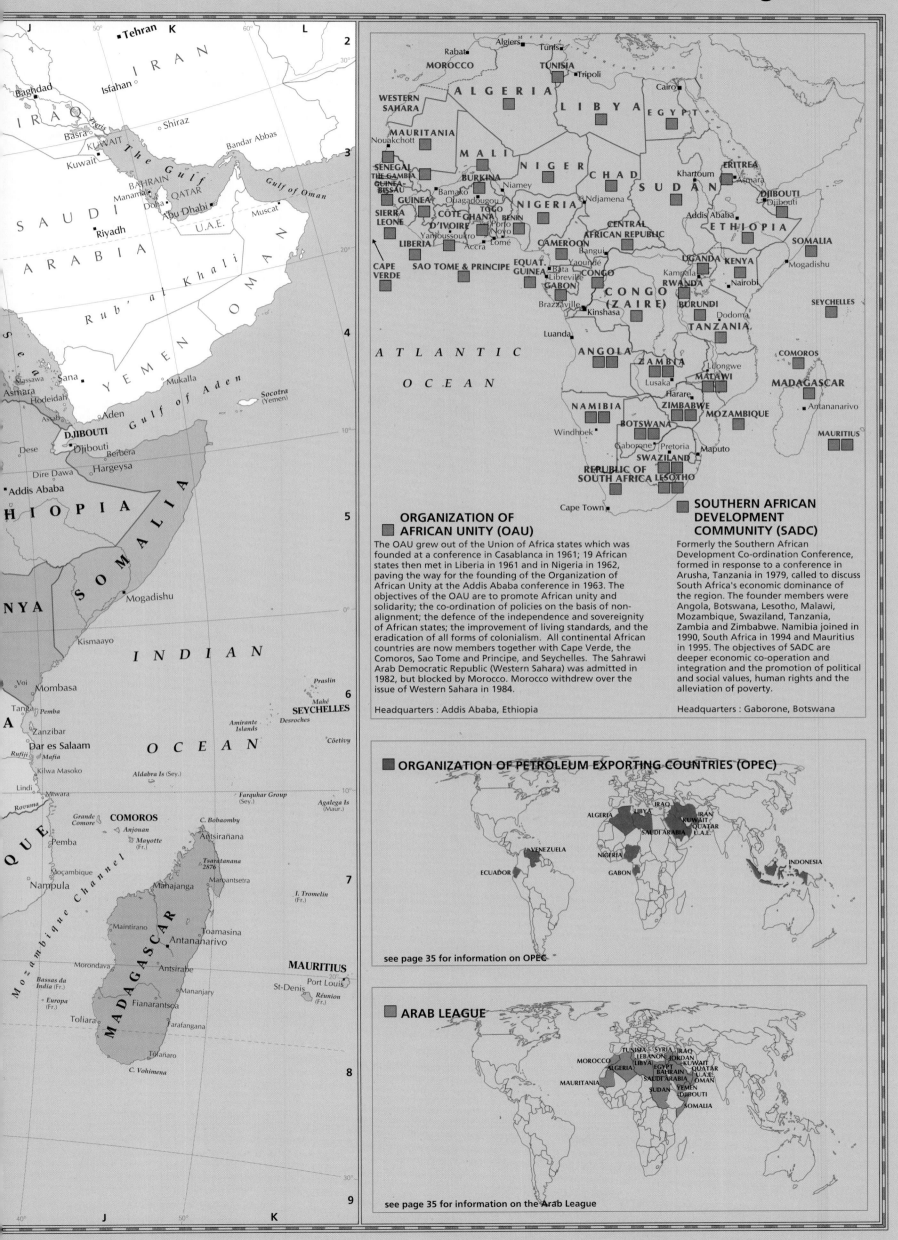

see page 35 for information on the Arab League

National Statistics

COUNTRY	AREA sq ml	AREA sq km	POPULATION total	density per sq ml	density per sq km	FORM OF GOVERNMENT	CAPITAL CITY	MAIN LANGUAGES	MAIN RELIGIONS	CURRENCY
ALGERIA	919 595	2 381 741	27 561 000	30	12	republic	Algiers	Arabic, French, Berber	Muslim, R.C.	Dinar
ANGOLA	481 354	1 246 700	10 674 000	22	9	republic	Luanda	Portuguese, local lang	R.C., Protestant, trad. beliefs	Kwanza
BENIN	43 483	112 620	5 387 000	124	48	republic	Porto Novo	French, Fon, Yoruba, Adja, local lang	Trad. beliefs, R.C., Muslim	CFA franc
BOTSWANA	224 468	581 370	1 443 000	6	2	republic	Gaborone	English (official), Setswana, Shona, local lang	Trad. beliefs, Protestant, R.C.	Pula
BURKINA	105 869	274 200	9 889 000	93	36	republic	Ouagadougou	French, More (Mossi), Fulani, local lang	Trad. beliefs, Muslim, R.C.	CFA franc
BURUNDI	10 747	27 835	6 134 000	571	220	republic	Bujumbura	Kirundi (Hutu, Tutsi), French	R.C., trad. beliefs, Protestant, Muslim	Franc
CAMEROON	183 569	475 442	12 871 000	70	27	republic	Yaoundé	French, English, Fang, Bamileke, local lang	Trad. beliefs, R.C., Muslim, Protestant	CFA franc
CAPE VERDE	1 557	4 033	381 000	245	94	republic	Praia	Portuguese, Portuguese Creole	R.C., Protestant, trad. beliefs	Escudo
C. A. R.	240 324	622 436	3 235 000	13	5	republic	Bangui	French, Sango, Banda, Baya, local lang	Protestant, R.C., trad. beliefs, Muslim	CFA franc
CHAD	495 755	1 284 000	6 214 000	13	5	republic	Ndjamena	Arabic, French, local lang	Muslim, trad. beliefs, R.C.	CFA franc
COMOROS	719	1 862	630 000	876	338	republic	Moroni	Comorian, French, Arabic	Muslim, R.C.	Franc
CONGO	132 047	342 000	2 516 000	19	7	republic	Brazzaville	French, Kongo, Monokutuba, local lang	R.C., Protestant, trad. beliefs, Muslim	CFA franc
CÔTE D'IVOIRE	124 504	322 463	13 695 000	110	42	republic	Yamoussoukro	French, Akan, Kru, Gur, local lang	Trad. beliefs, Muslim, R.C.	CFA franc
DJIBOUTI	8 958	23 200	566 000	63	24	republic	Djibouti	Somali, French, Arabic, Issa, Afar	Muslim, R.C.	Franc
EGYPT	386 199	1 000 250	57 851 000	150	58	republic	Cairo	Arabic, French	Muslim, Coptic Christian	Pound
EQUATORIAL GUINEA	10 831	28 051	389 000	36	14	republic	Malabo	Spanish, Fang	R.C., trad. beliefs	CFA franc
ERITREA	45 328	117 400	3 437 000	76	29	republic	Asmara	Tigrinya, Arabic, Tigre, English	Muslim, Coptic Christian	Ethiopian birr
ETHIOPIA	437 794	1 133 880	54 938 000	125	48	republic	Addis Ababa	Amharic, Oromo, local lang	Ethiopian Orthodox, Muslim, trad. beliefs	Birr
GABON	103 347	267 667	1 283 000	12	5	republic	Libreville	French, Fang, local lang	R.C., Protestant, trad. beliefs	CFA franc
GAMBIA	4 361	11 295	1 081 000	248	96	republic	Banjul	English, Malinke, Fulani, Wolof	Muslim, Protestant	Dalasi
GHANA	92 100	238 537	16 944 000	184	71	republic	Accra	English, Hausa, Akan, local lang	Protestant, R.C., Muslim, trad. beliefs	Cedi
GUINEA	94 926	245 857	6 501 000	68	26	republic	Conakry	French, Fulani, Malinke, local lang	Muslim, trad. beliefs, R.C.	Franc
GUINEA-BISSAU	13 948	36 125	1 050 000	75	29	republic	Bissau	Portuguese, Portuguese Creole, local lang	Trad. beliefs, Muslim, R.C.	Peso
KENYA	224 961	582 646	29 292 000	130	50	republic	Nairobi	Swahili, English, local lang	R.C., Protestant, trad. beliefs	Shilling
LESOTHO	11 720	30 355	1 996 000	170	66	monarchy	Maseru	Sesotho, English, Zulu	R.C., Protestant, trad. beliefs	Loti
LIBERIA	43 000	111 369	2 700 000	63	24	republic	Monrovia	English, Creole, local lang	Trad. beliefs, Muslim, Protestant, R.C.	Dollar
LIBYA	679 362	1 759 540	4 899 000	7	3	republic	Tripoli	Arabic, Berber	Muslim, R.C.	Dinar
MADAGASCAR	226 658	587 041	14 303 000	63	24	republic	Antananarivo	Malagasy, French	Trad. beliefs, R.C., Protestant, Muslim	Franc
MALAWI	45 747	118 484	9 461 000	207	80	republic	Lilongwe	English, Chichewa, Lomwe, local lang	Protestant, R.C., trad. beliefs, Muslim	Kwacha
MALI	478 821	1 240 140	10 462 000	22	8	republic	Bamako	French, Bambara, local lang	Muslim, trad. beliefs, R.C.	CFA franc
MAURITANIA	397 955	1 030 700	2 211 000	6	2	republic	Nouakchott	Arabic, French, local lang	Muslim	Ouguiya
MAURITIUS	788	2 040	1 113 000	1413	546	republic	Port Louis	English, French Creole, Hindi, Indian languages	Hindu, R.C., Muslim, Protestant	Rupee
MOROCCO	172 414	446 550	26 590 000	154	60	monarchy	Rabat	Arabic, Berber, French, Spanish	Muslim, R.C.	Dirham
MOZAMBIQUE	308 642	799 380	16 614 000	54	21	republic	Maputo	Portuguese, Makua, Tsonga, local lang	Trad. beliefs, R.C., Muslim	Metical
NAMIBIA	318 261	824 292	1 500 000	5	2	republic	Windhoek	English, Afrikaans, German, Ovambo, local lang	Protestant, R.C.	Dollar
NIGER	489 191	1 267 000	8 846 000	18	7	republic	Niamey	French, Hausa, Fulani, local lang	Muslim, trad. beliefs	CFA franc
NIGERIA	356 669	923 768	108 467 000	304	117	republic	Abuja	English, Creole, Hausa, Yoruba, Ibo, Fulani	Muslim, Protestant, R.C., trad. beliefs	Naira
RÉUNION	985	2 551	644 000	654	252	French territory	St-Denis	French, French Creole	R.C.	French franc
RWANDA	10 169	26 338	7 750 000	762	294	republic	Kigali	Kinyarwanda, French, English	R.C., trad. beliefs, Protestant, Muslim	Franc
SÃO TOMÉ AND PRÍNCIPE	372	964	125 000	336	130	republic	São Tomé	Portuguese, Portuguese Creole	R.C., Protestant	Dobra
SENEGAL	75 954	196 720	8 102 000	107	41	republic	Dakar	French, Wolof, Fulani, local lang	Muslim, R.C., trad. beliefs	CFA franc
SEYCHELLES	176	455	74 000	421	163	republic	Victoria	Seychellois, English	R.C., Protestant	Rupee
SIERRA LEONE	27 699	71 740	4 402 000	159	61	republic	Freetown	English, Creole, Mende, Temne, local lang	Trad. beliefs, Muslim, Protestant, R.C.	Leone
SOMALIA	246 201	637 657	9 077 000	37	14	republic	Mogadishu	Somali, Arabic	Muslim	Shilling
SOUTH AFRICA	470 689	1 219 080	40 436 000	86	33	republic	Pretoria/Cape Town	Afrikaans, English, local lang	Protestant, R.C., Muslim, Hindu	Rand
SUDAN	967 500	2 505 813	28 947 000	30	12	republic	Khartoum	Arabic, Dinka, Nubian, Beja, Nuer, local lang	Muslim, trad. beliefs, R.C., Protestant	Dinar
SWAZILAND	6 704	17 364	879 000	131	51	monarchy	Mbabane	Swazi, English	Protestant, R.C., trad. beliefs	Emalangeni
TANZANIA	364 900	945 087	28 846 000	79	31	republic	Dodoma	Swahili, English, Nyamwezi, local lang	R.C., Muslim, trad. beliefs, Protestant	Shilling
TOGO	21 925	56 785	3 928 000	179	69	republic	Lomé	French, Ewe, Kabre, local lang	Trad. beliefs, R.C., Muslim, Protestant	CFA franc
TUNISIA	63 379	164 150	8 814 000	139	54	republic	Tunis	Arabic, French	Muslim	Dinar
UGANDA	93 065	241 038	20 621 000	222	86	republic	Kampala	English, Swahili, Luganda, local lang	R.C., Protestant, Muslim, trad. beliefs	Shilling
ZAIRE (CONGO)	905 568	2 345 410	42 552 000	47	18	republic	Kinshasa	French, Lingala, Swahili, Kongo, local lang	R.C., Protestant, Muslim, trad. beliefs	Zaïre
ZAMBIA	290 586	752 614	9 196 000	32	12	republic	Lusaka	English, Bemba, Nyanja, Tonga, local lang	Protestant, R.C., trad. beliefs, Muslim	Kwacha
ZIMBABWE	150 873	390 759	11 150 000	74	29	republic	Harare	English, Shona, Ndebele	Protestant, R.C., trad. beliefs	Dollar

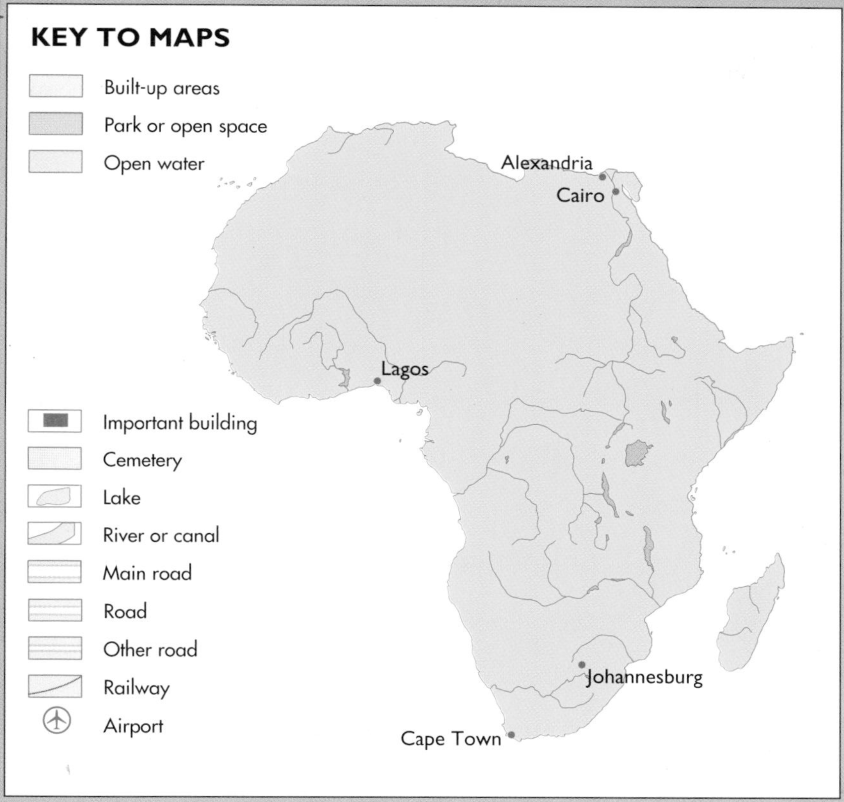
KEY TO MAPS
Built-up areas
Park or open space
Open water
Important building
Cemetery
Lake
River or canal
Main road
Road
Other road
Railway
Airport
Alexandria
Cairo
Lagos
Johannesburg
Cape Town

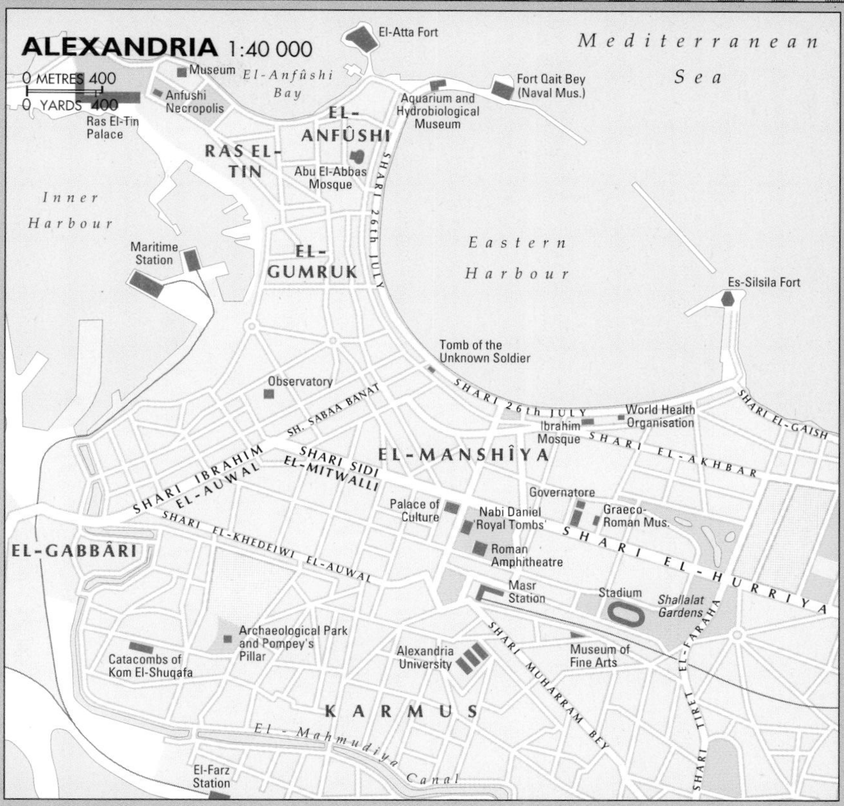
ALEXANDRIA 1:40 000
0 METRES 400
0 YARDS 400
Mediterranean Sea
El-Atta Fort
Museum
El-Anfûshi Bay
Anfushi Necropolis
Ras El-Tin Palace
EL-ANFÛSHI
RAS EL-TIN
Fort Qait Bey (Naval Mus.)
Aquarium and Hydrobiological Museum
Abu El-Abbas Mosque
Inner Harbour
Eastern Harbour
Maritime Station
EL-GUMRUK
SHARI 26th JULY
Es-Silsila Fort
Tomb of the Unknown Soldier
Observatory
SH. SABAA BANAT
World Health Organisation
Ibrahim Mosque
SHARI EL-GAISH
SHARI EL-AKHBAR
SHARI IBRAHIM EL-AUWAL
SHARI SIDI EL-MITWALLI
EL-MANSHÎYA
Governatore
EL-GABBÂRI
SHARI EL-KHEDEIWI EL-AUWAL
Palace of Culture
Nabi Daniel Royal Tombs
Graeco-Roman Mus.
SHARI EL-HURRIYA
Roman Amphitheatre
Masr Station
Stadium
Shallalat Gardens
Archaeological Park and Pompey's Pillar
Catacombs of Kom El-Shuqafa
Alexandria University
Museum of Fine Arts
SHARI MUHARRAM BEY
KARMUS
El-Mahmudiya Canal
El-Farz Station

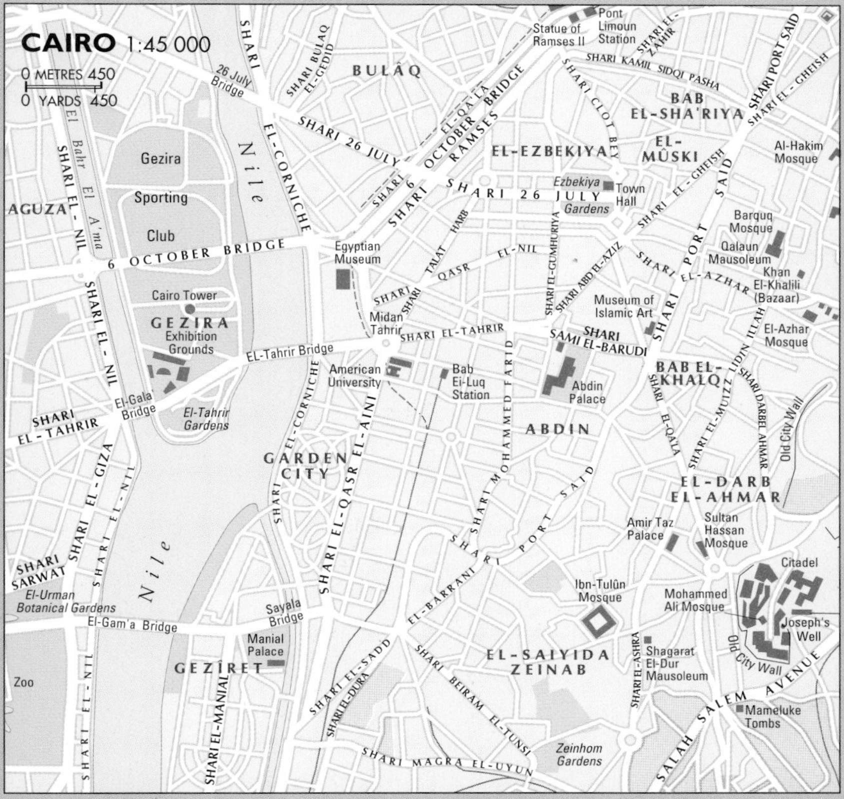
CAIRO 1:45 000
0 METRES 450
0 YARDS 450
Pont Limoun Station
Statue of Ramses II
BULÂQ
26 July Bridge
BAB EL-SHA'RIYA
SHARI 26 JULY
EL-EZBEKIYA
EL-MÛSKI
Al-Hakim Mosque
Gezira Sporting Club
AGUZA
Nile
Ezbekiya Gardens
Town Hall
6 OCTOBER BRIDGE
Egyptian Museum
Barquq Mosque
Qalaun Mausoleum
Khan El-Khalili (Bazaar)
Cairo Tower
GEZIRA
Exhibition Grounds
Midan Tahrir
Museum of Islamic Art
El-Azhar Mosque
El-Tahrir Bridge
SHARI EL-TAHRIR
American University
Bab El-Luq Station
SHARI SAMI EL-BARUDI
BAB EL-KHALQ
El-Gala Bridge
El-Tahrir Gardens
Abdin Palace
ABDIN
GARDEN CITY
EL-DARB EL-AHMAR
Amir Taz Palace
Sultan Hassan Mosque
Citadel
SHARI SARWAT
El-Urman Botanical Gardens
El-Gam'a Bridge
Ibn-Tulûn Mosque
Mohammed Ali Mosque
Joseph's Well
Sayala Bridge
Manial Palace
GEZIRET
EL-SAIYIDA ZEINAB
Shagarat El-Dur Mausoleum
Old City Wall
Zoo
SALAH SALEM AVENUE
Mameluke Tombs
Zeinhom Gardens
SHARI MAGRA EL-UYUN

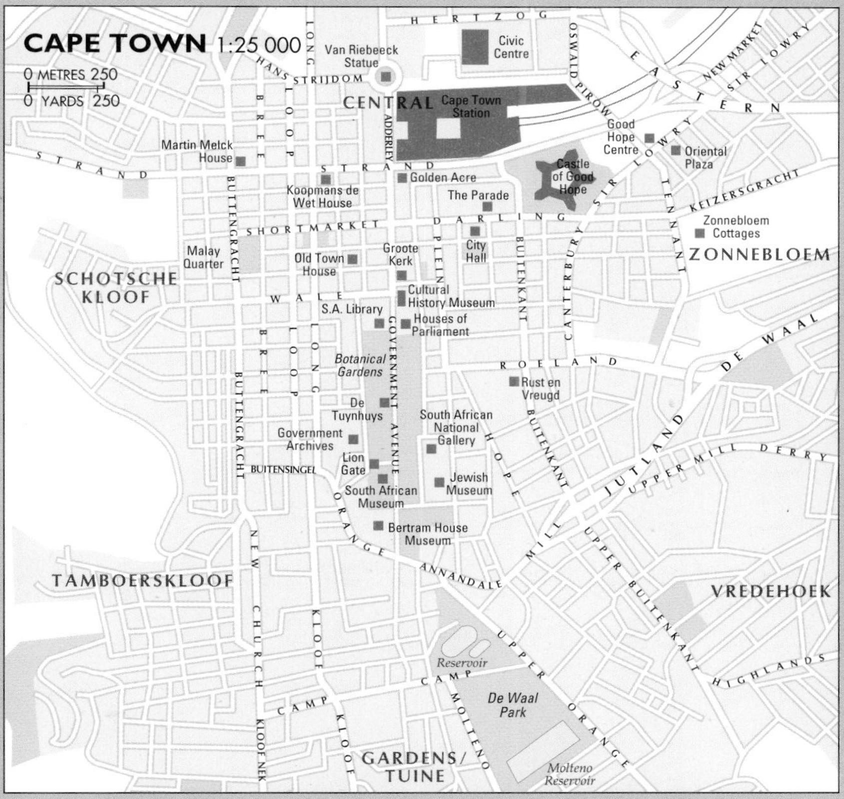
CAPE TOWN 1:25 000
0 METRES 250
0 YARDS 250
HERTZOG
Civic Centre
Van Riebeeck Statue
HANS STRIJDOM
CENTRAL
Cape Town Station
Martin Melck House
STRAND
Koopmans de Wet House
Golden Acre
Good Hope Centre
Oriental Plaza
Castle of Good Hope
The Parade
SHORTMARKET
DARLING
KEIZERSGRACHT
Zonnebloem Cottages
ZONNEBLOEM
SCHOTSCHE KLOOF
Malay Quarter
Old Town House
Groote Kerk
City Hall
S.A. Library
Cultural History Museum
Houses of Parliament
Botanical Gardens
ROELAND
Rust en Vreugd
DE WAAL
De Tuynhuys
South African National Gallery
Government Archives
BUITENSINGEL
Lion Gate
South African Museum
Jewish Museum
Bertram House Museum
ANNANDALE
JUTLAND
UPPER MILL
DERRY
TAMBOERSKLOOF
VREDEHOEK
Reservoir
De Waal Park
HIGHLANDS
GARDENS/TUINE
Molteno Reservoir

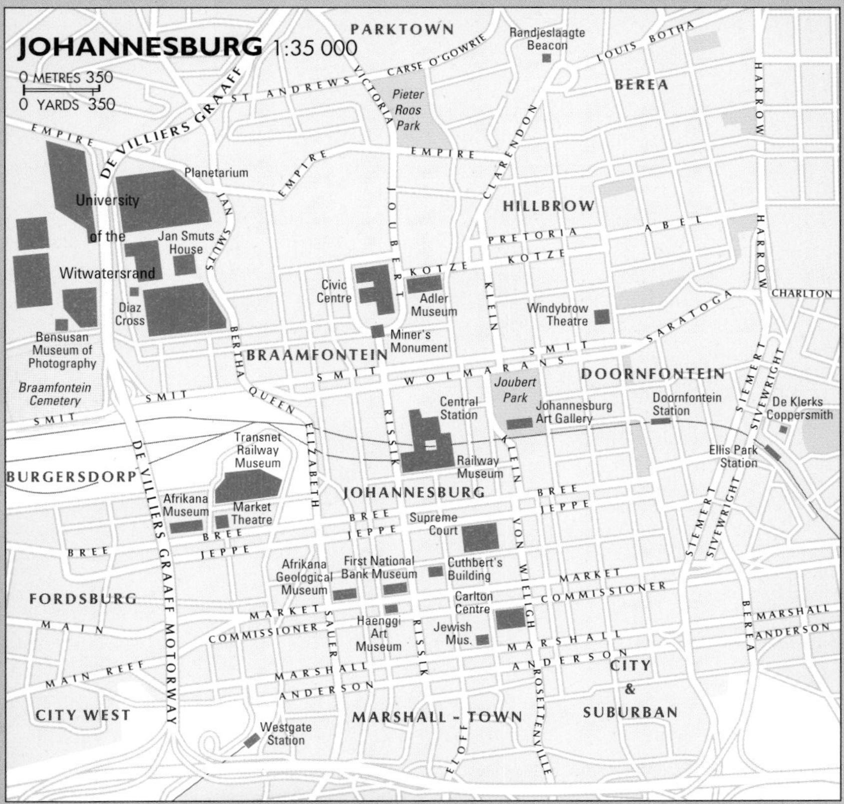
JOHANNESBURG 1:35 000
0 METRES 350
0 YARDS 350
PARKTOWN
Randjeslaagte Beacon
LOUIS BOTHA
BEREA
Pieter Roos Park
DE VILLIERS GRAAFF
Planetarium
University of the Witwatersrand
Jan Smuts House
HILLBROW
PRETORIA
KOTZE
Civic Centre
Adler Museum
Diaz Cross
Bensusan Museum of Photography
Windybrow Theatre
Miner's Monument
BRAAMFONTEIN
Braamfontein Cemetery
SMIT
WOLMARANS
Joubert Park
DOORNFONTEIN
De Klerks Coppersmith
Central Station
Johannesburg Art Gallery
Doornfontein Station
Transnet Railway Museum
Railway Museum
Ellis Park Station
BURGERSDORP
JOHANNESBURG
Afrikana Museum
Market Theatre
Supreme Court
BREE
JEPPE
Afrikana Geological Museum
First National Bank Museum
Cuthbert's Building
MARKET
COMMISSIONER
FORDSBURG
Carlton Centre
Haenggi Art Museum
Jewish Mus.
MARSHALL
ANDERSON
MAIN REEF
CITY & SUBURBAN
CITY WEST
Westgate Station
MARSHALL - TOWN
DE VILLIERS GRAAFF MOTORWAY

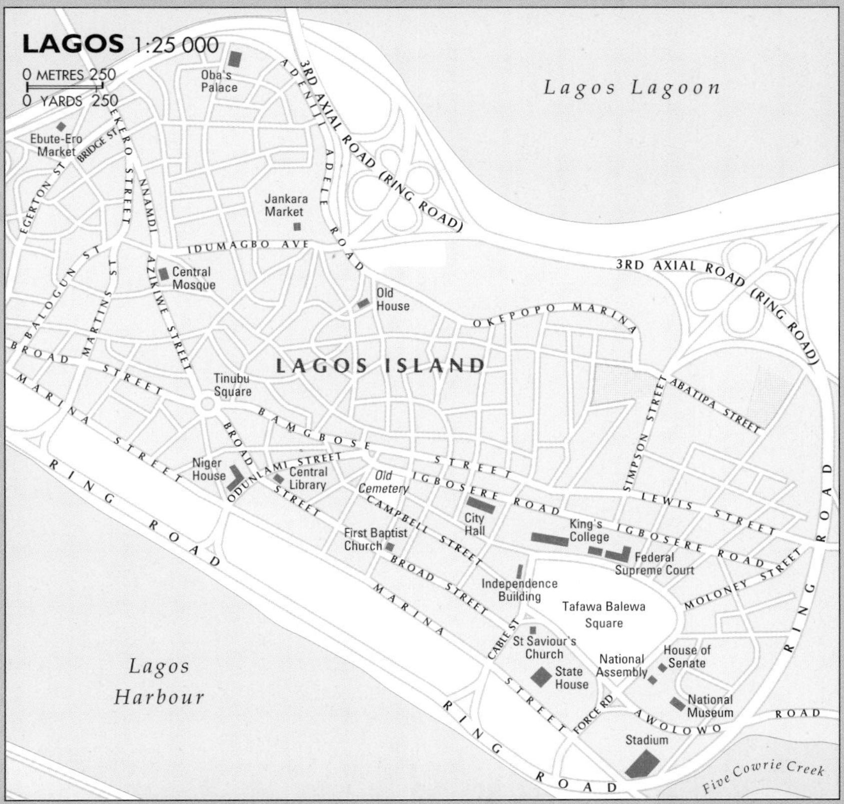
LAGOS 1:25 000
0 METRES 250
0 YARDS 250
Oba's Palace
Lagos Lagoon
3RD AXIAL ROAD (RING ROAD)
Ebute-Ero Market
Jankara Market
IDUMAGBO AVE
Central Mosque
Old House
OKEPOPO MARINA
LAGOS ISLAND
Tinubu Square
BROAD STREET
BAMGBOSE STREET
Niger House
Central Library
Old Cemetery
City Hall
First Baptist Church
King's College
Federal Supreme Court
Independence Building
Tafawa Balewa Square
St Saviour's Church
National Assembly
House of Senate
State House
Lagos Harbour
National Museum
Stadium
RING ROAD
MARINA
AWOLOWO ROAD
Five Cowrie Creek
LEWIS STREET
SIMPSON STREET
MOLONEY STREET

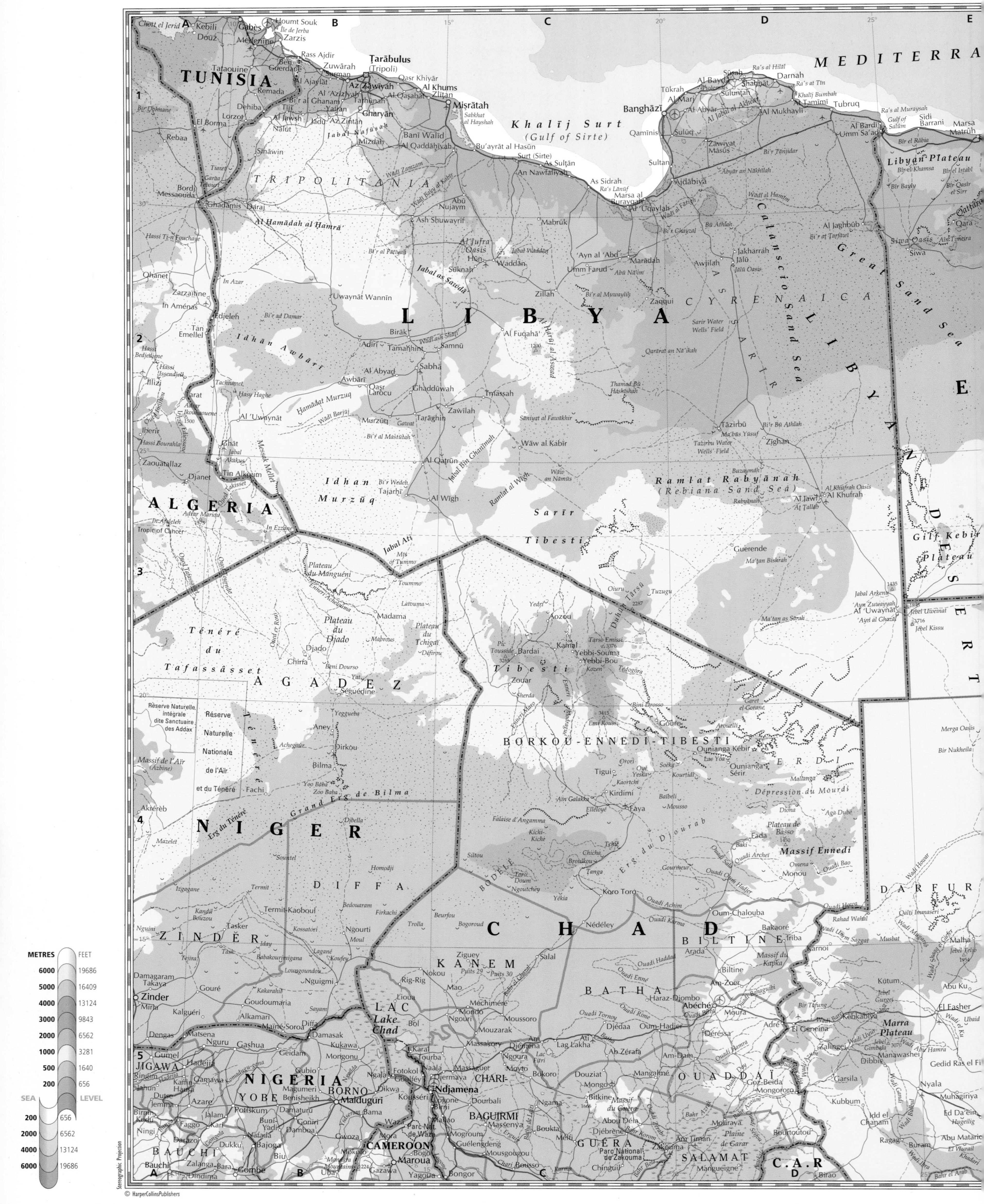
MEDITERRA
TUNISIA
LIBYA
ALGERIA
NIGER
CHAD
NIGERIA
CAMEROON
C.A.R
Ṭarābulus (Tripoli)
Banghāzī
Khalīj Surt (Gulf of Sirte)
Misrātah
Sabhā
Ndjamena
Lake Chad
Tibesti
Ramlat Rabyānah (Rebiana Sand Sea)
Great Sand Sea
Libyan Plateau
METRES
FEET
6000
19686
5000
16409
4000
13124
3000
9843
2000
6562
1000
3281
500
1640
200
656
SEA
LEVEL
200
656
2000
6562
4000
13124
6000
19686
Stereographic Projection

© HarperCollinsPublishers

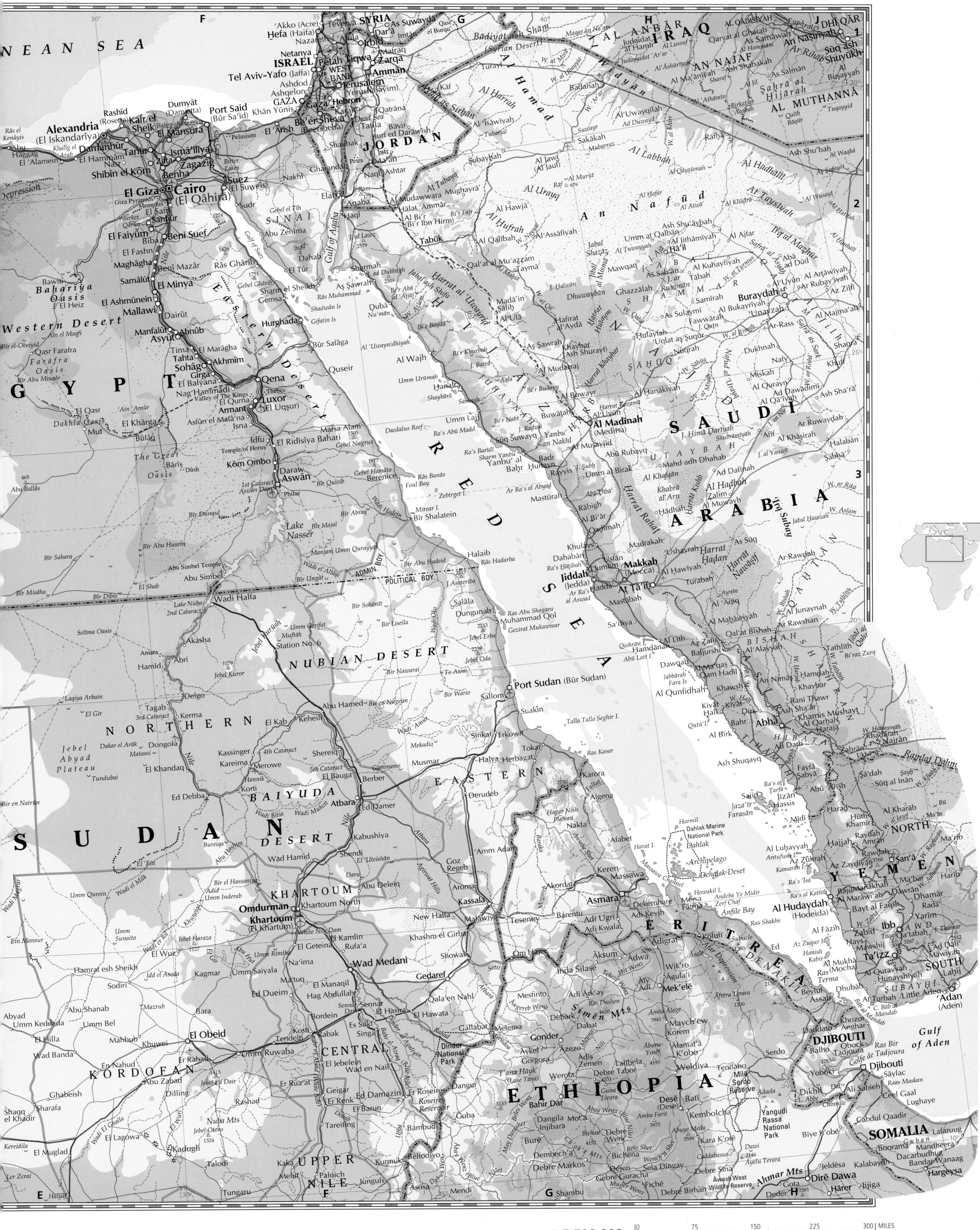

1:7 500 000

0	75	150	225	300	MILES		
0	75	150	225	300	375	450	KM

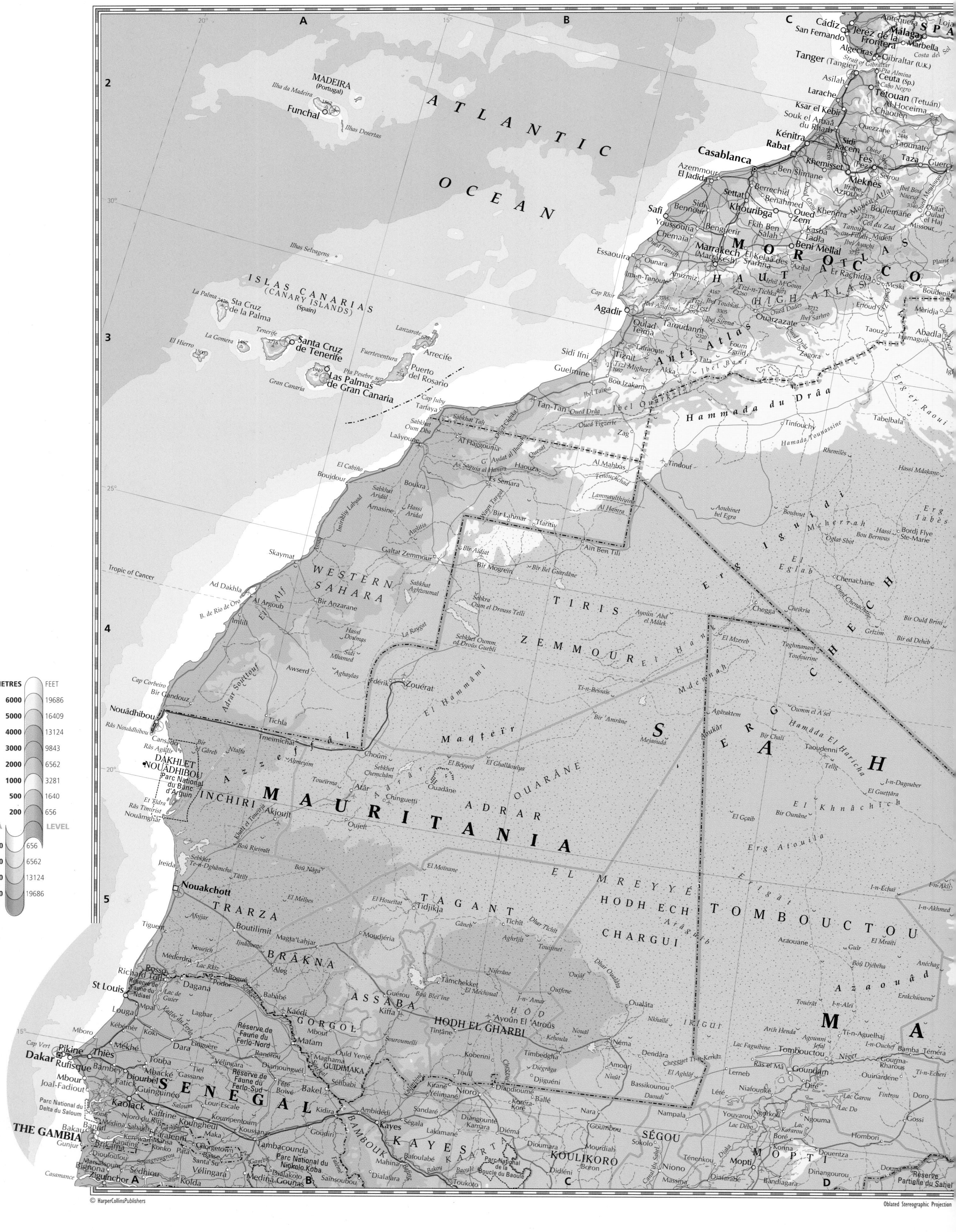
A
B
C
D
2
3
4
5
ATLANTIC
OCEAN
MADEIRA (Portugal)
Ilha da Madeira
Funchal
Ilhas Desertas
Ilhas Selvagens
ISLAS CANARIAS (CANARY ISLANDS) (Spain)
La Palma
Sta Cruz de la Palma
Tenerife
La Gomera
El Hierro
Santa Cruz de Tenerife
Lanzarote
Fuerteventura
Arrecife
Puerto del Rosario
Las Palmas de Gran Canaria
Gran Canaria
Cádiz
Jerez de la Frontera
San Fernando
Málaga
Algeciras
Marbella
Gibraltar (U.K.)
Strait of Gibraltar
Tanger (Tangier)
Ceuta (Sp.)
Tétouan (Tetuán)
Asilah
Larache
Al Hoceima
Chaouen
Ksar el Kebir
Souk el Arbaâ du Rharb
Kénitra
Rabat
Casablanca
Sidi Kacem
Khemisset
Fès (Fez)
Meknès
Taza
Azemmour
El Jadida
Ben Slimane
Settat
Berrechid
Benahmed
Khouribga
Oued Zem
Safi
Sidi Bennour
Youssoufia
Benguerir
Chemaïa
Fkih Ben Salah
Kasba Tadla
Beni Mellal
Essaouira
Marrakech (Marrakesh)
MOROCCO
HAUT ATLAS (HIGH ATLAS)
Er Rachidia
Ouarzazate
Agadir
Oulad Teïma
Taroudannt
Tiznit
Sidi Ifni
Guelmine
Anti Atlas
Tan-Tan
Tarfaya
Cap Juby
Laâyoune
Boujdour
Hammada du Drâa
Tindouf
Tabelbala
Smara
WESTERN SAHARA
Ad Dakhla
Tropic of Cancer
Skaymat
Bir Anzarane
Awserd
Cap Corbeiro
Bir Gandouz
Nouâdhibou
Râs Nouâdhibou
DAKHLET NOUÂDHIBOU
Parc National du Banc d'Arguin
Fdérik
Zouérat
TIRIS ZEMMOUR
Bir Mogreïn
Ain Ben Tili
MAURITANIA
INCHIRI
Akjoujt
Atâr
Chinguetti
Ouadâne
ADRAR
Maqteïr
OUARÂNE
Nouâmghâr
Nouakchott
TRARZA
Boutilimit
BRÂKNA
Aleg
Tidjikja
TAGANT
Tichît
HODH ECH CHARGUI
Néma
Oualâta
HODH EL GHARBI
Ayoûn el 'Atroûs
ASSABA
Kiffa
GORGOL
Kaédi
GUIDIMAKA
Sélibabi
Rosso
St Louis
Richard Toll
Podor
Dagana
Louga
Pikine
Dakar
Thiès
Rufisque
Mbour
Joal-Fadiout
Diourbel
Kaolack
SENEGAL
THE GAMBIA
Banjul
Brikama
Tambacounda
Kolda
Ziguinchor
Casamance
Parc National du Niokolo Koba
Bakel
Kayes
KAYES
KOULIKORO
SÉGOU
MOPTI
Mopti
Niono
Nioro
Diéma
Nara
TOMBOUCTOU
Tombouctou
Araouane
Taoudenni
Goundam
Niger
Léré
Tinfouchy
Erg Iguidi
Erg Chech
El Eglab
Chegga
Bir Chali
Erg Atouila
El Mreyyé
Azaouâd
METRES
FEET
6000
19686
5000
16409
4000
13124
3000
9843
2000
6562
1000
3281
500
1640
200
656
SEA
LEVEL
200
656
2000
6562
4000
13124
6000
19686
Oblated Stereographic Projection

1:7 500 000

0 75 150 225 300 MILES

0 75 150 225 300 375 450 KM

A
B
C
D
2
3
5
WESTERN SAHARA
Tropic of Cancer
TIRIS ZEMMOUR
MAURITANIA
INCHIRI
DAKHLET NOUÂDHIBOU
Parc National du Banc d'Arguin
ADRAR
TAGANT
TRARZA
BRAKNA
ASSABA
GORGOL
GUIDIMAKA
HODH EL GHARBI
HODH ECH CHARGUI
TOMBOUCTOU
MALI
KAYES
KOULIKORO
SÉGOU
MOPTI
SIKASSO
BURKINA
SENEGAL
THE GAMBIA
GUINEA-BISSAU
GUINEA
MOYENNE-GUINÉE
HAUTE-GUINÉE
GUINÉE-MARITIME
GUINÉE-FORESTIÈRE
SIERRA LEONE
NORTHERN
SOUTHERN
EASTERN
WESTERN AREA
LIBERIA
CÔTE D'IVOIRE
GHANA
UPPER WEST
UPPER EAST
NORTHERN
BRONG-AHAFO
ASHANTI
WESTERN
CENTRAL
EASTERN
ATLANTIC OCEAN
Ivory Coast
Grain Coast
Gold
Nouâdhibou
Nouakchott
Zouérat
Atâr
Akjoujt
Tidjikja
Kiffa
Néma
Rosso
St Louis
Dakar
Pikine
Thiès
Rufisque
Mbour
Kaolack
Tambacounda
Ziguinchor
Banjul
Bissau
Conakry
Freetown
Monrovia
Bamako
Kayes
Ségou
Mopti
Tombouctou
Labé
Kankan
Bobo Dioulasso
Ouagadougou
Korhogo
Bouaké
Yamoussoukro
Abidjan
Man
Daloa
Tamale
Kumasi
Accra
Takoradi
Sekondi
Cape Coast
Lake Volta
CAPE VERDE
Santo Antão
São Vicente
Mindelo
Santa Luzia
São Nicolau
Sal
Boa Vista
Maio
São Tiago
Fogo
Brava
Praia
at the same scale
METRES
FEET
6000
19686
5000
16409
4000
13124
3000
9843
2000
6562
1000
3281
500
1640
200
656
SEA
LEVEL
200
656
2000
6562
4000
13124
6000
19686
Oblated Stereographic Projection

© HarperCollinsPublishers

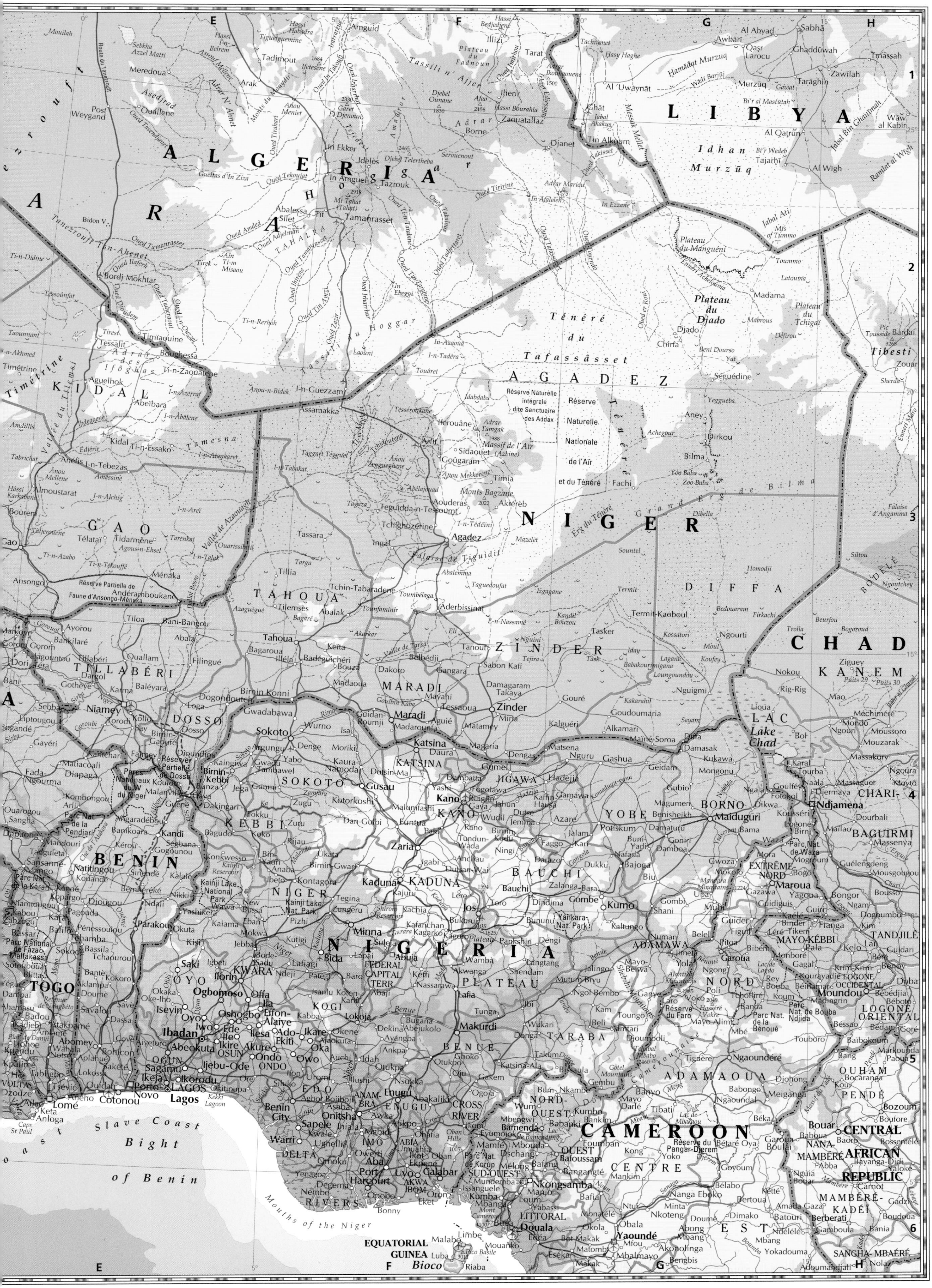

1:7 500 000

MILES	0	75	150	225	300

KM	0	75	150	225	300	375	450

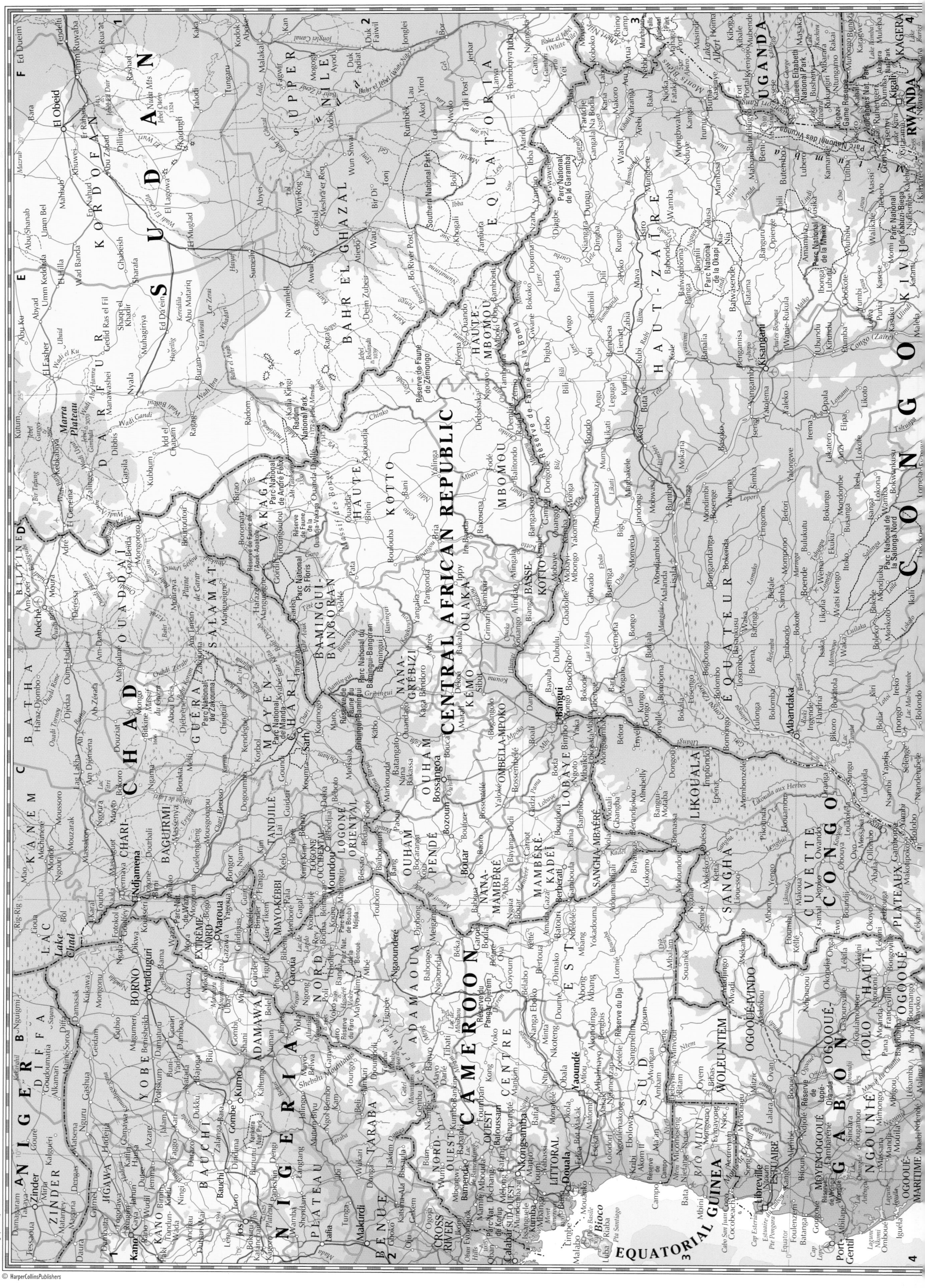
SUDAN
CHAD
CENTRAL AFRICAN REPUBLIC
CAMEROON
NIGERIA
NIGER
GABON
CONGO
UGANDA
RWANDA
EQUATORIAL GUINEA
KORDOFAN
DARFUR
BAHR EL GHAZAL
UPPER NILE
EQUATORIA
HAUT-ZAÏRE
ÉQUATEUR
KIVU
El Obeid
Abéché
Ndjamena
Maiduguri
Kano
Zinder
Bangui
Yaoundé
Douala
Libreville
Kisangani
Mbandaka
Lake Chad
Obliqued Stereographic Projection

METRES
FEET
6000
19686
5000
16409
4000
13124
3000
9843
2000
6562
1000
3281
500
1640
200
656
SEA
LEVEL
200
656
2000
6562
4000
13124
6000
19686

© HarperCollinsPublishers

1:7 500 000

MILES	0	75	150	225	300
KM	0	75	150	225	300	375	450

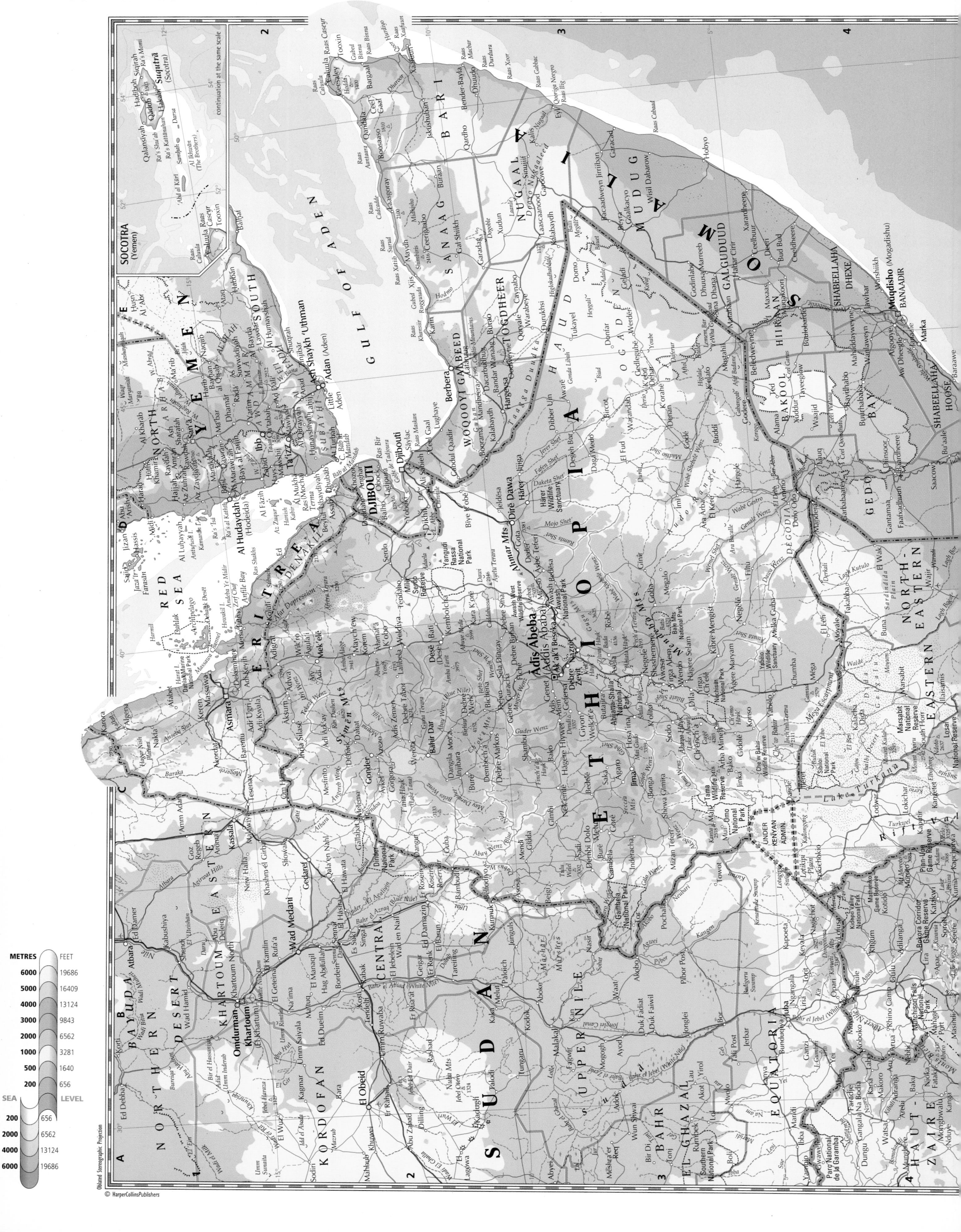
METRES
FEET
6000
19686
5000
16409
4000
13124
3000
9843
2000
6562
1000
3281
500
1640
200
656
SEA
LEVEL
200
656
2000
6562
4000
13124
6000
19686
SOCOTRA
(Yemen)
continuation at the same scale
GULF OF ADEN
RED SEA
YEMEN
ERITREA
DJIBOUTI
ETHIOPIA
SOMALIA
SUDAN
Khartoum
Adis Abeba
(Addis Ababa)
Asmara
Djibouti
Muqdisho (Mogadishu)
Obliated Stereographic Projection

© HarperCollinsPublishers

1:7 500 000

0 75 150 225 300 MILES

0 75 150 225 300 375 450 KM

ANGOLA
NAMIBIA
BOTSWANA
REPUBLIC OF
SOUTH AFRICA
ZAM
ATLANTIC OCEAN
BENGUELA
HUAMBO
BIÉ
MOXICO
HUÍLA
NAMIBE
CUNENE
CUANDO CUBANGO
NORTH - WESTERN
WESTERN
SOUTHERN
OHANGWENA
OMUSATI
OSHANA
OSHIKOTO
OKAVANGO
KUNENE
OTJOZONDJUPA
OMAHEKE
ERONGO
KHOMAS
HARDAP
KARAS
CAPRIVI
CHOBE
NGAMILAND
CENTRAL
GHANZI
KWENENG
KGALAGADI
NGWAKETSE
KGATLENG
SOUTH EAST
NORTH WEST
FREE STATE
NORTHERN CAPE
WESTERN CAPE
EASTERN CAPE
MATABELELAND NORTH
Kalahari Desert
Great Karoo
Little Karoo
Roggeveld
Namaqualand
Damaraland
Ovamboland
Okavango Delta
Makgadikgadi
Etosha Pan
Huíla Plateau
Skeleton Coast Game Park
Namib-Naukluft Park
Central Kalahari Game Reserve
Kalahari Gemsbok National Park
Gemsbok National Park
Tropic of Capricorn
Lubango
Namibe
Menongue
Mongu
Livingstone
Windhoek
Walvis Bay
Swakopmund
Lüderitz
Keetmanshoop
Rundu
Tsumeb
Maun
Ghanzi
Gaborone
Francistown
Mafikeng
Kimberley
Bloemfontein
Upington
Maseru
Cape Town
Port Elizabeth
Mossel Bay
East London
Soweto
Cape of Good Hope
Cape Agulhas
ASCENSION
(U.K.)
1:500 000
Georgetown
Green Mt
ST HELENA
(U.K.)
1:500 000
Jamestown
Longwood
TRISTAN DA CUNHA
(U.K.)
1:1.5M
Settlement of Edinburgh
Tristan da Cunha
Inaccessible I.
Nightingale I.
METRES
FEET
6000
19686
5000
16409
4000
13124
3000
9843
2000
6562
1000
3281
500
1640
200
656
SEA
LEVEL
200
656
2000
6562
4000
13124
6000
19686
Oblated Stereographic Projection

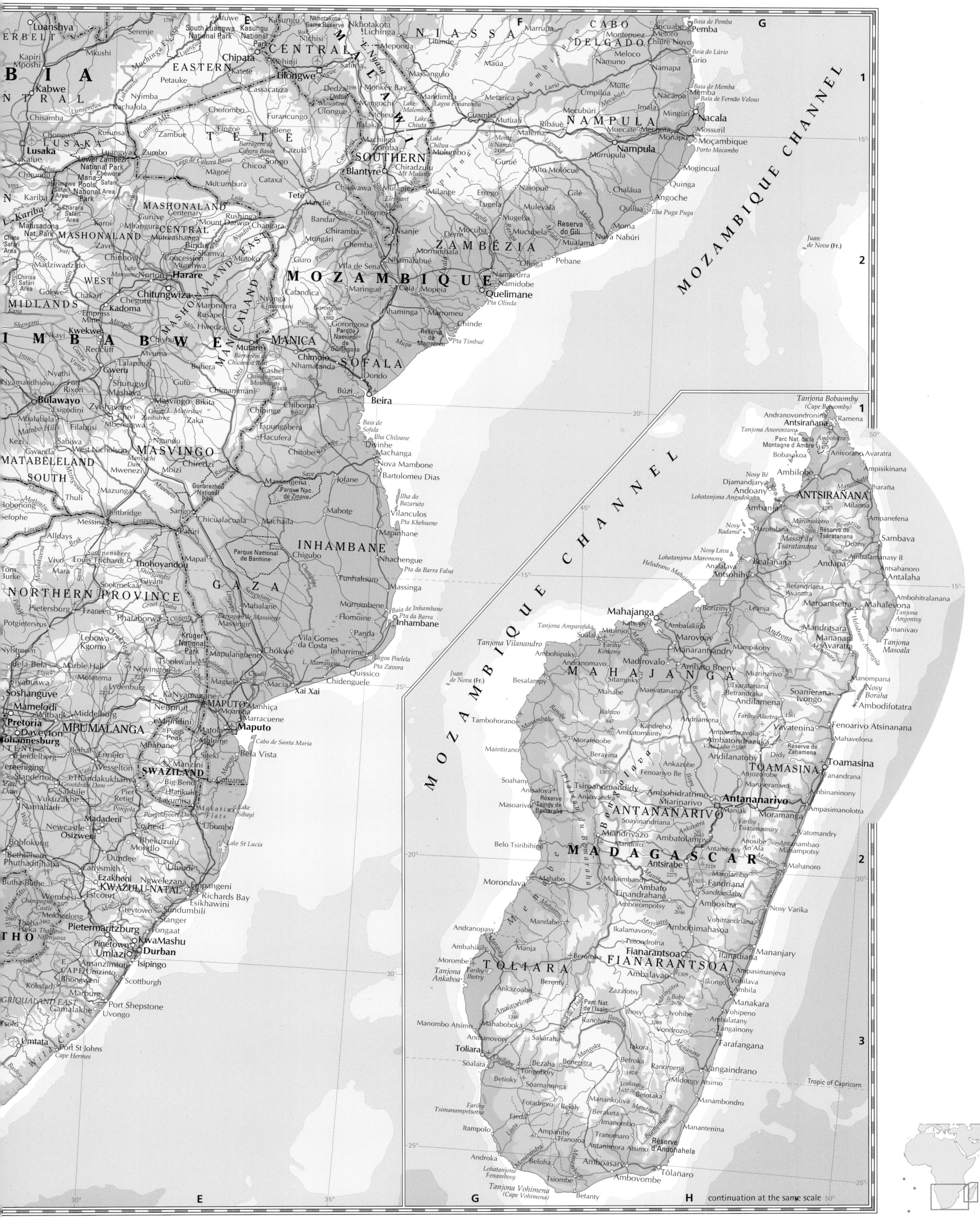

1:7 500 000

0 75 150 225 300 MILES

0 75 150 225 300 375 450 KM

Lambert Azimuthal Equal Area Projection

© HarperCollinsPublishers

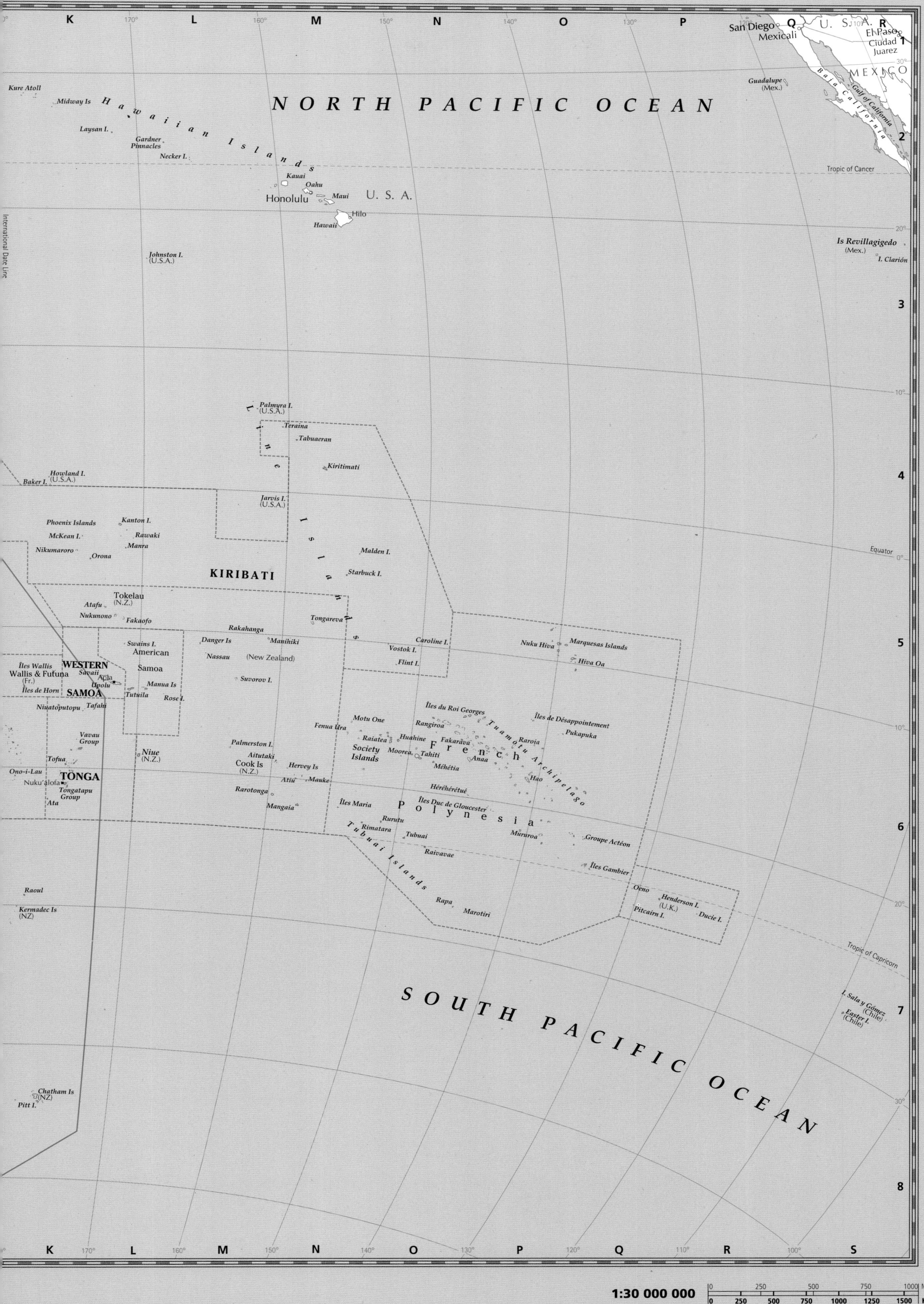
NORTH PACIFIC OCEAN
SOUTH PACIFIC OCEAN
Hawaiian Islands
Kure Atoll
Midway Is
Laysan I.
Gardner Pinnacles
Necker I.
Kauai
Oahu
Honolulu
Maui
U. S. A.
Hilo
Hawaii
Tropic of Cancer
Johnston I. (U.S.A.)
International Date Line
San Diego
Mexicali
El Paso
Ciudad Juarez
MEXICO
Guadalupe (Mex.)
Baja California
Gulf of California
Is Revillagigedo (Mex.)
I. Clarión
Palmyra I. (U.S.A.)
Line Islands
Teraina
Tabuaeran
Kiritimati
Howland I. (U.S.A.)
Baker I.
Jarvis I. (U.S.A.)
Phoenix Islands
Kanton I.
McKean I.
Rawaki
Nikumaroro
Manra
Orona
Malden I.
Starbuck I.
KIRIBATI
Equator
Tokelau (N.Z.)
Atafu
Nukunonu
Fakaofo
Tongareva
Rakahanga
Danger Is
Manihiki
Nassau
(New Zealand)
Caroline I.
Vostok I.
Flint I.
Nuku Hiva
Marquesas Islands
Hiva Oa
Swains I.
American Samoa
Manua Is
Tutuila
Rose I.
Îles Wallis
Wallis & Futuna (Fr.)
Îles de Horn
WESTERN SAMOA
Savaii
Apia
Upolu
Niuatoputapu
Tafahi
Suvorov I.
Vavau Group
Tofua
TONGA
Ono-i-Lau
Nuku'alofa
Tongatapu Group
Ata
Niue (N.Z.)
Palmerston I.
Aitutaki
Cook Is (N.Z.)
Hervey Is
Atiu
Mauke
Rarotonga
Mangaia
Îles du Roi Georges
Tuamotu Archipelago
Îles de Désappointement
Pukapuka
Motu One
Fenua Ura
Rangiroa
Raiatea
Huahine
Society Islands
Moorea
Tahiti
Fakarava
Raroja
Anaa
Méhétia
Hao
French Polynesia
Hérèhérètué
Îles Maria
Îles Duc de Gloucester
Rurutu
Rimatara
Tubuai
Tubuai Islands
Mururoa
Groupe Actéon
Raivavae
Îles Gambier
Rapa
Marotiri
Oeno
Henderson I. (U.K.)
Pitcairn I.
Ducie I.
Tropic of Capricorn
I. Sala y Gómez (Chile)
Easter I. (Chile)
Raoul
Kermadec Is (NZ)
Chatham Is (NZ)
Pitt I.
K L M N O P Q R S
1 2 3 4 5 6 7 8
170° 160° 150° 140° 130° 120° 110° 100°
30° 20° 10° 0°
1:30 000 000
0 250 500 750 1000 MILES
0 250 500 750 1000 1250 1500 KM

National Statistics: International Organizations

COUNTRY	AREA sq ml	AREA sq km	POPULATION total	density per sq ml	density per sq km	Form of Government	Capital City	MAIN LANGUAGES	MAIN RELIGIONS	CURRENCY
AMERICAN SAMOA	76	197	55 000	*723*	*279*	US territory	Pago Pago	Samoan, English	Protestant, RC	US dollar
AUSTRALIA	2 966 153	7 682 300	17 838 000	*6*	*2*	federation	Canberra	English, Italian, Greek, Aboriginal languages	Protestant, RC, Orthodox, Aboriginal beliefs	Dollar
FIJI	7 077	18 330	784 000	*111*	*43*	republic	Suva	English, Fijian, Hindi	Protestant, Hindu, RC, Sunni Muslim	Dollar
FRENCH POLYNESIA	1 261	3 265	215 000	*171*	*66*	French territory	Papeete	French, Polynesian languages	Protestant, RC, Mormon	Pacific franc
GUAM	209	541	146 000	*699*	*270*	US territory	Agana	Chamorro, English, Tagalog	RC	US dollar
KIRIBATI	277	717	77 000	*278*	*107*	republic	Bairiki	I-Kiribati (Gilbertese), English	RC, Protestant, Baha'i, Mormon	Austr. dollar
MARSHALL ISLANDS	70	181	54 000	*773*	*298*	republic	Dalap-Uliga-Darrit	Marshallese, English	Protestant, RC	US dollar
FED. STATES OF MICRONESIA	271	701	104 000	*384*	*148*	republic	Palikir	English, Trukese, Pohnpeian, local languages	Protestant, RC	US dollar
NAURU	8	21	11 000	*1357*	*524*	republic	Yaren	Nauruan, Gilbertese, English	Protestant, RC	Austr. dollar
NEW CALEDONIA	7 358	19 058	184 000	*25*	*10*	French territory	Nouméa	French, local languages	RC, Protestant, Sunni Muslim	Pacific franc
NEW ZEALAND	104 454	270 534	3 493 000	*33*	*13*	monarchy	Wellington	English, Maori	Protestant, RC	Dollar
NIUE	100	258	2 000	*20*	*8*	NZ territory	Alofi	English, Polynesian (Niuean)	Protestant, Mormon, RC	NZ dollar
NORTH. MARIANA IS.	184	477	47 000	*255*	*99*	US territory	Saipan	English, Chamorro, Tagalog, local languages	RC, Protestant	US dollar
PAPUA NEW GUINEA	178 704	462 840	3 997 000	*22*	*9*	monarchy	Port Moresby	English, Tok Pisin, many local languages	Protestant, RC, traditional beliefs	Kina
SOLOMON ISLANDS	10 954	28 370	366 000	*33*	*13*	monarchy	Honiara	English, Pidgin, many local languages	Protestant, RC	Dollar
TOKELAU	4	10	2 000	*518*	*200*	NZ territory		English, Tokelauan	Protestant, RC	NZ dollar
TONGA	289	748	98 000	*339*	*131*	monarchy	Nuku'alofa	Tongan, English	Protestant, RC, Mormon	Pa'anga
TUVALU	10	25	9 000	*932*	*360*	monarchy	Fongafale	Tuvaluan, English (official)	Protestant	Dollar
VANUATU	4 707	12 190	165 000	*35*	*14*	republic	Port-Vila	English, Bislama, French	Protestant, RC, traditional beliefs	Vatu
WALLIS AND FUTUNA	106	274	14 000	*132*	*51*	French territory	Mata-Utu	French, Polynesian	RC	Pacific franc
WESTERN SAMOA	1 093	2 831	164 000	*150*	*58*	monarchy	Apia	Samoan, English	Protestant, RC, Mormon	Tala

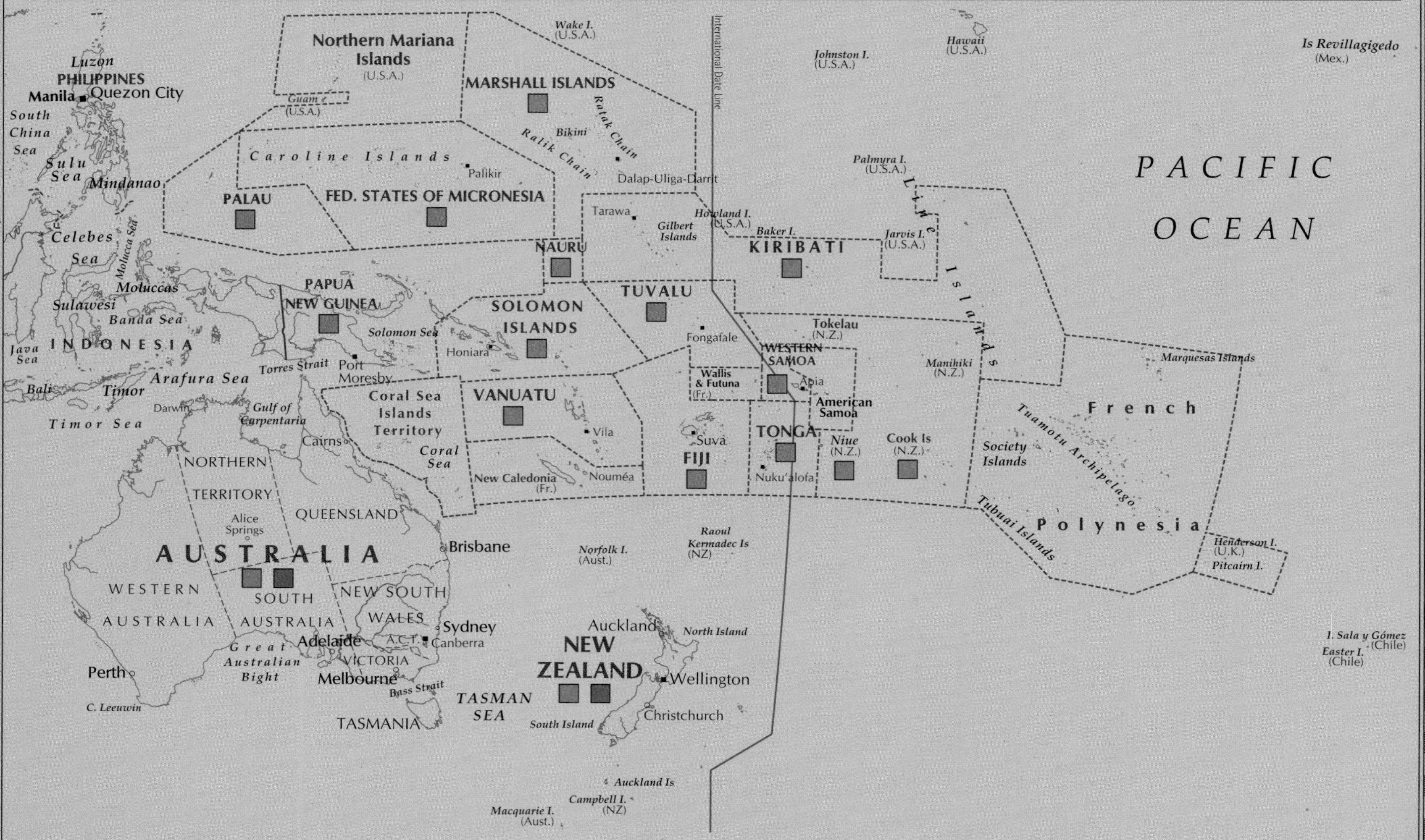

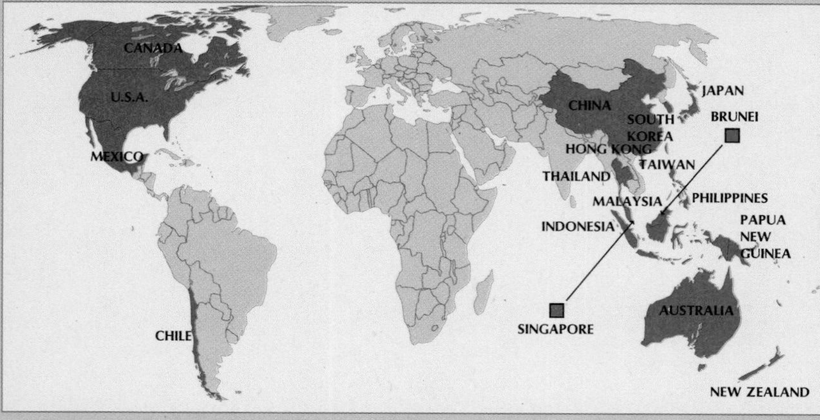

ASIA PACIFIC ECONOMIC CO-OPERATION FORUM (APEC)

Formed in 1989 to promote trade and economic co-operation, with the long term aim of the creation of a Pacific free trade area. The original members were Australia, Brunei, Canada, Indonesia, Japan, Malaysia, New Zealand, the Philippines, Singapore, South Korea, Thailand and U.S.A.. China, Hong Kong and Taiwan joined in 1991, Mexico and Papua New Guinea in 1993, and Chile in 1994.

Headquarters : Singapore

SOUTH PACIFIC FORUM

Originally established as a 'Trade Bureau' in 1972,it later became the South Pacific Bureau for Economic Co-operation (SPEC), before its current title was approved in 1988, and ratified in 1993. The objectives are to encourage and promote regional co-operation through trade and investment, and economic development including telecommunications and air transport. There are 16 members: Australia, the Cook Islands, Federated States of Micronesia, Fiji, Kiribati, Marshall Islands, Nauru, New Zealand, Niue, Palau, Papua New Guinea, Solomon Islands, Tonga, Tuvalu, Vanuatu and Western Samoa. In 1990 five of the smallest island states : Kiribati, the Cook Islands, Nauru, Niue and Tuvalu formed an economic sub-group to address their specific concerns.

© HarperCollinsPublishers

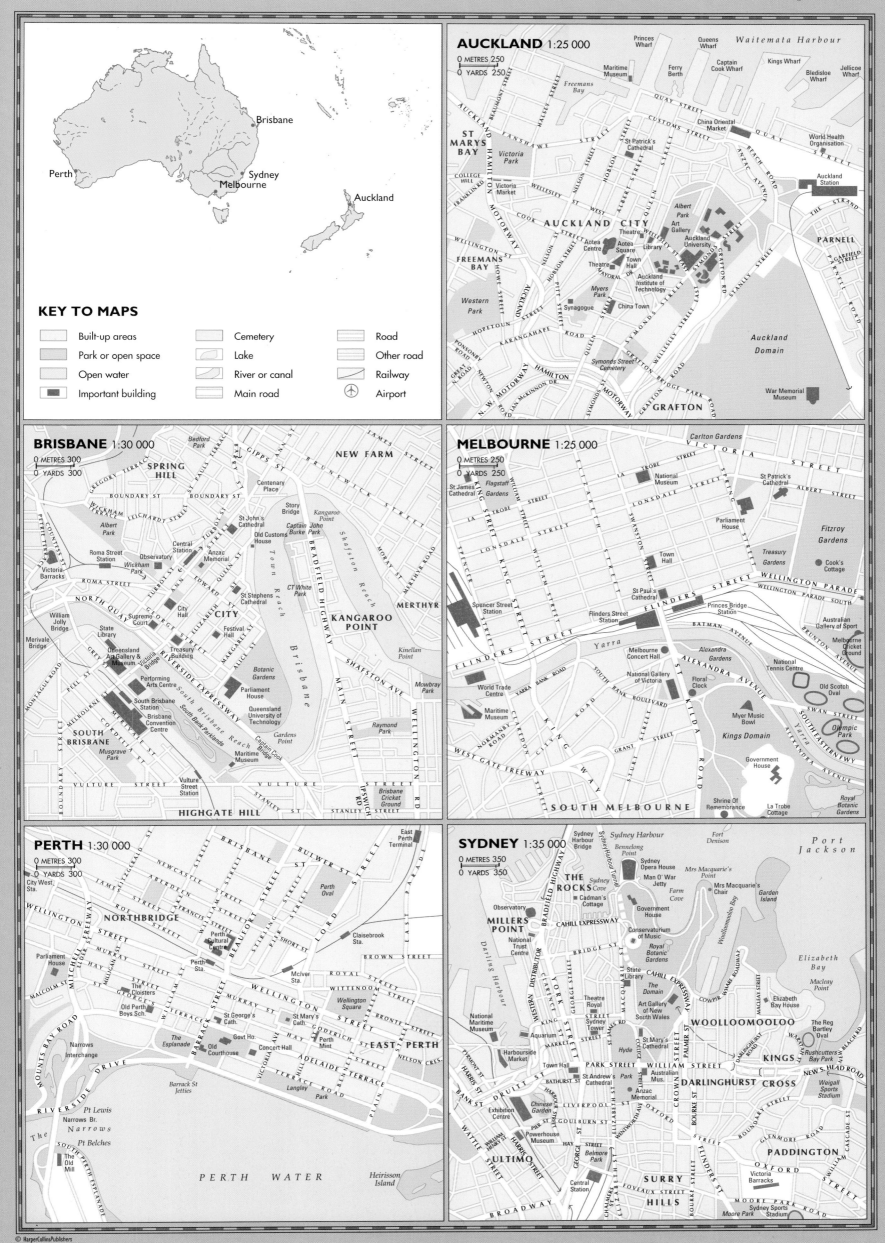

KEY TO MAPS

Built-up areas	Cemetery	Road
Park or open space	Lake	Other road
Open water	River or canal	Railway
Important building	Main road	Airport

AUCKLAND 1:25 000

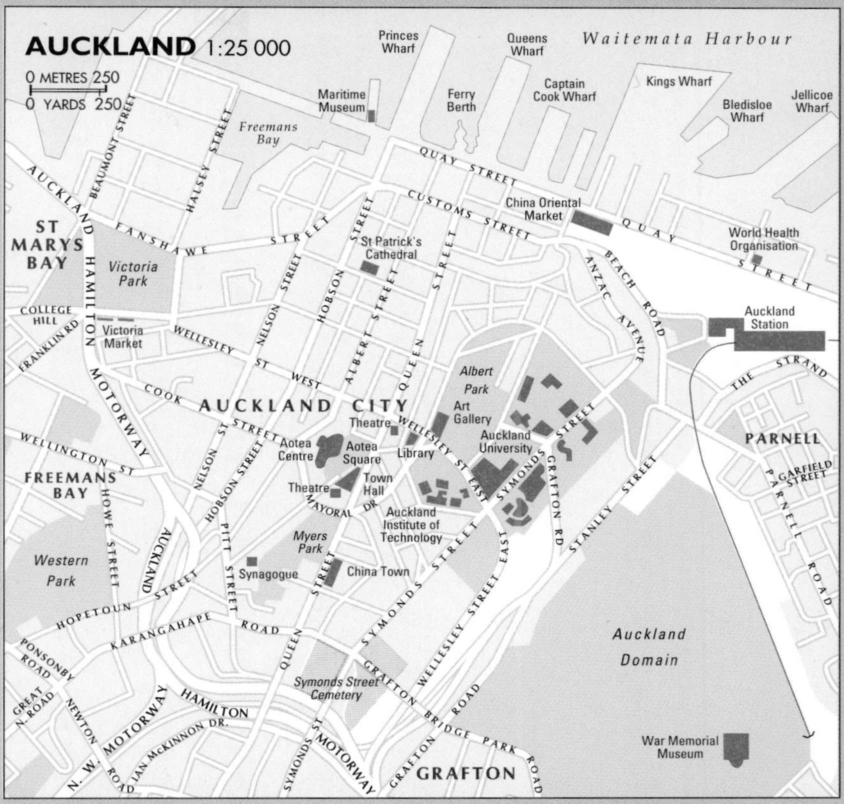

BRISBANE 1:30 000

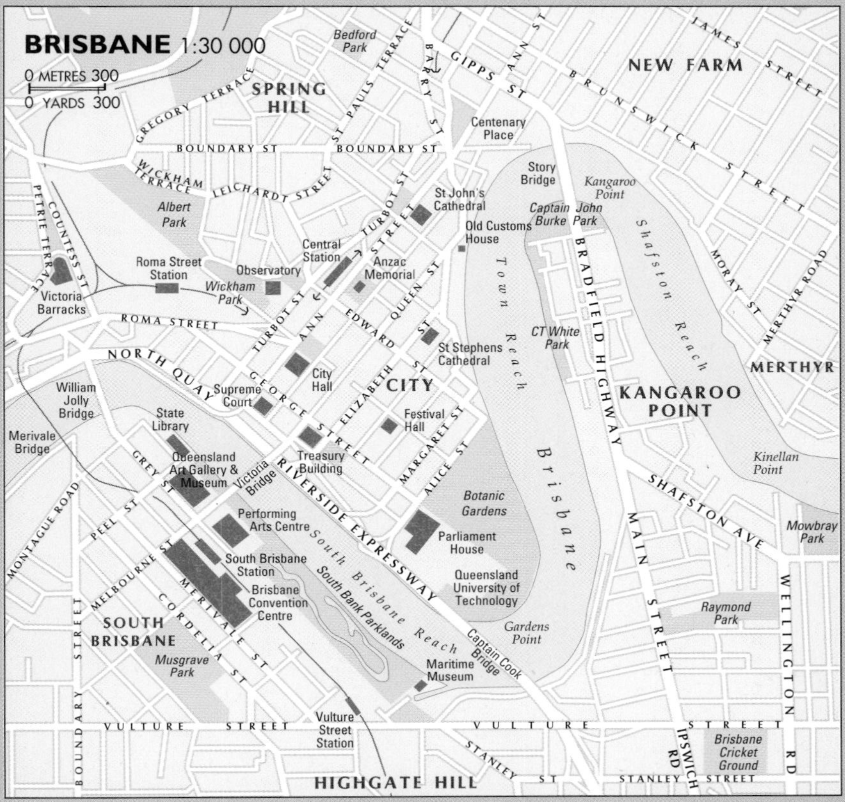

MELBOURNE 1:25 000

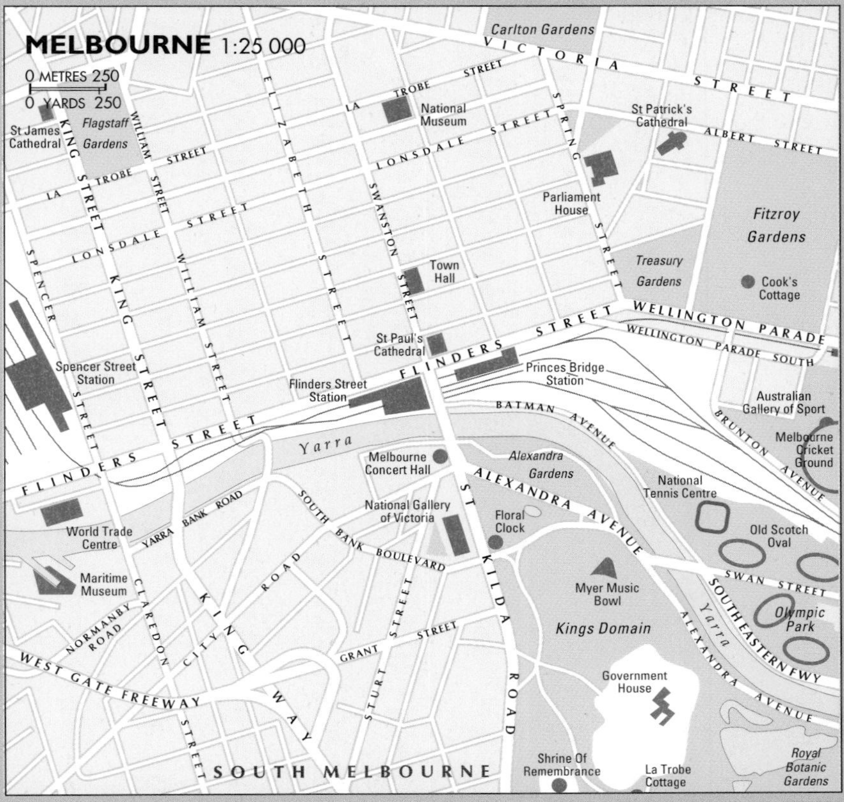

PERTH 1:30 000

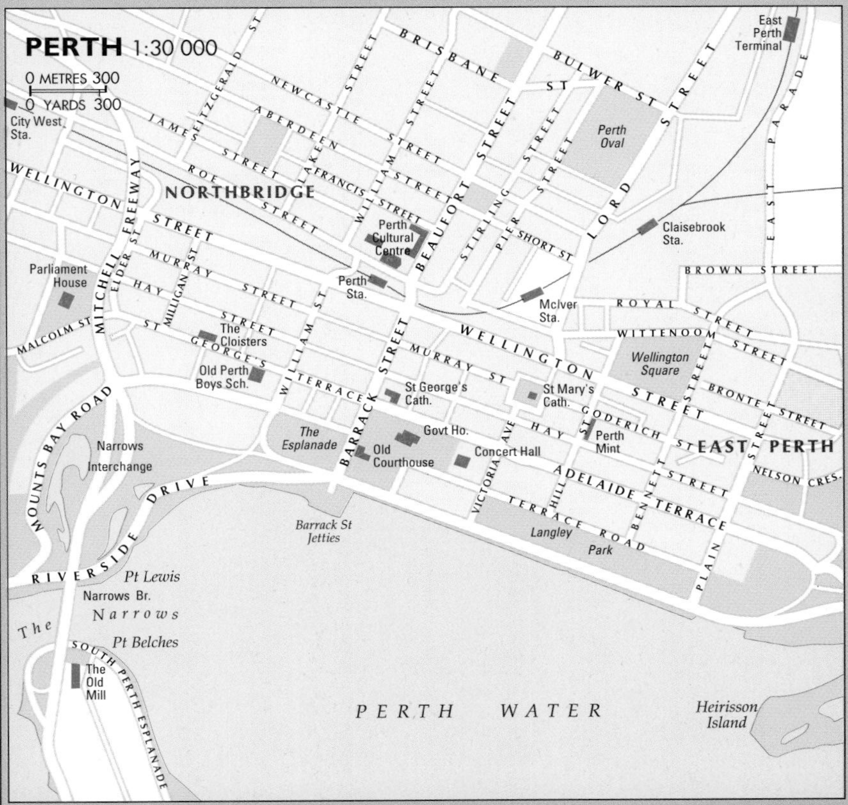

SYDNEY 1:35 000

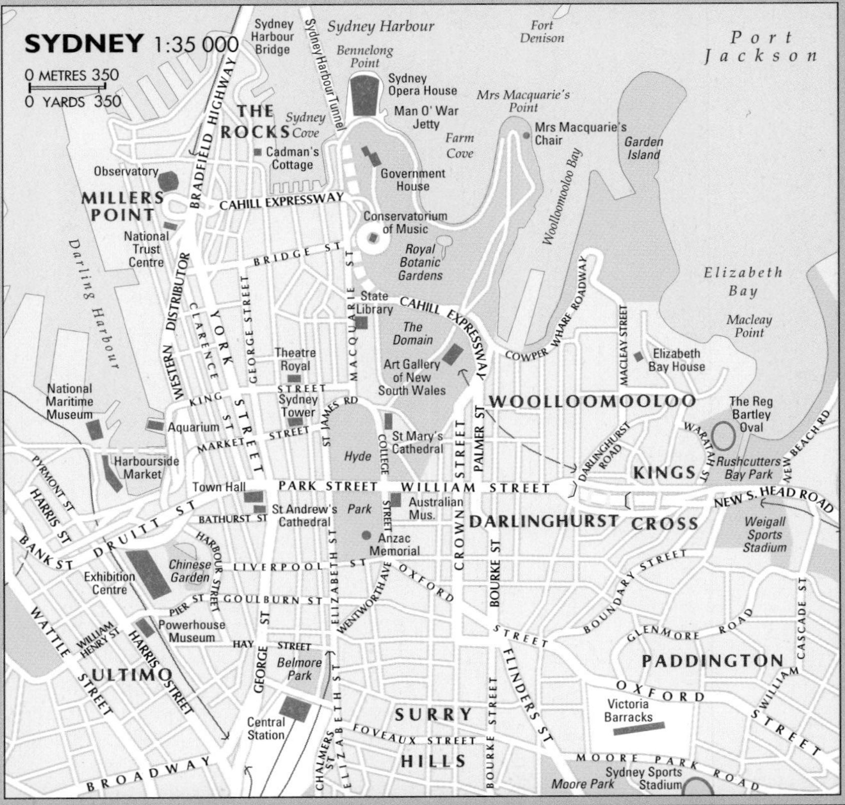

© HarperCollinsPublishers

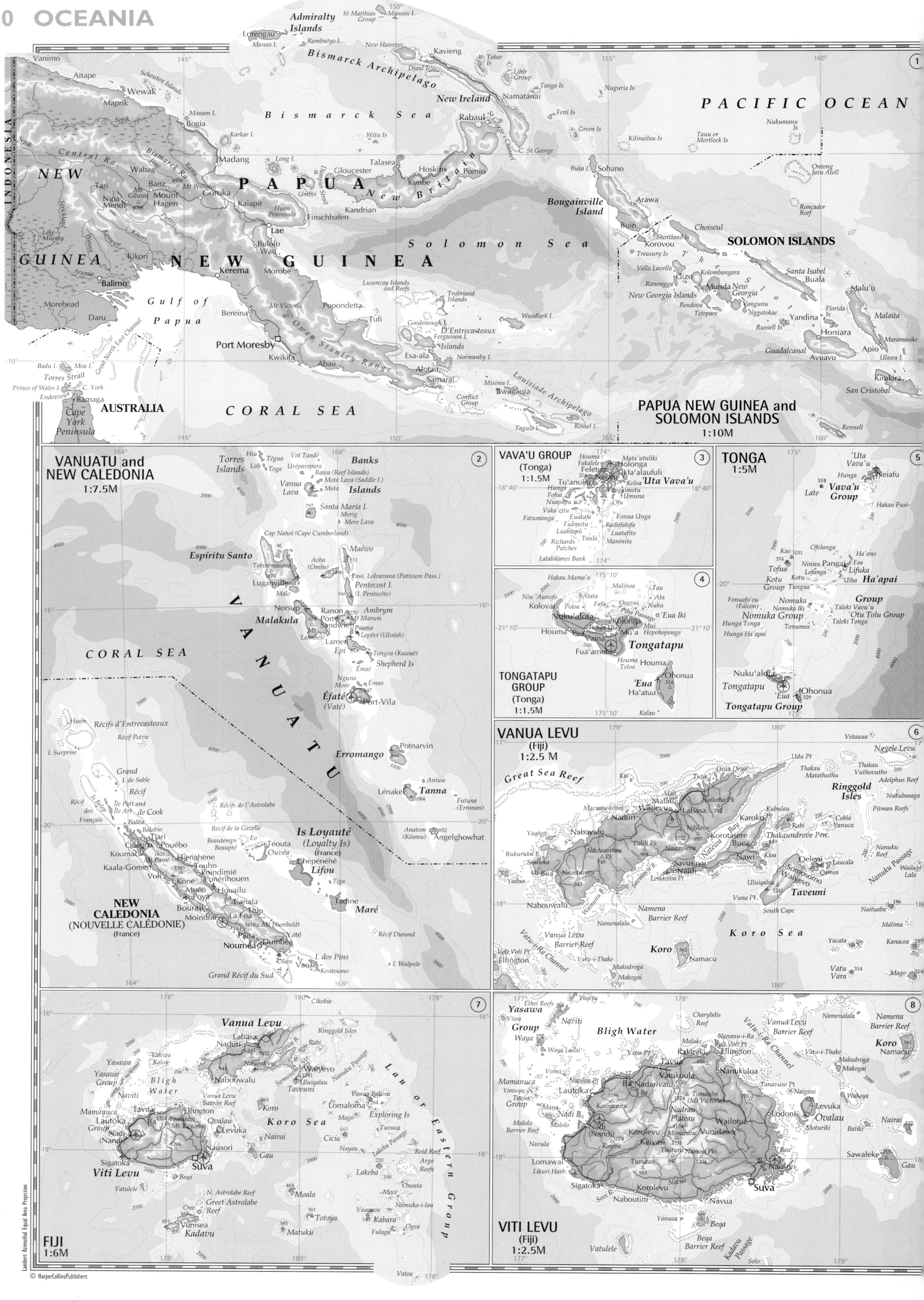
PAPUA NEW GUINEA and SOLOMON ISLANDS
1:10M
PACIFIC OCEAN
Bismarck Sea
Solomon Sea
CORAL SEA
Gulf of Papua
PAPUA NEW GUINEA
NEW GUINEA
INDONESIA
SOLOMON ISLANDS
AUSTRALIA
Admiralty Islands
St Matthias Group
Mussau I.
Lorengau
Manus I.
Rambutyo I.
New Hanover
Kavieng
Djaul I.
Bismarck Archipelago
Tabar Is
Lihir Group
Tanga Is
Nuguria Is
New Ireland
Namatanai
Feni Is
Green Is
Nukumanu Is
Rabaul
St George's Channel
C. St George
Kilinailau Is
Tauu or Mortlock Is
Ontong Java Atoll
Vanimo
Aitape
Schouten Islands
Wewak
Maprik
Sepik
Manam I.
Bogia
Karkar I.
Witu Is
Central Ra
Bismarck Ra
Madang
Long I.
Wabag
Ramu
Gloucester
Talasea
Hoskins
Pomio
Kimbe
New Britain
Tari
Banz
Mt Wilhelm
Nipa
Mendi
Mt Giluwe
Mount Hagen
Goroka
Kaiapit
Umboi
Dampier Strait
Huon Peninsula
Finschhafen
Kandrian
Buka I.
Sohano
Bougainville Island
Arawa
Roncador Reef
Strickland
Lake Murray
Purari
Kikori
Fly
Lae
Bulolo
Wau
Buin
Korovou
Shortland Is
Treasury Is
Choiseul
The Slot
Aramia
Balimo
Kerema
Morobe
Vella Lavella
Gizo
Kolombangara
Santa Isabel
Buala
Ranongga
Munda
New Georgia
New Georgia Islands
Vangunu
Rendova
Tetepare
Nggatokae
Malu'u
Malaita
Florida Is
Yandina
Russell Is
Honiara
Guadalcanal
Avuavu
Apio
Maramasike
Ulawa I.
Kirakira
San Cristobal
Rennell
Morehead
Daru
Great North East Channel
Lusancay Islands and Reefs
Trobriand Islands
Mt Victoria
Popondetta
Owen Stanley Range
Bereina
Tufi
Goodenough I.
D'Entrecasteaux Islands
Fergusson I.
Woodlark I.
Port Moresby
Kwikila
Abau
Esa-ala
Normanby I.
Alotau
Samarai
Misima I.
Bwagaoia
Louisiade Archipelago
Conflict Group
Tagula I.
Rossel I.
Badu I.
Moa I.
Torres Strait
Prince of Wales I.
Endeavour Strait
C. York
Bamaga
Cape York Peninsula
VANUATU and NEW CALEDONIA
1:7.5M
Torres Islands
Hiu
Tégua
Loh
Toga
Vot Tandé
Uréparapara
Banks Islands
Rowa (Reef Islands)
Mota Lava (Saddle I.)
Vanua Lava
Mota
Santa Maria I.
Merig
Mere Lava
Cap Nahoï (Cape Cumberland)
Espíritu Santo
Big B.
Tabwemasana
Maéwo
Aoba (Omba)
Pass. Lolvavana (Patteson Pass.)
Luganville
Malo
Pentecost I. (I. Pentecôte)
VANUATU
Norsup
Ranon
Port Sandwich
Ambrym
Mt Marum
Malakula
Paama
Lamen
Lopévi (Ulvéah)
Epi
Tongoa (Kuwaé)
Shepherd Is
Émaé
Nguna
Moso
Emao
Éfaté (Vaté)
Port-Vila
CORAL SEA
Huon
Récifs d'Entrecasteaux
Récif Petrie
I. Surprise
Erromango
Potnarvin
Aniwa
Tanna
Lénakel
Futuna (Erronan)
Grand Récif
I. de Sable
Récif des Français
Île Pott and Île Art
Îs Belep
de Cook
Récifs de l'Astrolabe
Récif de la Gazelle
Anatom (Kéamu)
Anelghowhat
Balabio
Tiari
Is Loyauté (Loyalty Is) (France)
Ouégoa
Pouébo
Téouta
Ouvéa
Beautemps Beaupré
Koumac
Hienghène
Chépénéhé
Lifou
Kaala-Gomen
Touho
Voh
Poindimié
Ponérihouen
Tiga
Kone
Houailou
Poya
Canala
Tadine
Maré
Bourail
Thio
Moindou
La Foa
Mt Humboldt
NEW CALEDONIA (NOUVELLE CALÉDONIE) (France)
Païta
Yaté
Nouméa
Dumbéa
Récif Durand
I. des Pins
Vao
I. Walpole
Grand Récif du Sud
VAVA'U GROUP (Tonga)
1:1.5M
Houma
Mata'utuliki
Holonga
Feletoa
Neiafu
Ha'alaufuli
Tu'anuku
'Uta Vava'u
Hunga
Fofoa
Nuapapu
Vaka'eitu
Fatumanga
Euakafa
Fonua Unga
Taula
Lualafitu
Maninita
Richards Patches
Lalalolomei Bank
TONGATAPU GROUP (Tonga)
1:1.5M
Hakau Mama'o
Malinoa
Niu 'Aunofo
Kolovai
Atata
Fafa
Onevai
Nuku
Pangaimotu
Nuku'alofa
Kolonga
'Eua Iki
Houma
Vaina
Mu'a
Fua'amotu
Tongatapu
Ohonua
'Eua
Ha'atua
Kalau
TONGA
1:5M
'Uta Vava'u
Hunga
Neiafu
Late
Vava'u Group
Hakau Fusi-
Kao
Tofua
Ofolanga
Ha'ano
Pangai
Foa
Lifuka
Ha'apai Group
Kotu Group
Tungua
Fonuafo'ou (Falcon)
Nomuka
Nomuka Iki
Nomuka Group
Tonumea
Hunga Tonga
Hunga Ha'apai
Taleki Vavu'u
'Otu Tolu Group
Taleki Tonga
Nuku'alofa
Tongatapu
'Eua
Ohonua
Tongatapu Group
VANUA LEVU (Fiji)
1:2.5 M
Vetauua
Naqelelevu
Thakau Vuthovutho
Adolphus Reef
Great Sea Reef
Udu Pt
Thakau Matathuthu
Ringgold Isles
Nukubasaga
Pitman Reefs
Mali
Dreketi
Labasa
Macuata-i-wai
Waileva
Naduri
Karoko Pt
Kubulau
Cobia
Yanuca
Nabavatu
Natewa Bay
Korotasere
Buca
Thakaundrove Pen.
Yaqaga
Valili Pk
Nasorolevu
Rukuruku B.
Savusavu
Nawi
Qeleni
Laucala
Qamea
Nanuku Reef
Nanuku Passage
Wailagi Lala
Bua
Navotuvotu
Lesiaceva Pt
Naidi
Somosomo
Waiyevo
Uluigalau
Taveuni
Yadua
Nabouwalu
Vuna Pt
South Cape
Naitauba
Namena Barrier Reef
Malima
Koro Sea
Vatu-i-Ra Channel
Vanua Levu Barrier Reef
Yacata
Kanacea
Koro
Namacu
Vatu Voli Pt
Ellington
Vatu-i-Thake
Makodroga
Makogai
Vatu Vara
Mago
FIJI
1:6M
Cikobia
Vanua Levu
Ringgold Isles
Labasa
Naduri
Rabi
Yasawa
Yasawa Group
Bligh Water
Savusavu
Nabouwalu
Somosomo
Waiyevo
Uluigalau
Taveuni
Nanuku Passage
Lau or Eastern Group
Naviti
Vanua Levu Barrier Reef
Vanua Balavu
Mamanuca
Tavua
Ellington
Koro
Lomaloma
Lautoka
Ovalau
Levuka
Exploring Is
Tuvuca
Nadi (Nandi)
Koro Sea
Nairai
Cicia
Nayau
Lakeba Passage
Nausori
Gau
Reid Reef
Argo Reefs
Sigatoka
Viti Levu
Suva
Beqa
Lakeba
Vatulele
Oneata
Moce
Namuka-i-lau
N. Astrolabe Reef
Great Astrolabe Reef
Moala
Ono
Vunisea
Kadavu
Totoya
Matuku
Kabara
Vuaqava
Ogea
Fulaga
Vatoa
VITI LEVU (Fiji)
1:2.5M
Ethel Reefs
Yaqeta
Yasawa Group
Viwa
Waya
Naviti
Bligh Water
Charybdis Reef
Vanua Levu Barrier Reef
Namenalala
Namena Barrier Reef
Koro
Namacu
Nananu-i-Ra
Rakiraki
Ellington
Vatu-i-Ra Channel
Vatu-i-Thake
Makodroga
Makogai
Tavua
Vatukoula
Nukuloa
Mamanuca
Lautoka
Ba
Nadarivatu
Tomanivi (Mt Victoria)
Tanavuso Pt
Naigani
Wakaya
Levuka
Ovalau
Moturiki
Batiki
Nairai
Nadi B.
Nadrau Plateau
Wailotua
Malolo
Malolo Barrier Reef
Nadi (Nandi)
Korolevu
Monasavu
Vunidawa
Navula
Keiyasi
Lodoni
Lomawai
Likuri Harb.
Namosi Pks
Nausori
Bau
Sawaleke
Gau
Sigatoka
Korolevu
Suva
Sovi B.
Naboutini
Navua
Yanuca
Beqa
Beqa Barrier Reef
Kadavu Passage
Vatulele
Solo

Lambert Azimuthal Equal Area Projection
© HarperCollinsPublishers

International Date Line
Tropic of Cancer
Equator
Tropic of Capricorn
HAWAII (U.S.A.)
Honolulu
Hilo
Kauai
Oahu
Maui
Hawaii
Hawaiian Islands
Hawaiian Ridge
Midway Is
Laysan I.
Gardner Pinnacles
Necker I.
Johnston I. (U.S.A.)
Wake I. (U.S.A.)
NORTHERN MARIANA ISLANDS (U.S.A.)
Pagan
Saipan
Tinian
Rota
Guam (U.S.A.)
Challenger Deep
Mariana Tr.
Ogasawara-shoto
Kazan-retto
MARSHALL ISLANDS
Bikini
Ratak Chain
Ralik Chain
Caroline Islands
Gaferut
Pikelot
Hall Is
Chuuk
Pohnpei
Nomoi Is
Kosrae
FED. STATES OF MICRONESIA
NAURU
Banaba
Nonouti
Beru
Nukunau
Tabiteuea
Onotoa
Arorae
Gilbert Islands
KIRIBATI
Howland I. (U.S.A.)
Baker I. (U.S.A.)
Phoenix Islands
Kanton I.
Rawaki
McKean I.
Manra
Nikumaroro
Orona
Palmyra I. (U.S.A.)
Teraina
Tabuaeran
Kiritimati (Christmas I.)
Jarvis I. (U.S.A.)
Line Islands
Malden I.
Starbuck I.
Caroline I.
Vostok I.
Flint I.
TUVALU
Nanumea
Nanumanga
Niutao
Nui
Vaitupu
Nukufetau
Tokelau (N.Z.)
Atafu
Nukunono
Fakaofo
Swains I.
W. SAMOA
Savaii
Upolu
American Samoa
Manua Is (U.S.A.)
Tutuila
Rose I.
Rakahanga
Danger Is
Manihiki
Nassau
Tongareva
Suvorov I.
Nuku Hiva
Marquesas Islands
Hiva Oa
Îles Wallis (Fr.)
Hoorn Is (Fr.)
Rotuma
Niuatoputapu
Tafahi
Vava'u Group
FIJI
Vanua Levu
Viti Levu
Suva
Koro
Gau
Kadavu
Tofua
TONGA
Tongatapu Group
Ata
Niue (N.Z.)
Palmerston I.
Aitutaki
Hervey Is
Mauke
Atiu
Cook Islands (N.Z.)
Rarotonga
Mangaia
Motu One
Raiatea
Huahine
Archipel de la Société
Tahiti
Mehetia
Rangiroa
Fakarava
Raroia
King George Is
Îles de Désappointement
Pukapuka
Archipel des Tuamotu
Anaa
Hao
FRENCH POLYNESIA (France)
Hérehérétué
Îles Duc de Gloucester
Îles Maria
Rimatara
Rurutu
Tubuai
Raivavae
Tubuai Islands
Mururoa
Groupe Actéon
Gambier Is
Rapa
Marotiri
Oeno (U.K.)
Henderson I. (U.K.)
Pitcairn I. (U.K.)
Ducie I. (U.K.)
Jayapura
Wewak
INDONESIA
Admiralty Is
New Hanover
New Ireland
Bismarck Sea
Madang
Rabaul
Mt Wilhelm
Lae
PAPUA NEW GUINEA
New Britain
Solomon Sea
Planet Deep
Bougainville
Tauu Is
Nukumanu Is
Ontong Java Atoll
Choiseul
Santa Isabel
New Georgia
Malaita
SOLOMON ISLANDS
Honiara
Guadalcanal
San Cristobal
Rennell
Duff Is
Santa Cruz Is
Tikopia
Cherry I.
Mitre I.
Kikori
G. of Papua
Daru
Port Moresby
Woodlark I.
D'Entrecasteaux Is
Louisiade Arch.
Torres Strait
Arafura Sea
C. York
C. Arnhem
Cape York Pen.
Gulf of Carpentaria
Wellesley Is
Cooktown
Cairns
Normanton
Townsville
CORAL SEA IS TERR.
Coral Sea
Great Barrier Reef
Banks Is
Espiritu Santo
Malakula
Ambrym
VANUATU
Éfaté
Erromango
Tanna
Anatom
Loyalty Is (Fr.)
New Caledonia (Fr.)
Nouméa
Île des Pins
Hunter I.
Horizon Depth
Mount Isa
Hughenden
Bowen
Mackay
Rockhampton
Gladstone
Maryborough
Gympie
Brisbane
Gold Coast
Toowoomba
Roma
Longreach
Simpson Desert
AUSTRALIA
Great Dividing Range
Cunnamulla
Bourke
Walgett
Grafton
Armidale
Tamworth
Taree
Newcastle
Broken Hill
Dubbo
Orange
Sydney
Wollongong
Canberra
Port Augusta
Woomera
Leigh Creek
Whyalla
Mildura
Albury
Mt Kosciusko
Port Lincoln
Adelaide
Horsham
Ballarat
Melbourne
Geelong
Bass Strait
King I.
Flinders I.
Devonport
Launceston
Tasmania
Hobart
South East C.
Tasman Sea
South Fiji Basin
Norfolk I. (Aust.)
Lord Howe I. (Aust.)
Raoul
Kermadec Tr.
C. Maria van Diemen
Kaitaia
Auckland
Great Barrier I.
Bay of Plenty
Hamilton
Rotorua
New Plymouth
Napier
Wanganui
North Island
NEW ZEALAND
Palmerston North
Wellington
Nelson
Greymouth
Mt Cook
Christchurch
South Island
Southern Alps
Kingston
Timaru
Dunedin
West C.
Invercargill
Stewart I.
Chatham Is (N.Z.)
Pitt I.
Auckland Is (N.Z.)
Campbell I. (N.Z.)
SOUTH PACIFIC OCEAN
1:40M
SAMOAN ISLANDS 1:6M
WESTERN SAMOA
Savaii
Asau
Samalaeulu
Puapua
Salelologa
Apia
Taga
Salailua
Falelima
Samatau
Lalomanu
Upolu
Lotofaga
Tutuila
Pago Pago
Tula
Leone
Ofu
Olosega
Tau
Manua Is
AMERICAN SAMOA (U.S.A.)
FRENCH POLYNESIA (France) 1:15M
Archipel de la Société
Archipel des Tuamotu
Îles sous le Vent
Îles du Vent
Motu Iti (Tupai)
Bora-Bora
Tahaa
Uturoa
Raiatea
Huahine
Tetiaroa
Moorea
Papeete
Tahiti
Presq'île de Taiarapu
Mehetia
Manihi
Ahé
Takaroa
Takapoto
Mataiva
Tikehau
Rangiroa
Arutua
Apataki
Îles Palliser
Kaukura
Makatea
Toau
Kauehi
Raraka
Rotoava
Fakarava
Faaite
Tahanea
Katiu
Makemo
Îles Raeffsky
Marutéa
Takumé
Fangatau
Fakahina
Tepoto
Napuka
Îles de Désappointement
Anaa
Haraiki
Hikuéru
Marokau
Amanu
Tauére
Hao
Ravahéré
Nengonengo
Manuhangi
Paraoa
Hérehérétué
Îles Duc de Gloucester
Ahunui
Anuanu Raro
TAHITI and MOOREA (French Polynesia) 1:1.5M
Pte Aroa
Pte Hauru
Papetoai
Pte Vénus
Mahina
Papenoo
Arue
Papava
Papeete
Tiarel
Mahaena
Hitiaa
Haapiti
Afareaitu
Faaa
Taunoa
Teavaro
Pte Tataa
Taapuma
Pte Nuupéré
Moorea
Punaauia
Aorai
Orohena
Tahiti
Utuofai
Faaone
Taravao
Afaahiti
Paéa
Maraa
Papara
Atimaono
Isthmus of Taravao
Mataiea
Vairao
Matiti
Teahupoo
Toaonao
Tepati
Pueu
Tautira
Pte Tatatua
Presqu'île de Taiarapu
Pte Vaiau
WESTERN SAMOA 1:2.5M
C. Puava
Safune
Safotu
Fagamalo
Samalaeulu
Sataua
Asau
Matavanu Crater
Falealupo
Falelima
Silisili
Savaii
Puapua
Tuasivi
Salailua
Vailoa
Salelologa
Satupaitea
C. Asuisui
Taga
Palauli B.
Malua
Falealeula
Vaiusu
Apia
Saluafata
Fagaloa Bay
Uafato
Tiavea
Mulifanua
Faleasiu
Afiamalu
Lauli'i
Fito
Salani
Falevai
Siumu
Samatau
C. Mulitapuili
Matautu
Safata B.
Poutasi
Lotofaga
Lalomanu
Upolu
AMERICAN SAMOA (U.S.A.) 1:2.5M
Tutuila
C. Matatula
Pago Pago
Tula
Aunuu
Leone
Steps Pt
Nuuuli
Vailogi
Ofu
Olosega
Maia
Luma
Manua Is
Tau
PITCAIRN I. (U.K.) 1:200 000
Young's Rock
Bounty Bay
Adamstown
Adam's Rock
Christian Pt
St Paul's Point
Tautama
See pp176-177 for location
Punta Salinas
Bahia Cumberland
San Juan Bautista
El Yunque
Santa Clara
ROBINSON CRUSOE, JUAN FERNÁNDEZ IS (Chile) 1:1.25M
EASTER I. (Chile) 1:750 000
Cabo Norte
Pta Rosalia
Bahia La Pérouse
Terevaka
Puhi
Katiki
C. O'Higgins
Motu Tautara
Rano Raraku
C. Roggeveen
Hanga Roa
Mataveri
Vaihu
Pta Cuidado
Rano Kao
Pta Baja
Motu Iti
Motu Nui
Cabo Sur
See pp150-151 for location

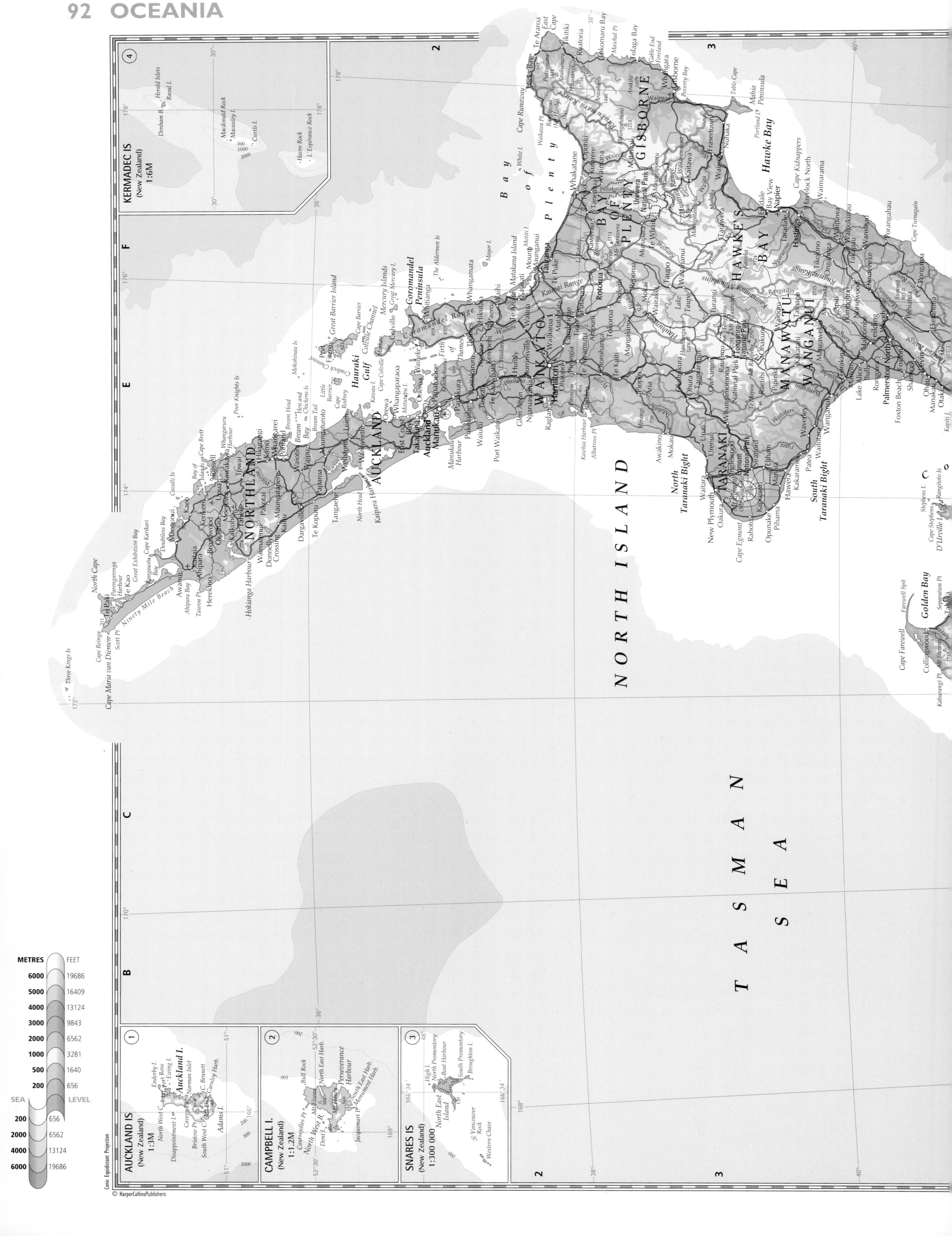
NORTH ISLAND
TASMAN SEA
NORTHLAND
AUCKLAND
WAIKATO
BAY OF PLENTY
GISBORNE
HAWKE'S BAY
TARANAKI
MANAWATU-WANGANUI
Bay of Plenty
Hawke Bay
North Taranaki Bight
South Taranaki Bight
Hauraki Gulf
Coromandel Peninsula
Auckland
Hamilton
Rotorua
Tauranga
Taupo
Lake Taupo
Napier
Hastings
Gisborne
New Plymouth
Palmerston North
Wanganui
Whangarei
North Cape
Cape Reinga
Cape Maria van Diemen
Ninety Mile Beach
Three Kings Is
East Cape
Cape Egmont
Golden Bay
Cape Farewell
KERMADEC IS (New Zealand) 1:6M
Raoul I.
Macauley I.
Curtis I.
L'Espérance Rock
AUCKLAND IS (New Zealand) 1:3M
Auckland I.
Adams I.
CAMPBELL I. (New Zealand) 1:1.2M
Perseverance Harbour
SNARES IS (New Zealand) 1:300 000
North East Island
Western Chain
METRES
FEET
6000 19686
5000 16409
4000 13124
3000 9843
2000 6562
1000 3281
500 1640
200 656
SEA LEVEL
200 656
2000 6562
4000 13124
6000 19686
Conic Equidistant Projection

© HarperCollinsPublishers

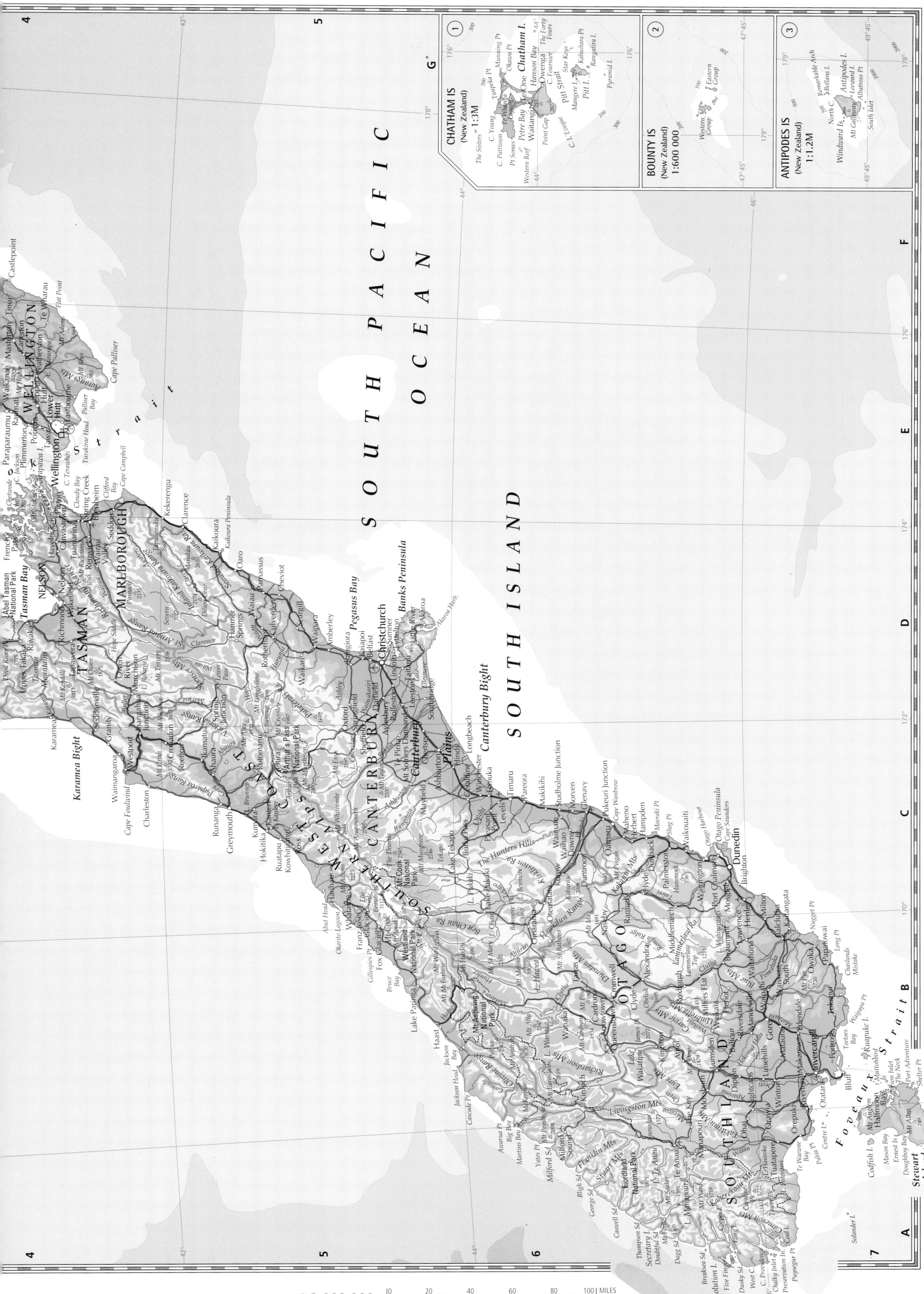
CHATHAM IS
(New Zealand)
1:3M
Chatham I.
Pitt I.
BOUNTY IS
(New Zealand)
1:600 000
ANTIPODES IS
(New Zealand)
1:1.2M
Antipodes I.
SOUTH PACIFIC
OCEAN
SOUTH ISLAND
Wellington
WELLINGTON
Cook Strait
NELSON
TASMAN
MARLBOROUGH
Tasman Bay
Karamea Bight
Blenheim
Kaikoura
Westport
Greymouth
Hokitika
Pegasus Bay
Christchurch
Banks Peninsula
Canterbury Bight
CANTERBURY
WEST COAST
Timaru
Oamaru
OTAGO
Dunedin
Queenstown
SOUTHLAND
Invercargill
Foveaux Strait
Stewart Island

1:3 000 000

0	20	40	60	80	100 MILES

0	20	40	60	80	100	120	140	160 KM

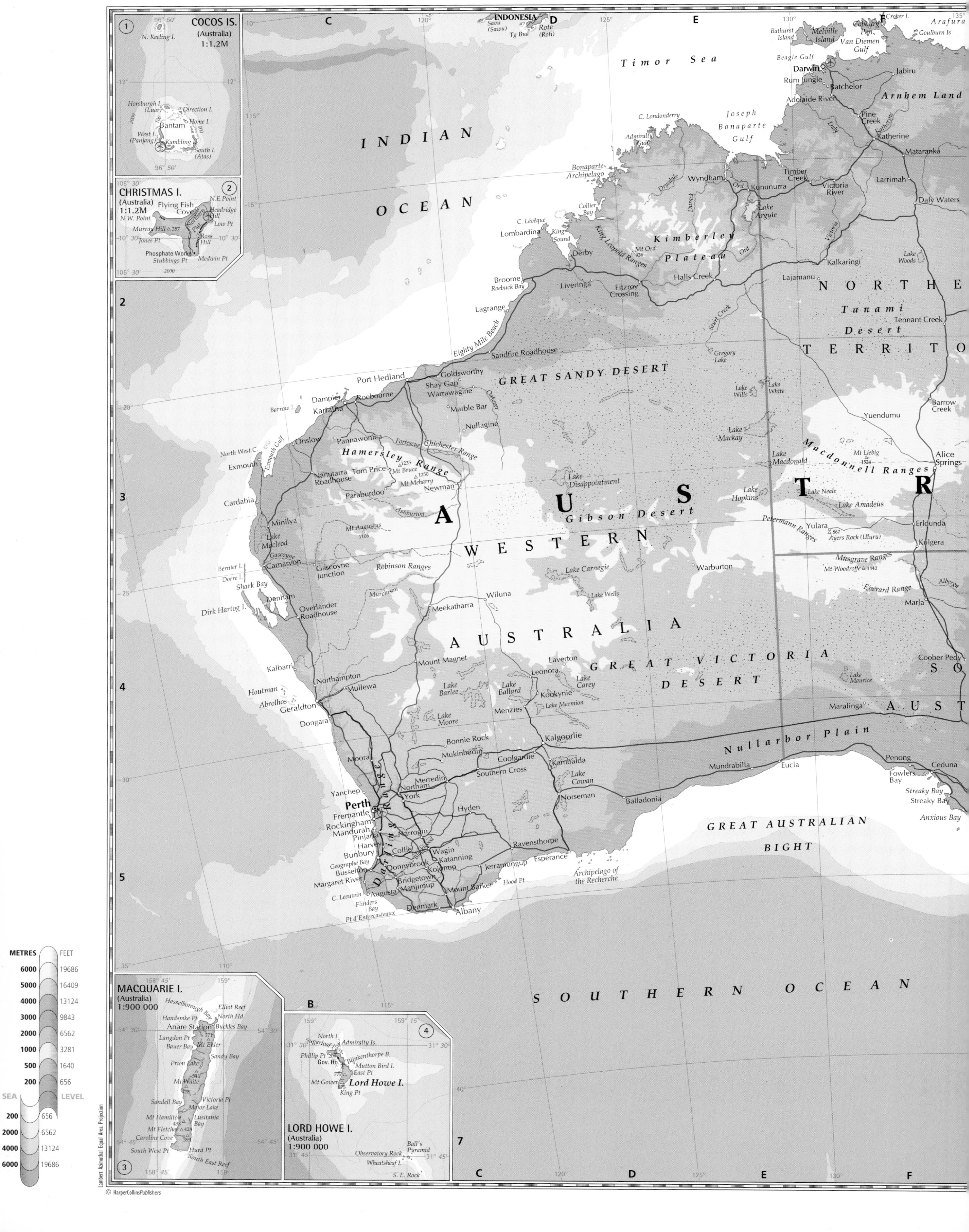

1 COCOS IS. (Australia) 1:1.2M
N. Keeling I.
Horsburgh I. (Luar)
Direction I.
Home I.
Bantam
West I. (Panjang)
Kambling
South I. (Atas)
2 CHRISTMAS I. (Australia) 1:1.2M
Flying Fish Cove
N.E. Point
Headridge Hill
N.W. Point
Low Pt
Murray Hill 357
Ross Hill
Jones Pt
Phosphate Works
Stubbings Pt
Medwin Pt
INDONESIA
Savu (Sawu)
Rote (Roti)
Tg Bua
Timor Sea
Arafura
Bathurst Island
Melville Island
Coburg Pen.
Croker I.
Goulburn Is
Van Diemen Gulf
Beagle Gulf
Darwin
Rum Jungle
Batchelor
Jabiru
Arnhem Land
Adelaide River
Pine Creek
Katherine
Mataranka
Larrimah
Daly Waters
Joseph Bonaparte Gulf
C. Londonderry
Admiralty Gulf
Bonaparte Archipelago
Wyndham
Kununurra
Timber Creek
Victoria River
Lake Argyle
Collier Bay
C. Lévêque
Lombardina
King Sound
Derby
Kimberley Plateau
King Leopold Ranges
Mt Ord 936
Halls Creek
Kalkaringi
Lake Woods
Broome
Roebuck Bay
Liveringa
Fitzroy Crossing
Lajamanu
NORTHERN TERRITORY
Tanami Desert
Tennant Creek
Lagrange
Eighty Mile Beach
Sandfire Roadhouse
Sturt Creek
Gregory Lake
INDIAN OCEAN
GREAT SANDY DESERT
Port Hedland
Goldsworthy
Shay Gap
Warrawagine
Marble Bar
Nullagine
Dampier
Roebourne
Karratha
Barrow I.
Lake Wills
Lake White
Lake Mackay
Yuendumu
Barrow Creek
North West C.
Exmouth Gulf
Onslow
Pannawonica
Exmouth
Hamersley Range
Fortescue
Chichester Range
Mt Bruce 1235
Tom Price
Nanutarra Roadhouse
Mt Meharry 1250
Newman
Paraburdoo
Ashburton
Lake Disappointment
Lake Macdonald
Macdonnell Ranges
Mt Liebig 1524
Alice Springs
Lake Hopkins
Lake Neale
Lake Amadeus
Cardabia
AUSTRALIA
Gibson Desert
Minilya
Lake Macleod
Mt Augustus 1106
WESTERN AUSTRALIA
Petermann Ranges
Yulara
867 Ayers Rock (Uluru)
Erldunda
Kulgera
Bernier I.
Dorre I.
Gascoyne
Carnarvon
Gascoyne Junction
Robinson Ranges
Lake Carnegie
Warburton
Musgrave Ranges
Mt Woodroffe 1440
Shark Bay
Dirk Hartog I.
Denham
Murchison
Wiluna
Lake Wells
Everard Range
Alberga
Marla
Overlander Roadhouse
Meekatharra
Kalbarri
Mount Magnet
Laverton
GREAT VICTORIA DESERT
Coober Pedy
Leonora
Lake Carey
Lake Maurice
Northampton
Mullewa
Houtman Abrolhos
Geraldton
Lake Barlee
Lake Ballard
Kookynie
Lake Marmion
Menzies
Maralinga
Dongara
Lake Moore
Bonnie Rock
Kalgoorlie
Nullarbor Plain
Moora
Mukinbudin
Coolgardie
Kambalda
Mundrabilla
Eucla
Penong
Ceduna
Merredin
Southern Cross
Lake Cowan
Fowlers Bay
Yanchep
Northam
York
Norseman
Balladonia
Streaky Bay
Perth
Fremantle
Rockingham
Mandurah
Pinjarra
Harvey
Darling Range
Hyden
Anxious Bay
GREAT AUSTRALIAN BIGHT
Narrogin
Bunbury
Collie
Wagin
Katanning
Ravensthorpe
Geographe Bay
Busselton
Donnybrook
Bridgetown
Kojonup
Jerramungup
Esperance
Margaret River
Manjimup
Mount Barker
Hood Pt
Archipelago of the Recherche
C. Leeuwin
Augusta
Flinders Bay
Pt d'Entrecasteaux
Denmark
Albany
SOUTHERN OCEAN
3 MACQUARIE I. (Australia) 1:900 000
Hasselborough Bay
Elliot Reef
North Hd
Handspike Pt
Anare Station
Buckles Bay
Langdon Pt
Bauer Bay
Mt Elder
Sandy Bay
Prion Lake
Mt Waite
Sandell Bay
Victoria Pt
Major Lake
Mt Hamilton
Lusitania Bay
Mt Fletcher 428
Caroline Cove
Hurd Pt
South West Pt
South East Reef
4 LORD HOWE I. (Australia) 1:900 000
North I.
Sugarloaf Pts
Admiralty Is.
Phillip Pt
Gov. Ho.
Blinkenthorpe B.
Mutton Bird I.
East Pt
Mt Gower
Lord Howe I.
King Pt
Observatory Rock
Ball's Pyramid
Wheatsheaf I.
S. E. Rock
METRES FEET
6000 19686
5000 16409
4000 13124
3000 9843
2000 6562
1000 3281
500 1640
200 656
SEA LEVEL
200 656
2000 6562
4000 13124
6000 19686
Lambert Azimuthal Equal Area Projection

© HarperCollinsPublishers

Gulf of Port Moresby
PAPUA
PAPUA NEW GUINEA
Owen Stanley Range
Kwikila
Abau
Tufi
D'Entrecasteaux Islands
Fergusson I.
Esa-ala
Alotau
Samarai
Normanby I.
Louisiade Archipelago
Misima I.
Conflict Group
Bwagaoia
Tagula I.
Rossel I.
Solomon Sea
Torres Strait
Badu I.
Moa I.
Prince of Wales I.
Endeavour Str.
C. York
Bamaga
Sea
C. Wessel
Wessel Is
Elcho I.
Buckingham B.
Melville B.
Arnhem B.
Nhulunbuy
C. Arnhem
C. Grenville
Cape York Peninsula
Albatross Bay
Weipa
C. Direction
Gulf of Carpentaria
Woodah I.
Bickerton I.
Alyangula
Groote Eylandt
Coen
Princess Charlotte Bay
C. Melville
Osprey Reef
Maria I.
Limmen Bight
Sir Edward Pellew Group
Vanderlin I.
C. Flattery
CORAL SEA
Borroloola
Mitchell
Laura
Cooktown
Weary B.
Mornington I.
Wellesley Islands
Bentinck I.
Karumba
Mossman
Mareeba
Cairns
Atherton
Mt Bartle Frere 1612
Ravenshoe
Innisfail
GREAT BARRIER REEF
CORAL SEA ISLANDS TERRITORY
Burketown
Normanton
Croydon
Georgetown
Forsayth
Tully
Hinchinbrook I.
Ingham
Barkly Tableland
Gregory Ra.
Magnetic I.
Townsville
Camooweal
Kajabbi
Ayr
Bowen
Whitsunday I.
Mount Isa
Cloncurry
Julia Creek
Richmond
Hughenden
Charters Towers
Proserpine
Dalrymple Lake
Mt Dalrymple 1277
Mackay
Sarina
Îles Chesterfield (New Caledonia)
QUEENSLAND
GREAT DIVIDING RANGE
Selwyn Range
Dajarra
Georgina
Winton
Percy Is
Arthur Pt
Swain Reefs
Capricorn Channel
Boulia
Diamantina
Clermont
Longreach
Barcaldine
Emerald
Rockhampton
Blackwater
Yeppoon
Keppel B.
Curtis I.
Gladstone
AUSTRALIA
Springsure
Laleham
Blackall
Yaraka
Moura
Biloela
Tropic of Capricorn
Simpson Desert
Birdsville
Bilpa Morea Claypan
Windorah
Buckland Tableland
Monto
Bundaberg
Hervey Bay
Sandy C.
Fraser I.
Maryborough
Warrego
Charleville
Gayndah
Quilpie
Mitchell
Roma
Miles
Murgon
Gympie
Tewantin
Nambour
Maroochydore
Caboolture
Moreton I.
Oodnadatta
Macumba
Warburton
Cooper Creek
Balonne
Condamine
Chinchilla
Kingaroy
Dalby
Glenmorgan
Toowoomba
Brisbane
Ipswich
Beaudesert
N. Stradbroke I.
Beenleigh
Gold Coast
Murwillumbah
Byron Bay
Ballina
Lake Eyre (North)
Sturt Desert
Grey Range
Cunnamulla
St George
Dirranbandi
Darling Downs
Goondiwindi
Inglewood
Warwick
Stanthorpe
Mungindi
Texas
Tenterfield
Lismore
Casino
Hungerford
Tibooburra
Goodooga
L. Eyre (South)
Lake Blanche
Moree
Warialda
Glen Innes
Grafton
Brewarrina
Bourke
Barwon
Lightning Ridge
Inverell
Leigh Creek
Lake Torrens
Woomera
Flinders Ranges
Lake Frome
Barrier Range
Walgett
Wee Waa
Narrabri
Armidale
Round Mt 1613
Coffs Harbour
Macksville
TASMAN SEA
Island Lagoon
Lake Macfarlane
Lake Gairdner
Darling
Macquarie
Coonamble
Coonabarabran
Gunnedah
Tamworth
Kempsey
Port Macquarie
Wauchope
Broken Hill
Wilcannia
NEW SOUTH WALES
Cobar
Nyngan
Warren
Gilgandra
Murrurundi
Port Augusta
Quorn
Whyalla
Port Pirie
Menindee
Menindee Lake
Narromine
Dubbo
Wellington
Muswellbrook
Mudgee
Mt Barrington 1585
Singleton
Taree
Forster
Lord Howe I. (Aust.)
Kyancutta
Peterborough
Jamestown
Burra
Ivanhoe
Condobolin
Burrendong Res.
Parkes
Orange
Cessnock
Maitland
Newcastle
Eyre Peninsula
Wallaroo
Lake Victoria
Garnpung Lake
Lake Cargelligo
Forbes
Bathurst
Lithgow
Gosford
Hillston
Lachlan
Booligal
Cowra
Katoomba
Sydney
Spencer Gulf
Yorke Peninsula
Port Lincoln
Adelaide
Gawler
Berri
Renmark
Wentworth
Mildura
Hay
Griffith
Leeton
West Wyalong
Young
Temora
Moss Vale
Botany Bay
Wollongong
C. Carnot
Gulf St Vincent
Yorketown
Murray Bridge
Tailem Bend
Robinvale
Balranald
Ouyen
Narrandera
Yass
Goulburn
Investigator Strait
Kingscote
Victor Harbour
Lake Alexandrina
Swan Hill
Wagga Wagga
Burrinjuck Res.
Canberra
A.C.T.
Nowra
Beecroft Pen.
Ulladulla
Kangaroo I.
Youngusband Pen.
Lake Tyrell
Kerang
Deniliquin
Cobram
Tumut
Nhill
Charlton
Echuca
Shepparton
Albury
Wodonga
Hume Res.
Tumbarumba
Batemans Bay
Moruya
Narooma
Horsham
Bendigo
Wangaratta
Mt Kosciusko 2230
Cooma
C. Jaffa
Naracoorte
Maryborough
Stawell
Castlemaine
Mt Bogong 1986
Bega
VICTORIA
GREAT DIVIDING RANGE
Mt William 1167
Ararat
Mt Macedon 1011
Ballarat
Melbourne
Bombala
Eden
Mount Gambier
Discovery Bay
Portland
Geelong
Port Phillip Bay
Bairnsdale
Orbost
C. Howe
Moe
Sale
C. Nelson
Warrnambool
Colac
Hastings
Ninety Mile Beach
C. Otway
Phillip I.
Wonthaggi
Corner Inlet
Wilson's Promontory
Bass Strait
Kent Group
Currie
King I.
Furneaux Group
Flinders I.
Hunter I.
Three Hummock I.
Hunter Is
Robbins I.
Whitemark
Cape Barren I.
Clarke I.
Banks Strait
Smithton
Burnie
George Town
Eddystone Pt
Devonport
Scottsdale
TASMANIA
Launceston
Rosebery
Mt Ossa 1617
Queenstown
Great L.
Fingal
Macquarie Harbour
Lake Gordon
Sorell
New Norfolk
Hobart
Port Arthur
Dover
Bruny I.
South East C.
Pt Vincent
Mt Bates 318
Anson B.
Burnt Pine
Rocky Pt
Cascade B.
Steel's Pt
Kingston
Collins Hd
Nepean I.
Sydney B.
Philip I.
NORFOLK I. (Australia) 1:900 000
G
H
K
L
1
2
3
4
5
6
1:11 000 000
MILES
KM

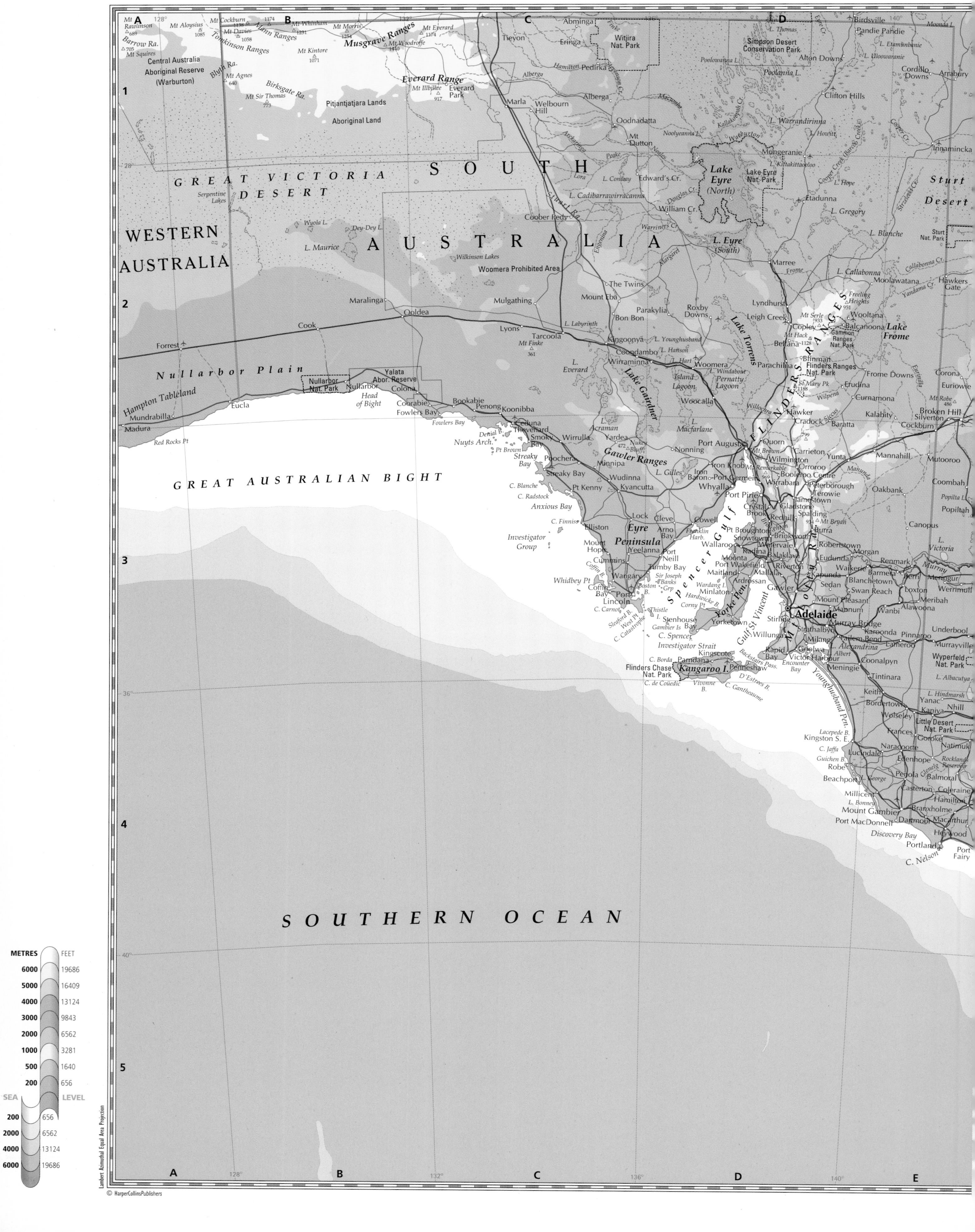
A
B
C
D
E
1
2
3
4
5
128°
132°
136°
140°
28°
36°
40°
Mt Rawlinson
Mt Aloysius
1085
Mt Cockburn
Mt Davies
Mann Ranges
Mt Whinham
Mt Morris
Musgrave Ranges
Mt Everard
Mt Woodroffe
1440
Barrow Ra.
Mt Squires
Tomkinson Ranges
Mt Kintore
1071
Central Australia Aboriginal Reserve (Warburton)
Blyth Ra.
Mt Agnes
Birksgate Ra.
Mt Sir Thomas
Everard Range
Mt Illbillee
Everard Park
Pitjantjatjara Lands
Aboriginal Land
Abminga
Tieyon
Eringa
Witjira Nat. Park
Simpson Desert Conservation Park
Birdsville
Pandie Pandie
L. Etamunbanie
L. Ulowaranie
Alton Downs
Poolowanna L.
Cordillo Downs
Arrabury
Hamilton
Pedirka
Alberga
Marla
Welbourn Hill
Clifton Hills
Oodnadatta
Mt Dutton
Nooyeanna L.
L. Warrandirinna
L. Howitt
Innamincka
Mungeranie
L. Kittakittaooloo
Lake Eyre (North)
Lake Eyre Nat. Park
L. Hope
Etadunna
L. Gregory
Sturt Desert
Sturt Nat. Park
L. Blanche
GREAT VICTORIA DESERT
Serpentine Lakes
SOUTH AUSTRALIA
WESTERN AUSTRALIA
L. Conway
Edward's Cr.
L. Cadibarrawirracanna
William Cr.
Coober Pedy
Wyola L.
Dey-Dey L.
L. Maurice
Wilkinson Lakes
Woomera Prohibited Area
L. Eyre (South)
Marree
L. Callabonna
Moolawatana
Hawkers Gate
The Twins
Mount Eba
Maralinga
Ooldea
Mulgathing
Parakylia
Roxby Downs
Lyndhurst
Leigh Creek
Copley
Beltana
Mt Serle
Freeling Heights
Wooltana
Balcanoona
Gammon Ranges Nat. Park
Lake Frome
Cook
Forrest
Bon Bon
L. Labyrinth
Lyons
Tarcoola
Mt Finke
361
Kingoonya
L. Younghusband
L. Hanson
Coondambo
Wirraminna
L. Hart
Woomera
L. Windabout
Pernatty Lagoon
Lake Torrens
Parachilna
Blinman
Flinders Ranges Nat. Park
FLINDERS RANGES
Frome Downs
Corona
Euriowie
Nullarbor Plain
Nullarbor Nat. Park
Nullarbor
Yalata Abor. Reserve
Colona
Head of Bight
Coorabie
Fowlers Bay
Bookabie
Penong
Koonibba
L. Everard
Lake Gairdner
Island Lagoon
Woocalla
Erudina
Curnamona
Kalabity
Broken Hill
Silverton
Cockburn
Hampton Tableland
Eucla
Mundrabilla
Madura
Red Rocks Pt
Ceduna
Thevenard
Denial B.
Nuyts Arch.
Smoky Bay
Pt Brown
Streaky Bay
L. Acraman
Wirrulla
Yardea
Nuckey Bluff
Gawler Ranges
Nonning
L. Macfarlane
Port Augusta
Hawker
Cradock
Baratta
Quorn
Carrieton
Yunta
Mannahill
Mutooroo
Coombah
Poochera
Minnipa
Wudinna
L. Gilles
Iron Knob
Iron Baron
Port Germein
Wilmington
Orroroo
Booleroo Centre
Wirrabara
Peterborough
Terowie
Oakbank
GREAT AUSTRALIAN BIGHT
C. Blanche
C. Radstock
Anxious Bay
Pt Kenny
Kyancutta
Whyalla
Port Pirie
Crystal Brook
Jamestown
Gladstone
Redhill
Spalding
Burra
Canopus
Popiltah
C. Finniss
Elliston
Lock
Cleve
Arno Bay
Cowell
Franklin Harb.
Pt Broughton
Snowtown
Brinkworth
Investigator Group
Mount Hope
Eyre Peninsula
Yeelanna
Cummins
Port Neill
Tumby Bay
Wallaroo
Moonta
Port Wakefield
Spencer Gulf
Robertstown
Morgan
Eudunda
Renmark
L. Victoria
Whidbey Pt
Coffin B.
Coffin Bay
Wangary
Sir Joseph Banks Grp
Maitland
Mallala
Riverton
Kapunda
Waikerie
Barmera
Berri
Loxton
Meningie
Port Lincoln
Boston B.
Wardang I.
Minlaton
Hardwicke B.
Ardrossan
Gawler
Sedan
Blanchetown
Swan Reach
Mount Pleasant
Werrimull
Meribah
Alawoona
C. Carnot
Thistle I.
Corny Pt
Yorke Pen.
Gulf St Vincent
Adelaide
Mannum
Wanbi
Slaeford B.
West Pt
C. Catastrophe
Gambier Is
Stenhouse Bay
Yorketown
Stirling
Strathalbyn
Murray Bridge
Karoonda
Pinnaroo
Tailem Bend
Lameroo
Underbool
Murrayville
C. Spencer
Investigator Strait
Willunga
Milang
Alexandrina
Kingscote
Rapid Bay
Goolwa
Victor Harbour
Albert
Coonalpyn
Wyperfeld Nat. Park
C. Borda
Parndana
Backstairs Pass.
Encounter Bay
Penneshaw
Flinders Chase Nat. Park
Kangaroo I.
Tintinara
L. Albacutya
C. de Couëdic
Vivonne B.
D'Estrees B.
C. Gantheaume
Youngshusband Pen.
Keith
L. Hindmarsh
Bordertown
Yanac
Kaniva
Nhill
Wolseley
Little Desert Nat. Park
Frances
Goroke
Lacepede B.
Kingston S. E.
C. Jaffa
Naracoorte
Natimuk
Lucindale
Guichen B.
Robe
Edenhope
Rocklands Reservoir
Beachport
L. George
Penola
Balmoral
Millicent
Casterton
Coleraine
L. Bonney
Hamilton
Mount Gambier
Branxholme
Port MacDonnell
Dartmoor
Macarthur
Heywood
Discovery Bay
Portland
Port Fairy
C. Nelson
SOUTHERN OCEAN
METRES
FEET
6000
19686
5000
16409
4000
13124
3000
9843
2000
6562
1000
3281
500
1640
200
656
SEA
LEVEL
200
656
2000
6562
4000
13124
6000
19686
Lambert Azimuthal Equal Area Projection

1:6 000 000

0 40 80 120 160 200 MILES

0 40 80 120 160 200 240 280 320 KM

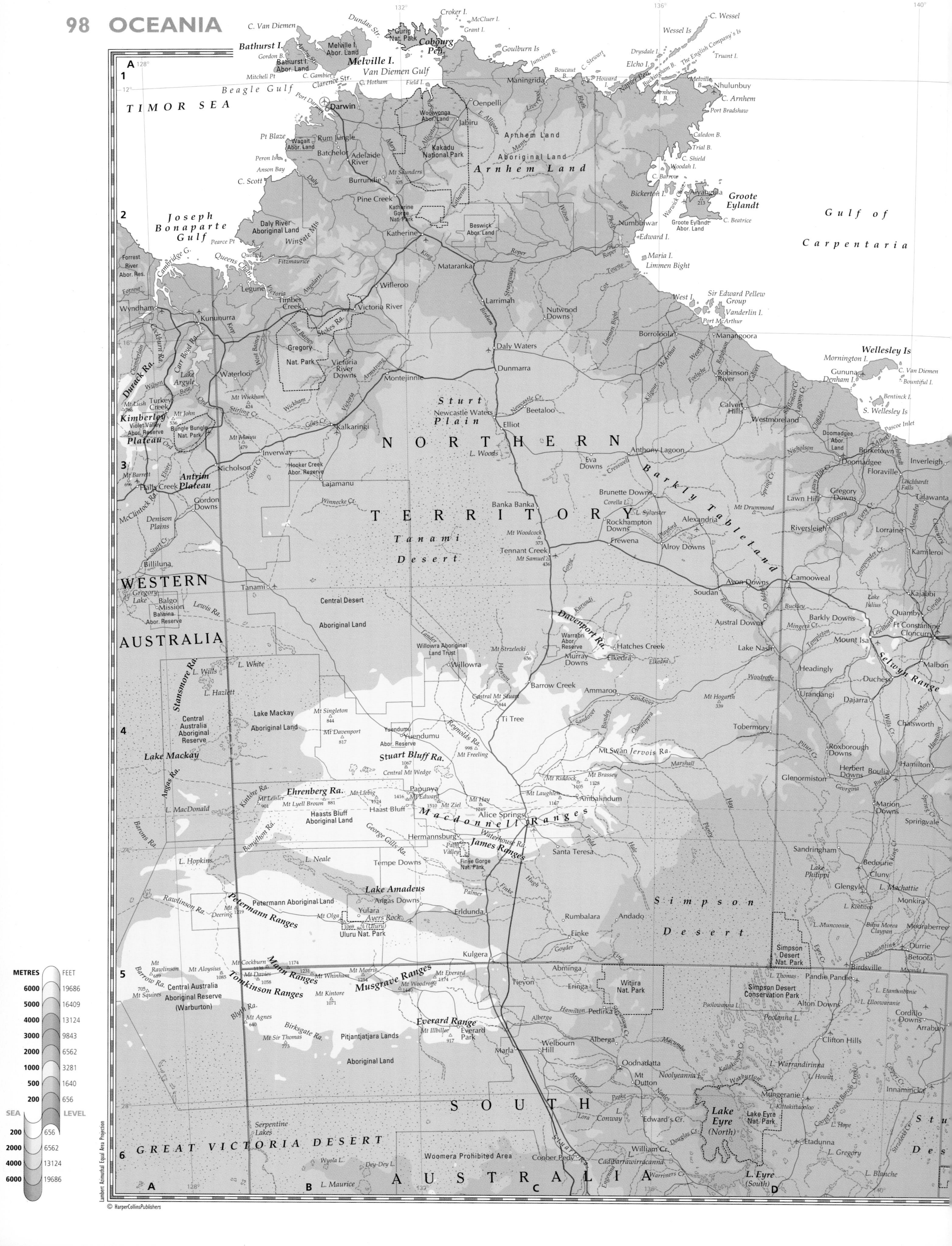
TIMOR SEA
Beagle Gulf
Bathurst I.
Melville I.
Melville I. Abor. Land
Bathurst I. Abor. Land
C. Van Diemen
Van Diemen Gulf
Clarence Str.
Dundas Str.
Croker I.
Cobourg Pen.
Gurig Nat. Park
Goulburn Is
Darwin
Port Darwin
Pt Blaze
Wagait Abor. Land
Rum Jungle
Batchelor
Adelaide River
Woolwonga Abor. Land
Jabiru
Oenpelli
Kakadu National Park
Maningrida
Arnhem Land
Aboriginal Land
Arnhem Land
C. Arnhem
Nhulunbuy
Wessel Is
C. Wessel
Elcho I.
Gove Pen.
Groote Eylandt
Groote Eylandt Abor. Land
Alyangula
Numbulwar
Bickerton I.
Gulf of Carpentaria
Joseph Bonaparte Gulf
C. Scott
Anson Bay
Peron Is
Burrundie
Pine Creek
Katherine Gorge Nat. Park
Katherine
Beswick Abor. Land
Daly River Aboriginal Land
Wingate Mts
Mataranka
Edward I.
Maria I.
Limmen Bight
Forrest River Abor. Res.
Cambridge G.
Queens Chan.
Legune
Timber Creek
Wifleroo
Victoria River
Larrimah
Nutwood Downs
Wyndham
Kununurra
Gregory Nat. Park
Stokes Ra.
Victoria River Downs
Daly Waters
Dunmarra
West I.
Sir Edward Pellew Group
Vanderlin I.
Port McArthur
Borroloola
Manangoora
Robinson River
Wellesley Is
Mornington I.
Gununa
Denham I.
Bentinck I.
S. Wellesley Is
Durack Ra.
Carr Boyd Ra.
Lake Argyle
Waterloo
Montejinnie
Turkey Creek
Mt Wickham
Sturt Plain
Newcastle Waters
Beetaloo
Elliot
Calvert Hills
Westmoreland
Kimberley Plateau
Violet Valley Abor. Reserve
Bungle Bungle Nat. Park
Kalkaringi
Mt Manu
Inverway
NORTHERN
L. Woods
Anthony Lagoon
Eva Downs
Doomadgee
Burketown
Floraville
Inverleigh
Nicholson
Hooker Creek Abor. Reserve
Antrim Plateau
Halls Creek
Lajamanu
Barkly Tableland
Brunette Downs
Gordon Downs
Banka Banka
TERRITORY
Rockhampton Downs
Alexandria
Gregory Downs
Lawn Hill
Talawanta
Denison Plains
Tanami Desert
Mt Woodcock
Frewena
Alroy Downs
Riversleigh
Lorraine
Tennant Creek
Kamileroi
Billiluna
WESTERN AUSTRALIA
Tanami
Gregory Lake
Balgo Mission
Balwina Abor. Reserve
Central Desert Aboriginal Land
Soudan
Avon Downs
Camooweal
Davenport Ra.
Warrabri Abor. Reserve
Hatches Creek
Murray Downs
Elkedra
Austral Downs
Barkly Downs
Mount Isa
Cloncurry
Kajabbi
Quamby
Willowra Aboriginal Land Trust
Willowra
Mt Strzelecki
Lake Nash
Headingly
Selwyn Range
Malbon
Duchess
Stansmore Ra.
L. White
L. Wills
L. Hazlett
Barrow Creek
Ammaroo
Urandangi
Dajarra
Central Mt Stuart
Mt Hogarth
Lake Mackay Aboriginal Land
Central Australia Aboriginal Reserve
Mt Singleton
Ti Tree
Chatsworth
4
Tobermory
Mt Davenport
Yuendumu
Yuendumu Abor. Reserve
Reynolds Ra.
Mt Freeling
Stuart Bluff Ra.
Mt Swan
Jervois Ra.
Roxborough Downs
Lake Mackay
Central Mt Wedge
Herbert Downs
Boulia
Hamilton
Angas Ra.
Kintore Ra.
Ehrenberg Ra.
Papunya
Mt Riddock
Mt Brassey
Glenormiston
Mt Leisler
Mt Lyell Brown
Mt Liebig
Mt Edward
Mt Ziel
Mt Hay
Mt Laughlen
Ambalindum
Haasts Bluff Aboriginal Land
Haast Bluff
Alice Springs
Macdonnell Ranges
L. MacDonald
Marion Downs
Springvale
Hermannsburg
Barons Ra.
Bonython Ra.
George Gills Ra.
Waterhouse Ra.
James Ranges
Palm Valley
Finke Gorge Nat. Park
Santa Teresa
Sandringham
L. Hopkins
L. Neale
Tempe Downs
Lake Philippi
Bedourie
Cluny
Lake Amadeus
Glengyle
L. Machattie
Angas Downs
Simpson
Monkira
Rawlinson Ra.
Petermann Aboriginal Land
Petermann Ranges
Mt Deering
Yulara
Mt Olga
Ayers Rock (Uluru)
Uluru Nat. Park
Erldunda
Rumbalara
Andado
Finke
Desert
Simpson Desert Nat. Park
Durrie
Betoota
Kulgera
Mt Rawlinson
Mt Aloysius
Mt Cockburn
Mt Davies
Mann Ranges
Mt Morris
Mt Whinham
Mt Everard
Musgrave Ranges
Mt Woodroffe
Abminga
Eringa
Witjira Nat. Park
Tieyon
Simpson Desert Conservation Park
Pandie Pandie
Birdsville
5
Barrow Ra.
Mt Squires
Central Australia Aboriginal Reserve (Warburton)
Tomkinson Ranges
Mt Kintore
Blyth Ra.
Mt Agnes
Birksgate Ra.
Everard Range
Mt Illbillee
Everard Park
Pedirka
Alton Downs
Cordillo Downs
Arrabury
Mt Sir Thomas
Pitjantjatjara Lands
Aboriginal Land
Marla
Welbourn Hill
Alberga
Clifton Hills
Oodnadatta
L. Warrandirinna
Mt Dutton
Noolyeanna L.
Innamincka
Mungeranie
SOUTH
Serpentine Lakes
GREAT VICTORIA DESERT
L. Conway
Edward's Cr.
Lake Eyre (North)
Lake Eyre Nat. Park
Etadunna
Woomera Prohibited Area
Coober Pedy
William Cr.
L. Gregory
L. Eyre (South)
L. Blanche
AUSTRALIA
L. Maurice
METRES
FEET
6000 19686
5000 16409
4000 13124
3000 9843
2000 6562
1000 3281
500 1640
200 656
SEA LEVEL
200 656
2000 6562
4000 13124
6000 19686
Lambert Azimuthal Equal Area Projection

© HarperCollinsPublishers

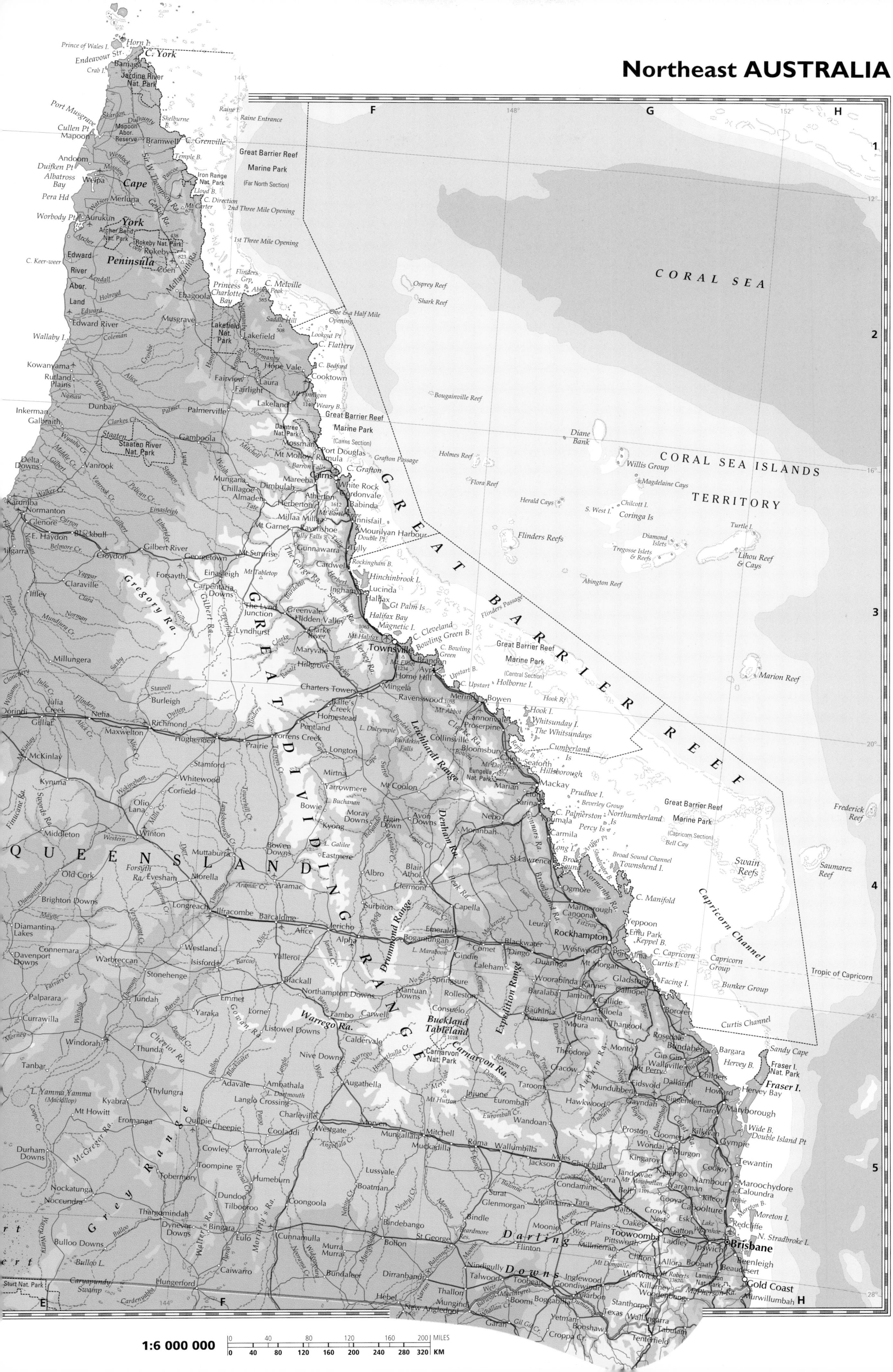
CORAL SEA
CORAL SEA ISLANDS TERRITORY
GREAT BARRIER REEF
Great Barrier Reef Marine Park (Far North Section)
Great Barrier Reef Marine Park (Cairns Section)
Great Barrier Reef Marine Park (Central Section)
Great Barrier Reef Marine Park (Capricorn Section)
QUEENSLAND
GREAT DIVIDING RANGE
Cape York Peninsula
C. York
Prince of Wales I.
Horn I.
Endeavour Str.
Crab I.
Bamaga
Jardine River Nat. Park
Port Musgrave
Cullen Pt
Mapoon
Mapoon Abor. Reserve
Shelburne B.
C. Grenville
Raine I.
Raine Entrance
Temple B.
Bramwell
Andoom
Duifken Pt
Albatross Bay
Weipa
Pera Hd
Iron Range Nat. Park
Lloyd B.
C. Direction
Mt Carter
2nd Three Mile Opening
1st Three Mile Opening
Merluna
Worbody Pt
Aurukun
Archer Bend Nat. Park
Rokeby Nat. Park
Rokeby
Coen
Edward River Abor. Land
C. Keer-weer
Holroyd
Ebagoola
Flinders Grp.
Princess Charlotte Bay
C. Melville
Musgrave
Edward River
Lakefield Nat. Park
Lakefield
Saddle Hill
One & a Half Mile Opening
Lookout Pt
C. Flattery
Wallaby I.
Coleman
Kowanyama
Rutland Plains
Hope Vale
C. Bedford
Cooktown
Fairview
Laura
Mt Finnigan
Weary B.
Nassau
Dunbar
Palmerville
Lakeland
Inkerman
Galbraith
Daintree Nat. Park
Mossman
Mt Molloy
Port Douglas
Rumula
Staaten River Nat. Park
Gamboola
Delta Downs
Vanrook
Mungana
Chillagoe
Almaden
Mareeba
Dimbulah
Atherton
Cairns
C. Grafton
Grafton Passage
Barron Falls
White Rock
Gordonvale
Babinda
Innisfail
Mourilyan Harbour
Double Pt.
Tully
Herberton
Millaa Millaa
Ravenshoe
Mt Garnet
Tully Falls
Gunnawarra
Karumba
Normanton
Glenore
Carron
Blackbull
E. Haydon
Belmore Cr.
Gilbert River
Croydon
Georgetown
Mt Surprise
Forsayth
Einasleigh
Mt Tabletop
Cardwell
Rockingham B.
Hinchinbrook I.
Lucinda
Ingham
Halifax
Gt Palm Is
Halifax Bay
Magnetic I.
Mt Halifax
C. Cleveland
Bowling Green B.
C. Bowling Green
Townsville
Brandon
Ayr
Mt Elliot
Home Hill
Upstart B.
C. Upstart
Holborne I.
Bowen
Merinda
Claraville
Iffley
Gregory Ra.
Carpentaria Downs
The Lynd Junction
Greenvale
Hidden Valley
Clarke River
Lyndhurst
Maryvale
Hillgrove
Charters Towers
Mingela
Ravenswood
Mt Abbot
Millungera
Cloncurry
Julia Creek
Nelia
Burleigh
Richmond
Maxwelton
Hughenden
Torrens Creek
Pentland
Balfe's Creek Homestead
Prairie
L. Dalrymple
Burdekin Falls
Collinsville
Cannonvale
Proserpine
Hook I.
Whitsunday I.
The Whitsundays
Cumberland Is
Bloomsbury
Eungella Nat. Park
Mt Dalrymple
Seaforth
C. Hillsborough
Mackay
Marian
Sarina
Prudhoe I.
Beverley Group
C. Palmerston
Northumberland Is
Percy Is
Koumala
Carmila
Long I.
Broad Sound
Broad Sound Channel
Townshend I.
St Lawrence
McKinlay
Stamford
Longton
Mirtna
Yarrowmere
Mt Coolon
Kynuna
Whitewood
Corfield
Olio
Lana
Winton
Middleton
Western
Buchanan
Moray Downs
Bowie
Kyong
Elgin Down
Avon Downs
L. Galilee
Eastmere
Nebo
Moranbah
Denham Ra.
Leichhardt Range
Muttaburra
Bowen Downs
Albro
Blair Athol
Clermont
Old Cork
Forsyth Ra.
Evesham
Morella
Aramac
Brighton Downs
Longreach
Ilfracombe
Barcaldine
Jericho
Alice
Alpha
Surbiton
Capella
Drummond Range
Emerald
Bogantungan
Comet
Blackwater
Dingo
Duaringa
Gindie
Leura
Marlborough
Ogmore
Yeppoon
Emu Park
Keppel B.
Rockhampton
Westwood
Mt Morgan
C. Manifold
C. Capricorn
Curtis I.
Facing I.
Gladstone
Capricorn Group
Bunker Group
Capricorn Channel
Tropic of Capricorn
Curtis Channel
Diamantina Lakes
Davenport Downs
Connemara
Westland
Warbreccan
Isisford
Yalleroi
Stonehenge
Blackall
Springsure
Rolleston
Northampton Downs
Mantuan Downs
L. Maraboon
Emerald
Comet
Woorabinda
Baralaba
Jambin
Callide
Biloela
Banana
Thangool
Moura
Calliope
Boyne
Bororen
Palparara
Jundah
Emmet
Yaraka
Lorne
Tambo
Carwell
Currawilla
Windorah
Listowel Downs
Warrego Ra.
Buckland Tableland
Consuelo
Expedition Range
Bauhinia Downs
Theodore
Dawson
Monto
Rosedale
Bundaberg
Bargara
Hervey B.
Sandy Cape
Fraser I. Nat. Park
Fraser I.
Hervey Bay
Childers
Gin Gin
Wallaville
Mt Perry
Eidsvold
Gayndah
Mundubbera
Biggenden
Howard
Maryborough
Tiaro
Tanbar
Thunda
Caldervale
Carnarvon Nat. Park
Carnarvon Ra.
Nive Downs
Augathella
Adavale
Ambathala
Thylungra
Langlo Crossing
L. Yamma Yamma (Mackillop)
Kyabra
Mt Howitt
Eromanga
Quilpie
Cheepie
Charleville
Westgate
Morven
Mungallala
Mitchell
Roma
Wallumbilla
Injune
Eurombah
Taroom
Hawkwood
Wandoan
Proston
Goomeri
Kilkivan
Gympie
Wide B.
Double Island Pt
Durham Downs
Cowley
Yarronvale
Cooladdi
Muckadilla
Jackson
Miles
Chinchilla
Wondai
Kingaroy
Murgon
Tewantin
Noosa
Nambour
Maroochydore
Caloundra
Cooroy
Toompine
Tobermory
Humeburn
Lussvale
Boatman
Surat
Condamine
Warra
Jandowae
Mt Mowbullan
Bell
Yarraman
Kilcoy
Caboolture
Moreton B.
Moreton I.
Nockatunga
Noccundra
McGregor Ra.
Grey Range
Dundoo
Tilbooroo
Coongoola
Glenmorgan
Meandarra
Tara
Dalby
Oakey
Crows Nest
Esk
Cooyar
Thargomindah
Dynevor Downs
Bingara
Eulo
Bindle
Moonie
Cecil Plains
Toowoomba
Gatton
Laidley
Ipswich
Redcliffe
Brisbane
N. Stradbroke I.
Bulloo Downs
Bulloo L.
Cunnamulla
Murra Murra
Bollon
Bindebango
St George
Beardmore Res.
Darling Downs
Flinton
Pittsworth
Millmerran
Clifton
Allora
Boonah
Beaudesert
Beenleigh
Gold Coast
Murwillumbah
Caiwarro
Bundaleer
Dirranbandi
Nindigully
Talwood
Toobeah
Goondiwindi
Inglewood
Warwick
Killarney
Woodenbong
Mt Roberts
Lamington Nat. Park
McPherson Ra.
Cariapundy Swamp
Hungerford
Sturt Nat. Park
Cardenyabba
Hebel
Thallon
Mungindi
New Angledool
Boomi
Boggabilla
Yelarbon
Stanthorpe
Texas
Wallangarra
Tabulam
Tenterfield
Yetman
Bonshaw
Croppa Cr.
Garah
Gil Gil Cr.
Osprey Reef
Shark Reef
Bougainville Reef
Diane Bank
Holmes Reef
Willis Group
Magdelaine Cays
Flora Reef
Herald Cays
S. West I.
Chilcott I.
Coringa Is
Flinders Reefs
Diamond Islets
Tregosse Islets & Reefs
Turtle I.
Lihou Reef & Cays
Abington Reef
Flinders Passage
Marion Reef
Hook Rf
Bell Cay
Swain Reefs
Frederick Reef
Saumarez Reef
F
G
H
E
1
2
3
4
5
144°
148°
152°
12°
16°
20°
24°
28°
1:6 000 000
0 40 80 120 160 200 MILES
0 40 80 120 160 200 240 280 320 KM

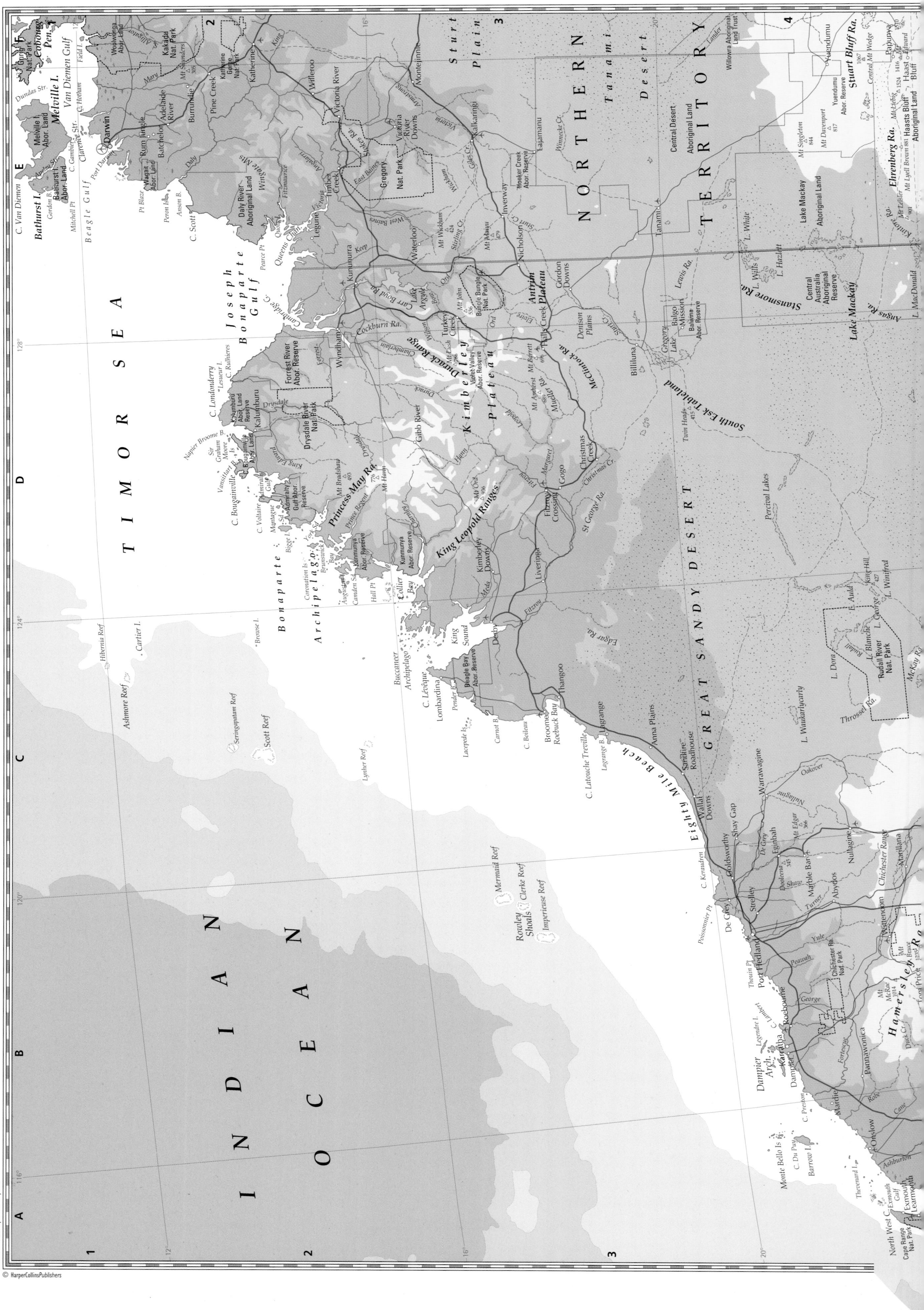
TIMOR SEA
INDIAN OCEAN
Joseph Bonaparte Gulf
Bonaparte Archipelago
Kimberley Plateau
King Leopold Ranges
Durack Range
Princess May Ra.
GREAT SANDY DESERT
Eighty Mile Beach
NORTHERN TERRITORY
Tanami Desert
Sturt Plain
Lake Mackay
Darwin
Melville I.
Bathurst I.
Van Diemen Gulf
Wyndham
Kununurra
Derby
Broome
Port Hedland
Dampier
King Sound
Rowley Shoals
Hamersley Ra.
Antrim Plateau
South Esk Tableland

METRES	FEET
6000	19686
5000	16409
4000	13124
3000	9843
2000	6562
1000	3281
500	1640
200	656
SEA	LEVEL
200	656
2000	6562
4000	13124
6000	19686

Lambert Azimuthal Equal Area Projection

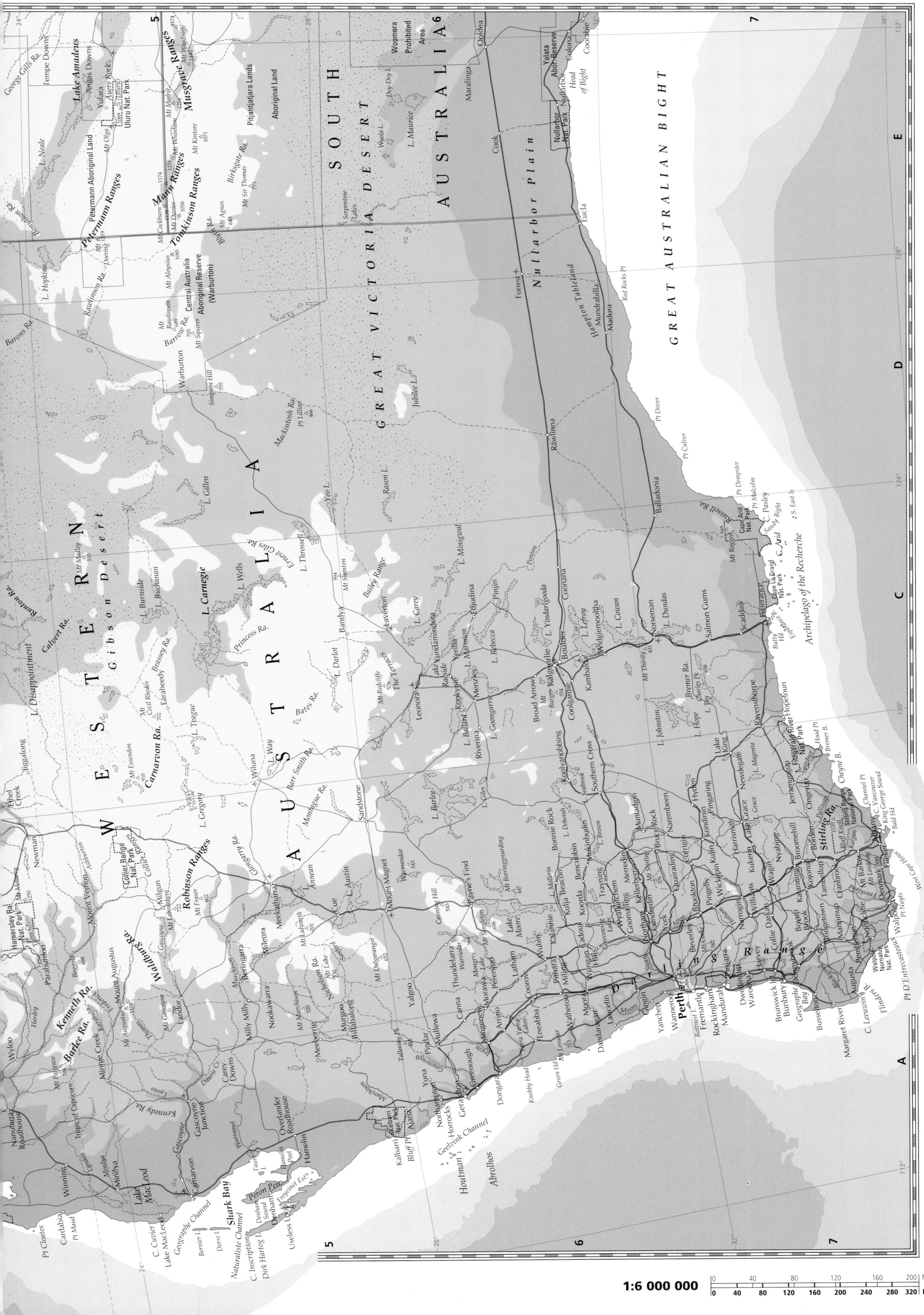
WESTERN AUSTRALIA
SOUTH AUSTRALIA
GREAT VICTORIA DESERT
Gibson Desert
Nullarbor Plain
GREAT AUSTRALIAN BIGHT
Archipelago of the Recherche
Perth
Fremantle
Rockingham
Mandurah
Bunbury
Busselton
Albany
Esperance
Kalgoorlie
Coolgardie
Norseman
Geraldton
Carnarvon
Wiluna
Meekatharra
Cue
Mount Magnet
Leonora
Laverton
Warburton
Eucla
Balladonia
Madura
Cook
Forrest
Rawlinna
Maralinga
Ooldea
Yulara
Uluru Nat. Park
Lake Amadeus
Petermann Ranges
Musgrave Ranges
Mann Ranges
Tomkinson Ranges
Robinson Ranges
Kenneth Ra.
Barlee Ra.
Carnarvon Ra.
Stirling Ra.
Darling Range
Shark Bay
Houtman Abrolhos
Geelvink Channel
Hampton Tableland
L. Disappointment
L. Carnegie
L. Barlee
L. Moore
Lake MacLeod
Pitjantjatjara Lands
Aboriginal Land
Central Australia Aboriginal Reserve (Warburton)
Woomera Prohibited Area
Nullarbor Nat. Park
Yalata Abor. Reserve
Head of Bight
Pt D'Entrecasteaux
C. Leeuwin
C. Naturaliste
Dirk Hartog I.
C. Inscription
Kalbarri Nat. Park
Cape Arid Nat. Park
Cape Le Grand Nat. Park
Fitzgerald River Nat. Park
Stirling Range National Park
Collier Range Nat. Park
Hamersley Ra. Nat. Park
Newman
Mount Vernon
Mount Augustus
Gascoyne Junction
Overlander Roadhouse
Hamelin
Denham
Nanutarra Roadhouse
Tropic of Capricorn

1:6 000 000

0 40 80 120 160 200 MILES
0 40 80 120 160 200 240 280 320 KM

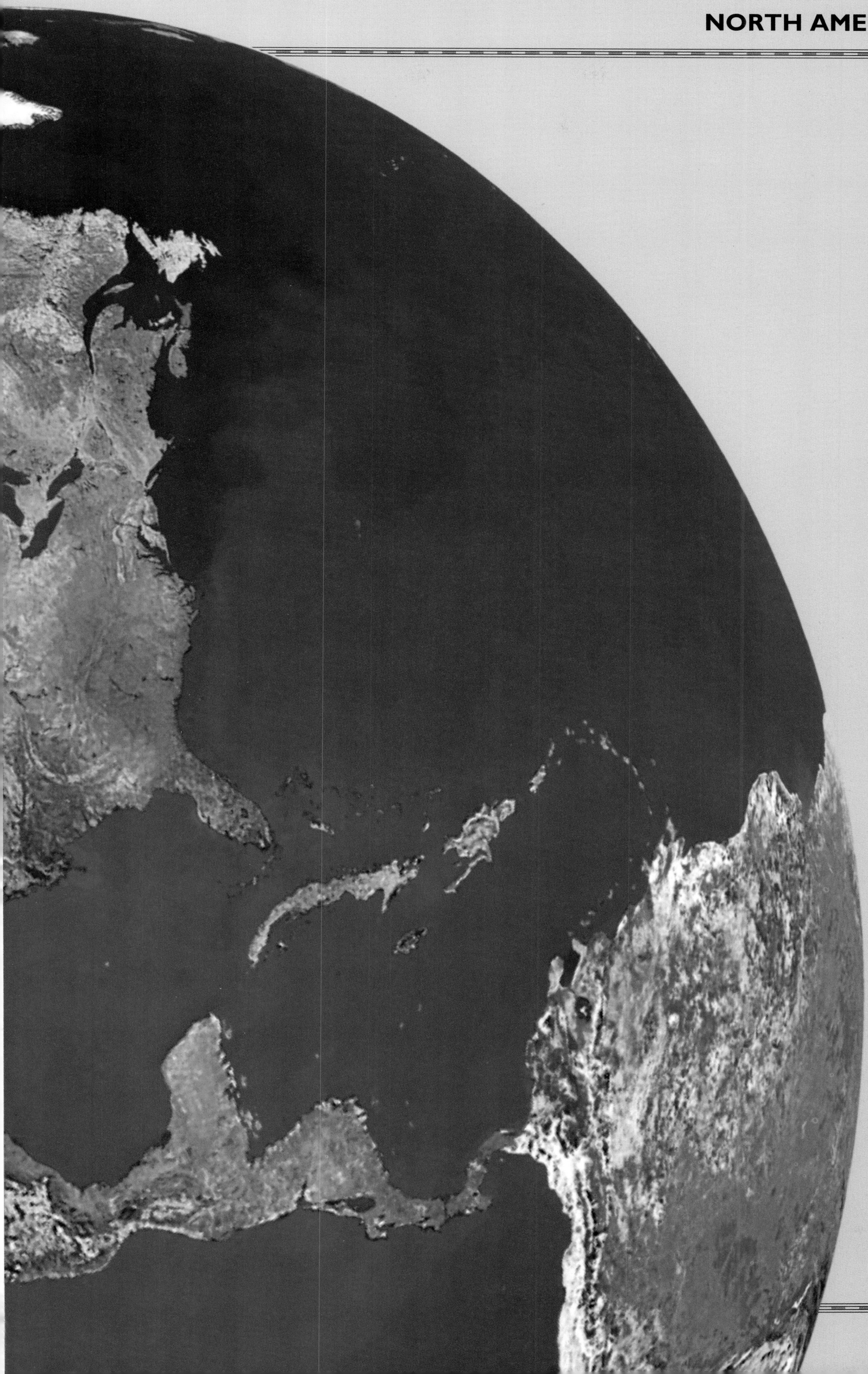

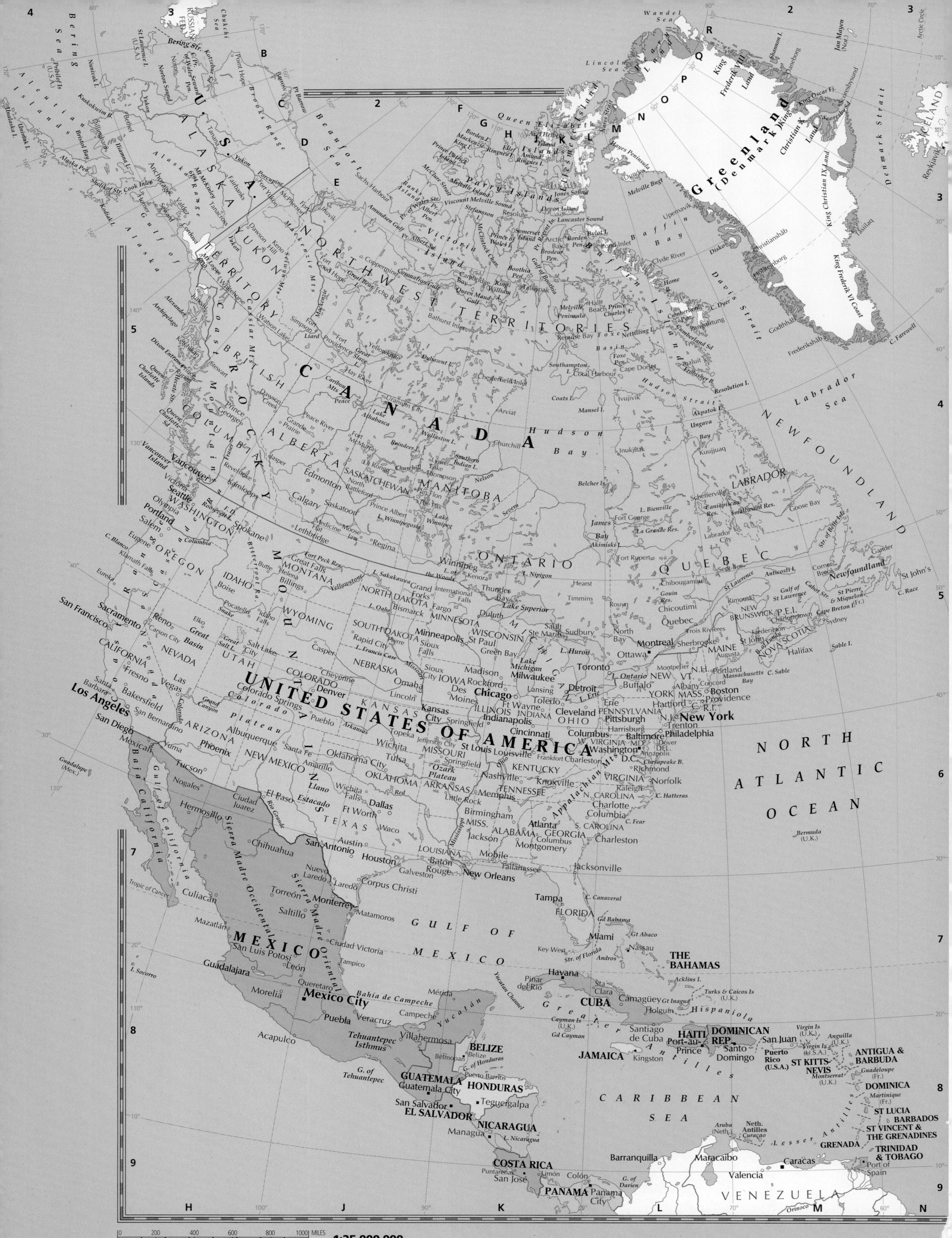

0 200 400 600 800 1000 MILES
0 200 400 600 800 1000 1200 1400 1600 KM

1:25 000 000

COUNTRY	AREA sqml	AREA sqkm	POPULATION total	density per sqml	density per sqkm	Form of Government	Capital City	MAIN LANGUAGES	MAIN RELIGIONS	CURRENCY
ANGUILLA	60	155	8 000	*134*	*52*	UK territory	The Valley	English	Protestant, RC	E. Carib. dollar
ANTIGUA & BARBUDA	171	442	65 000	*381*	*147*	monarchy	St John's	English, Creole	Protestant, RC	E. Carib. dollar
THE BAHAMAS	5 382	13 939	272 000	*51*	*20*	monarchy	Nassau	English, Creole, French Creole	Protestant, RC	Dollar
BARBADOS	166	430	264 000	*1590*	*614*	monarchy	Bridgetown	English, Creole (Bajan)	Protestant, RC	Dollar
BELIZE	8 867	22 965	211 000	*24*	*9*	monarchy	Belmopan	English, Creole, Spanish, Mayan	RC, Protestant, Hindu	Dollar
BERMUDA	21	54	63 000	*3022*	*1167*	UK territory	Hamilton	English	Protestant, RC	Dollar
CANADA	3 849 674	9 970 610	29 251 000	*8*	*3*	federation	Ottawa	English, French, Amerindian languages, Inuktitut (Eskimo)	RC, Protestant, Greek Orthodox, Jewish	Dollar
CAYMAN ISLANDS	100	259	31 000	*310*	*120*	UK territory	George Town	English	Protestant, RC	Dollar
COSTA RICA	19 730	51 100	3 071 000	*156*	*60*	republic	San José	Spanish	RC, Protestant	Colón
CUBA	42 803	110 860	10 960 000	*256*	*99*	republic	Havana	Spanish	RC, Protestant	Peso
DOMINICA	290	750	71 000	*245*	*95*	republic	Roseau	English, French Creole	RC, Protestant	E. Carib. dollar,
DOMINICAN REPUBLIC	18 704	48 442	7 769 000	*415*	*160*	republic	Santo Domingo	Spanish, French Creole	RC, Protestant	Peso
EL SALVADOR	8 124	21 041	5 641 000	*694*	*268*	republic	San Salvador	Spanish	RC, Protestant	Colón
GREENLAND	840 004	2 175 600	55 000			Danish territory	Nuuk	Greenlandic, Danish	Protestant	Danish krone
GRENADA	146	378	92 000	*630*	*243*	monarchy	St George's	English, Creole	RC, Protestant	E. Carib. dollar
GUADELOUPE	687	1 780	421 000	*613*	*237*	French territory	Basse-Terre	French, French Creole	RC, Hindu	French franc
GUATEMALA	42 043	108 890	10 322 000	*246*	*95*	republic	Guatemala City	Spanish, Mayan languages	RC, Protestant	Quetzal
HAITI	10 714	27 750	7 041 000	*657*	*254*	republic	Port-au-Prince	French, French Creole	RC, Protestant, Voodoo	Gourde
HONDURAS	43 277	112 088	5 770 000	*133*	*51*	republic	Tegucigalpa	Spanish, Amerindian languages	RC, Protestant	Lempira
JAMAICA	4 244	10 991	2 429 000	*572*	*221*	monarchy	Kingston	English, Creole	Protestant, RC, Rastafarian	Dollar
MARTINIQUE	417	1 079	375 000	*900*	*348*	French territory	Fort-de-France	French, French Creole	RC, Protestant, Hindu, traditional beliefs	French franc
MEXICO	761 604	1 972 545	93 008 000	*122*	*47*	republic	Mexico City	Spanish, many Amerindian languages	RC, Protestant	Peso
MONTSERRAT	39	100	11 000	*285*	*110*	UK territory	Plymouth	English	Protestant, RC	E. Carib. dollar
NETH. ANTILLES (North)	26	68	35 240	*1342*	*518*	Neth. territory		Dutch, Papiamento, English	RC, Protestant	Guilder
NICARAGUA	50 193	130 000	4 401 000	*88*	*34*	republic	Managua	Spanish, Amerindian languages	RC, Protestant	Córdoba
PANAMA	29 762	77 082	2 583 000	*87*	*34*	republic	Panama City	Spanish, English Creole, Amerindian languages	RC, Protestant, Sunni Muslim, Baha'i	Balboa
PUERTO RICO	3 515	9 104	3 686 000	*1049*	*405*	US territory	San Juan	Spanish, English	RC, Protestant	US dollar
ST KITTS & NEVIS	101	261	41 000	*407*	*157*	monarchy	Basseterre	English, Creole	Protestant, RC	E. Carib. dollar
ST LUCIA	238	616	141 000	*593*	*229*	monarchy	Castries	English, French Creole	RC, Protestant	E. Carib. dollar
ST PIERRE & MIQUELON	93	242	6 000	*64*	*25*	French territory	St-Pierre	French	RC	French franc
ST VINCENT & THE GRENADINES	150	389	111 000	*739*	*285*	monarchy	Kingstown	English, Creole	Protestant, RC	E. Carib. dollar
TURKS & CAICOS IS.	166	430	14 000	*84*	*33*	UK territory	Grand Turk	English	Protestant	US dollar
USA	3 787 425	9 809 386	260 660 000	*69*	*27*	republic	Washington	English, Spanish, Amerindian languages	Protestant, RC, Sunni Muslim, Jewish, Mormon	Dollar
VIRGIN ISLANDS (UK)	59	153	18 000	*305*	*118*	UK territory	Road Town	English	Protestant, RC	US dollar
VIRGIN ISLANDS (USA)	136	352	104 000	*765*	*295*	US territory	Charlotte Amalie	English, Spanish	Protestant, RC	US dollar

OECD

see page 7 for information

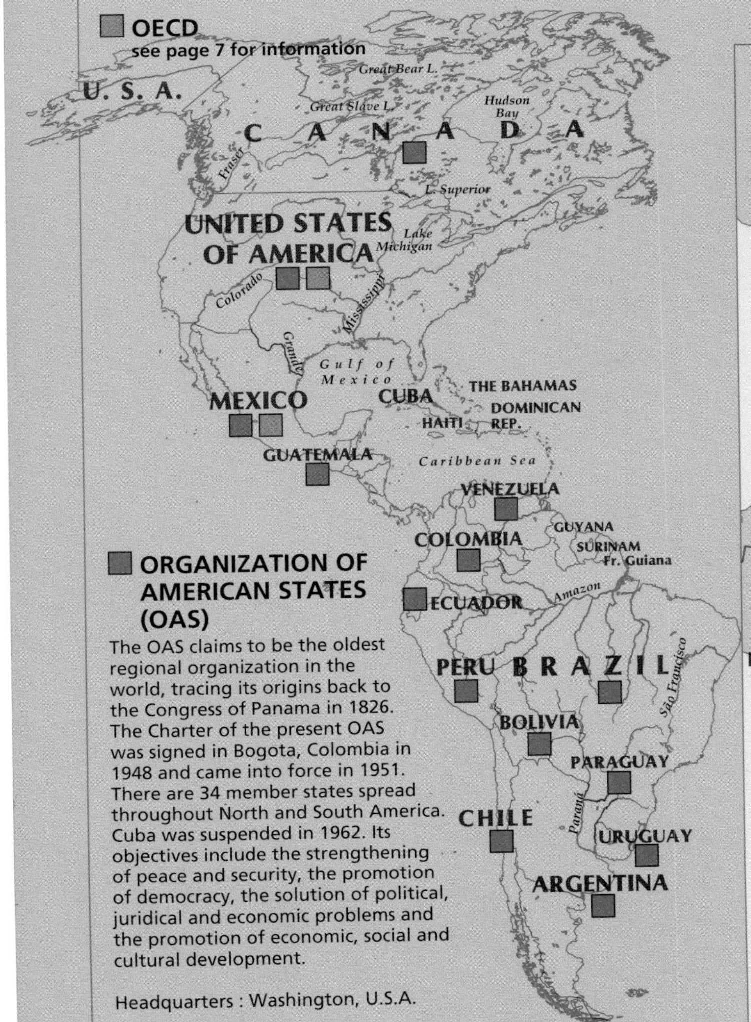

ORGANIZATION OF AMERICAN STATES (OAS)

The OAS claims to be the oldest regional organization in the world, tracing its origins back to the Congress of Panama in 1826. The Charter of the present OAS was signed in Bogota, Colombia in 1948 and came into force in 1951. There are 34 member states spread throughout North and South America. Cuba was suspended in 1962. Its objectives include the strengthening of peace and security, the promotion of democracy, the solution of political, juridical and economic problems and the promotion of economic, social and cultural development.

Headquarters : Washington, U.S.A.

CARIBBEAN COMMUNITY (CARICOM)

Following a series of initiatives in the 1960's to promote Caribbean regioinal co-operation CARICOM was established in 1973. The original members were Barbados, Guyana, Jamaica and Trindad and Tobago; in May 1974, Belize, Dominica, Grenada, Montserrat, St Lucia and St Vincent joined followed by Antigua and St Kitts-Nevis in August 1974, the Bahamas in 1984 and Surinam in 1995. The objectives of CARICOM are to foster co-operation, co-ordinate foreign policy, and to formulate and carry out common policies on health, education and culture, communications and industrial relations.

Headquarters: Georgetown, Guyana

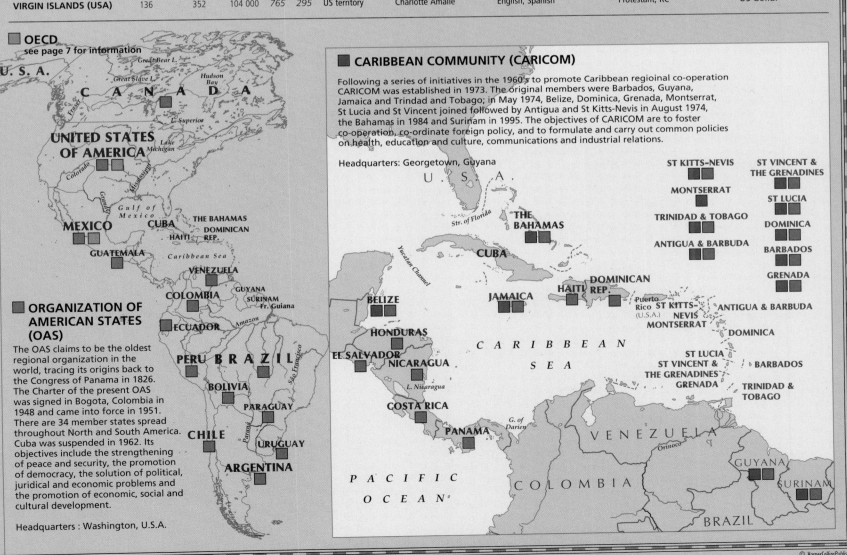

© HarperCollinsPublishers

KEY TO MAPS

- Built-up areas
- Park or open space
- Open water
- Important building
- Cemetery
- Lake
- River or canal
- Main road
- Road
- Other road
- Railway
- Airport

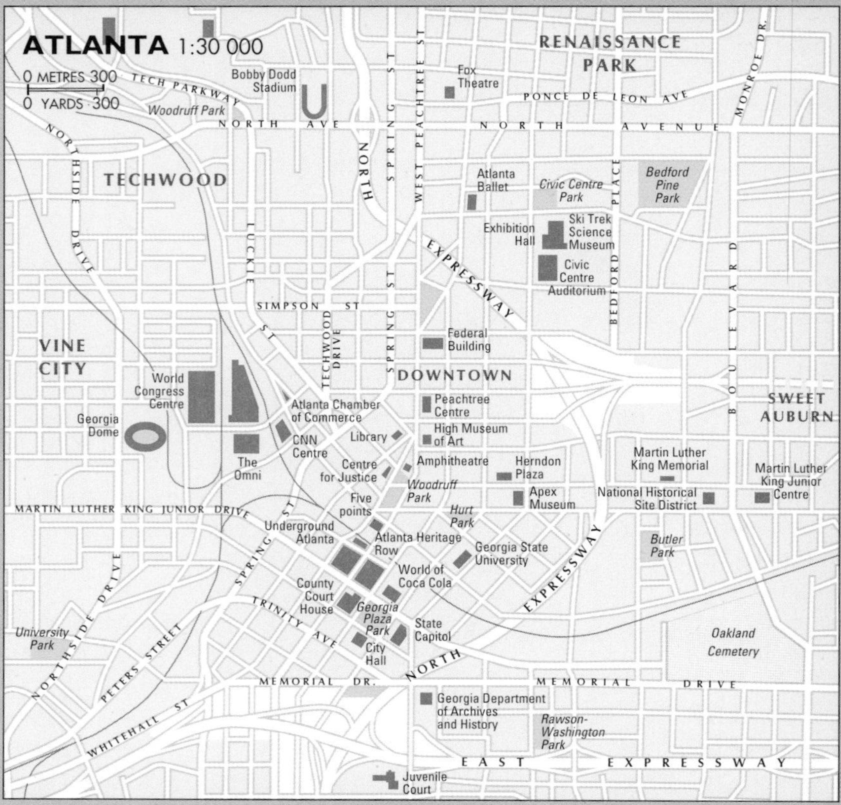

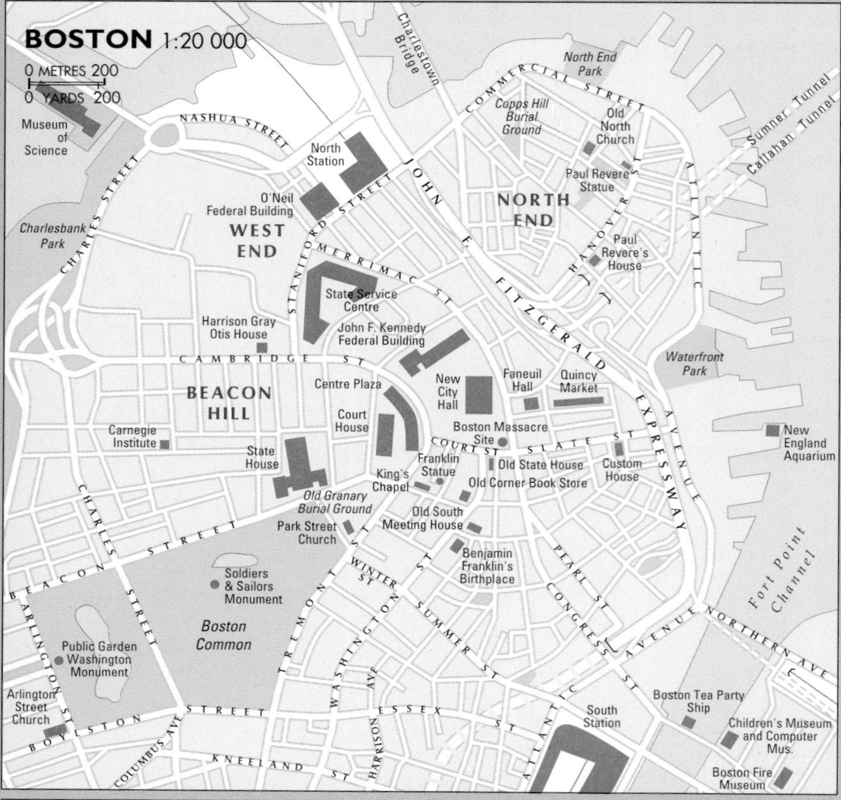

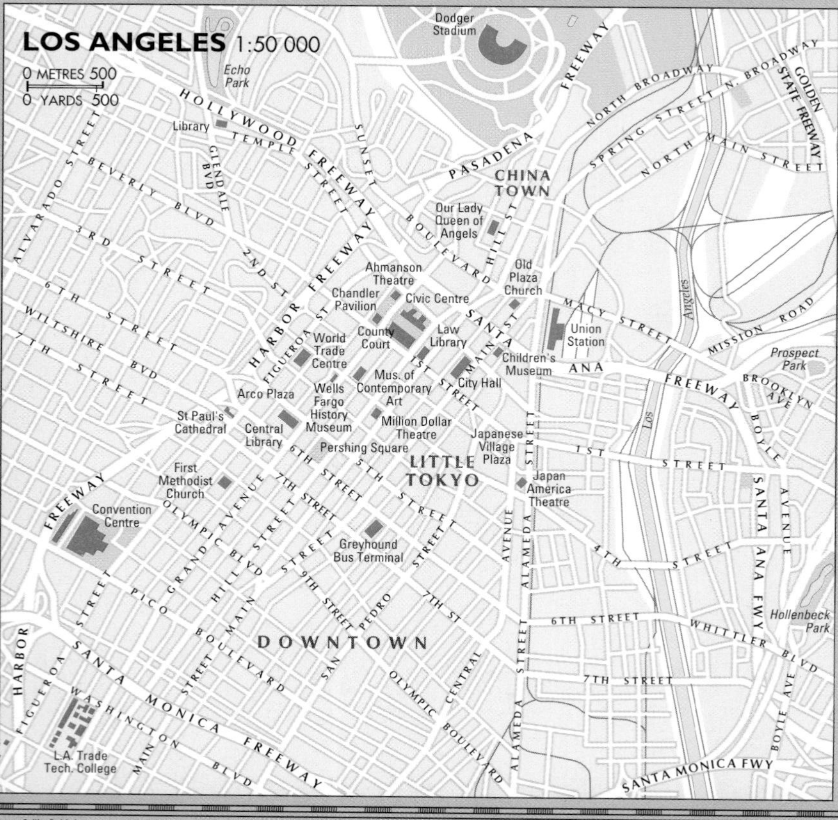

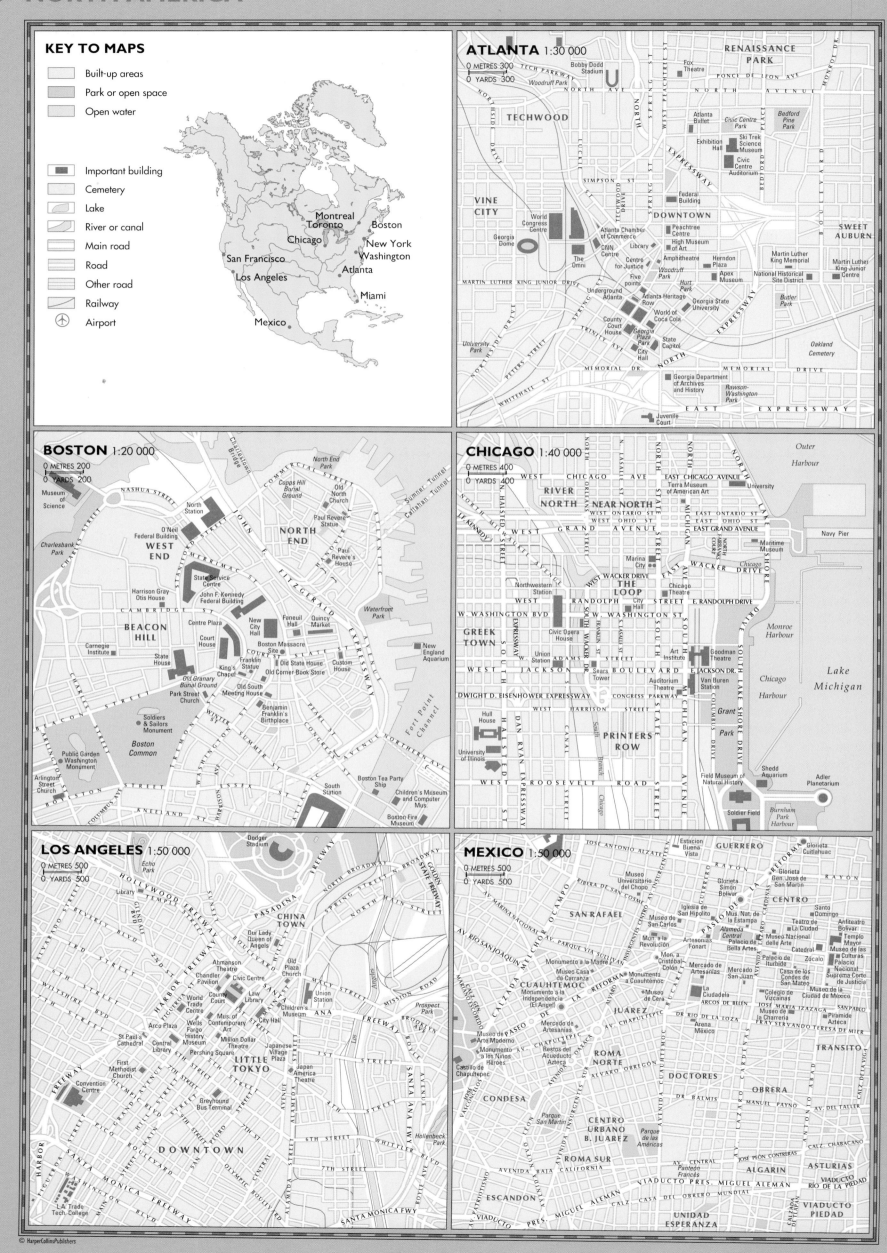

MIAMI 1:30 000
0 METRES 300
0 YARDS 300
South Florida Centre
N.W. 20TH STREET
NE 20TH ST
Museum of Modern Art
Biscayne Park
City Cemetery
Margaret Pace Park
Williams Park
Highland Park
Civic Centre Area
Dorsey Park
International Fine Arts College
VENETIAN CAUSEWAY
DOLPHIN EXPRESSWAY
Gibson Park
McARTHUR CAUSEWAY
Bicentennial Park
City Yatch Basin
Reeves Park
Miami Arena
Freedom Tower
N.W. 7TH ST
LITTLE HAVANA
Henderson Park
Old Fort Dallas
Lummus Park
Courthouse
Bayfront Park
HMS Bounty
Bayside Amphitheatre
Torch of Friendship
Christopher Columbus Mon.
Metro-Dade Cultural Centre
Miami Memorial Public Library
W. FLAGLER STREET
E. FLAGLER ST
S.W. 1ST STREET
S.E. 1ST ST
Gusman Centre
World Trade Centre
2ND ST
James Knight Convention Centre
Riverside Park
José Martí Riverfront Park
Brickell Point
NORTH - SOUTH EXPRESSWAY
NORTH MIAMI AVENUE
BISCAYNE BOULEVARD

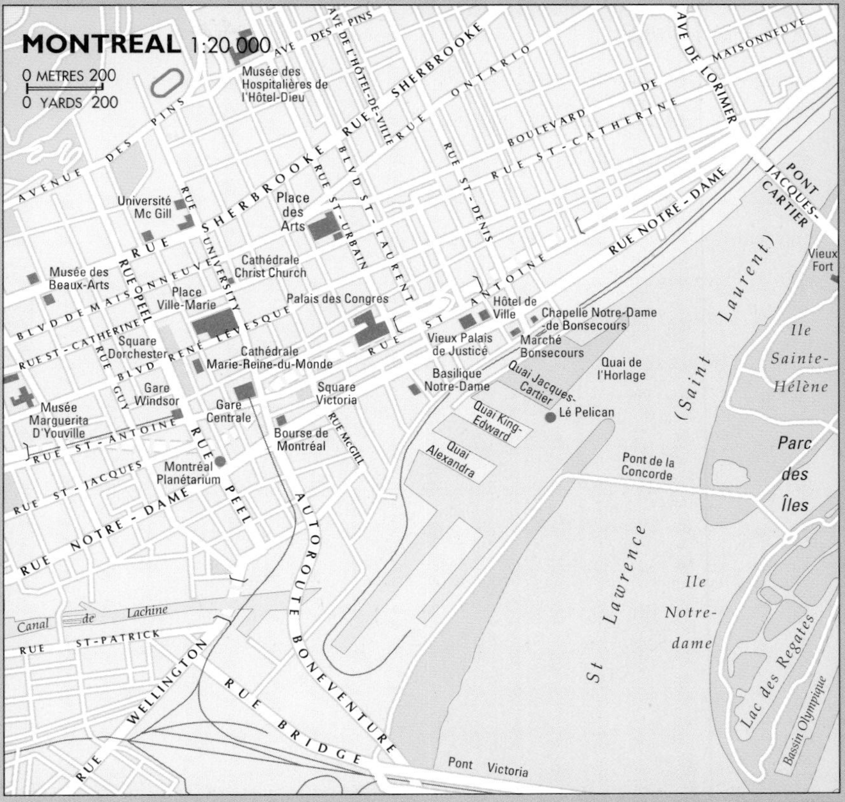
MONTREAL 1:20 000
0 METRES 200
0 YARDS 200
Musée des Hospitalières de l'Hôtel-Dieu
AVENUE DES PINS
RUE SHERBROOKE
RUE ONTARIO
BOULEVARD DE MAISONNEUVE
RUE STE-CATHERINE
RUE NOTRE-DAME
PONT JACQUES-CARTIER
AVE DE LORIMER
Université Mc Gill
Place des Arts
Musée des Beaux-Arts
Cathédrale Christ Church
Place Ville-Marie
Palais des Congrès
Hôtel de Ville
Chapelle Notre-Dame -de Bonsecours
Marché Bonsecours
Vieux Palais de Justice
Basilique Notre-Dame
Square Dorchester
Cathédrale Marie-Reine-du-Monde
Gare Windsor
Gare Centrale
Square Victoria
Bourse de Montréal
Musée Marguerita D'Youville
Montréal Planétarium
Quai Jacques-Cartier
Quai King-Edward
Quai Alexandra
Quai de l'Horlage
Lé Pelican
Pont de la Concorde
Vieux Fort
Ile Sainte-Hélène
Parc des Îles
Ile Notre-dame
St Lawrence (Saint Laurent)
Lac des Regates
Bassin Olympique
RUE ST-ANTOINE
RUE ST-JACQUES
AUTOROUTE BONEVENTURE
Canal de Lachine
RUE ST-PATRICK
RUE WELLINGTON
RUE BRIDGE
Pont Victoria

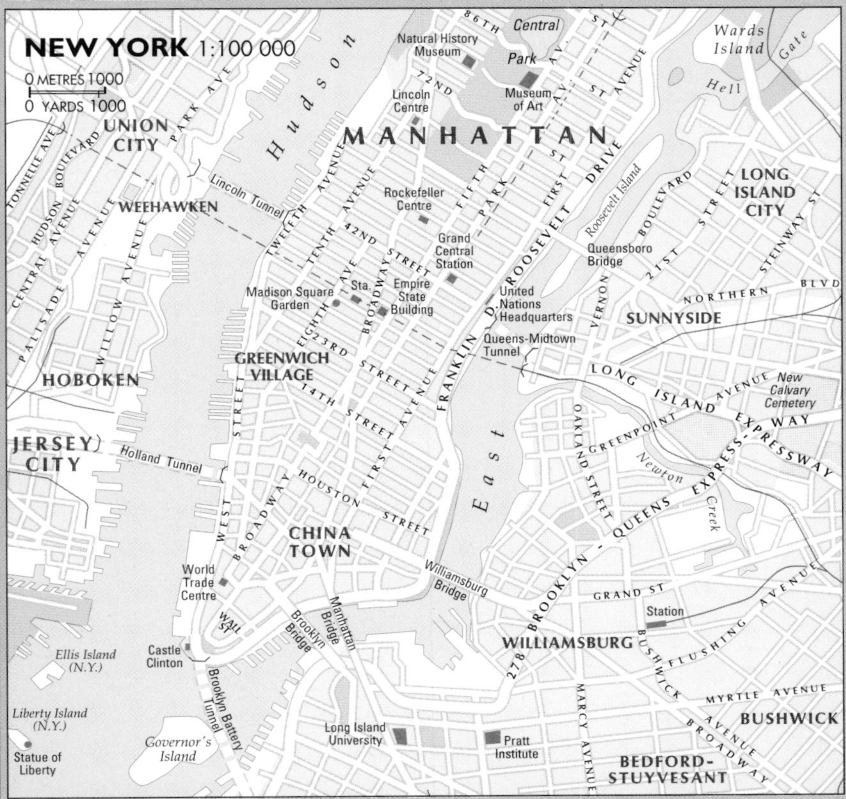
NEW YORK 1:100 000
0 METRES 1000
0 YARDS 1000
Natural History Museum
Central Park
Wards Island
Hell Gate
Museum of Art
Lincoln Centre
Hudson
UNION CITY
MANHATTAN
WEEHAWKEN
Lincoln Tunnel
Rockefeller Centre
Grand Central Station
LONG ISLAND CITY
Roosevelt Island
Queensboro Bridge
Madison Square Garden
Empire State Building
United Nations Headquarters
Queens-Midtown Tunnel
SUNNYSIDE
HOBOKEN
GREENWICH VILLAGE
New Calvary Cemetery
LONG ISLAND EXPRESSWAY
JERSEY CITY
Holland Tunnel
East
Newton Creek
CHINA TOWN
World Trade Centre
Williamsburg Bridge
BROOKLYN - QUEENS EXPRESSWAY
Manhattan Bridge
Brooklyn Bridge
Station
WILLIAMSBURG
Ellis Island (N.Y.)
Castle Clinton
Brooklyn Battery Tunnel
Liberty Island (N.Y.)
Statue of Liberty
Governor's Island
Long Island University
Pratt Institute
BUSHWICK
BEDFORD-STUYVESANT

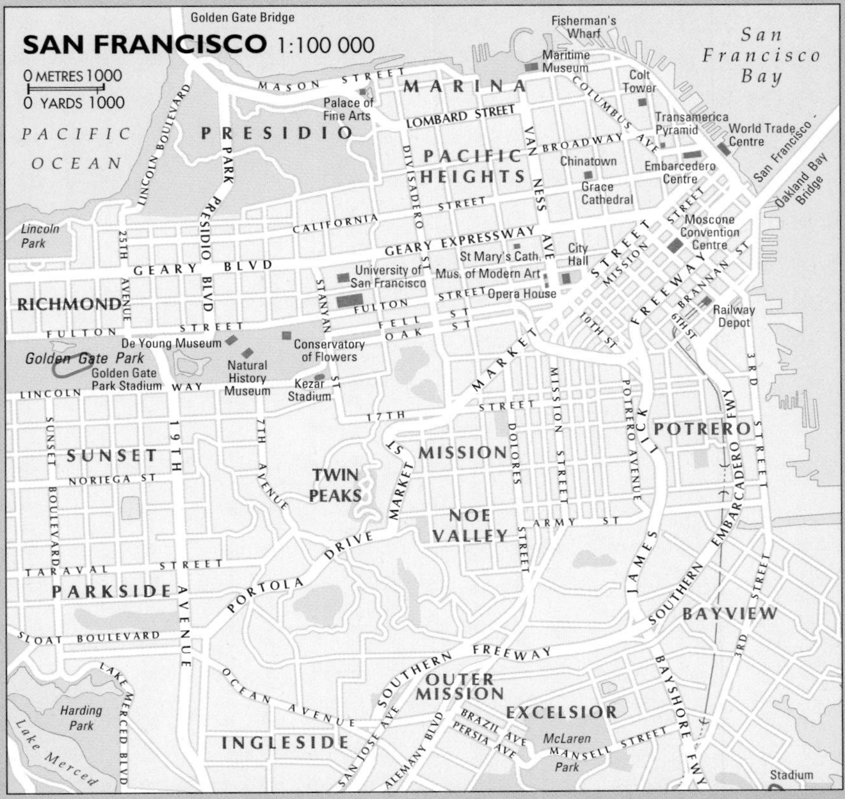
SAN FRANCISCO 1:100 000
0 METRES 1000
0 YARDS 1000
Golden Gate Bridge
Fisherman's Wharf
Maritime Museum
San Francisco Bay
Coit Tower
MARINA
PACIFIC OCEAN
PRESIDIO
Palace of Fine Arts
Transamerica Pyramid
World Trade Centre
Chinatown
Embarcadero Centre
PACIFIC HEIGHTS
Grace Cathedral
San Francisco - Oakland Bay Bridge
Lincoln Park
GEARY BLVD
St Mary's Cath
City Hall
Moscone Convention Centre
University of San Francisco
Mus. of Modern Art
Opera House
RICHMOND
Railway Depot
De Young Museum
Conservatory of Flowers
Golden Gate Park
Golden Gate Park Stadium
Natural History Museum
Kezar Stadium
SUNSET
MISSION
POTRERO
TWIN PEAKS
NOE VALLEY
PARKSIDE
BAYVIEW
OUTER MISSION
EXCELSIOR
Harding Park
Lake Merced
INGLESIDE
McLaren Park
Stadium

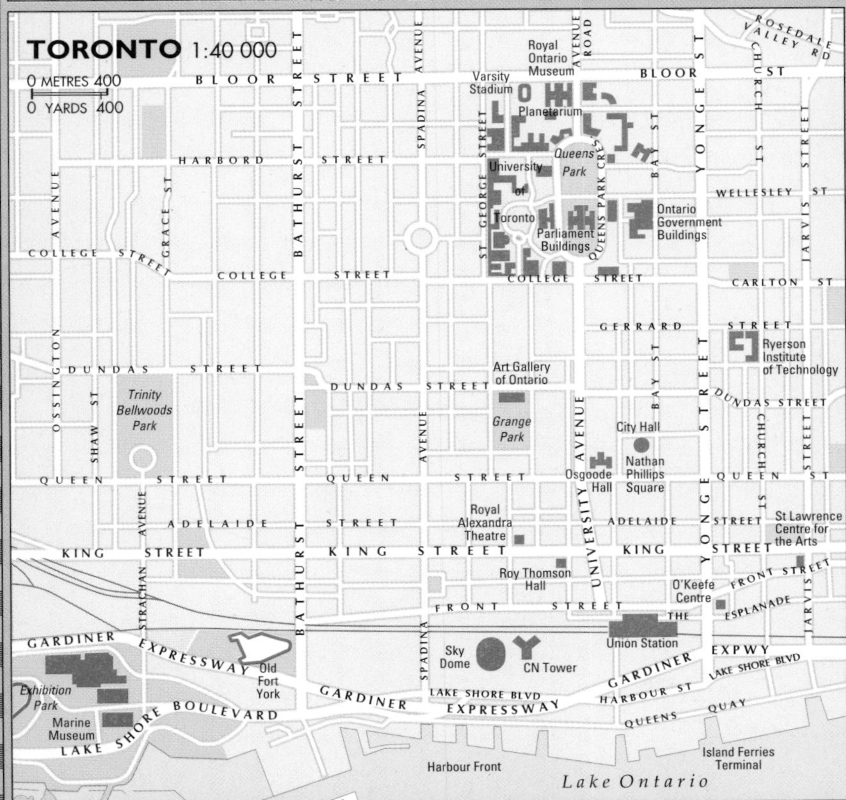
TORONTO 1:40 000
0 METRES 400
0 YARDS 400
BLOOR STREET
Royal Ontario Museum
Varsity Stadium
Planetarium
HARBORD STREET
Queens Park
University of Toronto
Ontario Government Buildings
Parliament Buildings
COLLEGE STREET
CARLTON ST
GERRARD ST
Ryerson Institute of Technology
DUNDAS STREET
Art Gallery of Ontario
Trinity Bellwoods Park
Grange Park
City Hall
Nathan Phillips Square
Osgoode Hall
QUEEN STREET
Royal Alexandra Theatre
ADELAIDE STREET
St Lawrence Centre for the Arts
KING STREET
Roy Thomson Hall
O'Keefe Centre
FRONT STREET
ESPLANADE
Union Station
Sky Dome
CN Tower
GARDINER EXPRESSWAY
Old Fort York
Exhibition Park
Marine Museum
LAKE SHORE BOULEVARD
HARBOUR ST
QUEENS QUAY
Harbour Front
Island Ferries Terminal
Lake Ontario
BATHURST STREET
SPADINA AVENUE
YONGE ST

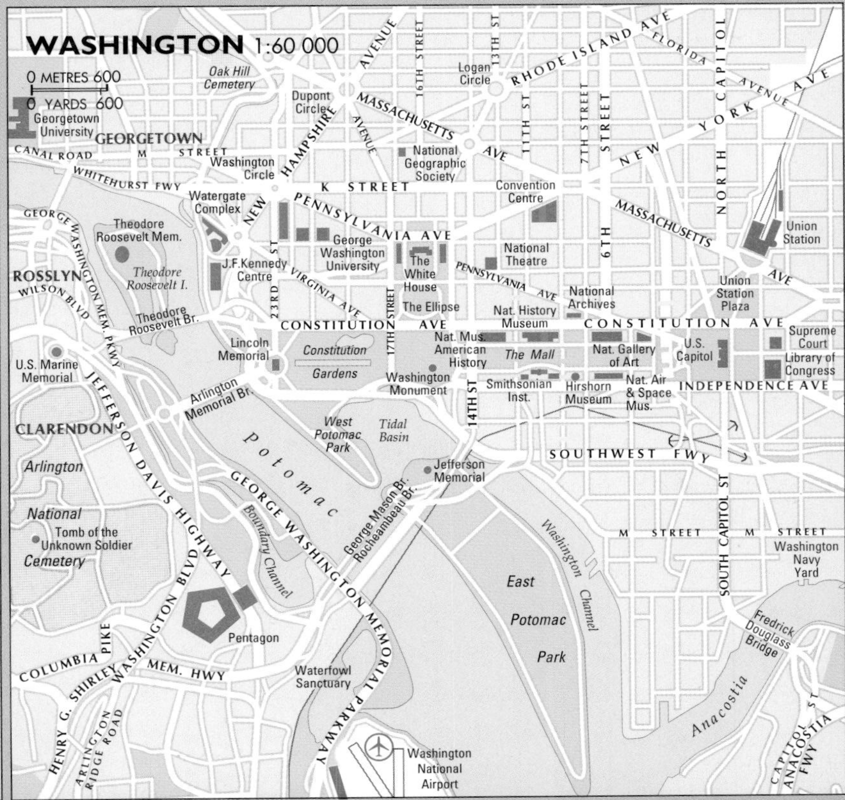
WASHINGTON 1:60 000
0 METRES 600
0 YARDS 600
Oak Hill Cemetery
Logan Circle
RHODE ISLAND AVE
FLORIDA AVENUE
Dupont Circle
Georgetown University
GEORGETOWN
MASSACHUSETTS AVE
National Geographic Society
NEW YORK AVE
Washington Circle
K STREET
Convention Centre
Union Station
Watergate Complex
Theodore Roosevelt Mem.
PENNSYLVANIA AVE
George Washington University
National Theatre
J.F. Kennedy Centre
ROSSLYN
Theodore Roosevelt I.
White House
The Ellipse
National Archives
Union Station Plaza
CONSTITUTION AVE
National History Museum
Supreme Court
Library of Congress
U.S. Marine Memorial
Lincoln Memorial
Constitution Gardens
Nat. Mus. American History
The Mall
Nat. Gallery of Art
U.S. Capitol
Washington Monument
Smithsonian Inst.
Hirshorn Museum
Nat. Air & Space Mus.
INDEPENDENCE AVE
Arlington Memorial Br.
CLARENDON
Arlington
West Potomac Park
Tidal Basin
Potomac
SOUTHWEST FWY
Jefferson Memorial
National Cemetery
Tomb of the Unknown Soldier
JEFFERSON DAVIS HIGHWAY
GEORGE WASHINGTON MEMORIAL PARKWAY
Boundary Channel
East Potomac Park
Washington Channel
M STREET
Washington Navy Yard
Pentagon
Fredrick Douglass Bridge
COLUMBIA PIKE
SHIRLEY MEM. HWY
Waterfowl Sanctuary
Anacostia
Washington National Airport
SOUTH CAPITOL ST

© HarperCollinsPublishers

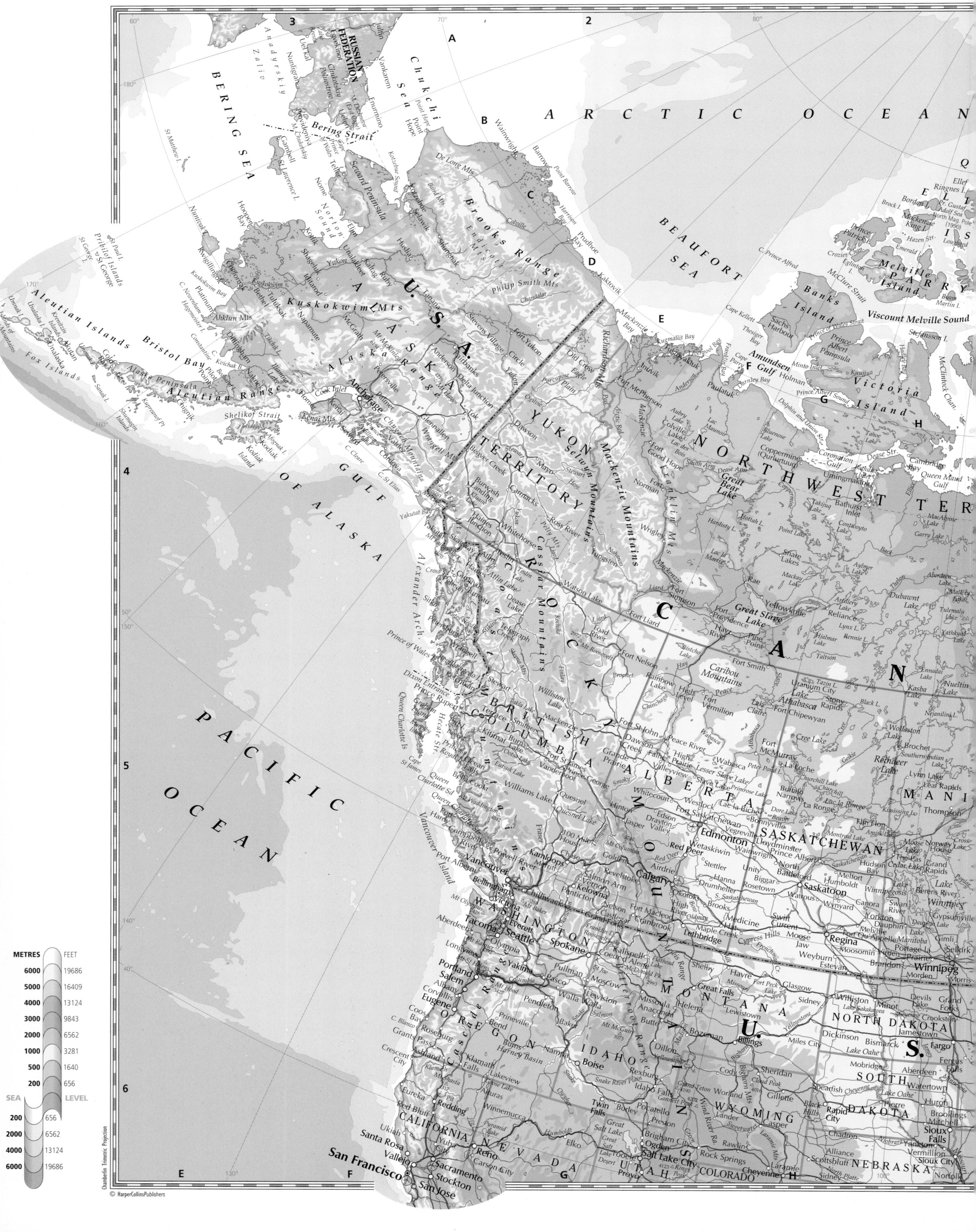
ARCTIC OCEAN
BEAUFORT SEA
Chukchi Sea
BERING SEA
Bering Strait
PACIFIC OCEAN
GULF OF ALASKA
RUSSIAN FEDERATION
U.S.A.
ALASKA
CANADA
YUKON TERRITORY
NORTHWEST TERRITORIES
BRITISH COLUMBIA
ALBERTA
SASKATCHEWAN
WASHINGTON
OREGON
IDAHO
MONTANA
WYOMING
NORTH DAKOTA
SOUTH DAKOTA
NEBRASKA
NEVADA
UTAH
COLORADO
CALIFORNIA
Brooks Range
Alaska Range
Aleutian Range
Aleutian Islands
Kuskokwim Mts
Mackenzie Mountains
Rocky Mountains
Cascade Range
Coast Mountains
Banks Island
Victoria Island
Melville Island
Great Bear Lake
Great Slave Lake
Anchorage
Fairbanks
Whitehorse
Yellowknife
Edmonton
Calgary
Saskatoon
Regina
Winnipeg
Vancouver
Victoria
Seattle
Tacoma
Spokane
Portland
Salem
Eugene
Boise
Billings
Helena
Great Falls
Salt Lake City
Reno
Sacramento
San Francisco
San Jose
METRES
FEET
6000 19686
5000 16409
4000 13124
3000 9843
2000 6562
1000 3281
500 1640
200 656
SEA LEVEL
200 656
2000 6562
4000 13124
6000 19686
Chamberlin Trimetric Projection

© HarperCollinsPublishers

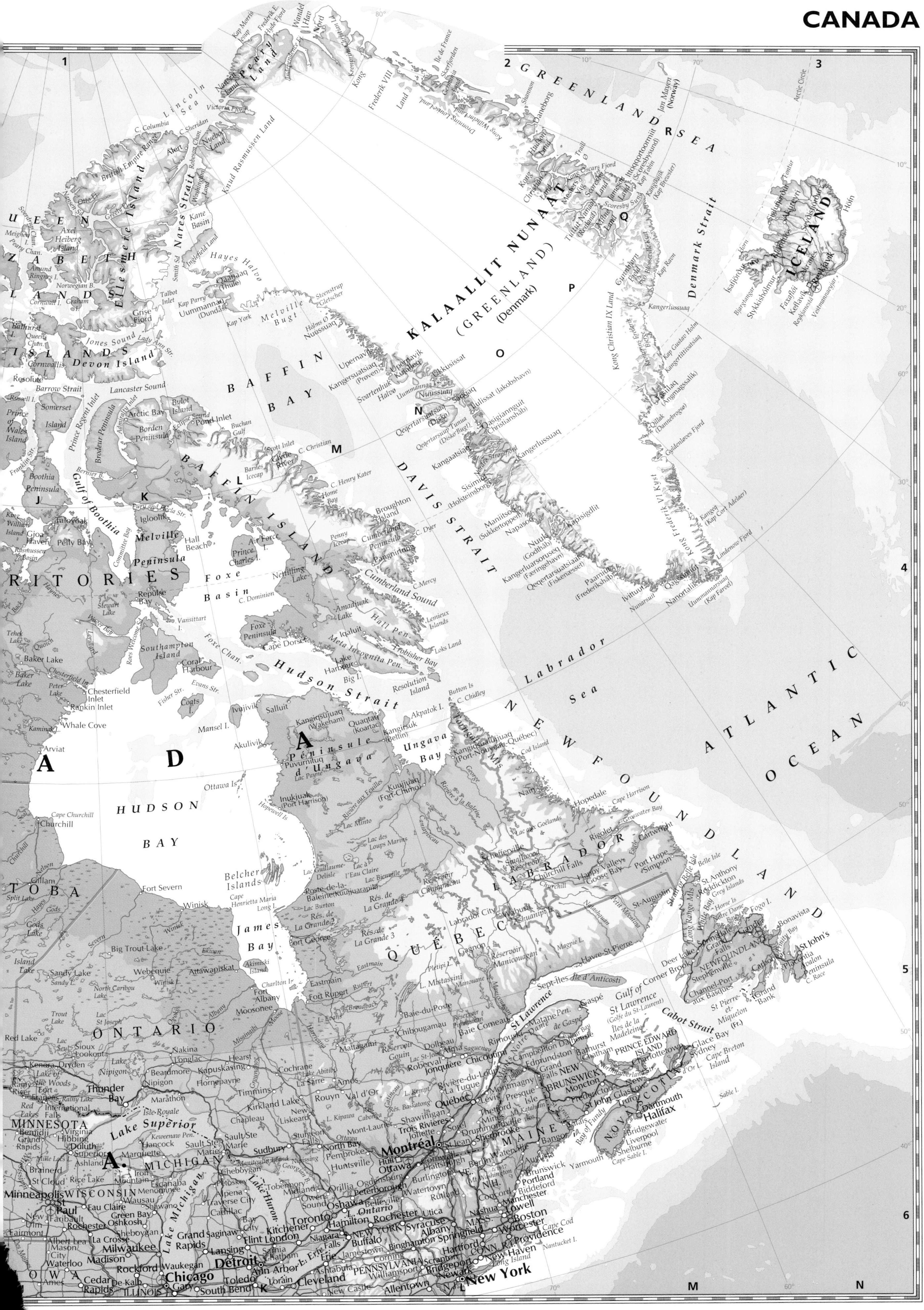

1:13 000 000

0	100	200	300	400	500	MILES

0	100	200	300	400	500	600	700	800	KM

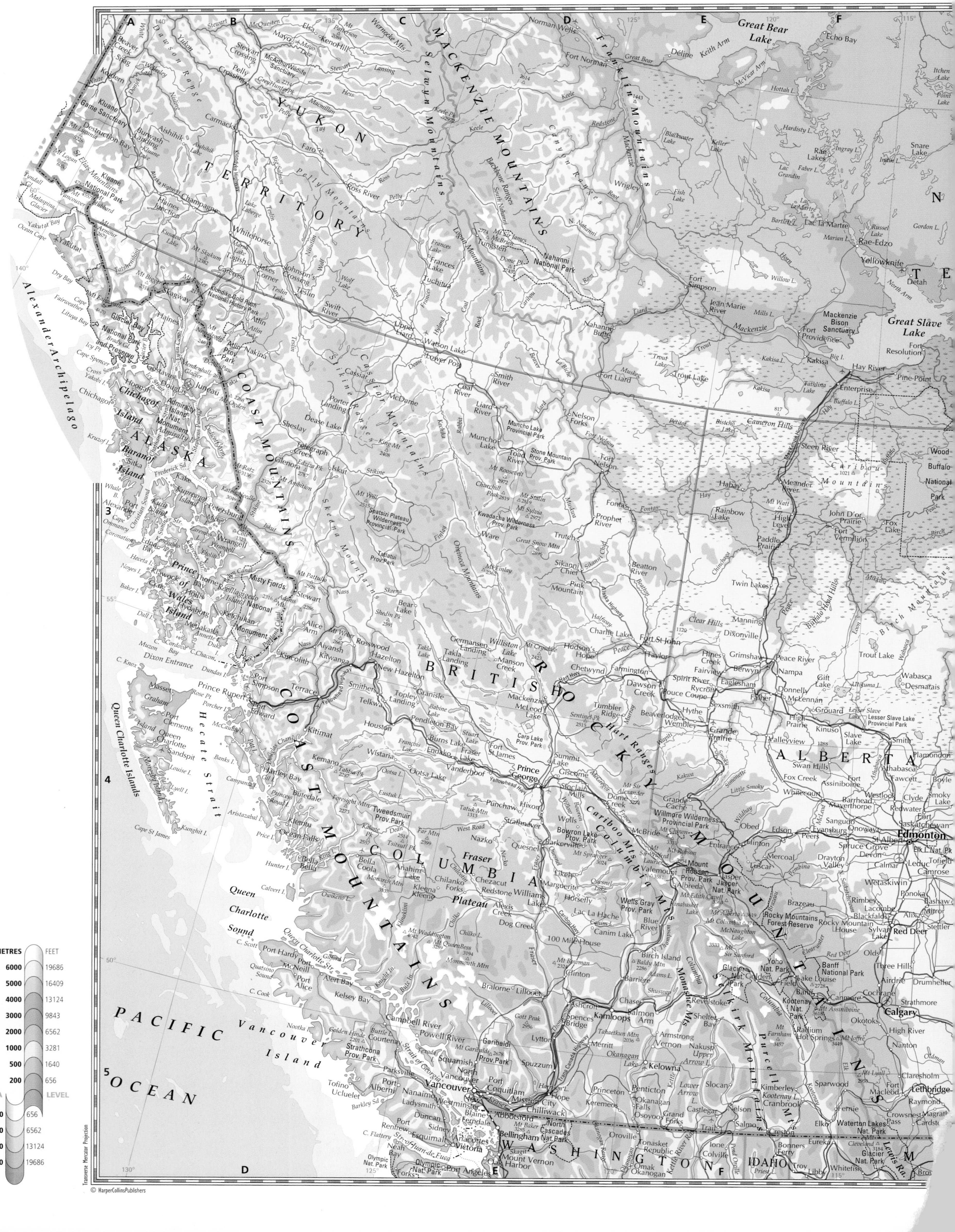
YUKON TERRITORY
MACKENZIE MOUNTAINS
Selwyn Mountains
Franklin Mountains
Great Bear Lake
Great Slave Lake
ALASKA
COAST MOUNTAINS
BRITISH COLUMBIA
ROCKY MOUNTAINS
ALBERTA
Cariboo Mts
Columbia Mts
Monashee Mts
Selkirk Mountains
Purcell Mts
Skeena Mountains
Cassiar Mountains
Fraser Plateau
Hart Ranges
Caribou Mountains
Queen Charlotte Islands
Hecate Strait
Dixon Entrance
Queen Charlotte Sound
Vancouver Island
Strait of Georgia
Alexander Archipelago
PACIFIC OCEAN
WASHINGTON
IDAHO
Whitehorse
Dawson Range
Yellowknife
Fort Simpson
Fort Nelson
Fort St John
Dawson Creek
Prince George
Prince Rupert
Kitimat
Juneau
Skagway
Haines
Sitka
Ketchikan
Wrangell
Petersburg
Yakutat
Watson Lake
Hay River
Peace River
Grande Prairie
Edmonton
Red Deer
Calgary
Lethbridge
Kamloops
Kelowna
Vernon
Penticton
Revelstoke
Vancouver
Victoria
Nanaimo
Bellingham
Port Angeles
Jasper
Banff
Lake Louise
Quesnel
Williams Lake
Prince Rupert
Terrace
Smithers
Hazelton
Port Hardy
Campbell River
Courtenay
Port Alberni
Tofino
Ucluelet
METRES
6000
5000
4000
3000
2000
1000
500
200
SEA
200
2000
4000
6000
FEET
19686
16409
13124
9843
6562
3281
1640
656
LEVEL
656
6562
13124
19686
A
B
C
D
E
F
3
4
5
140°
135°
130°
125°
120°
115°
60°
55°
50°
Transverse Mercator Projection

© HarperCollinsPublishers

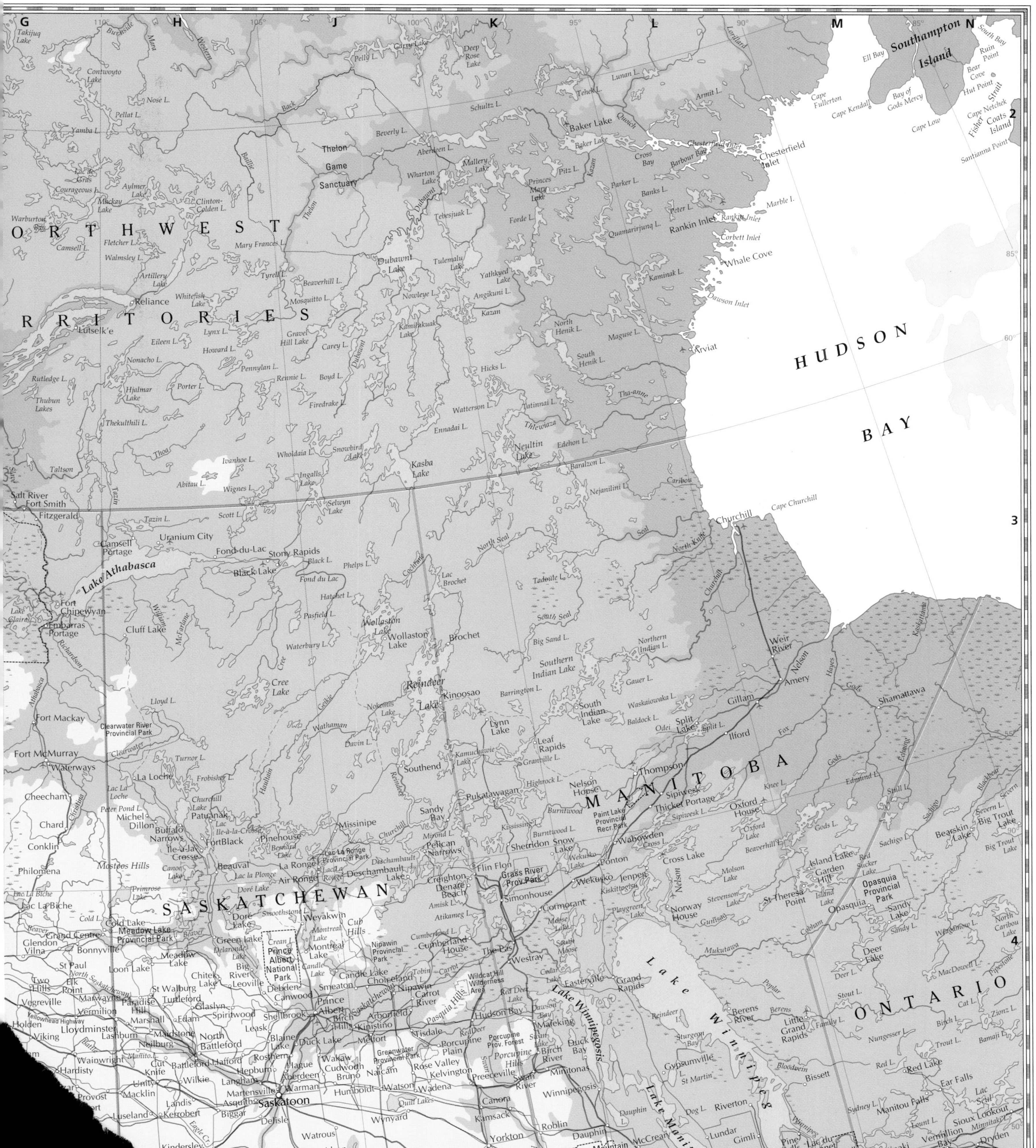

1:6 000 000

MILES	0	40	80	120	160	200

KM	0	40	80	120	160	200	240	280	320

A
B
C
D
E
2
3
4
5
HUDSON BAY
JAMES BAY
MANITOBA
ONTARIO
U.S.A.
WISCONSIN
MICHIGAN
LAKE SUPERIOR
LAKE MICHIGAN
LAKE HURON
LAKE ERIE
LAKE ONTA
Churchill
Cape Churchill
Gillam
Ilford
Split Lake
Weir River
Shamattawa
Oxford House
Fort Severn
Winisk
Peawanuck
Cape Henrietta Maria
Polar Bear Provincial Park
Opasquia Provincial Park
Island Lake
Red Lake
Big Trout Lake
Kasabonika
Webequie
Winisk River Provincial Park
Summer Beaver
Sandy Lake
Deer Lake
Pickle Lake
Attawapiskat
Akimiski Island
Kapiskau
Kashechewan
Fort Albany
Lake River
Moosonee
Moose Factory
Moose River
Smoky Falls
Otter Rapids
Fraserdale
Hearst
Kapuskasing
Cochrane
Timmins
Kirkland Lake
Sioux Lookout
Savant Lake
Dryden
Kenora
Ignace
Atikokan
Armstrong
Nakina
Longlac
Thunder Bay
Nipigon
Lake Nipigon
Marathon
Terrace Bay
Wawa
Chapleau
Sault Ste Marie
Sudbury
North Bay
Belcher Islands
Sanikiluaq
Inukjuak (Port Harrison)
Umiujaq
Poste-de-la-Baleine (Kuujjuarapik)
Whapmagoostui
Fort George
Chisasibi
Radisson
Wemindji (Nouveau-Comptoir)
Eastmain
Waskaganish
Fort Rupert
Matagami
Chibougamau
Val-d'Or
Rouyn
Amos
La Sarre
Mistassini
Duluth
Marquette
Green Bay
Milwaukee
Madison
Chicago
Rockford
Grand Rapids
Lansing
Flint
Detroit
Windsor
Toledo
Cleveland
Erie
Buffalo
Hamilton
Toronto
Mississauga
Kitchener
London
Oshawa
Barrie
Peterborough
Georgian Bay
Manitoulin I.
Isle Royale Nat. Park
Pukaskwa Nat. Park
Voyageurs Nat. Park
METRES
FEET
6000
5000
4000
3000
2000
1000
500
200
SEA
LEVEL
19686
16409
13124
9843
6562
3281
1640
656
Transverse Mercator Projection
© HarperCollinsPublishers

1:6 000 000

MILES 0 40 80 120 160 200

KM 0 40 80 120 160 200 240 280 320

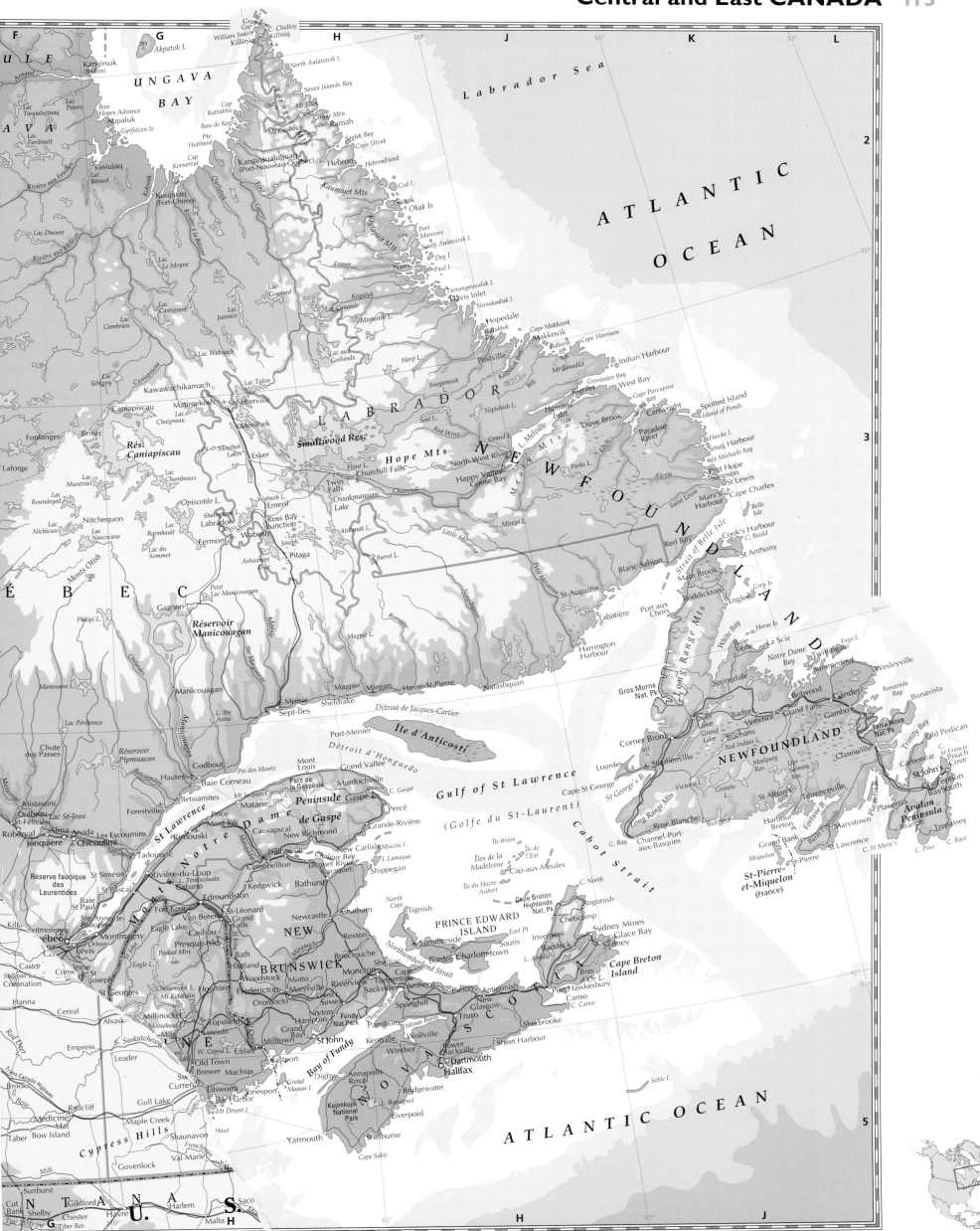

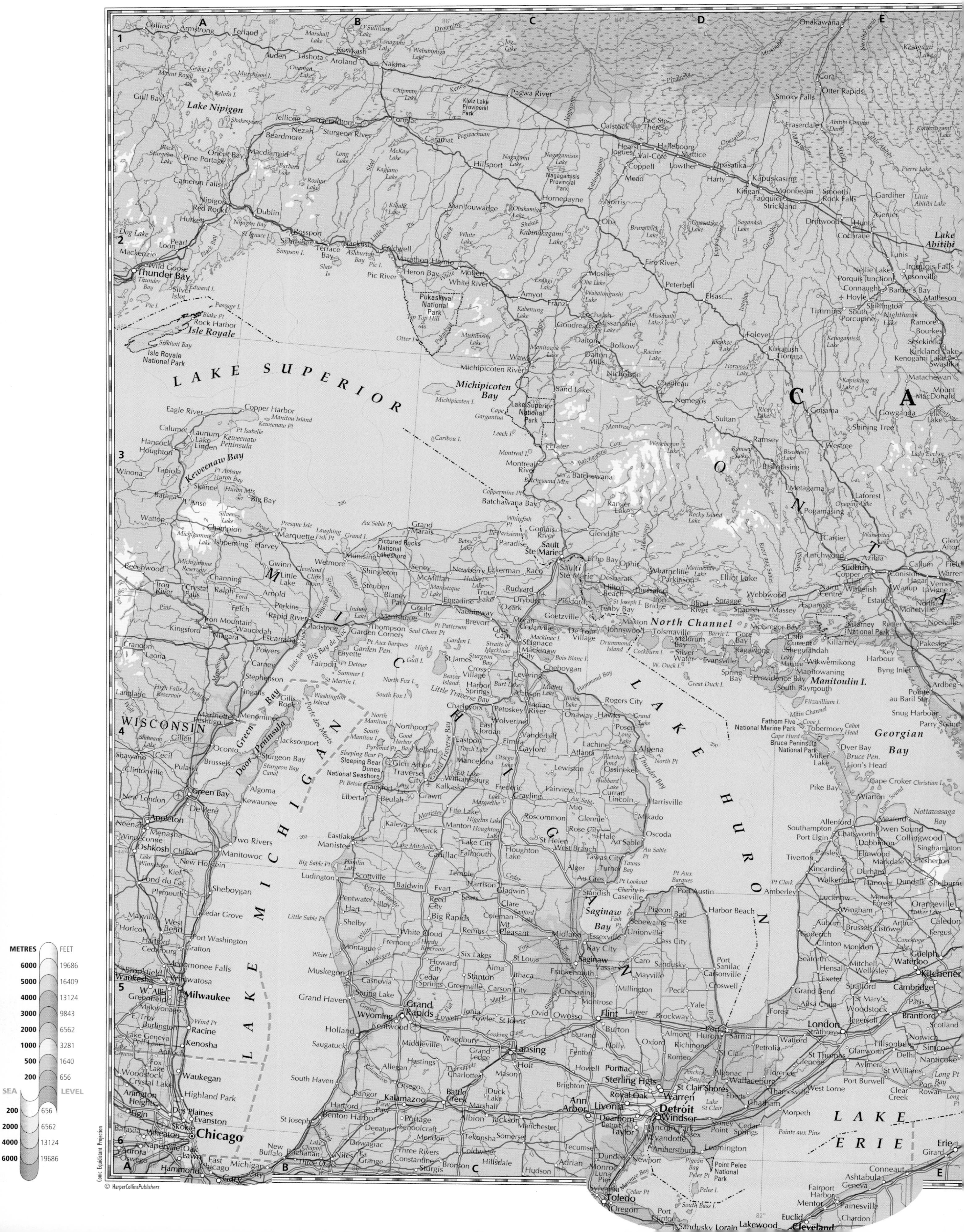
LAKE SUPERIOR
LAKE MICHIGAN
LAKE HURON
LAKE ERIE
MICHIGAN
ONTARIO
CANADA
WISCONSIN
North Channel
Georgian Bay
Saginaw Bay
Green Bay
Manitoulin I.
Isle Royale
Isle Royale National Park
Lake Nipigon
Lake Abitibi
Keweenaw Bay
Keweenaw Peninsula
Michipicoten Bay
Lake Superior National Park
Pukaskwa National Park
Pictured Rocks National Lakeshore
Sleeping Bear Dunes National Seashore
Bruce Peninsula National Park
Fathom Five National Marine Park
Killarney National Park
Point Pelee National Park
Thunder Bay
Sault Ste Marie
Sudbury
Marquette
Green Bay
Milwaukee
Chicago
Grand Rapids
Lansing
Flint
Saginaw
Detroit
Windsor
Toledo
London
Kitchener
Cleveland
METRES
FEET
6000
19686
5000
16409
4000
13124
3000
9843
2000
6562
1000
3281
500
1640
200
656
SEA
LEVEL
Conic Equidistant Projection

© HarperCollinsPublishers

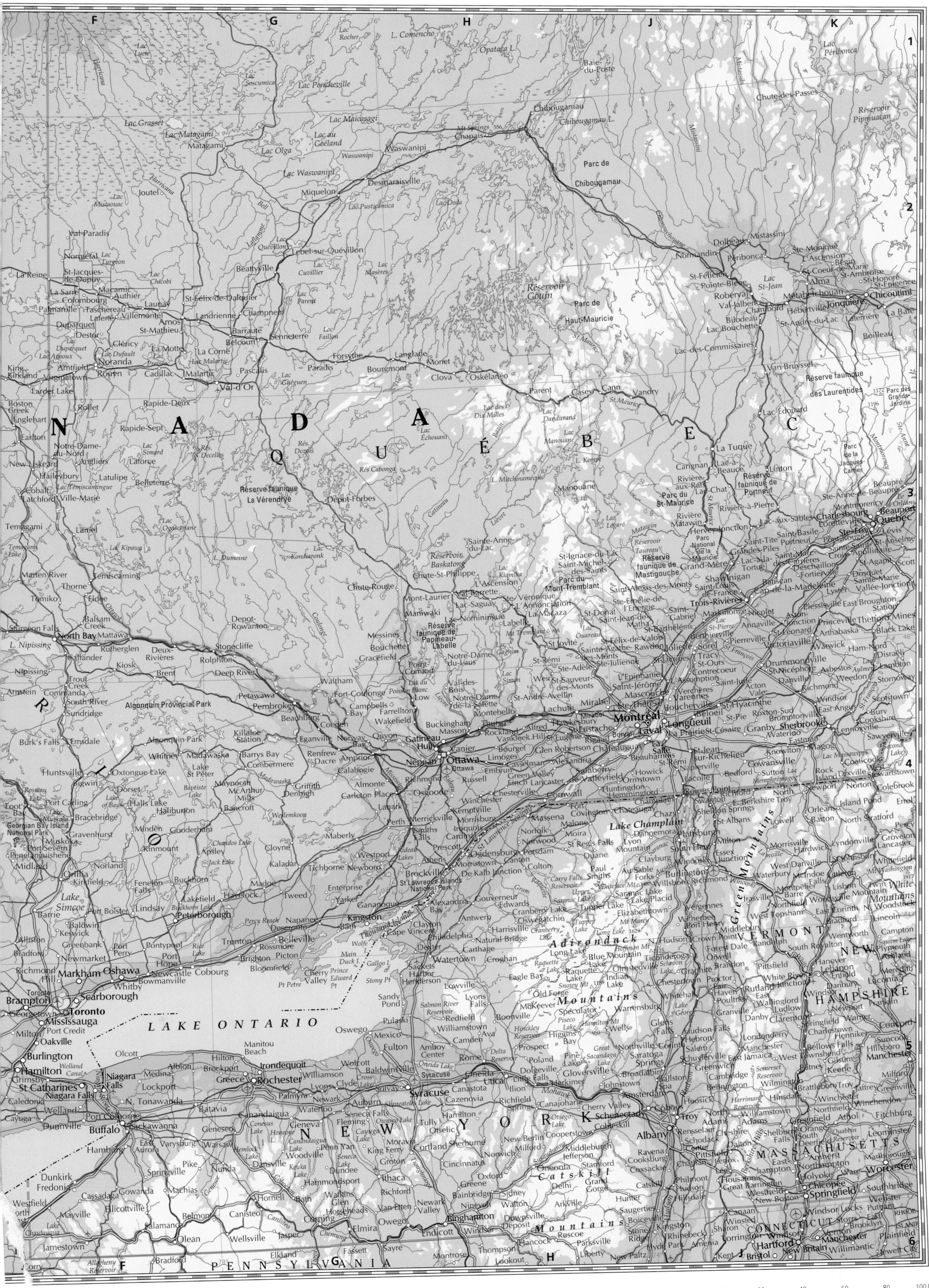

1:3 000 000

0	20	40	60	80	100 MILES
0	20 40	60 80	100 120	140 160	KM

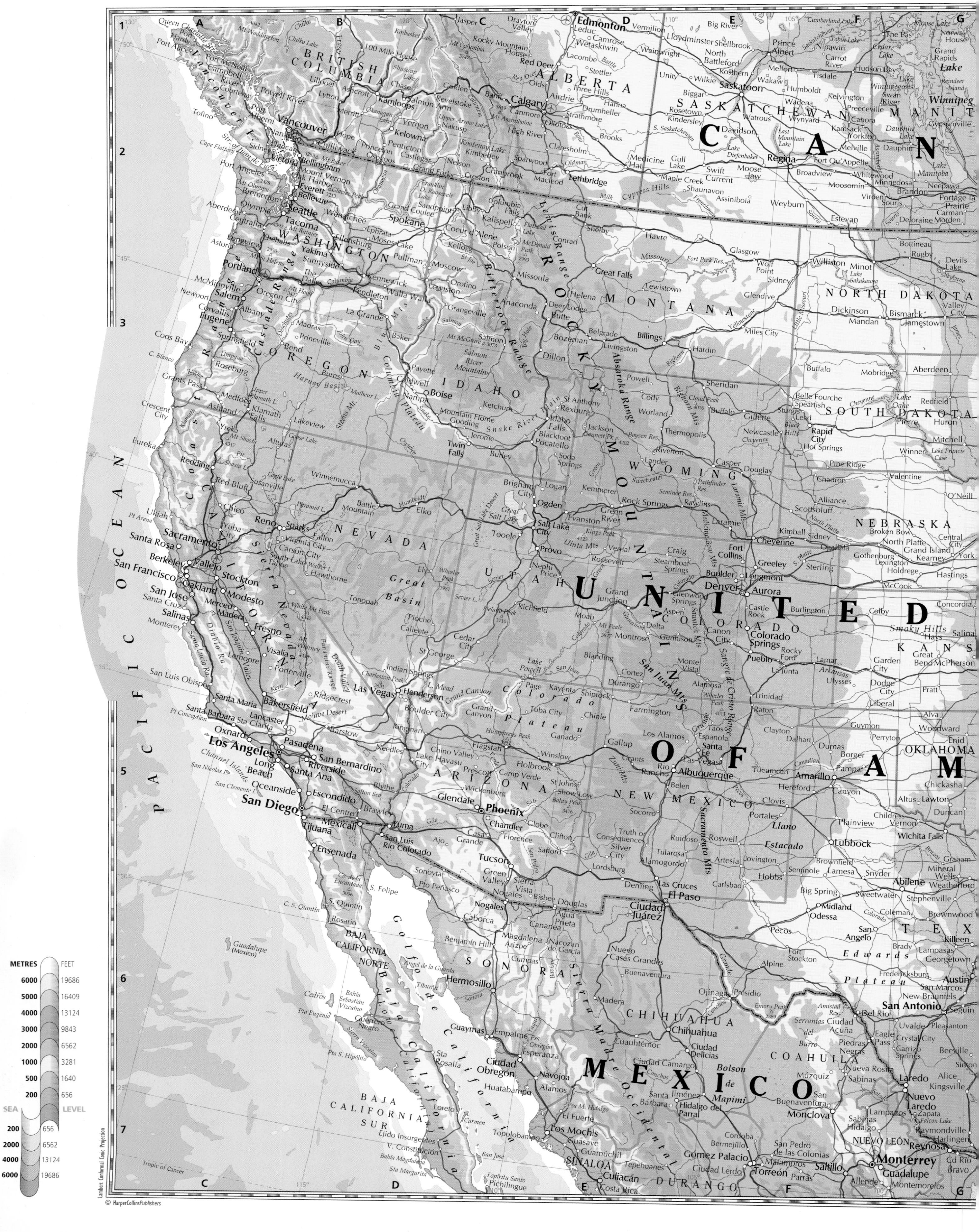
METRES
FEET
6000 19686
5000 16409
4000 13124
3000 9843
2000 6562
1000 3281
500 1640
200 656
SEA LEVEL
200 656
2000 6562
4000 13124
6000 19686
Lambert Conformal Conic Projection
CANADA
UNITED STATES OF AMERICA
MEXICO
PACIFIC OCEAN
BRITISH COLUMBIA
ALBERTA
SASKATCHEWAN
WASHINGTON
OREGON
IDAHO
MONTANA
NORTH DAKOTA
SOUTH DAKOTA
WYOMING
NEBRASKA
NEVADA
UTAH
COLORADO
CALIFORNIA
ARIZONA
NEW MEXICO
OKLAHOMA
SONORA
CHIHUAHUA
COAHUILA
NUEVO LEÓN
SINALOA
DURANGO
BAJA CALIFORNIA NORTE
BAJA CALIFORNIA SUR
ROCKY MOUNTAINS
Great Basin
Colorado Plateau
Golfo de California
Vancouver
Seattle
Portland
Calgary
Edmonton
Regina
Saskatoon
Winnipeg
San Francisco
Sacramento
Los Angeles
San Diego
Las Vegas
Phoenix
Tucson
Salt Lake City
Denver
Albuquerque
El Paso
Ciudad Juárez
Chihuahua
Hermosillo
Monterrey
San Antonio
Austin
Amarillo
Lubbock
Boise
Spokane
Tijuana
Mexicali

© HarperCollinsPublishers

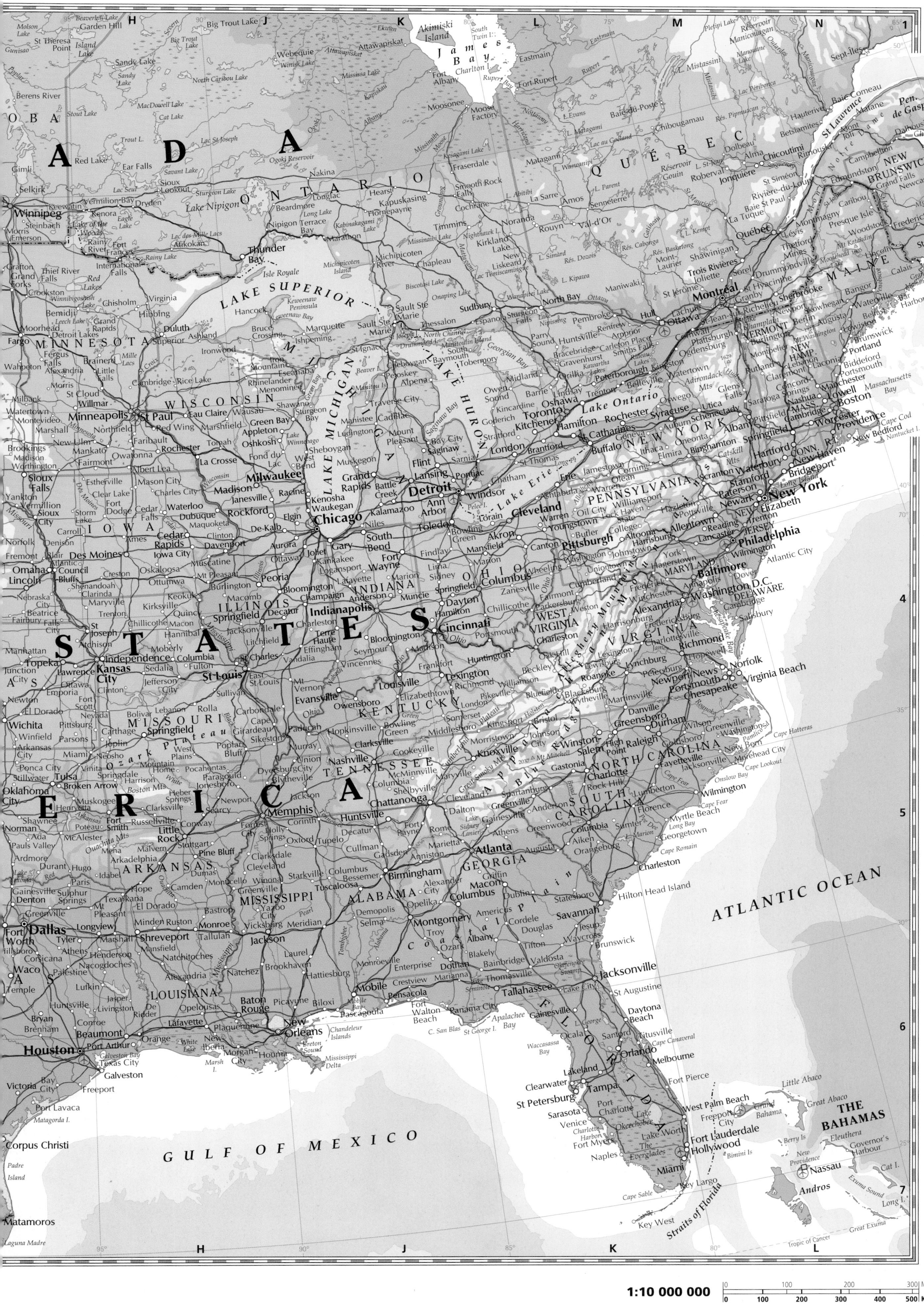

1:10 000 000

0 100 200 300 MILES
0 100 200 300 400 500 KM

ATLANTIC OCEAN
CANADA
ONTARIO
QUEBEC
NEW BRUNSWICK
MAINE
NEW HAMPSHIRE
VERMONT
MASSACHUSETTS
CONNECTICUT
RHODE ISLAND
NEW YORK
NEW JERSEY
PENNSYLVANIA
DELAWARE
MARYLAND
WASHINGTON D.C.
VIRGINIA
WEST VIRGINIA
OHIO
MICHIGAN
INDIANA
ILLINOIS
WISCONSIN
MINNESOTA
IOWA
MISSOURI
KENTUCKY
LAKE SUPERIOR
LAKE MICHIGAN
LAKE HURON
LAKE ERIE
LAKE ONTARIO
Georgian Bay
Long Island
Chesapeake Bay
Adirondack Mountains
Catskill Mts
St Lawrence

METRES	FEET
6000	19686
5000	16409
4000	13124
3000	9843
2000	6562
1000	3281
500	1640
200	656
SEA	LEVEL
200	656
2000	6562
4000	13124
6000	19686

Lambert Conformal Conic Projection

© HarperCollinsPublishers

1:6 000 000

MILES	0	40	80	120	160	200

KM	0	40	80	120	160	200	240	280	320

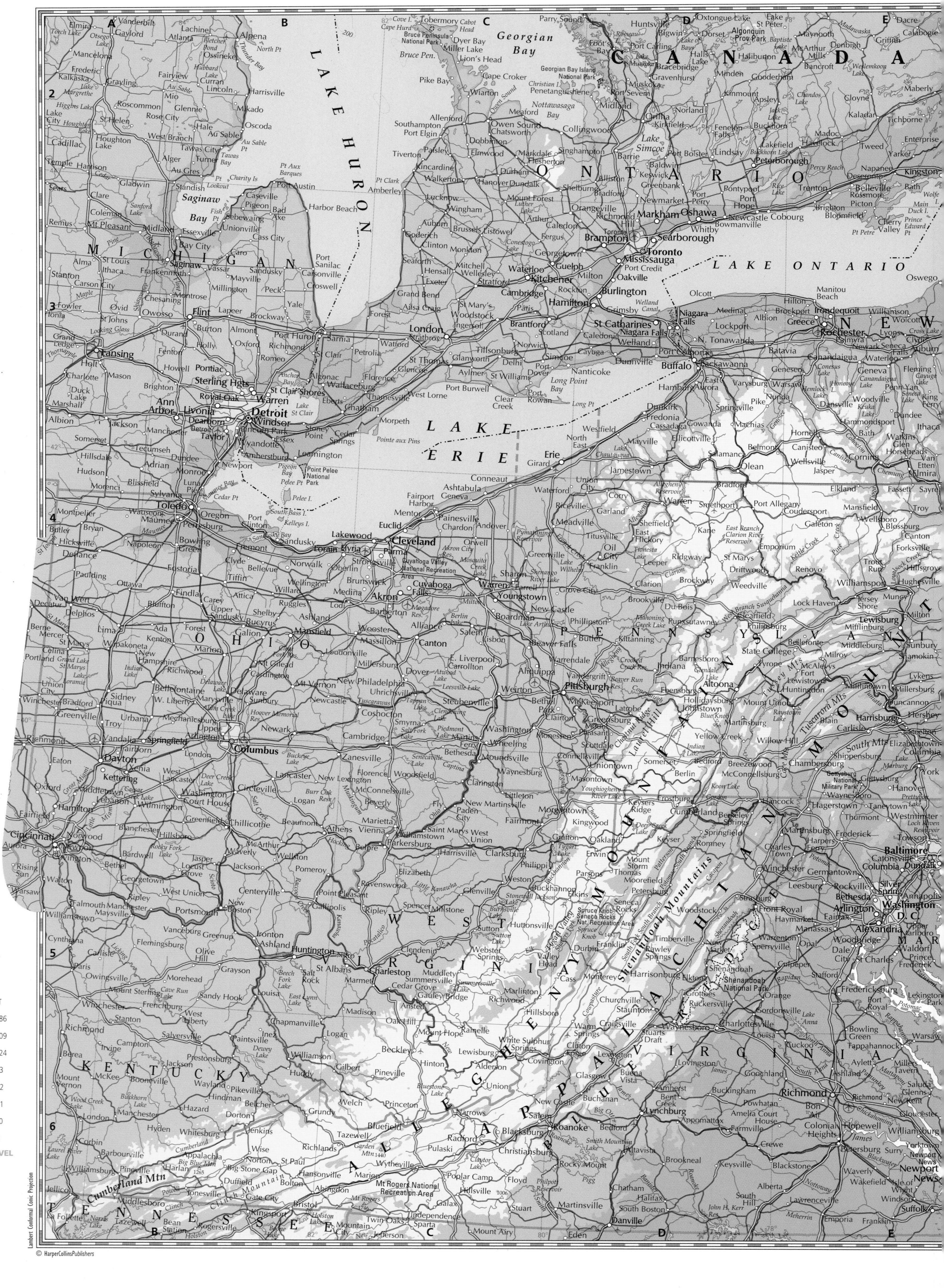

Lambert Conformal Conic Projection

METRES	FEET
6000	19686
5000	16409
4000	13124
3000	9843
2000	6562
1000	3281
500	1640
200	656
SEA	LEVEL
200	656
2000	6562
4000	13124
6000	19686

© HarperCollinsPublishers

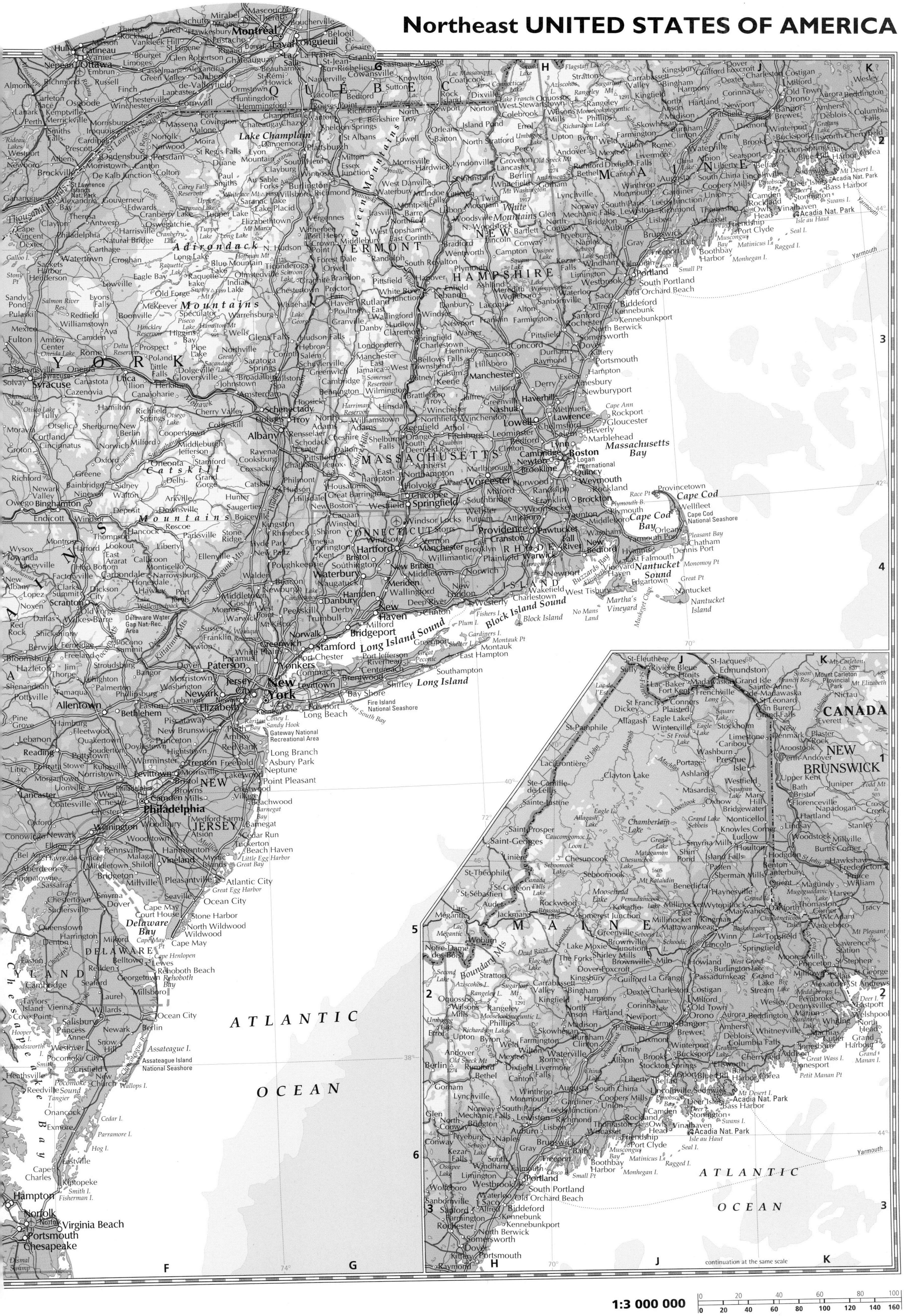

1:3 000 000

0 20 40 60 80 100 MILES

0 20 40 60 80 100 120 140 160 KM

LAKE SUPERIOR
LAKE MICHIGAN
MINNESOTA
WISCONSIN
MICHIGAN
IOWA
ILLINOIS
INDIANA
MISSOURI
Thunder Bay
Duluth
Minneapolis
St Paul
Green Bay
Milwaukee
Madison
Chicago
Grand Rapids
Lansing
Fort Wayne
Indianapolis
Springfield
Peoria
Rockford
Davenport
Cedar Rapids
Isle Royale
Isle Royale National Park
Apostle Islands National Lakeshore
Pictured Rocks National Lakeshore
Sleeping Bear Dunes National Seashore
Pukaskwa National Park
Lake Superior National Park
Michipicoten Bay
Keweenaw Bay
Sawtooth Mountains
Gogebic Range
Door Peninsula
Green Bay
METRES
FEET
6000
19686
5000
16409
4000
13124
3000
9843
2000
6562
1000
3281
500
1640
200
656
SEA
LEVEL
200
656
2000
6562
4000
13124
6000
19686
Lambert Conformal Conic Projection
© HarperCollinsPublishers

1:3 000 000

MILES	0	20	40	60	80	100

KM	0	20	40	60	80	100	120	140	160

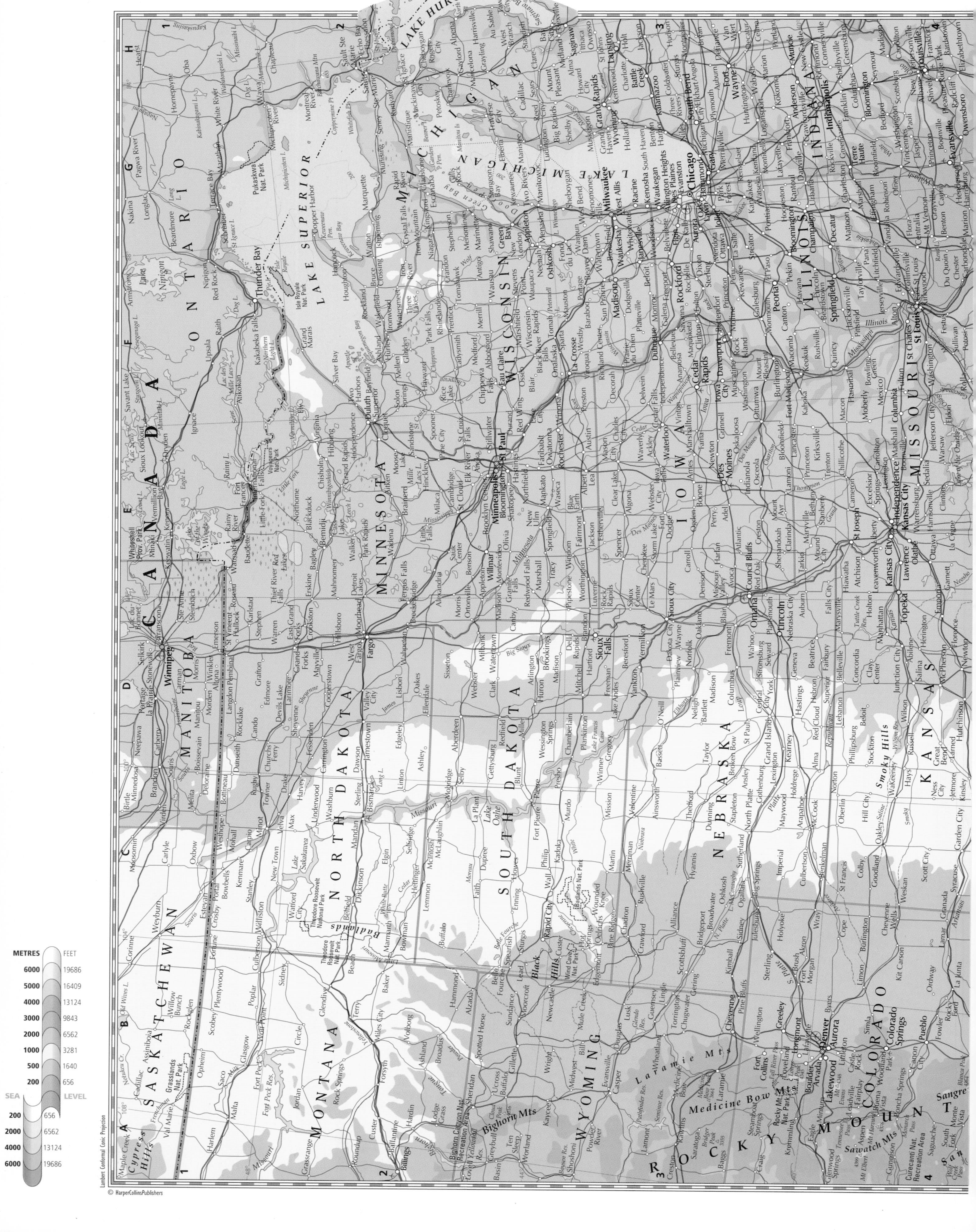
METRES
FEET
6000
19686
5000
16409
4000
13124
3000
9843
2000
6562
1000
3281
500
1640
200
656
SEA
LEVEL
200
656
2000
6562
4000
13124
6000
19686
Lambert Conformal Conic Projection
C A N A D A
O N T A R I O
MANITOBA
SASKATCHEWAN
NORTH DAKOTA
SOUTH DAKOTA
NEBRASKA
KANSAS
MINNESOTA
IOWA
MISSOURI
WISCONSIN
MICHIGAN
ILLINOIS
INDIANA
MONTANA
WYOMING
COLORADO
LAKE SUPERIOR
LAKE HURON
LAKE MICHIGAN
ROCKY MOUNT
Winnipeg
Thunder Bay
Duluth
Minneapolis
St Paul
Fargo
Bismarck
Sioux Falls
Sioux City
Omaha
Lincoln
Des Moines
Kansas City
Topeka
St Louis
Chicago
Milwaukee
Madison
Green Bay
Indianapolis
Denver
Cheyenne
Billings
Rapid City
Black Hills
Bighorn Mts
Medicine Bow Mts
Laramie Mts
Smoky Hills

© HarperCollinsPublishers

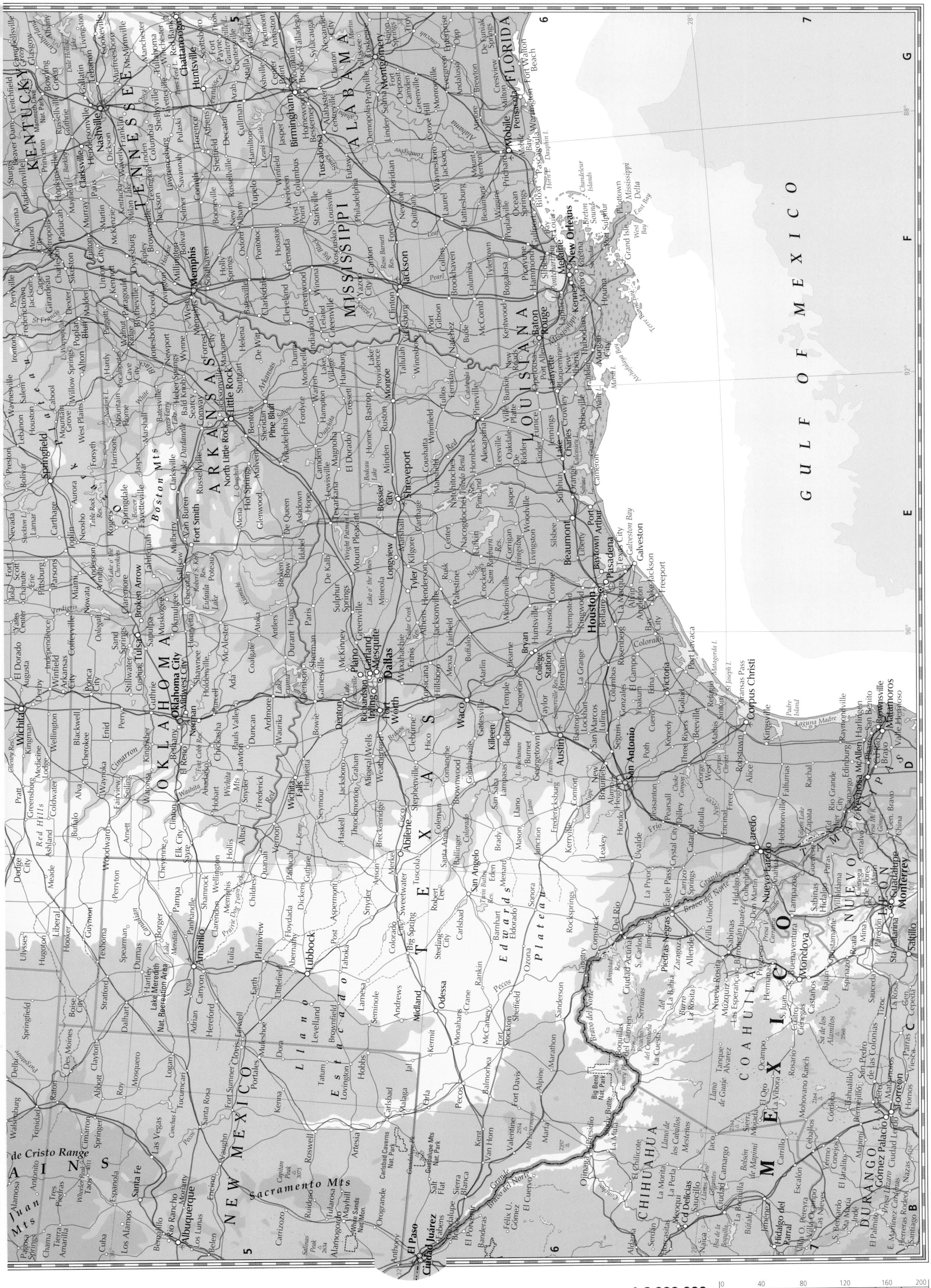

1:6 000 000

MILES	0	40	80	120	160	200			
KM	0	40	80	120	160	200	240	280	320

C A N A D A
BRITISH COLUMBIA
ALBERTA
SASKATCHEWAN
NORTH DAKOTA
SOUTH DAKOTA
NEBRASKA
MONTANA
WYOMING
IDAHO
WASHINGTON
OREGON
ROCKY MOUN
COAST MOUNTAINS
BITTERROOT RANGE
Snake River Plain
Columbia Plateau
Harney Basin
Great Salt Lake Desert
Vancouver Island
Calgary
Regina
Saskatoon
Vancouver
Seattle
Spokane
Portland
Boise
Salt Lake City
Denver
Sacramento
O C E A N
Lambert Conformal Conic Projection

METRES
FEET
6000
19686
5000
16409
4000
13124
3000
9843
2000
6562
1000
3281
500
1640
200
656
SEA
LEVEL
200
656
2000
6562
4000
13124
6000
19686

© HarperCollinsPublishers

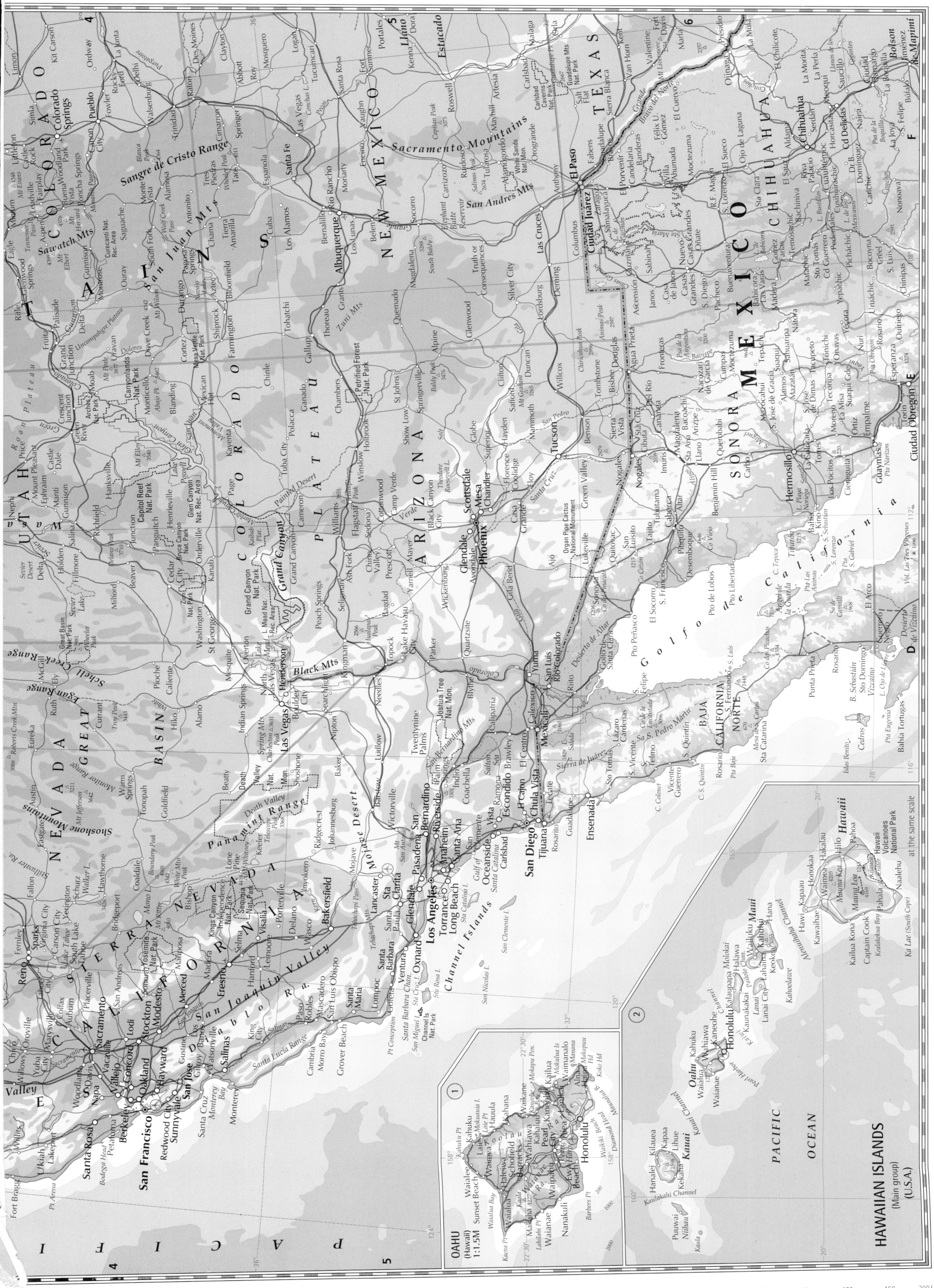

1:6 000 000

0		40		80		120	160	200	MILES
0	40	80	120	160	200	240	280	320	KM

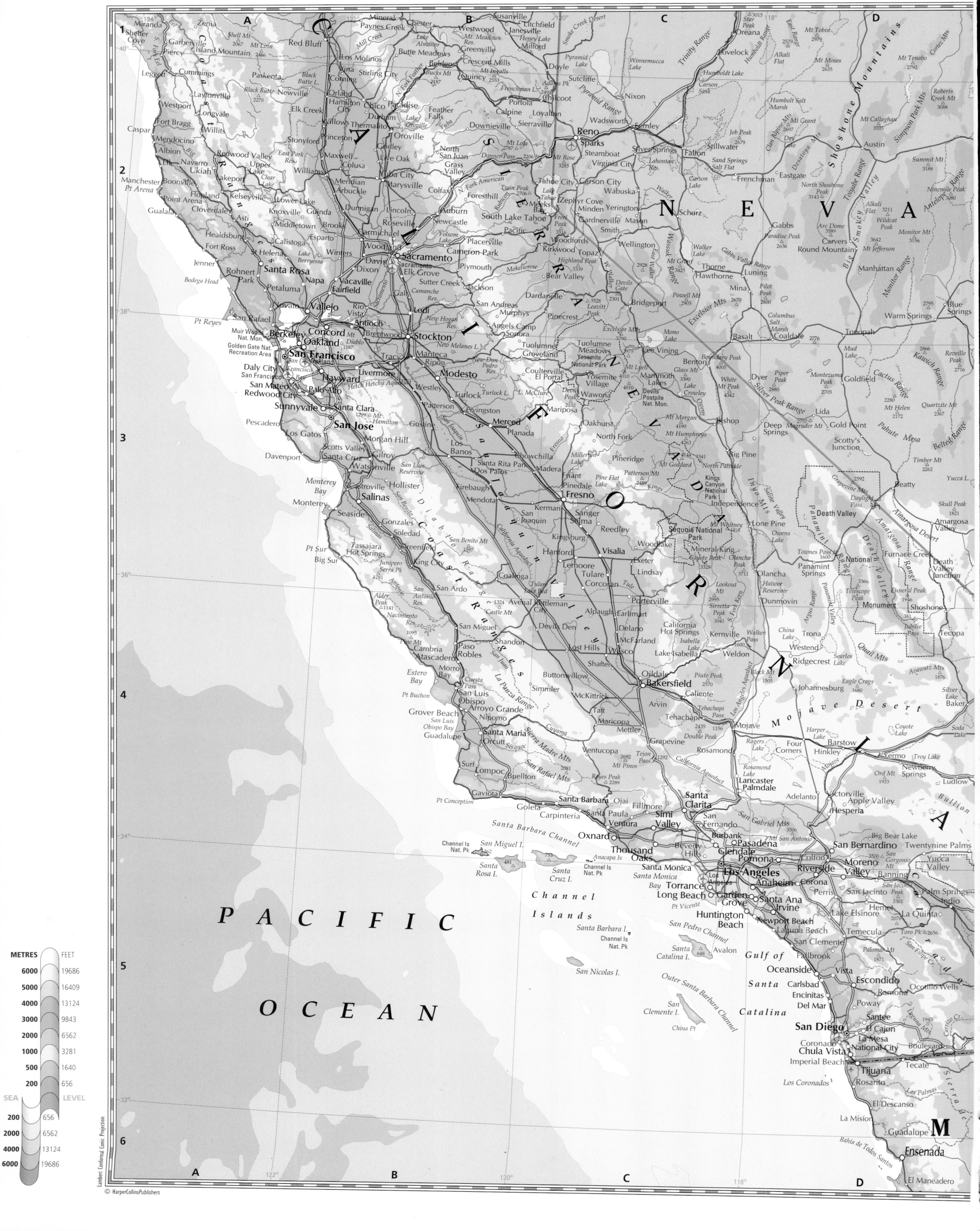
CALIFORNIA
NEVADA
SIERRA NEVADA
PACIFIC OCEAN
Channel Islands
Gulf of Santa Catalina
Mojave Desert
Coast Ranges
Diablo Range
San Joaquin Valley
Shoshone Mountains
San Francisco
Oakland
Berkeley
Sacramento
Stockton
Modesto
Fresno
Bakersfield
San Jose
Salinas
Monterey
Santa Rosa
Reno
Carson City
Los Angeles
Long Beach
Anaheim
Santa Ana
Riverside
San Bernardino
Oxnard
Santa Barbara
Oceanside
Escondido
San Diego
Chula Vista
Tijuana
Ensenada
Death Valley
Lake Tahoe
Santa Barbara Channel
Monterey Bay
A
B
C
D
1
2
3
4
5
6
122°
120°
118°
40°
38°
36°
34°
32°
METRES
FEET
6000
19686
5000
16409
4000
13124
3000
9843
2000
6562
1000
3281
500
1640
200
656
SEA
LEVEL
200
656
2000
6562
4000
13124
6000
19686
Lambert Conformal Conic Projection

© HarperCollinsPublishers

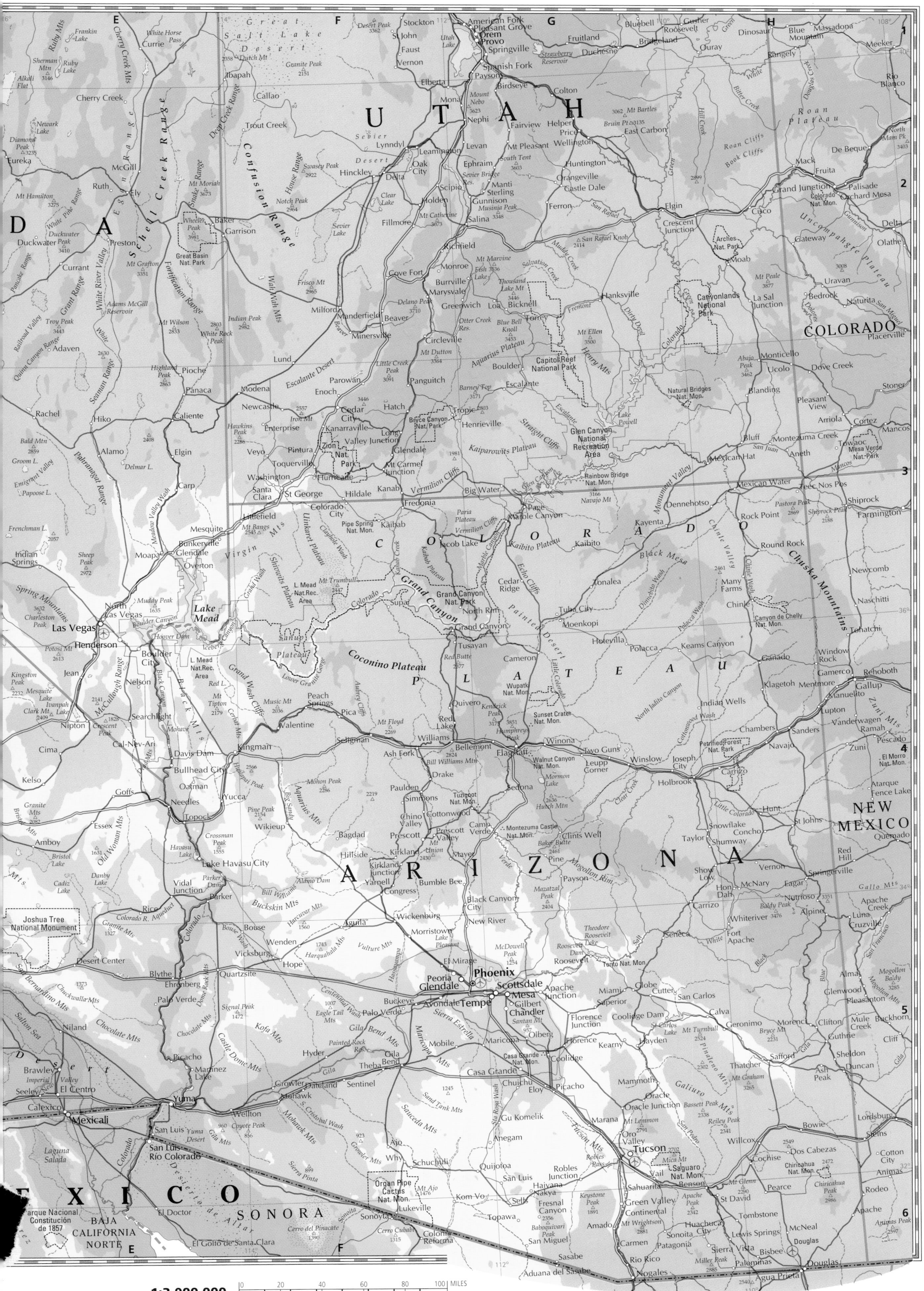

1:3 000 000

0 20 40 60 80 100 MILES
0 20 40 60 80 100 120 140 160 KM

ARIZONA
NEW MEXICO
UNITED
MEXICO
SONORA
CHIHUAHUA
COAHUILA
SINALOA
DURANGO
ZACATECAS
NAYARIT
JALISCO
BAJA CALIFORNIA NORTE
BAJA CALIFORNIA SUR
GOLFO DE CALIFORNIA
SIERRA MADRE OCCIDENTAL
PACIFIC OCEAN
CARIBBEAN SEA
HONDURAS
NICARAGUA
COSTA RICA
PANAMA
EL SALVADOR
Gulf of Honduras
Islas Revillagigedo (Mexico)
Guadalupe (Mex.)
Tijuana
Mexicali
Ensenada
Tucson
El Paso
Ciudad Juárez
Hermosillo
Chihuahua
Guaymas
Ciudad Obregón
Los Mochis
Culiacán
La Paz
Mazatlán
Durango
Torreón
Zacatecas
Aguascalientes
Tepic
Guadalajara
Colima
Tegucigalpa
San Pedro Sula
San Salvador
Managua
San José
Panamá
Colón
David
Limón
at the same scale
continuation at the same scale
Lambert Conformal Conic Projection
METRES
FEET
6000 19686
5000 16409
4000 13124
3000 9843
2000 6562
1000 3281
500 1640
200 656
SEA LEVEL
200 656
2000 6562
4000 13124
6000 19686

© HarperCollinsPublishers

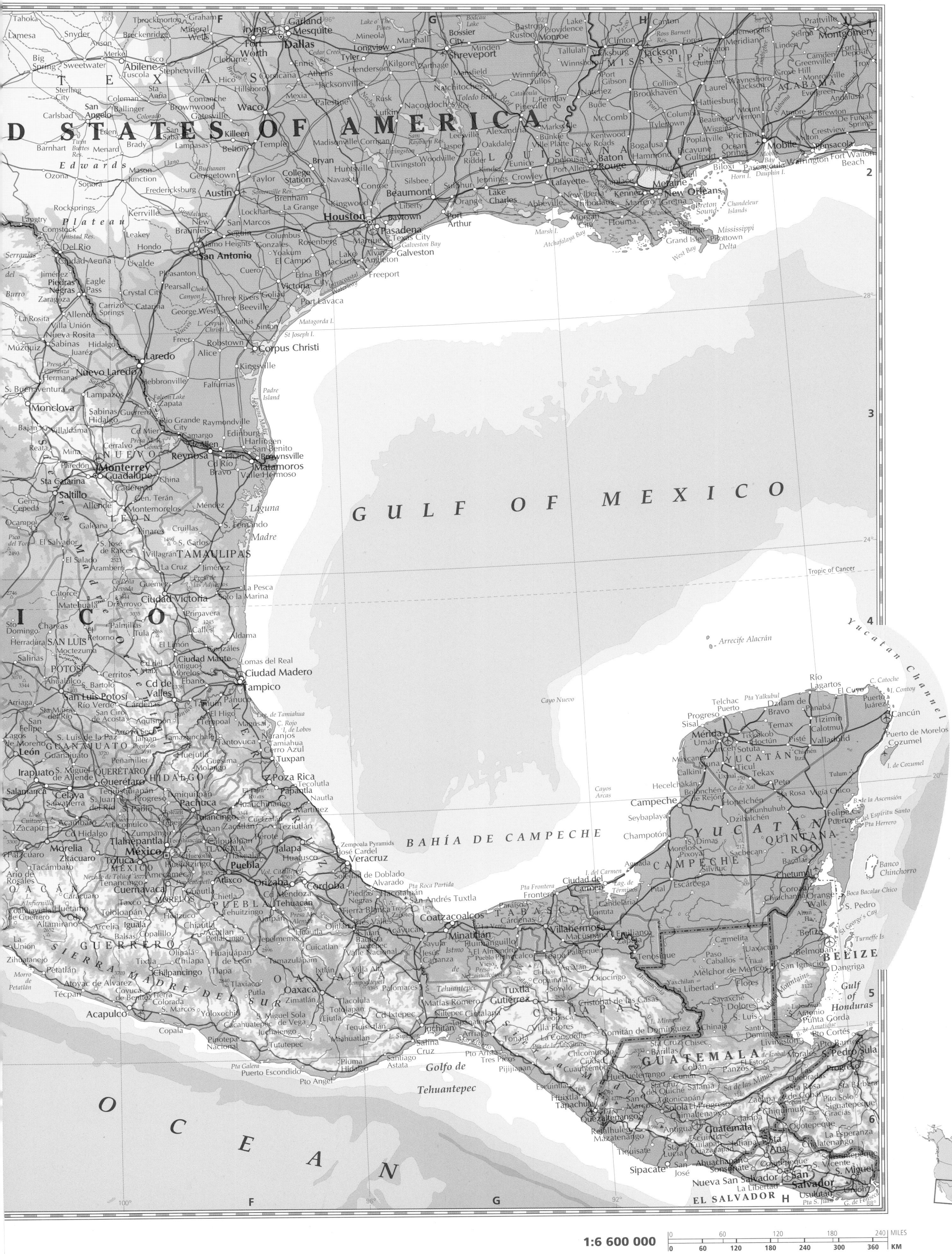

1:6 600 000

MILES 0 60 120 180 240

KM 0 60 120 180 240 300 360

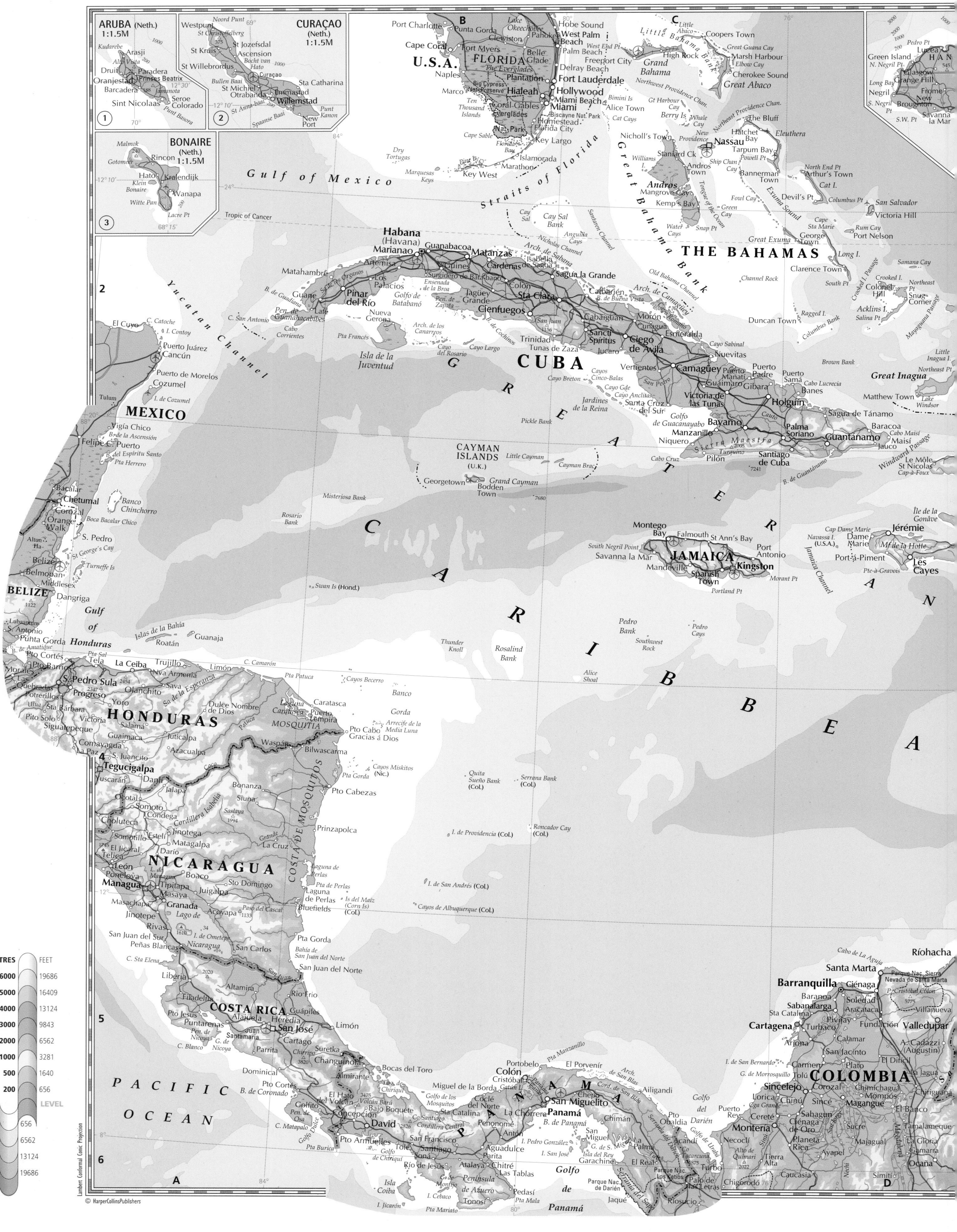

ARUBA (Neth.) 1:1.5M
Oranjestad
Sint Nicolaas
CURAÇAO (Neth.) 1:1.5M
Willemstad
BONAIRE (Neth.) 1:1.5M
Kralendijk
Gulf of Mexico
Tropic of Cancer
Straits of Florida
U.S.A.
FLORIDA
Port Charlotte
Punta Gorda
Cape Coral
Fort Myers
Naples
West Palm Beach
Palm Beach
Delray Beach
Fort Lauderdale
Hollywood
Hialeah
Miami Beach
Miami
Homestead
Florida City
Key Largo
Islamorada
Marathon
Key West
Grand Bahama
Great Abaco
Freeport City
Nassau
Andros
Eleuthera
THE BAHAMAS
Great Bahama Bank
Great Exuma
Long I.
San Salvador
Acklins I.
Great Inagua
Habana (Havana)
Marianao
Matanzas
Cárdenas
Pinar del Río
Isla de la Juventud
Santa Clara
Cienfuegos
Sancti Spíritus
Ciego de Ávila
Camagüey
Holguín
Bayamo
Santiago de Cuba
Guantánamo
CUBA
Yucatan Channel
MEXICO
Cancún
Cozumel
Chetumal
CAYMAN ISLANDS (U.K.)
Georgetown
Grand Cayman
Little Cayman
Cayman Brac
Windward Passage
Jérémie
Les Cayes
Port-à-Piment
Montego Bay
JAMAICA
Kingston
Spanish Town
Mandeville
Navassa I. (U.S.A.)
Jamaica Channel
CARIBBEAN SEA
Swan Is (Hond.)
Pedro Bank
Rosalind Bank
BELIZE
Belize
Belmopan
Dangriga
Gulf of Honduras
Islas de la Bahía
Roatán
Guanaja
La Ceiba
Trujillo
San Pedro Sula
HONDURAS
Tegucigalpa
Choluteca
Pto Cabezas
NICARAGUA
Managua
León
Granada
Lago de Nicaragua
Bluefields
COSTA DE MOSQUITOS
I. de San Andrés (Col.)
I. de Providencia (Col.)
COSTA RICA
San José
Limón
Puntarenas
Bocas del Toro
Colón
Panamá
PANAMA
David
Golfo de Panamá
PACIFIC OCEAN
Barranquilla
Cartagena
Santa Marta
Ríohacha
Valledupar
Sincelejo
Montería
COLOMBIA
Golfo del Darién
METRES FEET
6000 19686
5000 16409
4000 13124
3000 9843
2000 6562
1000 3281
500 1640
200 656
SEA LEVEL
200 656
2000 6562
4000 13124
6000 19686
Lambert Conformal Conic Projection
© HarperCollinsPublishers

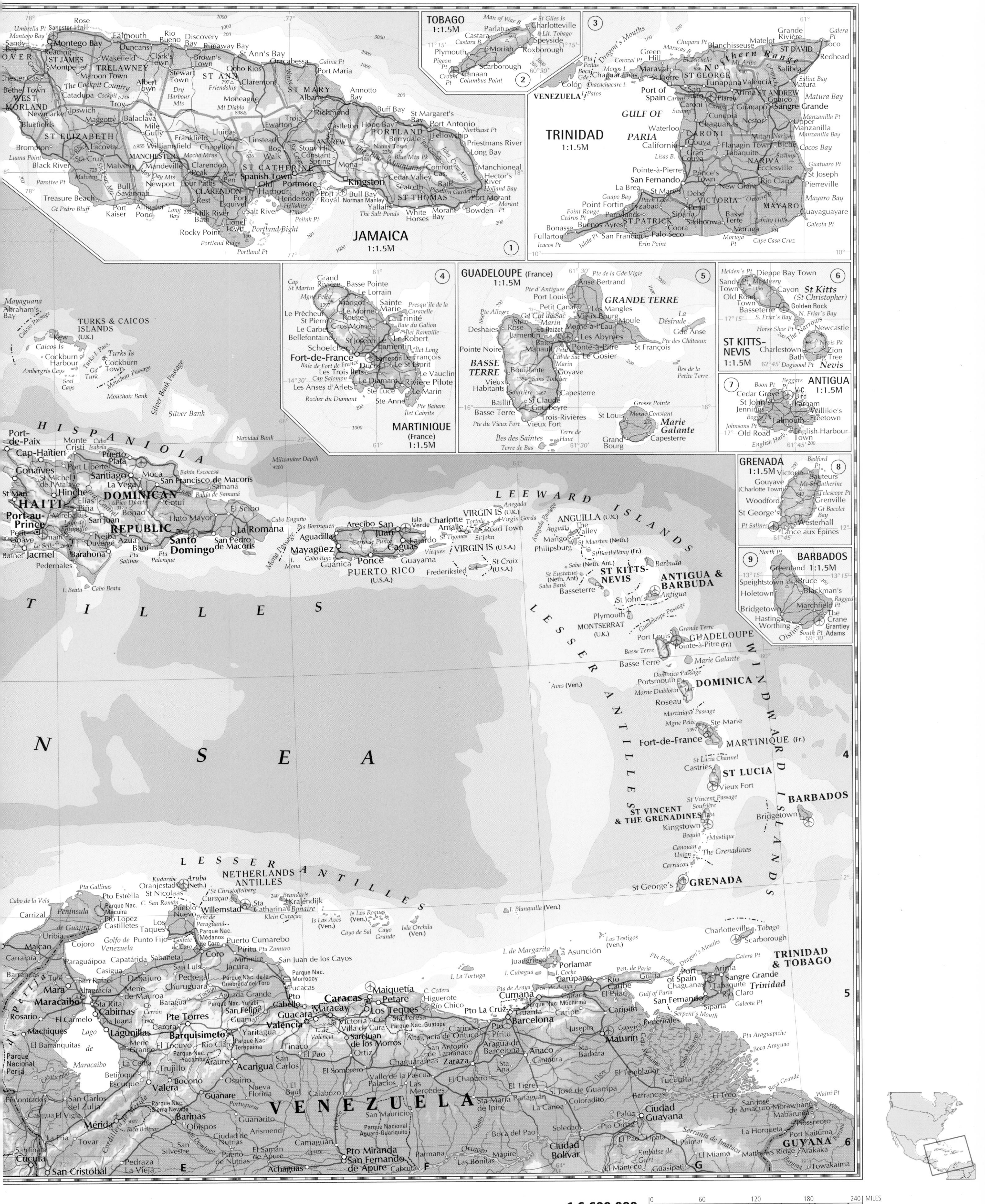
JAMAICA
1:1.5M
1
TOBAGO
1:1.5M
2
TRINIDAD
1:1.5M
3
MARTINIQUE
(France)
1:1.5M
4
GUADELOUPE (France)
1:1.5M
5
ST KITTS-NEVIS
1:1.5M
6
ANTIGUA
1:1.5M
7
GRENADA
1:1.5M
8
BARBADOS
1:1.5M
9
Montego Bay
Kingston
Spanish Town
ST ELIZABETH
ST CATHERINE
PORTLAND
ST THOMAS
CLARENDON
MANCHESTER
TRELAWNEY
ST JAMES
ST ANN
ST MARY
ST ANDREW
Port Antonio
Blue Mountains
Scarborough
Charlotteville
Port of Spain
San Fernando
GULF OF PARIA
Northern Range
VENEZUELA
Fort-de-France
BASSE TERRE
GRANDE TERRE
Pointe-à-Pitre
Marie Galante
St Kitts
(St Christopher)
Nevis
Basseterre
Charlestown
St John's
Bridgetown
St George's
TURKS & CAICOS ISLANDS
(U.K.)
HISPANIOLA
HAITI
Port-au-Prince
Cap-Haïtien
DOMINICAN REPUBLIC
Santo Domingo
Santiago
PUERTO RICO
(U.S.A.)
San Juan
Ponce
VIRGIN IS (U.K.)
VIRGIN IS (U.S.A.)
ANGUILLA (U.K.)
ST KITTS-NEVIS
ANTIGUA & BARBUDA
MONTSERRAT
(U.K.)
GUADELOUPE
DOMINICA
Roseau
MARTINIQUE (Fr.)
ST LUCIA
Castries
ST VINCENT & THE GRENADINES
Kingstown
BARBADOS
GRENADA
TRINIDAD & TOBAGO
LEEWARD ISLANDS
WINDWARD ISLANDS
LESSER ANTILLES
ANTILLES
N SEA
NETHERLANDS ANTILLES
Aruba
(Neth.)
Curaçao
Willemstad
Bonaire
Kralendijk
I. de Margarita
VENEZUELA
Caracas
Maracaibo
Lago de Maracaibo
Valencia
Barquisimeto
Maracay
Barcelona
Cumana
Maturín
Ciudad Guayana
Ciudad Bolívar
Mérida
San Cristóbal
GUYANA
E
F
G
4
5
6

1:6 600 000

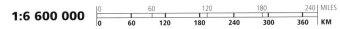

0 60 120 180 240 MILES
0 60 120 180 240 300 360 KM

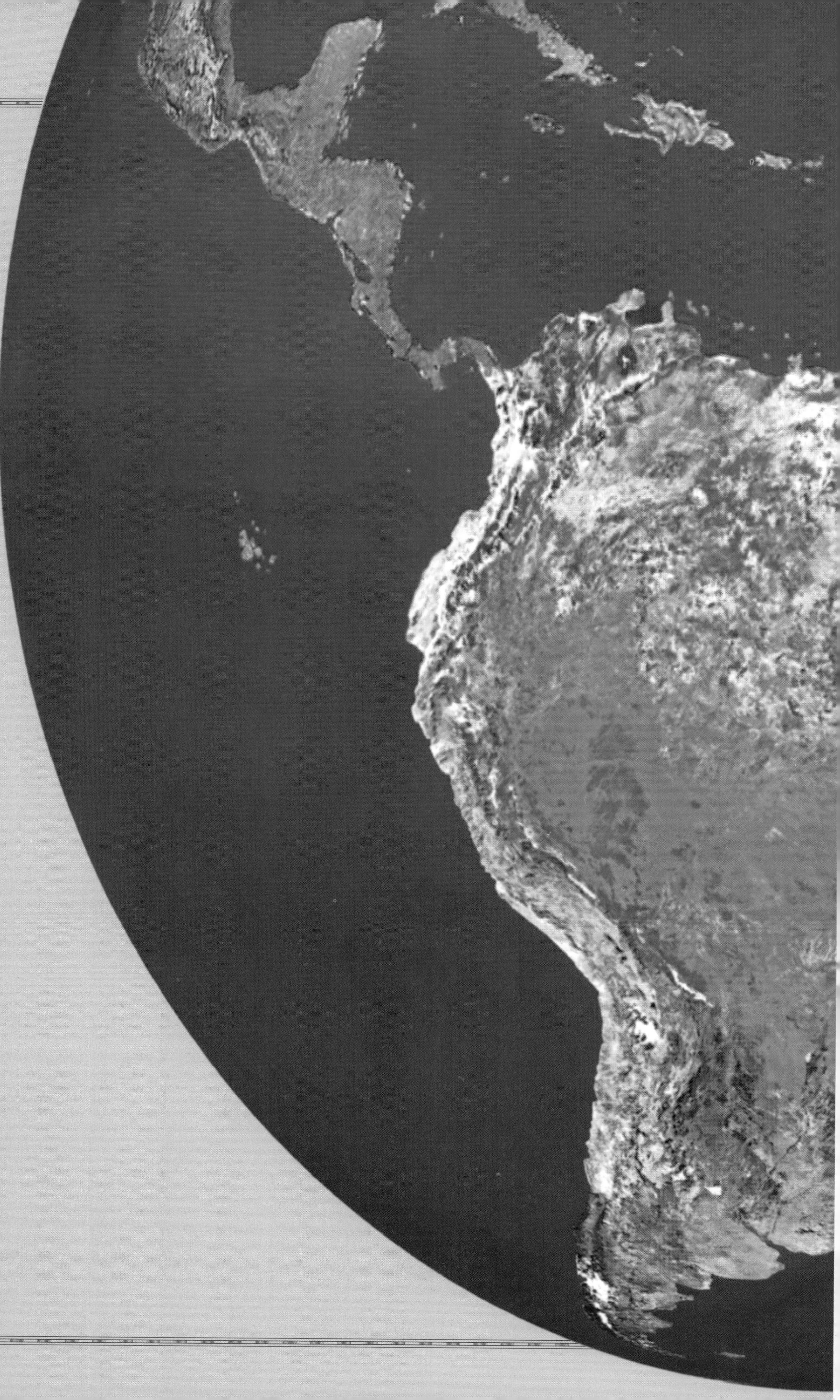

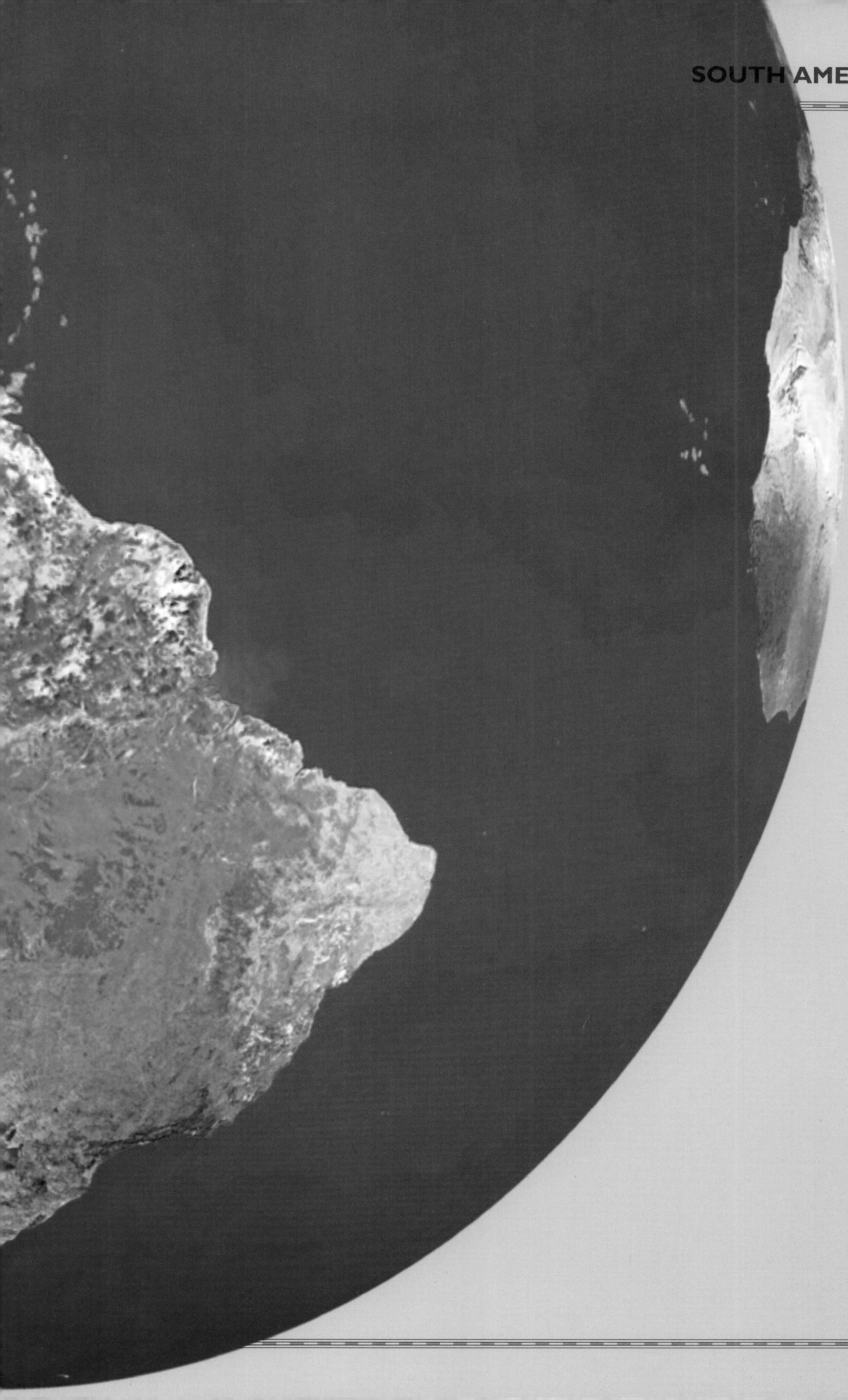

Countries : International Organizations

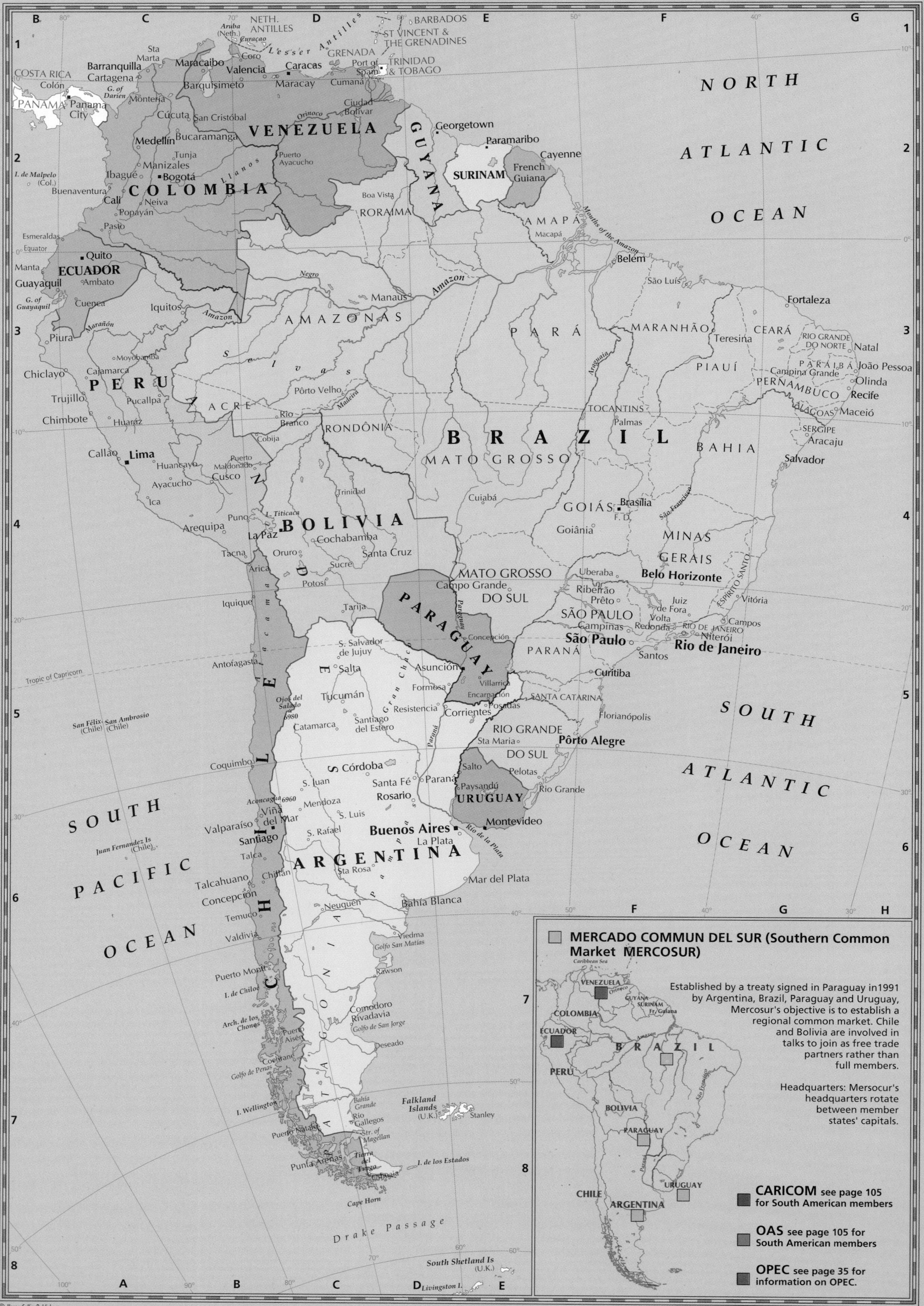

MERCADO COMMUN DEL SUR (Southern Common Market MERCOSUR)

Established by a treaty signed in Paraguay in1991 by Argentina, Brazil, Paraguay and Uruguay, Mercosur's objective is to establish a regional common market. Chile and Bolivia are involved in talks to join as free trade partners rather than full members.

Headquarters: Mersocur's headquarters rotate between member states' capitals.

CARICOM see page 105 for South American members

OAS see page 105 for South American members

OPEC see page 35 for information on OPEC.

0 200 400 600 800 MILES
0 200 400 600 800 1000 1200 1400 KM

1:25 000 000

COUNTRY	AREA sq ml	AREA sq km	POPULATION total	density per sq ml	density per sq km	FORM OF GOVERNMENT	CAPITAL CITY	MAIN LANGUAGES	MAIN RELIGIONS	CURRENCY
ARGENTINA	1 068 302	2 766 889	34 180 000	32	12	republic	Buenos Aires	Spanish, Italian, Amerindian languages	RC, Protestant, Jewish	Peso
ARUBA	75	193	69 000	926	358	Netherlands terr.	Oranjestad	Dutch , Papiamento, English	RC, Protestant	Florin
BOLIVIA	424 164	1 098 581	7 237 000	17	7	republic	La Paz	Spanish, Quechua, Aymara	RC, Protestant, Baha'i	Boliviano
BRAZIL	3 286 488	8 511 965	153 725 000	47	18	republic	Brasília	Portuguese, German, Japanese, Italian, Amerindian languages	RC, Spiritist, Protestant	Real
CHILE	292 258	756 945	13 994 000	48	18	republic	Santiago	Spanish, Amerindian languages	RC, Protestant	Peso
COLOMBIA	440 831	1 141 748	34 520 000	78	30	republic	Bogotá	Spanish, Amerindian languages	RC, Protestant	Peso
ECUADOR	105 037	272 045	11 221 000	107	41	republic	Quito	Spanish, Quechua, Amerind. lang.	RC, Protestant	Sucre
FALKLAND ISLANDS	4 699	12 170	2 000			UK territory	Stanley	English	Protestant, RC	Pound
FRENCH GUIANA	34 749	90 000	141 000	4	2	French territory	Cayenne	French, French Creole	RC, Protestant	French franc
GUYANA	83 000	214 969	825 000	10	4	republic	Georgetown	English, Creole, Hindi, Amerind. lang.	Protestant, Hindu, RC, Muslim	Dollar
NETH. ANTILLES (South)	283	732	158 206	560	216	Neth terr.	Willemstad	Dutch, Papiamento, English	RC, Protestant	Guilder
PARAGUAY	157 048	406 752	4 700 000	30	12	republic	Asunción	Spanish, Guaraní	RC, Protestant	Guaraní
PERU	496 225	1 285 216	23 088 000	47	18	republic	Lima	Spanish, Quechua, Aymara	RC, Protestant	Sol
SURINAM	63 251	163 820	418 000	7	3	republic	Paramaribo	Dutch, Surinamese, English, Hindi, Javanese	Hindu, RC, Protestant, Muslim	Guilder
TRINIDAD AND TOBAGO	1 981	5 130	1 250 000	631	244	republic	Port of Spain	English, Creole, Hindi	RC, Hindu, Protestant, Muslim	Dollar
URUGUAY	68 037	176 215	3 167 000	47	18	republic	Montevideo	Spanish	RC, Protestant, Jewish	Peso
VENEZUELA	352 144	912 050	21 177 000	60	23	republic	Caracas	Spanish, Amerindian languages	RC, Protestant	Bolivar

CITY PLANS

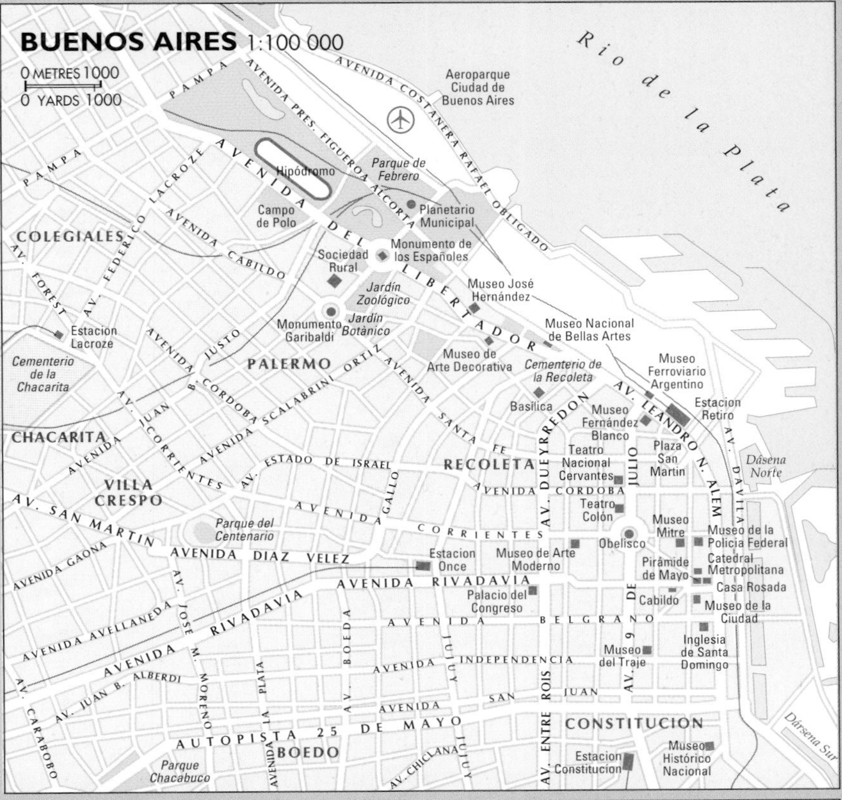

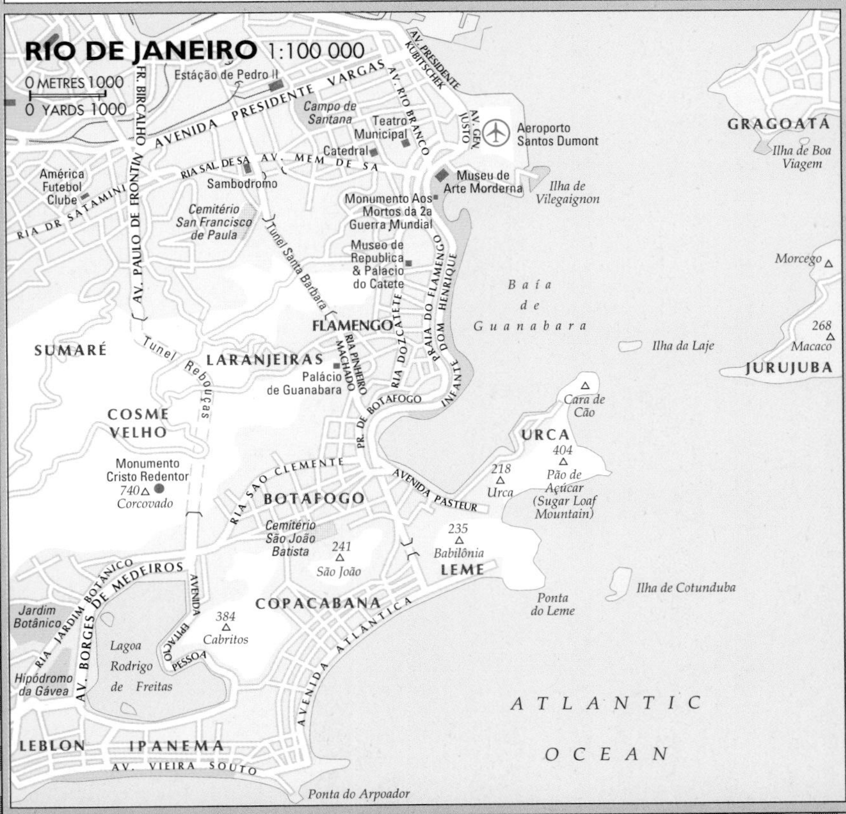

© HarperCollinsPublishers

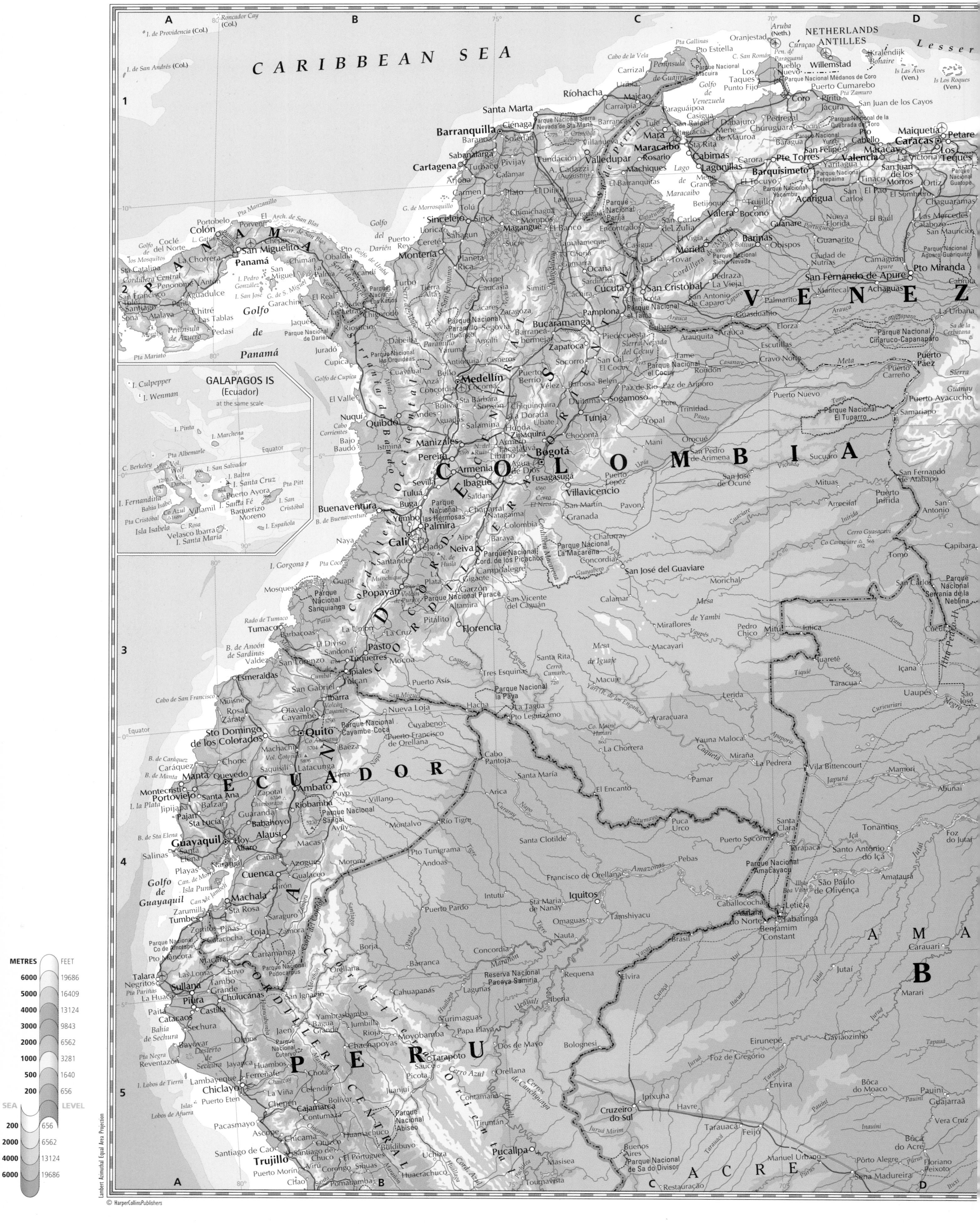
CARIBBEAN SEA
NETHERLANDS ANTILLES
PANAMA
COLOMBIA
VENEZ
ECUADOR
PERU
B
AMA
ACRE
GALAPAGOS IS
(Ecuador)
at the same scale
Golfo de Panamá
Golfo de Guayaquil
Bogotá
Medellín
Cali
Barranquilla
Cartagena
Caracas
Maracaibo
Quito
Guayaquil
Panamá
Iquitos
Trujillo
Equator
METRES
FEET
6000
19686
5000
16409
4000
13124
3000
9843
2000
6562
1000
3281
500
1640
200
656
SEA
LEVEL
200
656
2000
6562
4000
13124
6000
19686
Lambert Azimuthal Equal Area Projection

© HarperCollinsPublishers

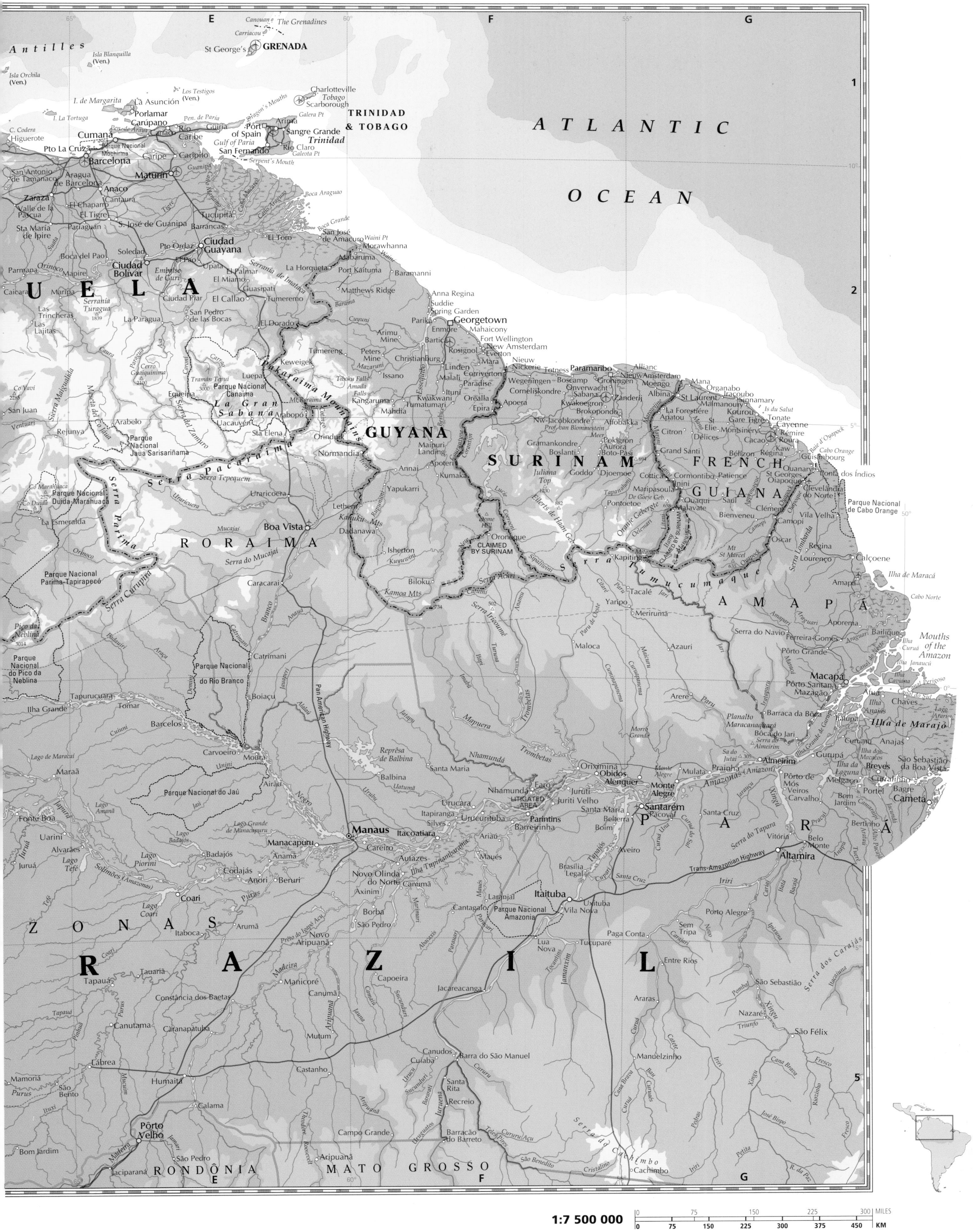

1:7 500 000

0 75 150 225 300 MILES

0 75 150 225 300 375 450 KM

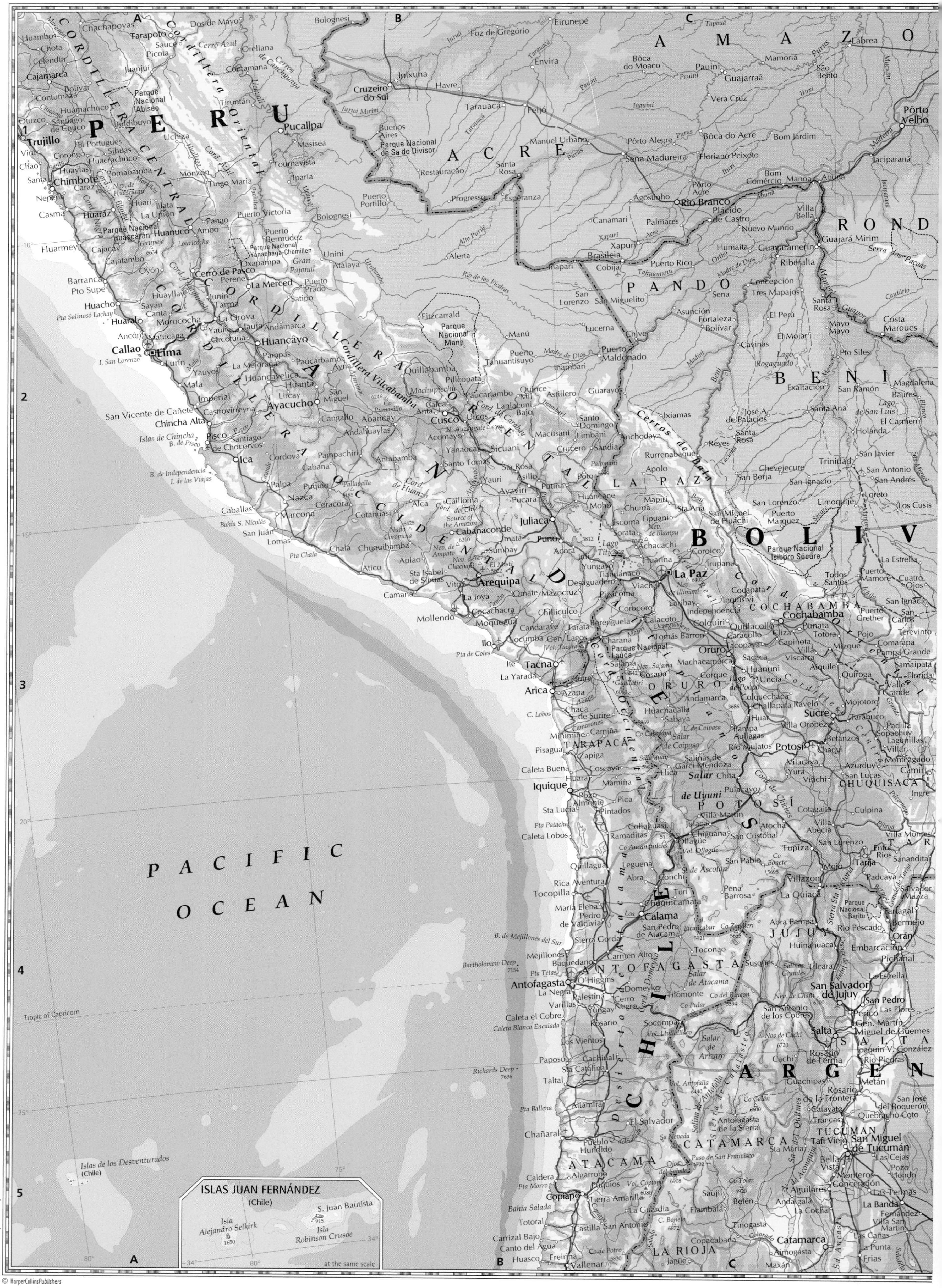
PERU
CORDILLERA CENTRAL
CORDILLERA ORIENTAL
CORDILLERA OCCIDENTAL
Cordillera Vilcabamba
ANDES
AMAZONAS
ACRE
PANDO
BENI
LA PAZ
COCHABAMBA
ORURO
POTOSÍ
CHUQUISACA
BOLIVIA
TARAPACÁ
ANTOFAGASTA
ATACAMA
CHILE
JUJUY
SALTA
CATAMARCA
LA RIOJA
TUCUMÁN
ARGENTINA
RONDÔNIA
PACIFIC OCEAN
Lima
Callao
Trujillo
Chimbote
Huaraz
Huánuco
Cerro de Pasco
Huancayo
Ayacucho
Huancavelica
Ica
Pisco
Nazca
Cusco
Arequipa
Juliaca
Puno
Moquegua
Ilo
Tacna
Arica
Iquique
Antofagasta
Calama
Chuquicamata
Tocopilla
Taltal
Copiapó
Caldera
Vallenar
La Paz
Oruro
Cochabamba
Sucre
Potosí
Tarija
Uyuni
Salar de Uyuni
Salar de Atacama
Desierto de Atacama
Lago Titicaca
Lago de Poopó
San Salvador de Jujuy
Salta
San Miguel de Tucumán
Catamarca
Pucallpa
Cruzeiro do Sul
Rio Branco
Porto Velho
Puerto Maldonado
Trinidad
Riberalta
Guayaramerín
Cobija
Tropic of Capricorn
Bartholomew Deep 7154
Richards Deep 7636
Islas de los Desventurados (Chile)
ISLAS JUAN FERNÁNDEZ (Chile)
Isla Alejandro Selkirk
Isla Robinson Crusoe
S. Juan Bautista
at the same scale
Lambert Azimuthal Equal Area Projection

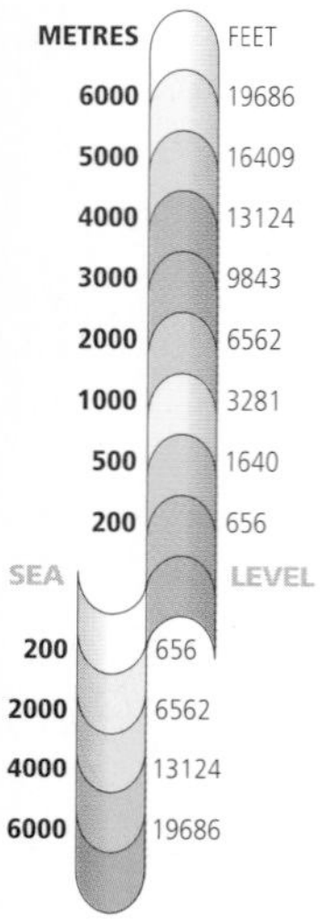
METRES
FEET
6000
19686
5000
16409
4000
13124
3000
9843
2000
6562
1000
3281
500
1640
200
656
SEA
LEVEL
200
656
2000
6562
4000
13124
6000
19686

© HarperCollinsPublishers

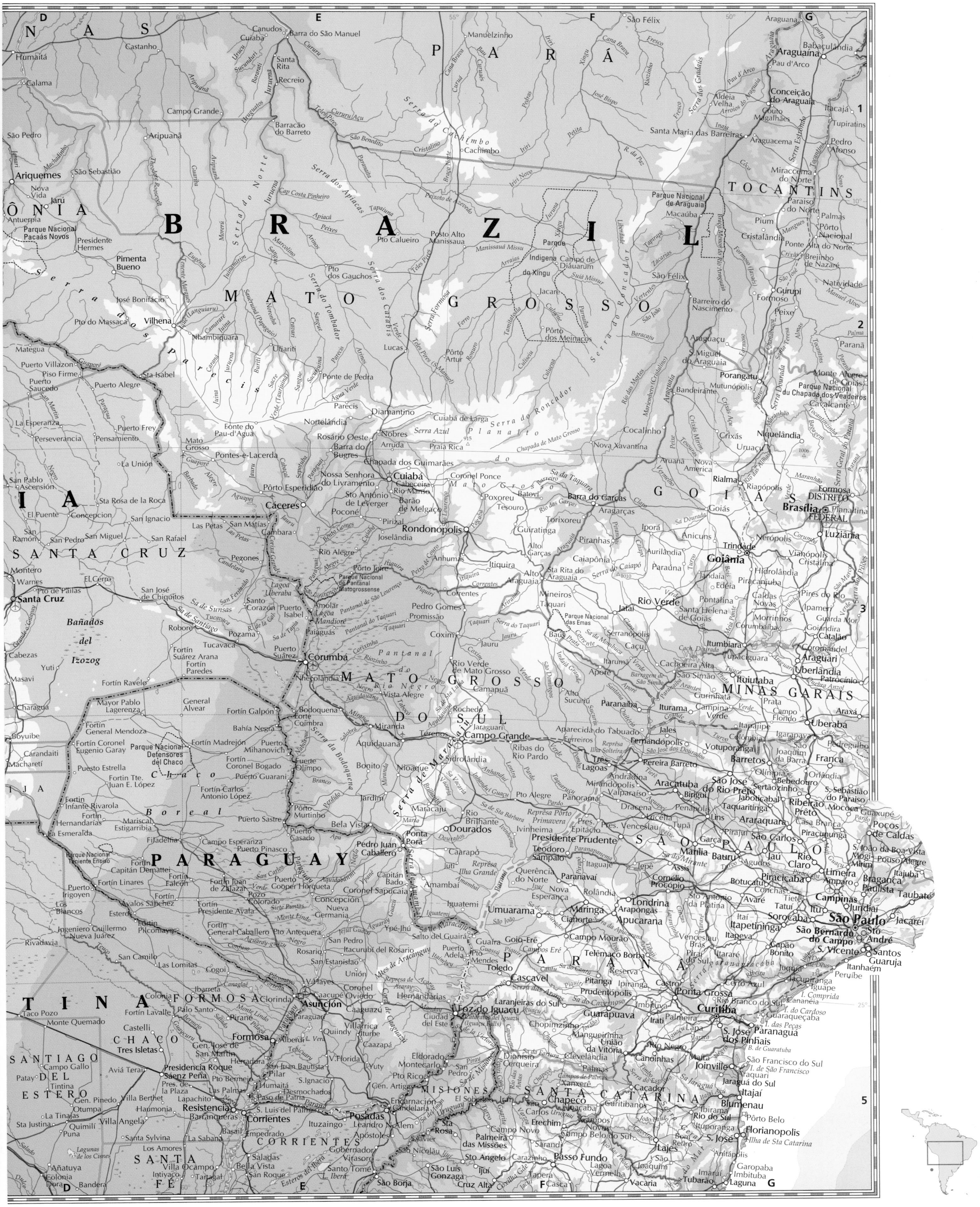

0 75 150 225 300 MILES
0 75 150 225 300 375 450 KM

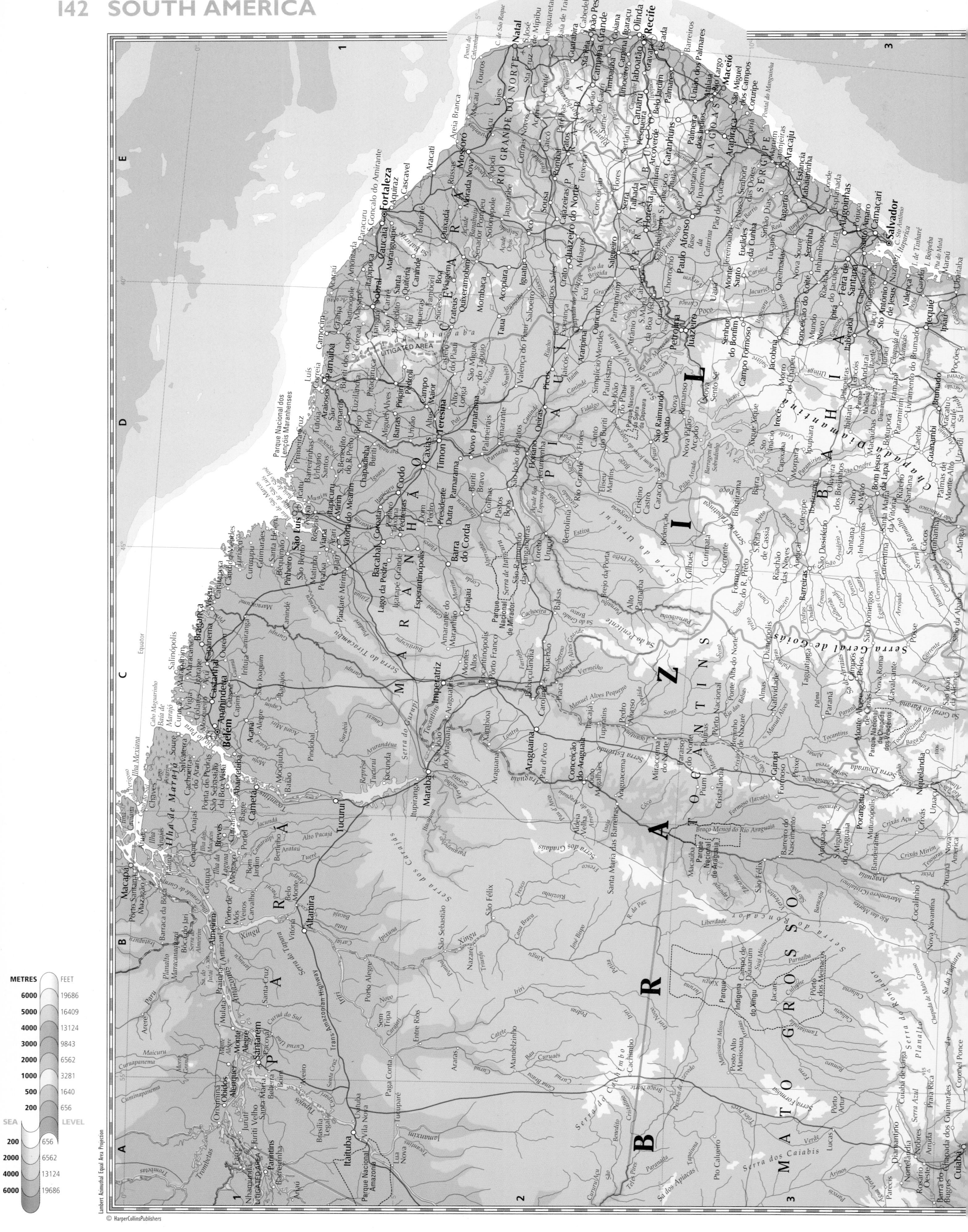
METRES
FEET
6000 19686
5000 16409
4000 13124
3000 9843
2000 6562
1000 3281
500 1640
200 656
SEA LEVEL
200 656
2000 6562
4000 13124
6000 19686
Lambert Azimuthal Equal Area Projection
B R A Z I L
P A R Á
M A R A N H Ã O
P I A U Í
C E A R Á
RIO GRANDE DO NORTE
P A R A Í B A
P E R N A M B U C O
A L A G O A S
S E R G I P E
B A H I A
T O C A N T I N S
MATO GROSSO
Ilha de Marajó
Belém
São Luís
Fortaleza
Natal
João Pessoa
Recife
Maceió
Aracaju
Salvador
Teresina
Santarém
Altamira
Marabá
Imperatriz
Macapá
Equator
Trans Amazonian Highway
Chapada Diamantina
Serra Geral de Goiás
LITIGATED AREA

© HarperCollinsPublishers

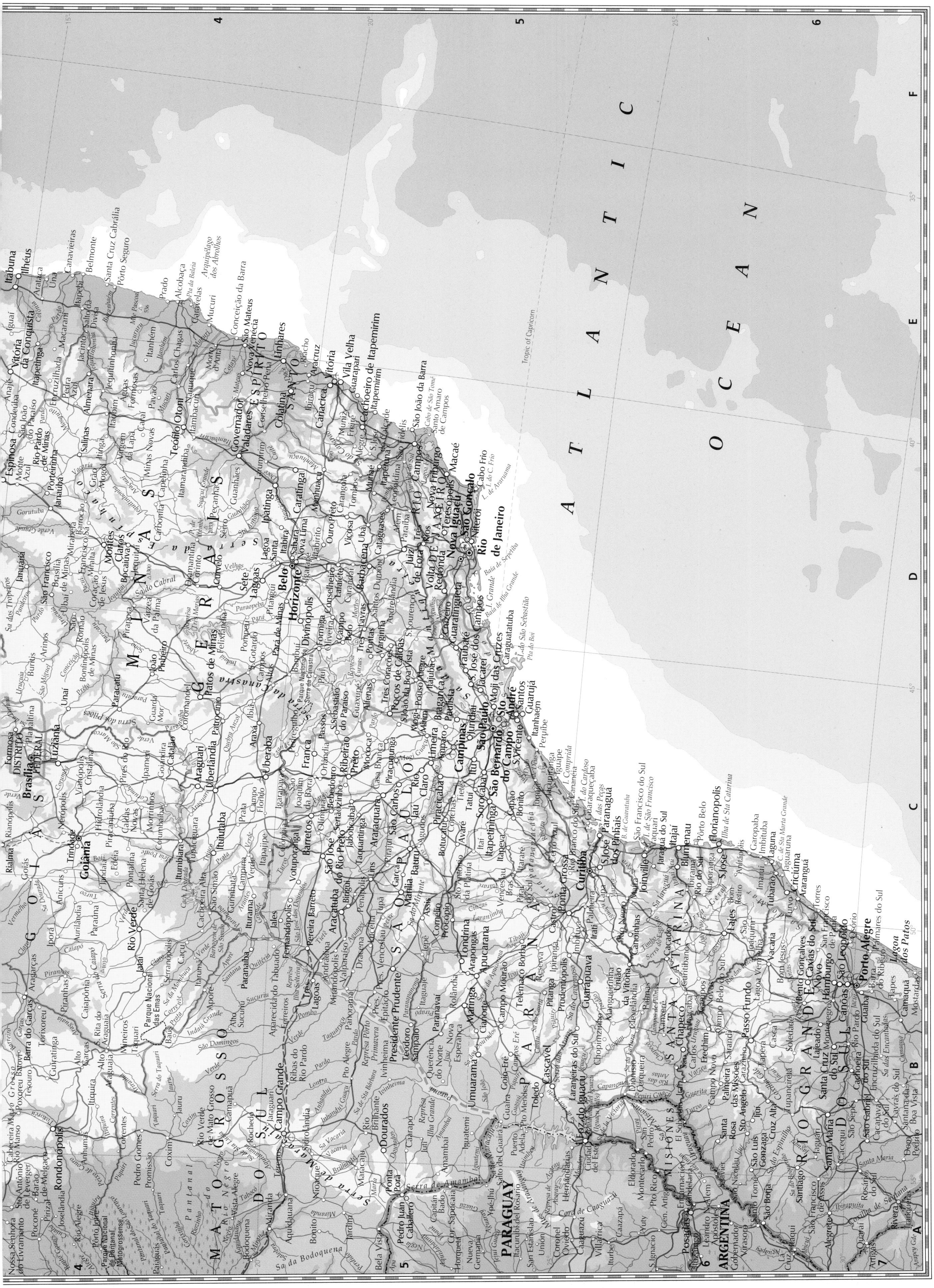
ATLANTIC OCEAN
Tropic of Capricorn
PARAGUAY
ARGENTINA
GOIÁS
MINAS GERAIS
ESPÍRITO SANTO
RIO DE JANEIRO
SÃO PAULO
PARANÁ
SANTA CATARINA
RIO GRANDE DO SUL
MATO GROSSO DO SUL
DISTRITO FEDERAL
Brasília
Belo Horizonte
Rio de Janeiro
São Paulo
Curitiba
Porto Alegre
Florianópolis
Vitória
Goiânia
Campo Grande
Campinas
Santos
Uberlândia
Juiz de Fora
Londrina
Lagoa dos Patos

1:7 500 000

0 75 150 225 300 MILES

0 75 150 225 300 375 450 KM

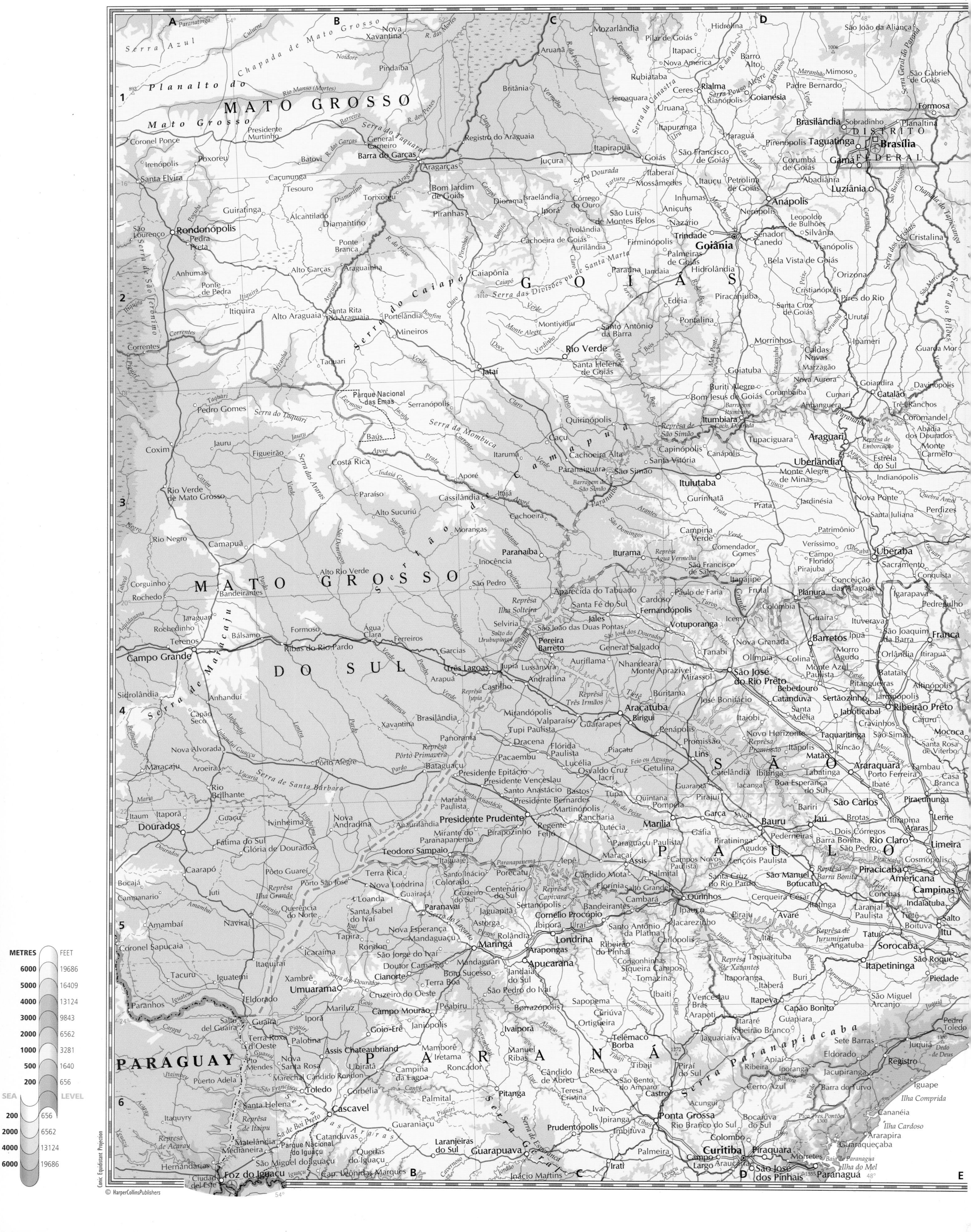
MATO GROSSO
Planalto do Mato Grosso
Chapada de Mato Grosso
Serra Azul
GOIÁS
MATO GROSSO DO SUL
SÃO PAULO
PARANÁ
PARAGUAY
DISTRITO FEDERAL
Brasília
Goiânia
Anápolis
Taguatinga
Gama
Luziânia
Formosa
Planaltina
Sobradinho
Brasilândia
Pirenópolis
Goiás
Rialma
Ceres
Goianésia
Uruana
Itapuranga
Jaraguá
Itapaci
Nova America
Rubiataba
Jeroaquara
Mozarlândia
Pilar de Goiás
Hidrolina
São João da Aliança
Mimoso
Padre Bernardo
São Gabriel de Goiás
Barro Alto
Aruanã
Britânia
Registro do Araguaia
Itapirapuã
Jussara
Itaberaí
Mossâmedes
Inhumas
Itauçu
Petrolina de Goiás
Nerópolis
Trindade
Senador Canedo
Leopoldo de Bulhões
Silvânia
Vianópolis
Cristalina
Bela Vista de Goiás
Orizona
Cristianópolis
Pires do Rio
Urutaí
Ipameri
Catalão
Goiandira
Davinópolis
Cumari
Anhanguera
Três Ranchos
Coromandel
Abadia dos Dourados
Monte Carmelo
Estrela do Sul
Araguari
Uberlândia
Monte Alegre de Minas
Indianópolis
Nova Ponte
Santa Juliana
Perdizes
Uberaba
Sacramento
Conquista
Patrimônio
Veríssimo
Campo Florido
Pirajuba
Conceição das Alagoas
Planura
Igarapava
Pedregulho
Franca
Ituverava
São Joaquim da Barra
Orlândia
Barretos
Guaíra
Colômbia
Frutal
Itapagipe
Iturama
São Francisco de Sales
Comendador Gomes
Campina Verde
Prata
Gurinhatã
Ituiutaba
Santa Vitória
Canápolis
Capinópolis
Tupaciguara
Itumbiara
Cachoeira Dourada
Bom Jesus de Goiás
Buriti Alegre
Goiatuba
Morrinhos
Caldas Novas
Marzagão
Nova Aurora
Corumbaíba
Pontalina
Edéia
Piracanjuba
Santa Cruz de Goiás
Hidrolândia
Palmeiras de Goiás
Paraúna
Jandaia
Firminópolis
São Luís de Montes Belos
Nazário
Anicuns
Córrego do Ouro
Israelândia
Iporá
Ivolândia
Cachoeira de Goiás
Aurilândia
Diorama
Bom Jardim de Goiás
Piranhas
Aragarças
Barra do Garças
Torixoréu
Caiapônia
Serra do Caiapó
Serra das Divisões ou de Santa Marta
Santo Antônio da Barra
Montividiu
Rio Verde
Santa Helena de Goiás
Jataí
Mineiros
Portelândia
Santa Rita do Araguaia
Alto Araguaia
Parque Nacional das Emas
Serranópolis
Baús
Quirinópolis
Caçu
Cachoeira Alta
Itarumã
Paranaiguara
São Simão
Represa de São Simão
Aporé
Cassilândia
Itajá
Cachoeira
Paranaíba
Inocência
São Pedro
Morangas
Alto Sucuriú
Paraíso
Costa Rica
Serra das Araras
Serra da Mombuca
Chapadão
Alto Rio Verde
Água Clara
Ferreiros
Ribas do Rio Pardo
Garcias
Três Lagoas
Arapuã
Jupiá
Castilho
Brasilândia
Xavantina
Bandeirantes
Corguinho
Rochedo
Jaraguari
Rochedinho
Terenos
Campo Grande
Bálsamo
Formoso
Sidrolândia
Anhanduí
Capão Seco
Nova Alvorada
Maracaju
Aroeira
Rio Brilhante
Serra de Maracaju
Serra de Santa Bárbara
Itaum
Itaporã
Dourados
Guaçu
Ivinhema
Nova Andradina
Fátima do Sul
Glória de Dourados
Caarapó
Pôrto Guarei
Juti
Bocajá
Campanario
Amambaí
Naviraí
Coronel Sapucaia
Itaquiraí
Tacuru
Iguatemi
Eldorado
Paranhos
Salto del Guairá
Guaíra
Terra Roxa d'Oeste
Palotina
Marechal Cândido Rondon
Toledo
Cascavel
Santa Helena
Puerto Adela
Itaquyry
Represa de Itaipu
Matelândia
Medianeira
Hernandarias
Ciudad del Este
Foz do Iguaçu
São Miguel do Iguaçu
Parque Nacional do Iguaçu
Quedas do Iguaçu
Catanduvas
Guaraniaçu
Laranjeiras do Sul
Guarapuava
Inácio Martins
Irati
Prudentópolis
Imbituva
Ipiranga
Ponta Grossa
Palmeira
Curitiba
Campo Largo
Araucária
Piraquara
São José dos Pinhais
Paranaguá
Morretes
Ilha do Mel
Guaraqueçaba
Cananéia
Ilha Comprida
Iguape
Registro
Jacupiranga
Eldorado
Juquiá
Pedro de Toledo
Sete Barras
Serra de Paranapiacaba
Apiaí
Iporanga
Ribeira
Capão Bonito
Itapeva
Itararé
Jaguariaíva
Piraí do Sul
Castro
Telêmaco Borba
Tibaji
Reserva
Ortigueira
Ivaiporã
Manuel Ribas
Cândido de Abreu
Pitanga
Palmital
Campina da Lagoa
Roncador
Mamborê
Campo Mourão
Goio-Erê
Assis Chateaubriand
Ubiratã
Umuarama
Cianorte
Cruzeiro do Oeste
Peabiru
Maringá
Apucarana
Arapongas
Londrina
Rolândia
Cornélio Procópio
Bandeirantes
Santo Antônio da Platina
Jacarezinho
Ourinhos
Cambará
Assis
Palmital
Cândido Mota
Paranavaí
Loanda
Santa Isabel do Ivaí
Nova Londrina
Terra Rica
Colorado
Santo Inácio
Porecatu
Teodoro Sampaio
Presidente Prudente
Presidente Epitácio
Presidente Venceslau
Presidente Bernardes
Santo Anastácio
Martinópolis
Rancharia
Regente Feijó
Pirapozinho
Mirante do Paranapanema
Euclides da Cunha
Anaurilândia
Batayporã
Pôrto Primavera
Bataguaçu
Pacaembu
Dracena
Tupi Paulista
Panorama
Mirandópolis
Valparaíso
Guararapes
Araçatuba
Birigui
Penápolis
Promissão
Lins
Getulina
Tupã
Bastos
Osvaldo Cruz
Lucélia
Flórida Paulista
Adamantina
Marília
Garça
Pompéia
Quintana
Bauru
Jaú
Pederneiras
Agudos
Lençóis Paulista
Botucatu
São Manuel
Avaré
Itapetininga
Sorocaba
Itu
Salto
Campinas
Americana
Piracicaba
Limeira
Rio Claro
Araras
Leme
Pirassununga
São Carlos
Araraquara
Matão
Jaboticabal
Ribeirão Prêto
Sertãozinho
Bebedouro
Catanduva
São José do Rio Prêto
Mirassol
Votuporanga
Fernandópolis
Jales
Santa Fé do Sul
Aparecida do Tabuado
Pereira Barreto
Ilha Solteira
Andradina
Auriflama
Nhandeara
General Salgado
Represa Três Irmãos
Coronel Ponce
Irenópolis
Poxoréu
Santa Elvira
Rondonópolis
São Lourenço
Pedra Preta
Guiratinga
Alcantilado
Diamantino
Tesouro
Caçununga
Batovi
General Carneiro
Presidente Murtinho
Nova Xavantina
Pindaíba
Ponte Branca
Araguainha
Alto Garças
Anhumas
Ponte de Pedra
Itiquira
Serra de São Jerônimo
Correntes
Taquari
Pedro Gomes
Serra do Taquari
Coxim
Jauru
Figueirão
Rio Verde de Mato Grosso
Rio Negro
Camapuã
A
B
C
D
E
1
2
3
4
5
6
METRES
FEET
6000
5000
4000
3000
2000
1000
500
200
19686
16409
13124
9843
6562
3281
1640
656
SEA
LEVEL
Conic Equidistant Projection

© HarperCollinsPublishers

1:3 750 000 | 0 20 40 60 80 100 120 MILES | 0 40 80 120 160 200 KM

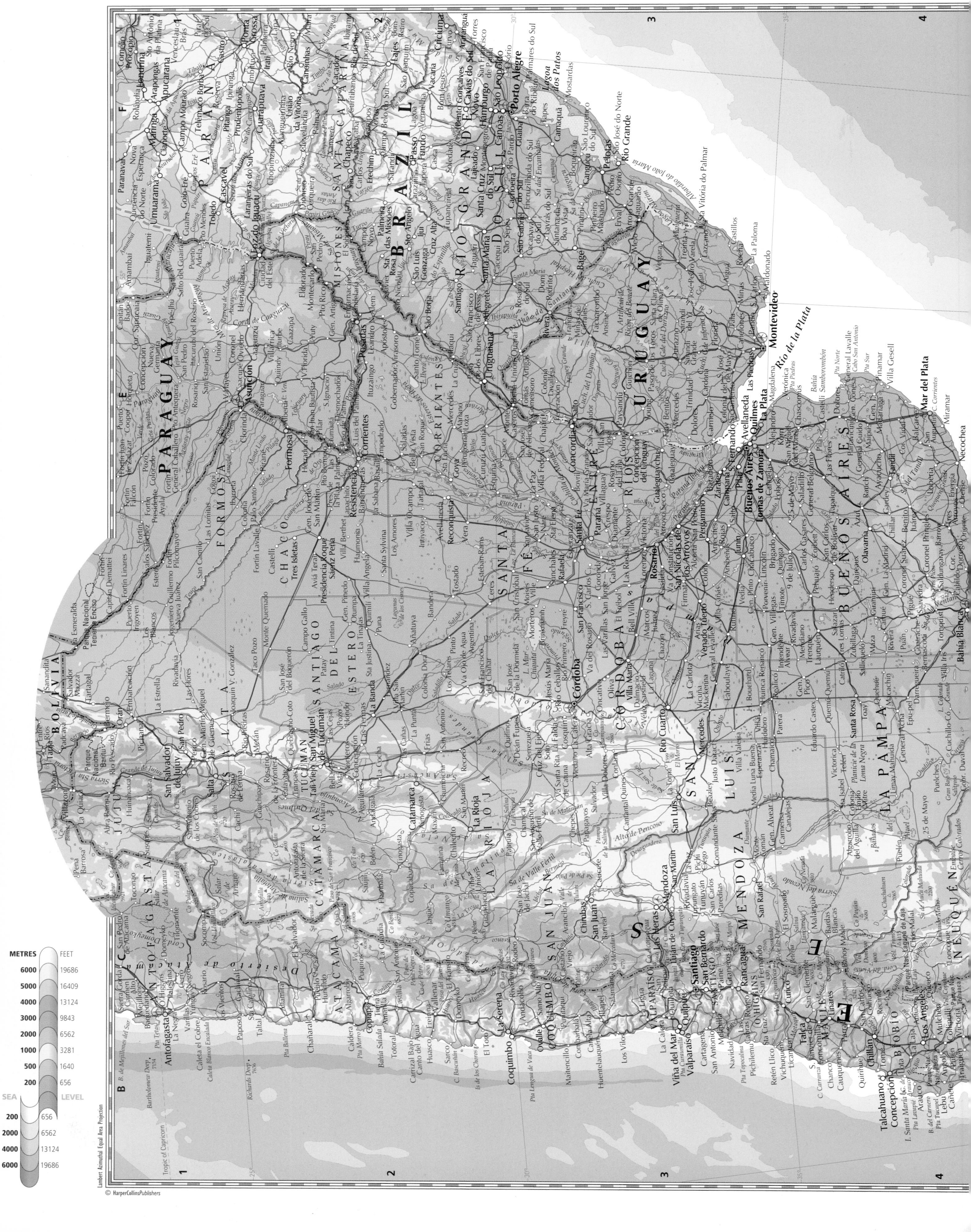
METRES FEET
6000 19686
5000 16409
4000 13124
3000 9843
2000 6562
1000 3281
500 1640
200 656
SEA LEVEL
200 656
2000 6562
4000 13124
6000 19686
Lambert Azimuthal Equal Area Projection
PARAGUAY
URUGUAY
BRAZIL
BOLIVIA
PARANÁ
SANTA CATARINA
RIO GRANDE DO SUL
MISIONES
CORRIENTES
ENTRE RÍOS
BUENOS AIRES
LA PAMPA
CÓRDOBA
SANTA FÉ
SANTIAGO DEL ESTERO
CHACO
FORMOSA
SALTA
JUJUY
TUCUMÁN
CATAMARCA
LA RIOJA
SAN JUAN
SAN LUIS
MENDOZA
NEUQUÉN
ANTOFAGASTA
ATACAMA
COQUIMBO
VALPARAÍSO
SANTIAGO
O'HIGGINS
MAULE
BÍO-BÍO
Río de la Plata
Tropic of Capricorn
Asunción
Montevideo
Buenos Aires
La Plata
Rosario
Córdoba
Mendoza
Santiago
Valparaíso
Porto Alegre
Mar del Plata
Bahía Blanca
Concepción

© HarperCollinsPublishers

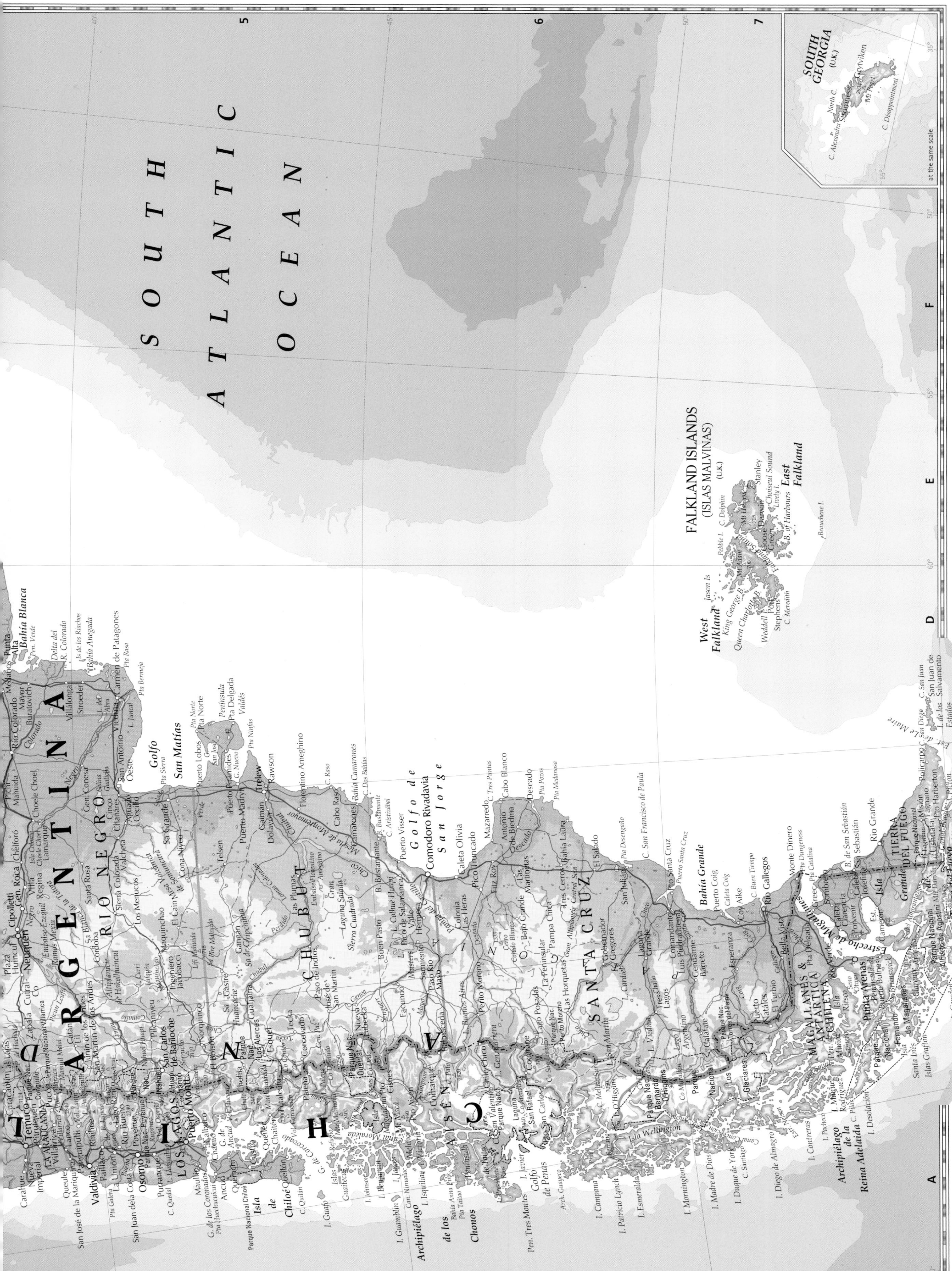
SOUTH ATLANTIC OCEAN
FALKLAND ISLANDS
(ISLAS MALVINAS)
(U.K.)
West Falkland
East Falkland
Stanley
SOUTH GEORGIA
(U.K.)
ARGENTINA
CHILE
RIO NEGRO
CHUBUT
SANTA CRUZ
TIERRA DEL FUEGO
Bahía Blanca
Golfo San Matías
Golfo San Jorge
Comodoro Rivadavia
Rawson
Trelew
Puerto Madryn
Neuquén
Temuco
Valdivia
Osorno
Puerto Montt
Isla de Chiloé
Archipiélago de los Chonos
Río Gallegos
Punta Arenas
Estrecho de Magallanes
Ushuaia
Cabo de Hornos
(C. Horn)

1:7 500 000

0	75	150	225	300	MILES
0	75	150	225	300	375	450	KM

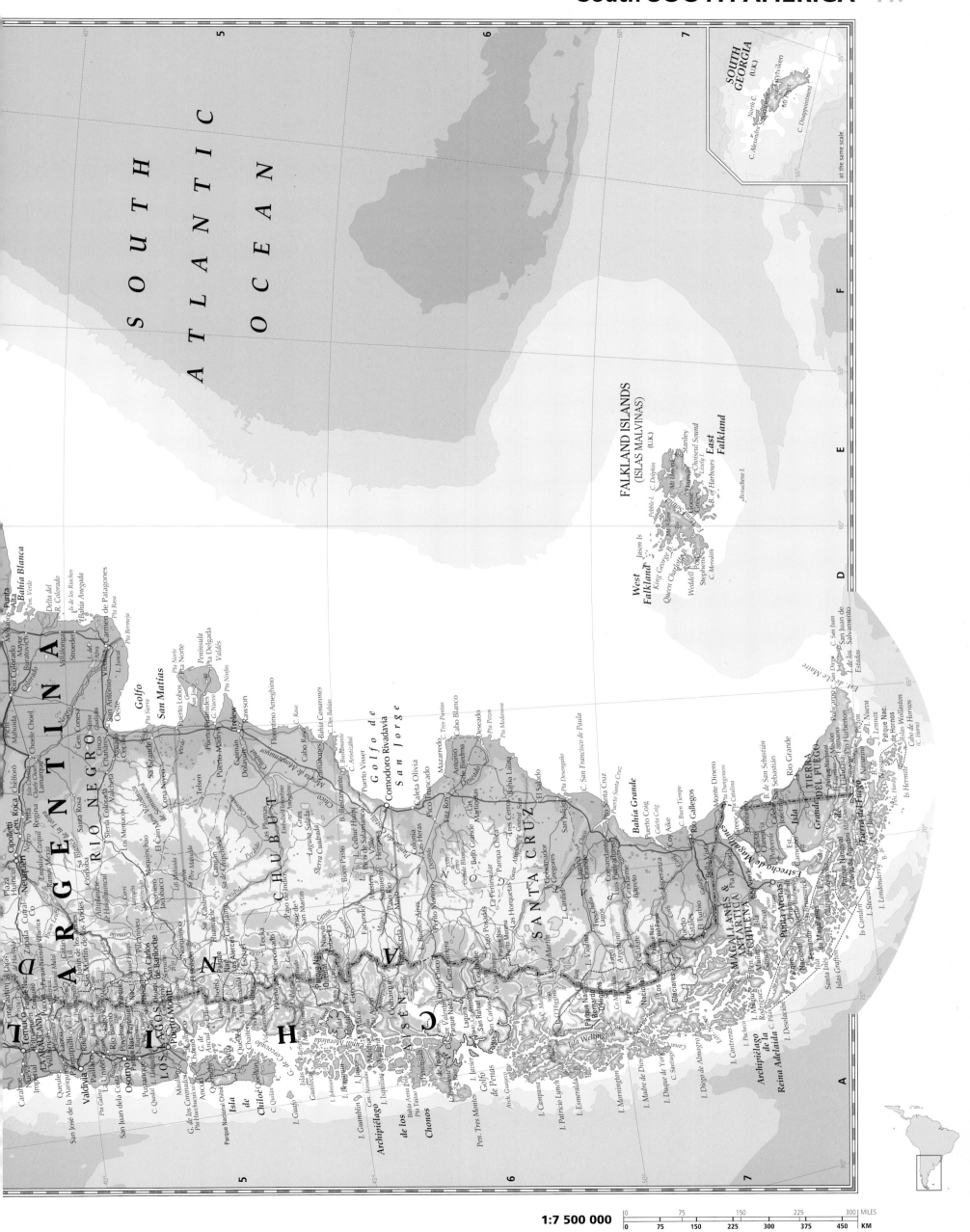

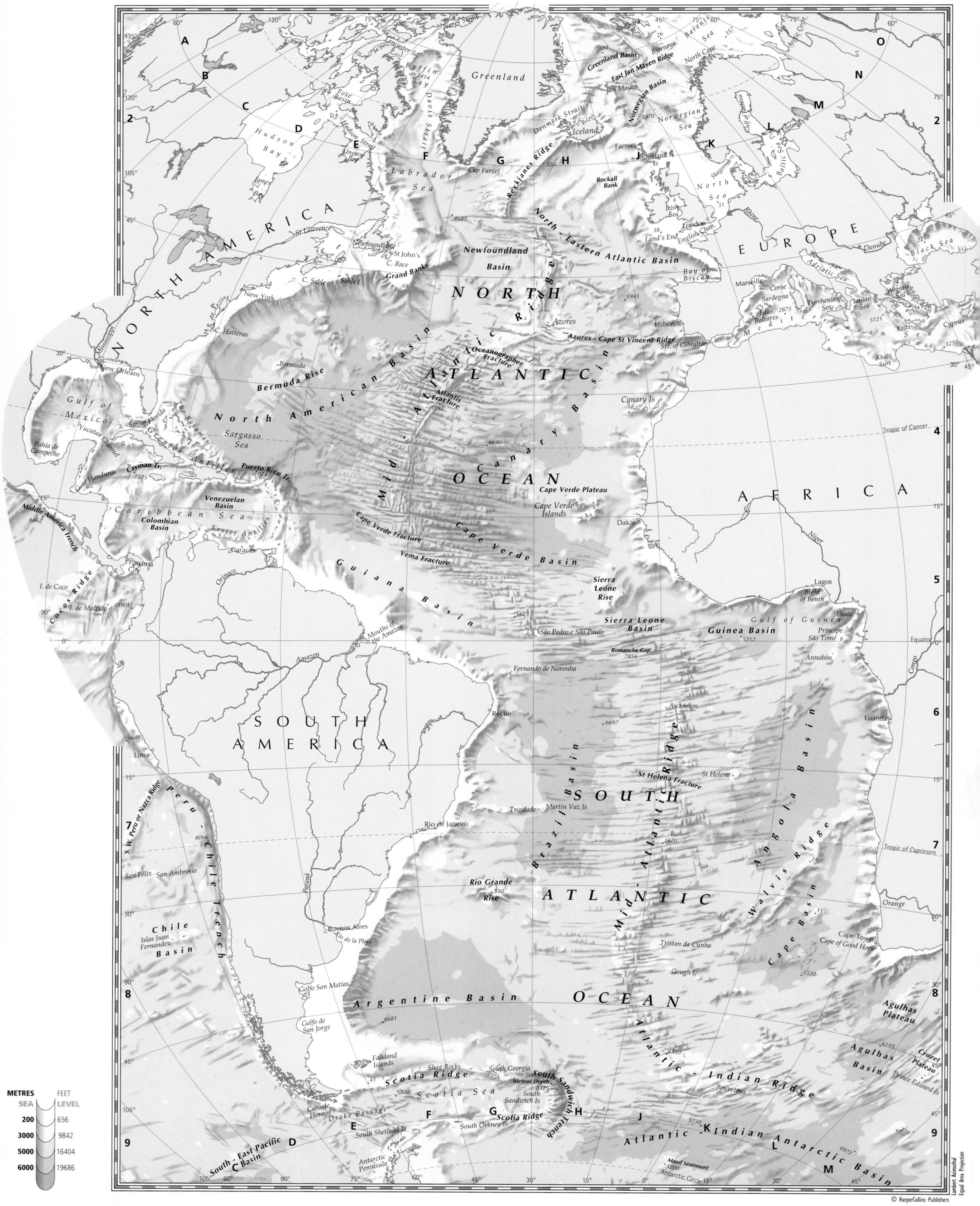

0 300 600 900 1200 1500 1800 MILES
0 500 1000 1500 2000 2500 3000 KM
1:48 000 000

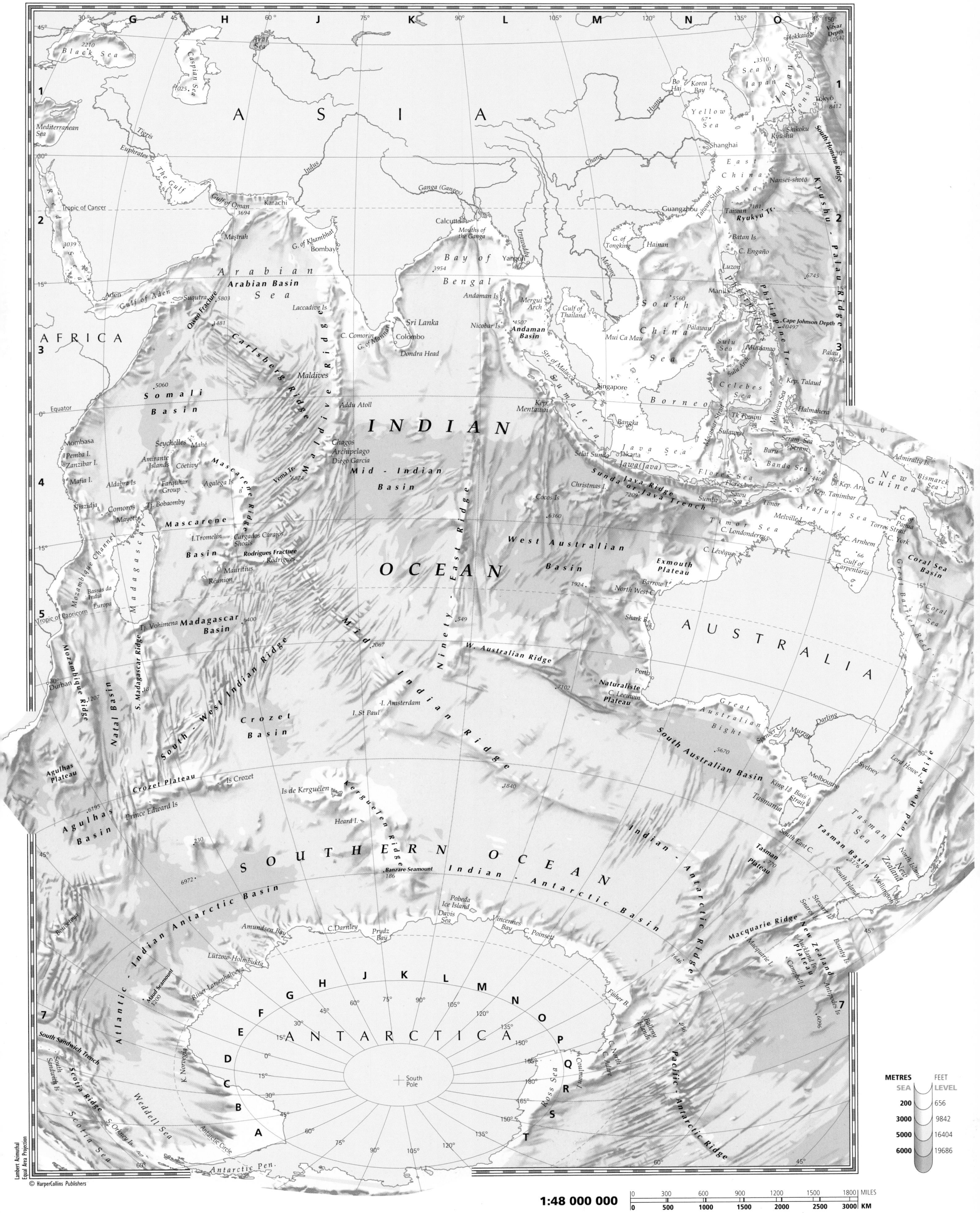
ASIA
AFRICA
AUSTRALIA
ANTARCTICA
INDIAN OCEAN
SOUTHERN OCEAN
Black Sea
Caspian Sea
Aral Sea
Mediterranean Sea
Red Sea
The Gulf
Gulf of Oman
Gulf of Aden
Arabian Sea
Arabian Basin
Bay of Bengal
Andaman Basin
Gulf of Thailand
South China Sea
Yellow Sea
East China Sea
Sea of Japan
Sulu Sea
Celebes Sea
Java Sea
Flores Sea
Banda Sea
Timor Sea
Arafura Sea
Gulf of Carpentaria
Coral Sea
Tasman Sea
Great Australian Bight
Weddell Sea
Ross Sea
Scotia Sea
Somali Basin
Mascarene Basin
Madagascar Basin
Mid - Indian Basin
West Australian Basin
Crozet Basin
Natal Basin
Agulhas Basin
Agulhas Plateau
South Australian Basin
Tasman Basin
Carlsberg Ridge
Maldive Ridge
Mascarene Ridge
Ninety - East Ridge
Mid - Indian Ridge
South - West Indian Ridge
Madagascar Ridge
Mozambique Ridge
W. Australian Ridge
Kerguelen Ridge
Indian - Antarctic Ridge
Pacific - Antarctic Ridge
Atlantic - Indian Antarctic Basin
Indian - Antarctic Basin
Macquarie Ridge
Lord Howe Rise
Sunda or Java Trench
Java Ridge
Philippine Tr.
Ryukyu Tr.
South Honshu Ridge
Kyushu - Palau Ridge
Cape Johnson Depth
Vityaz Depth
Owen Fracture
Rodrigues Fracture
Exmouth Plateau
Naturaliste Plateau
Crozet Plateau
Tasman Plateau
Kerguelen Plateau
Banzare Seamount
Maud Seamount
South Sandwich Trench
Scotia Ridge
Great Barrier Reef
Tropic of Cancer
Equator
Tropic of Capricorn
Antarctic Circle
South Pole
Karachi
Bombay
Calcutta
Colombo
Sri Lanka
Singapore
Jakarta
Shanghai
Guangzhou
Tokyo
Perth
Sydney
Melbourne
Mombasa
Durban
Aden
Madagascar
Mauritius
Réunion
Rodrigues
Seychelles
Maldives
Chagos Archipelago
Diego Garcia
Cocos Is
Christmas I.
I. Amsterdam
I. St Paul
Is de Kerguélen
Heard I.
Is Crozet
Prince Edward Is
Tasmania
New Zealand
New Guinea
Borneo
Sumatera
Java
Timor
Sumba
Hainan
Taiwan
Luzon
Mindanao
Hokkaido
Honshu
Shikoku
Kyushu
Comoros
Mayotte
Laccadive Is
Andaman Is
Nicobar Is
Amundsen Bay
Prydz Bay
Lützow-Holmbukta
Riiser-Larsenhalvøya
Antarctic Pen.
1:48 000 000
0 300 600 900 1200 1500 1800 MILES
0 500 1000 1500 2000 2500 3000 KM
METRES FEET
SEA LEVEL
200 656
3000 9842
5000 16404
6000 19686
Lambert Azimuthal Equal Area Projection

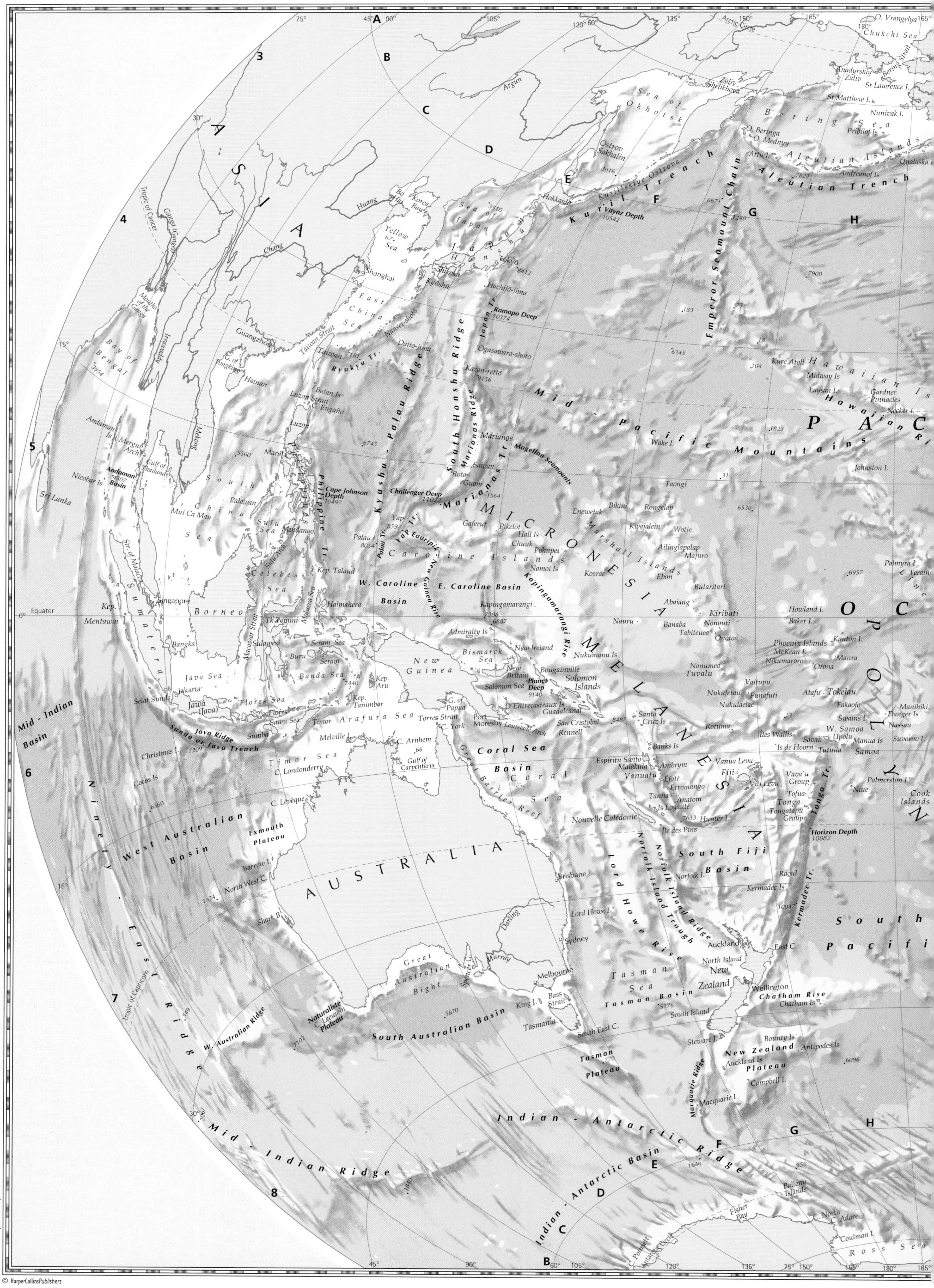

METRES	FEET
SEA	LEVEL
200	656
3000	9842
5000	16404
6000	19686

© HarperCollinsPublishers

NORTH AMERICA
SOUTH AMERICA
Hudson Bay
Gulf of Alaska
Kodiak I.
Alexander Archipelago
Queen Charlotte Islands
Vancouver Island
Vancouver
Columbia
Missouri
Mississippi
Colorado
Grande
New York
C. Hatteras
C. Sable
Sable I.
Bermuda
Bermuda Rise
North American Basin
Mid Atlantic Ridge
Atlantis Fracture
Mendocino Seascarp
C. Mendocino
San Francisco
Erben Tablemount
Los Angeles
Murray Seascarp
Guadalupe
Golfo de California
Molokai Fracture Zone
Kauai
Oahu
Maui
Hawaii
Clarion Fracture Zone
Clipperton Fracture Zone
Clipperton I.
Is Revillagigedo
I. Socorro
I. Clarión
East Pacific Rise
New Orleans
Gulf of Mexico
Bahía de Campeche
Str. of Florida
The Bahamas
Greater Antilles
Puerto Rico Tr.
Yucatan Channel
Cayman Tr.
G. of Honduras
G. de Tehuantepec
Tehuantepec Ridge
Middle America Trench
Venezuelan Basin
Caribbean Sea
Lesser Antilles
Colombian Basin
Caracas
Panama City
Orinoco
Guiana Basin
Cape Verde Fracture
Vemo Fracture
I. de Coco
Cocos Ridge
I. de Malpelo
Islas Galápagos
Carnegie Ridge
G. de Guayaquil
Mouths of the Amazon
Amazon
Tabuaeran
Kiritimati
Jarvis I.
Malden I.
Starbuck I.
Tongareva
Caroline I.
Flint I.
Nuku Hiva
Is Marquises
Hiva Oa
Is du Roi Georges
Îles de Désappointement
Is Tuamotu
Fenua Ura
Raiatea
Tahiti
Anaa
Raroia
Hao
Is de la Société
Hervey Is
Rarotonga
Mangaia
Îles Maria
Hereheretue
Îles Duc de Gloucester
Mururoa
Groupe Actéon
Is Gambier
Tubuai
Raivavae
Is Tubuai
Rapa
Henderson I.
Ducie I.
Pitcairn I.
Peru Basin
Lima
Peru Chile Trench
S. W. Peru or Nazca Ridge
Easter Island Fracture Zone
Easter I.
I. Sala y Gómez
San Félix
San Ambrosio
East Pacific Ridge
Challenger Fracture Zone
Chile Basin
Is Juan Fernández
Robinson Crusoe
Santiago
Paraná
Rio de Janeiro
Buenos Aires
Río de la Plata
Golfo San Matías
Golfo de San Jorge
Argentine Basin
Falkland Islands
Cabo de Hornos
Drake Passage
Scotia Sea
Scotia Ridge
Pacific Antarctic Ridge
Eltanin Fracture Zone
South-East Pacific Basin
Amundsen Sea
Peter I Øy

1:48 000 000

MILES	0	300	600	900	1200	1500	1800
KM	0	500	1000	1500	2000	2500	3000

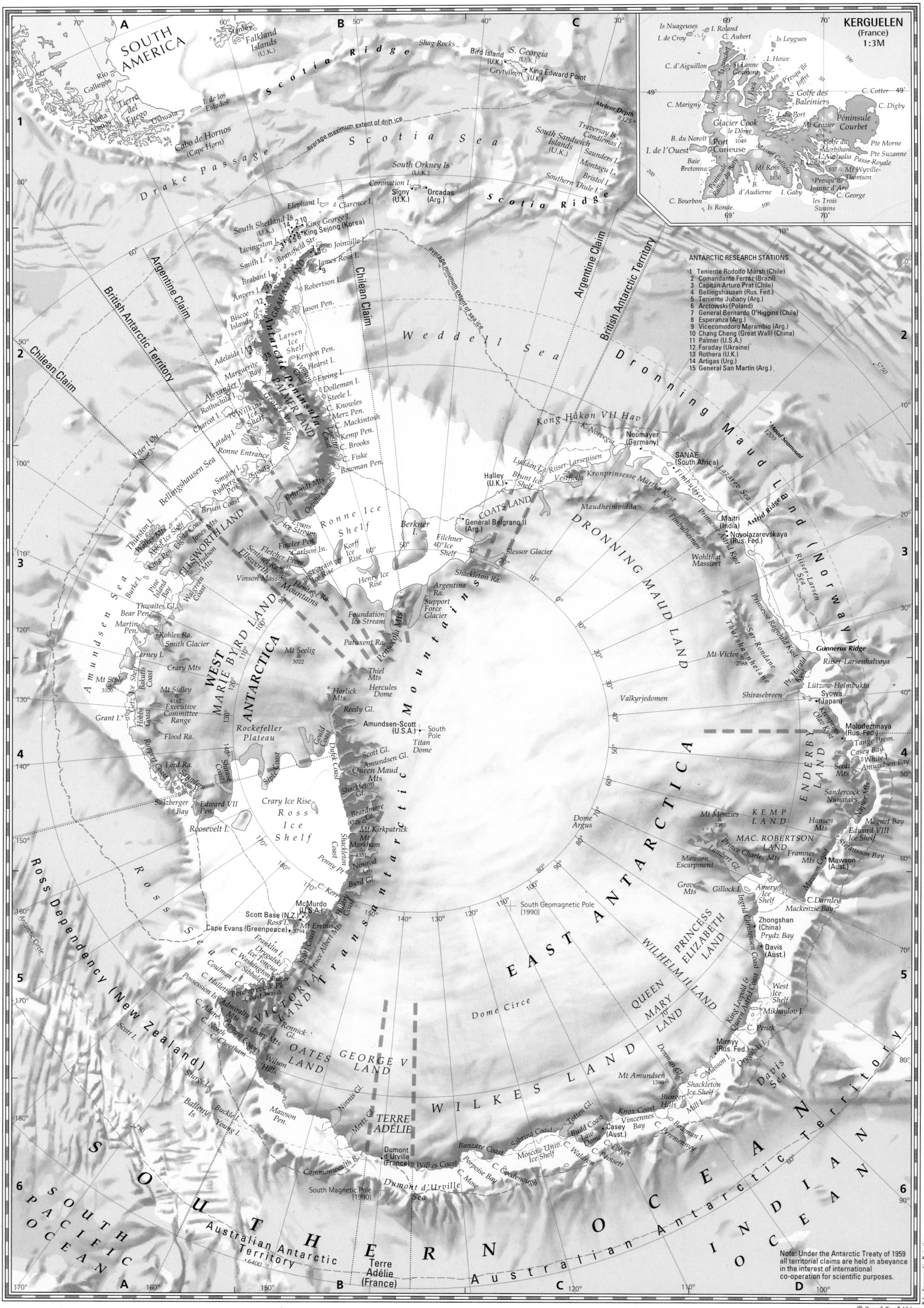

0 200 400 600 800 MILES
0 200 400 600 800 1000 1200 KM
1:24 000 000

© HarperCollins Publishers

THE INDEX INCLUDES the names on the maps in the ATLAS of the WORLD section. Names are indexed to the largest scale map on which they appear, and can be located using the grid reference letters and numbers around the map frame. Names on insets have a symbol: □, followed by the inset number. Although the maps have been revised to account for the change in name from Zaire to Congo and the reversion of Hong Kong to Chinese rule, this index reflects the prior situation.
Abbreviations used to describe features in the index are explained on the right. Abbreviations used in feature names on the maps and in the index, are explained on page 24. A glossary of alternative name forms is included on page 199.

A.C.T. Australian Capital Territory
b. bay
B.C. British Columbia
Bos.-Herz. Bosnia-Herzegovina
c. cape
chan. channel
div. division
est. estuary
g. gulf
gl. glacier
h. hill, hills
i., I. island
is, Is islands
l. lake
lag. lagoon
mt. mountain
mts mountains
N. North
nat. park. national park
N.W.T. Northwest Territories
pen. peninsula
plat. plateau
P.N.G. Papua New Guinea
pt point
r. river
reg. region
Rep. Republic
res. reserve
resr reservoir
Rus. Fed. Russian Federation
S. South
Str. Strait
Terr. Territory
U.A.E. United Arab Emirates
U.K. United Kingdom
U.S.A. United States of America
v. valley

A

18 C3 Aachen Germany
18 E4 Aalen Germany
18 B3 Aalst Belgium
21 J3 Aarau Switz.
21 H3 Aarberg Switz.
18 B3 Aarschot Belgium
50 C1 Aba China
77 F5 Aba Nigeria
78 F3 Aba Zaire
73 H2 Abā ad Dūd Saudi Arabia
139 F5 Abacaxis r. Brazil
57 B3 Abādān Iran
57 C3 Abādeh Iran
144 E3 Abadia dos Dourados Brazil
144 D2 Abadiânia Brazil
74 D2 Abadla Algeria
145 F3 Abaeté Brazil
145 F3 Abaeté r. Brazil
142 C1 Abaetetuba Brazil
49 F2 Abagaytuy Rus. Fed.
49 E4 Abag Qi China
24 B1 A Baiuca Spain
77 F5 Abaji Nigeria
127 E4 Abajo Pk summit U.S.A.
77 F5 Abakaliki Nigeria
65 M2 Abakan Rus. Fed.
65 L2 Abakan r. Rus. Fed.
65 L2 Abakanskiy Khrebet mt. ra. Rus. Fed.
78 C4 Abala Congo
77 E4 Abala Niger
77 F3 Abalak Niger
77 F3 Abalemma well Niger
75 E4 Abalessa Algeria
57 C3 Āb Anbār Iran
140 B2 Abancay Peru
78 B3 Abanga r. Gabon
25 F3 Abanilla Spain
57 C3 Abarqū Iran
46 K1 Abashiri Japan
46 K2 Abashiri-gawa r. Japan
46 K2 Abashiri-ko l. Japan
46 K1 Abashiri-wan b. Japan
81 C5 Abasula waterhole Kenya
65 H1 Abatskiy Rus. Fed.
90 □1 Abau P.N.G.
65 H3 Abay Kazak.
80 C3 Ābaya Hāyk' l. Ethiopia
65 M2 Abaza Rus. Fed.
78 C2 Abba C.A.R.
26 C4 Abbadia San Salvatore Italy
57 D2 Abbāsābād Iran
27 B5 Abbasanta Italy
122 C2 Abbaye, Pt pt U.S.A.
80 D2 Abbe, L. l. Ethiopia
20 E1 Abbeville France
125 E6 Abbeville U.S.A.
119 D5 Abbeville U.S.A.
99 F2 Abbey Peak h. Aust.
10 E2 Abborrträsk Sweden
152 A3 Abbot Ice Shelf ice feature Ant.
99 F4 Abbot, Mt mt. Aust.
110 E5 Abbotsford Can.
122 B3 Abbotsford U.S.A.
127 F4 Abbott U.S.A.
54 C2 Abbottabad Pakistan
60 D2 'Abd al 'Azīz, J. h. Syria
80 □ 'Abd al Kūrī i. Socotra Yemen
12 J4 Abdi Rus. Fed.
57 D2 Abdolabād Iran
57 D1 Abdollāhābād Iran
57 C2 Abdollāhābād Iran
64 D2 Abdulino Rus. Fed.
72 D5 Abéché Chad
57 D3 Āb-e Garm Iran
77 E3 Abeïbara well Mali
77 F5 Abejukolo Nigeria
77 F3 Abélajouad well Niger
93 D4 Abel Tasman National Park nat. park N.Z.
76 D5 Abengourou Côte d'Ivoire
24 D3 Abenójar Spain
11 C5 Åbenrå Denmark
18 E4 Abensberg Germany
77 E5 Abeokuta Nigeria
17 E5 Aberaeron U.K.
17 F6 Aberdare U.K.
97 G3 Aberdeen Aust.
111 H4 Aberdeen Can.
45 □ Aberdeen Hong Kong
82 C5 Aberdeen R.S.A.
16 F3 Aberdeen U.K.
121 E5 Aberdeen U.S.A.
125 F5 Aberdeen U.S.A.
124 D2 Aberdeen U.S.A.
126 B2 Aberdeen U.S.A.
111 J2 Aberdeen Lake l. Can.
16 E3 Aberfoyle U.K.
17 F6 Abergavenny U.K.
125 C5 Abernathy U.S.A.
17 E5 Aberystwyth U.K.
73 H4 Abhā Saudi Arabia
57 B1 Abhar r. Iran
57 B1 Abhar Iran
77 F5 Abia div. Nigeria
80 C3 Ābīata Hāyk' l. Ethiopia
57 B2 Ab-i Bazuft r. Iran
76 D5 Abidjan Côte d'Ivoire
57 G2 Ab-i-Istada l. Afghanistan
80 C3 Abijatta-Shalla National Park nat. park Ethiopia
57 D2 Ab-i-Kavir salt flat Iran
47 H6 Abiko Japan
124 D4 Abilene U.S.A.
125 D5 Abilene U.S.A.
17 G6 Abingdon U.K.
122 B5 Abingdon U.S.A.
120 C6 Abingdon U.S.A.
99 G3 Abington Reef reef Coral Sea Islands Terr. Pac. Oc.
13 F6 Abinsk Rus. Fed.
57 E2 Ab-i-Rahuk Afghanistan
57 F1 Ab-i-Safed r. Afghanistan
140 A1 Abiseo, Parque Nacional nat. park Peru
111 H2 Abitau Lake l. Can.
114 E2 Abitibi r. Can.
114 E2 Abitibi Canyon Dam dam Can.
114 E2 Abitibi, Lake l. Can.
13 G7 Abkhazia div. Georgia
96 C1 Abminga Aust.
73 F2 Abnûb Egypt
76 D5 Aboisso Côte d'Ivoire
80 B3 Aboke Sudan
77 E5 Abomey Benin
54 C3 Abonar India
78 B3 Abong Mbang Cameroon
76 D5 Abooso Ghana
41 A4 Aborlan Phil.
78 C1 Abou Déia Chad
60 F1 Abovyan Armenia
140 C4 Abra Chile
80 E1 Abrād, W. w Yemen
133 D2 Abraham's Bay The Bahamas
147 D5 Abra, L. del l. Arg.
146 C1 Abra Pampa Arg.
145 G4 Abre Campo Brazil
73 F3 'Abri Sudan
145 J2 Abrolhos, Arquipélago dos is Brazil
28 D1 Abrud Romania
27 D4 Abruzzo div. Italy
126 E2 Absaroka Range mt. ra. U.S.A.
59 H1 Abşeron Yarımdası pen. Azerbaijan
46 C6 Abu Japan
61 D2 Abū aḑ Ḑuhūr Syria
57 B4 Abū'Alī i. Saudi Arabia
57 C4 Abual Jirab i. U.A.E.
61 D5 Abu 'Amūd, W. w Jordan
73 H4 Abū 'Arīsh Saudi Arabia
61 C4 Abu 'Aweigîla well Egypt
73 E3 Abu Ballûs h. Egypt
73 F4 Abu Deleiq Sudan
73 G3 Abū Ḑībā' Saudi Arabia
61 B5 Abu Durba Egypt
61 B5 Abu Hâd, W. w Egypt
61 D3 Abu Hafrah, W. w Jordan
73 E1 Abu Haggag Egypt
61 D4 Abū Hallūfa, J. h. Jordan
73 F4 Abu Hamed Sudan
73 F4 Abu Hashim w Sudan
73 F5 Abu Hut w Sudan
77 F5 Abuja Nigeria
61 A4 Abu Kebîr Egypt
72 E5 Abu Ku Sudan
47 H5 Abukuma-gawa r. Japan
47 H5 Abukuma-kochi plat. Japan
73 G4 Abū Latt I. i. Saudi Arabia
78 E1 Abu Matariq Sudan
78 D3 Abumombazi Zaire
57 C4 Abū Mūsá i. U.A.E.
140 C1 Abunã r. Bolivia
140 C1 Abunã Brazil
138 D4 Abunai Brazil
72 C2 Abū Nā'im well Libya
80 C2 Ābune Yosēf mt. Ethiopia
72 C1 Abū Nujaym Libya
61 D2 Abū Qa'ţūr Syria
61 A6 Abu Qurqâs Egypt
78 F3 Aburo mt. Zaire
54 C4 Abu Road India
73 G3 Abū Rubayq Saudi Arabia
61 B5 Abu Rudeis Egypt
61 D5 Abu Sallah w Saudi Arabia
73 E5 Abu Shanab Sudan
73 F3 Abu Simbel Egypt
73 F3 Abu Simbel Temple Egypt
60 F4 Abū Şukhayr Iraq
93 C5 Abut Head hd N.Z.
61 D5 Abū Ujayyijāt well Saudi Arabia
80 C2 Abuye Meda mt. Ethiopia
41 C4 Abuyog Phil.
73 E5 Abu Zabad Sudan
57 C4 Abū Ẓabī U.A.E.
73 F2 Abu Zenîma Egypt
73 E5 Abyad Sudan
72 D1 Abyār an Nākhīlah well Libya
61 C5 Abyār Banī Murr well Saudi Arabia
100 B4 Abydos Aust.
78 E2 Abyei Sudan
72 C5 Ab Zérafa Chad
121 J2 Acadia Nat. Park nat. park U.S.A.
131 E4 Acambaro Mexico
131 H4 Acancéh Mexico
138 B2 Acandí Colombia
24 B1 A Cañiza Spain
130 D4 Acaponeta Mexico
131 F5 Acapulco Mexico
142 C1 Acará r. Brazil
142 C1 Acará Brazil
142 C1 Acará Miri r. Brazil
142 D1 Acaraú Brazil
142 D1 Acaraú r. Brazil
141 E5 Acaray r. Paraguay
142 E2 Acarí Brazil
145 F1 Acari r. Brazil
138 D2 Acarigua Venezuela
28 D1 Acâş Romania
131 F5 Acatlan Mexico
131 G5 Acayucán Mexico
76 D5 Accra Ghana
140 C3 Achacachi Bolivia
138 D2 Achaguas Venezuela
54 D5 Achalpur India
56 B2 Achampet India
63 T3 Achayvayam Rus. Fed.
77 G3 Achegour well Niger
29 C5 Acheloös r. Greece
49 H3 Acheng China
13 H6 Achikulak Rus. Fed.
17 B5 Achill Island i. Rep. of Ire.
63 L4 Achinsk Rus. Fed.
65 G4 Achisay Kazak.
64 E1 Achit Rus. Fed.
16 E3 Achnasheen U.K.
61 B2 Achno Cyprus
27 E7 Aci Castello Italy
27 E7 Aci Catena Italy
60 B2 Acıpayam Turkey
124 E3 Ackley U.S.A.
132 D2 Acklins I. i. The Bahamas
140 B2 Acomayo Peru
146 B3 Aconcagua, Cerro summit Arg.
142 E2 Acopiara Brazil
140 C3 Acora Peru
24 B1 A Coruña Spain
130 J7 Acoyapa Nicaragua
26 C4 Acquapendente Italy
26 B3 Acqui Terme Italy
96 C3 Acraman, L. salt flat Aust.
140 C2 Acre r. Brazil
140 B1 Acre div. Brazil
27 F6 Acri Italy
151 L7 Actéon, Groupe is Fr. Poly. Pac. Oc.
115 J4 Acton Vale Can.
142 E2 Açu Brazil
144 D6 Acungui Brazil
78 B3 Acurenam Equatorial Guinea
47 □2 Ada Japan
120 B4 Ada U.S.A.
125 D5 Ada U.S.A.
28 C2 Ada Yugo.
41 □2 Adacao Guam Pac. Oc.
80 D2 Adaela well Ethiopia
24 D2 Adaja r. Spain
80 E3 Adale well Ethiopia
78 B2 Adamaoua div. Cameroon
77 G5 Adamawa div. Nigeria
97 G4 Adaminaby Aust.
147 E7 Adam, Mt h. Falkland Is.
64 F2 Adamovka Rus. Fed.
19 L3 Adamów Poland
121 G3 Adams U.S.A.
122 C4 Adams U.S.A.
56 B4 Adam's Bridge reef India/Sri Lanka
92 □1 Adams I. i. Auckland Is N.Z.
110 F4 Adams L. l. Can.
129 E2 Adams McGill Reservoir resr U.S.A.
93 C5 Adams, Mt mt. N.Z.
93 E4 Adams, Mt h. N.Z.
110 C3 Adams Mt. mt. U.S.A.
126 B2 Adams, Mt mt. U.S.A.
128 B2 Adams Peak mt. U.S.A.
56 C5 Adam's Pk Sri Lanka
91 □14 Adam's Rock rock Pitcairn I. Pac. Oc.
91 □14 Adamstown Pitcairn I. Pac. Oc.
80 D2 'Adan Yemen
60 C2 Adana Turkey
61 C1 Adana div. Turkey
40 D2 Adang, Tk b. Indon.
17 C5 Adare Rep. of Ire.
152 A5 Adare, C. c. Ant.
99 F5 Adavale Aust.
129 E2 Adaven U.S.A.
78 D2 Adda w C.A.R./Sudan
26 B2 Adda r. Italy
73 H3 Ad Dafīnah Saudi Arabia
59 G4 Ad Dahnā reg. Saudi Arabia
74 A4 Ad Dakhla Western Sahara
80 D2 Aḑ Ḑāli' Yemen
57 B4 Ad Dammām Saudi Arabia
73 H4 Ad Darb Saudi Arabia
73 H3 Ad Dawādimī Saudi Arabia
57 B4 Ad Dawḩah Qatar
61 D2 Ad Daww plain Syria
77 F3 Addax, Réserve Naturelle intégrale dite Sanctuaire des res. Niger
59 G5 Ad Dir'īyah Saudi Arabia
121 K2 Addison U.S.A.
60 F4 Ad Dīwānīyah Iraq
149 J4 Addu Atoll atoll Maldives
61 D2 Ad Duraykīsh Syria
73 H1 Ad Duwayd well Saudi Arabia
119 D6 Adel U.S.A.
124 E3 Adel U.S.A.
96 D3 Adelaide Aust.
119 □2 Adelaide The Bahamas
152 B2 Adelaide I i. Ant.
98 B2 Adelaide River Aust.
128 D4 Adelanto U.S.A.
29 F6 Adelfoi i. Greece
59 G7 Aden, Gulf of g. Somalia/Yemen
77 F3 Aderbissinat Niger
80 D1 Adhanah, W. w Yemen
57 C4 Adh Dhayd U.A.E.
39 K7 Adi i. Indon.
80 C2 Ādī Ārk'ay Ethiopia
73 F4 'Adid Umm Inderab well Sudan
26 C3 Adige r. Italy
80 C2 Ādīgrat Ethiopia
80 C2 Adi Keyih Eritrea
80 C2 Adi Kwala Eritrea
56 B2 Adilabad India
80 B4 Adilanga Uganda
60 E2 Adilcevaz Turkey
126 B3 Adin U.S.A.
72 B2 Adīrī Libya
121 F2 Adirondack Mountains mt. ra. U.S.A.
80 C3 Ādīs Ābeba Ethiopia
80 C3 Ādīs Alem Ethiopia
80 C2 Ādīs Zemen Ethiopia
80 C2 Adi Ugri Eritrea
60 D2 Adıyaman Turkey
28 F1 Adjud Romania
119 □3 Adjuntas Puerto Rico
131 F4 Adjuntas, Presa de las resr Mexico
113 J3 Adlavik Islands is Can.
13 F7 Adler Rus. Fed.
100 D2 Admiralty Gulf b. Aust.
100 D2 Admiralty Gulf Abor. Reserve res. Aust.
109 K2 Admiralty Inlet inlet Can.
94 □4 Admiralty Is is Lord Howe I. Pac. Oc.
110 C3 Admiralty Island i. U.S.A.
110 C3 Admiralty Island Nat. Monument res. U.S.A.
90 □1 Admiralty Islands is P.N.G.
152 A5 Admiralty Mts mt. ra. Ant.
77 F5 Ado-Ekiti Nigeria
80 B3 Adok Sudan
90 □6 Adolphus Reef reef Fiji
56 B3 Adoni India
78 C3 Adoumandjali C.A.R.
20 D5 Adour r. France
24 E4 Adra Spain
78 F3 Adranga Zaire
27 E7 Adrano Italy
75 D3 Adrar Algeria
75 F4 Adrar mts Algeria
74 B4 Adrar div. Mauritania
74 B4 Adrâr h. Mauritania
77 E3 Adrar des Ifôghas reg. Mali
75 F3 Adrar Ikouhaouene mt. Algeria
75 F4 Adrar Mariou mt. Algeria
75 E3 Adrar N'Ahnet mts Algeria
74 A4 Adrar Souttouf mts Western Sahara
77 F3 Adrar Tamgak mt. Niger
61 B1 Adras D. mt. Turkey
57 E2 Adraskand r. Afghanistan
72 D5 Adré Chad
26 D3 Adria Italy
123 E5 Adrian U.S.A.
125 C5 Adrian U.S.A.
23 F3 Adriatic Sea sea Mediterranean Sea
129 G6 Aduana del Sasabe Mexico
11 G4 Aduliena Latvia
56 B4 Adur India
78 E3 Adusa Zaire
80 C2 Ādwa Ethiopia
63 P3 Adycha r. Rus. Fed.
13 F6 Adygeya div. Rus. Fed.
13 F6 Adygeysk Rus. Fed.
13 H6 Adyk Rus. Fed.
15 E2 Adzhamka Ukraine
76 D5 Adzopé Côte d'Ivoire
29 E5 Aegean Sea sea Greece/Turkey
18 D2 Aerzen Germany
24 B1 A Estrada Spain
91 □11 Afaahiti Fr. Poly. Pac. Oc.
80 C1 Afabet Eritrea
80 D3 Afaf Badane well Ethiopia
29 G6 Afantou Greece
75 F3 Afao mt. Algeria
80 D2 Afar Depression depression Eritrea/Ethiopia
91 □11 Afareaitu Fr. Poly. Pac. Oc.
76 D5 Afféri Côte d'Ivoire
139 F2 Affobakka Surinam
32 H6 Afghanistan country Asia
80 E4 Afgooye Somalia
91 □12 Afiamalu Western Samoa
73 H3 'Afīf Saudi Arabia
77 F5 Afikpo Nigeria
14 B1 Afim'ino Rus. Fed.
10 C3 Åfjord Norway
77 E5 Aflao Ghana
75 E2 Aflou Algeria
81 D4 Afmadow Somalia
108 C4 Afognak I. i. U.S.A.
74 A5 Afojjar well Mauritania
24 C1 A Fonsagrada Spain
145 H4 Afonso Cláudio Brazil
27 E5 Afragola Italy
142 D2 Afrânio Brazil
80 D2 Āfrēra Terara mt. Ethiopia
10 J2 Afrikanda Rus. Fed.
61 D1 'Afrīn Syria
61 D1 'Afrīn r. Syria/Turkey
60 D2 Afşin Turkey
18 B2 Afsluitdijk dam Netherlands
80 D3 Aftol well Ethiopia
126 E3 Afton U.S.A.
142 B1 Afuá Brazil
61 C3 'Afula Israel
60 B2 Afyon Turkey
61 A4 Aga Egypt
49 E2 Aga r. Rus. Fed.
49 E2 Aga Rus. Fed.
77 F2 Agadez div. Niger
77 F3 Agadez Niger
74 C2 Agadir Morocco
72 D4 Aga Dubé well Chad
65 H3 Agadyr' Kazak.
69 K7 Agalega Islands is Seychelles
41 □2 Agana Guam Pac. Oc.
54 D5 Agar India
76 C2 Agâraktem well Mali
80 C3 Āgaro Ethiopia
55 G5 Agartala India
56 A2 Agashi India
41 □2 Agat Guam Pac. Oc.
123 F2 Agate Can.
65 G3 Agat, G. h. Kazak.
29 F6 Agathonisi i. Greece
53 D8 Agatti i. India
77 F5 Agbor Bojiboji Nigeria
76 D5 Agboville Côte d'Ivoire
60 F1 Ağcabädi Azerbaijan
60 F1 Agdaş Azerbaijan
21 F5 Agde France
20 E4 Agen France
47 G5 Ageo Japan
80 C3 Āgere Maryam Ethiopia
14 C2 Ageyevo Rus. Fed.
74 B4 Aghaylas well Western Sahara
54 D1 Aghil Pass pass China
74 C5 Aghrîjît well Mauritania
29 F6 Agia Marina Notio Aigaio Greece
29 E7 Agia Vervara Greece
28 G2 Agighiol Romania
60 D2 Ağin Turkey
48 E2 Aginskiy-Buryatskiy Avt. Okr. Rus. Fed.
48 E2 Aginskoye Rus. Fed.
29 D6 Agioi Theodoroi Peloponnisos Greece
29 D5 Agiokampos Greece
29 D6 Agios Dimitrios Attiki Greece
29 E5 Agios Efstratios i. Greece
29 D6 Agios Georgios i. Greece
29 D5 Agios Konstantinos Sterea Ellas Greece
29 E7 Agios Nikolaos Kriti Greece
29 F5 Agios Paraskevi Greece
29 D6 Agios Petros Greece
73 G4 Agirwat Hills h. Sudan
29 C5 Agnantero Greece
96 B1 Agnes, Mt h. Aust.
76 D5 Agnibilékrou Côte d'Ivoire
28 E2 Agnita Romania
76 D5 Agogo Ghana
76 D5 Agona Swedru Ghana
48 B5 Agong China
140 C1 Agostinho Brazil
76 D3 Agounni Jefal well Mali
77 E3 Agous-n-Ehsel well Mali
54 D4 Agra India
13 H7 Agrakhanskiy Poluostrov pen. Rus. Fed.
25 F2 Agreda Spain
27 F5 Agri r. Italy
60 E2 Ağri Turkey
29 D7 Agria Gramvousa i. Greece
27 D7 Agrigento Italy
39 M3 Agrihan i. Northern Mariana Is Pac. Oc.
29 C5 Agrinio Greece
27 E5 Agropoli Italy
64 D1 Agryz Rus. Fed.
130 E4 Ags div. Mexico
60 G1 Ağsu Azerbaijan
145 G2 Água Boa Brazil
130 D4 Agua Brava, L. lag. Mexico
144 B4 Água Clara Brazil
131 H5 Aguada Mexico
133 E5 Aguada Grande Venezuela
138 B2 Aguadas Colombia
138 C3 Agua de Dios Colombia
119 □3 Aguadilla Puerto Rico
147 C5 Aguado Cecilio Arg.
130 K7 Aguadulce Panama
141 E3 Aguapei r. Brazil
146 E2 Aguapey r. Arg.
130 C2 Agua Prieta Mexico
141 E4 Aguaray-guazu r. Paraguay
141 E4 Aguaray Guazú r. Paraguay
24 B2 A Guardia Spain
138 D2 Aguaro-Guariquito, Parque Nacional nat. park Venezuela
130 E4 Aguascalientes Mexico
145 H2 Águas Formosas Brazil
145 H1 Águas Vermelhas Brazil
141 E2 Água Verde r. Brazil
144 D5 Agudos Brazil
24 B2 Águeda Portugal
77 E3 Aguelhok Mali
75 E3 Aguemour reg. Algeria
77 F4 Aguié Niger
129 F5 Aguila U.S.A.
24 D1 Aguilar de Campóo Spain
146 C2 Aguilares Arg.
25 F4 Águilas Spain
41 B4 Aguisan Phil.
119 □3 Agujereada, Pta pt Puerto Rico
80 C2 Āgula'i Ethiopia
149 F7 Agulhas Basin Indian Ocean
82 C5 Agulhas, Cape c. R.S.A.
145 F5 Agulhas Negras, Pico das mt. Brazil
149 F6 Agulhas Plateau Indian Ocean
40 C4 Agung, G. vol Indon.
41 C4 Agusan r. Phil.
41 B4 Agutaya Phil.
13 D7 Ağva Turkey
80 B3 Agwei r. Sudan
47 □2 Aha Japan
77 E5 Ahamasu Ghana
60 F2 Ahar Iran
93 C5 Ahaura r. N.Z.
93 C5 Ahaura N.Z.
18 C2 Ahaus Germany
91 □10 Ahé i. Fr. Poly. Pac. Oc.
92 F3 Ahimanawa Ra. mt. ra. N.Z.
92 D1 Ahipara N.Z.
92 D1 Ahipara Bay b. N.Z.
61 B1 Ahırlı Turkey
108 B4 Ahklun Mts U.S.A.
60 E2 Ahlat Turkey
18 C3 Ahlen Germany
54 C5 Ahmadabad India
57 D3 Ahmadī Iran
56 A2 Ahmadnagar India
54 B3 Ahmadnapur East Pakistan
54 B3 Ahmadpur Sial Pakistan
80 D3 Ahmar Mountains mt. ra. Ethiopia
29 F5 Ahmetli Turkey
74 B4 Aḩmeyim well Mauritania
54 C4 Ahore India
18 C3 Ahrweiler Germany
11 G3 Ähtäri Finland
11 G4 Ahtme Estonia
131 H6 Ahuachapán El Salvador
131 E4 Ahualulco Mexico
91 □10 Ahunui i. Fr. Poly. Pac. Oc.
93 B6 Ahuriri r. N.Z.
57 B3 Ahvāz Iran
54 C5 Ahwa India
82 B4 Ai-Ais Hot Springs and Fish River Canyon res. Namibia
48 D4 Aibag Gol r. China
46 J2 Aibetsu Japan
119 □3 Aibonito Puerto Rico
18 E4 Aichach Germany
47 F6 Aichi div. Japan
46 E6 Aida Japan
127 □1 Aiea U.S.A.
61 C2 Aigialousa Cyprus
29 D6 Aigina i. Greece
29 D6 Aigina Greece
29 D4 Aiginio Greece
29 D5 Aigio Greece
21 H3 Aigle Switz.
146 F3 Aiguá Uruguay
20 E4 Aiguillon France
152 □ Aiguillon, C. d' c. Kerguelen Indian Ocean
49 H2 Aihui China
47 G4 Aikawa Japan
119 D5 Aiken U.S.A.
50 C3 Ailao Shan mt. ra. China
130 L7 Ailigandi Panama
114 E5 Ailsa Craig Can.
40 E4 Aimere Indon.
146 C2 Aimogasta Arg.
145 H3 Aimorés Brazil
145 H3 Aimorés, Sa dos h. Brazil
73 F2 'Ain 'Amûr spring Egypt
75 F1 Aïn Beïda Algeria
75 D2 Aïn Beni Mathar Morocco
74 C3 'Aïn Ben Tili Mauritania
75 E1 Aïn Defla Algeria
75 E2 Aïn Deheb Algeria
61 B5 Ain el Bâgha well Egypt
61 C5 'Ain el Furtâga well Egypt
73 E2 Aîn el Maqfi spring Egypt
72 C4 Aïn Galakka spring Chad
42 A2 Ainggyi Myanmar
75 E3 Aïn Mezzer well Algeria
75 F1 Aïn-M'Lila Algeria
75 D2 Aïn Sefra Algeria
113 H4 Ainslie, Lake l. Can.
61 B5 Ain Sukhna Egypt
124 D3 Ainsworth U.S.A.
75 D1 Aïn Temouchent Algeria
72 E2 'Aîn Timeira spring Egypt
75 E4 Aïn Ti-m Misaou well Algeria
138 B3 Aipe Colombia
140 C3 Aiquile Bolivia
43 D7 Air i. Indon.
41 □1 Airai Palau
20 E2 Airaines France
139 E4 Airão Brazil
110 G4 Airdrie Can.
16 F4 Airdrie U.K.
21 G2 Aire r. France
20 D5 Aire-sur-l'Adour France
77 G3 Aïr et du Ténéré, Rés. Naturelle Nat. de l' res. Niger
109 L3 Air Force I. i. Can.
48 D4 Airgin Sum China
40 B2 Airhitam r. Indon.
40 B2 Airhitam, Tk b. Indon.
77 F3 Aïr, Massif de l' mts Niger
21 J3 Airolo Switz.
111 H3 Air Ronge Can.
20 D3 Airvault France
147 B6 Aisén div. Chile
147 B6 Aisén, Pto Chile
49 G5 Ai Shan h. China
110 B2 Aishihik Can.
110 B2 Aishihik Lake l. Can.
21 G2 Aisne r. France
75 D2 Aïssa, Djebel mt. Algeria
10 G2 Aitamännikkö Finland
90 □1 Aitape P.N.G.
124 E2 Aitken U.S.A.
87 L6 Aitutaki i. Cook Islands Pac. Oc.
28 D1 Aiud Romania
41 □1 Aiwokako Passage chan. Palau
21 F4 Aix r. France
21 F2 Aix-en-Othe France
21 G5 Aix-en-Provence France
20 E4 Aixe-sur-Vienne France
21 G4 Aix-les-Bains France
80 C2 Āīy Ādī Ethiopia
110 D3 Aiyansh Can.
55 F5 Aiyar Res. India
77 E5 Aiyetoro Nigeria
55 H5 Aizawl India
20 D3 Aizenay France
11 G4 Aizkraukle Latvia
11 F4 Aizpute Latvia
47 G5 Aizutakada Japan
47 G5 Aizu-wakamatsu Japan
60 F2 'Ajab Shīr Iran
21 J6 Ajaccio France
21 J6 Ajaccio, Golfe d' b. France
54 E4 Ajaigarh India
73 H2 Ajā, J. mts Saudi Arabia
131 F5 Ajalpán Mexico
101 A5 Ajana Aust.
54 C5 Ajanta India
77 F5 Ajaokuta Nigeria
13 G7 Ajaria div. Georgia
10 D2 Ajaureforsen Sweden
93 D5 Ajax, Mt mt. N.Z.
41 □2 Ajayan Bay b. Guam Pac. Oc.
72 D1 Ajdābiyā Libya
46 H3 Ajigasawa Japan
55 G4 Ājimganj India
19 H5 Ajka Hungary
57 C4 Ajman U.A.E.
54 C4 Ajmer India
129 F5 Ajo U.S.A.
129 F5 Ajo, Mt mt. U.S.A.
41 B4 Ajuy Phil.
46 J2 Akabira Japan
75 E3 Akabli Algeria
47 G5 Akadomari Japan
47 G4 Aka-gawa r. Japan
81 B5 Akagera National Park nat. park Rwanda
80 C3 Āk'ak'ī Beseka Ethiopia
72 B3 Akakus, Jabal mts Libya
56 B2 Akalkot India
46 K2 Akan Japan
46 K2 Akan National Park nat. park. Japan
61 B2 Akanthou Cyprus
46 D7 Akaoka Japan
47 □2 Akarie-Ue Japan
77 F3 Akarkar well Niger
29 C5 Akarnanika mt. ra. Greece
93 D5 Akaroa N.Z.
93 D5 Akaroa Har inlet N.Z.
55 H4 Akas reg. India
73 F3 Akasha Sudan
65 H3 Akbakay Kazak.
65 J3 Akbalyk Kazak.
55 E4 Akbarpur India
54 E4 Akbarpur India
64 F3 Akbasty Kazak.
65 H5 Akbaytal Tajikistan
65 H5 Akbaytal P. pass Tajikistan
75 E1 Akbou Algeria
64 E2 Akbulak Rus. Fed.
60 D2 Akçadağ Turkey
60 D2 Akçakale Turkey
60 B1 Akçakoca Turkey
61 D1 Akçakoyunlu Turkey
29 G6 Akçay r. Turkey
64 E4 Akchakaya, Vpadina depression Turkmenistan
65 H3 Akchatau Kazak.
29 G5 Akdağ mt. Turkey
60 C2 Akdağmadeni Turkey
11 E4 Åkersberga Sweden
11 C3 Akershus div. Norway
78 D3 Aketi Zaire
64 E5 Akhal div. Turkmenistan
13 G7 Akhalk'alak'i Georgia
13 G7 Akhalts'ikhe Georgia
59 J5 Akhḑar, Jabal mt. ra. Oman
61 D5 Akhḑar, W. al w Saudi Arabia
60 A2 Akhisar Turkey
73 F2 Akhmîm Egypt
54 C2 Akhnoor India
14 G4 Akhtuba Rus. Fed.
13 H5 Akhtubinsk Rus. Fed.
13 H7 Akhty Rus. Fed.
57 B2 Ākhvoreh-ye Bālā Iran
46 D7 Aki Japan
78 B4 Akiéni Gabon
49 E1 Akima Rus. Fed.
112 D3 Akimiski Island i. Can.
60 C2 Akıncı Br. pt Turkey
47 H4 Akita div. Japan
47 H4 Akita Japan
74 B5 Akjoujt Mauritania
74 C3 Akka Morocco
64 F3 Akkabak Kazak.
10 E2 Akkajaure l. Sweden
65 G3 Akkanse Kazak.
46 K2 Akkeshi Japan
46 K2 Akkeshi-ko l. Japan
46 K2 Akkeshi-wan b. Japan
61 C3 'Akko Israel
65 H4 Akkol' Kazak.
64 C3 Akkol' Kazak.
60 D1 Akkuş Turkey
64 D3 Akkystau Kazak.
77 E5 Aklampa Benin
54 D4 Aklera India
11 F4 Akmenrags pt Latvia
54 D1 Akmeqit China
65 H2 Akmola Kazak.
65 H2 Akmola div. Kazak.
46 E6 Akō Japan
80 B3 Akobo r. Ethiopia/Sudan
80 B3 Akobo Sudan
54 D5 Akola India
78 B3 Akom II Cameroon
78 B3 Akonolinga Cameroon
80 C1 Akordat Eritrea
60 C2 Akören Turkey
54 D5 Akot India
80 B3 Akot Sudan
76 D5 Akoupé Côte d'Ivoire
113 G1 Akpatok Island i. Can.
61 B1 Akpınar Turkey
65 J4 Akqi China
29 F5 Akra Agios Fokas pt Greece
29 E7 Akra Agios Ioannis pt Greece
29 C5 Akra Agiou Andreou pt Greece
29 E4 Akra Akrathos pt Greece
29 E4 Akra Arapis pt Greece
29 C5 Akra Araxos pt Greece
61 D1 Akrād, Jabal al mt. ra. Syria
29 D5 Akra Drepano pt Greece
29 C6 Akra Geraki pt Greece
61 C2 Akra, J. mt. Turkey
29 E5 Akra Kafireas pt Greece
29 D6 Akra Kapello pt Greece
29 D5 Akra Kassandras pt Greece
29 C6 Akra Katakolo pt Greece
29 E5 Akra Kymis pt Greece
29 G6 Akra Lindos pt Greece
29 E7 Akra Lithino pt Greece
29 D6 Akra Maleas i. Greece
29 F5 Akra Maleas pt Greece
29 E5 Akra Masticho pt Greece
29 E5 Akra Meston pt Greece
10 L2 Akranes Iceland
29 D5 Akra Paliouri pt Greece
29 F7 Akra Paraspori pt Greece
29 E4 Akra Pinnes pt Greece
29 F7 Akra Prasonisi pt Greece
29 F7 Akra Sideros pt Greece
29 E5 Akra Sigri pt Greece
29 D7 Akra Spatha pt Greece
29 E7 Akra Stavros pt Kriti Greece
29 D6 Akra Tainaro pt Greece
29 E7 Akra Trypiti pt Kriti Greece
29 F5 Akra Vamvakas pt Greece
29 F6 Akra Xodoto pt Greece
11 B4 Åkrehamne Norway
77 F3 Akrérèb Niger
57 F2 Ak Robat P. pass Afghanistan
126 G3 Akron U.S.A.
120 C4 Akron U.S.A.
120 C4 Akron City Reservoir resr U.S.A.
61 B2 Akrotirion B. b. Cyprus
54 D2 Aksai Chin reg. Jammu and Kashmir
29 G4 Aksakal Turkey
28 F3 Aksakovo Bulgaria
60 C2 Aksaray Turkey
13 F6 Aksay Rus. Fed.
54 D2 Aksayqin Hu l. China/Jammu and Kashmir
60 B2 Akşehir Turkey
60 B2 Akseki Turkey
57 C3 Aks-e Rostam r. Iran
48 E2 Aksha Rus. Fed.
64 F3 Akshiganak Kazak.
65 J4 Akshiy Kazak.
65 K4 Aksu China
65 K4 Aksu r. China
65 H2 Aksu Kazak.
65 J3 Aksu Kazak.
65 J3 Aksu r. Kazak.
60 B2 Aksu r. Turkey
64 F2 Aksuat Kustanay Kazak.
65 K3 Aksuat Semipalatinsk Kazak.
65 H3 Aksu-Ayuly Kazak.
65 H4 Aksuek Kazak.
80 C2 Āksum Ethiopia
65 G4 Aksumbe Kazak.
60 E2 Aktas Dāgh mt. Turkey
65 H2 Aktau Karaganda Kazak.
64 D4 Aktau Mangistau Kazak.
65 H3 Aktau Zhezkazgan Kazak.
65 J5 Akto China
65 J3 Aktogay Semipalatinsk Kazak.
65 H3 Aktogay Zhezkazgan Kazak.
13 D4 Aktsyabrski Belarus
65 G3 Aktuma Kazak.
64 E3 Aktumsyk Kazak.
64 E4 Aktumsyk, Mys pt Uzbekistan
64 E2 Aktyubinsk Kazak.
64 E3 Aktyubinsk div. Kazak.
109 L3 Akulivik Can.
46 C7 Akune Japan
77 F5 Akure Nigeria
10 M2 Akureyri Iceland
108 B4 Akutan U.S.A.
77 F6 Akwa Ibom div. Nigeria
77 F5 Akwanga Nigeria
55 G1 Akxokesay China
61 C1 Akyatan Gölü l. Turkey
65 H3 Akzhal Kazak.
65 G4 Akzhaykyn, Ozero salt l. Kazak.
11 C3 Ål Norway
57 B4 Al 'Abā Saudi Arabia
119 C6 Alabama r. U.S.A.
119 C5 Alabama div. U.S.A.
119 C5 Alabaster U.S.A.
41 B3 Alabat i. Phil.
72 B2 Al Abyaḑ Libya
72 D1 Al Abyār Libya
60 C1 Alaca Turkey
60 D2 Alacahan Turkey
60 C1 Alaçam Turkey
29 G5 Alaçam Dağları mt. ra. Turkey
131 H4 Alacrán, Arrecife atoll Mexico
60 C2 Ala Dağ mts Turkey
14 E2 Alad'ino Rus. Fed.
24 D2 Alaejos Spain
60 F1 Alagir Rus. Fed.
142 E2 Alagoas div. Brazil
142 E3 Alagoinhas Brazil
25 F2 Alagón Spain
10 F3 Alahärmä Finland
60 F4 Al Ahmadī Kuwait
25 J3 Alaior Spain
65 H5 Alai Range mt. ra. Kyrgyzstan
10 F3 Alajärvi Finland
72 B1 Al Ajaylāt Libya
73 H2 Al Ajfar Saudi Arabia
130 J7 Alajuela Costa Rica
61 D5 Al Akhḑar Saudi Arabia
61 A1 Alakır r. Turkey
65 K3 Alakol', Oz. salt l. Kazak.
12 D1 Alakurtti Rus. Fed.
139 E4 Alalaú r. Brazil
73 H4 Al'Alayyah Saudi Arabia
80 D4 Alama Somalia
39 M3 Alamagan i. Northern Mariana Is Pac. Oc.
60 F4 Al 'Amārah Iraq
80 C2 Ālamat'ā Ethiopia
55 H3 Alamdo China
41 A2 Alaminos Phil.
130 E3 Alamítos, Sa de los mt. Mexico
129 E3 Alamo U.S.A.
129 F4 Alamo Dam dam U.S.A.
127 F5 Alamogordo U.S.A.
125 D6 Alamo Heights U.S.A.
127 E6 Alamos Sonora Mexico
127 F4 Alamosa U.S.A.
56 B3 Alampur India
80 D2 Al 'Anad Yemen
10 D2 Alanäs Sweden
60 E3 Al Anbār div. Iraq
11 F3 Åland div. Finland
11 E3 Åland is Finland
56 B2 Aland India
60 F2 Aland r. Iran
11 E3 Åland div. Sweden
61 D2 Al Andarīn Syria
43 C7 Alang Besar i. Indon.
122 E3 Alanson U.S.A.
78 B2 Alantika Mountains mt. ra. Cameroon/Nigeria
60 C2 Alanya Turkey
73 H3 Al 'Aqīq Saudi Arabia
60 D3 Al Arak oasis Syria
25 E3 Alarcón, Embalse de resr Spain
74 A4 Al Argoub Western Sahara
73 J2 Al Arţāwīyah Saudi Arabia
40 D4 Alas Indon.
60 B2 Alaşehir Turkey
65 M2 Alash, Plato plat. Rus. Fed.
60 E4 Al 'Āshūrīyah well Iraq
108 C3 Alaska div. U.S.A.
108 D4 Alaska, Gulf of g. U.S.A.
110 E3 Alaska Highway Can./U.S.A.
108 B4 Alaska Peninsula pen. U.S.A.
108 C3 Alaska Range mt. ra. U.S.A.
73 G2 Al 'Assāfīyah Saudi Arabia
59 G2 Ălät Azerbaijan
64 F5 Alat Uzbekistan
60 E4 Al 'Athāmīn h. Iraq
27 D5 Alatri Italy
73 H2 Al Atwā' well Saudi Arabia
14 G2 Alatyr' r. Rus. Fed.
14 H2 Alatyr' Rus. Fed.
138 B4 Alausí Ecuador
60 F1 Alaverdi Armenia
57 B2 'Alavī Iran
10 G2 Alavieska Finland
11 F3 Alavus Finland
42 B1 Alawbum Myanmar
96 E3 Alawoona Aust.
14 H3 Alay r. Rus. Fed.
65 H4 Alaykuu Kyrgyzstan
13 H7 Alazani r. Azerbaijan/Georgia
60 F3 Al 'Azīzīyah Iraq
72 B1 Al 'Azīzīyah Libya
26 B3 Alba Italy
26 D4 Alba Adriatica Italy
61 D1 Al Bāb Syria
25 F3 Albacete Spain
96 E3 Albacutya, L. l. Aust.
61 C5 Al Bad' Saudi Arabia
24 D2 Alba de Tormes Spain
60 F4 Al Bādiyah al Janūbīyah h. Iraq
65 L2 Al'bagan, G. mt. Rus. Fed.
61 C2 Al Bahlūlīyah Syria
28 D1 Alba Iulia Romania
25 F2 Albalate de Arzobispo Spain
112 F3 Albanel, L. l. Can.
4 G4 Albania country Europe
27 D5 Albano Laziale Italy
101 B7 Albany Aust.
112 C3 Albany r. Can.
133 □1 Albany Jamaica
119 C6 Albany U.S.A.
122 E5 Albany U.S.A.
118 C4 Albany U.S.A.
121 G3 Albany U.S.A.
126 B2 Albany U.S.A.
146 F3 Albardão do João Maria Brazil
72 E1 Al Bardī Libya
60 F4 Al Başrah div. Iraq
60 F4 Al Başrah Iraq
99 E2 Albatross Bay b. Aust.
93 □3 Albatross Pt pt Antipodes Is N.Z.
92 E3 Albatross Pt pt N.Z.
72 D1 Al Bayḑā' Libya
80 E2 Al Bayda Yemen
138 □ Albemarle, Pta pt Galapagos Is Ecuador
119 E5 Albemarle Sd chan. U.S.A.
26 B3 Albenga Italy
24 D2 Alberche r. Spain
141 E5 Alberdi Paraguay
96 C1 Alberga Aust.
96 C1 Alberga w Aust.
24 B2 Albergaria-a-Velha Portugal
98 D3 Albert r. Aust.
20 F2 Albert France
110 F4 Alberta div. Can.
120 E6 Alberta U.S.A.
110 F4 Alberta, Mt mt. Can.
19 J5 Albertirsa Hungary
96 D3 Albert, L. l. Aust.
81 B4 Albert, Lake l. Uganda/Zaire
124 E3 Albert Lea U.S.A.
80 B4 Albert Nile r. Sudan/Uganda
147 B7 Alberto de Agostini, Parque Nacional nat. park Chile
133 □1 Albert Town Jamaica
21 H4 Albertville France
28 F1 Albeşti Romania
20 F5 Albi France
73 G3 Al Bi'ār Saudi Arabia
139 G2 Albina Surinam
26 B3 Albino Italy
128 A2 Albion U.S.A.
121 J2 Albion U.S.A.
122 E4 Albion U.S.A.
120 D3 Albion U.S.A.
73 G2 Al Bi'r Saudi Arabia
73 H4 Al Birk Saudi Arabia
11 C4 Ålborg Denmark
11 C4 Ålborg Bugt b. Denmark
25 E4 Albox Spain
110 F4 Albreda Can.
99 F4 Albro Aust.
18 D4 Albstadt Germany
57 B4 Al Budayyi Bahrain
24 B4 Albufeira Portugal
60 E3 Āl Bū Kamāl Syria
73 H2 Al Bukayrīyah Saudi Arabia
21 J3 Albula Alpen mt. ra. Switz.
127 F5 Albuquerque U.S.A.
61 D2 Al Burayj Syria
59 J5 Al Buraymī Oman
24 C3 Alburquerque Spain
97 F4 Albury Aust.
60 D4 Al Busayţā' plain Saudi Arabia
60 F4 Al Buşayyah Iraq
73 G3 Al Buwayr Saudi Arabia
140 B3 Alca Peru
24 B3 Alcácer do Sal Portugal
24 B3 Alcáçovas Portugal
25 G2 Alcalá de Chivert Spain
24 D4 Alcalá de Guadaira Spain
24 E2 Alcalá de Henares Spain
24 D4 Alcalá de los Gazules Spain
24 E4 Alcalá la Real Spain
27 D7 Alcamo Italy
25 G2 Alcanar Spain
25 F2 Alcañiz Spain
24 C3 Alcántara Spain
24 C3 Alcántara II, Embalse de resr Spain
25 F4 Alcantarilla Spain
144 B2 Alcantilado Brazil
25 E3 Alcaraz Spain
25 E3 Alcaraz, Sierra de mt. ra. Spain
24 D4 Alcaudete Spain
24 E3 Alcázar de San Juan Spain
13 F5 Alchevs'k Ukraine
24 D3 Alcoba Spain
145 J2 Alcobaça Brazil
24 C3 Alconchel Spain
25 F2 Alcora Spain
146 D3 Alcorta Arg.
25 F3 Alcoy Spain
25 H3 Alcúdia Spain
69 J6 Aldabra Islands is Seychelles
60 F3 Al Daghghārah Iraq
130 D2 Aldama Chihuahua Mexico
131 F4 Aldama Tamaulipas Mexico
63 P3 Aldan r. Rus. Fed.
63 O4 Aldan Rus. Fed.
17 H5 Aldeburgh U.K.
142 B2 Aldeia Velha Brazil
92 F2 Aldermen Is, The is N.Z.
17 F7 Alderney i. Channel Is.
128 B4 Alder Peak summit U.S.A.
120 C6 Alderson U.S.A.
28 C4 Aldinci Macedonia
122 B5 Aledo U.S.A.
74 B5 Aleg Mauritania
25 □ Alegranza i. Canary Is Spain
145 H4 Alegre Espírito Santo Brazil
142 C1 Alegre Pará Brazil
141 E3 Alegre r. Brazil
144 C2 Alegre, Monte r. Brazil
142 B1 Alegre, Monte h. Brazil
79 □ Alegre, Pto pt Sao Tome and Principe
143 A6 Alegrete Brazil
146 E4 Alejandro Korn Arg.
12 E2 Alekhovshchina Rus. Fed.
64 D4 Aleksandra Bekovicha-Cherkassogo, Zaliv b. Kazak.
14 E3 Aleksandro-Nevskiy Rus. Fed.
14 D1 Aleksandrov Rus. Fed.
28 C3 Aleksandrovac Yugo.
13 J5 Aleksandrov Gay Rus. Fed.
28 E3 Aleksandrovo Bulgaria
13 H6 Aleksandrovskoye Rus. Fed.
45 Q1 Aleksandrovsk-Sakhalinskiy Rus. Fed.
19 J2 Aleksandrów Kujawski Poland
19 J3 Aleksandrów Łódzki Poland
65 L3 Alekseyevka Kazak.
65 H2 Alekseyevka Kazak.
65 J2 Alekseyevka Kazak.
65 G2 Alekseyevka Kazak.
13 F5 Alekseyevka Rus. Fed.
14 H3 Alekseyevka Rus. Fed.
14 F4 Alekseyevka Rus. Fed.
15 G1 Alekseyevka Rus. Fed.
14 C2 Aleksin Rus. Fed.
28 C3 Aleksinac Yugo.
14 D2 Aleksino-Shatur Rus. Fed.
131 F5 Alemán, Presa, M. resr Mexico
78 B4 Alèmbé Gabon
145 G4 Além Paraíba Brazil
10 C3 Ålen Norway
20 E2 Alençon France
142 B1 Alenquer Brazil
24 C3 Alentejo reg. Portugal
127 □2 Alenuihaha Channel chan. U.S.A.
76 D5 Alépé Côte d'Ivoire
21 J5 Aléria France
109 M1 Alert Can.
140 B2 Alerta Peru
110 D4 Alert Bay Can.
21 G4 Alès France
28 D1 Aleşd Romania
26 B3 Alessandria Italy
10 B3 Ålesund Norway
21 H3 Aletschhorn mt. Switz.
108 B4 Aleutian Islands is U.S.A.
108 C4 Aleutian Range mt. ra. U.S.A.
151 G2 Aleutian Trench Pac. Oc.
63 R4 Alevina, Mys c. Rus. Fed.
121 K2 Alexander U.S.A.
108 E4 Alexander Archipelago is U.S.A.

82 B4 Alexander Bay R.S.A.
119 C5 Alexander City U.S.A.
152 A2 Alexander I. i. Ant.
98 E3 Alexandra r. Aust.
97 F4 Alexandra Aust.
93 B6 Alexandra N.Z.
147 G7 Alexandra, C. c. Atlantic Ocean
29 D4 Alexandreia Greece
98 D3 Alexandria Aust.
115 H4 Alexandria Can.
73 E1 Alexandria Egypt
28 E3 Alexandria Romania
122 E5 Alexandria U.S.A.
125 E6 Alexandria U.S.A.
124 E2 Alexandria U.S.A.
120 E5 Alexandria U.S.A.
121 F2 Alexandria Bay U.S.A.
96 D3 Alexandrina, L. l. Aust.
29 E4 Alexandroupoli Greece
113 J3 Alexis r. Can.
122 B5 Alexis U.S.A.
110 E4 Alexis Creek Can.
61 C3 'Āley Lebanon
65 K2 Aley r. Rus. Fed.
65 K2 Aleysk Rus. Fed.
25 F2 Alfambra r. Spain
25 F1 Alfaro Spain
60 F4 Al Farwānīyah Kuwait
28 F3 Alfatar Bulgaria
60 E3 Al Fatḩah Iraq
60 G4 Al Fāw Iraq
80 D2 Al Fāzih Yemen
18 D3 Alfeld (Leine) Germany
145 F4 Alfenas Brazil
19 K5 Alföld plain Hungary
26 D3 Alfonsine Italy
115 H4 Alfred Can.
121 H3 Alfred U.S.A.
145 H4 Alfredo Chaves Brazil
60 G4 Al Fuḩayḩīl Kuwait
57 D4 Al Fujayrah U.A.E.
72 C2 Al Fuqahā' Libya
64 E3 Alga Kazak.
64 D2 Algabas Kazak.
11 B4 Algård Norway
146 B2 Algarrobo Atacama Chile
146 C4 Algarrobo del Aguilla Arg.
24 B4 Algarve reg. Portugal
14 E3 Algasovo Rus. Fed.
24 D4 Algeciras Spain
25 F3 Algemesi Spain
80 C1 Algena Eritrea
75 E1 Alger Algeria
123 E3 Alger U.S.A.
68 D3 Algeria country Africa
60 F4 Al Ghammas Iraq
59 H6 Al Ghayḑah Yemen
27 B5 Alghero Italy
82 D5 Algoa Bay b. R.S.A.
122 D3 Algoma U.S.A.
124 E3 Algona U.S.A.
123 F4 Algonac U.S.A.
115 F4 Algonquin Park Can.
115 F4 Algonquin Provincial Park res. Can.
42 A4 Alguada Reef reef Myanmar
73 H3 Al Ḩadbah reg. Saudi Arabia
57 B4 Al Ḩadd Bahrain
73 H2 Al Hadhālīl plat. Saudi Arabia
61 D2 Al Ḩadīdīyah Syria
60 E3 Al Ḩadīthah Iraq
61 D4 Al Ḩadīthah Saudi Arabia
60 E3 Al Ḩaḑr Iraq
73 H2 Al Ḩafár well Saudi Arabia
74 B3 Al Haggounia Western Sahara
60 D3 Al Hamad plain Jordan/Saudi Arabia
72 B2 Al Ḩamādah al Ḩamrā' plat. Libya
24 E4 Alhama de Granada Spain
25 F4 Alhama de Murcia Spain
61 C2 Al Ḩamīdīyah Syria
60 F4 Al Hammām well Iraq
74 C3 Al Hamra w Western Sahara
61 D2 Al Ḩamrāt Syria
73 H3 Al Ḩanākīyah Saudi Arabia
73 J2 Al Ḩanbalī plain Saudi Arabia
73 G1 Al Ḩarrah h. Saudi Arabia
72 C2 Al Harūj al Aswad mt. ra. Libya
60 E2 Al Ḩasakah Syria
60 F3 Al Hāshimīyah Iraq
73 J2 Al Ḩatīfah plain Saudi Arabia
73 H3 Al Ḩawīyah Saudi Arabia
73 G2 Al Ḩawjā' Saudi Arabia
60 F3 Al Ḩayy Iraq
61 D5 Al Ḩazm Saudi Arabia
60 F3 Al Ḩillah Iraq
57 B4 Al Ḩinnāh Saudi Arabia
61 D4 Al Ḩinw mt. Saudi Arabia
61 C5 Al Ḩismā plain Saudi Arabia
74 D1 Al Hoceima Morocco
24 E5 Al Hoceima, Baie d' b. Morocco
80 D2 Al Hudaydah Yemen
73 G2 Al Ḩufrah reg. Saudi Arabia
57 B4 Al Hufuf Saudi Arabia
61 C5 Al Ḩumayḑah Saudi Arabia
80 E2 Al Ḩumayshah Yemen
57 B4 Al Ḩunayy Saudi Arabia
61 D2 Al Ḩuwayz Syria
54 D2 Ali China
57 E3 'Alīābād Iran
57 D2 'Ālīābād Iran
57 C1 'Alīābād Iran
57 C3 'Alīābād Iran
60 A2 Aliağa Turkey
29 D4 Aliakmonas r. Greece
60 F3 'Alī al Gharbī Iraq
29 D5 Aliartos Greece
56 A2 Alībāg India
54 B4 Ali Bandar Pakistan
60 G2 Äli Bayramlı Azerbaijan
29 F5 Alibey Adası i. Turkey
77 E4 Alibori r. Benin
28 C2 Alibunar Yugo.
25 F3 Alicante Spain
99 F4 Alice Aust.
99 E2 Alice r. Aust.
99 F4 Alice w Aust.
125 D7 Alice U.S.A.
110 D3 Alice Arm Can.
27 F6 Alice, Punta pt Italy
132 C3 Alice Shoal Caribbean
98 C4 Alice Springs Aust.
132 C1 Alice Town The Bahamas
65 H5 Alichur Tajikistan
41 B5 Alicia Phil.
99 E4 Alick Cr. r. Aust.
27 E6 Alicudi, Isola i. Italy
54 D4 Aligarh India
24 C2 Alijó Portugal
80 □ Al Ikhwān is Socotra Yemen
14 H2 Alikovo Rus. Fed.
78 C4 Alima r. Congo
29 F6 Alimia i. Greece
78 D2 Alindao C.A.R.
40 D2 Alindau Indon.
57 G2 Alinghar r. Afghanistan
11 D4 Alingsås Sweden
29 G5 Aliova r. Turkey
55 G4 Alipur Duar India
120 C4 Aliquippa U.S.A.
80 D2 Ali Sabieh Djibouti
61 D4 'Al 'Īsāwīyah Saudi Arabia
127 E6 Alisos r. Mexico
29 E5 Aliveri Greece
82 D5 Aliwal North R.S.A.
110 G4 Alix Can.
54 B2 Alizai Pakistan
72 D1 Al Jabal al Akhḑar mts Libya
57 B4 Al Jāfūrah desert Saudi Arabia
72 D2 Al Jaghbūb Libya
60 F4 Al Jahrah Kuwait
57 B4 Al Jamalīyah Qatar
72 D3 Al Jawf Libya
73 G2 Al Jawf Saudi Arabia
72 B1 Al Jawsh Libya
60 E3 Al Jazīrah reg. Iraq/Syria
57 B4 Al Jībān reg. Saudi Arabia
60 F4 Al Jil well Iraq
73 H2 Al Jilh escarpment Saudi Arabia
57 B4 Al Jishshah Saudi Arabia
73 H2 Al Jithāmīyah Saudi Arabia
57 B4 Al Jubayl Saudi Arabia
72 C2 Al Jufra Oasis oasis Libya
73 G3 Al Jumūm Saudi Arabia
73 H3 Al Junaynah Saudi Arabia
57 B4 Al Jurayd i. Saudi Arabia
24 B4 Aljustrel Portugal
61 D3 Al Juwayf depression Syria
61 D5 Al Kabid waterhole Jordan
77 G4 Alkamari Niger
59 J5 Al Khābūrah Oman
73 H2 Al Khaḑrā' well Saudi Arabia
73 H3 Al Khafqān salt pan Saudi Arabia
60 F3 Al Khālis Iraq
80 D1 Al Kharāb Yemen
57 D4 Al Khaşab Oman
73 H3 Al Khāşirah Saudi Arabia
57 B4 Al Khawr Qatar
57 B4 Al Khīşah well Saudi Arabia
72 D3 Al Khufrah Libya
72 D3 Al Khufrah Oasis oasis Libya
72 B1 Al Khums Libya
61 C3 Al Khushnīyah Syria
57 B4 Al Kir'ānah Qatar
61 D3 Al Kiswah Syria
18 B2 Alkmaar Netherlands
60 F3 Al Kūfah Iraq
73 H2 Al Kuhayfīyah Saudi Arabia
60 F3 Al Kumayt Iraq
60 F3 Al Kūt Iraq
60 F4 Al Kuwayt Kuwait
73 H2 Al Labbah plain Saudi Arabia
61 C2 Al Lādhiqīyah Syria
121 J1 Allagash U.S.A.
121 J1 Allagash r. U.S.A.
121 J1 Allagash Lake l. U.S.A.
55 E4 Allahabad India
61 D3 Al Lajā lava Syria
63 P3 Allakh-Yun' Rus. Fed.
42 A3 Allanmyo Myanmar
24 C1 Allariz Spain
83 D3 Alldays R.S.A.
122 E4 Allegan U.S.A.
120 D4 Allegheny r. U.S.A.
120 C6 Allegheny Mountains mt. ra. U.S.A.
120 D4 Allegheny Reservoir resr U.S.A.
133 □5 Allegre, Pte pt Guadeloupe Caribbean
119 D5 Allendale U.S.A.
131 E2 Allende Coahuila Mexico
131 E3 Allende Nuevo León Mexico
114 E4 Allenford Can.
17 C4 Allen, Lough l. Rep. of Ire.
93 A7 Allen, Mt h. N.Z.
121 F4 Allentown U.S.A.
56 B4 Alleppey India
25 F2 Allepuz Spain
18 E2 Aller r. Germany
18 E5 Allgäuer Alpen mt. ra. Austria/Germany
139 G2 Allianc Surinam
124 C3 Alliance U.S.A.
120 C4 Alliance U.S.A.
21 F4 Allier r. France
133 □1 Alligator Pond Jamaica
11 D5 Allinge-Sandvig Denmark
115 F4 Alliston Can.
73 H3 Al Līth Saudi Arabia
16 F3 Alloa U.K.
99 H5 Allora Aust.
21 H3 Allschwil Switz.
40 D3 Allu Indon.
80 D1 Al Luḩayyah Yemen
56 C3 Allur India
56 C3 Alluru Kottapatnam India
60 E4 Al Lussuf well Iraq
115 K2 Alma Can.
122 E4 Alma U.S.A.
124 D3 Alma U.S.A.
129 H5 Alma U.S.A.
60 E4 Al Ma'ānīyah Iraq
25 G2 Almacelles Spain
24 B3 Almada Portugal
61 D5 Al Madāfi' plat. Saudi Arabia
80 D1 Al Maḑāyā Saudi Arabia
99 F3 Almaden Aust.
24 D3 Almadén Spain
145 J1 Almadina Brazil
73 G3 Al Madīnah Saudi Arabia
73 H3 Al Maḩāwiyah Saudi Arabia
74 C3 Al Mahbas Western Sahara
73 G2 Al Maḩiā depression Saudi Arabia
73 J2 Al Majma'ah Saudi Arabia
57 B4 Al Malsūnīyah reg. Saudi Arabia
65 G4 Almalyk Uzbekistan
57 B4 Al Manāmah Bahrain
128 B1 Almanor, Lake l. U.S.A.
25 F3 Almansa Spain
73 H4 Al Ma'qaş Saudi Arabia
60 F4 Al Ma'qil Iraq
80 D2 Al Marāwi'ah Yemen
72 D1 Al Marj Libya
142 C3 Almas r. Brazil
142 C3 Almas Brazil
144 D1 Almas, R. das r. Brazil
65 J4 Almaty div. Kazak.
65 J4 Almaty Kazak.
60 E2 Al Mawşil Iraq
25 E2 Almazán Spain
63 N3 Almaznyy Rus. Fed.
142 B1 Almeirim Brazil
24 B3 Almeirim Portugal
18 C2 Almelo Netherlands
145 H2 Almenara Brazil
25 F3 Almenara Spain
24 C2 Almendra, Embalse de resr Spain
24 C3 Almendralejo Spain
18 B2 Almere Netherlands
25 E4 Almería Spain
25 E4 Almería, Golfo de b. Spain
64 D2 Al'met'yevsk Rus. Fed.
11 D4 Älmhult Sweden
24 D5 Almina, Pta pt Ceuta Spain
147 C7 Almirantazgo, S. del chan. Chile
130 K7 Almirante Panama
57 B3 Al Mish'āb Saudi Arabia
60 D3 Al Mismīyah Syria
24 B4 Almodôvar Portugal
25 F3 Almodóvar del Pinar Spain
123 F4 Almont U.S.A.
115 G4 Almonte Can.
24 D3 Almonte r. Spain
24 C4 Almonte Spain
54 D3 Almora India
25 F3 Almoradí Spain
24 D2 Almorox Spain
77 E3 Almoustarat Mali
57 B4 Al Mubarrez Saudi Arabia
73 G2 Al Mudarraj Saudi Arabia
60 C4 Al Mudawwara Jordan
57 B4 Al Muharraq Bahrain
61 D5 Al Muḩtaţab depression Saudi Arabia
59 G7 Al Mukallā Yemen
80 D2 Al Mukhā Yemen
72 D1 Al Mukhaylī Libya
24 E4 Almuñécar Spain
60 F3 Al Muqdādīyah Iraq
73 G2 Al Murūt well Saudi Arabia
73 G3 Al Musayjīd Saudi Arabia
60 F3 Al Musayyib Iraq
60 F4 Al Muthanná div. Iraq
73 H3 Al Muwayh Saudi Arabia
29 D5 Almyros Greece
127 □1 Alna Haina U.S.A.
17 G4 Alnwick U.K.
11 G4 Aloja Latvia
42 A2 Alon Myanmar
55 H3 Along India
49 G2 Alongshan China
29 D5 Alonnisos i. Greece
144 C6 Alonso r. Brazil
39 H8 Alor i. Indon.
24 D4 Álora Spain
39 H8 Alor, Kepulauan is Indon.
24 C4 Alosno Spain
18 B3 Alost Belgium
54 C5 Alot India
90 □1 Alotau P.N.G.
101 E5 Aloysius, Mt mt. Aust.
128 C4 Alpaugh U.S.A.
123 F3 Alpena U.S.A.
25 F3 Alpera Spain
142 C2 Alpercatas r. Brazil
21 G4 Alpes du Dauphiné mts France
21 H4 Alpes Maritimes mt. ra. France/Italy
99 F4 Alpha Aust.
21 H4 Alpi Cozie mt. ra. France/Italy
26 C2 Alpi Dolomitiche mt. ra. Italy
26 B2 Alpi Lepontine mt. ra. Italy/Switz.
129 H5 Alpine U.S.A.
125 C6 Alpine U.S.A.
126 E3 Alpine U.S.A.
145 E4 Alpinópolis Brazil
26 B2 Alpi Orobie mt. ra. Italy
26 A3 Alpi Pennine mt. ra. Italy/Switz.
22 E2 Alps Europe
59 G6 Al Qa'āmīyāt reg. Saudi Arabia
72 C1 Al Qaddāḩīyah Libya
60 F4 Al Qādisīyah div. Iraq
61 D2 Al Qadmūs Syria
73 H3 Al Qā'īyah Saudi Arabia
73 G2 Al Qalībah Saudi Arabia
60 E2 Al Qāmishlī Syria
73 H4 Al Qarḩah Saudi Arabia
61 D4 Al Qarqar Saudi Arabia
60 D3 Al Qaryatayn Syria
72 B1 Al Qaşabāt Libya
57 B4 Al Qaţīf Saudi Arabia
59 G6 Al Qaţn Yemen
72 B3 Al Qaţrūn Libya
73 H2 Al Qâyşūmah well Saudi Arabia
61 C3 Al Qunayţirah div. Syria
73 H4 Al Qunfidhah Saudi Arabia
73 H3 Al Qurayn Saudi Arabia
80 D2 Al Qurayyah Yemen
60 F4 Al Qurnah Iraq
61 D2 Al 'Quşayr Syria
61 D3 Al Quţayfah Syria
98 D3 Alroy Downs Aust.
21 H2 Alsace div. France
111 H4 Alsask Can.
18 D3 Alsfeld Germany
14 G3 Al'shanka Rus. Fed.
17 F4 Alston U.K.
11 F4 Alsunga Latvia
10 F1 Alta Norway
10 F1 Altaelva r. Norway
146 D3 Alta Gracia Arg.
138 C1 Altagracía Venezuela
133 F5 Altagracía de Orituco Venezuela
44 E2 Altai Mountains mt. ra. Asia
119 D6 Altamaha r. U.S.A.
142 B1 Altamira Brazil
146 C2 Altamira Chile
138 B3 Altamira Colombia
130 J7 Altamira Costa Rica
24 D3 Altamira, Sierra de mt. ra. Spain
93 B6 Alta, Mt mt. N.Z.
27 F5 Altamura Italy
48 D2 Altan Rus. Fed.
48 C3 Altanbulag Mongolia
48 C2 Altanbulag Mongolia
130 C2 Altar Mexico
130 B2 Altar, Desierto de desert Mexico
130 D3 Altata Mexico
120 D6 Altavista U.S.A.
65 L3 Altay China
48 A3 Altay Mongolia
65 L2 Altay, Respublika div. Rus. Fed.
65 L2 Altayskiy Rus. Fed.
65 K2 Altayskiy Kray div. Rus. Fed.
21 J3 Altdorf Switz.
25 F3 Altea Spain
10 F1 Alteidet Norway
19 F3 Altenberg Germany
18 F3 Altenburg Germany
55 H1 Altenqoke China
18 D4 Altensteig Germany
18 F2 Altentreptow Germany
24 C3 Alter do Chão Portugal
57 G2 Altimur P. pass Afghanistan
29 F5 Altınoluk Turkey
144 E4 Altinópolis Brazil
29 F5 Altınova Turkey
60 B2 Altıntaş Turkey
147 C5 Altiplanicie de Hakelhuincul plat. Arg.
140 C3 Altiplano plain Bolivia
18 E4 Altmühl r. Germany
144 B2 Alto Araguaia Brazil
79 C6 Alto Chicapa Angola
25 F2 Alto del Moncayo mt. Spain
146 C3 Alto de Pencoso h. Arg.
132 C5 Alto de Quimari mt. Colombia
144 B2 Alto Garças Brazil
142 D2 Alto Longá Brazil
83 F2 Alto Molócuè Mozambique
118 B4 Alton U.S.A.
125 F4 Alton U.S.A.
121 H3 Alton U.S.A.
124 D1 Altona Can.
96 D1 Alton Downs Aust.
120 D4 Altoona U.S.A.
142 B1 Alto Pacajá r. Brazil
142 C2 Alto Parnaíba Brazil
140 B2 Alto Purús r. Peru
145 G4 Alto Rio Doce Brazil
144 B3 Alto Rio Verde Brazil
142 D2 Altos Brazil
144 B3 Alto Sucuriú Brazil
18 F4 Altötting Germany
132 □1 Alto Vista h. Aruba Caribbean
14 B3 Altukhovo Rus. Fed.
131 H5 Altun Ha Belize
44 E4 Altun Shan mt. ra. China
126 B3 Alturas U.S.A.
125 D5 Altus U.S.A.
64 F3 Altynasar Kazak.
15 E1 Altynivka Ukraine
14 H2 Altyshevo Rus. Fed.
60 D1 Alucra Turkey
11 G4 Alūksne Latvia
73 G2 Al 'Ulā Saudi Arabia
80 E2 Al'ulah reg. Yemen
120 B4 Alum Creek Lake l. U.S.A.
13 E6 Alupka Ukraine
72 C1 Al 'Uqaylah Libya
57 B4 Al 'Uqayr Saudi Arabia
73 G2 Al Urayq desert Saudi Arabia
43 C6 Alur Setar Malaysia
13 E6 Alushta Ukraine
61 D5 Al Uthaylī Saudi Arabia
57 B4 Al 'Uthmānīyah Saudi Arabia
72 D3 Al 'Uwaynāt Libya
72 B2 Al 'Uwaynāt Libya
73 G2 Al 'Uwaynidhiyah i. Saudi Arabia
73 H1 Al 'Uwayqīlah Saudi Arabia
73 H2 Al 'Uyūn Saudi Arabia
73 G3 Al 'Uyūn Saudi Arabia
24 B2 Alva r. Portugal
125 D4 Alva U.S.A.
131 G5 Alvarado Mexico
139 E4 Alvarães Brazil
11 C3 Alvdal Norway
11 D3 Älvdalen Sweden
24 B3 Alverca do Ribatejo Portugal
11 D4 Alvesta Sweden
11 B3 Ålvik Norway
125 E6 Alvin U.S.A.
145 G4 Alvinópolis Brazil
11 D4 Älvsborg div. Sweden
10 F2 Älvsbyn Sweden
73 G2 Al Wajh Saudi Arabia
57 B4 Al Wakrah Qatar
57 B4 Al Wannān Saudi Arabia
73 J2 Al Waqbá well Saudi Arabia
54 D4 Alwar India
56 B4 Alwaye India
60 E4 Al Widyān desert Iraq/Saudi Arabia
72 B3 Al Wīgh Libya
73 H2 Al Wusayţ well Saudi Arabia
48 B5 Alxa Youqi China
48 C5 Alxa Zuoqi China
98 D2 Alyangula Aust.
11 G5 Alytus Lithuania
126 F2 Alzada U.S.A.
18 D4 Alzey Germany
138 C4 Amacayacu, Parque Nacional nat. park Colombia
78 C3 Amada Gaza C.A.R.
98 B5 Amadeus, Lake salt flat Aust.
60 E2 Amādīyah Iraq
109 M3 Amadjuak Lake l. Can.
129 G6 Amado U.S.A.
24 B3 Amadora Portugal
75 F4 Amadror plain Algeria
46 C7 Amagi Japan
139 F2 Amaila Falls waterfall Guyana
46 C7 Amakusa-Kami-shima i. Japan
46 B7 Amakusa-nada b. Japan
46 C7 Amakusa-Shimo-shima i. Japan
11 D4 Åmål Sweden
56 C2 Amalapuram India
138 B2 Amalfi Colombia
29 C6 Amaliada Greece
54 C5 Amalner India
39 L7 Amamapare Indon.
144 A5 Amambaí r. Brazil
144 A5 Amambaí Brazil
45 N6 Amami-guntō is Japan
45 N6 Amami-Ōshima i. Japan
78 E4 Amamula Zaire
139 E4 Amanã, Lago l. Brazil
26 D4 Amandola Italy
64 E3 Amangel'dy Aktyubinsk Kazak.
65 G2 Amangel'dy Turgay Kazak.
65 K4 Amankol China
27 F6 Amantea Italy
91 □10 Amanu i. Fr. Poly. Pac. Oc.
82 D2 Amanzamnyama r. Zimbabwe
83 E5 Amanzimtoti R.S.A.
139 G3 Amapá div. Brazil
139 G3 Amapá Brazil
139 G3 Amapari r. Brazil
73 F3 Amara Sudan
83 F1 Amaramba, Lagoa l. Mozambique
142 D2 Amarante Brazil
142 C2 Amarante do Maranhão Brazil
42 B2 Amarapura Myanmar
48 C3 Amardalay Mongolia
24 C3 Amareleja Portugal
128 D3 Amargosa Desert desert U.S.A.
128 D3 Amargosa Range mts U.S.A.
128 D3 Amargosa Valley U.S.A.
125 C5 Amarillo U.S.A.
54 E4 Amarpatan India
74 B3 Amasine Western Sahara
60 C1 Amasra Turkey
77 E3 Amâssine well Mali
60 C1 Amasya Turkey
131 G5 Amatán Mexico
138 D4 Amataurá Brazil
130 H6 Amatique, B. de b. Guatemala
130 D4 Amatlán de Cañas Mexico
49 G1 Amazar r. Rus. Fed.
139 D4 Amazonas div. Brazil
139 G4 Amazonas r. S. America
142 A1 Amazonia, Parque Nacional nat. park Brazil
139 G3 Amazon, Mouths of the river mouth Brazil
140 A2 Amazon, Source of the river source Peru
54 C2 Amb Pakistan
80 C2 Āmba Ālagē mt. Ethiopia
56 A2 Ambad India
80 C2 Amba Farit mt. Ethiopia
54 D4 Ambah India
83 G3 Ambahikily Madagascar
56 B2 Ambajogai India
54 D3 Ambala India
83 H2 Ambalakida Madagascar
83 H1 Ambalamanasy II Madagascar
56 C5 Ambalangoda Sri Lanka
83 H3 Ambalatany Madagascar
83 H3 Ambalavao Madagascar
98 C4 Ambalindum Aust.
78 B3 Ambam Cameroon
83 H1 Ambanja Madagascar
57 D3 Ambar Iran
40 B3 Ambarawa Indon.
63 S3 Ambarchik Rus. Fed.
12 E1 Ambarnyy Rus. Fed.
56 B4 Ambasamudram India
99 F5 Ambathala Aust.
138 B4 Ambato Ecuador
83 H2 Ambato Boeny Madagascar
83 H3 Ambato Finandrahana Madagascar
83 H2 Ambatolampy Madagascar
83 H2 Ambatomainty Madagascar
83 H2 Ambatondrazaka Madagascar
20 E4 Ambazac France
18 E4 Amberg Germany
133 E2 Ambergris Cays is Turks and Caicos Is Caribbean
21 G4 Ambérieu-en-Bugey France
114 E4 Amberley Can.
93 D5 Amberley N.Z.
21 F4 Ambert France
76 B4 Ambidédi Mali
55 E5 Ambikapur India
83 H3 Ambila Madagascar
83 H1 Ambilobe Madagascar
83 H2 Ambinaninony Madagascar
110 C3 Ambition, Mt mt. Can.
17 G4 Amble U.K.
18 B3 Amblève r. Belgium
140 A2 Ambo Peru
83 H3 Amboasary Madagascar
83 H2 Ambodifotatra Madagascar
83 H2 Ambohidratrimo Madagascar
83 H3 Ambohimahasoa Madagascar
83 G2 Ambohipaky Madagascar
83 H1 Ambohitra mt. Madagascar
83 H2 Ambohitralanana Madagascar
20 E3 Amboise France
39 J7 Ambon i. Indon.
39 J7 Ambon Indon.
83 H3 Amborompotsy Madagascar
81 C5 Amboseli National Park nat. park Kenya
83 H3 Ambositra Madagascar
83 H3 Ambovombe Madagascar
129 E4 Amboy U.S.A.
122 C5 Amboy U.S.A.
121 F3 Amboy Center U.S.A.
81 □4 Ambre, Isle d' i. Mauritius
79 B5 Ambriz Angola
90 □2 Ambrym i. Vanuatu
40 C3 Ambunten Indon.
56 B3 Ambur India
72 D5 Am-Dam Chad
62 H3 Amderma Rus. Fed.
77 D3 Amdillis well Mali
72 C5 Am Djéména Chad
55 G2 Amdo China
130 D4 Ameca Mexico
131 F5 Amecameca Mexico
18 B2 Ameland i. Netherlands
120 E6 Amelia Court House U.S.A.
27 F6 Amendolara Italy
121 G4 Amenia U.S.A.
144 E5 Americana Brazil
126 D3 American Falls U.S.A.
126 D3 American Falls Res. resr U.S.A.
129 G1 American Fork U.S.A.
87 L6 American Samoa terr. Pac. Oc.
119 C5 Americus U.S.A.
18 B2 Amersfoort Netherlands
111 L3 Amery Can.
152 D5 Amery Ice Shelf ice feature Ant.
124 E3 Ames U.S.A.
121 H3 Amesbury U.S.A.
54 C4 Amet India
55 E4 Amethi India
29 C5 Amfilochia Greece
29 D5 Amfissa Greece
63 P3 Amga Rus. Fed.
45 P2 Amgu China
75 F3 Amguid Algeria
63 P4 Amgun' r. Rus. Fed.
113 H4 Amherst Can.
121 J2 Amherst U.S.A.
121 G3 Amherst U.S.A.
120 D6 Amherst U.S.A.
114 D5 Amherstburg Can.
100 D3 Amherst, Mt h. Aust.
61 C2 Amicun Lebanon
20 F2 Amiens Somme France
60 E3 Amij, Wādī w Iraq
61 D1 Amik Ovası marsh Turkey
20 F3 Amilly France
57 C3 'Amīnābād Iran
56 A4 Amindivi Islands is India
80 D4 Amino Ethiopia
46 E6 Amino Japan
82 B3 Aminuis Namibia
60 F3 Amīrābād Iran
69 K6 Amirante Islands is Seychelles
57 E3 Amir Chah Pakistan
111 J4 Amisk L. l. Can.
125 C6 Amistad Res. resr Mexico/U.S.A.
74 C2 Amizmiz Morocco
54 D5 Amla Madhya Pradesh India
54 D5 Amla Madhya Pradesh India
77 E5 Amlamé Togo
55 F4 Amlekhganj Nepal
11 C4 Åmli Norway
17 E5 Amlwch U.K.
73 G4 'Amm Adam Sudan
60 C4 'Ammān Jordan
10 H2 Ämmänsaari Finland
80 E2 'Ammār reg. Yemen
10 E2 Ammarnäs Sweden
98 C4 Ammaroo Aust.
18 E5 Ammersee l. Germany
61 B2 Ammochostos Cyprus
61 B2 Ammochostos Bay b. Cyprus
50 C4 Amo r. China
54 C5 Amod India
57 C1 Amol Iran
141 E3 Amolar Brazil
14 B4 Amon' Rus. Fed.
142 E1 Amontada Brazil
29 E6 Amorgos i. Greece
115 F2 Amos Can.
74 C5 Amourj Mauritania
40 C2 Ampah Indon.
83 H1 Ampanefena Madagascar
83 G3 Ampanihy Madagascar
83 H2 Amparafaka, Tanjona c. Madagascar
83 H2 Amparafaravola Madagascar
56 C5 Amparai India
145 E5 Amparo Brazil
83 H3 Ampasimanjeva Madagascar
83 H2 Ampasimanolotra Madagascar
29 D5 Ampelonas Greece
40 D4 Ampenan Indon.
18 E4 Amper r. Germany
40 E2 Ampibaku Indon.
83 H1 Ampisikinana Madagascar
25 G2 Amposta Spain
80 D1 Amrān Yemen
54 D5 Amravati India
54 B5 Amreli India
54 B4 Amri Pakistan
55 H4 Amring India
54 C3 Amritsar India
54 D3 Amroha India
18 D1 Amrum i. Germany
10 E2 Åmsele Sweden
18 B2 Amsterdam Netherlands
121 F3 Amsterdam U.S.A.
149 K6 Amsterdam, Île i. Indian Ocean
19 G4 Amstetten Austria
78 D1 Am Timan Chad
64 F4 Amudar'ya r. Turkmenistan/Uzbekistan
109 J2 Amund Ringnes I. i. Can.
152 D4 Amundsen Bay b. Ant.
152 B4 Amundsen Gl. gl. Ant.
108 F2 Amundsen Gulf g. Can.
152 C5 Amundsen, Mt mt. Ant.
152 B4 Amundsen-Scott U.S.A. Base Ant.
152 A3 Amundsen Sea sea Ant.
40 C2 Amuntai Indon.
45 P1 Amur r. Rus. Fed.
45 P1 Amursk Rus. Fed.
49 J3 Amurzet Rus. Fed.
29 C5 Amvrakikos Kolpos b. Greece
13 F6 Amvrosiyivka Ukraine
29 C4 Amyntaio Greece
114 C2 Amyot Can.
72 D5 Am-Zoer Chad
42 A3 An Myanmar
29 F4 Ana r. Turkey
91 □10 Anaa i. Fr. Poly. Pac. Oc.
77 E4 Anaba Nigeria
40 E2 Anabanua Indon.
63 N2 Anabar r. Rus. Fed.
63 N2 Anabarskiy Zaliv b. Rus. Fed.
128 C4 Anacapa Is is U.S.A.
139 E2 Anaco Venezuela
126 D2 Anaconda U.S.A.
126 B1 Anacortes U.S.A.
125 D5 Anadarko U.S.A.
60 D1 Anadolu Dağları mt. ra. Turkey
63 T3 Anadyr' r. Rus. Fed.
63 T3 Anadyr' Rus. Fed.
108 A3 Anadyrskiy Zaliv b. Rus. Fed.
29 E6 Anafi i. Greece
25 □ Anaga, Pta de pt Canary Is Spain
60 E3 'Ānah Iraq
128 D5 Anaheim U.S.A.
110 D4 Anahim Lake Can.
125 C7 Anahuac Mexico
56 B4 Anaimalai Hills mts India
56 B4 Anai Mudi Pk mt. India
142 C1 Anajaś Brazil
142 B1 Anajás, Ilha i. Brazil
145 H1 Anajé Brazil
56 C2 Anakapalle India
83 H1 Analalava Madagascar
83 G3 Analavelona mts Madagascar
139 E4 Anamã Brazil
77 F5 Anambra div. Nigeria
122 B4 Anamosa U.S.A.
139 F3 Anamu r. Brazil
60 C2 Anamur Turkey
60 C2 Anamur Br. pt Turkey
46 E7 Anan Japan
43 D7 Anambas, Kepulauan is Indon.
54 C5 Anand India
55 F5 Ānandapur India
55 F5 Anandpur r. India
29 E6 Ananes i. Greece
142 C1 Ananindeua Brazil
56 B3 Anantapur India
54 C2 Anantnag India
15 C3 Anan'yiv Ukraine
13 F6 Anapa Rus. Fed.
144 D2 Anápolis Brazil
142 B1 Anapú r. Brazil
57 C3 Anār Iran
57 C2 Anārak Iran
57 B2 Anarbar r. Iran
57 E2 Anardara Afghanistan
94 □3 Anare Station Macquarie I. Pac. Oc.
119 □3 Añasco Puerto Rico
39 M3 Anatahan i. Northern Mariana Is Pac. Oc.
60 B2 Anatolia reg. Turkey
29 E4 Anatoliki Makedonia kai Thraki div. Greece
90 □2 Anatom i. Vanuatu
146 D2 Añatuya Arg.
139 E3 Anauá r. Brazil
144 B5 Anaurilândia Brazil
61 D5 Anaz mts Saudi Arabia
57 B1 Anbūh Iran
49 H5 Anbyon N. Korea
24 C1 Ancares, Serra dos mt. ra. Spain
146 C2 Ancasti, Sa mt. ra. Arg.
20 D3 Ancenis France
77 F4 Anchau Nigeria
145 H4 Anchieta Brazil
147 B7 Ancho, Can. chan. Chile
140 C2 Anchodaya Bolivia
108 D3 Anchorage U.S.A.
123 F4 Anchor Bay b. U.S.A.
82 A5 Anchorstock Pt pt Tristan da Cunha Atlantic Ocean
140 A2 Ancón Peru
26 D4 Ancona Italy
81 C7 Ancuabe Mozambique
147 B5 Ancud Chile
147 B5 Ancud, G. de g. Chile
49 H3 Anda China
146 B3 Andacollo Chile
98 C5 Andado Aust.
140 B2 Andahuaylas Peru
146 C2 Andalgalá Arg.
10 B3 Åndalsnes Norway
24 D4 Andalucía div. Spain
125 G6 Andalusia U.S.A.
43 A5 Andaman & Nicobar Islands div. India
149 L3 Andaman Basin Indian Ocean
43 A4 Andaman Islands is India
43 A5 Andaman Sea sea Asia
140 C3 Andamarca Bolivia
140 B2 Andamarca Peru
83 H1 Andapa Madagascar
57 G2 Andarāb Afghanistan
54 B2 Andarāb reg. Afghanistan
142 D3 Andaraí Brazil
80 D2 Andeba YeMidir Zerf Chaf pt Eritrea
10 E1 Andenes Norway
18 B3 Andenne Belgium
77 E3 Andéramboukane Mali
21 J3 Andermatt Switz.
20 D4 Andernos-les-Bains France
108 F3 Anderson r. Can.
108 D3 Anderson U.S.A.
122 E5 Anderson U.S.A.
125 E4 Anderson U.S.A.
119 D5 Anderson U.S.A.
97 F5 Anderson B. b. Aust.
138 B2 Andes Colombia
136 C3 Andes mt. ra. S. America
124 D3 Andes, Lake U.S.A.
10 E1 Andfjorden chan. Norway
56 B2 Andhra Pradesh div. India
83 H3 Andihahela, Réserve d' res. Madagascar
83 H2 Andilamena Madagascar
83 H2 Andilanatoby Madagascar
57 B2 Andīmeshk Iran
65 K5 Andirlangar China
13 H7 Andiyskoye Koysu r. Rus. Fed.
65 H4 Andizhan Uzbekistan
57 F1 Andkhui r. Afghanistan
57 F1 Andkhvoy Afghanistan
83 H1 Andoany Madagascar
138 B4 Andoas Peru
56 B2 Andol India
49 J5 Andong S. Korea
99 E2 Andoom Aust.
4 F4 Andorra country Europe
25 F2 Andorra Spain
25 G1 Andorra la Vella Andorra
17 G6 Andover U.K.
121 H2 Andover U.S.A.
120 C4 Andover U.S.A.
10 D1 Andøya i. Norway
145 E5 Andradas Brazil
144 C4 Andradina Brazil
83 H2 Andranomavo Madagascar
83 G3 Andranopasy Madagascar
83 H1 Andranovondronina Madagascar
83 G3 Andranovory Madagascar
104 A4 Andreanof Is U.S.A.
14 A1 Andreapol' Rus. Fed.
78 D2 Andre Felix, Parc National de nat. park C.A.R.
145 H1 André Fernandes Brazil
145 F4 Andrelândia Brazil
145 F3 Andrequicé Brazil
125 C5 Andrews U.S.A.
65 K3 Andreyevka Kazak.
14 G2 Andreyevka Rus. Fed.
14 E2 Andreyevo Rus. Fed.
14 A3 Andreykovichi Rus. Fed.
27 F5 Andria Italy
83 H2 Andriamena Madagascar
83 H3 Andringitra mts Madagascar
15 G3 Andrivka Ukraine
15 G2 Andriyivka Kharkiv Ukraine
15 G3 Andriyivka Zaporizhzhya Ukraine
83 G4 Androka Madagascar
83 H2 Androna reg. Madagascar
14 D1 Androniki Rus. Fed.
29 E6 Andros i. Greece
132 C1 Andros i. The Bahamas
121 H2 Androscoggin r. U.S.A.
132 C1 Andros Town The Bahamas
56 A4 Āndrott i. India
15 C1 Andrushivka Ukraine
15 C2 Andrushky Ukraine
19 J4 Andrychów Poland
10 E1 Andselv Norway
24 D3 Andújar Spain
79 C6 Andulo Angola
76 D3 Anéchag well Mali
77 E3 Anéfis Mali
119 □3 Anegada i. Virgin Is Caribbean
147 D5 Anegada, Bahía b. Arg.
133 G3 Anegada Passage chan. Virgin Is Caribbean
129 F5 Anegam U.S.A.
77 E5 Aného Togo
78 A4 Anengué, Lac l. Gabon
15 C3 Anenii Noi Moldova
129 H3 Aneth U.S.A.
25 G1 Aneto mt. Spain
77 G3 Aney Niger
80 D2 Anfile Bay b. Eritrea
51 F3 Anfu China
83 H1 Angadoka, Lohatanjona pt Madagascar
98 B2 Angalarri r. Aust.
49 G3 Ang'angxi China
63 L4 Angara r. Rus. Fed.
77 E4 Angaradébou Benin
48 B1 Angarsk Rus. Fed.
98 C5 Angas Downs Aust.
100 E4 Angas Ra. h. Aust.
41 B3 Angat Phil.
144 D5 Angatuba Brazil
41 □1 Angaur i. Palau
11 D3 Ånge Sweden
130 B2 Angel de la Guarda i. Mexico
41 B3 Angeles Phil.
90 □2 Angelghowhat Vanuatu
11 D4 Ängelholm Sweden
99 F5 Angellala Cr. r. Aust.
131 F6 Angel, Pto Mexico
128 B2 Angels Camp U.S.A.
80 C2 Āngereb Wenz r. Ethiopia
10 E2 Ångermanälven r. Sweden
19 G2 Angermünde Germany
20 D3 Angers France
142 D3 Angical Brazil
111 K2 Angikuni Lake l. Can.
43 C4 Angkor Cambodia
93 A7 Anglem, Mt mt. N.Z.
17 E5 Anglesey i. U.K.
125 E6 Angleton U.S.A.
115 F3 Angliers Can.
43 □ Ang Mo Kio Singapore
78 E3 Ango Zaire
83 F2 Angoche Mozambique
57 D4 Angohrān Iran
146 B4 Angol Chile
69 F7 Angola country Africa
122 E5 Angola U.S.A.
148 K7 Angola Basin Atlantic Ocean
83 H2 Agontsy, Tanjona c. Madagascar
131 G6 Angostura, Psa de la resr Chiapas Mexico
130 C2 Angostura, Psa de la resr Sonora Mexico
20 E4 Angoulême France
145 F5 Angra dos Reis Brazil
65 H4 Angren Uzbekistan
43 C4 Ang Thong Thailand
78 D3 Angu Zaire
49 G3 Anguang China
104 M8 Anguilla terr. Caribbean
132 C2 Anguilla Cays is The Bahamas
48 E4 Anguli Nur l. China
49 E5 Anguo China
144 A4 Anhanduí Brazil
144 A4 Anhanduí r. Brazil
144 D3 Anhanguera Brazil
11 C4 Anholt i. Denmark
51 E2 Anhua China
51 G1 Anhui div. China
144 A2 Anhumas Brazil
144 D2 Anicuns Brazil
27 D5 Aniene r. Italy
20 D5 Anie, Pic d' mt. France
49 G1 Anikino Rus. Fed.
12 G3 Anikovo Rus. Fed.
129 H6 Animas U.S.A.
129 H6 Animas Peak summit U.S.A.
130 B2 Animas, Pta Las pt Mexico
42 B4 Anin Myanmar
28 C2 Anina Romania
143 C6 Anitápolis Brazil
45 Q2 Aniva, Mys c. Rus. Fed.
45 Q2 Aniva, Zaliv b. Rus. Fed.
83 H1 Anivorano Avaratra Madagascar
90 □2 Aniwa i. Vanuatu
83 H2 Anjafy mt. Madagascar
11 G3 Anjalankoski Finland
56 B4 Anjengo India
51 G2 Anji China
54 D5 Anji India
47 F6 Anjō Japan
57 D2 Anjoman Iran
20 D3 Anjou reg. France
83 H2 Anjozorobe Madagascar
49 H5 Anjŭ N. Korea
83 G3 Ankaboa, Tanjona pt Madagascar
51 E1 Ankang China
60 C2 Ankara Turkey
83 H2 Ankaratra mts Madagascar
83 H2 Ankavandra Madagascar
83 G3 Ankazoabo Madagascar
83 H2 Ankazobe Madagascar
43 E4 An Khê Vietnam
19 F2 Anklam Germany
54 C5 Ankleshwar India
79 E5 Ankoro Zaire
14 D1 An'kovo Rus. Fed.
77 F5 Ankpa Nigeria
77 E5 Anloga Ghana
50 D3 Anlong China
43 D4 Ânlong Vêng Cambodia
51 F2 Anlu China
49 H5 Anmyŏn Do i. S. Korea
13 G5 Anna Rus. Fed.
75 F1 Annaba Algeria
18 F3 Annaberg-Buchholtz Germany
61 D4 An Nabk Saudi Arabia
60 D3 An Nabk Syria
73 H2 An Nafūd desert Saudi Arabia
139 F3 Annai Guyana
60 E4 An Najaf div. Iraq
60 F4 An Najaf Iraq
47 G5 Annaka Japan
120 E5 Anna, Lake l. U.S.A.
42 D3 Annam reg. Vietnam
61 C5 An Na'mī well Saudi Arabia
17 F4 Annan U.K.
17 F4 Annan r. U.K.
147 A6 Anna Pink, Bahía b. Chile
100 C3 Anna Plains Aust.
120 E5 Annapolis U.S.A.
113 G5 Annapolis Royal Can.
55 E3 Annapurna mt. Nepal
57 B4 An Naqīrah well Saudi Arabia
123 F4 Ann Arbor U.S.A.
139 F2 Anna Regina Guyana
60 F4 An Nāşirīyah Iraq
115 J3 Annaville Can.
72 C1 An Nawfalīyah Libya
121 H3 Ann, Cape hd U.S.A.
101 B5 Annean, L. salt flat Aust.
21 H4 Annecy France
21 H3 Annemasse France
110 C4 Annette I. i. U.S.A.
119 □1 Annie's Bay b. Bermuda
73 H4 An Nimāş Saudi Arabia
50 C3 Anning r. China
50 C3 Anning China
14 E3 Annino Rus. Fed.
119 C5 Anniston U.S.A.
148 K6 Annobón i. Equatorial Guinea
21 G4 Annonay France
133 □1 Annotto Bay Jamaica
57 B4 An Nu'ayrīyah Saudi Arabia
122 A3 Anoka U.S.A.
138 B3 Anoón de Sardinas, B. de b. Colombia
14 E2 Anopino Rus. Fed.
139 E4 Anori Brazil
83 H1 Anorontany, Tanjona hd Madagascar
83 H2 Anosibe An'Ala Madagascar
21 H2 Anould France
77 F3 Anou Mekkerene w Niger
77 E3 Ânou Mellene well Mali
75 E4 Anou Meniet well Algeria
75 E5 Anou-n-Bidek well Algeria
77 F3 Ânou Zeggueghene well Niger
29 E7 Ano Viannos Greece
51 E4 Anpu China
51 E4 Anpu Gang China
51 G2 Anqing China
49 F5 Anqiu China
51 F3 Anren China
48 D5 Ansai China
18 E4 Ansbach Germany
80 C1 Anseba Shet w Eritrea
133 □5 Anse Bertrand Guadeloupe Caribbean
81 □2 Anse Boileau Seychelles
81 □2 Anse Royal Seychelles
49 G4 Anshan China
50 D3 Anshun China
146 E3 Ansina Uruguay
124 D3 Ansley U.S.A.
125 D5 Anson U.S.A.
98 B2 Anson B. b. Aust.
95 □1 Anson B. b. Norfolk I. Pac. Oc.
77 E3 Ansongo Mali
77 E3 Ansongo-Ménaka, Réserve Partielle de Faune d' res. Mali
114 E2 Ansonville Can.
120 C5 Ansted U.S.A.
11 G4 Anstla Estonia
16 F3 Anstruther U.K.
54 D4 Anta India
140 B2 Anta Peru
140 B2 Antabamba Peru
83 H1 Antalaha Madagascar
60 B2 Antalya Turkey
60 B2 Antalya Körfezi g. Turkey
83 H2 Antanambao Manampotsy Madagascar
83 H2 Antananarivo Madagascar
83 H2 Antananarivo div. Madagascar
83 H2 Antanifotsy Madagascar
83 H3 Antanimora Atsimo Madagascar
152 B2 Antarctic Peninsula pen. Ant.
143 B6 Antas r. Brazil
143 B6 Antas, R. das r. Brazil
128 D2 Antelope Range mts U.S.A.
24 D4 Antequera Spain
127 F5 Anthony U.S.A.
98 C3 Anthony Lagoon Aust.
74 C3 Anti Atlas mt. ra. Morocco
21 H5 Antibes France
113 H4 Anticosti, Île d' i. Can.
20 E2 Antifer, Cap d' pt France
122 C3 Antigo U.S.A.
113 H4 Antigonish Can.
133 □7 Antigua i. Antigua and Barbuda
131 H6 Antigua Guatemala
25 □ Antigua Canary Is Spain
104 M8 Antigua and Barbuda country Caribbean
133 □5 Antigues, Pte d' pt Guadeloupe Caribbean
131 F4 Antiguo-Morelos Mexico
29 D5 Antikyra Greece
29 D7 Antikythira i. Greece
29 E6 Antimilos i. Greece
128 B3 Antioch U.S.A.
122 C4 Antioch U.S.A.
138 B2 Antioquia Colombia
29 E6 Antiparos i. Greece
29 C5 Antipaxoi i. Greece
93 □3 Antipodes I. i. Antipodes Is N.Z.
29 E5 Antipsara i. Greece
138 B4 Antisana, Co vol Ecuador
29 F6 Antitilos i. Greece
125 E5 Antlers U.S.A.
140 B4 Antofagasta Chile
140 C4 Antofagasta div. Chile
146 C2 Antofagasta de la Sierra Arg.
146 C2 Antofalla, Vol. vol Arg.
130 K7 Antón Panama
15 B2 Antoniny Ukraine
142 D3 Antônio r. Brazil
128 B3 Antonio r. U.S.A.
145 G4 Antônio Carlos Brazil
147 C6 Antonio de Biedma Arg.
145 G3 Antônio Dias Brazil
127 F4 Antonito U.S.A.
15 C2 Antoniv Ukraine
15 E1 Antonivka Chernihiv Ukraine
15 E3 Antonivka Kherson Ukraine
17 D4 Antrim U.K.
100 E3 Antrim Plateau plat. Aust.
27 D4 Antrodoco Italy
12 G3 Antropovo Rus. Fed.
83 H1 Antsahanoro Madagascar
83 G2 Antsalova Madagascar
83 H2 Antsirabe Madagascar
83 H1 Antsirañana div. Madagascar
83 H1 Antsirañana Madagascar
83 H1 Antsohihy Madagascar
10 F2 Anttis Sweden
11 G3 Anttola Finland
49 J4 Antu China
146 B4 Antuco Chile
141 D2 Antuerpia Brazil
80 D1 Antufush I. i. Yemen
121 F2 Antwerp U.S.A.
18 B3 Antwerpen div. Belgium
18 B3 Antwerpen Belgium
91 □10 Anuanu Raro i. Fr. Poly. Pac. Oc.
112 E2 Anuc, Lac l. Can.
55 F5 Anugul India
54 C3 Anupgarh India
56 C1 Anuppur India
56 C4 Anuradhapura Sri Lanka
57 C4 Anveh Iran
152 B2 Anvers I. i. Ant.
51 G3 Anxi China
44 G3 Anxi China
50 D2 An Xian China
51 F2 Anxiang China
49 E5 Anxin China
96 C3 Anxious Bay b. Aust.
76 D5 Anyama Côte d'Ivoire
48 E5 Anyang China
49 H5 Anyang S. Korea
40 A3 Anyar Indon.
29 E6 Anydro i. Greece
50 B1 A'nyêmaqên Shan mt. ra. China
51 F2 Anyi China
51 F3 Anyuan Jiangxi China
51 F3 Anyuan Jiangxi China
50 D2 Anyue China
63 S3 Anyuysk Rus. Fed.
138 B2 Anzá Colombia
48 E5 Anze China
62 K4 Anzhero-Sudzhensk Rus. Fed.
78 D4 Anzi Zaire
27 D5 Anzio Italy
90 □2 Aoba i. Vanuatu
43 B5 Ao Ban Don b. Thailand
49 F4 Aohan Qi China
46 H3 Aomori Japan
46 H3 Aomori div. Japan
91 □11 Aorai mt. Fr. Poly. Pac. Oc.
93 E4 Aorangi Mts mts N.Z.
92 D4 Aorere r. N.Z.
43 B5 Ao Sawi b. Thailand
26 A3 Aosta Italy
77 F3 Aouderas Niger
74 C3 Aouhinet bel Egra well Algeria
78 D1 Aoukalé r. C.A.R./Chad
78 D2 Aouk-Aoakole, Réserve de Faune de l' res. C.A.R.
74 C4 Aoukâr reg. Mali/Mauritania
75 E3 Aoulef Algeria
74 C2 Aoulime, Jbel mt. Morocco
46 E6 Aoya Japan
72 C3 Aozou Chad
141 E4 Apa r. Brazil
80 B4 Apac Uganda
129 H6 Apache U.S.A.
129 H5 Apache Creek U.S.A.
129 G5 Apache Junction U.S.A.
129 G6 Apache Peak summit U.S.A.
28 D1 Apahida Romania
144 D5 Apaiaí r. Brazil
119 C6 Apalachee Bay b. U.S.A.
119 C6 Apalachicola U.S.A.
131 F5 Apan Mexico
138 D4 Apaporis r. Colombia
144 C4 Aparecida do Tabuado Brazil
93 B6 Aparima r. N.Z.
41 B2 Aparri Phil.
40 D2 Apar, Tk b. Indon.
91 □10 Apataki i. Fr. Poly. Pac. Oc.
28 B2 Apatin Yugo.
62 E3 Apatity Rus. Fed.
139 G2 Apatou French Guiana
130 E5 Apatzingán Mexico
11 G4 Ape Latvia
18 B2 Apeldoorn Netherlands
54 E3 Api mt. Nepal
78 E3 Api Zaire
91 □12 Apia Western Samoa
141 E2 Apiacá r. Brazil
144 D6 Apiaí Brazil
90 □1 Apio Solomon Is.
26 D4 Apiro Italy
92 E3 Apiti N.Z.
77 E5 Aplahué Benin
140 B3 Aplao Peru
142 E2 Apodi r. Brazil
142 E2 Apodi Brazil
139 F2 Apoera Surinam
18 E3 Apolda Germany
97 E4 Apollo Bay Aust.
140 C2 Apolo Bolivia
41 C5 Apo, Mt vol Phil.
119 D6 Apopka, L. l. U.S.A.
144 C3 Aporé r. Brazil
144 C3 Aporé Brazil
139 G3 Aporema Brazil
118 B2 Apostle Is is U.S.A.
122 B2 Apostle Islands National Lakeshore res. U.S.A.
146 E2 Apóstoles Arg.
61 C2 Apostolos Andreas, C. hd Cyprus
15 E3 Apostolove Ukraine
139 F3 Apoteri Guyana
120 B6 Appalachia U.S.A.
120 C6 Appalachian Mountains mt. ra. U.S.A.
27 E5 Appennino Napoletano mt. ra. Italy
22 E3 Appennino mt. ra. Italy
27 D4 Appennino Abruzzese mt. ra. Italy
27 E5 Appennino Lucanose mt. ra. Italy
26 C4 Appennino Tosco-Emiliano mts Italy
26 D4 Appennino Umbro-Marchigiano mt. ra. Italy
17 F4 Appleby-in-Westmorland U.K.
16 E3 Applecross U.K.
124 D2 Appleton U.S.A.
122 C3 Appleton U.S.A.
128 D4 Apple Valley U.S.A.
120 D6 Appomattox U.S.A.
139 G3 Approuague r. French Guiana
41 □2 Apra Harb. inlet Guam Pac. Oc.
41 □2 Apra Heights Guam Pac. Oc.
14 C2 Aprelevka Rus. Fed.
27 D5 Aprilia Italy
55 H3 Aprunyi India
13 F6 Apsheronsk Rus. Fed.
115 F4 Apsley Can.
98 B1 Apsley Str. chan. Aust.
21 G5 Apt France
144 C5 Apucarana Brazil
41 A4 Apurahuan Phil.
138 D2 Apure r. Venezuela
140 B2 Apurimac r. Peru
60 C4 'Aqaba Jordan
61 C6 Aqaba, Gulf of chan. Africa/Asia
61 C5 'Aqaba, W. el w Egypt
57 C1 Aqbana Iran
57 F1 Āqchah Afghanistan
57 C2 Āqdā Iran
60 F2 Aqdoghmish r. Iran
73 G2 Aqla well Saudi Arabia
55 G1 Aqqikkol Hu salt l. China
61 D4 'Aqran h. Saudi Arabia
129 F4 Aquarius Mts mts U.S.A.
129 G3 Aquarius Plateau plat. U.S.A.

B

54 C4 Badnor India
51 E2 Badong China
43 D5 Ba Đông Vietnam
77 E5 Badou Togo
64 C5 Bädovan Burnu pt Azerbaijan
28 B2 Badovinci Yugo.
18 D3 Bad Pyrmont Germany
60 F3 Badrah Iraq
18 F5 Bad Reichenhall Germany
73 G3 Badr Ḩunayn Saudi Arabia
54 D3 Badrinath Peaks mts India
19 G5 Bad St Leonhard im Lavanttal Austria
18 D2 Bad Salzuflen Germany
18 E3 Bad Salzungen Germany
18 D3 Bad Schwalbach Germany
18 E2 Bad Schwartau Germany
18 E2 Bad Segeberg Germany
95 H1 Badu I. i. Aust.
56 C5 Badulla Sri Lanka
18 D5 Bad Waldsee Germany
49 K2 Badzhal Rus. Fed.
18 D2 Bad Zwischenahn Germany
10 L2 Bæir Iceland
24 D4 Baena Spain
138 B4 Baeza Ecuador
24 E4 Baeza Spain
78 B2 Bafang Cameroon
76 B4 Bafatá Guinea-Bissau
54 C2 Baffa Pakistan
109 M2 Baffin Bay sea Can./Greenland
109 L2 Baffin Island i. Can.
78 B3 Bafia Cameroon
77 E5 Bafilo Togo
76 B4 Bafing r. Guinea/Mali
76 B4 Bafing, Parc National du nat. park Mali
61 D1 Bafliyun Syria
76 B4 Bafoulabé Mali
78 B2 Bafoussam Cameroon
57 C3 Bāfq Iran
60 C1 Bafra Turkey
60 D1 Bafra Burun pt Turkey
57 D3 Bāft Iran
78 E3 Bafwamboma Zaire
78 E3 Bafwasende Zaire
142 C3 Bagagem r. Brazil
55 F4 Bagaha India
56 A2 Bagalkot India
81 C6 Bagamoyo Tanzania
43 C7 Bagan Datuk Malaysia
82 C2 Bagani Namibia
41 B5 Baganian Peninsula pen. Phil.
43 C6 Bagan Serai Malaysia
43 C7 Bagansiapiapi Indon.
29 F6 Bağarası Turkey
77 F3 Bagaré well Niger
77 E4 Bagaroua Niger
79 C4 Bagata Zaire
50 B1 Bag Belqer China
129 F4 Bagdad U.S.A.
146 F3 Bagé Brazil
126 F3 Baggs U.S.A.
54 C5 Bagh India
60 F3 Baghdād Iraq
57 B3 Bāgh-e Malek Iran
27 D6 Bagheria Italy
57 D3 Bāghīn Iran
57 G1 Baghlān Afghanistan
57 F2 Baghrān Afghanistan
124 E2 Bagley U.S.A.
55 E3 Baglung Nepal
20 E5 Bagnères-de-Bigorre France
20 E5 Bagnères-de-Luchon France
26 C4 Bagno di Romagna Italy
21 G4 Bagnols-sur-Cèze France
55 F4 Bagnuiti r. Nepal
48 D5 Bag Nur l. China
41 B4 Bago Phil.
76 C4 Bagoé r. Côte d'Ivoire/Mali
11 F5 Bagrationovsk Rus. Fed.
142 B1 Bagre Brazil
138 B5 Bagua Grande Peru
77 E4 Bagudo Nigeria
41 B2 Bagulo Phil.
77 F3 Bagzane, Monts mts Niger
55 E4 Bahadurganj Nepal
54 D3 Bahadurgarh India
104 L7 Bahamas, The country Caribbean
133 □4 Baham, Pte pt *Martinique* Caribbean
55 G4 Baharampur India
54 B4 Bahardipur Pakistan
73 E2 Bahariya Oasis oasis Egypt
43 C7 Bahau Malaysia
40 C2 Bahaur Indon.
54 C3 Bahawalnagar Pakistan
54 B3 Bahawalpur Pakistan
60 D2 Bahçe Turkey
54 D3 Baheri India
81 C6 Bahi Tanzania
145 H1 Bahia div. Brazil
146 D4 Bahía Blanca Arg.
130 J5 Bahía, Islas de la is Honduras
130 C2 Bahia Kino Mexico
147 C6 Bahía Laura Arg.
141 E4 Bahía Negra Paraguay
80 C2 Bahir Dar Ethiopia
57 B3 Bahmanyārī ye Pā'īn Iran
73 H4 Bahr Saudi Arabia
61 A4 Bahra el Burullus lag. Egypt
73 F1 Bahra el Manzala lag. Egypt
55 E4 Bahraich India
32 G7 Bahrain country Asia
57 B4 Bahrain, Gulf of g. Asia
55 E4 Bahramghat India
57 D3 Bahrāmjerd Iran
78 D2 Bahr Aouk r. C.A.R./Chad
61 D2 Baḩrat Ḩimş resr Syria
72 D5 Bahr Azoum w Chad
72 D5 Bahr Azrak w Chad
78 C1 Bahr Bola w Chad
78 C2 Bahr Dosséo r. Chad
80 B2 Bahr el Abiad r. Sudan/Uganda
78 E1 Bahr el Arab w Sudan
73 F5 Bahr el Azraq r. Ethiopia/Sudan
72 C5 Bahr el Ghazal r. Chad
78 E2 Bahr el Ghazal r. Sudan
78 E2 Bahr el Ghazal div. Sudan
80 B3 Bahr el Jebel r. Sudan/Uganda
80 B3 Bahr el Zeraf r. Sudan
78 C2 Bahr Kéita r. Chad
78 C1 Bahr Korom w Chad
54 D4 Bahror India
78 C2 Bahr Salamat r. Chad
61 D3 Baḩr Şayqal l. Syria
61 A5 Bahr Yûsef r. Egypt
57 E4 Bāhū Kālāt Iran
51 F1 Bai r. China
28 G2 Baia Romania
28 D2 Baia de Aramă Romania
28 D1 Baia de Arieș Romania
142 F2 Baía de Traição Brazil
79 B7 Baía dos Tigres Angola
28 D1 Baia Mare Romania
142 C1 Baião Brazil
28 D1 Baia Sprie Romania
57 C2 Baiazeh Iran
72 D4 Baïbeli well Chad
78 C2 Baïbokoum Chad
65 K4 Baicheng China
49 G3 Baicheng China
28 E2 Băicoi Romania
78 D2 Baïdou r. C.A.R.
113 G4 Baie Comeau Can.
115 J1 Baie du Poste Can.
133 □5 Baie-Mahault b. *Guadeloupe* Caribbean
113 F4 Baie Saint Paul Can.
113 J4 Baie Verte Can.
49 F5 Baigou r. China
50 B3 Baihanchang China
54 E5 Baihar India
49 J4 Baihe China
51 E1 Baihe China
60 E3 Baiji Iraq
65 L3 Baijiantan China
54 D2 Baijnath India
54 D3 Baijnath India
28 E2 Băile Govora Romania
28 D2 Băile Herculane Romania
24 E3 Bailén Spain
28 D2 Băilești Romania
28 E1 Băile Tușnad Romania
101 C6 Bailey Ra. h. Aust.
139 G3 Bailique Brazil
111 H2 Baillie r. Can.
133 □5 Baillif *Guadeloupe* Caribbean
50 C1 Bailong r. China
79 C6 Bailundo Angola
50 C1 Baima China
55 G3 Bainang China
119 C6 Bainbridge U.S.A.
121 F3 Bainbridge U.S.A.
20 D3 Bain-de-Bretagne France
133 D3 Bainet Haiti
55 G3 Baingoin China
24 B1 Baiona Spain
49 H3 Baiquan China
55 E2 Bairab Co l. China
55 F4 Bairagnia India
108 B3 Baird Mountains mt. ra. U.S.A.
49 F4 Bairing Qiao China
49 F4 Bairin Youqi China
49 F4 Bairin Zuoqi China
65 G4 Bairkum Kazak.
97 F4 Bairnsdale Aust.
60 D4 Bā'ir, Wādī w Jordan
41 B4 Bais Phil.
20 E5 Baïse r. France
50 E2 Baisha China
51 F3 Baisha China
51 E5 Baisha China
49 H4 Baishan China
50 D1 Baishui r. China
11 F5 Baisogala Lithuania
51 G3 Baisong Guan pass China
42 D3 Bai Thường Vietnam
49 F4 Baitle r. China
28 E1 Băiuț Romania
24 B3 Baixa da Banheira Portugal
49 G4 Baixingt China
145 H3 Baixo Guandu Brazil
79 C7 Baixo-Longa Angola
48 C5 Baiyin China
50 B2 Baiyü China
19 J5 Baja Hungary
130 B2 Baja California pen. Mexico
130 B2 Baja California Norte div. Mexico
130 B3 Baja California Sur div. Mexico
131 E3 Bajan Mexico
54 E3 Bajang Nepal
91 □16 Baja, Pta pt *Easter I.* Chile
130 A2 Baja, Pta pt Mexico
54 B2 Bajaur reg. Pakistan
39 H8 Bajawa Indon.
55 G5 Baj Baj India
57 D1 Bājgīrān Iran
80 D2 Bājil Yemen
28 B3 Bajina Bašta Yugo.
55 G4 Bajitpur Bangladesh
138 B2 Bajo Baudó Colombia
130 K7 Bajo Boquete Panama
77 G4 Bajoga Nigeria
147 C6 Bajo Grande Arg.
28 C3 Bajram Curri Albania
40 C2 Baka, Bukit mt. Indon.
64 E2 Bakal Rus. Fed.
78 D2 Bakala C.A.R.
65 J4 Bakanas Kazak.
72 D4 Bakaoré Chad
76 A4 Bakau The Gambia
40 D2 Bakaucengal Indon.
15 E1 Bakayivka Ukraine
76 B4 Bakel Senegal
128 D4 Baker U.S.A.
126 F2 Baker U.S.A.
129 E2 Baker U.S.A.
126 C2 Baker U.S.A.
129 G4 Baker Butte summit U.S.A.
87 K4 Baker I. i. Pac. Oc.
110 C3 Baker I. i. U.S.A.
111 K2 Baker Lake Can.
111 K2 Baker Lake l. Can.
126 B1 Baker, Mt vol U.S.A.
112 E2 Bakers Dozen Islands is Can.
128 C4 Bakersfield U.S.A.
43 D4 Bâ Kêv Cambodia
14 A3 Bakhany Rus. Fed.
64 E5 Bakharden Turkmenistan
64 E5 Bakhardok Turkmenistan
57 E2 Bākharz mt. ra. Iran
54 B4 Bakhasar India
13 E6 Bakhchysaray Ukraine
49 J2 Bakhirevo Rus. Fed.
15 E1 Bakhmach Ukraine
14 B1 Bakhmutovo Rus. Fed.
57 B2 Bakhtiari Country reg. Iran
55 F4 Bakhtiyarpur India
65 K3 Bakhty Kazak.
14 F2 Bakhtyzino Rus. Fed.
60 G1 Bakı Azerbaijan
72 D4 Baki well Chad
60 G2 Bakı Komissarı, 26 Azerbaijan
29 F5 Bakır r. Turkey
60 B1 Bakırköy Turkey
10 E1 Bakkejord Norway
76 C5 Bako Côte d'Ivoire
80 C3 Bako Ethiopia
80 C3 Bako Ethiopia
80 D4 Bakool div. Somalia
78 D2 Bakouma C.A.R.
78 B4 Bakoumba Gabon
76 B4 Bakoy r. Mali
13 G7 Baksan Rus. Fed.
19 L5 Baktalórántháza Hungary
78 F3 Baku Zaire
40 A1 Bakung i. Indon.
14 G3 Bakur r. Rus. Fed.
13 G7 Bakuriani Georgia
14 G3 Bakury Rus. Fed.
152 A4 Bakutis Coast Ant.
60 C2 Balâ Turkey
17 F5 Bala U.K.
41 A4 Balabac Phil.
41 A5 Balabac i. Phil.
41 A5 Balabac Strait str. Malaysia/Phil.
40 D2 Balabalangan, Kep. atolls Indon.
14 C2 Balabanovo Rus. Fed.
90 □2 Balabio i. Pac. Oc.
133 □1 Balaclava Jamaica
57 B3 Bālādeh Iran
57 B1 Baladeh Iran
54 E5 Balaghat India
56 A2 Balaghat Range h. India
25 G2 Balaguer Spain
57 D3 Bālā Ḩowẕ Iran
40 B2 Balaiberkuak Indon.
40 B1 Balaikarangan Indon.
40 B2 Balairiam Indon.
83 E1 Balaka Malawi
14 F1 Balakhna Rus. Fed.
14 D1 Balakirevo Rus. Fed.
96 D3 Balaklava Aust.
13 E6 Balaklava Ukraine
15 G2 Balakliya Ukraine
13 H4 Balakovo Rus. Fed.
41 A5 Balambangan i. Malaysia
57 E2 Bālā Morghāb Afghanistan
54 B4 Bālān India
28 E1 Bălan Romania
14 G4 Balanda r. Rus. Fed.
29 G6 Balan Dağı mt. Turkey
41 B3 Balanga Phil.
81 C5 Balangida, Lake l. Tanzania
55 E5 Balāngīr India
56 C5 Balangoda Sri Lanka
40 E2 Balase r. Indon.
14 C2 Balashikha Rus. Fed.
13 G5 Balashov Rus. Fed.
56 A1 Balasinor India
19 J4 Balassagyarmat Hungary
19 H5 Balaton l. Hungary
19 H5 Balatonfüred Hungary
19 H5 Balatonlelle Hungary
25 E3 Balazote Spain
19 L1 Balbieriškis Lithuania
139 F4 Balbina Brazil
17 D5 Balbriggan Rep. of Ire.
96 D2 Balcanoona Aust.
146 E4 Balcarce Arg.
28 G3 Balchik Bulgaria
93 B7 Balclutha N.Z.
101 B7 Bald Hd hd Aust.
145 G3 Baldim Brazil
125 F5 Bald Knob U.S.A.
129 E3 Bald Mtn mt. U.S.A.
111 K3 Baldock Lake l. Can.
115 F4 Baldwin Can.
119 D6 Baldwin U.S.A.
122 E4 Baldwin U.S.A.
122 A3 Baldwin U.S.A.
121 E3 Baldwinsville U.S.A.
129 H5 Baldy Peak mt. U.S.A.
48 D2 Bal'dzhikan Rus. Fed.
76 B4 Baléa Mali
25 H3 Baleares, Islas is Spain
40 C1 Baleh r. Malaysia
113 G2 Baleine, Rivière à la r. Can.
20 D3 Baleines, Pte des pt France
152 □ Baleiniers, Golfe de b. *Kerguelen* Indian Ocean
80 C3 Bale Mts National Park nat. park Ethiopia
28 E2 Băleni Romania
41 B3 Baler Phil.
41 B3 Baler Bay b. Phil.
55 F5 Bāleshwar India
11 B3 Balestrand Norway
49 F2 Baley Rus. Fed.
77 E4 Baléyara Niger
99 F4 Balfe's Creek Aust.
93 B6 Balfour N.Z.
48 A3 Balgatay Mongolia
48 A2 Balgazin Rus. Fed.
100 D4 Balgo Mission Aust.
81 C5 Balguda well Kenya
65 L4 Balguntay China
80 E2 Bālḩaf Yemen
80 D2 Balho Djibouti
54 C4 Bali India
40 C3 Bali i. Indon.
40 C4 Bali div. Indon.
38 C6 Balige Indon.
55 E5 Baliguda India
49 F4 Balihan China
61 C1 Balık r. Turkey
60 A2 Balıkesir Turkey
29 F5 Balıkesir div. Turkey
60 D2 Balīkh r. Syria/Turkey
29 F4 Balıklıçeşme Turkey
40 D2 Balikpapan Indon.
40 D2 Balikpapan, Tk b. Indon.
41 A5 Balimbing Phil.
56 C2 Balimila Reservoir resr India
90 □1 Balimo P.N.G.
49 G2 Balin China
18 D4 Balingen Germany
41 B2 Balintang Channel chan. Phil.
40 C3 Bali Sea g. Indon.
78 D2 Balitondo C.A.R.
41 B5 Baliungan i. Phil.
73 H4 Baljurshī Saudi Arabia
57 C1 Balkan div. Turkmenistan
65 G2 Balkashino Kazak.
57 F1 Balkh Afghanistan
57 F1 Balkhab r. Afghanistan
65 H3 Balkhash Kazak.
65 H3 Balkhash, Ozero l. Kazak.
13 H6 Balkuduk Kazak.
101 C7 Balladonia Aust.
17 C5 Ballaghaderreen Rep. of Ire.
10 E1 Ballangen Norway
126 E2 Ballantine U.S.A.
17 E4 Ballantrae U.K.
97 E4 Ballarat Aust.
101 C6 Ballard, L. salt flat Aust.
56 B2 Ballarpur India
16 F3 Ballater U.K.
76 C3 Ballé Mali
146 B2 Ballena, Pta pt Chile
152 A6 Balleny Is is Ant.
55 F4 Ballia India
80 E3 Balli Megali well Ethiopia
97 H2 Ballina Aust.
17 C4 Ballina Rep. of Ire.
17 C5 Ballinasloe Rep. of Ire.
125 D6 Ballinger U.S.A.
17 C5 Ballinrobe Rep. of Ire.
94 □4 Ball's Pyramid i. *Lord Howe I.* Pac. Oc.
121 G3 Ballston Spa U.S.A.
17 C5 Ballybunnion Rep. of Ire.
17 D5 Ballymahon Rep. of Ire.
17 D4 Ballymena U.K.
17 D4 Ballymoney U.K.
17 C4 Ballyshannon Rep. of Ire.
147 B6 Balmaceda Chile
24 E1 Balmaseda Spain
19 K5 Balmazújváros Hungary
96 E4 Balmoral Aust.
125 C6 Balmorhea U.S.A.
54 A3 Balochistān Pakistan
54 E5 Balod India
55 E5 Baloda Bazar India
40 A2 Balok, Tk b. Indon.
79 B6 Balombo Angola
99 G6 Balonne r. Aust.
54 C4 Balotra India
55 F4 Balpahari Res. resr India
55 E4 Balrampur India
97 E3 Balranald Aust.
28 E2 Balș Romania
115 F3 Balsam Creek Can.
144 B4 Bálsamo Brazil
25 G2 Balsareny Spain
142 C2 Balsas Brazil
130 E5 Balsas r. Mexico
131 F5 Balsas Mexico
142 C3 Balsas, Rio das r. Brazil
15 C3 Balta Ukraine
28 D3 Balta Berilovac Yugo.
12 J3 Baltasi Rus. Fed.
14 H3 Baltay Rus. Fed.
15 B3 Bălți Moldova
4 G3 Baltic Sea g. Europe
61 A4 Baltîm Egypt
120 E5 Baltimore U.S.A.
54 C2 Baltistan reg. Pakistan
11 E5 Baltiysk Rus. Fed.
138 □ Baltra, I. i. *Galapagos Is* Ecuador
55 H4 Balu India
57 D3 Baluch Ab well Iran
40 C2 Baluran, G. mt. Indon.
55 G4 Balurghat India
28 F1 Băluşeni Romania
41 C5 Balut i. Phil.
11 G4 Balvi Latvia
100 D4 Balwina Abor. Reserve res. Aust.
29 F5 Balya Turkey
48 D2 Balyaga Rus. Fed.
65 L2 Balyksa Rus. Fed.
64 D3 Balykshi Kazak.
48 A2 Balyktyg-Khem r. Rus. Fed.
15 B2 Balyn Ukraine
138 B4 Balzar Ecuador
48 E2 Bal'zino Rus. Fed.
57 D1 Bām Iran
57 D3 Bam Iran
50 D3 Bama China
77 G4 Bama Nigeria
99 E1 Bamaga Aust.
112 B3 Bamaji L. l. Can.
76 C4 Bamako Mali
76 D3 Bamba Mali
79 B4 Bambama Congo
41 B2 Bambang Phil.
79 D7 Bambangando Angola
78 D2 Bambari C.A.R.
18 E4 Bamberg Germany
119 D5 Bamberg U.S.A.
78 E3 Bambesa Zaire
76 A4 Bambey Senegal
78 E3 Bambili Zaire
78 C3 Bambio C.A.R.
82 D5 Bamboesberg mts R.S.A.
76 B4 Bambouk reg. Mali
81 □4 Bambou Mts h. Mauritius
78 E2 Bambouti C.A.R.
80 B2 Bambudi Ethiopia
145 F4 Bambuí Brazil
50 B2 Bamda China
78 B2 Bamenda Cameroon
78 B2 Bamendjing, Lac de l. Cameroon
57 F2 Bāmīān Afghanistan
49 H4 Bamiancheng China
78 D2 Bamingui C.A.R.
78 C2 Bamingui r. C.A.R.
78 D2 Bamingui-Bangoran div. C.A.R.
78 C2 Bamingui-Bangoran, Parc National du nat. park C.A.R.
42 C4 Bamnet Narong Thailand
57 E4 Bam Posht reg. Iran
57 E4 Bam Posht, Kūh-e mt. ra. Iran
57 E4 Bampūr Iran
57 D4 Bampūr w Iran
57 E2 Bamrūd Iran
80 E4 Banaadir div. Somalia
86 H5 Banaba i. Kiribati
142 E2 Banabuiu, Açude resr Brazil
146 C4 Bañados del Atuel marsh Arg.
141 D3 Bañados del Izozog swamp Bolivia
78 E3 Banalia Zaire
76 C4 Banamba Mali
99 G5 Banana Aust.
43 A6 Bananga *Andaman and Nicobar Is* India
56 D2 Bānapur India
43 C4 Ban Aranyaprathet Thailand
29 F4 Banarlı Turkey
54 D4 Banas r. India
80 E2 Bana, W. w Yemen
40 D3 Banawaya i. Indon.
60 B2 Banaz Turkey
42 C3 Ban Ban Laos
55 H3 Banbar China
43 C6 Ban Betong Thailand
17 D4 Banbridge U.K.
43 C4 Ban Bua Chum Thailand
42 C4 Ban Bua Yai Thailand
17 G5 Banbury U.K.
42 C2 Ban Cang Vietnam
74 A4 Banc d'Arguin, Parc National du nat. park Mauritania
42 C3 Ban Channabot Thailand
42 B3 Ban Chiang Dao Thailand
16 F3 Banchory U.K.
131 J5 Banco Chinchorro is Mexico
132 B4 Banco Gorda sand bank Honduras
41 A5 Bancoran i. Phil.
115 G4 Bancroft Can.
57 D2 Band Iran
78 B2 Banda Cameroon
54 E4 Banda India
78 E3 Banda Zaire
38 C5 Banda Aceh Indon.
54 B2 Banda Daud Shah Pakistan
47 H5 Bandai-Asahi National Park nat. park. Japan
76 B5 Bandajuma Sierra Leone
39 J7 Banda, Kepulauan is Indon.
76 D5 Bandama r. Côte d'Ivoire
76 C5 Bandama Blanc r. Côte d'Ivoire
57 E3 Bandān Iran
57 E3 Bandān Kūh mt. ra. Iran
83 E2 Bandar Mozambique
40 A3 Bandaragung Indon.
55 H5 Bandarban Bangladesh
57 D4 Bandar-e 'Abbās Iran
57 B1 Bandar-e Anzalī Iran
57 B3 Bandar-e Deylam Iran
57 C4 Bandar-e Khoemir Iran
57 C4 Bandar-e Lengeh Iran
57 C4 Bandar-e Māqām Iran
57 B3 Bandar-e Ma'shur Iran
57 B3 Bandar-e Rīg Iran
57 C1 Bandar-e Torkeman Iran
57 B3 Bandar Khomeynī Iran
38 F5 Bandar Labuan Malaysia
54 D3 Bandarpunch mt. India
38 F6 Bandar Seri Begawan Brunei
80 D3 Bandar Wanaag Somalia
39 J8 Banda Sea sea Indon.
57 D4 Band Bonī Iran
57 C4 Band-e Chārak Iran
145 H1 Bandeira Brazil
142 B3 Bandeirante Brazil
144 A3 Bandeirantes *Mato Grosso do Sul* Brazil
144 C5 Bandeirantes *São Paulo* Brazil
145 H4 Bandeiras, Pico de mt. Brazil
57 C4 Band-e Moghūyeh Iran
146 D2 Bandera Arg.
130 D2 Banderas Mexico
130 D4 Banderas, Bahía de b. Mexico
57 C2 Band-e Sar Qom Iran
54 C4 Bandi r. *Rajasthan* India
54 C4 Bandi r. *Rajasthan* India
56 C2 Bandia r. India
76 D4 Bandiagara Mali
57 F2 Band-i-Amir r. Afghanistan
57 E2 Band-i-Baba mt. ra. Afghanistan
54 D4 Bandikui India
54 C2 Bandipur India
55 F4 Bandipur Nepal
60 B1 Bandırma Turkey
57 E2 Band-i-Turkestan mt. ra. Afghanistan
17 C6 Bandon Rep. of Ire.
79 C4 Bandundu div. Zaire
79 C4 Bandundu Zaire
40 A3 Bandung Indon.
101 C5 Bandya Aust.
28 F2 Băneasa Romania
60 F3 Bāneh Iran
132 D2 Banes Cuba
110 F4 Banff Can.
16 F3 Banff U.K.
110 F4 Banff National Park nat. park Can.
76 D4 Banfora Burkina
78 C2 Bang C.A.R.
41 C5 Banga Phil.
79 D5 Banga Zaire
41 C5 Bangai Point pt Phil.
56 B3 Bangalore India
78 B2 Bangangté Cameroon
55 G5 Bangaon India
41 B2 Bangar Phil.
78 D3 Bangassou C.A.R.
55 E2 Bangdag Co salt l. China
39 H7 Banggai Indon.
39 H7 Banggai, Kepulauan is Indon.
41 A5 Banggi i. Malaysia
72 D1 Banghāzī Libya
40 C3 Bangil Indon.
40 A2 Bangka i. Indon.
40 C2 Bangkal Indon.
40 C3 Bangkalan Indon.
40 E1 Bangkir Indon.
55 G3 Bangkog Co l. China
43 C4 Bangkok Thailand
43 C4 Bangkok, Bight of b. Thailand
40 D4 Bangkulua Indon.
32 K7 Bangladesh country Asia
50 B4 Bangma Shan mt. ra. China
76 C5 Bangolo Côte d'Ivoire
54 D2 Bangong Co l. China
17 E5 Bangor U.K.
17 E4 Bangor U.K.
121 J2 Bangor U.S.A.
122 D4 Bangor U.S.A.
121 F4 Bangor U.S.A.
78 C2 Bangoran r. C.A.R.
40 D2 Bangsalsepulun Indon.
43 B5 Bang Saphan Yai Thailand
129 F3 Bangs, Mt mt. U.S.A.
10 C2 Bangsund Norway
41 B2 Bangued Phil.
78 C3 Bangui C.A.R.
41 B2 Bangui Phil.
78 C3 Bangui-Motaba Congo
78 E3 Banguru Zaire
79 E6 Bangweulu, Lake l. Zambia
43 C6 Ban Hat Yai Thailand
83 E3 Banhine, Parque Nacional de nat. park Mozambique
42 C3 Ban Hin Heup Laos
42 C2 Ban Houayxay Laos
43 B4 Ban Hua Hin Thailand
77 D4 Bani Burkina
78 D2 Bani C.A.R.
133 E3 Baní Dominican Rep.
76 C4 Bani r. Mali
78 C3 Bania C.A.R.
77 E3 Bani-Bangou Niger
76 C4 Banifing r. Mali
74 C3 Bani, Jbel ridge Morocco
77 E4 Banikoara Benin
79 B4 Banio, Lag. lag. Gabon
120 D6 Banister r. U.S.A.
73 H4 Banī Thawr Saudi Arabia
72 B1 Banī Walīd Libya
60 C3 Bāniyās Syria
61 C3 Bāniyās Syria
26 F3 Banja Luka Bos.-Herz.
54 D3 Banjar India
40 C2 Banjarbaru Indon.
40 C2 Banjarmasin Indon.
76 A4 Banjul The Gambia
55 F4 Banka India
98 C3 Banka Banka Aust.
43 D4 Ban Kadian Laos
43 B6 Ban Kantang Thailand
56 A3 Bankapur India
76 D4 Bankass Mali
43 B4 Ban Khao Yoi Thailand
42 D3 Ban Khemmarat Thailand
43 C4 Ban Khlung Thailand
43 B5 Ban Khok Kloi Thailand
42 B3 Ban Khun Yuam Thailand
55 F5 Banki India
77 E4 Bankilaré Niger
78 B2 Bankim Cameroon
76 B4 Banko Guinea
40 D3 Bankobankoang i. Indon.
76 B4 Banko, Massif de mt. Guinea
110 C4 Banks I. i. Can.
108 F2 Banks Island i. Can.
90 □2 Banks Islands is Vanuatu
126 C2 Banks L. l. U.S.A.
111 L2 Banks Lake l. Can.
93 D5 Banks Peninsula pen. N.Z.
97 G5 Banks Strait chan. Aust.
43 B4 Ban Kui Nua Thailand
55 F5 Bankura India
42 B3 Ban Mae La Luang Thailand
42 B3 Ban Mae Sariang Thailand
42 B3 Ban Mae Sot Thailand
42 B3 Ban Mae Thalop Thailand
42 A1 Banmauk Myanmar
54 B2 Banmi Pakistan
42 C3 Ban Mouang Laos
42 C4 Ban Muang Phon Thailand
17 D4 Bann r. U.K.
42 D3 Ban Na Kae Thailand
42 D3 Ban Nakham Laos
42 C3 Ban Na Noi Thailand
43 B5 Ban Na San Thailand
43 C6 Ban Na Thawi Thailand
122 C5 Banner U.S.A.
132 C1 Bannerman Town The Bahamas
128 D5 Banning U.S.A.
42 B3 Ban Noi Myanmar
76 B4 Banora Guinea
146 B4 Baños Maule Chile
19 J4 Bánovce nad Bebravou Slovakia
26 G3 Banovići Bos.-Herz.
42 C3 Ban Pak-Leng Laos
43 C5 Ban Pak Phanang Thailand
43 C4 Ban Pak Thong Chai Thailand
42 D3 Ban Phaeng Thailand
42 C4 Ban Phai Thailand
43 C4 Ban Phanat Nikhom Thailand
42 D4 Ban Phon Laos
42 C3 Ban Phon Thong Thailand
42 B4 Banphot Phisai Thailand
42 B3 Ban Phran Katai Thailand
43 B4 Ban Pong Thailand
42 C3 Ban Pua Thailand
42 B3 Ban Saraphi Thailand
43 C4 Ban Sattahip Thailand
43 B5 Ban Sawi Thailand
55 E4 Bansi India
43 B5 Ban Sichon Thailand
43 C4 Ban Si Racha Thailand
19 J4 Banská Bystrica Slovakia
19 J4 Banská Štiavnica Slovakia
28 D4 Bansko Bulgaria
42 B3 Ban Sop Prap Thailand
42 B3 Ban Sut Ta Thailand
56 B2 Banswada India
54 C5 Banswara India
40 D3 Bantaeng Indon.
42 C4 Ban Ta Khli Thailand
43 B5 Ban Takua Pa Thailand
94 □1 Bantam *Cocos Is* Indian Ocean
42 C3 Ban Taviang Laos
41 B4 Bantayan i. Phil.
77 E5 Bantè Benin
43 B5 Ban Tha Chang Thailand
42 B2 Ban Tha Don Thailand
43 B5 Ban Thai Muang Thailand
43 B5 Ban Tha Kham Thailand
42 B3 Ban Tha Song Yang Thailand
42 C4 Ban Tha Tako Thailand
42 C4 Ban Tha Tum Thailand
42 D3 Ban Tha Uthen Thailand
43 B4 Ban Thung Luang Thailand
41 B3 Banton i. Phil.
42 D3 Ban Tôp Laos
17 C6 Bantry Rep. of Ire.
17 C6 Bantry Bay b. Rep. of Ire.
40 B3 Bantul Indon.
56 A3 Bantval India
42 C3 Ban Woen Laos
43 D4 Ban Xepian Laos
42 C3 Ban Yang Talat Thailand
78 B2 Banyo Cameroon
25 H1 Banyoles Spain
40 A2 Banyuasin r. Indon.
40 C4 Banyuwangi Indon.
90 □1 Banz P.N.G.
152 C6 Banzare Coast Ant.
149 K7 Banzare Seamount Indian Ocean
48 B6 Bao'an China
49 E5 Baoding China
51 F1 Baofeng China
42 D2 Bao Hà Vietnam
50 D1 Baoji China
50 D1 Baoji China
51 E2 Baojing China
51 E2 Baokang China
43 D5 Bao Lôc Vietnam
49 K3 Baoqing China
78 C2 Baoro C.A.R.
50 B3 Baoshan China
48 D4 Baotou China
76 C4 Baoulé r. *Kayes/Koulikoro* Mali
76 C4 Baoulé r. *Sikasso* Mali
50 C2 Baoxing China
51 G1 Baoying China
54 C4 Bap India
56 C3 Bapatla India
20 F1 Bapaume France
115 F4 Baptiste Lake l. Can.
57 C2 Baqam Iran
55 H2 Baqêm China
55 H3 Baqên China
61 C5 Bāqir, J. mt. Jordan
60 F3 Ba'qūbah Iraq
140 C4 Baquedano Chile
138 □ Baquerizo Moreno *Galapagos Is* Ecuador
48 C2 Bar Rus. Fed.
15 B2 Bar Ukraine
28 B3 Bar Yugo.
55 E4 Bara India
77 G4 Bara Nigeria
73 F5 Bara Sudan
80 D4 Baraawe Somalia
40 C2 Barabai Indon.
54 E4 Bara Banki India
65 J1 Barabinsk Rus. Fed.
65 J2 Barabinskaya Step' plain Rus. Fed.
80 D4 Bar Abir well Ethiopia
122 B4 Baraboo r. U.S.A.
122 C4 Baraboo U.S.A.
142 B3 Baracaju r. Brazil
25 E1 Baracaldo Spain
132 D2 Baracoa Cuba
61 D3 Barada r. Syria
61 D2 Baradah Syria
146 E3 Baradero Arg.
97 G2 Baradine Aust.
97 G2 Baradine r. Aust.
122 C2 Baraga U.S.A.
55 E5 Baragarh India
138 D1 Baragua Venezuela
133 E3 Barahona Dominican Rep.
55 H4 Barail Range mt. ra. India
28 C2 Barajevo Yugo.
57 G1 Barak Afghanistan
55 H4 Barak r. India
80 C1 Baraka w Eritrea/Sudan
25 E1 Barakaldo Spain
57 G2 Barakī Barak Afghanistan
55 F5 Bārākot India
14 D2 Barakovo Rus. Fed.
65 G2 Barakpay Kazak.
99 G5 Baralaba Aust.
54 D2 Bara Lacha Pass pass India
60 E3 Bar al Milḩ l. Iraq
111 K3 Baralzon Lake l. Can.
139 F2 Barama r. Guyana
139 F2 Baramanni Guyana
56 A2 Baramati India
99 G5 Barambah r. Aust.
54 C2 Baramula India
54 D4 Baran India
54 A4 Baran r. Pakistan
12 C4 Baranavichy Belarus
76 D4 Barani Burkina
63 S3 Baranikha Rus. Fed.
15 B1 Baranivka Ukraine
57 E2 Bārān, Kūh-e mt. ra. Iran
138 C1 Baranoa Colombia
110 B3 Baranof Island i. U.S.A.
14 H3 Baranovka Rus. Fed.
143 A4 Barão de Melgaço Brazil
28 E1 Baraolt Romania
76 C4 Baraouéli Mali
139 F5 Bararati r. Brazil
14 F2 Barashevo Rus. Fed.
39 J8 Barat Daya, Kepulauan is Indon.
96 D3 Baratta Aust.
54 D3 Baraut India
138 B3 Baraya Colombia
145 G4 Barbacena Brazil
138 B3 Barbacoas Colombia
141 E3 Barbado r. Brazil
104 N8 Barbados country Caribbean
114 B2 Barbara Lake l. Can.
61 B5 Barbar, G. el mt. Egypt
25 G3 Barbaria, Cap de pt Spain
25 G1 Barbastro Spain
24 D4 Barbate de Franco Spain
114 E2 Barber's Bay Can.
127 □1 Barbers Pt pt U.S.A.
120 C4 Barberton U.S.A.
20 D4 Barbezieux-St-Hilaire France
138 C2 Barbosa Colombia
111 L2 Barbour Bay b. Can.
120 B6 Barbourville U.S.A.
41 B4 Barboza Phil.
133 G3 Barbuda i. Antigua and Barbuda
28 D3 Bârca Romania
132 □1 Barcadera *Aruba* Caribbean
99 F4 Barcaldine Aust.
27 E6 Barcellona Pozzo di Gotto Italy
25 H2 Barcelona Spain
139 E1 Barcelona Venezuela
119 □3 Barceloneta Puerto Rico
21 H4 Barcelonnette France
139 E4 Barcelos Brazil
19 H2 Barcin Poland
76 C6 Barclayville Liberia
99 E5 Barcoo w Aust.
19 H6 Barcs Hungary
19 K2 Barczewo Poland
60 F1 Bärdä Azerbaijan
72 C3 Bardai Chad
10 M2 Bárðarbunga mt. Iceland
146 C4 Bardas Blancas Arg.
55 F5 Barddhamān India
19 K4 Bardejov Slovakia
57 B4 Bardestān Iran
55 E4 Bardi India
43 D4 Bar Đôn Vietnam
26 A3 Bardonecchia Italy
17 E5 Bardsey Island i. U.K.
118 C4 Bardstown U.S.A.
120 B5 Bardwell U.S.A.
54 D3 Bareilly India
97 F3 Barellan Aust.
20 E2 Barentin France
62 C2 Barentsburg *Svalbard* Arctic Ocean
62 D2 Barentsøya i. *Svalbard* Arctic Ocean
62 E2 Barents Sea sea Arctic Ocean
80 C1 Barentu Eritrea
20 D2 Barfleur, Pte de pt France
54 E3 Barga China
26 C3 Barga Italy
80 F2 Bargaal Somalia
99 H5 Bargara Aust.
54 D5 Bargi India
18 E2 Bargteheide Germany
55 G5 Barguna Bangladesh
55 E4 Barhalganj India
121 J2 Bar Harbor U.S.A.
54 D4 Bari India
27 F5 Bari Italy
80 F2 Bari div. Somalia
78 C3 Bari Zaire
43 D5 Ba Ria Vietnam
75 F1 Barika Algeria
57 G2 Barikot Afghanistan
55 E3 Barikot Nepal
133 H6 Barima r. Guyana
138 C2 Barinas Venezuela
78 D3 Baringa Zaire
81 C4 Baringo, L. l. Kenya
144 D5 Bariri Brazil
73 F3 Bârîs Egypt
55 G5 Barisal Bangladesh
40 C2 Barito r. Indon.
146 D1 Baritu, Parque Nacional nat. park Arg.
21 H5 Barjols France
50 C2 Barkam China
57 B3 Barkan, Ra's-e pt Iran
11 G4 Barkava Latvia
110 E4 Barkerville Can.
54 B3 Barkhan Pakistan
55 F4 Barki Saraiya India
118 C4 Barkley, L. l. U.S.A.
110 D5 Barkley Sd inlet Can.
98 D4 Barkly Downs Aust.
82 D5 Barkly East R.S.A.
98 D3 Barkly Tableland reg. Aust.
82 C4 Barkly West R.S.A.
44 F3 Barkol China
57 D3 Barkūh Iran
28 F1 Bârlad Romania
21 G2 Bar-le-Duc France
101 B6 Barlee, L. salt flat Aust.
101 B4 Barlee Ra. h. Aust.
27 F5 Barletta Italy
19 G2 Barlinek Poland
97 F3 Barmedman Aust.
54 B4 Barmer India
96 E3 Barmera Aust.
17 E5 Barmouth U.K.
54 C5 Barnagar India
54 C3 Barnala India
17 G4 Barnard Castle U.K.
97 F2 Barnato Aust.
65 K2 Barnaul Rus. Fed.
121 F5 Barnegat U.S.A.
121 F5 Barnegat Bay b. U.S.A.
120 D4 Barnesboro U.S.A.
109 L2 Barnes Icecap ice cap Can.
20 D2 Barneville-Carteret France
129 G3 Barney Top mt. U.S.A.
125 C6 Barnhart U.S.A.
82 A5 Barn Long Pt pt *St Helena* Atlantic Ocean
17 G5 Barnsley U.K.
17 E6 Barnstaple U.K.
17 E6 Barnstaple Bay b. U.K.
119 D5 Barnwell U.S.A.
77 F5 Baro Nigeria
50 B2 Barong China
101 D4 Barons Ra. h. Aust.
80 B3 Baro Wenz r. Ethiopia
55 H4 Barpathar India
55 G4 Barpeta India
61 D5 Barqā 'Damaj well Saudi Arabia
61 C5 Barqa, G. mt. Egypt
122 D3 Barques, Pt Aux pt U.S.A.
123 F3 Barques, Pt Aux pt U.S.A.
138 D1 Barquisimeto Venezuela
142 D3 Barra Brazil
16 D3 Barra i. U.K.
97 G2 Barraba Aust.
144 D5 Barra Bonita Brazil
142 B1 Barraca da Bōca Brazil
141 E1 Barracão do Barreto Brazil
25 F2 Barracas Spain
145 E6 Barra de Santos inlet Brazil
145 H3 Barra de São Francisco Brazil
145 G5 Barra de São João Brazil
142 A4 Barra do Bugres Brazil
142 C2 Barra do Corda Brazil
79 B5 Barra do Cuanza Angola
144 B1 Barra do Garças Brazil
145 G5 Barra do Piraí Brazil
143 B7 Barra do Ribeiro Brazil
139 F5 Barra do São Manuel Brazil
144 D6 Barra do Turvo Brazil
83 F3 Barra Falsa, Pta da pt Mozambique
145 G4 Barra Longa Brazil
145 F5 Barra Mansa Brazil
138 B4 Barranca Peru
140 A2 Barranca Peru
138 C2 Barranca-bermeja Colombia
146 E3 Barrancas r. *Corrientes* Arg.
138 C1 Barrancas Colombia
139 E2 Barrancas Venezuela
24 C4 Barranco Velho Portugal
146 E2 Barranqueras Arg.
138 C1 Barranquilla Colombia
83 F3 Barra, Pta da pt Mozambique
142 D1 Barras Brazil
16 D3 Barra, Sound of chan. U.K.
115 G2 Barraute Can.
25 E3 Barrax Spain
121 G2 Barre U.S.A.
146 C3 Barreal Arg.
142 D3 Barreiras Brazil
142 A1 Barreirinha Brazil
142 D1 Barreirinhas Brazil
144 B1 Barreiro r. Brazil
142 B3 Barreiro do Nascimento Brazil
142 E2 Barreiros Brazil
43 A4 Barren I. i. *Andaman and Nicobar Is* India
144 D4 Barretos Brazil
100 D3 Barrett, Mt h. Aust.
110 G4 Barrhead Can.
115 F4 Barrie Can.
114 D4 Barrie I i. Can.
92 E2 Barrier, Cape c. N.Z.
110 E4 Barrière Can.
97 E2 Barrier Range h. Aust.
111 J3 Barrington Lake l. Can.
97 G3 Barrington, Mt mt. Aust.
144 D1 Barro Alto Brazil
145 G2 Barrocão Brazil
122 B3 Barron U.S.A.
99 F3 Barron Falls waterfall Aust.
145 G4 Barroso Brazil
125 C7 Barroterán Mexico
146 D4 Barrow Arg.
108 C2 Barrow U.S.A.
98 C2 Barrow, C. c. Aust.
98 C4 Barrow Creek Aust.
100 A4 Barrow I. i. Aust.
17 F4 Barrow-in-Furness U.K.
108 C2 Barrow, Point c. U.S.A.
101 D5 Barrow Ra. h. Aust.
109 J2 Barrow Strait str. Can.
101 C5 Barr Smith Ra. h. Aust.
17 F6 Barry U.K.
115 G4 Barrys Bay Can.
64 E3 Barsa-Kel'mes, O. i. Kazak.
54 C3 Barsalpur India
28 E1 Bârsana Romania
65 J3 Barshatas Kazak.
56 A2 Barsi India
54 D5 Barsi lakli India
128 D4 Barstow U.S.A.
14 C2 Barsuki Rus. Fed.
21 G2 Bar-sur-Aube France
21 G2 Bar-sur-Seine France
18 F1 Barth Germany
140 B4 Bartholomew Deep depth Chile
139 F2 Bartica Guyana
60 C1 Bartın Turkey
99 F3 Bartle Frere, Mt mt. Aust.
129 G2 Bartles, Mt mt. U.S.A.
124 D3 Bartlett U.S.A.
121 H2 Bartlett U.S.A.
110 F2 Bartlett Lake l. Can.
83 F3 Bartolomeu Dias Mozambique
121 G2 Barton U.S.A.
17 G5 Barton-upon-Humber U.K.
19 K1 Bartoszyce Poland
40 C4 Barung i. Indon.
48 C2 Baruunharaa Mongolia
48 C4 Baruunsuu Mongolia
48 E3 Baruun Urt Mongolia
130 K7 Barú, Volcán vol Panama
15 G2 Barvinkove Ukraine
54 D5 Barwah India
54 C3 Barwala India
54 C5 Barwani India
54 D4 Barwa Sagar India
19 H2 Barwice Poland
97 G2 Barwon r. Aust.
14 B2 Baryatino Rus. Fed.
19 H3 Barycz r. Poland
12 D4 Barysaw Belarus
14 H3 Barysh r. Rus. Fed.
14 H3 Barysh Rus. Fed.
15 D1 Baryshivka Ukraine
57 B2 Barzūk Iran
57 C4 Basaidu Iran
146 E2 Basail Arg.
99 F3 Basalt r. Aust.
128 C2 Basalt U.S.A.
45 □ Basalt I. i. Hong Kong
78 C3 Basankusu Zaire
56 B2 Basar India
15 C3 Basarabeasca Moldova
28 G2 Basarabi Romania
41 B1 Basco Phil.
24 E1 Basconcillos del Tozo Spain
146 B2 Bascuñán, C. c. Chile
21 H3 Basel Switz.
122 B1 Basewood Lake l. U.S.A.
57 D4 Bashākerd, Kūhhā-ye mt. ra. Iran
110 G4 Bashaw Can.
83 D5 Bashee r. R.S.A.
57 G2 Bashgul r. Afghanistan
64 E1 Bashkortostan div. Rus. Fed.
14 F3 Bashmakovo Rus. Fed.
57 B3 Bāsht Iran
15 E3 Bashtanka Ukraine
55 F5 Basia India
41 B5 Basilan i. Phil.
41 B5 Basilan Strait chan. Phil.
17 H6 Basildon U.K.
27 E5 Basilicata div. Italy
126 E2 Basin U.S.A.
17 G6 Basingstoke U.K.
55 G5 Basirhat India
121 K2 Baskahegan Lake l. U.S.A.
14 B2 Baskakovka Rus. Fed.
60 F2 Başkale Turkey
115 H3 Baskatong, Réservoir resr Can.
61 B1 Başköy Turkey
13 H5 Baskunchak, Ozero l. Rus. Fed.
40 A2 Baso i. Indon.
54 D5 Basoda India
78 D3 Basoko Zaire
25 E1 Basque Country div. Spain
26 C3 Bassano del Grappa Italy
77 E5 Bassar Togo
69 J8 Bassas da India is Indian Ocean
42 A3 Bassein Myanmar
42 A4 Bassein r. Myanmar
78 D3 Basse-Kotto div. C.A.R.
20 D2 Basse-Normandie div. France
133 □4 Basse Pointe *Martinique* Caribbean
76 B4 Basse Santa Su The Gambia
133 □5 Basse Terre i. *Guadeloupe* Caribbean
133 □5 Basse Terre *Guadeloupe* Caribbean
133 □6 Basseterre *St Kitts-Nevis* Caribbean
133 □3 Basse Terre Trin. and Tobago
124 D3 Bassett U.S.A.
129 G5 Bassett Peak summit U.S.A.
121 J2 Bass Harbor U.S.A.
74 C5 Bassikounou Mauritania
77 E5 Bassila Benin
72 D4 Basso, Plateau de plat. Chad
16 F3 Bass Rock i. U.K.
97 F4 Bass Strait str. Aust.
11 D4 Båstad Sweden
57 C4 Bastak Iran
60 F2 Bastānābād Iran
18 E3 Bastheim Germany
55 E4 Basti India
21 J5 Bastia France
142 E2 Bastioes r. Brazil
18 B3 Bastogne Belgium
144 C4 Bastos Brazil
125 F5 Bastrop U.S.A.
125 D6 Bastrop U.S.A.
57 F4 Basul r. Pakistan
40 A2 Basu, Tg pt Indon.
79 B5 Bas-Zaïre div. Zaire
78 A3 Bata Equatorial Guinea
132 B2 Batabanó, Golfo de b. Cuba
41 B2 Batac Phil.
63 P3 Batagay Rus. Fed.
63 P3 Batagay-Alyta Rus. Fed.
48 B1 Batagol Rus. Fed.
144 B4 Bataguaçu Brazil
28 E4 Batak Bulgaria
40 C3 Batakan Indon.
54 C3 Batala India
24 B3 Batalha Portugal
40 A1 Batam i. Indon.
78 E3 Batama Zaire
63 O3 Batamay Rus. Fed.
64 E2 Batamshinskiy Kazak.
41 B1 Batan i. Phil.
50 B2 Batang China
78 A4 Batanga Gabon
78 C2 Batangafo C.A.R.
41 B3 Batangas Phil.
40 A2 Batanghari r. Indon.
41 B1 Batan Islands is Phil.
144 E4 Batatais Brazil
122 C5 Batavia U.S.A.
120 D3 Batavia U.S.A.
14 A3 Batayeva Rus. Fed.
13 F6 Bataysk Rus. Fed.
114 C3 Batchawana r. Can.
114 C3 Batchawana Bay Can.
112 D4 Batchawana Mtn h. Can.
98 B2 Batchelor Aust.
114 C3 Batchewana Can.
114 C3 Batchewana Mtn mt. Can.
43 C4 Bătdâmbâng Cambodia
79 B4 Batéké, Plateaux plat. Congo
97 G3 Batemans Bay Aust.
47 □2 Baten Japan
95 □1 Bates, Mt h. *Norfolk I.* Pac. Oc.
101 C5 Bates Ra. h. Aust.
125 F5 Batesville U.S.A.
125 F5 Batesville U.S.A.
12 D3 Batetskiy Rus. Fed.
113 G4 Bath Can.
115 G4 Bath Can.
133 □6 Bath *St Kitts-Nevis* Caribbean
17 F6 Bath U.K.
121 J3 Bath U.S.A.
120 E3 Bath U.S.A.
72 C5 Batha w Chad
72 C5 Batha div. Chad
78 C1 Batha de Laïri w Chad
54 C3 Bathinda India
97 G3 Bathurst Aust.
113 G4 Bathurst Can.
98 B1 Bathurst I. i. Aust.
109 J2 Bathurst I. i. Can.
98 B1 Bathurst I. Abor. Land res. Aust.
108 H3 Bathurst Inlet inlet Can.
108 H3 Bathurst Inlet Can.
80 C2 Batī Ethiopia
76 D5 Batié Burkina
40 E2 Batikala, Tg pt Indon.
90 □8 Batiki i. Fiji
29 F6 Batı Menteşe Dağları mt. ra. Turkey
115 J3 Batiscan Can.
57 C2 Bāţlāq-e Gavkhūnī salt marsh Iran
97 G3 Batlow Aust.
60 E2 Batman Turkey
14 F1 Batmany Rus. Fed.
75 F1 Batna Algeria
125 F6 Baton Rouge U.S.A.
130 D3 Batopilas Mexico
78 B3 Batouri Cameroon
144 B1 Batovi Brazil
73 G2 Batrā, J. mt. Saudi Arabia
61 C5 Batrā, J. el mt. Jordan
61 C2 Batroûn Lebanon
10 H1 Båtsfjord Norway
48 A2 Bat-Sot Rus. Fed.
54 C3 Batti India
56 C5 Batticaloa Sri Lanka
43 A5 Batti Malv i. *Andaman and Nicobar Is* India
27 E5 Battipaglia Italy
111 G4 Battle r. Can.
122 E4 Battle Creek U.S.A.
111 H4 Battleford Can.
126 C3 Battle Mountain U.S.A.
54 C1 Battura Gl. gl. *Jammu and Kashmir*
80 C3 Batu mt. Ethiopia
40 C1 Batuayau, Bukit mt. Indon.
40 A2 Batubetumbang Indon.
40 C1 Batuesambang, Bukit mt. Indon.
43 C6 Batu Gajah Malaysia

133 □1 Brown's Town Jamaica
119 B5 Brownsville U.S.A.
125 D7 Brownsville U.S.A.
121 J2 Brownville U.S.A.
121 J2 Brownville Junction U.S.A.
125 D6 Brownwood U.S.A.
100 C2 Browse I. i. Aust.
24 C3 Brozas Spain
13 D4 Brozha Belarus
20 F1 Bruay-en-Artois France
133 □9 Bruce *Barbados* Caribbean
93 B5 Bruce Bay b. N.Z.
122 C2 Bruce Crossing U.S.A.
100 B4 Bruce, Mt mt. Aust.
114 E4 Bruce Pen. pen. Can.
114 E4 Bruce Peninsula National Park nat. park Can.
101 B6 Bruce Rock Aust.
18 D4 Bruchsal Germany
19 H4 Bruck an der Leitha Austria
19 G5 Bruck an der Mur Austria
18 A3 Brugge Belgium
129 G2 Bruin Pt summit U.S.A.
55 H3 Bruint India
61 B4 Brûk, W. el w Egypt
122 B2 Brule U.S.A.
145 F4 Brumadinho Brazil
142 D3 Brumado Brazil
11 C3 Brumunddal Norway
126 D3 Bruneau U.S.A.
126 D3 Bruneau r. U.S.A.
33 N9 Brunei country Asia
98 C3 Brunette Downs Aust.
10 D3 Brunflo Sweden
26 C2 Brunico Italy
93 C5 Brunner, L. l. N.Z.
111 H4 Bruno Can.
18 D2 Brunsbüttel Germany
119 D6 Brunswick U.S.A.
121 J3 Brunswick U.S.A.
120 C4 Brunswick U.S.A.
100 D2 Brunswick Bay b. Aust.
101 A7 Brunswick Jct. Aust.
114 D2 Brunswick Lake l. Can.
147 B7 Brunswick, Península de pen. Chile
19 H4 Bruntál Czech Rep.
152 C3 Brunt Ice Shelf ice feature Ant.
97 F5 Bruny I. i. Aust.
28 C3 Brus Yugo.
12 G2 Brusenets Rus. Fed.
126 G3 Brush U.S.A.
114 E5 Brussels Can.
122 D3 Brussels U.S.A.
19 H2 Brusy Poland
15 C1 Brusyliv Ukraine
97 F4 Bruthen Aust.
18 B3 Bruxelles Belgium
120 A4 Bryan U.S.A.
125 D6 Bryan U.S.A.
152 A3 Bryan Coast Ant.
96 D3 Bryan, Mt h. Aust.
14 A3 Bryansk div. Rus. Fed.
14 B3 Bryansk Rus. Fed.
13 H6 Bryanskoye Rus. Fed.
129 F3 Bryce Canyon Nat. Park nat. park U.S.A.
129 H5 Bryce Mt mt. U.S.A.
15 E3 Brylivka Ukraine
11 B4 Bryne Norway
13 F6 Bryukhovetskaya Rus. Fed.
19 H3 Brzeg Poland
19 H3 Brzeg Dolny Poland
19 L4 Brzozów *Krosno* Poland
73 J4 Bū well Yemen
90 □6 Bua Fiji
81 B7 Bua r. Malawi
80 D4 Bu'aale Somalia
90 □1 Buala Solomon Is.
94 D1 Bua, Tg pt Indon.
72 D2 Bū Athlah well Libya
72 C1 Bu'ayrāt al Hasūn Libya
76 A4 Buba Guinea-Bissau
81 A5 Bubanza Burundi
76 A4 Bubaque Guinea-Bissau
83 E3 Bubi r. Zimbabwe
60 G4 Būbīyān I. i. Kuwait
41 B5 Bubuan i. Phil.
90 □6 Buca Fiji
29 F5 Buca Turkey
60 B2 Bucak Turkey
61 B1 Bucakkışla Turkey
138 C2 Bucaramanga Colombia
41 C4 Bucas Grande i. Phil.
100 C3 Buccaneer Archipelago is Aust.
27 E5 Buccino Italy
15 A2 Buchach Ukraine
97 G4 Buchan Aust.
76 B5 Buchanan Liberia
122 D5 Buchanan U.S.A.
120 D6 Buchanan U.S.A.
99 F4 Buchanan, L. salt flat Aust.
101 C5 Buchanan, L. salt flat Aust.
125 D6 Buchanan, L. l. U.S.A.
109 L2 Buchan Gulf b. Can.
113 J4 Buchans Can.
18 D2 Bucholz in der Nordheide Germany
128 B4 Buchon, Point pt U.S.A.
97 F2 Buckambool Mt h. Aust.
129 F5 Buckeye U.S.A.
120 B5 Buckeye Lake l. U.S.A.
120 C5 Buckhannon r. U.S.A.
120 C5 Buckhannon U.S.A.
115 F4 Buckhorn Can.
129 H5 Buckhorn U.S.A.
115 F4 Buckhorn Lake l. Can.
120 B6 Buckhorn Lake l. U.S.A.
16 F3 Buckie U.K.
115 H4 Buckingham Can.
17 G5 Buckingham U.K.
120 D6 Buckingham U.S.A.
98 C2 Buckingham B. b. Aust.
99 G5 Buckland Tableland reg. Aust.
152 A6 Buckle I. i. Ant.
94 □3 Buckles Bay b. *Macquarie I.* Pac. Oc.
98 D4 Buckley w Aust.
129 F4 Buckskin Mts mts U.S.A.
128 B2 Bucks Mt mt. U.S.A.
121 J2 Bucksport U.S.A.
19 H4 Bučovice Czech Rep.
79 B4 Buco-Zau *Cabinda* Angola
28 E2 București Romania
120 B4 Bucyrus U.S.A.
14 B3 Buda Rus. Fed.
25 G2 Buda, Illa de i. Spain
42 A2 Budalin Myanmar
19 J5 Budapest Hungary
54 D3 Budaun India
80 E4 Bud Bud Somalia
152 C6 Budd Coast Ant.
80 D3 Buddi Ethiopia
27 B5 Buddusò Italy
17 E6 Bude U.K.
125 F6 Bude U.S.A.
13 H6 Budennovsk Rus. Fed.
28 F2 Budești Romania
54 B4 Budhapur Pakistan
61 B5 Budhîya, G. mt. ra. Egypt
54 C3 Budhlada India
78 C3 Budjala Zaire
54 D5 Budni India
12 E3 Budogoshch' Rus. Fed.
55 H2 Budongquan China
27 B5 Budoni Italy
28 B3 Budva Yugo.
78 A3 Buea Cameroon
21 G4 Buëch r. France
128 B4 Buellton U.S.A.
146 C3 Buena Esperanza Arg.
138 B3 Buenaventura Colombia
130 D2 Buenaventura Mexico
138 B3 Buenaventure, B. de b. Colombia
127 F4 Buena Vista U.S.A.
120 D6 Buena Vista U.S.A.
132 C2 Buena Vista, B. de b. Cuba
24 D1 Buenavista de Valdavia Spain
25 E2 Buendia, Embalse de resr Spain
79 C5 Buenga r. Angola
147 B5 Bueno r. Chile
145 F2 Buenópolis Brazil
146 D4 Buenos Aires div. Arg.
146 E3 Buenos Aires Arg.
140 B1 Buenos Aires Brazil
147 B6 Buenos Aires, L. l. Arg./Chile
133 □3 Buenos Ayres Trin. & Tobago
147 C6 Buen Pasto Arg.
147 C7 Buen Tiempo, C. hd Arg.
145 J1 Buerarema Brazil
24 B1 Bueu Spain
130 D3 Búfalo Mexico
110 G3 Buffalo r. Can.
120 D3 Buffalo U.S.A.
125 D4 Buffalo U.S.A.
124 C2 Buffalo U.S.A.
125 D6 Buffalo U.S.A.
122 B3 Buffalo U.S.A.
122 B3 Buffalo r. U.S.A.
126 F2 Buffalo U.S.A.
110 F3 Buffalo Head Hills h. Can.
110 F2 Buffalo Lake l. Can.
111 H3 Buffalo Narrows Can.
133 □1 Buff Bay Jamaica
82 B4 Buffels w R.S.A.
119 D5 Buford U.S.A.
28 E2 Buftea Romania
19 K2 Bug r. Poland
138 B3 Buga Colombia
77 F5 Bugana Nigeria
48 C2 Bugant Mongolia
40 B3 Bugel, Tg pt Indon.
24 □ Bugio i. *Madeira* Portugal
26 F3 Bugojno Bos.-Herz.
62 F3 Bugrino Rus. Fed.
41 A4 Bugsuk i. Phil.
49 G2 Bugt China
41 B2 Buguey Phil.
48 C1 Bugul'deyka Rus. Fed.
64 D2 Bugul'ma Rus. Fed.
64 F3 Bugun' Kazak.
64 D2 Buguruslan Rus. Fed.
48 A5 Buh r. China
57 C3 Būhābād Iran
29 G6 Buharkent Turkey
60 C3 Buḩayrat al Asad resr Syria
61 D3 Buḩayrat al Hījānah l. Syria
60 E3 Buḩayrat ath Tharthār l. Iraq
83 E2 Buhera Zimbabwe
41 B3 Buhi Phil.
18 D4 Bühl Germany
126 D3 Buhl U.S.A.
122 A2 Buhl U.S.A.
60 E2 Bühtan r. Turkey
81 C6 Buhu r. Tanzania
28 F1 Buhuși Romania
17 F5 Builth Wells U.K.
90 □1 Buin P.N.G.
76 D5 Bui National Park nat. park Ghana
12 J4 Buinsk Rus. Fed.
14 H2 Buinsk Rus. Fed.
57 B2 Bu'in Zahrā Iran
49 F3 Buir Nur l. Mongolia
82 B3 Buitepos Namibia
24 D4 Bujalance Spain
28 C3 Bujanovac Yugo.
28 E3 Bujoru Romania
81 A5 Bujumbura Burundi
19 H2 Buk Poland
49 F1 Bukachacha Rus. Fed.
90 □1 Buka I. i. P.N.G.
82 C2 Bukalo Namibia
79 E5 Bukama Zaire
14 B3 Bukan' Rus. Fed.
57 C3 Būkand Iran
79 E4 Bukavu Zaire
64 F5 Bukhara Uzbekistan
65 K3 Bukhtarminskoye Vdkhr. resr Kazak.
41 C6 Bukide i. Indon.
43 □ Bukit Batok Singapore
43 C7 Bukit Fraser Malaysia
40 C2 Bukitlidi Indon.
43 □ Bukit Panjang Singapore
43 □ Bukit Timah Singapore
38 D7 Bukittinggi Indon.
19 K4 Bükk mts Hungary
61 C4 Bukka, J. el mt. Jordan
81 B5 Bukoba Tanzania
81 B5 Bukombekombe Tanzania
14 D2 Bukrino Rus. Fed.
43 □ Bukum, P. i. Singapore
77 F5 Bukuru Nigeria
40 A2 Buku, Tg pt Indon.
15 D2 Buky Ukraine
39 K7 Bula Indon.
21 J3 Bülach Switz.
48 D2 Bulag Mongolia
48 C2 Bulagtay Mongolia
97 H3 Bulahdelal Aust.
41 B3 Bulan Phil.
60 D1 Bulancak Turkey
54 D3 Bulandshahr India
60 E2 Bulanık Turkey
73 F2 Bûlâq Egypt
83 D3 Bulawayo Zimbabwe
65 H2 Bulayevo Kazak.
60 B2 Buldan Turkey
54 D5 Buldana India
140 A1 Buldibuyo Peru
80 D3 Bulei well Ethiopia
48 B2 Bulgan *Bulgan* Mongolia
48 B2 Bulgan *Hövsgöl* Mongolia
48 B3 Bulgan *Ömnögovĭ* Mongolia
48 B2 Bulgan div. Mongolia
5 H4 Bulgaria country Europe
25 F3 Bullas Spain
133 □1 Bull Bay Jamaica
21 H3 Bulle Switz.
132 □2 Bullen Baai b. *Curaçao* Netherlands Ant.
93 D4 Buller r. N.Z.
97 F4 Buller, Mt mt. Aust.
129 E4 Bullhead City U.S.A.
128 D4 Bullion Mts mts U.S.A.
99 E6 Bulloo w Aust.
99 E6 Bulloo Downs Aust.
99 E6 Bulloo L. salt flat Aust.
92 □2 Bull Rock i. *Campbell I.* N.Z.
92 E4 Bulls N.Z.
133 □1 Bull Savannah Jamaica
43 □ Buloh, P. i. Singapore
90 □1 Bulolo P.N.G.
29 C4 Bulqizë Albania
41 C5 Buluan Phil.
40 E3 Bulubulu Indon.
80 C4 Buluk well Kenya
40 E3 Bulukumba Indon.
78 D4 Bulukutu Zaire
63 O2 Bulun Rus. Fed.
79 C4 Bulungu *Bandundu* Zaire
79 D5 Bulungu *Kasai-Occidental* Zaire
65 G5 Bulungur Uzbekistan
41 C3 Bulusan Phil.
78 B2 Bum Cameroon
79 C5 Bumba *Bandundu* Zaire
78 D3 Bumba *Équateur* Zaire
48 C3 Bumbat Mongolia
48 C4 Bumbat Sum China
28 D2 Bumbești-Jiu Romania
81 B5 Bumbire I. i. Tanzania
129 F4 Bumble Bee U.S.A.
41 A5 Bum-Bum i. Malaysia
42 B1 Bumhkang Myanmar
80 C4 Buna Kenya
79 C4 Buna Zaire
81 B5 Bunazi Tanzania
101 A7 Bunbury Aust.
17 D4 Buncrana Rep. of Ire.
81 B5 Bunda Tanzania
99 H5 Bundaberg Aust.
99 F6 Bundaleer Aust.
97 G2 Bundarra Aust.
98 C4 Bundey w Aust.
54 C4 Bundi India
81 B4 Bundibugyo Uganda
55 F5 Bundu India
80 B3 Bunduqiya Sudan
77 F4 Bunga w Nigeria
17 H5 Bungay U.K.
42 C4 Bung Boraphet l. Thailand
97 G3 Bungendore Aust.
152 C6 Bunger Hills h. Ant.
99 G5 Bungil Cr. r. Aust.
100 E3 Bungle Bungle Nat. Park nat. park Aust.
79 C5 Bungo Angola
46 D7 Bungo-suidō chan. Japan
46 C7 Bungo-takada Japan
78 F3 Bunia Zaire
79 D4 Bunianga Zaire
77 G4 Buni-Yadi Nigeria
54 C2 Bunji Pakistan
65 H5 Bunji *Jammu and Kashmir*
99 H4 Bunker Group atolls Aust.
129 E3 Bunkerville U.S.A.
79 E6 Bunkeya Zaire
125 E6 Bunkie U.S.A.
119 D6 Bunnell U.S.A.
25 F3 Buñol Spain
40 C2 Buntok Indon.
40 C2 Buntokecil Indon.
77 F5 Bununu Nigeria
60 C2 Bünyan Turkey
41 A6 Bunyu i. Indon.
77 E4 Bunza Nigeria
26 F3 Buoač Bos.-Herz.
57 B3 Bu ol Kheyr Iran
43 E4 Buôn Hô Vietnam
43 E4 Buôn Mê Thuôt Vietnam
63 P2 Buorkhaya, Guba b. Rus. Fed.
57 B4 Buqayq Saudi Arabia
81 C5 Bura Kenya
80 E2 Buraan Somalia
78 E1 Buram Sudan
65 L3 Buran Kazak.
54 E3 Burang China
145 J2 Buranhaém r. Brazil
145 H2 Buranhaém Brazil
80 E3 Burao Somalia
61 D3 Burāq Syria
14 H3 Burasy Rus. Fed.
41 C4 Burauen Phil.
73 H2 Buraydah Saudi Arabia
18 D3 Burbach Germany
128 C4 Burbank U.S.A.
97 F3 Burcher Aust.
99 F4 Burdekin r. Aust.
99 F4 Burdekin Falls waterfall Aust.
60 B2 Burdur Turkey
61 A1 Burdur div. Turkey
80 C2 Burē Ethiopia
80 B3 Burē Ethiopia
10 F2 Bureå Sweden
73 F4 Bureiqa well Sudan
49 K2 Bureiskiy Khrebet mt. ra. Rus. Fed.
48 A2 Buren-Khem Rus. Fed.
48 D3 Bürentsogt Mongolia
49 J2 Bureya Rus. Fed.
49 J2 Bureya r. Rus. Fed.
18 E1 Burg *Sachsen-Anhalt* Germany
28 F3 Burgas div. Bulgaria
28 F3 Burgas Bulgaria
119 E5 Burgaw U.S.A.
18 E2 Burg bei Magdeburg Germany
18 E4 Burgbernheim Germany
21 H3 Burgdorf Switz.
19 H5 Burgenland div. Austria
113 J4 Burgeo Can.
101 C6 Burges, Mt h. Aust.
18 A3 Burgh Netherlands
18 F4 Burghausen Germany
18 F4 Burglengenfeld Germany
24 E1 Burgos Spain
11 E4 Burgsvik Sweden
44 G4 Burhan Budai Shan mt. ra. China
60 A2 Burhaniye Turkey
54 D5 Burhanpur India
55 E5 Burhar-Dhanpuri India
55 F4 Burhi Gandak r. India
144 D5 Buri Brazil
41 B3 Burias i. Phil.
41 B3 Burias Pass. chan. Phil.
64 E2 Buribay Rus. Fed.
130 K7 Burica, Pta pt Costa Rica
81 B5 Burigi, Lake l. Tanzania
113 J4 Burin Peninsula pen. Can.
43 C4 Buriram Thailand
144 C4 Buritama Brazil
142 D1 Buriti Brazil
141 E2 Buriti r. Brazil
144 D3 Buriti Alegre Brazil
142 D2 Buriti Bravo Brazil
142 C2 Buriticupu r. Brazil
142 D1 Buriti dos Lopes Brazil
142 D3 Buritirama Brazil
145 E1 Buritis Brazil
145 F2 Buritizeiro Brazil
54 A3 Burj Pakistan
25 F3 Burjassot Spain
98 D4 Burke w Aust.
152 A3 Burke I. i. Ant.
93 C6 Burke Pass N.Z.
98 D3 Burketown Aust.
68 D4 Burkina country Africa
115 F4 Burk's Falls Can.
65 J2 Burla r. Rus. Fed.
65 J2 Burla Rus. Fed.
99 E4 Burleigh Aust.
126 D3 Burley U.S.A.
64 D2 Burlin Kazak.
115 F5 Burlington Can.
124 C4 Burlington U.S.A.
122 D5 Burlington U.S.A.
122 B5 Burlington U.S.A.
121 J2 Burlington U.S.A.
121 G2 Burlington U.S.A.
122 C4 Burlington U.S.A.
14 E3 Burminka Rus. Fed.
125 D6 Burnet U.S.A.
99 H5 Burnett r. Aust.
126 B3 Burney U.S.A.
121 J2 Burnham U.S.A.
97 F5 Burnie Aust.
65 H4 Burnoye Kazak.
126 C3 Burns U.S.A.
111 H1 Burnside r. Can.
101 C5 Burnside, L. salt flat Aust.
108 F4 Burns Lake Can.
120 C5 Burnsville Lake l. U.S.A.
119 F7 Burnt Ground The Bahamas
113 H3 Burnt Lake l. Can.
95 □1 Burnt Pine *Norfolk I.* Pac. Oc.
111 K3 Burntwood r. Can.
111 J3 Burnt Wood Lake l. Can.
65 L3 Burqin China
96 D3 Burra Aust.
28 C4 Burrel Albania
97 G3 Burrendong Reservoir resr Aust.
97 G2 Burren Jct. Aust.
25 F3 Burriana Spain
97 G3 Burrinjuck Aust.
97 G3 Burrinjuck Reservoir resr Aust.
120 B5 Burr Oak Reservoir resr U.S.A.
98 B2 Burrundie Aust.
129 G2 Burrville U.S.A.
29 G4 Bursa div. Turkey
60 B1 Bursa Turkey
73 F2 Bûr Safâga Egypt
15 A2 Burshtyn Ukraine
61 B5 Bûr Taufiq Egypt
122 E3 Burt Lake l. U.S.A.
123 F4 Burton U.S.A.
112 E3 Burton, Lac l. Can.
17 C4 Burtonport Rep. of Ire.
17 G5 Burton upon Trent U.K.
10 F2 Burträsk Sweden
121 K1 Burtts Corner Can.
97 E3 Burtundy Aust.
39 J7 Buru i. Indon.
69 G6 Burundi country Africa
81 A5 Bururi Burundi
110 B2 Burwash Landing Can.
16 F2 Burwick U.K.
115 K4 Bury Can.
48 B2 Buryatiya div. Rus. Fed.
15 E1 Buryn' Ukraine
64 D3 Burynshyk Kazak.
17 H5 Bury St Edmunds U.K.
54 C2 Burzil Pass pass *Jammu & Kashmir*
78 D4 Busanga Zaire
15 C2 Busha Ukraine
81 D5 Bushbush r. Kenya/Somalia
15 B1 Bushcha Ukraine
57 B3 Būshehr div. Iran
57 B3 Būshehr Iran
55 E2 Bushêngcaka China
81 B5 Bushenyi Uganda
122 B5 Bushnell U.S.A.
28 C4 Bushtricë Albania
49 F1 Bushuley Rus. Fed.
78 D3 Businga Zaire
43 □ Busing, P. i. Singapore
78 C4 Busira r. Zaire
15 A2 Bus'k Ukraine
11 C3 Buskerud div. Norway
19 K3 Busko-Zdrój Poland
61 D3 Buşrá ash Shām Syria
49 H2 Busse Rus. Fed.
101 A7 Busselton Aust.
78 E2 Busseri w Sudan
125 C7 Bustamante Mexico
147 C6 Bustamante, B. b. Arg.
28 E2 Buşteni Romania
130 D2 Bustillos, L. l. Mexico
26 B3 Busto Arsizio Italy
41 A3 Busuanga Phil.
41 A3 Busuanga i. Phil.
18 D1 Büsum Germany
78 D3 Buta Zaire
80 C3 Butajīra Ethiopia
43 B6 Butang Group is Thailand
81 A5 Butare Rwanda
16 E4 Bute i. U.K.
28 F1 Butea Romania
110 D4 Butedale Can.
110 D4 Bute In. inlet Can.
78 E3 Butembo Zaire
83 D4 Butha-Buthe Lesotho
42 A2 Buthidaung Myanmar
122 E5 Butler U.S.A.
120 D4 Butler U.S.A.
39 H8 Buton i. Indon.
15 G1 Butovo Rus. Fed.
126 D2 Butte U.S.A.
128 B1 Butte Meadows U.S.A.
43 C6 Butterworth Malaysia
82 D5 Butterworth R.S.A.
110 D5 Buttle L. l. Can.
16 D2 Butt of Lewis hd U.K.
109 M3 Button Is is Can.
128 C4 Buttonwillow U.S.A.
101 C7 Butty Hd pt Aust.
41 C4 Butuan Phil.
15 C3 Butuceni Moldova
50 C3 Butuo China
14 G2 Buturlino Rus. Fed.
13 G5 Buturlinovka Rus. Fed.
55 E4 Butwal Nepal
14 E2 Butylitsy Rus. Fed.
18 E2 Bützow Germany
80 E4 Buulobarde Somalia
81 D5 Buur Gaabo Somalia
80 D4 Buurhabaka Somalia
80 B4 Buvuma I. i. Uganda
61 C5 Buwārah, J. mt. Saudi Arabia
73 G3 Buwāţah Saudi Arabia
55 F4 Buxar India
18 D2 Buxtehude Germany
17 G5 Buxton U.K.
12 G3 Buy Rus. Fed.
48 D3 Buyant Mongolia
48 A3 Buyant Mongolia
48 A3 Buyant Gol r. Mongolia
48 C3 Buyant-Ovoo Mongolia
48 D3 Buyant-Uhaa Mongolia
122 A1 Buyck U.S.A.
13 H7 Buynaksk Rus. Fed.
76 C5 Buyo, Lac de l. Côte d'Ivoire
50 C4 Buyuan r. China
60 E2 Büyük Ağri mt. Turkey
61 B1 Büyük Egri D. mt. Turkey
29 F4 Büyükkarıştıran Turkey
29 G6 Büyükmenderes r. Turkey
29 G5 Büyükorhan Turkey
49 G4 Buyun Shan mt. China
64 D4 Buzachi, Pov. pen. Kazak.
20 E3 Buzançais France
28 F2 Buzău Romania
72 D3 Buzaymah oasis Libya
46 C7 Buzen Japan
14 E2 Buzha r. Rus. Fed.
83 E2 Búzi Mozambique
83 E3 Búzi r. Mozambique
28 C2 Buziaș Romania
145 H5 Buzios, Cabo dos hd Brazil
145 F5 Buzios, Ilha dos i. Brazil
14 G3 Buzovlevo Rus. Fed.
13 G5 Buzuluk r. Rus. Fed.
64 D2 Buzuluk Rus. Fed.
121 H4 Buzzards Bay b. U.S.A.
90 □1 Bwagaoia P.N.G.
55 G4 Byakar Bhutan
28 F3 Byala *Burgas* Bulgaria
28 E3 Byala *Razgrad* Bulgaria
28 D3 Byala Slatina Bulgaria
12 D4 Byalynichy Belarus
108 H2 Byam Martin I. i. Can.
13 C4 Byaroza Belarus
19 L3 Bychawa Poland
14 E3 Bychki Rus. Fed.
19 J3 Byczyna Poland
19 J2 Bydgoszcz Poland
12 D4 Byerazino Belarus
126 F4 Byers U.S.A.
12 D4 Byeshankovichy Belarus
11 B4 Bygland Norway
12 D4 Bykhaw Belarus
11 B4 Bykle Norway
13 H5 Bykovo Rus. Fed.
109 L2 Bylot Island i. Can.
114 E4 Byng Inlet Can.
152 B5 Byrd Gl. gl. Ant.
49 F2 Byrka Rus. Fed.
11 B3 Byrkjelo Norway
15 E1 Byrlivka Ukraine
97 F2 Byrock Aust.
122 C4 Byron U.S.A.
121 H2 Byron U.S.A.
97 H2 Byron Bay Aust.
97 H2 Byron, C. hd Aust.
14 A3 Byryne Ukraine
15 C1 Byshiv Ukraine
10 F2 Byske Sweden
19 H4 Bystřice nad Pernštejnem Czech Rep.
48 D2 Bystrinskiy Golets, G. mt. Rus. Fed.
63 P3 Bytantay r. Rus. Fed.
19 J4 Bytča Slovakia
19 J3 Bytom Poland
14 B3 Bytosh' Rus. Fed.
19 H1 Bytów Poland
81 B5 Byumba Rwanda
64 E5 Byuzmeyin Turkmenistan
19 K2 Bzura r. Poland

C

141 E5 Caacupé Paraguay
141 E5 Caagazú, Cordillera de h. Paraguay
141 E5 Caaguazú Paraguay
79 C6 Caála Angola
144 A5 Caarapó Brazil
145 H1 Caatiba Brazil
145 F2 Caatinga Brazil
141 E5 Caazapá Paraguay
141 E3 Cabaçal r. Brazil
132 C2 Cabaiguán Cuba
140 A2 Caballas Peru
138 C4 Caballococha Peru
130 D2 Caballos Mesteños, Llano de los plain Mexico
140 B2 Cabana Peru
140 B3 Cabanaconde Peru
24 D1 Cabañaquinta Spain
25 E4 Cabañas mt. Spain
41 B3 Cabanatuan Phil.
25 E4 Cabañas mt. Spain
41 B3 Cabanatuan Phil.
113 G4 Cabano Can.
140 C3 Cabaraya, Co mt. Bolivia
80 D2 Cabdul Qaadir Somalia
143 A4 Cabeceira Rio Manso Brazil
142 F2 Cabedelo Brazil
24 D3 Cabeza del Buey Spain
141 D3 Cabezas Bolivia
119 □3 Cabezas de San Juan pt Puerto Rico
24 C4 Cabezas Rubias Spain
146 D4 Cabildo Arg.
138 C1 Cabimas Venezuela
79 B5 Cabinda div. Angola
79 B5 Cabinda Angola
126 C1 Cabinet Mts mt. ra. U.S.A.
41 B5 Cabingan i. Phil.
119 □2 Cable Beach The Bahamas
147 C6 Cabo Blanco Arg.
81 C7 Cabo Delgado div. Mozambique
145 G5 Cabo Frio Brazil
145 H5 Cabo Frio, Ilha do c. Brazil
115 G3 Cabonga, Réservoir resr Can.
125 E4 Cabool U.S.A.
99 H5 Caboolture Aust.
139 G3 Cabo Orange, Parque Nacional de nat. park Brazil
138 B4 Cabo Pantoja Peru
147 C5 Cabo Raso Arg.
130 B2 Caborca Mexico
119 □3 Cabo Rojo Puerto Rico
114 E4 Cabot Head pt Can.
113 J4 Cabot Strait str. Can.
24 D4 Cabra Spain
27 B6 Cabras Italy
25 H3 Cabrera i. Spain
24 C1 Cabrera, Sierra de la mt. ra. Spain
25 F3 Cabriel r. Spain
133 □4 Cabrits, Ilet i. *Martinique* Caribbean
142 E2 Cabrobó Brazil
138 D2 Cabruta Venezuela
41 B2 Cabugao Phil.
26 F4 Čabulja mt. Bos.-Herz.
143 B6 Caçador Brazil
131 F5 Cacahuatepec Mexico
28 C3 Čačak Yugo.
139 G3 Cacao French Guiana
145 F5 Caçapava Brazil
143 B7 Caçapava do Sul Brazil
120 D5 Cacapon r. U.S.A.
138 B2 Cácares Colombia
27 B5 Caccia, Capo pt Italy
143 B6 Cacequi Brazil
141 E3 Cáceres Brazil
24 C3 Cáceres Spain
126 D3 Cache Peak summit U.S.A.
76 A4 Cacheu Guinea-Bissau
146 C2 Cachi Arg.
142 B2 Cachimbo Brazil
79 D5 Cachimo Angola
140 C4 Cachinal Chile
79 C6 Cachingues Angola
138 C2 Cáchira Colombia
142 E3 Cachoeira *Bahia* Brazil
144 C3 Cachoeira *Mato Grosso do Sul* Brazil
142 C2 Cachoeira r. Brazil
144 C3 Cachoeira Alta Brazil
144 C2 Cachoeira de Goiás Brazil
142 C1 Cachoeira do Arari Brazil
143 B7 Cachoeira do Sul Brazil
145 F5 Cachoeira Paulista Brazil
145 G5 Cachoeiras de Macacu Brazil
145 H4 Cachoeiro de Itapemirim Brazil
24 C4 Cachopo Portugal
76 A4 Cacine Guinea-Bissau
79 C6 Cacolo Angola
79 C6 Caconda Angola
79 B5 Cacongo *Cabinda* Angola
128 D3 Cactus Range mts U.S.A.
144 C3 Caçu Brazil
79 B5 Cacuaco Angola
142 D3 Caculé Brazil
145 J2 Cacumba, Ilha i. Brazil
144 B2 Caçununga Brazil
19 J4 Čadca Slovakia
80 D2 Caddabassa I. Ethiopia
18 D2 Cadenberge Germany
131 E3 Cadereyta Mexico
96 C2 Cadibarrawirracanna, L. salt flat Aust.
41 B3 Cadig Mts mt. ra. Phil.
115 F2 Cadillac Can.
111 H5 Cadillac Can.
20 D4 Cadillac France
122 E3 Cadillac U.S.A.
41 B4 Cadiz Phil.
24 C4 Cádiz Spain
24 C4 Cádiz, Golfo de g. Spain
129 E4 Cadiz Lake l. U.S.A.
101 B6 Cadoux Aust.
20 D2 Caen France
17 E5 Caernarfon U.K.
17 E5 Caernarfon Bay b. U.K.
120 B5 Caesar Creek Lake l. U.S.A.
61 C3 Caesarea Israel
142 D3 Caetité Brazil
146 C2 Cafayate Arg.
144 D4 Cafelândia Brazil
139 F3 Cafuini r. Brazil
41 B4 Cagayan i. Phil.
41 B2 Cagayan r. Phil.
41 C4 Cagayan de Oro Phil.
41 B4 Cagayan Islands is Phil.
26 D4 Cagli Italy
27 B6 Cagliari Italy
27 B6 Cagliari, Golfo di b. Italy
138 C3 Caguán r. Colombia
119 □3 Caguas Puerto Rico
119 C5 Cahaba r. U.S.A.
79 B7 Cahama Angola
17 C6 Caha Mts h. Rep. of Ire.
17 B6 Cahersiveen Rep. of Ire.
17 D5 Cahir Rep. of Ire.
83 E2 Cahora Bassa, Barragem de dam Mozambique
83 E2 Cahora Bassa, Lago de resr Mozambique
17 D5 Cahore Point pt Rep. of Ire.
20 E4 Cahors France
138 B5 Cahuapanas Peru
15 C3 Cahul Moldova
83 F2 Caia Mozambique
79 D6 Caianda Angola
144 C2 Caiapó r. Brazil
144 C2 Caiapônia Brazil
132 C2 Caibarién Cuba
43 D5 Cai Be Vietnam
139 D2 Caicara Venezuela
142 E2 Caicó Brazil
133 D2 Caicos Is is *Turks and Caicos Is* Caribbean
133 D2 Caicos Passage chan. *The Bahamas/Turks and Caicos Is* Caribbean
140 B3 Cailloma Peru
41 A3 Caiman Point pt Phil.
43 D5 Cai Nước Vietnam
16 F3 Cairngorm Mts mt. ra. U.K.
99 F3 Cairns Aust.
61 A4 Cairo Egypt
119 C6 Cairo U.S.A.
26 B3 Cairo Montenotte Italy
79 B6 Caitou Angola
79 C7 Caiundo Angola
99 F6 Caiwarro Aust.
51 G2 Caizi Hu l. China
140 A2 Cajacay Peru
119 □3 Caja de Muertos, I. i. Puerto Rico
138 B5 Cajamarca Peru
20 E4 Cajarc France
142 C1 Cajari Brazil
140 A2 Cajatambo Peru
142 E2 Cajàzeiras Brazil
28 B3 Čajetina Yugo.
41 B3 Cajidiocan Phil.
26 G4 Čajniče Bos.-Herz.
144 E4 Cajuru Brazil
48 A5 Caka China
48 A5 Caka Yanhu salt l. China
61 A1 Çakırlar Turkey
61 C1 Çakit r. Turkey
26 F2 Čakovec Croatia
60 B2 Çal Turkey
77 F6 Calabar Nigeria
115 G4 Calabogie Can.
138 D2 Calabozo Venezuela
27 F6 Calabria div. Italy
140 C3 Calacoto Bolivia
28 D3 Calafat Romania
147 B7 Calafate Arg.
25 H3 Cala Figuera, Cap de pt Spain
41 B3 Calagua Islands is Phil.
25 F1 Calahorra Spain
79 C7 Calai Angola
20 E1 Calais France
121 K2 Calais U.S.A.
146 C2 Calalasteo, Sierra de mt. ra. Arg.
141 D1 Calama Brazil
140 C4 Calama Chile
138 C1 Calamar *Bolívar* Colombia
138 C3 Calamar *Guaviare* Colombia
41 A3 Calamian Group is Phil.
25 F2 Calamocha Spain
28 D2 Călan Romania
24 C4 Calañas Spain
25 F2 Calanda Spain
79 C5 Calandula Angola
72 D2 Calanscio Sand Sea desert Libya
41 B3 Calapan Phil.
15 C3 Călărași Moldova
28 F2 Călărași Romania
25 F3 Calasparra Spain
27 D7 Calatafimi Italy
25 F2 Calatayud Spain
41 B3 Calauag Phil.
41 B3 Calavite, Cape c. Phil.
41 B2 Calayan i. Phil.
41 C3 Calbayog Phil.
41 C4 Calbiga Phil.
147 B5 Calbuco Chile
140 B2 Calca Peru
142 E1 Calcanhar, Ponta do pt Brazil
125 E6 Calcasieu L. l. U.S.A.
139 G3 Calçoene Brazil
55 G5 Calcutta India
28 E2 Căldăraru Romania
24 B3 Caldas da Rainha Portugal
144 D2 Caldas Novas Brazil
146 B2 Caldera Chile
99 F5 Caldervale Aust.
60 E2 Çaldıran Turkey
126 C3 Caldwell U.S.A.
114 E5 Caledon Can.
82 D5 Caledon r. Lesotho/R.S.A.
98 D2 Caledon B. b. Aust.
115 F5 Caledonia Can.
122 B4 Caledonia U.S.A.
99 G4 Calen Aust.
21 J5 Calenzana France
130 E4 Calera Mexico
24 D3 Calera y Chozas Spain
140 B4 Caleta Blanco Encalada b. Chile
140 B3 Caleta Buena Chile
147 B7 Caleta Clarencia Chile
147 C7 Caleta Coig inlet Arg.
140 B4 Caleta el Cobre Chile
147 C7 Caleta Josefina Chile
140 B4 Caleta Lobos Chile
147 C6 Caleta Olivia Arg.
129 E5 Calexico U.S.A.
17 E4 Calf of Man i. Isle of Man
110 G4 Calgary Can.
24 □ Calheta *Madeira* Portugal
119 C5 Calhoun U.S.A.
138 B3 Cali Colombia
41 C4 Calicoan i. Phil.
56 A4 Calicut India
128 C4 Caliente U.S.A.
129 E3 Caliente U.S.A.
133 □3 California Trin. & Tobago
128 B3 California div. U.S.A.
128 B3 California Aqueduct canal U.S.A.
130 B2 California, Golfo de g. Mexico
128 C4 California Hot Springs U.S.A.
60 G2 Cäilabad Azerbaijan
28 E2 Călimănești Romania
28 E1 Călimani, Munții mt. ra. Romania
127 D5 Calipatria U.S.A.
128 A2 Calistoga U.S.A.
82 C5 Calitzdorp R.S.A.
131 H4 Calkiní Mexico
96 E2 Callabonna Cr. w Aust.
96 D2 Callabonna, L. salt flat Aust.
20 C2 Callac France
128 D2 Callaghan, Mt mt. U.S.A.
119 D6 Callahan U.S.A.
115 F3 Callander Can.
16 E3 Callander U.K.
140 A2 Callao Peru
129 F2 Callao U.S.A.
131 F4 Calles Mexico
121 F4 Callicoon U.S.A.
99 G5 Callide Aust.
99 G5 Calliope Aust.
114 E3 Callum Can.
110 G4 Calmar Can.
122 B4 Calmar U.S.A.
129 E4 Cal-Nev-Ari U.S.A.
119 D7 Caloosahatchee r. U.S.A.
27 E5 Calore r. *Campania* Italy
131 H4 Calotmul Mexico
99 H5 Caloundra Aust.
25 G3 Calpe Spain
61 A1 Çalpınar Turkey
128 B2 Calpine U.S.A.
131 F5 Calpulálpan Mexico
141 E3 Cal, R. de la r. Bolivia
114 C2 Calstock Can.
27 E7 Caltagirone Italy
27 E7 Caltanissetta div. Italy
79 C6 Calucinga Angola
79 B5 Calulo Angola
122 C2 Calumet U.S.A.
79 D6 Calunda Angola
79 C7 Calunga Angola
79 B6 Caluquembe Angola
41 B4 Calusa i. Phil.
80 F2 Caluula Somalia
129 G5 Calva U.S.A.
98 D3 Calvert r. Aust.
98 D3 Calvert Hills Aust.
110 D4 Calvert I. i. Can.
101 C4 Calvert Ra. h. Aust.
21 J5 Calvi France
25 H3 Calvià Spain
130 E4 Calvillo Mexico
82 B5 Calvina R.S.A.
27 E5 Calvo, Monte mt. Italy
24 E3 Calzada de Calatrava Spain
17 H5 Cam r. U.K.
79 C5 Camabatela Angola
145 J1 Camacã Brazil
142 E3 Camaçari Brazil
128 B2 Camache Reservoir resr U.S.A.
130 E3 Camacho Mexico
79 B6 Camacuio Angola
79 C6 Camacupa Angola
138 D2 Camaguán Venezuela
132 C2 Camagüey Cuba
132 C2 Camagüey, Arch. de is Cuba
43 C6 Camah, Gunung mt. Malaysia
139 F5 Camaiú r. Brazil
130 B2 Camalli, Sa de mt. Mexico
140 B3 Camana Peru
79 D6 Camanongue Angola
144 A3 Camapuã Brazil
143 B7 Camaquã Brazil
143 B7 Camaquã r. Brazil
24 □ Câmara de Lobos *Madeira* Portugal
142 B1 Camaraipi r. Brazil
141 E2 Camararé r. Brazil
20 B2 Camaret-sur-Mer France
131 F3 Camargo Mexico
24 B1 Camariñas Spain
132 A4 Camarón, C. c. Honduras
130 D4 Camaronero, L. del lag. Mexico
147 C5 Camarones Arg.
140 C3 Camarones r. Chile
147 C5 Camarones, Bahía b. Arg.
126 B2 Camas U.S.A.
43 D5 Ca Mau Vietnam
141 E3 Cambara Brazil
144 C5 Cambará Brazil
33 M8 Cambodia country Asia
79 B6 Cambongo r. Angola
17 E6 Camborne U.K.
21 F1 Cambrai France
24 B1 Cambre Spain
128 B4 Cambria U.S.A.
17 F5 Cambrian Mountains mt. ra. U.K.
114 E5 Cambridge Can.
92 E2 Cambridge N.Z.
17 H5 Cambridge U.K.
122 B5 Cambridge U.S.A.
121 E5 Cambridge U.S.A.
121 H3 Cambridge U.S.A.
122 A3 Cambridge U.S.A.
121 G3 Cambridge U.S.A.
120 C4 Cambridge U.S.A.
108 H3 Cambridge Bay Can.
100 E2 Cambridge Gulf b. Aust.
113 G2 Cambrien, Lac l. Can.
25 G2 Cambrils de Mar Spain
145 E5 Cambuí Brazil
79 D5 Cambulo Angola
79 C6 Cambundi-Catembo Angola
145 F4 Cambuquira Brazil
97 G3 Camden Aust.
119 C5 Camden U.S.A.
125 E5 Camden U.S.A.
121 J2 Camden U.S.A.
121 F5 Camden U.S.A.
121 F3 Camden U.S.A.
119 D5 Camden U.S.A.
147 B7 Camden, Is i. Chile
100 D2 Camden Sd chan. Aust.
79 D6 Cameia Angola
79 D6 Cameia, Parque Nacional da nat. park Angola
15 C2 Camenca Moldova
129 G4 Cameron U.S.A.
125 E6 Cameron U.S.A.
124 E4 Cameron U.S.A.
125 D6 Cameron U.S.A.
122 B3 Cameron U.S.A.
114 A2 Cameron Falls Can.
43 C6 Cameron Highlands Malaysia
110 F3 Cameron Hills h. Can.
93 A7 Cameron Mts mts N.Z.
128 B2 Cameron Park U.S.A.
69 E5 Cameroon country Africa
78 A3 Cameroun, Mont mt. Cameroon
142 C1 Cametá Brazil
41 C4 Camiguin i. Phil.
41 B2 Camiguin i. Phil.
41 B3 Camiling Phil.
119 C6 Camilla U.S.A.
140 C3 Camiña Chile
142 C1 Camiranga Brazil
140 D4 Camiri Bolivia
79 D5 Camissombo Angola
61 C1 Çamlıyayla Turkey
130 C3 Camoa Mexico
142 D1 Camocim Brazil
98 D3 Camooweal Aust.
139 G3 Camopi Brazil
139 G3 Camopi r. French Guiana
43 A5 Camorta i. *Andaman and Nicobar Is* India
41 C4 Camotes Sea g. Phil.
146 E3 Campana Arg.
147 A6 Campana, I. i. Chile
145 H3 Campanário Brazil
144 A5 Campanario Brazil
145 F4 Campanha Brazil
27 E5 Campania div. Italy
110 D4 Campania I. i. Can.
93 E4 Campbell, Cape c. N.Z.
43 B5 Campbell I. i. Myanmar
92 □2 Campbell I. i. N.Z.
54 C2 Campbellpore Pakistan
110 D4 Campbell River Can.
115 G4 Campbells Bay Can.
118 C4 Campbellsville U.S.A.
113 G4 Campbellton Can.
97 F5 Campbell Town Aust.
17 E4 Campbeltown U.K.
131 H5 Campeche div. Mexico
131 H5 Campeche Mexico
131 G5 Campeche, Bahía de g. Mexico
97 E4 Camperdown Aust.
119 □2 Camperdown The Bahamas
28 D2 Câmpia Băileștilor plain Romania
15 B3 Câmpia Moldovei de Nord plain Moldova
15 C3 Câmpia Moldovei de Sud plain Moldova
28 D1 Câmpia Turzii Romania
24 D4 Campillos Spain
28 E2 Câmpina Romania
144 B6 Campina da Lagoa Brazil
142 E2 Campina Grande Brazil
144 E5 Campinas Brazil
144 D3 Campina Verde Brazil
78 A3 Campo Cameroon
138 B3 Campoalegre Colombia
27 E5 Campobasso Italy
145 F4 Campo Belo Brazil
143 B6 Campo Belo do Sul Brazil
24 E3 Campo de Criptana Spain
142 B3 Campó de Diauarum Brazil
26 B2 Campodolcino Italy
141 E4 Campo Esperanza Paraguay
144 D3 Campo Florido Brazil
142 D3 Campo Formoso Brazil
146 D2 Campo Gallo Arg.
141 E1 Campo Grande *Amazonas* Brazil
144 A4 Campo Grande *Mato Grosso do Sul* Brazil
144 D6 Campo Largo Brazil
142 D1 Campo Maior Brazil
24 C3 Campo Maior Portugal
144 B6 Campo Mourão Brazil
143 B6 Campo Novo Brazil
78 B3 Campo, Reserva de res. Cameroon
145 H4 Campos Brazil
145 E3 Campos Altos Brazil
142 C3 Campos Belos Brazil
143 B6 Campos de Palmas reg. Brazil
145 F5 Campos do Jordão Brazil
143 B5 Campos Eré reg. Brazil
145 F4 Campos Gerais Brazil
143 B6 Campos Novos Brazil
144 D5 Campos Novos Paulista Brazil
142 D2 Campos Sales Brazil
25 H1 Camprodon Spain
120 B6 Campton U.S.A.
121 H3 Campton U.S.A.
28 E2 Câmpulung Romania
28 E1 Câmpulung Moldovenesc Romania
129 G4 Camp Verde U.S.A.
43 E5 Cam Ranh Vietnam
110 G4 Camrose Can.
111 G2 Camsell Lake l. Can.
111 H3 Camsell Portage Can.
119 □3 Camuy Puerto Rico
60 A1 Çan Turkey
145 G4 Canaã Brazil
133 □2 Canaan *Tobago* Trin. & Tobago
121 G3 Canaan U.S.A.
142 A2 Cana Brava r. *Pará* Brazil
142 B2 Cana Brava r. *Pará* Brazil
145 F2 Canabrava Brazil
104 G4 Canada country N. America
121 H2 Canada Falls Lake l. U.S.A.
125 C5 Canadian r. U.S.A.
146 E2 Canaglaé, L. l. Arg.
139 E2 Canaima, Parque Nacional nat. park Venezuela
121 F3 Canajoharie U.S.A.
60 A1 Çanakkale Turkey
29 F5 Çanakkale div. Turkey
29 F4 Çanakkale Boğazı str. Turkey
90 □2 Canala Pac. Oc.
147 C7 Canal Beagle chan. Arg.
147 A7 Canal Concepción chan. Chile
27 B7 Canal de la Galite chan. Tunisia
25 E2 Canal de Trasvase canal Spain
139 G3 Canal do Norte chan. Brazil
142 B1 Canal do Sul chan. Brazil
76 C4 Canal du Sahel canal Mali
146 C4 Canalejas Arg.
147 B5 Canal Moraleda chan. Chile
142 C1 Canal Perigoso chan. Brazil
147 B7 Canal Smyth chan. Chile
25 E2 Cañamares Spain
140 C2 Canamari Brazil
120 E3 Canandaigua U.S.A.
120 E3 Canandaigua Lake l. U.S.A.
130 C2 Cananea Mexico
113 H2 Cananée, Lac l. Can.
144 E6 Cananéia Brazil
138 D3 Canapiare, Co h. Colombia
144 D3 Canápolis Brazil
138 B4 Cañar Ecuador
25 □ Canarias, Islas is Atlantic Ocean
25 □ Canarias, Islas div. Spain
132 B2 Canarreos, Arch. de los is Cuba
148 H4 Canary Basin Atlantic Ocean
121 F3 Canastota U.S.A.
142 D2 Canastra r. Brazil
130 D3 Canatlán Mexico
119 D6 Canaveral, Cape c. U.S.A.
25 E2 Cañaveras Spain
145 J1 Canavieiras Brazil
26 C2 Canazei Italy
97 F2 Canbelego Aust.
97 G3 Canberra Aust.
126 B3 Canby U.S.A.
124 D2 Canby U.S.A.
20 D2 Cancale France
131 J4 Cancún Mexico
140 B3 Candarave Peru
20 D3 Candé France
145 F4 Candeias Brazil
146 E2 Candelaria *Misiones* Arg.
141 E3 Candelaria r. Bolivia
131 H5 Candelaria *Campeche* Mexico
127 F6 Candelaria *Chihuahua* Mexico
24 D2 Candelario, Sa de mt. ra. Spain
24 D2 Candeleda Spain
97 G4 Candelo Aust.
144 C6 Cândido de Abreu Brazil
142 C1 Cândido Mendes Brazil
144 C5 Cândido Mota Brazil
145 H1 Cândido Sales Brazil
111 H4 Candle Lake Can.
111 H4 Candle Lake l. Can.
152 C1 Candlemas I. i. *S. Sandwich Is* Atlantic Ocean
121 G4 Candlewood, Lake l. U.S.A.
124 D1 Cando U.S.A.
41 B2 Candon Phil.
100 A4 Cane r. Aust.
146 B3 Canela Alta Chile
26 B3 Canelli Italy
146 E3 Canelones Uruguay
146 B4 Cañete Chile
25 F2 Cañete Spain
140 B2 Cangallo Peru
79 C6 Cangamba Angola
79 C5 Cangandala Angola
24 B1 Cangas Spain
24 C1 Cangas del Narcea Spain
24 D1 Cangas de Onís Spain
79 D6 Cangombe Angola
51 G1 Cangshan China
142 E2 Canguaretama Brazil
146 F3 Canguçu Brazil
146 F3 Canguçu, Sa do h. Brazil
51 E4 Cangwu China
49 F5 Cangzhou China
113 G3 Caniapiscau Can.
113 G2 Caniapiscau r. Can.
113 G3 Caniapiscau, Rés. resr Can.
27 D7 Canicattì Italy
41 C4 Canigao Channel chan. Phil.
25 E4 Caniles Spain
110 E4 Canim L. l. Can.
110 E4 Canim Lake Can.
142 C1 Canindé *Pará* Brazil
142 D2 Canindé r. Brazil
142 E1 Caninde Brazil
120 E3 Canisteo r. U.S.A.
120 E3 Canisteo U.S.A.
130 E4 Cañitas de Felipe Pescador Mexico
60 C1 Çankiri Turkey
81 B5 Cankuzo Burundi
41 B4 Canlaon Phil.
110 F4 Canmore Can.
115 J3 Cann Can.
101 A6 Canna Aust.
16 D3 Canna i. U.K.
56 A4 Cannanore India
56 A4 Cannanore Islands is India
21 H5 Cannes France
101 B6 Canning Hill h. Aust.
122 A3 Cannon r. U.S.A.
81 □4 Cannoniers Pt pt Mauritius
99 G4 Cannonvale Aust.
97 G4 Cann River Aust.
139 E2 Caño Araguao r. Venezuela
143 B6 Canõas Brazil
145 F3 Canoeiros Brazil
111 H3 Canoe L. l. Can.
143 B6 Canoinhas Brazil
139 E2 Caño Macareo r. Venezuela
139 E2 Caño Manamo r. Venezuela
127 F4 Canon City U.S.A.
99 G4 Canoona Aust.
96 E3 Canopus Aust.
111 J4 Canora Can.
133 G4 Canouan i. St Vincent
97 G3 Canowindra Aust.
74 A4 Cansado *Western Sahara*
113 H4 Canso, C. hd Can.
140 A2 Canta Peru
24 D1 Cantabria div. Spain
24 C1 Cantábrica, Cordillera mt. ra. Spain
139 F4 Cantagalo Brazil
24 E2 Cantalejo Spain
24 B2 Cantanhede Portugal
146 C3 Cantantal Arg.
139 E2 Cantaura Venezuela
121 K2 Canterbury Can.
93 C5 Canterbury div. N.Z.
17 H6 Canterbury U.K.
93 C6 Canterbury Bight b. N.Z.
93 C5 Canterbury Plains plain N.Z.
43 D5 Cần Thơ Vietnam
41 C4 Cantilan Phil.
146 B2 Canto del Agua Chile
142 D2 Canto do Buriti Brazil
122 B5 Canton U.S.A.
121 H2 Canton U.S.A.
125 F5 Canton U.S.A.
122 B5 Canton U.S.A.
121 F2 Canton U.S.A.
120 C4 Canton U.S.A.
120 E4 Canton U.S.A.
144 B6 Cantu r. Brazil
143 B5 Cantú, Sa do h. Brazil
139 F5 Canudos Brazil
146 E4 Cañuelas Arg.
139 E5 Canumã *Amazonas* Brazil
139 F4 Canumã *Amazonas* Brazil
139 E5 Canutama Brazil
93 D4 Canvastown N.Z.
20 E2 Cany-Barville France
125 C5 Canyon U.S.A.
126 C2 Canyon City U.S.A.
129 H3 Canyon de Chelly National Monument res. U.S.A.
126 D2 Canyon Ferry L. l. U.S.A.
129 H2 Canyonlands National Park nat. park U.S.A.
110 D2 Canyon Ranges mt. ra. Can.
126 B3 Canyonville U.S.A.
79 D5 Canzar Angola
42 D2 Cao Bằng Vietnam
65 K4 Caohu China
50 B3 Caojian China
79 C5 Caombo Angola
43 E4 Cao Nguyên Đắc Lắc plat. Vietnam
26 D3 Caorle Italy
49 H4 Caoshi China
51 F1 Cao Xian China
41 B5 Cap i. Phil.
27 E5 Capaccio Italy
132 D3 Cap-à-Foux c. Haiti
79 D5 Capaia Angola
138 D2 Capanaparo r. Venezuela
143 B6 Capanema r. Brazil
142 C1 Capanema Brazil
144 D6 Capão Bonito Brazil
144 A4 Capão Seco Brazil
143 D5 Caparaó, Sa do mt. ra. Brazil
138 C2 Caparo r. Venezuela
41 B3 Capas Phil.
133 E5 Capatárida Venezuela
113 H4 Cap-aux-Meules Can.
20 D5 Capbreton France
115 J3 Cap-de-la-Madeleine Can.
25 H3 Capdepera Spain
99 F4 Cape r. Aust.
101 C7 Cape Arid Nat. Park nat. park Aust.
97 G5 Cape Barren Island i. Aust.
148 K8 Cape Basin Atlantic Ocean
100 D2 Cape Bougainville Abor. Land res. Aust.
113 H4 Cape Breton Highlands Nat. Pk nat. park Can.
113 H4 Cape Breton Island i. Can.
113 J3 Cape Charles Can.
121 E6 Cape Charles U.S.A.
76 D5 Cape Coast Ghana
121 H4 Cape Cod Bay b. U.S.A.
121 J4 Cape Cod National Seashore res. U.S.A.
119 D7 Cape Coral U.S.A.
114 E4 Cape Croker Can.
109 L3 Cape Dorset Can.
152 B5 Cape Evans Antarctic Base Ant.
125 F4 Cape Girardeau U.S.A.
150 D5 Cape Johnson Depth depth Pac. Oc.
101 C7 Cape Le Grand Nat. Park nat. park Aust.
145 G2 Capelinha Brazil
99 G4 Capella Aust.
121 F5 Cape May U.S.A.
121 F5 Cape May Court House U.S.A.
121 F5 Cape May Pt pt U.S.A.
79 C5 Capenda-Camulemba Angola
100 A4 Cape Range Nat. Park nat. park Aust.
109 H5 Cape Sable Island i. Can.
113 J4 Cape St George Can.
133 □5 Capesterre *Guadeloupe* Caribbean
113 H4 Cape Tormentine Can.
82 B5 Cape Town R.S.A.
76 □ Cape Verde country Africa
148 G5 Cape Verde Basin Atlantic Ocean
148 F5 Cape Verde Fracture Atlantic Ocean
148 H4 Cape Verde Plateau Atlantic Ocean
121 E2 Cape Vincent U.S.A.
99 E2 Cape York pen. Aust.
133 D3 Cap-Haïtien Haiti
138 D3 Capibara Venezuela
142 E2 Capiberibe r. Brazil
142 C1 Capim Brazil
142 C1 Capim r. Brazil
144 D3 Capinópolis Brazil
140 C3 Capinota Bolivia
152 B2 Capitán Arturo Prat Chile Base Ant.
141 E4 Capitán Bado Paraguay
144 B6 Capitán Leônidas Marques Brazil
127 F5 Capitan Peak mt. U.S.A.
145 G2 Capitão Enéas Brazil
129 G2 Capitol Reef National Park nat. park U.S.A.

D

E

108 A3 Enurmino Rus. Fed.
140 B1 Envira Brazil
79 D4 Enyamba Zaire
78 C3 Enyéllé Congo
93 C5 Enys, Mt mt. N.Z.
26 C3 Enza r. Italy
47 G6 Enzan Japan
90 □2 Eo i. Pac. Oc.
78 C3 Epéna Congo
21 F2 Épernay France
129 G2 Ephraim U.S.A.
121 E4 Ephrata U.S.A.
126 C2 Ephrata U.S.A.
90 □2 Epi i. Vanuatu
21 G3 Épinac France
21 H2 Épinal France
139 F2 Epira Guyana
61 B2 Episkopi Cyprus
61 B2 Episkopi B. b. Cyprus
27 D5 Epomeo, Monte h. Italy
17 H6 Epping U.K.
17 G6 Epsom U.K.
146 D4 Epu-pel Arg.
57 C3 Eqlīd Iran
78 C3 Équateur div. Zaire
80 B3 Equatoria div. Sudan
69 E5 Equatorial Guinea country Africa
139 E2 Equeipa Venezuela
99 F5 Erac Cr. w Aust.
76 D3 Erakchiouene well Mali
41 A4 Eran Phil.
54 C5 Erandol India
60 D1 Erbaa Turkey
73 G3 Erba, Jebel mt. Sudan
18 F4 Erbendorf Germany
18 C4 Erbeskopf h. Germany
60 E2 Erçek Turkey
60 E2 Erciş Turkey
60 C2 Erciyes Daği mt. Turkey
19 J5 Érd Hungary
49 H4 Erdao r. China
55 H2 Erdaogou China
60 A1 Erdek Turkey
61 C1 Erdemli Turkey
48 C2 Erdenet Mongolia
48 A2 Erdenet Mongolia
48 C4 Erdenetsogt Mongolia
72 D4 Erdi reg. Chad
18 E4 Erding Germany
152 B5 Erebus, Mt mt. Ant.
60 F4 Erech Iraq
143 B6 Erechim Brazil
49 E2 Ereentsav Mongolia
60 C2 Ereğli Konya Turkey
60 B1 Ereğli Zonguldak Turkey
29 B5 Ereikoussa i. Greece
27 E7 Erei, Monti mts Italy
48 E4 Erenhot China
57 D2 Eresk Iran
24 D2 Eresma r. Spain
29 D5 Eretria Greece
74 D2 Erfoud Morocco
18 E3 Erfurt Germany
60 D2 Ergani Turkey
76 C2 Erg Atouila sand dunes Mali
74 C4 'Erg Chech sand dunes Algeria/Mali
72 C4 Erg du Djourab sand dunes Chad
77 G3 Erg du Ténéré sand dunes Niger
48 D4 Ergel Mongolia
60 A1 Ergene r. Turkey
74 D2 Erg er Raoui sand dunes Algeria
74 D3 Erg labès sand dunes Algeria
74 C3 Erg Iguidi sand dunes Algeria/Mauritania
75 F3 Erg Issaouane sand dunes Algeria
11 G4 Ergļi Latvia
78 C1 Erguig r. Chad
49 G2 Ergun Yougi China
49 G2 Ergun Zuoqi China
50 C3 Er Hai l. China
49 H4 Erhulai China
24 B3 Ericeira Portugal
16 E3 Ericht, Loch l. U.K.
122 B5 Erie U.S.A.
125 E4 Erie U.S.A.
120 C3 Erie U.S.A.
123 F5 Erie, Lake l. Can./U.S.A.
76 C3 'Erîgât sand dunes Mali
46 J2 Erimo Japan
46 J3 Erimo-misaki c. Japan
96 C1 Eringa Aust.
133 □3 Erin Point pt Trinidad Trin. & Tobago
68 H4 Eritrea country Africa
19 F2 Erkner Germany
73 G4 Erkowit Sudan
18 E4 Erlangen Germany
98 C5 Erldunda Aust.
49 J4 Erlong Shan mt. China
49 H4 Erlongshan Sk. resr China
48 E2 Ermana, Khr. mt. ra. Rus. Fed.
83 D4 Ermelo R.S.A.
61 B1 Ermenek Karaman Turkey
60 C2 Ermenek Turkey
29 D6 Ermioni Greece
29 E6 Ermoupoli Greece
56 B4 Ernakulam India
101 C5 Ernest Giles Ra. h. Aust.
93 A7 Ernest Is is N.Z.
56 B4 Erode India
99 E5 Eromanga Aust.
82 A3 Erongo div. Namibia
82 B3 Erongo Mts mts Namibia
74 D2 Er Rachidia Morocco
73 F5 Er Rahad Sudan
83 F2 Errego Mozambique
80 B2 Er Renk Sudan
17 C4 Errigal h. Rep. of Ire.
17 B4 Erris Head hd Rep. of Ire.
121 H2 Errol U.S.A.
90 □2 Erromango i. Vanuatu
80 B2 Er Roseires Sudan
73 F5 Er Rua'at Sudan
61 D3 Er Ruseifa Jordan
29 C4 Ersekë Albania
124 D2 Erskine U.S.A.
10 F3 Ersmark Sweden
14 E4 Ertil' Rus. Fed.
65 L3 Ertix r. China
96 D2 Erudina Aust.
60 E2 Eruh Turkey
146 F3 Erval Brazil
145 G4 Ervália Brazil
120 D5 Erwin U.S.A.
29 C6 Erymanthos r. Greece
29 D5 Erythres Greece
50 B3 Eryuan China
18 F3 Erzgebirge mt. ra. Czech Rep./Germany
49 H2 Erzhan China
48 A2 Erzin Rus. Fed.
61 D1 Erzin Turkey
60 D2 Erzincan Turkey
60 E2 Erzurum Turkey
90 □1 Esa-ala P.N.G.
46 H3 Esan-misaki pt Japan
46 J1 Esashi Japan
47 H4 Esashi Japan
46 H3 Esashi Japan
46 D7 Esawasaki Japan
11 C5 Esbjerg Denmark
142 E2 Escada Brazil
129 G3 Escalante U.S.A.
129 G3 Escalante r. U.S.A.
129 F3 Escalante Desert desert U.S.A.
25 G1 Escaló Spain
130 D3 Escalón Mexico
122 D3 Escanaba U.S.A.
131 H5 Escárcega Mexico
41 B2 Escarpada Point pt Phil.
25 F2 Escatrón Spain
21 F1 Escaut r. France
18 E2 Eschede Germany
18 B4 Esch-sur-Alzette Luxembourg
18 E3 Eschwege Germany
18 C3 Eschweiler Germany
133 E3 Escocesa, Bahía b. Caribbean
140 C3 Escoma Bolivia
128 D5 Escondido U.S.A.
130 D4 Escuinapa Mexico
131 H6 Escuintla Guatemala
131 G6 Escuintla Mexico
133 E5 Escuque Venezuela
145 E2 Escurso r. Brazil
138 C2 Escutillas Colombia
78 B3 Eséka Cameroon
57 C1 Esenguly Turkmenistan
18 C2 Esens Germany
57 B2 Eşfahan Iran
57 B2 Eşfahan div. Iran
57 C3 Esfandāran Iran
57 B3 Esfarjan Iran
64 E5 Eshāqābād Iran
57 C4 Eshkanān Iran
61 C4 Esh Sharā reg. Jordan
57 B2 Eshtehārd Iran
83 D3 Esigodini Zimbabwe
83 E4 Esikhawini R.S.A.
99 H5 Esk Aust.
97 F5 Esk r. Aust.
57 B2 Eskandarī Iran
92 F3 Eskdale N.Z.
113 G3 Esker Can.
15 G2 Eskhar Ukraine
10 N2 Eskifjörður Iceland
11 E4 Eskilstuna Sweden
60 C1 Eskipazar Turkey
60 B2 Eskişehir Turkey
24 D1 Esla r. Spain
60 F3 Eslamābād e Gharb Iran
11 D5 Eslöv Sweden
60 B2 Eşme Turkey
132 C2 Esmeralda Cuba
147 A6 Esmeralda, I. i. Chile
138 B3 Esmeraldas Ecuador
114 B1 Esnagami Lake l. Can.
114 C2 Esnagi Lake l. Can.
57 E4 Espakeh Iran
20 F4 Espalion France
114 E3 Espanola Can.
127 F4 Espanola U.S.A.
138 □ Española, I. i. Galapagos Is Ecuador
25 G2 Esparraguera Spain
128 A2 Esparto U.S.A.
101 C7 Esperance Aust.
101 C7 Esperance B. b. Aust.
92 □4 Espérance Rock, L' i. Kermadec Is N.Z.
142 D1 Esperantinópolis Brazil
152 B2 Esperanza Argentina Base Ant.
147 B7 Esperanza Santa Cruz Arg.
146 D3 Esperanza Santa Fé Arg.
130 C3 Esperanza Mexico
140 B1 Esperanza Peru
41 C4 Esperanza Phil.
119 □3 Esperanza Puerto Rico
130 J6 Esperanza, Sa de la mt. ra. Honduras
24 B3 Espichel, Cabo hd Portugal
24 D3 Espiel Spain
24 D1 Espigüete mt. Spain
125 C7 Espinazo Mexico
24 B2 Espinho Portugal
143 B6 Espinilho, Sa do h. Brazil
145 G1 Espinosa Brazil
145 H3 Espírito Santo div. Brazil
41 B2 Espiritu Phil.
90 □2 Espíritu Santo i. Vanuatu
131 J5 Espíritu Santo, B. del b. Mexico
130 C3 Espíritu Sto i. Mexico
142 E3 Esplanada Brazil
11 G3 Espoo Finland
83 E3 Espungabera Mozambique
147 B5 Esquel Arg.
110 E5 Esquimalt Can.
146 E3 Esquina Arg.
61 D3 Es Samrā Jordan
41 C5 Essang Indon.
74 C2 Essaouira Morocco
74 B3 Es Semara Western Sahara
18 C3 Essen Germany
101 C5 Essendon, Mt h. Aust.
139 F2 Essequibo r. Guyana
114 D5 Essex Can.
129 E4 Essex U.S.A.
121 G2 Essex Junction U.S.A.
123 F4 Essexville U.S.A.
18 D4 Esslingen am Neckar Germany
63 R4 Esso Rus. Fed.
73 F5 Es Suki Sudan
78 B3 Est div. Cameroon
24 C1 Estaca de Bares, Pta da pt Spain
147 D7 Estados, I. de los i. Arg.
57 C3 Eşţahbānāt Iran
114 E3 Estaire Can.
142 E3 Estância Brazil
147 C7 Estancia Camerón Chile
25 E4 Estancias, Sierra de las mt. ra. Spain
20 E5 Estats, Pic d' mt. France/Spain
83 D4 Estcourt R.S.A.
26 C3 Este Italy
146 D2 Esteban Rams Arg.
24 B2 Estela Portugal
130 J6 Estelí Nicaragua
25 E1 Estella Spain
24 D3 Estena r. Spain
24 D4 Estepa Spain
24 D4 Estepona Spain
119 □3 Este, Pta pt Puerto Rico
25 E2 Esteras de Medinaceli Spain
21 H5 Esterel reg. France
111 J4 Esterhazy Can.
78 A3 Esterias, Cap pt Gabon
128 B4 Estero Bay b. U.S.A.
141 D4 Esteros Paraguay
146 E2 Esteros del Iberá marsh Arg.
111 J5 Estevan Can.
124 E3 Estherville U.S.A.
113 H4 Est, Île de l' i. Can.
119 D5 Estill U.S.A.
142 D2 Estiva r. Brazil
145 E5 Estiva Brazil
121 J1 Est, Lac de l' l. Can.
142 D2 Estolado r. Brazil
5 H3 Estonia country Europe
145 F3 Estrêla do Indaiá Brazil
144 E3 Estrêla do Sul Brazil
24 C2 Estrela, Serra da mt. ra. Portugal
24 E3 Estrella mt. Spain
24 B3 Estremadura reg. Portugal
24 C3 Estremoz Portugal
78 B3 Estuaire div. Gabon
19 J5 Esztergom Hungary
20 C2 Étables-sur-Mer France
96 D2 Etadunna Aust.
54 D4 Etah India
21 G2 Étain France
20 F2 Étampes France
96 D1 Etamunbanie, L. salt flat Aust.
20 D4 Étang de Biscarrosse et de Parentis l. France
20 D4 Étang de Cazaux et de Sanguinet l. France
20 D4 Étang d'Hourtin-Carcans l. France
81 □5 Étang Salé Réunion Indian Ocean
20 E1 Étaples France
54 D4 Etawah India
83 E4 eThandakukhanya R.S.A.
101 C4 Ethel Creek Aust.
90 □8 Ethel Reefs reef Fiji
82 C4 E'Thembini R.S.A.
99 E3 Etheridge r. Aust.
69 H5 Ethiopia country Africa
60 C2 Etimesğut Turkey
16 E3 Etive, Loch inlet U.K.
27 E7 Etna, Monte vol Italy
11 B4 Etne Norway
110 C3 Etolin I. i. U.S.A.
99 G4 Eton Aust.
82 B2 Etosha National Park nat. park Namibia
82 B2 Etosha Pan salt pan Namibia
78 B3 Etoumbi Congo
28 E3 Etropole Bulgaria
56 B4 Ettaiyapuram India
18 C4 Ettelbruck Luxembourg
18 B3 Etten-Leur Netherlands
74 A5 Et Tidra i. Mauritania
78 E4 Etumba Zaire
130 D4 Etzatlán Mexico
90 □4 'Eua i. Tonga
97 F3 Euabalong Aust.
90 □4 'Eua Iki i. Tonga
90 □3 Euakafa i. Tonga
101 E6 Eucla Aust.
120 C4 Euclid U.S.A.
142 E3 Euclides da Cunha Brazil
97 G4 Eucumbene, L. l. Aust.
96 D3 Eudunda Aust.
119 C6 Eufaula U.S.A.
125 E5 Eufaula Lake resr U.S.A.
126 B2 Eugene U.S.A.
141 E2 Eugênia r. Brazil
130 B3 Eugenia, Pta c. Mexico
97 G3 Eugowra Aust.
99 F6 Eulo Aust.
97 G2 Eumungerie Aust.
99 G4 Eungella Nat. Park Aust.
125 E6 Eunice U.S.A.
60 F4 Euphrates r. Iraq
11 F3 Eura Finland
20 E2 Eure r. France
126 A3 Eureka U.S.A.
126 D1 Eureka U.S.A.
129 E2 Eureka U.S.A.
145 J2 Euriápolis Brazil
96 E2 Eurinilla w Aust.
96 E2 Euriowie Aust.
97 F4 Euroa Aust.
99 G5 Eurombah Aust.
99 G5 Eurombah Cr. r. Aust.
149 G5 Europa, Île i. Indian Ocean
24 D1 Europa, Picos de mt. ra. Spain
24 D4 Europa Point hd Gibraltar
97 E3 Euston Aust.
110 D4 Eustuk Lake l. Can.
119 C5 Eutaw U.S.A.
18 E1 Eutin Germany
98 C3 Eva Downs Aust.
119 □1 Evans Bay Bermuda
110 F4 Evansburg Can.
97 H2 Evans Head Aust.
152 B3 Evans Ice Stream ice feature Ant.
112 E3 Evans, L. l. Can.
127 F4 Evans, Mt mt. U.S.A.
126 D2 Evans, Mt mt. U.S.A.
109 K3 Evans Strait chan. Can.
122 D4 Evanston U.S.A.
126 E3 Evanston U.S.A.
114 D4 Evansville Can.
118 C4 Evansville U.S.A.
122 C4 Evansville U.S.A.
126 F3 Evansville U.S.A.
122 E4 Evart U.S.A.
82 D4 Evaton R.S.A.
57 C4 Evaz Iran
122 A2 Eveleth U.S.A.
63 R3 Evensk Rus. Fed.
93 □1 Eveque, Cape L' c. Chatham Is N.Z.
96 C2 Everard, L. salt flat Aust.
96 C1 Everard, Mt mt. Aust.
96 C1 Everard Park Aust.
96 C1 Everard Range h. Aust.
55 F4 Everest, Mt mt. China
121 K1 Everett Can.
126 B1 Everett U.S.A.
119 D7 Everglades Nat. Park nat. park. U.S.A.
119 D7 Everglades, The swamp U.S.A.
125 G6 Evergreen U.S.A.
139 F2 Everton Guyana
99 E4 Evesham Aust.
17 G5 Evesham U.K.
10 F3 Evijärvi Finland
78 B3 Evinayong Equatorial Guinea
11 B4 Evje Norway
24 C3 Évora Portugal
24 C3 Évora div. Portugal
45 P1 Evoron, Ozero l. Rus. Fed.
20 E2 Évreux France
20 D2 Évron France
29 F4 Evros r. Greece/Turkey
29 D6 Evrotas r. Greece
20 F2 Évry France
29 E5 Evvoia i. Greece
127 □1 Ewa Beach U.S.A.
133 □1 Ewarton Jamaica
81 C5 Ewaso Ngiro r. Kenya
49 F2 Ewenkizu Zizhiqi China
152 B2 Ewing I. i. Ant.
92 □1 Ewing I. i. Auckland Is N.Z.
78 B4 Ewo Congo
140 C2 Exaltación Bolivia
128 C2 Excelsior Mtn mt. U.S.A.
128 C2 Excelsior Mts mts U.S.A.
124 E4 Excelsior Springs U.S.A.
152 A4 Executive Committee Range mt. ra. Ant.
97 G3 Exeter Aust.
114 E5 Exeter Can.
17 F6 Exeter U.K.
128 C3 Exeter U.S.A.
121 H3 Exeter U.S.A.
17 F6 Exmoor reg. U.K.
121 F6 Exmore U.S.A.
100 A4 Exmouth Aust.
17 F6 Exmouth U.K.
100 A4 Exmouth Gulf b. Aust.
149 M5 Exmouth Plateau Indian Ocean
99 G5 Expedition Range mt. ra. Aust.
90 □7 Exploring Is is Fiji
24 D3 Extremadura div. Spain
78 B1 Extrême-Nord div. Cameroon
142 E2 Exú Brazil
132 C1 Exuma Sound chan. The Bahamas
78 D4 Eyangu Zaire
81 B5 Eyasi, Lake salt l. Tanzania
16 F4 Eyemouth U.K.
10 M2 Eyjafjörður b. Iceland
80 E3 Eyl Somalia
20 E4 Eymoutiers France
57 C2 Eyn or Rashid Iran
98 D5 Eyre Cr. w Aust.
93 B6 Eyre Mountains mt. ra. N.Z.
96 D2 Eyre (North), Lake salt flat Aust.
96 C3 Eyre Peninsula pen. Aust.
96 D2 Eyre (South), L. salt flat Aust.
18 D2 Eystrup Germany
16 D1 Eysturoy i. Faeroes
81 C5 Eyuku waterhole Kenya
78 A2 Eyumojok Cameroon
83 E4 Ezakheni R.S.A.
147 C4 Ezequil Ramos Mexia, Embalse resr Arg.
12 J2 Ezhva Rus. Fed.
60 A2 Ezine Turkey

F

91 □11 Faaa Fr. Poly. Pac. Oc.
53 D9 Faadhippolhu Atoll atoll Maldives
80 D4 Faafxadhuun Somalia
91 □10 Faaite i. Fr. Poly. Pac. Oc.
91 □11 Faaone Fr. Poly. Pac. Oc.
125 B6 Fabens U.S.A.
110 F2 Faber Lake l. Can.
43 □ Faber, Mt h. Singapore
24 C1 Fabero Spain
11 C5 Fåborg Denmark
26 D4 Fabriano Italy
138 C3 Facatativá Colombia
77 G3 Fachi Niger
99 G4 Facing I. i. Aust.
41 □2 Facpi Pt pt Guam Pac. Oc.
121 F4 Factoryville U.S.A.
147 B6 Facundo Arg.
72 D4 Fada Chad
77 E4 Fada-Ngourma Burkina
80 E2 Faḍli reg. Yemen
75 F3 Fadnoun, Plateau du plat. Algeria
26 C3 Faenza Italy
16 D1 Faeroes is Atlantic Ocean
78 C2 Fafa r. C.A.R.
90 □4 Fafa i. Tonga
39 K7 Fafanlap Indon.
24 B2 Fafe Portugal
80 D3 Fafen Shet' w Ethiopia
91 □12 Fagaloa Bay b. Western Samoa
91 □12 Fagamalo Western Samoa
28 E2 Făgăraş Romania
11 C3 Fagernes Norway
11 D4 Fagersta Sweden
28 D2 Făget Romania
77 F4 Faggo Nigeria
147 C7 Fagnano, L. l. Arg.
76 D3 Faguibine, Lac l. Mali
10 M3 Fagurhólsmýri Iceland
80 B3 Fagwir Sudan
57 D3 Fahraj Iran
24 □ Faial Madeira Portugal
115 G2 Faillon, Lac l. Can.
108 D3 Fairbanks U.S.A.
120 B5 Fairborn U.S.A.
124 D3 Fairbury U.S.A.
120 E5 Fairfax U.S.A.
128 A2 Fairfield U.S.A.
122 B5 Fairfield U.S.A.
120 A5 Fairfield U.S.A.
125 D6 Fairfield U.S.A.
121 G3 Fair Haven U.S.A.
41 A4 Fairie Queen sand bank Phil.
16 G2 Fair Isle i. U.K.
99 F2 Fairlight Aust.
124 E3 Fairmont U.S.A.
120 C5 Fairmont U.S.A.
127 F4 Fairplay U.S.A.
122 D3 Fairport U.S.A.
120 C4 Fairport Harbor U.S.A.
99 F2 Fairview Aust.
110 F3 Fairview Can.
123 E3 Fairview U.S.A.
125 D4 Fairview U.S.A.
129 G2 Fairview U.S.A.
45 □ Fairview Park Hong Kong
110 B3 Fairweather, Cape c. U.S.A.
110 B3 Fairweather, Mt mt. Can./U.S.A.
39 M5 Fais i. Fed. States of Micronesia
54 C3 Faisalabad Pakistan
124 C2 Faith U.S.A.
16 G1 Faither, The pt U.K.
55 E4 Faizabad India
119 □3 Fajardo Puerto Rico
91 □10 Fakaina i. Fr. Poly. Pac. Oc.
90 □3 Fakalele i. Tonga
87 K5 Fakaofo i. Tokelau Pac. Oc.
91 □10 Fakarava i. Fr. Poly. Pac. Oc.
17 H5 Fakenham U.K.
10 D3 Fåker Sweden
39 K7 Fakfak Indon.
57 C3 Fakhrabad Iran
49 G4 Faku China
76 B5 Falaba Sierra Leone
77 E4 Falagountou Burkina
20 D2 Falaise France
72 C4 Falaise d'Angamma cliff Chad
76 D4 Falaise de Bandiagara escarpment Mali
76 D4 Falaise de Banfora escarpment Burkina
77 F3 Falaise de Tiguidit escarpment Niger
55 G4 Falakata India
42 A2 Falam Myanmar
57 B2 Falavarjan Iran
28 G1 Fălciu Romania
26 D4 Falconara Marittima Italy
125 D7 Falcon Lake l. Mexico/U.S.A.
91 □12 Falealupo Western Samoa
91 □12 Faleasiu Western Samoa
91 □12 Falelima Western Samoa
76 B4 Falémé r. Mali/Senegal
12 J3 Falenki Rus. Fed.
91 □12 Falerai Western Samoa
15 B3 Făleşti Moldova
91 □12 Faleula Western Samoa
125 D7 Falfurrias U.S.A.
110 F3 Falher Can.
80 C1 Falkat r. Eritrea
11 D4 Falkenberg Sweden
18 F2 Falkensee Germany
16 F4 Falkirk U.K.
147 E7 Falkland Islands is Atlantic Ocean
147 D7 Falkland Sound chan. Falkland Is.
29 D6 Falkonera i. Greece
11 D4 Falköping Sweden
128 D5 Fallbrook U.S.A.
128 C2 Fallon U.S.A.
121 H4 Fall River U.S.A.
126 F3 Fall River Pass U.S.A.
124 E3 Falls City U.S.A.
77 E4 Falmey Niger
133 □7 Falmouth Antigua Caribbean
133 □1 Falmouth Jamaica
17 E6 Falmouth U.K.
120 A5 Falmouth U.S.A.
121 H3 Falmouth U.S.A.
122 E3 Falmouth U.S.A.
82 B5 False Bay b. R.S.A.
11 D5 Falster i. Denmark
28 F1 Fălticeni Romania
11 D3 Falun Sweden
146 C2 Famatina Arg.
146 C2 Famatina, Sa de mt. ra. Arg.
79 C4 Fambono Zaire
111 K4 Family L. l. Can.
76 C4 Fana Mali
83 H2 Fanandrana Madagascar
51 G2 Fanchang China
83 H3 Fandriana Madagascar
42 B3 Fang Thailand
91 □10 Fangatau i. Fr. Poly. Pac. Oc.
90 □4 Fanga Uta lag. Tonga
51 F1 Fangchēng China
50 E4 Fangcheng China
50 E2 Fangdou Shan mt. ra. China
51 H4 Fang-liao Taiwan
49 F5 Fangshan China
48 D5 Fangshan China
51 H4 Fangshan Taiwan
51 E1 Fang Xian China
49 J3 Fangzheng China
45 □ Fanling Hong Kong
16 E3 Fannich, Loch l. U.K.
57 D4 Fannūj Iran
26 D4 Fano Italy
51 H3 Fanshan China
48 E5 Fanshi China
42 C2 Fan Si Pan mt. Vietnam
49 E6 Fan Xian China
64 F5 Farab Turkmenistan
76 B4 Faraba Mali
152 B2 Faraday Ukraine Base Ant.
78 E3 Faradje Zaire
83 H3 Farafangana Madagascar
76 A4 Farafenni The Gambia
73 E2 Farafra Oasis oasis Egypt
57 C3 Farāgheh Iran
57 E2 Farah w Afghanistan
57 E2 Farāh Afghanistan
57 E2 Farah Rud r. Afghanistan
57 G2 Farakhulm Afghanistan
39 M2 Farallon de Pajaros i. Northern Mariana Is Pac. Oc.
76 B4 Faranah Guinea
92 D4 Farewell, Cape c. N.Z.
92 D4 Farewell Spit spit N.Z.
11 D4 Färgelanda Sweden
124 D2 Fargo U.S.A.
124 E2 Faribault U.S.A.
113 F2 Faribault, Lac l. Can.
54 D3 Faridabad India
54 C3 Faridkot India
55 G5 Faridpur Bangladesh
54 D3 Faridpur India
83 H2 Farihy Alaotra l. Madagascar
83 G3 Farihy Ihotry l. Madagascar
83 H2 Farihy Kinkony l. Madagascar
83 H2 Farihy Tsiazompaniry l. Madagascar
83 G3 Farihy Tsimanampetsotsa l. Madagascar
24 B3 Farilhões i. Portugal
57 D2 Farīmān Iran
142 C2 Farinha r. Brazil
61 A4 Fâriskûr Egypt
11 E4 Färjestaden Sweden
29 D5 Farkadonas Greece
65 G5 Farkhor Tajikistan
29 F6 Farmakonisi i. Greece
122 C5 Farmer City U.S.A.
112 D2 Farmer Island i. Can.
110 E3 Farmington Can.
122 B5 Farmington U.S.A.
122 B5 Farmington U.S.A.
121 H2 Farmington U.S.A.
121 H3 Farmington U.S.A.
129 H3 Farmington U.S.A.
126 E3 Farmington U.S.A.
110 D4 Far Mt. mt. Can.
120 D6 Farmville U.S.A.
17 G4 Farne Islands is U.K.
110 F4 Farnham, Mt mt. Can.
142 A1 Faro Brazil
110 C2 Faro Can.
24 C4 Faro Portugal
24 B4 Faro div. Portugal
11 E4 Fårö i. Sweden
78 B2 Faro, Réserve du res. Cameroon
24 C1 Faro, Serra do mt. ra. Spain
11 E4 Fårösund Sweden
69 K7 Farquhar Group is Seychelles
99 E5 Farrars Cr. w Aust.
57 C3 Farrāshband Iran
120 C4 Farrell U.S.A.
115 H4 Farrellton Can.
57 D2 Farrokhī Iran
57 C3 Fārs div. Iran
57 C2 Farsakh Iran
29 D5 Farsala Greece
57 E2 Fārsī Afghanistan
126 E3 Farson U.S.A.
11 B4 Farsund Norway
79 B6 Farta, Baia Angola
28 F2 Fărţăneşti Romania
144 C2 Fartura r. Brazil
143 B6 Fartura, Sa da mt. ra. Brazil
125 C5 Farwell U.S.A.
57 C3 Fasā Iran
27 F5 Fasano Italy
120 E4 Fassett U.S.A.
15 C1 Fastiv Ukraine
15 E1 Fastivtsi Ukraine
78 F3 Fataki Zaire
54 C3 Fatehabad India
54 D4 Fatehgarh India
54 C2 Fatehjang Pakistan
54 C4 Fatehnagar India
54 C4 Fatehpur Rajasthan India
54 E4 Fatehpur Uttar Pradesh India
54 B3 Fatehpur Pakistan
54 D4 Fatehpur Sikri India
14 B3 Fateyevka Rus. Fed.
14 B3 Fatezh Rus. Fed.
57 C3 Fatḫābād Iran
114 E4 Fathom Five National Marine Park nat. park Can.
76 A4 Fatick Senegal
144 A5 Fátima do Sul Brazil
90 □3 Fatumanga i. Tonga
79 C4 Fatundu Zaire
114 D2 Fauquier Can.
101 A5 Faure I. i. Aust.
28 F2 Făurei Romania
10 D2 Fauske Norway
129 F1 Faust U.S.A.
27 D7 Favignana, Isola i. Italy
110 G4 Fawcett Can.
112 C3 Fawn r. Can.
73 H2 Fawwārah Saudi Arabia
10 L2 Faxaflói b. Iceland
10 E3 Faxälven r. Sweden
50 C3 Faxian Hu l. China
72 C4 Faya Chad
122 D3 Fayette U.S.A.
125 E4 Fayetteville U.S.A.
119 E5 Fayetteville U.S.A.
119 C5 Fayetteville U.S.A.
73 H4 Fayfā Saudi Arabia
61 B4 Fâyid Egypt
60 G4 Faylakah i. Kuwait
61 D5 Fazair al Ghrazi w Saudi Arabia
77 E5 Fazao Malfakassa, Parc National de nat. park Togo
54 C3 Fazilka India
54 B3 Fazilpur Pakistan
57 B4 Fazrān, J. h. Saudi Arabia
74 B4 Fdérik Mauritania
119 E5 Fear, Cape c. U.S.A.
119 E5 Fear, Cape r. U.S.A.
128 B2 Feather Falls U.S.A.
93 E4 Featherston N.Z.
97 F4 Feathertop, Mt mt. Aust.
20 E2 Fécamp France
146 E3 Federación Arg.
77 F5 Federal Capital Territory div. Nigeria
16 K1 Fedje Norway
65 J2 Fedorovka Kazak.
64 F2 Fedorovka Kazak.
64 D2 Fedorovka Kazak.
15 F3 Fedotova Kosa spit Ukraine
19 L5 Fehérgyarmat Hungary
18 E1 Fehmarn i. Germany
145 H5 Feia, Lagoa lag. Brazil
51 G2 Feidong China
51 H1 Feihuanghe Kou river mouth China
140 B1 Feijó Brazil
92 E4 Feilding N.Z.
144 C4 Feio ou Aguapei r. Brazil
142 E3 Feira de Santana Brazil
24 C1 Feira do Monte Spain
61 B5 Feirân well Egypt
61 B5 Feirân, W. w Egypt
51 G2 Feixi China
51 G1 Fei Xian China
60 C2 Feke Turkey
25 H3 Felanitx Spain
122 D3 Felch U.S.A.
18 F2 Feldberg Mecklenburg-Vorpommern Germany
18 D5 Feldberg mt. Germany
18 D5 Feldkirch Austria
19 G5 Feldkirchen in Kärten Austria
28 E1 Feldru Romania
90 □3 Feletoa Tonga
146 E3 Feliciano r. Arg.
81 □1 Félicité I. i. Seychelles
53 D10 Felidu Atoll atoll Maldives
131 H5 Felipe C. Puerto Mexico
145 F3 Felixlândia Brazil
17 H6 Felixstowe U.K.
130 D2 Félix U. Gómez Mexico
26 D2 Fella r. Italy
133 □1 Fellowship Jamaica
26 C2 Feltre Italy
142 C3 Femeas r. Brazil
18 E1 Femer Bælt str. Denmark/Germany
11 C3 Femunden l. Norway
48 D5 Fen r. China
83 G4 Fenambosy, Lohatanjona pt Madagascar
129 H4 Fence Lake U.S.A.
115 F4 Fenelon Falls Can.
15 D1 Fenevychi Ukraine
29 E4 Fengari mt. Greece
49 H4 Fengcheng China
51 F2 Fengcheng China
50 D2 Fengdu China
50 D3 Fenggang China
51 H2 Fenghua China
51 E3 Fenghuang China
51 E2 Fengjie China
51 E4 Fengkai China
51 H4 Fenglin Taiwan
49 F5 Fengnan China
49 F4 Fengning China
50 B3 Fengqing China
51 F1 Fengqiu China
49 F5 Fengrun China
50 D3 Fengshan China
51 G4 Fengshun China
51 G1 Fengtai China
50 D1 Feng Xian China
51 F2 Fengxin China
51 G1 Fengyang China
48 E4 Fengzhen China
55 G5 Feni Bangladesh
90 □1 Feni Is is P.N.G.
122 B4 Fennimore U.S.A.
83 H2 Fenoarivo Atsinanana Madagascar
83 H2 Fenoarivo Be Madagascar
21 J6 Feno, Capo di pt France
17 G5 Fens, The reg. U.K.
123 F4 Fenton U.S.A.
151 J7 Fenua Ura is Fr. Poly. Pac. Oc.
48 D5 Fenxi China
48 D5 Fenyang China
13 E6 Feodosiya Ukraine
75 F1 Fer, Cap de hd Algeria
57 D2 Ferdows Iran
29 F4 Feres Greece
65 H4 Fergana Uzbekistan
65 H4 Fergana Too Tizmegi mt. ra. Kyrgyzstan
114 E5 Fergus Can.
124 D2 Fergus Falls U.S.A.
90 □1 Fergusson I. i. P.N.G.
75 F2 Fériana Tunisia
76 C5 Ferkessédougou Côte d'Ivoire
19 G5 Ferlach Austria
114 A1 Ferland Can.
76 B4 Ferlo Sud, Réserve de Faune du res. Senegal
76 A3 Ferlo, Vallée du w Senegal
26 D4 Fermo Italy
113 G3 Fermont Can.
24 C2 Fermoselle Spain
17 C5 Fermoy Rep. of Ire.
146 D2 Fernández Arg.
119 D6 Fernandina Beach U.S.A.
138 □ Fernandina, I. i. Galapagos Is Ecuador
147 B7 Fernando de Magallanes, Parque Nacional nat. park Chile
148 G6 Fernando de Noronha i. Atlantic Ocean
144 C4 Fernandópolis Brazil
145 F2 Fernão Dias Brazil
83 G1 Fernão Veloso, Baia de b. Mozambique
126 B1 Ferndale U.S.A.
17 G6 Ferndown U.K.
110 F5 Fernie Can.
128 C2 Fernley U.S.A.
121 F4 Fernridge U.S.A.
126 C2 Fernwood U.S.A.
26 C3 Ferrara Italy
27 B6 Ferrato, Capo pt Italy
24 B3 Ferreira do Alentejo Portugal
139 G3 Ferreira-Gomes Brazil
144 B4 Ferreiros Brazil
138 B5 Ferreñafe Peru
125 F6 Ferriday U.S.A.
142 B3 Ferro r. Brazil
27 B5 Ferro, Capo pt Italy
24 B1 Ferrol Spain
129 G2 Ferron U.S.A.
145 G3 Ferros Brazil
14 C2 Ferzikovo Rus. Fed.
74 D2 Fès Morocco
79 C5 Feshi Zaire
111 K5 Fessenden U.S.A.
124 F4 Festus U.S.A.
76 B4 Fété Bowé Senegal
28 F2 Feteşti Romania
60 B2 Fethiye Turkey
16 G1 Fetlar i. U.K.
113 F2 Feuilles, Rivière aux r. Can.
21 G4 Feurs France
61 D1 Fevzipaşa Turkey
57 G1 Feyzābād Afghanistan
57 D2 Feyẕābād Iran
146 C2 Fiambalá Arg.
76 D4 Fian Ghana
83 H3 Fianarantsoa Madagascar
83 H3 Fianarantsoa div. Madagascar
78 C2 Fianga Chad
80 C3 Fichē Ethiopia
142 D2 Fidalgo r. Brazil
26 C3 Fidenza Italy
110 F4 Field Can.
114 E3 Field Can.
98 C2 Field I. i. Aust.
28 E2 Fieni Romania
29 B4 Fier Albania
98 D3 Fiery Cr. r. Aust.
122 E3 Fife Lake U.S.A.
16 F3 Fife Ness pt U.K.
97 F3 Fifield Aust.
122 B3 Fifield U.S.A.
73 F4 5th Cataract rapids Sudan
20 F4 Figeac France
133 □6 Fig Tree St Kitts-Nevis Caribbean
24 B2 Figueira da Foz Portugal
144 B3 Figueirão Brazil
25 H1 Figueres Spain
75 D2 Figuig Morocco
78 B2 Figuil Cameroon
61 D5 Fiha al 'Ināb reg. Saudi Arabia
80 E2 Fi'i reg. Yemen
86 J6 Fiji country Pac. Oc.
83 D3 Filabusi Zimbabwe
130 J7 Filadelfia Costa Rica
141 D4 Filadélfia Paraguay
19 J4 Fiľakovo Slovakia
76 C4 Filamana Mali
152 B3 Filchner Ice Shelf ice feature Ant.
28 D2 Filiaşi Romania
29 C5 Filiates Greece
29 C6 Filiatra Greece
27 E6 Filicudi, Isola i. Italy
77 E4 Filingué Niger
14 F2 Filinskoye Rus. Fed.
29 C5 Filippiada Greece
11 D4 Filipstad Sweden
10 C3 Fillan Norway
128 C4 Fillmore U.S.A.
129 F2 Fillmore U.S.A.
80 D3 Filtu Ethiopia
152 C3 Fimbulheimen mt. ra. Ant.
152 C3 Fimbulisen ice feature Ant.
26 B3 Finale Ligure Italy
115 H4 Finch Can.
80 C3 Finch'a'ā Hayk' l. Ethiopia
16 E3 Findhorn r. U.K.
61 C1 Fındıkpınarı Turkey
120 B4 Findlay U.S.A.
97 G5 Fingal Aust.
112 E5 Finger Lakes lakes U.S.A.
83 E2 Fingoè Mozambique
60 B2 Finike Turkey
61 A1 Finike Kör. b. Turkey
98 C5 Finke w Aust.
98 C5 Finke Aust.
98 C5 Finke Gorge Nat. Park nat. park. Aust.
96 C2 Finke, Mt h. Aust.
5 H2 Finland country Europe
11 F4 Finland, Gulf of g. Europe
110 D3 Finlay r. Can.
110 D3 Finlay, Mt mt. Can.
97 F3 Finley Aust.
18 E3 Finne ridge Germany
99 F2 Finnigan, Mt h. Aust.
96 C3 Finniss, C. c. Aust.
62 D3 Finnland Finland
10 F1 Finnmark div. Norway
10 E1 Finnsnes Norway
90 □1 Finschhafen P.N.G.
11 D4 Finspång Sweden
19 F3 Finsterwalde Germany
17 D4 Fintona U.K.
76 D3 Fintrou well Mali
99 E4 Finucane Ra. h. Aust.
93 A6 Fiordland National Park nat. park N.Z.
26 B3 Fiorenzuola d'Arda Italy
60 D2 Fırat r. Turkey
128 B3 Firebaugh U.S.A.
111 J2 Firedrake Lake l. Can.
121 G4 Fire Island National Seashore res. U.S.A.
26 C4 Firenze Italy
114 D2 Fire River Can.
77 G3 Firkachi well Niger
146 D3 Firmat Arg.
145 J1 Firmino Alves Brazil
144 C2 Firminópolis Brazil
21 G4 Firminy France
12 E3 Firovo Rus. Fed.
54 B3 Firoza Pakistan
54 D4 Firozabad India
57 F2 Firozkoh reg. Afghanistan
54 D4 Firozpur India
54 C3 Firozpur India
73 F3 1st Cataract rapids Egypt
121 H2 First Connecticut L. l. U.S.A.
99 F2 1st Three Mile Opening chan. Aust.
92 E2 Firth of Thames b. N.Z.
57 C3 Firūzābād Iran
57 D1 Firūzeh Iran
57 C2 Fīrūzkūh Iran
57 D1 Firyuza Turkmenistan
82 B4 Fish w Namibia
150 E10 Fisher Bay b. Ant.
121 F6 Fisherman I. i. U.S.A.
121 H4 Fishers I. i. U.S.A.
111 N2 Fisher Strait chan. Can.
17 E6 Fishguard U.K.
110 E2 Fish Lake l. Can.
122 A2 Fish Lake l. U.S.A.
129 G2 Fish Lake l. U.S.A.
45 □ Fish Ponds lakes Hong Kong
123 F4 Fish Pt pt U.S.A.
152 B3 Fiske, C. c. Ant.
21 F2 Fismes France
24 B1 Fisterra, Cabo c. Spain
121 H3 Fitchburg U.S.A.
16 K2 Fitjar Norway
91 □12 Fito mt. Western Samoa
72 C5 Fitri, Lac l. Chad
140 B2 Fitzcarrald Peru
111 G3 Fitzgerald Can.
119 D6 Fitzgerald U.S.A.
101 B7 Fitzgerald River Nat. Park nat. park Aust.
98 B2 Fitzmaurice r. Aust.
147 C6 Fitz Roy Arg.
99 G4 Fitzroy r. Aust.
100 C3 Fitzroy r. Aust.
147 B6 Fitz Roy, Co mt. Arg.
100 D3 Fitzroy Crossing Aust.
114 E4 Fitzwilliam I. i. Can.
93 A6 Five Fingers Peninsula pen. N.Z.
26 C3 Fivizzano Italy
92 □2 Fizeau, Mt h. Campbell I. N.Z.
28 D1 Fizeşu Gherlii Romania
79 E4 Fizi Zaire
16 K1 Fjell Norway
74 C2 Fkih Ben Salah Morocco
11 C3 Flå Norway
129 G4 Flagstaff U.S.A.
82 A5 Flagstaff Bay b. St Helena Atlantic Ocean
121 H2 Flagstaff Lake l. U.S.A.
112 E2 Flaherty Island i. Can.
122 B3 Flambeau r. U.S.A.
17 G4 Flamborough Head hd U.K.
18 F2 Fläming h. Germany
126 E3 Flaming Gorge Res. l. U.S.A.
82 C5 Flaminksvlei l. R.S.A.
133 □3 Flanagin Town Trin. & Tobago
20 F1 Flandre reg. France
78 C4 Flandria Zaire
16 D2 Flannan Isles is U.K.
10 D2 Flåsjön l. Sweden
122 E4 Flat r. U.S.A.
126 D2 Flathead L. l. U.S.A.
81 □4 Flat I. i. Mauritius
93 E4 Flat Point pt N.Z.
99 F2 Flattery, C. c. Aust.
126 A1 Flattery, C. c. U.S.A.
119 □1 Flatts Village Bermuda
119 □2 Fleeming Pt pt The Bahamas
17 F5 Fleetwood U.K.
121 F4 Fleetwood U.S.A.
11 B4 Flekkefjord Norway
120 E3 Fleming U.S.A.
120 B5 Flemingsburg U.S.A.
11 E4 Flen Sweden
18 D1 Flensburg Germany
20 D2 Flers France
114 E4 Flesherton Can.
111 H2 Fletcher Lake l. Can.
94 □3 Fletcher, Mt h. Macquarie I. Pac. Oc.
123 F3 Fletcher Pond l. U.S.A.
152 B3 Fletcher Prom. hd Ant.
20 E5 Fleurance France
21 F5 Fleury France
20 E3 Fleury-les-Aubrais France
18 B2 Flevoland div. Netherlands
99 E3 Flinders r. Aust.
101 A7 Flinders B. b. Aust.
96 D3 Flinders Chase Nat. Park nat. park Aust.
99 F2 Flinders Grp is Aust.
97 G4 Flinders I. i. Aust.
99 G3 Flinders Passage chan. Aust.
96 D2 Flinders Ranges mt. ra. Aust.
96 D2 Flinders Ranges Nat. Park nat. park Aust.
99 G3 Flinders Reefs reef Coral Sea Islands Terr. Pac. Oc.
111 J4 Flin Flon Can.
17 F5 Flint U.K.
119 C6 Flint r. U.S.A.
123 F4 Flint U.S.A.
123 F4 Flint r. U.S.A.
87 M6 Flint Island i. Kiribati
99 G5 Flinton Aust.
11 D3 Flisa Norway
25 G2 Flix Spain
20 F1 Flixecourt France
18 F3 Flöha Germany
152 A4 Flood Ra. mt. ra. Ant.
122 A2 Floodwood U.S.A.
118 B4 Flora U.S.A.
21 F4 Florac France
99 F3 Flora Reef reef Coral Sea Islands Terr. Pac. Oc.
98 D3 Floraville Aust.
114 D5 Florence Can.
119 C5 Florence U.S.A.
129 G5 Florence U.S.A.
124 D4 Florence U.S.A.
120 C5 Florence U.S.A.
126 A3 Florence U.S.A.
119 E5 Florence U.S.A.
129 G5 Florence Junction U.S.A.
121 K1 Florenceville Can.
138 B3 Florencia Colombia
147 C5 Florentino Ameghino Arg.
147 C5 Florentino Ameghino, Embalse resr Arg.
146 E4 Flores r. Arg.
142 E2 Flores Pernambuco Brazil
142 D2 Flores Piauí Brazil
142 D2 Flores r. Brazil
131 H5 Flores Guatemala
40 E4 Flores i. Indon.
40 D3 Flores Sea sea Indon.
142 E2 Floresta Brazil
15 C3 Floreşti Moldova
142 D2 Floriano Brazil
140 C1 Floriano Peixoto Brazil
143 C6 Florianopolis Brazil
140 D3 Florida Bolivia
146 E3 Florida Uruguay
119 D6 Florida div. U.S.A.
119 D7 Florida Bay b. U.S.A.
119 D7 Florida City U.S.A.
90 □1 Florida Is is Solomon Is.
144 C4 Flórida Paulista Brazil
132 B2 Florida, Straits of str. The Bahamas/U.S.A.
29 C4 Florina Greece
144 C5 Florínia Brazil
11 B3 Florø Norway
113 H3 Flour Lake l. Can.
122 A4 Floyd U.S.A.
120 C6 Floyd U.S.A.
125 C5 Floydada U.S.A.
129 F4 Floyd, Mt mt. U.S.A.
25 F2 Flúmen r. Spain
27 B6 Flumendosa r. Italy
21 J3 Flums Switz.
25 H1 Fluvià r. Spain
90 □1 Fly r. P.N.G.
120 C5 Fly U.S.A.
94 □2 Flying Fish Cove Christmas I. Indian Ocean
90 □5 Foa i. Tonga
26 G4 Foča Bos.-Herz.
29 F5 Foça Turkey
152 □ Foch, I. i. Kerguelen Indian Ocean
28 F2 Focşani Romania
78 D2 Fodé C.A.R.
98 D3 Foelsche r. Aust.
90 □3 Fofoa i. Tonga
51 F4 Fogang China
65 G4 Fogelevo Kazak.
75 E3 Foggâret ez Zoûa Algeria
27 E5 Foggia Italy
76 □ Fogo i. Cape Verde
113 K4 Fogo I. i. Can.
77 F4 Fogolawa Nigeria
18 D1 Föhr i. Germany
20 E5 Foix France
14 B3 Fokino Rus. Fed.
77 E4 Fokku Nigeria
10 D2 Folda chan. Norway
10 D2 Foldereid Norway
10 C2 Foldfjorden chan. Norway
29 E6 Folegandros i. Greece
114 D2 Foleyet Can.
26 D4 Foligno Italy
17 H6 Folkestone U.K.
119 D6 Folkston U.S.A.
11 C3 Folldal Norway
26 C4 Follonica Italy
128 B2 Folsom Lake l. U.S.A.
81 D7 Fomboni Comoros
14 F2 Fominki Rus. Fed.
12 J1 Fominskaya Rus. Fed.
12 J2 Fominskiy Rus. Fed.
12 G3 Fominskoye Rus. Fed.
111 H3 Fond-du-Lac Can.
111 J3 Fond du Lac r. Can.
122 C4 Fond du Lac U.S.A.
81 □4 Fond du Sac Mauritius
24 B2 Fondevila Spain
27 D5 Fondi Italy
76 C5 Fon Going ridge Guinea
27 B5 Fonni Italy
130 H6 Fonseca, G. de b. Central America
20 F2 Fontainebleau France
113 F3 Fontanges Can.
110 E3 Fontas Can.
110 E3 Fontas r. Can.
139 D4 Fonte Boa Brazil
141 E2 Fonte do Pau-d'Agua Brazil
20 D3 Fontenay-le-Comte France
10 N2 Fontur pt Iceland
90 □5 Fonuafo'ou i. Tonga
90 □3 Fonua Unga i. Tonga
19 H5 Fonyód Hungary
115 F4 Foot's Bay Can.
50 E1 Foping China
97 G3 Forbes Aust.
55 F4 Forbesganj India
126 C1 Forbes, Mt mt. Can.
93 A6 Forbes, Mt mt. N.Z.
18 E4 Forchheim Germany
113 G2 Ford r. Can.
122 D2 Ford r. U.S.A.
11 B3 Førde Norway
111 K2 Forde Lake l. Can.
152 A4 Ford Ra. mt. ra. Ant.
97 F2 Fords Bridge Aust.
125 E5 Fordyce U.S.A.
76 B5 Forécariah Guinea
110 D4 Foresight Mtn mt. Can.
114 E5 Forest Can.
125 F5 Forest U.S.A.
120 B4 Forest U.S.A.
121 G3 Forest Dale U.S.A.
128 B2 Foresthill U.S.A.
97 G5 Forestier, C. hd Aust.
122 A3 Forest Lake U.S.A.
119 C5 Forest Park U.S.A.
113 G4 Forestville Can.
21 F2 Forêt d'Othe forest France
16 F3 Forfar U.K.
20 E2 Forges-les-Eaux France
126 A2 Forks U.S.A.
121 J2 Forks, The U.S.A.
120 E4 Forksville U.S.A.
26 D3 Forlì Italy
25 G3 Formentera i. Spain
25 H3 Formentor, Cap de pt Spain
27 D5 Formia Italy
145 F4 Formiga Brazil
146 E2 Formosa Arg.
146 D1 Formosa div. Arg.
144 E1 Formosa Brazil
142 C3 Formosa do R. Prêto Brazil
142 D3 Formoso r. Bahia Brazil
144 B3 Formoso r. Goiás Brazil
145 E1 Formoso Goiás Brazil
144 B4 Formoso Mato Grosso do Sul Brazil
142 C3 Formoso r. Tocantins Brazil
142 C3 Formoso Tocantins Brazil
16 F3 Forres U.K.
97 E4 Forrest Aust.
101 E6 Forrest Aust.
100 D2 Forrest r. Aust.
122 C5 Forrest U.S.A.
125 F5 Forrest City U.S.A.
122 C4 Forreston U.S.A.
100 D2 Forrest River Abor. Reserve res. Aust.
10 E3 Fors Sweden
99 E3 Forsayth Aust.
10 F2 Forsnäs Sweden
11 F3 Forssa Finland
19 G3 Forst Germany
97 H3 Forster Aust.
125 E4 Forsyth U.S.A.
126 F2 Forsyth U.S.A.
115 G2 Forsythe Can.
99 E4 Forsyth Ra. h. Aust.
54 C3 Fort Abbas Pakistan
112 D3 Fort Albany Can.
140 C2 Fortaleza Bolivia
142 E1 Fortaleza Brazil
129 H5 Fort Apache U.S.A.
110 G4 Fort Assiniboine Can.
122 C4 Fort Atkinson U.S.A.
16 E3 Fort Augustus U.K.
82 D5 Fort Beaufort R.S.A.
126 E2 Fort Benton U.S.A.
111 H3 Fort Black Can.
128 A2 Fort Bragg U.S.A.
111 G3 Fort Chipewyan Can.
125 D5 Fort Cobb Res. resr U.S.A.
126 F3 Fort Collins U.S.A.
98 E4 Fort Constantine Aust.
115 G4 Fort-Coulonge Can.
121 F2 Fort Covington U.S.A.
125 C6 Fort Davis U.S.A.
133 □4 Fort-de-France Martinique Caribbean
133 □4 Fort de France, Baie de b. Martinique Caribbean
119 C5 Fort Deposit U.S.A.
124 E3 Fort Dodge U.S.A.
141 E3 Forte Coimbra Brazil
100 B4 Fortescue r. Aust.
124 E1 Fort Frances U.S.A.
112 E3 Fort George Can.
108 F3 Fort Good Hope Can.
16 E3 Forth r. U.K.
16 F3 Forth, Firth of est. U.K.
115 J3 Fortierville Can.
129 E2 Fortification Range mts U.S.A.
141 D4 Fortín Ávalos Sánchez Paraguay
141 D4 Fortín Capitán Demattei Paraguay
141 E4 Fortín Carlos Antonio López Paraguay
141 E4 Fortín Coronel Bogado Paraguay
141 D4 Fortín Coronel Eugenio Garay Paraguay
141 E4 Fortín Falcón Paraguay
141 E3 Fortín Galpón Paraguay
141 E4 Fortín General Caballero Paraguay
141 D4 Fortín General Mendoza Paraguay
141 D4 Fortin Hernandarías Paraguay
141 D4 Fortin Infante Rivarola Paraguay
141 E4 Fortín Juan deZalazar Paraguay
146 D2 Fortín Lavalle Arg.
141 D4 Fortín Linares Paraguay
141 E4 Fortín Madrejón Paraguay
141 E3 Fortín Paredes Bolivia
146 D1 Fortin Pilcomayo Arg.
141 E4 Fortín Presidente Ayala Paraguay
141 D3 Fortín Ravelo Bolivia
141 D3 Fortín Suárez Arana Bolivia
141 D4 Fortin Tte. Juan E. López Paraguay
121 J1 Fort Kent U.S.A.
119 D7 Fort Lauderdale U.S.A.
110 E2 Fort Liard Can.
133 E3 Fort Liberté Haiti
111 G3 Fort Mackay Can.
110 G5 Fort Macleod Can.
122 B5 Fort Madison U.S.A.
122 B3 Fort McCoy U.S.A.
111 G3 Fort McMurray Can.
108 E3 Fort McPherson Can.
126 G3 Fort Morgan U.S.A.
54 B3 Fort Munro Pakistan
119 D7 Fort Myers U.S.A.
110 E3 Fort Nelson r. Can.
110 E3 Fort Nelson Can.
110 D2 Fort Norman Can.
119 C5 Fort Payne U.S.A.
126 F1 Fort Peck U.S.A.
126 F2 Fort Peck Res. resr U.S.A.
119 D7 Fort Pierce U.S.A.
124 C2 Fort Pierre U.S.A.
81 B4 Fort Portal Uganda
110 F2 Fort Providence Can.
111 J4 Fort Qu'Appelle Can.
110 G2 Fort Resolution Can.
83 D2 Fort Rixon Zimbabwe
93 B7 Fortrose N.Z.
16 E3 Fortrose U.K.
128 A2 Fort Ross U.S.A.
112 E3 Fort Rupert Can.
110 E4 Fort St James Can.
110 E3 Fort St John Can.
110 G4 Fort Saskatchewan Can.
125 E4 Fort Scott U.S.A.
112 C2 Fort Severn Can.
110 E2 Fort Simpson Can.
111 G2 Fort Smith Can.
125 E5 Fort Smith U.S.A.
125 C6 Fort Stockton U.S.A.
127 F5 Fort Sumner U.S.A.
126 A3 Fortuna U.S.A.
124 C1 Fortune U.S.A.
113 J4 Fortune B. b. Can.
110 F3 Fort Vermilion Can.
119 C6 Fort Walton Beach U.S.A.
122 E5 Fort Wayne U.S.A.
139 F2 Fort Wellington Guyana
42 A2 Fort White Myanmar
16 E3 Fort William U.K.
125 D5 Fort Worth U.S.A.
93 □1 Forty Fours, The is Chatham Is N.Z.
108 D3 Fort Yukon U.S.A.
10 D2 Forvik Norway
51 F4 Foshan China
76 D5 Foso Ghana
26 A3 Fossano Italy
97 F4 Foster Aust.
110 B3 Foster, Mt mt. Can./U.S.A.
120 B4 Fostoria U.S.A.
83 H3 Fotadrevo Madagascar
78 B1 Fotokol Cameroon
81 □3 Fouce, Pte de la pt Rodrigues I. Mauritius
20 B3 Fouesnant France
78 B4 Fougamou Gabon
20 D2 Fougères France

G

54 C2 Gurais Jammu and Kashmir
77 F5 Gurara r. Nigeria
78 E3 Gurba r. Zaire
48 B5 Gurban Hudag China
48 E4 Gurban Obo China
54 C2 Gurdaspur India
57 E4 Gurdim Iran
29 G5 Güre Turkey
54 D3 Gurgaon India
72 D5 Gurgei, Jebel mt. Sudan
142 D2 Gurgueia r. Brazil
54 B4 Gurha India
139 E2 Guri, Embalse de resr Venezuela
98 C1 Gurig Nat. Park nat. park Aust.
144 D3 Gurinhatã Brazil
13 H7 Gurjaani Georgia
57 D3 Gur Khar Iran
54 E3 Gurla Mandhata mt. China
64 F4 Gurlen Uzbekistan
83 E2 Guro Mozambique
29 G4 Gürsu Turkey
55 G3 Guru China
83 F2 Gurué Mozambique
60 D2 Gürün Turkey
142 B1 Gurupá Brazil
142 C3 Gurupi Brazil
142 C1 Gurupi r. Brazil
54 C4 Guru Sikhar mt. India
83 E2 Guruve Zimbabwe
65 L2 Gur'yevsk Rus. Fed.
11 F5 Gur'yevsk Rus. Fed.
14 E2 Gus' r. Rus. Fed.
77 F4 Gusau Nigeria
11 F5 Gusev Rus. Fed.
49 G5 Gushan China
129 H1 Gusher U.S.A.
57 E2 Gushgy Afghanistan
64 F5 Gushgy Turkmenistan
51 F1 Gushi China
76 D5 Gushiegu Ghana
47 □2 Gushikami Japan
47 □2 Gushikawa Japan
41 A5 Gusi Malaysia
63 M2 Gusikha Rus. Fed.
48 C2 Gusinoozersk Rus. Fed.
48 C2 Gusinoye Ozero Rus. Fed.
48 C2 Gusinoye, Ozero l. Rus. Fed.
14 E2 Gus'-Khrustal'nyy Rus. Fed.
27 B6 Guspini Italy
19 H5 Güssing Austria
109 P3 Gustav Holm, Kap c. Greenland
110 B3 Gustavus U.S.A.
128 B3 Gustine U.S.A.
18 F2 Güstrow Germany
14 E2 Gus'-Zheleznyy Rus. Fed.
50 A2 Gutang China
18 D3 Gütersloh Germany
129 H5 Guthrie U.S.A.
118 C4 Guthrie U.S.A.
125 D5 Guthrie U.S.A.
125 C5 Guthrie U.S.A.
51 G3 Gutian Fujian China
51 G3 Gutian Fujian China
55 F3 Gutsuo China
122 B4 Guttenberg U.S.A.
83 E2 Gutu Zimbabwe
55 G4 Guwahati India
60 E2 Guwēr Iraq
48 D5 Gu Xian China
136 E2 Guyana country S. America
48 D4 Guyang China
20 D4 Guyenne reg. France
125 C4 Guymon U.S.A.
57 C3 Gūyom Iran
97 G2 Guyra Aust.
49 E4 Guyuan China
48 C6 Guyuan China
65 G5 Guzar Uzbekistan
29 F5 Güzelhisar Barajı resr Turkey
61 A1 Güzelsu Turkey
51 E2 Guzhang China
51 G1 Guzhen China
130 D2 Guzmán Mexico
130 D2 Guzmán, L. de l. Mexico
11 F5 Gvardeysk Rus. Fed.
42 A3 Gwa Myanmar
97 G2 Gwabegar Aust.
77 F4 Gwadabawa Nigeria
57 E4 Gwadar Pakistan
57 E4 Gwadar West B. b. Pakistan
77 E4 Gwadu Nigeria
54 D3 Gwaldam India
54 D4 Gwalior India
83 D3 Gwanda Zimbabwe
78 E3 Gwane Zaire
54 A3 Gwash Pakistan
57 E4 Gwatar Bay b. Pakistan
78 E3 Gwawele Zaire
82 D2 Gwayi r. Zimbabwe
19 H2 Gwda r. Poland
42 A1 Gwedaukkon Myanmar
17 C4 Gweebarra Bay b. Rep. of Ire.
17 C4 Gweedore Rep. of Ire.
83 D2 Gweru Zimbabwe
83 D2 Gweru r. Zimbabwe
81 A5 Gweshe Zaire
82 D3 Gweta Botswana
122 D2 Gwinn U.S.A.
77 G4 Gwoza Nigeria
97 G2 Gwydir r. Aust.
55 H3 Gyaca China
50 C1 Gyagartang China
29 F6 Gyali i. Greece
55 F3 Gyangrang China
55 G3 Gyangzê China
50 B1 Gyaring China
55 G3 Gyaring Co l. China
50 B1 Gyaring Hu l. China
29 E6 Gyaros i. Greece
55 H3 Gyarubtang China
62 J2 Gydanskiy Poluostrov pen. Rus. Fed.
55 H3 Gyimda China
55 F3 Gyirong China
55 F3 Gyirong China
50 B2 Gyitang China
50 A1 Gyiza China
109 O3 Gyldenløves Fjord inlet Greenland
99 H5 Gympie Aust.
42 A3 Gyobingauk Myanmar
19 K5 Gyomaendrőd Hungary
19 J5 Gyöngyös Hungary
19 H5 Győr Hungary
111 K4 Gypsumville Can.
113 G2 Gyrfalcon Is i. Can.
29 D6 Gytheio Greece
19 K5 Gyula Hungary
60 E1 Gyumri Armenia
64 E5 Gyzylarbat Turkmenistan
14 B2 Gzhat' r. Rus. Fed.

H

90 □3 Ha'alaufuli Tonga
90 □5 Ha'ano i. Tonga
90 □5 Ha'apai Group is Tonga
10 G3 Haapajärvi Finland
10 G2 Haapavesi Finland
91 □11 Haapiti Fr. Poly. Pac. Oc.
11 F4 Haapsalu Estonia
18 B2 Haarlem Netherlands
18 C3 Haarstrang ridge Germany
93 B5 Haast N.Z.
93 B5 Haast r. N.Z.
98 B4 Haast Bluff Aust.
98 B4 Haasts Bluff Aboriginal Land res. Aust.
90 □4 Ha'atua Tonga
54 A4 Hab r. Pakistan
65 L3 Habahe China
132 B2 Habana Cuba
56 C4 Habarane Sri Lanka
80 E4 Habar Cirir Somalia
81 C4 Habaswein Kenya
73 H4 Ḩabawnāh, W. w Saudi Arabia
110 F3 Habay Can.
59 G7 Habbān Yemen
60 E3 Ḩabbānīyah Iraq
54 A4 Hab Chauki Pakistan
61 C4 Habesor w Israel
55 G4 Habiganj Bangladesh
49 E4 Habirag China
61 C4 Habīs, W. el w Jordan
138 B4 Hacha Colombia
147 B4 Hachado, Pico de pass Arg./Chile
47 G7 Hachijō-jima i. Japan
46 G3 Hachimori Japan
46 H3 Hachinohe Japan
47 G6 Hachiōji Japan
47 G3 Hachiryū Japan
60 G1 Hacı Zeynalabdin Azerbaijan
96 D2 Hack, Mt mt. Aust.
83 E3 Hacufera Mozambique
65 K4 Hadadong China
56 A3 Hadagalli India
47 G6 Hadano Japan
49 H2 Hadayang China
73 G3 Ḩaddā' Saudi Arabia
16 F4 Haddington U.K.
81 □1 Haddon Pt pt Seychelles
53 D10 Haddunmahti Atoll atoll Maldives
77 F4 Hadejia w Nigeria
77 G4 Hadejia Nigeria
61 C3 Hadera Israel
11 C5 Haderslev Denmark
73 H3 Ḩādhah Saudi Arabia
80 □ Hadībоh Socotra Yemen
61 D4 Hādi, J. el mts Jordan
60 C2 Hadım Turkey
108 H2 Hadley Bay b. Can.
46 A6 Hadong S. Korea
11 C4 Hadsund Denmark
15 E1 Hadyach Ukraine
49 H5 Haeju N. Korea
49 H5 Haeju-man b. S. Korea
49 H6 Haenam S. Korea
111 H4 Hafford Can.
60 D2 Hafik Turkey
73 G2 Hafirat al'Aydā Saudi Arabia
61 D4 Hafira, W. w Jordan
54 C2 Hafizabad Pakistan
55 H4 Hāflong India
10 L2 Hafnarfjörður Iceland
57 B3 Haft Gel Iran
10 L2 Hafursfjörður b. Iceland
73 F5 Hag Abdullah Sudan
114 E3 Hagar Can.
56 B3 Hagari r. India
80 C1 Hagar Nish Plateau plat. Eritrea
108 B4 Hagemeister I. i. U.S.A.
18 E2 Hagenow Germany
80 C3 Hāgere Hiywet Ethiopia
80 C3 Hāgere Selam Ethiopia
120 E5 Hagerstown U.S.A.
20 D5 Hagetmau France
11 D3 Hagfors Sweden
46 C6 Hagi Japan
42 D2 Ha Giang Vietnam
47 F6 Hagiwara Japan
17 C5 Hag's Head hd Rep. of Ire.
111 H4 Hague Can.
20 D2 Hague, Cap de la pt France
21 H2 Haguenau France
39 M1 Hahajima-rettō is Japan
49 F5 Hai r. China
81 C5 Hai Tanzania
51 H1 Hai'an China
49 G4 Haicheng China
55 E4 Haidargarh India
42 D2 Hai Dương Vietnam
61 C3 Haifa, B. of b. Israel
51 F4 Haifeng China
51 E4 Haikang China
51 E4 Haikou China
73 H2 Ha'il Saudi Arabia
55 H4 Hailakandi India
49 F2 Hailar China
49 F2 Hailar r. China
115 F3 Haileybury Can.
49 J3 Hailin China
49 H4 Hailong China
49 H3 Hailun China
10 G2 Hailuoto Finland
51 H2 Haimen China
51 E5 Hainan div. China
42 B2 Hai-nang Myanmar
18 B3 Hainaut div. Belgium
76 B5 Haindi Liberia
108 E4 Haines U.S.A.
110 B3 Haines U.S.A.
110 B2 Haines Junction Can.
18 E3 Hainleite ridge Germany
42 D2 Hai Phong Vietnam
49 K3 Haiqing Rus. Fed.
48 B5 Hairag China
48 B4 Hairhan Namag China
51 G3 Haitan Dao i. China
104 L8 Haiti country Caribbean
51 E5 Haitou China
129 G5 Haivana Nakya U.S.A.
128 D3 Haiwee Reservoir U.S.A.
49 F5 Haixing China
73 G4 Haiya Sudan
78 E1 Haiyaf pool Sudan
51 H2 Haiyan China
48 B5 Haiyan China
51 F4 Haiyan China
49 G5 Haiyang China
49 G5 Haiyang Dao i. China
48 C5 Haiyuan China
51 G1 Haizhou Wan b. China
19 K5 Hajdúböszörmény Hungary
19 K5 Hajdúszoboszló Hungary
57 G2 Hajigak P. pass Afghanistan
47 G4 Hajiki-zaki pt Japan
55 F4 Hajipur India
61 D5 Ḩājj Saudi Arabia
80 D1 Ḩajjah Yemen
57 C3 Ḩajjīābād Iran
57 C3 Ḩajjīābād Iran
57 C2 Ḩājjīābād-e Zarrīn Iran
59 J6 Hajmah Oman
19 L2 Hajnówka Poland
48 C3 Hajuu-Us Mongolia
42 A2 Haka Myanmar
80 □ Hakabi Socotra Yemen
127 □2 Hakalau U.S.A.
79 E5 Hakansson, Monts mts Zaire
90 □5 Hakau Fusi reef Tonga
60 E2 Hakkârı Turkey
10 F2 Hakkas Sweden
47 E6 Hakken-zan mt. Japan
46 J1 Hako-dake mt. Japan
46 H3 Hakodate Japan
82 B3 Hakos Mts mts Namibia
82 C4 Hakskeenpan l. R.S.A.
47 F5 Hakui Japan
47 F5 Haku-san vol Japan
47 F5 Haku-san National Park nat. park. Japan
54 B4 Hala Pakistan
61 D1 Ḩalab div. Syria
61 D1 Ḩalab Syria
73 H3 Halabān Saudi Arabia
60 F3 Halabja Iraq
49 H3 Halahai China
73 G3 Halaib Sudan
61 B4 Halâl, G. h. Egypt
61 D5 Ḩālat 'Ammār Saudi Arabia
127 □2 Halawa U.S.A.
61 D2 Halba Lebanon
48 A2 Halban Mongolia
18 E3 Halberstadt Germany
92 E4 Halcombe N.Z.
41 B3 Halcon, Mt mt. Phil.
11 C4 Halden Norway
18 E2 Haldensleben Germany
55 F5 Haldi r. India
55 G5 Haldia India
55 G4 Haldibari India
54 D3 Haldwani India
98 C4 Hale w Aust.
123 F3 Hale U.S.A.
60 D3 Halebiye Syria
127 □1 Haleiwa U.S.A.
76 D5 Half Assini Ghana
60 D2 Halfeti Turkey
93 B7 Halfmoon Bay N.Z.
110 E3 Halfway r. Can.
49 F3 Halhgol Mongolia
73 H4 Ḩalī Saudi Arabia
115 F4 Haliburton Can.
14 A3 Halichy Rus. Fed.
99 F3 Halifax Aust.
113 H5 Halifax Can.
17 G5 Halifax U.K.
120 D6 Halifax U.S.A.
99 F3 Halifax Bay b. Aust.
99 F3 Halifax, Mt mt. Aust.
61 D2 Halīmah mt. Lebanon/Syria
73 H4 Ḩalī, W. w Saudi Arabia
10 E3 Hälla Sweden
11 D4 Halland div. Sweden
109 K3 Hall Beach Can.
18 B3 Halle Belgium
18 E3 Halle Germany
114 D2 Hallebourg Can.
11 D4 Hällefors Sweden
18 F5 Hallein Austria
152 A5 Hallett, C. c. Ant.
152 C3 Halley U.K. Base Ant.
86 G4 Hall Is is Fed. States of Micronesia
10 E2 Hällnäs Sweden
124 D1 Hallock U.S.A.
109 M3 Hall Pen. pen. Can.
100 D2 Hall Pt pt Aust.
11 D4 Hallsberg Sweden
100 D3 Halls Creek Aust.
115 F4 Halls Lake Can.
10 D3 Hallviken Sweden
39 J6 Halmahera i. Indon.
28 D1 Halmeu Romania
11 D4 Halmstad Sweden
56 A1 Halol India
11 C4 Hals Denmark
10 G3 Halsua Finland
17 F4 Haltwhistle U.K.
57 C4 Ḩālūl i. Qatar
40 E4 Halura i. Indon.
54 B5 Halvad India
73 G2 Ḩalwān, J. mt. Saudi Arabia
15 A2 Halych Ukraine
15 E1 Halytsya Ukraine
21 F2 Ham France
46 D6 Hamada Japan
76 D2 Ḩamâda El Ḩaricha desert Mali
57 B2 Hamadān Iran
57 B2 Hamadān div. Iran
72 B2 Ḩamādat Murzuq plat. Libya
74 C3 Hamada Tounassine desert Algeria
74 D2 Hamaguir Algeria
61 D2 Ḩamah div. Syria
61 D2 Ḩamāh Syria
47 □2 Hamahika-jima i. Japan
47 F6 Hamakita Japan
61 D1 Hamam Turkey
46 H2 Hamamasu Japan
47 F6 Hamamatsu Japan
46 K2 Hamanaka-wan b. Japan
47 F6 Hamana-ko l. Japan
11 C3 Hamar Norway
10 D1 Hamarøy Norway
73 F3 Hamāta, Gebel mt. Egypt
46 J1 Hamatonbetsu Japan
56 C5 Hambantota Sri Lanka
119 □3 Ham Bluff pt Virgin Is Caribbean
18 D2 Hamburg Germany
125 F5 Hamburg U.S.A.
120 D3 Hamburg U.S.A.
121 F4 Hamburg U.S.A.
73 H4 Ḩamḑah Saudi Arabia
73 H4 Ḩamdānah Saudi Arabia
121 G4 Hamden U.S.A.
29 F5 Hamdibey Turkey
11 G3 Häme div. Finland
11 G3 Hämeenlinna Finland
101 A5 Hamelin Aust.
101 A5 Hamelin Pool b. Aust.
18 D2 Hameln Germany
100 B4 Hamersley Range mt. ra. Aust.
101 B4 Hamersley Ra. Nat. Park nat. park Aust.
49 H5 Hamhŭng N. Korea
44 F3 Hami China
57 B3 Ḩamīd Iran
73 F3 Hamīd Sudan
60 B2 Hamıdiye Turkey
98 E4 Hamilton w Aust.
98 E4 Hamilton Aust.
96 C1 Hamilton w Aust.
97 F5 Hamilton Aust.
96 E4 Hamilton Aust.
119 □1 Hamilton Bermuda
115 F5 Hamilton Can.
92 E2 Hamilton N.Z.
16 E4 Hamilton U.K.
119 C5 Hamilton U.S.A.
122 B5 Hamilton U.S.A.
126 D2 Hamilton U.S.A.
121 F3 Hamilton U.S.A.
120 A5 Hamilton U.S.A.
128 A2 Hamilton City U.S.A.
94 □3 Hamilton, Mt h. Macquarie I. Pac. Oc.
128 B3 Hamilton, Mt mt. U.S.A.
129 E2 Hamilton, Mt mt. U.S.A.
115 H5 Hamilton Mt h. U.S.A.
11 G3 Hamina Finland
54 D3 Hamirpur India
54 E4 Hamirpur India
113 J3 Hamiton Inlet inlet Can.
122 D3 Hamlin Lake l. U.S.A.
18 C3 Hamm Germany
74 C3 Hammada du Drâa plat. Algeria
27 C7 Hammamet Tunisia
75 G1 Hammamet, Golfe de g. Tunisia
10 E3 Hammarstrand Sweden
18 D3 Hammelburg Germany
10 D3 Hammerdal Sweden
10 F1 Hammerfest Norway
122 D5 Hammond U.S.A.
125 F6 Hammond U.S.A.
126 F2 Hammond U.S.A.
123 E3 Hammond Bay b. U.S.A.
120 E3 Hammondsport U.S.A.
121 F5 Hammonton U.S.A.
115 K4 Ham-Nord Can.
61 D1 Hamon Turkey
93 C6 Hampden N.Z.
113 G4 Hampton Can.
125 E5 Hampton U.S.A.
121 H3 Hampton U.S.A.
121 E6 Hampton U.S.A.
101 D6 Hampton Tableland reg. Aust.
73 E5 Hamrat esh Sheikh Sudan
43 D5 Ham Tân Vietnam
54 D2 Hamta P. pass India
57 D4 Hāmūn-e Jaz Mūrīān salt marsh Iran
57 E3 Hāmūn Helmand marsh Iran
59 L4 Hamun-i-Lora salt flat Pakistan
57 E3 Hāmūn Pu salt l. Afghanistan
127 □2 Hana U.S.A.
82 C3 Hanahai w Botswana/Namibia
73 G2 Ḩanalc Saudi Arabia
127 □2 Hanalei U.S.A.
47 H4 Hanamaki Japan
47 □1 Hanare-iwa is Japan
15 C3 Hâncești Moldova
51 E1 Hancheng China
51 F2 Hanchuan China
120 D5 Hancock U.S.A.
122 C2 Hancock U.S.A.
121 F4 Hancock U.S.A.
48 E5 Handan China
81 C6 Handeni Tanzania
19 J4 Handlová Slovakia
119 □2 Handover Sd chan. The Bahamas
94 □3 Handspike Pt pt Macquarie I. Pac. Oc.
128 C3 Hanford U.S.A.
56 A3 Hangal India
49 H5 Hangang r. S. Korea
91 □16 Hanga Roa Easter I. Chile
48 A3 Hangayn Nuruu mt. ra. Mongolia
48 C4 Hanggin Houqi China
48 D5 Hanggin Qi China
49 F5 Hangu China
54 B2 Hangu Pakistan
28 F1 Hangu Romania
51 F3 Hanguang China
51 H2 Hangzhou China
51 H2 Hangzhou Wan b. China
60 E2 Hani Turkey
57 B4 Ḩanīdh Saudi Arabia
29 G4 Hanife r. Turkey
80 D2 Hanish Kabir i. Eritrea
48 C5 Hanjiaoshui China
11 F4 Hanko Finland
129 G2 Hanksville U.S.A.
54 D2 Hanle India
93 D5 Hanmer Springs N.Z.
99 E2 Hann r. Aust.
100 D3 Hann r. Aust.
111 G4 Hanna Can.
112 D3 Hannah Bay b. Can.
122 B6 Hannibal U.S.A.
73 F4 Hannik well Sudan
15 E2 Hannivka Ukraine
100 D2 Hann, Mt h. Aust.
18 D2 Hannover Germany
11 D5 Hanöbukten b. Sweden
42 D2 Ha Nôi Vietnam
114 E4 Hanover Can.
133 □1 Hanover div. Jamaica
121 G3 Hanover U.S.A.
120 E5 Hanover U.S.A.
152 D4 Hansen Mts mts Ant.
51 E2 Hanshou China
51 F2 Han Shui r. China
54 D3 Hansi India
10 E1 Hansnes Norway
98 C4 Hanson w Aust.
93 □1 Hanson Bay b. Chatham Is N.Z.
96 D2 Hanson, L. salt flat Aust.
120 B6 Hansonville U.S.A.
11 C4 Hanstholm Denmark
49 F3 Han Sum China
65 K4 Hantengri Feng mt. Kyrgyzstan
13 C4 Hantsavichy Belarus
55 E4 Hanumana India
54 C3 Hanumangarh India
59 K4 Hamun-i-Mashkel salt flat Pakistan
48 B2 Hanuy Gol r. Mongolia
51 F2 Hanyang China
50 E1 Hanyin China
50 C2 Hanyuan China
50 D1 Hanzhong China
91 □10 Hao i. Fr. Poly. Pac. Oc.
55 G5 Hāora India
75 F2 Haoud el Hamra Algeria
74 B3 Haouza Western Sahara
10 G2 Haparanda Sweden
55 H4 Hāpoli India
98 D4 Happy Cr. w Aust.
113 H3 Happy Valley-Goose Bay Can.
49 J4 Hapsu N. Korea
54 D3 Hapur India
56 C5 Haputale Sri Lanka
61 C5 Ḩaql Saudi Arabia
80 D1 Ḩaraḑ Yemen
61 C5 Harad, J. el mt. Jordan
12 D4 Haradok Belarus
91 □10 Haraiki i. Fr. Poly. Pac. Oc.
73 H4 Ḩarajā Saudi Arabia
47 H5 Haramachi Japan
54 C2 Haramukh mt. India
54 C3 Harappa Road Pakistan
83 E2 Harare Zimbabwe
80 C1 Harat I. i. Eritrea
48 D3 Har-Ayrag Mongolia
73 F4 Haraza, Jebel mt. Sudan
72 C5 Haraz-Djombo Chad
78 D2 Haraze-Mangueigne Chad
73 G3 Harb reg. Saudi Arabia
76 B5 Harbel Liberia
147 C7 Harberton, Pto Arg.
49 H3 Harbin China
61 C6 Harb, J. mt. Saudi Arabia
54 A3 Harboi Hills mt. ra. Pakistan
123 F4 Harbor Beach U.S.A.
122 E3 Harbor Springs U.S.A.
113 J4 Harbour Breton Can.
147 E7 Harbours, B. of b. Falkland Is.
129 F5 Harcuvar Mts mts U.S.A.
54 D5 Harda Khās India
11 B3 Hardangervidda plat. Norway
11 B3 Hardangervidda Nasjonalpark nat. park. Norway
82 B3 Hardap div. Namibia
82 B3 Hardap Dam Namibia
16 K1 Hardbakke Norway
18 B2 Harderwijk Netherlands
82 B5 Hardeveld mt. ra. R.S.A.
101 B4 Hardey r. Aust.
126 F2 Hardin U.S.A.
111 G4 Hardisty Can.
110 F2 Hardisty Lake l. Can.
54 E4 Hardoi India
121 G2 Hardwick U.S.A.
96 D3 Hardwicke B. b. Aust.
125 F4 Hardy U.S.A.
147 C7 Hardy, Pen. pen. Chile
122 E4 Hardy Reservoir resr U.S.A.
61 C4 Hareidin, W. w Egypt
18 C2 Haren (Ems) Germany
80 D3 Hārer Ethiopia
80 D3 Hārer Wildlife Sanctuary res. Ethiopia
61 C3 Harf el Mreffi mt. Lebanon
121 F4 Harford U.S.A.
49 F2 Hargant China
80 D3 Hargele Ethiopia
80 D3 Hargeysa Somalia
61 C4 Har Harif mt. Israel
48 C5 Harhatan China
44 G4 Har Hu l. China
57 E2 Hari r. Afghanistan/Iran
25 □ Haría Canary Is Spain
80 E1 Harīb Yemen
54 D3 Haridwar India
56 A3 Harihar India
93 C5 Harihari N.Z.
46 E6 Harima-nada b. Japan
55 G5 Haringhat r. Bangladesh
54 C2 Haripur Pakistan
73 H4 Ḩarjab, W. w Saudi Arabia
11 F3 Harjavalta Finland
124 E3 Harlan U.S.A.
120 B6 Harlan U.S.A.
28 F1 Hârlău Romania
126 E1 Harlem U.S.A.
18 B2 Harlingen Netherlands
125 D7 Harlingen U.S.A.
17 H6 Harlow U.K.
126 E2 Harlowtown U.S.A.
60 B2 Harmancık Turkey
61 C3 Har Meron mt. Israel
80 D1 Harmil i. Eritrea
121 J2 Harmony U.S.A.
122 A4 Harmony U.S.A.
61 C4 Har Nafḩa h. Israel
54 A3 Harnai Pakistan
126 B3 Harney Basin basin U.S.A.
126 C3 Harney L. l. U.S.A.
11 E3 Härnösand Sweden
49 F2 Har Nuden China
49 G3 Har Nur China
44 F2 Har Nuur l. Mongolia
25 E1 Haro Spain
76 C6 Harper Liberia
128 D4 Harper Lake l. U.S.A.
120 E5 Harpers Ferry U.S.A.
113 H2 Harp Lake l. Can.
49 F4 Harqin China
49 F4 Harqin Qi China
129 F5 Harquahala Mts mts U.S.A.
73 G2 Ḩarrat al 'Uwayriḑ lava Saudi Arabia
61 D6 Ḩarrat ar Rahāh lava Saudi Arabia
61 D3 Ḩarrat er Rujeila lava Jordan
73 H3 Ḩarrat Ḩaḑan lava Saudi Arabia
73 H2 Ḩarrat Hutaym lava Saudi Arabia
73 G2 Ḩarrat Khaybar lava Saudi Arabia
73 H3 Ḩarrāt Kishb lava Saudi Arabia
73 H3 Ḩarrat Kuramā lava Saudi Arabia
73 H3 Ḩarrāt Nawāşīf lava Saudi Arabia
73 H3 Ḩarrat Rahaţ lava Saudi Arabia
115 F1 Harricana r. Can.
119 C5 Harriman U.S.A.
121 G3 Harriman Reservoir resr U.S.A.
121 F5 Harrington U.S.A.
113 J3 Harrington Harbour Can.
119 □1 Harrington Sound lag. Bermuda
118 B4 Harrisburg U.S.A.
120 E4 Harrisburg U.S.A.
101 B7 Harrismith Aust.
125 E4 Harrison U.S.A.
122 E3 Harrison U.S.A.
108 C2 Harrison Bay b. U.S.A.
120 D5 Harrisonburg U.S.A.
113 J3 Harrison, Cape c. Can.
110 E5 Harrison L. l. Can.
124 E4 Harrisonville U.S.A.
16 D3 Harris, Sound of chan. U.K.
123 F3 Harrisville U.S.A.
121 F2 Harrisville U.S.A.
120 C5 Harrisville U.S.A.
17 G5 Harrogate U.K.
61 C4 Har Saggi mt. Israel
50 B1 Har Sai Shan mt. China
28 E2 Hârseşti Romania
57 A2 Harsin Iran
60 D1 Harşit r. Turkey
28 F2 Hârşova Romania
10 E1 Harstad Norway
122 D4 Hart U.S.A.
49 G4 Hartao China
82 C4 Hartbees w R.S.A.
19 G5 Hartberg Austria
11 B3 Harteigan mt. Norway
121 G4 Hartford U.S.A.
122 D4 Hartford U.S.A.
124 D3 Hartford U.S.A.
122 C4 Hartford U.S.A.
110 E3 Hart Highway Can.
96 D2 Hart, L. salt flat Aust.
113 G4 Hartland Can.
121 J2 Hartland U.S.A.
17 E6 Hartland Point pt U.K.
17 G4 Hartlepool U.K.
125 C5 Hartley U.S.A.
110 D4 Hartley Bay Can.
11 G3 Hartola Finland
110 E4 Hart Ranges mts Can.
119 D5 Hartwell Res. resr U.S.A.
114 D2 Harty Can.
44 F2 Har Us Nuur l. Mongolia
57 E2 Harut w Afghanistan
48 B3 Haruuhin Gol r. Mongolia
122 C4 Harvard U.S.A.
127 F4 Harvard, Mt mt. U.S.A.
101 A7 Harvey Aust.
121 K2 Harvey Can.
122 D2 Harvey U.S.A.
124 C2 Harvey U.S.A.
17 H6 Harwich U.K.
54 C3 Haryana India
61 C4 Hāsā Jordan
60 D4 Ḩaşāh, Wādī al w Jordan
60 F2 Hasan Iran
60 C2 Hasan Daği mts Turkey
57 D4 Ḩasan Langī Iran
56 B2 Hasanparti India
61 C4 Hāsā, W. el w Jordan
60 E4 Ḩasb, Sha`īb w Iraq
55 E5 Hasdo r. India
18 C2 Hase r. Germany
48 C3 Hashaat Mongolia
47 F6 Hashima Japan
57 B2 Hashtgerd Iran
60 G2 Hashtpar Iran
125 D5 Haskell U.S.A.
17 G6 Haslemere U.K.
28 E1 Hăşmaşul Mare mt. Romania
20 D5 Hasparren France
56 B3 Hassan India
129 F5 Hassayampa r. U.S.A.
94 □3 Hasselborough Bay b. Macquarie I. Pac. Oc.
18 B3 Hasselt Belgium
74 B3 Hassi Aridal well Western Sahara
75 F3 Hassi Bedjedjene well Algeria
75 F3 Hassi Bel Guebbour Algeria
74 D3 Hassi Bou Bernous well Algeria
75 F3 Hassi Bourahla well Algeria
74 B4 Hassi Doumas well Western Sahara
75 E2 Hassi el Ahmar well Algeria
75 E3 Hassi el Krenig well Algeria
75 E2 Hassi Fahl well Algeria
75 E3 Hassi Habadra well Algeria
75 E3 Hassi I-n-Belrem well Algeria
75 E3 Hassi Inifel Algeria
75 F3 Hassi Issendjell well Algeria
77 D3 Hâssi Karkabane well Mali
74 D3 Hassi Mdakane well Algeria
75 F2 Hassi Messaoud Algeria
75 F2 Hassi M'Rara well Algeria
75 E3 Hassi Mseggeum well Algeria
75 E2 Hassi Nebka well Algeria
73 H4 Hassis Saudi Arabia
75 F2 Hassi Sebbakh well Algeria
75 F3 Hassi Tabelbalet well Algeria
75 E3 Hassi Teraga well Algeria
75 E3 Hassi Tiguentourine well Algeria
75 F3 Hassi Ti-n Fouchaye well Algeria
11 D4 Hässleholm Sweden
97 F4 Hastings Aust.
133 □9 Hastings Barbados Caribbean
92 F3 Hastings N.Z.
17 H6 Hastings U.K.
122 E4 Hastings U.S.A.
122 A3 Hastings U.S.A.
124 D3 Hastings U.S.A.
72 B2 Ḩasy Haghe well Libya
48 B3 Hatansuudal Mongolia
61 D1 Hatay div. Turkey
60 D2 Hatay Turkey
129 F3 Hatch U.S.A.
98 C4 Hatches Creek Aust.
132 C1 Hatchet Bay The Bahamas
111 J3 Hatchet Lake l. Can.
119 B5 Hatchie r. U.S.A.
28 D2 Haţeg Romania
97 E3 Hatfield Aust.
48 B2 Hatgal Mongolia
54 D4 Hathras India
55 F4 Hatia Nepal
43 D5 Ha Tiên Vietnam
119 □3 Hatillo Puerto Rico
42 D3 Ha Tĩnh Vietnam
55 G4 Hatisār Bhutan
132 □3 Hato Bonaire Netherlands Ant.
133 E3 Hato Mayor Dominican Rep.
46 D6 Hatsukaichi Japan
54 D4 Hatta India
97 E3 Hattah Aust.
119 F5 Hatteras, Cape c. U.S.A.
10 D2 Hattfjelldal Norway
56 C2 Hatti r. India
119 B6 Hattiesburg U.S.A.
19 J5 Hatvan Hungary
80 D3 Haud reg. Ethiopia
11 B4 Hauge Norway
11 B4 Haugesund Norway
92 E3 Hauhungaroa mt. N.Z.
92 E3 Hauhungaroa Ra. mt. ra. N.Z.
10 G2 Haukipudas Finland
11 H3 Haukivesi l. Finland
111 H3 Haultain r. Can.
146 D2 Haumonia Arg.
92 E2 Hauraki Gulf g. N.Z.
93 A7 Hauroko, L. l. N.Z.
91 □11 Hauru, Pte pt Fr. Poly. Pac. Oc.
74 C2 Haut Atlas mt. ra. Morocco
76 B4 Haute-Guinée div. Guinea
78 D2 Haute-Kotto div. C.A.R.
115 H2 Haute-Mauricie, Parc de res. Can.
78 E2 Haute-Mbomou div. C.A.R.
20 E2 Haute-Normandie div. France
113 G4 Hauterive Can.
21 G3 Haut-Folin h. France
121 J3 Haut, Isle au i. U.S.A.
78 B4 Haut-Ogooué div. Gabon
75 D2 Hauts Plateaux plat. Algeria
78 E3 Haut-Zaïre div. Zaire
127 □1 Hauula U.S.A.
19 F4 Hauzenberg Germany
122 B5 Havana U.S.A.
17 G6 Havant U.K.
129 E4 Havasu Lake l. U.S.A.
18 F2 Havel r. Germany
54 C3 Haveli Pakistan
54 C2 Haveliān Pakistan
115 G4 Havelock Can.
93 D4 Havelock N.Z.
119 E5 Havelock U.S.A.
43 A5 Havelock I. i. Andaman and Nicobar Is India
92 F3 Havelock North N.Z.
17 E6 Haverfordwest U.K.
121 H3 Haverhill U.S.A.
56 A3 Haveri India
19 G4 Havlíčkův Brod Czech Rep.
10 G1 Havøysund Norway
29 F5 Havran Turkey
140 B1 Havre Brazil
126 E1 Havre U.S.A.
113 H4 Havre Aubert, Île du i. Can.
121 E5 Havre de Grace U.S.A.
92 □4 Havre Rock i. Kermadec Is N.Z.
113 H3 Havre-St-Pierre Can.
15 G2 Havrylivka Dnipropetrovs'k Ukraine
15 G2 Havrylivka Kharkiv Ukraine
15 B2 Havrylivtsi Ukraine
29 F4 Havsa Turkey
60 C1 Havza Turkey
127 □2 Hawaii i. U.S.A.
150 H4 Hawaiian Islands is Pac. Oc.
150 H4 Hawaiian Ridge Pac. Oc.
127 □2 Hawaii Volcanoes National Park nat. park. U.S.A.
60 F4 Ḩawallī Kuwait
61 B5 Hawashîya, W. w Egypt
93 B6 Hawea, L. l. N.Z.
92 E3 Hawera N.Z.
17 F4 Hawes U.K.
127 □2 Hawi U.S.A.
17 F4 Hawick U.K.
93 B6 Hawkdun Range mt. ra. N.Z.
92 F3 Hawke Bay b. N.Z.
113 J3 Hawke Island i. Can.
96 D2 Hawker Aust.
96 E2 Hawkers Gate Aust.
92 F3 Hawke's Bay div. N.Z.
115 H4 Hawkesbury Can.
129 F3 Hawkins Peak summit U.S.A.
123 F3 Hawks U.S.A.
121 K2 Hawkshaw Can.
99 G5 Hawkwood Aust.
121 F4 Hawley U.S.A.
42 B2 Hawng Luk Myanmar
60 F4 Hawr al 'Awdah l. Iraq
60 E3 Hawr al Ḩabbānīyah l. Iraq
60 F4 Hawr al Ḩammār l. Iraq
60 F4 Hawr al Ḩawīzah l. Iraq
60 E3 Ḩawrān, Wādī w Iraq
60 F3 Hawr as Sa'dīyah l. Iraq
60 F3 Hawr as Suwayqīyah l. Iraq
61 C5 Hawşal h. Saudi Arabia
128 C2 Hawthorne U.S.A.
73 H3 Ḩawzah, Jabal h. Saudi Arabia
97 F3 Hay Aust.
98 D4 Hay w Aust.
110 F2 Hay r. Can.
122 B3 Hay r. U.S.A.
48 B4 Haya China
47 H4 Hayachine-san mt. Japan
46 C7 Hayasui-seto chan. Japan
15 G3 Haychur r. Ukraine
60 F2 Haydarābad Iran
129 G5 Hayden U.S.A.
126 C2 Hayden U.S.A.
111 L3 Hayes r. Can.
109 M2 Hayes Halvø pen. Greenland
48 E3 Haylaastay Mongolia
60 C2 Haymana Turkey
120 E5 Haymarket U.S.A.
98 C4 Hay, Mt mt. Aust.
109 J3 Haynes r. Can.
121 J2 Haynesville U.S.A.
29 F4 Hayrabolu Turkey
80 D1 Ḩayrān Yemen
110 F2 Hay River Can.
124 D4 Hays U.S.A.
80 D2 Ḩays Yemen
15 C2 Haysyn Ukraine
55 H3 Hayutang India
15 C2 Hayvoron Ukraine
128 A3 Hayward U.S.A.
122 B2 Hayward U.S.A.
17 G6 Haywards Heath U.K.
57 F2 Hazarajat reg. Afghanistan
120 B6 Hazard U.S.A.
55 F5 Hazārībāg India
55 E5 Hazaribagh Range h. India
20 F1 Hazebrouck France
110 D3 Hazelton Can.
121 F4 Hazelton U.S.A.
108 G2 Hazen Strait chan. Can.
57 F1 Hazhdanahr reg. Afghanistan
100 E4 Hazlett, L. salt flat Aust.
57 F1 Hazrat Sultan Afghanistan
51 E3 He r. China
98 D4 Headingly Aust.
96 B2 Head of Bight b. Aust.
128 A2 Healdsburg U.S.A.
97 F4 Healesville Aust.
149 J7 Heard Island i. Indian Ocean
125 D6 Hearne U.S.A.
114 D2 Hearst Can.
152 B2 Hearst I. i. Ant.
97 F4 Heathcote Aust.
121 E6 Heathsville U.S.A.
125 D7 Hebbronville U.S.A.
49 E5 Hebei div. China
99 F6 Hebel Aust.
125 E5 Heber Springs U.S.A.
115 K2 Hébertville Can.
48 E6 Hebi China
113 H2 Hebron Can.
61 C4 Hebron West Bank
122 D5 Hebron U.S.A.
124 D3 Hebron U.S.A.
121 G3 Hebron U.S.A.
113 H2 Hebron Fiord inlet Can.
110 C4 Hecate Strait chan. Can.
131 H4 Hecelchakán Mexico
110 C3 Heceta I. i. U.S.A.
50 E3 Hechi China
18 D4 Hechingen Germany
50 D2 Hechuan China
51 E4 Hechun China
93 E4 Hector, Mt mt. N.Z.
133 □1 Hector's River Jamaica
11 D3 Hede Sweden
11 D3 Hedemora Sweden
51 E4 Hede Sk. China
126 C2 He Devil Mt. mt. U.S.A.
11 C3 Hedmark div. Norway
47 □2 Hedo Japan
47 □2 Hedo-misaki c. Japan
122 A5 Hedrick U.S.A.
18 B2 Heerenveen Netherlands
18 B3 Heerlen Netherlands
61 C3 Ḩefa Israel
51 G2 Ḩefei China
51 E2 Hefeng China
49 J3 Hegang China
47 F5 Hegura-jima i. Japan
46 D7 Heguri-jima i. Japan
42 B2 Heho Myanmar
61 C4 Heidan w Jordan
18 D1 Heide Germany
18 D4 Heidelberg Germany
83 D4 Heidelberg R.S.A.
18 E4 Heidenheim an der Brenz Germany
18 D4 Heilbronn Germany
18 E1 Heiligenhafen Germany
45 □ Hei Ling Chau i. Hong Kong
49 H2 Heilong r. China/Rus. Fed.
49 H3 Heilongjiang div. China
48 A5 Heimahe China
10 C3 Heimdal Norway
11 G3 Heinola Finland
43 B4 Heinze Is is Myanmar
49 G4 Heishan China
49 F5 Hejian China
50 D2 Hejiang China
48 D6 Hejin China
65 L4 Hejing China
48 A6 Heka China
10 M2 Hekla vol Iceland
48 B5 Hekou China
50 C4 Hekou China
19 J1 Hel Poland
48 C5 Helan Shan mt. ra. China
133 □6 Helden's Pt pt St Kitts-Nevis Caribbean
55 H4 Helem India
125 F5 Helena U.S.A.
126 E2 Helena U.S.A.
128 D3 Helen, Mt mt. U.S.A.
16 E3 Helensburgh U.K.
18 C1 Helgoland i. Germany
18 D1 Helgoländer Bucht b. Germany
10 L3 Hella Iceland
81 □5 Hell-Bourg Réunion Indian Ocean
57 B3 Helleh r. Iran
10 F1 Helligskogen Norway
25 F3 Hellín Spain
126 C2 Hells Canyon gorge U.S.A.
133 □1 Hellshire Hills h. Jamaica
57 E3 Helmand r. Afghanistan/Iran
18 E3 Helme r. Germany
82 B4 Helmeringhausen Namibia
18 B3 Helmond Netherlands
16 F2 Helmsdale r. U.K.
16 F2 Helmsdale U.K.
18 E2 Helmstedt Germany
83 H2 Helodrano Antongila b. Madagascar
83 H2 Helodrano Mahajamba b. Madagascar
49 J4 Helong China
129 G2 Helper U.S.A.
11 D4 Helsingborg Sweden
11 D4 Helsingør Denmark
11 G3 Helsinki Finland
17 E6 Helston U.K.
145 J2 Helvécia Brazil
17 F4 Helvellyn mt. U.K.
61 A5 Helwân Egypt
128 D5 Hemet U.S.A.
114 C2 Hemlo Can.
120 E3 Hemlock Lake l. U.S.A.
115 J4 Hemmingford Can.
125 D6 Hempstead U.S.A.
11 E4 Hemse Sweden
50 C1 Henan China
51 F1 Henan div. China
92 E1 Hen and Chickens Is is N.Z.
24 E2 Henares r. Castilla - La Mancha Spain
46 G3 Henashi-zaki pt Japan
60 B1 Hendek Turkey
146 D4 Henderson Arg.
118 C4 Henderson U.S.A.
119 E4 Henderson U.S.A.
129 E3 Henderson U.S.A.
121 E3 Henderson U.S.A.
125 E5 Henderson U.S.A.
151 L7 Henderson Island i. Pitcairn Islands Pac. Oc.
119 D5 Hendersonville U.S.A.
119 C4 Hendersonville U.S.A.
57 B3 Hendījān Iran
57 C4 Hendorābī i. Iran
50 B2 Hengduan Shan mt. ra. China
18 C2 Hengelo Overijssel Netherlands
51 G2 Hengfeng China
51 F3 Hengshan China
49 J3 Hengshan China
48 E5 Heng Shan mt. China
48 D5 Hengshan China
49 E5 Hengshui China
51 E4 Heng Xian China
51 F3 Hengyang Hunan China
51 F3 Hengyang Hunan China
15 F3 Heniches'k Ukraine
93 C6 Henley N.Z.
17 G6 Henley-on-Thames U.K.
121 F5 Henlopen, Cape pt U.S.A.
47 □2 Henna Japan
20 C3 Hennebont France
18 C3 Hennef (Sieg) Germany
121 H3 Henniker U.S.A.
125 D5 Henrietta U.S.A.
112 D2 Henrietta Maria, Cape c. Can.
129 G3 Henrieville U.S.A.
122 C5 Henry U.S.A.
152 B3 Henry Ice Rise ice feature Ant.
109 M3 Henry Kater, C. hd Can.
43 A4 Henry Lawrence I. i. Andaman and Nicobar Is India
129 G2 Henry Mts mts U.S.A.
114 E5 Hensall Can.
82 A3 Hentiesbaai Namibia
48 D3 Hentiy div. Mongolia
47 □2 Hentona Japan
97 F3 Henty Aust.
42 A3 Henzada Myanmar
47 □2 Henza-jima i. Japan
111 H4 Hepburn Can.
51 F3 Heping China
51 E4 Hepu China
48 D5 Hequ China
10 N2 Héraðsflói b. Iceland
60 D3 Heraklia Syria
99 G3 Herald Cays atolls Coral Sea Islands Terr. Pac. Oc.
92 □4 Herald Islets is Kermadec Is N.Z.
92 E3 Herangi h. N.Z.
57 E2 Herāt Afghanistan
21 F5 Hérault r. France
73 G4 Herbagat Sudan
99 F3 Herbert r. Aust.
111 H4 Herbert Can.
93 C6 Herbert N.Z.
43 A5 Herbertabad Andaman and Nicobar Is India
98 D4 Herbert Downs Aust.
99 F3 Herberton Aust.
28 B3 Herceg-Novi Yugo.
152 B4 Hercules Dome ice feature Ant.
130 J7 Heredia Costa Rica
17 F5 Hereford U.K.
125 C5 Hereford U.S.A.
91 □10 Héréhérétué i. Fr. Poly. Pac. Oc.
92 D1 Herekino N.Z.
124 D4 Herington U.S.A.
93 B6 Heriot N.Z.
21 J3 Herisau Switz.
152 B3 Heritage Ra. mt. ra. Ant.
121 F3 Herkimer U.S.A.
49 E2 Herlen r. China
48 D3 Herlen Mongolia
18 F5 Hermagor Austria
15 B2 Hermakivka Ukraine
131 E3 Hermanas Mexico
16 G1 Herma Ness hd U.K.
98 C4 Hermannsburg Aust.
82 B5 Hermanus R.S.A.
61 D2 Hermel Lebanon
83 D5 Hermes, Cape c. R.S.A.
97 F2 Hermidale Aust.
25 □ Hermigua Canary Is Spain
126 C2 Hermiston U.S.A.
147 C7 Hermite, Is is Chile
138 B3 Hermosas, Parque Nacional las nat. park Colombia
130 C2 Hermosillo Mexico
19 K4 Hernád r. Hungary
141 F5 Hernandarias Paraguay
25 F1 Hernani Spain
18 C3 Herne Germany
11 C4 Herning Denmark
114 B2 Heron Bay Can.
20 D2 Hérouville-St-Clair France
146 E2 Herradura Arg.
131 E4 Herradura Mexico
24 D3 Herrera del Duque Spain
130 D3 Herreras Mexico
131 J5 Herrero, Pta pt Mexico
97 F5 Herrick Aust.
120 E4 Hershey U.S.A.
17 G6 Hertford U.K.
99 H5 Hervey B. b. Aust.
99 H5 Hervey Bay Aust.
151 J7 Hervey Islands is Cook Is Pac. Oc.
115 J3 Hervey-Jonction Can.
99 F3 Hervey Ra. mt. ra. Aust.
18 F3 Herzberg Brandenburg Germany
61 C3 Herzliyya Israel
18 E4 Herzogenaurach Germany
19 G4 Herzogenburg Austria
20 F1 Hesdin France
42 E2 Heshan China
51 F2 Heshengqia China
48 D6 Heshui China
48 E5 Heshun China
128 D4 Hesperia U.S.A.
110 C2 Hess r. Can.
18 D3 Hessen div. Germany
42 C2 Het r. Laos
128 B3 Hetch Hetchy Aqueduct canal U.S.A.
51 E4 Hetou China
124 C2 Hettinger U.S.A.
18 E3 Hettstedt Germany
20 E2 Hève, Cap de la pt France
19 K5 Heves Hungary
17 F4 Hexham U.K.
51 E3 He Xian China
51 G2 He Xian China
48 B5 Hexibao China
49 F4 Hexigten Qi China
51 E1 Heyang China
57 C3 Ḩeydarābād Iran
57 E3 Ḩeydarābād Iran
80 E3 Heygali well Ethiopia
17 F4 Heysham U.K.
96 E4 Heywood Aust.
122 C5 Heyworth U.S.A.
51 F1 Heze China
50 D3 Hezhang China
50 C1 Hezheng China
50 C1 Hezuozhen China
119 D7 Hialeah U.S.A.
124 E4 Hiawatha U.S.A.
73 H4 Hibata reg. Saudi Arabia
122 A2 Hibbing U.S.A.
97 F5 Hibbs, Pt hd Aust.
100 C2 Hibernia Reef reef Aust.
46 C6 Hibiki-nada b. Japan
119 D5 Hickory U.S.A.
92 G2 Hicks Bay N.Z.
111 K2 Hicks L. l. Can.
120 A4 Hicksville U.S.A.
125 D5 Hico U.S.A.
46 J2 Hidaka Japan
46 J2 Hidaka-sanmyaku mt. ra. Japan
131 F4 Hidalgo div. Mexico
131 F3 Hidalgo Mexico
130 D3 Hidalgo del Parral Mexico
130 C3 Hidalgo, Psa M. resr Mexico
18 F1 Hiddensee i. Germany
99 F3 Hidden Valley Aust.
144 D2 Hidrolândia Brazil
144 D1 Hidrolina Brazil
90 □2 Hienghène Pac. Oc.
46 D6 Higashi-Hiroshima Japan
47 □1 Higashi-iwa is Japan
47 G6 Higashi-izu Japan
47 H4 Higashine Japan
47 □2 Higashi-Onna Japan
47 E6 Higashi-ōsaka Japan
46 B7 Higashi-suidō chan. Japan
121 F3 Higgins Bay U.S.A.
122 E3 Higgins Lake l. U.S.A.
126 B3 High Desert desert U.S.A.
122 C3 High Falls Reservoir resr U.S.A.
92 □3 High I. i. Snares Is N.Z.
122 E3 High I. i. U.S.A.
45 □ High Island Res. resr Hong Kong
122 D4 Highland Park U.S.A.
128 C2 Highland Peak summit U.S.A.
129 E3 Highland Peak summit U.S.A.
110 F3 High Level Can.
82 A5 High Pk h. St Helena Atlantic Ocean
119 E5 High Point U.S.A.
110 F3 High Prairie Can.
110 G4 High River Can.
132 C1 High Rock The Bahamas
111 J3 Highrock Lake l. Can.
97 F5 High Rocky Pt hd Aust.
121 F4 Hightstown U.S.A.
17 G6 High Wycombe U.K.
80 D3 Higlale well Ethiopia
80 E3 Higlokadhacday well Somalia
130 C3 Higüera de Zaragoza Mexico
119 □3 Higuero, Pta pt Puerto Rico
139 D1 Higuerote Venezuela
61 A4 Hihya Egypt
80 E4 Hiiraan div. Somalia
11 F4 Hiiumaa i. Estonia
73 G2 Ḩijāz reg. Saudi Arabia
46 C7 Hikari Japan
129 E3 Hiko U.S.A.
47 F6 Hikone Japan
91 □10 Hikuéru i. Fr. Poly. Pac. Oc.
92 E1 Hikurangi N.Z.
92 G2 Hikurangi mt. N.Z.
92 E2 Hikutaia N.Z.
129 F3 Hildale U.S.A.
18 E3 Hildburghausen Germany
18 D2 Hildesheim Germany
55 G4 Hili Bangladesh
152 B5 Hillary Coast Ant.
124 D4 Hill City U.S.A.
129 H2 Hill Creek r. U.S.A.
11 D5 Hillerød Denmark
99 F3 Hillgrove Aust.
124 D2 Hillsboro U.S.A.
121 H3 Hillsboro U.S.A.
120 B5 Hillsboro U.S.A.
125 D5 Hillsboro U.S.A.
122 B4 Hillsboro U.S.A.
120 C5 Hillsboro U.S.A.
99 G4 Hillsborough, C. c. Aust.
122 E5 Hillsdale U.S.A.
121 G3 Hillsdale U.S.A.
120 E4 Hillsgrove U.S.A.
129 F4 Hillside U.S.A.
114 C2 Hillsport Can.
97 F3 Hillston Aust.
120 C6 Hillsville U.S.A.
16 G1 Hillswick U.K.
127 □2 Hilo U.S.A.
120 E3 Hilton U.S.A.
114 D3 Hilton Beach Can.
119 D5 Hilton Head Island U.S.A.
60 D2 Hilvan Turkey
18 B2 Hilversum Netherlands
54 D3 Himachal Pradesh India
73 H3 Ḩimā Ḑarīyah, J. mt. Saudi Arabia
55 F3 Himalchul mt. Nepal
10 F2 Himanka Finland
29 B4 Himarë Albania
54 C5 Himatnagar India
46 E6 Himeji Japan

I

60 B1 İnegöl Turkey
75 F4 In Ekker Algeria
40 E4 Inerie vol Indon.
28 C1 Ineu Romania
120 B6 Inez U.S.A.
75 G4 In Ezzane well Algeria
131 E5 Infiernillo, L. l. Mexico
24 D1 Infiesto Spain
12 E1 Inga Rus. Fed.
42 A3 Ingabu Myanmar
77 F3 Ingal Niger
122 D3 Ingalls U.S.A.
111 J2 Ingalls Lake l. Can.
128 B2 Ingalls, Mt mt. U.S.A.
65 H1 Ingaly Rus. Fed.
78 C4 Ingende Zaire
146 D1 Ingeniero Guillermo Nueva Juárez Arg.
147 C5 Ingeniero Jacobacci Arg.
25 □ Ingenio Canary Is Spain
114 E5 Ingersoll Can.
48 B2 Ingettolgoy Mongolia
99 F3 Ingham Aust.
109 L2 Inglefield Land reg. Greenland
99 G6 Inglewood Aust.
97 E4 Inglewood Aust.
92 E3 Inglewood N.Z.
48 E2 Ingoda r. Rus. Fed.
18 E4 Ingolstadt Germany
113 H4 Ingonish Can.
55 G4 Ingrāj Bāzār India
60 F2 Ingray Lake l. Can.
140 D4 Ingre Bolivia
152 D5 Ingrid Christensen Coast Ant.
75 F5 I-n-Guezzam Algeria
13 H7 Ingushetiya div. Rus. Fed.
83 F3 Inhambane Mozambique
83 E3 Inhambane div. Mozambique
83 F3 Inhambane, Baia de b. Mozambique
142 E3 Inhambupe Brazil
83 F2 Inhaminga Mozambique
145 G3 Inhapim Brazil
83 F3 Inharrime Mozambique
142 D3 Inhaúmas Brazil
145 H1 Inhobim Brazil
15 E3 Inhul r. Ukraine
15 E3 Inhulets' Ukraine
15 E3 Inhulets' r. Ukraine
144 D2 Inhumas Brazil
25 F3 Iniesta Spain
145 F3 Inimutaba Brazil
139 G3 Inini French Guiana
138 D3 Inírida r. Colombia
17 B5 Inishbofin i. Rep. of Ire.
17 C5 Inishmore i. Rep. of Ire.
17 C4 Inishmurray i. Rep. of Ire.
17 D4 Inishowen pen. Rep. of Ire.
17 D4 Inishtrahull i. Rep. of Ire.
17 B5 Inishturk i. Rep. of Ire.
49 F3 Injgan Sum China
80 C2 Injibara Ethiopia
99 G5 Injune Aust.
99 E3 Inkerman Aust.
57 E1 Inkylap Turkmenistan
93 D5 Inland Kaikoura Range mt. ra. N.Z.
42 B2 Inle, L. l. Myanmar
18 F4 Inn r. Austria/Germany
96 E1 Innamincka Aust.
10 D2 Inndyr Norway
16 E3 Inner Sound chan. U.K.
99 F3 Innisfail Aust.
49 J2 Innokent'yevka Rus. Fed.
46 D6 Innoshima Japan
18 E5 Innsbruck Austria
144 C3 Inocência Brazil
78 C4 Inongo Zaire
76 D3 I-n-Ouchef well Mali
19 J2 Inowrocław Poland
140 C3 Inquisivi Bolivia
75 D3 In Salah Algeria
14 G2 Insar r. Rus. Fed.
14 G3 Insar Rus. Fed.
101 A5 Inscription, C. c. Aust.
42 B3 Insein Myanmar
28 F2 Însurăţei Romania
83 D2 Insuza r. Zimbabwe
62 H3 Inta Rus. Fed.
77 F3 I-n-Tabakat well Niger
77 F2 I-n-Tadéra well Niger
77 E3 I-n-Talak well Mali
77 F3 I-n-Tebezas Mali
77 F3 I-n-Tédéini well Niger
146 D4 Intendente Alvear Arg.
29 F4 İntepe Turkey
124 E1 International Falls U.S.A.
43 A4 Interview I. i. Andaman and Nicobar Is India
146 D2 Intiyaco Arg.
28 F2 Întorsura Buzăului Romania
131 G2 Intracoastal Waterway canal U.S.A.
12 G1 Intsy Rus. Fed.
82 D2 Intundhla Zimbabwe
138 C4 Intutu Peru
47 H6 Inubō-zaki pt Japan
46 C7 Inukai Japan
65 L2 Inukjuak Can.
108 E3 Inuvik Can.
16 E3 Inveraray U.K.
16 F3 Inverbervie U.K.
93 B7 Invercargill N.Z.
97 G2 Inverell Aust.
98 E3 Inverleigh Aust.
113 H4 Inverness Can.
16 E3 Inverness U.K.
119 D6 Inverness U.S.A.
16 F3 Inverurie U.K.
98 B3 Inverway Aust.
43 B4 Investigator Chan. chan. Myanmar
96 C3 Investigator Group is Aust.
96 D3 Investigator Strait chan. Aust.
65 L2 Inya Rus. Fed.
65 K1 Inya r. Rus. Fed.
83 E2 Inyangani mt. Zimbabwe
127 C5 Inyokern U.S.A.
128 C3 Inyo Mts mts U.S.A.
81 B6 Inyonga Tanzania
14 H3 Inza r. Rus. Fed.
14 H3 Inza Rus. Fed.
64 E2 Inzer Rus. Fed.
14 F3 Inzhavino Rus. Fed.
29 C5 Ioannina Greece
39 M2 Iō-Jima i. Japan
125 E4 Iola U.S.A.
65 L2 Iolgo, Khr. mt. ra. Rus. Fed.
79 B7 Iona Angola
16 C4 Iona i. U.K.
79 B7 Iona, Parque Nacional do nat. park Angola
126 C1 Ione U.S.A.
28 E2 Ionești Romania
122 E4 Ionia U.S.A.
68 F2 Ionian Sea g. Greece/Italy
29 B5 Ionioi Nisoi div. Greece
13 H7 Iori r. Georgia
29 E6 Ios i. Greece
122 B5 Iowa r. U.S.A.
122 A4 Iowa div. U.S.A.
122 B5 Iowa City U.S.A.
122 A4 Iowa Falls U.S.A.
144 D2 Ipameri Brazil
145 H3 Ipanema Brazil
142 E2 Ipanema r. Brazil
140 B1 Iparía Peru
145 G2 Ipatinga Brazil
13 G6 Ipatovo Rus. Fed.
144 D5 Ipauçu Brazil
29 C5 Ipeiros div. Greece
19 J4 Ipel' r. Hungary/Slovakia
79 C4 Ipelegeng R.S.A.
138 B3 Ipiales Colombia
142 E3 Ipiaú Brazil
142 E3 Ipirá Brazil
144 C6 Ipiranga Brazil
140 B1 Ipixuna Amazonas Brazil
142 D1 Ipixuna Maranhão Brazil
142 B1 Ipixuna r. Brazil
43 C6 Ipoh Malaysia
142 E2 Ipojuca r. Brazil
144 C2 Iporá Brazil
144 B5 Iporã Brazil
144 D6 Iporanga Brazil
78 D2 Ippy C.A.R.
29 F4 İpsala Turkey
99 H5 Ipswich Aust.
133 □1 Ipswich Jamaica
17 H5 Ipswich U.K.
142 D1 Ipu Brazil
144 D4 Ipuã Brazil
142 D3 Ipueiras Brazil
142 D3 Ipupiara Brazil
109 M3 Iqaluit Can.
141 E2 Iquê r. Brazil
140 B4 Iquique Chile
138 C4 Iquitos Peru
14 F3 Ira r. Rus. Fed.
78 D2 Ira Banda C.A.R.
139 G2 Iracoubo French Guiana
57 E4 Īrafshān reg. Iran
47 F6 Irago-misaki pt Japan
143 B6 Iraí Brazil
29 D4 Irakleia Kentriki Makedonia Greece
29 E6 Irakleia i. Greece
29 E7 Irakleio Greece
142 D3 Iramaia Brazil
59 H3 Iran Asia
60 F2 Īrānshāh Iran
57 E4 Īrānshahr Iran
131 E4 Irapuato Mexico
32 F6 Iraq country Asia
142 E3 Irara Brazil
75 F3 Irarrarene reg. Algeria
121 G2 Irasville U.S.A.
139 G4 Iratapuru r. Brazil
144 C6 Irati Brazil
12 K1 Irayel' Rus. Fed.
60 C3 Irbid Jordan
142 E3 Irecê Brazil
78 C4 Irebu Zaire
119 □1 Ireland Island i. Bermuda
4 E3 Ireland, Republic of country Europe
78 D4 Irema Zaire
139 F3 Ireng r. Brazil
144 B6 Iretama Brazil
64 F3 Irgiz Kazak.
64 F3 Irgiz r. Kazak.
64 D2 Irgiz, B. r. Rus. Fed.
74 C2 Irhil M'Goun mt. Morocco
75 F3 Irhzer Ediessane w Algeria
49 H6 Iri S. Korea
39 L8 Irian Jaya div. Indon.
78 D1 Iriba Chad
41 B4 Iriga Phil.
76 C3 Irîgui reg. Mali/Mauritania
81 B6 Iringa div. Tanzania
81 C6 Iringa Tanzania
56 B4 Irinjalakuda India
142 B1 Iriri r. Brazil
142 B2 Iriri Novo r. Brazil
17 F5 Irish Sea sea Rep. of Ire./U.K.
142 C1 Irituia Brazil
65 H5 Irkeshtam Kyrgyzstan
15 E2 Irkliyiv Ukraine
48 B2 Irkut r. Rus. Fed.
48 C1 Irkutsk Rus. Fed.
48 B1 Irkutsk div. Rus. Fed.
20 B2 Iroise, Mer d' g. France
78 C1 Iro, Lac l. Chad
96 D3 Iron Baron Aust.
114 D3 Iron Bridge Can.
120 E3 Irondequoit U.S.A.
96 D3 Iron Knob Aust.
122 C3 Iron Mountain U.S.A.
129 F3 Iron Mt mt. U.S.A.
99 E2 Iron Range Nat. Park nat. park Aust.
122 C2 Iron River U.S.A.
125 F4 Ironton U.S.A.
120 B5 Ironton U.S.A.
122 B2 Ironwood U.S.A.
115 H4 Iroquois Can.
122 D5 Iroquois r. U.S.A.
114 E2 Iroquois Falls Can.
41 C3 Irosin Phil.
47 G6 Irō-zaki hd Japan
15 D1 Irpin' Ukraine
15 D1 Irpin' r. Ukraine
73 H2 Irq al Maẓhūr sand dunes Saudi Arabia
73 H3 'Irq Subay sand dunes Saudi Arabia
42 A4 Irrawaddy r. China/Myanmar
42 A3 Irrawaddy div. Myanmar
42 A4 Irrawaddy, Mouths of the river mouth Myanmar
15 C1 Irsha r. Ukraine
54 C1 Irshad P. Afghanistan/Pakistan
12 J2 Irta Rus. Fed.
65 H1 Irtysh r. Kazak./Rus. Fed.
65 H2 Irtysh Rus. Fed.
65 J2 Irtyshsk Kazak.
78 E3 Irumu Zaire
25 F1 Irún Spain
140 C3 Irupana Bolivia
17 E4 Irvine U.K.
128 D5 Irvine U.S.A.
120 B6 Irvine U.S.A.
125 D5 Irving U.S.A.
101 A6 Irwin r. Aust.
77 F4 Isa Nigeria
99 G4 Isaac r. Aust.
41 B5 Isabela Phil.
119 □3 Isabela Puerto Rico
133 E2 Isabela, Cabo pt Dominican Rep.
138 □ Isabela, Isla i. Galapagos Is Ecuador
138 □ Isabel, Bahía b. Galapagos Is Ecuador
130 J6 Isabela, Cordillera mt. ra. Nicaragua
122 B2 Isabella U.S.A.
132 B2 Isabela de Sagua Cuba
128 C4 Isabella Lake l. U.S.A.
122 D2 Isabelle, Pt pt U.S.A.
119 □3 Isabel Segunda Puerto Rico
28 G2 Isaccea Romania
10 L2 Ísafjarðardjúp est. Iceland
10 L2 Ísafjörður Iceland
54 D4 Isagarh India
46 C7 Isahaya Japan
78 D4 Isaka Zaire
54 B2 Isa Khel Pakistan
51 G1 Isakogorka Rus. Fed.
14 B2 Isakovo Rus. Fed.
28 D5 Işalniţa Romania
83 H3 Isalo, Parc National de l' nat. park Madagascar
79 D4 Isandja Zaire
18 D4 Isanga Zaire
77 F5 Isanlu Nigeria
18 F4 Isar r. Germany
16 G1 Isbister U.K.
24 D2 Iscar Spain
27 D5 Ischia, Isola d' i. Italy
47 F6 Ise Japan
78 D3 Isengi Zaire
26 C3 Iseo, Lago d' l. Italy
21 G4 Isère r. France
18 C3 Iserlohn Germany
27 E5 Isernia Italy
47 F6 Ise-shima National Park nat. park Japan
65 G1 Iset' r. Rus. Fed.
47 G5 Isetskoye Rus. Fed.
47 F6 Ise-wan b. Japan
77 E5 Iseyin Nigeria
65 G5 Isfana Kyrgyzstan
65 H4 Isfara Tajikistan
139 F3 Isherton Guyana
46 H2 Ishikari-gawa r. Japan
46 H2 Ishikari-wan b. Japan
47 F5 Ishikawa div. Japan
47 □2 Ishikawa Japan
65 G2 Ishim r. Kazak./Rus. Fed.
65 G1 Ishim Rus. Fed.
64 E2 Ishimbay Rus. Fed.
65 H1 Ishimskaya Step' plain Rus. Fed.
65 G2 Ishimskoye Kazak.
47 H4 Ishinomaki Japan
47 H4 Ishinomaki-wan b. Japan
47 G5 Ishioka Japan
46 D7 Ishizuchi-san mt. Japan
65 H5 Ishkoshim Tajikistan
54 C1 Ishkuman Pakistan
14 D1 Ishnya Rus. Fed.
122 D2 Ishpeming U.S.A.
65 G5 Ishtykhan Uzbekistan
55 G4 Ishurdi Bangladesh
140 C3 Isiboro Sécure, Parque Nacional nat. park Bolivia
20 D2 Isigny-sur-Mer France
65 H2 Isil'kul' Rus. Fed.
48 E1 Isinga Rus. Fed.
83 E5 Isipingo R.S.A.
78 E3 Isiro Zaire
99 F5 Isisford Aust.
60 D2 İskenderun Turkey
61 C1 İskenderun Körfezi b. Turkey
60 D1 İskilip Turkey
64 D3 Iskine Kazak.
65 K1 Iskitim Rus. Fed.
14 D2 Iskra Rus. Fed.
15 E2 Iskrivka Kirovohrad Ukraine
15 F2 Iskrivka Poltava Ukraine
28 E3 Iskŭr r. Bulgaria
80 F2 Iskushuban Somalia
110 C3 Iskut Can.
110 C3 Iskut r. Can.
25 G3 Isla Cristina Spain
60 D2 İslahiye Turkey
54 C2 Islamabad Pakistan
54 B4 Islamgarh Pakistan
54 B4 Islamkot Pakistan
119 D7 Islamorada U.S.A.
41 A4 Island Bay b. Phil.
121 J1 Island Falls U.S.A.
111 L4 Island L. l. Can.
96 D2 Island Lagoon salt flat Aust.
111 L4 Island Lake Can.
122 A2 Island Lake l. U.S.A.
128 A1 Island Mountain U.S.A.
126 E2 Island Park U.S.A.
121 H2 Island Pond U.S.A.
93 E1 Islands, Bay of b. N.Z.
16 C4 Islay i. U.K.
20 E4 Isle r. France
120 E6 Isle of Wight U.S.A.
122 C2 Isle Royale National Park nat. park U.S.A.
25 □ Isleta, La pen. Canary Is Spain
133 □3 Islote Pt pt Trinidad Trin. & Tobago
73 F1 Ismâ'ilîya Egypt
60 G1 İsmayıllı Azerbaijan
73 F2 Isna Egypt
13 G1 Isojoki Finland
81 B7 Isoka Zambia
10 G2 Isokylä Finland
10 F3 Isokyrö Finland
26 C3 Isola della Scala Italy
27 F6 Isola di Capo Rizzuto Italy
60 B2 Isparta Turkey
28 F3 Isperikh Bulgaria
54 A3 Ispikan Pakistan
60 E1 İspir Turkey
147 B6 Isquiliac, I. i. Chile
32 E6 Israel country Asia
144 C2 Israelândia Brazil
14 G3 Issa r. Mordoviya Rus. Fed.
12 D3 Issa Rus. Fed.
76 C5 Issia Côte d'Ivoire
139 F2 Issano Guyana
21 F4 Issoire France
20 E3 Issoudun France
21 G5 Is-sur-Tille France
65 J4 Issyk Kazak.
65 J4 Issyk-Kul' div. Kyrgyzstan
60 A1 İstanbul Turkey
29 G4 İstanbul div. Turkey
29 G4 İstanbul Boğazı chan. Turkey
57 B2 İstgāh-e Eznā Iran
91 □11 Isthmus of Taravao isth. Fr. Poly. Pac. Oc.
29 D5 Istiaia Greece
138 B2 Istmina Colombia
60 □ Istok Yugo.
119 D7 Istokpoga, L. l. U.S.A.
26 D3 Istra pen. Croatia
14 C2 Istra Rus. Fed.
21 G5 Istres France
14 C1 Istrinskoye Vdkhr. resr Rus. Fed.
55 G5 Iswaripur Bangladesh
142 E3 Itabaianinha Brazil
145 H4 Itabapoana r. Brazil
145 H4 Itabapoana Brazil
142 D3 Itaberaba Brazil
142 D4 Itaberaí Brazil
145 G3 Itabira Brazil
145 G4 Itabirito Brazil
142 E3 Itaboca Brazil
142 E5 Itaboraí Brazil
145 J1 Itabuna Brazil
142 B2 Itacaiuna r. Brazil
142 C2 Itacajá Brazil
145 F1 Itacarambi Brazil
142 E3 Itacaré Brazil
138 C5 Itacuaí r. Brazil
141 E4 Itacurubí del Rosario Paraguay
142 D3 Itaetê Brazil
142 D2 Itagmirim Brazil
142 D2 Itaguaçu Brazil
145 G5 Itaguaí Brazil
145 G3 Itaguajé Brazil
145 F4 Itaguara Brazil
144 D5 Itaí Brazil
142 D2 Itaim r. Brazil
144 C6 Itaiópolis Brazil
142 A1 Itaituba Brazil
144 C4 Itajá Brazil
143 C6 Itajaí Brazil
143 C6 Itajaí Açú r. Brazil
143 C6 Itajobi Brazil
145 F4 Itajubá Brazil
145 J1 Itaju de Colonia Brazil
145 J1 Itajuípe Brazil
55 E4 Itaki India
4 G4 Italy country Europe
145 G2 Itamarajú Brazil
145 G2 Itamarandiba Brazil
145 H3 Itambacuri r. Brazil
145 H3 Itambacuri Brazil
144 D4 Itambé Brazil
145 G2 Itambé, Pico de mt. Brazil
145 G1 Itamirim Brazil
83 G3 Itampolo Madagascar
55 H4 Itanagar India
42 C3 Itanguari r. Brazil
145 E6 Itanhaém Brazil
145 H2 Itanhandu Brazil
145 H2 Itanhém Brazil
145 H2 Itanhém r. Brazil
145 H2 Itanhomi Brazil
139 G3 Itany r. French Guiana
145 H3 Itaobim Brazil
145 G4 Itaocara Brazil
145 G4 Itapaci Brazil
142 D3 Itapajipe Brazil
142 E3 Itaparica, I. i. Brazil
145 J1 Itapebi Brazil
145 F4 Itapecerica Brazil
145 H4 Itapemirim Brazil
145 H4 Itaperuna Brazil
145 H1 Itapetinga Brazil
144 D5 Itapetininga Brazil
144 D5 Itapeva Brazil
139 F3 Itapi r. Brazil
142 E3 Itapicuru r. Bahia Brazil
142 D1 Itapicuru r. Maranhão Brazil
142 D3 Itapicuru Mirim r. Brazil
142 D1 Itapicuru Mirim Brazil
142 E1 Itapipoca Brazil
142 E3 Itapira Brazil
144 E4 Itapiranga Brazil
139 F4 Itapiranga Brazil
144 C1 Itapirapuã Brazil
144 D4 Itápolis Brazil
144 A5 Itaporã Brazil
144 D5 Itaporanga São Paulo Brazil
144 D1 Itapuranga Goiás Brazil
145 E5 Itaquaquecetuba Brazil
143 A6 Itaqui Brazil
145 F4 Itaquiraí Brazil
144 A6 Itaquyry Paraguay
142 D4 Itarana Brazil
145 H1 Itarantim Brazil
144 D5 Itararé r. Brazil
144 D6 Itararé Brazil
54 D5 Itarsi India
144 D3 Itarumã Brazil
145 E1 Itatá r. Brazil
145 E5 Itatiba Brazil
145 D5 Itatinga Brazil
142 B1 Itatupã Brazil
142 D4 Itaúçu Brazil
142 D2 Itaueira r. Brazil
144 A5 Itaum Brazil
145 F4 Itaúna Brazil
145 J3 Itaúnas r. Brazil
145 J3 Itaúnas Brazil
41 B1 Itbayat i. Phil.
110 G1 Itchen Lake l. Can.
138 B3 Ite Peru
29 D5 Itea Stereá Ellas Greece
78 E4 Itebero Zaire
79 E7 Itezhi-Tezhi Dam Zambia
122 E4 Ithaca U.S.A.
120 E3 Ithaca U.S.A.
29 C5 Ithaki i. Greece
61 D5 Ithil, W. al w Saudi Arabia
61 D4 Ithrîyat, Jebel h. Jordan
78 D3 Itimbiri r. Zaire
145 H2 Itinga Brazil
144 A2 Itiquira Brazil
144 A2 Itiquira r. Brazil
144 E4 Itirapina Brazil
142 D3 Itiúba Brazil
145 E3 Itmurinkol', Oz. l. Kazak.
47 G6 Itō Japan
47 F6 Itoigawa Japan
78 D5 Itoko Zaire
47 □2 Itoman Japan
145 H1 Itororó Brazil
20 F3 Itsa Egypt
82 B5 Ittiri Italy
109 Q2 Ittoqqortoormiit Greenland
144 E5 Itu Brazil
138 B2 Ituango Colombia
145 C5 Ituí r. Brazil
145 B2 Ituiutaba Brazil
145 E2 Itula Zaire
144 D3 Itumbiara Brazil
144 D3 Itumbiara, Barragem resr Brazil
139 F2 Ituni Guyana
142 C2 Itupiranga Brazil
144 D5 Ituporanga Brazil
144 D2 Iturama Brazil
141 E5 Iturbe Paraguay
78 E3 Ituri r. Zaire
49 P1 Iturup, Ostrov i. Rus. Fed.
144 C4 Ituverava Brazil
138 E5 Ituxi r. Brazil
146 E2 Ituzaingo Arg.
18 D2 Itzehoe Germany
138 D3 Iuaretê Brazil
108 A3 Iultin Rus. Fed.
145 H4 Iúna Brazil
145 D3 Iutica Brazil
145 B5 Ivaí r. Brazil
144 C6 Ivaí Brazil
144 C6 Ivaiporã Brazil
83 F3 Ivakoany mt. Madagascar
10 G1 Ivalo Finland
10 G1 Ivalojoki r. Finland
13 C4 Ivanava Belarus
12 F6 Ivanec Croatia
28 B3 Ivangrad Yugo.
97 F1 Ivanhoe Aust.
14 D2 Ivanhoe r. Can.
111 H2 Ivanhoe Lake l. Can.
114 D2 Ivanhoe Lake l. Can.
14 E2 Ivanishchi Rus. Fed.
15 D3 Ivanivka Kherson Ukraine
15 D3 Ivanivka Odesa Ukraine
15 D3 Ivanivtsi Ukraine
15 B2 Ivanjica Yugo.
15 C2 Ivankiv Ukraine
14 C2 Ivan'kovo Rus. Fed.
14 C2 Ivan'kovskoye Vdkhr. resr Rus. Fed.
49 K2 Ivankovtsy Rus. Fed.
15 A2 Ivano-Frankivs'k div. Ukraine
15 C2 Ivano-Frankivs'k Ukraine
15 C2 Ivanopil' Ukraine
14 F1 Ivanovka Rus. Fed.
64 D2 Ivanovka Rus. Fed.
14 F1 Ivanovo div. Rus. Fed.
14 F1 Ivanovo Rus. Fed.
14 E1 Ivanovo Rus. Fed.
14 B4 Ivanovskaya Rus. Fed.
14 D1 Ivanovskoye Rus. Fed.
14 D1 Ivanovskoye Rus. Fed.
129 E4 Ivanpah Lake l. U.S.A.
26 E3 Ivanščica mt. ra. Croatia
13 J4 Ivanteyevka Rus. Fed.
13 E1 Ivanytsya Ukraine
15 C4 Ivatsevichy Belarus
13 F4 Ivaylovgrad Bulgaria
62 H3 Ivdel' Rus. Fed.
14 F5 Iven'ye Rus. Fed.
28 F2 Ivești Galați Romania
28 F1 Ivești Vaslui Romania
78 B4 Ivindo r. Gabon
15 H3 Ivinheima r. Brazil
144 B5 Ivinheima Brazil
109 O3 Ivittuut Greenland
15 G1 Ivnya Rus. Fed.
83 H3 Ivohibe Madagascar
143 C2 Ivolândia Brazil
14 D3 Ivot Rus. Fed.
14 A4 Ivotka r. Ukraine
26 A3 Ivrea Italy
29 F5 İvrindi Turkey
109 L3 Ivujivik Can.
14 F3 Iwaizumi Japan
47 H5 Iwaki Japan
47 H5 Iwaki-san vol Japan
46 D6 Iwakuni Japan
46 H2 Iwamizawa Japan
47 G4 Iwanuma Japan
46 G3 Iwasaki Japan
47 G5 Iwasuge-yama vol Japan
47 F6 Iwata Japan
47 H4 Iwate div. Japan
47 H4 Iwate Japan
47 H4 Iwate-san vol Japan
47 E5 Iwo Nigeria
13 C4 Iwye Belarus
131 F4 Ixmiquilpán Mexico
130 D4 Ixtlán Nayarit Mexico
131 F5 Ixtlán Oaxaca Mexico
46 D7 Iyo Japan
46 D7 Iyomishima Japan
46 D7 Iyo-nada b. Japan
28 E1 Iza r. Romania
18 E1 Izabal, L. de l. Guatemala
131 H6 Izapa Mexico
46 H2 Izari-dake mt. Japan
81 C6 Izazi Tanzania
13 H7 Izberbash Rus. Fed.
14 A2 Izdeshkovo Rus. Fed.
57 B3 Īzeh Iran
77 F3 Izgagane well Niger
54 C2 Izgal Pakistan
62 G4 Izhevsk Rus. Fed.
12 H2 Izhma Rus. Fed.
62 G3 Izhma r. Rus. Fed.
62 G3 Izhma Rus. Fed.
14 C3 Izmalkovo Rus. Fed.
62 G3 Izmayil Ukraine
15 C3 Izmaylovo Rus. Fed.
60 A2 İzmir Turkey
29 F5 İzmir div. Turkey
29 F5 İzmir Körfezi b. Turkey
24 E5 Izmorene Morocco
14 F3 Iznair r. Rus. Fed.
24 E4 Iznalloz Spain
60 B1 İznik Turkey
14 B2 Iznoski Rus. Fed.
13 G6 Izobil'nyy Rus. Fed.
14 C1 Izoplit Rus. Fed.
61 D3 Izra' Syria
29 E4 Iztochni Rodopi mt. ra. Bulgaria
47 G6 Izu-hantō pen. Japan
46 B6 Izuhara Japan
46 C7 Izumi Japan
47 E6 Izumisano Japan
46 D6 Izumo Japan
47 G5 Izumozaki Japan
46 G7 Izu-Shotō is Japan
49 J2 Izvestkovyy Rus. Fed.
15 D2 Izyaslav Ukraine
15 G2 Izyum Ukraine

J

57 D2 Jaba r. Iran
24 E3 Jabalón r. Spain
54 D5 Jabalpur India
73 H4 Jabbārah Fara Is i. Saudi Arabia
98 C2 Jabiru Aust.
60 C3 Jablah Syria
26 F4 Jablanica Bos.-Herz.
28 C3 Jablanica r. Yugo.
19 G3 Jablonec nad Nisou Czech Rep.
19 J2 Jabłonowo Pomorskie Poland
19 J4 Jablunkov Czech Rep.
142 F2 Jaboatão Brazil
144 D4 Jaboticabal Brazil
26 E4 Jabuka i. Croatia
28 D2 Jabukovac Yugo.
40 A2 Jabung, Tg pt Indon.
25 F1 Jaca Spain
147 B5 Jacaf, Can. chan. Chile
145 G1 Jacaraci Brazil
138 F5 Jacaré Brazil
142 D3 Jacaré r. Brazil
139 F5 Jacareacanga Brazil
145 E5 Jacareí Brazil
144 D5 Jacarézinho Brazil
145 G4 Jaceaba Brazil
145 E1 Jacinto Brazil
141 D1 Jaciparaná Brazil
140 D2 Jaciparaná r. Brazil
114 B2 Jackfish Can.
114 G4 Jack Lake l. Can.
121 H2 Jackman U.S.A.
125 D5 Jacksboro U.S.A.
99 G5 Jackson Aust.
125 F5 Jackson U.S.A.
126 G6 Jackson U.S.A.
128 B2 Jackson U.S.A.
120 B6 Jackson U.S.A.
122 E4 Jackson U.S.A.
124 E3 Jackson U.S.A.
125 F5 Jackson U.S.A.
125 F5 Jackson U.S.A.
124 F4 Jackson U.S.A.
120 B5 Jackson U.S.A.
119 B5 Jackson U.S.A.
126 E3 Jackson U.S.A.
93 C5 Jackson, C. c. N.Z.
93 B5 Jackson Bay b. N.Z.
93 B5 Jackson Head hd N.Z.
126 E2 Jackson L. l. U.S.A.
125 E5 Jackson, Lake U.S.A.
122 D3 Jacksonport U.S.A.
125 E5 Jacksonville U.S.A.
119 D6 Jacksonville U.S.A.
122 B6 Jacksonville U.S.A.
119 E5 Jacksonville U.S.A.
125 E6 Jacksonville U.S.A.
119 D6 Jacksonville Beach U.S.A.
133 D3 Jacmel Haiti
130 D3 Jaco Mexico
54 B3 Jacobabad Pakistan
142 D3 Jacobina Brazil
129 F3 Jacob Lake U.S.A.
92 □2 Jacquemart I. i. Campbell I. N.Z.
113 H4 Jacques-Cartier, Détroit de chan. Can.
113 G4 Jacques Cartier, Mt mt. Can.
115 K3 Jacques Cartier, Parc de la res. Can.
113 G4 Jacquet River Can.
144 B3 Jacuba r. Brazil
144 E4 Jacuí Minas Gerais Brazil
143 B6 Jacuí r. Brazil
142 E3 Jacuipe r. Brazil
142 B1 Jacundá r. Brazil
142 B1 Jacundá Brazil
144 E6 Jacupiranga Brazil
138 D1 Jacura Venezuela
142 E1 Jacurici r. Brazil
26 G3 Jadar r. Bos.-Herz.
56 B2 Jadcherla India
57 E4 Jaddi, Ras pt Pakistan
19 F3 Jadovnik mt. Bos.-Herz.
73 F2 Jādū Libya
138 B5 Jaén Peru
25 F4 Jaén Spain
57 B2 Ja'farābād Iran
96 D4 Jaffa, C. c. Aust.
56 C4 Jaffna Sri Lanka
121 G3 Jaffrey U.S.A.
54 D3 Jagadhri India
56 B3 Jagalur India
56 D2 Jagdalpur India
49 H2 Jagdaqi China
82 D4 Jagersfontein R.S.A.
54 D2 Jaggang China
57 D4 Jagin w Iran
28 C2 Jagodina Yugo.
56 B2 Jagtial India
144 E3 Jaguapitã Brazil
146 F3 Jaguarão Brazil
143 B6 Jaguari r. Brazil
144 D6 Jaguariaíva Brazil
142 E2 Jaguaribe Brazil
142 E1 Jaguaribe r. Brazil
143 C6 Jaguaruna Brazil
132 B2 Jagüey Grande Cuba
54 B4 Jahanabad India
54 C4 Jahazpur India
60 F4 Jahmah well Iraq
57 C4 Jahrom Iran
77 F4 Jahun Nigeria
142 D2 Jaicós Brazil
48 B6 Jainca China
54 C4 Jaipur India
55 G4 Jaipurhat Bangladesh
55 E4 Jais India
54 B4 Jaisalmer India
55 F3 Jaisinghnagar India
55 G5 Jaitaran India
56 B1 Jaitgarh mt. India
55 D4 Jaitpur India
55 F4 Jajarkot Nepal
55 D1 Jajarm Iran
26 F3 Jajce Bos.-Herz.
40 A3 Jakarta Indon.
110 C2 Jakes Corner Can.
54 B5 Jakhan India
72 D2 Jakharrah Libya
10 E2 Jäkkvik Sweden
10 F3 Jakobstad Finland
28 C4 Jakupica mts Macedonia
125 C5 Jal U.S.A.
49 G3 Jalaid Qi China
57 G3 Jalālābād Afghanistan
54 D4 Jalalabad India
54 C3 Jalalabad India
65 H4 Jalal-Abad div. Kyrgyzstan
65 H4 Jalal-Abad Kyrgyzstan
55 E4 Jalalpur India
77 G4 Jalam Nigeria
54 C3 Jalandhar India
131 H6 Jalapa Guatemala
131 F5 Jalapa Mexico
130 J6 Jalapa Nicaragua
11 F3 Jalasjärvi Finland
54 D4 Jalaun India
55 G4 Jaldhaka r. Bangladesh
56 B2 Jaldrug India
144 C4 Jales Brazil
55 F5 Jalesar India
55 F5 Jaleshwar India
54 B5 Jalgaon India
56 B5 Jalgaon India
77 G5 Jalingo Nigeria
130 D5 Jalisco div. Mexico
54 C2 Jalkot Pakistan
56 A2 Jalna India
57 E4 Jālo Iran
25 F2 Jalón r. Spain
54 C4 Jalor India
130 D4 Jalostotitlán Mexico
28 B2 Jalovik Yugo.
130 E4 Jalpa Mexico
55 G4 Jalpaiguri India
131 F4 Jalpan Mexico
72 D2 Jālū Libya
60 F3 Jalūlā Iraq
72 D2 Jālū Oasis oasis Libya
57 E2 Jām r. Iran
57 E2 Jām reg. Iran
54 D5 Jamai India
118 L8 Jamaica country Caribbean
132 D3 Jamaica Channel chan. Haiti/Jamaica
57 B2 Jamālābād Iran
54 G4 Jamalpur Bangladesh
55 F4 Jamalpur India
132 □ Jamanota mt. Aruba Caribbean
139 F5 Jamanxim r. Brazil
141 D1 Jamari r. Brazil
138 A4 Jambeli, Can. de chan. Ecuador
40 A2 Jambi Indon.
40 A2 Jambi div. Indon.
99 G5 Jambin Aust.
54 C4 Jambo India
40 A5 Jambongan i. Malaysia
54 C5 Jambusar India
124 D2 James r. U.S.A.
120 D6 James r. U.S.A.
112 D3 James Bay b. Can.
147 B6 James, I. i. Chile
109 Q2 Jameson Land reg. Greenland
93 C6 James Peak mt. N.Z.
98 C5 James Ranges mt. ra. Aust.
152 B2 James Ross I. i. Ant.
84 E5 Jamestown St Helena Atlantic Ocean
96 D3 Jamestown Aust.
124 D2 Jamestown U.S.A.
120 D3 Jamestown U.S.A.
54 C5 Jamkhandi India
56 A2 Jamkhed India
55 E3 Jammalamadugu India
54 C2 Jammu India
54 D1 Jammu and Kashmir terr. Asia
54 B5 Jamnagar India
54 D4 Jamni r. India
40 A3 Jampang Kulon Indon.
54 B3 Jampur Pakistan
11 G3 Jämsä Finland
11 G3 Jämsänkoski Finland
55 F4 Jamshedpur India
77 G5 Jamtari Nigeria
10 D3 Jämtland div. Sweden
55 F4 Jamui India
55 G4 Jamuna r. Bangladesh
80 D4 Janaale Somalia
54 F4 Janakpur Nepal
145 G1 Janaúba Brazil
139 G3 Janaucú, Ilha i. Brazil
144 C2 Jandaia Brazil
144 C5 Jandaia do Sul Brazil
57 C2 Jandaq Iran
25 □ Jandía, Pta de pt Canary Is Spain
54 B2 Jandola Pakistan
78 D3 Jandongi Zaire
97 G5 Jandowae Aust.
142 C3 Janeiro r. Brazil
128 B1 Janesville U.S.A.
122 C4 Janesville U.S.A.
57 D2 Jangal Iran
56 B2 Jangaon India
40 A2 Jang, Tg pt Indon.
54 B4 Jani Khel Pakistan
19 J2 Janikowo Poland
55 F4 Janiópolis Brazil
26 G3 Janja Bos.-Herz.
109 S2 Jan Mayen i. Svalbard Arctic Ocean
60 F3 Jannah Iraq
57 E2 Jannatābād Iran
57 B2 Jannatabad Iran
130 C2 Janos Mexico
19 H5 Jánoshalma Hungary
19 K5 Jánossomorja Hungary
19 L3 Janów Lubelski Poland
19 K3 Janów Podlaski Poland
23 F3 Jantra r. Bulgaria
145 F1 Januária Brazil
54 C4 Jaora India
47 E6 Japan country Asia
47 F4 Japan, Sea of sea Asia
150 E4 Japan Trench sea feature Pac. Oc.
139 D4 Japurá r. Brazil
55 H4 Japvo Mt mt. India
130 L8 Jaqué Panama
60 D2 Jarābulus Syria
145 E4 Jaraguá Brazil
144 D1 Jaraguá do Sul Brazil
128 A2 Jaraguari Brazil
143 C6 Jaraguá, Sa mt. ra. Brazil
24 D3 Jaraicejo Spain
24 D2 Jaraíz de la Vera Spain
60 C3 Jarash Jordan
144 A5 Jarauçu r. Brazil
142 B1 Jardim Brazil
99 E1 Jardine River Nat. Park nat. park Aust.
132 C2 Jardines de la Reina is Cuba
144 D3 Jardinésia Brazil
144 E4 Jardinópolis Brazil
49 E3 Jargalant Mongolia
48 B3 Jargalant Mongolia
48 D3 Jargalant Mongolia
48 E3 Jargalant Mongolia
48 D3 Jargalthaan Mongolia
139 G3 Jari r. Brazil
78 D2 Jarmen Germany
11 E4 Järna Sweden
20 D4 Jarnac France
19 H3 Jarocin Poland
19 G3 Jaroměř Czech Rep.
19 L3 Jarosław Poland
10 D3 Järpen Sweden
57 B3 Jarrāhi w Iran
54 A2 Jartai China
141 D1 Jaru Brazil
48 D2 Jarud Qi China
11 G4 Järvakandi Estonia
11 G3 Järvenpää Finland
151 J6 Jarvis Island i. Pac. Oc.
55 E4 Jarwa India
54 B5 Jasdan India
55 F5 Jashpurnagar India
19 G3 Jasień Poland
81 D5 Jasiired Jasiira Somalia
19 K4 Jasło Poland
19 F1 Jasmund pen. Germany
147 D7 Jason Is is Falkland Is.
152 B2 Jason Pen. pen. Ant.
110 F4 Jasper Can.
119 C5 Jasper U.S.A.
125 E4 Jasper U.S.A.
119 D6 Jasper U.S.A.
118 C4 Jasper U.S.A.
120 E3 Jasper U.S.A.
120 B5 Jasper U.S.A.
125 E6 Jasper U.S.A.
110 F4 Jasper Nat. Park nat. park Can.
60 F3 Jaşşān Iraq
19 J1 Jastarnia Poland
26 E3 Jastrebarsko Croatia
19 J4 Jastrowie Poland
19 J4 Jastrzębie-Zdrój Poland
19 J5 Jászárokszállás Hungary
19 J5 Jászberény Hungary
144 C2 Jataí Brazil
139 F4 Jatapu r. Brazil
54 D4 Jatara India
54 B4 Jath India
54 B4 Jati Pakistan
40 B3 Jatibarang Indon.
40 B3 Jatoi Pakistan
144 D5 Jaú Brazil
145 E4 Jaú r. Brazil
146 E2 Jauaperi r. Brazil
139 E3 Jaua Sarisariñama, Parque Nacional nat. park Venezuela
132 D2 Jauco Cuba
140 A2 Jauja Peru
139 F5 Jauna r. Brazil
20 E3 Jaunay-Clan France
11 G4 Jaunlutriņi Latvia
11 G4 Jaunpiebalga Latvia
55 E4 Jaunpur India
144 B1 Jaú, Parque Nacional do nat. park Brazil
57 E3 Jauri Iran
141 E3 Jauru r. Mato Grosso Brazil
144 A3 Jauru r. Mato Grosso do Sul Brazil
144 A3 Jauru Brazil
54 B3 Javadi Hills mts India
25 F2 Javalambre, Sierra de mt. ra. Spain
57 F2 Javand Afghanistan
149 M4 Java Ridge Indian Ocean
48 E2 Javarthushuu Mongolia
40 B3 Java Sea sea Indon.
25 G3 Jávea Spain
147 B6 Javier, I. i. Chile
28 C3 Javor mts Yugo.
19 J4 Javorie mt. Slovakia
19 J4 Javorníky mts Slovakia
10 F2 Jävre Sweden
40 B4 Jawa i. Indon.
40 A3 Jawa Barat div. Indon.
54 C4 Jawad India
54 C4 Jawai r. India
40 B3 Jawa Tengah div. Indon.
40 C3 Jawa Timur div. Indon.
60 D2 Jawbān Bayk Syria
73 H4 Jawf, W. al w Yemen
56 A2 Jawhar India
80 E4 Jawhar Somalia
19 H3 Jawor Poland
138 B5 Jayanca Peru
55 G4 Jayanti India
39 L7 Jaya, Pk mt. Indon.
39 M7 Jayapura Indon.
54 B4 Jaynagar India
61 D3 Jayrūd Syria
73 H4 Jaza'ir Farasān is Saudi Arabia
57 C4 Jazīreh-ye Forūr i. Iran
57 C4 Jazīreh-ye Sīrrī i. Iran
61 C2 Jbail Lebanon
60 D3 Jdaide Syria
129 E4 Jean U.S.A.
111 E2 Jean Marie River Can.
152 □ Jeanne d'Arc, Presqu'île pen. Kerguelen Indian Ocean
113 G2 Jeannin, Lac l. Can.
57 D3 Jebāl Bārez, Kūh-e mt. ra. Iran
77 E5 Jebba Nigeria
28 C2 Jebel Romania
73 F4 Jebel Abyad Plateau plat. Sudan
24 D5 Jebha Morocco
40 A2 Jebus Indon.
16 F4 Jedburgh U.K.
26 D2 Jedeida Tunisia
19 K3 Jędrzejów Poland
19 L2 Jedwabne Poland
18 E2 Jeetze r. Germany
126 D2 Jefferson r. U.S.A.
120 C4 Jefferson U.S.A.
121 F3 Jefferson U.S.A.
122 C4 Jefferson U.S.A.
124 E4 Jefferson City U.S.A.
128 D2 Jefferson, Mt mt. U.S.A.
126 B2 Jefferson, Mt vol U.S.A.
124 C4 Jeffersonville U.S.A.
82 C5 Jeffrey's Bay R.S.A.
77 F4 Jega Nigeria
61 C4 Jeib, W. el w Israel/Jordan
141 E4 Jejuí Guazú r. Paraguay
11 G4 Jēkabpils Latvia
18 D3 Jelcz-Laskowice Poland
80 D3 Jeldēsa Ethiopia
19 H3 Jelenia Góra Poland
55 G4 Jelep La China
11 F4 Jelgava Latvia
28 C3 Jelica mts Yugo.
121 F5 Jellico U.S.A.
112 B4 Jellicoe Can.
43 D7 Jemaja i. Indon.
40 C4 Jember Indon.
55 H4 Jeminay China
77 F4 Jemma Nigeria
19 L4 Jempang, D. l. Indon.
18 E3 Jena Germany
26 D3 Jendouba Tunisia
61 C3 Jenin West Bank
120 B6 Jenkins U.S.A.
128 A2 Jenner U.S.A.
133 □7 Jennings Antigua Caribbean
125 E6 Jennings U.S.A.
97 G3 Jenolan Caves Aust.
111 K4 Jenpeg Can.
40 B3 Jepara Indon.
97 E3 Jeparit Aust.
142 E3 Jequié Brazil
145 G2 Jequitaí Brazil
145 G2 Jequitaí r. Brazil
145 H2 Jequitinhonha r. Brazil
145 H2 Jequitinhonha Brazil
43 C7 Jerantut Malaysia
75 G2 Jerba, Île de i. Tunisia
80 B3 Jerbar Sudan
133 E3 Jérémie Haiti
142 E3 Jeremoabo Brazil
80 D3 Jerer Shet' w Ethiopia
40 D4 Jereweh Indon.
130 E4 Jerez Mexico
24 C4 Jerez de la Frontera Spain
24 C3 Jerez de los Caballeros Spain
29 C5 Jergucat Albania
99 F4 Jericho Aust.
61 C3 Jericho Israel
97 F3 Jerilderie Aust.
144 C1 Jeroaquara Brazil
126 D3 Jerome U.S.A.
101 B7 Jerramungup Aust.
54 B3 Jerruck Pakistan
17 F7 Jersey i. Channel Is.
121 F4 Jersey City U.S.A.
120 E4 Jersey Shore U.S.A.
118 B4 Jerseyville U.S.A.
142 D2 Jerumenha Brazil
61 C4 Jerusalem Israel/West Bank
98 C4 Jervois Ra. h. Aust.
27 B6 Jerzu Italy
25 E2 Jesenice Slovenia
19 H3 Jeseník Czech Rep.
26 D4 Jesi Italy
18 F3 Jessen Germany
11 C3 Jessheim Norway
55 G5 Jessore Bangladesh
119 D6 Jesup U.S.A.
131 G5 Jesús Carranza Mexico
146 D3 Jesús María Arg.
76 A4 Jeta, Ilha de i. Guinea-Bissau
54 B5 Jetalsar India
124 D4 Jetmore U.S.A.
115 K6 Jewett City U.S.A.
19 K2 Jeziorany Poland
19 K2 Jezioro Dąbie l. Poland
19 K1 Jezioro Dargin l. Poland
19 H1 Jezioro Jamno lag. Poland
19 J2 Jezioro Jeziorak l. Poland
19 J3 Jezioro Jeziorsko l. Poland
19 H1 Jezioro Łebsko lag. Poland
19 K1 Jezioro Mamry l. Poland
19 K2 Jezioro Miedwie l. Poland
19 K2 Jezioro Narie l. Poland
19 K2 Jezioro Śniardwy l. Poland
19 J3 Jezioro Sulejowskie l. Poland
19 K2 Jezioro Zegrzyńskie l. Poland
61 C3 Jezzine Lebanon
55 F5 Jhabua India
54 F4 Jha Jha India
54 C4 Jhajju India
54 A3 Jhal Pakistan
55 G5 Jhalakati Bangladesh
54 D4 Jhalawar India
54 A4 Jhal Jhao Pakistan
54 D4 Jhalrapatan India
54 C3 Jhang Maghiana Pakistan
54 D4 Jhansi India
55 F5 Jharsuguda India
54 B3 Jhatpat Pakistan
54 F4 Jhawani Nepal
54 C3 Jhelum Pakistan
55 G5 Jhenida Bangladesh
57 G4 Jhimpir Pakistan
54 B3 Jhudo Pakistan
55 F4 Jhumritilaiya India
54 C3 Jhunjhunūn India
50 D1 Jiachuan China
51 H2 Jiading China
51 F3 Jiahe China
50 C2 Jiajiang China
51 F3 Jiamusi China
49 H4 Ji'an China
51 F3 Ji'an China
51 F3 Ji'an China
49 F4 Jianchang China
50 B3 Jianchuan China
51 G2 Jiande China
50 D2 Jiang r. China
50 D2 Jiang'an China
50 D2 Jiangbei China
50 C4 Jiangcheng China
51 G3 Jiangchuan China
50 D2 Jiangdu China
51 E4 Jianghong China
50 C3 Jianghua China
51 D2 Jiangjin China
50 E3 Jiangkou China
51 G3 Jiangle China
51 F2 Jiangling China
50 D1 Jiangluozhen China
51 F4 Jiangmen China
51 G2 Jiangshan China
51 G1 Jiangsu div. China
48 C6 Jiangtaibu China
49 G2 Jiangxi div. China
51 E1 Jiang Xian China
51 G2 Jiangxigou China
51 H2 Jiangyin China
51 G3 Jiangyong China
50 C2 Jiangyou China
51 G3 Jianhu China
51 F2 Jianli China
51 G3 Jianning China
51 G3 Jian'ou China
49 F4 Jianping China
49 F4 Jianping China
51 F2 Jianshan China
51 E2 Jianshi China
51 E3 Jianshui China
51 G3 Jianyang China
50 C2 Jianyang China
51 E2 Jiaocheng China
48 E5 Jiaocheng China
49 H4 Jiaohe China
49 F5 Jiaohe China
51 H2 Jiaojiang China
48 D5 Jiaokou China
49 E4 Jiaolai r. China
49 G5 Jiaolai r. China
49 F4 Jiaoling China
49 F6 Jiaonan China
49 G5 Jiao Xian China
49 G5 Jiaozhou Wan b. China
51 F1 Jiaozuo China
51 G1 Jiashan China
51 F2 Jiashan China
51 G1 Jiashan China
48 E5 Jiashi China
51 G1 Jia Xian China
50 D2 Jiaxing China
51 H2 Jiayi China
51 F2 Jiayin China
51 F4 Jiayu China
49 J2 Jiayuguan China
51 G4 Jiazi China
28 D1 Jibou Romania
130 K6 Jicarón, I. i. Panama
18 G3 Jičín Czech Rep.
73 G3 Jiddah Saudi Arabia
59 J6 Jiddat al Ḩarāsīs gravel area Oman
48 B5 Jiehebe China
51 E1 Jiehkkevárri mt. Norway
51 F4 Jieshi China
51 F4 Jieshi Wan b. China
51 F4 Jieshou China
10 G1 Jiešjávri l. Norway
51 F4 Jiexi China
51 F4 Jiexiu China
51 G4 Jieyang China
11 G4 Jieznas Lithuania
77 F4 Jigawa div. Nigeria
101 C4 Jiggalong Aust.
51 C1 Jigzhi China
51 F2 Jihār, W. al w Syria
19 H4 Jihlava r. Czech Rep.
19 H4 Jihlava Czech Rep.
19 G4 Jihočeský div. Czech Rep.
19 H4 Jihomoravský div. Czech Rep.
57 E2 Jija Sarai Afghanistan
75 F1 Jijel Algeria
80 D3 Jijiga Ethiopia
25 F3 Jijona Spain
50 C2 Jiju China
65 J6 Jilganang Kol, S. salt l. China/Jammu and Kashmir
81 D4 Jilib Somalia
49 H4 Jilin China
49 H4 Jilin div. China
49 J4 Jiling China
49 H4 Jilin Hada Ling mt. ra. China
49 G2 Jiliu r. China
25 F2 Jiloca r. Spain
80 C3 Jima Ethiopia
133 E3 Jimani Haiti
28 C2 Jimbolia Romania
50 C2 Jimda China
24 D4 Jimena de la Frontera Spain
130 D3 Jiménez Chihuahua Mexico
131 E2 Jiménez Coahuila Mexico
131 F3 Jiménez Tamaulipas Mexico
77 G5 Jimeta Nigeria
90 □1 Jimi r. P.N.G.
49 G5 Jimo China
44 E3 Jimsar China
121 F4 Jim Thorpe U.S.A.
51 F2 Jin r. China
49 F5 Jinan China
48 B5 Jinchang China
51 F1 Jincheng China
50 C2 Jinchuan China
54 D3 Jind India
97 G4 Jindabyne Aust.
19 G4 Jindřichův Hradec Czech Rep.
48 A5 Jinfosi China
50 E1 Jing r. China
51 G2 Jing'an China
48 D5 Jingbian China
50 D1 Jingchuan China
51 G2 Jingde China
51 G2 Jingdezhen China
50 C3 Jingdong China
51 F3 Jinggangshan China
51 G2 Jinggongqiao China
49 H4 Jinggu China
49 F5 Jinghai China
65 K4 Jinghe China
48 E5 Jingle China
51 F2 Jingmen China
50 D1 Jingning China
49 J4 Jingpo China
49 J4 Jingpo Hu resr China
48 B5 Jingtai China
50 D4 Jingxi China
51 E3 Jing Xian China
49 H4 Jingyu China
48 C5 Jingyuan China
49 G2 Jinhe China
51 G1 Jinhu China
51 G2 Jinhua China
49 F6 Jining China
48 E4 Jining China
80 C3 Jinka Ethiopia
50 C2 Jinkouhe China
49 G4 Jinlingsi China
51 E5 Jinmu Jiao China
50 C3 Jinning China
130 J6 Jinotega Nicaragua
130 J7 Jinotepe Nicaragua
50 C4 Jinping China
51 E3 Jinping China
50 C2 Jinping Shan r. China
51 E3 Jinsha China
50 D3 Jinsha Jiang r. China
51 H2 Jinshan China
51 E2 Jinshi China
48 A5 Jinta China
50 D2 Jintang China
41 B4 Jintotolo i. Phil.
41 B4 Jintotolo Channel chan. Phil.
56 B2 Jintur India
51 G3 Jinxi China
49 G4 Jinxi China
51 G2 Jin Xian China
51 G2 Jinxian China
51 G2 Jinxiang China
51 G1 Jinxiang China
51 H3 Jinyun China
50 C3 Jinyang China
51 H2 Jinzhai China
51 F2 Jinzhai China
49 G4 Jinzhou China
51 F5 Jipe, L. l. Tanzania
138 A4 Jipijapa Ecuador
51 J2 Jiquitaia Brazil
65 H5 Jirgatol Tajikistan
49 F3 Jirin Gol China
57 D3 Jīroft Iran
80 E3 Jirriiban Somalia
48 D6 Jishan China
51 E2 Jishou China
51 F3 Jishui China
60 D3 Jisr ash Shughūr Syria
43 E3 Jitra Malaysia
28 D3 Jiu r. Romania
51 E5 Jiudengkou China
50 C2 Jiuding Shan mt. China
50 D1 Jiufoping China
51 F2 Jiujiang China
51 G2 Jiujiang China
51 F2 Jiuling Shan mt. ra. China
50 C2 Jiulong China
49 G4 Jiumiao China
48 A5 Jiuquan China
50 D3 Jiuxu China
57 E4 Jiwani Pakistan
49 G2 Jiwen China
49 J3 Jixi China
51 G2 Jixi China
49 J3 Jixian China
49 E5 Ji Xian China
51 F1 Ji Xian China
51 F1 Jiyuan China
73 H4 Jīzān Saudi Arabia
73 G2 Jizl w Saudi Arabia
46 D6 Jizō-zaki pt Japan
143 B6 Joaçaba Brazil
142 F3 Joaíma Brazil
76 A4 Joal-Fadiout Senegal
142 F2 João Pessoa Brazil
144 D2 João Pinheiro Brazil
142 E2 Joaquim Felício Brazil
146 D2 Joaquín V. González Arg.
128 C2 Job Peak summit U.S.A.
55 F5 Joda India
54 C4 Jodhpur India
10 H3 Joensuu Finland
47 G5 Jōetsu Japan
83 F2 Jofane Mozambique
110 F4 Joffre, Mt mt. Can.
152 □ Joffre, Presqu'île pen. Kerguelen Indian Ocean
55 F4 Jogbani India
11 G4 Jõgeva Estonia
57 E2 Joghatāy Iran
55 G4 Jogighopa India
54 D3 Jogindarnagar India
114 C1 Jog Lake l. Can.
11 G4 Jõgua Estonia
114 D2 Jogues Can.
47 F5 Jōhana Japan
82 D3 Johannesburg R.S.A.
128 D4 Johannesburg U.S.A.
46 D7 Jōhen Japan
56 C1 Johilla r. India
133 □1 John Crow Mts Jamaica
126 C2 John Day U.S.A.
126 B2 John Day r. U.S.A.
110 F3 John D'Or Prairie Can.
120 D6 John H. Kerr Res. resr U.S.A.
100 E3 John, Mt h. Aust.
16 F2 John o'Groats U.K.
119 D4 Johnson City U.S.A.
147 B5 Johnson, I. i. Chile
110 C2 Johnson's Crossing Can.
133 □7 Johnsons Pt pt Antigua Caribbean
119 D5 Johnston U.S.A.
150 H4 Johnston I. Pac. Oc.
101 C7 Johnston, L. salt flat Aust.
121 F3 Johnstown U.S.A.
120 D4 Johnstown U.S.A.
123 F3 Johnswood U.S.A.
47 H3 Jōhōji Japan
43 C7 Johor div. Malaysia
43 C7 Johor Bahru Malaysia
11 G4 Jõhvi Estonia
21 F3 Joigny France
144 C6 Joinville Brazil
21 G2 Joinville France
152 B2 Joinville I. i. Ant.
10 E2 Jokkmokk Sweden
10 N2 Jökulsá á Brú r. Iceland

10 M2 Jökulsá á Fjöllum r. Iceland
10 N2 Jökulsá í Fljótsdal r. Iceland
60 F2 Jolfa Iran
122 C5 Joliet U.S.A.
115 J3 Joliette Can.
41 B5 Jolo Phil.
41 B5 Jolo i. Phil.
41 B3 Jomalig i. Phil.
40 C3 Jombang Indon.
11 G5 Jonava Lithuania
50 C1 Jonê China
125 F5 Jonesboro U.S.A.
121 K2 Jonesboro U.S.A.
152 A3 Jones Mts mts Ant.
121 K2 Jonesport U.S.A.
94 □2 Jones Pt pt *Christmas I.* Indian Ocean
109 K2 Jones Sound chan. Can.
120 B6 Jonesville U.S.A.
80 B3 Jonglei Sudan
80 B3 Jonglei Canal canal Sudan
55 E5 Jonk r. India
11 D4 Jönköping Sweden
11 D4 Jönköping div. Sweden
115 K2 Jonquière Can.
131 G5 Jonuta Mexico
20 D4 Jonzac France
125 E4 Joplin U.S.A.
121 E5 Joppatowne U.S.A.
54 D4 Jora India
61 C3 Jordan r. Asia
32 E6 Jordan country Asia
126 F2 Jordan U.S.A.
126 E3 Jordan r. U.S.A.
99 F4 Jordan Cr. w Aust.
145 H1 Jordânia Brazil
126 C3 Jordan Valley U.S.A.
143 B6 Jordão r. Brazil
11 D3 Jordet Norway
55 H4 Jorhat India
65 J5 Jor Hu l. China
57 G1 Jorm Afghanistan
10 F2 Jörn Sweden
11 G3 Joroinen Finland
11 B4 Jørpeland Norway
77 F5 Jos Nigeria
41 C5 Jose Abad Santos Phil.
140 C2 José A de Palacios Bolivia
142 B2 José Bispo r. Brazil
141 D2 José Bonifácio *Rondônia* Brazil
144 D4 José Bonifácio *São Paulo* Brazil
131 F5 José Cardel Mexico
147 B5 José de San Martin Arg.
143 A4 Joselândia Brazil
146 F3 José Pedro Varela Uruguay
100 E2 Joseph Bonaparte Gulf g. Aust.
129 G4 Joseph City U.S.A.
113 G3 Joseph, Lac l. Can.
54 D3 Joshimath India
47 G5 Jōshinetsu-kōgen National Park nat. park. Japan
129 E5 Joshua Tree National Monument res. U.S.A.
77 F5 Jos Plateau plat. Nigeria
20 C3 Josselin France
119 □3 Jost Van Dyke I. i. *Virgin Is* Caribbean
82 D4 Jouberton R.S.A.
61 C3 Joûnié Lebanon
115 F2 Joutel Can.
11 G3 Joutsa Finland
11 H3 Joutseno Finland
55 H4 Jowai India
19 L3 Józefów *Zamosć* Poland
74 A5 Jreïda Mauritania
130 E3 Juan Aldama Mexico
49 E6 Juancheng China
126 A1 Juan de Fuca, Str. of chan. U.S.A.
83 G2 Juan de Nova i. Indian Ocean
151 O8 Juan Fernández, Islas is Chile
133 G5 Juangriego Venezuela
138 B5 Juanjuí Peru
10 H3 Juankoski Finland
130 J7 Juan Santamaria airport Costa Rica
131 E3 Juaréz Mexico
130 A1 Juárez, Sierra de mt. ra. Mexico
142 D2 Juàzeiro Brazil
142 E2 Juàzeiro do Norte Brazil
76 C5 Juazohn Liberia
55 E5 Juba India
80 B4 Juba Sudan
80 D4 Jubba r. Somalia
81 D4 Jubbada Dhexe div. Somalia
81 D4 Jubbada Hoose div. Somalia
101 D6 Jubilee L. salt flat Aust.
128 D4 Jubilee Pass pass U.S.A.
74 B3 Juby, Cap pt Morocco
25 F3 Júcar r. Spain
132 C2 Jucaro Cuba
131 F5 Juchatengo Mexico
130 E4 Juchipila Mexico
131 G5 Juchitán Mexico
130 D4 Juchitlán Mexico
144 C1 Juçura Brazil
145 J2 Jucurucu Brazil
145 J2 Jucururu r. Brazil
60 E4 Judaidat al Hamir Iraq
60 E4 Judayyidat 'Ar'ar well Iraq
19 G5 Judenburg Austria
11 C5 Juelsminde Denmark
145 J2 Juerana Brazil
48 D5 Juh China
73 G2 Juhaynah reg. Saudi Arabia
49 G4 Juhua Dao i. China
130 J6 Juigalpa Nicaragua
141 E2 Juina r. Brazil
141 E2 Juinamirim r. Brazil
18 C2 Juist i. Germany
145 G4 Juiz de Fora Brazil
146 C1 Jujuy div. Arg.
140 C4 Julaca Bolivia
126 G3 Julesburg U.S.A.
140 C3 Juli Peru
140 B3 Juliaca Peru
99 E4 Julia Cr. r. Aust.
99 E4 Julia Cr. Aust.
139 F3 Juliana Top summit Surinam
26 D2 Julijske Alpe mts Slovenia
146 D4 Julio, 9 de Arg.
98 D4 Julius, Lake l. Aust.
20 D2 Jullouville France
50 B1 Jumanggoin China
138 B5 Jumbilla Peru
25 F3 Jumilla Spain
55 E3 Jumla Nepal
61 C4 Jum Suwwāna mt. Jordan
54 B5 Junagadh India
56 C2 Junagarh India
51 G1 Junan China
49 F3 Jun Bulen China
146 B3 Juncal mt. Chile
147 D5 Juncal, L. l. Arg.
119 □3 Juncos Puerto Rico
125 D6 Junction U.S.A.
127 D4 Junction U.S.A.
98 C1 Junction B. b. Aust.
124 D4 Junction City U.S.A.
99 E5 Jundah Aust.
145 E5 Jundiaí Brazil
110 C3 Juneau U.S.A.
61 C3 Jūn el Khudr b. Lebanon
65 L3 Junggar Pendi basin China
54 A4 Jungshahi Pakistan
80 B2 Junguls Sudan
120 E4 Juniata r. U.S.A.
146 D3 Junín Arg.
140 A2 Junín Peru
147 B4 Junín de los Andes Arg.
121 K1 Juniper Can.
128 B3 Junipero Serro Peak summit U.S.A.
47 H3 Jūnisho reg. Japan
50 D2 Junlian China
56 A2 Junnar India
10 E3 Junsele Sweden
51 G2 Junshan Hu l. China
126 C3 Juntura U.S.A.
51 E1 Jun Xian China
50 B1 Ju'nyunggoin China
11 G4 Juodupe Lithuania
145 H3 Juparanã, Lagoa l. Brazil
144 C4 Jupiá Brazil
144 E6 Juquiá r. Brazil
144 E6 Juquiá Brazil
78 E2 Jur r. Sudan
16 E4 Jura i. U.K.
142 D3 Jurací Brazil
138 B2 Juradó Colombia
145 G2 Juramento Brazil
16 E4 Jura, Sound of chan. U.K.
11 F5 Jurbarkas Lithuania
11 F5 Jurbarkas Lithuania
60 C4 Jurf ed Darāwīsh Jordan
49 G3 Jurh China
49 G3 Jurhe China
55 G2 Jurhen Ul Shan mt. ra. China
28 G2 Jurilovca Romania
142 A1 Juriti Velho Brazil
11 F4 Jūrmala Latvia
10 G2 Jurmu Finland
51 G2 Jurong China
43 □ Jurong Singapore
139 D4 Juruá Brazil
138 D5 Juruá r. Brazil
138 C5 Juruá Mirim r. Brazil
141 E1 Juruena r. Brazil
142 B3 Juruna r. Brazil
142 A1 Juruti Brazil
11 F3 Jurva Finland
46 H3 Jūsan-ko l. Japan
133 G5 Jusepín Venezuela
61 D2 Jūsīyah Syria
146 C3 Justo Daract Arg.
138 D5 Jutaí Brazil
138 D5 Jutaí r. Brazil
142 B1 Jutai, Sa do h. Brazil
18 F3 Jüterbog Germany
144 A5 Juti Brazil
131 H6 Jutiapa Guatemala
130 J6 Juticalpa Honduras
10 E2 Jutis Sweden
10 H3 Juuka Finland
11 G3 Juva Finland
132 B2 Juventud, Isla de la i. Cuba
57 E3 Juwain Afghanistan
40 B3 Juwana Indon.
49 F6 Ju Xian China
48 B4 Juyan China
51 G1 Juye China
57 D2 Jūymand Iran
57 C3 Jūyom Iran
82 C3 Jwaneng Botswana
11 G3 Jyväskylä Finland
11 G3 Jyväskylän mlk Finland

K

54 D2 K2 mt. China/Jammu and Kashmir
77 E4 Ka r. Nigeria
49 H5 Ka i. N. Korea
64 E5 Kaakhka Turkmenistan
127 □1 Kaala mt. U.S.A.
90 □2 Kaala-Gomen Pac. Oc.
81 D5 Kaambooni Kenya
11 F3 Kaarina Finland
76 C4 Kaarta reg. Mali
10 H3 Kaavi Finland
39 H8 Kabaena i. Indon.
64 F5 Kabakly Turkmenistan
76 B5 Kabala Sierra Leone
81 A5 Kabale Uganda
79 E5 Kabalo Zaire
79 E5 Kabamba, Lac l. Zaire
79 E4 Kabambare Zaire
79 D6 Kabangu Zaire
48 C2 Kabansk Rus. Fed.
90 □7 Kabara i. Fiji
13 G7 Kabardino-Balkariya div. Rus. Fed.
78 E4 Kabare Zaire
46 B7 Kaba-shima i. Japan
10 F2 Kåbdalis Sweden
46 D6 Kabe Japan
114 C2 Kabenung Lake l. Can.
75 E3 Kabertene Algeria
114 C2 Kabinakagami r. Can.
114 C2 Kabinakagami Lake l. Can.
79 D5 Kabinda Zaire
78 C2 Kabo C.A.R.
79 D6 Kabompo r. Zambia
79 D6 Kabompo Zambia
40 B1 Kabong Malaysia
79 E5 Kabongo Zaire
77 E5 Kabou Togo
57 E2 Kabūdeh Iran
57 D1 Kabūd Gonbad Iran
57 B2 Kabūd Rāhang Iran
41 B2 Kabugao Phil.
57 G2 Kabul r. Afghanistan
57 G2 Kābul Afghanistan
79 E6 Kabunda Zaire
40 D4 Kabunduk Indon.
41 C6 Kaburuang i. Indon.
73 F4 Kabushiya Sudan
79 E6 Kabwe Zambia
79 E5 Kabwe, Lac l. Zaire
64 F2 Kabyrga r. Kazak.
28 C3 Kačanik Yugo.
57 E3 Kacha Kuh mt. ra. Iran/Pakistan
13 H5 Kachalinskaya Rus. Fed.
54 B5 Kachchh, Gulf of g. India
54 A3 Kachh Pakistan
77 F5 Kachia Nigeria
42 B1 Kachin State div. Myanmar
81 B5 Kachira, Lake l. Uganda
65 J2 Kachiry Kazak.
44 J1 Kachug Rus. Fed.
60 E1 Kackar Daği mt. Turkey
14 H3 Kadada r. Rus. Fed.
42 B3 Kadaingti Myanmar
56 B4 Kadaiyanallur India
80 B4 Kadam mt. Uganda
57 F3 Kadanai r. Afghanistan/Pakistan
43 B4 Kadan Kyun i. Myanmar
40 C3 Kadapongan i. Indon.
54 D4 Kadaura India
90 □7 Kadavu i. Fiji
90 □8 Kadavu Passage chan. Fiji
49 F2 Kadaya Rus. Fed.
78 C3 Kadéï r. C.A.R.
47 □2 Kadena Japan
60 F3 Kādhimain Iraq
54 C5 Kadi India
60 B1 Kadıköy Turkey
96 D3 Kadina Aust.
60 C2 Kadınhanı Turkey
76 C4 Kadiolo Mali
76 B4 Kadiondola, Mt mt. Guinea
56 B3 Kadiri India
60 D2 Kadirli Turkey
77 E5 Kadjebi Ghana
53 D8 Kadmat i. India
12 G3 Kadnikov Rus. Fed.
124 C3 Kadoka U.S.A.
14 F2 Kadom Rus. Fed.
83 D2 Kadoma Zimbabwe
42 A4 Kadonkani Myanmar
14 G2 Kadoshkino Rus. Fed.
42 B1 Kadu Myanmar
78 E1 Kadugli Sudan
77 F4 Kaduna div. Nigeria
77 F4 Kaduna Nigeria
77 F5 Kaduna r. Nigeria
50 B2 Kadusam mt. China
12 F3 Kaduy Rus. Fed.
56 A2 Kadwa r. India
14 H2 Kadyshevo Rus. Fed.
12 G3 Kadyy Rus. Fed.
49 H5 Kaechon N. Korea
74 B5 Kaédi Mauritania
78 B1 Kaélé Cameroon
127 □1 Kaena Pt pt U.S.A.
92 D1 Kaeo N.Z.
49 H5 Kaesŏng N. Korea
73 G1 Kāf Saudi Arabia
79 D5 Kafakumba Zaire
77 F5 Kafanchan Nigeria
77 G4 Kaffin-Hausa Nigeria
76 A4 Kaffrine Senegal
78 D2 Kafia Kingi Sudan
61 D2 Kafr Buhum Syria
73 F1 Kafr el Sheik Egypt
61 A4 Kafr Sa'd Egypt
80 B4 Kafu r. Uganda
79 E7 Kafue r. Zambia
79 E7 Kafue Zambia
79 E6 Kafue National Park nat. park Zambia
47 F5 Kaga Japan
78 C2 Kaga Bandoro C.A.R.
54 C2 Kagan Pakistan
64 F5 Kagan Uzbekistan
50 C1 Kagang China
77 F5 Kagarko Nigeria
46 E6 Kagawa div. Japan
114 D4 Kagawong Can.
10 F2 Kåge Sweden
81 B5 Kagera div. Tanzania
114 B2 Kagiano Lake l. Can.
60 E1 Kağızman Turkey
73 F5 Kagmar Sudan
77 F5 Kagoro Nigeria
46 C8 Kagoshima Japan
46 C8 Kagoshima div. Japan
46 C8 Kagoshima-wan b. Japan
48 A2 Kagzhirba Rus. Fed.
57 B2 Kahak Iran
61 C6 Kahala, W. al w Saudi Arabia
127 □1 Kahaluu U.S.A.
81 B5 Kahama Tanzania
54 B3 Kahan Pakistan
127 □1 Kahana U.S.A.
15 D2 Kaharlyk Ukraine
82 A3 Kahawero waterhole Namibia
40 C2 Kahayan r. Indon.
79 C5 Kahemba Zaire
93 A6 Kaherekoau Mts mts N.Z.
57 D4 Kahnūj Iran
122 B5 Kahoka U.S.A.
127 □2 Kahoolawe i. U.S.A.
60 D2 Kahraman Maraş Turkey
54 B3 Kahror Pakistan
60 D2 Kahta Turkey
93 □1 Kahuitara Pt pt *Chatham Is* N.Z.
127 □1 Kahuku U.S.A.
127 □1 Kahuku Pt pt U.S.A.
127 □2 Kahului U.S.A.
57 D3 Kahurak Iran
92 D4 Kahurangi Point pt N.Z.
78 E4 Kahuzi-Biega, Parc National du nat. park Zaire
77 E5 Kaiama Nigeria
90 □1 Kaiapit P.N.G.
93 D5 Kaiapoi N.Z.
129 F3 Kaibab U.S.A.
127 D4 Kaibab Plat. plat. U.S.A.
46 E6 Kaibara Japan
39 K8 Kai Besar i. Indon.
129 G3 Kaibito U.S.A.
129 G3 Kaibito Plateau plat. U.S.A.
65 K4 Kaidu r. China
51 F1 Kaifeng China
51 F1 Kaifeng China
92 D1 Kaihu N.Z.
51 G2 Kaihua China
82 C4 Kaiingbulte reg. R.S.A.
50 D2 Kaijiang China
39 K8 Kai Kecil i. Indon.
39 K8 Kai, Kepulauan is Indon.
92 D1 Kaikohe N.Z.
93 D5 Kaikoura N.Z.
93 D5 Kaikoura Peninsula pen. N.Z.
45 □ Kai Kung Leng h. Hong Kong
76 B5 Kailahun Sierra Leone
55 G4 Kailāshahar India
50 D3 Kaili China
80 C4 Kailongong waterhole Kenya
49 G4 Kailu China
127 □1 Kailua U.S.A.
127 □2 Kailua Kona U.S.A.
92 E2 Kaimai Range h. N.Z.
39 K7 Kaimana Indon.
92 E3 Kaimanawa Mountains mt. ra. N.Z.
50 A1 Kaimar China
54 D4 Kaimganj India
55 E4 Kaimur Range h. India
11 F4 Käina Estonia
46 E7 Kainan Japan
47 E6 Kainan Japan
42 A2 Kaing Myanmar
77 E4 Kaingiwa Nigeria
77 F5 Kainji Lake National Park nat. park Nigeria
77 E4 Kainji Lake National Park nat. park Nigeria
77 E4 Kainji Reservoir resr Nigeria
56 D1 Kaintarāgarh India
92 E2 Kaipara Harbour inlet N.Z.
129 G3 Kaiparowits Plateau plat. U.S.A.
51 F4 Kaiping China
113 J3 Kaipokok Bay inlet Can.
54 D3 Kairana India
75 G1 Kairouan Tunisia
18 C4 Kaiserslautern Germany
49 J4 Kaishantun China
92 D1 Kaitaia N.Z.
93 B7 Kaitangata N.Z.
92 F3 Kaitawa N.Z.
54 D3 Kaithal India
40 A2 Kait, Tg pt Indon.
10 F2 Kaitum Sweden
39 J8 Kaiwatu Indon.
127 □2 Kaiwi Channel chan. U.S.A.
50 E2 Kai Xian China
50 D3 Kaiyang China
50 C4 Kaiyuan China
49 H4 Kaiyuan China
10 G2 Kajaani Finland
98 E4 Kajabbi Aust.
57 F2 Kajaki Afghanistan
40 E3 Kajang Indon.
43 C7 Kajang Malaysia
54 B3 Kajanpur Pakistan
57 F2 Kajrān Afghanistan
77 F4 Kajuru Nigeria
65 J4 Kajy-Say Kyrgyzstan
80 B2 Kaka Sudan
112 C4 Kakabeka Falls Can.
98 C2 Kakadu Nat. Park nat. park Aust.
82 C4 Kakamas R.S.A.
81 B4 Kakamega Kenya
47 F6 Kakamigahara Japan
43 A5 Kakana *Andaman and Nicobar Is* India
26 G3 Kakanj Bos.-Herz.
93 C6 Kakanui Mts mts N.Z.
77 G4 Kakarahil well Niger
92 E3 Kakaramea N.Z.
76 B5 Kakata Liberia
92 E3 Kakatahi N.Z.
55 H4 Kakching India
46 D6 Kake Japan
110 C3 Kake U.S.A.
47 G6 Kakegawa Japan
79 D4 Kakenge Zaire
15 E3 Kakhovka Ukraine
15 E3 Kakhovs'ke Vodoskhovyshche resr Ukraine
57 B3 Kākī Iran
56 C2 Kākināda India
110 F2 Kakisa Can.
110 F2 Kakisa r. Can.
110 F2 Kakisa Lake l. Can.
46 E6 Kakogawa Japan
19 L3 Kąkolewnica Wschodnia Poland
54 E4 Kakori India
79 E4 Kakoswa Zaire
76 D5 Kakpin Côte d'Ivoire
54 D4 Kakrala India
76 B4 Kakrima r. Guinea
108 D2 Kaktovik U.S.A.
47 H5 Kakuda Japan
110 F4 Kakwa r. Can.
54 B3 Kala Pakistan
81 B6 Kala Tanzania
54 B2 Kalabagh Pakistan
39 H8 Kalabahi Indon.
41 A5 Kalabakan Malaysia
80 E3 Kalabaydh *Nugaal* Somalia
80 D3 Kalabaydh *Woqooyi Galbeed* Somalia
96 E2 Kalabity Aust.
79 D6 Kalabo Zambia
13 G5 Kalach Rus. Fed.
57 F2 Kalacha Afghanistan
80 C4 Kalacha Dida Kenya
65 H2 Kalachinsk Rus. Fed.
13 G5 Kalach-na-Donu Rus. Fed.
42 A2 Kaladan r. India/Myanmar
115 G4 Kaladar Can.
127 □2 Ka Lae c. U.S.A.
40 E2 Kalaena r. Indon.
42 B2 Kalagwe Myanmar
82 C3 Kalahari Desert desert Botswana
82 C4 Kalahari Gemsbok National Park nat. park R.S.A.
64 F5 Kala-I-Mor Turkmenistan
10 G2 Kalajoki r. Finland
10 F2 Kalajoki Finland
77 E4 Kalalé Benin
54 C2 Kalam Pakistan
29 D4 Kalamaria Greece
29 D6 Kalamata Greece
122 E4 Kalamazoo U.S.A.
122 D4 Kalamazoo r. U.S.A.
40 C3 Kalambau i. Indon.
29 C5 Kalampaka Greece
29 E4 Kalampaki Greece
76 C4 Kalana Mali
54 C3 Kalanaur India
15 E3 Kalanchak Ukraine
57 E3 Kalandi Pakistan
81 B5 Kalangala Uganda
49 F2 Kalanguy Rus. Fed.
101 B6 Kalannie Aust.
54 C3 Kalanwali India
40 E3 Kalao i. Indon.
41 C5 Kalaong Phil.
56 C4 Kala Oya r. Sri Lanka
40 A2 Kalapa Indon.
57 E4 Kalar w Iran
60 F3 Kalār Iraq
14 B1 Kalashnikovo Rus. Fed.
54 A3 Kalat Pakistan
90 □4 Kalau i. Tonga
127 □2 Kalaupapa U.S.A.
13 G6 Kalaus r. Rus. Fed.
29 D5 Kalavryta Greece
42 B2 Kalaw Myanmar
101 A5 Kalbarri Aust.
101 A5 Kalbarri Nat. Park nat. park Aust.
57 D2 Kalbū Iran
15 G3 Kal'chyk r. Ukraine
29 G6 Kale *Denizli* Turkey
61 A1 Kale Turkey
61 A1 Kaleardı Br. pt Turkey
60 C1 Kalecik Turkey
78 E4 Kalehe Zaire
42 A3 Kaleindaung inlet Myanmar
79 D4 Kalema Zaire
79 E5 Kalémié Zaire
42 A2 Kalemyo Myanmar
122 D3 Kaleva U.S.A.
10 H2 Kalevala Rus. Fed.
42 A2 Kalewa Myanmar
60 F2 Kaleybar Iran
49 F2 Kalga Rus. Fed.
101 B7 Kalgan r. Aust.
101 C6 Kalgoorlie Aust.
77 G4 Kalguéri Niger
26 E3 Kali Croatia
54 E3 Kali r. India
40 A3 Kalianda Indon.
41 B4 Kalibo Phil.
55 E4 Kali Gadaki r. Nepal
14 D3 Kalikino Rus. Fed.
79 E4 Kalima Zaire
40 C2 Kalimantan reg. Indon.
40 B2 Kalimantan Barat div. Indon.
40 C2 Kalimantan Selatan div. Indon.
40 C2 Kalimantan Tengah div. Indon.
40 D1 Kalimantan Timur div. Indon.
55 G4 Kālimpang India
56 A3 Kalinadi r. India
54 D3 Kali Nadi r. India
64 E4 Kalinin Turkmenistan
11 F5 Kaliningrad Rus. Fed.
14 H2 Kalinino Rus. Fed.
13 H5 Kalininsk Rus. Fed.
13 F6 Kalininskaya Rus. Fed.
15 E3 Kalinins'ke Ukraine
13 D4 Kalinkavichy Belarus
64 E3 Kalinovka Kazak.
14 B4 Kalinovka Rus. Fed.
80 E3 Kalis Somalia
54 D5 Kali Sindh r. India
126 D1 Kalispell U.S.A.
19 J3 Kalisz Poland
19 G2 Kalisz Pomorski Poland
13 F5 Kalitva r. Rus. Fed.
81 B6 Kaliua Tanzania
10 F2 Kalix Sweden
10 F2 Kalixälven r. Sweden
54 D3 Kalka India
15 G3 Kalka r. Ukraine
60 B2 Kalkan Turkey
98 B3 Kalkaringi Aust.
122 E3 Kalkaska U.S.A.
82 B3 Kalkfeld Namibia
96 D1 Kallakoopah Cr. w Aust.
43 □ Kallang Singapore
11 G4 Kallaste Estonia
10 G3 Kallavesi l. Finland
29 C5 Kallifoni Greece
10 D3 Kallsedet Sweden
10 D3 Kallsjön l. Sweden
65 K2 Kalmanka Rus. Fed.
11 E4 Kalmar Sweden
11 D4 Kalmar div. Sweden
13 F6 Kal'mius r. Ukraine
57 D1 Kalmūkh Qaléh Iran
56 C5 Kalmunai Sri Lanka
13 H6 Kalmykiya div. Rus. Fed.
64 D3 Kalmykovo Kazak.
55 G4 Kalni r. Bangladesh
19 J5 Kalocsa Hungary
54 C5 Kalol India
41 C6 Kaloma i. Indon.
81 B6 Kaloma Tanzania
79 E7 Kalomo Zambia
110 D4 Kalone Pk summit Can.
61 B2 Kalopanagiotis Cyprus
54 D3 Kalpa India
56 A4 Kalpeni i. India
65 J4 Kalpin China
108 C3 Kaltag U.S.A.
65 L2 Kaltan Rus. Fed.
18 D2 Kaltenkirchen Germany
77 G5 Kaltungo Nigeria
54 C3 Kalu India
14 C2 Kaluga Rus. Fed.
14 B2 Kaluga div. Rus. Fed.
14 F3 Kalugino Rus. Fed.
15 E3 Kaluha Ukraine
40 D3 Kalukalukuang i. Indon.
40 D2 Kaluku Indon.
79 E6 Kalulushi Zambia
100 D2 Kalumburu Aust.
100 D2 Kalumburu Abor. Land Reserve res. Aust.
11 C5 Kalundborg Denmark
79 E5 Kalungwishi r. Zambia
54 B2 Kalur Kot Pakistan
15 A2 Kalush Ukraine
19 K2 Kałuszyn Poland
56 B5 Kalutara Sri Lanka
19 L1 Kalvarija Lithuania
10 F3 Kälviä Finland
56 A2 Kalyan India
14 C1 Kalyazin Rus. Fed.
29 F6 Kalymnos i. Greece
29 F6 Kalymnos Greece
15 D1 Kalynivka *Kyyiv* Ukraine
15 C2 Kalynivka *Vinnytsya* Ukraine
15 D1 Kalyta Ukraine
77 G5 Kam Nigeria
42 A3 Kama Myanmar
12 K3 Kama r. Rus. Fed.
79 E4 Kama Zaire
47 H4 Kamaishi Japan
47 □1 Kama-iwa i. Japan
47 G6 Kamakura Japan
76 B5 Kamakwie Sierra Leone
72 C3 Kamal Chad
54 C3 Kamalia Pakistan
42 B3 Kamamaung Myanmar
54 D4 Kaman India
60 C2 Kaman Turkey
78 E4 Kamande Zaire
82 A2 Kamanjab Namibia
79 E4 Kamanyola Zaire
80 D1 Kamaran Yemen
80 D1 Kamarān I. i. Yemen
57 F2 Kamard reg. Afghanistan
56 B2 Kamareddi India
29 C5 Kamares *Dytiki Ellas* Greece
57 E4 Kamarod Pakistan
76 B5 Kamaron Sierra Leone
15 D1 Kamaryn Belarus
65 G5 Kamashi Uzbekistan
82 D2 Kamativi Zimbabwe
42 B1 Kambaiti Myanmar
101 C6 Kambalda Aust.
56 B4 Kambam India
40 B4 Kambangan i. Indon.
64 D1 Kambarka Rus. Fed.
65 K4 Kamberdi China
76 B5 Kambia Sierra Leone
94 □1 Kambling I. i. *Cocos Is* Indian Ocean
49 J4 Kambo Ho mt. N. Korea
79 E6 Kambove Zaire
40 E2 Kambuno, Bukit mt. Indon.
63 R4 Kamchatka r. Rus. Fed.
63 S4 Kamchatka pen. Rus. Fed.
57 G2 Kamdesh Afghanistan
13 J5 Kamelik r. Rus. Fed.
28 E3 Kamen Bulgaria
79 D5 Kamende Zaire
19 G4 Kamenice nad Lipou Czech Rep.
64 D2 Kamenka Kazak.
12 H1 Kamenka Rus. Fed.
14 G3 Kamenka Rus. Fed.
13 F5 Kamenka Rus. Fed.
14 A2 Kamenka Rus. Fed.
14 G1 Kamenka Rus. Fed.
14 E3 Kamenka Rus. Fed.
14 B2 Kamenka Rus. Fed.
65 K2 Kamen'-na-Obi Rus. Fed.
14 D1 Kamenniki Rus. Fed.
11 H3 Kamennogorsk Rus. Fed.
28 F3 Kameno Bulgaria
13 G6 Kamenolomni Rus. Fed.
49 K3 Kamen'-Rybolov Rus. Fed.
63 S3 Kamenskoye Rus. Fed.
14 D3 Kamenskoye Rus. Fed.
13 G5 Kamensk-Shakhtinskiy Rus. Fed.
64 F1 Kamensk-Ural'skiy Rus. Fed.
19 G3 Kamenz Germany
14 E1 Kameshkovo Rus. Fed.
54 D3 Kamet mt. China
29 B4 Kamëz Albania
46 B6 Kamiagata Japan
19 H3 Kamienna Gora Poland
19 G2 Kamień Pomorski Poland
46 J2 Kamikawa Japan
46 B8 Kami-Koshiki-jima i. Japan
98 E3 Kamileroi Aust.
111 J2 Kamilukuak Lake l. Can.
79 D5 Kamina Zaire
79 E5 Kamina Base Zaire
111 L2 Kaminak Lake l. Can.
15 A1 Kamin'-Kashyrs'kyy Ukraine
46 H3 Kaminokuni Japan
47 H4 Kaminoyama Japan
26 E2 Kaminške in Savinjske Alpe mt. ra. Slovenia
14 E1 Kaminskiy Rus. Fed.
47 F5 Kamioka Japan
29 F6 Kamiros Greece
46 J2 Kamishihoro Japan
46 B6 Kamitsushima Japan
79 E4 Kamituga Zaire
47 □2 Kamiyama-jima i. Japan
55 H4 Kamjong India
55 F4 Kamla r. India
65 L2 Kamlak Rus. Fed.
110 E4 Kamloops Can.
47 G5 Kamo Japan
92 E1 Kamo N.Z.
139 F3 Kamoa Mts mts Guyana
46 H2 Kamoenai Japan
47 H6 Kamogawa Japan
54 C3 Kamoke Pakistan
79 D5 Kamonia Zaire
19 G4 Kamp r. Austria
81 B4 Kampala Uganda
43 C6 Kampar Malaysia
18 B2 Kampen Netherlands
79 E4 Kampene Zaire
42 B3 Kamphaeng Phet Thailand
56 B3 Kampli India
79 E6 Kampolombo, Lake l. Zambia
43 D5 Kâmpóng Cham Cambodia
43 D4 Kâmpóng Chhnăng Cambodia
43 D4 Kâmpóng Khleăng Cambodia
43 D5 Kâmpóng Spoe Cambodia
43 D4 Kâmpóng Thum Cambodia
43 D5 Kâmpong Tranch Cambodia
43 D5 Kâmpôt Cambodia
76 D4 Kampti Burkina
39 K7 Kamrau, Teluk b. Indon.
111 J4 Kamsack Can.
76 B4 Kamsar Guinea
12 J4 Kamskoye Ust'ye Rus. Fed.
62 G4 Kamskoye Vdkhr. resr Rus. Fed.
81 D4 Kamsuuma Somalia
111 J3 Kamuchawie Lake l. Can.
81 B4 Kamuli Uganda
15 B1 Kam"yane *Rivne* Ukraine
15 F1 Kam"yane *Sumy* Ukraine
15 B2 Kam"yanets'-Podil's'kyy Ukraine
15 E2 Kam"yanka *Cherkasy* Ukraine
15 G2 Kam"yanka *Kharkiv* Ukraine
15 D3 Kam"yanka *Odesa* Ukraine
15 A1 Kam"yanka-Buz'ka Ukraine
15 F3 Kam"yanka-Dniprovs'ka Ukraine
28 G2 Kam"yans'ke Ukraine
13 B4 Kamyanyets Belarus
15 B1 Kam"yanyy Brid Ukraine
15 D3 Kam"yanyy Mist Ukraine
60 F3 Kāmyārān Iran
13 F6 Kamyshevatskaya Rus. Fed.
13 H5 Kamyshin Rus. Fed.
64 F3 Kamyshlybash Kazak.
64 F3 Kamyslybas, Oz. l. Kazak.
13 J6 Kamyzyak Rus. Fed.
57 D4 Kamzar Oman
80 B3 Kan Sudan
78 F3 Kana Zaire
83 D2 Kana r. Zimbabwe
112 F3 Kanaaupscow r. Can.
129 F3 Kanab U.S.A.
129 F3 Kanab Creek r. U.S.A.
90 □6 Kanacea i. Fiji
47 G6 Kanagawa div. Japan
54 A3 Kanak Pakistan
29 C5 Kanallaki Greece
79 D5 Kananga Zaire
97 G3 Kanangra Nat. Park nat. park Aust.
129 F3 Kanarraville U.S.A.
14 H2 Kanash Rus. Fed.
120 C5 Kanawha r. U.S.A.
47 F6 Kanayama Japan
47 F5 Kanazawa Japan
47 F5 Kanazu Japan
42 A2 Kanbalu Myanmar
43 B4 Kanchanaburi Thailand
56 B3 Kanchipuram India
19 L4 Kańczuga Poland
54 A3 Kand mt. Pakistan
57 F3 Kandahār Afghanistan
10 J2 Kandalaksha Rus. Fed.
12 E1 Kandalakshskiy Zaliv g. Rus. Fed.
40 C2 Kandangan Indon.
77 E5 Kandé Togo
54 B3 Kandhkot Pakistan
54 B2 Kandhura Pakistan
77 E4 Kandi Benin
54 A3 Kandi Pakistan
54 B4 Kandiaro Pakistan
29 C5 Kandila *Sterea Ellas* Greece
77 G3 Kandil Bouzou well Niger
60 B1 Kandıra Turkey
54 B5 Kandla India
97 G3 Kandos Aust.
83 H2 Kandreho Madagascar
90 □1 Kandrian P.N.G.
56 B3 Kandukur India
56 C5 Kandy Sri Lanka
120 D4 Kane U.S.A.
109 M2 Kane Basin b. Greenland
57 C4 Kaneh w Iran
72 C5 Kanem div. Chad
127 □1 Kaneohe U.S.A.
127 □1 Kaneohe Bay b. U.S.A.
12 F1 Kanevka Rus. Fed.
13 F6 Kanevskaya Rus. Fed.
47 H4 Kaneyama Japan
82 C3 Kang Botswana
55 G5 Kanga r. Bangladesh
78 F3 Kanga Zaire
109 N3 Kangaatsiaq Greenland
76 C4 Kangaba Mali
60 D2 Kangal Turkey
57 D4 Kangān Iran
57 C4 Kangan Iran
43 C6 Kangar Malaysia
96 D3 Kangaroo I. i. Aust.
139 F2 Kangaruma Guyana
11 H3 Kangaslampi Finland
11 G3 Kangasniemi Finland
57 A2 Kangāvar Iran
49 E4 Kangbao China
55 G4 Kangchenjunga mt. Nepal
50 C2 Kangding China
49 H5 Kangdong N. Korea
40 C3 Kangean i. Indon.
40 C3 Kangean, Kep. is Indon.
80 B3 Kangen r. Sudan
109 O3 Kangeq hd Greenland
109 N3 Kangerluarsoruseq Greenland
109 N3 Kangerlussuaq Greenland
109 P3 Kangerlussuaq inlet Greenland
109 N2 Kangersuatsiaq Greenland
109 P3 Kangertittivatsiaq inlet Greenland
80 C4 Kangetet Kenya
49 H4 Kanggye N. Korea
109 Q2 Kangikajik c. Greenland
49 F1 Kangil Rus. Fed.
113 G2 Kangiqsualujjuaq Can.
109 L3 Kangiqsujuaq Can.
113 G1 Kangirsuk Can.
46 A6 Kangjon S. Korea
50 C1 Kangle China
55 F3 Kangmar China
55 G3 Kangmar China
49 J5 Kangnŭng S. Korea
78 B3 Kango Gabon
47 □1 Kangoku-iwa i. Japan
49 G4 Kangping China
54 D2 Kangra India
55 H3 Kangri Karpo Pass India
55 E3 Kangrinboqê Feng mt. China
55 H4 Kangto mt. China
55 F2 Kangtog China
50 D1 Kang Xian China
54 D1 Kangxiwar China
42 A3 Kangyidaung Myanmar
56 B1 Kanhan r. India
55 E4 Kanhar r. India
76 C5 Kani Côte d'Ivoire
42 A2 Kani Myanmar
79 D5 Kaniama Zaire
93 C5 Kaniere N.Z.
93 C5 Kaniere, L. l. N.Z.
76 A4 Kanifing The Gambia
56 B3 Kanigiri India
54 B2 Kaniguram Pakistan
62 F3 Kanin Nos Rus. Fed.
62 F3 Kanin Nos, Mys c. Rus. Fed.
62 F3 Kanin, P-ov pen. Rus. Fed.
46 H3 Kanita Japan
15 D2 Kaniv Ukraine
96 E4 Kaniva Aust.
28 C1 Kanjiža Yugo.
11 F3 Kankaanpää Finland
122 D5 Kankakee U.S.A.
122 C5 Kankakee r. U.S.A.
76 C4 Kankan Guinea
76 C5 Kankan, Réserve Naturelle de res. Guinea
55 E5 Kanker India
56 C4 Kankesanturai Sri Lanka
54 C1 Kankhun P. pass Afghanistan/Pakistan
43 B5 Kanmaw Kyun i. Myanmar
54 D4 Kannanj India
119 D5 Kannapolis U.S.A.
56 B4 Kanniyakumari India
54 D5 Kannod India
10 G3 Kannonkoski Finland
10 F3 Kannus Finland
46 C6 Kano Japan
77 F4 Kano div. Nigeria
77 F4 Kano Nigeria
46 D6 Kan-onji Japan
40 C1 Kanowit Malaysia
46 C8 Kanoya Japan
54 E4 Kanpur India
54 B3 Kanpur Pakistan
54 A4 Kanrach reg. Pakistan
124 D4 Kansas r. U.S.A.
124 D4 Kansas div. U.S.A.
124 E4 Kansas City U.S.A.
124 E4 Kansas City U.S.A.
63 L4 Kansk Rus. Fed.
65 J5 Kansu China
65 H4 Kant Kyrgyzstan
80 C3 Kanta mt. Ethiopia
43 D4 Kantaralak Thailand
77 E4 Kantchari Burkina
13 F5 Kantemirovka Rus. Fed.
55 F5 Kānthi India
55 F4 Kanti India
150 H6 Kanton Island i. Kiribati
47 G6 Kanto-sanchi mt. ra. Japan
17 C5 Kanturk Rep. of Ire.
139 F3 Kanuku Mts mts Guyana
47 G5 Kanuma Japan
82 B4 Kanus Namibia
90 □1 Kanuwe r. P.N.G.
83 E4 KaNyamazane R.S.A.
82 D3 Kanye Botswana
14 A2 Kanyutino Rus. Fed.
90 □5 Kao i. Tonga
43 C5 Kaôh Kŏng i. Cambodia
43 C5 Kaôh Rŭng i. Cambodia
51 H4 Kao-hsiung Taiwan
43 C5 Kaôh Smăch i. Cambodia
82 A2 Kaokoveld plat. Namibia
76 A4 Kaolack Senegal
79 D6 Kaoma Zambia
72 C4 Kaortchi well Chad
78 D2 Kaouadja C.A.R.
127 □2 Kapaa U.S.A.
127 □2 Kapaau U.S.A.
65 J3 Kapal Kazak.
79 D5 Kapanga Zaire
81 B6 Kapatu Zambia
65 J4 Kapchagay Kazak.
65 J4 Kapchagayskoye Vdkhr. resr Kazak.
80 B4 Kapchorwa Uganda
19 G5 Kapfenberg Austria
55 H4 Kapili r. India
150 F5 Kapingamarangi Rise Pac. Oc.
54 B3 Kapip Pakistan
79 E6 Kapiri Mposhi Zambia
109 N3 Kapisigdlit Greenland
112 D3 Kapiskau Can.
112 D3 Kapiskau r. Can.
114 E3 Kapiskong Lake l. Can.
40 C1 Kapit Malaysia
15 D2 Kapitanivka Ukraine
92 E4 Kapiti I. i. N.Z.
139 F3 Kapiting Brazil
72 D5 Kapka, Massif du mts Chad
19 G4 Kaplice Czech Rep.
43 B5 Kapoe Thailand
80 B4 Kapoeta Sudan
92 E3 Kaponga N.Z.
19 H5 Kaposvár Hungary
57 E4 Kappar Pakistan
18 D1 Kappeln Germany
18 E5 Kappl Austria
81 C4 Kapsabet Kenya
49 J4 Kapsan N. Korea
49 F2 Kaptsegaytuy Rus. Fed.
40 B1 Kapuas r. *Kalimantan Barat* Indon.
40 C2 Kapuas r. *Kalimantan Tengah* Indon.
96 D3 Kapunda Aust.
54 C4 Kapūriya India
54 C3 Kapurthala India
114 D2 Kapuskasing Can.
114 D2 Kapuskasing r. Can.
13 H5 Kapustin Yar Rus. Fed.
15 D1 Kapustyntsi Ukraine
97 G2 Kaputar mt. Aust.
80 C4 Kaputir Kenya
19 H5 Kapuvár Hungary
12 C4 Kapyl' Belarus
14 A2 Kapyrevshchina Rus. Fed.
77 E5 Kara Togo
60 E2 Kara r. Turkey
29 F6 Kara Ada i. Turkey
29 F5 Kara Ada i. Turkey
65 H4 Kara-Balta Kyrgyzstan
14 D1 Karabanovo Rus. Fed.
64 F5 Karabekaul Turkmenistan
60 A1 Karabiga Turkey
64 D4 Kara-Bogaz-Gol Turkmenistan
64 D4 Kara-Bogaz Gol, Zaliv b. Turkmenistan
60 C1 Karabük Turkey
14 E2 Karabukhino Rus. Fed.
65 J4 Karabulak Kazak.
65 K3 Karabulak Kazak.
65 J3 Karabulakskaya Kazak.
29 F5 Karaburun Turkey
64 F3 Karabutak Kazak.
29 G4 Karacabey Turkey
60 B1 Karacaköy Turkey
60 D2 Karacalı Dağ mt. Turkey
61 B1 Karaçal T. mt. Turkey
29 G6 Karacasu Turkey
13 G7 Karachayevo-Cherkesiya div. Rus. Fed.
13 G7 Karachayevsk Rus. Fed.
14 B3 Karachev Rus. Fed.
54 A4 Karachi Pakistan
56 A2 Karad India
60 C2 Kara Dağ mt. Turkey
65 H4 Kara-Darya r. Kyrgyzstan
76 D5 Karaga Ghana
65 H3 Karaganda Kazak.
65 J3 Karagayly Kazak.
63 S4 Karaginskiy, O. i. Rus. Fed.
63 S4 Karaginskiy Zaliv b. Rus. Fed.
81 B5 Karagwe Tanzania
28 F4 Karahalil Turkey
29 G6 Karahisar Turkey
56 B4 Kāraikāl India
56 B4 Karaikkudi India
65 K3 Kara Irtysh r. Kazak.
60 C2 Karaisalı Turkey
57 B2 Karaj Iran
60 C4 Karak Jordan
64 E5 Kara Kala Turkmenistan
64 E4 Karakalpakiya Uzbekistan
65 J5 Karakax r. China
41 C5 Karakelong i. Indon.
41 C6 Karakitang i. Indon.
60 E2 Karakoçan Turkey
65 G3 Karakoin, Oz. salt l. Kazak.
64 D3 Karakol' Kazak.
65 H4 Kara-Köl Kyrgyzstan
65 J4 Karakol Kyrgyzstan
54 D2 Karakoram Pass pass China/Jammu and Kashmir
54 C1 Karakoram Range mt. ra. Asia
80 C2 Kara K'orē Ethiopia
49 E2 Karaksar Rus. Fed.
64 F5 Karakul' Uzbekistan
65 H5 Karakul', Ozero l. Tajikistan
78 B1 Karal Chad
11 F4 Karala Estonia
40 D2 Karama r. Indon.
61 B1 Karaman div. Turkey
60 C2 Karaman Turkey
65 K3 Karamay China
65 H5 Karambar Pass pass Afghanistan/Pakistan
40 D2 Karambu Indon.
93 D4 Karamea N.Z.
93 C4 Karamea Bight b. N.Z.
93 D4 Karamea River r. N.Z.
57 F1 Karamet-Niyaz Turkmenistan
40 C3 Karamian i. Indon.
55 F1 Karamiran China
55 F1 Karamiran Shankou pass China
12 D3 Karamyshevo Rus. Fed.
57 G1 Karan r. Afghanistan
57 B4 Karān i. Saudi Arabia
60 F3 Karand Iran
40 A2 Karangagung Indon.
40 A3 Karangan Indon.
40 C4 Karangasem Indon.
40 B4 Karangbolong, Tg pt Indon.
40 D2 Karang, Tg pt Indon.
54 D5 Karanja India
56 B2 Karanja r. India
55 F5 Karanjia India
65 J2 Karaoba Kazak.
29 F6 Karaova Turkey
65 H3 Karaoy Kazak.
28 F3 Karapelit Bulgaria
60 C2 Karapınar Turkey
29 G5 Karapürçek Turkey
82 B4 Karas div. Namibia
55 E1 Karasay China
65 J4 Kara-Say Kyrgyzstan
82 B4 Karasburg Namibia
14 D1 Karash Rus. Fed.
10 G1 Karasjok Norway
65 G2 Karasu Kazak.
64 F2 Karasu Kazak.
65 H2 Karasu r. Kazak.
61 D1 Karasu r. Turkey
13 D7 Karasu Turkey
65 K2 Karasuk r. Rus. Fed.
65 J2 Karasuk Rus. Fed.
65 H4 Kara-Suu Kyrgyzstan
15 A1 Karasyn Ukraine
57 E2 Karāt Iran
65 L3 Karatan Kazak.
60 C2 Karataş Turkey
61 C1 Karataş Burun c. Turkey
65 H4 Karatau Kazak.
65 G4 Karatau, Khr. mt. ra. Kazak.
54 E2 Karatax Shan mt. ra. China
43 B5 Karathuri Myanmar
56 B4 Karativu i. Sri Lanka
64 D3 Karatobe Kazak.
64 F4 Karatobe, Mys pt Kazak.
65 J3 Karatol r. Kazak.
64 D3 Karaton Kazak.
55 G4 Karatoya r. Bangladesh
46 B7 Karatsu Japan
41 C5 Karatung i. Indon.
65 G2 Karaturgay r. Kazak.
65 J3 Karaul Kazak.
54 D4 Karauli India
64 E4 Karauzyak Uzbekistan
65 H4 Karavan Kyrgyzstan
29 D6 Karavi i. Greece
29 F7 Karavonisia i. Greece
61 B2 Karavostasi Cyprus
40 A3 Karawang Indon.
14 F4 Karay r. Rus. Fed.
65 K4 Karayulgan China
65 H3 Karazhal Kazak.
64 E4 Karazhar Uzbekistan
65 H3 Karazhingil Kazak.
60 E3 Karbalā' div. Iraq
60 F3 Karbalā' Iraq
65 J3 Karbushevka Kazak.
19 K5 Karcag Hungary
28 G3 Kardam Bulgaria
29 C5 Karditsa Greece
11 F4 Kärdla Estonia
14 A2 Kardymovo Rus. Fed.
73 F4 Kareima Sudan
54 D5 Kareli India
12 D1 Kareliya div. Rus. Fed.
12 E1 Karel'skiy Bereg Rus. Fed.
81 B6 Karema Tanzania
54 D4 Karera India
10 F1 Karesuando Sweden
57 E4 Kārevāndar Iran
13 H7 Kargalinskaya Rus. Fed.
64 E2 Kargalinskoye Kazak.
61 D1 Kargamiş Turkey
64 F1 Kargapol'ye Rus. Fed.
65 K1 Kargat r. Rus. Fed.
65 K1 Kargat Rus. Fed.
13 E7 Kargı Turkey
54 D2 Kargil *Jammu and Kashmir*
14 H3 Kargino Rus. Fed.
12 F2 Kargopol' Rus. Fed.
19 G2 Kargowa Poland
11 E3 Karholmsbruk Sweden
77 G4 Kari Nigeria
14 E3 Karian Rus. Fed.
83 D2 Kariba Zimbabwe
83 D2 Kariba, Lake resr Zambia/Zimbabwe
46 G2 Kariba-yama vol Japan
82 B3 Karibib Namibia
82 C5 Kariega w R.S.A.
10 G1 Karigasniemi Finland
11 F3 Karijoki Finland
46 J2 Karikachi Pass pass Japan
92 D1 Karikari, Cape c. N.Z.
57 C2 Karīmābād Iran
40 B2 Karimata i. Indon.
40 B2 Karimata, P.P. is Indon.
57 B2 Karim Khanch Iran
56 B2 Karimnagar India
40 B3 Karimunjawa i. Indon.
40 B3 Karimunjawa, P.P. is Indon.
80 E2 Karin Somalia
57 D2 Karit Iran
47 F6 Kariya Japan
56 A2 Karjat India
55 F5 Karkai r. India
56 A3 Karkal India
65 J3 Karkaralinsk Kazak.
41 C5 Karkaralong, Kepulauan is Indon.
90 □1 Karkar I. i. P.N.G.
57 B3 Karkheh r. Iran
57 D4 Kārkīn Dar Iran
13 E6 Karkinits'ka Zatoka g. Ukraine
11 G3 Kärkölä Finland
19 G1 Karlino Poland
60 E2 Karlıova Turkey
15 F2 Karlivka Ukraine
65 H5 Karl Marks mt. Tajikistan
26 E3 Karlovac Croatia
28 E3 Karlovo Bulgaria
18 F3 Karlovy Vary Czech Rep.
11 D4 Karlsborg Sweden
11 D4 Karlshamn Sweden
11 D4 Karlskoga Sweden
11 D4 Karlskrona Sweden
18 D4 Karlsruhe Germany
11 D4 Karlstad Sweden
124 D1 Karlstad U.S.A.
18 D4 Karlstadt Germany
13 D4 Karma Belarus
78 C1 Karma r. Chad
77 E4 Karma Niger
56 A2 Karmala India
14 B2 Karmanovo Rus. Fed.
11 B4 Karmøy i. Norway
55 H5 Karnafuli Reservoir resr Bangladesh
54 D3 Karnal India
55 E3 Karnali r. Nepal
54 D3 Karnaprayag India
56 A3 Karnataka div. India
28 F3 Karnobat Bulgaria
72 D4 Karnoi Sudan
19 F5 Kärnten div. Austria
54 A4 Karodi Pakistan
83 D2 Karoi Zimbabwe
90 □6 Karoko Fiji
42 B4 Karokpi Myanmar
55 G3 Karo La China
55 H4 Karong India
81 B6 Karonga Malawi
81 A5 Karonje mt. Rwanda
96 D3 Karoonda Aust.
54 B3 Karor Pakistan
80 C1 Karora Eritrea
40 D2 Karossa Indon.
40 D4 Karossa, Tg pt Indon.
29 F7 Karpathos Greece
29 F7 Karpathos i. Greece
29 C5 Karpenisi Greece
12 H1 Karpogory Rus. Fed.
61 A1 Karpuz r. Turkey
29 F6 Karpuzlu *Aydın* Turkey
29 F4 Karpuzlu *Edirne* Turkey
15 B1 Karpylivka Ukraine
100 B4 Karratha Aust.
57 E2 Karrukh Afghanistan
57 E1 Karrychirla Turkmenistan
60 E1 Kars Turkey
10 G3 Kärsämäki Finland
11 G4 Kārsava Latvia
64 D4 Karshi Turkmenistan
65 G5 Karshi Uzbekistan
29 F5 Karşıyaka Turkey
62 G3 Karskiye Vorota, Proliv chan. Rus. Fed.
62 J2 Karskoye More sea Rus. Fed.
18 E2 Karstädt Germany
10 G3 Karstula Finland
14 H2 Karsun Rus. Fed.
60 B1 Kartal Turkey
81 D7 Kartala crater Comoros
64 F2 Kartaly Rus. Fed.
12 K1 Kartayel' Rus. Fed.
10 G3 Karttula Finland
19 J1 Kartuzy Poland
99 E3 Karumba Aust.
57 B3 Kārūn r. Iran
81 B5 Karungu Bay b. Kenya
40 D4 Karuni Indon.
56 B4 Karur India
11 F3 Karvia Finland
11 F3 Karvianjoki r. Finland
19 J4 Karviná Czech Rep.
56 A3 Karwar India
29 C5 Karya Greece
48 E2 Karymskoye Rus. Fed.
29 E5 Karystos Greece
14 G3 Karzhimant Rus. Fed.
112 C3 Kasabonika Can.
112 C3 Kasabonika Lake l. Can.
46 E6 Kasai Japan
79 C4 Kasai r. Zaire
79 D5 Kasai Occidental div. Zaire
79 D5 Kasai Oriental div. Zaire
79 D6 Kasaji Zaire
47 H5 Kasama Japan
81 B7 Kasama Zambia
65 G5 Kasan Uzbekistan
82 D2 Kasane Botswana
79 C4 Kasangulu Zaire
65 H4 Kasansay Uzbekistan
56 A3 Kasaragod India
111 J2 Kasba Lake l. Can.
74 C2 Kasba Tadla Morocco
46 C8 Kaseda Japan
79 E6 Kasempa Zambia
79 E6 Kasenga Zaire
79 E5 Kasengu Zaire
78 F3 Kasenye Zaire
81 B4 Kasese Uganda
78 E4 Kasese Zaire
54 D4 Kasganj India
57 B2 Kāshān Iran
13 G5 Kashary Rus. Fed.
112 D3 Kashechewan Can.
65 J5 Kashi China
47 E6 Kashihara Japan
46 C7 Kashima Japan
47 H5 Kashima-nada b. Japan
14 C1 Kashin Rus. Fed.
14 C1 Kashinka r. Rus. Fed.
54 D3 Kashipur India
14 D2 Kashira Rus. Fed.
13 F5 Kashirskoye Rus. Fed.
47 G5 Kashiwazaki Japan
65 H3 Kashkanteniz Kazak.
12 F1 Kashkarantsy Rus. Fed.
15 G3 Kashlahach r. Ukraine
14 F3 Kashma r. Rus. Fed.
57 D2 Kāshmar Iran
54 B3 Kashmor Pakistan
57 G2 Kashmund reg. Afghanistan
79 E5 Kashyukulu Zaire
55 E4 Kasia India
14 A3 Kasilovo Rus. Fed.
40 D2 Kasimbar Indon.
14 E2 Kasimov Rus. Fed.
118 B4 Kaskaskia r. U.S.A.
111 L3 Kaskattama r. Can.
65 J4 Kaskelen Kazak.
11 F3 Kaskinen Finland
64 F1 Kasli Rus. Fed.
40 C2 Kasongan Indon.
79 E4 Kasongo Zaire
79 C5 Kasongo-Lunda Zaire
29 F7 Kasos i. Greece
13 H7 Kaspi Georgia
13 H7 Kaspiysk Rus. Fed.
73 G4 Kassala Sudan
29 D4 Kassandra pen. Greece
29 D4 Kassandreia Greece
18 D3 Kassel Germany
75 F1 Kasserine Tunisia
73 F4 Kassinger Sudan
122 A3 Kasson U.S.A.
60 C1 Kastamonu Turkey
29 E7 Kastelli *Kriti* Greece
29 D7 Kastelli *Kriti* Greece
29 C4 Kastoria Greece
14 D4 Kastornoye Rus. Fed.
29 C5 Kastos i. Greece
46 C7 Kasuga Japan
47 F6 Kasugai Japan
78 E4 Kasuku Zaire
81 B5 Kasulu Tanzania
79 E6 Kasumbalesa Zaire
46 E6 Kasumi Japan
47 H5 Kasumiga-ura l. Japan
13 J7 Kasumkent Rus. Fed.
81 B7 Kasungu Malawi
81 B7 Kasungu National Park nat. park Malawi
54 C3 Kasur Pakistan
121 J2 Katahdin, Mt mt. U.S.A.
54 D2 Kataklik *Jammu and Kashmir*
79 D4 Katako-Kombe Zaire
80 B4 Katakwi Uganda
54 D5 Katangi India
101 B7 Katanning Aust.
78 E4 Katanti Zaire
29 C6 Katastari Greece
81 B6 Katavi National Park nat. park Tanzania
64 E2 Katav Ivanovsk Rus. Fed.
57 G2 Katawaz Afghanistan
64 F1 Kataysk Rus. Fed.
43 A6 Katchall i. *Andaman and Nicobar Is* India
79 E5 Katea Zaire
79 D5 Katenge Zaire
29 D4 Katerini Greece
15 D2 Katerynopil' Ukraine
81 C5 Katesh Tanzania
110 C3 Kate's Needle mt. Can./U.S.A.
81 B7 Katete Zambia
55 E5 Katghora India
42 B1 Katha Myanmar
61 B5 Katherîna, G. mt. Egypt
98 C2 Katherine r. Aust.
98 C2 Katherine Aust.
99 E4 Katherine Cr. w Aust.
98 C2 Katherine Gorge Nat. Park nat. park Aust.
54 B5 Kathiawar India
61 B4 Kathîb el Henu h. Egypt
61 B4 Kathîb el Makhâzin sand dunes Egypt
56 C4 Kathiraveli Sri Lanka
55 F4 Kathmandu Nepal
82 C4 Kathu R.S.A.
54 C2 Kathua India
81 C5 Kathua w Kenya
76 C4 Kati Mali
55 F4 Katihar India
92 E2 Katikati N.Z.

15 C1 Kocheriv Ukraine
14 G4 Kochetovka Rus. Fed.
14 E3 Kochetovka Rus. Fed.
46 D7 Kōchi div. Japan
46 D7 Kōchi Japan
47 □2 Kochinada Japan
65 K2 Kochki Rus. Fed.
65 J4 Kochkor Kyrgyzstan
14 G2 Kochkurovo Rus. Fed.
13 H6 Kochubey Rus. Fed.
13 G6 Kochubeyevskoye Rus. Fed.
19 L3 Kock Poland
56 B4 Kodaikanal India
15 D1 Kodaky Ukraine
56 D2 Kodala India
55 F4 Kodari Nepal
55 F4 Kodarma India
19 L3 Kodeń Poland
108 C4 Kodiak U.S.A.
108 C4 Kodiak Island i. U.S.A.
12 F2 Kodino Rus. Fed.
80 B3 Kodok Sudan
46 H3 Kodomari-misaki pt Japan
13 G7 Kodori r. Georgia
15 C1 Kodra Ukraine
15 C3 Kodyma r. Ukraine
15 C2 Kodyma Ukraine
29 E4 Kodzhaele mt. Bulgaria/Greece
55 E4 Koel r. India
55 F5 Koel, S. r. India
82 B4 Koës Namibia
129 F5 Kofa Mts mts U.S.A.
28 F4 Kofçaz Turkey
82 C4 Koffiefontein R.S.A.
19 G5 Köflach Austria
76 D5 Koforidua Ghana
47 G6 Kōfu Japan
112 E2 Kogaluc r. Can.
112 E2 Kogaluc, Baie de b. Can.
113 H2 Kogaluk r. Can.
11 D5 Køge Denmark
77 F5 Kogi div. Nigeria
76 B4 Kogon r. Guinea
46 A6 Kogŭm do i. S. Korea
46 C6 Kogushi Japan
54 A4 Kohan Pakistan
54 B2 Kohat Pakistan
57 F2 Koh-i-Hisar mt. ra. Afghanistan
11 G4 Kohila Estonia
55 H4 Kohima India
57 F2 Koh-i-Mazar mt. Afghanistan
54 A4 Koh-i-Patandar mt. Pakistan
57 F2 Koh-i-Sangan mt. Afghanistan
57 G2 Kohistan reg. Afghanistan
54 C2 Kohistan reg. Pakistan
57 E3 Koh-i-Sultan mt. Pakistan
57 B3 Kohkīlūyeh va Būyer Ahmadī div. Iran
152 A3 Kohler Ra. mt. ra. Ant.
54 B3 Kohlu Pakistan
57 F2 Kohsan Afghanistan
11 G4 Kohtla-Järve Estonia
92 E2 Kohukohunui h. N.Z.
46 D6 Kohŭng S. Korea
93 C6 Kohurau mt. N.Z.
47 G5 Koide Japan
110 A2 Koidern Can.
43 A5 Koihoa Andaman and Nicobar Is India
56 B3 Koilkuntla India
60 F2 Koi Sanjaq Iraq
49 J6 Kōje do i. S. Korea
47 G7 Ko-jima i. Japan
46 G3 Ko-jima i. Japan
101 B7 Kojonup Aust.
42 B3 Kok r. Thailand
121 J2 Kokadjo U.S.A.
64 F3 Kokalaat Kazak.
64 A3 Kokand Uzbekistan
11 F4 Kökar Finland
57 G1 Kokcha r. Afghanistan
11 F3 Kokemäenjoki r. Finland
80 C3 K'ok' Hāyk' l. Ethiopia
14 E1 Kokhma Rus. Fed.
76 A3 Koki Senegal
57 C4 Kokkilai Sri Lanka
10 F3 Kokkola Finland
65 L3 Kok Kuduk well China
77 E4 Koko Nigeria
76 C4 Kokofata Mali
127 □1 Koko Hd hd U.S.A.
122 D5 Kokomo U.S.A.
46 C7 Kokonoe Japan
14 B3 Kokorevka Rus. Fed.
77 E5 Kokoro Benin
76 B4 Kokou mt. Guinea
65 K3 Kokpekty Kazak.
65 G4 Koksaray Kazak.
65 J4 Kokshaal-Tau mt. ra. China/Kyrgyzstan
65 G2 Kokshetau div. Kazak.
65 G2 Kokshetau Kazak.
112 G2 Koksoak r. Can.
83 D5 Kokstad R.S.A.
10 D2 Kokstranda Norway
65 J4 Koktal Kazak.
65 G2 Kokterek Kazak.
46 C8 Kokubu Japan
45 C5 Ko Kut i. Thailand
49 F1 Kokuy Rus. Fed.
10 J1 Kola Rus. Fed.
54 A4 Kolachi r. Pakistan
54 C2 Kolahoi mt. India
39 H7 Kolaka Indon.
43 B6 Ko Lanta Thailand
43 B6 Ko Lanta i. Thailand
56 C2 Kolar India
56 B3 Kolar India
54 D4 Kolaras India
56 B3 Kolar Gold Fields India
10 F2 Kolari Finland
28 B3 Kolašin Yugo.
54 C4 Kolayat India
19 K3 Kolbuszowa Poland
14 D1 Kol'chugino Rus. Fed.
76 A4 Kolda Senegal
76 F5 Koldere Turkey
11 C5 Kolding Denmark
78 E3 Kole Haute-Zaïre Zaire
79 D4 Kole Kasai-Oriental Zaire
10 F2 Koler Sweden
67 F3 Kolguyev, O. i. Rus. Fed.
55 F5 Kolhan India
56 A2 Kolhapur India
43 B6 Ko Libong i. Thailand
76 B3 Kolimbiné w Mali/Mauritania
19 G3 Kolín Czech Rep.
80 C3 K'olīto Ethiopia
11 F4 Kõljala Estonia
11 F4 Kolkasrags pt Latvia
65 G5 Kolkhozobod Tajikistan
15 A1 Kolky Ukraine
56 B3 Kollegal India
56 C2 Kolleru L. l. India
77 E4 Kollo Niger
18 C3 Köln Germany
19 K2 Kolno Łomża Poland
19 J2 Koło Poland
79 B5 Kolo Zaire
93 □2 Koloa i. Tonga
14 E1 Kolobovo Rus. Fed.
19 G1 Kołobrzeg Poland
15 A2 Kolodne Ukraine
12 H3 Kologriv Rus. Fed.
14 G4 Kologrivovka Rus. Fed.
76 C4 Kolokani Mali
14 D1 Koloksha r. Rus. Fed.
15 F2 Kolomak Ukraine
15 F2 Kolomak r. Ukraine
90 □1 Kolombangara i. Solomon Is.
14 D2 Kolomna Rus. Fed.
15 A2 Kolomyya Ukraine
76 C4 Kolondiéba Mali
76 A4 Kolondiéba Mali
90 □4 Kolonga Tonga
29 B4 Kolonjë Albania
15 F2 Kolontayiv Ukraine
65 H1 Kolosovka Rus. Fed.
90 □4 Kolovai Tonga
64 D2 Kolovertnoye Kazak.
14 E2 Kolp' Rus. Fed.
62 K4 Kolpashevo Rus. Fed.
14 C3 Kolpny Rus. Fed.
29 D4 Kolpos Agiou Orous b. Greece
29 D7 Kolpos Chanion b. Greece
29 D4 Kolpos Ierissou b. Greece
29 E7 Kolpos Irakleiou b. Greece
29 D4 Kolpos Kassandras b. Greece
29 E4 Kolpos Kavalas b. Greece
29 D7 Kolpos Kissamou b. Greece
29 D4 Kolpos Orfanou b. Greece
29 D6 Kolpos Ydras chan. Greece
62 E3 Kol'skiy Poluostrov pen. Rus. Fed.
14 G3 Koltovskoye Rus. Fed.
28 B2 Kolubara r. Yugo.
80 D2 Koluli Eritrea
53 D10 Kolumadulu Atoll atoll Maldives
65 G2 Koluton Kazak.
56 A2 Kolvan India
10 C2 Kolvereid Norway
10 G1 Kolvik Norway
12 E1 Kolvitskoye, Ozero l. Rus. Fed.
57 F4 Kolwa reg. Pakistan
79 E6 Kolwezi Zaire
14 D3 Kolybel'skoye Rus. Fed.
63 R3 Kolyma r. Rus. Fed.
63 R3 Kolymskaya Nizmennost lowland Rus. Fed.
63 S3 Kolymskiy, Khrebet mt. ra. Rus. Fed.
14 G3 Kolyshley Rus. Fed.
14 G3 Kolyshley r. Rus. Fed.
65 K1 Kolyvan' Rus. Fed.
77 G4 Komadugu-gana w Nigeria
47 F6 Komagane Japan
46 H2 Komaga-take vol Japan
82 B4 Komaggas Mts mts R.S.A.
19 L4 Komańcza Poland
63 S4 Komandorskiye Ostrova is Rus. Fed.
14 B3 Komarichi Rus. Fed.
15 B2 Komariv Ukraine
19 J5 Komárno Slovakia
15 A1 Komarove Ukraine
47 F5 Komatsu Japan
46 E6 Komatsushima Japan
79 E4 Kombe Zaire
76 D4 Kombissiri Burkina
77 E4 Kombongou Burkina
55 H3 Komdi mt. India
41 □1 Komebail Lagoon lag. Palau
81 B5 Kome Channel chan. Uganda
81 B5 Kome I. i. Uganda
81 B5 Kome Island i. Tanzania
40 A2 Komering r. Indon.
12 J1 Komi div. Rus. Fed.
46 H3 Kominato Japan
15 D3 Kominternivs'ke Ukraine
26 F4 Komiža Croatia
19 J5 Komló Hungary
14 E1 Kommunar Rus. Fed.
65 L2 Kommunar Rus. Fed.
40 D4 Komodo i. Indon.
76 C5 Komodou Guinea
76 D5 Komoé r. Côte d'Ivoire
76 D5 Komoé r. Côte d'Ivoire
73 F3 Kôm Ombo Egypt
79 B4 Komono Congo
47 G5 Komoro Japan
29 E4 Komotini Greece
12 E5 Kompaniyivka Ukraine
82 C5 Komsberg mts R.S.A.
64 F2 Komsomolets Kazak.
63 M1 Komsomolets, O. i. Rus. Fed.
64 D3 Komsomolets, Zaliv b. Kazak.
14 E1 Komsomol'sk Rus. Fed.
64 F5 Komsomol'sk Turkmenistan
15 E2 Komsomol's'k Ukraine
15 G2 Komsomol's'ke Ukraine
13 H6 Komsomol'skiy Rus. Fed.
12 H4 Komsomol'skiy Rus. Fed.
45 P1 Komsomol'sk-na-Amure Rus. Fed.
64 E4 Komsomol'sk-na-Ustyurte Uzbekistan
64 F2 Komsomol'skoye Kazak.
48 D1 Komsomol'skoye Rus. Fed.
14 H2 Komsomol'skoye Rus. Fed.
28 E4 Komuniga Bulgaria
13 G7 Kömürlü Turkey
129 F6 Kom Vo U.S.A.
28 B3 Kom Vojnik mts Yugo.
15 E1 Komyshnya Ukraine
15 E3 Komyshuvakha Ukraine
55 E4 Kon India
14 D3 Konakovo Rus. Fed.
55 F6 Konārka India
55 F5 Konar Res. India
57 B3 Konār Takhteh Dālakī Iran
24 D4 Konch India
56 C2 Kondagaon India
76 B5 Kondembaia Sierra Leone
115 G3 Kondiaronk, Lac l. Can.
101 B7 Kondinin Aust.
81 C5 Kondoa Tanzania
13 G3 Kondol' Rus. Fed.
28 E3 Kondolovo Bulgaria
12 G3 Kondopoga Rus. Fed.
14 B2 Kondrovo Rus. Fed.
57 G1 Kondūz Afghanistan
90 □2 Kone Pac. Oc.
78 B2 Kong Cameroon
109 P3 Kong Christian IX Land reg. Greenland
109 Q2 Kong Christian X Land reg. Greenland
109 Q2 Kong Frederik VIII Land reg. Greenland
109 O3 Kong Frederik VI Kyst Greenland
152 C2 Kong Håkon VII Hav sea Ant.
62 D2 Kong Karl's Land is Svalbard Arctic Ocean
40 D1 Kongkemul mt. Indon.
82 C2 Kongola Namibia
79 E5 Kongolo Zaire
109 Q2 Kong Oscar Fjord inlet Greenland
76 D4 Kongoussi Burkina
11 C4 Kongsberg Norway
11 D3 Kongsvinger Norway
43 D4 Kông, T. r. Cambodia
65 J5 Kongur Shan mt. China
81 C6 Kongwa Tanzania
109 Q2 Kong Wilhelm Land reg. Greenland
19 J3 Koniecpol Poland
18 E4 Königsbrunn Germany
19 G5 Königs Wusterhausen Germany
19 J2 Konin Poland
29 C4 Konitsa Greece
26 F4 Konjic Bos.-Herz.
26 G3 Konjuh mts Bos.-Herz.
82 B4 Konkiep w Namibia
14 D3 Kon'-Kolodez' Rus. Fed.
77 E4 Konkwesso Nigeria
76 D4 Konna Mali
11 G3 Konnevesi Finland
76 D5 Konongo Ghana
15 E1 Kononivka Ukraine
12 G2 Konosha Rus. Fed.
47 G5 Kōnosu Japan
15 E1 Konotop Ukraine
43 E4 Kon Plong Vietnam
41 □1 Konrei Palau
19 K3 Końskie Poland
80 C3 Konso Ethiopia
49 H2 Konstantinovka Rus. Fed.
14 D1 Konstantinovo Rus. Fed.
13 G6 Konstantinovsk Rus. Fed.
14 D1 Konstantinovskiy Rus. Fed.
18 D5 Konstanz Germany
77 F4 Kontagora Nigeria
42 B2 Kontha Myanmar
10 H3 Kontiolahti Finland
10 G2 Konttila Finland
43 D4 Kon Tum Vietnam
43 E4 Kontum, Plateau du plat. Vietnam
12 G1 Konushin, Mys pt Rus. Fed.
61 B1 Konya div. Turkey
60 C2 Konya Turkey
14 B4 Konyshevka Rus. Fed.
101 C6 Kookynie Aust.
127 □1 Koolau Range mt. ra. U.S.A.
98 D5 Koolivoo, L. salt flat Aust.
101 B6 Koolyanobbing Aust.
97 F3 Koondrook Aust.
96 C2 Koonibba Aust.
120 D5 Koon Lake l. U.S.A.
97 G4 Koorawatha Aust.
101 B6 Koorda Aust.
82 A3 Koosa waterhole Namibia
126 C2 Kooskia U.S.A.
110 F5 Kootenay r. Can./U.S.A.
110 F5 Kootenay L. l. Can.
110 F4 Kootenay Nat. Park nat. park Can.
28 C3 Kopaonik mt. ra. Yugo.
56 A2 Kopargaon India
77 E5 Kopargo Benin
10 M2 Kópasker Iceland
15 B2 Kopayhorod Ukraine
65 J3 Kopbirlik Kazak.
26 D3 Koper Slovenia
16 K2 Kopervik Norway
64 E5 Kopet Dag, Khrebet mt. ra. Turkmenistan
64 F1 Kopeysk Rus. Fed.
43 C5 Ko Phangan i. Thailand
43 B5 Ko Phra Thong i. Thailand
43 B6 Ko Phuket i. Thailand
11 E4 Köping Sweden
28 B3 Koplik Albania
10 E3 Köpmanholmen Sweden
14 B2 Koporikha Rus. Fed.
56 B3 Koppal India
11 C3 Koppang Norway
11 D3 Kopparberg Sweden
11 D4 Kopparberg div. Sweden
26 F2 Koprivnica Croatia
60 B2 Köprü r. Turkey
29 G5 Köprübaşı Turkey
15 A2 Kopychyntsi Ukraine
57 B3 Kor w Iran
28 C4 Korab mt. ra. Albania/Macedonia
14 E3 Korablino Rus. Fed.
80 E3 Korf well Ethiopia
80 D3 K'orahē Ethiopia
54 A4 Korak Pakistan
112 E1 Korak, Baie b. Can.
81 C5 Kora National Reserve res. Kenya
56 B2 Korangal India
54 A4 Korangi Pakistan
57 G1 Korān va Monjan Afghanistan
56 C2 Koraput India
76 D3 Korarou, Lac l. Mali
55 E5 Korba India
75 G1 Korba Tunisia
18 D3 Korbach Germany
78 C2 Korbol Chad
43 C6 Korbu, Gunung mt. Malaysia
29 C4 Korçë Albania
15 B2 Korchivka Ukraine
26 F4 Korčula i. Croatia
26 F4 Korčula Croatia
26 F4 Korčulanski Kanal chan. Croatia
57 A2 Kördestan div. Iran
57 C1 Kord Kūy Iran
73 E5 Kordofan div. Sudan
57 E4 Kords reg. Iran
57 C3 Kord Sheykh Iran
49 G5 Korea Bay g. China/North Korea
46 B6 Korea Strait str. Japan/South Korea
76 B4 Koréba Burkina
56 A2 Koregaon India
80 C2 Korem Ethiopia
15 D1 Koren' r. Rus. Fed.
14 C3 Korenevo Rus. Fed.
13 F6 Korenovsk Rus. Fed.
76 C4 Koréra-Koré Mali
15 B1 Korets' Ukraine
12 J3 Kort' Rus. Fed.
60 B1 Körfez Turkey
152 B3 Korff Ice Rise ice feature Ant.
55 F1 Korgan China
10 D2 Korgen Norway
76 C5 Korhogo Côte d'Ivoire
54 C4 Kori Creek r. India
29 D5 Korinthiakos Kolpos chan. Greece
29 D6 Korinthos Greece
19 H5 Kőris-hegy mt. Hungary
47 H5 Kōriyama Japan
64 F2 Korkino Rus. Fed.
60 B2 Korkuteli Turkey
65 L4 Korla China
14 H1 Korlyaki Rus. Fed.
61 B2 Kormakitis, C. c. Cyprus
19 H5 Körmend Hungary
65 H1 Kormilovka Rus. Fed.
26 F3 Kornat i. Croatia
65 G2 Korneyevka Kazak.
13 J5 Korneyevka Rus. Fed.
15 C1 Kornyn Ukraine
90 □8 Koro i. Fiji
76 D4 Koro Mali
90 □8 Koroba mt. Fiji
14 B3 Korobets Rus. Fed.
15 G1 Korocha Rus. Fed.
60 B1 Köroğlu Tepesi mt. Turkey
80 D4 Korogo well Ethiopia
81 C6 Korogwe Tanzania
97 E4 Koroit Aust.
90 □8 Korolevu Fiji
90 □8 Korolevu Fiji
97 E4 Korong Vale Aust.
29 C6 Koroni Greece
29 D4 Koronia, L. l. Greece
19 J2 Koronowo Poland
15 E1 Korop Ukraine
41 □1 Koror i. Palau
19 K5 Körös r. Hungary
90 □6 Koro Sea sea Fiji
15 C1 Korosten' Ukraine
15 C1 Korostyshiv Ukraine
90 □6 Korotasere Fiji
14 H1 Korotni Rus. Fed.
72 C4 Koro Toro Chad
90 □1 Korovou Solomon Is.
15 E1 Korovyntsi Ukraine
90 □8 Koroyanitu mt. Fiji
15 G2 Korozhechna r. Rus. Fed.
11 H3 Korpilahti Finland
11 F3 Korpo Finland
45 Q2 Korsakov Rus. Fed.
14 C3 Korsakovo Rus. Fed.
14 A3 Korsika Rus. Fed.
11 F3 Korsnäs Finland
11 D5 Korsør Denmark
15 D2 Korsun'-Shevchenkivs'kyy Ukraine
19 K1 Korsze Poland
10 F3 Kortesjärvi Finland
73 F4 Korti Sudan
12 J2 Kortkeros Rus. Fed.
18 A3 Kortrijk Belgium
78 A2 Korup, Parc National de nat. park Cameroon
10 G2 Korvala Finland
54 D4 Korwai India
63 R4 Koryakskaya Sopka vol Rus. Fed.
63 S3 Koryakskiy Khrebet mt. ra. Rus. Fed.
12 H2 Koryazhma Rus. Fed.
19 L2 Korycin Poland
15 D1 Koryukivka Ukraine
14 H2 Korzhevka Rus. Fed.
29 F6 Kos i. Greece
29 F6 Kos Greece
13 E6 Kosa Arabats'ka Strilka spit Ukraine
15 D1 Kosachivka Ukraine
43 C5 Ko Samui i. Thailand
14 C2 Kosaya Gora Rus. Fed.
64 D3 Koschagyl Kazak.
19 H2 Kościan Poland
19 J2 Kościerzyna Poland
19 H1 Kościerzyna Poland
125 F5 Kosciusko U.S.A.
110 C3 Kosciusko I. i. U.S.A.
97 G4 Kosciusko, Mt mt. Aust.
97 G4 Kosciusko National Park nat. park Aust.
60 D1 Köse Dağı mt. Turkey
56 B2 Kosgi India
44 E2 Kosh-Agach Rus. Fed.
15 E1 Koshary Ukraine
46 B8 Koshikijima-rettō is Japan
46 B8 Koshiki-kaikyō chan. Japan
46 K2 Koshimizu Japan
57 E2 Koshkak Iran
57 E2 Koshk-e-Kohneh Afghanistan
12 J4 Koshki Rus. Fed.
122 C4 Koshkoning, Lake l. U.S.A.
15 B2 Koshlyaky Ukraine
15 F2 Koshmanivka Ukraine
64 D4 Koshoba Turkmenistan
47 G5 Kōshoku Japan
54 D4 Kosi India
54 D3 Kosi r. India
19 K4 Košice Slovakia
56 B3 Kosigi India
64 E2 Kos-Istek Kazak.
15 A2 Kosiv Ukraine
15 A2 Kosivka Ukraine
28 B3 Kosjerić Yugo.
29 G6 Köşk Turkey
14 A2 Koski Rus. Fed.
65 G3 Koskol' Kazak.
12 J2 Koslan Rus. Fed.
46 A5 Kosŏng N. Korea
14 C3 Kosorzha Rus. Fed.
28 C3 Kosovo div. Yugo.
28 C3 Kosovo Polje plain Yugo.
28 C3 Kosovska Kamenica Yugo.
28 C3 Kosovska Mitrovica Yugo.
86 H4 Kosrae i. Fed. States of Micronesia
65 J5 Kosrap China
77 G3 Kossatori well Niger
41 □1 Kossol Passage chan. Palau
41 □1 Kossol Reef reef Palau
76 C5 Kossou, Lac de l. Côte d'Ivoire
28 D3 Kostenets Bulgaria
14 D2 Kosterevo Rus. Fed.
73 F5 Kosti Sudan
28 D3 Kostinbrod Bulgaria
62 K3 Kostino Rus. Fed.
28 D3 Kostolac Yugo.
10 H2 Kostomuksha Rus. Fed.
15 B1 Kostopil' Ukraine
12 G3 Kostroma r. Rus. Fed.
12 G3 Kostroma div. Rus. Fed.
14 E1 Kostroma Rus. Fed.
19 G2 Kostrzyn Gorzów Poland
13 F5 Kostyantynivka Donets'k Ukraine
15 F2 Kostyantynivka Kharkiv Ukraine
15 F2 Kostyantynivka Zaporizhzhya Ukraine
14 A2 Kostyri Rus. Fed.
19 J1 Koszalin Poland
19 H5 Kőszeg Hungary
55 E5 Kota India
54 C4 Kota India
40 A3 Kotaagung Indon.
40 B2 Kotabaru Indon.
40 D2 Kotabaru Indon.
40 D2 Kotabaru Indon.
40 C2 Kotabesi Indon.
40 B2 Kota Bharu Malaysia
40 A3 Kotabumi Indon.
54 B3 Kot Addu Pakistan
38 G5 Kota Kinabalu Malaysia
43 B5 Ko Tao i. Thailand
56 C2 Kotapārh India
43 C6 Kota Tinggi Malaysia
54 B4 Kot Diji Pakistan
54 D4 Kotdwara India
12 J3 Kotel'nich Rus. Fed.
13 G6 Kotel'nikovo Rus. Fed.
63 P2 Kotel'nyy, O. i. Rus. Fed.
15 F1 Kotel'va Ukraine
56 C2 Kotgar India
56 C2 Kotgarh India
18 E3 Köthen Germany
56 A2 Kothi India
81 B4 Kotido Uganda
53 C3 Kot Kapura India
12 J2 Kotlas Rus. Fed.
18 E3 Kotlik U.S.A.
108 B3 Kotlik U.S.A.
10 M3 Kötlutangi pt Iceland
11 H4 Kotly Rus. Fed.
77 F5 Koton-Karifi Nigeria
77 F4 Kotorkoshi Nigeria
28 B3 Kotor Varoš Bos.-Herz.
76 D5 Kotouba Côte d'Ivoire
13 H5 Kotovo Rus. Fed.
14 F4 Kotovsk Rus. Fed.
15 C3 Kotovs'k Ukraine
54 D4 Kot Putli India
54 B4 Kotri r. India
54 B4 Kotri Pakistan
54 A5 Kot Sarae Pakistan
15 A2 Kotsyubyns'ke Ukraine
56 C2 Kottagudem India
56 B4 Kottarakara India
56 B4 Kottayam India
57 C5 Kotte Sri Lanka
78 D2 Kotto r. C.A.R.
56 B3 Kotturu India
90 □5 Kotu i. Tonga
90 □5 Kotu Group is Tonga
63 M2 Kotuy r. Rus. Fed.
108 B3 Kotzebue U.S.A.
108 B3 Kotzebue Sound b. U.S.A.
77 E4 Kouandé Benin
78 D3 Kouango C.A.R.
76 D4 Koubia Guinea
76 D4 Koudougou Burkina
29 D6 Koufalia Greece
77 G4 Koufey well Niger
29 F7 Koufonisi i. Greece
82 C5 Kougaberg mts R.S.A.
78 D3 Kouki C.A.R.
79 B4 Kouilou div. Congo
76 D4 Kouka Burkina
78 C2 Koukourou r. C.A.R.
76 B5 Koulamoutou Gabon
76 C4 Koulikoro div. Mali
76 C4 Koulikoro Mali
77 G3 Koulou Niger
76 B4 Koulountou r. Guinea/Senegal
78 B2 Koum Cameroon
78 C2 Kouma r. C.A.R.
90 □2 Koumac Pac. Oc.
99 G4 Koumala Aust.
76 B4 Koumbia Guinea
78 C2 Koumogo Chad
76 B4 Koumpentoum Senegal
78 C2 Koumra Chad
76 B4 Koundâra Guinea
76 D4 Koundougou Burkina
76 B4 Koungheul Senegal
29 F6 Kounoupoi i. Greece
65 H3 Kounradskiy Kazak.
76 D4 Koupéla Burkina
65 K2 Kourak Rus. Fed.
76 C5 Kourandou mt. Guinea
78 C2 Kourayadjé Chad
76 C4 Kourémalé Mali
47 □2 Kouri-jima i. Japan
139 G2 Kourou French Guiana
76 C4 Kouroussa Guinea
72 D4 Kourtidi well Chad
76 B4 Koussanar Senegal
78 C1 Kousséri Cameroon
76 C4 Koutiala Mali
90 □2 Koutoumo i. Pac. Oc.
29 F6 Koutsomyti i. Greece
11 G3 Kouvola Finland
78 C4 Kouyou r. Congo
28 C2 Kovačica Yugo.
82 B2 Kovallberget Sweden
10 H2 Kovdor Rus. Fed.
10 H2 Kovdozero, Oz. l. Rus. Fed.
15 A1 Kovel' Ukraine
14 F1 Kovernino Rus. Fed.
56 B4 Kovilpatti India
28 C1 Kovin Yugo.
14 C1 Kovrov Rus. Fed.
15 F2 Kov"yahy Ukraine
14 G2 Kovylkino Rus. Fed.
12 F2 Kovzhskoye, Ozero l. Rus. Fed.
99 E2 Kowanyama Aust.
82 A2 Kowares waterhole Namibia
93 C5 Kowhitirangi N.Z.
114 B1 Kowkash Can.
45 □ Kowloon Hong Kong
45 □ Kowloon Pk h. Hong Kong
65 K5 Koxlax China
65 J5 Koxtag China
46 C6 Kōyama-misaki pt Japan
43 B5 Ko Yao Yai i. Thailand
60 B2 Köyceğiz Turkey
29 G6 Köyceğiz Gölü l. Turkey
55 E4 Koyda Rus. Fed.
12 J2 Koygorodok Rus. Fed.
28 E3 Koynare Bulgaria
56 A2 Koyna Res. resr India
12 H1 Koynas Rus. Fed.
47 H4 Koyoshi-gawa r. Japan
62 G4 Kozacha Lopan' Ukraine
46 B6 Kō-zaki pt Japan
46 D6 Kōzan Japan
60 C2 Kozan Turkey
29 C4 Kozani Greece
26 F3 Kozara mt. ra. Bos.-Herz.
76 B4 Kozats'ke Ukraine
15 D1 Kozelets' Ukraine
15 E2 Kozel'shchyna Ukraine
14 B2 Kozel'sk Rus. Fed.
15 C3 Kozen well Chad
64 F3 Kozhabakhy Kazak.
62 G3 Kozhanka Ukraine
53 N2 Kozhevnikovo Rus. Fed.
65 K3 Kozhukliv Ukraine
19 K3 Kozienice Poland
14 G1 Kozikovo Rus. Fed.
15 D1 Koziliyivka Ukraine
15 E4 Kozloduy Bulgaria
14 E2 Kozlovka Rus. Fed.
14 G2 Kozlovka Rus. Fed.
12 J4 Kozlovka Rus. Fed.
14 C1 Kozlovo Rus. Fed.
60 B1 Kozlu Turkey
26 G3 Kozluk Bos.-Herz.
19 J3 Koźmin Poland
14 H1 Koz'modem'yansk Rus. Fed.
15 A2 Kozova Ukraine
19 G3 Kożuchów Poland
29 D4 Kožuf mts Greece/Macedonia
47 G6 Kōzu-shima i. Japan
15 C2 Kozyatyn Ukraine
15 D2 Kozyn Kyyiv Ukraine
15 D1 Kozyn Kyyiv Ukraine
29 F4 Kozyörük Turkey
77 E5 Kpalimé Togo
76 D5 Kpandae Ghana
77 E5 Kpandu Ghana
43 B5 Krabi Thailand
43 B5 Kra Buri Thailand
43 D4 Krâcheh Cambodia
11 D5 Kraddsele Sweden
40 B3 Kragan Indon.
11 C4 Kragerø Norway
28 C2 Kragujevac Yugo.
43 B5 Kra, Isthmus of isth. Thailand
19 H2 Krajenka Poland
40 A3 Krakatau i. Indon.
43 D4 Krâkôr Cambodia
19 J4 Kraków Poland
19 J3 Kraków Poland
43 C4 Krâlănh Cambodia
132 □3 Kralendijk Bonaire Netherlands Ant.
26 E3 Kraljevica Croatia
28 C3 Kraljevo Yugo.
19 K4 Kráľova hoľa mt. Slovakia
18 F4 Kralovice Czech Rep.
19 K4 Kráľovský Chlmec Slovakia
18 G3 Kralupy nad Vltavou Czech Rep.
15 G2 Kramators'k Ukraine
10 E3 Kramfors Sweden
29 D6 Kranidi Greece
26 F2 Kranj Slovenia
43 □ Kranji Res. resr Singapore
15 E3 Kranoznam"yans'kyy Kanal canal Ukraine
13 H5 Krasnoarmeysk Rus. Fed.
26 E4 Krapanj Croatia
26 E2 Krapinske Toplice Croatia
65 L1 Krapivinskiy Rus. Fed.
14 C2 Krapivna Rus. Fed.
19 H3 Krapkowice Poland
12 H2 Krasavino Rus. Fed.
12 H2 Krasavino Rus. Fed.
15 A2 Krasenivka Ukraine
28 B2 Krasino Rus. Fed.
14 F3 Krasivka Rus. Fed.
11 G5 Krāslava Latvia
18 F3 Kraslice Czech Rep.
15 G3 Krasna Polyana Ukraine
15 B1 Krasna Slobidka Ukraine
13 D4 Krasnaya Gora Rus. Fed.
14 E2 Krasnaya Gorbatka Rus. Fed.
65 H3 Krasnaya Polyana Kazak.
13 G7 Krasnaya Polyana Rus. Fed.
15 F1 Krasnaya Yaruga Rus. Fed.
14 C3 Krasnaya Zarya Rus. Fed.
14 F3 Krasnaya Znamya Rus. Fed.
15 D1 Krasne Chernihiv Ukraine
15 A2 Krasne L'viv Ukraine
15 C2 Krasne Vinnytsya Ukraine
19 L3 Kraśnik Poland
15 C3 Krasni Okny Ukraine
63 N4 Krasnoarmeysk Rus. Fed.
13 H5 Krasnoarmeysk Rus. Fed.
14 D1 Krasnoarmeysk Rus. Fed.
13 F6 Krasnoarmeyskaya Rus. Fed.
63 T3 Krasnoarmeyskiy Rus. Fed.
14 H2 Krasnoarmeyskoye Rus. Fed.
15 G2 Krasnoarmiys'k Ukraine
12 H2 Krasnoborsk Rus. Fed.
65 L2 Krasnobrodskiy Rus. Fed.
13 F6 Krasnodar div. Rus. Fed.
13 F6 Krasnodar Rus. Fed.
13 F5 Krasnodon Ukraine
12 D3 Krasnogorodskoye Rus. Fed.
14 C2 Krasnogorsk Rus. Fed.
45 Q2 Krasnogorsk Rus. Fed.
64 F2 Krasnogorskiy Rus. Fed.
14 E1 Krasnogvardeyskiy Rus. Fed.
13 G6 Krasnogvardeyskoye Rus. Fed.
15 F2 Krasnohrad Ukraine
13 E6 Krasnohvardiys'ke Ukraine
49 F2 Krasnokamensk Rus. Fed.
65 J2 Krasnokutsk Kazak.
15 F1 Krasnokuts'k Ukraine
14 D4 Krasnolesnyy Rus. Fed.
14 H1 Krasnooktyabr'skiy Rus. Fed.
15 G2 Krasnopavlivka Ukraine
13 E6 Krasnoperekops'k Ukraine
15 D2 Krasnopilka Ukraine
15 F1 Krasnopillya Ukraine
12 F1 Krasnoshchel'ye Rus. Fed.
15 B2 Krasnosilka Ukraine
64 B2 Krasnoslobodsk Rus. Fed.
14 F2 Krasnoslobodsk Rus. Fed.
14 F2 Krasnoslobodsk Rus. Fed.
12 J3 Krasnovobodnoye Rus. Fed.
62 H4 Krasnotur'insk Rus. Fed.
64 E1 Krasnoufimsk Rus. Fed.
64 E2 Krasnousol'skiy Rus. Fed.
62 G3 Krasnovishersk Rus. Fed.
64 D4 Krasnovodsk Turkmenistan
64 D5 Krasnovodsk Zaliv b. Turkmenistan
64 D4 Krasnovodsk, Mys pt Turkmenistan
64 D4 Krasnovodskoye Plato plat. Turkmenistan
64 E2 Krasnoyar Kazak.
49 J2 Krasnoyarovo Rus. Fed.
63 L4 Krasnoyarsk Rus. Fed.
65 M2 Krasnoyarskoye Vdkhr. resr Rus. Fed.
14 A3 Krasnoye Rus. Fed.
14 D3 Krasnoye Rus. Fed.
15 G1 Krasnoye Rus. Fed.
14 E1 Krasnoye-na-Volge Rus. Fed.
14 D1 Krasnoye Plamya Rus. Fed.
14 B1 Krasnoye Znamya Rus. Fed.
15 A2 Krasnoyil's'k Ukraine
12 J2 Krasnozatonskiy Rus. Fed.
16 D2 Krasnozavodsk Rus. Fed.
65 J2 Krasnozerskoye Rus. Fed.
15 E3 Krasnoznam"yanka Ukraine
19 L3 Krasnystaw Poland
14 A2 Krasnyy Rus. Fed.
14 E1 Krasnyy Bogatyr' Rus. Fed.
48 D2 Krasnyy Chikoy Rus. Fed.
14 G1 Krasnyy Baki Rus. Fed.
13 H6 Krasnyye Barrikady Rus. Fed.
14 H2 Krasnyye Chetai Rus. Fed.
14 D1 Krasnyye Tkachi Rus. Fed.
14 C1 Krasnyy Kholm Rus. Fed.
15 F1 Krasnyy Kolyadyn Ukraine
13 H5 Krasnyy Kut Rus. Fed.
13 D2 Krasnyy Luch Rus. Fed.
13 F5 Krasnyy Lyman Ukraine
14 H1 Krasnyy Most Rus. Fed.
14 D1 Krasnyy Oktyabr' Rus. Fed.
14 E1 Krasnyy Oktyabr' Rus. Fed.
14 G4 Krasnyy Oktyabr' Rus. Fed.
14 E1 Krasnyy Profintern Rus. Fed.
14 A3 Krasnyy Rog Rus. Fed.
13 H5 Krasnyy Yar Rus. Fed.
14 G3 Krasnyy Yar Rus. Fed.
12 J4 Krasnyy Yar Rus. Fed.
14 H4 Krasnyy Yar Rus. Fed.
13 J6 Krasnyy Yar Rus. Fed.
15 B2 Krasyliv Ukraine
28 D3 Kratovo Macedonia
13 H7 Kraynovka Rus. Fed.
18 C3 Krefeld Germany
29 C5 Kremaston, Techniti Limni resr Greece
15 E2 Kremenchuk Ukraine
15 E2 Kremenchuts'ka Vodoskhovshche resr Ukraine
15 A1 Krements' Ukraine
15 E1 Kremenki Rus. Fed.
14 C2 Kremenki Rus. Fed.
15 G2 Kremenskoye Rus. Fed.
19 G4 Křemešník h. Czech Rep.
15 A2 Kremintsi Ukraine
126 F3 Kremmling U.S.A.
19 G4 Krems an der Donau Austria
19 G4 Kremsmünster Austria
108 B4 Krenitzin Islands is U.S.A.
12 J2 Kreshchenka Rus. Fed.
28 D4 Kresna Bulgaria
108 A3 Kresta, Zaliv b. Rus. Fed.
12 E3 Krestovka Rus. Fed.
12 E3 Kresttsy Rus. Fed.
14 D3 Kresty Rus. Fed.
11 F5 Kretinga Lithuania
18 E5 Kreuth Germany
21 J3 Kreuzlingen Switz.
78 A3 Kribi Cameroon
28 E3 Krichim Bulgaria
19 G5 Krieglach Austria
29 C5 Krikellos Greece
45 Q2 Kril'on, Mys c. Rus. Fed.
78 C2 Krim-Krim Chad
56 B2 Krishna r. India
56 B3 Krishnagiri India
56 C3 Krishna, Mouths of the river mouth India
55 G5 Krishnanagar India
56 B3 Krishnaraja Sagara l. India
11 B4 Kristiansand Norway
11 D4 Kristianstad Sweden
11 D4 Kristianstad div. Sweden
10 B3 Kristiansund Norway
11 E3 Kristinehamn Sweden
11 D4 Kristinestad Finland
29 E7 Kriti div. Greece
58 B3 Kriti i. Greece
14 D2 Kriusha Rus. Fed.
14 F2 Kriusha Rus. Fed.
26 G3 Krivaja r. Bos.-Herz.
28 D3 Kriva Palanka Macedonia
12 E1 Krivoy Porog Rus. Fed.
13 F5 Krivozer'ye Rus. Fed.
26 F2 Križevci Croatia
26 E3 Krk i. Croatia
26 E3 Krk Croatia
26 F3 Krka r. Croatia
26 F3 Krka r. Slovenia
19 G3 Krkonoše mt. ra. Czech Rep.
19 H3 Krnov Czech Rep.
28 B3 Krnovo pass Yugo.
19 H3 Krobia Poland
10 D3 Krokom Sweden
40 B1 Krokong Malaysia
10 C3 Krokstadøra Norway
15 E1 Krolevets' Ukraine
14 B3 Kroma r. Rus. Fed.
14 B3 Kromy Rus. Fed.
18 E3 Kronach Germany
43 C5 Krŏng Kaôh Kŏng Cambodia
11 D4 Kronoberg div. Sweden
10 F3 Kronoby Finland
109 Q1 Kronprins Christian Ld reg. Greenland
109 P3 Kronprins Frederik Bjerge nunatak Greenland
18 E1 Kronshagen Germany
42 B4 Kronwa Myanmar
82 D4 Kroonstad R.S.A.
13 G6 Kropotkin Rus. Fed.
15 C1 Kropyvnya Ukraine
19 K4 Krosno Poland
19 G3 Krosno Odrzańskie Poland
19 H3 Krotoszyn Poland
40 B3 Kroya Indon.
26 E3 Krško Slovenia
14 D3 Kruchi Rus. Fed.
83 E3 Kruger National Park nat. park R.S.A.
40 A3 Krui Indon.
82 C5 Kruisfontein R.S.A.
29 B4 Krujë Albania
29 E4 Krumovgrad Bulgaria
28 B2 Krupanj Yugo.
14 B4 Krupets Rus. Fed.
19 J4 Krupina Slovakia
12 D4 Krupki Belarus
15 E2 Krupodernytsi Ukraine
28 C3 Kruševac Yugo.
29 C4 Kruševo Macedonia
18 F3 Krušné Hory mt. ra. Czech Rep.
19 J2 Kruszwica Poland
65 K2 Krutikha Rus. Fed.
65 H1 Krutinka Rus. Fed.
14 C3 Krutoye Rus. Fed.
15 E1 Kruty Ukraine
110 B3 Kruzof I. i. U.S.A.
12 D4 Krychaw Belarus
15 B1 Krylov Ukraine
13 E6 Krym' pen. Ukraine
13 F6 Krymsk Rus. Fed.
13 E6 Kryms'ki Hori mt. ra. Ukraine
19 K4 Krynica Poland
19 J1 Krynica Morska Poland
15 F2 Krynychky Ukraine
29 E6 Krytiko Pelagos sea Greece
15 E2 Kryva Ruda Ukraine
15 C2 Kryvchunka Ukraine
15 D3 Kryve Ozero Ukraine
15 E2 Kryvyy Rih Ukraine
15 C2 Kryzhopil' Ukraine
19 J3 Krzepice Poland
19 H2 Krzyż Wielkopolski Poland
75 D3 Ksabi Algeria
75 E1 Ksar Chellala Algeria
75 D1 Ksar el Boukhari Algeria
74 C1 Ksar el Kebir Morocco
24 D5 Ksar Sghir Morocco
62 G3 Ksenofontova Rus. Fed.
14 C4 Kshen' r. Rus. Fed.
14 C4 Kshenskiy Rus. Fed.
75 G1 Ksour Essaf Tunisia
75 D2 Ksour, Monts des mts Algeria
14 G1 Kstovo Rus. Fed.
14 B3 Ktsyn' Rus. Fed.
43 B6 Kuah Malaysia
40 B2 Kualajelai Indon.
43 C6 Kuala Kangsar Malaysia
40 C2 Kualakapuas Indon.
43 C6 Kuala Kerai Malaysia
40 C2 Kualakuayan Indon.
40 C7 Kuala Kubu Baharu Malaysia
43 C6 Kuala Lipis Malaysia
43 C6 Kuala Lumpur Malaysia
43 C6 Kuala Nerang Malaysia
40 C2 Kualapembuang Indon.
43 C7 Kuala Pilah Malaysia
43 C7 Kuala Rompin Malaysia
43 B6 Kualasimpang Indon.
43 C6 Kuala Terengganu Malaysia
40 C2 Kualatungal Indon.
41 A5 Kuamut Malaysia
49 F4 Kuancheng China
49 H4 Kuandian China
51 H4 Kuanshan Taiwan
43 C7 Kuantan Malaysia
13 H7 Kuba Azer.
15 C1 Kuban' r. Rus. Fed.
61 D2 Kubaybāt Syria
73 E5 Kubbum Sudan
78 D1 Kubenskoye, Ozero l. Rus. Fed.
12 F3 Kubnya r. Rus. Fed.
12 H4 Kubokawa Japan
46 D7 Kubrat Bulgaria
28 F3 Kubu Indon.
40 C4 Kubuhut Pt pt Fiji
90 □6 Kubumesaäi Indon.
40 C2 Kučevo Yugo.
28 C2 Kuchāman India
54 C4 Kuchema Rus. Fed.
12 G1 Kucherivka Ukraine
15 E1 Kuching Malaysia
40 C2 Kuchinotsu Japan
46 C7 Kuchinotsu Japan
46 C7 Kuchnay Darwēsh Afghanistan
57 E4 Kuchukskoye, Oz. salt l. Rus. Fed.
65 J2 Kuchurhan r. Ukraine
15 C3 Kuçovë Albania
29 B4 Kudaka-jima i. Japan
47 □2 Kudal India
56 A3 Kudamatsu Japan
46 C7 Kudap Malaysia
41 A5 Kudara Rus. Fed.
48 D1 Kudarebe pt Aruba Caribbean
132 □1 Kudligi India
56 B3 Kud'ma r. Rus. Fed.
14 G1 Kudremukh mt. India
56 A3 Kudrinskaya Rus. Fed.
14 D2 Kudryavtsivka Ukraine
15 D3 Kudus Indon.
40 B3 Kuei-shan Tao i. Taiwan
51 H2 Kufstein Austria
18 F5 Kugaly Kazak.
65 J4 Kugesi Rus. Fed.
14 H1 Kugmallit Bay b. Can.
108 E3 Kūhak Iran
57 E4 Kūhbonān Iran
57 D3 Kūhdasht Iran
57 A2 Kūh-e Sahand mt. Iran
60 F2 Kūhhaye Sabalan mt. Iran
57 E4 Kūhlab, Ra's pt Iran
10 H2 Kuhmo Finland
11 G3 Kuhmoinen Finland
57 D4 Kūh, Ra's-al pt Iran
82 B3 Kuiseb w Namibia
82 B3 Kuiseb Pass Namibia
79 C6 Kuito Angola
110 B3 Kuiu Island i. U.S.A.
10 G2 Kuivaniemi Finland
40 C2 Kujang Indon.
45 H5 Kujang-Dong N. Korea
47 H3 Kuji Japan
47 H5 Kuji-gawa r. Japan
46 C7 Kuji-wan b. Japan
47 H3 Kujū-san vol. Japan
49 K2 Kukan Rus. Fed.
77 G4 Kukawa Nigeria
101 B7 Kukerin Aust.
29 B3 Kukës Albania
15 A1 Kukhits'ka Volya Ukraine
12 J3 Kukmor Rus. Fed.
40 C1 Kukup Malaysia
57 C4 Kūl r. Iran
28 E3 Kula Bulgaria
60 B2 Kula Turkey
28 B2 Kula Yugo.
54 B3 Kulachi Pakistan
64 D3 Kulagino Kazak.
55 G3 Kula Kangri mt. Bhutan
80 C4 Kulal, Mount mt. Kenya
64 D4 Kulaly, O. i. Kazak.
65 J4 Kulanak Kyrgyzstan
64 E3 Kulandy Kazak.
57 E4 Kulaneh reg. Pakistan
57 F3 Kulao r. Pakistan
63 P2 Kular Rus. Fed.
41 B5 Kulassein i. Phil.
43 D1 Kulat, G. mt. Indon.
55 H4 Kulaura Bangladesh
40 D2 Kulawi Indon.
15 F1 Kul'baki Rus. Fed.
11 F4 Kuldīga Latvia
49 J2 Kul'dur Rus. Fed.
12 F4 Kulebaki Rus. Fed.
43 D4 Kulen Cambodia
14 C3 Kuleshi Rus. Fed.
19 L2 Kulesze Kościelne Poland
12 E4 Kulevatovo Rus. Fed.
98 C4 Kulgera Aust.
12 H2 Kulikovo Rus. Fed.
43 C6 Kulim Malaysia
101 B7 Kulin Aust.
65 H5 Kuli Sarez l. Tajikistan
101 B6 Kulja Aust.
64 F4 Kulkuduk Uzbekistan
97 F2 Kulkyne w Aust.
54 D3 Kullu India
18 E3 Kulmbach Germany
65 G5 Kŭlob Tajikistan
13 G1 Kuloy r. Rus. Fed.
12 G1 Kuloy Rus. Fed.
121 F4 Kulpsville U.S.A.
64 D3 Kul'sary Kazak.
48 D1 Kul'skiy Rus. Fed.
60 C2 Kulu Turkey
65 J2 Kulunda Rus. Fed.
65 K2 Kulunda r. Rus. Fed.
65 J2 Kulundinskaya Step' plain Kazak./Rus. Fed.
65 J2 Kulundinskoye, Oz. salt l. Rus. Fed.
49 E2 Kulusutay Rus. Fed.
57 C3 Kūlvand Iran
97 E3 Kulwin Aust.
15 F4 Kulyabovka Rus. Fed.
15 E2 Kulykivka Ukraine
49 H5 Kŭm r. S. Korea
46 D7 Kuma Japan
13 H6 Kuma r. Rus. Fed.
47 G5 Kumagaya Japan
40 B2 Kumai Indon.
46 G2 Kumaishi Japan
40 B2 Kumai, Tk b. Indon.
64 E2 Kumak r. Rus. Fed.
139 F3 Kumaka Guyana
49 F1 Kumakanda Rus. Fed.
46 C7 Kumamoto Japan
46 C7 Kumamoto div. Japan
47 F7 Kumano Japan
28 C3 Kumanovo Macedonia
93 C5 Kumara N.Z.
49 H2 Kumara Rus. Fed.
76 D5 Kumasi Ghana
78 A3 Kumba Cameroon
60 B2 Kumbağ Turkey
56 B4 Kumbakonam India
78 B2 Kumbo Cameroon
57 C2 Kumel well Iran
12 J3 Kumeny Rus. Fed.
64 E2 Kumertau Rus. Fed.
55 G4 Kumguri India
46 D6 Kŭmho r. S. Korea
49 J5 Kumi S. Korea
80 B4 Kumi Uganda
29 F5 Kumkale Turkey
11 E4 Kumla Sweden
61 A1 Kumluca Turkey
18 F2 Kummerower See l. Germany
77 G4 Kumo Nigeria
49 H6 Kŭmo do i. S. Korea
42 B1 Kumon Range mt. ra. Myanmar
42 C3 Kumphawapi Thailand
56 A3 Kumta India
78 E3 Kumu Zaire
61 C4 Kumub Israel
13 H7 Kumukh Rus. Fed.
14 H1 Kum'ya Rus. Fed.
13 G5 Kumylzhenskiy Rus. Fed.
42 B3 Kun r. Myanmar
57 G2 Kunar r. Afghanistan
65 K4 Künas Chang China
64 F1 Kunashak Rus. Fed.
45 R3 Kunashir, Ostrov i. Rus. Fed.
42 B2 Kunchaung Myanmar
55 F3 Kunchha Nepal
55 E2 Kunchuk Tso salt l. China
11 G4 Kunda Estonia
55 E4 Kunda India
79 C5 Kunda-dia-Baze Angola
56 A3 Kundāpura India
54 B3 Kundar r. Afghanistan/Pakistan
79 E6 Kundelungu, Monts mts Zaire
79 E6 Kundelungu Ouest, Parc National de nat. park Zaire
79 E6 Kundelungu, Parc National de nat. park Zaire
54 B2 Kundian Pakistan
64 F2 Kundravy Rus. Fed.
40 A1 Kundur i. Indon.
57 G1 Kunduz r. Afghanistan
82 A2 Kunene r. Namibia
82 A2 Kunene div. Namibia
65 K4 Künes r. China
11 D4 Kungälv Sweden
65 J4 Kungei-Tau mt. ra. Kazak./Kyrgyzstan
110 C4 Kunghit I. i. Can.
64 E4 Kungrad Uzbekistan
11 D4 Kungsbacka Sweden
11 D4 Kungshamn Sweden
78 C3 Kungu Zaire
78 B6 Kunguta Tanzania
42 A3 Kungyangon Myanmar
19 K5 Kunhegyes Hungary
42 B2 Kunhing Myanmar
51 F1 Kunimi-dake mt. Japan
40 A3 Kuningan Indon.
55 F5 Kunjabar India
42 B2 Kunlong Myanmar
55 F4 Kunlui r. India
55 E2 Kunlun Shan mt. ra. China
19 K5 Kunmadaras Hungary
50 C3 Kunming China
100 D3 Kunmunya Abor. Reserve res. Aust.
100 D2 Kunmunya Abor. Reserve res. Aust.
54 D4 Kuno r. India
46 D5 Kunsan S. Korea
51 F3 Kunshan China
19 K5 Kunszentmárton Hungary
19 J5 Kunszentmiklós Hungary
11 G2 Kununurra Aust.
49 G5 Kunyu Shan h. China
18 D4 Künzelsau Germany
79 C4 Kunzulu Zaire
51 H2 Kuocang Shan mt. ra. China
11 G3 Kuohijärvi l. Finland
10 H2 Kuolayarvi Rus. Fed.
10 G3 Kuopio div. Finland
10 G3 Kuopio Finland
10 F3 Kuortane Finland
26 F3 Kupa r. Croatia/Slovenia
39 H8 Kupang Indon.
15 B2 Kupil' Ukraine
65 J2 Kupino Rus. Fed.
11 G5 Kupiškis Lithuania
110 C3 Kupreanof Island i. U.S.A.
108 C4 Kupreanof Pt pt U.S.A.
15 G2 Kup"yans'k Ukraine
65 K4 Kuqa China
60 G1 Kür r. Azerbaijan
49 K2 Kur r. Rus. Fed.
13 G7 Kura r. Azerbaijan/Georgia
101 B4 Kurabuka r. Aust.
46 D6 Kurahashi-jima i. Japan
60 F1 Kurakh Rus. Fed.
15 G3 Kurakhove Ukraine
14 B3 Kurakino Rus. Fed.
13 G3 Kurakino Rus. Fed.
11 F4 Kura Kurk chan. Estonia/Latvia
26 D6 Kurashiki Japan
55 E5 Kurasia India
46 D6 Kurayoshi Japan
65 L2 Kurayskiy Khr. mt. ra. Rus. Fed.
48 D1 Kurba r. Rus. Fed.
48 D2 Kurba, Nov. Rus. Fed.
14 B4 Kurchatov Rus. Fed.
65 K3 Kurchum Kazak.
60 G1 Kürdämir Azerbaijan
60 F2 Kür Dili pen. Azerbaijan
56 A2 Kurduvadi India
14 F1 Kurdyum Rus. Fed.
28 E4 Kŭrdzhali Bulgaria
46 D6 Kure Japan
60 C1 Küre Turkey
87 K2 Kure Atoll atoll U.S.A.
11 F4 Kuressaare Estonia
65 H2 Kurgal'dzhinskiy Kazak.
65 G1 Kurgan Rus. Fed.
13 G6 Kurganinsk Rus. Fed.
65 G3 Kurgasyn Kazak.
57 G1 Kuri Afghanistan
54 B4 Kuri India
11 F3 Kurikka Finland
47 H4 Kurikoma-yama vol Japan
13 J5 Kurilovka Rus. Fed.
47 E2 Kuril'sk Japan
63 Q5 Kuril'skiye Ostrova is Rus. Fed.
14 D3 Kurkino Rus. Fed.
49 F1 Kurleya Rus. Fed.
14 E2 Kurlovskiy Rus. Fed.
64 D2 Kurmanayevka Rus. Fed.
80 B2 Kurmuk Sudan
14 H2 Kurmysh Rus. Fed.
56 B3 Kurnool India
47 F5 Kurobe Japan
46 C7 Kurogi Japan
46 H3 Kuroishi Japan
47 H5 Kuroiso Japan
46 H2 Kuromatsunai Japan
73 F3 Kurour, Jebel mt. Sudan
48 E2 Kurort-Darasun Rus. Fed.
15 F3 Kuroshany r. Ukraine
12 C2 Kurovskoy Rus. Fed.
14 D2 Kurovskoye Rus. Fed.
93 C6 Kurow N.Z.
19 J3 Kurów Poland
54 B2 Kurram r. Afghanistan/Pakistan
97 G3 Kurri Kurri Aust.
13 G6 Kursavka Rus. Fed.
55 F4 Kursela India
11 F5 Kuršių Marios b. Lithuania
14 C4 Kursk div. Rus. Fed.
14 C4 Kursk Rus. Fed.
13 G6 Kurskaya Rus. Fed.
14 B4 Kurskoye Vdkhr. resr Rus. Fed.
28 C3 Kuršumlija Yugo.
60 C1 Kurşunlu Turkey
60 E2 Kurtalan Turkey
64 F2 Kurtamysh Rus. Fed.
29 G6 Kurtoğlu Burnu pt Turkey
65 J4 Kurty r. Kazak.
55 G4 Kuru r. Bhutan
80 B3 Kuru w Sudan
60 D2 Kuruçay Turkey
54 D3 Kurukshetra India
13 E3 Kuruktag mt. ra. China
82 C4 Kuruman w R.S.A.
82 C4 Kuruman R.S.A.
46 C7 Kurume Japan
45 K1 Kurumkan Rus. Fed.
80 B3 Kurun r. Sudan
98 C4 Kurundi w Aust.
57 C5 Kurunegala Sri Lanka
49 F2 Kurunzulay Rus. Fed.
73 F3 Kurūsh, Jebel h. Sudan
65 K2 Kur'ya Rus. Fed.
29 F6 Kuşadası Turkey
29 F6 Kuşadası Körfezi b. Turkey
110 B2 Kusawa Lake l. Can.
15 C1 Kushalino Rus. Fed.
57 D2 Kūshank Iran
13 F6 Kushchevskaya Rus. Fed.
47 □2 Kushi Japan
47 F6 Kushida-gawa r. Japan
46 C8 Kushikino Japan
46 C8 Kushima Japan
47 E7 Kushimoto Japan
46 J2 Kushiro Japan
46 K2 Kushiro-Shitsugen National Park nat. park. Japan
64 F5 Kushka r. Turkmenistan
64 F2 Kushmurun Kazak.
64 F2 Kushmurun, Ozt. salt l. Kazak.
56 B3 Kushtagi India
55 G5 Kushtia Bangladesh
15 F3 Kushuhum Ukraine
48 C5 Kushui r. China
64 D2 Kushum r. Kazak.
64 D2 Kushum Kazak.
108 B3 Kuskokwim r. U.S.A.
108 B4 Kuskokwim Bay U.S.A.
108 C3 Kuskokwim Mountains mt. ra. U.S.A.
14 B2 Kuskovo Rus. Fed.
49 H5 Kusŏng N. Korea
46 K2 Kussharo-ko l. Japan
64 F2 Kustanay div. Kazak.
64 F2 Kustanay Kazak.
14 F2 Kustarevka Rus. Fed.
15 B2 Kustivtsi Ukraine
60 B2 Kütahya Turkey
13 G7 K'ut'aisi Georgia
13 H6 Kutan Rus. Fed.
92 E3 Kutarere N.Z.
46 H2 Kutchan Japan
77 F5 Kutigi Nigeria
72 F3 Kutina Croatia
19 G4 Kutná Hora Czech Rep.
19 J2 Kutno Poland
40 B3 Kutoarjo Indon.
82 C3 Kutse Game Reserve res. Botswana
79 C4 Kutu Zaire
55 G5 Kutubdia I. i. Bangladesh
72 D5 Kutum Sudan
18 B1 Kutty Ukraine
108 G2 Kuujjua r. Can.
113 G2 Kuujjuaq Can.
64 D4 Kuuli-Mayak Turkmenistan
11 G2 Kuusamo Finland
11 G3 Kuusankoski Finland
14 H2 Kuvakino Rus. Fed.
14 H2 Kuvak-Nikol'skoye Rus. Fed.
79 C6 Kuvango Angola
14 B1 Kuvshinovo Rus. Fed.
57 B4 Kuwait country Asia
47 F6 Kuwana Japan
12 G1 Kuya Rus. Fed.
14 H1 Kuyar Rus. Fed.
65 J1 Kuybyshev Rus. Fed.
15 G3 Kuybysheve Donets'k Ukraine
15 G3 Kuybysheve Zaporizhzhya Ukraine
65 G2 Kuybyshevskiy Kazak.
12 J4 Kuybyshevskoye Vdkhr. resr Rus. Fed.
48 D5 Kuye r. China
65 H3 Kuyeda Rus. Fed.
65 H3 Kuygan Kazak.
65 L4 Kuytun China
29 G6 Kuyucak Turkey
139 F3 Kuyuwini r. Guyana
65 L2 Kuzbass reg. Rus. Fed.
15 F1 Kuzemyn Ukraine

26 F2 Lendava Slovenia
57 D3 Lengbarūt Iran
65 G4 Lenger Kazak.
48 B5 Lenglong Ling mt. ra. China
78 C3 Lengoué r. Congo
51 E3 Lengshuijiang China
51 E3 Lengshuitan China
146 B3 Lengua de Vaca, Pta hd Chile
11 D4 Lenhovda Sweden
65 G5 Lenin Tajikistan
64 E4 Leninabad Uzbekistan
13 E6 Lenine Krym Ukraine
15 E3 Lenine Mykolayiv Ukraine
11 H3 Leningrad div. Rus. Fed.
13 F6 Leningradskaya Rus. Fed.
63 T3 Leningradskiy Rus. Fed.
65 H5 Leningradskiy Tajikistan
65 K2 Leninogorsk Kazak.
64 D2 Leninogorsk Rus. Fed.
64 F3 Leninsk Kazak.
13 H5 Leninsk Rus. Fed.
64 E4 Leninsk Turkmenistan
14 C2 Leninskiy Rus. Fed.
65 L2 Leninsk-Kuznetskiy Rus. Fed.
65 G4 Leninskoye Kazak.
65 G2 Leninskoye Kazak.
49 K3 Leninskoye Rus. Fed.
12 H3 Leninskoye Rus. Fed.
18 C3 Lenne r. Germany
147 C7 Lennox, I. i. Chile
115 K4 Lennoxville Can.
119 D5 Lenoir U.S.A.
121 G3 Lenox U.S.A.
63 N3 Lensk Rus. Fed.
60 E1 Lentekhi Georgia
19 H5 Lenti Hungary
76 D4 Léo Burkina
17 F5 Leominster U.K.
121 H3 Leominster U.S.A.
20 D5 Léon France
131 E4 León Mexico
130 J6 León Nicaragua
24 D1 León Spain
82 B3 Leonardville Namibia
61 C2 Leonarisson Cyprus
91 □13 Leone American Samoa Pac. Oc.
27 E7 Leonforte Italy
97 F4 Leongatha Aust.
29 D6 Leonidi Greece
24 C1 León, Montes de mt. ra. Spain
101 C6 Leonora Aust.
100 D3 Leopold r. Aust.
145 G4 Leopoldina Brazil
144 D2 Leopoldo de Bulhões Brazil
28 F1 Leorda Romania
15 C3 Leova Moldova
111 H4 Leoville Can.
20 C3 Le Palais France
40 A2 Lepar i. Indon.
82 D3 Lephepe Botswana
51 G2 Leping China
115 J4 L'Epiphanie Can.
21 G4 Le Pont-de-Claix France
81 □5 Le Port Réunion Indian Ocean
28 C3 Leposavić Yugo.
10 G3 Leppävirta Finland
65 J3 Lepsy Kazak.
29 D4 Leptokarya Greece
21 F4 Le-Puy-en-Velay France
133 □5 Le Raizet airport Guadeloupe Caribbean
27 D7 Lercara Friddi Italy
78 B2 Léré Chad
77 F4 Lere Nigeria
138 C4 Lerida Colombia
25 G2 Lérida Spain
60 G2 Lerik Azerbaijan
24 E1 Lerma Spain
13 G6 Lermontov Rus. Fed.
49 K3 Lermontovka Rus. Fed.
76 D3 Lerneb Mali
133 □4 Le Robert Martinique Caribbean
29 F6 Leros i. Greece
122 C5 Le Roy U.S.A.
11 D4 Lerum Sweden
16 G1 Lerwick U.K.
78 E1 Ler Zerai well Sudan
133 □5 Les Abymes Guadeloupe Caribbean
133 □4 Le St Esprit Martinique Caribbean
20 F3 Les Aix-d'Angillon France
133 □4 Les Anses d'Arlets Martinique Caribbean
81 C5 Lesatima mt. Kenya
81 □5 Les Avirons Réunion Indian Ocean
25 G2 Les Borges Blanques Spain
25 H1 L'Escala Spain
81 □4 L'Escalier Mauritius
132 D3 Les Cayes Haiti
20 D2 Les Coëvrons h. France
21 H3 Le Sentier Switz.
25 G1 Les Escaldes Andorra
113 G4 Les Escoumins Can.
121 J1 Les Étroits Can.
50 C2 Leshan China
20 D3 Les Herbiers France
12 H1 Leshukonskoye Rus. Fed.
78 E2 Lesi w Sudan
90 □6 Lesiaceva Pt pt Fiji
27 E5 Lesina, Lago di lag. Italy
19 L4 Lesko Poland
28 C3 Leskovac Yugo.
29 C4 Leskovik Albania
15 E2 Les'ky Ukraine
133 □5 Les Mangles Guadeloupe Caribbean
14 D1 Lesnaya Polyana Rus. Fed.
20 B2 Lesneven France
14 E2 Lesnoy Rus. Fed.
12 K3 Lesnoy Rus. Fed.
12 E3 Lesnoye Rus. Fed.
14 F2 Lesogorsk Rus. Fed.
62 L4 Lesosibirsk Rus. Fed.
69 G8 Lesotho country Africa
49 K3 Lesozavodsk Rus. Fed.
20 D4 Lesparre-Médoc France
20 D3 Les Ponts-de-Cé France
20 D3 Les Sables-d'Olonne France
133 G3 Lesser Antilles is Caribbean
110 F3 Lesser Slave Lake l. Can.
110 G3 Lesser Slave Lake Provincial Park res. Can.
10 G3 Lestijärvi Finland
10 G3 Lestijärvi l. Finland
133 □4 Les Trois Îlets is Martinique Caribbean
152 □ les Trois Swains is Kerguelen Indian Ocean
100 D2 Lesueur I. i. Aust.
101 A6 Lesueur, Mt h. Aust.
21 G4 Les Vans France
29 E5 Lesvos i. Greece
19 H3 Leszno Poland
81 □5 Le Tampon Réunion Indian Ocean
19 H5 Letenye Hungary
54 D4 Leteri India
42 A2 Letha Range mt. ra. Myanmar
110 G5 Lethbridge Can.
139 F3 Lethem Guyana
21 H3 Le Thillot France
138 D4 Leticia Colombia
39 J8 Leti, Kepulauan is Indon.
49 F5 Leting China
82 D3 Letlhakane Botswana
82 D3 Letlhakeng Botswana
12 F1 Letniy Navolok Rus. Fed.
14 F1 Letnyaya Baza Rus. Fed.
20 E1 Le Touquet-Paris-Plage France
42 A3 Letpadan Myanmar
20 E1 Le Tréport France
43 B5 Letsok-aw Kyun i. Myanmar
17 D4 Letterkenny Rep. of Ire.
43 D7 Letung Indon.
15 B2 Letychiv Ukraine
79 D6 Léua Angola
28 E1 Leud Romania
12 G1 Leunovo Rus. Fed.
129 G4 Leupp Corner U.S.A.
99 G4 Leura Aust.
18 E5 Leutkirch im Allgäu Germany
18 B3 Leuven Belgium
29 D5 Levadeia Greece
29 B4 Levan Albania
129 G2 Levan U.S.A.
10 C3 Levanger Norway
26 B3 Levanto Italy
27 D6 Levanzo, Isola di i. Italy
13 H7 Levashi Rus. Fed.
133 □4 Le Vauclin Martinique Caribbean
125 C5 Levelland U.S.A.
93 C6 Levels N.Z.
16 F3 Leven U.K.
21 H5 Levens France
100 C3 Lévêque, C. c. Aust.
122 E3 Levering U.S.A.
18 C3 Leverkusen Germany
20 F4 Lévézou mts France
19 J4 Levice Slovakia
29 D6 Levidi Greece
92 E4 Levin N.Z.
115 K3 Lévis Can.
29 F6 Levitha i. Greece
121 G4 Levittown U.S.A.
121 F4 Levittown U.S.A.
19 K4 Levoča Slovakia
20 E3 Levroux France
28 E3 Levski Bulgaria
14 D3 Lev Tolstoy Rus. Fed.
90 □8 Levuka Fiji
20 D2 Lévy, Cap pt France
40 D4 Lewa Indon.
42 B3 Lewe Myanmar
17 H6 Lewes U.K.
121 F5 Lewes U.S.A.
19 H3 Lewin Brzeski Poland
16 D2 Lewis i. U.K.
120 E4 Lewisburg U.S.A.
120 C6 Lewisburg U.S.A.
93 D5 Lewis Pass pass N.Z.
100 E4 Lewis Ra. h. Aust.
126 D1 Lewis Range mt. ra. U.S.A.
119 C5 Lewis Smith, L. l. U.S.A.
129 G6 Lewis Springs U.S.A.
126 C2 Lewiston U.S.A.
121 H2 Lewiston U.S.A.
114 C4 Lewiston U.S.A.
122 B4 Lewiston U.S.A.
122 B5 Lewistown U.S.A.
126 E2 Lewistown U.S.A.
120 E4 Lewistown U.S.A.
125 E5 Lewisville U.S.A.
125 D5 Lewisville, Lake l. U.S.A.
122 C5 Lexington U.S.A.
118 C4 Lexington U.S.A.
124 E4 Lexington U.S.A.
119 D5 Lexington U.S.A.
124 D3 Lexington U.S.A.
119 B5 Lexington U.S.A.
120 D6 Lexington U.S.A.
120 E5 Lexington Park U.S.A.
50 D3 Leye China
152 □ Leygues, Is is Kerguelen Indian Ocean
41 C4 Leyte i. Phil.
41 C4 Leyte Gulf g. Phil.
19 L3 Leżajsk Poland
28 B4 Lezhë Albania
50 D2 Lezhi China
14 E1 Lezhnevo Rus. Fed.
25 E3 Lezuza Spain
14 B4 L'gov Rus. Fed.
55 H3 Lhari China
55 G4 Lhasa Tibet China
55 F3 Lhazê China
55 F3 Lhazhong China
20 C3 l'Herbaudière, Pte de pt France
38 C5 Lhokseumawe Indon.
50 A2 Lhorong China
55 H3 Lhünzê China
55 G3 Lhünzhub China
51 E3 Li r. China
82 C2 Liambezi, Lake l. Namibia
51 G3 Liancheng China
41 C4 Lianga Phil.
41 C4 Lianga Bay b. Phil.
51 F2 Liangaz Hu l. China
48 E4 Liangcheng China
50 D1 Liangdang China
50 D1 Lianghekou China
50 D2 Liangping China
40 C1 Liangpran, Bukit mt. Indon.
49 E6 Liangshan China
51 E4 Liangtian China
50 C3 Liangwang Shan mt. ra. China
48 D5 Liangzhen China
51 F3 Lianhua China
51 F4 Lianhua Shan mt. ra. China
51 G3 Lianjiang China
51 E4 Lianjiang China
51 F3 Liannan China
51 F3 Lianping China
51 F3 Lianshan China
51 G1 Lianshui China
43 C4 Liant, C. c. Thailand
51 F3 Lian Xian China
49 G1 Lianyin China
51 E3 Lianyuan China
51 G1 Lianyungang Jiangsu China
51 G1 Lianyungang Jiangsu China
49 J3 Lianzhushan China
49 G4 Liao r. China
49 E5 Liaocheng China
49 G4 Liaodong Bandao pen. China
49 G4 Liaodong Wan b. China
49 G4 Liaoning div. China
49 G4 Liaoyang China
49 H4 Liaoyuan China
49 G4 Liaozhong China
29 B5 Liapades Greece
54 B2 Liaqatabad Pakistan
110 E2 Liard r. Can.
110 D3 Liard River Can.
54 A4 Liari Pakistan
61 C3 Liban, Jebel mt. ra. Lebanon
138 B3 Libano Colombia
126 D1 Libby U.S.A.
78 C3 Libenge Zaire
125 C4 Liberal U.S.A.
145 F5 Liberdade Brazil
142 B3 Liberdade r. Brazil
19 G3 Liberec Czech Rep.
69 C5 Liberia country Africa
130 J7 Liberia Costa Rica
130 B2 Libertad, Pto Mexico
122 B6 Liberty U.S.A.
121 J2 Liberty U.S.A.
124 E4 Liberty U.S.A.
121 F4 Liberty U.S.A.
125 E6 Liberty U.S.A.
41 B3 Libmanan Phil.
50 D3 Libo China
29 C4 Libohovë Albania
20 D4 Libourne France
29 C4 Librazhd Albania
78 A3 Libreville Gabon
41 C5 Libuganon r. Phil.
68 F3 Libya country Africa
72 D2 Libyan Desert desert Egypt/Libya
72 E1 Libyan Plateau plat. Egypt
140 C4 Licancabur, Vol. vol Chile
146 B3 Licantén Chile
27 D7 Licata Italy
60 E2 Lice Turkey
48 E5 Licheng China
17 G5 Lichfield U.K.
81 C7 Lichinga Mozambique
18 E3 Lichte Germany
82 D4 Lichtenburg R.S.A.
18 E3 Lichtenfels Germany
51 E2 Lichuan China
51 G3 Lichuan China
145 G1 Licinio de Almeidà Brazil
120 B5 Licking r. U.S.A.
26 E3 Lički Osik Croatia
12 C4 Lida Belarus
128 D3 Lida U.S.A.
11 D4 Lidköping Sweden
10 D2 Lidsjöberg Sweden
19 J2 Lidzbark Poland
19 K1 Lidzbark Warmiński Poland
18 F2 Liebenwalde Germany
98 B4 Liebig, Mt mt. Aust.
4 F4 Liechtenstein country Europe
18 B3 Liège div. Belgium
18 B3 Liège Belgium
10 H3 Lieksa Finland
11 G4 Lielvārde Latvia
10 E3 Lien Sweden
78 E3 Lienart Zaire
18 F5 Lienz Austria
11 F4 Liepāja Latvia
11 B4 Liervik Norway
16 K2 Liervik Norway
25 F3 Liétor Spain
20 F1 Liévin France
115 H3 Lièvre r. Can.
19 G5 Liezen Austria
78 D3 Lifanga Zaire
17 D5 Liffey r. Rep. of Ire.
17 D4 Lifford Rep. of Ire.
20 D2 Liffré France
147 C5 Lifi Mahuida mt. Arg.
90 □2 Lifou i. Pac. Oc.
90 □5 Lifuka i. Tonga
41 B3 Ligao Phil.
11 G4 Līgatne Latvia
11 G4 Līgatne Latvia
97 F2 Lightning Ridge Aust.
83 F2 Ligonha r. Mozambique
122 E5 Ligonier U.S.A.
130 C3 Ligui Mexico
26 B3 Liguria div. Italy
26 B4 Ligurian Sea sea Italy
81 C7 Lihehe Tanzania
90 □1 Lihir Group is P.N.G.
99 G3 Lihou Reef & Cays reef Coral Sea Islands Terr. Pac. Oc.
127 □2 Lihue U.S.A.
50 C3 Lijiang China
49 F5 Lijin China
79 E6 Likasi Zaire
78 D3 Likati r. Zaire
78 D3 Likati Zaire
110 E4 Likely Can.
14 B1 Likhoslavl' Rus. Fed.
78 D4 Likolia Zaire
78 D4 Likoto Zaire
78 C3 Likouala r. Congo
78 C3 Likouala div. Congo
78 C3 Likouala aux Herbes r. Congo
40 B1 Liku Indon.
90 □8 Likuri Harb. b. Fiji
21 J5 L'Île-Rousse France
19 G4 Lilienfeld Austria
18 D2 Lilienthal Germany
51 F3 Liling China
54 C2 Lilla Pakistan
11 D4 Lilla Edet Sweden
21 F1 Lille Nord France
11 C5 Lille Bælt chan. Denmark
11 C3 Lillehammer Norway
11 C4 Lillesand Norway
11 C4 Lillestrøm Norway
122 E4 Lilley U.S.A.
10 D3 Lillholmsjö Sweden
101 D5 Lillian, Pt h. Aust.
110 E4 Lillooet r. Can.
110 E4 Lillooet Can.
55 H4 Lilong India
81 B7 Lilongwe Malawi
83 E1 Lilongwe r. Malawi
81 □1 L'Îlot i. Seychelles
41 B4 Liloy Phil.
147 B5 Lilpela, P. pass Arg./Chile
97 F5 Lilydale Aust.
140 A2 Lima Peru
126 D2 Lima U.S.A.
120 A4 Lima U.S.A.
145 G4 Lima Duarte Brazil
57 D4 Līmah Oman
13 H6 Liman Rus. Fed.
40 B3 Liman, G. mt. Indon.
19 K4 Limanowa Poland
55 E2 Lima Ringma Tso l. China
40 A1 Limas Indon.
17 D4 Limavady U.K.
147 B5 Limay r. Arg.
146 C4 Limay Mahuida Arg.
18 F3 Limbach-Oberfrohna Germany
140 C2 Limbani Peru
27 B5 Limbara, Monte mt. ra. Italy
11 G4 Limbaži Latvia
78 A3 Limbe Cameroon
40 C2 Limbungan Indon.
18 B3 Limburg div. Belgium
18 B3 Limburg div. Netherlands
18 D3 Limburg an der Lahn Germany
43 □ Lim Chu Kang h. Singapore
43 □ Lim Chu Kang Singapore
82 C4 Lime Acres R.S.A.
93 B7 Limehills N.Z.
144 E5 Limeira Brazil
17 C5 Limerick Rep. of Ire.
122 A4 Lime Springs U.S.A.
121 K1 Limestone U.S.A.
11 C4 Limfjorden chan. Denmark
24 C1 Limia r. Spain
10 D2 Limingen l. Norway
10 D2 Limingen Norway
121 H3 Limington U.S.A.
10 G2 Liminka Finland
98 D2 Limmen Bight b. Aust.
98 C3 Limmen Bight R. r. Aust.
29 D5 Limni Greece
29 C4 Limni Aliakmonas l. Greece
29 D4 Limni Kerkinitis l. Greece
29 C5 Limni Trichonida l. Greece
29 E4 Limni Vistonida lag. Greece
29 E5 Limnos i. Greece
142 E2 Limoeiro Brazil
115 H4 Limoges Can.
20 E4 Limoges France
130 K7 Limón Costa Rica
130 J6 Limón Honduras
127 G4 Limon U.S.A.
81 □3 Limon, Mt h. Rodrigues I. Mauritius
140 D3 Limoquije Bolivia
20 E4 Limousin reg. France
20 E4 Limousin div. France
20 E4 Limousin, Monts du h. France
20 E4 Limousin, Plateaux du plat. France
20 F5 Limoux France
83 E3 Limpopo r. Africa
51 E3 Limu China
10 H1 Linakhamari Rus. Fed.
51 G2 Lin'an China
41 A4 Linapacan i. Phil.
41 A4 Linapacan Strait chan. Phil.
146 B4 Linares Chile
131 F3 Linares Mexico
24 E3 Linares Spain
27 B6 Linas, Monte mt. Italy
50 C4 Lincang China
48 E5 Lincheng China
51 G3 Linchuan China
146 D3 Lincoln Arg.
93 D5 Lincoln N.Z.
17 G5 Lincoln U.K.
128 B2 Lincoln U.S.A.
122 C5 Lincoln U.S.A.
121 J2 Lincoln U.S.A.
123 F3 Lincoln U.S.A.
124 D3 Lincoln U.S.A.
121 H2 Lincoln U.S.A.
126 A2 Lincoln City U.S.A.
123 F4 Lincoln Park U.S.A.
109 M1 Lincoln Sea sea Can./Greenland
17 G5 Lincolnshire Wolds reg. U.K.
121 J2 Lincolnville U.S.A.
14 F1 Linda r. Rus. Fed.
14 G1 Linda Rus. Fed.
16 K1 Lindas Norway
142 D3 Linda, Sa h. Brazil
18 D5 Lindau (Bodensee) Germany
139 F2 Linden Guyana
119 C5 Linden U.S.A.
119 C5 Linden U.S.A.
122 A2 Linden Grove U.S.A.
109 O3 Lindenow Fjord inlet Greenland
101 B7 Lindesay, Mt h. Aust.
11 B4 Lindesnes c. Norway
81 C6 Lindi div. Tanzania
81 C6 Lindi Tanzania
78 E4 Lindi r. Zaire
49 H3 Lindian China
141 E4 Lindo, Monte r. Paraguay
29 G6 Lindos Greece
121 K1 Lindsay Can.
115 F4 Lindsay Can.
128 C3 Lindsay U.S.A.
87 M5 Line Islands is Pac. Oc.
65 K2 Linevo Rus. Fed.
48 D5 Linfen China
56 A3 Linganamakki Reservoir resr India
51 E5 Lingao China
41 B2 Lingayen Phil.
41 B2 Lingayen Gulf b. Phil.
51 E1 Lingbao China
51 G1 Lingbi China
48 E6 Lingchuan China
51 E3 Lingchuan China
82 D5 Lingelihle R.S.A.
18 C2 Lingen (Ems) Germany
40 A2 Lingga i. Indon.
40 B1 Lingga Malaysia
40 A2 Lingga, Kepulauan is Indon.
41 C4 Lingig Phil.
126 F3 Lingle U.S.A.
78 D3 Lingomo Zaire
48 E5 Lingqiu China
51 E4 Lingshan China
49 G6 Lingshan Dao i. China
48 D5 Lingshi China
51 E5 Lingshui China
56 B2 Lingsugur India
50 D1 Lingtai China
50 E5 Lingtou China
76 A3 Linguère Senegal
51 E3 Lingui China
48 C5 Lingwu China
51 F3 Ling Xian China
49 F4 Lingyuan China
50 D3 Lingyun China
54 D2 Lingzi Thang Plains plain China/Jammu and Kashmir
51 H2 Linhai China
145 H3 Linhares Brazil
42 D3 Linh Cam Vietnam
48 C4 Linhe China
121 H1 Linière Can.
49 H4 Linjiang China
11 D4 Linköping Sweden
49 J3 Linkou China
51 E2 Linli China
16 E3 Linnhe, Loch inlet U.K.
128 A1 Linn, Mt mt. U.S.A.
27 D7 Linosa, Isola di i. Italy
49 E5 Linqing China
49 F5 Linqu China
51 F1 Linquan China
51 F1 Linru China
144 D4 Lins Brazil
51 G1 Linshu China
50 D2 Linshui China
133 □1 Linstead Jamaica
83 G3 Linta r. Madagascar
50 C1 Lintan China
50 C1 Lintao China
21 J3 Linthal Switz.
115 J3 Linton Can.
124 C2 Linton U.S.A.
51 E1 Lintong China
49 F4 Linxi China
48 B6 Linxia China
48 D5 Lin Xian China
51 F2 Linxiang China
82 C2 Linyanti r. Botswana/Namibia
82 C2 Linyanti Swamp Namibia
49 F5 Linyi China
51 E1 Linyi China
51 G1 Linyi China
51 F1 Linying China
19 G4 Linz Austria
48 B5 Linze China
19 L3 Lioboml' Ukraine
15 A1 Lioboml' Ukraine
133 □1 Lionel Town Jamaica
21 F5 Lion, Golfe du g. France
114 E4 Lion's Head Can.
121 F4 Lionville U.S.A.
72 B5 Lioua Chad
78 C3 Liouesso Congo
41 B3 Lipa Phil.
27 E6 Lipari Italy
27 E6 Lipari, Isola i. Italy
27 E6 Lipari, Isole is Italy
15 B2 Lipcani Moldova
14 D3 Lipetsk div. Rus. Fed.
14 D3 Lipetsk Rus. Fed.
12 F2 Lipin Bor Rus. Fed.
51 E3 Liping China
14 C3 Lipitsy Rus. Fed.
14 C3 Lipki Rus. Fed.
28 C3 Lipljan Yugo.
19 H4 Lipník nad Bečvou Czech Rep.
19 J2 Lipno Włocławek Poland
28 C1 Lipova Romania
18 C3 Lippe r. Germany
18 D3 Lippstadt Germany
19 L2 Lipsk Poland
19 K3 Lipsko Poland
54 E3 Lipti Lekh pass Nepal
77 E4 Liptougou Burkina
19 J4 Liptovská Osada Slovakia
19 J4 Liptovský Hrádok Slovakia
97 F4 Liptrap, C. hd Aust.
14 B2 Liptsy Rus. Fed.
51 E3 Lipu China
28 C3 Liqeni i Fierzes resr Albania
28 B3 Liqeni i Shkodrës l. Albania/Yugo.
80 B4 Lira Uganda
78 C4 Liranga Congo
140 B2 Lircay Peru
27 D5 Liri r. Italy
80 B4 Liria Sudan
41 C6 Lirung Indon.
64 F2 Lisakovsk Kazak.
78 D3 Lisala Zaire
83 H3 l'Isalo, Massif de mts Madagascar
133 □3 Lisas B. b. Trinidad Trin. & Tobago
24 B3 Lisboa Portugal
24 B3 Lisboa div. Portugal
122 C5 Lisbon U.S.A.
121 H2 Lisbon U.S.A.
124 D2 Lisbon U.S.A.
121 H2 Lisbon U.S.A.
120 C4 Lisbon U.S.A.
17 D4 Lisburn U.K.
17 C5 Liscannor Bay b. Rep. of Ire.
17 C5 Lisdoonvarna Rep. of Ire.
15 C1 Lishchyn Ukraine
50 C3 Lishe r. China
48 D5 Lishi China
49 H4 Lishu China
51 G2 Lishui China
51 E2 Li Shui r. China
20 E2 Lisieux France
17 E6 Liskeard U.K.
13 F5 Liski Rus. Fed.
54 D3 Liskot India
97 H2 Lismore Aust.
17 D5 Lismore Rep. of Ire.
15 C3 Lisne Ukraine
114 E5 Listowel Can.
99 F5 Listowel Downs Aust.
48 C2 Listvyanka Rus. Fed.
10 D3 Lit Sweden
50 C2 Litang China
51 E4 Litang China
50 C2 Litang Qu r. China
61 C3 Līṭāni r. Lebanon
139 G3 Litani r. Surinam
128 B1 Litchfield U.S.A.
118 B4 Litchfield U.S.A.
20 D4 Lit-et-Mixe France
97 G3 Lithgow Aust.
5 H3 Lithuania country Europe
121 E4 Lititz U.S.A.
29 D4 Litochoro Greece
19 G3 Litoměřice Czech Rep.
19 H4 Litovel Czech Rep.
132 C1 Little Abaco i. The Bahamas
114 E2 Little Abitibi r. Can.
114 E2 Little Abitibi Lake l. Can.
80 D2 Little Aden Yemen
43 A5 Little Andaman i. Andaman and Nicobar Is India
132 C1 Little Bahama Bank sand bank The Bahamas
92 E2 Little Barrier i. N.Z.
122 D3 Little Bay de Noc b. U.S.A.
126 E2 Little Belt Mts mt. ra. U.S.A.
132 B3 Little Cayman i. Cayman Is Caribbean
43 A4 Little Coco I. i. Cocos Is Indian Ocean
129 H4 Little Colorado r. U.S.A.
129 F3 Little Creek Peak summit U.S.A.
114 E4 Little Current Can.
112 C3 Little Current r. Can.
96 E4 Little Desert Nat. Park nat. park Aust.
121 F5 Little Egg Harbor inlet U.S.A.
119 F7 Little Exuma i. The Bahamas
124 E2 Little Falls U.S.A.
121 F3 Little Falls U.S.A.
129 F3 Littlefield U.S.A.
125 C5 Littlefield U.S.A.
124 E1 Little Fork U.S.A.
122 A1 Little Fork r. U.S.A.
111 K4 Little Grand Rapids Can.
132 D2 Little Inagua I. i. The Bahamas
120 C5 Little Kanawha r. U.S.A.
82 C5 Little Karoo plat. R.S.A.
122 D2 Little Lake U.S.A.
113 H3 Little Mecatina r. Can.
120 A5 Little Miami r. U.S.A.
16 D3 Little Minch str. U.K.
124 C2 Little Missouri r. U.S.A.
43 A6 Little Nicobar i. Andaman and Nicobar Is India
114 B2 Little Pic r. Can.
110 D2 Little Rancheria r. Can.
54 B5 Little Rann India
93 D5 Little River N.Z.
125 E5 Little Rock U.S.A.
122 D4 Little Sable Pt pt U.S.A.
119 F7 Little San Salvador i. The Bahamas
110 F4 Little Smoky r. Can.
119 □1 Little Sound inlet Bermuda
133 □2 Little Tobago i. Tobago Trin. & Tobago
127 F4 Littleton U.S.A.
121 H2 Littleton U.S.A.
120 C5 Littleton U.S.A.
122 E3 Little Traverse Bay b. U.S.A.
60 E3 Little Zab r. Iraq
78 B3 Littoral div. Cameroon
81 C7 Litunde Mozambique
110 B3 Lituya Bay b. U.S.A.
15 C2 Lityn Ukraine
49 F4 Liu r. China
49 G4 Liu r. China
50 D1 Liuba China
50 D3 Liuchong r. China
49 G4 Liugu r. China
49 H4 Liuhe China
51 E2 Liujiachang China
51 E3 Liujiang China
48 B6 Liujiaxia Sk. l. China
48 C6 Liupan Shan mt. ra. China
50 D3 Liupanshui China
79 D6 Liuwa Plain plain Zambia
79 D6 Liuwa Plain Nat. Park nat. park Zambia
51 F2 Liuyang China
49 H2 Liuzhan China
51 E3 Liuzhou China
28 D1 Livada Romania
11 G4 Līvāni Latvia
26 F3 Livanjsko Polje plain Bos.-Herz.
147 E7 Lively I. i. Falkland Is.
128 B2 Live Oak U.S.A.
119 D6 Live Oak U.S.A.
100 D3 Liveringa Aust.
128 B3 Livermore U.S.A.
121 H2 Livermore Falls U.S.A.
125 B6 Livermore, Mt mt. U.S.A.
98 C2 Liverpool r. Aust.
113 H5 Liverpool Can.
17 F5 Liverpool U.K.
108 E3 Liverpool Bay b. Can.
97 G2 Liverpool Plains plain Aust.
97 G2 Liverpool Ra. mt. ra. Aust.
131 H6 Livingston Guatemala
128 B3 Livingston U.S.A.
126 E2 Livingston U.S.A.
119 C4 Livingston U.S.A.
125 E6 Livingston U.S.A.
79 E7 Livingstone Zambia
152 B2 Livingston I. i. S. Shetland Is Ant.
81 B7 Livingstonia Malawi
125 E6 Livingston, L. l. U.S.A.
93 B6 Livingston Mts mt. ra. N.Z.
26 F4 Livno Bos.-Herz.
14 C3 Livny Rus. Fed.
12 C1 Livojoki r. Finland
123 F4 Livonia U.S.A.
26 C4 Livorno Livorno Italy
21 F4 Livradois, Monts du mt. ra. France
142 D3 Livramento do Brumado Brazil
61 D3 Liwā' w Syria
81 C6 Liwale Tanzania
50 C2 Li Xian China
51 E2 Li Xian China
50 D1 Li Xian China
51 G1 Lixin China
29 C5 Lixouri Greece
51 G2 Liyang China
17 E7 Lizard Point pt U.K.
20 E4 Lizonne r. France
28 C2 Ljig Yugo.
26 F3 Ljubija Bos.-Herz.
28 B3 Ljubišnja mts Yugo.
26 E2 Ljubljana Slovenia
26 F4 Ljubuša mts Bos.-Herz.
11 E4 Ljugarn Sweden
11 E3 Ljungan r. Sweden
11 E3 Ljungaverk Sweden
11 D4 Ljungby Sweden
11 E3 Ljusdal Sweden
11 D3 Ljusnan r. Sweden
11 E3 Ljusne Sweden
26 F2 Ljutomer Slovenia
25 H1 Llançà Spain
17 F6 Llandovery U.K.
17 F5 Llandrindod Wells U.K.
17 F5 Llandudno U.K.
24 D1 Llanes Spain
17 F5 Llangollen U.K.
130 C2 Llano Mexico
125 D6 Llano r. U.S.A.
125 D6 Llano U.S.A.
130 E3 Llano de Guaje plain Mexico
125 C5 Llano Estacado plain U.S.A.
136 C2 Llanos reg. Colombia/Venezuela
147 B5 Llanquihue, L. l. Chile
140 A1 Llata Peru
25 G2 Lleida Spain
24 C3 Llerena Spain
140 C3 Llica Bolivia
25 F3 Lliria Spain
25 E1 Llodio Spain
99 E2 Lloyd B. b. Aust.
111 H3 Lloyd Lake l. Can.
111 G4 Lloydminster Can.
25 H3 Llucmajor Spain
133 □1 Lluidas Vale Jamaica
140 C4 Llullaillaco, Vol. vol Chile
42 D2 Lô r. China/Vietnam
140 C4 Loa r. Chile
129 G2 Loa U.S.A.
40 D2 Loakulu Indon.
144 B5 Loanda Brazil
26 B3 Loano Italy
14 B1 Lob' r. Rus. Fed.
12 J3 Loban' r. Rus. Fed.
14 D3 Lobanovo Rus. Fed.
82 D4 Lobatse Botswana
19 G3 Löbau Germany
78 C3 Lobaye r. C.A.R.
78 C3 Lobaye div. C.A.R.
146 E4 Loberia Arg.
19 G2 Łobez Poland
79 B6 Lobito Angola
14 C1 Lobnya Rus. Fed.
146 E4 Lobos Arg.
140 B3 Lobos, C. c. Chile
138 A5 Lobos de Afuera, Islas is Peru
138 A5 Lobos de Tierra, I. i. Peru
131 F4 Lobos, I. de Mexico
130 B2 Lobos, Pto de Mexico
18 F2 Loburg Germany
19 H2 Łobżenica Poland
21 J3 Locarno Switz.
42 D2 Lôc Binh Vietnam
114 C2 Lochalsh Can.
20 E3 Loches France
16 E3 Lochgilphead U.K.
16 E2 Lochinver U.K.
19 K2 Łochów Poland
120 E5 Loch Raven Reservoir resr U.S.A.
16 E3 Lochy, Loch l. U.K.
96 C3 Lock Aust.
17 F4 Lockerbie U.K.
97 F3 Lockhart Aust.
125 D6 Lockhart U.S.A.
120 E4 Lock Haven U.S.A.
120 D3 Lockport U.S.A.
20 C3 Locminé France
43 D5 Lôc Ninh Vietnam
140 B3 Locumba Peru
120 B5 Locust Grove U.S.A.
61 C4 Lod Israel
97 E4 Loddon r. Aust.
21 F5 Lodève France
12 E2 Lodeynoye Pole Rus. Fed.
126 F2 Lodge Grass U.S.A.
54 B3 Lodhran Pakistan
26 B3 Lodi Italy
128 B2 Lodi U.S.A.
120 B4 Lodi U.S.A.
10 D2 Løding Norway
10 D1 Lødingen Norway
79 D4 Lodja Zaire
90 □8 Lodoni Fiji
25 E1 Lodosa Spain
80 C4 Lodwar Kenya
19 J3 Łódź Poland
57 G2 Loe Dakka Afghanistan
76 B5 Lofa r. Liberia
90 □5 Lofanga i. Tonga
10 D1 Lofoten is Norway
96 D3 Lofty Ra., Mt mt. ra. Aust.
80 B4 Lofusa Sudan
13 G5 Log Rus. Fed.
77 E4 Loga Niger
127 G5 Logan U.S.A.
120 B5 Logan U.S.A.
126 E3 Logan U.S.A.
120 C6 Logan U.S.A.
99 F4 Logan Cr. r. Aust.
110 D2 Logan Mountains mt. ra. Can.
110 A2 Logan, Mt mt. Can.
122 D5 Logansport U.S.A.
26 E3 Logatec Slovenia
79 B5 Loge r. Angola
78 C1 Logone r. Africa
78 C1 Logone Birni Cameroon
78 C2 Logone Occidental div. Chad
78 C2 Logone Oriental div. Chad
76 C5 Logoualé Côte d'Ivoire
25 E1 Logroño Spain
55 H4 Logtak L. l. India
90 □2 Loh i. Vanuatu
55 F5 Lohardaga India
18 F4 Lohberg Germany
10 G2 Lohiniva Finland
55 H4 Lohit r. India
11 F3 Lohjanjärvi l. Finland
18 D2 Löhne Germany
18 D2 Lohne (Oldenburg) Germany
10 F3 Lohtaja Finland
42 B3 Loikaw Myanmar
50 B5 Loi Lan mt. Myanmar/Thailand
78 D4 Loile r. Zaire
11 F3 Loimaa Finland
20 E3 Loir r. France
20 F3 Loire r. France
42 B2 Loi Sang mt. Myanmar
138 B4 Loja Ecuador
24 D4 Loja Spain
15 A1 Lokachi Ukraine
78 D4 Lokako Zaire
79 E4 Lokandu Zaire
10 G2 Lokan tekojärvi l. Finland
18 B3 Lokeren Belgium
15 E1 Lokhvytsya Ukraine
80 C4 Lokichar Kenya
80 B4 Lokichokio Kenya
40 E2 Lokilalaki, G. mt. Indon.
11 C4 Løkken Denmark
10 C3 Løkken Norway
12 D3 Loknya Rus. Fed.
15 A1 Loknytsya Ukraine
78 D4 Lokofe Zaire
77 F5 Lokoja Nigeria
79 C4 Lokolama Zaire
78 D4 Lokolo r. Zaire
78 C3 Lokomo Cameroon
78 D4 Lokona Zaire
78 C3 Lokosafa C.A.R.
77 E5 Lokossa Benin
14 B3 Lokot' Rus. Fed.
109 M3 Loks Land i. Can.
78 E2 Lol Sudan
78 E2 Lol w Sudan
79 B6 Lola Angola
76 C5 Lola Guinea
128 B2 Lola, Mt mt. U.S.A.
11 C5 Lolland i. Denmark
80 B3 Lolle w Sudan
81 C5 Lollondo Tanzania
126 D2 Lolo U.S.A.
78 B3 Lolodorf Cameroon
90 □2 Lolvavana, Pass. chan. Vanuatu
28 D3 Lom Bulgaria
11 C3 Lom Norway
14 D1 Lom Rus. Fed.
78 D3 Lomako r. Zaire
90 □7 Lomaloma Fiji
78 D4 Lomami r. Zaire
76 B5 Loma Mountains mts Sierra Leone
146 C4 Loma Negra, Planicie de la plain Arg.
57 F2 Lomar P. pass Afghanistan
140 B3 Lomas Peru
147 C5 Lomas Coloradas plat. Arg.
131 F4 Lomas del Real Mexico
146 E3 Lomas de Zamora Arg.
90 □8 Lomawai Fiji
79 D7 Lomba r. Angola
26 B3 Lombardia div. Italy
100 C3 Lombardina Aust.
39 H8 Lomblen i. Indon.
40 D4 Lombok i. Indon.
40 D4 Lombok Indon.
77 E5 Lomé Togo
78 D4 Lomela r. Zaire
78 D4 Lomela Zaire
78 B3 Lomié Cameroon
18 C3 Lommel Belgium
16 E3 Lomond, Loch l. U.K.
65 G2 Lomonosovka Kazak.
21 H3 Lomont reg. France
11 H4 Lomoriosov Rus. Fed.
14 F2 Lomovka Rus. Fed.
12 G1 Lomovoye Rus. Fed.
40 D3 Lompobattang, G. mt. Indon.
128 B4 Lompoc U.S.A.
49 F1 Lomy Rus. Fed.
19 L2 Łomża Poland
56 B2 Lonar India
146 B4 Loncopue Arg.
114 E5 London Can.
17 G6 London U.K.
120 A6 London U.S.A.
120 B5 London U.S.A.
17 D4 Londonderry U.K.
121 G3 Londonderry U.S.A.
100 D2 Londonderry, C. c. Aust.
147 B7 Londonderry, I. i. Chile
144 C5 Londrina Brazil
79 C6 Londuimbali Angola
128 C3 Lone Pine U.S.A.
50 E3 Long r. China
79 B6 Longa r. Angola
79 C6 Longa Angola
79 C6 Longa r. Angola
29 C6 Longa Greece
50 D4 Long'an China
63 T2 Longa, Proliv chan. Rus. Fed.
26 D2 Longarone Italy
146 B4 Longavi mt. Chile
133 □1 Long Bay b. Jamaica
133 □1 Long Bay Jamaica
119 E5 Long Bay b. U.S.A.
93 C6 Longbeach N.Z.
128 C5 Long Beach U.S.A.
121 G4 Long Beach U.S.A.
40 C1 Longboh Indon.
121 F4 Long Branch U.S.A.
122 A6 Long Branch Lake l. U.S.A.
50 D2 Longchang China
50 B3 Long chuan r. China
51 F3 Longchuan China
17 G5 Long Eaton U.K.
93 D5 Longfellow, Mt mt. N.Z.
97 F5 Longford Aust.
17 D5 Longford Rep. of Ire.
51 G3 Longhai China
45 □ Long Harbour inlet Hong Kong
49 F4 Longhua China
51 E3 Longhui China
81 C5 Longido Tanzania
40 D2 Longikis Indon.
133 □4 Long, Îlet i. Martinique Caribbean
40 C2 Longiram Indon.
99 G4 Long Island i. Aust.
112 E3 Long Island i. Can.
109 L4 Long Island i. Can.
93 A6 Long Island i. N.Z.
90 □1 Long Island i. P.N.G.
132 D2 Long Island i. The Bahamas
121 G4 Long Island i. U.S.A.
121 G4 Long Island Sound chan. U.S.A.
49 G3 Longjiang China
55 H3 Longju China
49 G5 Longkou Wan b. China
114 B2 Longlac Can.
114 B2 Long Lake l. Can.
121 J1 Long Lake l. U.S.A.
122 E3 Long Lake l. U.S.A.
123 F3 Long Lake l. U.S.A.
124 C2 Long Lake l. U.S.A.
121 F3 Long Lake U.S.A.
121 F2 Long Lake l. U.S.A.
82 A5 Long Ledge i. St Helena Atlantic Ocean
50 D3 Longli China
50 D3 Longlin China
50 B3 Longling China
49 H2 Longmen China
50 D1 Longmen Shan mt. ra. China
126 F3 Longmont U.S.A.
51 F3 Longnan China
40 C1 Longnawan Indon.
79 C6 Longonjo Angola
43 D5 Long Phu Vietnam
20 E5 Long, Pic mt. France
114 E5 Long Point pt Can.
93 B7 Long Point pt N.Z.
119 □2 Long Point pt The Bahamas
114 E5 Long Point Bay b. Can.
51 G2 Longquan China
51 G2 Longquan Xi r. China
113 J4 Long Range Mts h. Can.
99 F4 Longreach Aust.
50 C1 Longriba China
51 E2 Longshan China
51 E3 Longsheng China
126 F3 Longs Peak summit U.S.A.
51 E2 Longtian China
99 F4 Longton Aust.
17 F4 Longtown U.K.
152 □ Longue, I. i. Kerguelen Indian Ocean
20 D3 Longué-Jumelles France
115 J4 Longueuil Can.
128 A2 Longvale U.S.A.
129 F3 Long Valley Junction U.S.A.
125 E5 Longview U.S.A.
126 B2 Longview U.S.A.
82 A5 Longwood St Helena Atlantic Ocean
50 D1 Longxi China
50 D1 Long Xian China
51 G3 Longxi Shan mt. China
43 D5 Long Xuyên Vietnam
51 G3 Longyan China
49 H2 Longzhen China
50 D4 Longzhou China
26 F3 Lonjsko Polje plain Croatia
11 D4 Lönsboda Sweden
21 G3 Lons-le-Saunier France
10 N2 Lónsvík b. Iceland
42 B1 Lonton Myanmar
144 B4 Lontra r. Brazil
142 C2 Lontra r. Brazil
41 B3 Looc Phil.
122 E4 Looking Glass r. U.S.A.
121 F4 Lookout U.S.A.
112 D2 Lookout, Cape c. Can.
119 E5 Lookout, Cape c. U.S.A.
128 C3 Lookout Mt mt. U.S.A.
99 F2 Lookout Pt pt Aust.
123 F3 Lookout, Pt pt U.S.A.
81 C5 Loolmalasin crater Tanzania
114 A2 Loon Can.
110 F3 Loon r. Can.
111 H4 Loon Lake Can.
121 J1 Loon Lake l. U.S.A.
17 C5 Loop Head hd Rep. of Ire.
54 E1 Lop China
14 G3 Lopatino Rus. Fed.
63 R4 Lopatka, Mys c. Rus. Fed.
15 A1 Lopatyn Ukraine
43 C4 Lop Buri Thailand
78 B4 Lopé-Okanda, Réserve de res. Gabon
90 □2 Lopévi i. Vanuatu
41 B3 Lopez Phil.
121 E4 Lopez U.S.A.
78 A4 Lopez, Cap pt Gabon
44 F3 Lop Nur l. China
78 D3 Lopori r. Zaire
10 F1 Lopphavet b. Norway
12 J2 Loptyuga Rus. Fed.
14 G4 Lopukhovka Rus. Fed.
57 F3 Lora r. Afghanistan
96 C2 Lora w Aust.
24 D4 Lora del Río Spain
120 B4 Lorain U.S.A.
54 B3 Loralai Pakistan
54 B3 Loralai r. Pakistan
120 A4 Loramie, Lake l. U.S.A.
152 □ Loranchet, Péninsule pen. Kerguelen Indian Ocean
25 F4 Lorca Spain
41 A4 Lord Auckland sand bank Phil.
57 B3 Lordegān Iran
94 □4 Lord Howe Island i. Aust.
149 P6 Lord Howe Rise Pac. Oc.
43 B5 Lord Loughborough I. i. Myanmar
129 H5 Lordsburg U.S.A.
145 F5 Lorena Brazil
90 □1 Lorengau P.N.G.
39 L7 Lorentz r. Indon.
57 B2 Lorestān div. Iran
140 D3 Loreto Bolivia
142 C2 Loreto Brazil
26 D4 Loreto Italy
130 C3 Loreto Mexico
41 C4 Loreto Phil.
115 K3 Loretteville Can.
138 B2 Lorica Colombia
20 C3 Lorient France
111 L1 Lorillard r. Can.
99 F5 Lorne Aust.
97 E4 Lorne Aust.
16 D3 Lorn, Firth of est. U.K.
55 H3 Loro r. China
76 D4 Loropéni Burkina
18 C5 Lörrach Germany
98 D3 Lorraine Aust.
21 H2 Lorraine div. France
21 H2 Lorrain, Plateau plat. France
75 G2 Lorzot Tunisia
80 C4 Losai National Reserve res. Kenya
127 F5 Los Alamos U.S.A.
147 B5 Los Alerces, Parque Nacional nat. park Arg.
146 D2 Los Amores Arg.
146 B4 Los Angeles Chile
128 C5 Los Angeles U.S.A.
128 C5 Los Angeles airport U.S.A.
128 C4 Los Angeles Aqueduct canal U.S.A.
128 B3 Los Banos U.S.A.
146 D1 Los Blancos Arg.
130 C3 Los Burros Mexico
25 □ Los Canarios Canary Is Spain
147 A6 Los Chonos, Archipiélago de is Chile
146 D2 Los Cisnes, Lagunas de salt l. Arg.
128 D5 Los Coronados is Mexico
24 D1 Los Corrales de Buelna Spain
140 D3 Los Cusis Bolivia
13 G5 Losevo Rus. Fed.
81 C5 Loseya well Tanzania
128 B3 Los Gatos U.S.A.
147 B7 Los Glacieres, Parque Nacional nat. park Chile
19 L2 Łosice Poland
76 B5 Los, Îles de is Guinea
26 E3 Lošin i. Croatia
11 G4 Loska Estonia
138 B2 Los Katios, Parque Nacional nat. park Colombia
147 B5 Los Lagos div. Chile
25 □ Los Llanos de Aridane Canary Is Spain
127 F5 Los Lunas U.S.A.
147 C5 Los Menucos Arg.
14 B2 Los'mino Rus. Fed.
130 C3 Los Mochis Mexico
128 A1 Los Molinos U.S.A.
78 C3 Losombo Zaire
132 B2 Los Palacios Cuba
24 D4 Los Palacios y Villafranca Spain
24 D3 Los Pedroches plat. Spain
25 F3 Los Pedrones Spain
130 C2 Los Pocitos Mexico
25 □ Los Realejos Canary Is Spain
130 E5 Los Reyes Mexico
138 D1 Los Roques, Is is Venezuela
25 □ Los Sauces Canary Is Spain
16 F3 Lossiemouth U.K.
138 C1 Los Taques Venezuela
146 D2 Los Telares Arg.
138 D1 Los Teques Venezuela
139 E1 Los Testigos is Venezuela
128 C4 Lost Hills U.S.A.
126 D2 Lost Trail Pass pass U.S.A.
140 C4 Los Vientos Chile
146 B3 Los Vilos Chile
24 E3 Los Yébenes Spain
15 D1 Losynivka Ukraine
20 E4 Lot r. France
146 B4 Lota Chile
80 B4 Lotagipi Swamp swamp Kenya/Sudan
57 D1 Lotfābād Iran
80 B4 Lotikipi Plain plain Kenya
79 D4 Loto Zaire
91 □12 Lotofaga Western Samoa
78 C4 Lotoi r. Zaire
14 B1 Lotoshino Rus. Fed.
82 D3 Lotsane w Botswana
15 E3 Lotskyne Ukraine
10 H1 Lotta r. Rus. Fed.
42 C2 Louang Namtha Laos
42 C3 Louangphrabang Laos
79 B4 Loubomo Congo
20 C2 Loudéac France
51 E3 Loudi China
79 B4 Loudima Congo
120 B4 Loudonville U.S.A.
20 E3 Loudun France
79 B4 Louéssé r. Congo
152 □ l'Ouest, I. de i. Kerguelen Indian Ocean
76 A3 Louga Senegal
17 G5 Loughborough U.K.
108 H2 Lougheed I. i. Can.
17 C5 Loughrea Rep. of Ire.
21 G3 Louhans France
120 B5 Louisa U.S.A.
120 E5 Louisa U.S.A.
110 C4 Louise I. i. Can.
90 □1 Louisiade Archipelago is P.N.G.
125 E6 Louisiana div. U.S.A.
83 D3 Louis Trichardt R.S.A.
119 D5 Louisville U.S.A.
118 C4 Louisville U.S.A.
125 F5 Louisville U.S.A.
112 E3 Louis-XIV, Pointe c. Can.
12 E1 Loukhi Rus. Fed.
78 C4 Loukoléla Congo
79 B4 Loukouo Congo
24 B4 Loulé Portugal
78 A3 Loum Cameroon
79 C4 Louna r. Congo
77 G4 Loungoundou well Niger
112 B3 Lount L. l. Can.
19 F3 Louny Czech Rep.
124 D3 Loup r. U.S.A.
112 F2 Loups Marins, Lacs des l. Can.
113 J4 Lourdes Can.
20 D5 Lourdes France
139 G3 Lourenço Brazil
76 B4 Lour-Escale Senegal
140 A2 Louricocha, Lago l. Peru
24 B3 Lourinhã Portugal
24 B2 Lousã Portugal
97 F2 Louth Aust.
17 G5 Louth U.K.
29 D5 Loutra Aidipsou Greece
29 D6 Loutraki Peloponnisos Greece
18 B3 Louvain Belgium
20 E2 Louviers France
10 F2 Lövånger Sweden
12 D3 Lovat' r. Rus. Fed.
28 E3 Lovech Bulgaria
28 E3 Lovech div. Bulgaria
126 F3 Loveland U.S.A.
126 E2 Lovell U.S.A.
128 C1 Lovelock U.S.A.
11 G3 Loviisa Finland
120 D6 Lovingston U.S.A.
122 C6 Lovington U.S.A.
125 C5 Lovington U.S.A.
26 E3 Lovran Croatia
28 C2 Lovrin Romania
14 D2 Lovtsy Rus. Fed.
79 D6 Lôvua Angola
115 H4 Low Can.
78 E4 Lowa r. Zaire
78 E4 Lowa Zaire
111 M2 Low, Cape c. Can.
121 H3 Lowell U.S.A.
122 E4 Lowell U.S.A.
121 G2 Lowell U.S.A.
110 F5 Lower Arrow L. l. Can.
129 F4 Lower Granite Gorge gorge U.S.A.
93 E4 Lower Hutt N.Z.
128 A2 Lower Lake U.S.A.
17 D4 Lower Lough Erne l. U.K.
43 □ Lower Peirce Res. resr Singapore
110 D3 Lower Post Can.
113 H5 Lower Sackville Can.
79 E7 Lower Zambezi National Park nat. park Zambia
17 H5 Lowestoft U.K.
57 G2 Lowgar r. Afghanistan
19 J2 Łowicz Poland
112 E3 Low, Lac l. Can.
94 □2 Low Pt pt Christmas I. Indian Ocean
97 F5 Low Rocky Pt hd Aust.
114 D2 Lowther Can.
121 F3 Lowville U.S.A.
96 E3 Loxton Aust.
82 C5 Loxton R.S.A.
16 E2 Loyal, Loch l. U.K.
120 E4 Loyalsock Creek r. U.S.A.
128 B2 Loyalton U.S.A.
90 □2 Loyauté, Îs is Pac. Oc.
15 D1 Loyew Belarus
12 K3 Loyno Rus. Fed.
21 F4 Lozère, Mont mt. France
28 B2 Loznica Yugo.
28 F3 Loznitsa Bulgaria
15 G1 Loznoye Rus. Fed.
15 G2 Lozova Ukraine
65 J2 Lozovoye Kazak.
24 E2 Lozoya Spain
15 G3 Lozuvatka r. Ukraine
78 C3 Lua r. Zaire
79 D6 Luacano Angola
79 D5 Luachimo r. Angola/Zaire
90 □3 Luahiapu i. Tonga
83 F2 Luala r. Mozambique
79 D6 Luampa r. Zambia
51 G2 Lu'an China
49 F4 Luan r. China
133 □1 Luana Point pt Jamaica
51 E1 Luanchuan China
79 B5 Luanda div. Angola
79 B5 Luanda Angola
79 C6 Luando r. Angola
79 C6 Luando Angola
79 C6 Luando, Reserva Natural Integral do res. Angola
79 D6 Luanginga r. Zambia
79 D6 Luanguinga r. Angola
79 F6 Luangwa r. Central/Eastern Zambia
81 B6 Luangwa r. Northern Zambia
55 H2 Luanhaizi China
111 L2 Luan Lake l. Can.
49 F5 Luannan China
142 A1 Lua Nova Brazil
49 F4 Luanping China
79 E6 Luanshya Zambia
49 F5 Luan Xian China
79 E5 Luanza Zaire
79 E6 Luapula div. Zambia
24 C1 Luarca Spain
40 C1 Luar, D. l. Indon.
79 D6 Luashi Zaire
90 □3 Luatafito i. Tonga
81 C7 Luatize r. Mozambique
79 D6 Luau Angola
78 C3 Lua Vindu r. Zaire
78 A3 Luba Equatorial Guinea
131 H5 Lubaantum Belize
19 L3 Lubaczów Poland
79 C5 Lubalo Angola
19 G3 Lubań Poland
11 G4 Lubānas l. Latvia
41 B3 Lubang i. Phil.
41 B3 Lubang Phil.
41 A3 Lubang Islands is Phil.
79 B6 Lubango Angola
79 E5 Lubao Zaire
19 L3 Lubartów Poland
19 J2 Lubawa Poland
19 F3 Lübben Germany
19 F3 Lübbenau Germany
82 B4 Lubbeskolk l. R.S.A.
125 C5 Lubbock U.S.A.
18 E2 Lübeck Germany
79 D4 Lubefu Zaire
64 D2 Lubenka Kazak.
78 E4 Lubero Zaire
21 G5 Lubéron, Montagne du ridge France
20 E4 Lubersac France
19 J2 Lubień Kujawski Poland
79 D5 Lubilash r. Zaire
19 H3 Lubin Legnica Poland
79 E4 Lubirizi Zaire
19 L3 Lublin Poland
19 J3 Lubliniec Poland
15 E1 Lubny Ukraine
40 B1 Lubok Antu Malaysia
19 H2 Luboń Poland
14 E2 Lubonos Rus. Fed.

M

N

54 D3 Nabha India
57 D3 Nabīd Iran
141 E4 Nabileque r. Brazil
39 L7 Nabire Indon.
61 C3 Nablus *West Bank*
76 D4 Nabolo Ghana
90 □8 Naboutini Fiji
90 □6 Nabouwalu Fiji
61 C5 Nabq Egypt
54 D2 Nabra r. India
43 B4 Nabule Myanmar
83 G1 Nacala Mozambique
130 J6 Nacaome Honduras
83 F1 Nacaroa Mozambique
126 B2 Naches U.S.A.
81 C7 Nachingwea Tanzania
54 B4 Nāchna India
19 H3 Náchod Czech Rep.
90 □8 Nacilau Pt pt Fiji
128 B4 Nacimiento Reservoir resr U.S.A.
125 E6 Nacogdoches U.S.A.
130 C2 Nacozari de García Mexico
47 G5 Nadachi Japan
90 □8 Nadarivatu Fiji
90 □8 Nadi Fiji
54 C5 Nadiad India
90 □8 Nadi B. b. Fiji
57 C3 Nadīk Iran
28 C1 Nădlac Romania
75 D1 Nador Morocco
90 □8 Nadrau Plateau plat. Fiji
90 □6 Naduri Fiji
15 A2 Nadvirna Ukraine
12 E2 Nadvoitsy Rus. Fed.
62 J3 Nadym Rus. Fed.
54 C4 Naenwa India
11 C5 Næstved Denmark
77 G4 Nafada Nigeria
29 C5 Nafpaktos Greece
29 D6 Nafplio Greece
60 F3 Naft r. Iraq
57 B3 Naft-e Safīd Iran
60 F3 Naft Khanen Iraq
60 F3 Naft Shahr Iran
73 H2 Nafud al 'Urayq sand dunes Saudi Arabia
72 B1 Nafūsah, Jabal h. Libya
73 H2 Nafy Saudi Arabia
41 B3 Naga Phil.
114 C2 Nagagami r. Can.
114 C2 Nagagami Lake l. Can.
114 C2 Nagagamisis Lake l. Can.
114 C2 Nagagamisis Provincial Park res. Can.
47 H8 Nagagusuku-wan b. Japan
46 D7 Nagahama Japan
47 F6 Nagahama Japan
55 H4 Naga Hills mt. ra. India
47 H4 Nagai Japan
55 H4 Nagaland India
47 □2 Nagannu-jima i. Japan
47 G5 Nagano Japan
47 F5 Nagano div. Japan
47 G5 Nagaoka Japan
55 H4 Nagaon India
56 B4 Nagappattinam India
54 D4 Nagar India
52 E4 Nagar India
56 B2 Nāgārjuna Sāgar Reservoir resr India
54 B4 Nagar Parkar Pakistan
55 G3 Nagarzê China
46 B7 Nagasaki Japan
46 B7 Nagasaki div. Japan
46 C7 Nagashima Japan
46 C7 Naga-shima i. Japan
46 D7 Naga-shima i. Japan
46 C6 Nagato Japan
54 C4 Nagaur India
56 C2 Nagavali r. India
55 G2 Nag, Co salt l. China
54 C5 Nagda India
56 B4 Nagercoil India
57 F4 Nagha Kalat Pakistan
73 F2 Nag 'Hammâdi Egypt
80 B4 Nagichot Sudan
54 D3 Nagina India
55 E3 Nagma Nepal
47 □2 Nago Japan
54 E4 Nagod India
50 A2 Nagong Chu r. China
12 J3 Nagorsk Rus. Fed.
14 D1 Nagor'ye Rus. Fed.
47 □2 Nago-wan b. Japan
47 F6 Nagoya Japan
54 D5 Nagpur India
55 H3 Nagqu China
119 □3 Naguabo Puerto Rico
41 C3 Nagumbuaya Point pt Phil.
62 F1 Nagurskoye Rus. Fed.
19 H5 Nagyatád Hungary
19 K4 Nagyhalász Hungary
19 K5 Nagykálló Hungary
19 H5 Nagykanizsa Hungary
19 J5 Nagykáta Hungary
19 J5 Nagykőrös Hungary
47 □2 Naha Japan
57 E4 Nahang r. Iran/Pakistan
110 E2 Nahanni Butte Can.
110 D2 Nahanni National Park nat. park Can.
61 C3 Naharayim Israel
61 C3 Nahariyya Israel
57 B2 Nahāvand Iran
18 C4 Nahe r. Germany
90 □2 Nahoï, Cap c. Vanuatu
61 D1 Nahr Sājūr r. Syria
146 B4 Nahuelbuta, Parque Nacional nat. park Chile
147 B5 Nahuel Huapí, L. l. Arg.
147 B5 Nahuel Huapi, Parque Nacional nat. park Arg.
119 D6 Nahunta U.S.A.
57 F1 Naibabad Afghanistan
130 D3 Naica Mexico
28 C2 Naidăș Romania
90 □6 Naidi Fiji
42 B1 Nai Ga Myanmar
90 □8 Naigani i. Fiji
55 H2 Naij Tal China
90 □6 Nailotha Pk h. Fiji
73 F5 Na'ima Sudan
49 G4 Naiman Qi China
113 H2 Nain Can.
57 C2 Nā'īn Iran
54 D3 Naini Tal India
54 E5 Nainpur India
83 F2 Naiopué Mozambique
90 □8 Nairai i. Fiji
16 F3 Nairn U.K.
114 E3 Nairn Centre Can.
81 C5 Nairobi Kenya
90 □6 Naituaba i. Fiji
81 C5 Naivasha Kenya
81 C5 Naivasha, L. l. Kenya
49 H4 Naizishan China
57 B2 Najafābād Iran
73 H2 Najd reg. Saudi Arabia
25 E1 Nájera Spain
54 D3 Najibabad India
49 J4 Najin N. Korea
73 H4 Najrān Saudi Arabia
46 A6 Naju S. Korea
46 B7 Nakadōri-shima i. Japan
46 J1 Nakagawa Japan
47 H5 Naka-gawa r. Japan
46 E7 Naka-gawa r. Japan
47 □2 Nakagusuku-wan b. Japan
46 C7 Nakama Japan
76 D4 Nakambé w Burkina/Ghana
46 D7 Nakamura Japan
63 M3 Nakanno Rus. Fed.
47 G5 Nakano Japan
46 D5 Nakano-shima i. Japan
46 D6 Nakanoumi lag. Japan
47 □2 Nakaoshi Japan
81 B4 Nakasangola Uganda
46 H3 Nakasato Japan
46 J2 Nakasatsunai Japan
46 K2 Nakashibetsu Japan
46 C7 Nakatsu Japan
47 F6 Nakatsugawa Japan
80 C1 Nakfa Eritrea
73 F2 Nakhl Egypt
45 O3 Nakhodka Rus. Fed.
55 H4 Nakhola India
43 C4 Nakhon Nayok Thailand
43 C4 Nakhon Pathom Thailand
43 C4 Nakhon Ratchasima Thailand
43 B5 Nakhon Si Thammarat Thailand
42 C3 Nakhon Thai Thailand
54 B5 Nakhtarana India
110 C3 Nakina Can.
114 B1 Nakina Can.
19 H2 Nakło nad Notecią Poland
108 C4 Naknek U.S.A.
54 C3 Nakodar India
81 B6 Nakonde Zambia
11 C5 Nakskov Denmark
49 J6 Naktong r. S. Korea
81 C5 Nakuru Kenya
110 F4 Nakusp Can.
54 A4 Nal Pakistan
57 F4 Nal r. Pakistan
48 C3 Nalayh Mongolia
55 G4 Nalbari India
13 G7 Nal'chik Rus. Fed.
54 D3 Naldera India
56 B2 Naldurg India
19 L3 Nałęczów Poland
76 D4 Nalerigu Ghana
56 B2 Nalgonda India
55 F4 Nalhati India
56 B3 Nallamala Hills h. India
60 B1 Nallıhan Turkey
72 B1 Nālūt Libya
90 □8 Namacu Fiji
79 C7 Namacunde Angola
83 F2 Namacurra Mozambique
83 D4 Namahadi R.S.A.
41 □1 Namai Bay b. Palau
57 D3 Namakzar-e Shadad salt flat Iran
40 A2 Namang Indon.
81 C5 Namanga Kenya
65 H4 Namangan Uzbekistan
90 □8 Namanu-i-Ra i. Fiji
81 C7 Namapa Mozambique
82 B4 Namaqualand reg. Namibia
82 B4 Namaqualand reg. R.S.A.
90 □1 Namatanai P.N.G.
42 C2 Nam Beng r. Laos
55 H4 Nambol India
99 H5 Nambour Aust.
97 H2 Nambucca Heads Aust.
43 D5 Năm Căn Vietnam
55 H3 Namcha Barwa mt. China
55 F4 Namche Bazar Nepal
49 H5 Namch'ŏn N. Korea
55 G3 Nam Co salt l. China
10 D2 Namdalen v. Norway
10 C2 Namdalseid Norway
42 D2 Nam Đinh Vietnam
122 B3 Namekagon r. U.S.A.
41 □1 Namelakl Passage chan. Palau
90 □8 Namena Barrier Reef reef Fiji
90 □8 Namenalala i. Fiji
19 J4 Námestovo Slovakia
49 J6 Namhae Do i. S. Korea
42 B2 Nam Hka r. Myanmar
42 B2 Namhkam Myanmar
42 B2 Nam Hsin r. Myanmar
82 A3 Namib Desert desert Namibia
79 B7 Namibe Angola
79 B7 Namibe div. Angola
79 B7 Namibe, Reserva de res. Angola
69 F8 Namibia country Africa
82 B4 Namib-Naukluft Park res. Namibia
83 F2 Namidobe Mozambique
47 H5 Namie Japan
42 C3 Nam Khan r. Laos
42 B2 Namlan Myanmar
42 B2 Namlang r. Myanmar
39 J7 Namlea Indon.
42 C3 Nam Lik r. Laos
42 C2 Nam Loi r. Myanmar
42 B3 Nammekon Myanmar
42 C2 Nam Na r. China/Vietnam
42 C3 Nam Ngum r. Laos
97 G2 Namoi r. Aust.
90 □8 Namosi Pks mts Fiji
42 C2 Nam Ou r. Laos
110 F3 Nampa Can.
126 C3 Nampa U.S.A.
76 C3 Nampala Mali
42 C3 Nam Pat Thailand
42 C3 Nam Phong Thailand
49 H5 Namp'o N. Korea
83 F1 Nampula div. Mozambique
83 F2 Nampula Mozambique
55 G2 Namru Co salt l. China
55 H4 Namrup India
42 B1 Namsai Myanmar
42 D3 Nam Sam r. Laos/Vietnam
55 E3 Namsê La Nepal
10 D2 Namsen r. Norway
55 H4 Namsi India
10 C2 Namsos Norway
42 B2 Nam Teng r. Myanmar
42 C2 Nam Tha r. Laos
42 B3 Namtok Myanmar
43 B4 Nam Tok Thailand
42 B2 Namton Myanmar
63 O3 Namtsy Rus. Fed.
42 B2 Namtu Myanmar
90 □7 Namuka-i-lau i. Fiji
83 F2 Namuli, Monte mt. Mozambique
81 C7 Namuno Mozambique
18 B3 Namur Belgium
18 B3 Namur div. Belgium
82 B2 Namutoni Namibia
79 E7 Namwala Zambia
49 H6 Namwŏn S. Korea
42 B1 Namya Ra Myanmar
42 B2 Nam Yi Tu r. Myanmar
19 H3 Namysłów Poland
78 C2 Nana Bakassa C.A.R.
78 C2 Nana Barya r. C.A.R./Chad
78 C2 Nana-Grébizi div. C.A.R.
110 E5 Nanaimo Can.
127 □1 Nanakuli U.S.A.
78 C2 Nana-Mambéré div. C.A.R.
51 G3 Nan'an China
99 H5 Nanango Aust.
47 F5 Nanao Japan
47 F5 Nanao-wan b. Japan
47 F5 Nanatsu-shima i. Japan
50 D2 Nanbu China
49 J3 Nancha China
51 F2 Nanchang China
51 F2 Nanchang China
51 G3 Nancheng China
50 D2 Nanchong China
50 D2 Nanchuan China
43 A6 Nancowry i. *Andaman and Nicobar Is* India
21 H2 Nancy France
54 E3 Nanda Devi mt. India
54 E3 Nanda Kot mt. India
50 D3 Nandan China
46 E6 Nandan Japan
56 B2 Nānded India
97 G2 Nandewar Range mt. ra. Aust.
54 C5 Nandgaon India
50 B4 Nanding r. China/Myanmar
51 E5 Nandu r. China
54 C5 Nandurbar India
56 B3 Nandyal India
51 G3 Nanfeng China
51 E4 Nanfeng China
78 B3 Nanga Eboko Cameroon
40 C1 Nangahbunut Indon.
40 B2 Nangah Dedai Indon.
40 C1 Nangahembaloh Indon.
40 B1 Nangahkantuk Indon.
40 C2 Nangahkemangai Indon.
40 B1 Nangahketungau Indon.
40 B1 Nangah Merakai Indon.
40 B2 Nangahpinoh Indon.
40 C1 Nangahtempuai Indon.
49 J4 Nangang Shan mts China
54 C2 Nanga Parbat mt. *Jammu and Kashmir*
40 B2 Nangatayap Indon.
77 E5 Nangbéto, Retenue de res. Togo
43 B5 Nangin Myanmar
49 H5 Nangnim Sanmaek mt. ra. S. Korea
46 C8 Nangō Japan
49 E5 Nangong China
50 B1 Nangqên China
81 C6 Nangulangwa Tanzania
55 H3 Nang Xian China
48 A5 Nanhua China
50 C3 Nanhua China
51 H2 Nanhui China
57 G2 Nani Afghanistan
56 B3 Nanjangud India
50 C3 Nanjian China
50 D1 Nanjiang China
51 G3 Nanjing China
51 G1 Nanjing China
50 B4 Nanka r. China
51 F3 Nankang China
46 D7 Nankoku Japan
79 C7 Nankova Angola
49 E5 Nanle China
50 B4 Nanlei r. China
51 E3 Nan Ling mt. ra. China
51 G2 Nanling China
51 E4 Nanliu r. China
50 E4 Nanning China
133 □1 Nanny Town Jamaica
109 O3 Nanortalik Greenland
50 D3 Nanpan r. China
55 E4 Nanpara India
49 G4 Nanpiao China
50 D1 Nanping China
51 G3 Nanping China
51 G3 Nanri Dao i. China
45 N6 Nansei-shotō is Japan
149 N2 Nansei-shotō Trench Pac. Oc.
109 O1 Nansen Land reg. Greenland
109 J1 Nansen Sound chan. Can.
81 B5 Nansio Tanzania
20 D3 Nantes France
56 C4 Nanthi Kadal lag. Sri Lanka
40 A3 Nanti, Bukit mt. Indon.
114 E5 Nanticoke Can.
121 F5 Nanticoke r. U.S.A.
110 G4 Nanton Can.
51 H1 Nantong China
51 H2 Nantong China
51 H4 Nant'ou Taiwan
121 H4 Nantucket U.S.A.
121 H4 Nantucket I. i. U.S.A.
121 H4 Nantucket Sound g. U.S.A.
90 □8 Nanukuloa Fiji
90 □6 Nanuku Passage chan. Fiji
90 □6 Nanuku Reef reef Fiji
86 J5 Nanumanga i. Tuvalu
150 G6 Nanumea i. Tuvalu
145 H2 Nanuque Brazil
41 C5 Nanusa, Kepulauan is Indon.
101 A4 Nanutarra Roadhouse Aust.
50 D2 Nanxi China
51 F2 Nan Xian China
51 F3 Nanxiong China
51 F1 Nanyang China
47 H4 Nanyō Japan
81 C5 Nanyuki Kenya
49 H4 Nanzamu China
51 E2 Nanzhang China
51 F1 Nanzhao China
25 G3 Nao, Cabo de la hd Spain
113 F3 Naococane, Lac l. Can.
55 G4 Naogaon Bangladesh
54 C2 Naoshera India
51 E4 Naozhou Dao China
128 A2 Napa U.S.A.
121 K1 Napadogan Can.
108 C3 Napamute U.S.A.
115 G4 Napanee Can.
54 C4 Napasar India
109 N3 Napasoq Greenland
122 C5 Naperville U.S.A.
92 F3 Napier N.Z.
100 D2 Napier Broome B. b. Aust.
152 D4 Napier Mts mt. ra. Ant.
98 C2 Napier Pen. pen. Aust.
115 J4 Napierville Can.
119 D7 Naples U.S.A.
121 H3 Naples U.S.A.
50 D4 Napo China
138 C4 Napo r. Ecuador/Peru
120 A4 Napoleon U.S.A.
27 E5 Napoli Italy
27 E5 Napoli, Golfo di b. Italy
122 E5 Nappanee U.S.A.
91 □10 Napuka i. *Fr. Poly.* Pac. Oc.
60 C4 Naqb Ashtar Jordan
61 B5 Naqb Malha mt. Egypt
80 E2 Naqūb Yemen
47 E6 Nara div. Japan
47 E6 Nara Japan
76 C3 Nara Mali
14 C2 Nara r. Rus. Fed.
96 E4 Naracoorte Aust.
97 F3 Naradhan Aust.
56 C2 Narainpur India
48 E2 Naranbulag Mongolia
138 B4 Naranjal Ecuador
130 C3 Naranjo Mexico
131 F4 Naranjos Mexico
46 B7 Narao Japan
56 D2 Narasannapeta India
56 C2 Narasapatnam, Pt pt India
56 C2 Narasapur India
56 C2 Narasaraopet India
48 E2 Narasun Rus. Fed.
43 C6 Narathiwat Thailand
55 G5 Narayanganj Bangladesh
56 A2 Narayangaon India
55 F4 Narayanghat Nepal
20 F5 Narbonne France
43 A4 Narcondam I. i. *Andaman and Nicobar Is* India
57 C1 Nardin Iran
27 G5 Nardò Italy
146 D3 Nare Arg.
54 B3 Narechi r. Pakistan
101 B7 Narembeen Aust.
109 L2 Nares Strait str. Can./Greenland
19 L2 Narew Poland
19 K2 Narew r. Poland
57 F3 Nari r. Pakistan
82 B3 Narib Namibia
13 H6 Narimanov Rus. Fed.
65 K3 Narimskiy Khr. mt. ra. Kazak.
57 G1 Narin Afghanistan
47 H6 Narita Japan
133 □3 Nariva div. *Trinidad* Trin. Trinidad and Tobago Tobago
133 □3 Nariva Swamp swamp *Trinidad* Trin. and Tobago
130 C3 Narizon, Pta pt Mexico
55 F4 Narkatiaganj India
61 D1 Narlı Turkey
54 C5 Narmada r. India
54 D3 Narnaul India
26 D4 Narni Italy
15 C1 Narodychi Ukraine
14 C2 Naro-Fominsk Rus. Fed.
81 C5 Narok Kenya
97 G4 Narooma Aust.
14 F3 Narovchat Rus. Fed.
15 C1 Narowlya Belarus
11 F3 Närpes Finland
97 G2 Narrabri Aust.
121 H4 Narragansett Bay b. U.S.A.
97 F2 Narran r. Aust.
97 F3 Narrandera Aust.
97 F2 Narran L. l. Aust.
101 B7 Narrogin Aust.
97 G3 Narromine Aust.
120 C6 Narrows U.S.A.
121 F4 Narrowsburg U.S.A.
133 □6 Narrows, The chan. *St Kitts-Nevis* Caribbean
54 D5 Narsimhapur India
55 G5 Narsingdi Bangladesh
54 D5 Narsinghgarh India
56 C2 Narsipatnam India
49 E4 Nart China
48 C2 Nart Mongolia
14 G2 Naruksovo Rus. Fed.
46 E6 Naruto Japan
11 H4 Narva Estonia
11 G4 Narva Bay b. Estonia/Rus. Fed.
41 B2 Narvacan Phil.
10 E1 Narvik Norway
11 H4 Narvskoye Vdkhr. resr Rus. Fed.
54 D3 Narwana India
54 D4 Narwar India
62 G3 Naryan'-Mar Rus. Fed.
65 J4 Naryn div. Kyrgyzstan
65 J4 Naryn Kyrgyzstan
65 H4 Naryn r. Kyrgyzstan
48 A2 Naryn Rus. Fed.
14 B3 Naryshkino Rus. Fed.
10 E3 Näsåker Sweden
28 E1 Năsăud Romania
129 H3 Naschitti U.S.A.
93 C6 Naseby N.Z.
122 A4 Nashua U.S.A.
121 H3 Nashua U.S.A.
119 C4 Nashville U.S.A.
122 A2 Nashwauk U.S.A.
60 D3 Nasib Syria
26 G3 Našice Croatia
19 K2 Nasielsk Poland
11 F3 Näsijärvi l. Finland
54 C5 Nasik India
40 B1 Nasilat Indon.
80 B3 Nasir Sudan
54 C4 Nasirabad India
54 B3 Nasirabad Pakistan
55 F4 Nasmganj India
79 E6 Nasondoye Zaire
90 □6 Nasorolevu mt. Fiji
73 F1 Nasr Egypt
57 B2 Naşrābād *Eşfahān* Iran
57 D2 Naşrābād *Khorāsān* Iran
61 D3 Naşrānī, J. an mt. ra. Syria
60 F3 Nasrīān-e-Pā'īn Iran
110 D3 Nass r. Can.
77 F5 Nassarawa Nigeria
99 E2 Nassau r. Aust.
150 J6 Nassau i. *Cook Islands* Pac. Oc.
119 □2 Nassau airport The Bahamas
119 □2 Nassau The Bahamas
147 C7 Nassau, B. de b. Chile
119 □2 Nassau Village The Bahamas
73 F3 Nasser, Lake resr Egypt
11 D4 Nässjö Sweden
112 E2 Nastapoca r. Can.
112 E2 Nastapoka Islands is Can.
47 G5 Nasu-dake vol Japan
41 B3 Nasugbu Phil.
12 D3 Nasva Rus. Fed.
82 D3 Nata Botswana
82 D2 Nata w Botswana/Zimbabwe
81 B5 Nata Tanzania
138 B3 Natagaima Colombia
142 E2 Natal Brazil
149 G6 Natal Basin Indian Ocean
57 B2 Naţanz Iran
113 H3 Natashquan r. Can.
113 H3 Natashquan Can.
125 F6 Natchez U.S.A.
125 E6 Natchitoches U.S.A.
90 □6 Natewa Bay b. Fiji
97 F4 Nathalia Aust.
54 C4 Nathdwara India
96 E4 Natimuk Aust.
128 D5 National City U.S.A.
92 E3 National Park N.Z.
82 A3 National West Coast Tourist Recreation Area res. Namibia
77 E4 Natitingou Benin
145 H4 Natividade *Rio de Janeiro* Brazil
142 C3 Natividade *Tocantins* Brazil
42 A2 Natogyi Myanmar
130 C2 Nátora Mexico
47 H4 Natori Japan
81 C5 Natron, Lake salt l. Tanzania
47 H5 Natsui-gawa r. Japan
42 A3 Nattalin Myanmar
57 E2 Na'tū Iran
43 E6 Natuna Besar i. Indon.
43 D7 Natuna, Kepulauan is Indon.
121 F2 Natural Bridge U.S.A.
129 G3 Natural Bridges National Monument res. U.S.A.
101 A5 Naturaliste Channel chan. Aust.
149 M6 Naturaliste Plateau Indian Ocean
129 H2 Naturita U.S.A.
122 E2 Naubinway U.S.A.
20 F4 Naucelle France
82 B3 Nauchas Namibia
18 F2 Nauen Germany
121 G4 Naugatuck U.S.A.
41 B3 Naujan Phil.
41 B3 Naujan, L. l. Phil.
11 F4 Naujoji Akmenė Lithuania
54 C4 Naukh India
79 B7 Naulila Angola
18 E3 Naumburg *Sachsen-Anhalt* Germany
42 B3 Naungpale Myanmar
61 C4 Na'ūr Jordan
54 A3 Nauroz Kalat Pakistan
86 H5 Nauru country Pac. Oc.
54 B4 Naushahro Firoz Pakistan
54 B4 Naushara Pakistan
90 □8 Nausori Fiji
11 B3 Naustdal Norway
138 C4 Nauta Peru
131 F4 Nautla Mexico
55 E4 Nautonwa India
57 F2 Nauzad Afghanistan
24 D3 Navahermosa Spain
12 C4 Navahrudak Belarus
129 H4 Navajo U.S.A.
127 F4 Navajo Lake l. U.S.A.
129 G3 Navajo Mt mt. U.S.A.
41 C4 Naval Phil.
24 D2 Navalcarnero Spain
25 E2 Navalero Spain
24 D3 Navalmoral de la Mata Spain
24 D3 Navalvillar de Pela Spain
17 D5 Navan Rep. of Ire.
12 D4 Navapolatsk Belarus
63 T3 Navarin, Mys c. Rus. Fed.
147 C7 Navarino, I. i. Chile
25 F1 Navarra div. Spain
25 F3 Navarrés Spain
128 A2 Navarro U.S.A.
14 F2 Navashino Rus. Fed.
125 D6 Navasota U.S.A.
132 D3 Navassa I. terr. Caribbean
10 D3 Näverede Sweden
14 C3 Navesnoye Rus. Fed.
24 C1 Navia Spain
146 B3 Navidad Chile
133 E2 Navidad Bank Caribbean
142 E2 Navio r. Brazil
144 A5 Naviraí Brazil
90 □8 Naviti i. Fiji
15 A1 Naviz Ukraine
14 B3 Navlya r. Rus. Fed.
14 B3 Navlya Rus. Fed.
28 G2 Năvodari Romania
65 G5 Navoi Uzbekistan
130 C3 Navojoa Mexico
12 G3 Navoloki Rus. Fed.
90 □6 Navotuvotu h. Fiji
54 C5 Navsari India
90 □8 Navua r. Fiji
90 □8 Navua Fiji
90 □8 Navula i. Fiji
54 C4 Nawa India
60 D3 Nawá Syria
55 G4 Nawabganj Bangladesh
55 E4 Nawabganj India
54 B4 Nawabshah Pakistan
55 F4 Nawada India
57 F2 Nāwah Afghanistan
54 C4 Nawalgarh India
54 B3 Nawan Kot Pakistan
54 D3 Nawashahr India
54 C2 Nawashahr Pakistan
90 □6 Nawi Fiji
42 B2 Nawnghkio Myanmar
42 B2 Nawngleng Myanmar
60 F2 Naxçıvan Azerbaijan
50 D2 Naxi China
29 E6 Naxos i. Greece
29 E6 Naxos Greece
138 B3 Naya Colombia
55 F5 Nayagarh India
57 F2 Nayak Afghanistan
130 D4 Nayar Mexico
130 D4 Nayarit div. Mexico
90 □7 Nayau i. Fiji
57 C4 Nāy Band Iran
46 J1 Nayoro Japan
56 B3 Nāyudupeta India
73 G2 Nayyāl, W. w Saudi Arabia
142 E3 Nazaré *Bahia* Brazil
142 B2 Nazaré *Pará* Brazil
56 B4 Nazareth India
61 C3 Nazareth Israel
144 D2 Nazário Brazil
14 E2 Nazarovka Rus. Fed.
125 B7 Nazas Mexico
140 B2 Nazca Peru
57 E3 Nāzīl Iran
60 B2 Nazilli Turkey
54 A4 Nazimabad Pakistan
76 D4 Nazinon r. Burkina
55 H4 Nazira India
55 G5 Nazir Hat Bangladesh
110 E4 Nazko Can.
110 E4 Nazko r. Can.
13 H7 Nazran' Rus. Fed.
80 C3 Nazrēt Ethiopia
59 J5 Nazwá Oman
65 H1 Nazyvayevsk Rus. Fed.
79 E5 Nchelenge Zambia
82 C3 Ncojane Botswana
78 B3 Ncue Equatorial Guinea
79 B5 N'dalatando Angola
77 E5 Ndali Benin
77 F5 Ndeji Nigeria
90 □6 Ndelanathau Pk h. Fiji
78 D2 Ndélé C.A.R.
78 B3 Ndélélé Cameroon
78 B4 Ndendé Gabon
76 A3 Ndiael, Réserve de Faune du res. Senegal
90 □6 Ndikeva h. Fiji
78 C1 Ndjamena Chad
78 D2 Ndji r. C.A.R.
78 B4 Ndjolé Gabon
78 B4 Ndjounou Gabon
79 E6 Ndola Zambia
80 C4 Ndoto mt. Kenya
78 E3 Nduye Zaire
10 C3 Nea r. Norway
29 E7 Nea Alikarnassos Greece
29 D5 Nea Anchialos Greece
29 D5 Nea Artaki Greece
99 F5 Neabul Cr. r. Aust.
94 □2 Neadridge Hill h. *Christmas I.* Indian Ocean
17 D4 Neagh, Lough l. U.K.
126 A1 Neah Bay U.S.A.
98 B5 Neale, L. salt flat Aust.
96 D1 Neales w Aust.
29 D5 Nea Liosia Greece
29 D5 Nea Makri Greece
29 D4 Nea Moudania Greece
29 E7 Neapoli *Kriti* Greece
29 D6 Neapoli *Peloponnisos* Greece
29 D4 Nea Roda Greece
17 F6 Neath U.K.
29 D4 Nea Zichni Greece
80 B4 Nebbi Uganda
76 D4 Nebbou Burkina
12 J1 Nebdino Rus. Fed.
99 F5 Nebine Cr. r. Aust.
64 D5 Nebitdag Turkmenistan
99 G4 Nebo Aust.
12 E3 Nebolchi Rus. Fed.
129 G2 Nebo, Mount mt. U.S.A.
124 C3 Nebraska div. U.S.A.
124 E3 Nebraska City U.S.A.
27 E7 Nebrodi, Monti mt. ra. Italy
15 D3 Nechayane Ukraine
14 G3 Nechayevka Rus. Fed.
125 E6 Neches r. U.S.A.
138 C2 Nechi r. Colombia
80 C3 Nechisar National Park nat. park Ethiopia
18 D4 Neckarsulm Germany
150 J4 Necker I. U.S.A.
93 B7 Neck, The pen. N.Z.
146 E4 Necochea Arg.
132 C5 Necoclí Colombia
29 C6 Nedas r. Greece
112 F2 Neddouc, Lac l. Can.
72 C4 Nédéley Chad
14 C2 Nedel'noye Rus. Fed.
15 B2 Nedoboyivtsi Ukraine
55 G3 Nêdong China
10 F1 Nedre Soppero Sweden
15 E1 Nedryhayliv Ukraine
129 E4 Needles U.S.A.
17 G6 Needles, The stack U.K.
122 C3 Neenah U.S.A.
111 K4 Neepawa Can.
60 G2 Neftçala Azerbaijan
64 D1 Neftekamsk Rus. Fed.
13 H6 Neftekumsk Rus. Fed.
62 J3 Nefteyugansk Rus. Fed.
27 B7 Nefza Tunisia
79 C5 Negage Angola
76 C4 Négala Mali
57 D3 Negār Iran
40 C4 Negara *Bali* Indon.
40 C2 Negara *Kalimantan Selatan* Indon.
40 C2 Negara r. Indon.
80 C3 Negēlē Ethiopia
80 C3 Negele Ethiopia
43 C7 Negeri Sembilan div. Malaysia
61 C4 Negev desert Israel
141 E4 Negla r. Paraguay
81 C7 Negomane Mozambique
56 B5 Negombo Sri Lanka
28 D2 Negotin Yugo.
140 A1 Negra, Cord. mt. ra. Peru
42 A4 Negrais, Cape c. Myanmar
138 A5 Negra, Pta pt Peru
25 E2 Negredo Spain
24 B1 Negreira Spain
20 E4 Nègrepelisse France
28 F1 Negrești Romania
28 D1 Negrești-Oaș Romania
28 F1 Negri Romania
133 □1 Negril Jamaica
75 F2 Négrine Algeria
138 A4 Negritos Peru
147 D5 Negro r. Arg.
146 E2 Negro r. Arg.
141 E3 Negro r. *Mato Grosso do Sul* Brazil
143 C6 Negro r. *Paraná/Santa Catarina* Brazil
141 E4 Negro r. Paraguay
138 E4 Negro r. S. America
24 D5 Negro, Cabo c. Morocco
74 C1 Negro, Cap hd Morocco
41 B4 Negros i. Phil.
28 G3 Negru Vodă Romania
57 E3 Nehbandān Iran
49 H2 Nehe China
28 F2 Nehoiu Romania
79 C7 Nehone Angola
90 □3 Neiafu Tonga
133 E3 Neiba Dominican Rep.
50 D2 Neijiang China
111 H4 Neilburg Can.
43 A5 Neill I. i. *Andaman and Nicobar Is* India
49 E3 Nei Monggol Zizhiqu div. China
138 B3 Neiva Colombia
51 E1 Neixiang China
111 K3 Nejanilini Lake l. Can.
80 C3 Nek'emtē Ethiopia
13 G5 Nekhayevskiy Rus. Fed.
15 E1 Nekhayivka Ukraine
14 G1 Neklyudovo Rus. Fed.
14 E2 Neklyudovo Rus. Fed.
14 E1 Nekrasovskoye Rus. Fed.
11 D5 Neksø Denmark
99 E4 Nelia Aust.
14 A1 Nelidovo Rus. Fed.
124 D3 Neligh U.S.A.
63 P4 Nel'kan Rus. Fed.
63 Q3 Nel'kan Rus. Fed.
114 E2 Nellie Lake Can.
56 B3 Nellore India
110 F5 Nelson Can.
111 L3 Nelson r. Can.
93 D4 Nelson N.Z.
93 D4 Nelson div. N.Z.
129 E4 Nelson U.S.A.
96 E4 Nelson, C. c. Aust.
147 A7 Nelson, Estrecho str. Chile
110 E3 Nelson Forks Can.
111 K3 Nelson House Can.
83 E4 Nelspruit R.S.A.
74 C5 Néma Mauritania
12 J3 Nema Rus. Fed.
122 A2 Nemadji r. U.S.A.
11 F5 Neman Rus. Fed.
60 D3 Nemara Syria
77 F6 Nembe Nigeria
12 G3 Nemda r. Rus. Fed.
29 D6 Nemea Greece
12 K2 Nemed Rus. Fed.
114 D3 Nemegos Can.
75 F2 Nementcha, Monts des mts Algeria
10 J1 Nemetskiy, Mys c. Rus. Fed.
15 D1 Nemishayeve Ukraine
49 H2 Nemor r. China
20 F2 Nemours France
46 K2 Nemuro-hantō pen. Japan
46 K2 Nemuro-kaikyō chan. Japan
46 K2 Nemuro-wan b. Japan
15 C2 Nemyriv *Vinnytsya* Ukraine
15 B2 Nemyryntsi Ukraine
49 G3 Nen r. China
17 C5 Nenagh Rep. of Ire.
14 C2 Nenashevo Rus. Fed.
17 G5 Nene r. U.K.
91 □10 Nengonengo i. *Fr. Poly.* Pac. Oc.
49 H2 Nenjiang China
47 F6 Neo Japan
29 C5 Neochori *Thessalia* Greece
29 F6 Neo Karlovasi Greece
124 E4 Neosho r. U.S.A.
125 E4 Neosho U.S.A.
29 D4 Neos Marmaras Greece
32 K7 Nepal country Asia
55 E3 Nepalganj Nepal
115 H4 Nepean Can.
95 □1 Nepean I. i. *Norfolk I.* Pac. Oc.
140 A1 Nepeña Peru
14 D2 Nepetsyno Rus. Fed.
129 G2 Nephi U.S.A.
17 C4 Nephin h. Rep. of Ire.
78 E3 Nepoko r. Zaire
14 D3 Nepryadva r. Rus. Fed.
121 F4 Neptune U.S.A.
19 J2 Ner r. Poland
20 E4 Nérac France
49 F2 Nerchinsk Rus. Fed.
49 F2 Nerchinskiy Khr. mt. ra. Rus. Fed.
49 F2 Nerchinskiy Zavod Rus. Fed.
14 E1 Nerekhta Rus. Fed.
26 G4 Neretva r. Bos.-Herz./Croatia
26 F4 Neretvanski Kanal chan. Croatia
79 D7 Neriquinha Angola
11 G5 Neris r. Lithuania
14 E1 Nerl' Rus. Fed.
14 D1 Nerl' r. Rus. Fed.
14 D1 Nerl' Rus. Fed.
14 D1 Nero, Ozero l. Rus. Fed.
144 D2 Nerópolis Brazil
25 E3 Nerpio Spain
15 D3 Nerubays'ke Ukraine
14 C3 Neruch' r. Rus. Fed.
14 B3 Nerussa r. Rus. Fed.
63 O4 Neryungri Rus. Fed.
11 C3 Nes Norway
12 H1 Nes' r. Rus. Fed.
12 H1 Nes' Rus. Fed.
11 C3 Nesbyen Norway
28 F3 Nesebŭr Bulgaria
10 D2 Nesna Norway
14 E2 Nesnanovo Rus. Fed.
124 D4 Ness City U.S.A.
110 C3 Nesselrode, Mt mt. Can./U.S.A.
16 E3 Ness, Loch l. U.K.
19 L1 Nesterov Rus. Fed.
14 G1 Nestiary Rus. Fed.
133 □3 Nestor Trin. Trinidad and Tobago Tobago
29 E4 Nestos r. Greece
61 C3 Netanya Israel
111 N2 Netchek, Cape c. Can.
4 F3 Netherlands country Europe
104 M8 Netherlands Antilles terr. Caribbean
15 B1 Netishyn Ukraine
54 C5 Netrang India
109 L3 Nettilling Lake l. Can.
122 A1 Nett Lake l. U.S.A.
122 A1 Nett Lake U.S.A.
131 G5 Netzahualcóyotl, Presa resr Mexico
80 B3 Neubari r. Sudan
18 F2 Neubrandenburg Germany
18 E4 Neuburg an der Donau Germany
21 H3 Neuchâtel Switz.
21 H3 Neuchâtel, Lac de l. Switz.
19 F2 Neuenhagen Berlin Germany
18 B4 Neufchâteau Belgium
21 G2 Neufchâteau France
20 E2 Neufchâtel-en-Bray France
18 D3 Neuhof Germany
111 K2 Neultin Lake l. Can.
18 E4 Neumarkt in der Oberpfalz Germany
152 C2 Neumayer Germany Base Ant.
18 D1 Neumünster Germany
19 H5 Neunkirchen Austria
18 C4 Neunkirchen *Saarland* Germany
146 B4 Neuquén r. Arg.
147 C4 Neuquén Arg.
18 F2 Neuruppin Germany
119 E5 Neuse r. U.S.A.
19 H5 Neusiedler See l. Austria/Hungary
18 D2 Neustadt am Rübenberge Germany
18 D4 Neustadt an der Weinstraße Germany
18 E1 Neustadt in Holstein Germany
19 G3 Neustadt in Sachsen Germany
18 F2 Neustrelitz Germany
21 H2 Neuves-Maisons France
18 D2 Neuwerk i. Germany
18 C3 Neuwied Germany
125 E4 Nevada U.S.A.
128 D2 Nevada div. U.S.A.
146 C4 Nevada, Co mt. Arg.
146 C2 Nevada, Sierra mt. Arg.
24 E4 Nevada, Sierra mt. ra. Spain
140 B2 Nevado Auzangate mt. Peru
146 B4 Nevado Chillán mt. ra. Chile
146 C2 Nevado de Aconquija mt. ra. Arg.
140 B3 Nevado de Ampato mt. Peru
140 B3 Nevado de Chachani mt. Peru
146 C1 Nevado de Chañi mt. Arg.
130 E5 Nevado de Colima vol Mexico
138 B3 Nevado de Cumbal mt. Colombia
140 A1 Nevado de Huascaran mt. Peru
138 B3 Nevado de Huila mt. Colombia
140 C3 Nevado de Illampu mt. Bolivia
140 C3 Nevado de Illimani mt. Bolivia
138 B3 Nevado del Ruiz vol Colombia
131 F5 Nevado de Tolúca mt. Mexico
140 C3 Nevado Sajama mt. Bolivia
146 C4 Nevado, Sierra del mt. ra. Arg.
12 D3 Nevel' Rus. Fed.
14 H3 Neverkino Rus. Fed.
21 F3 Nevers France
97 F2 Nevertire Aust.
26 G4 Nevesinje Bos.-Herz.
13 G6 Nevinnomyssk Rus. Fed.
133 □6 Nevis i. *St Kitts-Nevis* Caribbean
133 □6 Nevis Pk mt. *St Kitts-Nevis* Caribbean
60 C2 Nevşehir Turkey
49 K3 Nevskoye Rus. Fed.
139 F3 New r. Guyana
129 E5 New r. U.S.A.
120 C6 New r. U.S.A.
81 C7 Newala Tanzania
118 C4 New Albany U.S.A.
125 F5 New Albany U.S.A.
121 E4 New Albany U.S.A.
139 F2 New Amsterdam Guyana
97 F2 New Angledool Aust.
121 F5 Newark U.S.A.
121 F5 Newark U.S.A.
121 F4 Newark U.S.A.
120 E3 Newark U.S.A.
120 B4 Newark U.S.A.
129 E2 Newark Lake l. U.S.A.
17 G5 Newark-on-Trent U.K.
121 E3 Newark Valley U.S.A.
121 H4 New Bedford U.S.A.
126 B2 Newberg U.S.A.
121 F3 New Berlin U.S.A.
119 E5 New Bern U.S.A.
122 E2 Newberry U.S.A.
119 D5 Newberry U.S.A.
128 D4 Newberry Springs U.S.A.
115 G4 Newboro Can.
121 G3 New Boston U.S.A.
120 B5 New Boston U.S.A.
125 D6 New Braunfels U.S.A.
90 □1 New Britain i. P.N.G.
121 G4 New Britain U.S.A.
133 □1 New Broughton Jamaica
113 G4 New Brunswick div. Can.
121 F4 New Brunswick U.S.A.
122 D5 New Buffalo U.S.A.
16 F3 Newburgh U.K.
121 F4 Newburgh U.S.A.
17 G6 Newbury U.K.
121 H3 Newburyport U.S.A.
77 E5 New Bussa Nigeria
86 H7 New Caledonia terr. Pac. Oc.
113 G4 New Carlisle Can.
97 G3 Newcastle Aust.
113 G4 Newcastle Can.
115 F5 Newcastle Can.
133 □6 Newcastle *St Kitts-Nevis* Caribbean
83 D4 Newcastle R.S.A.
17 E4 Newcastle U.K.
128 B2 Newcastle U.S.A.
122 E6 New Castle U.S.A.
120 B4 Newcastle U.S.A.
120 C4 New Castle U.S.A.
129 F3 Newcastle U.S.A.
120 C6 New Castle U.S.A.
126 F3 Newcastle U.S.A.
98 C3 Newcastle Cr. r. Aust.
17 E5 Newcastle Emlyn U.K.
17 F4 Newcastleton U.K.
17 F5 Newcastle-under-Lyme U.K.
17 G4 Newcastle upon Tyne U.K.
98 C3 Newcastle Waters Aust.
17 C5 Newcastle West Rep. of Ire.
121 F6 New Church U.S.A.
129 H3 Newcomb U.S.A.
101 B7 Newdegate Aust.
121 K1 New Denmark Can.
128 B3 New Don Pedro Reservoir resr U.S.A.
97 G2 New England Ra. mt. ra. Aust.
108 B4 Newenham, C. c. U.S.A.
113 J4 Newfoundland div. Can.
148 G2 Newfoundland Basin Atlantic Ocean
17 E4 New Galloway U.K.
90 □1 New Georgia i. Solomon Is.
90 □1 New Georgia Islands is Solomon Is.
113 H4 New Glasgow Can.
133 □3 New Grant Trin. and Tobago
39 M8 New Guinea i. Indon.
73 G4 New Halfa Sudan
121 G3 New Hampshire div. U.S.A.
120 B4 New Hampshire U.S.A.
122 A4 New Hampton U.S.A.
90 □1 New Hanover i. P.N.G.
121 G4 New Haven U.S.A.
110 D3 New Hazelton Can.
128 B2 New Hogan Reservoir resr U.S.A.
122 C4 New Holstein U.S.A.
125 F6 New Iberia U.S.A.
83 E3 Newington R.S.A.
90 □1 New Ireland i. P.N.G.
121 F5 New Jersey div. U.S.A.
120 E6 New Kent U.S.A.
120 B5 New Lexington U.S.A.
122 B4 New Lisbon U.S.A.
115 F3 New Liskeard Can.
121 G4 New London U.S.A.
122 B5 New London U.S.A.
122 B6 New London U.S.A.
122 C3 New London U.S.A.
101 B4 Newman Aust.
122 D6 Newman U.S.A.
115 F4 Newmarket Can.
133 □1 Newmarket Jamaica
17 H5 Newmarket U.K.
120 D5 New Market U.S.A.
17 C5 Newmarket on-Fergus Rep. of Ire.
120 C5 New Martinsville U.S.A.
126 C2 New Meadows U.S.A.
128 B3 New Melanes L. l. U.S.A.
127 F5 New Mexico div. U.S.A.
119 C5 Newnan U.S.A.
97 F5 New Norfolk Aust.
125 F6 New Orleans U.S.A.
121 F4 New Paltz U.S.A.
120 C4 New Philadelphia U.S.A.
92 E3 New Plymouth N.Z.
133 □1 Newport Jamaica
132 □2 New Port *Curaçao* Netherlands Ant.
17 G6 Newport U.K.
17 F6 Newport U.K.
125 F5 Newport U.S.A.
120 A5 Newport U.S.A.
121 J2 Newport U.S.A.
123 F5 Newport U.S.A.
121 G3 Newport U.S.A.
126 A2 Newport U.S.A.
121 H4 Newport U.S.A.
121 G2 Newport U.S.A.
126 C1 Newport U.S.A.
128 D5 Newport Beach U.S.A.
120 E6 Newport News U.S.A.
119 □2 New Providence i. The Bahamas
17 E6 Newquay U.K.
113 G4 New Richmond Can.
122 A3 New Richmond U.S.A.
129 F5 New River U.S.A.
125 F6 New Roads U.S.A.
17 D5 New Ross Rep. of Ire.
17 D4 Newry U.K.
122 A5 New Sharon U.S.A.
119 D6 New Smyrna Beach U.S.A.
97 F3 New South Wales div. Aust.
45 □ New Territories reg. Hong Kong
124 E3 Newton U.S.A.
124 D4 Newton U.S.A.
121 H3 Newton U.S.A.
125 F5 Newton U.S.A.
121 F4 Newton U.S.A.
17 F6 Newton Abbot U.K.
16 E3 Newtonmore U.K.
17 E4 Newton Stewart U.K.
124 C1 New Town U.S.A.
17 E4 Newtownabbey U.K.
17 E4 Newtownards U.K.
17 D4 Newtownstewart U.K.
124 E2 New Ulm U.S.A.
128 A2 Newville U.S.A.
110 E5 New Westminster Can.
121 E3 New York div. U.S.A.
121 G4 New York U.S.A.
121 G4 New York-John F. Kennedy airport U.S.A.
121 F4 New York-Newark airport U.S.A.
86 J9 New Zealand country Australasia
149 Q7 New Zealand Plateau Pac. Oc.
12 G3 Neya r. Rus. Fed.
12 G3 Neya Rus. Fed.
57 C2 Neyestānak Iran
57 C3 Neyrīz Iran
57 D1 Neyshābūr Iran
56 B4 Neyyattinkara India
114 B2 Nezah Can.
15 G1 Nezhegol' r. Rus. Fed.
14 F1 Nezhitino Rus. Fed.
15 A2 Nezvys'ko Ukraine
40 B1 Ngabang Indon.
79 C4 Ngabé Congo
43 B4 Nga Chong, Kh. mt. Myanmar/Thailand
77 G4 Ngadda w Nigeria
40 D4 Ngadubolu Indon.
42 B1 Ngagahtawng Myanmar
77 G4 Ngala Nigeria
41 C6 Ngalipaëng Indon.
40 E4 Ngalu Indon.
78 C1 Ngam Chad
78 C1 Ngama Chad
41 □1 Ngamegei Passage chan. Palau
82 C3 Ngami, Lake l. Botswana
82 C2 Ngamiland div. Botswana
55 F3 Ngamring China
80 B4 Ngangala Sudan
55 E3 Ngangla Ringco salt l. China
54 E2 Nganglong Kangri mt. China
55 E2 Nganglong Kangri mt. ra. China
79 B6 N'gangula Angola
55 F3 Ngangzê Co salt l. China
40 B3 Nganjuk Indon.
42 B3 Ngao Thailand
78 B2 Ngaoundal Cameroon
78 B2 Ngaoundéré Cameroon
55 H5 Ngape Myanmar
42 A3 Ngaputaw Myanmar
81 B5 Ngara Tanzania
40 A3 Ngaras Indon.
41 □1 Ngardmau Palau
41 □1 Ngardmau Bay b. Palau
41 □1 Ngardololok Palau
41 □1 Ngaregur i. Palau
92 E2 Ngaruawahia N.Z.
92 F3 Ngaruroro r. N.Z.
92 E2 Ngatea N.Z.
41 □1 Ngateguil, Pt pt Palau
42 A3 Ngathainggyaung Myanmar
92 E3 Ngauruhoe, Mt vol N.Z.
40 B3 Ngawi Indon.
78 E3 Ngayu r. Zaire
78 B3 Ngbala Congo
41 □1 Ngemelis Is is Palau
41 □1 Ngeregong i. Palau
41 □1 Ngergoi i. Palau
41 □1 Ngesebus i. Palau
90 □1 Nggatokae i. Solomon Is.
90 □6 Nggele Levu i. Fiji
82 C3 Nghabe r. Botswana
42 C3 Ngiap r. Laos
79 C4 Ngo Congo
41 □1 Ngobasangel i. Palau
43 D4 Ngoc Linh mt. Vietnam
55 F3 Ngoin, Co l. China
78 C4 Ngoko Congo
77 G5 Ngol Bembo Nigeria
78 B3 Ngomedzap Cameroon
50 A1 Ngom Qu r. China
78 B2 Ngong Cameroon
55 F2 Ngoqumaima China
50 B1 Ngoring China
50 B1 Ngoring Hu l. China
76 D3 Ngorkou Mali
81 C5 Ngorongoro Conservation Area res. Tanzania
79 C4 Ngoso Zaire
78 C3 Ngoto C.A.R.
78 B3 Ngoulémakong Cameroon
76 D3 Ngouma Mali
78 B4 Ngounié r. Gabon
78 B4 Ngounié div. Gabon
78 B4 Ngouoni Gabon
78 C1 Ngoura Chad
72 C5 Ngouri Chad
77 G3 Ngourti Niger
72 C4 Ngoutchey well Chad
78 E2 Ngouyo C.A.R.
78 B2 Nguia Bouar C.A.R.
77 G4 Nguigmi Niger
77 F3 Nguini well Niger
39 L5 Ngulu i. Fed. States of Micronesia
90 □2 Nguna i. Vanuatu
83 E3 Ngundu Zimbabwe
40 C4 Ngunut Indon.
77 G4 Nguru Nigeria
42 D2 Nguy ên Binh Vietnam
82 C3 Ngwaketse div. Botswana
82 C3 Ngwako Pan salt pan Botswana
83 E4 Ngwelezana R.S.A.
79 E7 Ngweze r. Zambia
83 F3 Nhachengue Mozambique
42 D3 Nhac Sơn Vietnam
83 F2 Nhamalabué Mozambique
83 E2 Nhamatanda Mozambique
141 E2 Nhambiquara Brazil
142 A1 Nhamundá Brazil
139 F4 Nhamundá r. Brazil
144 C4 Nhandeara Brazil
79 C6 N'harea Angola
43 E4 Nha Trang Vietnam
141 E3 Nhecolândia Brazil
79 B6 Nhia r. Angola
96 E4 Nhill Aust.
42 D2 Nho Quan Vietnam
98 D2 Nhulunbuy Aust.
78 E4 Niabembe Zaire
111 J4 Niacam Can.
76 D3 Niafounké Mali
122 D3 Niagara U.S.A.
115 F5 Niagara Falls Can.
120 D3 Niagara Falls U.S.A.
123 H4 Niagara River r. Can./U.S.A.
76 C4 Niagassola Guinea
76 C4 Niagouelé, Mt du h. Guinea
54 D2 Niagzu China/Jammu and Kashmir
76 C5 Niakaramandougou Côte d'Ivoire
77 E4 Niamey Niger
41 C5 Niampak Indon.
77 E5 Niamtougou Togo
76 C5 Niandan r. Guinea
76 C4 Niandankoro Guinea
78 E3 Niangara Zaire
76 D4 Niangoloko Burkina
78 E3 Nia-Nia Zaire
49 G3 Nianzishan China
79 B4 Niari div. Congo
38 C6 Nias i. Indon.
81 C7 Niassa div. Mozambique
11 F4 Nīca Latvia
104 K8 Nicaragua country Central America
130 J7 Nicaragua, Lago de l. Nicaragua
27 F6 Nicastro Italy
21 H5 Nice France
113 F3 Nichicun, Lac l. Can.
46 C6 Nichihara Japan
46 C8 Nichinan Japan
55 E4 Nichlaul India
132 B2 Nicholas Channel chan. The Bahamas/Cuba
132 C1 Nicholl's Town The Bahamas
98 D3 Nicholson r. Aust.
100 E3 Nicholson Aust.
114 D3 Nicholson Can.
101 B5 Nicholson Ra. h. Aust.
43 A5 Nicobar Islands is *Andaman and Nicobar Is* India
28 G2 Nicolae Bălcescu Romania
115 J3 Nicolet Can.
27 E7 Nicosia Italy
27 E6 Nicotera Italy
130 J7 Nicoya, G. de b. Mexico
130 J7 Nicoya, Pen. de pen. Costa Rica
121 K1 Nictau Can.
28 G2 Niculiţel Romania
11 F5 Nida Lithuania
19 K3 Nida r. Poland
18 D3 Nidder r. Germany
29 C4 Nidže mt. Greece/Macedonia
19 K2 Nidzica Poland
18 D1 Niebüll Germany
18 D3 Niederaula Germany
19 F5 Niedere Tauern mts Austria
19 F3 Niederlausitz reg. Germany
19 G4 Niederösterreich div. Austria
18 D2 Niedersachsen div. Germany
19 L3 Niedrzwica Duża Poland
78 B3 Niefang Equatorial Guinea
79 E5 Niemba Zaire
18 F2 Niemegk Germany
76 C4 Niéna Mali
18 D2 Nienburg (Weser) Germany
76 C5 Niénokoué, Mt h. Côte d'Ivoire
18 C3 Niers r. Germany
19 G3 Niesky Germany
139 F2 Nieuw Amsterdam Surinam
139 F3 Nieuw-Jacobkondre Surinam
139 F2 Nieuw Nickerie Surinam
18 A3 Nieuwpoort Belgium
25 □ Nieves, Pico de las mt. *Canary Is* Spain
60 C2 Niğde Turkey
68 E4 Niger country Africa
76 F5 Niger r. Africa
77 F4 Niger div. Nigeria
69 E5 Nigeria country Africa
77 F6 Niger, Mouths of the river mouth Nigeria
76 B5 Niger, Source of the Guinea
93 B6 Nightcaps N.Z.
114 E2 Nighthawk Lake l. Can.
82 A5 Nightingale I. i. *Tristan da Cunha* Atlantic Ocean
47 H5 Nihonmatsu Japan
47 G5 Niigata div. Japan
47 G5 Niigata Japan
46 D7 Niihama Japan
127 □2 Niihau i. U.S.A.
47 G6 Nii-jima i. Japan
46 J2 Niikappu Japan
46 D6 Niimi Japan
47 G5 Niitsu Japan
25 E4 Níjar Spain
74 C5 Nijerâne well Mauritania
18 B3 Nijmegen Netherlands
29 D5 Nikaia Greece
10 H1 Nikel' Rus. Fed.
13 F5 Nikitovka Rus. Fed.
77 E5 Nikki Benin
47 G5 Nikkō Nat. Park nat. park Japan
65 G2 Nikolayevka Kazak.
64 F2 Nikolayevka Rus. Fed.
49 K2 Nikolayevka Rus. Fed.
14 H3 Nikolayevka Rus. Fed.
13 H5 Nikolayevsk Rus. Fed.
63 Q4 Nikolayevsk-na-Amure Rus. Fed.
12 H3 Nikol'sk Rus. Fed.
14 H3 Nikol'sk Rus. Fed.
12 G3 Nikol'skoye Rus. Fed.
63 S4 Nikol'skoye Rus. Fed.

28 E3 **Nikopol** Bulgaria
15 F3 **Nikopol'** Ukraine
57 B1 **Nik Pey** Iran
60 D1 **Niksar** Turkey
57 E4 **Nikshahr** Iran
28 B3 **Nikšić** Yugo.
150 H6 **Nikumaroro i.** Kiribati
150 G6 **Nikunau i.** Kiribati
54 C2 **Nila** Pakistan
55 F5 **Nilagiri** India
129 E5 **Niland** U.S.A.
53 D10 **Nilande Atoll atoll** Maldives
54 D3 **Nilang** India
56 B2 **Nilanga** India
73 F2 **Nile r.** Africa
122 D5 **Niles** U.S.A.
56 A3 **Nileswaram** India
56 B4 **Nilgiri Hills mts** India
80 C2 **Nili r.** Ethiopia
57 F2 **Nil P. pass** Afghanistan
10 H3 **Nilsiä** Finland
131 G5 **Niltepec** Mexico
54 C4 **Nimach** India
54 C4 **Nimbahera** India
76 C5 **Nimba, Monts mt.** Côte d'Ivoire
21 G5 **Nîmes** France
97 G4 **Nimmitabel** Aust.
152 B4 **Nimrod Gl. gl.** Ant.
80 B4 **Nimule** Sudan
60 E3 **Nīnawá div.** Iraq
79 D6 **Ninda** Angola
99 G6 **Nindigully** Aust.
53 D9 **Nine Degree Channel chan.** India
128 D2 **Ninemile Peak summit** U.S.A.
45 □ **Ninepin Group is** Hong Kong
149 K5 **Ninety-East Ridge** Indian Ocean
97 F4 **Ninety Mile Beach beach** Aust.
92 D1 **Ninety Mile Beach beach** N.Z.
60 E2 **Nineveh** Iraq
121 F3 **Nineveh** U.S.A.
147 D5 **Ninfas, Pta pt** Arg.
49 J3 **Ning'an** China
51 H2 **Ningbo** China
49 F4 **Ningcheng** China
51 G3 **Ningde** China
51 F3 **Ningdu** China
51 F3 **Ninggang** China
51 G2 **Ningguo** China
51 H2 **Ninghai** China
49 F5 **Ninghe** China
51 G3 **Ninghua** China
77 F4 **Ningi** Nigeria
50 B2 **Ningjing Shan mt. ra.** China
50 C3 **Ninglang** China
51 F1 **Ningling** China
50 D4 **Ningming** China
50 C3 **Ningnan** China
50 D1 **Ningqiang** China
50 E1 **Ningshan** China
48 E5 **Ningwu** China
48 C5 **Ningxia div.** China
50 D1 **Ning Xian** China
51 F2 **Ningxiang** China
49 F6 **Ningyang** China
51 E3 **Ningyuan** China
42 D2 **Ninh Binh** Vietnam
43 E4 **Ninh Hoa** Vietnam
90 □5 **Niniva i.** Tonga
152 B6 **Ninnis Gl. gl.** Ant.
47 H3 **Ninohe** Japan
147 B6 **Ninualac, Can. chan.** Chile
143 A5 **Nioaque** Brazil
124 C3 **Niobrara r.** U.S.A.
78 F3 **Nioka** Zaire
79 C4 **Nioki** Zaire
55 H4 **Nioko** India
76 B4 **Niokolo Koba, Parc National du nat. park** Senegal
76 C4 **Niono** Mali
76 C3 **Nioro** Mali
76 A4 **Nioro du Rip** Senegal
20 D3 **Niort** France
74 C5 **Nioût well** Mauritania
90 □1 **Nipa** P.N.G.
56 A2 **Nipani** India
111 J4 **Nipawin** Can.
111 J4 **Nipawin Provincial Park res.** Can.
114 A2 **Nipigon** Can.
114 A2 **Nipigon Bay b.** Can.
114 A2 **Nipigon, Lake l.** Can.
113 H3 **Nipishish Lake l.** Can.
115 F3 **Nipissing** Can.
115 F3 **Nipissing, L. l.** Can.
128 B4 **Nipomo** U.S.A.
129 E4 **Nipton** U.S.A.
142 C3 **Niquelândia** Brazil
132 C2 **Niquero** Cuba
60 F2 **Nir** Iran
56 A2 **Nira r.** India
47 G6 **Nirasaki** Japan
73 H3 **Nīr, J. an h.** Saudi Arabia
56 B2 **Nirmal** India
55 F4 **Nirmali** India
56 B2 **Nirmal Range h.** India
28 C3 **Niš** Yugo.
24 C3 **Nisa** Portugal
27 E7 **Niscemi** Italy
46 H2 **Niseko** Japan
47 G5 **Nishiaizu** Japan
46 K2 **Nishibetsu-gawa r.** Japan
46 C8 **Nishikata** Japan
47 H4 **Nishikawa** Japan
46 E6 **Nishino-shima i.** Japan
46 D5 **Nishino-shima i.** Japan
46 B7 **Nishi-Sonogi-hantō pen.** Japan
46 B6 **Nishi-suidō chan.** S. Korea
46 E6 **Nishiwaki** Japan
19 L3 **Nisko** Poland
110 B2 **Nisling r.** Can.
15 C3 **Nisporeni** Moldova
11 D4 **Nissan r.** Sweden
15 C3 **Nistru r.** Moldova
110 C2 **Nisutlin r.** Can.
29 F6 **Nisyros i.** Greece
57 B4 **Niţā** Saudi Arabia
113 F3 **Nitchequon** Can.
145 G5 **Niterói** Brazil
17 F4 **Nith r.** U.K.
19 J4 **Nitra** Slovakia
120 C5 **Nitro** U.S.A.
90 □4 **Niu' Aunofo pt** Tonga
87 L6 **Niue i.** Pac. Oc.
150 G6 **Niulakita i.** Tuvalu
50 C3 **Niulan r.** China
86 J5 **Niutao i.** Tuvalu
49 G4 **Niuzhuang** China
10 G3 **Nivala** Finland
99 F5 **Nive w** Aust.
99 F5 **Nive Downs** Aust.
12 K2 **Nivshera** Rus. Fed.
54 C4 **Niwāi** India
128 C2 **Nixon** U.S.A.
65 K5 **Niya r.** China
46 D7 **Niyodo-gawa r.** Japan
40 B1 **Niyut, G. mt.** Indon.
56 B2 **Nizamabad** India
56 B2 **Nizam Sagar l.** India
64 D1 **Nizhnekamsk** Rus. Fed.
64 D1 **Nizhnekamskoye Vdkhr. resr** Rus. Fed.
63 S3 **Nizhnekolymsk** Rus. Fed.
63 L4 **Nizhneudinsk** Rus. Fed.
62 J3 **Nizhnevartovsk** Rus. Fed.
63 P2 **Nizhneyansk** Rus. Fed.
13 G5 **Nizhniy Chir** Rus. Fed.
14 F3 **Nizhniy Lomov** Rus. Fed.
14 F1 **Nizhniy Novgorod div.** Rus. Fed.
12 K2 **Nizhniy Odes** Rus. Fed.
14 F3 **Nizhniy Shibryay** Rus. Fed.
14 G3 **Nizhniy Shkaft** Rus. Fed.
62 G4 **Nizhniy Tagil** Rus. Fed.
49 E2 **Nizhniy Tsasuchey** Rus. Fed.
12 H3 **Nizhniy Yenangsk** Rus. Fed.
12 H1 **Nizhnyaya Mgla** Rus. Fed.
65 H1 **Nizhnyaya Omka** Rus. Fed.
49 F2 **Nizhnyaya Shakhtama** Rus. Fed.
12 G1 **Nizhnyaya Zolotitsa** Rus. Fed.
15 D1 **Nizhyn** Ukraine
19 K2 **Nizina reg.** Poland
60 D2 **Nizip** Turkey
61 D1 **Nizip r.** Turkey
19 K4 **Nízke Beskydy reg.** Slovakia
19 J4 **Nízke Tatry mts** Slovakia
26 B3 **Nizza Monferrato** Italy
10 E2 **Njavve** Sweden
81 D7 **Njazidja i.** Comoros
28 B3 **Njegoš mts** Yugo.
81 C6 **Njinjo** Tanzania
79 D7 **Njoko r.** Zambia
81 B6 **Njombe** Tanzania
81 B6 **Njombe r.** Tanzania
11 E3 **Njurundabommen** Sweden
78 B2 **Nkambe** Cameroon
81 B6 **Nkasi** Tanzania
76 D5 **Nkawkaw** Ghana
83 D2 **Nkayi** Zimbabwe
74 C5 **Nkhaïlé well** Mauritania
81 B7 **Nkhata Bay** Malawi
81 B7 **Nkhotakota** Malawi
81 B7 **Nkhotakota Game Reserve res.** Malawi
78 A4 **Nkomi, Lagune lag.** Gabon
81 B6 **Nkondwe** Tanzania
78 A3 **Nkongsamba** Cameroon
76 D5 **Nkoranza** Ghana
78 B3 **Nkoteng** Cameroon
81 B6 **Nkundi** Tanzania
82 B2 **Nkurenkuru** Namibia
82 D5 **Nkwenkwezi** R.S.A.
42 B1 **Nmai Hka r.** Myanmar
55 H4 **Noa Dihing r.** India
55 G5 **Noakhali** Bangladesh
55 F5 **Noamundi** India
46 C7 **Nobeoka** Japan
46 H2 **Noboribetsu** Japan
142 A3 **Nobres** Brazil
99 E5 **Noccundra** Aust.
99 E5 **Nockatunga** Aust.
114 E3 **Noelville** Can.
130 C2 **Nogales** Mexico
20 D5 **Nogaro** France
46 C7 **Nōgata** Japan
20 E2 **Nogent-le-Rotrou** France
20 F2 **Nogent-sur-Oise** France
20 F3 **Nogent-sur-Vernisson** France
14 D2 **Noginsk** Rus. Fed.
63 L3 **Noginsky** Rus. Fed.
99 G5 **Nogo r.** Aust.
99 F5 **Nogoa r.** Aust.
47 F6 **Nōgōhaku-san mt.** Japan
146 E3 **Nogoyá** Arg.
146 E3 **Nogoya r.** Arg.
25 G1 **Noguera Pallaresa r.** Spain
49 J5 **Nogwak-san mt.** S. Korea
54 C3 **Nohar** India
46 H3 **Noheji** Japan
18 C4 **Nohfelden** Germany
24 B1 **Noia** Spain
144 B1 **Noidore r.** Brazil
133 □5 **Noire, Pointe pt** *Guadeloupe* Caribbean
24 E5 **Noire, Pte pt** Morocco
20 C2 **Noires, Montagnes h.** France
20 C3 **Noirmoutier-en-l'Île** France
20 C3 **Noirmoutier, Île de i.** France
47 G6 **Nojima-zaki c.** Japan
54 C4 **Nokha** India
57 E3 **Nok Kundi** Pakistan
111 J3 **Nokomis Lake l.** Can.
72 B5 **Nokou** Chad
55 G4 **Nokrek Pk. mt.** India
78 C3 **Nola** C.A.R.
12 J3 **Nolinsk** Rus. Fed.
46 C8 **Noma-misaki pt** Japan
121 H4 **No Mans Land i.** U.S.A.
108 B3 **Nome** U.S.A.
48 C4 **Nomgon** Mongolia
46 D6 **Nōmi-jima i.** Japan
86 G4 **Nomoi Islands is** Fed. States of Micronesia
82 D5 **Nomonde** R.S.A.
46 B7 **Nomo-zaki pt** Japan
90 □5 **Nomuka i.** Tonga
90 □5 **Nomuka Group is** Tonga
90 □5 **Nomuka Iki i.** Tonga
12 G3 **Nomzha** Rus. Fed.
111 H2 **Nonacho Lake l.** Can.
49 H3 **Nong'an** China
42 D3 **Nông Hèt** Laos
43 C4 **Nong Hong** Thailand
42 C3 **Nong Khai** Thailand
55 G4 **Nongstoin** India
96 D3 **Nonning** Aust.
130 D3 **Nonoava** Mexico
150 G6 **Nonouti i.** Kiribati
49 H5 **Nonsan** S. Korea
43 C4 **Nonthaburi** Thailand
20 E4 **Nontron** France
82 C5 **Nonzwakazi** R.S.A.
101 B5 **Nookawarra** Aust.
96 D1 **Noolyeanna L. salt flat** Aust.
99 F6 **Noorama Cr. w** Aust.
18 A3 **Noordbeveland i.** Netherlands
18 B3 **Noord-Brabant div.** Netherlands
18 B2 **Noord-Holland div.** Netherlands
18 B2 **Noordoost Polder reclaimed land** Netherlands
132 □2 **Noord Punt pt** *Curaçao* Netherlands Ant.
110 D5 **Nootka I. i.** Can.
79 B5 **Nóqui** Angola
65 G5 **Norak** Tajikistan
41 C5 **Norala** Phil.
115 F2 **Noranda** Can.
11 D3 **Norberg** Sweden
78 B2 **Nord div.** Cameroon
109 R1 **Nord** Greenland
62 D2 **Nordaustlandet i.** *Svalbard* Arctic Ocean
18 C2 **Norden** Germany
63 L2 **Nordenshel'da, Arkhipelag is** Rus. Fed.
18 C2 **Norderney i.** Germany
18 C2 **Norderney** Germany
18 E2 **Norderstedt** Germany
11 B3 **Nordfjordeid** Norway
10 D2 **Nordfold** Norway
18 D1 **Nordfriesische Inseln is** Germany
18 E3 **Nordhausen** Germany
16 K1 **Nordhorland chan.** Norway
18 C2 **Nordhorn** Germany
10 G1 **Nordkapp c.** Norway
10 E1 **Nordkjosbotn** Norway
10 H1 **Nordkynhalvøya i.** Norway
10 D2 **Nordland div.** Norway
10 D2 **Nordlii** Norway
18 E4 **Nördlingen** Germany
10 E3 **Nordmaling** Sweden
78 B2 **Nord-Ouest div.** Cameroon
20 F1 **Nord-Pas-de-Calais div.** France
109 N3 **Nordre Strømfjord inlet** Greenland
18 C3 **Nordrhein-Westfalen div.** Germany
18 D1 **Nordstrand i.** Germany
10 C2 **Nord-Trøndelag div.** Norway
10 L2 **Norðurland Vestra div.** Iceland
63 N2 **Nordvik** Rus. Fed.
17 D5 **Nore r.** Rep. of Ire.
124 D3 **Norfolk** U.S.A.
121 F2 **Norfolk** U.S.A.
121 E6 **Norfolk airport** U.S.A.
95 □1 **Norfolk I. i.** Pac. Oc.
150 G7 **Norfolk Island Ridge** Pac. Oc.
150 F7 **Norfolk Island Trough** Pac. Oc.
125 E4 **Norfork L. l.** U.S.A.
11 B3 **Norheimsund** Norway
47 F5 **Norikura-dake vol** Japan
62 K3 **Noril'sk** Rus. Fed.
14 A3 **Norino** Rus. Fed.
115 F4 **Norland** Can.
122 C5 **Normal** U.S.A.
99 E3 **Norman r.** Aust.
125 D5 **Norman** U.S.A.
99 F2 **Normanby r.** Aust.
90 □1 **Normanby I. i.** P.N.G.
99 G4 **Normanby Ra. h.** Aust.
139 F3 **Normandia** Brazil
115 J2 **Normandin** Can.
119 □3 **Norman I. i.** *Virgin Is* Caribbean
92 □1 **Norman Inlet inlet** *Auckland Is* N.Z.
119 D5 **Norman, L. l.** U.S.A.
133 □1 **Norman Manley airport** Jamaica
99 E3 **Normanton** Aust.
110 D1 **Norman Wells** Can.
115 F2 **Normétal** Can.
152 □ **Noroît, Baie b.** *Kerguelen* Indian Ocean
141 E2 **Noronha r.** Brazil
147 B5 **Ñorquinco** Arg.
10 F3 **Norra Kvarken str.** Finland/Sweden
10 D2 **Norra Storfjället mts** Sweden
10 E2 **Norrbotten div.** Sweden
114 C2 **Norris** Can.
120 B6 **Norris Lake l.** U.S.A.
121 F4 **Norristown** U.S.A.
11 E4 **Norrköping** Sweden
11 E4 **Norrtälje** Sweden
101 C7 **Norseman** Aust.
92 F4 **Norsewood** N.Z.
10 E2 **Norsjö** Sweden
90 □2 **Norsup** Vanuatu
139 G3 **Norte, Cabo pt** Brazil
91 □16 **Norte, Cabo c.** *Easter I.* Chile
142 A3 **Nortelândia** Brazil
146 E4 **Norte, Pta pt** *Buenos Aires* Arg.
147 D5 **Norte, Pta pt** *Chubut* Arg.
121 G3 **North Adams** U.S.A.
17 G4 **Northallerton** U.K.
101 B6 **Northam** Aust.
148 F4 **North American Basin** Atlantic Ocean
101 A6 **Northampton** Aust.
17 G5 **Northampton** U.K.
121 G3 **Northampton** U.S.A.
99 F5 **Northampton Downs** Aust.
43 A4 **North Andaman i.** *Andaman and Nicobar Is* India
120 E5 **North Anna r.** U.S.A.
121 J2 **North Anson** U.S.A.
110 G2 **North Arm b.** Can.
90 □7 **North Astrolabe Reef reef** Fiji
119 D5 **North Augusta** U.S.A.
113 H2 **North Aulatsivik Island i.** Can.
41 A4 **North Balabac Strait chan.** Phil.
111 H4 **North Battleford** Can.
115 F3 **North Bay** Can.
112 E2 **North Belcher Islands is** Can.
126 A3 **North Bend** U.S.A.
16 F3 **North Berwick** U.K.
121 H3 **North Berwick** U.S.A.
122 A3 **North Branch** U.S.A.
152 A5 **North, C. c.** Ant.
147 G7 **North C. c.** Atlantic Ocean
113 H4 **North, C. c.** Can.
93 □3 **North C. c.** *Antipodes Is* N.Z.
113 H4 **North Cape pt** *Prince Edward I.* Can.
92 D1 **North Cape c.** N.Z.
112 B3 **North Caribou Lake l.** Can.
119 D5 **North Carolina div.** U.S.A.
126 B1 **North Cascades Nat. Park** U.S.A.
119 □2 **North Cay i.** The Bahamas
114 D3 **North Channel chan.** Can.
17 E4 **North Channel str.** U.K.
101 B7 **Northcliffe** Aust.
121 H2 **North Conway** U.S.A.
124 C2 **North Dakota div.** U.S.A.
17 G6 **North Downs h.** U.K.
82 D3 **North East div.** Botswana
120 D3 **North East** U.S.A.
82 □1 **North East Bay b.** *Ascension* Atlantic Ocean
80 D4 **North-Eastern div.** Kenya
148 H2 **North-Eastern Atlantic Basin** Atlantic Ocean
92 □2 **North East Harb. inlet** *Campbell I.* N.Z.
92 □3 **North East Island i.** *Snares Is* N.Z.
94 □2 **North East Point pt** *Christmas I.* Indian Ocean
133 □1 **Northeast Point pt** Jamaica
132 D2 **Northeast Point pt** The Bahamas
132 D2 **Northeast Point pt** The Bahamas
132 C1 **Northeast Providence Chan. chan.** The Bahamas
18 D3 **Northeim** Germany
132 D1 **North End Pt pt** The Bahamas
41 □1 **North Entrance chan.** Palau
76 D5 **Northern div.** Ghana
81 B7 **Northern div.** Malawi
76 B5 **Northern div.** Sierra Leone
73 E4 **Northern div.** Sudan
81 B7 **Northern div.** Zambia
54 C1 **Northern Areas div.** Pakistan
82 C5 **Northern Cape div.** R.S.A.
111 K3 **Northern Indian Lake l.** Can.
17 D4 **Northern Ireland div.** U.K.
112 B4 **Northern Light L. l.** Can.
86 F3 **Northern Mariana Islands terr.** Pac. Oc.
94 □2 **Northern Plateau plat.** *Christmas I.* Indian Ocean
83 D3 **Northern Province div.** R.S.A.
133 □3 **Northern Range mt. ra.** *Trinidad* Trin. and Tobago
98 C3 **Northern Territory div.** Aust.
16 F3 **North Esk r.** U.K.
121 G3 **Northfield** U.S.A.
122 A3 **Northfield** U.S.A.
121 G2 **Northfield** U.S.A.
17 H6 **North Foreland c.** U.K.
128 C3 **North Fork** U.S.A.
128 B2 **North Fork American r.** U.S.A.
128 B2 **North Fork Feather r.** U.S.A.
122 E3 **North Fox I. i.** U.S.A.
114 E1 **North French r.** Can.
133 □6 **North Friar's Bay b.** *St Kitts-Nevis* Caribbean
121 K2 **North Head** Can.
92 E2 **North Head hd** N.Z.
94 □3 **North Head pt** *Macquarie I.* Pac. Oc.
111 K2 **North Henik Lake l.** Can.
121 G3 **North Hudson** U.S.A.
94 □4 **North I. i.** *Lord Howe I.* Pac. Oc.
81 □1 **North I. i.** Seychelles
41 B1 **North Is i.** Phil.
92 E3 **North Island i.** N.Z.
41 B4 **North Islet reef** Phil.
129 G4 **North Jadito Canyon** U.S.A.
122 D5 **North Judson** U.S.A.
94 □1 **North Keeling I. i.** *Cocos Is* Indian Ocean
111 K3 **North Knife r.** Can.
33 O5 **North Korea country** Asia
55 H4 **North Lakhimpur** India
92 E1 **Northland div.** N.Z.
129 E3 **North Las Vegas** U.S.A.
125 E5 **North Little Rock** U.S.A.
81 B7 **North Luangwa National Park nat. park** Zambia
129 H2 **North Mam Peak summit** U.S.A.
122 E5 **North Manchester** U.S.A.
122 D3 **North Manitou I. i.** U.S.A.
114 E3 **North Monetville** Can.
110 D2 **North Nahanni r.** Can.
133 □1 **North Negril Pt pt** Jamaica
111 L5 **Northome** U.S.A.
128 C3 **North Palisade summit** U.S.A.
124 C3 **North Platte r.** U.S.A.
124 C3 **North Platte** U.S.A.
82 A4 **North Point pt** *Ascension* Atlantic Ocean
82 A5 **North Point pt** *Tristan da Cunha* Atlantic Ocean
97 F4 **North Point pt** Aust.
133 □9 **North Point pt** *Barbados* Caribbean
45 □ **North Point** Hong Kong
81 □2 **North Point pt** Seychelles
118 D2 **North Point pt** U.S.A.
122 E3 **Northport** U.S.A.
92 □3 **North Promontory pt** *Snares Is* N.Z.
43 A4 **North Reef I. i.** *Andaman and Nicobar Is* India
129 F3 **North Rim** U.S.A.
16 F2 **North Ronaldsay i.** U.K.
128 B2 **North San Juan** U.S.A.
111 G4 **North Saskatchewan r.** Can.
4 F3 **North Sea sea** Europe
111 J3 **North Seal r.** Can.
43 A5 **North Sentinel I. i.** *Andaman and Nicobar Is* India
128 D2 **North Shoshone Peak summit** U.S.A.
17 H5 **North Somercotes** U.K.
99 H5 **North Stradbroke I. i.** Aust.
121 H2 **North Stratford** U.S.A.
92 E3 **North Taranaki Bight b.** N.Z.
110 F4 **North Thompson r.** Can.
120 D3 **North Tonawanda** U.S.A.
54 D3 **North Tons r.** India
93 A7 **North Trap reef** N.Z.
121 G2 **North Troy** U.S.A.
112 D3 **North Twin I. i.** Can.
17 F4 **North Tyne r.** U.K.
16 D3 **North Uist i.** U.K.
99 G4 **Northumberland Is is** Aust.
113 H4 **Northumberland Strait chan.** Can.
110 E5 **North Vancouver** Can.
121 F3 **Northville** U.S.A.
17 H5 **North Walsham** U.K.
82 D4 **North West div.** R.S.A.
92 □2 **North West B. b.** *Campbell I.* N.Z.
100 A4 **North West C. c.** Aust.
92 □1 **North West C. c.** *Auckland Is* N.Z.
79 D6 **North-Western div.** Zambia
54 C2 **North West Frontier** Pakistan
94 □2 **North West Point pt** *Christmas I.* Indian Ocean
132 C1 **Northwest Providence Chan. chan.** The Bahamas
113 J3 **North West River** Can.
108 H3 **Northwest Territories** Can.
121 F5 **North Wildwood** U.S.A.
121 H2 **North Woodstock** U.S.A.
17 G4 **North York Moors h.** U.K.
113 G4 **Norton** Can.
124 D4 **Norton** U.S.A.
121 H2 **Norton** U.S.A.
120 B6 **Norton** U.S.A.
83 E2 **Norton** Zimbabwe
108 B3 **Norton Sound b.** U.S.A.
18 D1 **Nortorf** Germany
20 D3 **Nort-sur-Erdre** France
152 C2 **Norvegia, C. c.** Ant.
121 G4 **Norwalk** U.S.A.
120 B4 **Norwalk** U.S.A.
4 F2 **Norway country** Europe
121 H2 **Norway** U.S.A.
115 G4 **Norway Bay** Can.
111 K4 **Norway House** Can.
148 J1 **Norwegian Basin** Atlantic Ocean
109 J2 **Norwegian Bay b.** Can.
148 K1 **Norwegian Sea** Atlantic Ocean
114 E5 **Norwich** Can.
17 H5 **Norwich** U.K.
121 G4 **Norwich** U.S.A.
121 F3 **Norwich** U.S.A.
121 H3 **Norwood** U.S.A.
121 F2 **Norwood** U.S.A.
120 A5 **Norwood** U.S.A.
46 K2 **Nosapu-misaki pt** Japan
146 C1 **Nos de Cachi mt.** Arg.
111 H1 **Nose Lake l.** Can.
28 F3 **Nos Emine pt** Bulgaria
28 F3 **Nos Galata pt** Bulgaria
46 H1 **Noshappu-misaki hd** Japan
47 G3 **Noshiro** Japan
12 J2 **Noshul'** Rus. Fed.
15 D1 **Nosivka** Ukraine
28 G3 **Nos Kaliakra pt** Bulgaria
15 B2 **Noskivtsi** Ukraine
82 C4 **Nosop r.** Botswana
14 G1 **Nosovaya** Rus. Fed.
57 D3 **Noṣratābād** Iran
142 E3 **Nossa Senhora das Dores** Brazil
143 A4 **Nossa Senhora do Livramento** Brazil
11 D4 **Nossebro** Sweden
18 F3 **Nossen** Germany
28 G3 **Nos Shabla pt** Bulgaria
16 G1 **Noss, Isle of i.** U.K.
82 C4 **Nossob r.** Namibia/R.S.A.
76 C4 **Nossombougou** Mali
83 H1 **Nosy Bé i.** Madagascar
83 H2 **Nosy Boraha i.** Madagascar
83 H1 **Nosy Lava i.** Madagascar
83 H1 **Nosy Radama i.** Madagascar
83 H3 **Nosy Varika** Madagascar
129 F2 **Notch Peak summit** U.S.A.
19 G2 **Noteć r.** Poland
29 C5 **Notia Pindos mt. ra.** Greece
29 E6 **Notio Aigaio div.** Greece
29 D5 **Notios Evvoïkos Kolpos chan.** Greece
29 C5 **Notio Steno Kerkyras chan.** Greece
47 F5 **Noto** Japan
11 C4 **Notodden** Norway
27 E7 **Noto, Golfo di g.** Italy
47 F5 **Noto-hantō pen.** Japan
47 F5 **Noto-jima i.** Japan
46 K1 **Notoro-ko l.** Japan
113 K4 **Notre Dame Bay b.** Can.
115 H4 **Notre-Dame-de-la-Salette** Can.
121 H2 **Notre-Dame-des-Bois** Can.
115 H3 **Notre-Dame-du-Laus** Can.
115 F3 **Notre-Dame-du-Nord** Can.
113 G4 **Notre Dame, Monts mt. ra.** Can.
77 E5 **Notsé** Togo
46 K2 **Notsuke-saki pt** Japan
46 K2 **Notsuke-suidō chan.** Japan
114 E4 **Nottawasaga Bay b.** Can.
112 E3 **Nottaway r.** Can.
17 G5 **Nottingham** U.K.
120 E6 **Nottoway r.** U.S.A.
111 H5 **Notukeu Cr. r.** Can.
74 A4 **Nouâdhibou** Mauritania
74 A5 **Nouakchott** Mauritania
74 C5 **Noual well** Mauritania
74 A5 **Nouâmghâr** Mauritania
42 D4 **Nouei** Vietnam
74 A5 **Noueïch well** Mauritania
90 □2 **Nouméa** Pac. Oc.
78 B3 **Noun r.** Cameroon
76 D4 **Nouna** Burkina
82 C5 **Noupoort** R.S.A.
10 H2 **Nousu** Finland
65 G4 **Nov** Tajikistan
145 H4 **Nova Almeida** Brazil
144 A4 **Nova Alvorada** Brazil
144 D1 **Nova America** Brazil
144 B5 **Nova Andradina** Brazil
13 F5 **Nova Astrakhan'** Ukraine
144 D3 **Nova Aurora** Brazil
19 J4 **Nová Baňa** Slovakia
15 C1 **Nova Borova** Ukraine
79 B5 **Nova Caipemba** Angola
28 D2 **Novaci** Romania
145 G3 **Nova Era** Brazil
144 B5 **Nova Esperança** Brazil
145 G5 **Nova Friburgo** Brazil
26 F3 **Nova Gradiška** Croatia
144 D4 **Nova Granada** Brazil
145 G5 **Nova Iguaçu** Brazil
15 E3 **Nova Kakhovka** Ukraine
145 G3 **Nova Lima** Brazil
144 B5 **Nova Londrina** Brazil
12 D4 **Novalukoml'** Belarus
83 F3 **Nova Mambone** Mozambique
15 E3 **Nova Mayachka** Ukraine
83 F2 **Nova Nabúri** Mozambique
15 D3 **Nova Odesa** Ukraine
19 G3 **Nová Paka** Czech Rep.
28 C2 **Nova Pazova** Yugo.
142 D2 **Nova Pilão Arcado** Brazil
144 E3 **Nova Ponte** Brazil
15 E2 **Nova Praha** Ukraine
26 B3 **Novara** Italy
142 D2 **Nova Remanso** Brazil
145 E4 **Nova Resende** Brazil
142 C3 **Nova Roma** Brazil
144 B6 **Nova Santa Rosa** Brazil
113 H5 **Nova Scotia div.** Can.
142 D2 **Nova Sento Sé** Brazil
145 F3 **Nova Serrana** Brazil
15 F1 **Nova Sloboda** Ukraine
142 E3 **Nova Soure** Brazil
128 A2 **Novato** U.S.A.
26 F3 **Nova Topola** Bos.-Herz.
15 B2 **Nova Ushytsya** Ukraine
28 B3 **Nova Varoš** Yugo.
145 H3 **Nova Venécia** Brazil
145 J2 **Nova Viçosa** Brazil
141 D2 **Nova Vida** Brazil
15 F2 **Nova Vodolaha** Ukraine
144 B1 **Nova Xavantina** Brazil
14 H3 **Novaya Bekshanka** Rus. Fed.
64 C3 **Novaya Kazanka** Kazak.
12 E2 **Novaya Ladoga** Rus. Fed.
14 E3 **Novaya Lyada** Rus. Fed.
63 R2 **Novaya Sibir', O. i.** Rus. Fed.
62 G2 **Novaya Zemlya i.** Rus. Fed.
28 E3 **Nova Zagora** Bulgaria
15 E3 **Nova Zbur"yivka** Ukraine
15 E2 **Nove** Ukraine
25 F3 **Novelda** Spain
19 H3 **Nové Město nad Metuj** Czech Rep.
19 J5 **Nové Zámky** Slovakia
12 D3 **Novgorod div.** Rus. Fed.
12 D3 **Novgorod** Rus. Fed.
15 E2 **Novhorodka** Ukraine
14 A4 **Novhorod-Sivers'kyy** Ukraine
28 C2 **Novi Bečej** Yugo.
15 C1 **Novi Bilokorovychi** Ukraine
15 D1 **Novi Borovychi** Ukraine
15 A1 **Novi Chervyshcha** Ukraine
28 D3 **Novi Iskŭr** Bulgaria
26 B3 **Novi Ligure** Italy
26 F2 **Novi Marof** Croatia
15 E1 **Novi Mlyny** Ukraine
28 F3 **Novi Pazar** Bulgaria
28 C3 **Novi Pazar** Yugo.
28 B2 **Novi Sad** Yugo.
15 F2 **Novi Sanzhary** Ukraine
26 E3 **Novi Vinodolski** Croatia
14 E1 **Novki** Rus. Fed.
14 E2 **Novlyanka** Rus. Fed.
142 B1 **Novo r.** Brazil
13 G6 **Novoaleksandrovsk** Rus. Fed.
14 B2 **Novoaleksandrovskiy** Rus. Fed.
64 E2 **Novoalekseyevka** Kazak.
65 K2 **Novoaltaysk** Rus. Fed.
13 G5 **Novoanninskiy** Rus. Fed.
139 E5 **Novo Aripuanã** Brazil
15 D2 **Novoarkhanel's'k** Ukraine
13 F6 **Novoazovs'k** Ukraine
15 F3 **Novobohdanivka** Ukraine
14 E3 **Novobokino** Rus. Fed.
14 H1 **Novocheboksarsk** Rus. Fed.
13 G6 **Novocherkassk** Rus. Fed.
145 H2 **Novo Cruzeiro** Brazil
15 F3 **Novodanylivka** Ukraine
14 F2 **Novodmitriyevka** Rus. Fed.
15 B2 **Novodnistrovs'k** Ukraine
65 H2 **Novodolinka** Kazak.
15 G2 **Novodonets'ke** Ukraine
14 B2 **Novodugino** Rus. Fed.
12 G1 **Novodvinsk** Rus. Fed.
15 C2 **Novofastiv** Ukraine
49 H2 **Novogeorgiyevka** Rus. Fed.
14 B3 **Novognezdilovo** Rus. Fed.
14 C2 **Novogurovskiy** Rus. Fed.
143 B6 **Novo Hamburgo** Brazil
144 D4 **Novo Horizonte** Brazil
15 E3 **Novohradivka** Ukraine
15 B1 **Novohrad-Volyns'kyy** Ukraine
15 G2 **Novohrodivka** Ukraine
48 D2 **Novoil'insk** Rus. Fed.
15 F3 **Novoivanivka** Ukraine
14 D4 **Novokastornoye** Rus. Fed.
64 F3 **Novokazalinsk** Kazak.
49 J2 **Novokiyevskiy Uval** Rus. Fed.
13 G6 **Novokubansk** Rus. Fed.
12 J4 **Novokuybyshevsk** Rus. Fed.
65 L2 **Novokuznetsk** Rus. Fed.
15 E3 **Novokyyivka** Ukraine
152 D3 **Novolazarevskaya Rus. Fed. Base** Ant.
63 M2 **Novoletov'ye** Rus. Fed.
15 F2 **Novomar"yivka** Ukraine
26 E3 **Novo Mesto** Slovenia
14 D2 **Novomichurinsk** Rus. Fed.
13 F6 **Novomikhaylovskiy** Rus. Fed.
12 F4 **Novomoskovsk** Rus. Fed.
15 F2 **Novomoskovs'k** Ukraine
15 F3 **Novomykhaylivka** Ukraine
15 F3 **Novomykolayivka** Ukraine
15 D2 **Novomyrhorod** Ukraine
15 E3 **Novonatalivka** Ukraine
13 G5 **Novonikolayevskiy** Rus. Fed.
13 H5 **Novonikol'skoye** Rus. Fed.
15 F3 **Novooleksiyivka** Ukraine
139 F4 **Novo Olinda do Norte** Brazil
64 E2 **Novoorsk** Rus. Fed.
15 E1 **Novoorzhyts'ke** Ukraine
15 C1 **Novoozeryanka** Ukraine
142 D2 **Novo Parnarama** Brazil
15 D3 **Novopavlivka** Ukraine
48 D2 **Novopavlovka** Rus. Fed.
14 E1 **Novopistsovo** Rus. Fed.
15 F2 **Novopokrovka** Ukraine
13 G6 **Novopokrovskaya** Rus. Fed.
14 F4 **Novopokrovskoye** Rus. Fed.
15 E3 **Novopoltavka** Ukraine
14 D3 **Novopolyan'ye** Rus. Fed.
13 F5 **Novopskov** Ukraine
49 J1 **Novorossiyka** Rus. Fed.
13 F6 **Novorossiysk** Rus. Fed.
63 M2 **Novorybnoye** Rus. Fed.
12 D3 **Novorzhev** Rus. Fed.
15 C3 **Novoselivka** Ukraine
14 F2 **Novoselki** Rus. Fed.
29 D4 **Novo Selo** Macedonia
15 B2 **Novoselytsya** Ukraine
64 D2 **Novosergiyevka** Rus. Fed.
13 F6 **Novoshakhtinsk** Rus. Fed.
65 K1 **Novosibirsk** Rus. Fed.
65 K2 **Novosibirsk** Rus. Fed.
63 P2 **Novosibirskiye Ostrova is** Rus. Fed.
14 C3 **Novosil'** Rus. Fed.
14 D4 **Novosil'skoye** Rus. Fed.
64 F1 **Novosineglazovskiy** Rus. Fed.
12 D3 **Novosokol'niki** Rus. Fed.
64 E2 **Novotroitsk** Rus. Fed.
65 H4 **Novotroitskoye** Kazak.
14 A3 **Novotroitskoye** Rus. Fed.
14 G2 **Novotroitskoye** Rus. Fed.
15 F3 **Novotroyits'ke** Ukraine
15 D2 **Novoukrayinka** *Kirovohrad* Ukraine
15 A1 **Novoukrayinka** *Rivne* Ukraine
13 J5 **Novouzensk** Rus. Fed.
15 F3 **Novovasylivka** Ukraine
15 A1 **Novovolyns'k** Ukraine
13 F5 **Novovoronezh** Rus. Fed.
15 E3 **Novovorontsovka** Ukraine
14 F1 **Novovyazniki** Rus. Fed.
14 D3 **Novoye Dubovoye** Rus. Fed.
14 E1 **Novoye Leushino** Rus. Fed.
14 E3 **Novoyur'yevo** Rus. Fed.
14 C1 **Novozavidovskiy** Rus. Fed.
15 C2 **Novozhyvotiv** Ukraine
13 D4 **Novozybkov** Rus. Fed.
19 G3 **Nový Bor** Czech Rep.
19 H4 **Nový Jičín** Czech Rep.
63 M2 **Novyy** Rus. Fed.
15 E3 **Novyy Buh** Ukraine
15 D1 **Novyy Bykiv** Ukraine
14 H2 **Novyye Aybesi** Rus. Fed.
14 H3 **Novyye Burasy** Rus. Fed.
14 A3 **Novyye Ivaytenki** Rus. Fed.
14 D1 **Novyy Nekouz** Rus. Fed.
15 G1 **Novyy Oskol** Rus. Fed.
62 J3 **Novyy Port** Rus. Fed.
14 C3 **Novyy Sinets** Rus. Fed.
15 E2 **Novyystarodub** Ukraine
12 J3 **Novyy Tor'yal** Rus. Fed.
62 J3 **Novyy Urengoy** Rus. Fed.
49 K2 **Novyy Urgal** Rus. Fed.
64 D4 **Novyy Uzen'** Kazak.
57 C3 **Now** Iran
19 K3 **Nowa Dęba** Poland
19 H3 **Nowa Ruda** Poland
19 G3 **Nowa Sól** Poland
125 E4 **Nowata** U.S.A.
57 B2 **Nowbarān** Iran
19 J2 **Nowe** Poland
19 K3 **Nowe Miasło nad Pilicą** Poland
19 G3 **Nowe Miasteczko** Poland
19 J2 **Nowe Miasto Lubawskie** Poland
54 D4 **Nowgong** India
60 G2 **Nowjeh Deh** Iran
57 C1 **Now Kharegan** Iran
111 J2 **Nowleye Lake l.** Can.
19 G2 **Nowogard** Poland
19 K2 **Nowogród** Poland
19 G3 **Nowogród Bobrzański** Poland
97 G3 **Nowra** Aust.
57 B1 **Now Shahr** Iran
60 G2 **Nowshahr** Iran
54 C2 **Nowshera** Pakistan
19 J1 **Nowy Dwór Gdański** Poland
19 K2 **Nowy Dwór Mazowiecki** Poland
19 K4 **Nowy Sącz** Poland
19 K4 **Nowy Targ** Poland
19 H2 **Nowy Tomyśl** Poland
121 E4 **Noxen** U.S.A.
62 J3 **Noyabr'sk** Rus. Fed.
110 C3 **Noyes I. i.** U.S.A.
20 F2 **Noyon** France
20 D3 **Nozay** France
78 C4 **Nsambi** Zaire
83 F2 **Nsanje** Malawi
76 D5 **Nsawam** Ghana
78 B3 **Nsoc** Equatorial Guinea
79 E6 **Nsombo** Zambia
76 D5 **Nsuatre** Ghana
77 F5 **Nsukka** Nigeria
74 A4 **Ntalfa well** Mauritania
78 C4 **Ntandembele** Zaire
83 E1 **Ntcheu** Malawi
81 B7 **Ntchisi** Malawi
78 B3 **Ntem r.** Africa
78 A3 **Ntoum** Gabon
78 B3 **Ntui** Cameroon
81 B5 **Ntungamo** Uganda
82 D3 **Ntwetwe Pan salt pan** Botswana
50 B3 **Nu r.** China
152 □ **Nuageuses, Is is** *Kerguelen* Indian Ocean
90 □3 **Nuapapu i.** Tonga
59 J5 **Nu'aym reg.** Oman
73 F3 **Nuba, Lake l.** Sudan
80 B2 **Nuba Mountains mts** Sudan
73 F3 **Nubian Desert desert** Sudan
146 B4 **Nuble r.** Chile
48 D4 **Nüden** Mongolia
140 B3 **Nudo Coropuna mt.** Peru
125 D6 **Nueces r.** U.S.A.
130 J6 **Nueva Armenia** Honduras
138 D2 **Nueva Florida** Venezuela
141 E4 **Nueva Germania** Paraguay
132 B2 **Nueva Gerona** Cuba
147 C7 **Nueva, I. i.** Chile
147 B4 **Nueva Imperial** Chile
138 B3 **Nueva Loja** Ecuador
147 B5 **Nueva Lubecka** Arg.
131 E3 **Nueva Rosita** Mexico
131 H6 **Nueva San Salvador** El Salvador
132 C2 **Nuevitas** Cuba
130 D2 **Nuevo Casas Grandes** Mexico
147 D5 **Nuevo, G. g.** Arg.
130 D3 **Nuevo Ideal** Mexico
131 F3 **Nuevo Laredo** Mexico
131 F3 **Nuevo León div.** Mexico
140 C2 **Nuevo Mundo** Bolivia
80 E3 **Nugaal div.** Somalia
80 E3 **Nugaal w** Somalia
93 B7 **Nugget Pt pt** N.Z.
73 F3 **Nugrus, Gebel mt.** Egypt
90 □1 **Nuguria Is is** P.N.G.
92 F3 **Nuhaka** N.Z.
150 G6 **Nui i.** Tuvalu
11 G4 **Nuia** Estonia
21 G3 **Nuits-St-Georges** France
96 C3 **Nukey Bluff h.** Aust.
90 □4 **Nuku i.** Tonga
90 □4 **Nuku'alofa** Tonga
90 □6 **Nukubasaga reef** Fiji
150 G6 **Nukufetau i.** Tuvalu
151 K6 **Nuku Hiva i.** *Fr. Poly.* Pac. Oc.
150 G6 **Nukulaelae i.** Tuvalu
90 □1 **Nukumanu Is is** P.N.G.
87 K5 **Nukunono atoll** *Tokelau* Pac. Oc.
64 E4 **Nukus** Uzbekistan
100 C4 **Nullagine** Aust.
100 C4 **Nullagine r.** Aust.
96 B2 **Nullarbor** Aust.
96 B2 **Nullarbor Nat. Park nat. park** Aust.
96 B2 **Nullarbor Plain plain** Aust.
49 F4 **Nulu'erhu Shan mt. ra.** China
77 G5 **Numan** Nigeria
73 G2 **Nu'mān i.** Saudi Arabia
47 G5 **Numata** *Gunma* Japan
46 H2 **Numata** *Hokkaido* Japan
78 E2 **Numatinna w** Sudan
47 G6 **Numazu** Japan
98 C2 **Numbulwar** Aust.
11 C3 **Numedal v.** Norway
39 K7 **Numfor i.** Indon.
49 H3 **Numin r.** China
97 F4 **Numurkah** Aust.
113 H2 **Nunaksaluk Island i.** Can.
109 O3 **Nunarsuit i.** Greenland
111 M2 **Nunavut reg.** Can.
120 E3 **Nunda** U.S.A.
79 E4 **Nunda** Zaire
97 G2 **Nundle** Aust.
112 B3 **Nungesser L. l.** Can.
49 F3 **Nungnain Sum** China
108 B4 **Nunivak I.** U.S.A.
54 D2 **Nunkun mt.** India
108 A3 **Nunligran** Rus. Fed.
24 C2 **Nuñomoral** Spain
49 G2 **Nuomin r.** China
27 B5 **Nuoro** Italy
73 H2 **Nuqrah** Saudi Arabia
138 B2 **Nuquí** Colombia
54 E1 **Nur** China
65 H2 **Nura r.** Kazak.
65 H3 **Nura** Kazak.
64 C5 **Nūrābād** Iran
57 B3 **Nūrābād** Iran
65 G4 **Nurata** Uzbekistan
65 G4 **Nuratau, Khr. mt. ra.** Uzbekistan
61 D1 **Nur Dağları mt. ra.** Turkey
26 B3 **Nure r.** Italy
57 G2 **Nūr Gal** Afghanistan
54 A3 **Núr Gamma** Pakistan
130 C2 **Nuri** Mexico
57 G2 **Nuristan reg.** Afghanistan
40 B2 **Nuri, Tk b.** Indon.
54 D2 **Nurla** India
12 J4 **Nurlat** Rus. Fed.
10 H3 **Nurmes** Finland
10 F3 **Nurmo** Finland
18 E4 **Nürnberg** Germany
54 B3 **Nurpur** Pakistan
97 F2 **Nurri, Mt h.** Aust.
55 H1 **Nur Turu** China
40 D4 **Nusa Tenggara Barat div.** Indon.
40 D4 **Nusa Tenggara Timur div.** Indon.
60 E2 **Nusaybin** Turkey
61 D2 **Nuşayrīyah, Jabal al mt. ra.** Syria
50 B3 **Nu Shan mt. ra.** China
54 A3 **Nushki** Pakistan
113 H2 **Nutak** Can.
129 H5 **Nutrioso** U.S.A.
54 B3 **Nuttal** Pakistan
98 C2 **Nutwood Downs** Aust.
109 N3 **Nuuk** Greenland
10 G2 **Nuupas** Finland
91 □11 **Nuupéré, Pte pt** *Fr. Poly.* Pac. Oc.
109 N2 **Nuussuaq** Greenland
109 N2 **Nuussuaq pen.** Greenland
91 □13 **Nuuúli** *American Samoa* Pac. Oc.
56 C5 **Nuwara Eliya** Sri Lanka
61 C5 **Nuweiba el Muzeina** Egypt
14 G2 **Nuya r.** Rus. Fed.
96 C3 **Nuyts Arch. is** Aust.
101 B7 **Nuyts, Pt pt** Aust.
101 B7 **Nyabing** Aust.
83 E2 **Nyadire r.** Zimbabwe
62 H3 **Nyagan'** Rus. Fed.
81 C4 **Nyahururu** Kenya
97 E3 **Nyah West** Aust.
55 G3 **Nyainqêntanglha Feng mt.** China
55 G3 **Nyainqêntanglha Shan mt. ra.** China
55 H2 **Nyainrong** China
81 B5 **Nyakaliro** Tanzania
10 E3 **Nyaker** Sweden
72 D5 **Nyala** Sudan
55 F3 **Nyalam** China
83 D2 **Nyamandhiovu** Zimbabwe
78 E2 **Nyamlell** Sudan
12 G2 **Nyandoma** Rus. Fed.
12 F2 **Nyandomskiy Vozvyshennost' h.** Rus. Fed.
79 B4 **Nyanga** Congo
79 B4 **Nyanga div.** Gabon
83 E2 **Nyanga** Zimbabwe
55 G3 **Nyang Qu r.** *Tibet* China
55 H3 **Nyang Qu r.** *Tibet* China
76 D5 **Nyankpala** Ghana
81 B5 **Nyanza div.** Kenya
81 A5 **Nyanza** Rwanda
40 D1 **Nyapa, G. mt.** Indon.
81 B6 **Nyasa, Lake l.** Africa
83 D2 **Nyathi** Zimbabwe
42 B3 **Nyaunglebin** Myanmar
42 A2 **Nyaungu** Myanmar
64 E1 **Nyazepetrovsk** Rus. Fed.
10 H1 **Nyborg** Norway
11 D4 **Nybro** Sweden
109 N1 **Nyeboe Land reg.** Greenland
55 G3 **Nyêmo** China
81 C5 **Nyeri** Kenya
81 B7 **Nyika National Park nat. park** Malawi
55 F3 **Nyima** China
81 B7 **Nyimba** Zambia
55 H3 **Nyingchi** China
19 L5 **Nyírbátor** Hungary
19 L5 **Nyírbéltek** Hungary
19 K5 **Nyíregyháza** Hungary
80 C4 **Nyiru, Mount mt.** Kenya
10 F3 **Nykarleby** Finland
11 C5 **Nykøbing** Denmark
11 C5 **Nykøbing Sjælland** Denmark
10 E3 **Nyland** Sweden
83 D3 **Nylstroom** R.S.A.
97 F3 **Nymagee** Aust.
97 H2 **Nymboida r.** Aust.
19 G3 **Nymburk** Czech Rep.
11 E4 **Nynäshamn** Sweden
97 F2 **Nyngan** Aust.
12 B4 **Nyoman r.** Belarus/Lithuania
21 H3 **Nyon** Switz.
19 H3 **Nysa** Poland
19 H3 **Nysa Kłodzka r.** Poland
12 J2 **Nyuchpas** Rus. Fed.
47 G4 **Nyūdō-zaki pt** Japan
12 H2 **Nyukhcha** Rus. Fed.
12 H2 **Nyuksenitsa** Rus. Fed.
79 E5 **Nyunzu** Zaire
63 N3 **Nyurba** Rus. Fed.
12 J2 **Nyuvchim** Rus. Fed.
19 L4 **Nyzhankovychi** Poland
15 F3 **Nyzhni Sirohozy** Ukraine
15 F3 **Nyzhni Torhayi** Ukraine
15 F1 **Nyzhnya Syrovatka** Ukraine
15 F1 **Nyzy** Ukraine
79 B4 **Nzambi** Congo
78 E3 **Nzara** Sudan
76 C5 **Nzébéla** Guinea
81 B5 **Nzega** Tanzania
76 C5 **Nzérékoré** Guinea
79 B5 **N'zeto** Angola
76 D5 **Nzi r.** Côte d'Ivoire
79 E6 **Nzilo, Lac l.** Zaire
79 E4 **Nzingu** Zaire
81 B4 **Nzoia r.** Kenya
78 E3 **Nzoro r.** Zaire
81 D7 **Nzwani i.** Comoros

O

124 C2 **Oahe, Lake l.** U.S.A.
127 □1 **Oahu i.** U.S.A.
96 E3 **Oakbank** Aust.
129 F2 **Oak City** U.S.A.
125 E6 **Oakdale** U.S.A.
124 D2 **Oakes** U.S.A.
99 G5 **Oakey** Aust.
17 G5 **Oakham** U.K.
126 B1 **Oak Harbor** U.S.A.
120 C6 **Oak Hill** U.S.A.
128 C3 **Oakhurst** U.S.A.
122 B2 **Oak I. i.** U.S.A.
128 A3 **Oakland airport** U.S.A.
128 A3 **Oakland** U.S.A.
120 D5 **Oakland** U.S.A.
124 D3 **Oakland** U.S.A.
126 B3 **Oakland** U.S.A.
122 D5 **Oak Lawn** U.S.A.
124 C4 **Oakley** U.S.A.
100 C4 **Oakover r.** Aust.
126 B3 **Oakridge** U.S.A.
119 C4 **Oak Ridge** U.S.A.
92 D3 **Oakura** N.Z.
115 F5 **Oakville** Can.
93 C6 **Oamaru** N.Z.
17 D4 **Oa, Mull of hd** U.K.
93 D5 **Oaro** N.Z.
41 B3 **Oas** Phil.
46 D6 **Ōasa** Japan
126 D3 **Oasis** U.S.A.
28 D1 **Oașului, Munții mts** Romania
152 B5 **Oates Land reg.** Ant.
97 F5 **Oatlands** Aust.
129 E4 **Oatman** U.S.A.
131 F5 **Oaxaca div.** Mexico
131 F5 **Oaxaca** Mexico
5 O3 **Ob' r.** Rus. Fed.
114 C2 **Oba** Can.
114 C2 **Obakamiga Lake l.** Can.
78 B3 **Obala** Cameroon
114 C2 **Oba Lake l.** Can.
47 E6 **Obama** Japan
77 F5 **Oban** Nigeria
16 E3 **Oban** U.K.
47 H4 **Obanazawa** Japan
77 F5 **Oban Hills mt.** Nigeria
24 C1 **O Barco** Spain
112 F4 **Obatogama L. l.** Can.
110 F4 **Obed** Can.
93 B6 **Obelisk mt.** N.Z.
18 E5 **Oberau** Germany
18 F5 **Oberdrauburg** Austria
124 C4 **Oberlin** U.S.A.
120 B4 **Oberlin** U.S.A.
21 H2 **Obernai** France
19 F4 **Oberösterreich div.** Austria
18 F4 **Oberpfälzer Wald mts** Germany
19 H5 **Oberpullendorf** Austria
15 A2 **Obertyn** Ukraine
19 H5 **Oberwart** Austria
14 B4 **Obesta r.** Rus. Fed.
39 J7 **Obi i.** Indon.
142 A1 **Obidos** Brazil
65 G5 **Obigarm** Tajikistan
46 J2 **Obihiro** Japan
13 H6 **Obil'noye** Rus. Fed.
46 H1 **Obira** Japan
138 C2 **Obispos** Venezuela
13 G5 **Oblivskaya** Rus. Fed.
49 J2 **Obluch'ye** Rus. Fed.
14 C2 **Obninsk** Rus. Fed.
78 E2 **Obo** C.A.R.
48 B5 **Obo** China
80 D2 **Obock** Djibouti
78 E4 **Obokote** Zaire
24 C1 **O Bolo** Spain
15 E2 **Obolon'** Ukraine
19 H2 **Oborniki** Poland
78 C4 **Obouya** Congo
15 G1 **Oboyan'** Rus. Fed.
12 G2 **Obozerskiy** Rus. Fed.
55 E4 **Obra** India
19 G2 **Obra r.** Poland
130 C3 **Obregón, Psa resr** Mexico
28 F3 **Obrochishte** Bulgaria
19 H2 **Obrzycko** Poland
94 □4 **Observatory Rock i.** *Lord Howe I.* Pac. Oc.
14 A2 **Obsha r.** Rus. Fed.
64 D2 **Obshchiy Syrt h.** Rus. Fed.
62 J3 **Obskaya Guba chan.** Rus. Fed.
15 E1 **Obtove** Ukraine
76 D5 **Obuasi** Ghana
15 D1 **Obukhiv** Ukraine
12 J2 **Ob''yachevo** Rus. Fed.
15 G3 **Obytichna Kosa spit** Ukraine
15 F3 **Obytichna Zakota b.** Ukraine
14 F1 **Obzherikha** Rus. Fed.
119 D6 **Ocala** U.S.A.
130 E3 **Ocampo** *Coahuila* Mexico
131 E3 **Ocampo** *Coahuila* Mexico
138 C2 **Ocaña** Colombia
24 E3 **Ocaña** Spain
26 C3 **Occhiobello** Italy
140 C3 **Occidental, Cordillera mt. ra.** Chile
138 B3 **Occidental, Cordillera mt. ra.** Colombia
140 A2 **Occidental, Cordillera mt. ra.** Peru
110 B3 **Ocean Cape pt** U.S.A.
121 F5 **Ocean City** U.S.A.
121 F5 **Ocean City** U.S.A.
110 D4 **Ocean Falls** Can.
148 G3 **Oceanographer Fracture** Atlantic Ocean
128 D5 **Oceanside** U.S.A.
125 F6 **Ocean Springs** U.S.A.
15 D3 **Ochakiv** Ukraine
13 G7 **Och'amch'ire** Georgia
46 D6 **Ōchi** Japan
46 K2 **Ochiishi-misaki pt** Japan
16 F3 **Ochil Hills h.** U.K.
14 A3 **Ochkyne** Ukraine
133 □1 **Ocho Rios** Jamaica
18 E4 **Ochsenfurt** Germany
29 E5 **Ochthonia** Greece
11 E3 **Ockelbo** Sweden
28 D2 **Ocna Sibiului** Romania
15 B2 **Ocnița** Moldova
131 G5 **Ococingo** Mexico
122 C4 **Oconomowoc** U.S.A.
122 D3 **Oconto** U.S.A.
24 C1 **O Corgo** Spain
130 J6 **Ocotal** Nicaragua
130 H6 **Ocotepeque** Honduras
128 D5 **Ocotillo Wells** U.S.A.
130 E4 **Ocotlán** Mexico
76 D5 **Oda** Ghana
46 D6 **Ōda** Japan
10 M2 **Ódáðahraun lava** Iceland
73 G3 **Oda, Jebel mt.** Sudan
47 H3 **Ōdate** Japan
47 G6 **Odawara** Japan
11 B3 **Odda** Norway
24 B4 **Odeceixe** Portugal
111 K3 **Odei r.** Can.
122 C5 **Odell** U.S.A.
24 B4 **Odemira** Portugal
60 A2 **Ödemiş** Turkey
11 C5 **Odense** Denmark
19 G1 **Oderbucht b.** Germany
19 G2 **Oderhaff b.** Germany
26 D3 **Oderzo** Italy
15 C3 **Odesa div.** Ukraine
13 D6 **Odesa** Ukraine
11 D4 **Ödeshog** Sweden
125 C6 **Odessa** U.S.A.
65 H2 **Odesskoye** Rus. Fed.
24 C4 **Odiel r.** Spain
76 C5 **Odienné** Côte d'Ivoire
14 C2 **Odintsovo** Rus. Fed.
28 F2 **Odobești** Romania
19 H3 **Odolanów** Poland
43 D5 **Ôdôngk** Cambodia
28 E1 **Odorheiu Secuiesc** Romania
14 C3 **Odoyev** Rus. Fed.
19 H3 **Odra r.** Germany/Poland
28 B2 **Odžaci** Yugo.
83 E2 **Odzi r.** Zimbabwe
142 D2 **Oeiras** Brazil
139 G3 **Oelemari r.** Surinam
124 C3 **Oelrichs** U.S.A.
18 F3 **Oelsnitz** *Sachsen* Germany
122 B4 **Oelwein** U.S.A.
87 P7 **Oeno atoll** *Pitcairn Islands* Pac. Oc.
98 C2 **Oenpelli** Aust.
60 E1 **Of** Turkey
27 F5 **Ofanto r.** Italy
61 C4 **Ofaqim** Israel
77 E5 **Offa** Nigeria
18 D3 **Offenbach am Main** Germany
18 C4 **Offenburg** Germany
78 B4 **Offoué r.** Gabon
29 F6 **Ofidoussa i.** Greece
77 E5 **Ofiki r.** Nigeria
90 □5 **Ofolanga i.** Tonga
91 □13 **Ofu i.** *American Samoa* Pac. Oc.
90 □3 **Ofu i.** Tonga
47 H4 **Ōfunato** Japan
46 H2 **Ofuyu-misaki pt** Japan
40 C1 **Oga r.** Indon.
47 G4 **Oga** Japan
47 H4 **Ogachi** Japan
80 E3 **Ogadēn reg.** Ethiopia
47 G4 **Oga-hantō pen.** Japan
47 F6 **Ōgaki** Japan
124 C3 **Ogallala** U.S.A.
40 A2 **Ogan r.** Indon.
39 M1 **Ogasawara-shotō is** Japan
115 F3 **Ogascanane, Lac l.** Can.
47 H5 **Ōgawa** Japan
46 H3 **Ogawara-ko l.** Japan
77 E5 **Ogbomoso** Nigeria
124 E3 **Ogden** U.S.A.
126 E3 **Ogden** U.S.A.
110 C3 **Ogden, Mt mt.** Can.
121 F2 **Ogdensburg** U.S.A.
90 □7 **Ogea i.** Fiji
47 G5 **Ogi** Japan
14 H1 **Ogibnoye** Rus. Fed.
108 E3 **Ogilvie r.** Can.
47 □2 **Ogimi** Japan
74 D3 **Oglat Sbot well** Algeria
119 C5 **Oglethorpe, Mt mt.** U.S.A.
26 C3 **Oglio r.** Italy
99 G4 **Ogmore** Aust.
40 D1 **Ogoamas, G. mt.** Indon.
77 F5 **Ogoja** Nigeria
112 C3 **Ogoki r.** Can.
112 C3 **Ogoki Res. resr** Can.
78 B4 **Ogooué r.** Gabon
78 B3 **Ogooué-Ivindo div.** Gabon
78 B4 **Ogooué-Lolo div.** Gabon
78 A4 **Ogooué-Maritime div.** Gabon
46 C6 **Ogōri** Japan
46 C7 **Ogōri** Japan
11 G4 **Ogre** Latvia
26 E3 **Ogulin** Croatia
77 E5 **Ogun r.** Nigeria
77 E5 **Ogun div.** Nigeria
64 D5 **Ogurchinskiy, O. i.** Turkmenistan
60 F1 **Oğuz** Azerbaijan
61 D1 **Oğuzeli** Turkey
77 F5 **Ohafia** Nigeria
93 A6 **Ohai** N.Z.
92 E3 **Ohakune** N.Z.
75 F3 **Ohanet** Algeria
82 B2 **Ohangwena div.** Namibia
46 H3 **Ōhata** Japan
92 E4 **Ohau** N.Z.
93 B6 **Ohau, L. l.** N.Z.
92 E2 **Ohaupo** N.Z.
140 B4 **O'Higgins** Chile
146 B3 **O'Higgins div.** Chile
91 □16 **O'Higgins, C. c.** *Easter I.* Chile
147 B6 **O'Higgins, L. l.** Arg.
118 C4 **Ohio r.** U.S.A.
120 B4 **Ohio div.** U.S.A.
15 F2 **Ohiyivka** Ukraine
18 D3 **Ohm r.** Germany
90 □4 **Ohonua** Tonga
18 F3 **Ohre r.** Czech Rep.
18 E2 **Ohre r.** Germany
29 C4 **Ohrid** Macedonia
29 C4 **Ohrid, Lake l.** Albania/Macedonia
92 E3 **Ohura** N.Z.
139 G3 **Oiapoque r.** Brazil
139 G3 **Oiapoque** Brazil
55 H3 **Oiga** China
120 D4 **Oil City** U.S.A.
128 C4 **Oildale** U.S.A.
50 B2 **Oi Qu r.** China
46 H3 **Oirase-gawa r.** Japan
21 F2 **Oise r.** France
133 □9 **Oistins** *Barbados* Caribbean
46 C7 **Ōita div.** Japan
46 C7 **Ōita** Japan
29 D5 **Oiti mt.** Greece

P

19 J5 Paks Hungary
57 G2 Paktīkā Afghanistan
40 A2 Paku, Tg pt Indon.
43 D4 Pakxé Laos
78 B2 Pala Chad
43 B4 Pala Myanmar
40 A3 Palabuhanratu Indon.
40 A3 Palabuhanratu, Tk b. Indon.
133 F5 Palacios Venezuela
25 H2 Palafrugell Spain
26 F4 Palagruža i. Croatia
29 F7 Palaikastro Greece
29 D7 Palaiochora Greece
29 C5 Palairos Greece
20 F2 Palaiseau France
83 D3 Palala r. R.S.A.
55 F5 Pāla Laharha India
43 A5 Palalankwe *Andaman and Nicobar Is* India
29 D5 Palamas Greece
25 H2 Palamós Spain
54 C4 Palana India
63 R4 Palana Rus. Fed.
41 B2 Palanan Phil.
41 B2 Palanan Point pt Phil.
57 E3 Palangān, Kūh-e mt. ra. Iran
40 C2 Palangkaraya Indon.
56 B4 Palani India
54 C4 Palanpur India
57 F4 Palantak Pakistan
41 C3 Palapag Phil.
82 D3 Palapye Botswana
56 B3 Palar r. India
54 C2 Palas Pakistan
40 E1 Palasa Indon.
55 G4 Palasbari India
63 R3 Palatka Rus. Fed.
86 E4 Palau country Pac. Oc.
41 B2 Palaui i. Phil.
41 A3 Palauig Phil.
43 B4 Palauk Myanmar
91 □12 Palauli B. b. Western Samoa
150 E5 Palau Tr. Pac. Oc.
43 B4 Palaw Myanmar
41 A4 Palawan i. Phil.
41 A4 Palawan Passage str. Phil.
41 B3 Palayan Phil.
27 E7 Palazzolo Acreide Italy
11 G4 Paldiski Estonia
14 E1 Palekh Rus. Fed.
40 A2 Palembang Indon.
147 B5 Palena *Los Lagos* Chile
147 B5 Palena r. Chile
147 B5 Palena, L. l. Chile
24 D1 Palencia Spain
131 G5 Palenque Mexico
133 E3 Palenque, Pta pt Dominican Rep.
27 D6 Palermo Italy
140 C4 Palestina Chile
61 C4 Palestine reg. Asia
125 E6 Palestine U.S.A.
42 A2 Paletwa Myanmar
56 B4 Palghat India
101 A4 Palgrave, Mt h. Aust.
82 A3 Palgrave Point pt Namibia
54 C4 Pali India
41 C5 Palimbang Phil.
27 E5 Palinuro, Capo c. Italy
129 H2 Palisade U.S.A.
18 B4 Paliseul Belgium
54 B5 Palitana India
11 F4 Palivere Estonia
56 B4 Palk Bay b. Sri Lanka
11 H4 Palkino Rus. Fed.
56 C2 Pālkohda India
56 B3 Palkonda Range mt. ra. India
56 B4 Palk Strait str. India/Sri Lanka
140 B2 Pallapalla mt. Peru
13 H5 Pallasovka Rus. Fed.
56 C3 Pallavaram India
56 B2 Palleru r. India
101 B7 Pallinup r. Aust.
81 B4 Pallisa Uganda
93 E4 Palliser Bay b. N.Z.
93 E4 Palliser, Cape c. N.Z.
91 □10 Palliser, Îles is *Fr. Poly.* Pac. Oc.
54 C3 Pallu India
142 C3 Palma r. Brazil
81 D7 Palma Mozambique
24 D4 Palma del Río Spain
25 H3 Palma de Mallorca *Mallorca* Spain
27 D7 Palma di Montechiaro Italy
25 □ Palma, La i. *Canary Is* Spain
140 C2 Palmares *Acre* Brazil
142 E2 Palmares *Pernambuco* Brazil
143 B7 Palmares do Sul Brazil
138 C2 Palmarito Venezuela
27 D5 Palmarola, Isola i. Italy
115 F2 Palmarolle Can.
143 B6 Palmas *Paraná* Brazil
142 C3 Palmas *Tocantins* Brazil
76 C6 Palmas, Cape c. Liberia
142 D3 Palmas de Monte Alto Brazil
132 D2 Palma Soriano Cuba
119 D7 Palm Bay U.S.A.
119 D7 Palm Beach U.S.A.
128 C4 Palmdale U.S.A.
144 D6 Palmeira Brazil
143 B6 Palmeira das Missões Brazil
142 E2 Palmeira dos Índios Brazil
142 D2 Palmeirais Brazil
142 C3 Palmeiras r. Brazil
142 D3 Palmeiras Brazil
144 D2 Palmeiras de Goiás Brazil
79 B5 Palmeirinhas, Pta das hd Angola
152 B2 Palmer U.S.A. Base Ant.
98 C5 Palmer w Aust.
99 E3 Palmer r. Aust.
108 D3 Palmer U.S.A.
152 B2 Palmer Land reg. Ant.
93 C6 Palmerston N.Z.
99 G4 Palmerston, C. c. Aust.
150 J7 Palmerston Island i. *Cook Islands* Pac. Oc.
92 E4 Palmerston North N.Z.
121 F4 Palmerton U.S.A.
99 F2 Palmerville Aust.
119 E7 Palmetto Pt pt The Bahamas
27 E6 Palmi Italy
131 F4 Palmillas Mexico
138 B3 Palmira Colombia
144 B6 Palmital *Paraná* Brazil
144 C5 Palmital *São Paulo* Brazil
128 D5 Palm Springs U.S.A.
99 G5 Palm Tree Cr. r. Aust.
98 C5 Palm Valley v. Aust.
122 B6 Palmyra U.S.A.
120 E3 Palmyra U.S.A.
122 C4 Palmyra U.S.A.
150 J5 Palmyra I. i. Pac. Oc.
55 F5 Palmyras Point pt India
128 A3 Palo Alto U.S.A.
138 B2 Palo de las Letras Colombia
80 B2 Paloich Sudan
10 F1 Palojärvi Finland
10 F1 Palojoensuu Finland
10 G1 Palomaa Finland
140 C2 Palomani mt. Peru
131 G5 Palomares Mexico
128 D5 Palomar Mt mt. U.S.A.
129 G6 Palominas U.S.A.
56 C2 Paloncha India
40 E2 Palopo Indon.
146 E2 Palo Santo Arg.
25 F4 Palos, Cabo de c. Spain
133 □3 Palo Seco Trin. and Tobago
144 B6 Palotina Brazil
129 F5 Palo Verde U.S.A.
129 E5 Palo Verde U.S.A.
140 A2 Palpa Peru
99 E5 Palparara Aust.
10 G2 Paltamo Finland
28 F1 Păltiniș Romania
14 B3 Pal'tso Rus. Fed.
40 D2 Palu Indon.
40 D2 Palu r. Indon.
60 E2 Palu Turkey
133 G5 Palúa Venezuela
41 B3 Paluan Phil.
64 F5 Pal'vart Turkmenistan
54 D3 Palwal India
63 T3 Palyavaam r. Rus. Fed.
78 C3 Pama r. C.A.R.
138 C4 Pamar Colombia
56 B4 Pamban Channel chan. India
97 G4 Pambula Aust.
40 C3 Pamekasan Indon.
40 A3 Pameungpeuk Indon.
19 H5 Pamhagen Austria
56 B3 Pamidi India
20 E5 Pamiers France
65 H5 Pamir r. Afghanistan
65 H5 Pamir mt. ra. Asia
119 E5 Pamlico Sound chan. U.S.A.
125 C5 Pampa U.S.A.
140 C3 Pampa Aullagas Bolivia
147 C6 Pampa Chica Arg.
140 B2 Pampachiri Peru
146 C3 Pampa de la Salinas salt pan Arg.
147 C6 Pampa del Castillo h. Arg.
140 D3 Pampa Grande Bolivia
40 E3 Pampanua Indon.
146 D3 Pampas reg. Arg.
140 B2 Pampas Peru
61 A1 Pamphylia reg. Turkey
81 □4 Pamplemousses Mauritius
138 C2 Pamplona Colombia
41 B4 Pamplona Phil.
25 F1 Pamplona Spain
40 D2 Pamukan, Tk b. Indon.
29 F5 Pamukçu Turkey
120 E6 Pamunkey r. U.S.A.
14 G1 Pamyat' Parizhskoy Kommuny Rus. Fed.
54 D2 Pamzal *Jammu and Kashmir*
78 B4 Pana Gabon
118 B4 Pana U.S.A.
131 H4 Panabá Mexico
41 C5 Panabo Phil.
129 E3 Panaca U.S.A.
29 E4 Panagia i. Greece
41 A4 Panagtaran Point pt Phil.
28 E3 Panagyurishte Bulgaria
40 A3 Panaitan i. Indon.
56 A3 Panaji India
104 K9 Panama country Central America
130 L7 Panamá Panama
130 L7 Panamá, B. de b. Panama
130 L7 Panama Canal canal Panama
119 C6 Panama City U.S.A.
130 L8 Panamá, Golfo de g. Panama
128 D3 Panamint Range mt. ra. U.S.A.
128 D3 Panamint Springs U.S.A.
128 D3 Panamint Valley U.S.A.
140 A1 Panao Peru
41 C4 Panaon i. Phil.
55 F4 Panar r. India
27 E6 Panarea, Isola i. Italy
43 E7 Panarik Indon.
26 C3 Panaro r. Italy
41 B4 Panay i. Phil.
41 C3 Panay i. Phil.
41 B4 Panay Gulf b. Phil.
129 E2 Pancake Range mts U.S.A.
145 H3 Pancas Brazil
28 C2 Pančevo Yugo.
40 C1 Pancingapan, Bukit mt. Indon.
28 F2 Panciu Romania
83 E3 Panda Mozambique
41 C3 Pandan Phil.
41 B4 Pandan Phil.
41 B4 Pandan B. b. Phil.
43 □ Pandan Res. resr Singapore
55 E5 Pandaria India
40 A3 Pandeglang Indon.
145 F1 Pandeiros r. Brazil
56 A2 Pandharpur India
54 D5 Pandhurna India
96 D1 Pandie Pandie Aust.
140 C2 Pando div. Bolivia
146 E3 Pando Uruguay
54 A3 Pandran Pakistan
11 G5 Panevėžys Lithuania
15 D1 Panfyly Ukraine
49 G1 Pang r. China
78 E3 Panga Zaire
90 □5 Pangai Tonga
90 □3 Pangaimotu i. Tonga
40 B3 Pangandaran Indon.
81 C6 Pangani Tanzania
40 D2 Pangean Indon.
42 B2 Panghsang Myanmar
79 E4 Pangi Zaire
55 H3 Pangin India
54 C2 Pangi Range mt. ra. Pakistan
40 D3 Pangkajene Indon.
40 B3 Pangkalanbuun Indon.
38 C6 Pangkalansusu Indon.
40 A2 Pangkalpinang Indon.
39 H7 Pangkalsiang, Tg pt Indon.
42 B1 Panglang Myanmar
109 M3 Pangnirtung Can.
79 B5 Pango Aluquém Angola
62 J3 Pangody Rus. Fed.
78 D2 Pangonda C.A.R.
54 D2 Pangong Tso l. India
40 A3 Pangrango vol Indon.
147 B4 Panguipulli Chile
147 B4 Panguipulli, L. l. Chile
129 F3 Panguitch U.S.A.
41 B5 Pangutaran i. Phil.
41 B5 Pangutaran Group is Phil.
125 C5 Panhandle U.S.A.
79 E5 Pania-Mwanga Zaire
90 □2 Panié, Mt mt. Pac. Oc.
54 B5 Pānikoita i. India
14 E4 Panino Rus. Fed.
14 B1 Panino Rus. Fed.
54 D3 Panipat India
41 A4 Panitan Phil.
57 G1 Panj Tajikistan
57 F2 Panjāb Afghanistan
65 G5 Panjakent Tajikistan
43 E7 Panjang i. Indon.
40 A3 Panjang Indon.
57 F4 Panjgur Pakistan
54 C5 Panjhra r. India
54 B3 Panjnad r. Pakistan
10 H3 Pankakoski Finland
65 J2 Pankrushikha Rus. Fed.
77 F5 Pankshin Nigeria
54 E4 Panna India
54 E4 Panna reg. India
100 B4 Pannawonica Aust.
144 C4 Panorama Brazil
65 H1 Panovo Rus. Fed.
14 E3 Panovy Kusty Rus. Fed.
56 B4 Panruti India
49 G4 Panshan China
49 H4 Panshi China
40 D2 Pantai Indon.
143 A4 Pantanal de São Lourenço marsh Brazil
143 A4 Pantanal do Rio Negro marsh Brazil
143 A4 Pantanal do Taquari marsh Brazil
143 A4 Pantanal Matogrossense, Parque Nacional de nat. park Brazil
28 F2 Pantelimon Romania
27 C7 Pantelleria Italy
27 D7 Pantelleria, Isola di i. Italy
39 H8 Pantemakassar Indon.
41 C5 Pantukan Phil.
131 F4 Pánuco *Veracruz* Mexico
131 F4 Pánuco r. Mexico
56 A2 Panvel India
50 D3 Pan Xian China
51 F4 Panyu China
15 G2 Panyutyne Ukraine
79 C5 Panzi Zaire
131 H6 Panzos Guatemala
142 E2 Pão de Açúcar Brazil
27 F6 Paola Italy
118 C4 Paoli U.S.A.
91 □11 Paopao *Fr. Poly.* Pac. Oc.
78 C2 Paoua C.A.R.
65 H4 Pap Uzbekistan
19 H5 Pápa Hungary
29 D6 Papadianika Greece
145 F3 Papagaios Brazil
146 C3 Papagayos Arg.
92 E2 Papakura N.Z.
27 E5 Papa, Monte del mt. Italy
131 F4 Papantla Mexico
138 B5 Papa Playa Peru
91 □11 Papara *Fr. Poly.* Pac. Oc.
56 C2 Pāparhāhandi India
92 E2 Paparoa N.Z.
93 C5 Paparoa Range mt. ra. N.Z.
16 G1 Papa Stour i. U.K.
92 E2 Papatoetoe N.Z.
93 B7 Papatowai N.Z.
91 □11 Papava *Fr. Poly.* Pac. Oc.
16 F2 Papa Westray i. U.K.
91 □11 Papeete *Fr. Poly.* Pac. Oc.
18 C2 Papenburg Germany
91 □11 Papenoo r. *Fr. Poly.* Pac. Oc.
91 □11 Papenoo *Fr. Poly.* Pac. Oc.
91 □11 Papetoai *Fr. Poly.* Pac. Oc.
115 H3 Papineau-Labelle, Réserve faunique de res. Can.
129 E3 Papoose L. l. U.S.A.
146 B2 Paposo Chile
90 □1 Papua, Gulf of g. P.N.G.
86 F5 Papua New Guinea country Australasia
42 B3 Papun Myanmar
98 B4 Papunya Aust.
57 C3 Pa Qal'eh Iran
142 B1 Pará div. Brazil
145 F3 Pará r. Brazil
14 E3 Para r. Rus. Fed.
101 B4 Paraburdoo Aust.
41 B3 Paracale Phil.
145 G5 Paracambi Brazil
139 F4 Paracari r. Brazil
145 F2 Paracatu r. *Minas Gerais* Brazil
145 E2 Paracatu *Minas Gerais* Brazil
145 F2 Paracatu r. Brazil
38 F3 Paracel Islands is S. China Sea
96 D2 Parachilna Aust.
54 B2 Parachinar Pakistan
28 C3 Paraćin Yugo.
142 E1 Paracuru Brazil
145 F3 Pará de Minas Brazil
132 □1 Paradera *Aruba* Caribbean
115 G2 Paradis Can.
139 F2 Paradise Guyana
128 B2 Paradise U.S.A.
122 E2 Paradise U.S.A.
111 H4 Paradise Hill Can.
119 □2 Paradise I. i. The Bahamas
128 D2 Paradise Peak summit U.S.A.
113 J3 Paradise River Can.
125 F4 Paragould U.S.A.
141 D2 Paragua r. Bolivia
139 E2 Paragua r. Venezuela
142 D3 Paraguaçu r. Brazil
144 C5 Paraguaçu Paulista Brazil
141 E3 Paraguai r. Brazil
138 C1 Paraguáipoa Venezuela
138 D1 Paraguaná, Pen. de pen. Venezuela
141 E5 Paraguarí Paraguay
141 E5 Paraguay r. Arg./Paraguay
136 D5 Paraguay country S. America
57 E4 Parahadab Pakistan
142 E2 Paraíba r. Brazil
142 E2 Paraíba div. Brazil
145 G5 Paraíba do Sul Brazil
145 H4 Paraíba do Sul r. Brazil
144 B3 Paraíso Brazil
131 G5 Paraíso Mexico
142 C3 Paraíso do Norte Brazil
145 F5 Paraisópolis Brazil
14 H2 Parakino Rus. Fed.
77 E5 Parakou Benin
57 D4 Parākūn Iran
96 D2 Parakylia Aust.
56 D2 Parālākhemundi India
29 D5 Paralia *Stereá Ellás* Greece
56 C2 Paralkot India
56 B4 Paramakkudi India
139 F2 Paramaribo Surinam
138 B2 Paramillo mt. Colombia
138 B2 Paramillo, Parque Nacional nat. park Colombia
142 D3 Paramirim r. Brazil
142 D3 Paramirim Brazil
14 C3 Paramonovo Rus. Fed.
121 F4 Paramus U.S.A.
63 R4 Paramushir, O. i. Rus. Fed.
29 C5 Paramythia Greece
61 C4 Paran w Israel
146 D3 Paraná r. Arg.
146 D3 Paraná Arg.
142 C3 Paranã Brazil
142 C3 Paranã r. Brazil
144 B6 Paraná div. Brazil
144 D6 Paranaguá Brazil
144 D6 Paranagua, Baia de b. Brazil
144 C3 Paranaíba Brazil
144 B3 Paranaíba r. Brazil
146 E3 Paraná Ibicuy r. Arg.
144 C3 Paranaiguara Brazil
141 E1 Paranaíta r. Brazil
144 C5 Paranapanema r. Brazil
143 C4 Paranã, Sa do h. Brazil
144 A1 Paranatinga r. Brazil
144 B5 Paranavaí Brazil
57 B2 Parandak Iran
40 B3 Parang i. Indon.
41 B5 Parang Phil.
56 B4 Parangipettai India
144 A5 Paranhos Brazil
54 C5 Paranoli i. India
91 □10 Paraoa i. *Fr. Poly.* Pac. Oc.
145 F3 Paraopeba Brazil
145 F3 Paraopeba r. Brazil
93 E4 Paraparaumu N.Z.
142 C1 Para, Rio do r. Brazil
125 D7 Paras Mexico
55 G5 Parashunam Bangladesh
145 F5 Parati Brazil
55 B4 Paratwada India
142 B2 Parauapebas r. Brazil
139 F5 Parauari r. Brazil
144 C2 Paraúna Brazil
21 G3 Paray-le-Monial France
54 D5 Parbati r. India
55 G4 Parbatipur Bangladesh
56 B2 Parbhani India
18 E2 Parchim Germany
19 L3 Parczew Poland
122 C4 Pardeeville U.S.A.
28 G2 Pardina Romania
55 G2 Parding China
145 J1 Pardo r. *Bahia/Minas Gerais* Brazil
144 B4 Pardo r. *Mato Grosso do Sul* Brazil
145 F1 Pardo r. *Minas Gerais* Brazil
144 D6 Pardo r. *Paraná/São Paulo* Brazil
144 D4 Pardo r. *São Paulo* Brazil
19 G3 Pardubice Czech Rep.
40 C3 Pare Indon.
142 A3 Parecis Brazil
141 E2 Parecis r. Brazil
24 D1 Paredes de Nava Spain
146 C3 Pareditas Arg.
131 E3 Paredón Mexico
60 F2 Pareh Iran
142 E2 Parelhas Brazil
92 D1 Parengarenga Harbour inlet N.Z.
115 H3 Parent Can.
20 D4 Parentis-en-Born France
115 G2 Parent, Lac l. Can.
93 C6 Pareora N.Z.
40 D3 Parepare Indon.
146 D4 Parera Arg.
29 C5 Parga Greece
11 F3 Pargas Finland
27 E6 Parghelia Italy
139 E2 Pariaguán Venezuela
133 □3 Paria, Gulf of g. Trinidad/Venezuela
139 E1 Paria, Península de pen. Venezuela
129 F3 Paria Plateau plat. U.S.A.
40 E2 Parigi Indon.
139 F2 Parika Guyana
11 H3 Parikkala Finland
139 D3 Parima-Tapirapecó, Parque Nacional nat. park Venezuela
138 A4 Pariñas, Pta pt Peru
142 A1 Parintins Brazil
114 E5 Paris Can.
20 F2 Paris France
120 A5 Paris U.S.A.
119 B4 Paris U.S.A.
125 E5 Paris U.S.A.
114 C3 Parisienne, Île i. Can.
130 K8 Parita Panama
43 C6 Parit Buntar Malaysia
57 C3 Pārīz Iran
57 D4 Parkā Bandar Iran
56 B2 Parkal India
11 F3 Parkano Finland
113 J3 Parke Lake l. Can.
65 G4 Parkent Uzbekistan
129 E4 Parker U.S.A.
129 E4 Parker Dam dam U.S.A.
111 K2 Parker Lake l. Can.
45 □ Parker, Mt h. Hong Kong
122 A4 Parkersburg U.S.A.
120 C5 Parkersburg U.S.A.
97 G3 Parkes Aust.
122 B3 Park Falls U.S.A.
122 D5 Park Forest U.S.A.
133 □7 Parkham *Antigua* Caribbean
114 D3 Parkinson Can.
124 E2 Park Rapids U.S.A.
110 E5 Parksville Can.
121 F4 Parksville U.S.A.
54 D2 Parkutta Pakistan
65 J5 Parkutta *Jammu and Kashmir*
24 E2 Parla Spain
56 D2 Parla Kimedi India
133 □2 Parlatuvier *Tobago* Trin. and Tobago
56 B2 Parli Vaijnath India
26 C3 Parma *Parma* Italy
26 C3 Parma r. Italy
126 C3 Parma U.S.A.
120 C4 Parma U.S.A.
139 D2 Parmana Venezuela
142 B3 Parnaíba r. Brazil
142 D1 Parnaíba r. Brazil
142 C2 Parnaíba r. Brazil
142 D1 Parnaíba Brazil
142 C2 Parnaibinha r. Brazil
142 E2 Parnamirim Brazil
142 D2 Parnarama Brazil
29 D5 Parnassos mt. Greece
93 D5 Parnassus N.Z.
96 D3 Parndana Aust.
122 A5 Parnell U.S.A.
29 D6 Parnon mts Greece
11 G4 Pärnu Estonia
11 G4 Pärnu-Jagupi Estonia
55 G4 Paro Bhutan
97 F2 Paroo w Aust.
97 E2 Paroo Channel w Aust.
57 E2 Paropamisus mt. ra. Afghanistan
29 E6 Paros i. Greece
29 E6 Paros Greece
133 □1 Parottee Pt pt Jamaica
129 F3 Parowan U.S.A.
146 B4 Parral Chile
121 F6 Parramore I. i. U.S.A.
130 E3 Parras Mexico
146 E4 Parravicini Arg.
17 F6 Parrett r. U.K.
130 J7 Parrita Costa Rica
113 H4 Parrsboro Can.
108 F2 Parry, Cape pt Can.
108 G2 Parry Islands is Can.
109 L2 Parry, Kap c. Greenland
133 □3 Parrylands Trin. and Tobago
114 E4 Parry Sound Can.
19 H2 Parsęta r. Poland
14 E3 Parskiy Ugol Rus. Fed.
125 E4 Parsons U.S.A.
120 D5 Parsons U.S.A.
55 E5 Partabpur India
27 D7 Partanna Italy
20 D3 Parthenay France
27 D6 Partinico Italy
19 J4 Partizánske Slovakia
14 F2 Partsa r. Rus. Fed.
15 F3 Partyzany Ukraine
139 G4 Paru r. Brazil
139 F3 Paru de Oeste r. Brazil
15 D3 Parutyne Ukraine
56 C2 Parvatipuram India
54 C4 Parvatsar India
54 D4 Parwan r. India
55 E3 Paryang China
128 C4 Pasadena U.S.A.
125 E6 Pasadena U.S.A.
29 F4 Paşalimanı Adası i. Turkey
40 D2 Pasangkayu Indon.
42 B3 Pasawng Myanmar
125 F6 Pascagoula U.S.A.
115 G2 Pascalis Can.
28 F1 Pașcani Romania
126 C2 Pasco U.S.A.
145 J2 Pascoal, Monte h. Brazil
99 E2 Pascoe r. Aust.
98 D3 Pascoe Inlet inlet Aust.
41 B3 Pascual Phil.
19 G2 Pasewalk Germany
111 H3 Pasfield Lake l. Can.
12 E2 Pasha Rus. Fed.
65 K1 Pashino Rus. Fed.
49 J2 Pashkovo Rus. Fed.
14 F3 Pashkovo Rus. Fed.
41 B3 Pasig Phil.
55 H3 Pasighat India
60 E2 Pasinler Turkey
43 □ Pasir Gudang Malaysia
40 C4 Pasirian Indon.
43 C6 Pasir Mas Malaysia
43 □ Pasir Panjang Singapore
43 C6 Pasir Putih Malaysia
128 A2 Paskenta U.S.A.
64 F3 Paskevicha, Zaliv b. Kazak.
57 E4 Paskūh Iran
19 J1 Pasłęk Poland
101 C7 Pasley, C. c. Aust.
57 E4 Pasni Pakistan
131 H5 Paso Caballos Guatemala
147 C5 Paso de Indios Arg.
146 E2 Paso de los Libres Arg.
146 E3 Paso de los Toros Uruguay
141 E5 Paso de Patria Paraguay
146 C2 Paso de Peña Negra Chile
42 A2 Pasok Myanmar
147 B6 Paso Río Mayo Arg.
128 B4 Paso Robles U.S.A.
111 J4 Pasquia Hills h. Can.
57 C3 Pasrūdak Iran
121 J2 Passadumkeag U.S.A.
122 C1 Passage I. i. U.S.A.
145 F4 Passa Tempo Brazil
18 F4 Passau Germany
152 □ Passe Royale chan. *Kerguelen* Indian Ocean
41 B4 Passi Phil.
143 B6 Passo Fundo Brazil
145 E4 Passos Brazil
12 C4 Pastavy Belarus
138 B4 Pastaza r. Peru
111 J4 Pas, The Can.
138 B3 Pasto Colombia
129 H3 Pastora Peak summit U.S.A.
142 D2 Pastos Bons Brazil
41 B2 Pasuquin Phil.
40 C3 Pasuruan Indon.
11 G4 Pasvalys Lithuania
19 J5 Pásztó Hungary
78 D2 Pata C.A.R.
41 B5 Pata i. Phil.
76 B4 Pata Senegal
140 B4 Patache, Pta pt Chile
147 B6 Patagonia reg. Arg.
129 G6 Patagonia U.S.A.
40 A3 Patah, G. mt. Indon.
55 G4 Patakata India
57 E3 Patambar Iran
54 D5 Patan India
54 C5 Patan India
55 F4 Patan Nepal
146 D2 Patay Arg.
97 E3 Patchewollock Aust.
92 E3 Patea r. N.Z.
92 E3 Patea N.Z.
77 F5 Pategi Nigeria
81 D5 Pate I. i. Kenya
55 G5 Patenga Pt pt Bangladesh
19 F5 Paternion Austria
27 E7 Paternò Italy
97 G3 Paterson Aust.
121 F4 Paterson U.S.A.
93 B7 Paterson Inlet inlet N.Z.
55 E5 Pathalgaon India
54 C2 Pathankot India
52 E4 Pathankot India
126 F3 Pathfinder Res. resr U.S.A.
43 B5 Pathiu Thailand
56 B2 Pathri India
43 C4 Pathum Thani Thailand
40 B3 Pati Indon.
138 B3 Patía r. Colombia
54 D3 Patiala India
139 G3 Patience French Guiana
41 □2 Pati Pt pt *Guam* Pac. Oc.
40 E3 Patiro, Tg pt Indon.
55 H4 Pātkai Bum mt. ra. India
29 F6 Patmos i. Greece
55 F4 Patna India
55 F5 Patnagarh India
41 B3 Patnanongan i. Phil.
60 E2 Patnos Turkey
147 B6 Pato, C. mt. Chile
54 E3 Paton India
29 B4 Patos Albania
142 E2 Patos Brazil
145 E3 Patos de Minas Brazil
133 □3 Patos, I. i. *Trinidad* Trin. and Tobago
143 B7 Patos, Lagoa dos lag. Brazil
144 D1 Patos, R. dos r. Brazil
146 C3 Patquia Arg.
29 C5 Patra Greece
28 F1 Pătrăuți Romania
10 K2 Patreksfjörður Iceland
147 A6 Patricio Lynch, I. i. Chile
144 D3 Patrimônio Brazil
141 G3 Patrocínio Brazil
10 H1 Patsoyoki r. Rus. Fed.
43 C6 Pattani r. Thailand
43 C6 Pattani Thailand
43 C4 Pattaya Thailand
121 J2 Patten U.S.A.
128 B3 Patterson U.S.A.
120 D5 Patterson r. U.S.A.
110 C2 Patterson, Mt mt. Can.
128 C3 Patterson Mt mt. U.S.A.
122 E3 Patterson, Pt pt U.S.A.
55 E4 Patti India
10 G2 Pattijoki Finland
10 F1 Pättikkä Finland
56 B3 Pattikonda India
93 □1 Pattison, C. c. *Chatham Is* N.Z.
110 D3 Pattullo, Mt mt. Can.
55 G5 Patuakhali Bangladesh
111 H3 Patuanak Can.
130 J6 Patuca r. Honduras
130 J6 Patuca, Pta pt Honduras
120 E5 Patuxent r. U.S.A.
152 B3 Patuxent Ra. mt. ra. Ant.
131 E5 Pátzcuaro Mexico
20 D5 Pau France
145 J1 Pau-Brasil Brazil
140 B2 Paucarbamba Peru
140 B2 Paucartambo Peru
142 C2 Pau d'Arco r. Brazil
142 C2 Pau d'Arco Brazil
20 D4 Pauillac France
138 D5 Pauiní r. Brazil
140 C1 Pauini Brazil
42 A2 Pauk Myanmar
42 A3 Paukkaung Myanmar
42 A2 Pauktaw Myanmar
108 F3 Paulatuk Can.
129 F4 Paulden U.S.A.
120 A4 Paulding U.S.A.
113 H2 Paul Island i. Can.
142 D2 Paulistana Brazil
142 E2 Paulo Afonso Brazil
144 D4 Paulo de Faria Brazil
121 F4 Paul Smiths U.S.A.
125 D5 Pauls Valley U.S.A.
28 F1 Păunești Romania
42 A3 Paungde Myanmar
54 D3 Pauri India
138 C2 Pauto r. Colombia
145 H2 Pavão Brazil
60 F3 Pāveh Iran
14 D3 Pavelets Rus. Fed.
26 B3 Pavia Italy
11 F4 Pāvilosta Latvia
12 H3 Pavino Rus. Fed.
28 E3 Pavlikeni Bulgaria
14 A2 Pavlinovo Rus. Fed.
15 A1 Pavlivka *Volyn* Ukraine
15 F1 Pavlivka Ukraine
65 J2 Pavlodar div. Kazak.
65 J2 Pavlodar Kazak.
15 F2 Pavlohrad Ukraine
15 F3 Pavlopillya Ukraine
65 H2 Pavlovka Kazak.
14 H3 Pavlovka Rus. Fed.
14 F2 Pavlovo Rus. Fed.
13 G5 Pavlovsk Rus. Fed.
65 K2 Pavlovsk Rus. Fed.
13 F6 Pavlovskaya Rus. Fed.
14 D2 Pavlovskiy Posad Rus. Fed.
14 E1 Pavlovskoye Rus. Fed.
15 E2 Pavlysh Ukraine
138 C3 Pavon Colombia
26 C3 Pavullo nel Frignano Italy
40 B2 Pawan r. Indon.
54 E3 Pawayan India
122 E4 Paw Paw U.S.A.
121 H4 Pawtucket U.S.A.
43 B4 Pawut Myanmar
29 E7 Paximadia i. Greece
29 C5 Paxoi i. Greece
122 C5 Paxton U.S.A.
55 E4 Payagpur India
38 D7 Payakumbuh Indon.
43 □ Paya Lebar Singapore
138 C3 Paya, Parque Nacional la nat. park Colombia
21 H3 Payerne Switz.
126 C2 Payette U.S.A.
49 J2 Paykan Rus. Fed.
62 H3 Pay-Khoy, Khrebet h. Rus. Fed.
112 F2 Payne, Lac l. Can.
128 B1 Paynes Creek U.S.A.
101 B6 Payne's Find Aust.
146 E3 Paysandú Uruguay
20 D5 Pays Basque reg. France/Spain
20 D3 Pays de la Loire div. France
20 B2 Pays de Léon reg. France
129 G4 Payson U.S.A.
129 G1 Payson U.S.A.
146 C4 Payún, Co vol Arg.
57 B3 Pāzanān Iran
60 E1 Pazar Turkey
28 E3 Pazardzhik Bulgaria
29 G5 Pazarlar Turkey
130 C3 Paz, B. de la b. Mexico
138 C2 Paz de Ariporo Colombia
138 C2 Paz de Rio Colombia
26 D3 Pazin Croatia
142 B2 Paz, R. da r. Brazil
28 C3 Pčinja r. Macedonia
43 B4 Pe Myanmar
90 □4 Pea Tonga
144 B5 Peabiru Brazil
110 G3 Peace r. Can.
110 F3 Peace River Can.
129 F4 Peach Springs U.S.A.
96 C2 Peake w Aust.
113 G4 Peaked Mt. h. U.S.A.
41 A4 Peaked Point pt Phil.
97 G3 Peak Hill Aust.
99 G4 Peak Ra. h. Aust.
82 A4 Peak, The summit *Ascension* Atlantic Ocean
129 H2 Peale, Mt mt. U.S.A.
129 H6 Pearce U.S.A.
98 B2 Pearce Pt pt Aust.
114 A2 Pearl Can.
125 F6 Pearl r. U.S.A.
127 □1 Pearl City U.S.A.
127 □1 Pearl Harbor inlet U.S.A.
125 D6 Pearsall U.S.A.
119 D6 Pearson U.S.A.
109 J2 Peary Channel chan. Can.
109 P1 Peary Land reg. Greenland
100 B4 Peawah r. Aust.
112 C2 Peawanuck Can.
83 F2 Pebane Mozambique
138 C4 Pebas Peru
147 E7 Pebble I. i. Falkland Is.
40 E2 Pebengko Indon.
28 C3 Peć Yugo.
145 G3 Peçanha Brazil
143 C6 Peças, I. das i. Brazil
10 H1 Pechenga Rus. Fed.
15 G2 Pechenihy Ukraine
15 A2 Pechenizhyn Ukraine
14 D2 Pecherniki Rus. Fed.
62 G3 Pechora r. Rus. Fed.
62 G3 Pechora Rus. Fed.
62 G2 Pechorskoye More sea Rus. Fed.
11 G4 Pechory Rus. Fed.
28 G3 Pecineaga Romania
76 A4 Pecixe, Ilha de i. Guinea-Bissau
123 F4 Peck U.S.A.
27 B6 Pecora, Capo pt Italy
125 C6 Pecos r. U.S.A.
125 C6 Pecos U.S.A.
19 J5 Pécs Hungary
132 B6 Pedasí Panama
133 E3 Pedernales Haiti
130 D2 Pedernales Mexico
133 G5 Pedernales Venezuela
144 D5 Pederneiras Brazil
10 F3 Pedersöre Finland
96 C1 Pedirka Aust.
79 B7 Pediva Angola
55 E3 Pedo La pass China
145 H1 Pedra Azul Brazil
76 □ Pedra Lume Cape Verde
144 A2 Pedra Preta Brazil
142 C3 Pedras r. *Bahia* Brazil
142 B2 Pedras r. *Pará* Brazil
145 F1 Pedras de Maria da Cruz Brazil
138 C2 Pedraza La Vieja Venezuela
138 C1 Pedregal Venezuela
144 E4 Pedregulho Brazil
142 D1 Pedreiras *Maranhão* Brazil
145 E5 Pedreiras *São Paulo* Brazil
130 E3 Pedriceña Mexico
142 C2 Pedro Afonso Brazil
132 C3 Pedro Bank Caribbean
132 C3 Pedro Cays i. Caribbean
138 C3 Pedro Chico Colombia
140 C4 Pedro de Valdivia Chile
143 B4 Pedro Gomes *Mato Grosso do Sul* Brazil
144 A3 Pedro Gomes *Mato Grosso do Sul* Brazil
130 L7 Pedro González, I. i. Panama
138 D3 Pedro II, Ilha reg. Brazil
141 E4 Pedro Juan Caballero Paraguay
145 F3 Pedro Leopoldo Brazil
142 D1 Pedroll Brazil
130 B2 Pedro Mártir, Sa S. mt. ra. Mexico
25 E3 Pedro Muñoz Spain
146 F3 Pedro Osorio Brazil
133 □1 Pedro Pt pt Jamaica
56 C4 Pedro, Pt pt Sri Lanka
24 B2 Pedroso Portugal
144 E6 Pedro Toledo Brazil
119 E5 Pee Dee r. U.S.A.
121 G4 Peekskill U.S.A.
97 G2 Peel r. Aust.
108 E3 Peel r. Can.
17 E4 Peel Isle of Man
18 F2 Peene r. Germany
110 F4 Peers Can.
97 E2 Peery L. salt flat Aust.
93 D5 Pegasus Bay b. N.Z.
42 B3 Pegu Myanmar
42 A3 Pegu div. Myanmar
40 A2 Pegunungan Barisan mt. ra. Indon.
40 C1 Pegunungan Iran mt. ra. Indon.
40 C1 Pegunungan Kapuas Hulu mt. ra. Indon./Malaysia
39 L7 Pegunungan Maoke mt. ra. Indon.
40 C2 Pegunungan Meratus mt. ra. Indon.
40 C1 Pegunungan Muller mt. ra. Indon.
40 C2 Pegunungan Schwaner mt. ra. Indon.
39 L7 Pegunungan Van Rees mt. ra. Indon.
42 A3 Pegu Yoma mt. ra. Myanmar
12 J2 Pegysh Rus. Fed.
29 F4 Pehlivanköy Turkey
146 D4 Pehuajó Arg.
51 H4 Peikang Taiwan
18 E2 Peine Germany
11 G4 Peipus, Lake l. Estonia/Rus. Fed.
29 D6 Peiraias Greece
144 D2 Peixe r. *Goiás* Brazil
142 B3 Peixe r. *Goiás* Brazil
142 C3 Peixe Brazil
144 C5 Peixe, Rio do r. *São Paulo* Brazil
144 B2 Peixe, Rio do r. *Goiás* Brazil
141 E2 Peixes r. *Mato Grosso* Brazil
145 G4 Peixes r. *Minas Gerais* Brazil
144 B1 Peixes, Rio dos r. *Mato Grosso* Brazil
51 G1 Pei Xian China
51 G1 Pei Xian China
141 E3 Peixo de Couro r. Brazil
141 E2 Peixoto de Azevedo r. Brazil
40 A1 Pejantan i. Indon.
40 B3 Pekalongan Indon.
43 C7 Pekan Malaysia
14 E3 Pekhlets Rus. Fed.
122 C5 Pekin U.S.A.
14 A3 Peklino Rus. Fed.
14 D1 Peksha r. Rus. Fed.
43 C7 Pelabuhan Kelang Malaysia
27 D7 Pelagie, Isole is Italy
29 C4 Pelagonija plain Macedonia
40 C2 Pelaihari Indon.
21 H4 Pelat, Mont mt. France
40 D1 Pelawanbesar Indon.
19 G2 Pełczyce Poland
114 D6 Pelee I. i. Can.
133 □4 Pelée, Montagne vol *Martinique* Caribbean
114 D6 Pelee Pt pt Can.
41 □1 Peleliu i. Palau
39 H7 Peleng i. Indon.
19 G4 Pelhřimov Czech Rep.
108 E4 Pelican U.S.A.
99 E3 Pelican Cr. r. Aust.
122 A1 Pelican Lake l. U.S.A.
122 C3 Pelican Lake l. U.S.A.
111 J3 Pelican Narrows Can.
15 B3 Pelinia Moldova
26 F4 Pelješac pen. Croatia
10 G2 Pelkosenniemi Finland
111 H1 Pellat Lake l. Can.
26 A3 Pellice r. Italy
122 C4 Pell Lake U.S.A.
10 F2 Pello Finland
18 D1 Pellworm i. Germany
110 B2 Pelly r. Can.
109 K3 Pelly Bay Can.
110 B2 Pelly Crossing Can.
111 J1 Pelly Lake l. Can.
110 C2 Pelly Mountains mt. ra. Can.
40 D3 Pelokang is Indon.
29 C6 Peloponnisos div. Greece
27 E7 Peloritani, Monti mts Italy
27 E6 Peloro, Capo c. Italy
93 D4 Pelorus Sd chan. N.Z.
146 F3 Pelotas Brazil
143 B6 Pelotas, R. das r. Brazil
19 J2 Pelplin Poland
73 F1 Pelusium Egypt
21 H4 Pelvoux, Massif du mts France
21 H4 Pelvoux, Mt mt. France
14 G2 Pelya-Khovanskaya Rus. Fed.
121 J2 Pemadumcook Lake l. U.S.A.
40 B3 Pemalang Indon.
40 B1 Pemangkat Indon.
43 B7 Pematangsiantar Indon.
81 D7 Pemba Mozambique
79 E7 Pemba Zambia
81 D7 Pemba, Baia de b. Mozambique
81 C6 Pemba Channel chan. Tanzania
81 C6 Pemba I. i. Tanzania
101 A7 Pemberton Aust.
110 F4 Pembina r. Can.
124 D1 Pembina U.S.A.
115 G4 Pembroke Can.
17 E6 Pembroke U.K.
121 K2 Pembroke U.S.A.
93 A6 Pembroke, Mt mt. N.Z.
40 C2 Pembuanghulu Indon.
40 B2 Pemuar Indon.
56 A2 Pen India
42 A2 Pen r. Myanmar
15 G1 Pena r. Rus. Fed.
140 C4 Pena Barrosa Bolivia
24 D2 Peñafiel Spain
24 D4 Peñaflor Spain
133 □3 Penal Trin. Trinidad and Tobago Tobago
142 C1 Penalva Brazil
131 F4 Peñamiller Mexico
131 F4 Peña Nevada, Co mt. Mexico
144 C4 Penápolis Brazil
24 D2 Peñaranda de Bracamonte Spain
24 D3 Peñarroya-Pueblonuevo Spain
130 J7 Peñas Blancas Nicaragua
24 D1 Peñas, Cabo de c. Spain
130 B2 Peñasco, Pto Mexico
147 A6 Penas, Golfo de g. Chile
133 G5 Peñas, Pta pt Venezuela
56 B1 Pench r. India
152 D5 Penck, C. c. Ant.
40 C2 Pendadahian Indon.
78 C2 Pendé r. C.A.R.
76 B5 Pendembu Sierra Leone
100 C3 Pender B. b. Aust.
29 G4 Pendik Turkey
77 E4 Pendjari, Parc National de la nat. park Benin
126 C2 Pendleton U.S.A.
110 D4 Pendleton Bay Can.
40 A2 Pendopo Indon.
126 C1 Pend Oreille r. U.S.A.
126 C2 Pend Oreille L. l. U.S.A.
55 E5 Pendra India
77 E5 Pénessoulou Benin
115 F4 Penetanguishene Can.
50 D2 Peng'an China
56 B2 Penganga r. India
45 □ Peng Chau i. Hong Kong
51 H3 P'eng-chia Hsü i. Taiwan
51 G4 P'eng-hu Lieh-tao is Taiwan
51 G4 Peng-hu Tao i. Taiwan
40 B1 Pengiki i. Indon.
43 □ Peng Kang h. Singapore
49 G5 Penglai China
50 C2 Pengshan China
50 E2 Pengshui China
50 D2 Pengxi China
51 G2 Pengze China
24 B3 Peniche Portugal
40 C4 Penida h. Indon.
12 E2 Peninga Rus. Fed.
43 D7 Peninsular Malaysia pen. Malaysia
142 C2 Penitente, Sa do reg. Brazil
60 F3 Penjwin Iraq
20 B3 Penmarc'h, Pte de pt France
26 D4 Penne Italy
152 A5 Pennell Coast Ant.
56 B3 Penner r. India
96 D3 Penneshaw Aust.
17 F4 Pennines h. U.K.
121 F5 Pennsville U.S.A.
120 D4 Pennsylvania div. U.S.A.
120 E3 Penn Yan U.S.A.
109 M3 Penny Icecap ice cap Can.
111 H2 Pennylan Lake l. Can.
152 B4 Penny Pt pt Ant.
14 A1 Peno Rus. Fed.
121 J2 Penobscot r. U.S.A.
121 J2 Penobscot Bay b. U.S.A.
96 E4 Penola Aust.
96 C2 Penong Aust.
130 K7 Penonomé Panama
17 F4 Penrith U.K.
119 C6 Pensacola U.S.A.
152 B3 Pensacola Mts mts Ant.
141 D2 Pensamiento Bolivia
97 E4 Penshurst Aust.
90 □2 Pentecost I. i. Vanuatu
110 F5 Penticton Can.
17 E6 Pentire Point pt U.K.
99 F4 Pentland Aust.
16 F2 Pentland Firth chan. U.K.
16 F4 Pentland Hills h. U.K.
122 D4 Pentwater U.S.A.
40 A2 Penuba Indon.
56 B3 Penukonda India
42 B3 Penwegon Myanmar
15 F1 Peny Rus. Fed.
17 F5 Penygadair h. U.K.
14 F3 Penza div. Rus. Fed.
14 G3 Penza Rus. Fed.
17 E6 Penzance U.K.
63 S3 Penzhino Rus. Fed.
63 S3 Penzhinskaya Guba b. Rus. Fed.
129 F5 Peoria U.S.A.
122 C5 Peoria U.S.A.
146 F2 Pepiri Guaçú r. Arg./Brazil
29 B4 Pëqin Albania
99 E2 Pera Hd hd Aust.
43 C6 Perai Malaysia
43 B6 Perak i. Malaysia
43 C6 Perak div. Malaysia
43 C6 Perak r. Malaysia
25 F2 Perales del Alfambra Spain
29 E7 Perama *Kriti* Greece
56 B4 Perambalur India
10 F2 Perämeri Bottenviken g. Finland/Sweden
11 F3 Peräseinäjoki Finland
113 H4 Percé Can.
100 D4 Percival Lakes salt flat Aust.
121 H2 Percy U.S.A.
99 G4 Percy Is is Aust.
115 G4 Percy Reach l. Can.
142 C2 Perdida r. Brazil
147 C5 Perdido r. *Chubut* Arg.
141 E4 Perdido r. Brazil
29 C5 Perdika Greece
144 E3 Perdizes Brazil
145 F4 Perdões Brazil
19 L4 Perechyn Ukraine
62 H3 Peregrebnoye Rus. Fed.
138 B3 Pereira Colombia
144 C4 Pereira Barreto Brazil
24 C4 Pereiro Portugal
12 D3 Perekhoda r. Rus. Fed.
15 E1 Perekopivka Ukraine
13 G5 Perelazovskiy Rus. Fed.
64 D2 Perelyub Rus. Fed.
122 D4 Pere Marquette r. U.S.A.
152 C6 Peremennyy, C. c. Ant.
14 F2 Peremilovskiye Gory h. Rus. Fed.
15 G2 Peremoha *Kharkiv* Ukraine
15 D1 Peremoha *Kyyiv* Ukraine
14 C2 Peremyshl' Rus. Fed.
15 A2 Peremyshlyany Ukraine
140 A2 Perene Peru
101 B6 Perenjori Aust.
15 F2 Pereshchepyne Ukraine
14 D1 Pereslavl' Zalesskiy Rus. Fed.
14 F3 Peresypkino Pervoye Rus. Fed.
14 F3 Perevesinka Rus. Fed.
15 E1 Perevid r. Ukraine
64 D2 Perevolotskiy Rus. Fed.
14 G2 Perevoz Rus. Fed.
49 K3 Pereyaslavka Rus. Fed.
15 D1 Pereyaslav-Khmel'nyts'kyy Ukraine
19 G4 Perg Austria
146 D3 Pergamino Arg.
61 A1 Perge Turkey
26 D4 Pergola Italy
15 B1 Perha Ukraine
43 C6 Perhentian Besar i. Malaysia
10 G3 Perho Finland
115 J2 Péribonca Can.
115 K1 Péribonca, Lac l. Can.
146 C1 Perico Arg.
130 D3 Pericos Mexico
28 F1 Perieni Romania
20 D2 Périers France
20 E4 Périgueux France
138 C2 Perijá, Parque Nacional nat. park Venezuela
29 E5 Peristera i. Greece
147 B6 Perito Moreno Arg.
147 B6 Perito Moreno, Parque Nacional nat. park Arg.
142 D1 Peritoró Brazil
122 D3 Perkins U.S.A.
15 B2 Perkivtsi Ukraine
130 K6 Perlas, Laguna de lag. Nicaragua
130 K6 Perlas, Pta de pt Nicaragua
18 E2 Perleberg Germany
19 L2 Perlejewo Poland
14 D4 Perlevka Rus. Fed.
43 C6 Perlis div. Malaysia
62 G4 Perm' Rus. Fed.
12 H3 Permas Rus. Fed.
29 C4 Përmet Albania
14 G2 Permisi Rus. Fed.
26 E3 Permuda i. Croatia
142 E2 Pernambuco div. Brazil
96 D2 Pernatty Lagoon salt flat Aust.
28 D3 Pernik Bulgaria
98 B2 Peron Is is Aust.
20 F2 Péronne France
101 A5 Peron Pen. pen. Aust.
131 F5 Perote Mexico
20 F5 Perpignan France
128 D5 Perris U.S.A.
20 C2 Perros-Guirec France
119 D6 Perry U.S.A.
119 D5 Perry U.S.A.
124 E3 Perry U.S.A.
125 D4 Perry U.S.A.
120 B4 Perrysburg U.S.A.
125 C4 Perryton U.S.A.
125 F4 Perryville U.S.A.
92 □2 Perseverance Harbour inlet *Campbell I.* N.Z.
141 D2 Perseverancia Bolivia
15 E2 Pershe Travnya Ukraine
15 G2 Pershotravens'k Ukraine
15 G3 Pershotravneve *Donets'k* Ukraine
15 C1 Pershotravneve *Zhytomyr* Ukraine
60 D2 Pertek Turkey
97 F5 Perth Aust.
101 A6 Perth Aust.
115 G4 Perth Can.
16 F3 Perth U.K.
121 F4 Perth Amboy U.S.A.
121 K1 Perth-Andover Can.
12 F1 Pertominsk Rus. Fed.
21 G5 Pertuis France
20 D3 Pertuis Breton chan. France
20 D3 Pertuis d'Antioche chan. France
11 G3 Pertunmaa Finland
136 C3 Peru country S. America
122 C5 Peru U.S.A.
151 O6 Peru Basin Pac. Oc.
148 E7 Peru-Chile Trench Pac. Oc.
26 F4 Peručko Jezero l. Croatia
26 D4 Perugia Italy
146 E2 Perugorría Arg.
143 C5 Peruíbe Brazil
14 F2 Pervomaysk Rus. Fed.
14 G2 Pervomaysk Rus. Fed.
15 D2 Pervomays'k Ukraine
12 K2 Pervomayskaya Rus. Fed.
15 E3 Pervomays'ke Ukraine
65 K2 Pervomayskiy Kazak.
14 C2 Pervomayskiy Rus. Fed.
49 E2 Pervomayskiy Rus. Fed.
14 E3 Pervomayskiy Rus. Fed.
15 G2 Pervomays'kyy Ukraine
64 E1 Pervoural'sk Rus. Fed.
40 B2 Pesaguan Indon.
40 B2 Pesaguan r. Indon.
26 D4 Pesaro Italy
128 A3 Pescadero U.S.A.
129 H4 Pescado U.S.A.
26 E4 Pescara Italy
28 C2 Pescari Romania
13 G6 Peschanokopskoye Rus. Fed.
64 D4 Peschanyy, Mys pt Kazak.
27 F5 Peschici Italy
74 B3 Pesebre, Pta pt *Canary Is* Spain
43 □ Pesek, P. i. Singapore
54 B2 Peshawar Pakistan
28 C4 Peshkopi Albania
28 E3 Peshtera Bulgaria
122 D3 Peshtigo U.S.A.
122 C3 Peshtigo r. U.S.A.
14 D2 Peski Rus. Fed.
64 F5 Peski Turkmenistan
64 E3 Peski Bol'shiye Barsuki desert Kazak.
64 D4 Peski Chil'mamedkum desert Turkmenistan
64 D3 Peski Karakum desert Kazak.
64 E5 Peski Karakumy desert Turkmenistan
64 D4 Peski Karynzharyk desert Kazak.
64 F4 Peski Kyzylkum desert Uzbekistan
65 G3 Peski Moinkum desert Kazak.
65 G4 Peski Muyunkum desert Kazak.
64 F3 Peski Priaral'skiye Karakumy desert Kazak.
64 F5 Peski Sundukli desert Turkmenistan
65 H4 Peski Taukum desert Kazak.
64 D3 Peski Taysoygan desert Kazak.
12 K3 Peskovka Rus. Fed.
26 E2 Pesnica Slovenia
14 D1 Pesochnoye Rus. Fed.
14 E2 Pesochnya Rus. Fed.
14 A3 Pesochnya Rus. Fed.
24 C2 Peso da Regua Portugal
142 E2 Pesqueira Brazil
20 D4 Pessac France
12 E3 Pestovo Rus. Fed.
14 H3 Pestrovka Rus. Fed.
14 F1 Pestyaki Rus. Fed.
14 E2 Pet r. Rus. Fed.
130 E5 Petacalco, B. de b. Mexico
61 C3 Petah Tiqwa Israel
29 C6 Petalidi Greece
29 E5 Petalioi i. Greece
128 A2 Petaluma U.S.A.
40 C2 Petangis Indon.
138 D1 Petare Venezuela
131 E5 Petatlán Mexico
81 B7 Petauke Zambia
115 G4 Petawawa Can.
122 C3 Petenwell Lake l. U.S.A.
114 D2 Peterbell Can.
96 D3 Peterborough Aust.
97 E4 Peterborough Aust.
115 F4 Peterborough Can.
17 G5 Peterborough U.K.
16 G3 Peterhead U.K.
152 A3 Peter 1 I. i. Ant.
119 □3 Peter I. i. *Virgin Is* Caribbean
111 L2 Peter Lake l. Can.
98 B5 Petermann Aboriginal Land res. Aust.
98 B5 Petermann Ranges mt. ra. Aust.
146 B4 Peteroa, Vol. vol Chile
111 H3 Peter Pond L. l. Can.
110 C3 Petersburg U.S.A.
122 C6 Petersburg U.S.A.
120 E6 Petersburg U.S.A.
120 D5 Petersburg U.S.A.
18 D2 Petershagen *Nordrhein-Westfalen* Germany
113 F2 Peters, Lac l. Can.
139 F2 Peters Mine Guyana
108 C3 Petersville U.S.A.
27 F6 Petilia Policastro Italy
142 B2 Petita r. Brazil
133 □5 Petit Canal *Guadeloupe* Caribbean
133 □5 Petit Cul de Sac Marin b. *Guadeloupe* Caribbean
81 □5 Petite-Île *Réunion* Indian Ocean
112 E2 Petite Rivière de la Baleine r. Can.
133 □5 Petite Terre, Îles de la is *Guadeloupe* Caribbean
133 D3 Petit-Goâve Haiti
113 G3 Petit Lac Manicouagan l. Can.
121 K2 Petit Manan Pt pt U.S.A.
113 J3 Petit Mécatina r. Can.
110 E3 Petitot r. Can.
54 C5 Petlad India
131 F5 Petlalcingo Mexico
54 C5 Petlawad India
131 H4 Peto Mexico
122 E3 Petoskey U.S.A.
60 C4 Petra Jordan
45 O3 Petra Velikogo, Zaliv b. Rus. Fed.
93 □1 Petre Bay b. *Chatham Is* N.Z.
115 G5 Petre, Pt pt Can.
29 D4 Petrich Bulgaria
90 □2 Petrie, Récif reef Pac. Oc.
129 H4 Petrified Forest Nat. Park nat. park U.S.A.
28 D2 Petrila Romania
26 F3 Petrinja Croatia
15 F3 Petrivka *Kherson* Ukraine
15 F3 Petrivka *Luhans'k* Ukraine
15 D3 Petrivka *Odesa* Ukraine
15 D3 Petrivka *Odesa* Ukraine
15 G3 Petrivs'ke Ukraine
15 E2 Petrivtsi Ukraine
146 C2 Petro, Co de mt. Chile
114 D5 Petrolia Can.
142 D2 Petrolina Brazil
144 D2 Petrolina de Goiás Brazil
15 G2 Petropavlivka Ukraine
48 C2 Petropavlovka Rus. Fed.
13 G5 Petropavlovka Rus. Fed.
65 G2 Petropavlovsk Kazak.
63 R4 Petropavlovsk-Kamchatskiy Rus. Fed.
145 G5 Petrópolis Brazil
28 D2 Petroșani Romania
15 E2 Petrove Ukraine
14 G3 Petrovsk Rus. Fed.
14 E1 Petrovskiy Rus. Fed.
14 E3 Petrovskoye Rus. Fed.
14 D1 Petrovskoye Rus. Fed.
14 C1 Petrovskoye Rus. Fed.
48 D2 Petrovsk-Zabaykal'skiy Rus. Fed.
13 H5 Petrov Val Rus. Fed.
12 E2 Petrozavodsk Rus. Fed.
15 B3 Petrușeni Moldova
65 G1 Petukhovo Rus. Fed.
14 D2 Petushki Rus. Fed.
18 F5 Petzeck mt. Austria
63 T3 Pevek Rus. Fed.
12 H1 Peza r. Rus. Fed.
21 F5 Pézenas France
19 H4 Pezinok Slovakia
141 E3 Pezones Bolivia
54 B2 Pezu Pakistan
18 E4 Pfaffenhofen an der Ilm Germany
18 F4 Pfarrkirchen Germany
18 D4 Pforzheim Germany
18 E5 Pfunds Austria
18 D4 Pfungstadt Germany
82 D4 Phahameng R.S.A.
83 E3 Phalaborwa R.S.A.
54 C2 Phalia Pakistan
54 C4 Phalodi India

Q

R

143 C5 São Bernardo do Campo Brazil
143 A6 São Borja Brazil
143 B6 São Carlos *Santa Catarina* Brazil
144 E5 São Carlos *São Paulo* Brazil
142 D3 São Desidério Brazil
142 D3 São Desidério r. Brazil
144 C3 São Domingos r. *Goiás* Brazil
144 B3 São Domingos r. *Mato Grosso do Sul* Brazil
145 E1 São Domingos r. *Minas Gerais* Brazil
142 C3 São Domingos Brazil
142 B3 São Félix *Mato Grosso* Brazil
142 B2 São Félix *Pará* Brazil
145 H4 São Fidélis Brazil
76 □ São Filipe Cape Verde
144 A6 São Francisco r. *Paraná* Brazil
142 E2 São Francisco r. Brazil
145 F1 São Francisco Brazil
143 A6 São Francisco de Assis Brazil
144 D1 São Francisco de Goiás Brazil
144 D3 São Francisco de Sales Brazil
143 C6 São Francisco do Sul Brazil
143 C6 São Francisco, I. de i. Brazil
146 F3 São Gabriel Brazil
145 H3 São Gabriel da Palha Brazil
144 E1 São Gabriel de Goiás Brazil
145 G5 São Gonçalo Brazil
145 F3 São Gonçalo do Abaeté Brazil
142 E1 São Gonçalo do Amirante Brazil
145 F4 São Gonçalo do Sapucaí Brazil
145 E3 São Gotardo Brazil
142 B3 São João r. *Mato Grosso* Brazil
143 B5 São João r. *Paraná* Brazil
144 E1 São João da Aliança Brazil
145 H4 São João da Barra Brazil
145 E4 São João da Boa Vista Brazil
24 B2 São João da Madeira Portugal
145 F1 São João da Ponte Brazil
144 C4 São João das Duas Pontas Brazil
145 F4 São João del Rei Brazil
142 C2 São João do Araguaia Brazil
142 E2 São João do Cariri Brazil
145 G1 São João do Paraíso Brazil
142 D2 São João do Piauí Brazil
142 D2 São João dos Patos Brazil
145 G3 São João Evangelista Brazil
145 G4 São João Nepomuceno Brazil
142 C1 São Joaquim *Pará* Brazil
143 C6 São Joaquim *Santa Catarina* Brazil
144 E4 São Joaquim da Barra Brazil
144 B5 São Jorge do Ivaí Brazil
138 D4 São José *Amazonas* Brazil
143 C6 São José *Santa Catarina* Brazil
142 C3 São José r. Brazil
142 D1 São José, Baia de b. Brazil
142 E2 São José de Mipibu Brazil
143 D5 São José do Calçado Brazil
145 H3 São José do Divino Brazil
145 G3 São José do Jacurí Brazil
146 F3 São José do Norte Brazil
145 E4 São José do Rio Pardo Brazil
144 D4 São José do Rio Prêto Brazil
145 F5 São José dos Campos Brazil
144 C4 São José dos Dourados r. Brazil
144 D6 São José dos Pinhais Brazil
143 B6 São Leopoldo Brazil
145 F5 São Lourenço Brazil
141 F3 São Lourenço r. Brazil
144 A2 São Lourenço Brazil
146 F3 São Lourenço do Sul Brazil
142 D1 São Luís Brazil
144 C2 São Luis de Montes Belos Brazil
145 F5 São Luís do Paraitinga Brazil
143 B6 São Luís Gonzaga Brazil
142 D1 São Luís, Ilha de i. Brazil
144 D5 São Manuel Brazil
144 E2 São Marcos r. Brazil
142 D1 São Marcos, Baia de b. Brazil
145 H3 São Mateus r. Brazil
145 J3 São Mateus Brazil
145 E1 São Miguel r. Brazil
144 E5 São Miguel Arcanjo Brazil
144 A6 São Miguel do Iguaçu Brazil
142 E2 São Miguel dos Campos Brazil
142 D2 São Miguel do Tapuio Brazil
21 G3 Saône r. France
140 A3 Sã Nicolás, Bahía b. Peru
142 D2 São Nicolau r. Brazil
143 A6 São Nicolãu Brazil
76 □ São Nicolau i. Cape Verde
145 E5 São Paulo Brazil
144 D4 São Paulo div. Brazil
138 D4 São Paulo de Olivença Brazil
139 F4 São Pedro *Amazonas* Brazil
144 C3 São Pedro *Mato Grosso do Sul* Brazil
141 D1 São Pedro *Rondônia* Brazil
144 E5 São Pedro *São Paulo* Brazil
142 D2 São Pedro r. Brazil
145 G5 São Pedro da Aldeia Brazil
144 C5 São Pedro do Ivaí Brazil
24 B2 São Pedro do Sul Portugal
148 H5 São Pedro e São Paulo is Atlantic Ocean
142 C2 São Raimundo das Mangabeiras Brazil
142 D2 São Raimundo Nonato Brazil
145 F2 São Romão Brazil
144 E5 São Roque Brazil
142 E2 São Roque, C. de c. Brazil
145 E4 São Roque de Minas Brazil
142 B2 São Sebastião *Pará* Brazil
141 D1 São Sebastião *Rondônia* Brazil
145 F5 São Sebastião *São Paulo* Brazil
142 C1 São Sebastião da Boa Vista Brazil
145 E4 São Sebastião do Paraíso Brazil
145 F5 São Sebastião, Ilha do i. Brazil
143 B7 São Sepé Brazil
144 E4 São Simão Brazil
144 C3 São Simão Brazil
144 C3 São Simão, Barragem de resr Brazil
39 J6 Sao-Siu Indon.
145 F4 São Tiago Brazil
76 □ São Tiago i. Cape Verde
79 □ São Tomé i. Sao Tome and Principe
79 □ São Tomé Sao Tome and Principe
69 E5 Sao Tome and Principe country Africa
145 H4 São Tomé, Cabo de c. Brazil
143 C5 São Vicente Brazil
76 □ São Vicente i. Cape Verde
24 B4 São Vicente, Cabo de c. Portugal
60 B1 Sapanca Turkey
142 C3 Sapão r. Brazil
39 J7 Saparua Indon.
77 F5 Sapele Nigeria
29 E4 Sapes Greece
147 C5 Sa Pire Mahuida mt. ra. Arg.
25 H3 Sa Pobla Spain
76 C5 Sapo National Park nat. park Liberia
144 C5 Sapopema Brazil
19 L2 Sapotskina Belarus
14 E3 Sapozhok Rus. Fed.
46 H2 Sapporo Japan
27 E5 Sapri Italy
145 F4 Sapucai r. *Minas Gerais* Brazil
144 E4 Sapucai r. *São Paulo* Brazil
40 C3 Sapudi i. Indon.
125 D4 Sapulpa U.S.A.
40 C3 Sapulu Indon.
57 D2 Sāqī Iran
109 N2 Saqqaq Greenland
60 F2 Saqqez Iran
138 B4 Saquisilí Ecuador
60 F2 Sarāb Iran
61 B5 Sarabît el Khâdim Egypt
43 C4 Sara Buri Thailand
25 F2 Saragossa *Zaragoza* Spain
138 B4 Saraguro Ecuador
14 E3 Sarai Rus. Fed.
54 C3 Sarai Sidhu Pakistan
26 G4 Sarajevo Bos.-Herz.
57 E1 Sarakhs Iran
29 E5 Sarakino i. Greece
64 E2 Saraktash Rus. Fed.
65 L2 Sarala Rus. Fed.
55 H4 Saramati mt. India
65 H3 Saran' Kazak.
121 G2 Saranac r. U.S.A.
121 F2 Saranac Lake U.S.A.
112 E5 Saranac Lakes lakes U.S.A.
29 C5 Sarandë Albania
143 B6 Sarandi Brazil
146 E3 Sarandí del Yí Uruguay
146 E3 Sarandí Grande Uruguay
40 B2 Saran, G. mt. Indon.
41 C5 Sarangani i. Phil.
41 C5 Sarangani Bay b. Phil.
41 C5 Sarangani Islands is Phil.
41 C5 Sarangani Str. chan. Phil.
55 E5 Sarangarh India
54 D5 Sarangpur India
14 G2 Saransk Rus. Fed.
64 D1 Sarapul Rus. Fed.
119 D7 Sarasota U.S.A.
54 B5 Saraswati r. India
15 C3 Sarata Ukraine
15 C3 Sărătenii Vechi Moldova
126 F3 Saratoga U.S.A.
121 G3 Saratoga Springs U.S.A.
40 B1 Saratok Malaysia
14 G4 Saratov Rus. Fed.
14 H4 Saratov div. Rus. Fed.
64 C2 Saratovskoye Vdkhr. resr Rus. Fed.
57 E4 Saravan Iran
42 D4 Saravan Laos
43 B4 Sarawa r. Myanmar
40 B1 Sarawak div. Malaysia
60 A1 Saray Turkey
76 B4 Saraya Senegal
61 C2 Sarāyā Syria
60 B2 Sarayköy Turkey
60 C2 Sarayönü Turkey
57 E4 Sarbāz Iran
57 E4 Sarbāz r. Iran
55 G4 Sarbhāng Bhutan
57 D2 Sarbīsheh Iran
19 J5 Sárbogárd Hungary
26 C3 Sarca r. Italy
146 B2 Sarco Chile
54 E3 Sarda r. India/Nepal
54 C5 Sardarpur India
54 C3 Sardarshahr India
60 F2 Sar Dasht Iran
27 C5 Sardegna i. Italy
27 B5 Sardegna div. Italy
138 C2 Sardinata Colombia
80 C4 Sardindida Plain plain Kenya
57 B4 Sareb, Rās-as pt U.A.E.
40 D3 Sarege i. Indon.
10 E2 Sareks National Park nat. park Sweden
10 E2 Sarektjåkkå mt. Sweden
40 C2 Sarempaka, G. mt. Indon.
57 F1 Sar-e Pol Afghanistan
57 C3 Sare Yazd Iran
148 E4 Sargasso Sea sea Atlantic Ocean
65 H1 Sargatskoye Rus. Fed.
54 C2 Sargodha Pakistan
78 C2 Sarh Chad
57 E3 Sarhad reg. Iran
74 C2 Sarhro, Jbel mts Morocco
57 C1 Sārī Iran
29 F7 Saria i. Greece
57 F2 Sar-i-Bum Afghanistan
28 G2 Sarichioi Romania
39 M3 Sarigan i. *Northern Mariana Is* Pac. Oc.
60 B2 Sarıgöl Turkey
60 E1 Sarıkamış Turkey
60 C2 Sarıkaya Turkey
29 F6 Sarıkemer Turkey
29 F4 Sarıköy Turkey
43 □ Sarimbun Res. resr Singapore
99 G4 Sarina Aust.
25 F2 Sariñena Spain
57 F2 Sar-i-Pul Afghanistan
57 C1 Sāri Qamīsh Iran
72 C3 Sarīr Tibesti desert Libya
72 D2 Sarir Water Wells' Field well Libya
49 H5 Sariwŏn N. Korea
60 B1 Sarıyer Turkey
55 E4 Sarju r. India
17 F7 Sark i. Channel Islands
65 K3 Sarkand Kazak.
54 B4 Sarkāri Tala India
60 B2 Şarkikaraağaç Turkey
60 D2 Şarkışla Turkey
60 A1 Şarköy Turkey
57 F3 Sarlath Ra. mt. ra. Afghanistan/Pakistan
20 E4 Sarlat-la-Canéda France
14 F2 Sarma r. Rus. Fed.
28 E1 Sărmașu Romania
39 L7 Sarmi Indon.
147 C6 Sarmiento Arg.
11 D3 Särna Sweden
21 J3 Sarnen Switz.
114 D5 Sarnia Can.
27 E5 Sarno Italy
15 B1 Sarny Ukraine
38 D7 Sarolangun Indon.
46 J1 Saroma-ko l. Japan
29 D6 Saronikos Kolpos g. Greece
29 F4 Saros Körfezi b. Turkey
19 K4 Sárospatak Hungary
54 C4 Sarotra India
14 F2 Sarova Rus. Fed.
57 G2 Sarowbī Afghanistan
13 H6 Sarpa, Oz. l. *Kalmykiya* Rus. Fed.
13 H5 Sarpa, Ozero l. *Volgograd* Rus. Fed.
41 □1 Sar Passage chan. Palau
28 C4 Šar Planina mt. ra. Macedonia/Yugo.
11 C4 Sarpsborg Norway
21 H2 Sarrebourg France
21 H2 Sarreguemines France
24 C1 Sarria Spain
21 G2 Sarry France
21 J6 Sartène France
20 D3 Sarthe r. France
57 B2 Sarud r. Iran
46 J2 Saru-gawa r. Japan
29 F5 Saruhanlı Turkey
46 D6 Sarumasa-yama mt. Japan
54 A4 Saruna Pakistan
60 F2 Şärur Azerbaijan
61 D2 Sarūt r. Syria
19 H5 Sárvár Hungary
57 C3 Sarvestān Iran
54 C4 Sarwar India
65 G4 Saryagach Kazak.
64 F3 Sarybasat Kazak.
65 J3 Sary-Ishikotrau, Peski desert Kazak.
64 D3 Sarykamys Kazak.
64 E4 Sarykamyshkoye Ozero salt l. Turkmenistan
65 H2 Sarykiyak Kazak.
65 H5 Sarykol Range mt. ra. China/Tajikistan
65 H3 Sarykomey Kazak.
65 J4 Saryozek Kazak.
65 H3 Saryshagan Kazak.
65 G3 Sarysu r. Kazak.
65 H5 Sary Tash Kyrgyzstan
57 E1 Sary Yazikskoye Vdkhr. resr Turkmenistan
26 B3 Sarzana Italy
20 C3 Sarzeau France
129 G6 Sasabe U.S.A.
55 F4 Sasaram India
40 E4 Sasar, Tg pt Indon.
15 E1 Saschnivka Ukraine
46 B7 Sasebo Japan
15 E2 Sasivka Ukraine
111 J4 Saskatchewan r. Can.
108 H4 Saskatchewan div. Can.
111 H4 Saskatoon Can.
63 N2 Saskylakh Rus. Fed.
130 J6 Saslaya mt. Nicaragua
14 E2 Sasovo Rus. Fed.
121 F5 Sassafras U.S.A.
76 C6 Sassandra Côte d'Ivoire
76 C5 Sassandra r. Côte d'Ivoire
27 B5 Sassari Italy
19 F1 Sassnitz Germany
26 D4 Sassocorvaro Italy
26 D4 Sassoferrato Italy
76 C6 Sass Town Liberia
26 C3 Sassuolo Italy
65 K3 Sasykkol', Oz. l. Kazak.
13 H6 Sasykoli Rus. Fed.
76 B4 Satadougou Mali
46 C8 Sata-misaki c. Japan
54 C5 Satana India
15 B2 Sataniv Ukraine
91 □12 Satapuala Western Samoa
56 A2 Satara India
91 □12 Sataua Western Samoa
40 D3 Satengar i. Indon.
14 E3 Satinka Rus. Fed.
140 B2 Satipo Peru
14 F2 Satis r. Rus. Fed.
14 F2 Satis Rus. Fed.
64 E1 Satka Rus. Fed.
55 G5 Satkhira Bangladesh
56 B2 Satmala Range h. India
54 E4 Satna India
19 K4 Sátoraljaújhely Hungary
65 G3 Satpayev Kazak.
54 C5 Satpura Range mt. ra. India
46 C8 Satsuma-hantō pen. Japan
46 J2 Satsunai-gawa r. Japan
47 G5 Satte Japan
54 D2 Satti *Jammu and Kashmir*
28 D1 Satu Mare Romania
43 C6 Satun Thailand
91 □12 Satupaitea Western Samoa
146 E3 Sauce Arg.
138 B5 Sauce Peru
125 C7 Sauceda Mexico
129 F5 Sauceda Mts mts U.S.A.
130 D2 Saucillo Mexico
11 B4 Sauda Norway
10 M2 Sauðárkrókur Iceland
32 F7 Saudi Arabia country Asia
141 E2 Sauêruiná r. Brazil
122 D4 Saugatuck U.S.A.
121 G3 Saugerties U.S.A.
21 F4 Saugues France
146 C2 Saujil Arg.
20 D4 Saujon France
124 E2 Sauk Center U.S.A.
122 C4 Sauk City U.S.A.
139 G3 Saul French Guiana
18 D4 Saulgau Germany
21 G3 Saulieu France
114 C3 Sault Ste Marie Can.
122 E2 Sault Ste Marie U.S.A.
99 H4 Saumarez Reef reef *Coral Sea Islands Terr.* Pac. Oc.
39 K8 Saumlakki Indon.
20 D3 Saumur France
93 C6 Saunders, Cape c. N.Z.
152 A4 Saunders Coast Ant.
152 C1 Saunders I. i. *S. Sandwich Is* Atlantic Ocean
98 B2 Saunders, Mt h. Aust.
43 B5 Saung Thailand
42 B1 Saungka Myanmar
64 D4 Saura Rus. Fed.
79 D5 Saurimo Angola
40 E2 Sausu Indon.
79 C6 Sautar Angola
133 □8 Sauters *Grenada* Caribbean
26 G3 Sava r. Europe
130 J6 Sava Honduras
91 □12 Savaii i. Western Samoa
14 E4 Savala r. Rus. Fed.
77 E5 Savalou Benin
122 B4 Savanna U.S.A.
119 D6 Savannah U.S.A.
119 D5 Savannah r. U.S.A.
119 B5 Savannah U.S.A.
119 E7 Savannah Sound The Bahamas
42 D3 Savannakhét Laos
133 □1 Savanna la Mar Jamaica
112 B3 Savant Lake Can.
56 A3 Savanur India
10 F3 Sävar Sweden
60 A2 Savaştepe Turkey
77 E5 Savè Benin
83 E3 Save r. Mozambique
57 B2 Sāveh Iran
76 D5 Savelugu Ghana
20 D3 Savenay France
28 F1 Săveni Romania
21 H2 Saverne France
10 H3 Saviaho Finland
28 F1 Săvinești Romania
14 E1 Savino Rus. Fed.
12 G2 Savinskiy Rus. Fed.
28 B3 Šavnik Yugo.
26 B3 Savona Italy
11 H3 Savonranta Finland
15 D2 Savran' Ukraine
15 C2 Savranka r. Ukraine
11 D4 Sävsjö Sweden
39 H8 Savu i. Indon.
10 H2 Savukoski Finland
60 E2 Savur Turkey
90 □6 Savusavu Fiji
90 □6 Savusavu B. b. Fiji
82 C2 Savuti Botswana
49 F2 Savvo-Borzya Rus. Fed.
15 E1 Savynky Ukraine
15 G2 Savyntsi Ukraine
42 A2 Saw Myanmar
54 D4 Sawai Madhopur India
90 □8 Sawaleke Fiji
40 C2 Sawan Indon.
42 B3 Sawankhalok Thailand
47 G5 Sawasaki-bana pt Japan
47 G5 Sawata Japan
127 F4 Sawatch Mts mt. ra. U.S.A.
72 B2 Sawdā', Jabal as h. Libya
19 L3 Sawin Poland
122 B2 Sawtooth Mountains h. U.S.A.
39 H8 Sawu Sea g. Indon.
115 K4 Sawyerville Can.
99 E3 Saxby r. Aust.
10 D2 Saxnäs Sweden
18 F3 Saxony div. Germany
77 E4 Say Niger
65 J3 Sayak Kazak.
77 G4 Sayam well Niger
140 A2 Sayán Peru
65 M2 Sayanogorsk Rus. Fed.
64 F5 Sayat Turkmenistan
131 H5 Sayaxché Guatemala
73 H4 Şayḩ well Yemen
58 H6 Sayḩūt Yemen
13 H5 Saykhin Kazak.
80 D2 Säylac Somalia
48 D3 Saynshand Mongolia
65 K4 Sayram Hu salt l. China
125 D5 Sayre U.S.A.
120 E4 Sayre U.S.A.
130 E5 Sayula *Jalisco* Mexico
131 G5 Sayula *Veracruz* Mexico
64 D4 Say-Utes Kazak.
29 B4 Sazan i. Albania
15 G1 Sazhnoye Rus. Fed.
54 C2 Sazin Pakistan
12 E3 Sazonovo Rus. Fed.
75 D3 Sbaa Algeria
75 F1 Sbeitla Tunisia
101 C7 Scaddan Aust.
17 F4 Scafell Pike mt. U.K.
27 E6 Scalea Italy
16 G1 Scalloway U.K.
26 C4 Scansano Italy
28 F2 Scânteia Romania
16 F2 Scapa Flow inlet U.K.
115 F5 Scarborough Can.
133 □2 Scarborough *Tobago* Trin. & Tobago
17 G4 Scarborough U.K.
41 A3 Scarborough Shoal sand bank Phil.
93 D5 Scargill N.Z.
43 D6 Scawfell Shoal sand bank S. China Sea
26 F4 Šćedro i. Croatia
21 J3 Schaffhausen Switz.
18 B2 Schagen Netherlands
57 E3 Schao w Afghanistan
18 E1 Scharbeutz Germany
18 F4 Schärding Austria
18 D2 Scharhörn sand bank Germany
113 G3 Schefferville Can.
19 G4 Scheibbs Austria
18 B3 Schelde r. Belgium
129 E2 Schell Creek Range mt. ra. U.S.A.
121 G3 Schenectady U.S.A.
18 D2 Schenefeld *Niedersachsen* Germany
18 D5 Schesaplana mt. Austria/Swit.
18 F4 Schierling Germany
18 C2 Schiermonnikoog i. Netherlands
29 D5 Schimatari Greece
26 C3 Schio Italy
28 F1 Schitu Duca Romania
18 C3 Schleiden Germany
18 D1 Schleswig Germany
18 D1 Schleswig-Holstein div. Germany
18 D3 Schlüchtern Germany
18 D2 Schneverdingen Germany
121 G3 Schodack Center U.S.A.
133 □4 Schoelcher *Martinique* Caribbean
122 C3 Schofield U.S.A.
127 □1 Schofield Barracks U.S.A.
18 E2 Schönebeck *Sachsen-Anhalt* Germany
18 E2 Schöningen Germany
121 J2 Schoodic Lake l. U.S.A.
122 E4 Schoolcraft U.S.A.
97 G5 Schouten I. i. Aust.
90 □1 Schouten Islands is P.N.G.
114 B2 Schreiber Can.
19 G4 Schrems Austria
18 E4 Schrobenhausen Germany
121 G3 Schroon Lake l. U.S.A.
129 F5 Schuchuli U.S.A.
17 C6 Schull Rep. of Ire.
111 K2 Schultz Lake l. Can.
128 C2 Schurz U.S.A.
121 G3 Schuylerville U.S.A.
18 E4 Schwabach Germany
18 D4 Schwäbische Alb mts Germany
18 D4 Schwäbisch Gmünd Germany
18 D4 Schwäbisch Hall Germany
18 E4 Schwabmünchen Germany
21 J3 Schwanden Switz.
18 F4 Schwandorf Germany
18 E5 Schwangau Germany
18 E2 Schwarzenbek Germany
18 F3 Schwarzenberg Germany
82 B4 Schwarzrand mts Namibia
18 D4 Schwarzwald mts Germany
18 E5 Schwaz Austria
19 G2 Schwedt Germany
18 E3 Schweinfurt Germany
18 D4 Schwenningen Germany
18 E2 Schwerin Germany
18 E2 Schweriner See l. Germany
21 J3 Schwyz Switz.
27 D7 Sciacca Italy
27 E7 Scicli Italy
17 D7 Scilly, Isles of is U.K.
120 B5 Scioto r. U.S.A.
129 F2 Scipio U.S.A.
126 F1 Scobey U.S.A.
97 G3 Scone Aust.
109 Q2 Scoresby Land reg. Greenland
109 Q2 Scoresby Sund chan. Greenland
28 E2 Scornicești Romania
152 B1 Scotia Ridge Atlantic Ocean
148 G9 Scotia Sea sea Atlantic Ocean
114 E5 Scotland Can.
16 E3 Scotland div. U.K.
115 K4 Scotstown Can.
115 K3 Scott Can.
152 B5 Scott Base N.Z. Base Ant.
83 E5 Scottburgh R.S.A.
98 B2 Scott, C. c. Aust.
110 D4 Scott, C. c. Can.
124 C4 Scott City U.S.A.
152 B5 Scott Coast Ant.
120 D4 Scottdale U.S.A.
152 B4 Scott Gl. gl. Ant.
109 L2 Scott Inlet inlet Can.
152 A5 Scott Island i. Ant.
111 H3 Scott Lake l. Can.
152 D4 Scott Mts mt. ra. Ant.
92 D1 Scott Pt pt N.Z.
100 C2 Scott Reef reef Aust.
124 C3 Scottsbluff U.S.A.
119 C5 Scottsboro U.S.A.
118 C4 Scottsburg U.S.A.
97 F5 Scottsdale Aust.
127 E5 Scottsdale U.S.A.
128 A3 Scotts Valley U.S.A.
122 D4 Scottville U.S.A.
128 D3 Scotty's Junction U.S.A.
16 E2 Scourie U.K.
121 F4 Scranton U.S.A.
17 G5 Scunthorpe U.K.
21 K3 Scuol Switz.
101 B6 Seabrook, L. salt flat Aust.
121 F5 Seaford U.S.A.
99 G4 Seaforth Aust.
114 E5 Seaforth Can.
133 □1 Seaforth Jamaica
41 A4 Seahorse Bank sand bank Phil.
111 K3 Seal r. Can.
97 E3 Sea Lake Aust.
82 A5 Seal Bay b. *Tristan da Cunha* Atlantic Ocean
82 C5 Seal, Cape c. R.S.A.
133 E2 Seal Cays is *Turks and Caicos Is* Caribbean
121 J3 Seal I. i. U.S.A.
113 H3 Seal Lake l. Can.
129 E3 Seaman Range mts U.S.A.
129 E4 Searchlight U.S.A.
125 F5 Searcy U.S.A.
128 D4 Searles Lake l. U.S.A.
122 E4 Sears U.S.A.
121 J2 Searsport U.S.A.
128 B3 Seaside U.S.A.
126 B2 Seaside U.S.A.
126 B2 Seattle U.S.A.
99 F3 Seaview Ra. mt. ra. Aust.
121 F5 Seaville U.S.A.
93 D5 Seaward Kaikoura Ra. mt. ra. N.Z.
121 H3 Sebago Lake l. U.S.A.
40 D2 Sebakung Indon.
40 C2 Sebangan, Tk b. Indon.
40 A1 Sebangka i. Indon.
130 B2 Sebastián Vizcaíno, B b. Mexico
121 J2 Sebasticook r. U.S.A.
41 A5 Sebatik i. Indon.
77 E4 Sebba Burkina
75 D2 Sebdou Algeria
76 C4 Sébékoro Mali
28 D2 Sebeş Romania
40 A3 Sebesi i. Indon.
123 F4 Sebewaing U.S.A.
12 D3 Sebezh Rus. Fed.
82 D3 Sebina Botswana
60 D1 Şebin Karahisar Turkey
28 D1 Sebiş Romania
75 E3 Sebkha Azzel Matti salt pan Algeria
74 B4 Sebkhet Chemchâm salt l. Mauritania
75 G1 Sebkhet de Sidi El Hani salt pan Tunisia
74 B3 Sebkhet Oum ed Droûs Telli salt flat Mauritania
74 B4 Sebkhet Oum ed Droûs Guebli salt l. Mauritania
74 A5 Sebkhet Te-n-Dghâmcha salt marsh Mauritania
121 J2 Seboeis Lake l. U.S.A.
121 J2 Seboomook U.S.A.
121 J2 Seboomook Lake l. U.S.A.
119 D7 Sebring U.S.A.
40 D2 Sebuku i. Indon.
40 B1 Sebuyau Malaysia
80 C3 Seccia Mts mts Ethiopia
14 G2 Sechenovo Rus. Fed.
138 A5 Sechura Peru
138 A5 Sechura, Bahía de b. Peru
73 F3 2nd Cataract rapids Sudan
121 H2 Second Lake l. U.S.A.
99 E2 2nd Three Mile Opening chan. Aust.
114 C5 Secord Lake l. U.S.A.
93 A6 Secretary Island i. N.Z.
56 B2 Secunderabad India
140 C3 Sécure r. Bolivia
124 E4 Sedalia U.S.A.
56 B2 Sedam India
96 D3 Sedan Aust.
21 G2 Sedan France
93 E4 Seddon N.Z.
93 C4 Seddonville N.Z.
60 A1 Seddülbahir Turkey
61 C4 Sede Boqer Israel
57 D2 Sedeh Iran
61 C4 Sederot Israel
121 J2 Sedgwick U.S.A.
76 A4 Sédhiou Senegal
19 G4 Sedlčany Czech Rep.
15 A1 Sedlyshche Ukraine
15 D1 Sedniv Ukraine
61 C4 Sedom Israel
129 G4 Sedona U.S.A.
27 A7 Sédrata Algeria
40 D1 Sedulang Indon.
11 F5 Šeduva Lithuania
19 G2 Seebad Heringsdorf Germany
18 E2 Seehausen Germany
82 B4 Seeheim Namibia
18 D4 Seeheim-Jugenheim Germany
129 E5 Seeley U.S.A.
152 B3 Seelig, Mt mt. Ant.
19 G2 Seelow Germany
20 E2 Sées France
18 E3 Seesen Germany
18 E2 Seevetal Germany
76 B5 Sefadu Sierra Leone
29 F5 Seferihisar Turkey
57 B2 Sēfīd Dasht Iran
83 D3 Sefophe Botswana
74 D2 Sefrou Morocco
76 B4 Ségala Mali
11 C3 Segalstad Norway
41 A5 Segama r. Malaysia
43 C7 Segamat Malaysia
24 E5 Segangane Morocco
28 D2 Şegarcea Romania
77 E4 Ségbana Benin
40 D3 Segeri Indon.
12 E2 Segezha Rus. Fed.
57 G1 Seghnān Afghanistan
25 F3 Segorbe Spain
76 C4 Ségou Mali
76 C4 Ségou div. Mali
138 C2 Segovia Colombia
24 D2 Segovia Spain
12 E2 Segozerskoye, Oz. l. Rus. Fed.
20 D3 Segré France
77 G2 Séguédine Niger
76 C5 Séguéla Côte d'Ivoire
76 C5 Séguélon Côte d'Ivoire
125 D6 Seguin U.S.A.
146 D3 Segundo r. Arg.
25 E3 Segura r. Spain
25 E4 Segura, Sierra de mt. ra. Spain
82 C3 Sehithwa Botswana
54 D5 Sehore India
54 A4 Sehwan Pakistan
42 A2 Seikpyu Myanmar
10 F1 Seiland i. Norway
125 D4 Seiling U.S.A.
10 F3 Seinäjoki Finland
112 B4 Seine r. Can.
21 G3 Seine r. France
20 D2 Seine, Baie de b. France
20 F2 Seine, Val de v. France
28 D1 Seini Romania
40 C2 Seipinang Indon.
19 L1 Sejny Poland
40 B1 Sekadau Indon.
40 A2 Sekanak, Tk b. Indon.
41 A6 Sekatak Bengara Indon.
40 A2 Sekayu Indon.
47 F6 Seki Japan
76 D6 Sekondi Ghana
14 G3 Sekretarka Rus. Fed.
57 E3 Seküheh Iran
40 B1 Sekura Indon.
80 C3 Sela Dingay Ethiopia
126 B2 Selah U.S.A.
40 B1 Selakau Indon.
43 C7 Selangor div. Malaysia
39 K8 Selaru i. Indon.
40 D4 Selat Alas chan. Indon.
40 C3 Selatan, Tg pt Indon.
40 C4 Selat Bali chan. Indon.
40 A2 Selat Bangka chan. Indon.
40 A2 Selat Berhala chan. Indon.
39 K7 Selat Dampir chan. Indon.
40 A2 Selat Gaspar chan. Indon.
43 □ Selat Johor chan. Malaysia/Singapore
43 □ Selat Jurong chan. Singapore
40 B2 Selat Karimata str. Indon.
40 C2 Selat Laut chan. Indon.
40 C4 Selat Lombok chan. Indon.
40 C3 Selat Madura chan. Indon.
43 □ Selat Pandan chan. Singapore
40 E3 Selat Salayar chan. Indon.
40 D4 Selat Sape chan. Indon.
40 D4 Selat Sumba chan. Indon.
40 A3 Selat Sunda chan. Indon.
39 L7 Selat Yapen chan. Indon.
108 B3 Selawik U.S.A.
10 C3 Selbekken Norway
10 C3 Selbu Norway
17 G5 Selby U.K.
124 C2 Selby U.S.A.
29 F6 Selçuk Turkey
27 E5 Sele r. Italy
82 D3 Selebi-Phikwe Botswana
29 C4 Selečka Planina mt. ra. Macedonia
29 G5 Selendi Turkey
48 C2 Selenduma Rus. Fed.
48 C1 Seleng r. Rus. Fed.
48 B2 Selenge Mongolia
48 C2 Selenge div. Mongolia
78 C4 Selenge Zaire
48 C2 Selenge Mörön r. Mongolia
48 C2 Selenginsk Rus. Fed.
29 B4 Selenicë Albania
21 H2 Sélestat France
43 □ Seletar Singapore
43 □ Seletar, P. i. Singapore
43 □ Seletar Res. resr Singapore
65 H2 Seletinskoye Kazak.
65 H2 Selety r. Kazak.
65 H2 Seletyteniz, Oz. salt l. Kazak.
124 C2 Selfridge U.S.A.
12 J2 Selib Rus. Fed.
74 B5 Sélibabi Mauritania
14 B3 Selichnya Rus. Fed.
14 A1 Seliger, Oz. l. Rus. Fed.
129 F4 Seligman U.S.A.
73 E3 Selīma Oasis oasis Sudan
40 C1 Selimbau Indon.
61 A1 Selimiye *Antalya* Turkey
29 F6 Selimiye *Muğla* Turkey
76 C4 Sélingué, Lac de l. Mali
123 J5 Selinsgrove U.S.A.
14 A1 Selishche Rus. Fed.
14 F2 Selishchi Rus. Fed.
13 H6 Selitrennoye Rus. Fed.
14 A1 Selizharovo Rus. Fed.
11 C4 Seljord Norway
111 K4 Selkirk Can.
110 F4 Selkirk Mountains mt. ra. Can.
129 G6 Sells U.S.A.
119 C5 Selma U.S.A.
128 C3 Selma U.S.A.
119 B5 Selmer U.S.A.
40 D4 Selong Indon.
21 G3 Selongey France
76 B4 Sélouma Guinea
81 C6 Selous Game Reserve res. Tanzania
57 E3 Selseleh-ye Pīr Shūrān mt. ra. Iran
17 G6 Selsey Bill hd U.K.
14 B3 Sel'tso *Bryansk* Rus. Fed.
14 B3 Sel'tso *Bryansk* Rus. Fed.
144 C4 Selviria Brazil
111 J3 Selwyn Lake l. Can.
110 C2 Selwyn Mountains mt. ra. Can.
98 D4 Selwyn Range h. Aust.
15 A3 Selyatyn Ukraine
15 G2 Selydove Ukraine
29 B4 Seman r. Albania
40 A3 Semangka, Tk b. Indon.
40 B3 Semarang Indon.
40 B1 Sematan Malaysia
40 C2 Semayang, D. l. Indon.
41 A6 Sembakung r. Indon.
43 □ Sembawang Singapore
78 B3 Sembé Congo
40 C4 Semenanjung Blambangan pen. Indon.
79 C4 Semendua Zaire
14 D1 Semendyayevo Rus. Fed.
13 E4 Semenivka *Chernihiv* Ukraine
15 E2 Semenivka *Poltava* Ukraine
14 G1 Semenov Rus. Fed.
14 D1 Semibratovo Rus. Fed.
12 G3 Semigorodnyaya Rus. Fed.
14 G3 Semiley Rus. Fed.
14 F2 Semilovo Rus. Fed.
14 D4 Semiluki Rus. Fed.
126 F3 Seminoe Res. resr U.S.A.
125 C5 Seminole U.S.A.
119 C6 Seminole, L. l. U.S.A.
65 L2 Seminskiy Khrebet mt. ra. Rus. Fed.
14 E2 Semion Rus. Fed.
64 F2 Semiozernoye Kazak.
48 D2 Semiozer'ye Rus. Fed.
65 K2 Semipalatinsk Kazak.
65 J3 Semipalatinsk div. Kazak.
41 B3 Semirara i. Phil.
41 B4 Semirara Islands is Phil.
57 B3 Semīrom Iran
40 B1 Semitau Indon.
65 J2 Semiyarka Kazak.
65 H2 Semiz-Bugu Kazak.
57 C2 Semnān div. Iran
57 C2 Semnān Iran
48 B5 Sêmnyi China
18 B4 Semois r. Belgium
41 A5 Semporna Malaysia
40 C4 Sempu i. Indon.
142 B1 Sem Tripa Brazil
14 A3 Semtsy Rus. Fed.
21 G3 Semur-en-Auxois France
12 H1 Semzha Rus. Fed.
140 C2 Sena Bolivia
144 D2 Senador Canedo Brazil
142 E2 Senador Pompeu Brazil
41 A5 Senaja Malaysia
140 C1 Sena Madureira Brazil
56 C5 Senanayake Samudra l. Sri Lanka
79 D7 Senanga Zambia
40 B1 Senaning Indon.
21 G5 Sénas France
15 E1 Sencha Ukraine
47 H4 Sendai Japan
46 C8 Sendai Japan
46 C8 Sendai-gawa r. Japan
18 E4 Senden Germany
50 A2 Sêndo China
43 C7 Senebui, Tanjung pt Indon.
129 G5 Seneca U.S.A.
122 C5 Seneca U.S.A.
126 C2 Seneca U.S.A.
120 E3 Seneca Falls U.S.A.
120 E3 Seneca Lake l. U.S.A.
120 D5 Seneca Rocks U.S.A.
120 C5 Senecaville Lake l. U.S.A.
68 C4 Senegal country Africa
76 B3 Sénégal r. Mauritania/Senegal
122 E2 Seney U.S.A.
19 G3 Senftenberg Germany
81 B6 Senga Hill Zambia
54 D4 Sengar r. India
40 D1 Sengata Indon.
81 B5 Sengerema Tanzania
12 J4 Sengiley Rus. Fed.
64 D4 Sengiri, Mys pt Kazak.
147 B6 Senguerr r. Arg.
83 D2 Sengwa r. Zimbabwe
142 D3 Senhor do Bonfim Brazil
19 H4 Senica Slovakia
26 D4 Senigallia Italy
26 E3 Senj Croatia
10 E1 Senja i. Norway
76 C5 Senko Guinea
15 G2 Sen'kove Ukraine
54 D2 Senku India
20 F2 Senlis France
43 D4 Senmonorom Cambodia
47 E6 Sennan Japan
73 F5 Sennar Sudan
73 F5 Sennar Dam dam Sudan
115 G2 Senneterre Can.
14 H3 Sennoy Rus. Fed.
147 B7 Seno Otway b. Chile
83 D5 Senqu r. Lesotho
21 F2 Sens France
130 H6 Sensuntepeque El Salvador
28 C2 Senta Yugo.
129 F5 Sentinel U.S.A.
110 E3 Sentinel Pk summit Can.
152 B3 Sentinel Ra. mt. ra. Ant.
43 □ Sentosa i. Singapore
40 D1 Senyiur Indon.
60 E2 Şenyurt Turkey
46 C6 Senzaki Japan
46 D7 Sen-zaki pt Japan
54 D5 Seoni India
55 E5 Seorinarayan India
40 C3 Sepanjang i. Indon.
92 D4 Separation Pt pt N.Z.
40 D1 Sepasu Indon.
40 B1 Sepauk Indon.
143 D5 Sepetiba, Baía de b. Brazil
57 B3 Sepidān Iran
90 □1 Sepik r. P.N.G.
40 D1 Sepinang Indon.
27 E5 Sepino Italy
19 H2 Sępólno Krajeńskie Poland
141 E3 Sepotuba r. Brazil
113 G3 Sept-Îles Can.
20 C2 Sept-Îles, Les is France
40 A3 Seputih r. Indon.
128 C3 Sequoia National Park nat. park U.S.A.
13 G5 Serafimovich Rus. Fed.
57 E1 Serakhs Turkmenistan
39 J7 Seram i. Indon.
39 J7 Seram Sea g. Indon.
40 A3 Serang Indon.
43 □ Serangoon Harbour chan. Singapore
43 □ Serangoon, P. i. Singapore
43 E7 Serasan i. Indon.
43 E7 Seraya i. Indon.
43 □ Seraya, P. i. Singapore
61 B5 Serbâl, G. mt. Egypt
130 D2 Serdán Mexico
80 D2 Serdo Ethiopia
14 G3 Serdoba r. Rus. Fed.
14 G3 Serdobsk Rus. Fed.
65 K3 Serebryansk Kazak.
14 D2 Serebryanyye Prudy Rus. Fed.
19 H4 Sered' Slovakia
14 E1 Sereda Rus. Fed.
14 B2 Seredeyskiy Rus. Fed.
11 H4 Seredka Rus. Fed.
14 D2 Serednikovo Rus. Fed.
19 L4 Serednye Ukraine
14 B3 Seredyna-Buda Ukraine
60 C2 Şereflikoçhisar Turkey
21 F3 Serein r. France
43 C7 Seremban Malaysia
24 D3 Serena, Embalse de la resr Spain
81 B5 Serengeti National Park nat. park Tanzania
81 C5 Serengeti Plains plain Kenya
81 B7 Serenje Zambia
142 C2 Sereno r. Brazil
80 B4 Serere Uganda
15 A2 Seret r. Ukraine
14 F2 Serezha r. Rus. Fed.
14 G2 Sergach Rus. Fed.
48 D3 Sergelen Mongolia
48 E2 Sergelen Mongolia
65 G2 Sergeyevka Kazak.
142 E3 Sergipe div. Brazil
14 D1 Sergiyev Posad Rus. Fed.
64 D2 Sergiyevsk Rus. Fed.
14 C3 Sergiyevskoye Rus. Fed.
14 D3 Sergiyevskoye Rus. Fed.
15 E1 Serhiyivka *Chernihiv* Ukraine
15 D3 Serhiyivka *Odesa* Ukraine
15 D3 Serhiyivka *Odesa* Ukraine
38 F6 Seria Brunei
40 B1 Serian Malaysia
29 E6 Serifos i. Greece
113 G2 Sérigny, Lac l. Can.
60 B2 Serik Turkey
65 J5 Serikbuya China
100 C2 Seringapatam Reef reef Aust.
96 D2 Serle, Mt h. Aust.
39 J8 Sermata, Kepulauan is Indon.
12 J3 Sernur Rus. Fed.
64 E5 Sernyy Zavod Turkmenistan
132 □1 Seroe Colorado *Aruba* Caribbean
13 H6 Seroglazovka Rus. Fed.
25 E4 Serón Spain
82 C2 Seronga Botswana
75 F4 Serouenout well Algeria
62 H4 Serov Rus. Fed.
82 D3 Serowe Botswana
24 C4 Serpa Portugal
96 B2 Serpentine Lakes salt flat Aust.
139 E2 Serpent's Mouth chan. Trinidad/Venezuela
14 B2 Serpeysk Rus. Fed.
25 F3 Serpis r. Spain
15 C3 Serpneve Ukraine
14 E3 Serpovoye Rus. Fed.
14 C2 Serpukhov Rus. Fed.
145 H4 Serra Brazil
139 F3 Serra Acari h. Brazil/Guyana
144 A1 Serra Azul h. Brazil
145 E1 Serra Bonita Brazil
139 E3 Serra Curupira mt. ra. Brazil
143 B5 Serra da Apucarana h. Brazil
145 F5 Serra da Bocaina, Parque Nacional da nat. park Brazil
143 A5 Serra da Bodoquena h. Brazil
145 H2 Serra da Cana Brava h. Brazil
144 C1 Serra da Canastra mts *Goiás* Brazil
145 E3 Serra da Canastra mt. ra. *Minas Gerais* Brazil
145 E4 Serra da Canastra, Parque Nacional da nat. park Brazil
143 D4 Serra da Espinhaco mt. ra. Brazil
142 D1 Serra da Ibiapaba h. Brazil
145 F5 Serra da Mantiqueira mt. ra. Brazil
144 B3 Serra da Mombuca h. Brazil
144 B6 Serra das Araras mt. ra. Brazil
145 F1 Serra das Araras Brazil
144 B3 Serra das Araras h. Brazil
144 C2 Serra das Divisões ou de Santa Marta mt. ra. Brazil
142 D3 Serra da Tabatinga h. Brazil
141 E4 Serra de Amambaí h. Brazil/Paraguay
144 C6 Serra de Esperanca mt. ra. Brazil
142 C2 Serra de Itapicuru h. Brazil
144 A4 Serra de Maracaju h. Brazil
24 B1 Serra de Outes Spain
144 B4 Serra de Santa Bárbara h. Brazil
145 E1 Serra de Santa Maria h. Brazil
145 F1 Serra de São Felipe h. Brazil
144 A2 Serra de São Jerônimo h. Brazil
27 E7 Serra di Burgio h. Italy
142 B1 Serra do Almeirim h. Brazil
145 F2 Serra do Cabral mts Brazil
142 A2 Serra do Cachimbo h. Brazil
144 B2 Serra do Caiapó mts Brazil
145 H2 Serra do Chifre mt. ra. Brazil
140 B1 Serra do Divisor, Parque Nacional de nat. park Brazil
142 D2 Serra do Dois Irmãos h. Brazil
143 B6 Serra do Espigao mts Brazil
145 G2 Serra do Espinhaco mt. ra. Brazil
142 C1 Serra do Gurupi h. Brazil
144 B5 Serra do Lagarto h. Brazil
145 G5 Serra do Mar mt. ra. *Rio de Janeiro* Brazil
143 B6 Serra do Mar mt. ra. *Rio Grande do Sul/Santa Catarina* Brazil
145 F5 Serra do Mar mt. ra. *São Paulo* Brazil
139 E3 Serra do Mucajaí mt. ra. Brazil
139 G3 Serra do Navio Brazil
141 E2 Serra do Norte h. Brazil
142 D3 Serra do Ramalho h. Brazil
145 E2 Serra do Rio Prêto h. Brazil
142 B3 Serra do Roncador h. Brazil
145 H2 Serra dos Aimorés Brazil
142 A3 Serra dos Apiacas h. Brazil
142 A3 Serra dos Caiabis h. Brazil
142 B2 Serra dos Carajás h. Brazil
144 E2 Serra dos Cristais mts Brazil
144 B5 Serra dos Dourados h. Brazil
142 B2 Serra dos Gradaús h. Brazil
140 D2 Serra dos Pacaás h. Brazil
141 D2 Serra dos Parecis h. Brazil
144 E2 Serra dos Pilões mt. ra. Brazil
145 F1 Serra dos Tropeiros h. Brazil
142 B1 Serra do Tapara h. Brazil
144 B1 Serra do Taquaral h. Brazil
144 B3 Serra do Taquari h. Brazil
142 C1 Serra do Tiracambu h. Brazil
141 E2 Serra do Tombador h. Brazil
142 C3 Serra Dourada mt. ra. Brazil
144 C2 Serra Dourada h. Brazil
142 C2 Serra do Uruçuí h. Brazil
142 C2 Serra Estrondo h. Brazil
142 A3 Serra Formosa h. Brazil
144 C6 Serra Geral mt. ra. *Paraná* Brazil
143 B6 Serra Geral mt. ra. *Santa Catarina* Brazil
142 C3 Serra Geral de Goiás h. Brazil
144 E1 Serra Geral do Paraná h. Brazil
139 F3 Serra Iricoumé h. Brazil
139 G3 Serra Lombarda h. Brazil
132 B4 Serrana Bank Colombia
145 G3 Serra Negra mts Brazil
138 B2 Serranía de Abibe mt. ra. Colombia
138 B2 Serranía de Baudo mt. ra. Colombia
25 E2 Serranía de Cuenca mt. ra. Spain
139 E2 Serranía de Imataca mt. ra. Venezuela
138 D3 Serranía de la Neblina, Parque Nacional nat. park Venezuela
130 L7 Serranía del Darién mt. ra.. Panama
132 C6 Serranía del Sapo mt. ra. Panama
24 D4 Serranía de Ronda mt. ra. Spain
131 E2 Serranías del Burro mt. ra. Mexico
139 E2 Serranía Turagua mt. Venezuela
147 B6 Serrano i. Chile
144 B3 Serranópolis Brazil
139 E3 Serra Pacaraima mt. ra. Brazil
144 D6 Serra Paranapiacaba mt. ra. Brazil
139 E3 Serra Parima mt. ra. Brazil
144 D1 Serra Pouso Alegre mts Brazil
142 E2 Serra Talhada Brazil
139 E3 Serra Tepequem mt. ra. Brazil
139 F3 Serra Tumucumaque h. Brazil
29 D4 Serres Greece
146 C3 Serrezuela Arg.
142 E3 Serrinha Brazil
145 G3 Sêrro Brazil
147 B5 Serrucho mt. Arg.
27 B7 Sers Tunisia
142 E2 Sertânia Brazil
144 C5 Sertanópolis Brazil
144 B3 Sertão de Camapuã reg. Brazil
144 E4 Sertãozinho Brazil
50 C1 Sêrtar China
11 H3 Sertolovo Rus. Fed.
40 A3 Sertung i. Indon.
39 L7 Serui Indon.
82 D3 Serule Botswana
40 C2 Seruyan r. Indon.
29 D4 Servia Greece
50 B1 Sêrxu China
41 A6 Sesayap r. Indon.
41 A6 Sesayap Indon.
112 B3 Seseganaga L. l. Can.
81 B5 Sese Is i. Uganda
114 E2 Sesekinika Can.
90 □6 Seseleka h. Fiji
82 A2 Sesfontein Namibia
14 A3 Seshcha Rus. Fed.
79 D7 Sesheke Zambia
29 F6 Sesklio i. Greece
47 □2 Sesoko Japan
47 □2 Sesoko-jima i. Japan
25 G3 S'Espalmador i. Spain
79 D6 Sessa Angola
27 D5 Sessa Aurunca Italy
26 B3 Sestri Levante Italy
11 H3 Sestroretsk Rus. Fed.
46 G2 Setana Japan
21 F5 Sète France
144 E6 Sete Barras Brazil
145 F3 Sete Lagoas Brazil
10 E1 Setermoen Norway
11 B4 Setesdal v. Norway
55 F3 Seti r. *Gandakhi* Nepal
54 E3 Seti r. *Seti* Nepal
75 F1 Sétif Algeria
73 G5 Setit r. Africa
47 F6 Seto Japan
46 D7 Seto-naikai sea Japan
42 A4 Setsan Myanmar
74 C2 Settat Morocco
79 A4 Setté Cama Gabon
26 B3 Settepani, Monte mt. Italy
26 A3 Settimo Torinese Italy
17 F4 Settle U.K.
98 D3 Settlement Cr. r. Aust.
145 G2 Setubal r. Brazil
24 B3 Setúbal Portugal
24 B3 Setúbal div. Portugal
24 B3 Setúbal, Baía de b. Portugal
122 E3 Seul Choix Pt pt U.S.A.
112 B3 Seul, Lac l. Can.
21 G3 Seurre France
14 B3 Sev r. Rus. Fed.
60 F1 Sevan Armenia
60 F1 Sevana Lich l. Armenia
13 E6 Sevastopol' Ukraine
113 H2 Seven Islands Bay b. Can.
21 F4 Sévérac-le-Château France
14 D2 Severka r. Rus. Fed.
97 G2 Severn r. Aust.
112 B3 Severn r. Can.
93 D5 Severn mt. N.Z.
17 F5 Severn r. U.K.
12 G2 Severnaya Dvina r. Rus. Fed.
13 G7 Severnaya Osetiya div. Rus. Fed.
63 M2 Severnaya Zemlya is Rus. Fed.
112 B3 Severn L. l. Can.
64 D2 Severnoye Rus. Fed.
65 J1 Severnoye Rus. Fed.
62 H3 Severnyy Rus. Fed.
14 G1 Severnyy Rus. Fed.
15 G1 Severnyy Rus. Fed.
64 E3 Severnyy Chink Ustyurta escarpment Kazak.
19 G3 Severočeský div. Czech Rep.
65 L2 Severo-Chuyskiy Khrebet mt. ra. Rus. Fed.
12 F1 Severodvinsk Rus. Fed.
65 G2 Severo-Kazakhstan div. Kazak.
63 R4 Severo-Kuril'sk Rus. Fed.
19 H4 Severomoravský div. Czech Rep.
10 J1 Severomorsk Rus. Fed.
12 F2 Severoonezhsk Rus. Fed.
63 L3 Severo-Yeniseyskiy Rus. Fed.
15 G1 Severskiy Donets r. Rus. Fed.
127 D4 Sevier r. U.S.A.
129 G2 Sevier Bridge Reservoir resr U.S.A.
129 F2 Sevier Desert desert U.S.A.
129 F2 Sevier Lake salt l. U.S.A.
138 B3 Sevilla Colombia
24 D4 Sevilla Spain
28 E3 Sevlievo Bulgaria
14 B3 Sevsk Rus. Fed.
76 B5 Sewa r. Sierra Leone
54 C3 Sewāni India
108 D3 Seward U.S.A.
124 D3 Seward U.S.A.
108 B3 Seward Peninsula pen. U.S.A.
110 F3 Sexsmith Can.
57 E2 Seyah Band Koh mt. ra. Afghanistan
62 J2 Seyakha Rus. Fed.
131 H5 Seybaplaya Mexico
81 □1 Seychelles country Indian Ocean
64 F5 Seydi Turkmenistan
60 B2 Seydişehir Turkey
10 N2 Seyðisfjörður Iceland
60 C2 Seyhan r. Turkey
61 C1 Seyhan Barajı resr Turkey
60 B2 Seyitgazi Turkey
14 B4 Seym r. Rus. Fed.
15 G1 Seym Rus. Fed.
15 E1 Seym r. Ukraine
63 R3 Seymchan Rus. Fed.
97 F4 Seymour Aust.
118 C4 Seymour U.S.A.
125 D5 Seymour U.S.A.
57 G2 Seyyedābād Afghanistan
21 F2 Sézanne France
14 B2 Sezha r. Rus. Fed.
27 D5 Sezze Italy
29 E7 Sfakia Greece
28 E2 Sfântu Gheorghe Romania
28 G2 Sfântu Gheorghe Romania
75 G2 Sfax Tunisia
18 B2 's-Gravenhage Netherlands
48 E5 Sha r. China
48 D6 Shaanxi div. China
79 E5 Shaba div. Zaire
80 E4 Shabeellaha Dhexe div. Somalia
80 D4 Shabeellaha Hoose div. Somalia
60 F2 Shabestar Iran
61 C5 Shabibī, J. esh mt. Jordan
28 G3 Shabla Bulgaria
14 B3 Shablykino Rus. Fed.
113 G3 Shabogamo Lake l. Can.
79 E4 Shabunda Zaire
65 J5 Shache China
152 B4 Shackleton Coast Ant.
152 B4 Shackleton Gl. gl. Ant.
152 D6 Shackleton Ice Shelf ice feature Ant.
152 C3 Shackleton Ra. mt. ra. Ant.
54 A4 Shadadkot Pakistan
57 F3 Shadikhak P. pass Afghanistan
57 C3 Shādkām w Iran
64 F1 Shadrinsk Rus. Fed.

T

42 B3 To or China Bakir r. Myanmar
99 G5 Toowoomba Aust.
80 F2 Tooxin Somalia
129 G6 Topawa U.S.A.
128 C2 Topaz U.S.A.
81 □3 Topaze B. b. Rodrigues I. Mauritius
65 K2 Topchikha Rus. Fed.
124 E4 Topeka U.S.A.
130 D3 Topia Mexico
14 D2 Topkanovo Rus. Fed.
65 L1 Topki Rus. Fed.
110 D4 Topley Landing Can.
23 C3 Toplica r. Yugo.
28 E1 Toplița Romania
146 B3 Topocalma, Pta pt Chile
129 E4 Topock U.S.A.
28 C2 Topola Yugo.
19 J4 Topoľčany Slovakia
130 C3 Topolobampo Mexico
28 G2 Topolog Romania
28 E2 Topoloveni Romania
28 F3 Topolovgrad Bulgaria
15 B1 Topory Ukraine
12 D1 Topozero, Oz. l. Rus. Fed.
126 B2 Toppenish U.S.A.
121 K2 Topsfield U.S.A.
129 F3 Toquerville U.S.A.
80 B3 Tor Ethiopia
60 A2 Torbalı Turkey
57 D2 Torbat-e Heydarīyeh Iran
57 E2 Torbat-e Jām Iran
14 F2 Torbeyevo Rus. Fed.
14 B2 Torbeyevo Rus. Fed.
14 E1 Torchino Rus. Fed.
122 E3 Torch Lake l. U.S.A.
15 A1 Torchyn Ukraine
24 D2 Tordesillas Spain
25 F2 Tordesilos Spain
10 F2 Töre Sweden
25 H1 Torelló Spain
24 C1 Toreno Spain
24 C2 Torey Rus. Fed.
18 F3 Torgau Germany
19 G2 Torgelow Germany
13 H5 Torgun r. Rus. Fed.
20 D2 Torigni-sur-Vire France
130 C3 Torin Mexico
26 A3 Torino Italy
86 F2 Tori-shima i. Japan
80 B4 Torit Sudan
144 B2 Torixoreu Brazil
24 D2 Tormes r. Spain
19 K4 Tornaľa Slovakia
10 F2 Torneälven r. Sweden
10 E1 Torneträsk l. Sweden
10 E1 Torneträsk Sweden
113 H2 Torngat Mountains mt. ra. Can.
10 G2 Tornio Finland
146 D4 Tornquist Arg.
77 F4 Toro Niger
24 D2 Toro Spain
146 C2 Toro, Co del mt. Chile
77 E4 Torodi Niger
72 C4 Toro Doum well Chad
19 K4 Törökszentmiklós Hungary
97 G3 Toronto Aust.
115 F5 Toronto Can.
115 F5 Toronto airport Can.
12 D3 Toropets Rus. Fed.
128 D5 Toro Pk summit U.S.A.
81 B4 Tororo Uganda
61 B1 Toros Dağları mt. ra. Turkey
17 F6 Torquay U.K.
128 C5 Torrance U.S.A.
24 B3 Torrão Portugal
24 C2 Torre mt. Portugal
27 E5 Torre Annunziata Italy
25 G2 Torreblanca Spain
27 G5 Torre Cavallo, Capo di pt Italy
27 E5 Torre del Greco Italy
24 C2 Torre de Moncorvo Portugal
24 E4 Torredonjimeno Spain
24 D3 Torrejón-Tajo, Emb. de resr Spain
24 E2 Torrelaguna Spain
24 D1 Torrelavega Spain
24 D4 Torremolinos Málaga Spain
99 F4 Torrens Cr. w Aust.
99 F4 Torrens Creek Aust.
96 D2 Torrens, Lake salt flat Aust.
25 F3 Torrent Spain
130 E3 Torreón Mexico
27 E5 Torre Orsaia Italy
25 F4 Torre-Pacheco Spain
143 C6 Torres Brazil
130 D3 Torres Mexico
147 B7 Torres del Paine, Parque Nacional nat. park Chile
90 □2 Torres Islands is Vanuatu
24 B3 Torres Novas Portugal
95 H1 Torres Strait str. Aust./P.N.G.
24 B3 Torres Vedras Portugal
25 F4 Torrevieja Spain
129 G2 Torrey U.S.A.
17 E6 Torridge r. U.K.
16 E3 Torridon, Loch inlet U.K.
26 B3 Torriglia Italy
24 D3 Torrijos Spain
121 G4 Torrington U.S.A.
126 F3 Torrington U.S.A.
25 H1 Torroella de Montgrí Spain
24 E4 Torrox Spain
55 G4 Torsa r. Bhutan
11 D3 Torsby Sweden
16 D1 Tórshavn Faeroes
119 □3 Tortola i. Virgin Is Caribbean
146 C2 Tórtolas, Co Las mt. Chile
27 B6 Tortolì Italy
26 B3 Tortona Italy
25 G2 Tortosa Spain
130 B3 Tortugas, Bahía Mexico
60 E1 Tortum Turkey
57 C2 Ţorūd Iran
60 D1 Torul Turkey
19 J2 Toruń Poland
17 C4 Tory Island i. Rep. of Ire.
19 K4 Toryša r. Slovakia
14 B1 Torzhok Rus. Fed.
56 D7 Tosa Japan
46 D7 Tosashimizu Japan
46 D7 Tosa-wan b. Japan
10 D2 Tosbotn Norway
82 C4 Tosca R.S.A.
26 C4 Toscana div. Italy
27 C4 Toscano, Arcipelago is Italy
47 H3 Tōshima-yama mt. Japan
12 D3 Tosno Rus. Fed.
48 A2 Tosontsengel Mongolia
146 D2 Tostado Arg.
18 D2 Tostedt Germany
46 C7 Tosu Japan
60 C1 Tosya Turkey
25 F4 Totana Spain
12 G3 Tot'ma Rus. Fed.
139 F2 Totness Surinam
131 F5 Totolapan Mexico
131 G4 Totonicapán Guatemala
140 C3 Totora Bolivia
146 B2 Totoral Chile
76 C5 Totota Liberia
90 □7 Totoya i. Fiji
152 C6 Totten Glacier gl. Ant.
97 F3 Tottenham Aust.
46 D6 Tottori div. Japan
46 E6 Tottori Japan
77 F2 Touârat well Niger
76 C5 Touba Côte d'Ivoire
76 A4 Touba Senegal
74 C2 Toubkal, Jbel mt. Morocco
78 C2 Touboro Cameroon
21 F3 Toucy France
48 C5 Toudaohu China
74 B4 Toueïrma well Mauritania
76 D3 Touérât well Mali
76 D2 Toufourine well Mali
76 D4 Tougan Burkina
75 F2 Touggourt Algeria
76 D4 Tougouri Burkina
76 B4 Tougué Guinea
90 □2 Touho Pac. Oc.
74 C5 Touijinet well Mauritania
74 B5 Touil Mauritania
76 D3 Toukoto Mali
21 G2 Toul France
76 C5 Toulépleu Côte d'Ivoire
21 G5 Toulon Var France
20 E5 Toulouse Haute-Garonne France
77 F3 Toumbélaga well Niger
77 G2 Toummo well Niger
76 C5 Toumodi Côte d'Ivoire
77 F3 Tounfaminir well Niger
77 G5 Toungo Nigeria
42 B3 Toungoo Myanmar
51 E3 Toupai China
20 E3 Touraine reg. France
42 C3 Tourakom Laos
78 C1 Tourba Chad
24 B1 Touriñán, Cabo c. Spain
20 D2 Tourlaville France
18 A3 Tournai Belgium
140 B1 Tournavista Peru
21 G4 Tournon-sur-Rhône France
21 G3 Tournus France
142 E2 Touros Brazil
20 E3 Tours France
20 E2 Toury France
76 D4 Toussiana Burkina
72 C3 Tousside, Pic mt. Chad
78 D2 Toussoro, Mt mt. C.A.R.
82 C5 Touws River R.S.A.
18 F3 Toužim Czech Rep.
48 G3 Tövar div. Mongolia
138 C2 Tovar Venezuela
14 B2 Tovarkovo Rus. Fed.
14 D3 Tovarkovskiy Rus. Fed.
60 F1 Tovuz Azerbaijan
47 H3 Towada Japan
46 H3 Towada-Hachimantai National Park nat. park. Japan
47 H3 Towada-ko l. Japan
92 E1 Towai N.Z.
133 H6 Towakaima Guyana
121 E4 Towanda U.S.A.
129 H3 Towaoc U.S.A.
122 A2 Tower U.S.A.
99 F4 Towerhill Cr. w Aust.
93 A7 Tower Pk summit N.Z.
111 J5 Towner U.S.A.
128 D3 Townes Pass pass U.S.A.
98 C2 Towns r. Aust.
126 E2 Townsend U.S.A.
99 G4 Townshend I. i. Aust.
99 F4 Townsville Aust.
39 H7 Towori, Teluk b. Indon.
80 B3 Towot Sudan
120 E5 Towson U.S.A.
65 J4 Toxkan r. China
46 F2 Tōya-ko l. Japan
47 F5 Toyama Japan
47 F5 Toyama div. Japan
47 F5 Toyama-wan b. Japan
15 A1 Toykut Ukraine
46 D7 Tōyo Japan
47 F6 Toyohashi Japan
47 F6 Toyokawa Japan
47 E6 Toyonaka Japan
46 E6 Toyooka Japan
46 C6 Toyota Japan
47 F6 Toyota Japan
46 H2 Toyotomi Japan
65 G4 Toytepa Uzbekistan
75 F2 Tozeur Tunisia
63 G7 Tqibuli Georgia
13 G7 Tqvarch'eli Georgia
61 C2 Trâblous Lebanon
28 D4 Trabotivište Macedonia
60 E1 Trabzon Turkey
121 K2 Tracy Can.
115 J3 Tracy Can.
128 B3 Tracy U.S.A.
124 E2 Tracy U.S.A.
122 A4 Traer U.S.A.
24 C4 Trafalgar, Cabo pt Spain
82 D5 Tragacete Spain
146 B4 Traiguén Chile
110 F5 Trail Can.
109 Q2 Traill Ø i. Greenland
126 E3 Trairas r. Brazil
19 G4 Traisen r. Austria
145 G5 Trajano de Morais Brazil
11 G5 Trakai Lithuania
12 J2 Trakt Rus. Fed.
17 C5 Tralee Rep. of Ire.
139 E2 Tramán Tepuí mt. Venezuela
17 D5 Tramore Rep. of Ire.
25 H3 Tramuntana, Serra de mt. ra. Spain
11 D4 Tranås Sweden
146 C2 Trancas Arg.
145 J2 Trancoso Brazil
11 D4 Tranemo Sweden
43 B6 Trang Thailand
39 K8 Trangan i. Indon.
97 G3 Trangie Aust.
27 F5 Trani Italy
83 H3 Tranomaro Madagascar
83 H3 Tranoroa Madagascar
146 E3 Tranqueras Uruguay
152 B5 Transantarctic Mountains mts Ant.
111 G4 Trans Canada Highway Can.
111 K5 Transcona Can.
27 D6 Trapani Italy
20 F2 Trappes France
97 F4 Traralgon Aust.
74 A5 Trarza div. Mauritania
26 D4 Trasimeno, Lago l. Italy
24 C2 Trás-os-Montes reg. Portugal
14 A3 Tratsino Rus. Fed.
43 C4 Trat Thailand
19 G4 Traun Austria
19 F5 Traunreut Germany
19 F5 Traunsee l. Austria
18 F5 Traunstein Germany
57 E3 Travellers L. l. Aust.
152 C1 Traversay Is is S. Sandwich Is Atlantic Ocean
122 E3 Traverse City U.S.A.
93 D5 Travers, Mt mt. N.Z.
43 D5 Tra Vinh Vietnam
126 D5 Travis, L. l. U.S.A.
26 F3 Travnik Bos.-Herz.
101 B6 Trayning Aust.
26 E2 Trbovlje Slovenia
133 □1 Treasure Beach Jamaica
90 □1 Treasury Is is Solomon Is.
26 B3 Trebbia r. Italy
19 G4 Třebíč Czech Rep.
26 G4 Trebinje Bos.-Herz.
27 F6 Trebisacce Italy
19 K4 Trebišov Slovakia
26 E3 Trebnje Slovenia
19 G4 Třeboň Czech Rep.
122 B3 Trego U.S.A.
20 C2 Trégorrois reg. France
99 G3 Tregosse Islets & Reefs is Coral Sea Islands Terr. Pac. Oc.
146 F3 Treinta-y-Tres Uruguay
133 □1 Trelawney div. Jamaica
20 D3 Trélazé France
147 C5 Trelew Arg.
11 D5 Trelleborg Sweden
115 H3 Tremblant, Mt h. Can.
81 □5 Tremblet Réunion Indian Ocean
27 E4 Tremiti, Isole is Italy
126 D3 Tremonton U.S.A.
18 F4 Třemošná Czech Rep.
25 G1 Tremp Spain
122 B3 Trempealeau r. U.S.A.
146 D4 Trenque Lauquén Arg.
17 G5 Trent r. U.K.
26 C2 Trentino Alto Adige div. Italy
26 C2 Trento Italy
115 G4 Trenton Can.
124 E3 Trenton U.S.A.
121 F4 Trenton U.S.A.
113 K4 Trepassey Can.
146 D4 Tres Arroyos Arg.
147 C6 Tres Cerros Arg.
145 F4 Três Corações Brazil
138 B3 Tres Esquinas Colombia
146 D2 Tres Isletas Arg.
26 G4 Treskavica mts Bos.-Herz.
14 G3 Treskino Rus. Fed.
144 C4 Três Lagoas Brazil
147 B6 Tres Lagos Arg.
146 D4 Tres Lomas Arg.
140 C2 Tres Mapajos Bolivia
145 F3 Três Marias Brazil
147 A6 Tres Montes, Pen. pen. Chile
131 E5 Tres Picos Mexico
146 D4 Tres Picos, Co mt. Arg.
127 F4 Tres Piedras U.S.A.
145 F4 Três Pontas Brazil
144 D6 Três Pontões, Pico mt. Brazil
147 C6 Tres Puntas, C. c. Arg.
144 E3 Três Ranchos Brazil
145 G5 Três Rios Brazil
131 F5 Tres Valles Mexico
130 B3 Tres Vírgenes, Vol. Las vol. Mexico
131 G5 Tres Zapotes Mexico
11 C3 Tretten Norway
11 C4 Treungen Norway
26 B3 Treviglio Italy
26 D3 Treviso Italy
81 □1 Trevor Pt pt Seychelles
17 E6 Trevose Head hd U.K.
28 D3 Trgovište Yugo.
97 F5 Triabunna Aust.
98 D2 Trial B. b. Aust.
42 B1 Triangle, The mt. ra. Myanmar
29 F6 Tria Nisia i. Greece
29 G6 Trianta Greece
54 B2 Tribal Areas div. Pakistan
27 G6 Tricase Italy
56 B4 Trichur India
97 F3 Trida Aust.
19 G5 Trieben Austria
18 C4 Trier Germany
26 D3 Trieste Italy
26 D3 Trieste, Golfo di g. Italy
20 E5 Trie-sur-Baïse France
29 C5 Trikala Greece
29 D5 Trikeri, D. chan. Greece
61 B2 Trikomon Cyprus
39 L7 Trikora, Pk mt. Indon.
26 F4 Trilj Croatia
56 C4 Trincomalee Sri Lanka
144 D2 Trindade Brazil
148 G7 Trindade, Ilha da i. Atlantic Ocean
140 D2 Trinidad Bolivia
138 C2 Trinidad Colombia
132 C2 Trinidad Cuba
133 □3 Trinidad i. Trin. & Tobago
146 E3 Trinidad Uruguay
127 F4 Trinidad U.S.A.
104 M8 Trinidad and Tobago country Caribbean
113 K4 Trinity Bay b. Can.
133 □3 Trinity Hills h. Trinidad Trin. & Tobago
128 C1 Trinity Range mts U.S.A.
81 □4 Triolet Mauritius
119 C5 Trion U.S.A.
27 E5 Trionto, Capo c. Italy
29 D6 Tripoli Greece
75 D1 Tripolitania reg. Libya
55 G5 Tripunittura India
55 G5 Tripura div. India
18 D1 Trischen i. Germany
82 A5 Tristan da Cunha i. Atlantic Ocean
76 A4 Tristao, Îles is Guinea
54 D3 Trisul mt. India
82 B2 Triunfo r. Brazil
56 B4 Trivandrum India
27 E5 Trivento Italy
19 H4 Trnava Slovakia
90 □1 Trobriand Islands is P.N.G.
19 G5 Trofaiach Austria
10 D2 Trofors Norway
26 F4 Trogir Croatia
27 E5 Troia Italy
27 E7 Troina Italy
81 □5 Trois Bassins Réunion Indian Ocean
18 C3 Troisdorf Germany
75 D1 Trois Fourches, Cap des hd Morocco
115 J3 Trois-Rivières Can.
133 □5 Trois-Rivières Guadeloupe Caribbean
14 C2 Troitsk Rus. Fed.
14 F2 Troitsk Rus. Fed.
64 F2 Troitsk Rus. Fed.
62 G3 Troitsko-Pechorsk Rus. Fed.
13 H6 Troitskoye Rus. Fed.
65 K2 Troitskoye Rus. Fed.
65 J2 Troitskoye Rus. Fed.
133 □1 Troja Jamaica
72 B4 Trolla well Chad
11 D4 Trollhättan Sweden
139 F4 Trombetas r. Brazil
149 H5 Tromelin, Île i. Indian Ocean
146 C4 Tromen, Volcán vol Arg.
146 B4 Tromen, Volcán vol Arg.
10 E1 Troms div. Norway
10 E1 Tromsø Norway
128 D4 Trona U.S.A.
10 C3 Trondheim Norway
10 C3 Trondheimsfjorden chan. Norway
26 D4 Tronto r. Italy
61 B2 Troodos Cyprus
29 C6 Tropaia Greece
143 C4 Tropeiros, Sa dos h. Brazil
129 F3 Tropic U.S.A.
14 B3 Trosna Rus. Fed.
18 F4 Trostberg Germany
15 F1 Trostyanets' Sumy Ukraine
15 C2 Trostyanets' Vinnytsya Ukraine
15 A1 Trostyanets' Volyn Ukraine
110 E2 Trout r. Can.
115 F4 Trout Creek Can.
129 F2 Trout Creek U.S.A.
112 B3 Trout L. l. Can.
110 G3 Trout Lake Can.
110 E2 Trout Lake Can.
110 E2 Trout Lake l. Can.
122 E2 Trout Lake U.S.A.
122 C2 Trout Lake l. U.S.A.
126 E2 Trout Peak summit U.S.A.
120 E4 Trout Run U.S.A.
20 E2 Trouville-sur-Mer France
17 F6 Trowbridge U.K.
97 F5 Trowutta Aust.
133 □1 Troy Jamaica
60 A2 Troy Turkey
119 C6 Troy U.S.A.
126 D2 Troy U.S.A.
121 G3 Troy U.S.A.
121 G3 Troy U.S.A.
120 A4 Troy U.S.A.
120 E4 Troy U.S.A.
28 E3 Troyan Bulgaria
15 D2 Troyanka Ukraine
14 C3 Troyekurovo Rus. Fed.
14 D3 Troyekurovo Rus. Fed.
21 G2 Troyes France
15 E3 Troyits'ke Ukraine
15 E3 Troyits'ko-Safonove Ukraine
128 D4 Troy Lake l. U.S.A.
129 E2 Troy Peak summit U.S.A.
28 C3 Trstenik Yugo.
98 D1 Truant I. i. Aust.
14 A3 Trubchevsk Rus. Fed.
14 D3 Trubetchino Rus. Fed.
15 D1 Trubizh r. Ukraine
24 C1 Truchas Spain
57 C4 Trucial Coast U.A.E.
49 K4 Trudovoye Rus. Fed.
14 C3 Trudy r. Rus. Fed.
130 J6 Trujillo Honduras
140 A1 Trujillo Peru
24 D3 Trujillo Spain
138 C2 Trujillo Venezuela
121 G4 Trumbull U.S.A.
129 F3 Trumbull, Mt mt. U.S.A.
28 D3 Trŭn Bulgaria
97 F3 Trundle Aust.
42 D4 Trung Hiệp Vietnam
42 D2 Trung Khanh Vietnam
131 H4 Truro Can.
17 E6 Truro U.K.
28 F1 Truşeşti Romania
15 E2 Trushivtsi Ukraine
28 E3 Trŭstenik Bulgaria
110 E3 Trutch Can.
127 F5 Truth or Consequences U.S.A.
19 G3 Trutnov Czech Rep.
20 F4 Truyère r. France
28 E3 Tryavna Bulgaria
15 A2 Trybukhivtsi Ukraine
11 D3 Trysil Norway
19 H2 Trzcianka Piła Poland
19 G2 Trzciel Poland
19 H2 Trzebiatów Poland
19 J3 Trzebinia Poland
19 H3 Trzebnica Poland
19 H2 Trzemeszno Poland
19 H2 Trzcińsko-Zdrój Poland
44 E2 Tsagaannuur Bayan Ölgiy Mongolia
49 F3 Tsagaannuur Dornod Mongolia
48 A3 Tsagaan-Olom Mongolia
48 D3 Tsagaan Ovoo Mongolia
13 H6 Tsagan Aman Rus. Fed.
48 D2 Tsagan Khurtey, Khr. mt. ra. Rus. Fed.
13 H6 Tsagan-Nur Rus. Fed.
54 D2 Tsaka La China
78 B4 Tsama I Congo
83 H2 Tsaratanana Madagascar
83 H1 Tsaratanana, Massif du mts Madagascar
83 H2 Tsaratanana, Réserve de res. Madagascar
14 B2 Tsarevo-Zaymishche Rus. Fed.
14 G3 Tsarevshchino Rus. Fed.
82 B3 Tsaris Mts mts Namibia
15 F2 Tsarychanka Ukraine
14 C1 Tsatsa Rus. Fed.
81 C5 Tsavo r. Kenya
81 C5 Tsavo National Park nat. park Kenya
15 D3 Tsebrykove Ukraine
65 L2 Tselinnoye Rus. Fed.
48 B2 Tsengel Mongolia
12 J3 Tsenogora Rus. Fed.
11 J3 Tsentral'nyy Rus. Fed.
14 D1 Tsentral'nyy Rus. Fed.
82 B4 Tses Namibia
82 C3 Tsetseng Botswana
48 B3 Tsetserleg Mongolia
77 E5 Tsévié Togo
74 C3 Tshabong Botswana
82 C4 Tshako Zaire
79 D5 Tshane Botswana
13 F6 Tshchikskoye Vdkhr. resr Rus. Fed.
79 B4 Tshela Zaire
79 D5 Tshibala Zaire
79 D5 Tshibwika Zaire
79 D5 Tshikapa r. Zaire
79 D5 Tshikapa Zaire
79 E5 Tshilenge Zaire
79 E5 Tshimbo Zaire
79 D5 Tshimbulu Zaire
79 D5 Tshinsenda Zaire
79 E5 Tshitanzu Zaire
79 C5 Tshofa Zaire
83 E3 Tshokwane R.S.A.
83 D5 Tsholotsho Zimbabwe
82 D3 Tshootsha Botswana
82 C3 Tshopo r. Zaire
78 D4 Tshuapa r. Zaire
13 G6 Tsimlyansk Rus. Fed.
13 G5 Tsimlyanskoye Vdkhr. resr Rus. Fed.
82 C4 Tsineng R.S.A.
83 G2 Tsingy de Bemaraha, Réserve res. Madagascar
45 □ Tsing Yi i. Hong Kong
83 H3 Tsiombe Madagascar
83 H2 Tsiroanomandidy Madagascar
83 H3 Tsitondroina Madagascar
110 D4 Tsitsutl Pk summit Can.
14 H2 Tsivil' r. Rus. Fed.
14 H2 Tsivil'sk Rus. Fed.
13 G7 Ts'khinvali Georgia
14 E3 Tsna r. Rus. Fed.
83 E2 Tsodilo Hills Botswana
54 D2 Tsokr Chumo l. India
83 D5 Tsolo R.S.A.
54 D2 Tso Morari L. l. India
13 G7 Tsqaltubo Georgia
47 F6 Tsu Japan
46 E2 Tsubetsu Japan
47 H5 Tsuchiura Japan
45 □ Tsuen Wan Hong Kong
46 H3 Tsugaru-kaikyō chan. Japan
47 G5 Tsugawa Japan
47 □2 Tsuha Japan
47 E6 Tsukechi Japan
47 □2 Tsuken-jima i. Japan
46 H2 Tsukigata Japan
47 H5 Tsukuba Japan
46 C7 Tsukumi Japan
48 C3 Tsul-Ulaan Mongolia
15 A1 Tsuman' Ukraine
82 B2 Tsumeb Namibia
82 B3 Tsumis Park Namibia
82 C2 Tsumkwe Namibia
46 C7 Tsuno Japan
46 C6 Tsuno-shima i. Japan
47 F6 Tsuruga Japan
46 E7 Tsurugi-san mt. Japan
46 D7 Tsurumi-zaki pt Japan
47 G4 Tsuruoka Japan
46 B6 Tsushima i. Japan
46 E6 Tsuwano Japan
46 E6 Tsuyama Japan
15 D2 Tsvitkove Ukraine
15 E2 Tsvitne Ukraine
82 D4 Tswelelang R.S.A.
15 C2 Tsybuliv Ukraine
10 J1 Tsyp-Navolok Rus. Fed.
15 E3 Tsyurupyns'k Ukraine
92 E2 Tuakau N.Z.
39 K8 Tual Indon.
17 C5 Tuam Rep. of Ire.
93 D4 Tuamarina N.Z.
91 □10 Tuamotu, Archipel des is Fr. Poly. Pac. Oc.
42 C2 Tuân Giao Vietnam
90 □3 Tu'anuku Tonga
13 F6 Tuapse Rus. Fed.
43 □ Tuas Singapore
91 □12 Tuasivi Western Samoa
93 A7 Tuatapere N.Z.
129 G3 Tuba City U.S.A.
40 C3 Tuban Indon.
143 C6 Tubarão Brazil
73 G1 Tubarjal Saudi Arabia
61 C3 Tubas Israel
41 A4 Tubbataha Reefs reef Phil.
18 D4 Tübingen Germany
76 B5 Tubmanburg Liberia
41 B4 Tubod Phil.
72 D1 Tubruq Libya
151 K7 Tubuai, Îles is Fr. Poly. Pac. Oc.
130 C2 Tubutama Mexico
133 E5 Tucacas Venezuela
142 E3 Tucano Brazil
146 B4 Tucapel, Pta hd Chile
141 E3 Tucavaca r. Bolivia
141 E3 Tucavaca Bolivia
110 D2 Tuchitua Can.
14 C2 Tuchkovo Rus. Fed.
19 H2 Tuchola Poland
19 K4 Tuchów Poland
15 B1 Tuchyn Ukraine
119 □1 Tucker's Town Bermuda
121 F5 Tuckerton U.S.A.
129 G5 Tucson U.S.A.
130 C1 Tucson airport U.S.A.
129 G5 Tucson Mts mts U.S.A.
146 C2 Tucuman div. Arg.
127 G5 Tucumcari U.S.A.
142 A2 Tucuparé Brazil
139 E2 Tucupita Venezuela
142 C1 Tucuruí Brazil
25 F1 Tudela Spain
24 D2 Tudela de Duero Spain
28 F2 Tudor Vladimirescu Romania
14 A1 Tudovka r. Rus. Fed.
24 C2 Tuela r. Portugal
45 □ Tuen Mun Hong Kong
55 H4 Tuensang India
142 B1 Tuerê r. Brazil
14 B1 Tufanovo Rus. Fed.
57 B4 Ţufayḩ Saudi Arabia
90 □1 Tufi P.N.G.
83 E4 Tugela r. R.S.A.
41 C4 Tugnug Point pt Phil.
14 D2 Tugolesskiy Bor Rus. Fed.
14 E4 Tugolukovo Rus. Fed.
50 C3 Tuguancun China
40 D1 Tuguan Maputi i. Indon.
41 B2 Tuguegarao Phil.
63 P4 Tugur Rus. Fed.
48 C1 Tugutuy Rus. Fed.
83 E3 Tugwi r. Zimbabwe
49 F5 Tuhai r. China
42 B1 Tuhtong Myanmar
24 B1 Tui Spain
25 □ Tuineje Canary Is Spain
130 L7 Tuira r. Panama
39 H8 Tukangbesi, Kepulauan is Indon.
112 E2 Tukarak Island i. Can.
81 D3 Tukayel Ethiopia
110 C2 Tukehe Nepal
61 A4 Tûkh Egypt
92 F3 Tukituki r. N.Z.
72 D1 Tükrah Libya
108 E3 Tuktoyaktuk Can.
11 F4 Tukums Latvia
40 B2 Tukung, Bukit mt. Indon.
81 B6 Tukuyu Tanzania
131 F4 Tula Mexico
91 □13 Tula American Samoa Pac. Oc.
14 C2 Tula Rus. Fed.
14 C2 Tula div. Rus. Fed.
55 G1 Tulagt Ar Gol r. China
54 E1 Tulai China
48 A5 Tulai Shan mt. ra. China
131 F4 Tulancingo Mexico
40 A3 Tulangbawang r. Indon.
128 C3 Tulare U.S.A.
128 C3 Tulare Lake Bed l. U.S.A.
127 F5 Tularosa U.S.A.
56 C2 Tulasi mt. India
138 B3 Tulcán Ecuador
28 G2 Tulcea Romania
15 C2 Tul'chyn Ukraine
128 C3 Tule r. U.S.A.
138 C1 Tule Venezuela
57 C2 Tuleh Iran
111 J2 Tulemalu Lake l. Can.
49 G3 Tule Mod China
28 E1 Tulgheș Romania
54 C4 Tulia U.S.A.
49 G2 Tulihe China
55 G3 Tuling P. China
19 J2 Tuliszków Poland
61 C3 Tulkarm West Bank
119 C5 Tullahoma U.S.A.
17 D4 Tullamore Aust.
97 F3 Tullamore Aust.
17 D5 Tullamore Rep. of Ire.
20 E4 Tulle France
10 D3 Tulleråsen Sweden
97 F3 Tullibigeal Aust.
19 H4 Tulln Austria
125 E6 Tullos U.S.A.
17 D5 Tullow Rep. of Ire.
99 F3 Tully Aust.
99 F3 Tully r. Aust.
121 E3 Tully U.S.A.
99 F3 Tully Falls waterfall Aust.
28 F2 Tulnici Romania
12 D5 Tulos Rus. Fed.
125 D4 Tulsa U.S.A.
90 □6 Tulu i. Fiji
138 B3 Tuluá Colombia
28 G2 Tulucești Romania
108 B3 Tuluksak U.S.A.
61 D3 Tulul el Ashaqif reg. Jordan
131 J4 Tulum Mexico
146 C3 Tulum, Valle de v. Arg.
44 H1 Tulun Rus. Fed.
40 D4 Tulungagung Indon.
55 H4 Tulung La China
41 A4 Tuluran i. Phil.
80 B3 Tulu Welel mt. Ethiopia
15 E1 Tulyholove Ukraine
14 E2 Tuma Rus. Fed.
138 B3 Tumaco Colombia
82 D4 Tumahole R.S.A.
55 G2 Tumain China
13 J6 Tumak Rus. Fed.
57 E2 Tūmān Āqā Iran
139 F2 Tumatumari Guyana
11 E4 Tumba Sweden
79 D4 Tumba Zaire
78 C4 Tumba, Lac l. Zaire
40 C2 Tumbangsamba Indon.
40 B2 Tumbangtiti Indon.
41 C5 Tumbao Phil.
97 G3 Tumbarumba Aust.
138 A4 Tumbes Peru
110 E3 Tumbler Ridge Can.
14 F2 Tumbotino Rus. Fed.
96 D3 Tumby Bay Aust.
48 D4 Tumd Youqi China
48 D4 Tumd Zuoqi China
49 J4 Tumen China
49 J4 Tumen r. China/North Korea
48 B5 Tumenzi China
139 E2 Tumeremo Venezuela
139 G3 Tumereng Guyana
41 A5 Tumindao i. Phil.
145 H3 Tumiritinga Brazil
56 B3 Tumkur India
72 B3 Tummo, Mountains of mts Libya/Niger
41 □2 Tumon Bay b. Guam Pac. Oc.
57 E4 Tump Pakistan
40 C2 Tumpah Indon.
97 G3 Tumut Aust.
65 J4 Tumxuk China
78 D3 Tuna, Pta pt Puerto Rico
133 □3 Tunapuna Trin. & Tobago
132 C2 Tunas de Zaza Cuba
57 C4 Tunb al Kubrá i. Iran
57 C4 Ţunb as Şughrá i. Iran
17 H6 Tunbridge Wells, Royal U.K.
60 D2 Tunceli Turkey
51 E5 Tunchang China
97 H3 Tuncurry Aust.
73 E4 Tundubai well Sudan
77 F4 Tundun-Wada Nigeria
81 C6 Tunduru Tanzania
28 F3 Tundzha r. Bulgaria
108 C3 Tunga Rus. Fed.
77 F5 Tunga Nigeria
56 B3 Tungabhadra r. India
56 B3 Tungabhadra Reservoir resr India
55 H3 Tunga Pass pass China/India
83 G3 Tungaru Sudan
41 B5 Tungawan Phil.
45 □ Tung Chung Wan b. Hong Kong
10 B2 Tungnaá r. Iceland
110 D2 Tungsten Can.
90 □5 Tungua i. Tonga
40 C1 Tungun, Bukit mt. Indon.
63 L3 Tunguska, Nizhnyaya r. Rus. Fed.
45 □ Tung Wan b. Hong Kong
56 C2 Tuni India
54 B4 Tuni r. India
114 E2 Tunis Can.
75 G1 Tunis Tunisia
75 G1 Tunis, Golfe de g. Tunisia
70 E2 Tunisia country Africa
138 C2 Tunja Colombia
48 B2 Tunka Rus. Fed.
48 B2 Tunkinskiye Gol'tsy mt. ra. Rus. Fed.
48 E5 Tunliu China
10 D2 Tunnsjøen l. Norway
11 C4 Tunoshna Rus. Fed.
10 H2 Tuntsa Finland
10 H2 Tuntsayoki r. Rus. Fed.
113 H2 Tunungayualok Island i. Can.
146 C3 Tunuyán Arg.
146 C3 Tunuyán r. Arg.
51 G1 Tuo r. China
50 D2 Tuo r. China
49 G5 Tuoji Dao i. China
43 D5 Tuôl Khpos Cambodia
128 B3 Tuolumne U.S.A.
128 C3 Tuolumne Meadows U.S.A.
50 D3 Tuoniang r. China
52 G2 Tuotuo r. China
55 H2 Tuotuoyan China
144 C4 Tupã Brazil
144 D3 Tupaciguara Brazil
143 B6 Tuparanceti Brazil
125 F5 Tupelo U.S.A.
143 B4 Tupinambarama, Ilha i. Brazil
144 C4 Tupi Paulista Brazil
142 C2 Tupiratins Brazil
140 C4 Tupiza Bolivia
121 F2 Tupper Lake l. U.S.A.
121 F2 Tupper Lake U.S.A.
146 C3 Tupungato Arg.
146 C3 Tupungato vol Arg.
60 F4 Tuqayyid well Iraq
49 G3 Tuquan China
138 B3 Túquerres Colombia
55 E5 Tuqu Wan China
55 G4 Tura India
63 M3 Tura Rus. Fed.
73 H3 Turabah Saudi Arabia
92 E4 Turakina N.Z.
93 E4 Turakirae Head hd N.Z.
57 D2 Turan Iran
48 B2 Turan Rus. Fed.
49 J2 Turana, Khrebet mt. ra. Rus. Fed.
92 E3 Turangi N.Z.
64 E5 Turan Lowland plain Asia
73 G1 Turayf Saudi Arabia
138 B1 Turbaco Colombia
80 D1 Turbah Yemen
57 E4 Turbat Pakistan
15 C2 Turbiv Ukraine
138 B2 Turbo Colombia
19 J4 Turčianske Teplice Slovakia
28 D2 Turcoaia Romania
18 D3 Turda Romania
14 D2 Turdey Rus. Fed.
101 B4 Turee Cr. r. Aust.
19 J2 Turek Poland
65 H2 Turgay Akmola Kazak.
64 F3 Turgay Turgay Kazak.
64 F2 Turgay r. Kazak.
65 G2 Turgay div. Kazak.
64 F2 Turgayskaya Dolina v. Kazak.
64 F2 Turgayskaya Stolovaya Strana reg. Kazak.
14 F2 Turgenevo Rus. Fed.
115 F2 Turgeon, Lac l. Can.
28 F3 Türgovishte Bulgaria
60 A2 Turgutlu Turkey
29 F6 Turgutreis Turkey
64 F1 Turhal Turkey
140 C4 Turi Chile
11 G4 Türi Estonia
25 F3 Turia r. Spain
142 C1 Turiaçu r. Brazil
142 C1 Turiaçu Brazil
62 H4 Turinsk Rus. Fed.
15 A1 Turiya r. Ukraine
49 J3 Turiy Rog Rus. Fed.
15 A1 Turiys'k Ukraine
44 J1 Turka Rus. Fed.
19 L4 Turka Ukraine
80 C4 Turkana, Lake salt l. Ethiopia/Kenya
60 F4 Türkeli Adası i. Turkey
65 G4 Turkestan Kazak.
65 G5 Turkestan Range mt. ra. Asia
32 E6 Turkey country Asia
122 B4 Turkey r. U.S.A.
100 E3 Turkey Creek Aust.
14 F4 Turki Rus. Fed.
60 B2 Türkmen Daği mt. Turkey
32 G6 Turkmenistan country Asia
57 E1 Turkmen-Kala Turkmenistan
64 D5 Turkmenskiy Zaliv b. Turkmenistan
60 D2 Türkoğlu Turkey
104 L8 Turks and Caicos Islands terr. Caribbean
133 E2 Turks I. Pass. chan. Turks and Caicos Is Caribbean
133 E2 Turks Is is Turks and Caicos Is Caribbean
11 F3 Turku Finland
11 F3 Turku-Pori div. Finland
80 C4 Turkwel r. Kenya
128 B3 Turlock U.S.A.
128 B3 Turlock L. l. U.S.A.
145 G2 Turmalina Brazil
73 H2 Turmus, W. at w Saudi Arabia
92 F4 Turnagain, Cape c. N.Z.
129 G5 Turnbull, Mt mt. U.S.A.
131 J5 Turneffe Is is Belize
100 B4 Turner r. Aust.
123 F3 Turner U.S.A.
18 B3 Turnhout Belgium
19 G5 Türnitz Austria
111 H3 Turnor Lake l. Can.
18 G3 Turnov Czech Rep.
28 E3 Turnu Măgurele Romania
65 L2 Turochak Rus. Fed.
97 G3 Turon r. Aust.
44 E3 Turpan China
44 E3 Turpan Pendi depression China
132 C3 Turquino mt. Cuba
16 F3 Turriff U.K.
60 F3 Tursāq Iraq
64 F4 Turtkul' Uzbekistan
122 B2 Turtle Flambeau Flowage resr U.S.A.
111 H4 Turtleford Can.
99 H3 Turtle I. i. Coral Sea Islands Terr. Pac. Oc.
41 A5 Turtle Islands is Phil.
76 B5 Turtle Islands is Sierra Leone
122 A3 Turtle Lake U.S.A.
65 J4 Turugart Pass pass China/Kyrgyzstan
62 K3 Turukhansk Rus. Fed.
139 F3 Turuna r. Brazil
48 C1 Turuntayevo Rus. Fed.
144 C2 Turvo r. Goiás Brazil
143 B6 Turvo r. Rio Grande do Sul Brazil
144 D5 Turvo r. São Paulo Brazil
144 D4 Turvo r. São Paulo Brazil
143 C6 Turvo Brazil
129 F4 Tusayan U.S.A.
119 C5 Tuscaloosa U.S.A.
27 C4 Tuscania Italy
120 C4 Tuscarawas r. U.S.A.
120 E4 Tuscarora Mts h. U.S.A.
122 C6 Tuscola U.S.A.
125 D5 Tuscola U.S.A.
57 D2 Tusharīk Iran
14 C4 Tuskar' r. Rus. Fed.
119 C5 Tuskegee U.S.A.
120 E4 Tussey Mts h. U.S.A.
19 J3 Tuszyn Poland
57 D3 Tūtak Iran
60 E2 Tutak Turkey
14 D1 Tutayev Rus. Fed.
56 B4 Tuticorin India
142 D1 Tutóia Brazil
28 F2 Tutrakan Bulgaria
124 D4 Tuttle Creek Res. resr U.S.A.
18 D5 Tuttlingen Germany
109 Q2 Tuttut Nunaat reg. Greenland
91 □13 Tutuila i. American Samoa Pac. Oc.
82 D3 Tutume Botswana
131 F5 Tututepec Mexico
48 C2 Tuul Gol r. Mongolia
49 H4 Tuun, Mt mt. N. Korea
10 H3 Tuupovaara Finland
10 H3 Tuusniemi Finland
91 □16 Tuutapu h. Easter I. Chile
86 J5 Tuvalu country Pac. Oc.
90 □8 Tuvuca i. Fiji
90 □7 Tuvutau h. Fiji
10 D1 Tuwau r. Indon.
61 D4 Tuweiyil esh Shiqāq mt. Jordan
130 E5 Tuxpan Jalisco Mexico
131 F4 Tuxpan Veracruz Mexico
131 G5 Tuxtla Gutiérrez Mexico
43 D4 Tuy Đuc Vietnam
42 D2 Tuyên Quang Vietnam
43 E4 Tuy Hoa Vietnam
64 D2 Tuymazy Rus. Fed.
57 B2 Tūysarkān Iran
60 C2 Tuz Gölü salt l. Turkey
14 H3 Tuzha Rus. Fed.
28 B3 Tuzi Yugo.
129 F4 Tuzigoot National Monument res. U.S.A.
60 F3 Tuz Khurmātū Iraq
28 G3 Tuzla Bos.-Herz.
28 G3 Tuzla Romania
60 E2 Tuzla r. Turkey
60 D2 Tuzla Turkey
13 F6 Tuzlov r. Rus. Fed.
72 G3 Tuzugu well Libya
11 C4 Tvedestrand Norway
14 B1 Tver' div. Rus. Fed.
14 B1 Tver' Rus. Fed.
14 B1 Tvertsa r. Rus. Fed.
16 D1 Tvøroyri Faeroes
28 E3 Tvŭrditsa Bulgaria
19 H3 Twardogóra Poland
115 G4 Tweed Can.
16 F4 Tweed r. U.K.
110 D4 Tweedsmuir Prov. Park res. Can.
24 B4 Twentynine Palms U.S.A.
113 K4 Twillingate Can.
126 D2 Twin Bridges U.S.A.
126 D3 Twin Buttes Res. resr U.S.A.
113 H3 Twin Falls Can.
126 D3 Twin Falls U.S.A.
100 D4 Twin Heads h. Aust.
126 D3 Twin Lakes Can.
121 H2 Twin Mountain U.S.A.
120 C6 Twin Oaks U.S.A.
128 B2 Twin Peak summit U.S.A.
96 C2 Twins, The Aust.
97 G4 Twofold B. b. Aust.
129 G4 Two Guns U.S.A.
122 B2 Two Harbors U.S.A.
111 G4 Two Hills Can.
126 D1 Two Medicine r. U.S.A.
122 D3 Two Rivers U.S.A.
28 D1 Tyachiv Ukraine
55 H5 Tyao r. India
15 E2 Tyasmyn r. Ukraine
46 L1 Tyatya mt. Rus. Fed.
19 L4 Tyczyn Poland
10 C3 Tydal Norway
120 D5 Tygart Lake l. U.S.A.
120 D5 Tygart Valley v. U.S.A.
49 H1 Tygda Rus. Fed.
29 F4 Tykhero Greece
125 E5 Tyler U.S.A.
125 F6 Tylertown U.S.A.
15 D3 Tylihul r. Ukraine
15 E2 Tymchenky Ukraine
29 C5 Tymfi mts Greece
15 F3 Tymoshivka Ukraine
29 E7 Tympaki Greece
63 O4 Tynda Rus. Fed.
110 A2 Tyndall Gl. gl. U.S.A.
15 D2 Tynivka Ukraine
15 B1 Tynne Ukraine
11 C3 Tynset Norway
97 E3 Tyrell, L. l. Aust.
111 H2 Tyrell Lake l. Can.
49 K2 Tyrma Rus. Fed.
49 J2 Tyrma r. Rus. Fed.
10 G2 Tyrnävä Finland
29 D5 Tyrnavos Greece
14 D2 Tyrnovo Rus. Fed.
120 D4 Tyrone U.S.A.
97 E3 Tyrrell r. Aust.
97 E3 Tyrrell, L. l. Aust.
27 C5 Tyrrhenian Sea sea Italy
28 D1 Tysa r. Romania/Ukraine
15 D2 Tyshkivka Ukraine
15 A2 Tysmenytsya Ukraine
15 D2 Tysmenytsya r. Ukraine
16 K1 Tysnesøy i. Norway
16 K1 Tysse Norway
19 L3 Tyszowce Poland
65 J4 Tyubelyakh Rus. Fed.
64 C3 Tyub-Karagan, Mys hd Kazak.
65 H1 Tyukalinsk Rus. Fed.
64 D4 Tyulen'i, Ostrova is Kazak.
64 E2 Tyul'gan Rus. Fed.
65 G1 Tyumen' Rus. Fed.
62 H4 Tyumen' Rus. Fed.
65 G4 Tyumen'-Aryk Kazak.
65 K2 Tyumentsevo Rus. Fed.
63 N3 Tyung r. Rus. Fed.
10 J1 Tyuva-Guba Rus. Fed.
48 A2 Tyva div. Rus. Fed.
15 C2 Tyvriv Ukraine
17 E6 Tywi r. U.K.
83 E3 Tzaneen R.S.A.

U

139 E3 Uacauyén Venezuela
91 □12 Uafato Western Samoa
79 D7 Uamanda Angola
139 D4 Uarini Brazil
139 F4 Uatumã r. Brazil
142 E2 Uauá Brazil
142 B2 Uaupés Brazil
138 D3 Uaupés r. Brazil
131 H5 Uaxactún Guatemala
28 C2 Ub Yugo.
145 G4 Ubá Brazil
65 K2 Uba r. Kazak.
77 G4 Uba Nigeria
65 F2 Ubagan r. Kazak.
145 F4 Ubaí Brazil
72 F5 Ubaid well Sudan
145 H4 Ubaitaba Brazil
64 E4 Ubal Karabaur h. Uzbekistan
78 C3 Ubangi r. C.A.R./Zaire
15 C1 Ubarts r. Belarus
138 C2 Ubate Colombia
145 F5 Ubatuba Brazil
80 D2 Ubaydīyah Yemen
21 H4 Ubaye r. France
60 E4 Ubayyia, Wādī al w Iraq/Saudi Arabia
60 E3 Ubayyid, Wādī al w Iraq
46 C7 Ube Japan
24 E3 Úbeda Spain
144 D3 Uberaba r. Brazil
144 E3 Uberaba Brazil
141 E3 Uberaba, Lagoa l. Brazil
144 D3 Uberlândia Brazil
18 D5 Überlingen Germany
43 □ Ubin, Pulau i. Singapore
65 J1 Ubinskoye Rus. Fed.
65 K1 Ubinskoye, Ozero l. Rus. Fed.
144 B6 Ubiratã Brazil
42 C3 Ubolratna Res. resr Thailand
83 E4 Ubombo R.S.A.
43 D4 Ubon Ratchathani Thailand
15 B1 Ubort' r. Ukraine
24 D4 Ubrique Spain
79 E4 Ubundu Zaire
64 F1 Ucar Azerbaijan
61 B1 Uçarı Turkey
138 C5 Ucayali r. Peru
24 E2 Ucero r. Spain
57 E1 Uch-Adzhi Turkmenistan
64 E2 Uchaly Rus. Fed.
57 E3 Üchān Iran
65 K3 Ucharal Kazak.
47 D7 Uchiko Japan
46 C8 Uchinoura Japan
47 C1 Uchinskoye Vdkhr. resr Rus. Fed.
46 H2 Uchiura-wan b. Japan
41 A1 Uchiza Peru
64 F4 Uchkuduk Uzbekistan
57 F1 Uchkyay Uzbekistan
64 F4 Uchsay Uzbekistan
54 A4 Uchto r. Pakistan
17 H6 Uckfield U.K.
110 D5 Ucluelet Can.
129 H3 Ucolo U.S.A.
126 F2 Ucross U.S.A.
18 D1 Uda r. Rus. Fed.
15 E2 Uda r. Ukraine
64 C3 Udachnoye Rus. Fed.
63 N3 Udachnyy Rus. Fed.
56 B4 Udagamandalam India
55 G5 Udaipur India
54 C4 Udaipur India
54 D5 Udaipura India
55 F4 Udaipur Garhi Nepal
55 H4 Udalguri India
55 E5 Udanti r. India/Myanmar
15 E1 Uday r. Ukraine
56 B3 Udayagiri India
56 B4 Uddevalla Sweden
10 E2 Uddjaure l. Sweden
56 B2 Udgir India
54 C2 Udhampur India
12 H2 Udimskiy Rus. Fed.
26 D2 Udine Italy
21 Q2 Udjuktok Bay b. Can.
12 E3 Udomlya Rus. Fed.
42 C3 Udon Thani Thailand
63 P4 Udskaya Guba b. Rus. Fed.
56 B4 Udumalaippetai India
56 A3 Udupi India
90 □6 Udu Pt pt Fiji
15 G1 Udy Ukraine
63 P4 Udyl', Ozero l. Rus. Fed.
19 F2 Uecker r. Germany
19 G2 Ueckermünde Germany
47 G5 Ueda Japan
40 E2 Uekuli Indon.
78 D3 Uele r. Zaire
108 B3 Uelen Rus. Fed.
108 A3 Uel'kal Rus. Fed.
18 E2 Uelzen Germany
47 F6 Ueno Japan
78 E3 Uere r. Zaire
64 E1 Ufa r. Rus. Fed.
64 E2 Ufa Rus. Fed.
80 B2 Uffat r. Sudan
18 E4 Uffenheim Germany
82 B3 Ugab w Namibia
81 B6 Ugalla r. Tanzania
81 B6 Ugalla River Game Reserve res. Tanzania
69 H5 Uganda country Africa
48 E1 Ugdan Rus. Fed.
27 G6 Ugento Italy
16 K1 Uggdal Norway
79 F5 Ughelli Nigeria
45 Q2 Uglegorsk Rus. Fed.
14 D1 Uglich Rus. Fed.
26 E3 Ugljan i. Croatia
14 J2 Uglovoye Rus. Fed.
65 K2 Uglovskoye Rus. Fed.
63 Q3 Ugol'naya Zyryanka Rus. Fed.
63 T3 Ugol'nyye Kopi Rus. Fed.
14 B2 Ugra r. Rus. Fed.
14 B2 Ugra Rus. Fed.
19 H4 Uherské Hradiště Czech Rep.
18 F4 Úhlava r. Czech Rep.
19 L3 Uhniv Ukraine
120 C4 Uhrichsville U.S.A.
15 F1 Uhroyidy Ukraine
79 C5 Uige Angola
79 C5 Uíge div. Angola
90 □5 'Uiha i. Tonga
49 H5 Ŭijŏngbu S. Korea
14 E3 Uiju N. Korea
65 E3 Uil r. Kazak.
64 D3 Uil Kazak.
13 G7 Uilpata mt. Rus. Fed.
10 H3 Uimaharju Finland
129 F3 Uinkaret Plateau plat. U.S.A.
116 D3 Uinta Mts mts U.S.A.
46 B6 Ŭiryŏng S. Korea
82 A3 Uis Mine Namibia
49 J5 Ŭisŏng S. Korea
82 D5 Uitenhage R.S.A.
18 C2 Uithuizen Netherlands
113 H2 Uivak, Cape hd Can.
19 K5 Újfehértó Hungary
54 D4 Ujhani India
47 E6 Uji Japan
46 B8 Uji-guntō is Japan
81 A5 Ujiji Tanzania
54 C5 Ujjain India
19 H2 Ujście Poland
40 D4 Ujung Pandang Indon.
47 □2 Uka Japan
77 F4 Ukata Nigeria
81 B5 Ukerewe I. i. Tanzania
73 H4 Ukhdūd Saudi Arabia
14 E3 Ukholovo Rus. Fed.
55 H4 Ukhrul India
12 K2 Ukhta r. Rus. Fed.
12 E1 Ukhtokhma r. Rus. Fed.
128 A2 Ukiah U.S.A.
126 C2 Ukiah U.S.A.
109 N2 Ukkusissat Greenland
11 G5 Ukmergė Lithuania
5 H4 Ukraine country Europe
15 D1 Ukrayinka Ukraine
26 F4 Ukrina r. Bos.-Herz.
12 J2 Uktym Rus. Fed.
79 B6 Uku Angola
46 B7 Uku-jima i. Japan
82 C3 Ukwi Pan salt pan Botswana
54 D2 Ul r. India
29 G6 Ula Turkey
48 C3 Ulaanbaatar Mongolia
48 D3 Ulaan-Ereg Mongolia
44 F2 Ulaangom Mongolia
48 B3 Ulaanhudag Mongolia
48 B3 Ulaan Nuur l. Mongolia
48 D3 Ulaan-Uul Mongolia
15 C2 Uladivka Ukraine
97 G3 Ulan Aust.
52 J3 Ulan China
65 H4 Ulanbel' Kazak.
48 C3 Ulan Buh Shamo desert China
48 C1 Ulan-Burgasy, Khr. mt. ra. Rus. Fed.
13 H6 Ulan Erge Rus. Fed.
15 C2 Ulaniv Ukraine
48 B4 Ulanove Rus. Fed.
48 B4 Ulansuhai Nur l. China
49 B4 Ulan Tohoi China
48 C2 Ulan-Ude Rus. Fed.
53 D2 Ulan Ul Hu l. China
60 D2 Ulaş Sivas Turkey
29 F4 Ulaş Tekirdağ Turkey
90 □1 Ulawa I. i. Solomon Is.
65 K2 Ul'ba Kazak.
49 J5 Ulchin S. Korea
28 B4 Ulcinj Yugo.
48 D2 Uldz r. Mongolia
48 D2 Uldz Mongolia
11 C4 Ulefoss Norway
11 G4 Ülenurme Estonia
48 G2 Ulety Rus. Fed.
49 F3 Ulgain Gol r. China
65 G2 Ul'gili Kazak.
56 A2 Ulhasnagar India
48 A3 Uliastay Mongolia
78 E4 Ulindi r. Zaire
39 L4 Ulithi i. Fed. States of Micronesia
64 F3 Ul'kayak r. Kazak.
97 G3 Ulladulla Aust.
16 E3 Ullapool U.K.
16 F3 Ullava Finland
25 G2 Ulldecona Spain
17 F4 Ullswater l. U.K.
49 J5 Ullŭng S. Korea
49 K5 Ullŭng do i. S. Korea
18 D4 Ulm Germany
49 J2 Ul'ma r. Rus. Fed.
97 F2 Ulmarra Aust.
28 F2 Ulmeni Călăraşi Romania
28 D1 Ulmeni Maramureș Romania
26 G4 Ulog Bos.-Herz.
83 E1 Ulongue Mozambique
96 D1 Uloowaranie, L. salt flat Aust.
11 D4 Ulricehamn Sweden
49 J6 Ulsan S. Korea
10 C3 Ulsberg Norway
17 D4 Ulster reg. Rep. of Ire./U.K.
97 E3 Ultima Aust.
29 G4 Ulubat Gölü l. Turkey
60 B2 Uluborlu Turkey
60 B1 Uludağ mt. Turkey
50 F5 Ulugqat China
90 □6 Ulugalau mt. Fiji
43 C7 Ulu Kali, Gunung mt. Malaysia
60 C2 Ulukışla Turkey
83 E4 Ulundi R.S.A.
65 L3 Ulungur Hu l. China
43 □ Ulu Pandan Singapore
98 B5 Uluru Nat. Park nat. park Aust.
13 E7 Ulus Turkey
17 F4 Ulverston U.K.
97 F5 Ulverstone Aust.
11 D3 Ulvsjön Sweden

14 C1 Ul'yanikha Rus. Fed.
12 H4 Ul'yankovo Rus. Fed.
15 D2 Ul'yanovka Ukraine
14 B3 Ul'yanovo Rus. Fed.
12 J4 Ul'yanovsk Rus. Fed.
14 H3 Ul'yanovsk div. Rus. Fed.
65 H2 Ul'yanovskiy Kazak.
49 F2 Ulyatuy Rus. Fed.
125 C4 Ulysses U.S.A.
65 G3 Ulytau Kazak.
65 G3 Ulyzhilanshik r. Kazak.
49 G1 Uma Rus. Fed.
131 H4 Umán Mexico
15 D2 Uman' Ukraine
146 C2 Umango, Co mt. Arg.
54 A3 Umarao Pakistan
54 E5 Umaria India
56 B2 Umarkhed India
56 C2 Umarkot India
54 B4 Umarkot Pakistan
41 □2 Umatac *Guam* Pac. Oc.
126 C2 Umatilla U.S.A.
12 E1 Umba Rus. Fed.
121 H2 Umbagog Lake l. U.S.A.
78 D2 Umbelasha w Sudan
26 D4 Umbertide Italy
90 □1 Umboi i. P.N.G.
93 B6 Umbrella Mts mts N.Z.
133 □1 Umbrella Pt pt Jamaica
26 D4 Umbria div. Italy
83 D2 Ume r. Zimbabwe
10 F3 Umeå Sweden
10 D2 Umeälven r. Sweden
61 C3 Um ed Daraj, J. mt. Jordan
14 F3 Umet Rus. Fed.
14 F2 Umet Rus. Fed.
108 H3 Umingmaktok Can.
112 E2 Umiujaq Can.
83 E4 Umlazi R.S.A.
73 G3 Umm al Birak Saudi Arabia
57 C4 Umm al Qaywayn U.A.E.
73 H2 Umm at Qalbān Saudi Arabia
57 B4 Umm Bāb Qatar
73 E5 Umm Bel Sudan
61 B5 Umm Bugma Egypt
72 C2 Umm Farud Libya
73 F3 Umm Gerifat waterhole Sudan
73 E5 Umm Keddada Sudan
73 G2 Umm Lajj Saudi Arabia
61 C5 Umm Mafrûd, G. mt. Egypt
61 C5 Umm Nukhaylah well Saudi Arabia
60 F4 Umm Qasr Iraq
73 E4 Umm Qurein well Sudan
73 F5 Umm Rimtha well Sudan
73 F5 Umm Ruwaba Sudan
72 E1 Umm Sa'ad Libya
73 F5 Umm Saiyala Sudan
61 D5 Umm Shajtiya waterhole Saudi Arabia
61 B5 Umm Shomar, G. mt. Egypt
73 E4 Umm Sunaita well Sudan
61 B5 Umm Tinâṣṣib, G. mt. Egypt
73 G2 Umm Urūmah i. Saudi Arabia
61 B5 Umm Zanatir mt. Egypt
104 B4 Umnak I. i. U.S.A.
83 F1 Umpilua Mozambique
126 A3 Umpqua r. U.S.A.
79 C6 Umpulo Angola
54 D5 Umred India
56 A1 Umreth India
83 D5 Umtata R.S.A.
77 F5 Umuahia Nigeria
144 B5 Umuarama Brazil
90 □3 Umuna i. Tonga
29 F4 Umurbey Turkey
83 E5 Umzinto R.S.A.
26 F3 Una r. Bos.-Herz./Croatia
145 J1 Una Brazil
61 D4 'Unāb, W. al w Jordan
145 E2 Unaí Brazil
57 G2 Unai P. pass Afghanistan
108 B3 Unalakleet U.S.A.
108 B4 Unalaska U.S.A.
108 B4 Unalaska I. i. U.S.A.
81 C7 Unango Mozambique
60 C4 'Unayzah Jordan
73 H2 'Unayzah Saudi Arabia
54 E4 Unchahra India
140 C3 Uncia Bolivia
127 E4 Uncompahgre Plateau plat. U.S.A.
49 F2 Unda r. Rus. Fed.
49 F2 Unda Rus. Fed.
96 E3 Underbool Aust.
124 C2 Underwood U.S.A.
40 E4 Undu, Tg pt Indon.
13 D4 Unecha Rus. Fed.
14 H2 Unga r. Rus. Fed.
108 B4 Unga I. i. U.S.A.
97 F3 Ungarie Aust.
113 G2 Ungava Bay b. Can.
112 F1 Ungava, Péninsule d' pen. Can.
49 J4 Unggi N. Korea
15 B3 Ungheni Moldova
28 E1 Unguraşi Romania
81 D5 Ungwana Bay b. Kenya
12 J3 Uni Rus. Fed.
142 D1 União Brazil
143 B6 União da Vitória Brazil
142 E2 União dos Palmares Brazil
54 D4 Uniara India
19 J3 Uniejów Poland
108 B4 Unimak I. i. U.S.A.
139 E4 Unini r. Brazil
140 B2 Unini Peru
141 E4 Unión Paraguay
133 G4 Union i. St Vincent
121 J2 Union U.S.A.
119 D5 Union U.S.A.
120 C6 Union U.S.A.
120 A4 Union City U.S.A.
120 D4 Union City U.S.A.
119 B4 Union City U.S.A.
129 F4 Union, Mt mt. U.S.A.
119 C5 Union Springs U.S.A.
120 D5 Uniontown U.S.A.
81 □4 Union Vale Mauritius
123 F4 Unionville U.S.A.
126 E3 Unita Mts. mts U.S.A.
32 G7 United Arab Emirates country Asia
4 E3 United Kingdom country Europe
104 H6 United States of America country N. America
111 H4 Unity Can.
121 J2 Unity U.S.A.
126 C2 Unity U.S.A.
82 A3 Unjab w Namibia
54 C5 Unjha India
54 E4 Unnão India
49 H5 Ŭnp'a N. Korea
49 H5 Ŭnsan N. Korea
16 G1 Unst i. U.K.
47 □2 Unten Japan
55 G2 Unuli Horog China
46 C7 Unzen-dake vol Japan
47 F5 Uozu Japan
14 C2 Upa r. Rus. Fed.
55 F5 Upar Ghat India
139 E2 Upata Venezuela
79 E5 Upemba, Lac l. Zaire
79 E5 Upemba, Parc National de l' nat. park Zaire
109 N2 Upernavik Greenland
109 N2 Upernavik Kujalleq Greenland
41 C5 Upi Phil.
138 C3 Upía r. Colombia
82 C4 Upington R.S.A.
54 B5 Upleta India
10 H2 Upoloksha Rus. Fed.
91 □12 Upolu i. Western Samoa
120 B4 Upper Arlington U.S.A.
110 F4 Upper Arrow L. l. Can.
76 D4 Upper East div. Ghana
93 E4 Upper Hutt N.Z.
122 B4 Upper Iowa r. U.S.A.
121 K1 Upper Kent Can.
126 B3 Upper Klamath L. l. U.S.A.
126 B3 Upper L. l. U.S.A.
128 A2 Upper Lake U.S.A.
110 D2 Upper Liard Can.
17 D4 Upper Lough Erne l. U.K.
133 □3 Upper Manzanilla Trin. & Tobago
120 E5 Upper Marlboro U.S.A.
80 B3 Upper Nile div. Sudan
43 □ Upper Peirce Res. resr Singapore
113 J4 Upper Salmon Reservoir resr Can.
120 B4 Upper Sandusky U.S.A.
121 F2 Upper Saranac Lake l. U.S.A.
93 D4 Upper Takaka N.Z.
76 D4 Upper West div. Ghana
11 E4 Uppsala div. Sweden
11 E4 Uppsala Sweden
112 B4 Upsala Can.
54 D2 Upshi India
99 F3 Upstart B. b. Aust.
99 F3 Upstart, C. hd Aust.
121 H2 Upton U.S.A.
92 E1 Upua N.Z.
61 D2 'Uqayribāt Syria
61 C4 'Uqeiqa, W. w Jordan
60 F4 Uqlat al 'Udhaybah well Iraq
73 H2 'Uqlat aş Şuqūr Saudi Arabia
138 B2 Urabá, Golfo de b. Colombia
48 D4 Urad Qianqi China
48 D4 Urad Zhonghou Lianheqi China
57 D3 Ūrāf Iran
47 G6 Uraga-suid ō chan. Japan
47 G5 Uragawara Japan
46 J2 Urahoro Japan
144 C5 Uraí Brazil
46 J2 Urakawa Japan
97 F3 Ural h. Aust.
64 D2 Ural r. Kazak./Rus. Fed.
97 G2 Uralla Aust.
64 D2 Ural'sk Kazak.
62 G4 Ural'skiy Khrebet mt. ra. Rus. Fed.
81 B6 Urambo Tanzania
97 F3 Urana Aust.
97 F3 Urana, L. l. Aust.
98 D4 Urandangi Aust.
145 G1 Urandi Brazil
111 H3 Uranium City Can.
139 E3 Uraricoera Brazil
139 E3 Uraricuera r. Brazil
47 □2 Urasoe Japan
129 H2 Uravan U.S.A.
14 G2 Urazovka Rus. Fed.
122 C5 Urbana U.S.A.
120 B4 Urbana U.S.A.
142 D1 Urbano Santos Brazil
26 D4 Urbino Italy
140 B2 Urcos Peru
13 H5 Urda Kazak.
24 E3 Urda Spain
12 J2 Urdoma Rus. Fed.
65 K3 Urdzhar Kazak.
17 G4 Ure r. U.K.
12 H3 Uren' Rus. Fed.
62 J3 Urengoy Rus. Fed.
14 H2 Ureno-Karlinskoye Rus. Fed.
92 E3 Urenui N.Z.
90 □2 Uréparapara i. Vanuatu
92 F3 Urewera National Park nat. park N.Z.
61 B6 'Urf, G. el mt. Egypt
14 G2 Urga r. Rus. Fed.
49 K2 Urgal r. Rus. Fed.
64 F4 Urgench Uzbekistan
60 C2 Ürgüp Turkey
65 L3 Urho China
10 G1 Urho Kekkosen kansallispuisto nat. park Finland
54 C2 Uri India
93 C5 Uriah, Mt mt. N.Z.
138 C1 Uribia Colombia
97 E2 Urisino Aust.
65 G2 Uritskiy Kazak.
14 D4 Uritskoye Rus. Fed.
80 C2 Urī Wenz r. Ethiopia
11 F3 Urjala Finland
60 A2 Urla Turkey
28 F2 Urlaţi Romania
48 C2 Urluk Rus. Fed.
49 K2 Urmi r. Rus. Fed.
45 □ Urmston Road chan. Hong Kong
77 F5 Uromi Nigeria
28 C3 Uroševac Yugo.
65 G5 Ŭroteppa Tajikistan
55 F3 Urru Co salt l. China
14 E2 Urshel'skiy Rus. Fed.
19 L3 Urszulin Poland
48 B4 Urt Mongolia
144 D1 Uru r. Brazil
130 C3 Uruáchic Mexico
142 C3 Uruaçu Brazil
144 D1 Uruana Brazil
130 E5 Uruapan Mexico
140 B2 Urubamba r. Peru
139 F4 Urubu r. Brazil
144 C4 Urubupungá, Salto do waterfall Brazil
139 F4 Urucara Brazil
14 A3 Uruch'ye Rus. Fed.
139 F5 Urucu r. Brazil
145 J1 Uruçuca Brazil
142 D2 Uruçuí Brazil
145 F2 Urucuia r. Brazil
145 F2 Urucuia Brazil
142 C2 Uruçuí Prêto r. Brazil
139 F4 Urucurituba Brazil
143 B6 Uruguai r. Brazil
146 E2 Uruguaiana Brazil
139 F5 Uruguatos r. Brazil
146 E3 Uruguay r. Arg./Uruguay
136 E6 Uruguay country S. America
49 H2 Uruhe China
41 □1 Urukthapel i. Palau
61 D1 Urūmaş Şughrá Syria
44 E3 Ürümqi China
97 H2 Urunga Aust.
13 G6 Urup r. Rus. Fed.
63 R5 Urup, O. i. Rus. Fed.
13 H7 Urus-Martan Rus. Fed.
14 F3 Urusovo Rus. Fed.
64 D2 Urussu Rus. Fed.
144 D2 Urutaí Brazil
92 E3 Uruti N.Z.
65 L3 Uryl' Kazak.
46 H2 Uryūgawa r. Japan
49 G1 Uryupino Rus. Fed.
13 G5 Uryupinsk Rus. Fed.
12 J3 Urzhum Rus. Fed.
28 F2 Urziceni Romania
46 C7 Usa Japan
12 J4 Usa r. Rus. Fed.
29 G5 Uşak div. Turkey
60 B2 Uşak Turkey
82 B3 Usakos Namibia
152 B5 Usarp Mts mts Ant.
147 E7 Usborne, Mt h. Falkland Is.
28 C3 Ušće Yugo.
19 F2 Usedom Germany
19 G2 Usedom i. Germany
101 A5 Useless Loop Aust.
73 G3 Usfān Saudi Arabia
62 J1 Ushakova, O. i. Rus. Fed.
73 H3 'Ushayrah Saudi Arabia
48 A2 Ush-Bel'dyr Rus. Fed.
46 C7 Ushibuka Japan
14 F3 Ushinka Rus. Fed.
14 E2 Ushna Rus. Fed.
14 E2 Ushna r. Rus. Fed.
65 J3 Ushtobe Kazak.
147 C7 Ushuaia Arg.
49 H1 Ushumun Rus. Fed.
55 E4 Uska India
14 D3 Usman' r. Rus. Fed.
14 D3 Usman' Rus. Fed.
11 F4 Usmas Ezers l. Latvia
24 D3 Uso r. Spain
12 J2 Usogorsk Rus. Fed.
44 H1 Usol'ye-Sibirskoye Rus. Fed.
14 B3 Usozha r. Rus. Fed.
15 G3 Uspenivka Ukraine
65 J2 Uspenka Kazak.
15 E1 Uspenka Ukraine
65 H3 Uspenskiy Kazak.
13 G6 Uspenskoye Rus. Fed.
20 F4 Ussel *Limousin* France
49 J4 Ussuriysk Rus. Fed.
12 H3 Usta r. Rus. Fed.
65 M2 Ust'-Abakan Rus. Fed.
12 H2 Ust'- Alekseyevo Rus. Fed.
54 B3 Usta Muhammad Pakistan
64 F1 Ust'-Bagaryak Rus. Fed.
45 J1 Ust'-Barguzin Rus. Fed.
12 K2 Ust'-Chernaya Rus. Fed.
49 F1 Ust'-Chernaya Rus. Fed.
13 G6 Ust'-Donetskiy Rus. Fed.
27 D6 Ustica, Isola di i. Italy
63 M4 Ust'Ilimsk Rus. Fed.
48 E2 Ust'-Ilya Rus. Fed.
62 G3 Ust'-Ilych Rus. Fed.
19 G3 Ústí nad Labem Czech Rep.
19 H4 Ústí nad Orlicí Czech Rep.
19 H1 Ustka Poland
63 S4 Ust'-Kamchatsk Rus. Fed.
65 K3 Ust'-Kamenogorsk Kazak.
65 K2 Ust'-Kan Rus. Fed.
49 F1 Ust'-Karsk Rus. Fed.
64 E2 Ust'-Katav Rus. Fed.
65 L2 Ust'-Koksa Rus. Fed.
12 K2 Ust'-Kulom Rus. Fed.
63 M4 Ust'-Kut Rus. Fed.
63 P2 Ust'-Kuyga Rus. Fed.
13 F6 Ust'-Labinsk Rus. Fed.
49 G1 Ust'-Lubiya Rus. Fed.
11 H4 Ust'-Luga Rus. Fed.
63 P3 Ust'-Maya Rus. Fed.
62 K3 Ust-Mukduyka Rus. Fed.
49 F1 Ust'-Nachin Rus. Fed.
63 Q3 Ust'-Nera Rus. Fed.
49 K2 Ust'-Niman Rus. Fed.
63 N2 Ust'-Olenek Rus. Fed.
63 Q3 Ust'omchug Rus. Fed.
48 C1 Ust'-Ordynskiy Buryatskiy Avt. Okrug div. Rus. Fed.
63 S3 Ust' Penzhino Rus. Fed.
28 F3 Ustrem Bulgaria
19 L4 Ustrzyki Dolne Poland
14 F4 Ust'-Shcherbedino Rus. Fed.
65 J1 Ust'-Tarka Rus. Fed.
49 J2 Ust'-Tyrma Rus. Fed.
49 K2 Ust'-Umalta Rus. Fed.
12 H2 Ust'-Ura Rus. Fed.
49 K2 Ust'-Urgal Rus. Fed.
64 F2 Ust'-Uyskoye Kazak.
12 G2 Ust'-Vayen'ga Rus. Fed.
12 H2 Ust'-Vyyskaya Rus. Fed.
12 H2 Ust'ya r. Rus. Fed.
14 D1 Ust'ye r. Rus. Fed.
14 E3 Ust'ye Rus. Fed.
12 F3 Ust'ye Rus. Fed.
19 L3 Ustyluh Ukraine
15 A1 Ustyluh Ukraine
15 E3 Ustynivka Ukraine
64 D4 Ustyurta escarpment Kazak.
64 E4 Ustyurt, Plato plat. Uzbekistan
12 F3 Ustyuzhna Rus. Fed.
65 K4 Usu China
47 G5 Usuda Japan
46 C7 Usuki Japan
130 H6 Usulután El Salvador
131 H5 Usumacinta r. Mexico
12 D4 Usvyaty Rus. Fed.
129 G2 Utah div. U.S.A.
129 G1 Utah Lake l. U.S.A.
10 G2 Utajärvi Finland
46 J2 Utashinai Japan
46 K1 Utashinai Rus. Fed.
90 □3 'Uta Vava'u i. Tonga
73 H3 'Utaybah reg. Saudi Arabia
57 B4 Utayyiq Saudi Arabia
25 F2 Utebo Spain
79 D7 Utembo r. Angola
11 G5 Utena Lithuania
81 C6 Utete Tanzania
54 A4 Uthal Pakistan
61 D2 'Uthmānīyah Syria
43 B4 U Thong Thailand
141 E2 Utiariti Brazil
121 F3 Utica U.S.A.
25 F3 Utiel Spain
110 F3 Utikuma Lake l. Can.
142 D3 Utinga r. Brazil
15 F3 Utlyuks'kyy Lyman est. Ukraine
46 C7 Uto Japan
55 E4 Utraula India
18 B2 Utrecht Netherlands
18 B2 Utrecht div. Netherlands
24 D4 Utrera Spain
16 K2 Utsira Norway
10 G1 Utsjoki Finland
47 G5 Utsunomiya Japan
13 H6 Utta Rus. Fed.
42 C3 Uttaradit Thailand
54 D3 Uttarkashi India
54 D4 Uttar Pradesh India
119 □3 Utuado Puerto Rico
65 L3 Utubulak China
91 □11 Utuofai *Fr. Poly.* Pac. Oc.
91 □10 Uturoa *Fr. Poly.* Pac. Oc.
64 D2 Utva r. Kazak.
109 M2 Uummannaq Greenland
109 N2 Uummannaq Fj. inlet Greenland
109 O4 Uummannarsuaq c. Greenland
11 G3 Uurainen Finland
48 B2 Üür Gol r. Mongolia
11 F3 Uusikaupunki Finland
11 G3 Uusimaa div. Finland
82 A2 Uutapi Namibia
125 D6 Uvalde U.S.A.
14 B2 Uvarovka Rus. Fed.
14 F4 Uvarovo Rus. Fed.
14 G3 Uvarovo Rus. Fed.
81 B6 Uvinza Tanzania
79 E4 Uvira Zaire
14 E1 Uvod' r. Rus. Fed.
83 E5 Uvongo R.S.A.
44 F1 Uvs Nuur salt l. China
46 D7 Uwa Japan
46 D7 Uwajima Japan
72 B2 'Uwaynāt Wannīn Libya
72 E3 Uweinat, Jebel mt. Sudan
40 A1 Uwi i. Indon.
48 D5 Uxin Ju China
48 D5 Uxin Qi China
142 A1 Uxituba Brazil
131 H4 Uxmal Mexico
64 F2 Uy r. Rus. Fed.
64 F4 Uyaly Kazak.
48 C3 Üydzin Mongolia
63 Q3 Uyega Rus. Fed.
77 F5 Uyo Nigeria
42 A1 Uyu Chaung r. Myanmar
65 H4 Uyuk Kazak.
61 B5 'Uyûn Mûsa spring Egypt
13 H4 Uza r. Rus. Fed.
32 H5 Uzbekistan country Asia
64 D4 Uzen' Kazak.
20 E4 Uzerche France
21 G4 Uzès France
15 C1 Uzh r. Ukraine
13 B5 Uzhhorod Ukraine
14 G2 Uzhovka Rus. Fed.
14 D3 Uzlovaya Rus. Fed.
14 F1 Uzola r. Rus. Fed.
60 B2 Üzümlü Turkey
65 J4 Uzunagach Kazak.
60 A1 Uzunköprü Turkey
15 D2 Uzyn Ukraine
64 F4 Uzynkair Kazak.

V

78 D2 Va r. C.A.R.
82 C4 Vaal r. R.S.A.
10 G2 Vaala Finland
83 D4 Vaal Dam dam R.S.A.
10 F3 Vaasa Finland
10 F3 Vaasa div. Finland
64 F4 Vabkent Uzbekistan
14 A3 Vablya r. Rus. Fed.
19 J5 Vác Hungary
145 F4 Vacaré r. Brazil
145 G2 Vacaria r. Brazil
143 B6 Vacaria Brazil
144 A4 Vacaria r. Brazil
143 B5 Vacaria, Serra h. Brazil
128 B2 Vacaville U.S.A.
14 F2 Vacha Rus. Fed.
81 □4 Vacoas Mauritius
14 F2 Vad r. Rus. Fed.
14 G2 Vad Rus. Fed.
56 A2 Vada India
28 F2 Vădeni Romania
14 F3 Vadinsk Rus. Fed.
11 B4 Vadla Norway
54 C5 Vadodara India
10 H1 Vadsø Norway
18 D5 Vaduz Liechtenstein
10 D2 Værøy i. Norway
12 G2 Vaga r. Rus. Fed.
11 C3 Vågåmo Norway
26 E3 Vaganski Vrh mt. Croatia
16 D1 Vágar i. Faeroes
24 B2 Vagos Portugal
10 E2 Vägsele Sweden
19 H4 Váh r. Slovakia
10 F3 Vähäkyrö Finland
91 □11 Vaiau, Pte pt *Fr. Poly.* Pac. Oc.
11 G4 Vaida Estonia
56 B4 Vaigai r. India
91 □16 Vaihu *Easter I.* Chile
129 G5 Vail U.S.A.
91 □12 Vailoa Western Samoa
90 □4 Vaina Tonga
91 □11 Vairao *Fr. Poly.* Pac. Oc.
21 G4 Vaison-la-Romaine France
91 □13 Vaitogi *American Samoa* Pac. Oc.
150 G6 Vaitupu i. Tuvalu
91 □12 Vaiusu Western Samoa
90 □3 Vaka'eitu i. Tonga
78 D2 Vakaga div. C.A.R.
62 K3 Vakh r. Rus. Fed.
54 C1 Vakhan Tajikistan
65 G5 Vakhsh Tajikistan
57 D3 Vakīlābād Iran
56 C5 Valachchenai Sri Lanka
12 K3 Valamaz Rus. Fed.
29 D4 Valandovo Macedonia
19 J4 Valašské Klobouky Czech Rep.
19 H4 Valašské Meziříčí Czech Rep.
29 E5 Valaxa i. Greece
115 H3 Val-Barrette Can.
147 C5 Valcheta Arg.
114 D2 Val-Côté Can.
26 C3 Valdagno Italy
21 H3 Valdahon France
24 D1 Valdavia r. Spain
12 E3 Valday Rus. Fed.
14 A1 Valdayskaya Vozvyshennost' h. Rus. Fed.
24 D3 Valdecañas, Embalse de resr Spain
11 F4 Valdemārpils Latvia
11 E4 Valdemarsvik Sweden
21 G2 Val-de-Meuse France
24 E2 Valdemoro Spain
24 E3 Valdepeñas Spain
24 D1 Valderaduey r. Spain
24 D1 Valderas Spain
20 E2 Val-de-Reuil France
115 H4 Val-des-Bois Can.
147 D5 Valdés, Península pen. Arg.
138 B3 Valdez Ecuador
108 D3 Valdez U.S.A.
21 H4 Val-d'Isère France
147 B4 Valdivia Chile
26 C3 Valdobbiadene Italy
115 G2 Val-d'Or Can.
119 D6 Valdosta U.S.A.
11 C3 Valdres v. Norway
13 G7 Vale Georgia
126 C2 Vale U.S.A.
28 D1 Valea lui Mihai Romania
110 F4 Valemount Can.
145 G5 Valença Brazil
142 E3 Valença Brazil
142 D2 Valença do Piauí Brazil
20 E3 Valençay France
21 G4 Valence *Rhône-Alpes* France
25 F3 Valencia Spain
25 F3 Valencia div. Spain
133 □3 Valencia Trin. & Tobago
138 D1 Valencia Venezuela
24 C3 Valencia de Alcántara Spain
24 D1 Valencia de Don Juan Spain
25 G3 Valencia, Golfo de g. Spain
17 B6 Valencia Island i. Rep. of Ire.
133 F5 Valencia, L. de l. Venezuela
21 F1 Valenciennes France
28 F2 Vălenii de Munte Romania
21 H5 Valensole, Plateau de plat. France
129 F4 Valentine U.S.A.
124 C3 Valentine U.S.A.
125 B6 Valentine U.S.A.
26 B3 Valenza Italy
41 B3 Valenzuela Phil.
11 C3 Våler Norway
138 C2 Valera Venezuela
145 J2 Vale Verde Brazil
20 E5 Valier, Mont mt. France
90 □6 Valili Pk h. Fiji
21 J6 Valinco, Golfe de b. France
115 J2 Val-Jalbert Can.
28 B2 Valjevo Yugo.
11 G4 Valka Estonia
11 G4 Valka Latvia
11 G3 Valkeakoski Finland
18 B3 Valkenswaard Netherlands
15 F2 Valky Ukraine
152 C4 Valkyrjedomen ice feature Ant.
131 H4 Valladolid Mexico
24 D2 Valladolid Spain
130 D4 Vallarta, Pto Mexico
21 H5 Vallauris France
25 F3 Vall de Uxó Spain
11 B4 Valle Norway
24 D1 Valle Spain
26 A3 Valle d'Aosta div. Italy
139 D2 Valle de la Pascua Venezuela
138 C1 Valledupar Colombia
115 K3 Vallée-Jonction Can.
146 C3 Valle Fértil, Sa de mt. ra. Arg.
140 D3 Valle Grande Bolivia
147 C6 Valle Hermosa Arg.
131 F3 Valle Hermoso Mexico
25 □ Vallehermoso *Canary Is* Spain
128 A2 Vallejo U.S.A.
27 D7 Vallelunga Pratameno Italy
131 F5 Valle Nacional Mexico
146 B2 Vallenar Chile
27 E7 Valletta Malta
124 D2 Valley City U.S.A.
126 B3 Valley Falls U.S.A.
41 B2 Valley Head pt Phil.
120 C5 Valley Head U.S.A.
73 F2 Valley of The Kings Egypt
133 G3 Valley, The *Anguilla* Caribbean
110 F3 Valleyview Can.
25 G2 Valls Spain
111 H5 Val Marie Can.
11 G4 Valmiera Latvia
20 D2 Valognes France
24 C2 Valpacos Portugal
115 F2 Val-Paradis Can.
144 C4 Valparaíso Brazil
146 B3 Valparaíso div. Chile
146 B3 Valparaíso Chile
130 E4 Valparaíso Mexico
122 D5 Valparaiso U.S.A.
26 G3 Valpovo Croatia
21 G4 Valréas France
54 C5 Valsād India
28 C2 Valška Yugo.
82 C4 Valspan R.S.A.
39 L8 Vals, Tg c. Indon.
12 H1 Val'tevo Rus. Fed.
10 H3 Valtimo Finland
81 □4 Valton Mauritius
29 C5 Valtou mt. ra. Greece
26 A3 Valtournenche Italy
90 □8 Valukoula Fiji
14 A3 Valuyets Rus. Fed.
13 F5 Valuyki Rus. Fed.
25 □ Valverde *Canary Is* Spain
24 C4 Valverde del Camino Spain
19 H3 Vamberk Czech Rep.
43 D5 Vam Co Tay r. Vietnam
81 D7 Vamizi, Ilha i. Mozambique
11 F3 Vammala Finland
56 C2 Vamsadhara r. India
60 E2 Van Turkey
60 F1 Vanadzor Armenia
63 M3 Vanavara Rus. Fed.
115 J3 Van Bruyssel Can.
125 E5 Van Buren U.S.A.
121 K1 Van Buren U.S.A.
43 E4 Vân Canh Vietnam
121 K2 Vanceboro U.S.A.
120 B5 Vanceburg U.S.A.
110 E5 Vancouver Can.
126 B2 Vancouver U.S.A.
101 B7 Vancouver, C. c. Aust.
110 D5 Vancouver Island i. Can.
110 B2 Vancouver, Mt mt. Can./U.S.A.
92 □3 Vancouver Rock i. *Snares Is* N.Z.
118 B4 Vandalia U.S.A.
120 A5 Vandalia U.S.A.
25 G2 Vandellós Spain
82 D4 Vanderbijlpark R.S.A.
122 E3 Vanderbilt U.S.A.
120 D4 Vandergrift U.S.A.
110 E4 Vanderhoof Can.
98 D2 Vanderlin I. i. Aust.
129 H4 Vanderwagen U.S.A.
98 B1 Van Diemen, C. c. Aust.
98 D3 Van Diemen, C. c. Aust.
98 C1 Van Diemen Gulf b. Aust.
11 G4 Vändra Estonia
115 J3 Vandry Can.
11 D4 Vänern b. Sweden
11 D4 Vänersborg Sweden
120 E3 Van Etten U.S.A.
83 H3 Vangaindrano Madagascar
60 E2 Van Gölü salt l. Turkey
90 □1 Vangunu i. Solomon Is.
125 B6 Van Horn U.S.A.
115 H4 Vanier Can.
90 □1 Vanimo P.N.G.
45 Q2 Vanino Rus. Fed.
56 B3 Vanivilasa Sagara resr India
56 B3 Vaniyambadi India
28 D2 Vânju Mare Romania
108 A3 Vankarem Rus. Fed.
115 H4 Vankleek Hill Can.
10 E1 Vanna i. Norway
10 E3 Vännäs Sweden
20 C3 Vannes France
65 H4 Vannovka Kazak.
21 H4 Vanoise, Massif de la mts France
82 B5 Vanrhynsdorp R.S.A.
99 E3 Vanrook Aust.
99 E3 Vanrook Cr. r. Aust.
11 D3 Vansbro Sweden
100 D2 Vansittart B. b. Aust.
109 K3 Vansittart I. i. Can.
11 G3 Vantaa Finland
90 □7 Vanua Bailavu i. Fiji
90 □2 Vanua Lava i. Vanuatu
90 □6 Vanua Levu i. Fiji
90 □8 Vanua Levu Barrier Reef reef Fiji
86 H6 Vanuatu country Pac. Oc.
120 A4 Van Wert U.S.A.
82 C5 Vanwyksvlei l. R.S.A.
82 C5 Vanwyksvlei R.S.A.
42 D2 Văn Yên Vietnam
90 □2 Vao Pac. Oc.
15 C2 Vapnyarka Ukraine
21 H5 Var r. France
56 A3 Varada r. India
11 G4 Varakļāni Latvia
76 D5 Varalé Côte d'Ivoire
26 B3 Varallo Italy
57 B2 Varāmīn Iran
55 E4 Varanasi India
10 H1 Varangerfjorden chan. Norway
10 H1 Varangerhalvøya pen. Norway
26 F2 Varaždin Croatia
26 B3 Varazze Italy
11 D4 Varberg Sweden
57 B2 Varcheh Iran
29 C5 Varda Greece
56 B2 Vardannapet India
28 C4 Vardar r. Macedonia
11 C5 Varde Denmark
60 F1 Vardenis Armenia
10 H1 Vardø Norway
14 D1 Varegovo Rus. Fed.
18 D2 Varel Germany
11 G5 Varėna Lithuania
115 J4 Varennes Can.
26 G3 Vareš Bos.-Herz.
26 B3 Varese Italy
28 D1 Vârful Bihor mt. Romania
28 E1 Vârful Bivolu mt. Romania
28 E2 Vârful Cozia mt. Romania
15 A3 Vârful Harghita-Mădăra mt. Romania
28 C2 Vârful Leordişu mt. Romania
28 E2 Vârful Moldoveanu mt. Romania
28 D2 Vârful Padeşu mt. Romania
15 B3 Vârful Şandru Mare mt. Romania
28 D1 Vârful Vlădeasa mt. Romania
11 D4 Vårgårda Sweden
142 E2 Vargem r. Brazil
145 E4 Vargem Grande do Sul Brazil
145 F4 Varginha Brazil
140 B4 Varillas Chile
62 D3 Varkaus Finland
11 D4 Värmland div. Sweden
28 F3 Varna div. Bulgaria
28 F3 Varna Bulgaria
64 F2 Varna Rus. Fed.
11 D4 Värnamo Sweden
11 D3 Värnäs Sweden
14 G1 Varnavino Rus. Fed.
61 B2 Varosia Cyprus
26 F3 Varoška Rijeka Bos.-Herz.
10 G3 Varpaisjärvi Finland
19 J5 Várpalota Hungary
57 G1 Varsaj Afghanistan
60 E2 Varto Turkey
28 D2 Vârtop Romania
55 E4 Varuna r. India
15 E1 Varva Ukraine
28 C3 Varvarin Yugo.
15 G1 Varvarivka *Kharkiv* Ukraine
15 B1 Varvarivka *Khmel'nyts'kyy* Ukraine
120 D3 Varysburg U.S.A.
57 C2 Varzaneh Iran
60 F2 Varzaqān Iran
143 C6 Varzea r. *Paraná* Brazil
143 B6 Varzea r. *Rio Grande do Sul* Brazil
145 F2 Várzea da Palma Brazil
145 F1 Varzelândia Brazil
26 B2 Varzo Italy
12 F1 Varzuga Rus. Fed.
142 E3 Vasa Barris r. Brazil
19 L4 Vásárosnamény Hungary
28 D1 Vaşcău Romania
12 H1 Vashka r. Rus. Fed.
15 A2 Vashkivtsi Ukraine
12 H2 Vasilevo Rus. Fed.
14 H1 Vasil'sursk Rus. Fed.
14 B1 Vasil'yevskiy Mokh Rus. Fed.
14 G1 Vasil'yevskoye Rus. Fed.
14 E1 Vasil'yevskoye Rus. Fed.
11 G4 Vasknarva Estonia
15 C1 Vas'kovychi Ukraine
28 F1 Vaslui Romania
123 F4 Vassar U.S.A.
145 G5 Vassouras Brazil
11 E4 Västerås Sweden
10 E2 Västerbotten div. Sweden
11 D3 Västerdalälven r. Sweden
10 E2 Västerfjäll Sweden
11 E4 Vasterhaninge Sweden
10 E3 Västernorrland div. Sweden
11 E4 Västervik Sweden
11 D4 Västmanland div. Sweden
27 E4 Vasto Italy
19 H5 Vasvár Hungary
15 E2 Vasylivka *Kirovohrad* Ukraine
15 F1 Vasylivka *Sumy* Ukraine
15 F3 Vasylivka *Zaporizhzhya* Ukraine
15 D1 Vasyl'kiv Ukraine
15 G2 Vasyl'kivka Ukraine
15 B2 Vasyutyntsi Ukraine
20 E3 Vatan France
56 A2 Vathar India
90 □8 Vatia Pt pt Fiji
27 D5 Vatican City country Europe
10 M2 Vatnajökull ice cap Iceland
90 □7 Vatoa i. Fiji
83 H2 Vato Loha mt. Madagascar
83 H2 Vatomandry Madagascar
28 E1 Vatra Dornei Romania
28 E1 Vatra Moldoviţei Romania
11 D4 Vättern l. Sweden
90 □8 Vatu-i-Ra Channel chan. Fiji
90 □8 Vatu-i-Thake i. Fiji
90 □8 Vatulele i. Fiji
15 D2 Vatutine Ukraine
90 □6 Vatu Vara i. Fiji
21 G5 Vaucluse, Monts de mts France
21 G2 Vaucouleurs France
127 F5 Vaughn U.S.A.
138 C3 Vaupés r. Colombia
21 G5 Vauvert France
83 H2 Vavatenina Madagascar
90 □3 Vava'u Group is Tonga
76 C5 Vavoua Côte d'Ivoire
56 C4 Vavuniya Sri Lanka
12 C4 Vawkavysk Belarus
11 D4 Växjö Sweden
56 B3 Vāyalpād India
62 G2 Vaygach, O. i. Rus. Fed.
145 E2 Vazante Brazil
12 H1 Vazhgort Rus. Fed.
14 B2 Vazuza r. Rus. Fed.
14 B2 Vazuzskoye Vdkhr. resr Rus. Fed.
65 K1 Vdovino Rus. Fed.
43 C4 Veal Vêng Cambodia
18 D2 Vechta Germany
18 C2 Vechte r. Germany
56 B4 Vedaranniyam India
11 D4 Veddige Sweden
28 E2 Vedea r. Romania
28 E3 Vedea Romania
60 F2 Vedi Armenia
146 D3 Vedia Arg.
12 E2 Vedlozero Rus. Fed.
122 D5 Veedersburg U.S.A.
18 C2 Veendam Netherlands
18 B2 Veenendaal Netherlands
10 C2 Vega i. Norway
125 C5 Vega U.S.A.
119 □3 Vega Baja Puerto Rico
24 C1 Vegadeo Spain
111 G4 Vegreville Can.
11 G3 Vehkalahti Finland
54 B3 Vehoa r. Pakistan
142 B1 Veiros Brazil
57 G4 Veirwaro Pakistan
19 L1 Veisiejis Lithuania
11 C5 Vejle Denmark
57 E1 Vekīl'-Bazar Turkmenistan
138 C1 Vela, Cabo de la pt Colombia
26 F4 Vela Luka Croatia
56 B4 Velanai I. i. Sri Lanka
138 □ Velasco Ibarra *Galapagos Is* Ecuador
146 C2 Velasco, Sa de mt. ra. Arg.
26 E3 Velebit mt. ra. Croatia
26 E3 Velebitski Kanal chan. Croatia
18 C3 Velen Germany
26 E2 Velenje Slovenia
28 C4 Veles Macedonia
14 F2 Velet'ma Rus. Fed.
26 F4 Velež mts Bos.-Herz.
138 C2 Vélez Colombia
24 D4 Vélez-Málaga Spain
25 E4 Vélez-Rubio Spain
145 E3 Velhas r. *Minas Gerais* Brazil
145 F2 Velhas r. *Minas Gerais* Brazil
13 H6 Velichayevskoye Rus. Fed.
15 A2 Velika Berezovytsya Ukraine
26 F3 Velika Gorica Croatia
15 A1 Velika Hlusha Ukraine
26 E3 Velika Kapela mt. ra. Croatia
28 C3 Velika Kruša Yugo.
15 B1 Velika Ozera Ukraine
28 C2 Velika Plana Yugo.
12 J3 Velikaya r. *Kirov* Rus. Fed.
12 D3 Velikaya r. *Pskov* Rus. Fed.
12 E2 Velikaya Guba Rus. Fed.
15 A2 Veliki Birky Ukraine
28 C3 Veliki Jastrebac mts Yugo.
12 D3 Velikiye Luki Rus. Fed.
15 A2 Velikiy Hlybochok Ukraine
15 D1 Velikiy Lystven Ukraine
12 H2 Velikiy Ustyug Rus. Fed.
15 B2 Velikiy Zhvanchyk Ukraine
14 E2 Velikodvorskiy Rus. Fed.
28 C2 Veliko Gradište Yugo.
56 B3 Velikonda Ra. h. India
14 A1 Velikooktyabr'skiy Rus. Fed.
28 E3 Veliko Tŭrnovo Bulgaria
14 D1 Velikoye Rus. Fed.
14 C1 Velikoye, Oz. l. Rus. Fed.
14 E2 Velikoye, Oz. l. Rus. Fed.
26 E3 Veli Lošinj Croatia
76 B4 Vélingara *Kolda* Senegal
76 B3 Vélingara *Louga* Senegal
28 D3 Velingrad Bulgaria
27 D4 Velino, Monte mt. Italy
12 D4 Velizh Rus. Fed.
19 J4 Veľká Fatra mts Slovakia
19 L4 Veľké Kapušany Slovakia
19 H4 Velké Meziříčí Czech Rep.
19 J4 Veľký Krtíš Slovakia
19 H5 Veľký Meder Slovakia
90 □1 Vella Lavella i. Solomon Is.
56 B4 Vellar r. India
56 B3 Vellore India
29 D6 Velopoula i. Greece
12 G2 Vel'sk Rus. Fed.
18 F2 Velten Germany
111 J5 Velva U.S.A.
14 C2 Vel'yaminovo Rus. Fed.
15 E2 Velyka Bahachka Ukraine
15 F3 Velyka Bilozerka r. Ukraine
15 E2 Velyka Burimka Ukraine
15 D3 Velyka Korenykha Ukraine
15 E3 Velyka Lepetykha Ukraine
15 C3 Velyka Mykhaylivka Ukraine
15 G3 Velyka Novosilka Ukraine
15 E3 Velyka Oleksandrivka Ukraine
15 F1 Velyka Pysarivka Ukraine
15 F2 Velyka Rublivka Ukraine
15 B1 Velyka Tsvilya Ukraine
15 D2 Velyka Vys' r. Ukraine
15 D2 Velyka Vyska Ukraine
15 C2 Velyki Korovyntsi Ukraine
15 E2 Velyki Krynky Ukraine
15 A1 Velyki Mosty Ukraine
15 E1 Velyki Sorochyntsi Ukraine
15 E2 Velykiy Khutir Ukraine
15 D3 Velykodolyns'ke Ukraine
15 G3 Velykomykhaylivka Ukraine
15 G1 Velykyy Burluk Ukraine
28 E1 Velykyy Bychkiv Ukraine
148 G5 Vema Fracture Atlantic Ocean
149 J4 Vema Trough Indian Ocean
56 B4 Vembanād L. l. India
146 D3 Venado Tuerto Arg.
27 E5 Venafro Italy
26 A3 Venaria Italy
144 D5 Venceslau Brás Brazil
145 H4 Venda Nova Brazil
12 H2 Vendinga Rus. Fed.
20 E3 Vendôme France
15 B2 Vendychany Ukraine
26 D3 Veneta, Laguna lag. Italy
26 C3 Veneto div. Italy
12 F4 Venev Rus. Fed.
26 D3 Venezia Italy
26 D3 Venezia, Golfo di g. Italy
136 D2 Venezuela country S. America
138 C1 Venezuela, Golfo de g. Venezuela
56 A3 Vengurla India
119 D7 Venice U.S.A.
21 G4 Vénissieux France
56 B3 Venkatagiri India
56 C2 Venkatapuram India
11 B4 Vennesla Norway
26 C2 Venosta, Val v. Italy
18 B3 Venray Netherlands
11 F4 Venta r. Lithuania
11 F4 Venta Lithuania
24 D2 Venta de Baños Spain
146 D4 Ventan, Serra de la h. Arg.
91 □10 Vent, Îles du is *Fr. Poly.* Pac. Oc.
91 □10 Vent, Îles sous le is *Fr. Poly.* Pac. Oc.
147 B5 Ventisquero mt. Arg.
17 G6 Ventnor U.K.
27 D5 Ventotene, Isola i. Italy
21 G4 Ventoux, Mont mt. France
49 J3 Ventselevo Rus. Fed.
11 F4 Ventspils Latvia
139 D3 Ventuari r. Venezuela
128 C4 Ventucopa U.S.A.
128 C4 Ventura U.S.A.
97 F4 Venus B. b. Aust.
91 □11 Vénus, Pte pt *Fr. Poly.* Pac. Oc.
26 D2 Venzone Italy
146 D2 Vera Arg.
25 F4 Vera Spain
140 C1 Vera Cruz Brazil
131 F4 Veracruz div. Mexico
131 F5 Veracruz Mexico
141 E5 Verá, L. l. Paraguay
54 B5 Veraval India
15 A1 Verba *Rivne* Ukraine
26 B3 Verbania Italy
14 C1 Verbilki Rus. Fed.
15 F3 Verbove Ukraine
15 A2 Verbovets' Ukraine
14 E2 Verbovskiy Rus. Fed.
15 F3 Verby Ukraine
26 B3 Vercelli Italy
115 J4 Verchères Can.
21 G4 Vercors reg. France
14 E3 Verda r. Rus. Fed.
10 C3 Verdalsøra Norway
147 C5 Verde r. Arg.
142 D3 Verde r. *Bahia* Brazil
144 C2 Verde r. *Goiás* Brazil
144 D1 Verde r. *Goiás* Brazil
144 C3 Verde r. *Goiás* Brazil
144 E2 Verde r. *Goiás/Minas Gerais* Brazil
141 E2 Verde r. *Mato Grosso* Brazil
141 E2 Verde r. *Mato Grosso* Brazil
144 B4 Verde r. *Mato Grosso do Sul* Brazil
144 D3 Verde r. *Minas Gerais* Brazil
145 F4 Verde r. *Minas Gerais* Brazil
146 E1 Verde r. Paraguay
129 G4 Verde r. U.S.A.
145 G2 Verde Grande r. Brazil
133 F3 Verde, Isla airport Puerto Rico
41 B3 Verde Island Pass. chan. Phil.
18 D2 Verden (Aller) Germany
147 D4 Verde, Pen. pen. Arg.
145 G1 Verde Pequeno r. Brazil
125 E4 Verdigris r. U.S.A.
144 C2 Verdinho r. Brazil
21 G2 Verdun France
20 E5 Verdun-sur-Garonne France
83 D4 Vereeniging R.S.A.
15 E2 Veremiyivka Ukraine
115 G3 Vérendrye, Réserve faunique La res. Can.
14 C2 Vereya Rus. Fed.
76 B4 Verga, Cap pt Guinea
146 F3 Vergara Uruguay
99 E4 Vergemont Cr. w Aust.
121 G2 Vergennes U.S.A.
14 D1 Verigino Rus. Fed.
24 C2 Verín Spain
144 D3 Veríssimo Brazil
15 F2 Verkhivtseve Ukraine
64 E2 Verkhne-Avzyan Rus. Fed.
14 A2 Verkhnedneprovskiy Rus. Fed.
62 K3 Verkhneimbatskoye Rus. Fed.
12 H3 Verkhnespasskoye Rus. Fed.
10 H1 Verkhnetulomskiy Rus. Fed.
14 D4 Verkhneturovo Rus. Fed.
64 E2 Verkhneural'sk Rus. Fed.
63 O3 Verkhnevilyuysk Rus. Fed.
14 A1 Verkhnevolzhskoye Vdkhr. resr Rus. Fed.
14 G2 Verkhneye Talyzino Rus. Fed.
13 H5 Verkhniy Baskunchak Rus. Fed.
15 G2 Verkhniy Byshkyn Ukraine
13 J5 Verkhniy Kushum Rus. Fed.
14 F1 Verkhniy Landekh Rus. Fed.
14 F3 Verkhniy Lomov Rus. Fed.
15 F3 Verkhniy Rohachyk Ukraine
48 D2 Verkhniy Shergol'dzhin Rus. Fed.
64 F1 Verkhniy Ufaley Rus. Fed.
48 E2 Verkhniy Ul'khun Rus. Fed.
12 E1 Verkhniy Vyalozerskiy Rus. Fed.
15 F2 Verkhn'odniprovs'k Ukraine
15 D2 Verkhnyachka Ukraine
14 C4 Verkhnyaya Grayvoronka Rus. Fed.
65 K2 Verkhnyaya Irmen' Rus. Fed.
14 D4 Verkhnyaya Khava Rus. Fed.
49 E2 Verkhnyaya Khila Rus. Fed.
10 J2 Verkhnyaya Pirenga, Oz. l. Rus. Fed.
12 H2 Verkhnyaya Toyma Rus. Fed.
14 C1 Verkhnyaya Troitsa Rus. Fed.
12 J3 Verkhoshizhem'ye Rus. Fed.
12 G2 Verkhovazh'ye Rus. Fed.
14 C3 Verkhov'ye Rus. Fed.
15 A2 Verkhovyna Ukraine
63 P3 Verkhoyansk Rus. Fed.
63 O2 Verkhoyanskiy Khrebet mt. ra. Rus. Fed.
14 H3 Verkhozim Rus. Fed.
49 E1 Verkh-Usugli Rus. Fed.
10 H2 Verkneye Kuyto, Oz. l. Rus. Fed.
12 H2 Verkola Rus. Fed.
142 C2 Vermelho r. Brazil
144 C1 Vermelho r. Brazil
142 C2 Vermelho r. Brazil
111 G4 Vermilion Can.
122 C5 Vermilion r. U.S.A.
129 F3 Vermilion Cliffs cliff U.S.A.
122 A2 Vermilion Lake l. U.S.A.
122 A2 Vermilion Range h. U.S.A.
124 D3 Vermillion U.S.A.
112 B4 Vermillion Bay Can.
121 G3 Vermont div. U.S.A.
14 F3 Vernadovka Rus. Fed.
126 E3 Vernal U.S.A.
114 E3 Verner Can.
20 E2 Verneuil-sur-Avre France
110 F4 Vernon Can.
20 E2 Vernon France
129 H4 Vernon U.S.A.
121 G4 Vernon U.S.A.
125 D5 Vernon U.S.A.
129 F1 Vernon U.S.A.
119 D7 Vero Beach U.S.A.
29 D4 Veroia Greece
26 C3 Verona Italy
146 E4 Verónica Arg.
26 A3 Verres Italy
22 D2 Versailles France
49 E1 Vershino-Darasunskiy Rus. Fed.
76 A4 Vert, Cap c. Senegal
142 B3 Vertentes r. Brazil
132 C2 Vertientes Cuba
15 D1 Vertiyivka Ukraine
20 D3 Vertou France
18 B3 Verviers Belgium
21 F2 Vervins France
21 J5 Vescovato France
64 E2 Veselaya, G. mt. Rus. Fed.
15 F3 Vesele Ukraine
14 C2 Veselevo Rus. Fed.
19 G4 Veselí nad Lužnicí Czech Rep.
19 H4 Veselí nad Moravou Czech Rep.
15 C1 Veselivka Ukraine
13 G6 Veselovskoye Vdkhr. resr Rus. Fed.
15 D3 Veselynove Ukraine
13 G6 Veselyy Rus. Fed.
13 G5 Veshenskaya Rus. Fed.
14 H2 Veshkayma Rus. Fed.
12 G1 Veshkoma Rus. Fed.
21 G2 Vesle r. France
21 H3 Vesoul France
11 B4 Vest-Agder div. Norway
10 D1 Vesterålen is Norway
10 D1 Vesterålsfjorden chan. Norway
10 G1 Vestertana Norway
10 L2 Vestfirðir div. Iceland
152 C3 Vestfjella mts Ant.
10 D2 Vestfjorden chan. Norway
11 C4 Vestfold div. Norway
16 D1 Vestmanna Faeroes
10 L3 Vestmannaeyjar Iceland
10 L3 Vestmannaeyjar is Iceland
10 N2 Vesturhorn c. Iceland
10 L2 Vesturland div. Iceland
27 E5 Vesuvio vol Italy
12 F3 Ves'yegonsk Rus. Fed.
19 H5 Veszprém Hungary
90 □6 Vetauua i. Fiji
10 F3 Veteli Finland
11 D4 Vetlanda Sweden
14 H1 Vetluga r. Rus. Fed.
12 H3 Vetluga Rus. Fed.
14 G1 Vetluzhskiy Rus. Fed.
28 F3 Vetovo Bulgaria
26 D4 Vettore, Monte mt. Italy
18 A3 Veurne Belgium
21 H3 Vevey Switz.
21 G4 Veynes France
129 F3 Veyo U.S.A.
20 E4 Vézère r. France
60 C1 Vezirköprü Turkey
11 E3 Vi Sweden
140 C3 Viacha Bolivia
140 A2 Viajas, I. de las i. Peru
79 B5 Viana Angola
145 H4 Viana *Espírito Santo* Brazil
142 D1 Viana *Maranhão* Brazil
24 C3 Viana do Alentejo Portugal
24 C1 Viana do Bolo Spain
24 B2 Viana do Castelo Portugal
24 B2 Viana do Castelo div. Portugal
42 C3 Viangchan Laos
42 C2 Viangphoukha Laos
144 D2 Vianópolis Brazil
24 D4 Viar r. Spain
26 C4 Viareggio Italy
20 F4 Viaur r. France
11 C4 Viborg Denmark
27 F6 Vibo Valentia Italy
25 H2 Vic Spain
152 B2 Vicecomodoro Marambio Argentina Base Ant.
20 E5 Vic-en-Bigorre France
130 A2 Vicente Guerrero Mexico
128 C5 Vicente, Pt pt U.S.A.
26 C3 Vicenza Italy
20 E5 Vic-Fezensac France
138 D3 Vichada r. Colombia
146 C2 Vichina r. Arg.
14 E1 Vichuga Rus. Fed.
146 B3 Vichuquén Chile
21 F3 Vichy France
129 F5 Vicksburg U.S.A.
125 F5 Vicksburg U.S.A.
21 F4 Vic-le-Comte France
145 G4 Viçosa Brazil
20 F4 Vic-sur-Cère France
122 A5 Victor U.S.A.
96 D3 Victor Harbour Aust.
146 D3 Victoria Arg.
98 B2 Victoria r. Aust.
97 F4 Victoria div. Aust.
110 E5 Victoria Can.
133 □8 Victoria *Grenada* Caribbean
146 B4 Victoria Chile
130 J6 Victoria Honduras
27 E7 Victoria Malta
28 F2 Victoria *Brăila* Romania
28 E2 Victoria *Braşov* Romania
81 □2 Victoria Seychelles
133 □3 Victoria div. *Trinidad* Trin. & Tobago
125 D6 Victoria U.S.A.
132 C2 Victoria de las Tunas Cuba
79 E7 Victoria Falls waterfall Zambia/Zimbabwe
82 D2 Victoria Falls Zimbabwe
109 O1 Victoria Fjord inlet Greenland
45 □ Victoria Harbour chan. Hong Kong
132 D1 Victoria Hill The Bahamas
147 B6 Victoria, Isla i. Chile
108 H2 Victoria Island i. Can.
81 B5 Victoria, Lake l. Africa
96 E3 Victoria, Lake l. Aust.
113 J4 Victoria Lake l. Can.
152 B5 Victoria Land reg. Ant.
42 A2 Victoria, Mt mt. Myanmar
93 D5 Victoria, Mt mt. N.Z.
90 □1 Victoria, Mt mt. P.N.G.
81 B4 Victoria Nile r. Sudan/Uganda
94 □3 Victoria Pt pt *Macquarie I.* Pac. Oc.
93 D5 Victoria Range mt. ra. N.Z.
98 B2 Victoria River Aust.
98 B3 Victoria River Downs Aust.
146 F2 Victoria, Sa de la h. Arg.
115 K3 Victoriaville Can.
82 C5 Victoria West R.S.A.
146 C4 Victorica Arg.
152 D3 Victor, Mt mt. Ant.
128 D4 Victorville U.S.A.
146 D3 Vicuña Mackenna Arg.
129 E4 Vidal Junction U.S.A.
28 E2 Videle Romania
28 D3 Vidin Bulgaria
54 D5 Vidisha India
12 E2 Vidlitsa Rus. Fed.
14 C2 Vidnoye Rus. Fed.
26 G4 Viduša mts Bos.-Herz.
12 J2 Vidz'yuyar Rus. Fed.
18 F4 Viechtach Germany
147 D5 Viedma Arg.
147 B6 Viedma, L. l. Arg.
24 B3 Vieira de Leiria Portugal
130 B2 Viejo, Co mt. Mexico
25 G1 Vielha Spain
18 B3 Vielsalm Belgium
18 E3 Vienenburg Germany
118 B4 Vienna U.S.A.
121 F5 Vienna U.S.A.
120 C5 Vienna U.S.A.
20 E3 Vienne r. France
21 G4 Vienne France
146 B4 Viento, C. del mt. ra. Arg.
146 B4 Viento, Cordillera del mt. ra. Arg.
133 F3 Vieques i. Puerto Rico
119 □3 Vieques, Isla de i. Puerto Rico
10 G3 Vieremä Finland
21 J3 Vierwaldstätter See l. Switz.
20 F3 Vierzon France
125 C7 Viesca Mexico
11 G4 Viesīte Latvia
27 F5 Vieste Italy
10 E2 Vietas Sweden
33 M8 Vietnam country Asia
42 D2 Việt Tri Vietnam
133 □5 Vieux Bourg *Guadeloupe* Caribbean
133 □5 Vieux Fort *Guadeloupe* Caribbean
133 G4 Vieux Fort St Lucia
133 □5 Vieux Fort, Pte du pt *Guadeloupe* Caribbean
133 □5 Vieux Habitants *Guadeloupe* Caribbean
41 B2 Vigan Phil.
26 B3 Vigevano Italy
142 C1 Vigia Brazil
131 J5 Vigía Chico Mexico
20 F1 Vignacourt France
26 C3 Vignola Italy
24 B1 Vigo Spain
10 G2 Vihanti Finland
54 C3 Vihari Pakistan
19 L4 Vihorlat mt. Slovakia
11 G3 Vihti Finland
10 G3 Viitasaari Finland
54 C3 Vijainagar India
56 A2 Vijayadurg India
56 C2 Vijayawada India
10 M3 Vík Iceland
10 G2 Vikajärvi Finland
111 G4 Viking Can.
10 C2 Vikna i. Norway
11 B3 Vikøyri Norway
15 D3 Viktorivka Ukraine
65 H1 Vikulovo Rus. Fed.
138 D4 Vila Bittencourt Brazil
140 C3 Vilacaya Bolivia
76 □ Vila da Ribeira Brava Cape Verde
76 □ Vila de Sal Rei Cape Verde
83 F2 Vila de Sena Mozambique
24 B2 Vila do Conde Portugal
76 □ Vila do Tarrafal Cape Verde
24 C2 Vila Flor Portugal
25 G2 Vilafranca del Penedès Spain

W

18 C3 Westerwald reg. Germany
147 D7 West Falkland i. Falkland Is.
124 D2 West Fargo U.S.A.
122 D5 Westfield U.S.A.
121 K1 Westfield U.S.A.
121 G3 Westfield U.S.A.
120 D3 Westfield U.S.A.
99 F5 Westgate Aust.
121 K2 West Grand Lake l. U.S.A.
16 F3 Westhill U.K.
124 C1 Westhope U.S.A.
98 D2 West I. i. Aust.
94 □1 West I. i. *Cocos Is* Indian Ocean
152 D5 West Ice Shelf ice feature Ant.
45 □ West Lamma Chan. chan. Hong Kong
120 B5 West Lancaster U.S.A.
99 E4 Westland Aust.
93 C5 Westland National Park nat. park N.Z.
128 B3 Westley U.S.A.
120 B6 West Liberty U.S.A.
120 B4 West Liberty U.S.A.
110 G4 Westlock Can.
114 E5 West Lorne Can.
79 D6 West Lunga r. Zambia
79 D6 West Lunga National Park nat. park Zambia
125 F5 West Memphis U.S.A.
120 E5 Westminster U.S.A.
119 D5 Westminster U.S.A.
98 D3 Westmoreland Aust.
133 □1 Westmorland div. Jamaica
83 D3 West Nicholson Zimbabwe
120 C5 Weston U.S.A.
17 F6 Weston-super-Mare U.K.
121 F5 Westover U.S.A.
119 D7 West Palm Beach U.S.A.
125 F4 West Plains U.S.A.
96 C3 West Point pt Aust.
97 F5 West Point pt Aust.
125 F5 West Point U.S.A.
121 F4 West Point U.S.A.
115 G4 Westport Can.
93 C4 Westport N.Z.
17 C5 Westport Rep. of Ire.
128 A2 Westport U.S.A.
132 □2 Westpunt *Curaçao* Netherlands Ant.
111 J4 Westray Can.
16 F2 Westray i. U.K.
114 E3 Westree Can.
110 E4 West Road r. Can.
97 F4 West Sister I. i. Aust.
121 H2 West StewartstownU.S.A.
18 B2 West-Terschelling Netherlands
121 H4 West Tisbury U.S.A.
121 G2 West Topsham U.S.A.
121 G3 West Townshend U.S.A.
122 B4 West Union U.S.A.
120 B5 West Union U.S.A.
120 C5 West Union U.S.A.
122 D5 Westville U.S.A.
120 C5 West Virginia div. U.S.A.
18 A3 West-Vlaanderen div. Belgium
128 C2 West Walker r. U.S.A.
99 G4 Westwood Aust.
128 B1 Westwood U.S.A.
97 F3 West Wyalong Aust.
126 E2 West Yellowstone U.S.A.
39 J8 Wetar i. Indon.
110 G4 Wetaskiwin Can.
81 C6 Wete Tanzania
122 D2 Wetmore U.S.A.
18 D3 Wetzlar Germany
90 □1 Wewak P.N.G.
17 D5 Wexford Rep. of Ire.
111 H4 Weyakwin Can.
122 C3 Weyauwega U.S.A.
111 J5 Weyburn Can.
19 G5 Weyer Markt Austria
18 D2 Weyhe Germany
17 F6 Weymouth U.K.
121 H3 Weymouth U.S.A.
92 F3 Whakatane r. N.Z.
92 F2 Whakatane N.Z.
43 B5 Whale B. b. Myanmar
110 B3 Whale B. b. U.S.A.
132 C1 Whale Cay i. The Bahamas
111 L2 Whale Cove Can.
97 G2 Whallan Cr. r. Aust.
16 G1 Whalsay i. U.K.
92 E3 Whangaehu r. N.Z.
92 E2 Whangamata N.Z.
92 E3 Whangamomona N.Z.
92 E2 Whangaparaoa N.Z.
92 G3 Whangara N.Z.
92 E1 Whangarei N.Z.
92 E1 Whangaruru Harbour b. N.Z.
112 E2 Whapmagoostui Can.
17 G5 Wharfe r. U.K.
114 D3 Wharncliffe Can.
111 J2 Wharton Lake l. Can.
93 C5 Whataroa N.Z.
122 A5 What Cheer U.S.A.
126 F3 Wheatland U.S.A.
122 C5 Wheaton U.S.A.
94 □4 Wheatsheaf I. i. *Lord Howe I.* Pac. Oc.
129 E2 Wheeler Peak summit U.S.A.
127 F4 Wheeler Peak summit U.S.A.
120 C4 Wheeling U.S.A.
17 F4 Whernside h. U.K.
96 C3 Whidbey Pt pt Aust.
96 B1 Whinham, Mt mt. Aust.
126 B3 Whiskeytown-Shasta-Trinity Nat. Recreation Area res. U.S.A.
115 F5 Whitby Can.
17 G4 Whitby U.K.
93 C5 Whitcombe, Mt mt. N.Z.
114 C2 White r. Can.
110 A2 White r. Can./U.S.A.
133 □1 White r. Jamaica
129 G5 White r. U.S.A.
125 E4 White r. U.S.A.
126 E3 White r. U.S.A.
118 C4 White r. U.S.A.
122 D4 White r. U.S.A.
129 E2 White r. U.S.A.
124 C3 White r. U.S.A.
122 B2 White r. U.S.A.
113 J3 White Bay b. Can.
124 C2 White Butte mt. U.S.A.
97 E2 White Cliffs Aust.
122 E4 White Cloud U.S.A.
110 F4 Whitecourt Can.
122 A2 Whiteface Lake l. U.S.A.
115 H4 Whiteface Mt mt. U.S.A.
121 H2 Whitefield U.S.A.
114 E3 Whitefish Can.
122 D3 Whitefish r. U.S.A.
126 D1 Whitefish U.S.A.
111 H2 Whitefish Lake l. Can.
122 E2 Whitefish Pt pt U.S.A.
121 G3 Whitehall U.S.A.
122 B3 Whitehall U.S.A.
17 F4 Whitehaven U.K.
110 B2 Whitehorse Can.
129 E1 White Horse Pass pass U.S.A.
133 □1 White Horses Jamaica
152 D4 White I. i. Ant.
92 F2 White I. i. N.Z.
98 B4 White, L. salt flat Aust.
125 E6 White L. l. U.S.A.
122 D4 White L. l. U.S.A.
114 C2 White Lake l. Can.
97 G5 Whitemark Aust.
121 H2 White Mountains mt. ra. U.S.A.
128 C3 White Mt Peak summit U.S.A.
73 F4 White Nile Dam dam Sudan
82 B3 White Nossob w Namibia
129 E2 White Pine Range mts U.S.A.
121 G4 White Plains U.S.A.
114 C2 White River Can.
129 H5 Whiteriver U.S.A.
121 G3 White River Junction U.S.A.
118 F3 White River Junction U.S.A.
129 E2 White River Valley v. U.S.A.
99 F3 White Rock Aust.
129 E2 White Rock Peak summit U.S.A.
127 F5 White Sands Nat. Mon. res. U.S.A.
120 B6 Whitesburg U.S.A.
111 K4 Whiteshell Prov. Park res. Can.
126 E2 White Sulphur Springs U.S.A.
120 C6 White Sulphur Springs U.S.A.
119 E5 Whiteville U.S.A.
76 D5 White Volta r. Ghana
122 C4 Whitewater U.S.A.
112 C3 Whitewater L. l. Can.
99 E4 Whitewood Aust.
111 J4 Whitewood Can.
17 E4 Whithorn U.K.
92 E2 Whitianga N.Z.
121 K2 Whiting U.S.A.
119 D5 Whitmire U.S.A.
115 F4 Whitney Can.
128 C3 Whitney, Mt mt. U.S.A.
121 K2 Whitneyville U.S.A.
99 G4 Whitsunday I. i. Aust.
99 G4 Whitsundays, The is Aust.
97 F3 Whitton Aust.
99 E5 Whitula w Aust.
111 H2 Wholdaia Lake l. Can.
129 F5 Why U.S.A.
96 D3 Whyalla Aust.
42 B2 Wiang Phran Thailand
42 C3 Wiang Sa Thailand
114 E4 Wiarton Can.
76 D4 Wiasi Ghana
76 D5 Wiawso Ghana
125 D4 Wichita U.S.A.
125 D5 Wichita Falls U.S.A.
125 D5 Wichita Mts mts U.S.A.
16 F2 Wick U.K.
129 F5 Wickenburg U.S.A.
101 B7 Wickepin Aust.
98 B3 Wickham r. Aust.
97 E4 Wickham, C. c. Aust.
98 B3 Wickham, Mt h. Aust.
17 D5 Wicklow Rep. of Ire.
17 E5 Wicklow Head hd Rep. of Ire.
17 D5 Wicklow Mountains mts Rep. of Ire.
19 J3 Widawka r. Poland
99 H5 Wide B. b. Aust.
99 F6 Widgeegoara w Aust.
101 C6 Widgiemooltha Aust.
49 H6 Wi Do i. S. Korea
19 H2 Więcbork Poland
18 C3 Wiehl Germany
19 H3 Wielka Sowa mt. Poland
19 J3 Wieluń Poland
19 H4 Wien Austria
19 H5 Wiener Neustadt Austria
19 L3 Wieprz r. Poland
18 B2 Wieringermeer Polder reclaimed land Netherlands
19 J3 Wieruszów Poland
18 D3 Wiesbaden Germany
18 D4 Wiesloch Germany
17 F5 Wigan U.K.
125 F6 Wiggins U.S.A.
17 G6 Wight, Isle of i. U.K.
111 H2 Wignes Lake l. Can.
17 E4 Wigtown U.K.
18 B3 Wijchen Netherlands
129 F4 Wikieup U.S.A.
80 C2 Wik'ro Ethiopia
114 E4 Wikwemikong Can.
21 J3 Wil Switz.
126 C2 Wilbur U.S.A.
97 E2 Wilcannia Aust.
111 J4 Wildcat Hill Wilderness Area res. Can.
128 D2 Wildcat Peak summit U.S.A.
83 D5 Wild Coast R.S.A.
114 A2 Wild Goose Can.
110 F4 Wildhay r. Can.
21 H3 Wildhorn mt. Switz.
19 G5 Wildon Austria
122 A2 Wild Rite Lake l. U.S.A.
97 F5 Wild Rivers Nat. Park nat. park Aust.
119 D6 Wildwood U.S.A.
121 F5 Wildwood U.S.A.
83 D4 Wilge r. R.S.A.
152 C5 Wilhelm II Land reg. Ant.
120 C4 Wilhelm, Lake l. U.S.A.
90 □1 Wilhelm, Mt mt. P.N.G.
18 D2 Wilhelmshaven Germany
133 □1 Wiliamsfield Jamaica
121 F4 Wilkes-Barre U.S.A.
152 B6 Wilkes Coast Ant.
152 B6 Wilkes Land reg. Ant.
111 H4 Wilkie Can.
152 B2 Wilkins Coast Ant.
152 B2 Wilkins Ice Shelf ice feature Ant.
96 C2 Wilkinson Lakes salt flat Aust.
126 B2 Willamette r. U.S.A.
97 F3 Willandra Billabong w Aust.
126 B1 Willapa B. b. U.S.A.
120 B4 Willard U.S.A.
121 F5 Willards U.S.A.
129 H5 Willcox U.S.A.
132 □2 Willemstad *Curaçao* Netherlands Ant.
98 B2 Willeroo Aust.
111 H3 William r. Can.
96 D2 William Cr. Aust.
97 E4 William, Mt mt. Aust.
99 E4 Williams r. Aust.
101 B7 Williams Aust.
129 F4 Williams U.S.A.
128 A2 Williams U.S.A.
122 A5 Williamsburg U.S.A.
120 A6 Williamsburg U.S.A.
122 E3 Williamsburg U.S.A.
120 E6 Williamsburg U.S.A.
132 C1 Williams I. i. The Bahamas
110 E4 Williams Lake Can.
113 H1 William Smith, Cap c. Can.
120 E3 Williamson U.S.A.
120 B6 Williamson U.S.A.
122 D5 Williamsport U.S.A.
120 E4 Williamsport U.S.A.
119 E5 Williamston U.S.A.
120 A5 Williamstown U.S.A.
121 G3 Williamstown U.S.A.
121 F3 Williamstown U.S.A.
120 C5 Williamstown U.S.A.
133 □7 Willikie's *Antigua* Caribbean
121 G4 Willimantic U.S.A.
99 G3 Willis Group atolls *Coral Sea Islands Terr.* Pac. Oc.
82 C5 Williston R.S.A.
119 D6 Williston U.S.A.
124 C1 Williston U.S.A.
110 E3 Williston Lake l. Can.
128 A2 Willits U.S.A.
124 E2 Willmar U.S.A.
110 F4 Willmore Wilderness Prov. Park res. Can.
110 D3 Will, Mt mt. Can.
96 D2 Willochra w Aust.
110 E4 Willow r. Can.
111 H5 Willow Bunch Can.
120 E4 Willow Hill U.S.A.
110 F2 Willow Lake l. Can.
82 C5 Willowmore R.S.A.
98 C4 Willowra Aust.
98 C4 Willowra Aboriginal Land Trust res. Aust.
122 C3 Willow Reservoir resr U.S.A.
128 A2 Willows U.S.A.
125 F4 Willow Springs U.S.A.
121 G2 Willsboro U.S.A.
98 D4 Wills Cr. w Aust.
100 E4 Wills, L. salt flat Aust.
96 D3 Willunga Aust.
96 D3 Wilmington Aust.
121 F5 Wilmington U.S.A.
119 E5 Wilmington U.S.A.
120 B5 Wilmington U.S.A.
121 G3 Wilmington U.S.A.
96 D2 Wilpena w Aust.
100 D3 Wilson r. Aust.
124 D4 Wilson U.S.A.
119 E5 Wilson U.S.A.
152 B5 Wilson Hills h. Ant.
127 F4 Wilson, Mt mt. U.S.A.
129 E2 Wilson, Mt mt. U.S.A.
124 D4 Wilson Res. resr U.S.A.
121 H2 Wilsons Mills U.S.A.
97 F4 Wilson's Promontory pen. Aust.
98 C2 Wilton r. Aust.
122 B5 Wilton U.S.A.
121 H2 Wilton U.S.A.
18 B4 Wiltz Luxembourg
101 C5 Wiluna Aust.
20 E1 Wimereux France
122 D5 Winamac U.S.A.
81 B5 Winam G. b. Kenya
17 F6 Wincanton U.K.
121 G3 Winchendon U.S.A.
115 H4 Winchester Can.
93 C6 Winchester N.Z.
17 G6 Winchester U.K.
122 B6 Winchester U.S.A.
122 E5 Winchester U.S.A.
120 A6 Winchester U.S.A.
121 G3 Winchester U.S.A.
119 C5 Winchester U.S.A.
120 D5 Winchester U.S.A.
126 E3 Wind r. U.S.A.
96 D2 Windabout, L. salt flat Aust.
124 C3 Wind Cave Nat. Park nat. park. U.S.A.
17 F4 Windermere U.K.
17 F4 Windermere l. U.K.
82 B3 Windhoek Namibia
19 G5 Windischgarsten Austria
124 E3 Windom U.S.A.
99 E5 Windorah Aust.
129 H4 Window Rock U.S.A.
122 D4 Wind Pt pt U.S.A.
126 E3 Wind River Range mt. ra. U.S.A.
97 G3 Windsor Aust.
113 J4 Windsor Can.
113 H5 Windsor Can.
114 D5 Windsor Can.
115 J4 Windsor Can.
17 G6 Windsor U.K.
121 G4 Windsor U.S.A.
119 E5 Windsor U.S.A.
121 F3 Windsor U.S.A.
121 G3 Windsor U.S.A.
120 E6 Windsor U.S.A.
132 D2 Windsor, Lake l. The Bahamas
121 G4 Windsor Locks U.S.A.
93 □3 Windward Is is *Antipodes Is* N.Z.
133 G4 Windward Islands is Caribbean
132 D3 Windward Passage chan. Cuba/Haiti
119 C5 Winfield U.S.A.
122 B5 Winfield U.S.A.
125 D4 Winfield U.S.A.
98 B2 Wingate Mts h. Aust.
97 G2 Wingen Aust.
97 H2 Wingham Aust.
114 E5 Wingham Can.
100 C4 Winifred, L. salt flat Aust.
112 C2 Winisk Can.
112 C2 Winisk r. Can.
112 C3 Winisk L. l. Can.
112 C3 Winisk River Provincial Park res. Can.
42 B4 Winkana Myanmar
111 K5 Winkler Can.
121 J2 Winn U.S.A.
76 D5 Winneba Ghana
122 C3 Winnebago, Lake l. U.S.A.
98 B3 Winnecke Cr. w Aust.
122 C3 Winneconne U.S.A.
126 C3 Winnemucca U.S.A.
128 C1 Winnemucca Lake l. U.S.A.
18 D4 Winnenden Germany
124 D3 Winner U.S.A.
125 E6 Winnfield U.S.A.
124 E2 Winnibigoshish L. l. U.S.A.
101 A4 Winning Aust.
111 K5 Winnipeg Can.
111 K4 Winnipeg r. Can.
111 K4 Winnipeg, Lake l. Can.
111 J4 Winnipegosis Can.
111 J4 Winnipegosis, Lake l. Can.
121 H3 Winnipesaukee, L. l. U.S.A.
125 F5 Winnsboro U.S.A.
129 G4 Winona U.S.A.
122 C2 Winona U.S.A.
122 B3 Winona U.S.A.
125 F5 Winona U.S.A.
121 G2 Winooski r. U.S.A.
121 G2 Winooski U.S.A.
18 D2 Winsen (Aller) Germany
18 E2 Winsen (Luhe) Germany
129 G4 Winslow U.S.A.
121 G4 Winsted U.S.A.
119 D4 Winston-Salem U.S.A.
18 D3 Winterberg Germany
119 D6 Winter Haven U.S.A.
121 J2 Winterport U.S.A.
128 B2 Winters U.S.A.
18 C3 Winterswijk Netherlands
21 J3 Winterthur Switz.
121 J1 Winterville U.S.A.
121 J2 Winthrop U.S.A.
99 E4 Winton Aust.
93 B7 Winton N.Z.
119 □2 Winton The Bahamas
40 A2 Wiralaga Indon.
96 D3 Wirrabara Aust.
17 F5 Wirral pen. U.K.
96 D2 Wirraminna Aust.
96 C3 Wirrulla Aust.
17 H5 Wisbech U.K.
121 J2 Wiscasset U.S.A.
122 B4 Wisconsin r. U.S.A.
122 C3 Wisconsin div. U.S.A.
122 C4 Wisconsin Dells U.S.A.
122 C4 Wisconsin, Lake l. U.S.A.
122 C3 Wisconsin Rapids U.S.A.
120 B6 Wise U.S.A.
80 E3 Wisil Dabarow Somalia
19 K3 Wisła r. Poland
19 K3 Wisłoka r. Poland
18 E2 Wismar Germany
122 B3 Wissota L. l. U.S.A.
110 D4 Wistaria Can.
19 L3 Wisznice Poland
83 D4 Witbank R.S.A.
17 G5 Witham r. U.K.
121 G2 Witherbee U.S.A.
17 H5 Withernsea U.K.
96 C1 Witjira Nat. Park nat. park Aust.
19 H2 Witkowo *Konin* Poland
17 G6 Witney U.K.
19 G2 Witnica *Gorzów* Poland
21 G2 Witry-lès-Reims France
122 C3 Wittenberg U.S.A.
18 E2 Wittenberge Germany
18 E2 Wittenburg Germany
21 H3 Wittenheim France
100 B4 Wittenoom Aust.
132 □3 Witte Pan salt pan *Bonaire* Netherlands Ant.
18 E2 Wittingen Germany
18 C4 Wittlich Germany
18 C2 Wittmund Germany
18 F1 Wittow pen. Germany
18 F2 Wittstock Germany
90 □1 Witu Is is P.N.G.
82 B3 Witvlei Namibia
18 D3 Witzenhausen Germany
99 H5 Wivenhoe, Lake l. Aust.
114 C5 Wixom Lake l. U.S.A.
19 L2 Wizna Poland
19 K2 Wkra r. Poland
19 J1 Władysławowo Poland
19 J2 Włocławek Poland
19 L3 Włodawa Poland
19 J3 Włoszczowa Poland
121 H2 Woburn Can.
97 F4 Wodonga Aust.
19 J3 Wodzisław Śląski Poland
19 L3 Wojsławice Poland
39 K8 Wokam i. Indon.
49 J3 Woken r. China
55 H4 Wokha India
17 G6 Woking U.K.
99 E4 Wokingham w Aust.
122 D5 Wolcott U.S.A.
120 E3 Wolcott U.S.A.
19 J3 Wołczyn Poland
19 F2 Woldegk Germany
78 B3 Woleu-Ntem div. Gabon
110 C2 Wolf r. Can.
122 C3 Wolf r. U.S.A.
126 D2 Wolf Creek U.S.A.
127 F4 Wolf Creek Pass pass U.S.A.
121 H3 Wolfeboro U.S.A.
115 G4 Wolfe I. i. Can.
18 F3 Wolfen Germany
18 E2 Wolfenbüttel Germany
110 C2 Wolf Lake l. Can.
126 F1 Wolf Point U.S.A.
19 G5 Wolfsberg Austria
18 E2 Wolfsburg Germany
18 C4 Wolfstein Germany
113 H4 Wolfville Can.
138 □ Wolf, Vol. vol *Galapagos Is* Ecuador
19 F1 Wolgast Germany
19 G2 Wolin i. Poland
19 G2 Wolin Poland
147 C7 Wollaston, Islas is Chile
111 J3 Wollaston Lake Can.
111 J3 Wollaston Lake l. Can.
97 G3 Wollongong Aust.
18 E2 Wolmirstedt Germany
76 B5 Wologizi Mts mts Liberia
19 K2 Wołomin Poland
19 H3 Wołów Poland
96 E4 Wolseley Aust.
19 H2 Wolsztyn Poland
18 C2 Wolvega Netherlands
17 F5 Wolverhampton U.K.
122 E3 Wolverine U.S.A.
99 G5 Wondai Aust.
101 B6 Wongan Hills Aust.
78 A4 Wonga Wongué, Réserve de res. Gabon
45 □ Wong Chuk Hang Hong Kong
49 H5 Wŏnju S. Korea
97 E2 Wonominta w Aust.
40 B3 Wonosari Indon.
40 B3 Wonosobo Indon.
49 H5 Wŏnsan N. Korea
97 F4 Wonthaggi Aust.
96 D2 Woocalla Aust.
98 D2 Woodah I. i. Aust.
120 E5 Woodbridge U.S.A.
110 G3 Wood Buffalo National Park nat. park Can.
97 H2 Woodburn Aust.
126 B2 Woodburn U.S.A.
122 E4 Woodbury U.S.A.
121 F5 Woodbury U.S.A.
98 C3 Woodcock, Mt h. Aust.
120 A6 Wood Creek Lake l. U.S.A.
97 H2 Woodenbong Aust.
133 □8 Woodford *Grenada* Caribbean
128 C2 Woodfords U.S.A.
128 C3 Woodlake U.S.A.
128 B2 Woodland U.S.A.
127 F4 Woodland Park U.S.A.
43 □ Woodlands Singapore
90 □1 Woodlark I. i. P.N.G.
98 D4 Woodroffe w Aust.
96 B1 Woodroffe, Mt mt. Aust.
126 E3 Woodruff U.S.A.
120 C5 Woodsfield U.S.A.
98 C3 Woods, L. salt flat Aust.
112 B4 Woods, Lake of the l. Can./U.S.A.
97 F4 Woods Pt Aust.
113 G4 Woodstock Can.
114 E5 Woodstock Can.
122 C4 Woodstock U.S.A.
120 D5 Woodstock U.S.A.
121 F5 Woodstown U.S.A.
121 G2 Woodsville U.S.A.
92 E4 Woodville N.Z.
120 E3 Woodville U.S.A.
125 E6 Woodville U.S.A.
125 D4 Woodward U.S.A.
17 F4 Wooler U.K.
97 H2 Woolgoolga Aust.
96 D2 Wooltana Aust.
98 C2 Woolwonga Abor. Land res. Aust.
96 D2 Woomera Aust.
96 C2 Woomera Prohibited Area res. Aust.
121 H4 Woonsocket U.S.A.
99 G5 Woorabinda Aust.
101 A5 Wooramel r. Aust.
120 C4 Wooster U.S.A.
80 D2 Woqooyi Galbeed div. Somalia
21 H3 Worb Switz.
99 E2 Worbody Pt pt Aust.
82 B5 Worcester R.S.A.
17 F5 Worcester U.K.
121 H3 Worcester U.S.A.
18 F5 Wörgl Austria
17 F4 Workington U.K.
126 F2 Worland U.S.A.
18 D4 Worms Germany
17 E6 Worms Head hd U.K.
76 C5 Worofla Côte d'Ivoire
18 D4 Wörth am Rhein Germany
133 □9 Worthing *Barbados* Caribbean
17 G6 Worthing U.K.
124 E3 Worthington U.S.A.
40 E2 Wotu Indon.
124 C3 Wounded Knee U.S.A.
39 H7 Wowoni i. Indon.
110 C3 Wrangell U.S.A.
110 C3 Wrangell I. i. U.S.A.
108 D3 Wrangell Mountains mt. ra. Can./U.S.A.
16 E2 Wrath, Cape c. U.K.
124 C3 Wray U.S.A.
82 B4 Wreck Point pt R.S.A.
17 F5 Wrexham U.K.
19 G2 Wriezen Germany
41 C4 Wright Phil.
126 F3 Wright U.S.A.
43 A5 Wrightmyo *Andaman and Nicobar Is* India
125 E5 Wright Patman L. l. U.S.A.
129 G6 Wrightson, Mt mt. U.S.A.
110 E2 Wrigley Can.
19 H3 Wrocław Poland
19 H2 Wronki Poland
19 H2 Września Poland
19 H3 Wschowa Poland
50 E2 Wu r. China
48 E5 Wu'an China
101 B6 Wubin Aust.
48 D5 Wubu China
49 G3 Wuchagou China
49 H3 Wuchang China
51 F2 Wuchang China
51 E4 Wuchuan China
48 D4 Wuchuan China
50 D2 Wuchuan China
48 C5 Wuda China
51 E1 Wudang Shan mt. ra. China
51 E1 Wudang Shan mt. China
49 G5 Wudao China
55 H2 Wudaoliang China
49 F5 Wudi China
77 F4 Wudil Nigeria
50 C3 Wuding China
48 D5 Wuding r. China
96 C3 Wudinna Aust.
50 D1 Wudu China
51 E2 Wufeng China
51 E3 Wugang China
50 E1 Wugong China
48 C5 Wuhai China
51 F2 Wuhan China
51 G1 Wuhe China
51 G2 Wuhu China
51 F4 Wuhua China
54 D2 Wūjang China
51 E4 Wujia China
77 F5 Wukari Nigeria
50 A2 Wulang China
54 C2 Wular L. l. India
49 G5 Wuleidao Wan l. China
49 F6 Wulian China
50 C2 Wulian Feng mt. ra. China
50 C3 Wuliang Shan mt. ra. China
39 K8 Wuliaru i. Indon.
51 E2 Wuling Shan mt. ra. China
78 B2 Wum Cameroon
50 C3 Wumeng Shan mt. ra. China
50 E4 Wuming China
50 C2 Wungda China
51 F2 Wuning China
78 E2 Wun Rog Sudan
78 E2 Wun Shwai Sudan
18 F3 Wunsiedel Germany
42 A2 Wuntho Myanmar
129 G4 Wupatki National Monument res. U.S.A.
51 G3 Wuping China
18 C3 Wuppertal Germany
48 D5 Wuqi China
49 F5 Wuqiao China
77 F4 Wurno Nigeria
18 D4 Würzburg Germany
18 F3 Wurzen Germany
50 D1 Wushan China
51 E2 Wushan China
50 D2 Wusheng China
51 F2 Wusheng Guan pass China
51 E4 Wushi China
65 J4 Wushi China
18 D3 Wüstegarten h. Germany
49 K3 Wusuli r. China/Rus. Fed.
48 E5 Wutai China
48 E5 Wutai Shan mt. China
39 M7 Wuvulu I. i. P.N.G.
51 G2 Wuwei China
48 B5 Wuwei China
51 E2 Wuxi China
51 H2 Wuxi China
50 E4 Wuxu China
51 E4 Wuxuan China
51 F1 Wuyang China
51 G2 Wuyi China
49 J2 Wuyiling China
51 G3 Wuyi Shan mt. ra. China
48 D4 Wuyuan China
51 G2 Wuyuan China
48 D5 Wuzhai China
51 E5 Wuzhi Shan mt. China
48 C5 Wuzhong China
51 E4 Wuzhou China
99 E3 Wyaaba Cr. r. Aust.
122 B5 Wyaconda r. U.S.A.
101 B6 Wyalkatchem Aust.
123 F4 Wyandotte U.S.A.
122 C5 Wyanet U.S.A.
19 L2 Wydminy Poland
17 F5 Wye r. U.K.
101 B6 Wyemandoo h. Aust.
18 D1 Wyk auf Föhr Germany
101 B4 Wyloo Aust.
17 H5 Wymondham U.K.
100 E2 Wyndham Aust.
125 F5 Wynne U.S.A.
97 F5 Wynyard Aust.
111 J4 Wynyard Can.
96 B2 Wyola L. salt flat Aust.
122 C5 Wyoming U.S.A.
122 E4 Wyoming U.S.A.
126 E3 Wyoming div. U.S.A.
126 E3 Wyoming Peak summit U.S.A.
97 G3 Wyong Aust.
96 E3 Wyperfeld Nat. Park nat. park Aust.
19 H2 Wysoka *Piła* Poland
19 L2 Wysokie Mazowieckie Poland
121 E4 Wysox U.S.A.
19 K2 Wyszków Poland
120 C6 Wytheville U.S.A.
121 J2 Wytopitlock U.S.A.
152 □ Wyville-Thomson, Mt h. *Kerguelen* Indian Ocean
19 L3 Wyżyna Lubelska reg. Poland

X

80 F2 Xaafuun Somalia
60 G1 Xaçmaz Azerbaijan
55 H3 Xagquka China
54 D1 Xaidulla China
55 G3 Xainza China
83 E4 Xai Xai Mozambique
131 H4 Xal, Co de h. Mexico
142 C2 Xambioa Brazil
144 B5 Xambrê r. Brazil
144 B5 Xambrê Brazil
42 D2 Xam Hua Laos
79 C5 Xá-Muteba Angola
42 C3 Xan r. Laos
82 C3 Xanagas Botswana
48 B4 Xangd China
48 D4 Xangdin Hural China
79 B7 Xangongo Angola
60 F2 Xankändi Azerbaijan
13 H7 Xanlar Azerbaijan
29 E4 Xanthi Greece
143 B6 Xanxerê Brazil
140 C2 Xapuri r. Brazil
140 C2 Xapuri Brazil
65 J5 Xaqung China
80 E4 Xarardheere Somalia
60 G2 Xärä Zirä Adasi is Azerbaijan
55 F3 Xarba La China
64 C5 Xaraba Sähär Sayı i. Azerbaijan
48 C4 Xar Burd China
48 E3 Xar Hudag China
48 D4 Xar Moron r. *Inner Mongolia* China
49 F4 Xar Moron r. *Inner Mongolia* China
29 C5 Xarrë Albania
25 F3 Xátiva Spain
82 C2 Xaudum w Botswana/Namibia
82 C3 Xau, Lake l. Botswana
144 B4 Xavantina Brazil
43 D5 Xa Vo Đat Vietnam
65 K4 Xayar China
65 L3 Xazgat China
42 D3 Xé Bangfai r. Laos
42 D3 Xé Banghiang r. Laos
42 D4 Xé Don r. Laos
43 D4 Xé Kamon r. Laos
42 D4 Xé Kong r. Laos
120 B5 Xenia U.S.A.
42 D3 Xé Noy r. Laos
43 D4 Xé Xan r. Vietnam
82 C3 Xhorodomo Pan salt pan Botswana
82 C3 Xhumo Botswana
51 E4 Xi r. *Guangdong* China
48 B4 Xi w *Inner Mongolia* China
49 G4 Xi r. *Liaoning* China
49 H2 Xiabole Shan mt. China
51 F4 Xiachuan Dao China
50 C1 Xiahe China
51 F3 Xiajiang China
49 F5 Xiajin China
51 G3 Xiamen China
51 E1 Xi'an China
51 F1 Xiancheng China
48 C5 Xianchengbu China
51 E2 Xianfeng China
51 F3 Xiang r. China
51 F1 Xiangcheng China
50 B2 Xiangcheng China
51 F1 Xiangfan China
48 D6 Xiangfen China
48 E4 Xianghuang Qi China
42 C3 Xiangkhoang Laos
48 D6 Xiangning China
54 E3 Xiangquan r. China
51 H2 Xiangshan China
51 F3 Xiangtan China
51 F3 Xiangxiang China
51 F2 Xiangyin China
48 E5 Xiangyuan China
50 C3 Xiangyun China
51 H2 Xianju China
51 F2 Xianning China
50 C2 Xianshui r. China
51 G3 Xianxia Ling mt. ra. China
49 F5 Xian Xian China
50 E1 Xianyang China
51 G3 Xianyou China
50 E4 Xiaodong China
49 G2 Xiao'ergou China
51 F2 Xiaogan China
49 H2 Xiao Hinggan Ling mt. ra. China
50 C2 Xiaojin China
51 G3 Xiaomei China
55 H2 Xiaonanchuan China
51 H2 Xiaoshan China
50 B1 Xiao Surmang China
51 G3 Xiaotao China
49 E5 Xiaowutai Shan mt. China
51 G1 Xiao Xian China
50 C2 Xiaoxiang Ling mt. ra. China
48 D5 Xiaoyi China
51 H3 Xiapu China
48 D6 Xiayukou China
50 C3 Xichang China
51 E4 Xichang China
50 D2 Xichong China
50 D4 Xichou China
51 E1 Xichuan China
50 C2 Xide China
51 E4 Xieyang Dao China
51 G1 Xifei r. China
49 H4 Xifeng China
50 D3 Xifeng China
48 C6 Xifengzhen China
55 G3 Xigazê China
50 D1 Xihan Shui r. China
50 D1 Xihe China
51 F1 Xihua China
48 C6 Xiji China
55 G2 Xijir China
55 G2 Xijir Ulan Hu salt l. China
48 B5 Xijishui China
49 G1 Xikouzi Rus. Fed.
48 E4 Xil China
49 G3 Xilaotou Shan mt. China
49 G4 Xiliao r. China
50 D3 Xilin China
51 E2 Xiling Xia r. China
49 F4 Xilinhot China
48 D3 Xilin Qagan Obo China
48 B4 Ximiao China
51 G2 Xin r. China
51 G2 Xin'anjiang Sk. resr China
49 F2 Xin Barag Youqi China
49 F2 Xin Barag Zuoqi China
49 H4 Xinbin China
49 F2 Xin Bulag Dong China
51 F1 Xincai China
50 E3 Xincheng China
48 C5 Xincheng China
48 D5 Xinchengbu China
51 E5 Xincun China
49 H3 Xindian China
50 D2 Xindu China
51 E4 Xindu China
51 F3 Xinfeng China
51 F3 Xinfeng China
51 F4 Xinfengjiang Sk. resr China
51 F3 Xingan China
51 E3 Xing'an China
49 G4 Xingcheng China
51 F3 Xingguo China
48 A6 Xinghai China
48 E4 Xinghe China
51 G1 Xinghua China
51 G3 Xinghua Wan b. China
49 K3 Xingkai China
49 K3 Xingkai Hu l. China/Rus. Fed.
49 H2 Xinglong China
49 F4 Xinglong China
49 H3 Xinglongzhen China
51 F3 Xingning China
51 F2 Xingou China
50 E1 Xingping China
50 D3 Xingren China
50 C1 Xingsagoinba China
51 E2 Xingshan China
48 E5 Xingtai China
48 E5 Xingtang China
142 B1 Xingu r. Brazil
142 B3 Xingu, Parque Indigena do nat. park Brazil
50 D2 Xingwen China
48 D5 Xing Xian China
51 F1 Xingyang China
50 D3 Xingyi China
51 G2 Xingzi China
49 E5 Xinhe China
65 K4 Xinhe China
51 E3 Xinhua China
48 B5 Xinhuacun China
51 E3 Xinhuang China
51 F4 Xinhui China
48 B5 Xining China
51 F2 Xinjian China
48 D6 Xinjiang China
65 J4 Xinjiang Uygur Zizhiqu div. China
48 D5 Xinjie China
50 B3 Xinjie China
50 C2 Xinjin China
49 G5 Xinjin China
49 G3 Xinkai r. China
49 H2 Xinlitun China
50 C2 Xinlong China
49 G4 Xinmin China
51 E3 Xinning China
50 C3 Xinping China
49 J2 Xinqing China
51 G3 Xinquan China
49 F6 Xintai China
51 F3 Xintian China
51 F2 Xin Xian China
48 E5 Xin Xian China
51 F1 Xinxiang China
51 F4 Xinxing China
51 F1 Xinyang China
51 F1 Xinyang China
51 H1 Xinyang Gang r. China
51 F1 Xinye China
51 G1 Xinye r. China
51 G1 Xinyi China
51 E4 Xinyi China
51 E5 Xinying China
51 F3 Xinyu China
65 K4 Xinyuan China
48 E5 Xinzhou China
24 C1 Xinzo de Limia Spain
49 G4 Xiongyuecheng China
51 E1 Xiping China
51 F1 Xiping China
50 C1 Xiqing Shan mt. ra. China
142 D3 Xique Xique Brazil
50 D2 Xishui China
51 F2 Xishui China
76 B4 Xitole Guinea-Bissau
49 F3 Xi Ujimqin Qi China
51 G2 Xiuning China
51 E2 Xiushan China
51 F2 Xiushui China
51 F2 Xiu Shui r. China
50 D3 Xiuwen China
51 F1 Xiuwu China
49 G4 Xiuyan China
51 E5 Xiuying China
50 B1 Xiwu China
55 F3 Xixabangma Feng mt. China
51 E1 Xixia China
51 F1 Xi Xian China
48 D5 Xi Xian China
50 D1 Xi Xiang China
50 D4 Xiyang r. China
51 H3 Xiyang Dao i. China
55 F2 Xizang Gaoyuan plat. China
55 F3 Xizang Zizhiqu China
49 G5 Xizhong Dao i. China
80 E2 Xjis Somalia
55 H3 Xoka China
43 D5 Xom An Lôc Vietnam
43 D5 Xom Dưc Hanh Vietnam
51 G2 Xuancheng China
51 E2 Xuan'en China
50 D2 Xuanhan China
48 C5 Xuanhepu China
49 E4 Xuanhua China
43 D5 Xuân Lôc Vietnam
50 D3 Xuanwei China
51 F1 Xuchang China
60 G1 Xudat Azerbaijan
80 D4 Xuddur Somalia
80 E3 Xudun Somalia
51 E3 Xuefeng Shan mt. ra. China
55 H2 Xugui China
50 B1 Xümatang China
51 E1 Xun r. China
51 E4 Xun r. China
49 J2 Xun r. China
50 C3 Xundian China
55 E2 Xungba China
55 F3 Xungru China
49 H2 Xunhe China
49 J2 Xunke Rus. Fed.
51 F3 Xunwu China
48 E6 Xun Xian China
51 E1 Xunyang China
50 E1 Xunyi China
51 E3 Xupu China
55 F3 Xuru Co l. China
49 E5 Xushui China
51 E4 Xuwen China
51 G1 Xuyi China
50 D2 Xuyong China
51 G1 Xuzhou China
29 D5 Xylokastro Greece

Y

50 C2 Ya'an China
97 E3 Yaapeet Aust.
78 A3 Yabassi Cameroon
80 C4 Yabēlo Ethiopia
80 C4 Yabēlo Wildlife Sanctuary res. Ethiopia
28 E3 Yablanitsa Bulgaria
28 F3 Yablanovo Bulgaria
14 E3 Yablonovets Rus. Fed.
48 D2 Yablonovyy Khrebet mt. ra. Rus. Fed.
15 A2 Yabluniv Ukraine
77 F4 Yabo Nigeria
48 B5 Yabrai Shan mt. ra. China
48 B5 Yabrai Yanchang China
61 D3 Yabrūd Syria
119 □3 Yabucoa Puerto Rico
49 J3 Yabuli China
15 C1 Yabunets' Ukraine
138 D2 Yacambu, Parque Nacional nat. park Venezuela
90 □6 Yacata i. Fiji
51 E5 Yacheng China
97 F4 Yackandandah Aust.
140 C2 Yacuma r. Bolivia
78 C2 Yadé, Massif du mts C.A.R.
56 B2 Yadgir India
55 G4 Yadong China
14 H2 Yadrin Rus. Fed.
90 □6 Yadua i. Fiji
72 B1 Yafran Libya
76 D4 Yagaba Ghana
47 □2 Yagaji-jima i. Japan
62 J3 Yagel'naya Rus. Fed.
46 H1 Yagishiri-tō i. Japan
63 Q3 Yagodnoye Rus. Fed.
14 B3 Yagodnoye Rus. Fed.
78 C1 Yagoua Cameroon
55 E3 Yagra China
50 A1 Yagradagzê Shan mt. China
43 C6 Yaha Thailand
47 F6 Yahagi-gawa r. Japan
78 D3 Yahuma Zaire
60 C2 Yahyalı Turkey
57 G3 Yahya Wana Afghanistan
47 G5 Yaita Japan
25 □ Yaiza *Canary Is* Spain
47 G6 Yaizu Japan
50 C2 Yajiang China
78 C3 Yaka C.A.R.
49 G2 Yakeshi China
57 F3 Yakhehal Afghanistan
14 C1 Yakhroma Rus. Fed.
126 B2 Yakima U.S.A.
126 B2 Yakima r. U.S.A.
57 C2 Yakinish Iran
57 E3 Yakmach Pakistan
76 D4 Yako Burkina
110 B3 Yakobi I. i. U.S.A.
78 D3 Yakoma Zaire
28 D4 Yakoruda Bulgaria
14 H3 Yakovlevka Rus. Fed.
15 G1 Yakovlevo Rus. Fed.
46 H2 Yakumo Japan
108 E4 Yakutat U.S.A.
108 D4 Yakutat Bay b. U.S.A.
63 O3 Yakutsk Rus. Fed.
15 F3 Yakymivka Ukraine
43 C6 Yala Thailand
96 B2 Yalata Abor. Reserve res. Aust.
123 F4 Yale U.S.A.
78 D3 Yaleko Zaire
90 □7 Yalewa Kalou i. Fiji
14 G2 Yalga Rus. Fed.
101 B6 Yalgoo Aust.
29 F6 Yalıkavak Turkey
78 D2 Yalinga C.A.R.
131 H4 Yalkubul, Pta pt Mexico
133 □1 Yallahs Jamaica
99 F5 Yalleroi Aust.
78 C2 Yaloké C.A.R.
50 C3 Yalong r. China
78 D3 Yalongwe Zaire
60 B1 Yalova Turkey
15 G3 Yalta *Donets'k* Ukraine
13 E6 Yalta *Krym* Ukraine
15 B2 Yaltushkiv Ukraine
49 G3 Yalu r. China
49 H4 Yalu r. China/North Korea
49 H5 Yalujiang Kou river mouth N. Korea
65 G1 Yalutorovsk Rus. Fed.
60 B2 Yalvaç Turkey
47 H4 Yamada Japan
47 G4 Yamagata div. Japan
47 H4 Yamagata Japan
46 C8 Yamagawa Japan
46 C6 Yamaguchi div. Japan
46 C6 Yamaguchi Japan
62 H2 Yamal, Poluostrov pen. Rus. Fed.
47 G6 Yamanashi div. Japan
48 D2 Yamarovka Rus. Fed.
47 H5 Yamatsuri Japan
97 H2 Yamba Aust.
97 E4 Yambacoona Aust.
111 G2 Yamba Lake l. Can.
78 E3 Yambio Sudan
14 F2 Yambirno Rus. Fed.
28 F3 Yambol Bulgaria
138 B5 Yambrasbamba Peru
62 J3 Yamburg Rus. Fed.
86 E5 Yamdena i. Indon.
46 C7 Yame Japan
48 B5 Yamenzhuang China
42 B2 Yamethin Myanmar
41 B1 Y'ami i. Phil.
47 H5 Yamizo-san mt. Japan
11 H4 Yamm Rus. Fed.
99 E5 Yamma Yamma, L. salt flat Aust.
61 C4 Yammit Egypt
76 C5 Yamoussoukro Côte d'Ivoire
126 E3 Yampa r. U.S.A.
15 B2 Yampil' *Khmel'nyts'kyy* Ukraine
14 A4 Yampil' *Sumy* Ukraine
15 C2 Yampil' *Vinnytsya* Ukraine
54 E4 Yamuna r. India
54 D3 Yamunanagar India
65 J2 Yamyshevo Kazak.
55 G3 Yamzho Yumco l. China
48 D5 Yan r. China
63 P3 Yana r. Rus. Fed.
76 B5 Yana Sierra Leone
96 E4 Yanac Aust.
140 A2 Yanachaga-Chemillen, Parque Nacional nat. park Peru
47 □2 Yanaha-jima i. Japan
46 D7 Yanai Japan
56 C2 Yanam India
48 D5 Yan'an China
140 B2 Yanaoca Peru
64 E1 Yanaul Rus. Fed.
50 C3 Yanbian China
73 G3 Yanbu' al Baḩr Saudi Arabia
73 G3 Yanbu' an Nakhl reg. Saudi Arabia
51 H1 Yancheng China
101 A6 Yanchep Aust.
48 C5 Yanchi China
48 D5 Yanchuan China
97 F2 Yanda w Aust.
96 E2 Yandama Cr. w Aust.
90 □1 Yandina Solomon Is.
78 C4 Yandja Zaire
42 A3 Yandoon Myanmar
76 C4 Yanfolila Mali
49 E4 Yang r. China
78 D2 Yangalia C.A.R.
78 D3 Yangambi Zaire
55 H3 Ya'ngamdo China
76 C4 Yangasso Mali
55 G3 Yangbajain China
50 B3 Yangbi China
51 F1 Yangcheng China
51 E4 Yangchun China
49 H5 Yangdok N. Korea
48 E4 Yanggao China
49 E5 Yanggu China
54 D2 Yangi Davan pass China
57 B1 Yangi Kand Iran
65 G4 Yangirabad Uzbekistan
65 G4 Yangiyul' Uzbekistan
51 E4 Yangjiang China
42 B3 Yangon div. Myanmar
42 B3 Yangon Myanmar
51 E2 Yangping China
48 E5 Yangquan China
51 F3 Yangshan China
51 E3 Yangshuo China
50 C3 Yangtouyan China
80 D2 Yangudi Rassa National Park nat. park Ethiopia
50 D1 Yang Xian China
48 E4 Yangyuan China
51 G1 Yangzhou China
50 E2 Yanhe China
55 E2 Yanhuqu China
11 H3 Yanis'yarvi, Ozero l. Finland
49 J4 Yanji China
50 D2 Yanjin China
50 B2 Yanjing China
77 G5 Yankara Nat. Park nat. park Nigeria
124 D3 Yankton U.S.A.
63 Q2 Yano-Indigirskaya Nizmennost' lowland Rus. Fed.
14 A2 Yanovo Rus. Fed.
62 K3 Yanov Stan Rus. Fed.
56 C4 Yan Oya r. Sri Lanka
44 E3 Yanqi China
49 E4 Yanqing China
49 F5 Yanshan China
51 G2 Yanshan China
50 D4 Yanshan China
49 F4 Yan Shan mt. ra. China
55 H2 Yanshiping China
49 J3 Yanshou China
63 P2 Yanskiy Zaliv g. Rus. Fed.
97 F2 Yantabulla Aust.
49 G5 Yantai China
11 E5 Yantarnyy Rus. Fed.
49 H4 Yantongshan China
28 E3 Yantra r. Bulgaria
90 □8 Yanuca i. Fiji
90 □6 Yanuca reef Fiji
73 H3 Yanūfī, J. al h. Saudi Arabia
90 □8 Yanuya i. Fiji
50 B3 Yanwa China
65 G4 Yany-Kurgan Kazak.
50 C3 Yanyuan China
49 F6 Yanzhou China
50 C3 Yao'an China
78 B3 Yaoundé Cameroon
51 E1 Yao Xian China
49 H2 Yaoxiaoling China
39 L5 Yap i. Fed. States of Micronesia
39 L7 Yapen i. Indon.
99 E3 Yappar r. Aust.
150 E5 Yap Tr. Pac. Oc.
139 F3 Yapukarri Guyana
90 □6 Yaqaga i. Fiji
90 □8 Yaqetu i. Fiji
130 C2 Yaqui r. Mexico
12 K3 Yar Rus. Fed.
99 F5 Yaraka Aust.
14 H1 Yaransk Rus. Fed.
96 C3 Yardea Aust.
60 B2 Yardımcı Burnu pt Turkey
60 G2 Yardımlı Azerbaijan
17 H5 Yare r. U.K.
12 K2 Yarega Rus. Fed.
15 A2 Yaremcha Ukraine
12 J2 Yarensk Rus. Fed.
138 C3 Yari r. Colombia
47 F5 Yariga-take mt. Japan
80 D2 Yarīm Yemen
139 G3 Yaripo Brazil
138 D1 Yaritagua Venezuela
65 J5 Yarkant r. China
115 G4 Yarker Can.
54 C1 Yarkhun r. Pakistan
55 H3 Yarlung Zangbo r. China
15 B2 Yarmolyntsi Ukraine
113 G5 Yarmouth Can.
121 H4 Yarmouth Port U.S.A.
129 F4 Yarnell U.S.A.
14 E3 Yarok Rus. Fed.
15 E1 Yaroslavets' Ukraine
14 C1 Yaroslavl' div. Rus. Fed.
14 D1 Yaroslavl' Rus. Fed.
97 F4 Yarram Aust.
99 G5 Yarraman Aust.
101 A6 Yarra Yarra Lakes salt flat Aust.
99 F5 Yarronvale Aust.
99 F4 Yarrowmere Aust.
55 H3 Yartö Tra La China
14 A2 Yartsevo Rus. Fed.
138 B2 Yarumal Colombia
50 B2 Yarzhong China
79 C4 Yasa Zaire
90 □7 Yasawa i. Fiji
90 □8 Yasawa Group is Fiji
28 F3 Yasenkovo Bulgaria
77 F4 Yashi Nigeria
77 E5 Yashikera Nigeria
65 H5 Yashilkŭl l. Tajikistan
46 D7 Ya-shima i. Japan
47 H4 Yashima Japan
46 D7 Yashiro-jima i. Japan
13 H6 Yashkul' Rus. Fed.
28 F3 Yasna Polyana Bulgaria
49 E2 Yasnogorsk Rus. Fed.
14 C2 Yasnogorsk Rus. Fed.
15 D1 Yasnohorodka Ukraine
64 E2 Yasnyy Rus. Fed.
97 G3 Yass Aust.
46 D6 Yasugi Japan
57 B3 Yāsūj Iran
15 G2 Yasynuvata Ukraine
77 G2 Yat well Niger
78 D2 Yata r. C.A.R.
60 B2 Yatağan Turkey
81 C5 Yata Plateau plat. Kenya
90 □2 Yaté Pac. Oc.
125 E4 Yates Center U.S.A.
93 A6 Yates Pt pt N.Z.
111 K2 Yathkyed Lake l. Can.
78 D3 Yatolema Zaire
47 G6 Yatsuga-take vol Japan
46 C7 Yatsushiro Japan
46 C7 Yatsushiro-kai b. Japan
61 C4 Yatta Israel
119 □3 Yauco Puerto Rico
140 A2 Yauli Peru
138 C4 Yauna Maloca Colombia
140 B2 Yauri Peru
45 □ Yau Tong Hong Kong
140 A2 Yauyos Peru
138 C4 Yavari r. Brazil
130 C3 Yavaros Mexico
14 F2 Yavas r. Rus. Fed.
14 F2 Yavas Rus. Fed.
54 D5 Yavatmāl India
139 D2 Yaví, Co mt. Venezuela
15 E3 Yavkyne Ukraine
15 A2 Yavoriv *Ivano-Frankivs'k* Ukraine
13 B5 Yavoriv *L'viv* Ukraine
46 D7 Yawatahama Japan
65 K5 Yawatongguz r. China
65 K5 Yawatongguzlangar China
50 B4 Yawng-hwe Myanmar
76 B5 Yawri Bay b. Sierra Leone
131 H5 Yaxchilan Guatemala
61 D2 Yayladaği Turkey
14 G2 Yaz Rus. Fed.
42 A2 Yazagyo Myanmar
57 C3 Yazd div. Iran
57 C3 Yazd Iran
57 E2 Yazdān Iran
57 C3 Yazd-e Khvāst Iran
125 F5 Yazoo r. U.S.A.
125 F5 Yazoo City U.S.A.
14 H2 Yazykovo Rus. Fed.
14 H2 Yazykovo Rus. Fed.
19 G5 Ybbs r. Austria
19 G4 Ybbs an der Donau Austria
29 D6 Ydra Greece
29 D6 Ydra i. Greece
42 B4 Ye Myanmar
43 B4 Ye r. Myanmar
97 F4 Yea Aust.
72 C3 Yebbi-Bou Chad
72 C3 Yebbi-Souma Chad
65 J5 Yecheng China
25 F3 Yecla Spain
130 C2 Yécora Mexico
42 B3 Yedashe Myanmar
12 H2 Yedoma Rus. Fed.
72 C3 Yedri well Chad
119 D7 Yeehaw Junction U.S.A.
96 C3 Yeelanna Aust.
14 F2 Yefanovo Rus. Fed.
12 E3 Yefimovskiy Rus. Fed.
14 D3 Yefremov Rus. Fed.
77 G3 Yeggueba well Niger
60 F2 Yeghegnadzor Armenia
65 J3 Yegindybulak Kazak.
13 G6 Yegorlykskaya Rus. Fed.
14 A2 Yegor'ye Rus. Fed.
49 H2 Yegor'yevka Rus. Fed.
14 D2 Yegor'yevsk Rus. Fed.
77 E5 Yégué Togo
78 F2 Yei r. Sudan
80 B4 Yei Sudan
76 D5 Yeji Ghana
51 F2 Yejiaji China
64 F1 Yekaterinburg Rus. Fed.
49 J2 Yekaterinoslavka Rus. Fed.
14 G3 Yekaterinovka Rus. Fed.
14 D3 Yekaterinovka Rus. Fed.
72 C4 Yékia well Chad
14 A2 Yekimovichi Rus. Fed.
42 A3 Ye Kyun i. Myanmar
64 D1 Yelabuga Rus. Fed.
13 G5 Yelan' Rus. Fed.
14 F4 Yelan' r. Rus. Fed.
15 D3 Yelanets' Ukraine
99 G6 Yelarbon Aust.
14 H1 Yelasy Rus. Fed.
14 E2 Yelat'ma Rus. Fed.
64 F5 Yelbarsli Turkmenistan
14 B3 Yelenskiy Rus. Fed.
14 D3 Yelets Rus. Fed.
76 B3 Yélimané Mali
14 D2 Yelino Rus. Fed.
63 R4 Yelizovo Rus. Fed.
12 J4 Yelkhovka Rus. Fed.
16 G1 Yell i. U.K.
56 C2 Yellandu India
56 A3 Yellapur India
122 B3 Yellow r. U.S.A.
120 D4 Yellow Creek U.S.A.
108 G3 Yellowknife Can.
97 F3 Yellow Mt h. Aust.
49 G6 Yellow Sea sea Asia
126 F2 Yellowstone r. U.S.A.
126 E2 Yellowstone L. l. U.S.A.
126 E2 Yellowstone Nat. Park nat. park. U.S.A.
126 E2 Yellowtail Res. resr U.S.A.
16 G1 Yell Sound chan. U.K.
14 F2 Yel'niki Rus. Fed.
14 A2 Yel'nya Rus. Fed.
65 G1 Yeloshnoye Rus. Fed.
64 F5 Yeloten Turkmenistan
15 C1 Yel'sk Belarus
65 L2 Yel'tsovka Rus. Fed.
15 G3 Yelyseyivka Ukraine
15 E2 Yelyzavethradka Ukraine
64 F2 Yemanzhelinsk Rus. Fed.
32 F8 Yemen country Asia
65 G1 Yemets r. Rus. Fed.
12 G2 Yemetsk Rus. Fed.
15 B1 Yemil'chyne Ukraine
12 G2 Yemtsa Rus. Fed.
12 J2 Yemva Rus. Fed.
10 H2 Yena Rus. Fed.
77 F6 Yenagoa Nigeria
13 F5 Yenakiyeve Ukraine
42 A2 Yenangyat Myanmar
42 A2 Yenangyaung Myanmar

Z

Abergwaun *see* Fishguard
Abertawe *see* Swansea
Abkhazskaya Respublika *see* Abkhazia
Abqaiq *see* Buqayq
Abu Dhabi *see* Abū Ẓabī
Acre *see* 'Akko
A.C.T. div. *see* Australian Capital Territory
Adalia *see* Antalya
Aden *see* 'Adan
Adzharia *see* Ajaria
Adzharskaya Respublika *see* Ajaria
Afal w *see* 'Ifāl, W.
Agdash *see* Agdaş
Agdzhabedi *see* Ağcabädi
Aguapei r. *see* Feio ou Aguapei
Ahwāz *see* Ahvāz
Ajanta Range h. *see* Sahyadriparvat
a-Jiddét gravel area *see* Jiddat al Ḥarāsīs
Akhsu *see* Ağsu
Akyab *see* Sittwe
Alagez mt. *see* Aragats Lerr
Alappuzha *see* Alleppey
Alataw Shankou pass *see* Dzungarian Gate
Aleppo *see* Ḥalab
Alevisik *see* Samandağı
Alexandretta *see* İskenderun
Algiers *see* Alger
Alma-Ata *see* Almaty
Amazon r. *see* Amazonas
Amboina *see* Ambon
Amherst *see* Kyaikkami
Amirabad *see* Fūlād Maialleh
Amne Machin Range mt. ra. *see* A'nyêmaqên Shan
Amoy *see* Xiamen
Anadyrskiy Khrebet mt. ra. *see* Chukotskiy Khrebet
Anaypazari *see* Gülnar
An Cóbh *see* Cóbh
Anda *see* Daqing
Angmagssalik *see* Tasiilaq
Anhwei *see* Anhui
Anjouan i. *see* Nzwani
An Muileann gCearr *see* Mullingar
An Nás *see* Naas
An Tairbeart *see* Tarbert
Antakya *see* Hatay
An tAonach *see* Nenagh
Anti-Lebanon mt. ra. *see* Sharqi, Jebel esh
An tInbhear Mór *see* Arklow
Antioch *see* Hatay
Antwerp *see* Antwerpen
An Uaimh *see* Navan
Anvers *see* Antwerpen
Aoraki, Mt *mt. see* Cook, Mt
Araks r. *see* Araz
Araks r. *see* Aras
Aral'skoye More salt l. *see* Aral Sea
Ararat, Mt mt. *see* Büyük Ağri
Archangel *see* Arkhangel'sk
Armageddon *see* Megiddo
Armavir *see* Hoktemberyan
Ashkhabad *see* Ashgabat
Ash Shurayf *see* Khaybar
Astalu I. i. *see* Astola I.
Asterabad *see* Gorgān
Astin Tagh mt. ra. *see* Altun Shan
Astipalaia i. *see* Astypalaia
Astrakhan' Bazar *see* Cälilabad
Atas I. i. *see* South Island
Athens *see* Athina
Attalea *see* Antalya
Azbine mts *see* Aïr, Massif de l'
Badaojiang *see* Hunjiang
Bago *see* Pegu
Bagrax Hu l. *see* Bosten Hu
Bahāmabād *see* Rafsanjān
Baikal, Lake l. *see* Baykal, Ozero
Baile Átha Cliath *see* Dublin
Baile Átha Luain *see* Athlone
Baku *see* Bakı
Baky *see* Bakı
Balearic Islands *see* Baleares, Islas
Balkan Mts mts *see* Stara Planina
Balmer *see* Barmer
Balykchy *see* Ysyk-Köl
Bandar *see* Machilipatnam
Bandar-e Pahlavi *see* Bandar-e Anzalī
Bandar-e Shāhpūr *see* Bandar Khomeynī
Ban Don *see* Surat Thani
Banow *see* Andarāb
Ban Pla Soi *see* Chon Buri
Ba'oan *see* Shenzhen
Barak *see* Kargamiş
Barcoo Creek w *see* Cooper Cr.
Baroda *see* Vadodara
Basle *see* Basel
Basra *see* Al Başrah
Basuo *see* Dongfang
Batum *see* Bat'umi
Bay *see* Baicheng
Béal an Átha *see* Ballina
Béal Átha na Sluaighe *see* Ballinasloe
Beersheba *see* Be'ér Sheva'
Beinn na Faoghla i. *see* Benbecula
Belgrade *see* Beograd
Bellin *see* Kangirsuk
Beyrouth *see* Beirut
Bezwada *see* Vijayawada
Bhādrachalam Road Sta. *see* Kottagudem
Bhatnair *see* Hanumangarh
Biblos *see* Jbail
Bideford Bay b. *see* Barnstaple Bay
Billabong r. *see* Moulamein
Bi'r Ibn Hirmās *see* Al Bi'r
Bishbek *see* Bishkek
Black Pagoda *see* Konārka
Black River r. *see* Sông Đa
Black Rock h. *see* El 'Ināb
Black Volta r. *see* Mouhoun
Blue Nile r. *see* Bahr el Azraq
Bokombayevskoye *see* Bökönbaev
Bol'shoy Kavkaz mt. ra. *see* Caucasus
Bonin Is is *see* Ogasawara-shotō
Bortala *see* Bole
Borzhomi *see* Borjomi
Bosporus str. *see* İstanbul Boğazı
Bowo *see* Bomi
Bozyaka *see* Beskonak
Bré *see* Bray
Brewster, Kap c. *see* Kangikajik
Brezhnev *see* Naberezhnyye Chelny
Brittany div. *see* Bretagne
Brothers, The is *see* Al Ikhwān
Bruges *see* Brugge
Brussel *see* Bruxelles
Brussels *see* Bruxelles
Bucharest *see* Bucureşti
Buckner Bay b. *see* Nakagusuku-wan
Bügür *see* Luntai
Burgundy div. *see* Bourgogne
Burma *see* Myanmar
Būr Sa'īd *see* Port Said
Būr Sudan *see* Port Sudan
Burultokay *see* Fuhai
Bushire *see* Būshehr
Cabora Bassa Dam *dam see* Cahora Bassa, Barragem de
Caerdydd *see* Cardiff
Caerfyrddin *see* Carmarthen
Caergybi *see* Holyhead
Caisleán an Bharraigh *see* Castlebar
Çamalan *see* Gülek
Cambay *see* Khambhat
Cambay, Gulf of b. *see* Khambhat, Gulf of
Canary Islands is *see* Canarias, Islas
Cantabrian Mountains mt. ra. *see* Cantábrica, Cordillera
Canton *see* Guangzhou
Carraig na Siuire *see* Carrick-on-Suir
Casnewydd *see* Newport
Castell-y-Nedd *see* Neath
Ceanannus Mór *see* Kells
Ceatharlach *see* Carlow
Celebes i. *see* Sulawesi
Cephalonia i. *see* Kefallonia
Chanda *see* Chandrapur
Charleville *see* Rathluirc
Charlotte Town *see* Gouyave
Chayek *see* Chaek
Chechenia div. *see* Chechnya
Chefoo *see* Yantai
Chekiang *see* Zhejiang
Chengchow *see* Zhengzhou
Chengtu *see* Chengdu
Chernobyl *see* Chornobyl'
Chicacole *see* Srikakulam
Chihli, Gulf of g. *see* Bo Hai
Chonggye *see* Qonggyai
Christianshåb *see* Qasigiannguit
Christmas Island i. *see* Kiritimati
Chudskoye Ozero l. *see* Peipus, Lake
Chungking *see* Chongqing
Churubay Nura *see* Abay
Cill Airne *see* Killarney
Cill Chainnigh *see* Kilkenny
Cill Mhantáin *see* Wicklow
Cluain Meala *see* Clonmel
Cocanada *see* Kākināda
Colair L. l. *see* Kolleru L.
Cologne *see* Köln
Coney I. i. *see* Serangoon, P.
Coondapoor *see* Kundāpura
Copenhagen *see* København
Coracesium *see* Alanya
Corcaigh *see* Cork
Cordova *see* Córdoba
Corfu i. *see* Kerkyra
Corn Is i. *see* Maíz, Is del
Correntina r. *see* Éguas
Corsica i. *see* Corse
Cort Adelaer, Kap hd *see* Kangeq
Crete i. *see* Kriti
Crete div. *see* Kriti
Crimea pen. *see* Krym'
Cristalino r. *see* Mariembero
Cumberland, Cape c. *see* Nahoï, Cap
Cuzco *see* Cusco
Cyclades is *see* Kyklades
Dabba *see* Daocheng
Dagxoi *see* Yidun
Dairen *see* Dalian
Dalmatia reg. *see* Dalmacija
Damascus *see* Dimashq
Damietta *see* Dumyât
Dammam *see* Ad Dammām
Damqoq Kanbab r. *see* Maquan
Dangla mt. ra. *see* Tanggula Shan
Dannebrogsø i. *see* Qillak
Dantu *see* Zhenjiang
Danube r. *see* Donau
Danube r. *see* Dunav
Danube r. *see* Dunaj
Dardanelles str. *see* Çanakkale Boğazı
Dardo *see* Kangding
Dashkesan *see* Daşkäsän
Daulatabad *see* Malāyer
Dawei *see* Tavoy
Dawukou *see* Shizuishan
Deh Barez *see* Rudan
Deir-ez-Zor *see* Dayr az Zawr
Den Haag *see* 's-Gravenhage
Derry *see* Londonderry
Dhahran *see* Aẓ Ẓahrān
Dilizhan *see* Dilijan
Disappointment Is is *see* Désappointement, Îles de
Disko i. *see* Qeqertarsuatsiaq
Disko Bugt b. *see* Qeqertarsuup Tunua
Divichi *see* Däväci
Dizak *see* Dāvar Panāh
Dnieper r. *see* Dnypro
Dnieper r. *see* Dnepr
Dnieper r. *see* Dnipro
Dniester r. *see* Dnister
Dodecanese is *see* Dodekanisos
Doha *see* Ad Dawḥah
Dohad *see* Dāhod
Dolonnur *see* Duolon
Domel I. i. *see* Letsok-aw Kyun
Dorbiljin *see* Emin
Dorbod Qi *see* Siziwang Qi
Droichead Átha *see* Drogheda
Dubai *see* Dubayy
Duke of Gloucester Is is *see* Duc de Gloucester, Îles
Dundas *see* Uummannaq
Dún Dealgan *see* Dundalk
Dún Garbhán *see* Dungarvan
Dunkirk *see* Dunkerque
Dura Europos *see* Qal'at as Ṣāliḥīyah
Durlas *see* Thurles
Duzdab *see* Zāhedān
Dzhalalabad *see* Cälilabad
Dzhalal-Abad *see* Jalal-Abad
Dzhul'fa *see* Culfa
Dzungarian Basin basin *see* Junggar Pendi
East Cape c. *see* Dezhneva, Mys
Eastern Group is *see* Lau Group
East Retford *see* Retford
East Siberian Sea sea *see* Vostochno-Sibirskoye More
Echmiadzin *see* Ejmiadzin
Edwardesabad *see* Banmi
Eilat *see* Elat
Eilean Barraigh i. *see* Barra
Eilean Leodhais i. *see* Lewis
Eksere *see* Gündoğmuş
El Iskandarîya *see* Alexandria
El Khartum *see* Khartoum
El Qâhira *see* Cairo
El Suweis *see* Suez
El Uqşur *see* Luxor
Elvanlı *see* Tömük
Engaños, R. de los r. *see* Yari
Eochaill *see* Youghal
Epirus div. *see* Ipeiros
Erevan *see* Yerevan
Ergun r. *see* Argun'
Erronan i. *see* Futuna
Euboea i. *see* Evvoia
Eynihal *see* Kale
Færingehavn *see* Kangerluarsoruseq
Falcon i. *see* Fonuafo'ou
Famagusta *see* Ammochostos
Farrukhabad *see* Fatehgarh
Farvel, Kap c. *see* Uummannarsuaq
Fener Burun c. *see* Karataş Burun
Fergana Range mt. ra. *see* Fergana Too Tizmegi
Fez *see* Fès
Finisterre, Cape c. *see* Fisterra, Cabo
Firuzabad *see* Rāsk
Fiskenæsset *see* Qeqertarsuatsiaat
Florence *see* Firenze
Foochow *see* Fuzhou
Formosa *see* Taiwan
Føroyar is *see* Faeroes
Fort-Chimo *see* Kuujjuaq
Fort Hertz *see* Putao
Fort Sandeman *see* Zhob
Franz Josef Land is *see* Zemlya Frantsa-Iosifa
Frederikshåb *see* Paamiut
Frunze *see* Bishkek
Fujairah *see* Al Fujayrah
Fukien *see* Fujian
Fuxian *see* Wafangdian
Gaillimh *see* Galway
Galilee, Sea of l. *see* Tiberias, L.
Gand *see* Gent
Gandzha *see* Gäncä
Ganges r. *see* Ganga
Gaoxiong *see* Kao-hsiung
Gargunsa *see* Gar
Gartar *see* Qianning
Gartok *see* Garyarsa
Gascuña, Golfo de g. *see* Gascogne, Golfe de
Geneva *see* Genève
Geneva, Lake l. *see* Léman, Lac
Genoa *see* Genova
Gey *see* Nikshahr
Ghent *see* Gent
Gılındire *see* Aydıncık
Godthåb *see* Nuuk
Godwin-Austen, Mt mt. *see* K2
Gogra r. *see* Ghaghara
Gomel' *see* Homyel'
Gonabad *see* Jūymand
Goradiz *see* Horadiz
Gor'kiy *see* Nizhniy Novgorod
Graham Bell I. i. *see* Greem Bell,O.
Grande Comore i. *see* Njazidja
Grodno *see* Hrodna
Guanghua *see* Laohekou
Guanyinqiao *see* Chuosijia
Gulja *see* Yining
Güma *see* Pishan
Gurdzhaani *see* Gurjaani
Gyaisi *see* Jiulong
Gyandzha *see* Gäncä
Gyangtse *see* Gyangzê
Hague, The *see* 's-Gravenhage
Haifa *see* Ḥefa
Hainan Strait *see* Qiongzhou Haixia
Hakha *see* Haka
Hangchow *see* Hangzhou
Hanjiang *see* Yangzhou
Hanoi *see* Ha Nôi
Hardy, Mt mt. *see* Rangipoua
Havana *see* Habana
Heihe *see* Aihui
Hengnan *see* Hengyang
Herlen Gol r. *see* Kerulen
Hermon, Mt mt. *see* Shaykh, Jabal esh
High Atlas mt. ra. *see* Haut Atlas
Hingol r. *see* Girdar Dhor
Hobot Xar Qi *see* Xianghuang Qi
Hodeida *see* Al Hudaydah
Hofuf *see* Al Hufuf
Hokang *see* Hegang
Holsteinsborg *see* Sisimiut
Homs *see* Ḥimş
Horn, C. c. *see* Hornos, Cabo de
Hpa-an *see* Pa-an
Huang Hai sea *see* Yellow Sea
Huhehot *see* Hohhot
Huiyang *see* Huizhou
Hulun *see* Hailar
Hupeh div. *see* Hubei
Hwlffordd *see* Haverfordwest
Ibiza i. *see* Eivissa
Ibiza *see* Eivissa
Iguaçu Falls rapids *see* Iguazú, Cataratas del
Il'ichevsk *see* Şärur
imeni 26 Bakinskikh Komissarov *see* Bakı Komissarı, 26
Imishli *see* İmişli
Indur *see* Nizamabad
Inguri r. *see* Enguri
Inis *see* Ennis
Inis Córthaidh *see* Enniscorthy
Inland Sea *see* Seto-naikai
Inner Mongolian Aut. Region div. *see* Nei Monggol Zizhiqu
Ionian Islands div. *see* Ionioi Nisoi
Iraklion *see* Irakleio
Iranshahr *see* Fahraj
Isfahan *see* Eşfahan
Isfandaqeh *see* Gāv Koshī
Ismailly *see* İsmayıllı
Issyk-Kul', Ozero salt l. *see* Ysyk-Köl
Istria pen. *see* Istra
Ithaca *see* Ithaki
Iwo Jima i. *see* Iō-Jima
Jacobshavn *see* Ilulissat
Jaffa *see* Tel Aviv-Yafo
Jagok Tso salt l. *see* Urru Co
Japan Alps Nat. Park *see* Chibu-Sangaku Nat. Park
Java i. *see* Jawa
Javaés r. *see* Formoso
Jedda *see* Jiddah
Jethro *see* Maghā'ir Shu'ayb
Jiaji *see* Qionghai
Jiayi *see* Chia-i
Jilong *see* Chi-lung
Jing *see* Jinghe
Jogjakarta *see* Yogyakarta
Kaba *see* Habahe
Kadzhi-Say *see* Kajy-Say
Kahnu *see* Kahnūj
Kailas mt. *see* Kangrinboqê Feng
Kailas Range mt. ra. *see* Gangdisê Shan
Kakhi *see* Qax
Kalaallit Nunaat terr. *see* Greenland
Kalāt *see* Kabūd Gonbad
Kalgan *see* Zhangjiakou
Kalinino *see* Tashir
Kâmpóng Saôm *see* Sihanoukville
Kampuchea country *see* Cambodia
Kang-ma *see* Kangmar
Kanniya Kumari c. *see* Comorin, Cape
Kannur *see* Cannanore
Kansu div. *see* Gansu
Kara Deniz sea *see* Black Sea
Karaklis *see* Vanadzor
Kara Sea sea *see* Karskoye More
Karaxahar r. *see* Kaidu
Karghalik *see* Yecheng
Karl-Marx-Stadt *see* Chemnitz
Karpaty mt. ra. *see* Carpathian Mts
Kashgar *see* Kashi
Kashmir terr. *see* Jammu and Kashmir
Kaspiyskoye More sea *see* Caspian Sea
Kazakh *see* Qazax
Kazi Magomed *see* Qazımämmäd
Kéamu i. *see* Anatom
Keferdiz *see* Sakçagöze
Keriya *see* Yutian
Kerulen r. *see* Herlen
Khabis *see* Shahdāb
Khachmas *see* Xaçmaz
Khankendi *see* Xankändi
Khan Tengri mt. *see* Hantengri Feng
Kharari *see* Abu Road
Khar'kov *see* Kharkiv
Khudat *see* Xudat
Kiangsu *see* Jiangsu
Kiev *see* Kyyiv
Kilyazi *see* Gilazi
King I. i. *see* Kadan Kyun
Kingisseppa *see* Kuressaare
Kirgizskiy Khrebet mt. ra. *see* Kirghiz Range
Kirobasi *see* Mağara
Kirovabad *see* Gäncä
Kirovakan *see* Vanadzor
Kishinev *see* Chişinău
Kisseraing I. i. *see* Kanmaw Kyun
Kistna r. *see* Krishna
Koartac *see* Quaqtaq
Kochi *see* Cochin
Koktokay *see* Fuyun
Kolab r. *see* Sābari
Kola Peninsula pen. *see* Kol'skiy Poluostrov
Kollam *see* Quilon
Korat *see* Nakhon Ratchasima
Kozhikode *see* Calicut
Krivoy Rog *see* Kryvyy Rih
Krungkao *see* Ayutthaya
Krung Thep *see* Bangkok
Kuba *see* Quba
Kumayri *see* Gyumri
Künes *see* Xinyuan
Kura r. *see* Kür
Kuril Is is *see* Kuril'skiye Ostrova
Kurinskaya Kosa pen. *see* Kür Dili
Kurskiy Zaliv lag. *see* Courland Lagoon
Kusary *see* Qusar
Kut-al-Imara *see* Al Kūt
Kuujjuarapik *see* Poste-de-la-Baleine
Kuwaé i. *see* Tongoa
Kuwait *see* Al Kuwayt
Kuybyshev *see* Samara
Kvareli *see* Qvareli
Kwangsi div. *see* Guangxi
Kwangtung div. *see* Guangdong
Kweichow *see* Guizhou
Kweiyang *see* Guiyang
Kyurdamir *see* Kürdämir
Ladoga, Lake l. *see* Ladozhskoye Ozero
Lanchow *see* Lanzhou
Langmusi *see* Dagcanglhamo
Languiaru r. *see* Iquê
Laowohi *see* Khardung La
Laptev Sea sea *see* Laptevykh, More
Laranda *see* Karaman
Latakia *see* Al Lādhiqīyah
Leghorn *see* Livorno
Leizhou *see* Haikang
Leninakan *see* Gyumri
Leningrad *see* Sankt-Peterburg
Lesbos i. *see* Lesvos
Lesser Caucasus mt. ra. *see* Malyy Kavkaz
Lianzhou *see* Hepu
Lima Is is *see* Wanshan Qundao
Limassol *see* Lemesos
Lindisfarne i. *see* Holy Island
Lisbon *see* Lisboa
Loch Garman *see* Wexford
Lohil r. *see* Zavū Qu
Lower California pen. *see* Baja California
Loyalty Is is *see* Loyauté, Îs
Loyang *see* Luoyang
Luar I. i. *see* Horsburgh I.
Lucerne *see* Luzern
Lüda *see* Dalian
Luik *see* Liège
Luimneach *see* Limerick
Lyallpur *see* Faisalabad
Macar *see* Gebiz
Macintyre r. *see* Barwon
Mackillop, L. salt flat *see* Yamma Yamma, L.
Magas *see* Zābolī
Magway *see* Magwe
Mahabalipuram *see* Māmallapuram
Makharadze *see* Ozurget'i
Makran Coast Range mt. ra. *see* Talar-i-Band
Mala *see* Mallow
Malawi, Lake l. *see* Nyasa, Lake
Malvinas, Islas is *see* Falkland Islands
Mamisonskiy Pereval pass *see* Mamisonis Ugheltekhili
Manche, La str. *see* English Channel
Mangshi *see* Luxi
Manikgarh *see* Rajura
Manipur *see* Imphal
Mar Cantábrico *see* Biscay, Bay of
Marjan *see* Wazi Khwa
Marmara, Sea of sea *see* Marmara Denizi
Marquesas Islands is *see* Marquises, Îles
Marrakesh *see* Marrakech
Mashtagi *see* Maştağa
Masulipatam *see* Machilipatnam
Matapan, Cape pt *see* Akra Tainaro
Matturai *see* Matara
Matun *see* Khowst
Mawlamyine *see* Moulmein
Mecca *see* Makkah
Medina *see* Al Madīnah
Medu Kongkar *see* Maizhokunggar
Meilü *see* Wuchuan
Mei Xian *see* Meizhou
Mekong r. *see* Mênam Khong
Mersin *see* İçel
Merv *see* Mary
Meshed *see* Mashhad
Midway *see* Thamarīt
Milan *see* Milano
Mindzhivan *see* Mincivan
Mingechaur *see* Mingäçevir
Mingechaurskoye Vdkhr. l. *see* Mingäçevir Su Anbarı
Min-Kush *see* Ming-Kush
Minya Konka mt. *see* Gongga Shan
Mobutu, Lake l. *see* Albert, Lake
Mocha *see* Al Mukhā
Mogadishu *see* Muqdisho
Moḥammadābād *see* Darreh Gaz
Moheli i. *see* Mwali
Moluccas is *see* Maluku
Môn i. *see* Anglesey
Monggolküre *see* Zhaosu
Monze, C. c. *see* Mauri, Ras
Mortes r. *see* Rio Manso
Morvi *see* Morbi
Mosul *see* Al Mawşil
Mughalbhin *see* Jati
Muineachán *see* Monaghan
Mukden *see* Shenyang
Mumbai *see* Bombay
Munich *see* München
Muscat *see* Masqaṭ
Nada *see* Dan Xian
Nagorno-Karabakh div. *see* Qarabağ
Nagornyy Karabakh div. *see* Qarabağ
Nai-tung *see* Nêdong
Nakhichevan' *see* Naxçıvan
Nam Mao r. *see* Shweli
Nandi *see* Nadi
Nanking *see* Nanjing
Naples *see* Napoli
Narbada r. *see* Narmada
Nasirabad *see* Mymensingh
Nasosnyy *see* Hacı Zeynalabdin
Nasratabad *see* Zābol
Neftechala *see* Neftçala
New Siberia Islands is *see* Novosibirskiye Ostrova
Ngawa *see* Aba
Niassa, L. l. *see* Nyasa, Lake
Nicosia *see* Lefkosia
Nimbhera *see* Nimbahera
Ningsia div. *see* Ningxia
Nippon Hai sea *see* Japan, Sea of
Nīshāpūr *see* Neyshābūr
Niya *see* Minfeng
Nonni r. *see* Nen
Normandes, Îles is *see* Channel Islands
Northern Sporades is *see* Voreioi Sporades
Nouveau-Comptoir *see* Wemindji
Nouvelle Calédonie terr. *see* New Caledonia
Nowgong *see* Nagaon
Nyagquka *see* Yajiang
Nyagrong *see* Xinlong
Nyenchen Tanglha Range mt. ra. *see* Nyainqêntanglha Shan
Oder r. *see* Odra
Odessa *see* Odesa
Okhotsk, Sea of sea *see* Okhotskoye More
Oktemberyan *see* Hoktemberyan
Omba i. *see* Aoba
Onega, Lake l. *see* Onezhskoye Ozero
Oporto *see* Porto
Oranje r. *see* Orange
Ordu *see* Yayladağı
Ordzhonikidze *see* Vladikavkaz
Orontes r. *see* Asi
Ostend *see* Oostende
Padua *see* Padova
Paknampho *see* Muang Nakhon Sawan
Palakkat *see* Palghat
Palmyra *see* Tadmur
Panama City *see* Panamá
Panjang I. i. *see* West I.
Panjim *see* Panaji
Papagaio r. *see* Sauêruiná
Paphos *see* Pafos
Pascua, Isla de i. *see* Easter I.
Pas de Calais str. *see* Dover, Strait of
Patan *see* Somnath
Pathein *see* Bassein
Patteson Pass. chan. *see* Lolvavana, Pass.
Pechora Sea sea *see* Pechorskoye More
Peipsi Järve l. *see* Peipus, Lake
Peking *see* Beijing
Pelusium, B. of b. *see* Khalīg el Tîna
Pentecôte, Î. i. *see* Pentecost I.
Pereval Bedel pass *see* Bedel Pass
Pereval Torugart pass *see* Turugart Pass
Persia *see* Iran
Persian Gulf g. *see* Gulf, The
Pescadores is *see* P'eng-hu Lieh-tao
Phnom Penh *see* Phnum Penh
Pindu Pass pass *see* Pedo La
Pindus Mountains mt. ra. *see* Pindos
Pingdong *see* P'ing-tun
Piraeus *see* Peiraias
Pishpek *see* Bishkek
Pomo Tso l. *see* Puma Yumco
Poona *see* Pune
Port Arthur *see* Lüshun
Port Harrison *see* Inukjuak
Port Klang *see* Pelabuhan Kelang
Port Láirgé *see* Waterford
Port-Nouveau-Québec *see* Kangiqsualujjuaq
Porto Novo *see* Parangipettai
Port Taufiq *see* Būr Taufiq
Prague *see* Praha
Pripet r. *see* Prypyats'
Pripet r. *see* Pryp"yat'
Prome *see* Pyè
Prøven *see* Kangersuatsiaq
Przheval'sk *see* Karakol
Pudai w *see* Dor
Puducherri *see* Pondicherry
Pushkino *see* Biläsuvar
Qagchêng *see* Xiangcheng
Qarkilik *see* Ruoqiang
Qarqan *see* Qiemo
Qogir Feng mt. *see* K2
Qomolangma Feng mt. *see* Everest, Mt
Qoqek *see* Tacheng
Queen Maud Land reg. *see* Dronning Maud Land
Quelpart I. i. *see* Cheju Do
Quemoy *see* Chinmen
Quqên *see* Jinchuan
Qurlurtuuq *see* Coppermine
Qu Xian *see* Quzhou
Qyteti Stalin *see* Kuçovë
Rabkob *see* Dharmjaygarh
Rahaeng *see* Tak
Raibu i. *see* Air
Ramnad *see* Ramanathapuram
Rampur Boalia *see* Rajshahi
Rangoon *see* Yangon
Razdan *see* Hrazdan
Rebiana Sand Sea desert *see* Ramlat Rabyānah
Red River r. *see* Hông, S.
Red Volta r. *see* Nazinon
Reef Islands is *see* Rowa
Renland reg. *see* Tuttut Nunaat
Rhine r. *see* Rhein
Rhodes i. *see* Rodos
Rhum i. *see* Rum
Rīgas Jūras Līcis b. *see* Riga, Gulf of
Riia Laht g. *see* Riga, Gulf of
Riyadh *see* Ar Riyāḍ
Rome *see* Roma
Rongzhag *see* Danba
Rosetta *see* Rashîd
Ross Island i. *see* Daung Kyun
Roti i. *see* Rote
Routh Bank sand bank *see* Seahorse Bank
Rubha Robhanais hd *see* Butt of Lewis
Rybach'ye *see* Ysyk-Köl
Saatly *see* Saatlı
Sabzawar *see* Shindand
Sabzvārān *see* Jīroft
Saddle I. i. *see* Mota Lava
Safad *see* Ẕefat
Sagaredzho *see* Sagarejo
Saharan Atlas mt. ra. *see* Atlas Saharien
Sahyadri mt. ra. *see* Western Ghats
Saigon *see* Hô Chi Minh
Saīn Qal'eh *see* Sa'īndezh
St Christopher i. *see* St Kitts
St Christopher *see* Fig Tree
St Luke's i. *see* Zadetkale Kyun
St Matthew's I. i. *see* Zadetkyi Kyun
St Petersburg *see* Sankt-Peterburg
St Vincent, Cape c. *see* São Vicente, Cabo de
Sal'yany *see* Salyan
Samirum *see* Yazd-e Khvāst
Sangachaly *see* Sanqaçal
Santorini i. *see* Thira
Sardinia i. *see* Sardegna
Sar Eskandar *see* Āzarān
Sarıoğlan *see* Belören
Sāūjbolāgh *see* Mahābād
Savanat *see* Eşṭahbānāt
Sawu i. *see* Savu
Scarpanto i. *see* Karpathos
Scheldt r. *see* Schelde
Scoresbysund *see* Ittoqqortoormiit
Seleucia *see* Silifke
Seleucia Pieria *see* Samandağı
Sellore I. i. *see* Saganthit Kyun
Seoul *see* Sŏul
Serbia div. *see* Srbija
Sevan, Ozero l. *see* Sevana Lich
Seven Pagodas *see* Māmallapuram
Seville *see* Sevilla
Seyhan *see* Adana
Shāhpūr *see* Salmās
Shahrezā *see* Qomisheh
Shakhagach *see* Şahağac
Shakhbuz *see* Şahbuz
Shamkhor *see* Şämkir
Shangxian *see* Shangzhou
Shantung div. *see* Shandong
Shan Xian *see* Sanmenxia
Sharjah *see* Ash Shāriqah
Sharur *see* Şärur
Sheikh Othman *see* Ash Shaykh 'Uthman
Sheki *see* Şäki
Shemakha *see* Şamaxı
Shensi div. *see* Shaanxi
Shiliu *see* Changjiang
Shiquanhe *see* Ali
Shohi Pass pass *see* Tal Pass
Shuicheng *see* Liupanshui
Shusha *see* Şuşa
Sian *see* Xi'an
Siazan' *see* Siyäzän
Sicily i. *see* Sicilia
Side *see* Selimiye
Sidon *see* Saïda
Silistat *see* Bozkır
Simbirsk *see* Ul'yanovsk
Simbor i. *see* Pānikoita
Sinai, Mount mt. *see* Katherîna,G.
Sind *see* Thul
Singora *see* Songkhla
Sinkiang Uighur Aut. Region div. *see* Xinjiang Uygur Zizhiqu
Sinneh *see* Sanandaj
Sirjan *see* Sa'īdābād
Sirte *see* Surt
Sirte, Gulf of g. *see* Khalīj Surt
Sis *see* Kozan
Sligeach *see* Sligo
Society Islands is *see* Société, Archipel de la
Socotra i. *see* Suquṭrā
Sofia *see* Sofiya
Soochow *see* Suzhou
South Cape c. *see* Ka Lae
Stalingrad *see* Volgograd
Stampalia i. *see* Astypalaia
Stepanakert *see* Xankändi
Sui Xian *see* Suizhou
Sukhumi *see* Sokhumi
Sukkertoppen *see* Maniitsoq
Sulaymaniyah *see* As Sulaymānīyah
Sullivan I. i. *see* Lanbi Kyun
Sultanabad *see* Arāk
Sumatra i. *see* Sumatera
Sumgait *see* Sumqayıt
Sungari r. *see* Songhua
Sungqu *see* Songpan
Su Xian *see* Suzhou
Sverdlovsk *see* Yekaterinburg
Syracuse *see* Siracusa
Syrian Desert desert *see* Bādiyat ash Shām
Szechwan div. *see* Sichuan
Taganrogskiy Zaliv g. *see* Taganrog, Gulf of
Tagus r. *see* Tejo
Taibei *see* T'ai-pei
Taiwan Haixia str. *see* Taiwan Strait
Taizhong *see* T'ai-chung
Taklimakan Desert desert *see* Taklimakan Shamo
Talas Range mt. ra. *see* Talas Ala-Too
Taldysu *see* Taldy-Suu
Talyshskiye Gory mts *see* Talış Dağları
Tangdan *see* Dongchuan
Tangier *see* Tanger
Tanintharyi *see* Tenasserim
Tanjore *see* Thanjavur
Taranaki, Mt vol *see* Egmont, Mt
Tarim Basin basin *see* Tarim Pendi
Tashi Chho *see* Thimphu
Tāshqurghān *see* Kholm
Tauriuiná r. *see* Verde
Tauz *see* Tovuz
Tavoy I. i. *see* Mali Kyun
Teheran *see* Tehrān
Tehri *see* Tikamgarh
Terter r. *see* Tärtär
Tetuán *see* Tétouan
Tha Hin *see* Lop Buri
Thalassery *see* Tellicherry
Thanlwin r. *see* Salween
Thiruvananthapuram *see* Trivandrum
Thrissur *see* Trichur
Thule *see* Qaanaaq
Tian Shan mt. ra. *see* Tien Shan
Tiber r. *see* Tevere
Tiberias *see* Teverya
Tibet Aut. Region *see* Xizang Zizhiqu
Tibet, Plateau of plat. *see* Xizang Gaoyuan
Tientsin *see* Tianjin
Tiflis *see* T'bilisi
Tirana *see* Tiranë
Tkibuli *see* Tqibuli
Tkvarcheli *see* Tqvarch'eli
Tokkuztara *see* Gongliu
Toksu *see* Xinhe
Toling *see* Zanda
Tomur Feng mt. *see* Pobedy, Pik
Tongshan *see* Xuzhou
Trá Lí *see* Tralee
Trá Mhór *see* Tramore
Transylvanian Alps mts *see* Carpaţii Meridionali
Trefaldwyn *see* Montgomery
Tripoli *see* Ţarābulus
Truk is *see* Chuuk
Tsinan *see* Jinan
Tsinghai div. *see* Qinghai
Tsingtao *see* Qingdao
Tsiteli Tskaro *see* Dedoplis Tsqaro
Tsitsihar *see* Qiqihar
Tskhaltubo *see* Tsqaltubo
Tsona *see* Cona
Tsushima-kaikyō str. *see* Korea Strait
Tulach Mhór *see* Tullamore
Tunxi *see* Huangshan
Tupai i. *see* Motu Iti
Turfan *see* Turpan
Turin *see* Torino
Tuva div. *see* Tyva
Tuz, L. salt l. *see* Tuz Gölü
Tyre *see* Soûr
Tyuratam *see* Leninsk
Udzhary *see* Ucar
Uibhist a' Deas i. *see* South Uist
Uibhist a' Tuath i. *see* North Uist
Ulan Bator *see* Ulaanbaatar
Ulanhad *see* Chifeng
Ulanhot *see* Horqin Youyi Qianqi
Uluru h. *see* Ayers Rock
Ulvéah i. *see* Lopévi
Upper Chindwin *see* Mawlaik
Upturpan *see* Wushi
Uracas i. *see* Farallon de Pajaros
Ural Mountains mt. ra. *see* Ural'skiy Khrebet
Urmia *see* Orūmīyeh
Urmia, L. salt l. *see* Daryācheh-ye Orūmīyeh
Uruk *see* Erech
Urumchi *see* Ürümqi
Ussuri r. *see* Wusuli
Ustinov *see* Izhevsk
Utu *see* Miao'ergou
Van, L. salt l. *see* Van Gölü
Vartashen *see* Oğuz
Vasht *see* Khāsh
Vaté i. *see* Éfaté
Venice *see* Venezia
Vesuvius vol *see* Vesuvio
Victoria, Mt mt. *see* Tomanivi
Vienna *see* Wien
Vientiane *see* Viangchan
Vistula r. *see* Wisła
Vizagapatam *see* Vishakhapatnam
Volcano Bay b. *see* Uchiura-wan
Volcano Is. is *see* Kazan-rettō
Volta Blanche w *see* Nakambé
Volta Rouge r. *see* Nazinon
Voroshilovgrad *see* Luhans'k
Wakeham *see* Kangiqsujuaq
Wang Mai Khon *see* Sawankhalok
Warsaw *see* Warszawa
Western Dvina r. *see* Zapadnaya Dvina
White Sea g. *see* Beloye More
White Volta w *see* Nakambé
Wrangel I. i. *see* Vrangelya, O.
Wrecsam *see* Wrexham
Wujin *see* Changzhou
Wuxing *see* Huzhou
Xangdoring *see* Xungba
Xianguan *see* Dali
Xiangyang *see* Xiangfan
Xiaoshi *see* Benxi
Xinzhu *see* Hsin-chu
Xulun Hobot Qagan Qi *see* Zhengxiangbai Qi
Xulun Hoh Qi *see* Zhenglan Qi
Yacha *see* Baisha
Yangtse, Mouth of the river mouth *see* Changjiang Kou
Yangtze r. *see* Jinsha
Yangtze r. *see* Chang
Yardymly *see* Yardımlı
Yarkant *see* Shache
Yaxian *see* Sanya
Yekhegnadzor *see* Yeghegnadzor
Yeotmal *see* Yavatmāl
Yeo Yeo r. *see* Bland
Yerushalayim *see* Jerusalem
Yevlakh *see* Yevlax
Y-Fenni *see* Abergavenny
Yin Xian *see* Ningbo
Yr Wyddfa mt. *see* Snowdon
Yugo-Osetinskaya Avtonomnaya Oblast' *see* South Ossetia
Yushuwan *see* Huaihua
Zainlha *see* Xiaojin
Zakataly *see* Zaqatala
Zante i. *see* Zakynthos
Zestafoni *see* Zestap'oni
Zhaggo *see* Luhuo
Zhangde *see* Anyang
Zhanghua *see* Chang-hua
Zhi Qu r. *see* Tongtian
Zhiziluo *see* Bijiang
Zhuji *see* Shangqiu
Zogainrawar *see* Huashixia
Zongga *see* Gyirong